MORALS

AND

POLITICS

MORALS
AND
POLITICS

VITTORIO HÖSLE

Translated by Steven Rendall

UNIVERSITY OF NOTRE DAME PRESS

Notre Dame, Indiana

Translated by Steven Rendall from *Moral und Politik: Grundlagen einer
Politischen Ethik für das 21. Jahrhundert* by Vittorio Hösle,
copyright © C. H. Beck'sche Verlagsbuchhandlung (Oscar Beck), 1997.

The University of Notre Dame Press gratefully acknowledges the generous support
in the publication of this book of the George W. Strake Endowment
in the College of Arts and Letters, University of Notre Dame.

Library of Congress Cataloging-in-Publication Data
Hösle, Vittorio, 1960–
[Moral und Politik. English]
Morals and politics / Vittorio Hösle ; translated by Steven Rendall.
p.   cm.
Includes bibliographical references and index.
ISBN 0-268-03065-0 (alk. paper)
1. Political ethics.   2. Sociology—Philosophy.   I. Title.

JA79.H6313   2004
172—dc22
2004053650

∞ *This book is printed on acid-free paper.*

Contents

Preface to the English Translation   xi
Introduction   xiv

I. NORMATIVE FOUNDATIONS

1. **Outline of the Problem's Background in Intellectual History**   **3**

1.1.   Political Feeling in Archaic Cultures   5
1.2.   Reflections on the State in Advanced Cultures   6
1.3.   Greek Political Philosophy   8
1.4.   Hellenistic and Roman Political Philosophy   18
1.5.   Christianity and Medieval Political Philosophy   21
1.6.   Modern Political Philosophy   27
1.6.1.   Thomas Hobbes and the Sovereignty of the Modern State   32
1.6.2.   The Separation of Powers and the "Superstructure"   40
1.6.3.   Rousseau and the French Revolution   44
1.6.4.   The Political Philosophy of Kant and of German Idealism   48
1.6.5.   Democracy, Nationalism, and the Welfare State   53
1.6.6.   What Is the Starting Point for Political Philosophy Today?   58

2. **The Relationship between Morals and Politics**   **62**

2.1.   Concepts of the Political and Concepts of the Moral   62
2.1.1.   The Political and the Cratic   62
2.1.2.   Morals, Ethics, Mores, Morality   70
2.2.   Rejection of Certain Objections to a Moral Evaluation of Politics   76

3. **Principles of Ethics**   **89**

3.1.   On Intentionalism   93
3.1.1.   The Limits of Intentionalism   93
3.1.2.   What Is Morally Attributable?   99

3.2.   On Universalism   105

3.2.1.   Universalism and the Postulate of Universalizability: Kantianism,
Utilitarianism, and Discourse Ethics   107

3.2.2.   Formalism and Material Ethics: The Problem of Grounding Ethics   112

3.2.3.   Comparative and Metrical Concepts in Ethics: The Tragic   117

3.3.   A Priori and Empirical Knowledge in Ethics   121

3.3.1.   The Subsumption Problem   122

3.3.2.   Means and Ends   123

3.3.2.1.   Technical, Strategic, and Communicative Rationality   126

3.3.2.2.   The Ideal and the Non-Ideal Part of Ethics   129

3.3.2.3.   Intrinsic and Extrinsic Value   131

3.3.3.   The Importance of Decision Theory and Game Theory for Ethics   133

3.3.3.1.   Moral Preferences in Decision Theory and Game Theory   136

3.3.3.2.   The Status of Probabilities   138

3.3.3.3.   Actions and Omissions   144

3.3.3.4.   The Finitude of Human Knowledge; "Satisficing" and Maximizing;
Political Genius and a "Political Topics"   146

3.3.3.5.   Criteria for Decisions That Are Morally Right   149

3.4.   Ontology, Science, and Ethics   153

3.4.1.   On the Relation between Descriptive Analysis and Analysis of Values   153

3.4.2.   Methodology of the Social Sciences   155

3.4.2.1.   Social Being as the Fourth Sphere of Being: Explanation and
Understanding in the Social Sciences   158

3.4.2.2.   Philosophical Interpretation and the Self-Interpretation of Social
Structures: The Problem of Methodological Individualism   162

3.4.2.3.   Social Sciences and Historical Sciences: The Sources of Knowledge
in the Social Sciences   165

3.4.2.4.   Pre-Scientific Knowledge and Knowledge through Art   173

3.5.   Morals and History   174

3.5.1.   The Greatness and Limits of Moral Evolutionism   176

3.5.2.   Moral and Religious Consciousness   183

II.   FOUNDATIONS OF A THEORY OF THE SOCIAL WORLD

4.   **Man**   **189**

4.1.   The Human and the Organic   192

4.1.1.   The Nature of the Organic   194

4.1.2.   Ethics and Sociobiology   197

4.1.3.   The Evolution of the Organic: Forms of Animal Behavior   210

4.1.4.   The Biological Bases of the Human Sense of the Moral   218

4.2.   The Human Identity Problem   222

4.2.1.   Life and Spirit   222

4.2.2.	Elements of Self-Consciousness	227
4.2.2.1.	Memory, Thinking, Feelings	230
4.2.2.2.	Principles of the Theory of Action	240
4.2.2.3.	Descriptive and Normative Self-Images: The "Me"	247
4.3.	Man and Culture	254
4.3.1.	Man as a Symbolic Being: Language	255
4.3.2.	Custom, Social Orders, Social Subsystems	260
4.3.3.	Collective Identities	271
4.4.	The Moral Element in Man	276
4.4.1.	Intrinsic Values in Pre-Human Nature	276
4.4.2.	Human Dignity, Personality, and Basic Goods	278
4.4.3.	The System of Virtues	281
4.4.3.1.	The Pre-Social Virtues	283
4.4.3.2.	Social Virtues	287
4.4.3.2.1.	Justice	289
4.4.3.2.2.	Friendship and Love	291
4.4.4.	The System of the Vices	295
4.4.4.1.	Pre-Social Vices	296
4.4.4.2.	Social Vices	299

5.	**Power**	**305**
5.1.	The Essence and Appearance of Power	308
5.1.1.	On the Concept of Power	308
5.1.2.	Phenomenology of the Genesis of Power	313
5.1.2.1.	Struggles over Interests, Recognition, and Values	315
5.1.2.2.	Means of Struggle	321
5.1.2.2.1.	Force and Ruse: Enslavement	321
5.1.2.2.2.	Threats	327
5.1.2.2.3.	The Third Party	331
5.1.2.2.4.	Positive Sanctions	340
5.1.2.2.4.1.	Diplomatic Abilities	343
5.1.2.2.4.2.	Supply and Demand: The Relationship between Positive and Negative Sanctions	345
5.1.2.2.5.	Power and Opinion	348
5.1.2.2.5.1.	Manipulation	350
5.1.2.2.5.2.	Persuading and Convincing: Weakness as a Power Factor	352
5.1.2.2.5.3.	Authority	357
5.2.	Political Man and His Maxims	362
5.2.1.	On the Psychology of the Striving for Power	363
5.2.2.	The Ambivalence of Cratology	370
5.2.3.	The Logic of Power	374
5.2.3.1.	Maxims of the Aspirant to Power	377

5.2.3.2. Maxims for Fighting Enemies   382

5.2.3.3. Maxims of the Power-Holder   393

5.2.4. The Loneliness of the Power-Holder   401

5.3. Power and Morals   405

5.3.1. The Impossibility of Doing without Power   406

5.3.2. The Conditions of Moral Striving for Power   410

5.3.3. On the Moral Evaluation of the Political Man's Maxims   417

5.3.4. On the Moral Evaluation of the Forms of Power   423

5.3.4.1. The Morals of Consensus   423

5.3.4.2. The Morals of Forms of Power Based on Opinion   426

5.3.4.3. The Morals of Positive Sanctions   430

5.3.4.4. The Morals of Negative Sanctions   431

6. **The State and Its History**   **436**

6.1. From the Power Relationship to the State   440

6.1.1. Forms of Pre-Political Domination   442

6.1.1.1. Domination in the Family   442

6.1.1.2. Obedience on the Part of Those Subjected by Force   444

6.1.1.3. Domination by Contract: The Aporias of the Genetic Contract Theory   446

6.1.1.4. Domination on the Basis of Authority That Is Not Based on Kinship   449

6.1.2. The Basic Social Functions and Political Domination   451

6.1.2.1. Reproduction   451

6.1.2.2. Economic Life   456

6.1.2.3. The Military Function   459

6.1.2.4. The Legal Order and Political Domination   462

6.1.2.5. Religion   467

6.1.3. Elements of the State   471

6.1.3.1. State Population (*Staatsvolk*)   473

6.1.3.2. State Territory   480

6.1.3.3. State Power: Inner Sovereignty   484

6.1.3.4. The Legal Forms of Relationships between States: External Sovereignty   493

6.1.3.5. State Apparatus and State Organs   498

6.1.3.6. The Tasks of the State   503

6.1.3.7. Constitution, Legislative, Executive, Judiciary   514

6.1.3.8. The Forms of the State   526

6.1.3.9. State and Society   539

6.2. On the History of the State   542

6.2.1. Basic Problems of the Philosophy of History   543

6.2.2. Stages in World History   554

6.2.2.1. Hunters and Gatherers 555

6.2.2.2. Agrarian Societies 558

6.2.2.2.1. Phoenicians and Greeks 564

6.2.2.2.2. The Roman Empire 568

6.2.2.2.3. The Western Middle Ages 571

6.2.2.3. Modernity 577

6.2.2.3.1. Non-Political Changes 578

6.2.2.3.2. Changes in Internal Policy 586

6.2.2.3.3. Changes in Foreign Policy 598

6.3. The Current World Political Situation 602

6.3.1. The Structural Conditions of Foreign Policy 603

6.3.2. The Structural Conditions of Internal Policy 609

6.3.3. Religious Structural Conditions 618

III.   POLITICAL ETHICS

7. **The Just State**   **625**

7.1. The Justification of Statehood in General 627

7.2. The Concept of Natural Law 631

7.2.1. Natural Law and Positive Law 632

7.2.2. Natural Law and Morals 637

7.2.2.1. The Basic Idea, Forms, and Limits of Liberalism 638

7.2.2.2. Natural Law as the Nucleus of Morals 644

7.3. The System of Natural Law 654

7.3.1. Principles of Civil Law: Person, Property, Contract 655

7.3.1.1. Who Has Rights? 656

7.3.1.2. Legitimate Sources of Property 665

7.3.1.3. The Importance and Limits of Contracts 673

7.3.2. Principles of Criminal Law 678

7.3.3. The Law of the Most Important Social Institutions 692

7.3.3.1 Principles of Family Law 693

7.3.3.2. Principles of the Law of Society 704

7.3.3.2.1. The State and the Economy 705

7.3.3.2.2. The State and Religions 719

7.3.3.3. Principles of Consitutional Law 724

7.3.3.3.1. The Problem of the State Form 724

7.3.3.3.2. The Special Status of Constitutional Norms 729

7.3.3.3.3. The Federal Principle 734

7.3.3.3.4. The Legislative 737

7.3.3.3.5. The Executive 747

7.3.3.3.6. The Judiciary 758

7.3.3.3.7. A Universal State or a Plurality of States? 762

8.   **Just Politics**   772
8.1.   Moral Principles of Domestic Politics   774
8.1.1.   The Morals of Mores   774
8.1.2.   The Morals of Positive Law   776
8.1.3.   The Subjectively Moral in Immoral Mores   779
8.1.4.   Fundamental Moral Tasks of Politics within Stable Mores   783
8.1.5.   The Morals of Violations of the Law within Stable Mores   794
8.1.5.1.   Violations of the Law in a Constitutional State Founded on the Rule of Law   797
8.1.5.2.   Violations of the Law and Cooperation in States That Are Not Constitutional States   800
8.1.5.3.   Secession   807
8.1.6.   The Morals of Morality   811
8.1.7.   Fundamental Moral Tasks of Politics in Times of Radical Change   818
8.1.8.   The Morals of Violations of the Law in Times of Radical Change   822
8.2.   Moral Principles of Foreign Policy   824
8.2.1.   Moral Foreign Policy in Times of Peace   826
8.2.1.1.   Cultural Relations Policy   828
8.2.1.2.   Policy regarding Transnational Economic and Environmental Issues   832
8.2.1.3.   Aid for Development   834
8.2.2.   Just Wars   837
8.2.2.1.   Just Grounds for War   841
8.2.2.2.   Just Conduct of War   853
8.2.2.3.   Just Post-War Policy   863

9.   **Outline of a Political Ethic for the Twenty-First Century**   865
9.1.   The Politics of International Organizations   866
9.1.1.   The United Nations   867
9.1.2.   Religions   876
9.1.3.   Economics   878
9.2.   Foreign Policy in the Broader Sense   881
9.2.1.   Foreign Policy in the Narrower Sense   881
9.2.2.   Defense Policy   892
9.2.3.   Development Policy   895
9.3.   Domestic Policy in the Broader Sense   902
9.3.1.   Environmental Policy   903
9.3.2.   Economic Policy and Social Policy   911
9.3.3.   Domestic Policy in the Narrower Sense   916
9.3.4.   Educational and Research Policy   921

Bibliography   932
Index of Names   948
Index of Subjects   962

Preface to the English Translation

It is with great joy and pride that I see this work published in what has become the universal language of the world, and by the press of a university to which I am particularly proud to belong. This book was published for the first time in 1997 by C. H. Beck in Munich, and a paperback edition appeared in 2000. The book received many reviews and also triggered an interview in *Der Speigel* (46 [1997]: 247–252). In 2001 Bernd Goebel and Manfred Wetzel published a collection of essays about it with my response to my critics, *Eine moralische Politik? Vittorio Hösles Politische Ethik in der Diskussion*. Recently I published under the title *Philosophie und Öffentlichkeit* a series of papers that deal in a more detailed form with some aspects of political ethics neglected in the book (for example, bioethical issues, education, and foreign policy).

The English version of the book is basically a translation of the German original. Only in the ninth chapter were paragraphs dropped that related too narrowly to the German situation. Some mistakes were corrected, and a few additions alluding to later events were made. But the changes of the last years, both in the real world and in its philosophical analysis, have not been so momentous that a restructuring of the book appeared necessary. Still, the book will appear in some ways teutonic to the English-speaking reader (albeit written by a German alienated by the contemporary situation of his country's university system). Classical German philosophy from Kant through Fichte to Hegel, the philosophical sociology of Max Weber, the philosophical anthropology of Scheler, Plessner, and Gehlen, Hermann Heller's and Carl Schmitt's doctrine of the state, Hans Jonas's philosophical biology, and the interpretation of the history of political thought that we owe to Leo Strauss and Eric Voegelin all play an important role in the synthesis proposed here. Treating the ancient philosophers Plato and Aristotle and some modern thinkers, traditionally dear to the German tradition, such as Machiavelli, Hobbes, Vico and Montesquieu, again and again as intellectual contemporaries, will also appear quite Germanic. Nevertheless, the reader will find in the book a strong presence of contemporary British and American thinkers, such as Dworkin, Hare, Rawls, and Walzer, and will find recognition, even if on the basis of a teutonic thinking, of the political mission that Britain, and especially the United States, have played and continue to play in world history. When I was the Max Kade Professor at Ohio State University in 1996, I learned much from regular lunches with Daniel Farrell; I owe him special gratitude for all he taught me about American philosophy of law.

Even more than in the field of philosophy, I am aware that in the field of law my examples are predominantly German. This is partly owing to the limits of my education. But it is also based on my conviction that the German legal system is one of the fairest and most rational in the world. If what I defend as natural law in the seventh chapter on the whole—but by no means on all points—comes closer to continental than to common law, this is not due solely to the influence that was exerted upon me in Germany, where the links between philosophy and law have always been strong. I do indeed think that the common law doctrine of consideration in contract law, the doctrine of sovereign immunity, which strongly limits the state's liability, the discretion of the prosecutor, the plea bargain, the adversarial nature of the criminal process, and the fact that mens rea is not a necessary condition for punishment—to mention only a few things—are institutions no closer to sound reason and justice than are their continental counterparts. And I most certainly think that the lack of a more comprehensive ecological orientation in American law and politics endangers America's mission—one need think only of the energy and resource consumption per capita in the United States, which is the second highest in the world, could not be universalized to the whole world population, and is therefore unfair and immoral.

Many people have to be thanked for having made the publication of this book possible. First and foremost, the translator, Steven Rendall, did an excellent job. He worked with great competence, speed, and dedication. Given the difficulties of the book—of my German syntax, of the various disciplines dealt with, and of the many books quoted—I worked closely with Steven Rendall in revising the translation and in checking the many quotations in English translation, since only I had access to a good American library. This work took at least half of the year I was fortunate to spend at the Erasmus Institute of the University of Notre Dame. I thank the directors, James Turner and the Reverend Robert Sullivan, for having granted me the necessary time—originally planned for other purposes—and for having advised me again and again, together with other Erasmus fellows such as Brad Gregory, the Reverend Karl Morrison, and Dorothea Rice, on how to translate the technical terms of the work. (Robert Sullivan's generosity in time and knowledge was exceptional.) Several other colleagues at Notre Dame were kind enough to help me with their expertise: I mention only Georges Enderle, Edward Goerner, Jan Hagens, Jennifer Herdt, Donald Kommers, David O'Connor, Steven Smith, Catherine and Michael Zuckert. Donald Kommers's familiarity with both German and American law proved particularly helpful. Still, despite all efforts, there may be some mistranslations of technical terms; they are, of course, my own responsibility.

This translation could not have been financed without a very generous grant by the George W. Strake Endowment in the College of Arts and Letters at the University of

Notre Dame. To Mr. Strake and the Dean of the College, Mark Roche, who allocated this grant, I owe much, and I can only hope that this book proves worthy of their endeavors and of the mission of the great Catholic university they support. My secretary Claire Dettling-Shafer procured from the library with great efficiency and friendliness all the books I needed. Last, but not least, I want to thank my wife and our children for having borne with me when I was even more absentminded than usual due to the translation choices Steven Rendall and I had to make.

Notre Dame, August 2002

Introduction

S ince 1989 we have lived through lightning-fast historical transformations of vast significance, such as no one born after the Second World War has ever before experienced. And yet the current disorientation of politics does not have its deepest roots in the end of the Cold War. Rather, the end of the Cold War unveiled what the Cold War itself simply concealed: that a politics that wants to be taken seriously from a moral and intellectual point of view has to set goals and assume forms very different from those it has long taken for granted. It is no longer possible to resolve the problems of the twenty-first century with ideas of order borrowed from the nineteenth.

There are good grounds for thinking that the collapse of communism, instead of strengthening the First World, is in reality only a symptom of a more profound crisis of modernity that will soon have broader repercussions and will certainly affect the West. In many respects the promise with which modernity, in the form of present-day science and the Enlightenment, began its triumphal conquest of the planet has turned into a threat. The peace the modern state has produced through its monopoly on force, gives it (together with contemporary technology) a power that has resulted in an unprecedented explosion of violence in those cases in which international conflicts are settled by wars. The enormous wealth of one part of the world, which it owes to the combination of science, technology, and capitalism, has caused (because of the necessity of economic growth) needs to rise even faster than the means of satisfying them; thus it has not made people in wealthy countries happier than they were before; on the contrary, if poverty is measured by the difference between desire and fulfillment, it has made them even poorer.

The fraternal solidarity that was supposed to result from the tearing down of social barriers increasingly amounts to no more than general indifference and an inability to perceive differences in value in any terms other than monetary ones. The historically unprecedented equality achieved in the societies of the so-called First World has brought about a no less unprecedented inequality between these societies and those that have not yet come to terms with the process of modernization—an inequality that flagrantly contradicts the principle of inner equality from which it paradoxically springs. The broadening of individual human freedom culminates in a situation where the state is becoming increasingly reactive because of the exceptional complexity and interlacing of social systems, and is itself no longer free to do what is required for survival.

The progress of knowledge, because it not only describes but also changes the world, has helped produce a society that is less clear and comprehensible to its members than traditional societies were. Scientific and technological mastery over nature could end in an absorption of the spiritual and higher life by simpler natural forms—something that was not possible in cultures more closely connected with nature and that challenges the idea of progress in an unparalleled way. In fact, the rationalization of our society's subsystems is increasingly unable to keep us from feeling that reason is in decline—indeed, one can hardly avoid the impression of being at the mercy of a collective psychosis that becomes even more uncanny because disorientation regarding the goals to be achieved is combined with methodological perfection in employing the means to achieve them. The Enlightenment seems ultimately to have produced intellectuals who believe they have finally seen through everything and have concluded that it is no more possible to know reality than to have a normative preference for one type of action over another.

It is these last two assumptions that philosophy must criticize (though this is only its starting point). So long as we have not developed a theory of the current state of the world that is more appropriate to the phenomena concerned, more consistent logically, and structurally simpler than the one currently available, and so long as we have not succeeded in combining sureness of judgment with differentiation in analysis, politics will not be able to overcome its pompous helplessness. However, insight into the principles and developmental tendencies of present-day culture is clearly not sufficient. Without normative ideas concerning what may and should be striven for in politics, the latter can be no more than a narrow-minded struggle for power. In fact, the lack of a guiding model is even more worrisome than the lack of suitable descriptions of reality and its developmental tendencies. Because of the nature of human knowledge, beyond certain quite narrow limits we cannot know how the political world will look fifty years from now; and this is also desirable for the sake of the freedom of human action. But on the other hand, the fact that we have scarcely any idea how it *should* reasonably look is an index of the poverty of this culture, which is even more embarrassing for its intellectuals than for its politicians.

Here, however, we encounter an objection that is both theoretically important and itself a social fact that must be taken into account in any analysis of the current situation. This objection holds that in the modern world, politics is successful to the degree that it has nothing to do with morals, and that a moralization of politics not only does not help us resolve our problems, but ultimately makes them more difficult. Morals and politics are supposed to be independent spheres whose mixture is theoretically absurd and practically dangerous. This conception is the basic hallmark of modern political theory; present in an embryonic form in Machiavelli and Hobbes, it has become an axiom of the modern social sciences. The number of philosophers who have challenged this axiom, particularly in the twentieth century, is small. Most of them are open to two objections: first, they have not sufficiently reflected on the theoretical importance of this axiom; second, because they have not incorporated into their approach to a political ethics the relevant insights of social scientists regarding the laws governing the functioning of social systems, their approach is necessarily doomed to remain abstract.

The goals of the present work are implicit in the two preceding reflections. First, this book raises once again the metaethical question of the relationship between morals and politics and proposes a relatively complex answer to it. This answer involves a search for a synthesis between the classical, ancient European conviction that political philosophy must be based on ethics and the more modern notion that ethical arguments themselves have a political function. Thus it is not surprising that the classics of ancient European thought are constantly present in this book, though in constant dialogue with more recent authors. It will seem to many readers that the latter are given less attention, and in fact a greater familiarity with contemporary thinkers, particularly in the social sciences, would certainly be desirable. Nonetheless, it may be conceded that these classics have enduring value, whereas it is an open question how many current authors will still be read fifty years from now. In any case, the idea that the new is necessarily better than the old is a superstition, at least in philosophy. It arose from the religion of progress, and like any superstition, it has outlived its origin. It is partly responsible for the credulity with regard to intellectual fashions apparently evinced by so many intellectuals in our time. The second goal of this work is to propose, on the previously mentioned bases, a concrete political ethics for the situation in which humanity finds itself today. In this context, "today" is not an arbitrary indexical, but instead refers to the moment in world history in which the project of the modern has encountered its immanent limits and exhausted itself or even, in a certain sense, collapsed.

To develop a political ethics for the twenty-first century we must first deal with several preliminary questions, including three sets of problems that are of particular importance. First, we must explain what meaningful principles of ethical evaluation are. Second, these principles must be applied to political actions and to the political institutions that are the object of these actions; to do this, we must have the outlines of a theory of human beings and the state. Third, we need to determine, from the point of view of the philosophy of history, the situation in which humanity now finds itself. The work is divided into three parts: a normative foundation; a descriptive theory of the field of objects with which political philosophy is concerned and of its presuppositions; and a concrete political ethics that represents, so to speak, the conclusion drawn from a normative and a descriptive premise.

The first part begins with a historical overview of the various positions that have been adopted in the history of philosophy with regard to the relationship between morals and politics (chapter 1). Since throughout the twentieth century it was widely held that politics could not be subjected to moral evaluation, the concepts of the political and the moral have to be rethought, and certain popular objections to a moral evaluation of the political refuted (chapter 2). Then, in the framework of a metaethical examination of the most important ethical theories, the principles of ethics that underlie this book are developed (chapter 3). In the following chapters, I leave the strictly normative level to describe the objects involved in political ethics and use the ethical principles I have developed to evaluate the individual structures to be described at the end of chapters 4 and 5. First, I consider human beings, for example, against the background of organic evolution, though I can consider only those human qualities that are relevant to political philosophy (chapter 4). The most important of these qualities is the human striving for power. A phenomenology of power and an outline of a pure "cratology," that is, a discussion of the principles of the technique of power, constitute the center of the subsequent chapter (chapter 5). It is followed by a theory of the state and of its historical development (chapter 6). These three chapters sketch out a theory of the social and make up the second part of the book. Of course, they do not attempt to discuss all social phenomena, but focus primarily on those essential for understanding the political. Whereas a human being is a *substance* and power is a social *relation,* in the case of the state we are dealing with a *corporate group* in which relationships are substantialized.

Following these discussions, in the third part of the book I attempt to offer a legitimation of the state in general and to describe an ideal state (chapter 7). Then the question of what constitutes a just politics has to be addressed; while my answer to this question presupposes the blueprint developed in the preceding chapter, it cannot be reduced to this blueprint, since an ideal situation certainly does not yet exist. Here the problem of political ethics in the true sense arises, for if social institutions are as they should be, politics is essentially reduced to administration. Thus there are good arguments for a universal state, but so long as a plurality of states exists, their foreign policies must also be subjected to moral norms. We should mention in particular one political problem that arises in all periods of crisis—and not just in our own: How is political leadership possible in a situation in which moral paradigms are changing? In the context of the discussion of foreign policy, we will also touch upon the question of what normative criteria should be applied in shaping the political relationships between cultures with differing value systems (chapter 8). Clearly, answering such questions is a condition for survival in a situation like ours, in which global politics is emerging as a desideratum, although the differences between individual cultures have probably never been greater than they are today, and although the identity crisis that is troubling not only the former Second World but also the Third and First Worlds is of an almost unparalleled violence. The ninth and last chapter draws the consequences from everything that has been developed up to that point and outlines a political ethics for the twenty-first century. Whereas the seventh chapter deals with the ideal state *in general,* and the eighth discusses the *particular* problems that confront politics in non-ideal situations, the subject of the ninth chapter is politics in the *individual* historical situation of today. It will be objected that this chapter is more akin to intellectual journalism than to philosophy. I accept the objection if it is conceded that the proposals made in it are mediated by a justifying context not found in every kind of political journalism. It goes without saying that the competence of the philosopher declines as problems become more specialized; it would be dangerously naive to imagine that a philosopher is the person best qualified to draw up programs for political parties. Conversely, however, it is also correct to say that a community is hardly in a position to make significant political achievements if it lacks moral strength and conceptual clarity, which it is also the task of philosophy to convey.

The desire to be concrete means that this book cannot pursue its questioning by philosophical means alone. To illustrate ideas, I have repeatedly cited not only the relevant social sciences but also historians and poets. The fact that I cite with inordinate frequency examples taken from ancient historians is connected with my educational background, but since Machiavelli this has also become something of a tradition. However, independently of this tradition, it can hardly be denied that we owe the idea of political philosophy to the Greeks, and that the Romans were the people who demonstrated the greatest political capabilities. Quoting poets may seem strange, because it departs from current scholarly practice, but one observation regarding its justification should suffice. It is scarcely an accident that the two high points of political philosophy—which occurred in Greece in the fourth century BC and in seventeenth-century England—followed the composition of humanity's most important political tragedies: those of Aeschylus, Euripides, and Sophocles, on one hand, and those of Shakespeare on the other. (The historical tragedies of German classicism, which are aesthetically not comparable to those of the Greeks and Shakespeare, were nonetheless followed by German idealism's philosophy of the state.) The greatest political philosophers have not thought much more deeply about the problem of morals and politics than did these poets, and it would be a sign of intellectual arrogance to spurn their insights. Poets do not offer arguments, of course, but they point to phenomena that philosophy can undertake to analyze. One can learn from analytical philosophy that the use of examples aids thought—but we do not necessarily have to think up stories about Sally and Sam when our poets offer us far more complex and more deeply significant ones.

This book is characterized by the use of various methods—discussions of intellectual history as well as reflections based on conceptual analysis, phenomenological observations no less than recourse to the findings of the empirical and formal sciences—with the unwelcome consequence that its terminology is not entirely uniform. The book's thematic and methodological variety makes it even harder to read; it is not intended as an introduction to its subject, presupposes a great deal of knowledge, and is often too dense. In fact, I would recommend that anyone who is chiefly interested in concrete questions of application read the book from back to front—that is, begin with chapter 9, then work through chapter 8, and finally turn to the presuppositions of the whole argument. A subsequent run through the book might show that its construction does begin with what is in itself the simplest, even if it is not the simplest for us. And perhaps the reader might even agree that in view of the complexity of the subject matter, a methodological pluralism alone could do justice to the plethora of problems. Admittedly, I am only too painfully aware that the breadth of the subjects dealt with has sometimes been achieved at the cost of the required depth. Nonetheless, I may say that I know somewhat more than I have indicated in my deliberately limited footnotes; I am fully aware of the divergence from many current theories in the social sciences and historical studies that I have not explicitly addressed. But it is hard to deny that in our time there is above all a lack of an overview, of a vision of the whole, on the basis of which further progress can be made. Without such a vision, thoroughness in detail often becomes misleading and even dangerous. Thus an elaborate theory of the welfare state, such as we find for instance in Rawls's excellent *Theory of Justice*, is odd if it has nothing to say about the international dimension of social issues. Even if it is not always as precise as it might be, the present book is voluminous, and in a time when people's attention span is so short an even more voluminous book would probably remain unread.

To anyone familiar with the structure of philosophy it must seem surprising that after my brief outline of the systematic features of philosophy in *Die Krise der Gegenwart und die Verantwortung der Philosophie*, I did not next turn to the elaboration of a theoretical philosophy. This surprise is only too well justified, for it is inevitable that in the present book I have constantly had to presuppose things about which I have neither published nor yet achieved the necessary clarity. This is all the more dangerous because I am dealing with an area in which it is only too easy to make enemies—particularly when one departs from current prejudices by proposing new theses, thus putting in question unstable identities and repeatedly putting forward political views that are not in accord with those of any party. So far as the latter are concerned, I can say in good conscience that I have never consciously sought to wound other people—but that I consider it my duty to accept that result if it is an inevitable consequence of a primary interest in knowing and in the communication of knowledge. Intellectual relentlessness is a philosopher's first duty, even though it certainly remains desirable that it be tempered by friendliness. Regarding the first point, I might offer the excuse that we live in a time that surprises and displeases us in many respects, and that it seemed to me so urgent to clarify the relationship between morals and politics that I believed I had to sacrifice to it the purity of philosophical structure. Hobbes published the third part of his *De Cive* first because he hoped this appeal to reason would forestall the outbreak of civil war.[1] His hope was not fulfilled, but it is a testimony to this man's civic sense that he left nothing undone that was in his power and that might have preserved the peace, subordinating the orderly development of his philosophical work to the public good. What is now threatening humanity is far worse than the English Civil War, and the temporality of our existence sets unavoidable limits to the ability, which is constitutive of philosophizing, to distance oneself from social reality. If we waited to act (and publishing a book, and especially a book on political philosophy, *is* an act) until we were fully satisfied with the extent of our knowledge, we would never act—and thus never come to know anything. But this question itself is one of those that constitute the subject of this book.

The ideas put forth in this work matured during several journeys undertaken over the past few years. From the outset, these journeys were directed toward the problems dealt with in this book and took me to various European countries, the United States, the former Soviet Union, Latin America, India, and to Korea. Whether they have allowed

---

1. Foreword to the Reader (1839 ff. b; 2:151).

me to overcome a certain German provincialism, I cannot say; but in any event I have tried my best to do so. I am indebted for many, often crucial, insights to countless colleagues and friends, of whom I can name only a few. Gerardo Marotta, president of the Istituto Italiano per gli Studi Filosofici in Naples, and his collaborators, Dr. Antonio Gargano and Dr. Giuseppe Orsi, drew my attention to the subject and through their detailed knowledge of Italian political parties opened my eyes to a form of politics very different from German politics. Concerning the ethical dimension of the relationship between developing countries and developed countries, I learned a great deal from Professor Carlos Roberto Cirne-Lima (Porto Alegre) and Professor Manfredo Araújo de Oliveira (Ceará), as well as from the members of the Centre for the Study of Developing Societies in Delhi, especially Suresh Sharma; concerning the conditions for "successful" development, I am indebted to Professor Sokjin Lim (Seoul). My Moscow colleagues Professor Nelli Motrošilova and Professor Erich Solovyev, the younger philosophers Dr. Dmitri Nikulin and Dr. Sergey Poceluev, and the painter Maxim Kantor taught me a great deal about the ethical problems that arise in a totalitarian state and during its breakdown. I am also indebted for many essential insights to the ever-watchful eye of my teacher Professor Imre Tóth, who has personally experienced and battled totalitarianism in its various forms. The implications for ethics and politics of the scientific and technological transformation of the world were the subject of a stimulating interdisciplinary seminar hosted by the Department of Environmental Sciences at the ETH (Swiss Federal Institute of Technology) in Zurich and organized by my friends Professor Carlo Jaeger and Matthias Wächter. This seminar was attended by several colleagues in the natural sciences, notably Professor Hans Primas and Professor Walter Schneider. I benefited from their ideas as well as from those of Professor Anton Leist of the University of Zurich. Most of the references to great literary works on my subject I owe to my friends Professor Jan-Lüder Hagens and Professor Mark Roche, and to my father, Professor Johannes Hösle. Many specifically philosophical insights go back to conversations with my colleagues at the New School for Social Research, Professors Richard Bernstein, Agnes Heller, and Jerome Kohn, as well as to my friend Reiner Schürmann, who died much too young but whom I have never forgotten; to my Norwegian colleagues and friends Professor Audun Østi, Professor Egil, and Professor Truls Wyller (Universities of Oslo and Trondheim); and to my revered teacher, Professor Dieter Wandschneider. I am immensely indebted to discussions with friends involved in practical responsibilities, Dr. Matthias Hartwig, Leif Hovelsen, Dr. Christoph Jermann, Dr. Thomas Kesselring, Burghard and Waltraut Kreft, Professor Klaus Leisinger, Renato Parascandalo, Davide Scelzo, Dr. Heinz-Ulrich Schmidt, Rev. Valson Thampu, and Dr. Thomas Unnerstall, to my students at the Universities of Tübingen and Essen, and to the former vice-president of the German Constitutional Court, Professor Gottfried Mahrenholz. It hardly needs to be said that Hans Jonas and Karl-Otto Apel are the contemporary thinkers who have most influenced me—through the conversations I was able to have with them even more than through their writings: it becomes obvious in this book that in many respects I have sought to produce a synthesis of their two intellectual worlds. The arduous work of reading the manuscript and helping me correct many errors (no doubt others remain, for which I am solely responsible) was carried out by the following colleagues and friends: Professor Paul Münch (Essen), Professor Mark Roche (University of Notre Dame), Professor Georg Scherer (Essen), Professor Ulrich Steinvorth (Hamburg), Professor Dieter Wandschneider (Aachen), and two former government ministers, Professor Klaus-Michael Meyer-Abich and Reinhard Ueberhorst, whose criticism of my excessive belief in the state in an earlier version of the book I found helpful. My assistant Dr. Christian Illies and the theologian Dr. Bernd Goebel conscientiously worked through the text to eliminate the many linguistic shortcomings and possible imprecisions in content. My research student Matthias Donath, M.A., reliably and indefatigably found me the necessary books, and the final technical emendations were made by Mr. Florian Riedler. Without this selfless work, for which I heartily thank all those mentioned, the book would have had even more shortcomings. Among the institutions to which I am indebted for help, I owe the most gratitude to the Deutsche Forschungsgemeinschaft, which generously financed my travels by giving me a Heisenberg grant, the Fritz-Winter-Stiftung, which awarded me, on the recommendation of the Bavarian Academy of Sciences, the Fritz Winter Prize, and The Kulturwissenschaftliches Institut in Essen, where I was freed of all teaching duties for a year, which enabled me to complete the book in my colleague Klaus-Michael Meyer-Abich's study group.

But the simultaneously alarming and delightful feeling of witnessing the beginning of one of the greatest historical crises experienced by humankind was conveyed to me by the politics of Mikhail Gorbachev, a man who felt obligated to change the world in a radical way, and who has had the intellectual ability and the will power to do it. It is clear that the tragic dimension of his partial failure in no way diminishes his greatness; indeed, it lends his politics a special solemnity. No one who has made history ever really willed what he caused to happen; but being the tool of a power greater than oneself is perhaps a greater honor than merely imposing one's own will. If, to borrow Tocqueville's famous phrase, a new world requires a new political science,[2] then political philosophy is deeply indebted to this statesman for having awakened it, by his courage, from its long slumber. However, the overthrow of Soviet totalitarianism was possible only because there were also people who, in the name of the highest moral values, battled the system's structures of domination from the outside; the miracle of a non-violent end of Soviet totalitarianism became possible only because various people inside and outside these structures were guided in very different ways by certain moral standards. The great writer and politician Václav Havel represents the other moment in the binomial "morals and politics." This book is dedicated to him and to Mikhail Sergeyevitch Gorbachev, with a gratitude that I feel not only as a citizen of this planet but also as a philosopher.

---

2. "Il faut une science politique nouvelle à un monde tout nouveau" (1835 ff.; 1:62).

I

Normative Foundations

1

Outline of the Problem's Background in Intellectual History

The historical consciousness of our time clearly does not have positive consequences alone. The inability to understand directly questions related to the issue itself and the tendency to transform them into questions about *opinions* connected with specific problems is one of the historicism's most dangerous legacies for philosophy—from which analytical philosophy is free, in ways that are sometimes naive but always enviable. But this legacy cannot be overcome by ignoring it. When one can interpret the currently most widespread position with regard to the relationship between morals and politics as merely the momentary result of a process of development in intellectual history that has passed through various stages, it becomes easier to regard it as a position that has no claim to be conclusive, and it will be possible to escape from its influence—especially if a certain logic becomes discernible in this development. On one hand, it follows from this that the current position is not a mere accident that can be simply overcome. On the other hand, the discovery of a necessary development in the history of human consciousness also means that the latter does not collapse into a series of arbitrary events; and this discovery can encourage us to assume that the human mind is capable of grasping necessary truths, even if only by passing through a series of errors. Four other reasons make a short survey of the history of our problem useful, even if it will inevitably be far too superficial. First, the characterization of the most important ideas about our problem will provide a brief introduction to the issues that will later be discussed from a purely systematic point of view; moreover, it will make possible a more orderly arrangement of the historical references that will often be required in the following chapters. Second, the survey of intellectual history will enable us to clarify a thesis in the philosophy of history that will later prove useful in interpreting the modern world: a thesis regarding the rise of modern subjectivity. Third, even if German culture suffers from an excess of historical consciousness, the other extreme, which one sees in the United States, is no less dangerous—theoretically and practically. In any case, the inability to grasp the reasonableness of pre-modern forms of life is the source of many of America's errors in foreign policy. Fourth, it must be noted that earlier stages in history are past only in a certain sense: the psychic mechanisms of archaic peoples also emerge in modern peoples when they are confronted by crisis situations, for example, wars; and the unity of the individual and the polis in Greece has remained, even after its demise, an ideal without which the modern philosophy of the state cannot be understood.

In my *Philosophie der ökologischen Krise* (*Philosophy of the Ecological Crisis*) I distinguished five concepts of nature, as they are produced by an increasing abstraction of humans from their natural environment, culminating in Descartes's opposition between a pure consciousness and a nature without subjectivity to which this consciousness does not belong.[1] In an analogous way, I want to show here how the strict separation of morals and politics is the final result of a development that begins with their unity and leads to an increasingly sharp opposition between them. Whereas it is the relationship between physical being and consciousness that reaches its most extreme treatment in the Cartesian dualism of *res cogitans* and *res extensa*, in the opposition we will analyze here it is a question of the elaboration of the dualism between *Is* and *Ought*. Despite all the differences between them, the two dualisms are connected, and from this it follows that the ecological crisis has much to do with the current understanding of the relationship between morals and politics.

For sensitive modern people who have had the good fortune to be able to study ancient Greek culture, the latter remains the object of nostalgic ideas even if we clearly recognize that this world is not only irretrievably lost but lacked moral values of which moderns have a right, and even a duty, to be proud.[2] This ambivalent relationship with Greek culture is particularly characteristic of politics, even more than of the fine arts, poetry, and philosophy. On one hand, the lack of a universalist ideal in the classical Greek philosophy of the state is unacceptable to a modern person who does not allow himself to be completely dazzled by the charm of this culture: the complacency with which Plato and especially Aristotle[3] take slavery for granted, the unspeakable arrogance with which the Greeks look down on barbarians, the position (even though Plato challenges it) of women in the Greek state, and finally the limitation of the state to the city-state and the absence of more comprehensive attempts to humanize international relations, constantly show how much the Greek polis lacked. And yet, on the other hand, no other culture elaborated with comparable intensity a conception of the exceptional moral relevance of political action. The Greeks of classical times were deeply

---

1. (1991), 48 ff.

2. Even the most profound apologist for modernity, Hegel, cannot forgo the following statement regarding Greece in his *Vorlesungen über die Geschichte der Philosophie* (*Lectures on the History of Philosophy*)—as a counterfactual conditional, of course: "Wenn es erlaubt wäre, eine Sehnsucht zu haben, so nach solchem Lande, solchem Zustande" (1969 ff.; 18:173). ("If nostalgia were allowed, it would be for such a land, for such a condition.")

3. Cf., for example, *Politics* 1253b15 ff.

convinced that moral action could be completely carried out only by participating in political activity; the conception of a purely individual ethics without relation to political ethics does not emerge until the Hellenistic period.[4] Moreover, the classical understanding of politics includes the view, complementary to the one mentioned first, that politics itself must conform to moral norms if it is not to lose its inner dignity. Taken together, these two views represent (to simplify slightly) the specific difference between classical Greek political philosophy and all later forms of political thought—and all earlier ones, for if political *philosophy* is a Greek achievement, a pre-philosophical *reflection* on the state is found before the Greeks as well.

1.1. Political Feeling in Archaic Cultures

We have no contemporary written testimony regarding the archaic cultures that preceded high cultures. We could ignore such cultures here; one can speak of a "state" in them only if one adopts an extremely broad concept of what constitutes a state. However, since it is in fact important for political philosophy that the enduring organized state and especially individualism are late products of historical development, a few brief observations are appropriate.

In these archaic cultures the subject is absorbed into the community; outside of the latter the subject can neither physically survive nor preserve its identity. Religion and politics are not yet differentiated institutionally, or are only beginning to be so differentiated; and above all morals are reduced to the norms the group considers valid. These norms are felt to be immediately valuable, and even to be the paradigm of all values, among other reasons because they exercise a terrible power within the group, which violators of these norms experience in themselves. Archaic people can distinguish between *Is* and *Ought* still less than between animate and inanimate. The only justification of rule they know is reference to ancestral traditions that were ultimately founded by the gods; however, these traditions may contain the seed of a critique of the present. The rites of archaic cultures celebrate their own institutions, to which they owe their survival in a threatening natural environment, yet the meaning of these institutions is also anchored in this environment. The only way beyond the insularity of these cultures is via the problem posed by the existence of other cultures. For the norms of others are often valued negatively; and even if the reflection that follows probably emerged only much later and presupposes intellectual operations that must have taken place over hundreds of thousands of years, this negative valuation could lead a given culture to the idea that its own norms must appear just as valueless to others as theirs appear to it. It is far more likely that people became aware that, with regard to other groups, their own group observed norms that were not only different from but partly

---

4. Cf. the two classical loci: Plato, *Republic* 368c ff. and Aristotle, *Nicomachean Ethics* 1094b8 ff.

opposed to those they considered valid in dealing with members of their own group. To be sure, this contradiction is all too easily concealed by the fact that they were called upon to obey the most demanding norm governing internal relationships—self-sacrifice for the community—chiefly in situations that were connected with killing people from other groups, that is, in war.

1.2. Reflections on the State in Advanced Cultures

Advanced cultures did not lead solely to the emergence of the state as an enduring center of action for the society as a whole that at the same time performs specific, clearly distinguished functions. Every advanced culture also has a justification of its ruling order, though it is usually formulated in the language of myth. The social order is interpreted as an image of the cosmic order and traced back to the will of the gods; but this type of justification is pre-philosophical in nature. However, in some advanced cultures politics becomes for the first time an object for analytical examination. The so-called Chinese legalists[5] and the Indian authors of *Arthaśāstra* literature[6] are the best known example of this kind of political thought. The insights into the necessary means of maintaining and extending power found in these works are astonishingly detailed and have in many respects not lost their relevance. These writings are obviously based on experience gained in the centuries-long processes of state-building and in the political power struggles connected with them. In particular, the best known and doubtless also most important Indian text of this kind, the *Kauṭilīya-Arthaśāstra,* can also claim to have provided a major systematization of such insights; the theory of foreign relations developed in book 7 remains an exceptional intellectual achievement to which nothing in Greek or Roman culture is comparable. Max Weber's famous statement that compared with the *Arthaśāstra* Machiavelli is harmless[7] is all the more apt in that the collection goes far beyond Machiavelli in the dry, matter-of-fact way in which it offers detailed advice on liquidating opponents by trickery and force, constructing a network of in-

---

5. On the ancient and later philosophers of the state and law in ancient Chinese philosophy, who were themselves active as statesmen, see A. Forke (1964), 60 ff., 441 ff. The most important of these are Shang Yang and Han-fei-tzu.

6. Since at the beginning of the *Kauṭilīya-Arthaśāstra* (*Kautiliya's Treatise on Utility*) it is explained that the text is a compilation of earlier works, and earlier sources are constantly cited, thematically related works must have been produced long before it (cf. F. Wilhelm [1960]). Even if it is attributed to King Candragupta Maurya's minister Kauṭilya or Cāṇakya (end of the fourth century BC), the final version of this work, which was probably written over a long period of time, was produced in the first centuries AD. Today it can be consulted in the easily accessible three-volume edition translated by R. P. Kangle (1988). Kāmandaka's *Nītisāra* (probably eighth-century) is also important.

7. (1919b), 445.

formers, and even sacrificing one's own spies if this proves advantageous.[8] I cite only one typical recommendation: In order to silence an enemy of the king, an agent should draw the enemy's attention to a particularly beautiful woman. When the enemy has abducted this woman, another agent disguised as a Brahman should pretend to be a relative of the woman and complain to the enemy's allies. If the latter turn against their ally, the king should support him and thus split the group opposing him. If, on the other hand, the enemy's allies accept his misdeed, the king should have the false Brahman murdered, and blame the crime on his enemy—for the latter's allies cannot remain indifferent to the murder of a Brahman.[9] What is particularly brutal about this suggestion is the planned murder of one's own faithful agent—one thinks of the way British Intelligence instrumentalizes its own agent in John Le Carré's justly famous novel, *The Spy Who Came in from the Cold*, which made him a celebrity.

And yet none of this alters the previous claim that the Greeks were not the first to found political science but the first to found political philosophy.[10] For they were the first to ask not just why certain political institutions and certain modes of political action serve to maintain a given ruler's power but also why they are morally better than other possible alternatives, and even why the political sphere is necessary at all on moral grounds; and they sought rational answers to these questions. It is true that one finds in the *Kauṭilīya-Arthaśāstra* the moral argument—which reminds us of later attempts to justify the state—that if the state lacks the power to punish, the "law of fishes," by which the bigger eat the smaller, will hold sway;[11] but this argument is the only moral one in the book, a tiny island in a sea of purely descriptive statements or hypothetical imperatives: a sea in which recommendations regarding raising elephants seem to have the same moral status as those regarding the liquidation of opponents.

The use of the concepts "descriptive statement" and "hypothetical imperative" is in a certain sense misleading—they use our language to speak of a culture that was still far

---

8. See only 9.6.39. In order to win the trust of the enemy, a false defector should betray the incompetent agents on his own side.

9. 11.1.44 ff., at least if we follow J. J. Meyer and R. P. Kangle in reading *dūṣyasamghamukhya-madhye* instead of *duṣyaḥ*, which would make no sense. For how could one use an enemy for such an operation? Moreover, it is not difficult to explain why most manuscripts adopted this variant reading: the recommended sacrifice of the pawn evidently struck the copyists as too repellent.

10. Since I am able to read only Indian and not Chinese literature in the original, and since I am only slightly familiar with the latter in translation, I can compare only India and Greece with a reasonable degree of competence. Nonetheless, similar observations regarding China are also made by Sinologists, though some disagree, e.g., H. Roetz (1992), to whom we owe an admirable reconstruction of Chinese ethics in the "axial age," to use Jaspers's term. But however much we are willing to grant Roetz's claim that the level of thought in Chinese practical philosophy has thus far been underestimated, the qualitative difference between Chinese and Greek writings about the state still seems to me undeniable: pure reflection on legitimacy, such as we encounter in Plato's *Republic,* is not to be found in the texts cited by Roetz.

11. 1.4.13. See also 1.13.5. This idea is found in many Indian texts.

from becoming aware of such categories. The modern view that the social world consists of facts without inherent value is essentially alien to these advanced cultures; in all innocence, they presuppose that the social order within which state power is exercised has an intrinsic value and that its religious justification is acceptable[12]—but they simply *presuppose* this. It is not grounded, and no attempt to provide such a grounding is even seen as desirable. According to Indian tradition, Kauṭilya, to whom this classical Arthaśāstra is attributed, was a Brahman; and the image of him found in later literature (where he embodies, as Machiavelli does in European literature, the quintessence of the highly intelligent politician) lacks—unlike the European image of Machiavelli—any demonic characteristics. He is seen as a traditionalist of exceptional intelligence, no less pious than crafty: for example, in Viśākhadatta's drama, "Mudrārākṣasa," Kauṭilya is an exclusively positive hero despite, or perhaps because of, his lack of scruples. The *Arthaśāstras* and the works of the Chinese Legalists seek, within a social system that is thoroughly questioned, to formulate techniques for use in power struggles—that is essentially their interest, and it is very far from the positions of Machiavelli and Hobbes, though some of the concrete insights in these texts may remind us of these later thinkers.

1.3. Greek Political Philosophy

One can understand a great deal about the essence of ancient European cultures—Greek, Roman, and medieval—by noting that they did not produce the kind of unprejudiced analyses of power struggles found in the advanced cultures we have just discussed, despite the state-building achievements of the Romans in particular, which far surpass the achievements not only of the Indians, but of the Chinese as well. Not until the beginning of modern times do we find a similarly sober examination of the phenomenon of power—an examination which is nonetheless, despite all its superficial similarities to those produced by the previously mentioned Asian cultures, utterly different from them in nature. For our subject, the innovation of early European thinkers is crucial—it can be rejected, but it cannot be ignored.

Their innovation consists in the fact that for the first time in the history of humankind the question of legitimacy is raised as such—and this is, in fact, the fundamental precondition for political philosophy. In the Sophistic movement, the first movement of enlightenment to succeed within a culture,[13] social institutions, religious

---

12. The use of magical practices is justified by the maintenance of the four castes. See 14.1.1. This does not, however, exclude an instrumentalization of superstitions for political ends: see, for example, 5.2.39 f., 10.3.33, 13.1.3 and 8, 13.2.1 ff.

13. To be sure, other cultures also experienced the beginnings of movements of enlightenment—but they never became decisive for intellectual life. Consider, for instance, the fate of the atheistic Nāstikas in India, whose ideas have survived—in a much reduced number—chiefly thanks to the polemics directed against them.

beliefs, and forms of rule are presented not as unquestionable facts but rather as requiring justification. The focus is not on the most effective ways of achieving certain
goals, but rather on the ultimate goals of individual and collective action. This is not the
place to explain why it was Greek culture that took this step, perhaps the most momentous in human history; let us note only that the emergence of political philosophy
among the Greeks was based on at least three non-philosophical presuppositions.[14]
First, there is Attic drama—especially tragedy, which by representing conflicts between
institutions (Aeschylus) or between individuals and institutions (Sophocles and Euripides) raised the question of which of two parties, both apparently appealing to currently
valid norms, was right.[15] But through its institutionalized ironizing of the Greeks'
own social reality, comedy also promoted the development of a political philosophy
that examined this social reality. This is also true in cases where comedy is directed not
against currently accepted social practices but rather against critical and utopian social
thought, as in Aristophanes' "Clouds" (*Nephelai*) and in his "Women at the Ecclesia"
(*Ekklesiazousai*), which anticipated Plato's society in which property and wives are held
in common—for in doing so it raised these issues and encouraged thought about the
state and society. Second, we must mention historiography. In Herodotus we can see
clearly how much the encounter with other cultures must have stimulated moral and
political thinking;[16] in addition, his work also contains the first normative discussion
of various forms of government.[17] Finally, Thucydides understood the logic of political
power struggles better than any of his predecessors and better than most of his successors. He banished all mythical explanations from historical writing, but he nonetheless
saw history as a meaningful series of events.[18] Third—or rather first, considering its
significance for our subject—the democratic tradition of some Greek states played a
decisive role. The pride in this new form of government, unknown to other peoples, as

---

14. On the following points, see, among other works, C. Meier's remarkable book (1980a).

15. See my analysis of ancient tragedy (1984b).

16. See the well-known Anecdote III 38 (as well as VII 152) and its reflection in the *Dissoi Logoi*
2, 18 (H. Diels and W. Kranz [1954], 2:409).

17. III 80 ff. It throws a dazzling light on the birth of political philosophy that this alleged debate is supposed to have taken place after the murder of the false Smerdis (if he really was the false
one) and his brother: the rational search for a form of government is particularly necessary in a situation where there is a vacuum of political power, and the most far-reaching power vacuum is produced after a coup. Shedding blood and political thought are closely connected, as the example of
Hobbes also shows.

18. Since Thucydides is sometimes seen as the forerunner of a value-free historiography, I should
say here why I consider this interpretation to be an error. Thucydides judges, just as Tocqueville does—
but both authors try to do justice to both the advantages and the disadvantages of the system in question. The greatness of Athens seems to Thucydides just as objective a fact as its moral failings; and his
own interest is, as it will later be Plato's, to understand precisely how brilliance and guilt are connected.
This can be called "tragic consciousness," but the tragic can be experienced only by a person who is fully
conscious of the objectivity of the opposed values. See below, chap. 2, n. 39.

well as the possibility it offered for many persons to participate in political life, doubt-less encouraged theoretical reflection on politics. An excellent work in political science such as the *Constitution of Athens* (transmitted among Xenophon's works, but clearly not written by him), with its sober analyses of power relationships, could only have been written in a democracy, despite all its criticism of democracy.

To be sure, the Sophistic school has a striking parallel in the European Enlighten-ment of the seventeenth and eighteenth centuries.[19] However, the later movement took place under different circumstances, which we will discuss later on, and which were re-sponsible for the fact that in the modern period morals and politics were much more strictly separated from one another than would have been possible in antiquity, even though the question of legitimation was first raised in that period. Probably no work shows us more clearly the difference between ancient and modern political philosophy, especially regarding the relationship between morals and politics, than Plato's *Repub-lic*. On one hand, Plato's key experience was the execution of the man who sought to an-swer the Sophists' question by developing an ethics that was to be both grounded in human reason and absolutely binding. Hardly any event is more symptomatic of the emerging opposition between politics and morals than the fact that the founder of ethics was killed by his state—and for offenses connected with his activity as an ethi-cist.[20] And yet on the other hand, it is just as clear that Socrates saw himself primarily as a servant of his state[21]—he thinks he has earned the right, through his philosophizing, to be maintained by the state, and he hopes that even in Hades he will be able to con-tinue the intersubjective dialogue he has carried on throughout his life.[22] In any case, a purely subjective salvation was never his goal.

As we have said, a similar ambivalence characterizes Plato's *Republic*. On one hand, it is the first time in Western history that a distance is taken from the practical social world, a distance that must have been virtually incomprehensible to Plato's con-temporaries and is therefore justified by thoroughgoing epistemological and ontologi-cal investigations. In actuality, one can hardly understand the marvelous, almost cycli-cal structure of the *Republic* unless one constantly keeps in mind that here, for the first time in human history, possible suggestions regarding what should be considered valid are no longer to be assessed on the basis of the values accepted in one's own culture; in-stead, these values are themselves to be measured against ideal norms. This is a genu-

---

19. I discussed the similarities between these two movements in an earlier book (1984a; 225 ff.), but neglected the distinction between them. In a subsequent essay (1993) I sought to correct and com-plement my earlier discussion of this point.

20. This distinguishes Socrates from other philosophers who died opposing tyranny, as Zeno of Elea (cf. Diogenes Laertius IX 26 f.) is supposed to have done. For if there is a historical basis for the story about Zeno, he tried to overthrow a specific tyranny *as a citizen*, and not *as a philosopher*; in con-trast, Socrates sought to bring about a radical transformation of his countrymen's mentality.

21. See the interpretation of the *Apology* in C. Jermann's fine book on Plato (1986), 62 ff.

22. *Apology* 36d ff.; 40e ff.

ine "turnaround of the soul"[23] that is probably more radical than any that preceded it, and influenced European culture to an extent that can hardly be overestimated. It is well known that Plato speaks of this "turnaround of the soul" in the allegory of the cave, the third of the three allegories constituting the center of the epistemological and ontological books V–VII, which themselves stand at the center of Plato's masterwork.[24] In these books Plato develops his doctrine of Ideas with a thoroughness not found in any earlier dialogue, and this confirms the claim that one of the functions of the doctrine of Ideas (in addition to grounding mathematics) consists in anticipating what was later to be known as the distinction between *Is* and *Ought*. Nowhere was it so urgent to offer a detailed explanation of this doctrine of Ideas as in the political context, precisely because it was much harder for Greeks to accept that their polis experienced as immediately valuable needed to be normatively grounded in an authority that transcended it than that such a grounding was necessary for mathematics. The importance Plato ascribes to mathematics in the education of the philosopher-king,[25] at which later readers have usually smiled,[26] results from this relationship: it is mathematics that can bring about this turnaround of the soul because it alone prepares the way for the idea that the world of facts—including the social world in which we live—is not the true reality. However, the mathematical method cannot solve the final problem of the grounding of politics. For its nature consists in the fact that it starts out from concepts and propositions that it can no longer ground itself. But a grounding that remains hypothetical does not satisfy the ultimate demands of reason. That is the point of the second of Plato's three allegories, which, despite its brevity and inferior appeal to the imagination, has a certain claim to be the most important philosophically, because of its central position.[27] Plato's more detailed reflections on this question, which in our own time corresponds to the problem of the ultimate foundation, are not relevant here. However, it should be noted that this question first arose in a work of political philosophy, apparently because Plato believed that a political philosophy that did not raise this question lacked a center. Perhaps he was less incorrect in thinking so than most later political philosophers seem to have believed.

Nonetheless, in order to arrive at an adequate understanding of Plato's place in history, it is equally important to emphasize that the separation of *Is* from *Ought* that he introduces is infinitely less radical than the one that we find in modern thought, and especially in Kant. The marvelous tension of the *Republic* consists in the fact that after

---

23. *Republic* 518c ff.

24. On the special function of the central part in Plato's dialogues, see E. Wyller's impressive study (1970), for example p. 30.

25. 524d ff. For Plato, the practical utility of mathematical knowledge—in military matters, for instance—is completely secondary in comparison to the change in consciousness produced through the recognition of ideal entities.

26. See, for instance, Hobbes (1651), 407.

27. 509c ff.

opening up an unprecedented dualism, Plato devotes all his intellectual energy to a construction that will bring the philosophers back into the polis.[28] This is true on two levels.

First, the distinction between Ideas and appearances is not an absolute dualism, because the former are the models for the latter. The empirical world—to which nature,
the individual soul, and the polis belong—does not lack any order and any value, but
rather reflects the ideal order that has value in the highest degree and in whose value the
empirical world participates. The world of appearances does not derive its value from itself, but it has—through participation—a value all the same; even the rule-governed
movement that produces the diverse forms of government, including the negative ones,
is grounded in the Ideas and is the expression of an affirmative structure. Whereas in the
modern period the value-positing subjectivity confronts a social world emptied of value
in its facticity, in Plato the individual subjectivity is in no way the source of values; instead, the latter have their source in the ideal world. The individual subjectivity is no less
inadequate than the individual polis, and for that reason the Platonic model cannot release the utopian energies that we find in modern times, after subjectivity has repressed
any consciousness of its ultimate finiteness and is prepared to use the authority it has
granted itself to create the political world anew. Moreover, one of the most important
differences between Platonic and modern utopias consists in the fact that Plato's battle
against the individualism that was emerging in his time—and which led him to go so far
as to demand that the Guardians share women and property—is guided by a conception
of community that had only shortly before his time become moribund. The moral obligation he defines is in many ways modeled on the past being of his own culture.[29] On the
other hand, the striving of modern utopias to transcend individualism radically contradicts the essence of the modern, and thereby overlooks the fact that the modern utopia is
itself the result of a form of individualism, without which this kind of resolute distancing from one's own culture would not be possible at all. In order to understand the differences between ancient and modern utopias it is also important to take their relationship to history into account. Plato would have found incomprehensible the idea that the
course of history could validate values; and even the notion that history could produce
an approach to a normatively justified goal is alien to him. It is true that in Plato we find
a differentiated philosophy of history.[30] But for him, any intellectual or political development occurs within a structure that repeats itself cyclically: the concept of progress

---

28. The movement out of the polis and then back to it characterizes not only Plato's basic intellectual operation—as it is described in the allegory of the cave, for instance—but also determines
the structure of the *Republic,* whose central books concern the vision of the Ideas, but whose beginning and end deal with traditional political questions. Thus the *Republic* itself recapitulates the movement that is its subject. It is a work of art in which form and content coincide, and whose very structure expresses the relationships between art and the state.

29. This was rightly pointed out by Hegel, for example, in the preface to the *Philosophy of Right*
(1969 ff.; 7:24). The influence of ancient Greek morality is particularly evident in Plato's *Laws.*

30. See K. Gaiser (1968), 203 ff., and V. Hösle (1984a), 589 ff.

therefore cannot have the meaning it has in modern political philosophy, and moreover, within a cycle intellectual progress goes hand in hand with the dissolution of inherited mores, so that the philosopher necessarily comes too late to realize his ideas. Plato's utopia is not a direct recipe for action; his consciousness of the transcendental difference between Idea and appearance, as well as his pessimistic philosophy of history, force him to acknowledge that the true state exists only in heaven,[31] no matter how much political reality may copy it in various forms.

Second, in the concrete formulation of Plato's ideal the decisive point consists in the mutual interpenetration of soul and state. Nowhere is Plato more Greek than in the idea that soul and state are strictly parallel to each other, and this means that individual ethics and political ethics are also parallel. As is well known, according to Plato the classes in the ideal state should correspond to the parts of the soul, and even the degenerate forms taken by the state, which are investigated in the eighth and ninth books of the *Republic*, are each correlated with a specific human type. The virtue of the state proceeds from the virtue of its citizens; Machiavelli's idea that the virtue—that is, the performance—of the state is directly related to the vices of its citizens would have been incomprehensible for Plato and Aristotle. Yet the soul and the state not only correspond to each other, they are also in harmony with the cosmos.[32] No matter how strange some of the elaborations of this idea may seem to us,[33] it is important to emphasize that the state is not considered a phenomenon involving solely relations among humans; it also has its place in a comprehensive natural order[34]—a further essential difference from modern political philosophy. A decisive consequence of the idea of order is that nature, soul, and state appear to be hierarchically structured. This is particularly important for the soul. According to Plato, the value of a soul depends on how "just" it is, that is, how far it "performs its own task"—for justice consists, for Plato, in a properly ordered relationship among the parts of a whole.[35] The difference between this conception and that of modern thinkers such as Hobbes is immediately clear: whereas for the latter, justice consists in obeying the laws of the state, for Plato, justice is first of all a concept that makes it possible to evaluate states. Second, he conceives justice on the basis of the conditions for the functioning of

---

31. *Republic* 592a f.; cf. 499cf., 502af.

32. The idea that the order of the state mirrors that of the cosmos is not peculiar to Greek culture, but is also found in many high cultures. Plato's new discovery consists in the insight that the state and the *soul* are homologous (cf. Voegelin [1952], 93 ff.); but this discovery is mediated by old convictions.

33. I am thinking, for example, of the idea that one should emulate the revolutions of the cosmos (*Timaeus* 90cf.).

34. The greatest literary expression of this conception is found at the end of Cicero's *De Republica*, in the "Somnium Scipionis," at the end of a work in whose first book (chapter 13 ff.) astronomical questions are discussed as well. Cosmophilosophical arguments are also common in medieval political theory; I mention here only the fifteenth chapter of Al-Farabi's work on the perfect state (1985; 228 ff.) and Dante's *De Monarchia* (see, for example, I 7, I 9 [1950; 42 ff., 46 ff.]).

35. 433a–445e.

the whole, not on that of an individual's rights and claims. Third, even if an individualistic notion of right is alien to Plato, we should note that his state is ultimately founded on an individual virtue, namely, the soul's just relationship to itself. A just and temperate soul is one in which the lower part is subordinated to the higher. This in no way means only—as in many parts of modern ethics—that reason should somehow control the impulses so that they do not result in actions that contradict the interest in self-preservation. In Plato, reason is far more a faculty that enjoys knowledge of the truth not for its utility in some respect, but rather as a goal in itself; and the value of a person is directly dependent on the degree to which knowledge—and not, for example, the satisfaction of ambition or even sensual desires—is a goal in itself. Rather than the appropriation of information, it is this attitude toward knowledge, namely the experience of the cognition of truth as an end in itself, that is the goal of the process of education; and education is both the condition and the task of the state.

Before engaging in political activity, one must first establish a just hierarchy within one's soul; anyone who has not put his soul's house in order will ultimately do nothing but harm in the house of the state, unless he is ruled by those who have succeeded in establishing such a hierarchy in their souls. For Plato, the ideal state is one in which political power is exercised by those in whom the higher part of the soul rules. But this means that the ideal state is one in which philosophers are kings or kings are philosophers.[36] However, here Plato encounters a very peculiar problem. For those who should really rule because they have the most elevated insights have no interest in ruling, because for them knowledge is the highest goal in itself.[37] They must be compelled to rule; but who could compel them? Obviously, only they themselves could do so—but then they would have to sacrifice their justified striving for happiness to the happiness of a community that will know how to resist being forced to be happy. Thus the philosopher is confronted by a thankless task for which he is poorly prepared; because he is guided by the ideal world, he lacks any instinct for power. In this respect, philosophical talent seems more a curse than a blessing, and Socrates's fate not an unfortunate accident but an inevitable result.[38] The image of the tormented and ultimately impaled just man, who is indeed moral, but does not seem to be so and therefore calls down on himself passionate hatred[39]—an image in which the whole of Greek culture perhaps comes closest to Jewish culture and most deeply anticipates Christianity—endangers the program of a unity of individual and political ethics.

This is precisely the point at which Aristotle begins, and we owe to him the first critique of excessively utopian thought. As mistaken as it is to compare Plato with modern

---

36. 473cff.

37. 519bff.

38. Similarly, Plato's experience in Syracuse can claim a certain general validity; the Seventh Letter, which describes, among other things, the complicated web of relationships among Plato, Dion, and Dionysius II, can compete with the greatest political tragedies.

39. 361ef.

totalitarianism,[40] the inhumane aspects of his vision of the state that suppress the individual are even more undeniable in the bitter work of his old age, the *Laws*, than they are in the *Republic*. In any case, Aristotle can claim—for instance, on the basis of his empirical analyses of existing constitutions[41]—to have produced insights into political science and the sociology of the state that we find lacking in Plato, and this is particularly true with regard to democracy, to which Plato seldom does justice (even though in making such judgments we must constantly keep in mind that ancient democracy was essentially different from modern democracy). Nonetheless, Plato and Aristotle are in agreement insofar as they distinguish the various forms of the state not only in terms of whether power is held by one person, by several persons, or by all, but also, intersecting this formal criterion, in terms of whether power is exercised well or badly, in accordance with the laws or in violation of them. As a result of the combinations of these two criteria, for the Greeks, after Plato's *Statesman*,[42] the state could take any one of six forms (in addition to an ideal one). It is worth noting that Plato and Aristotle are at pains to bring good and bad monarchies together under a general concept: for them, these are fundamentally different forms of the state, because the substantive question regarding the moral legitimacy of the corresponding political systems enters into their conception of the form of the state. It is symptomatic of Jean Bodin's radical modernity that he breaks with this moral assessment of political structures and treats monarchy, aristocracy, and democracy as forms of the state that are characterized solely by the way in which power is exercised—without any reference to their greater or lesser justice.[43]

Another great achievement of Aristotle's is to have arrived at a precise understanding of the *categorial* and not merely quantitative distinction separating the family and the state[44] (between which he locates the village); this is one of the grounds on which he can provide a convincing criticism of Plato's communism.[45] Whereas in Plato the state threatens partly to absorb the family, and partly to be itself conceived on the model of a large family, Aristotle develops a theory of different social structures with

---

40. See Popper (1945), whose sense of history and familiarity with the most important foundational strategies of practical philosophy in no way equals his theoretical achievements. It is precisely the moral obligation of politicians in Plato that shows the distance between his approach and that of modern totalitarianism, which in both its forms is the result of the subversion of Western belief in an objective morality whose ultimate foundation transcends society.

41. Of 158 studies of this kind, only the "Constitution of Athens" is still largely extant. On Aristotle's *Politics*, the history of whose genesis is extremely complex, see, for example, E. Schütrumpf (1980).

42. 291cff., 302bff. Similar passages in Aristotle, *Nicomachean Ethics* 1160a31ff., *Politics* 1279a22 ff.

43. See the beginning of the first chapter of the second book of Bodin's *Les Six Livres de la République*. The normative, substantive criterion is considered a detail which one must move beyond if one wants to arrive at useable definitions (1576; 251f.). See also Hobbes (1651), 239f., in the nineteenth chapter of *Leviathan*.

44. 1252a7ff.

45. 1261a16ff.

their own organizing principles, of which the state is only one, even if it is doubtless the most important. Since Aristotle, political philosophy has had to deal with the question of how the state is related to pre-political institutions. Here we should also emphasize the importance of Aristotle's rejection of Plato's extreme demands by noting that because of human nature, even institutions based on the noblest ideals inevitably produce certain negative consequences. With great soberness Aristotle reminds us that people feel less responsible for public property,[46] and foresees conflicts between persons of differing abilities.[47] On the other hand, we must acknowledge that in comparison with Plato, Aristotle has a significantly inferior understanding of the nature of normative statements and their logical independence from descriptive statements. That goes for his whole practical philosophy—that is, not just for political philosophy but for ethics as well. From the point of view of justification, Aristotle's philosophy is in many respects a step backward with regard to Plato's. Combining his substantively correct insights, and especially his persuasive critique of utopianism, with a position that maintains the independence of *Is* and *Ought* remains an important task.

However, all Aristotle's differences with Plato cannot change the fact that the two greatest Greek philosophers are much closer than the former's polemics often suggest. The precedence of the theoretical over the practical form of life is even greater in Aristotle than it is in Plato,[48] but results in fewer systematic problems because Aristotle abandons the thesis of the philosopher-ruler and limits himself to the notion that philosophers should advise those who hold political power.[49] (However, Aristotle also fails to offer a convincing explanation as to why the philosopher is supposed to dedicate himself to politics.) Plato and Aristotle both see a narrow connection between morals and politics.[50] In Aristotle too, the state, even though it has been established solely in the interest of survival, has as its goal the good life.[51] However, Aristotle's conception of the good life is more eudaemonistic than Plato's: for Aristotle, the good life is by definition one that leads to happiness. On the other hand, in a remarkably circular way, Aristotle's concept of happiness is not free from normative connotations. For him, it is by no means true that every human being could become happy if his needs were satisfied, because an individual's capacity for happiness depends on his needs and his virtues. In any case,

---

46. 1261b33 f.

47. 1263a11 ff.

48. *Nicomachean Ethics* 1177a12 ff; *Politics* 1324a13 ff.

49. See the circular sent to Alexander the Great περί βασίλεὶς (*Peri basileias*), frag. 2 in W. D. Ross's collection of fragments (1955).

50. See for example *Politics* 1276b16 ff, where all restrictions are formulated against the background of a fundamental harmony of individual and political virtues, at least among the rulers of the good forms of the state. Even clearer is 1323b33 ff., where it is said in general that the best life for the individual and for the state coincide. The first passage is cited with approval by Thomas Aquinas, who sums up thus: "Unde impossibile est quod bonum commune civitatis bene se habeat, nisi cives sint virtuosi, ad minus illi quibus convenit principari" (*Summa theologica* I/II, q.92 a.1 ad tertium).

51. 1252b27 ff., 1280b39 ff.

happiness is not possible without a comprehensive education like that described in the two final books of the *Politics*. A state truly worthy of the name must be concerned with the virtues of its citizens.[52]

On this basis, it goes without saying that the law of the state has to be rooted in natural law; the latter is based on moral intuitions.[53] There is a criterion anterior to positive law that makes it possible to distinguish just forms of the state from perverted ones: whether priority is given to the common good (which implies the good life for as many people as possible) or to the particular interest of the rulers.[54] These two possibilities are also present when the majority holds power—and only when the majority is concerned to promote the common good and does not tyrannize the minority is the result a good form of the state, namely the polity, for which Aristotle feels strong sympathies. Here Aristotle argues as a typical representative of ancient philosophy, insofar as he refers to the republic's ability to resolve certain problems of substance. For example, he offers the argument that a large number people of average intelligence can surpass a smaller number of people of outstanding intelligence,[55] or he emphasizes the greater stability of democratic constitutions.[56] However, we hardly find the idea that every individual as such has a right to participate in political decision making,[57] and in any event in Athenian democracy the citizens were only a small part of the population. The whole comes before the parts;[58] like Plato, Aristotle starts out from the conditions for the functioning of the polis, not from the basic rights of individuals. In general it can be said, first, that Aristotle is seeking a compromise between the *formal* principle of the broadest possible equality and the demands of *substantively* correct decisions between quantity and quality; hence he opts for a mixed constitution combining democratic and oligarchic elements.[59] Second, Aristotle is completely undoctrinaire to the extent that for him the question about the form of the state has to be answered differently depending on the historical context: when a very superior individual is involved, a monarchy may also be justified.[60]

A good life presupposes virtue, and one of the most important virtues throughout all the ethical works in Aristotle's corpus is friendship, which finds expression within the polis in the form of political friendship.[61] The latter refers to feelings of solidarity and

---

52. 1280b5 ff.

53. *Nicomachean Ethics* 1134b18 ff. and *Rhetoric* 1373b1 ff.

54. *Politics* 1279a28 ff.

55. 1281a42 ff.

56. 1281b29 ff., 1295a25 ff.

57. Nonetheless, regarding the ideology of certain democracies, Aristotle reports that only this form of the state is able to guarantee freedom (1217a40 ff.) and equality (1318a3 ff.); however, his reservations are obvious.

58. 1253a18 ff.

59. 1296b17 ff.

60. 1288a15 ff.

61. *Nicomachean Ethics*, 1159b25 ff.

sympathy among citizens, as they are possible, naturally, only in a political structure the size of the polis, where—as has been rightly pointed out—every citizen may not know every other, but is nonetheless bound to every other by common acquaintances.[62] This constitutes one of the most important limitations of the classical Greek philosophy of the state, namely, that it can conceive the state only as a city-state. In Aristotle this is all the more striking because he was the teacher of the man who caused the downfall of the city-state. This enormous political transformation left hardly any traces in his work,[63] and neither will one find any discussion of the ethical problems raised by the collision of very different cultures resulting from Alexander's conquests.[64] In fact, neither Plato nor Aristotle worked out a concrete normative theory of foreign relations even within the Greek world. The soul's turning away from the world of appearances and toward the heaven of normativity put Plato in a position to conceive institutions that contradicted the mores of his time and were in part far ahead of it (such as the idea of educating men and women in the same way[65]); but it did not enable him to challenge the idea of the polis itself. Perhaps there is nothing that honors this early form of the state so much as the fact that even Plato could imagine the state only as a polis.

1.4. HELLENISTIC AND ROMAN POLITICAL PHILOSOPHY

The Hellenistic and Roman periods produced no philosophy comparable in level to that of Plato and Aristotle, and this is especially true for political philosophy. But these were nonetheless important times for political philosophy, because during them new political structures sprang up that were to be crucial for later thought, and that even in their own time stimulated philosophy. Here we should mention in particular the emergence of larger territorial states, such as we already find in the Hellenistic period and especially in the Roman Empire. It is certainly true that the complex constitutional structure of the Roman Empire reflects its source in the idea of city-states, because for a long time it consisted of an alliance of cities and granted Roman citizenship even to the Italians only after the Social War, and to all those living in the empire only under Caracalla, that is, immediately before the great crisis in the empire. But the actual historical development

---

62. On the size of the ideal state, see *Politics* 1326a5 ff. Aristotle insists on the fact that certain qualities of the state can be achieved only if a quantitative limit is not exceeded: like plants and animals, states also have their measure. Only in 1327b32 f. is there an allusion to pan-Hellenic ideals.

63. Here I am setting aside a vision of a universal state that is extant only in an Arabic translation, and may also go back to *De Monarchia*, but whose attribution to Aristotle is not sufficiently proven. See S. M. Stern (1968).

64. Cf. the Helleno-centrism in *Politics* 1327b20 ff. Even if Xenophon cannot be considered an original philosopher, it is nonetheless remarkable that in *The Education of Cyrus* he represented a Persian ruler as a model, albeit in an idealized form that does not do justice to what is specifically Persian in Cyrus.

65. *Republic* 451c ff.

proves that in this period ideas that looked beyond the polis became increasingly influential. Cosmopolitan ideas in Hellenistic philosophy, particularly among the Stoics, prepared the way for the conception of a universal state.[66] On one hand, this was the result,
negatively, of the development of an interest in individual subjectivity that loosened the
bonds that had bound the Greeks of the classical period to the polis. But this general
state of being thrown back on oneself constituted a kind of universal equality that was
capable of laying the foundations for a world culture and thus for a world state.[67] At the
same time, the new individualism forced the state and the philosophy of the state to take
the basic rights of individuals more seriously than the Greek polis had. It is no accident
that Stoicism saw slavery as a moral problem in a way completely different from classical Greek thought—it demanded that the treatment of slaves be at least humanized.[68]
Moreover, this individualism confronted the state with a private sphere that was, it is
true, publicly protected, but which saw itself as the ultimate goal toward which a fulfilled
life must tend.[69] Catullus's love-hate relationship with Lesbia, the inner turmoil and boredom described by Lucretius (III 1053 ff.)—these are feelings of a subjectivity that has
grown deeper, and that were alien to the Greeks; it remains an open question of whether
one ought for this reason to pity them or envy them.

No less important than these intellectual and emotional developments was the
politics of the nation that saw its own merits neither in art nor philosophy (or political
philosophy), but in real politics.[70] This relationship to true political reality is what is
new in the Roman philosophy of the state: No matter how slight the philosophical originality of Cicero's writings on political philosophy, his conviction that the ideal state
had been realized in the Roman Constitution, because of its perfect synthesis of the
monarchical, aristocratic, and democratic elements,[71] is not merely the expression of a
great national pride but also represents a new step forward in the determination of the
relation between the ideal and the real. For no matter how much Cicero seeks to provide
a philosophical justification for the state, he remains aware that reasonable constitutions

---

66. See Zeno's fragment I 262 in J. von Arnim's edition of the *Stoicorum veterum fragmenta* (60 f.),
which is taken from Plutarch's work *De Alex. virt.* I 6. Plutarch correctly notes connections between
Alexander and Hellenistic political philosophy that do not exist between Alexander's politics and the
political though of his teacher Aristotle. From the Epicurean tradition, cf. Diogenes of Oenoanda's
fragment 30. II.3–11 in M. F. Smith's edition.

67. The idea of the *vijigiṣu* in the *Kauṭilīya-Arthaśāstra*, that is, of the person who wants to conquer the whole world, concerns only the Indian world. See R. P. Kangle's commentary (1988; 3:262).

68. See Seneca's forty-seventh letter to Lucilius, where we find the crucial reference to the moral
dimension that is accessible to everyone and can be acquired by each individual himself: "Non min-
isteriis illos aestimabo sed moribus: sibi quisque dat mores, ministeria casus adsignat" (15).

69. Consider Epicurus's attitude toward the state: the wise man will not get involved in politics
(Diogenes Laertius X 119).

70. Virgil, *Aeneid* VI 847 ff.

71. This idea goes back to Polybius (VI 11 ff.). On the idea of a mixed constitution in Polybius,
see the fundamental study by K. von Fritz (1954).

cannot spring from the brain of a single individual, but have to develop over centuries; and in his interest in the concrete historical development of his own state, he himself sees a distinction between his approach and that of Plato's *Republic*.[72]

The Roman world empire was not, any more than the British Empire, the result of a policy that sought from the outset what was ultimately actually produced, partly as a result of favorable conditions in foreign relations. But it is nonetheless correct to say that various specifically Roman factors promoted this development, of which one of the most important was a very special ability in matters of law. Roman civil law is one of the greatest human achievements in abstract thought, comparable to Pāṇini's *Aṣṭādhyāyī* and Euclid's *Elements,* and the Romans' construction of a peculiar juridical rationality deeply influenced later political philosophy. In the realm of constitutional law, it remains truly amazing how much the Romans were able to combine the principle of the separation of powers with the demands of great power politics, even if successes in foreign policy ultimately caused the breakdown of the republican state. No less impressive are Roman achievements in administration; it was by no means self-evident, given the crushing power of Rome, that its administration would be governed by law even in the provinces.[73] We find here what may be Rome's most important discovery: If it aimed at long-term rule, it could not allow the law to be broken, because law provided its most important support. The significance of the Roman concept of law consists in the fact that the Romans, far more than the Greeks, conceived justice in legal terms, and at the same time did not deny the connection between positive law and a natural law that transcends the state.[74] Even wars were seen essentially as means of enforcing the laws; and no matter how much deception and self-deception may have occurred in the course of them,[75] probably no other great power has considered it so important to justify its wars. Finally, the pacifying function of the empire was clearly perceived and used as a moral argument justifying Roman policy.

---

72. *De re publica,* book II, chap. 1.

73. To be sure, terrible abuses of power occurred (particularly in the chaotic final years of the Republic), but the fact that Verres had to go into exile is perhaps even more surprising than what he did. Mommsen is unfortunately right in saying, in the introduction to the fifth volume of his *Römische Geschichte,* that "Still today there are many parts of the East as well as of the West, for which the period of the Roman Empire represents the apex of good government—a modest apex, but one that was never reached before or after; and if a divine angel should ever try to decide whether or not the area ruled by Severus Antoninus was then governed with greater understanding and humanity than it is today, and whether cultured behavior and the happiness of the people in general has today progressed or regressed, it is very doubtful whether his judgment would be in favor of the present" (1976; 6:14). Cicero's letter to his brother Quintus (I 1) concerning his duties as a governor is a justly famed testimony to this moral and legal acknowledgment of norms for Roman administration.

74. See, for example, Cicero, *De legibus* book I.

75. See Livy, 9.8 f., 42.47 (though the resistance by the older senators is worthy of note). The justification of Roman imperialism was considered by its victims as ideological window dressing for a brutal will to power, as we know—thanks to Roman historians who provided objective reports on this subject. See Caesar, *De bello gallico* VII 77; Sallust, *De bello Iugurthino* 81; Tacitus, *Agricola* 30 ff.

However, the deep roots of Roman thought in juridical categories were also responsible for its limits. In its precise and persistent search for conclusiveness and clear
decisions, it lacked any sense for the sometimes insoluble moral complexity of political
relationships: The feeling for the tragic, which the Greeks had discovered, had no place
in Roman nature. (Seneca's bloody dramas have nothing in common with tragedy in
the strict sense of the word.) Similarly, the Romans lacked the sovereignty that, even in
the face of external defeat, is bestowed by a high intellectual level and a strong relationship to transcendence (as is the case with the Jews). Their historical success was what ultimately proved to them that they were right; hardly any people has found it so hard to
deal with setbacks. Perhaps this explains why the Romans had greater capacities as
statesmen and at the same time less intellectual ability than the Greeks, and this observation may show quite fundamentally why an excessively differentiated perception of
reality is not compatible with the virtues needed by a man of action.

1.5. CHRISTIANITY AND MEDIEVAL POLITICAL PHILOSOPHY

The connection between the rise of Christianity and the breakdown of the ancient
world was already a subject of controversy in antiquity: Augustine's *City of God* has
its point of departure in this controversy. In a certain sense, the relationship between
Christianity and Rome is similar to that between Socrates and Athens. Both were symptoms of a grave identity crisis in the corresponding cultures, but they were attempts at
regeneration on a new level, although this regeneration first presupposed the complete
collapse of an outmoded system of legitimation. Wherein consists the significance of
Christianity for political philosophy, and especially for the question that concerns us
here, the relation between morals and politics? Machiavelli and Rousseau grasped it
very precisely: Christianity deepened the gulf between morals and politics.[76] Through
the opposition between the transcendent *civitas Dei* (which in Augustine is not identical
with the church[77]) and the *civitas terrena*, the political world has been devalued in a way
compared with which Plato's "turnaround of the soul" is harmless. Not only did this religion, whose God died the most humiliating of all deaths, accelerate the estrangement
of Christians from their state,[78] but also provided, through the idea of all human beings

---

76. Machiavelli, *Discorsi sopra la prima deca di Tito Livio* II 2, 26 ff. (1984; 298 ff.); Rousseau, *Du
contrat social* IV 8 (1975; 329 ff.). See also the last chapter of N. D. Fustel de Coulanges' s classic work
(1864; 519 ff.), of which I have made extensive use in the following pages.

77. On one hand, angels as well as several human beings who lived before the Incarnation belong to the City of God, and on the other hand, damned people belong to the church (*De civitate Dei*
XVIII 49).

78. See Hegel (1969 ff.), 17:290: "Wenn das Kreuz zum Panier erhoben ist, und zwar zum
Panier, dessen *positiver* Inhalt zugleich das Reich Gottes ist, so ist die innere Gesinnung in ihrem tief-
sten Grunde dem bürgerlichen und Staatsleben entzogen und die substantielle Grundlage desselben

as God's children,[79] a broader as well as existentially deeper diffusion of the universalistic and individualistic ideals of Hellenism—and thereby eliminated a possible identification with any state that does not include all human beings and is not constituted in accord with the principles of Christianity.[80] This is not in any way altered by all the calls for obedience to state power found from Paul's Letter to the Romans onward.[81] The crucial point, which critics have pinpointed with great exactitude, is that this obedience is merely external, and conceals an infinite inner distance that slowly but surely erodes the vital marrow of the state. Can one imagine a greater distance from the institutions of the state—which to the Greeks was divine—than the one implicit in Augustine's famous questions and in his comparison of the pirate with Alexander the Great in *De civitate Dei?*[82] Can one conceive a more radical devaluation of the political and cultural achievements of the Roman Empire than Augustine's, when he refers to Rome's bloody origin in a fratricide[83] and to the price paid for the construction of the Roman Empire,[84] and even wonders whether a great empire is in principle worth striving for?[85] Finally, can one imagine a more fundamental turning away from the ancients' anthropological optimism, which had emphasized the social nature of human beings, than Augustine's doctrine of original sin? What Nietzsche only dreamed of actually happened in the first centuries AD: a transvaluation of values, such as no other epoch has ever experienced again.[86]

---

hinweggenommen, so daß das ganze Gebäude keine Wirklichkeit mehr, sondern eine leere Erscheinung ist, die bald krachend zusammenstürzen . . . muß." ("When the Cross is raised as a banner, and as a banner whose *positive* content is at the same time the Kingdom of God, then civil and governmental life is deprived of the inner conviction in its deepest ground, and the substantial foundation of the same is taken away, so that the whole structure no longer has any reality, but is an empty appearance that must soon crash down. . . .")

79. See, for example, Galatians 3:28.

80. Tertullian, *Apologeticum* 38.3: "nobis . . . nec ulla magis res aliena quam publica. Unam omnium rempublicam agnoscimus, mundum."

81. Romans 13:1 ff.

82. "Remota itaque iustitia quid sunt regna nisi magna latrocinia? quia et latrocinia quid sunt nisi parva regna? . . . Eleganter enim et veraciter Alexandro illi Magno quidam comprehensus pirata respondit. Nam cum idem rex hominem interrogaret, quid ei videretur, ut mare haberet infestum, ille libera contumacia: Quod tibi, inquit, ut orbem terrarum; sed quia <id> ego exiguo navigio facio, latro vocor; quia tu magna classe, imperator" (IV 4). D. Sternberger rightly says about this passage: "No later condemnation of the state, including the "bourgeois" or "capitalist" state, and including those of Marx and Lenin, equals this one in its immense curtness" (1978; 1:318).

83. XV 5. There are similar passages in Minucius Felix, *Octavius* 25.

84. XIX 7: "sed hoc quam multis et quam grandibus bellis, quanta strage hominum, quanta effusione humani sanguinis comparatum est?"

85. Cf. IV 5: "Videant ergo ne forte non pertineat ad viros bonos gaudere de regni latitudine."

86. It has to be admitted that Augustine's dualistic definition of the relationship between the state and religion was not the only one within Christianity. One has only to think of Eusebius's imperial theology, which even in recent times has been the focus of a great debate between Erik Peterson and Carl Schmitt (1970) regarding the possibility of a political theology. But Augustine's conception has been the most momentous and influential.

Even if one refuses to believe in a transcendent god, one has to acknowledge that this belief alone has produced two basic preconditions for modernity. First, the opposition between *res extensa* and *res cogitans*, which is constitutive for modern science, would never have entered the history of consciousness if a god had not been conceived that did not himself—unlike the Greek divinities—belong to nature, and whose place could later be taken by a subject external to the world. Second, only through reflection on the transcendent god did humans emerge from their immediate unity with their political community, and no matter how much this god at first bound this community to a religious value world whose claims were even more unconditional than those of the polis, his ultimate decline left behind a social world in which even the values of one's own community appear to be objective facts that have no claim of their own to be loved or even merely obeyed. At the same time, this belief afforded a strong upswing, even an infinite emotion, to universal ideals, according to which all human beings should be regarded as equal. For if there is only one god, then he can hardly be the god of one's own people alone. In any case, Christianity owes its success in comparison with Judaism to the fact that, among other things, it overcame its awkward if not contradictory combination of monotheism with the doctrine of a chosen people. Judaism and Christianity are not the only monotheistic religions, and Christianity's specific difference can be understood only if it is seen as the sole monotheistic religion of salvation: Islam is not a religion of salvation, and Buddhism is a non-monotheistic religion of salvation. Religions of salvation accord great significance to the individual in his particularity, and also and especially in his suffering or now guilty subjectivity. Because in Christianity there is only one god who is fundamentally concerned with every individual person's salvation, it paves the way for modern individualism, which culminates in the assumption that the individual has inalienable basic rights.[87] In fact, even the dogma of original sin ought not to be evaluated in merely negative terms. One can feel sinful only if one has ideals that point beyond factual reality, and one experiences the political sphere as controlled by evil only if one demands that it be more moral.

Thus we arrive at the second problem that Christianity poses for political philosophy. If Christianity demanded only a retreat from the world, it would be in a sense less threatening than it actually is. The difficulty with Christianity, however, consists in the fact that it not only devalues politics, but also makes demands on politics, based on its universalistic and individualistic ethics. The relationship between church and state thus becomes the greatest political problem for politics, just as it was for medieval political philosophy. Compared with pre-monotheistic religions, Christianity represents an intensification as well as a diminution of the religious—the one not despite, but because

---

87. To be sure, a transformation of law and the state were not among the concerns of Jesus of Nazareth or even the early Christians—to assume that it was would be absurd, if only because of the imminent eschatology. But Christianity was a necessary (though in no way sufficient) condition for the modern idea of general human rights.

of the other. It is a diminution because the Christian god, who no longer exists within *physis*, rules out a whole realm—nature—as profane.[88] It is an intensification because the transcendent god, the creator of the world, and the source of all value, possesses an omnipotence that would have been unthinkable in Greek or Roman religion, and acts in history, which is therefore no longer seen as determined by cyclical structures but increasingly seen as a linear process with a clear goal. The Incarnation becomes the model for a unique, non-repeatable event.[89] Christianity is therefore responsible for two things. On one hand, through a process lasting several centuries, it made possible a politics that was finally free of all religious and especially ritual considerations. On the other hand, through an extremely intensive moralization of the religious, it demanded an influence on politics that went far beyond what was conceivable for the ancients. The *fetiales* (Roman priestly officials) were supposed to see to it that the necessary formalities were correctly performed before a declaration of war or a peace treaty. The augurs might advise a commander against engaging the enemy in battle because the sacred hens had not eaten; and if the commander disregarded this advice, as did P. Clodius Pulcher, the augurs' prediction might become a self-fulfilling prophecy, because the soldiers would fight fearfully and against their will.[90] However, Bishop Ambrose's exclusion of the emperor Theodosius from Communion until he had done public penance for the massacre he had caused in Thessalonika shows in a very striking way the difference between the non-monotheistic religions and Christianity, which insisted that moral principles be observed in politics.[91] Only in Judaism, in the framework of prophecy, but not in Greek or Roman religion, can we find analogies. Ultimately, early Christianity decisively influenced later politics because its novel understanding of history was a necessary condition for the development of historicism, one of modernity's most powerful systems of political

---

88. This does not mean that the Judeo-Christian concept of creation directly devalued nature: the idea of creation was originally connected with the assumption of God's immanence in the world. Therefore the Christian transformation of nature into something profane has not been complete, as the Orthodox churches or St. Francis of Assisi show. But compared with pre-Christian religions, this transformation was well advanced, and was completed by the voluntaristic and nominalist theology of the late Middle Ages.

89. See M. Eliade (1966). Let us recall here Augustine's polemic against a cyclical conception of history, which culminates in the statement that "Semel enim Christus mortuus est pro peccatis nostris" (*De civitate dei* XII 14).

90. At least this is what later Roman tradition reports (Cicero, *De natura deorum* II 7; Suetonius, *Tiberius* 2), although not Polybius (I 52); if the anecdote is not historical, it is nonetheless well invented.

91. Cf. also Ambrose's letter to Theodosius (no. LI in Migne, *PL* 16, 1209 ff.). Ambrose's behavior outraged the proponents of the modern theory of sovereignty (cf. Hobbes, *Leviathan* chap. 42 [1651; 608]; Spinoza, *Tractatus theologico-politicus* chap. 19 [n.d.; 3:228]). But it not only aroused enthusiasm in Augustine (*De civitate Dei* V 26), it even compelled Montesquieu's partial respect (*Lettres persanes* LXI [1949; 220 f.]).

legitimation, from which it is nevertheless separated not only by long periods of time, but even more by great intellectual differences.[92]

Despite religion's direct intervention in politics, we must emphasize that in a certain sense religion was not the ultimate normative authority in the Middle Ages. Many, but certainly not all medieval philosophers recognized that it was desirable that religion be justified, at least in part, by something that transcended its facticity; that is, they sought to provide a rational reconstruction of religion. And even if they assumed that this rational search necessarily ended in a justification of religion, it was nonetheless seen as valuable in itself, and religion was transformed through this process. Since there were no accepted criteria for an appropriate historical interpretation, the three monotheistic religions were always interpreted by means of categories indebted to philosophy; in this way the ancient conception of the three types of theology could continue to operate.[93] Thus, positive religion was distinguished from its philosophical interpretation in the form of a rational theology as well as from its political function; and precisely because positive religion could be considered the image of an absolute truth grounded in reason, the reference to its political utility was not, as it was in the counter-Enlightenment of the nineteenth and twentieth centuries, a simple instrumentalization of an ideology people no longer believed to be true or in which they were simply no longer interested, but was rather seen as moral and thus legitimate if its assertions were not taken literally. In one of the most impressive works of Islamic philosophy, Al-Farabi's *On the Perfect State* (tenth century AD), we already find a discussion of religion as a way of knowing the truth that is deficient in comparison with philosophy, but that is nonetheless politically indispensable;[94] and even if this position was in many respects the *opinio communis* of ancient intellectuals (particularly in the Platonic tradition), applying it to a revealed religion is a remarkable achievement on Al-Farabi's part. Within the Judaic[95] and Christian[96] traditions we find analogous ideas as well. The decline of this position is one of the most

---

92. See Löwith (1949) on the connections between Christian theology of history and modern philosophy of history. No matter how deep the breach between them, which Löwith elucidates in an impressive way, it remains correct that *without* Christianity it is difficult to explain the fundamental distinction between the archaic and the modern understanding of history.

93. The division of theology into poetic-mythical, philosophical or natural, and political is already implicit in Aristotle (*Metaphysics* 1074a38 ff.), and was influential throughout antiquity and on into the modern age (cf. among many other authors Augustine, *De civitate Dei* VI 5 ff. on Varro). However, it is clear that monotheistic religions' claim to be revealed is not immediately compatible with the devaluation of positive, originally mythical religion implicit in this tripartite division: Vico, for example, combines the latter with political theology as the first level, and ranks revealed religion over the philosophers' natural theology (*Scienza nuova* para. 366).

94. Chap. 17 (1985; 276 ff.)

95. I am thinking especially of Maimonides, even if L. Strauss probably went too far in his interpretation of *A Guide for the Perplexed* as an esoteric text (1952; 38–94). Unfortunately, I am able to read Al-Farabi and Maimonides only in translation.

96. Here we should mention especially Nicholas of Cusa, who carries out, in *Dialogus de genesi*, an evaluation of positive religion reminiscent of Al-Farabi (1964 ff.; 408 ff.).

striking characteristics of early modern philosophy of the state and of religion: hence-forth, religion is considered either as a simple error, in the worst case as a deception, or else as direct truth in its unmediated and, as is assumed, revealed literal sense. The subtly differentiated position taken by a both rational and political theology—which assessed actual religion in accord with criteria immanent to reason and was at the same time aware of its social and political significance—gradually died out (although not entirely) in part because of the crisis of Platonism, and in part because of the emergence of a hermeneu-tics that prided itself on precise historical understanding.[97] Even though the importance of modern hermeneutics for the development of modern philology and historiography is undeniable, it should be noted that it was ultimately this hermeneutics that made it impossible for people to develop traditions further in an unreflected way and at the same time to feel that they still belonged to them.

These deep roots in antiquity are one of the reasons why, despite their basically re-ligious character, the Middle Ages stand in many respects closer to the Greek concept of reason than does modernity, and especially why the main trends in legal and political philosophy recognized a connection between reason and natural law, that is, the higher paradigm by which postive law is to be judged. In Thomas Aquinas,[98] for instance, the ultimate ground of all law is the *lex aeterna*, which is grounded in God's wisdom, and is known to all human beings, even if in varying degrees;[99] a rational being's participation in this *lex aeterna* is what Aquinas calls *lex naturalis*.[100] The *lex naturalis* is inalterable and one and the same in all human beings;[101] to it are also added positive human and posi-tive divine law. Whereas the latter requires its own revelation, the *lex naturalis* is acces-sible to all humans—it is indeed grounded in God, but not in a positive religion. Legiti-mate positive law must not contradict natural law, and must itself be directed toward the common good, but at the same time the positivization of natural law is inevitable: on one hand, only this positivization leads to the necessary determination; and on the other, positive law's power to sanction, which goes beyond the ideal validity of the *lex naturalis*, is necessary in order to overcome resistance to the law for the sake of peace.[102]

The universalism of the Middle Ages ultimately allowed the development of norms for relations between different states (even between states with very different cultural backgrounds), and in particular the development of a theory of just war that has no par-allel in ancient thought. Vitoria's lectures "De Jure Belli" and "De Indis," which deal with the problems of international law that resulted from the conquest of the Americas, are among the most significant intellectual achievements not only of Renaissance Scholasti-cism, but of political philosophy as a whole. The debate between Las Casas and Sepúlveda

---

97. In this connection, the classic work is Spinoza's *Tractatus theologico-politicus.*
98. On the following points, see *Summa theologica* I/II, q.90 ff.
99. I/II q.93 a.1–3.
100. I/II q.91 a.2.
101. I/II q.94 a.4–5.
102. I/II q.95 a.1–2.

about the rights of the Indians provides a striking illustration of how far Christianity represents a moral advance over the ancients, for Sepúlveda's justification of the treatment of the Indians is based on Aristotle's teaching regarding natural slavery.[103]

According to the theory of imperial theology, the highest political authority of the Middle Ages—corresponding to the universalistic ideals of Christianity—was the Holy Roman Empire, which was considered a continuation of the Roman Empire. Yet this political structure was not sovereign, for three reasons. First, its claim to rule had to be harmonized with countless special rights that drew their validity not from the empire itself, but rather from manifold personal relationships that had developed through history, especially feudal ties between lords and vassals. After the collapse of the Western Roman Empire, such particular and local relationships of loyalty between weaker people who needed protection and the stronger ones who were able to provide it had laid the foundations for the development of new relationships of rule. Second, the imperial claim to rule was contested by the rising territorial states. Third, the church repeatedly claimed sovereignty over the state. As late as the fourteenth century a pope claimed the right to dismiss the emperor. The determination of the precise relationship between church and state thus constituted one of the chief tasks of medieval political philosophy and its novelty with regard to antiquity. Whereas in John of Salisbury's *Policraticus,* for example, the state is subordinate to the church, the rejection of the church's claim to control over the state and the doctrine of the two powers' independence from each other (in Dante's *De Monarchia,* for instance, as well as in earlier works[104]), is a step toward the development of the modern state. Marsilius of Padua's *Defensor pacis* paves the way for the modern doctrine of sovereignty with its subordination of the church to the state, which alone is allowed to make laws.[105] It is noteworthy that in the fourteenth century it was precisely the theory of the people's sovereignty that supported imperial power against that of the pope.

1.6. Modern Political Philosophy

The thesis that modern political philosophy continues the previous line of development in the deepening cleft between social being (*Is*) and moral obligation (*Ought*)

---

103. See L. Hanke (1974).

104. The historical development is not simply linear, but oscillating; but this in no way alters the fact that in an overall perspective a basic tendency is discernible.

105. It is characteristic of the transition to the modern age that in the tenth chapter of the first part of his book (§ 4) Marsilius distinguishes among the various meanings of the word "law" and singles out the law in force that is provided with the power to sanction, quite independently of whether it is just or not. "Et sic accepta lex dupliciter considerari potest: uno modo secundum se, ut per ipsam solum ostenditur quid iustum aut iniustum, conferens aut nocivum. . . . Alio modo considerari potest, secundum quod de ipsius observacione datur preceptum coactum per penam aut premium in presenti seculo distribuenda . . . ; et hoc modo considerata propriissime lex vocatur et est" (1932 f.; 1:49 f.).

may appear illusory, insofar as it initially devoted almost all its energy to overcoming the dualism in which the opposition between morals and politics had manifested itself during the Middle Ages—that is, the dualism of state and church. This fact might—for example, in Machiavelli, the most original and most important thinker of the Italian Renaissance—leave precisely that impression, as if after arriving at an extreme dualistic opposition the movement reversed itself and modernity rediscovered the unity of morals and politics that had characterized ancient philosophy. Yet although that is correct in a certain sense, it is one-sided. The concept of the political, which Machiavelli thinks through with a passion similar to that of the ancients, has undergone a sea change in relation to its Greek and Roman version. While the transcendence of the medieval God moves out of modern political philosophy's field of vision, this does not mean a return to the immanence of the Greek world. This transcendence continues to influence modernity in the form of a subjectivity that frees itself from everything through reflection. For the modern state, this may be a still more serious problem than the church was for the medieval state, and the success of Hobbes's solution cannot be understood unless we understand the relief that must have been felt by those who thought they had overcome modern subjectivity through this subjectivity itself. We can see with particular clarity the continuing influence of medieval innovations in the anthropology of the two fathers of modern political philosophy, Machiavelli and Hobbes. Their emphasis on human egoism and their denial that human beings are naturally social is reminiscent of Augustine;[106] but they lack the immediate belief in the Redeemer. The evil that Christianity had discovered has remained, but it is no longer be overcome through a savior, but only through the Leviathan. Obviously, Protestantism—in the genesis of which it is no accident that Augustine played an important role—also makes clear the great distance separating modern and ancient political philosophy. Although by means of Luther's two realms theory[107] Protestantism threw off the yoke that had subordinated the state to the church during the Middle Ages (and thus provided a model for all the Catholic states that were earnestly seeking political power), it opposed to the state a subjective pole to whose interests or conscience the state had to be reduced if it expected to be obeyed, and which in its privacy demanded an absolute dignity that did not proceed from the commitment to an intersubjective whole.

The other major difference between ancient and modern political philosophy has to do with the respective political structures to which they are related. Modernity is no longer concerned with the polis, and thus it is not concerned with the emotional forces that bind people together and that gave life to this manageable structure. However, neither is it the Holy Roman Empire, whose abstract universalism lacked real political

---

106. See B. Qviller and B. Thommessen (1991–92) on the relationships between Machiavelli and Augustine.

107. The term "two realms theory" does not stem from Luther himself, who developed his conception only in occasional writings. In any case, his doctrine promoted more than almost anything else the autonomization of the political.

power, against which the modern state is measured.[108] Rather, it is the territorial state, lacking in poetry and moral solemnity with its awkward interposing of itself between the familiar, everyday environment represented by the city and the high ideal of empire. The territorial state's sober prose has made possible a concentration of power that would have been impossible, for different reasons, in a polis or an empire; and it is the necessity of the battle against the rights, anterior to the state, of medieval society and the church, on one hand, and, on the other, against other territorial states that required the systematization of the rules of the political struggle for power—that is, the doctrine of the *raison d'État*.[109] However, in this case the latter is based on ethical arguments that are not found in the Arthaśāstras, and that remain ethical in nature even when they urge that moralizing be limited in politics.

Nothing indicates more clearly the dawn of a new era in political philosophy than two short books written within a few years of each other during the second decade of the sixteenth century: Thomas More's *Utopia* and Niccolò Machiavelli's *Il Principe*. It is crucial to understand that these two works, despite the contrast between them or rather because of it, are an expression of the same new development in intellectual history and complement each other. For with More's work began not utopian literature—to which his work gave its name—but rather a new phase in the history of this genre. We have already seen that a deep gulf separates at least Plato's *Republic* from modern utopias.[110] Even if More stands closer to the classical world than writers like Campanella and Andreae,[111] his work also lacks any epistemological discussion of the necessary distance between the ideal and reality, and More's initial discussion of the unjust conditions in England shows how powerfully utopian energy is directed toward concrete social reforms. Machiavelli's acute examination of the logic of power struggles seems very far removed from this utopian orientation. But in truth pure utopianism and amoral analysis of political reality are two end products of one and the same process of dissociation.

---

108. Thus from Pufendorf's *De statu imperii germanici* (cap. VI, § 9 [1910; 126]) to Hegel's essay on the German constitution (1969 ff.; 1:461) the Holy Roman Empire of the German Nation was described, because of its lack of a sovereign center, as a monstrous structure with an irregular constitution or as no longer being a state at all.

109. The expression "reasons of state" (*raison d'État*) is not found in Machiavelli, but appeared for the first time in the written language in his lifetime (in Guiccardini, for instance). The first text containing the phrase in its title is G. Botero's *Della ragion di stato* (1589), which was directed against Machiavelli, but was nonetheless deeply influenced by him. On the history of the concept of reasons of state, see F. Meinecke's classic work (1924), R. Schnur (1975), and M. Stolleis (1990).

110. I ignore here Hellenistic utopias such as those of Iambulus, which take an intermediate form. On one hand, Iambulus moved much farther away from reality than did Plato—the comprehensive literary genre to which his work belongs is the romance, which sprang from the collapse of the closed worldview of epic; on the other hand, his work lacks the political seriousness we sense in not only Plato, but also in modern utopias: Iambulus does not seek to realize any political program.

111. I cannot discuss here the logic of the development of the modern utopia, for example, the often emphasized transition from spatial to temporal utopias. See W. Braungart's learned book (1989).

Only after Christianity had fundamentally estranged the individual from the state in which he lived did it become possible to hit upon the idea of analyzing one's own political reality as a complex of value-free facts, on one hand, and on the other of opposing to it a world that is a wholly subjective creation. To be sure, these two positions are not, at the beginning of the sixteenth century, worked out in the systematic way that we first find after Kant, in the value-free social sciences and the utopianism based on pure intentions of our own century. But on the basis of our current knowledge we recognize in these writings the seed of a development that had a decisive influence on later history.

Machiavelli is best known as the author of a systematic account of "Machiavellian" techniques of maintaining and expanding power. Even if this is not his true significance, the uninhibited construction of a strategic rationality within the framework of political philosophy must be recognized as one of the important innovations of the modern age. Since strategic rationality culminates in the ability to deceive, and since in Machiavelli lying is almost more important than force, it is likely that the modern interest in an autonomous strategic rationality is linked to Descartes's typically modern theory of the mind-body relation, according to which consciousness stands in an external relationship to its body. One result of this theory is that the old physiognomic doctrine of a direct expression of thought in the body loses its plausibility. In any case, it is clear that the Cartesian theory of the *res cogitans*, whose connection with the whole world of extension is denied, opens up endless possibilities for deception whose association with the interest in a comprehensive use of strategic rationality is hardly accidental.[112] However, Machiavelli would not be a philosopher but only a political scientist if his achievement consisted solely in collecting such techniques. His deeply disturbing originality, which proves that he belongs to the old European tradition, consists rather in the fact that he raised the use of strategic rationality—that is, first and foremost, the disengagement of politics from individual morality—to the level of a moral demand.[113] This sounds paradoxical, and in fact one cannot spare Machiavelli the reproach that he did not really succeed in resolving this paradox, no matter how rationally his insight can be reconstructed. It was not without a certain painful surprise, which results from his familiarity with the classical tradition, and also not without a peculiar form of pleasure we will examine later, that the Florentine state secretary discovered that political action in accord with rules that are generally considered binding on the conduct of private individuals may have dreadful consequences, whereas conversely, a situation we welcome on moral grounds is often enough produced by a kind of behavior that seems morally objectionable. The classic examples of this are the benevolent ruler who allows a power vacuum to emerge that leads to bloody power struggles or even to civil war, and the power-hungry tyrant who, for despicable motives, brings peace to a war-torn state or even founds a new one. From this point of

---

112. *Larvatus prodeo,* says Descartes of himself (1964 ff.; 10:213).
113. See V. Hösle (1990a).

view, a figure like Cesare Borgia seems a blessing.[114] Since Machiavelli in no way sought only to evaluate or even merely to describe reality the way it is, but rather to set forth concrete norms for the guidance of good statesmen, it is important to emphasize that he recommended the use of force only in cases where it was necessary to achieve political goals. Although Machiavelli is deeply convinced that in certain situations the refusal to resort to force necessarily leads to a state of affairs that is far more violent than a timely use of violence would have been, and is just as convinced that this refusal has to be regarded as a sign of contemptible cowardice, he is also capable of distinguishing between force used in the service of the common good and force used in the service of an individual's cruelty.[115] It cannot be denied that he never justified the latter. But it also cannot be denied that according to Machiavelli, the final normative standard for the good statesman is not his own happiness, but rather the happiness of his state, to which the happiness of other people and states may, and even should, be unhesitatingly sacrificed.[116] From this ambivalence in his argumentation proceeds that of its reception—and that of his name, which is one of the very few to have become common noun: Machiavelli is indeed the prototype of a human type without which modern politics can no longer function. Yet, as we said, the connotations attached to this noun differ: whereas in Elizabethan culture "Machiavel" stands for the unscrupulous and immoral man of power,[117] in Goethe's *Egmont*, Machiavell, the political advisor to Margarete of Parma, is a pleasing figure who offers a sober assessment of the situation and sincerely seeks to prevent a greater evil. The historical Machiavelli was certainly first of all a concerned and skillful servant of his state—no matter how much the attentive reader finds it hard not to suspect that the substantive and objective argumentation for unusual measures that characterizes his writings is connected with a disturbing delight in the fact that one may, for instance, instrumentalize other people with a good conscience.[118] One of Machiavelli's most repulsive traits as a person is that he seems to have had no sense of the tragic dimension of his discovery. All the dramas he wrote are comedies.[119]

---

114. See *Il Principe* 7.1f., esp. 8 (1986; 107 ff., esp. 112) and 17.1 (151f.): "Era tenuto Cesare Borgia crudele; nondimanco, quella sua crudeltà aveva racconcia la Romagna, unitola, ridottola in pace e in fede. Il che se si considerrà bene, si vedrà quello essere stato molto più pietoso che il populo fiorentino, il quale, per fuggire el nome del crudele, lasciò destruggere Pistoia." ("Cesare Borgia was considered strict, but his strictness had brought order to Romagna, united it, and reduced it to peace and fealty. If this is considered well, it will be seen that he was really much more merciful than the Florentine people, who, to avoid the name of strictness, allowed Pistoia to be destroyed." Trans. L. Ricci and E. R. P. Vincent, 60. The translation has been slightly revised; see the following note.)

115. The word *crudeltà* must therefore not be translated by "cruelty," but rather by "strictness."

116. *Discorsi* III 41 (1984; 563).

117. Cf., among many other instances, Christopher Marlowe's prologue to *The Famous Tragedy of the Rich Jew of Malta*, in which "Machevill" personally appears.

118. At least Machiavelli made it easier for later sadistic politicians to conceal their cruelty from themselves and from others by making use of secondary rationalizations.

119. As was rightly pointed out by L. Strauss (1958; 292).

Here we can offer not even a rough outline of Machiavelli's extremely complex political theory. The greatest difficulty in adequately understanding it consists in the very tense relationship between *Il Principe* and the *Discorsi sopra la prima deca di Tito Livio*, the less often read but more fundamental work for the philosophy of the state, whose deep insight into the meaning of republican institutions seems to stand in contradiction to the absolutist options of *Il Principe*. The most sensible explanation of this alleged contradiction[120] is that Machiavelli intended to justify tyrannical measures only for historically exceptional situations, the prevention of which he considered, moreover, to be one of the tasks of normal politics. No matter how insufficient his remarks on this problem may be in detail, Machiavelli's often underestimated achievement is to have grasped two sets of problems that many of his critics do not perceive at all. First, he recognizes that our usual ethics functions only because there is a public framework that guarantees its continuation. From this it follows that we cannot simply presuppose for the actions that create this framework the same normative principles as those that operate within this framework that protects them. Second, and more generally, Machiavelli has an extraordinary sense of the necessity, in a normative theory, of conceiving political decisions in relation to their historical situation. One looks in vain for such a sense of history among the seventeenth-century natural law theorists, while in Machiavelli we still lack the connection between political philosophy and the program of modern science.

1.6.1. Thomas Hobbes and the Sovereignty of the Modern State

The next great figure in the modern philosophy of the state, and indeed probably the one who is most consistently modern—and also, as his rejection of the Greek and Roman classics shows,[121] the one most distant from ancient political theory—is Thomas Hobbes. In his century, the seventeenth, the project of modernity emerged. Even more than Machiavelli, it is difficult correctly to judge Hobbes. That he was the most important political philosopher since Plato is as undeniable as that he is one of those terrible simplifiers who contributed, through their marvelous one-sidedness, to the enormous expansion of the power of the modern state, as well as to its dangerous limitation.[122] The diametrical opposite of Plato in philosophy and in personality, Hobbes fascinates and estranges us by his plebeian directness, which lacks any sense for the subtlety of allusion that constitutes the grace and elegance not only of Plato's but also of Cicero's dialogues on political philosophy. A comparison of his intellectual style with that of Locke is also highly informative. On the whole, Locke's political theory is certainly more

---

120. See G. Sasso's fundamental study (1980).
121. See, among many other passages, *Leviathan* chap. 29 (1651; 369 f.).
122. Richelieu is probably the most impressive and eeriest example of the deformation of personality that the construction of the modern state demanded of its founders.

acceptable and more plausible than Hobbes's; his common sense recognized in Hobbes's approach problems which, although they are obvious enough, Hobbes himself stubbornly failed to see. Thus it is no accident that Locke played a greater role in history. He is one of the very few great political philosophers—perhaps even the only one—who made a direct contribution to a concrete political coup, the Glorious Revolution. His *Treatises of Government* were written before, not after, the revolution,[123] with the specific intention of promoting it; moreover, Locke's ideas also influenced the American revolution.[124] In spite of that fact, or perhaps precisely because of it, Locke's ideas are less original and fundamental than Hobbes's. For Locke borrows most of Hobbes's principles and deviates from them only in some consequences; and although the consequences Locke draws from these principles are sometimes more reasonable than those Hobbes draws, the latter are the ones that follow from the premises common to the two thinkers. Locke was more prudent politically than Hobbes. But if philosophy is concerned to deduce the largest possible number of theorems from axioms that are as few and as simple as possible, then it is less damaging for philosophy (though not for practice) to arrive at substantive errors on the basis of correct deductions than to present clever insights as the results of premises from which they do not follow; and to this extent, Hobbes is a more important political thinker than Locke. Here we discern an important aspect of the political: a person who thinks clearly and consistently will seldom have the flexibility and capacity for compromise that usually characterize the successful politician. Locke was infinitely subtler in dealing with the sensitivities of the powerful, infinitely more capable of disguising himself than were Machiavelli and Hobbes; but precisely because this disguise had become a second nature in him, he lost his eye for the nakedly political.

Three factors contribute to Hobbes's modernity. First, Hobbes continues the line of cool observation of the phenomenon of power that Machiavelli inaugurated. He also subsumes under the concept of power all possible theories with a claim to truth. In no author do we find an equal obsession with discovering whose struggle for power any given theory supports—a question that stands in the way, to say the least, of an unprejudiced analysis of that theory's claim to be true.[125] Second, at the center of Hobbes's theory of the state stands the category of sovereignty, which Jean Bodin's *Six livres de la république* had already elevated to the status of an essential concept, and which finally demolished the medieval doctrine of the two powers. In general, following Bodin, Hobbes connects the juridical question, which in Machiavelli's political theory remained remarkably

---

123. We owe this point to P. Laslett. See his extraordinarily learned introduction to Locke (1690), 45 ff.

124. However, it is in the nature of the subject that even Locke's ideas exercised their influence through various dilutions, and were combined with other components of the tradition (as with republicanism based on the Roman model); the worldview of the fathers of the American revolution was eclectic. Great ideas produce their effects only through refractions.

125. *Leviathan* chap. 47 (1651; 704 ff.); *Behemoth* (1682; 16): "I think that neither the preaching of friars nor monks, nor of parochial priests, tended to teach men what, but whom to believe."

undiscussed, with the problem of power. Third, Hobbes adopts the axiomatic method of modern science.[126] Whereas Machiavelli proceeds inductively, generalizing political rules from his readings of historical texts, Hobbes outlines the program for a deductive political philosophy that deduces many conclusions from the smallest possible number of assumptions. Yet it is not only this idea that connects Hobbes with modern natural science. Just as the latter is underpinned by the *verum-factum* principle—that is, by the assumption that only what we ourselves can reproduce is true—Hobbes interprets the state as a human artifact, and no longer as a structure that reflects the harmony of the cosmos, as did the ancient polis.[127] Modern science's rejection of teleological thinking explodes any possibility of orienting human beings toward nature's goals.

As is well known, Hobbes's basic political experience was the English Civil War, which was fought for denominational reasons, among others. This monster, which he calls "Behemoth," after the fortieth chapter of the Book of Job, can only be controlled by an even more powerful monster—Leviathan, that is, the modern state holding a monopoly on force. With unprecedented clarity, Hobbes sees what has since become self-evident for most philosophers, and even for most citizens of modern states, namely, that conflicts between people in a hypothetical condition anterior to the state, as well as among citizens and the state or between organs of the state, are unavoidable, and are likely to lead inevitably to war or civil war if it is not clear from the outset who is to make the final decision regarding questions of law and the legal use of force. It is characteristic of Hobbes that he does not assess morally conflicts in the situation anterior to the establishment of the state. In contrast to Locke, for him there is no condemnable aggressor and no innocent victim of aggression. For when there is no monopoly on force everyone must reckon with the possibility of attack, so that striking first can be seen as a form of preventive defense.[128] For that very reason the foundation of a sovereign state is indispensable if one wants to achieve peace. The sovereignty of the state is valid in particular with regard to the church. To this end Hobbes uses religious expressions to transfigure the state in order to transfer to the latter the loyalty traditionally given the church.[129] What form the sovereign state organ takes—whether it is a monarch or a representative assembly—remains for

---

126. On his encounter with Euclid's method, see his *Vita* (1839 ff. b; 1:xiv). In the "Foreword to the Reader" in *De cive*, Hobbes programmatically states that "Non enim dissero, sed computo" (1839 ff. b; 2:151).

127. (1839 ff. a), 7:183 f. (in the dedicatory letter to *Six Lessons to the Professors of the Mathematics*).

128. Compare *Leviathan* chap. 13 with Locke's *Second Treatise* chap. 16.

129. See the famous passage at the end of the seventeenth chapter of *Leviathan:* "This is the Generation of that great LEVIATHAN, or rather (to speak more reverently) of that *Mortall God,* to which wee owe under the *Immortal God,* our peace and defence" (1651; 227). Hobbes can still only prove that there cannot be two sovereigns, but this does not logically determine whether the church should be subordinate to the state or vice versa. A theocracy would be entirely compatible with Hobbes's approach—and it is his deep anti-religious feelings, rather than his political-philosophical arguments, that lead him to reject this solution.

Hobbes a secondary question, even if he opts for an absolutist solution to the problem.[130] However, Hobbes himself made a precise distinction between his central political-
philosophical insight regarding the importance of sovereignty and his concrete political preferences. there can be no doubt that for him an assembly can also be sovereign,
and even that he always considered a truly sovereign democracy preferable to a weak absolute monarchy. Even his preference for monarchy is strongly influenced by his political-
philosophical premises, and deviates radically from the legitimist ideas of the monar-
chists of his time. For, on one hand, Hobbes attributes to monarchs more powers than
even the constitutional law most favorable to monarchy in his time did. This is particularly true of his notion that the sovereign head of state could name his own successor,
and was thus not bound by the law of succession.[131] On the other hand, this also means
an abandonment of any idea that the law of succession accords the king any special personal right: in Hobbes, monarchy does not exist by the grace of God, but only because
it is the most efficient way of ensuring civil peace. From this it follows that the rule of a
usurper who produces the same result is legitimate, and that efforts to restore the earlier ruler are not permissible—at least so long as they are not successful.

Hobbes's strict distinction between private and public is just as modern. The view
held by a traditionalist proponent of absolute monarchy like Robert Filmer, who maintained that king's power proceeds from the patriarchal relationship that set Adam over
his wife and his descendents,[132] is very far from that of Hobbes, according to whom the
sovereign, and thus also the king, is not an especially powerful private person, but rather
a *representative*—a representative of the state, which Hobbes does not conceive as a large
family. From this function of representing the general, Hobbes derives the principles that
still constitute a well-ordered state: protection of the people; concern for the general
welfare; education of the population; equality before the law; general taxation; public
support for those unable to work; limitation of laws to what is necessary and clarity in
formulating them; a distinction between public punishment and revenge; and finally, political advisors chosen for their qualifications in the relevant subject matter.[133] This suffices to explain the Stuarts' limited enthusiasm for Hobbes's writings. However, it is an
indication of the exceptional importance of Hobbes's political thought that in time it became a commonplace, even though it had pleased few in the seventeenth century.

Yet all this still does not completely explain Hobbes's modernity. That the state guarantees civil and external peace is a thoroughly classical insight, even if it had never before
appeared in the foreground of political philosophy. Rather, what is specifically modern in
Hobbes is the figure of the social contract, the individualistic legitimation of the importance of peace and of legal positivism. To be sure, we sometimes encounter a contract

---

130. Chap. 19 (1651; 239 ff.).
131. (1651), 247 ff.
132. The text is easily accessible in P. Laslett's 1949 edition of Filmer's works.
133. Chap. 30 (1651; 376 ff.).

theory among the ancients—it is already there in the Sophists, for instance.[134] But its goal is usually to deprive the state of its legitimacy, insofar as it is not produced by nature, but is rather a human artifact, the precise opposite of modern contract theory's goal.[135] Analogously, among the ancients there are also undeveloped ideas according to which self-interest is the ultimate motive of the clever politician. But what distinguishes Hobbes's philosophy from this kind of approach—as discussed, for instance, in the first book of Plato's *Republic* and at the beginning of the second book—is the universalistic character of egoism in his work. Thrasymachus (in the *Republic*) or Callicles (in the *Gorgias*), with their power positivism, can see themselves as aristocratic exceptions. In contrast, Hobbes starts out from the assumption that all human beings are rational egoists, or at least ought to be, and that this is not harmful to the state, indeed, that it may be of great use to it. Despite (or precisely because) of his sympathy with absolutism, Hobbes thinks in a radically egalitarian way insofar as for him there are no better or worse men—they are all the same in their desire for self-preservation and their impulse to satisfy their needs; there are no more higher social classes in his society than there are higher parts of the soul in his image of human beings. In principle, he regards all drives as being equally justified and as having a right to be satisfied. Hobbes can no longer understand the traditional meaning of the concepts of vice and sin; in his work, ethics is reduced to the calculation of utility. It is true that he recognizes many of the traditional virtues, but what is absolutely modern in him is that he deprives them of their intrinsic value and functionalizes them in relation to the maintenance of the state: they are politically useful, nothing else. The capacity for forgiveness, for instance, is certainly prized by Hobbes, but not because he sees something that is in itself valuable in reconciliation with enemies and the overcoming of hatred, as Christianity teaches, but rather because it contributes to civil peace.[136] The state is no longer justified, as it was among the ancients, by the fact that it provides a framework within which individual and public virtues can develop. Rather, what is virtuous is what serves the state, and the state is a legitimate institution because it is in the rational self-interest of all. At most, moral superiority might consist in recognizing, more honestly than do those who deceive themselves and others, that everyone strives to satisfy his own self-interest, even if the degree of rationality with which one pursues self-interest varies. But why, on the basis of rational self-interest, should one recognize the equality of all? Hobbes bluntly notes that in principle any person can kill any other and therefore each individual represents a threat to be taken seriously.[137]

---

134. Cf. H. Diels and W. Kranz (1954), 2:307 (i.e., 83, 3) on Lycophron.

135. Cf. L. Strauss (1953), 123. Those familiar with this splendid work will have recognized how much the first chapter of the present book owes to it.

136. Chap. 15 (1651; 210).

137. Chap. 13 (1651; 183). "Nature hath made men so equall, in the faculties of body, and mind; as that though there bee found one man sometimes manifestly stronger in body, or of quicker mind then another; yet when all is reckoned together, the difference between man, and man, is not so considerable, as that one man can thereupon claim to himselfe any benefit, to which another may not pretend, as

Finally, so far as Hobbes's theory of law is concerned, the forgoing indicates its peculiar intermediate position between natural law theory and legal positivism. On one
hand, Hobbes never tires of emphasizing that the validity of law is not due to its moral
qualities or even its relation to metaphysical or religious truths, but rather to the authority of those who make the laws: "Authoritas, non veritas, facit legem."[138] After the
subordination to the state, justice consists in nothing more than obedience to the laws
in force.[139] The voluntarism of this approach stands in a clear relationship to the theological voluntarism of the late Middle Ages, which estranged God even more radically
from the natural and social world than the doctrine of his transcendence had already
done; just as God can create the world in its concrete determination in accordance with
his arbitrary will, so can the lawgiver create the laws that proceed from his will, not his
reason. On the other hand, it is extremely important to recognize that Hobbes is very
far from modern legal positivism (for example, that of Hans Kelsen).[140] For Hobbes,
there is a reason why we should not question the justice of a law—or at least why our
answer to this question should not influence our conduct. We must not allow this to
happen because the ultimate consequence of this kind of questioning would be a refusal to obey, even civil war, and we must reject that for the sake of our survival, the
ensuring of which is the task of the state, indeed, its central task. To this task, as to all
natural laws and all the previously mentioned principles of the rational state, law is undoubtedly bound, though paradoxically in such a way that the individual may not make
his own decision as to how far the laws are adequate to this task, because such a decision, were it made universally, would make it impossible for law to fulfill its task. One
may have doubts about Hobbes's argument, but we must first of all recognize formally
that like Machiavelli's, it is an *ethical* argument for the limitation of morals in politics.
And, second, even if there certainly are good reasons for assuming that Hobbes exaggerated, on the level of content one has to concede that his fundamental insight remains worthy of consideration even if one's ethical presuppositions are quite different
from his. If each individual were to assume the right to resist the state whenever a law
seemed immoral to him, the consequences would in fact be dreadful.

As we have seen, according to Hobbes peace is a value only because it serves the drive
to self-preservation more than war does, for the individual can only be expected to act in
his own enlightened self-interest. Precisely therein consists the simplicity of Hobbes's approach: the duty to obey the state requires no metaphysical or religious presuppositions.

---

well as he. For as to the strength of body, the weakest has strength enough to kill the strongest, either by
secret machination, or by confederacy with others, that are in the same danger with himselfe."

138. Quoted from the Latin translation of *Leviathan* (1839 ff. b; 3:202).

139. It is true that in Hobbes the concept of justice is closely connected with the principle that
agreements are to be honored, and we will return to this point later on (chap. 15 [1651; 201 ff.]); but
since the most important agreement is precisely subordination to a state whose laws are thereby recognized, he can say that "Lawes are the Rules of Just, and Unjust" (chap. 26 [1651; 312]).

140. See the beautiful passage in chap. 26 (1651; 324).

No matter how much Hobbes seeks to show that Christian religion does not contradict his conclusions drawn from entirely different assumptions, he nonetheless hints that, fundamentally, any religious quest that goes beyond the religion recognized by the state is not merely unnecessary but even dangerous, because it could lead people to refuse to obey. According to Hobbes, rational striving to realize self-interest is necessary and sufficient for an emergence out of the natural state of war of each against all and for the prevention of a relapse such as occurs in the case of a civil war, no matter on what well-meant and allegedly moral grounds the cessation of obedience may be based.

Another question that has greatly preoccupied Hobbes's critics is of less interest here, namely, whether there actually ever was at the beginning of history a state of nature that preceded the emergence of the state. For Hobbes's argumentation it suffices to show that the state of nature represented by civil war is a real and constant danger that cannot be in anyone's enlightened interest, and that emergence from a natural condition anterior to the state, if there ever was one, would always have been prudent. The construction of the state is supposed to occur in the form of a contract. However, this is a contract only among those who subordinate themselves to the sovereign, and not between them and the sovereign himself, whose sovereignty would otherwise be restricted.[141] To be sure, it goes without saying that the state also has a responsibility to provide something in exchange for the obedience of its citizens: protection, and above all protection from a relapse into the state of nature. The state can ensure this protection only if all citizens renounce their right of resistance, to which they can appeal, however, if the state no longer fulfills its duty to protect them.[142] Thus in general Hobbes condones resistance to the state only when the latter is too weak; and against a state that is too strong only when its power is turned against oneself, not when it is turned against another person.

Here arises one of the greatest problems for Hobbes's argument. His third law of nature says that contracts are to be honored. But why? If the ultimate ground of the validity of all ethical precepts consists in rational striving to realize one's own self-interest, to which they can and should be traced back,[143] then contracts should not be honored when it is advantageous to break them. The contract would thus express only a present agreement of interests, not a peculiar source of legitimation independent of self-interest. But does not Hobbes's whole argument hinge on the notion that contracts are to be honored even if they are the result of a threat of violence, and it might therefore be in one's own self-interest to renounce them?[144] Scholars differ on this question. Some attempt to save

---

141. Chap. 18 (1651; 230 f.).

142. Chap. 21 (1651; 272 ff.).

143. See the definition of natural law in chap. 14 (1651; 189): "A LAW OF NATURE, (*Lex Naturalis*) is a Precept, or generall Rule, found out by Reason, by which a man is forbidden to do, that, which is destructive of his life, or taketh away the means of preserving the same; and to omit, that, by which he thinketh it may be best preserved."

144. Cf., for example, chaps. 14 and 20 (1651; 198, 252). In this, Hobbes falls beneath the level of reflection already found in Roman civil law: consider the *actio quod metus causa*.

Hobbes's construction by attributing an absolute status to the principle that contracts are to be honored,[145] no matter how patently it emerges from Hobbes's work that he recognizes only hypothetical, and not categorical, imperatives (i.e., that he does not recognize unconditional duties). In my view, the contradiction among the exegetes reflects a contradiction within Hobbes's work itself. On one hand, Hobbes's claim to originality consists in the idea that rational self-interest suffices to explain the functioning of the state, while on the other hand, it is impossible on this basis to prove what he is aiming at if this principle at least is not granted categorical status—which in the course of the work seems in fact to happen, but sub rosa and without the point of departure ever being explicitly corrected. Within his system, Hobbes can only repeatedly argue that the attempt to escape subordination to governmental authority is very risky.[146] But apart from the fact that this risk is not always and everywhere of the same dimensions (and a rational egoist may not care about the consequences of the bad example he sets, insofar as they do not come back to affect him), it is certainly not irrational to make an attempt to seize state power, even when one has little chance of succeeding, if one considers a success in this attempt to be of exceptionally high worth. Given his great fear of dying,[147] Hobbes's refusal to risk his life under any circumstances may seem perfectly rational— if one shares his preferences. But why one should have these preferences, why the fear of death should be greater than the fear of an unjust state, or even than fear of a mere loss of personal power, remains unclear, even if it is evident that Hobbes's theory, after having abandoned the category of the *summum bonum*,[148] desperately needs death as a *summum malum,* and even if we can also understand why Hobbes heaps abuse on those who have other preferences. It is certainly in his self-interest that everyone think as he does. But is it also in the interest of those whose preferences differ from his?

Since the question as to whether the state can be traced back to self-interest will be probed in detail in the systematic part of this book, only a few suggestions are called for here. Obviously, one must distinguish between interest and self-interest. We can consider a person who strives to realize his preferences in the most rational possible way as maximizing his interests—quite independently of what his preferences are, whether they are egoistic or altruistic. However, the whole structure of Hobbes's philosophy depends on rational actors having specific preferences, and in particular on their seeing their *own* death as the greatest evil. Hobbes knows that not all people are like that, otherwise he could hardly explain how civil wars happen at all; and perhaps it also sometimes occurred to him that the voluntary death of God incarnate in a human being stands at the center of Christianity. Yet Hobbes seems to believe that it would be far

---

145. See in particular H. Warrender (1957). Here I must leave aside the question whether Hobbes's philosophy of religion can provide a basis for the categorical status of his natural laws.

146. Chap. 15 (1651; 203 ff.).

147. Which he freely admitted: see, in *Vita carmine expressa,* the lines: "Atque metum tantum concepit tunc mea mater, / Ut pareret geminos, meque metumque simul" (1839 ff. b; 1:lxxxvi).

148. Chap. 11 (1651; 160).

better if all people thought as he does. He regards with particular suspicion the belief in a life beyond death, because in his view this belief lends an extraordinary power, which could endanger civil peace, to those who provide access to this life.[149] But even if all people in his state shared Hobbes's preferences, it is not difficult to see that this state would quickly be subjugated to another in which some people were willing to risk their lives—paradoxically, a state that consisted of Hobbesian rational egoists would thus lose at the very least its independence. In fact, Hobbes cannot ultimately explain why in extreme situations the state could ask its citizens, or even its soldiers, to put their lives at risk.[150] Hobbes never grasped the terrible dialectic about protecting human life through the readiness to risk one's own life and to endanger the lives of others. He thus committed major errors on the descriptive level and led his followers to commit still greater errors. On the normative level he helped to trivialize human existence.[151]

In addition, subjugation to Leviathan can be considered an advance over the state of nature only if it is accompanied by certain guarantees that there will be no abuse of power and that although individual freedom will be limited, it will thereby also be protected. A war of each against all is certainly risky. But it is hard to see why anyone who is not yet subjugated should deliver himself over to another person who he has reason to fear will kill him—especially if we assume that fear of death is the strongest motive. As John Locke pointed out, a person who is afraid of foxes should not trust a lion: "As if when Men quitting the State of Nature entered into Society, they agreed that all of them but one, should be under the restraint of Law, but that he should still retain all the Liberty of the State of Nature, increased with Power, and made licentious by Impunity. This is to think that Men are so foolish that they take care to avoid what Mischiefs may be done them by *Pole-cats*, or *Foxes*, but are content, nay think it Safety, to be devoured by *Lions*."[152]

1.6.2. The Separation of Powers and the "Superstructure"

With this observation John Locke opened a new chapter in the history of modern philosophy of the state. However, it is important to emphasize that all later philosophy of the state sought merely to complement Hobbes's doctrine of sovereignty, not really

---

149. Chap. 38 (1651; 478).

150. In the final part of his book Hobbes even considered introducing an additional natural law in order to ground the duty of citizens to defend their state in time of war (1651; 718 ff.). But the question is not whether one should postulate such a natural law, but rather whether the content of such a natural law would be compatible with Hobbes's conception of natural law.

151. In this set of problems may lie the deepest explanation for Hobbes's extremely cursory discussion of foreign policy. In any case, the necessity of a universal state seems to follow from his principles, especially since Hobbes's extreme individualism is incapable of dealing with the concept of a community of values constituting a people. (However, it might be objected that for Hobbes the state of nature among states is not as dangerous as the one that obtained before the founding of the state.)

152. Locke, Second Treatise § 93 (1690; 328).

to challenge it. The demand for basic rights and representation, as well as the theory of the separation of powers, especially as elaborated by Montesquieu,[153] seek institutional guarantees *within* the state against abuse of power by the state—they do not abolish the state's monopoly on legislation or its on the use of force. This is also, indeed especially, true with regard to the mechanisms for changing the law, which will always interest some people. What is crucial is that the modern state offers *legal* opportunities to change the laws and thus binds these dissatisfied people to itself. Only the state can limit or change the state; the establishment of authorities outside the state with a claim to obedience can only result in chaos and anarchy. On the whole, the concrete connection of the idea of sovereignty with that of the separation of powers is one of the major achievements of modern political philosophy and of the modern state, as well as one of the secrets of the latter's success. Combining the "horizontal" separation of powers into the legislative, executive, and judicial with the "vertical" separation of powers in the federal state remains the epoch-making contribution of the constitution that was able to realize the principles of the modern state in their purest form, because it was least hindered by past history, as was also the case with its theoretical justification in the *Federalist Papers* of Alexander Hamilton, John Madison, and John Jay (1787 f.). The greatness of this achievement is clear from the mere fact that the Constitution of the United States—the oldest written constitution in the world—is still in force, with only a few amendments, even though the country's role in foreign affairs and its domestic political tasks have radically changed in the two hundred years of its existence. On one hand, sovereignty and the separation of powers are, as we have already said, more closely connected with each other than it may at first seem. Normally, a person is loyal to a sovereign state only when the fear of an abuse of power is slight, that is, only when there are mechanisms for the separation of powers does the sovereign state usually have its beneficial pacifying effect. On the other hand, it is no accident that those responsible for the idea of sovereignty historically preceded the theorists of the separation of powers. The idea of sovereignty is more fundamental; that of the separation of powers already presupposes it, if it is not to lead back to the polyarchy of the Middle Ages.

Sovereignty and the separation of powers, representation and the recognition of general civil and human rights, the distinction of society from the state, and finally legal means of changing the laws, are the characteristic marks of the modern state based on the rule of law that is the historical result of the American and the French revolutions. Yet we should not overlook the fact that the power and efficiency of the modern state is also indebted to factors external to politics. The "superstructure" of modernity, as Arnold Gehlen has called it,[154] goes back to the association of science, technology, and economics; and modern political philosophy early on assigned to the state the task of promoting this structure and using it for its own purposes. So far as science and technology

---

153. See especially *Esprit des lois* 11.6 (1748; 1:294 ff.).
154. Gehlen (1957), 11 f.

are concerned, *the* classic work is the *New Atlantis* by Francis Bacon (whom Hobbes served for a time as an amanuensis), a utopia that came true in the course of the following century and was even surpassed. What is striking in this work is the decisiveness with which shaping scientific and technological policies is declared to be a central task of the state. While it is true that in Plato's *Republic* the highest officials are also engaged in scientific activity, the difference between the two thinkers' conceptions of science could not be greater. For Plato, science, in its highest form, is metaphysical contemplation, followed by mathematics (pure mathematics, not applied). In contrast, Bacon has the empirical sciences in view, not as ends in themselves, but as serving practical ends, the goal being the greatest possible expansion of human control.[155] A state is considered ideal if, in order to achieve this goal, it collects all the relevant knowledge and directs programs of research that are to further expand knowledge. The religious background of Bacon's utopia is fascinating: the central scientific institution of his utopian island is called "Solomon's House." Like the fathers of modern science, Bacon regards his program as truly Christian. The idea that modern science would dissolve Christianity would have struck Bacon and Descartes as absurd. For them, as for the religious reformers, it was a matter of realizing the truth of Christianity.

Still closer are the relationships between modern political philosophy and capitalist economics. No matter how problematic Hobbes's attempt to trace the state back to rational self-interest, this approach is far more plausible for capitalist economics. Indeed, Machiavelli's painful recognition of the bad consequences of good actions and the good consequences of bad actions is valid for capitalist economics as well. Mandeville's *Fable of the Bees* is analogous to *Il Principe* insofar as Mandeville shows—this time for the economy—that repellent motives can have beneficial effects: it is better for the whole to give egoism free rein than to try to suppress it.[156] Even the genuine philosophers of the state, Hobbes and Locke, make an important contribution to legitimating capitalism: the characterization of their approach as "possessive individualism"[157] has become well-known. In Hobbes we already find the later neo-classical theory that the price set by the market is by definition fair. Whereas tradition introduced the concept of value in order to distinguish just from unjust prices, Hobbes reduces value to price; for Hobbes, even the value of a human being is identical with his market price.[158] In con-

---

155. See (1857f.), 3:156: "The End of our Foundation is the knowledge of Causes, and secret motions of things; and the enlarging of the bounds of Human Empire, to the effecting of all things possible." In *Magnalia naturae, praecipue quoad usus humanos* (3:167f.), Bacon lists the scientific and technological innovations he wants to achieve. In addition to prolonging life, partially restoring youth, and delaying aging, he also mentions increasing the ability to withstand torture—as if the efficiency of torture could not also be correspondingly increased; and in fact, he puts on his wish list for the coming centuries "instruments of destruction, as of war and poison."

156. "Fraud, Luxury, and Pride must live, / Whilst we the Benefits receive: . . . So Vice is beneficial found, / When its by justice lopt and bound" (1714; 19). Cf. Montesquieu, *Esprit des lois* 19.11.

157. C. B. Macpherson (1962).

158. Chap. 10 (1651; 151f.).

trast, Locke's theory of value is the first fully worked-out labor theory of value;[159] yet his possessive individualism does not take second place to Hobbes's. Like Hobbes, Locke starts out from the assumption that, at least since the introduction of a money economy, human needs are unlimited. for Hobbes and Locke, humans are characterized by a constant striving for more power or money, whereas for Plato and Aristotle the nature of happiness sets natural limits to this striving.[160] In general, Locke shares Hobbes's view that the state exists for the sake of the rational self-interest of individuals, and thus the *First Treatise* is directed against Filmer, not against Hobbes, whose methodological and ethical individualism he shares. But whereas in Hobbes it is only life that the state must protect, Locke assumes a property order that precedes the state and which it is the state's task to protect. The political serves economic ends, and the right to participate in politics is primarily demanded in order to see to it that the state performs its duty in this regard, not, as in the ancient polis, because it is enjoyed as an end in itself. Since Locke's state of nature is less brutal than Hobbes's, his theory lacks the emotional ground for the negative legitimation of the political that we still find in Hobbes. For both thinkers the state is not an end in itself, but there is still a difference between supporting it because it prevents bloodshed and supporting it because it makes economic progress possible. Thus we can say that the diminution of the dignity of the state in Locke is far more advanced than in Hobbes; and it is no accident that Carl Schmitt and other thinkers who seek, even in the era of the triumph of economics, to re-establish the dignity of politics, draw on Hobbes, not on Locke. However, they generally overlook what is justified in Locke's criticism of Hobbes, and in particular they fail to recognize that without a more comprehensive moral orientation of the state, which Hobbes was the first to set aside, this dignity cannot be recovered.

Locke's inconsistency mentioned above consists in the fact that on one hand, like Hobbes, he adheres to an empiricist theory of knowledge, but, on the other hand, his concept of natural law requires far more explicitly than does Hobbes's an ethical and epistemological foundation that transcends empiricism and rational egoism; this foundation is not to be found in the *Essay Concerning Human Understanding*.[161] It is true that Locke understands that natural law entails demands that cannot be grounded in terms of rational egoism; but only the reference to God and to the divine power to punish allows him to make the legitimacy of these demands comprehensible. The unsatisfying oscillation between egoistic prudence and moral demands that go beyond it, so characteristic of bourgeois morality, was first overcome by Kant. Like no other modern thinker before him, he understood that morals cannot be reduced to rules of prudence

---

159. *Second Treatise* § 40 (1690; 296).

160. Contrast Hobbes (chap. 11 [1651; 160 f.]) and Locke (§ 37 ff. [1690; 294 ff.]) with Aristotle, *Politics* 1256b27 ff., 1257b41 ff.

161. A Locke scholar as learned as P. Laslett hypothesizes that the incompatibility of the *Essay*'s epistemology with the natural law theory in the two *Treatises of Government* may be one of the reasons for why Locke concealed his authorship of the latter (see Locke [1690], 82).

without thereby becoming heteronomous, that is, grounded in something non-human—a recognition that is of basic importance for political philosophy as well. While in Hobbes egoistic self-determination, and in Locke a natural law dependent on God, were the ultimate principles of practical philosophy, Kant succeeds in overcoming egoism by remaining committed to the autonomy of the *I*.

1.6.3. Rousseau and the French Revolution

The path to Kant's recognition was prepared by Rousseau, the first great opponent of rational possessive individualism of early modernity in political philosophy. To him we are indebted for the idea, indispensable for the development of a democracy, that a state is more than the sum of its members, that it must have a collective identity that underlies the individual identities of its citizens rather than simply consisting of them. The self-commitment of everyone in this collective is the primordial ethical and political act from which the legitimacy of the state arises. While in antiquity it was the cosmos and in the Middle Ages it was God that legitimated the state, in modernity it is the human being. But whereas in Hobbes and Locke single individuals are the ultimate legitimating authority, Rousseau developed an emphatic concept of the political collective that was to become very important for the development of nationalism. Just as Kant connects the validity of the moral law with the self-commitment of the human will, in Rousseau freedom and commitment are united in the people, that is, in the "general will" (*volonté générale*) that is more than the will of all (*volonté de tous*). In many respects the general will reminds us of Kant's higher faculty of desire: it refers to the rational will, which is universalizable, whereas the will of all is merely the sum of actual strivings. Out of the collectivist interpretation of the general will proceeds the idea of popular sovereignty. The people, who are subject to the laws and free only in this way, must also be their initiators.[162]

However, the flipside of Rousseau's justification of popular sovereignty is his inability to guarantee the inviolability of the individual's basic rights. Thus Rousseau offered an intellectual foundation for totalitarianism, even if the other elements of totalitarianism were still alien to him. Characteristic of this are Rousseau's demands for a religious legitimation of the act of producing the constitution and for a civic religion.[163] Certainly, Rousseau is not without grounds in arguing that the binding powers that every state needs if it is to be more than an individualistic association must be supplied by a religion. But his criticism of Christianity (though he also subscribes to a form of

---

162. *Contrat social* II 3, II 6 (1975; 252 f., 257 ff.). However, Rousseau is aware of the difficulties involved in the democratic form of the state, which he considers too perfect for human beings (III 4 [1975; 281]): popular sovereignty does not necessarily imply that the state is democratic in form.

163. II 7, IV 8 (1975 [262 f., 327 ff.]).

Christianity) suggests that religions could have simply appeared, or even been created. The basic paradox of all critics of the possessive-individualistic state appears for the first time in his work. Such criticisms, if they are to be taken seriously, themselves require something sacred, something that is not simply utilizable but must be made available for one's own ends if one wants to be politically active.[164] Precisely therein lies the crucial problem that has bedeviled all opponents of possessive individualism—from Robespierre's instauration of a possessive cult of the Supreme Being and Comte's Esperanto religion to the Marxist-Leninist attempt to give "scientific" socialism a quasi-religious status. And it is a dreadful error to believe that we are in a better position today. No matter how questionable an increasing number of people may find possessive individualism with regard to the ecological crisis in which it has played a crucial role, the problem of civic religion has inevitably proven to be the rock on which all attempts to overcome it have thus far run aground.

It is not accidental that Rousseau's reaction against his time was connected with a return to the ideal of the ancient polis. In general we can say that modern metaphysics, ethics, and political philosophy represent a "quarrel between the ancients and the moderns" in which thinkers who seek to plumb the ultimate consequences of the principles of modernity are opposed by others trying to produce a synthesis of the typically modern with the basic principles of ancient thought; Hegel is certainly the most important of the latter group. However, it is of the utmost importance to see that not all political philosophers who invoke Greece or Rome can really claim to have contributed to the taming of modern subjectivity. This is obvious precisely in the case of Rousseau. To be sure, his suffering at the hands of the highly scientific and hypocritical society of his time was just as genuine as his longing for a truer community. But this kind of longing is far from sufficient to produce such a community. On the contrary, it is thoroughly modern, because instead of leading the subject that laments the estrangement of modern society toward a new community, it actually estranges it from the last remaining bonding forces that still persist in the society of possessive individualism. It is an exaggerated subjectivism that enabled Rousseau to see his time as even more negative than it really was; and his overexcited and hard-to-predict nature, which longed for once to do something that was not in his rational self-interest, made him even less able to identify with an institution than were Hobbes and Locke. Rousseauian subjectivity is only a deepening of the modern subjectivity with whose overcoming it confuses itself. Its criticism of modern society is for the most part only too justified, but what it itself represents is even more dangerous than what it criticizes. Since the triumph of Rousseauian

---

164. Cf. Arendt (1963), 134 f.: "The need for gods in the body politic of a republic appeared in the course of the French Revolution in Robespierre's desperate attempt at founding an entirely new cult, the cult of a Supreme Being. . . . In terms of the French Revolution, he needed an ever-present transcendent source of authority that could not be identified with the general will of either the nation or the Revolution itself."

sensitivity, which has spread to the farthest corners of Western democracy, governments have been confronted with the problem of how to deal with people who have an aversion to the incredible efficiency of the modern state but nonetheless want to enjoy all the advantages of a system that alone allows them to luxuriate in their inner life. An aesthetic sensibility that can always imagine something better, indulges in dreamy constructions of archaizing political systems, and periodically breaks into emotional tears over its own goodness, is truly not easy to govern. We can only pity those entrusted with that thankless task! But we could still consider them fortunate if they were confronted only with ingratitude. Since the simultaneously sublime and dreadful events that followed 1789, every politician—at least in the European cultural context—must know that modern moralism brooks no opposition when favorable circumstances seem to give it a chance to realize the idea of community for which it longs. Resistance is not tolerated, and the most delicate compassion turns into mistrust and terror. Machiavelli and Hobbes never justified the cruelty of which the Jacobins, who were inspired by Rousseau and animated by love for the fatherland and for humanity, proved themselves capable.[165] Nothing can elicit more fear of the fanaticism of pure hearts than the strange connection between the declaration of civil and human rights on one hand, and the Reign of Terror on the other—a connection that only a few modern intellectuals have really grasped. There seem to me to be good reasons for saying that Terror had its ultimate roots in the Rousseauian conviction that human beings are good by nature, and that it is only society that makes them bad.[166] This doctrine does not lead back to the naive anthropological optimism of the ancients; instead, it merely absolves the individual of any guilt and of any duty to improve himself, while at the same time legitimating the craziest attitude that everything should be provided by someone else as well as the most unbridled hatred of "others," "society," and "the system."[167] The Christian dogma of original sin, at least in the crude version in which it was usually taught, is surely an

---

165. Tocqueville trenchantly summed up the course of the French Revolution in these words: "Au début, c'est Montesquieu qu'on cite et qu'on commente; à la fin, on ne parle plus que de Rousseau" (1953; 107). ("At the outset, it was Montesquieu who was cited and commented upon; at the end, people were talking only about Rousseau").

166. See the ninth note in the second *Discours sur l'inégalité:* "Les hommes sont méchants . . . ; cependant l'homme est naturellement bon, je crois l'avoir démontré" (1975; 100). ("Men are wicked . . . ; yet man is naturally good, as I believe I have demonstrated.")

167. Cf., among Burckhardt's splendid letters to Friedrich von Preen, which contain one of the most profound analyses of the intellectual composition of the late nineteenth century and the catastrophes that were to occur in the twentieth century, the one written on 2 July 1871 (1949 ff.; 5:129–131): "Das große Unheil ist im vorigen Jahrhundert angezettelt worden, hauptsächlich durch Rousseau mit seiner Lehre von der Güte der menschlichen Natur. Plebs und Gebildete destillirten hieraus die Doctrin eines goldenen Zeitalters, welches ganz unfehlbar kommen müßte, wenn man das edle Menschthum nur gewähren ließe. Die Folge war, wie jades Kind weiß, die völlige Auflösung des Begriffes Autorität in den Köpfen de Sterblichen, worauf man freilich periodisch der bloßen Gewalt anheimfiel. In den intelligenten Schichten der abendländischen Nationen war inzwischen die Idee von der Naturgüte umgeschlagen in die des Fortschritts, d. h. des unbedingten Geldverdienens

unreasonable intellectual imposition. But the great social significance of this dogma, which had taught human beings to have a healthy distrust of themselves,[168] should not be underestimated by an age that can no longer understand the idea of salvation, and whose best representatives feel at most an abstract intellectual discomfort on finding that they can no longer experience the pain medieval people felt on Good Friday, in which empathy with the crucified Christ and shame for one's own guilt, which had rendered this crucifixion necessary, were combined in the soul in a purifying way.

At a time when nearly all important European intellectuals were intoxicated with the ideals of the French Revolution as well as by the formal fact that the institutions corresponding to these ideals were not the result of a natural development but rather, in accord with the *verum-factum* principle of modernity, consciously established through the common action of all people of good will,[169] at this very time, Edmund Burke (who had urged reconciliation between Great Britain and the American colonies, but immediately discerned the differences between the American and the French Revolutions) made one of the greatest achievements in the history of political theory, first, by recognizing as early as 1790 where the path taken must lead and second, by foreseeing the Reign of Terror, the threat to all of Europe, and finally the rise of a popular general.[170]

---

und Comforts, mit Gewissensbeschwichtigung durch Philanthropie. . . . Die einzige denkbare Heilung wäre: daß endlich der verrückte Optimismus bei Groß und Klein wieder aus den Gehirnen verschwände. Auch unser jetziges Christentum genügt hiezu nicht, da es sich seit 100 Jahren viel zu stark mit diesem Optimismus eingelassen und verquickt hat. Kommen wird und muß die Veränderung, aber nach Gott weiß wie vielen Leiden" (130). ("The great disaster was hatched in the last century, chiefly by Rousseau's theory of the goodness of human nature. The common people and the educated distilled from this theory the doctrine of a golden age that must unfailingly come if noble humanity was simply allowed to do as it pleased. The consequence was, as every child knows, the complete dissolution of the concept of authority in the heads of mortals, with the result that people periodically fell into mere violence. In the meantime, among the intelligent strata of Western countries the idea of good human nature was transformed into that of progress, that is, an unlimited ability to accumulate money and comforts while salving one's conscience through philanthropy. . . . The sole conceivable cure would be for this mad optimism finally to disappear from the brains of great and small. Even our current Christianity is not sufficient to achieve this, since for the past hundred years it has been much too strongly mixed up and combined with this optimism. Change must and will come, but only after God knows how much suffering.")

168. Even N. Luhmann, who can hardly be said to have any sense for metaphysics or ethics, recognizes—in the framework of his sociological reductionism—the social significance of the dogma of original sin: "It had demanded . . . moral self-judgment and thus moderation in moral criticism. . . . A modern functional equivalent of original sin is not yet in sight" (1986; 231).

169. Thomas Paine had nearly religious expectations of the American and the French Revolutions because both involved a radically new, man-made beginning. "We have it in our power to begin the world over again. A situation, similar to the present, hath not happened since the days of Noah until now. The birth-day of a new world is at hand" (1776; 120). "A scene so new, and so transcendently unequalled by any thing in the European world, that the name of a revolution is diminutive of its character, and it rises into a regeneration of man" (1791; 353, cf. 383, 505).

170. Burke (1790), 236 f.

Since Burke's *Reflections on the Revolution in France,* conservatism has existed as a specific political position, and mistrust with regard to a kind of moralism that overthrows whole kingdoms and launches historical processes whose ultimate results it cannot foresee, has had a theoretical basis. Burke is not a true political philosopher; his defense of the British hereditary monarchy, for example, is weak, to put it mildly.[171] But he has an eye for the political consequences that specific normative theories will necessarily have in certain historical contexts that is completely lacking in his counterpart Paine, or even in Kant and Fichte, who are undeniably superior to him as philosophers.

1.6.4. The Political Philosophy of Kant and of German Idealism

One of the reasons that Kant and Fichte are superior to Burke as philosophers is that they clearly saw (as Hume had already done) that normative propositions do not follow from descriptive ones. This holds not only for empirical propositions concerning nonhuman nature, but also for propositions concerning actual human behavior. For the fact that people behave in a given way does not mean that they *should* behave in this way. But how should they behave? According to Kant, a guiding authority for one's own conduct is not to be found in the natural or social worlds or in God (who is believed in for ethical reasons and who therefore cannot ground ethics itself). Self-consciousness can find such an authority only in its own practical reason, in the form of the categorical imperative. The latter grounds a formal, universalist, intentionalist ethics: what counts for ethics are the maxims of the will, not the success of an action, but also not the moral feelings that accompany an action. The morality of a maxim is not primarily dependent on substantive goals, but rather on whether it can provide the basis for a general legislation. For political philosophy, this implies that the state founded on the rule of law can be considered morally excellent because all citizens are treated equally, quite independently of Hobbes's question of whether it is in one's enlightened self-interest.[172] While in Hobbes universalism followed from the empirical assumption that every person could kill every other, in Kant it enjoys an absolute, that is, categorical, moral dignity. However, it is of great importance to recognize that Kant thinks no less individualistically than Hobbes. The idea that intersubjective institutions could be an end in themselves is just as alien to Kant (at least in the political realm) as it is to Hobbes: the state has the obligation to delimit each individual's sphere of rights and thereby to secure the maximum private space of free-

---

171. Cf. Burke (1790), 26 ff. Burke argues exclusively on the basis of the English constitution in force, while Paine (1791; 277 ff.) asks the extraordinarily important question of what right the parliament that had opted in 1688 for a constitutional monarchy had to bind future generations as well.

172. Kant agrees with Hobbes that even for a nation of devils entry into the state would be rational, and that such a state would be capable of functioning (1976 f.; 11:224), but that does not mean that for him there is no other justification of the state.

dom for each one.[173] Yet whereas in Hobbes it is the drive to self-preservation that motivates support for the state in carrying out this task, in Kant it is self-respect. Moreover,
on the basis of his ethics, Kant promotes republican institutions, and even the development toward a league of nations, because that would be the only way to stop war. In *Zum
ewigen Frieden* (*Perpetual Peace*) he gave the ideal of a world republic a moral justification
that it never had before—or after, with the same degree of freshness and clarity. Kant regards action on behalf of what the categorical imperative demands in the realm of politics as a moral duty not in the least affected by commonplaces such as that what is true
in theory does not apply to practice. However, Kant considers such action permissible
only if, first, it takes place in the framework of the laws currently in force (he rejects the
right to resist even more energetically than does Hobbes[174]), and second, if it does not
contradict the categorical imperative. For instance, he regards lying as categorically prohibited; and therefore it would not be permissible to establish the world republic if it
could be done only by means of lies.[175] Indeed, anyone who considered himself no longer
bound by the categorical imperative in the realm of politics would be committing a sin
that could be forgiven in neither this life nor the next.[176]

Even if Kant has a fully worked-out ethical and political theory, there is reason to
wonder whether substantive assumptions regarding goods and values that do not follow
from the categorical principle alone did not make their way into the *Doctrine of Right* as

---

173. Cf. *Metaphysik der Sitten: Einleitung in die Rechtslehre* § B: "Das Recht ist also der Inbegriff
der Bedingungen, unter denen die Willkür des einen mit der Willkür des anderen nach einem allgemeinen Gesetze der Freiheit zusammen vereinigt werden kann" (8:337). ("Right is therefore the sum
of the conditions under which the choice of one can be united with the choice of another in accordance with a universal law of freedom." Trans. M. Gregor (1994), 24.)

174. 8:437 ff.; 11:154 ff., 229 f.

175. Cf. his essay "Über ein vermeintes Recht aus Menschenliebe zu lügen" ("On a Supposed
Right to Lie out of Charity").

176. See the sublime passage in *Zum ewigen Frieden* (11:232): "Ich kann mir zwar einen moralischen Politiker (der die Politick nach der Moral) aber auf keine Weise einen politischen Moralisten
(der die Moral nach der Politik vorschreibt) denken und obgleich den Übertretungen welche bei (in-
nerer Verehr der) im Allgemeinen auf das was Recht ist gegründeter Maxime doch der Neigung dann
und wann obgleich ungern Ausnahmen erlauben allenfalls zur Gnade der Verzeihung vor dem höchsten Gericht Hoffnung gegeben werden könnte so ist doch diejenige welche die Idee der Pflicht selbst
vorsetzlich verfälscht oder als Pedanterei verächtlich macht eine so ungeheure Verletzung (iniuria
atrox) der obersten in uns Gesetz gebenden Gewalt daß sie für die einzige gehalten werden muß die
soweit wir urteilen können weder in dieser noch in einer künftigen Welt vergeben werden kann." ("I
can imagine a moral politician (one who prescribes politics according to moral principles), but in no
way can I imagine a political moralist (one who prescribes moral principles according to political
needs); and although there may be hope that violations that are occasional and grudging exceptions
to inclination, recognizing (and even internally revering) a maxim which in general is based on what
is just, may find the grace of forgiveness before the highest court, a violation that intentionally coun-
terfeits the idea of duty or ridicules it as something pedantic and an enormous violation (*iniuria
atrox*) of the supreme legislative power within us has to be regarded as the only one that—so far as we
can judge—cannot be forgiven in either this world or in a future world.")

well as into the *Doctrine of Virtue* in the *Metaphysics of Morals*. However that may be, one point has to be conceded: Kant's irrevocable separation of *Is* from *Ought* conceals both a philosophical opportunity and a terrible political danger. It is an opportunity because it forces philosophy to make efforts to provide a theoretical foundation whose difficulties are counterbalanced by the peculiar attraction of this work, in which reason is wholly thrown back on its own resources. It is a danger, because those who are not capable of dealing with these difficulties fall into a normative vacuum that teaches them that in dealing with all socially produced values and norms (including those of their own culture) they should ask the skeptical question of why these norms and values should be considered valid, but it does not always teach them how to answer this question. Heine's famous comparison of Kant with Robespierre[177] absolutely hits the nail on the head: probably no person on earth so increased the potential for subversion as much as did this radical from Königsberg who had been raised in pietism and lived a middle-class life.

It was this recognition, among other things, that motivated Hegel's criticism of Kant. His *Elements of the Philosophy of Right* is, in my opinion, the greatest work in modern political philosophy—a synthesis of ancient and modern thought regarding the state whose depth and breadth can hardly be surpassed.[178] Despite important recent insights regarding particular points, there has been no later work that one would be inclined unhesitatingly to describe as a classic of political philosophy, yet research in the social sciences relevant to political science has become even more important—work whose integration with specifically philosophical investigation is clearly the problem whose magnitude cripples present-day political philosophy. This integration is so difficult partly because of the relationship between normative and descriptive propositions; and we can say that our dissatisfaction with Hegel's *Philosophy of Right* has to do with precisely this question. However, we must first note Hegel's crucial deviation from the modern philosophy of the state. Whereas in Kant, and even more strongly in Fichte,[179] practical philosophy is divided into two parts, philosophy of law and individual ethics, and the philosophy of the state becomes part of the philosophy of law, Hegel recognizes that the state is more than a legislative institution that is itself constructed in accord with law. In his conception the state is, after the family and civil society, the third and final institution composing mores, which he interprets as a synthesis of abstract law and morality. Without subjective animation through individual action, the state

---

177. (1835), 239: "Wenn aber Immanuel Kant, dieser große Zerstörer im Reiche der Gedanken, an Terrorismus den Maximilian Robespierre weit übertraf . . . ("But if Immanuel Kant, that great destroyer in the realm of thought, far surpassed Maximilian Robespierre in his terrorism . . .")

178. On the following, see C. Jermann (1987) and V. Hösle (1987a), 412–587.

179. Cf. the introduction to *Grundlage des Naturrechts* (*The Foundations of Natural Law*) II 5: "Es ist in dieser ganzen Darstellung des Rechtsbegriffes unterlassen worden, diejenigen ausführlich zu widerlegen, welche die Rechtslehre vom Sittengesetze abzuleiten versuchen" (1971; 3:10). ("In this whole exposition of the concept of law we have refrained from expressly confuting those who seek to derive the doctrine of law from the moral law.")

cannot survive: the state is more than the sum of its juristically analyzable components; as in the case of the Greeks, it presupposes an individual morality. Yet the point of Hegel's concept of ethical life (*Sittlichkeit*) is not directed solely, or even primarily, against a juristic limitation of the concept of the state. He polemicizes still more strongly against an understanding of morals as a pure relationship within the self: for him, any ethic that does not culminate in a normative theory of institutions is incomplete, or worse yet, misconceived from the beginning. For human beings can be truly good—and here Hegel also goes back to the Greeks—only within the state; a moral reasoning conceiving itself as being, in the excellence of its own conscience, outside all institutions leads to what is called "evil."[180] It is crucial, according to Hegel, that one experience the institutions of the family and the state as ends in themselves that transcend rational self-interest. The higher of the two, the state, even has in extreme cases the right to demand the sacrifice of one's own life.[181] However, the mature Hegel recognizes that the modern state is functional only because it provides a social realm between the family and the state that is still lacking in Aristotle and in which the individual himself is in fact the ultimate goal: civil society, to which the sphere of economics in particular belongs.[182] By granting this civil society autonomy, Hegel avoids Rousseau's temptations and integrates into his own conception the approach of Locke and Hobbes; yet while he steadfastly maintains that the state presupposes civil society but cannot be conceived on its model, Hegel succeeds in reconnecting with the ancient ideal of the state. Since he finally subordinates objective spirit to the absolute, to which religion (from which the state draws its ultimate legitimation[183]) in particular belongs, medieval insights also find a place in Hegel's political philosophy.

A further achievement of Hegel's political philosophy is to have done full justice to the historically conditioned nature of the various forms taken by the state. Whereas Hobbes and Locke lack any sense that human nature and thus also human institutions have qualitatively changed in the course of time, and whereas it would in particular never have occurred to them that the extreme individualism of modern subjectivity is a very late product of human history and not at all an anthropological constant, Hegel understands the historical situation of the modern state based on the rule of law, and especially its Christian presuppositions.[184] The European thinker who first grasped the historical development of human cultures is Vico. Yet no matter how marvelous his philosophy of culture and history[185] or how significant the consequences of his approach for political philosophy, we cannot count him among the genuine political philosophers.

---

180. Cf. §§ 135 ff. (1969 ff.; 7:252 ff.).

181. § 324 (1969 ff.; 7:491 ff.).

182. §§ 182 ff. (1969 ff.; 7:339 ff.).

183. § 270 (1969 ff.; 7:415 ff.), as well as § 552 (10:353 ff.) in *Enzyklopädie der philosophischen Wissenschaften* (*Encyclopedia of the Philosophical Sciences*).

184. *Enzyklopädie* § 482 (10:301 f.).

185. See V. Hösle (1990b).

52 NORMATIVE FOUNDATIONS

Hegel, in contrast, is the first who combined political philosophy with philosophy of history, though Kant had also made some modest progress in this direction. However, we must note that neither Kant nor Hegel granted history a legitimating function. An institution is not reasonable because it was established in the course of history; at most we can say that (according to them) it was established because it is reasonable. Moving toward the idea of a state based on the rule of law, which is grounded in the consciousness of freedom that human beings possess qua human beings, is for Hegel the measure of historical progress.[186] Moreover, although he rejected the ideal of a world republic, Hegel's sense of history did not lead him to endorse the romantic glorification of the historically evolved nation: nationalistic ideas are alien to him.[187]

Hegel's approach is questionable chiefly in the following ways. First, the brevity and heterogeneity of the second part of the *Philosophy of Right*, entitled "Morality," is striking. In fact, it could even be said that this part includes almost everything except an individual ethics, which moreover has no place in Hegel's system as a whole, and this is lethal for Hegel's claim to have achieved a synthesis between ethics and political philosophy. Second, the absence of an ethics in Hegel is explained by deeper reasons connected with his metaphysics. Certainly nothing would be more absurd than to interpret Hegel's *Philosophy of Right* as a descriptive work. Hegel obviously proceeds not empirically, but a priori. Indeed, he can even claim to have developed a method of a priori knowledge that, although not without problems, is amazingly productive. It is the "self-movement of the concept" that generates his argumentation. And yet Hegel's basic problem consists in the fact that it is the same self-movement of the concept that produces nature and objective spirit: both are as they ought to be. That the world is ultimately as it ought to be does not follow, for Hegel, from the elimination—as in positivism—of an *Ought* transcending the empirical world. On the contrary, Hegel, like Kant and Fichte, takes as his point of departure an ideal being's independence from any empirical being; but unlike Kant he assumes that this ideal being determines the empirical world, which can only correspond to it—at least in the approximation of the historical process, which he clearly sees as culminating in the modern state founded upon the rule of law after the French Revolution and in the philosophical understanding of this state. In Hegel, practical philosophy's task is not to guide our future conduct; it is a theoretical discipline that discovers the reasonable in what has emerged through history. The lack of any view of the future in Hegel necessarily leads to a playing down of the problems that were not resolved by the states of his time, such as the lack of a genuine democracy, the intensification of the social question, and the continuation of wars, which as a result of nineteenth-century nationalism became considerably more violent than they had been in the eighteenth century.

---

186. (1969 ff.), 12:32: "Die Weltgeschichte ist der Fortschritt im Bewußtsein der Freiheit." ("World history is progress in the consciousness of freedom.")

187. On this question see D. Losurdo's learned book (1997).

1.6.5. Democracy, Nationalism, and the Welfare State

After Hegel, both political battles and thinking about the state were concerned primarily with the introduction of democracy and the resolution of the social problem. While it is true that the divine right of kings had been theoretically overthrown by Hobbes and Locke, in reality it survived for a long time afterward, and the establishment of the principle of popular sovereignty required difficult struggles from which the idea of the nation, among other things emerged. Hand in hand with this political battle went a social change that drove the old aristocracy from the leading roles in politics. The equality of all, particularly with regard to political rights, became a principle whose rise could certainly be delayed, but ultimately not prevented; in its inexorable triumph the Catholic aristocrat de Tocqueville saw even the will of Providence.[188] As much as he approved of this social and political process and considered it futile and counterproductive to try to resist it,[189] Tocqueville recognized just as clearly its dangers: on the political level, the tyranny of the majority over the minority, which can be countered only by ever more differentiated institutions of the separation of powers, such as are found in an exemplary form in the Constitution of the United States of America.[190] Where such institutions are lacking, the modern state, with the power of its centralism to which have fallen victim all the traditional intermediate authorities inherited from feudalism, threatens to turn into the most fearful despotism—not despite, but rather precisely because of its democratic legitimation.[191] But even where it is possible to forestall this danger—which Tocqueville regards as completely possible and an important task—it is hard to prevent a flattening of human culture in a society of mass democracy consisting of individualists without civic virtues who devote themselves entirely to satisfying their economic needs. Distrust of outstanding personalities is so constitutive of modern mass democracy, and pressure on deviant views is so lethal, despite external tolerance, that one must prepare oneself for a leveling of intellectual life. In democracy, pre-modern political societies' opposition between great vices and great virtues turns into a peaceful middle way for which the security of property and one's own self-important activity are the ultimate criteria. Tocqueville cannot be

---

188. (1835 ff.), 1:60 f.

189. Cf. (1835 ff.), 2:6: "On s'étonnera peut-être qu'étant fermement de cette opinion que la révolution démocratique dont nous sommes témoins est un fait irrésistible contre lequel il ne serait ni désirable ni sage de lutter, il me soit arrivé souvent, dans ce livre, d'adresser des paroles si sévères aux sociétés démocratiques que cette révolution a créées. Je répondrai simplement que c'est parce que je n'étais point un adversaire de la démocratie que j'ai voulu être sincère envers elle." ("The reader may be surprised that being firmly convinced that the democratic revolution that we are witnessing is an irresistible fact against which it would be neither desirable nor wise to struggle, I have so often addressed, in this book, such severe words to the democratic societies that this revolution has created. I would reply simply that it is because I was not at all an adversary of democracy that I have tried to be sincere toward it.")

190. (1835 ff.), 1:343 ff., 361 ff.

191. (1835 ff.), 2:131.

considered a genuine political philosopher because he does not attempt to legitimate the state or his own value judgments. But he can claim to have developed what is still the most significant political sociology, which does not consider only the state in itself, but also examines the influence of political institutions on non-political spheres of society such as religion, art, etc., and vice versa. Like that of his forerunners, Vico and Montesquieu, Tocqueville's sociology, into which are integrated juristic and historical analyses, is a descriptive-normative synthesis, since Tocqueville does not hesitate to make value judgments even if he is still far from later sociology's postulate of "ethical neutrality." This may reflect a certain naiveté, but it is a naiveté that makes his work even more stimulating.

In addition to the demand for democracy, the social question played a decisive role in the further development of thinking about the state in the nineteenth and twentieth centuries. However, the ideas expressed by the philosophy of the state that emerged from the related debate did not correspond to the importance of the actual political changes.[192] The same can be said for the triumph of nationalism, with which the development of the welfare state is closely connected. This gap between practice and theory is not surprising. Nationalism obviously stands in radical contradiction to the universalistic principles of modernity; and even if it is pragmatically plausible that democracy and the welfare state initially required a particular collective identity in order to establish themselves, this is far from meaning that the idea of the nation (which is notoriously hard to define) can claim the kind of dignity that was attributed to it in the nineteenth and twentieth centuries. It is typical of the theoretically precarious situation of nationalism that the first important work on this issue written in Germany, Fichte's *Reden an die deutsche Nation* (*Addresses to the German Nation*), is the popular work of a thinker whose writings on ethics and on the philosophy of the state *stricto sensu* are based on a clear universalism, such that his national interests and the principles of his philosophy cannot be successfully reconciled. Nonetheless, the undeniable moral significance of nationalism consists in the fact that it united—though by excluding other nations—its own people and elevated the reconciliation of social oppositions to the level of a duty. However, the social question is not a purely political problem; indeed, precisely because it was increasingly presented as the central political task, it has contributed to both the decline of political philosophy and political catastrophes of enormous dimensions. This is Hannah Arendt's well-known thesis (1963), which is exaggerated but nonetheless perceives something crucial. Even if it is an important political decision not to allow excessively large social oppositions, among other reasons because a certain economic equality is a precondition for efficient democracy, the

---

192. This also holds for the two most influential theories of contemporary political philosophy, that of John Rawls and that of Jürgen Habermas. To be sure, Rawls legitimates the welfare state, and Habermas legitimates democracy at a high level of abstraction (it is hardly an accident that these justifications were written by the former in the United States and by the latter in Germany, since the United States is deficient as a welfare state and Germany as a democracy). But the formalism and thematic limitation of their theories prevents them from being as significant as the earlier, classic political philosophies.

question of *how* this goal is best achieved is primarily for economists to answer; overlooking this fact can only confuse political thinking.

All the same, the retreat from extreme economic liberalism and the recognition that the state has a social responsibility are connected with deeper philosophical changes insofar as they correspond to the gradual substitution of the category of intersubjectivity for that of subjectivity that can be seen in the first philosophy of the late nineteenth and twentieth centuries. The discovery of the middle path between extreme economic liberalism and socialism constituted by the welfare state remains a significant theoretical achievement, accomplished in Germany by Lorenz von Stein and others.[193] That it proved possible to realize this ideal in the democracies of Western Europe is one of the reasons for the latter's amazing ability to survive. In order to be able to distribute wealth, however, the welfare state presupposes a corresponding social product—and to this extent it benefits very much from a flourishing economy, whose development was one of the chief tasks of liberal possessive individualism. Conversely, the economy requires stability in order to succeed, and that also means social peace. Welfare-state and market-oriented economics are therefore complementary; they differ more in emphasis than in kind. However, it is no more accidental that liberal economic ideas preceded welfare-state ideas than that the ideal of sovereignty is older than that of the separation of powers. Something has to exist before it can be separated or distributed.

The true achievement of the modern state consists in its having realized to an increasing degree both liberal economic and welfare-state ideas. The economic liberalism of Wilhelm von Humboldt's *Ideen zu einem Versuch, die Grenzen der Wirksamkeit des Staats zu bestimmen* (*The Limits of State Action*, 1792) and John Stuart Mill's *On Liberty* (1859) goes far beyond Locke's because it purges his conception of its theological relics and actually reduces the state to what is necessary for the maintenance of external and internal security (and in some situations for the flourishing of the economy);[194] in particular, the demand for even a minimal religious homogeneity drops out. The state is supposed to have a legitimate interest only in restraining actions that harm others; nothing else concerns the state, and especially not the inner thoughts of its citizens, so long as they remain—for whatever reasons—within the law. Harming oneself and harming others with their consent may not be punished by the state under any circumstances.[195] The welfare state then compensates, through a certain economic equality, for

---

193. See especially his introduction to *Geschichte der socialen Bewegung in Frankreich* (1850).

194. Humboldt goes so far as to deny that the state has a welfare function: "*Der Staat enthalte sich aller Sorgfalt für den positiven Wohlstand der Bürger, und gehe keinen Schritt weiter, als zu ihrer Sicherstellung gegen sich selbst, und gegen auswärtige Feinde nothwendig ist; zu keinem andren Endzwekke beschränke er ihre Freiheit*" (1903; 129). ("The state must abstain from any concern for the positive welfare of its citizens, and must not go one step further than is required to ensure their own security against themselves and against external enemies; for no other ultimate goal may it abridge their freedom.") The state has no right to control either religion or education (177).

195. Mill (1972), 131 ff., 149 ff.

the increasing differentiation of society that individualism entails. Moreover, no matter how much a more complete conception of the individual is to be found in Humboldt and even in Mill than in present-day economic liberalism; no matter how much, on the other hand, the idea of the welfare state also has its source in feelings of solidarity rooted in the idea of the nation, we must still soberly observe that over time the positions of liberal economics and welfare-statism have dwindled into a simple matter of economic policy. The classical question of the philosophy of the state regarding the correct relationship between state and individual is reduced to the question of what degree of economic inequality is permissible in order to satisfy the greatest number of needs of the greatest possible number of citizens in one's own state.

Marx too strongly influenced political history and is too important a philosophical sociologist and economic theorist to remain unmentioned here; yet one can hardly call a political philosopher a thinker who took as his starting point the withering away of the state. Even if it follows from this that Marx is not directly responsible for the totalitarianism practiced in his name, by not working out a political theory he nonetheless did not forestall several errors that represent for all critics of possessive individualism an obvious temptation. The success of Marxism can be understood only if one sees that the politicization of the social question had much deeper grounds than those previously mentioned. The refusal to see this question in merely technical-economic terms had to do with the fact that mass poverty following industrialization posed a fundamental challenge to the ideas of modernity. There had always been poverty, and it had repeatedly become a political issue. But the fact that from the process of industrialization a new form of poverty emerged[196] that was more terrible because it destroyed familiar ways of life, and at the same time more dangerous politically and more demoralizing because of the loss of the belief in the meaning of the social order to which people belonged, was paradoxical insofar as this same process of industrialization had begun by claiming that it would overcome poverty. A great deal of the self-evidence and the legitimacy of modernity depended on the possibility of being able to interpret this paradoxical result as a mere temporary interim result and to surmount it once and for all. So far as Marx and Marxism's fundamental rejection of the capitalist market economy is concerned, their accusation that it was crisis-prone was merely a pretext. In reality, they rejected it because its possessive individualism seemed to establish forever the alienation that sensitive intellectuals since Rousseau had striven to overcome. Whereas the system-immanent solution to the social question satisfied the workers, who had been interested in nothing else, it outraged many of the intellectuals who had intended to use the social question as a lever for the realization of more far-reaching aspirations.

But this does not yet suffice to explain the historical power of Marxism-Leninism. I have discussed elsewhere other factors that contributed to its attractiveness.[197] What

---

196. The most striking description of this process is still found in Marx and Engels's *Communist Party Manifesto* (1961 ff.; 4:464 ff.).

197. (1990c), 63–71.

is important in the context of these observations is that its essence consists in a combination of abstract utopianism and value-free *Realpolitik,* that is, of the two aspects that we distinguished in early modern political philosophy, using the examples of Machiavelli's and More's work, and at the same time recognized to be two different results of the same process. Marxism-Leninism is absolutely modern; and its collapse is probably the harbinger of a crisis of the form of political philosophy that began to emerge at the beginning of the modern age. Marxism is modern through the pathos of a radical change in human history that is to be achieved through a collective effort. The suggestive, almost hypnotic effect that the word "revolution" has exercised for decades, despite Burke and despite a global situation that made the outbreak of revolutions highly unlikely, can be understood only on the basis of the identity that modernity derives from its most important principle. Only what one has oneself made can be acknowledged (*verum factum, bonum factum*). Yet this extreme subjectivism, which makes political salvation spring from one's own revolutionary action, is only one side of Marxist ideology. Just as much an expression of modernity and its concept of nature is the objectivism found in Marxism that transforms human beings into cogwheels in history, deprives them of their dignity, and prides itself on its unprejudiced recognition of the logic of power. This results in an elimination of individual responsibility, and in its intensified form, of any individual ethics—i.e., of the idea that one must first work on one's own moral improvement in order to earn the right to seek to improve the world—that is one of the most awkward and repellent characteristics of the totalitarianisms of our century. Nonetheless, communist totalitarianism demonstrated the continuing influence of universalistic, supranational ideals that the other totalitarian ideology, National Socialism, expressly rejected; and in these ideals there is certainly something that must be included in a factually more convincing theory of the relationship between morals and politics.

One of the paradoxes of the twentieth century is that although it produced political events and structures that are unique in world history, such as the two totalitarianisms, the two world wars, and the world civil war known as the Cold War, it did not produce any theory, at least any adequate theory, justifying these events and structures. Even comprehensive explanations in terms of the philosophy of history as to how such events could happen are lacking. However, it is clear that the complete negation of universalistic ideals expressed in National Socialism would not have been possible without the spread of ethical nihilism in the late nineteenth century and in the twentieth century. A steadily increasing number of intellectuals have adopted the view that the basic values of Western culture are social facts without any special claim to validity; at least Kant's insight that descriptive and normative propositions are logically independent of each other was extended to the more far-reaching view that normative propositions and value judgments had no role in the sciences—and especially not in the social sciences. According to Max Weber, the social sciences must deal with values (though the latter are regarded solely as social facts); any attempt to determine which of these values are the right ones is considered unscientific, and ultimately—and this is a further step—irrational. Only insights into means-end relationships are supposed to be scientific.[198] Thus in the twentieth century politics increasingly finds itself confronted by a social science (including political science) that has at its disposal manifold knowledge of causal relationships in social systems, but cannot answer, and ultimately no longer understands, the question as to which political goals are legitimate. With the decreasing consensus regarding values and the "polytheism of values" in modern societies, which are increasingly falling apart into subsystems each with its own logic, politics is losing, both in practice and in theory, the function of a guiding authority for society. The concept of politics is even becoming detached from the state and, after power was raised to the status of the ultimate and most fundamental category in Nietzsche, it has been associated with general power struggles and ultimately with friend-foe relationships—as in *Der Begriff des Politischen* (*The Concept of the Political*) by Carl Schmitt, who is the most original political philosopher of the twentieth century and at the same time the most horrifying expression of the decoupling of politics from morals.[199] Even the shame of all power, the use of physical force, is openly examined, and even celebrated as an end in itself.[200] If in Hobbes politics was still connected with the rational self-interest of beings with a drive to self-preservation, the twentieth century has produced an increasing number of people whose complete indifference with regard to all values includes the acceptance of their own self-destruction, which makes it impossible to predict how they will behave. It is in this negation of all traditional moral restrictions on the use of force, as well in the taking of risks that remained incomprehensible to those who regarded the will to self-preservation as a general anthropological principle, that we find the secret of Hitler's rise to power.

1.6.6. What Is the Starting Point for Political Philosophy Today?

If we ask where political philosophy must begin today, we first encounter the riddle represented by the modern state founded on the rule of law. The latter is a riddle because after being greatly threatened by the two totalitarianisms, it seems to have risen from the ashes of the end of the twentieth century and now to dominate the whole world without serious competition. The breakdown of socialism as it existed in reality seems to show, a hundred and fifty years later, that Hegel was right, and that the liberal state founded on the rule of law whose concept he defined is the historically unsur-

---

198. Weber (1917) and (1919a).

199. It is no accident that many of the most original exponents of political philosophy in the twentieth century are Catholics or Jews who have become estranged from their religion, after centuries in which the most important works were written by Protestants. The modern state has an essential relation to Protestantism; and its crisis is easier to understand for people who belong to religions that are full of a deep mistrust for the project of modernity. However, a certain estrangement from these religions is necessary in order to understand the project of modernity at all.

200. Sorel (1908).

passable expression of reason coagulated into institutions, at least after it had incorporated the democratic welfare state and made war between modern states less likely through the construction of international institutions. In the summer of 1989, just before the collapse of the Iron Curtain, Francis Fukuyama, who was influenced by the Hegelian thinker Alexandre Kojève, spoke of the end of history.[201]

Nonetheless, this thesis is not convincing, no matter how impressive the achievements of the modern state or how much Hegel, of all modern philosophers of the state, has the best claim to have grasped its inner structure. It is not convincing for five reasons. In the first place, it is not easy to interpret the political cataclysms of the twentieth century as merely superficial phenomena that ultimately belong to the past. Ethical nihilism, without which they cannot be explained, has by no means been surmounted; in fact, the uncanny thing about the current situation is that on one hand the modern state continues to make further external advances—for instance, regarding the international codification of human rights—while on the other hand the foundation of its worldview is eroding with increasing speed. If one appeals to Hegel, one must not forget that he connected the modern state with Christianity, or rather with the latter's subsumption in a rational theology; and one has understood little about the essence of early modernity if one believes that the crisis in the foundation of its worldview will have no consequences for the modern state based on the rule of law. It is no accident that the literary genre so characteristic of the optimism of modernity, the utopia, was transformed in the course of the twentieth century into a dystopia. The classic works written by Zamyatin, Huxley, and Orwell show in different ways how the increase in the power of the modern state, which it owes to the systematic application of modern science and technology, can end in a nightmare because in these over-technologized worlds the traditional values that constituted the humane necessarily die out.

But, second, independently of the value vacuum in which an increasing number of people in the politically dominant parts of the world live, the real condition of the planet does not bode well for the future. The risk of a war in which weapons of mass destruction would be used remains great; and the paradox that, because of its great power, the same state that has managed more than any earlier political structure to establish internal peace through its monopoly on force, uses force as never before in history in its clashes with other states, may explain why since the nineteenth century anarchist ideas have had a certain attraction even for intelligent people. It is true that a world state with a monopoly on force was never more necessary than it is today; yet unfortunately it is just as true that it was never more difficult to achieve, because—and this is my third point— of the difference between modern states and the political structures that only bear the name of "states" and actually have little to do with the modern state. In any event, the inequality between the so-called developed and so-called developing countries will

---

201. (1989). In the revised book version published in 1992, Fukuyama elaborated his thesis in greater detail.

increase over the next decades, and be in increasingly flagrant contradiction with modernity's universalistic ideas. In the fourth place, we must mention the ecological question, which indicates a deep shortcoming in modern political philosophy's fundamental approach and puts in question the superstructure to which the modern state owes its power. The fifth problem, finally, is the crisis in political leadership virtually all over the world. That the course the world is taking must be changed in some way is as widely recognized as it is undecided what the morally required policy is; and it is no less unclear what institutional changes modern democracy needs to make in order to survive.

The problems mentioned above are not only unresolved in practice, but are also, at least in part, categorially different from the questions that occupied earlier political philosophy, or at least that of the modern age. Modern nihilism is a logical outcome of the changes in direction undertaken at the beginning of the modern age—an outcome, however, that puts in question the project that owes its existence to precisely these changes. There have always been wars, but wars that could annihilate humanity are something qualitatively new, which the right to self-defense can no longer justify as easily as it justified earlier wars. The problem of the developing countries confronts the modern state with political structures different from its own, and which modern political philosophy has ignored because the legitimation of the modern state was already hard enough. The ecological problem points to the concept of nature—and nature has been fundamentally eliminated, at least from modern political philosophy. The associated problem of possible duties toward coming generations questions many things that are taken for granted by modern philosophy of law and theory of democracy, especially the idea that rights and duties are symmetrical. The principle of growth is so closely connected with the dynamics of the capitalist economy and the welfare state that surmounting it, no matter how indispensable this is on ecological grounds, is impossible without profound changes in the modern state. The lack of competent leadership, finally, has to do with the fact that the concept of leadership creates difficulties in an era that is convinced that everyone is equal and does not know what to do with the idea that not all interests and needs are equally valuable.

It is thus absolutely necessary to move beyond the horizon of modern political philosophy. However, an attempt to do so has a chance of succeeding only if it patiently develops further the intellectual achievements of political philosophy up to this point—perhaps taking its stimulus from the study of the ancient political philosophy that modern philosophy has too hastily rejected.[202] The past and the future are more closely connected to each other than a naive belief in progress assumed. In general, the task that political thought and active politicians over the next decades must carry out (so long as there is still time to do so) is this: to separate everything in the modern state that

---

202. To this extent the writers who have revived classical political philosophy, L. Strauss and E. Voegelin, are very important for systematic political thought, no matter how little they themselves did justice to the political demands of our time.

is in fact an expression of a deeply impressive reason from what the modern state—and modernity in general—contains that is destructive, and even self-destructive. But the two sides of modernity—the affirmative and the destructive—are so closely associated that it will require expert intellectual surgery to separate them; and since the operation is being carried out on our *own* heart—for it is our own identity that is at issue in the criticism of modernity—it will not be easy to keep our hands from shaking. The courage required to make such an attempt will grow out of the conviction that politics involves something that has a high moral value, and that indifference to the public sphere is not compatible with the effort to be a moral person.

2

The Relationship between Morals
and Politics

2.1. Concepts of the Political and Concepts of the Moral[1]

2.1.1. The Political and the Cratic

In democracies with political parties one sometimes hears professional politicians say they do not understand a bill proposed by a member of their party (who is also an intra-party opponent), "either as a substantial matter on its merits or as a political matter." The association of the "substantial" and the "political," which is not meant as redundant, is remarkable. The substance of legislative bills is concerned with what is good for the state, and since in Greek the state is called the *polis,* one might assume that in this context "a substantial matter on its merits" and "a political matter" amounted to the same thing. However, this is obviously not the case. So what does "political" mean? A hint is provided by the fact that today people talk about the "politics" not only of states but also of private enterprises, and even of criminal organizations subversive of the state: "the politics of the Mafia" is an expression whose meaning is immediately clear. Conversely, the concept of a "political trial" assumes that not every governmental activity can be considered "political," since most trials conducted before a court are governmental.[2] Evidently the word "politics" is used to refer to all activities of an institution (or in some cases a person) that are intended to serve its power interests;[3] analogously, a "political"

---

1. In order to forestall mistaken expectations, I want to make clear at the outset that this section is concerned solely with the clarification of concepts, not with the legitimation of the political or with the justification of the moral as an autonomous sphere. The latter will be possible only when it has been made clear how these concepts are being used.

2. Not even all trials for high treason are considered "political trials."

3. In his *Politik als Beruf* (*Politics as a Profession*), Max Weber refers in his definition to the striving for power within the state or between states: "'Politik' würde für uns also heißen: Streben

trial is one in which either power interests and not truly legal arguments determine the decision, or whose result has major effects on the allocation of power (especially in the state). In the initial example, the intended meaning is that a certain proposed law is neither good for the state (that is, it lacks merit) nor in the interest of maintaining or extending power. Naturally, the concept of power implies a subject who holds power, and this formulation consciously or unconsciously leaves open the question of whose power is concerned—the power of the politician's party ally (or personal opponent), his own power, or the power of the party as a whole within the state. Presumably it is at least claimed that the latter is concerned—for the one voicing the criticism can hardly demand that his opponent take measures to increase his own power; and if he were thinking of his opponent's power, he would just give him a bit of friendly advice. Thus if this criticism is publicly made, it can only mean that the proposed law would not be good for the state, and would not be approved by the voters on whom the party's power depends.

This reference to linguistic usage (which is often but not always a litmus test for far-reaching changes in the history of consciousness) may be informative because it puts to the test the thesis mentioned previously regarding the development of the relationship between morals and politics. A Greek would not have understood this expression at first;[4] and if it were explained to him, he would be saddened by the fact that the concept of the political had been detached from that of what is right for the state in a substantial way. This does not mean that the Greeks were unfamiliar with power struggles; but they did not apply the concept of the political to them. In order to avoid conceptual confusions, in the following the concept of the political will henceforth be limited to certain activities that have to do with the state, whereas the term "cratic" will be used to refer to phenomena that have to do with power struggles. I derive the term "cratic" from the Greek word that most closely corresponds to "power" (as is well known, there is no precise equivalent). In addition, we should note the distinction between "cratic" and "cratological," which corresponds to that between "politics" and "political science": political men have cratic talent, and those that analyze them are cratologists.[5] It is obvious that not all cratic persons ("crats") have cratological ability, nor do all cratologists have cratic talent, just as a good political scientist is not necessarily a good politician, and vice versa.

The cratic and the political are very closely related—so closely, in fact, that it is not hard to see why the term "political" has been used for both. On one hand, so far as the legal situation is concerned, the state is the ultimate power authority, at least in the

---

nach Machtanteil oder nach Beeinflussung der Machtverteilung, sei es zwischen Staaten, sei es innerhalb eines Staates zwischen den Menschengruppen, die er umschließt" (1919b; 506). ("For us, then, 'politics' means: striving for a share of power or for influence on the allocation of power, whether between states or within a state among the groups that it includes.") H. D. Lasswell and A. Kaplan equate the political with the aspect of power in an interactive social whole (1969; xvii), without expressly taking the state into account.

    4. See, for instance, H. G. Liddell and R. Scott (1961), 1435, s.v. πολιτικός.

    5. I owe this distinction to my friend Davide Scelzo's criticism.

modern state with its monopoly on the use of force. Anyone who seeks power is almost necessarily compelled to seek state power as well; to this extent the cratic inevitably refers to the political. Conversely, however, politics cannot be practiced without cratic abilities, if only because we still have a plurality of states that are locked in a power struggle. Even in a world state, the rise to power in the state and the defense of power against competitors once it is won cannot take place without power struggles, and it is not even desirable that it should (at least if we consider the principle of competition meaningful).

Yet even if the cratic and the political overlap, it is clear that they are not coterminous. On one hand, the cratic is more general than the political: some power struggles are conducted neither for power within the state nor between states, and thus they cannot be "political" (as the latter term is defined in this book). Political power struggles are a special case of the cratic, albeit, as we have already said, an extremely important special case, since all power struggles ultimately culminate in them. The distinction and the connection between the political and the cratic become clear if we consider, for instance, the popularity sometimes enjoyed in management training programs by certain East Asian military writings, such as the classical Chinese text on war by Sun-tzu or Musashi's Japanese work on sword-fighting, as well as by Clausewitz's *Vom Krieg* (*On War*). Since Sun-tzu's work is primarily political-military in nature and Musashi's deals only with techniques of sword-fighting and has nothing to do with politics, their success among managers who have never been on a battlefield is not easy to explain. However, their popularity shows that many of the insights they develop in a military context are generally cratological in nature: they hold true not only for power struggles between states that make use of physical force but also for power struggles within a business firm. Musashi's recommendation "to bring your mind back to observe your adversary's condition," that is, to understand "the perception of impulses and incipient actions of adversaries as the first sword, understand the weapon that strikes according to what they do as the second sword," is valid for any power struggle, whether it is conducted with swords or with words.[6] It is striking, and a proof of the intercultural validity of several of these recommendations, that they are found in almost identical form in texts from completely different cultures. Thus the insight that one should not too violently badger an enemy who is already almost defeated, for fear that despair might lend him new strength, is encountered in Sun-tzu,[7] in the *Kauṭilīya-Arthaśāstra*,[8] in Herodotus,[9] and in the European master of cratology, Machiavelli.[10] However, the crucial point is that this advice can be considered purely cratological only if it is derived from insights into the nature of power

---

6. See M. Musashi (2000), 362, 359.

7. (1988), 35; (1989), 55 f. This text is accessible to me only in German and English translations. Since these sometimes differ considerably, I have given references to both editions.

8. 10.3.57.

9. VIII 108.

10. *Discorsi* III 12.18 f. (1984; 505 f.).

struggles rather than moral reflection. In actuality, a supplement to Sun-tzu's text supports this cratological interpretation. In this supplement we read that the physical annihilation of the opponent may be expedient when there is no reason to expect him to gain new strength from despair.[11] Thus amorality is an essential mark of pure cratology. It is compatible with two things that might at first seem to contradict it. First, cratological recommendations may well be in accord with moral rules—what matters is that this accord is *accidental;* the heterogeneity of cratological and moral principles remains unaffected. The cratologist seeks to discover what is useful for the maintenance or expansion of power; the moralist is concerned with what ought to be done, independently of concrete interests. If under certain conditions the sparing of an opponent's life furthers one's own power interests, the cratologist will not mind if the moralist demands the same thing independently of all individual interests; and if one allowed this accord to lead to an act that flew in the face of morality and was at the same time directed against one's own interests, one would not be acting in a way that was consistently cratological, but primarily immoral. (It is obvious that there are such people, and this is related to deeper connections in the human mind that will be examined in chapter 4.4.4.2. They are not important here because we are concerned at this point only with the concept of the cratic, not with the question of whether there are people who act in a purely cratic way, and even less with how a nearly pure cratic attitude might be produced in its origin.) Second, we should note that the previously mentioned accord between cratic and the moral demands is no longer accidental if we mean by the moral something different from what I have meant by it up to this point. As we will show later, the word "morals," like the word "politics," refers to more than one concept. If "morals" designates simply the actual convictions of a culture with regard to the ultimate norms that are valid, then in a normal case cratology may—indeed, must—recommend adopting, or at least seeming to adopt, these morals, not, of course, because one objectively identifies with these norms, but rather because violating them too blatantly would damage one's own reputation and thus usually one's power as well.[12] It is quite compatible with this that under certain circumstances it may be morally permissible and even advisable to acquire cratic skills. The exercise of power as such is not immoral, and it can even become a duty; the task then consists in reconciling the demands of morality with those of cratology. But it is not cratology itself that assigns this task.

The concept of the cratic is thus both more and less comprehensive than the full concept of politics. The concept of politics, at least as it will be used in the following pages, is not at all limited to power struggles. In general, power struggles usually but not always occur for the sake of a goal that goes beyond the power struggle itself, and it is essential to the ideology of all *political* battles for power to claim that they are fought over substantial differences. As we will see later on, the concept of power is sometimes

11. Sun-tzu (1988), 47 f. This passage is not included in the German translation.
12. Cf. Machiavelli, *Il Principe* 18.4 f. (1986; 157 f.).

used in such a way that any intersubjective structure can be described as "power-determined"; but this makes it lose its edge and its differentiating power. Naturally one can say that power is also at issue in decisions about economic policy, because they usually determine the redistribution of power; but first, power is only one of the considerations involved in such decisions (economic efficiency or fair distribution are also desiderata), and second, in general these decisions do not directly concern the power of the economic policy decision maker, even if a new distribution of power presumably affects his own position. What is involved here is the relatively trivial insight that the actual capabilities needed in politics cannot be reduced to cratic abilities. Making policy in the areas of law, economics, health, the environment, defense, and foreign affairs requires specialized knowledge (in law, economics, medicine, ecology, and military matters) that is a result of the logic of the corresponding areas and that goes beyond the ability to impose one's own will—no matter how much it can also be said that the authority resulting from this specialized knowledge may itself be a power factor. (Nonetheless, in the case of foreign policy it must be conceded that cratology not only teaches how to impose the right policy but is also itself relevant, in part, to the determination of the right policy, precisely because foreign policy involves power struggles between states, among other things.[13] This is one of the two reasons why great politicians almost always have a special gift for foreign policy. The second reason has to do with the extraordinary importance of the good protected by foreign policy: peace.) In this connection it is important to note that the forgoing presupposes no specific theory regarding what the state's morally legitimate goals are; it presupposes only that what is actually recognized by citizens as a goal of the state cannot generally be reduced to victory in a power struggle. For the moment, we need not concern ourselves with the question of whether economic growth is a legitimate goal of state economic policy; what is crucial here is only that voluntary promotion or obstruction of economic growth is not possible without some knowledge of economics. Just as one can ascribe cratic abilities to someone who succeeds in climbing the ranks in a firm, without being convinced that he also has real competence in economics, the fact that someone holds high state office does not necessarily imply that he is competent in the field for which he is responsible, but for the most part it does imply that he has cratic intelligence (at least so long as there are many competitors for his office and its holder is not merely a puppet of more powerful figures behind the scenes who in this case are the persons who have this kind of intelligence). However, it is not easy to say wherein political competence in its highest form consists—for it is clearly not solely economic, legal or military. We might sug-

---

13. Because H. J. Morgenthau also understands foreign policy, and even politics in general, essentially in terms of the problematics of power, he does not ascribe a political character to all a state's activities with regard to another state (1985; 31 f.). Thus for him the only foreign policy worthy of the name is one that deals explicitly with questions of the distribution of power—in contradistinction to foreign policy motivated purely by economic interests, for example. Nevertheless, in the latter case I will speak of "foreign policy," and refer to the former as "critically motivated foreign policy."

gest that it is an ability to *correctly mediate* among the various goals of the state. A person who does not have this ability may be a good department head, but he could never become a major head of government. We should also mention here that because of the typically modern inclination toward reflexive structures, "policy par excellence" is sometimes (but not in this book) interpreted to designate what might be called, in distinction from economic, scientific, or foreign policy, *Politikpolitik* (to use an ugly but necessary term) or "meta-policy."[14] This term refers to a policy that is concerned with state organs themselves and with governmental regulation of the framework within which politics is practiced. For instance, demands for a law regarding parties or election reform, or more generally, for changes not in civil or criminal law but in constitutional law, would fall within the realm of meta-policy. It is clear that such a meta-policy would for the most part be immediately more relevant cratically than economic policy, for instance; but it cannot be reduced to the cratic, because in it, too, principles related to substance are important.

It is obvious, however, that even the greatest understanding of a subject can produce nothing *without* cratic abilities, and that only those who have both can become great politicians.[15] Moreover, it should not be assumed that there are general cratic abilities that can succeed in all social systems. To be sure, there are certain qualities that are necessary everywhere in order to rise to positions of power. But that does not mean that there is a combination of qualities that would be sufficient to ensure success everywhere. It may very well be that someone who wants to succeed in a royal court needs a certain quality that would necessarily lead to his downfall in a democracy, and vice versa. In any case, an investigation of both cratic abilities and political competence is indispensable for a satisfactory theory of politics. If Plato's error was to have nearly erased the cratic dimension of politics, most political thinkers of our own century have ignored the political dimension proper, and this is a still more disastrous form of one-sidedness. For example, in his *Begriff des Politischen* (*The Concept of the Political*), Carl Schmitt deals only with aspects of the concept of the cratic in which the opposition between friend and foe does in fact play a central role.

---

14. Despite her glorification of the ancient polis, the admirable Hannah Arendt demonstrates her modernity by seeing politics primarily as meta-policy and completely ignoring politically relevant issues such as economic and scientific policy. The term *Politikpolitik* is used by R. Ueberhorst (1986), among others.

15. In current usage the term "statesman" refers to persons who have both competence in their subject and cratic abilities, whereas "politician" is usually used for people who have cratic abilities alone. I have not adopted this usage and call careerists who are able to establish themselves in the state apparatus without being able to deal with matters of substance "political crats" (*politischen Kratiker*). Much the same holds for other spheres. A head physician, for example, needs not only medical knowledge but also leadership qualities, that is, cratic abilities; among artists, the same is particularly true of theater and film directors. This is objectively necessary and thus not to be lamented. It is only unfortunate when the crucial positions in a clinic, the arts, or science fall into the hands of medical, aesthetic, or scientific crats.

Thus I use the word "politics" to refer to acts that are directed toward the determination and/or implementation of state goals in the context of power struggles.[16] What goals are involved can remain an open question here. Protection from civil and foreign violence is certainly such a goal, but not the only one. Since the determination of goals is a theoretical task, this definition implies that public concern with questions of political philosophy must also be considered political. Thus the view toward which Plato seems to have inclined,[17] that Socrates was the most important Athenian politician, at least of his generation, is not untenable on formal grounds, and in terms of content it can be claimed with good reason that Socrates had significantly greater influence on the political destiny of Athens and even of all European states than did the politicians who condemned him. Similarly, when toward the end of the Roman Empire many scions of the Roman aristocracy decided to make a career in the church their decision may have been partly political in nature. There are situations in which founding a monastic order may be a greater contribution to a future state than preserving an empire,[18] and it could very well be that in current Western democracies shifts in perspective crucial for the politics of the coming decades are occurring not in the ministries but rather in the society. If the most urgent political task is the delegitimation of the existing order, then it must be carried out primarily outside the organs of the state. In any case, it would be a serious mistake to believe that political action is possible only through organs of the state; and nothing is more detrimental to a permanent transformation of the state than pressure to hold public offices before the necessary changes in society have been introduced. This is one of the many lessons that can be drawn not only from the collapse of Bolshevist experiments but also from Gorbachev's *perestroika*.

What precisely makes a goal a public goal? A necessary but not sufficient condition is that it concerns many, and sometimes all, the inhabitants of a certain area. However, scientific discoveries show that not all goals of this kind are public in nature. Scientific discoveries can have far-ranging consequences that cannot be considered public: Edward Jenner was a great physician, but that did not make him a great politician. A further important aspect of public goals is that they are seen by many people as being relevant to many people, and that a plurality is organized and cooperating in order to achieve them. But this sort of thing is already found in society, and not only in the state—consider private associations for the improvement of public health. On the other hand, a state goal in the narrower sense is involved when legal coercion is threatened as the ultimate means— whether against citizens or against members of the bureaucracy who do not apply cer-

---

16. One problem with this definition consists in the fact that not all cultures have a state, although they are all politically active. Cf. below, chap. 6, esp. chap. 6.2.2.1. The definition of politics as "the processes of human action by which conflict between the common good and the interests of groups is carried on or settled, always involving the use of or struggle for power" (M. J. Schwartz, V. W. Turner, and A. Tuden [1976], 189) escapes this problem; however, it is crucial that the concluding phrase be applied to a collective use of force that is felt to be legitimate.

17. *Gorgias* 521d.

18. Cf. MacIntyre's striking conclusion (1981), 244 f.

tain laws. With the introduction of obligatory vaccination, and even with the mere offer of voluntary but free vaccination paid for by public tax monies, Jenner's discovery became a state goal; and the definition we have given above indicates that such demands should be described as "political." If even the most remote relationship to legal coercion is lacking, I would speak of "public" rather than "political" goals: an athletic club that has millions of members is still not a political entity so long as it exercises no influence on the state's decisions and is not a corporation under public law (with compulsory membership, for instance). This distinction between "political" and "public" is obviously not intended to suggest that non-political public goals are any less important for the welfare of a people than are political goals. They are merely different in kind, because in principle no coercive measures are available to enforce them.

Even more than the determination of legitimate state goals, the battle for their actual implementation is generally regarded as the core of politics. We have already seen that it is not necessary that state organs be the agents of political activities. However, as a rule[19] it will be an intermediate goal of such activities that their own ends be pursued by state organs (perhaps after a political upheaval).[20] Even a non-parliamentary opposition or a revolutionary movement can be politically active, and parties are to be characterized as "political" organizations even if one considers the parties' infiltration of the state one of the greatest dangers to modern democracies. Conversely, not every governmental activity is political in the sense adopted here. The opposition between politics and the public bureaucracy does not consist in the fact that the public bureaucracy fulfills no state functions; but ideally it obeys commands and carries out only those state goals that have been set by politics. Naturally, bureaucracy is no less important than politics for the functioning of a good state, and thus every comprehensive politics must also include a policy of public bureaucracy; but then public bureaucracy is the object, not the subject of politics. Very roughly, we can say that public bureaucracy is related to politics as theorems are related to the axioms of an incomplete system; the latter are fundamental, the former are derived—no matter how great the degree of freedom enjoyed in administrative decisions in comparison with deductions of theorems from axioms.

---

19. It is a difficult terminological question of whether one can ascribe political goals to anarchists as well, since what they seek is the destruction of the state. I would like to answer the question in the affirmative, since their goal, even if in a negative way, is still related to the state.

20. In his precise language, Max Weber differentiates in the following way: "Der Sprachgebrauch nennt freilich 'politische Verbände' nicht nur die Träger der als legitim geltenden Gewaltsamkeit selbst, sondern z. B. auch Parteien und Klubs, welche die . . . Beeinflussung des politischen Verbandshandelns bezwecken. Wir wollen diese Art des sozialen Handelns als 'politisch orientiert' von dem eigentlich 'politischen' Handeln (dem *Verband*shandeln der politischen Verbände selbst . . .) scheiden." (1980; 30). ("It is, of course, true that every-day usage applies the term 'political,' not only to groups which are the direct agents of the legitimate use of force itself, but also to other . . . groups, which attempt to influence politically corporate action. It seems best for present purposes to distinguish this type of social action, 'politically oriented' action, from political action as such, the actual *corporate* action of political groups." Trans. A. R. Henderson and T. Parsons, 155 f.).

Since in this context we are not concerned with a distinction between politics and public bureaucracy as defined by constitutional law, my use of these terms in no way excludes the possibility that the true politics in a state might be practiced where in constitutional terms one would speak of bureaucracy. When rising to a ministerial post increasingly requires more and more cratic abilities and less and less expertise, and when ministers are ever more rapidly rotated from one ministry to another and end up performing their roles as if they were on acting on stage, then in a modern state the real policy is almost inevitably made by high administrative officials, that is, by the *political bureaucracy*. This does not necessarily mean that the quality of the policy is not good, even if this situation is not foreseen by the constitution of the state concerned.

The dynamic element in the concept of the power struggle indicates that there are people who are interested in changing the status quo, and others who defend it. In an age in which the political threatens to be reduced to the cratic, it is no accident that the most important political oppositions are no longer ignited by opposed recommendations for resolving concrete problems, but rather by the formal issue of whether one is for or against the status quo, conservative or progressive. In this context where it is still exclusively a question of clarifying the concept of the political, the point is only that conservative politics is easier (which says nothing about whether it is right or wrong). The status quo has a determinate character that does not characterize the possible alternative situations. Precisely for that reason, a successful politics of changing the status quo presupposes greater formal skills than one that seeks to preserve it. In the former we can see the highest form of politics, which could be defined as all those actions that seek, in the context of power struggles, to change the definition of the state's goals and to implement them. It will have been noticed that this concept of politics is still ethically neutral. According to this definition, Lenin, Stalin, and Hitler were highly successful politicians and not merely political crats. They not only held onto power for years (in Stalin's case even for decades), but also assigned new tasks to the state and were able to carry them out for a time against great resistance.

2.1.2. Morals, Ethics, Mores, Morality

The question inevitably arises as to which state goals and what means for realizing them are morally legitimate. It is this question with which this book is concerned; yet before we can answer it, and even before we can ask whether it is a meaningful question at all, two other concepts must be clarified. In this book, "morals" is used as a *normative* concept: an act, an institution, or an emotion are moral when they are as they ought to be.[21] The morals of a specific action, a specific institution, a specific act of the will, or

---

21. "Moral" can also mean "related to morals." A moral argument is not an argument that is as it should be, but rather one that seeks to discover what should be. "Moral feeling" correspondingly has two meanings.

a specific emotion is thus that about it which is as it should be.[22] If we are talking not about a specific activity but rather a type of behavior, then by its "morals" we mean the quintessence of what it should be. A book about the morals of politics deals with what is involved in politics and in what forms it should take place.[23] The discipline that is concerned with how human acts of will, feelings, actions, and institutions ought to be called "practical philosophy" (or sometimes "ethics"); its most important elements are individual ethics and political philosophy. Practical philosophy alone can make well-founded assertions concerning the moral nature of an action or an institution.

The basis for the division of practical philosophy into individual ethics and political philosophy results from the following observations. Moral norms clearly describe a behavior that should be, but that is not, necessary. How does a moral person react to immoral behavior? The severest possible sanction is physical coercion, and norms which it is permissible to enforce by resort to coercion, if it proves necessary, must be distinguished from those that it is not permissible to enforce in this way. Philosophy of law is the normative discipline concerned with norms whose violation should entail coercive measures on moral grounds. (Actual legal systems may deviate from the system of norms set forth by the philosophy of law just as actual individual behavior may deviate from what individual ethics requires.) Political philosophy is based on the philosophy of law insofar as the concept of the state presupposes that of law; but this does not mean that in political philosophy only the norms of the philosophy of law play a role. For example, patriotism cannot be enforced, but that does not mean that it is without importance. Another important difference between individual ethics and political philosophy is that in the former institutions play only a peripheral role as part of the contextual framework of individual behavior, whereas in the latter a normative theory of institutions, and in particular a normative theory of the state, is central. This is a consequence of the idea of coercion, among other things, which is morally permissible only when it is exercised impersonally, that is, as a function of an institution. However, it is clear that these institutions have to be realized through actions, and a normative theory, not of the institutions themselves, but of the actions involved in establishing and maintaining them makes up that part of political philosophy sometimes called "political ethics." Whereas the classical philosophy of the state can essentially be reduced to a normative theory of political institutions, Machiavelli's *Il Principe* is a good example of political ethics. In view of the great importance of the governmental framework for moral action, it is obvious that an ethics that does not include political philosophy is incomplete—and incomplete to a radical extent. To limit oneself to being a good husband while one's own state is committing crimes is morally insufficient, no matter how

---

22. The expression "about it" does not imply that only part of an actual action, etc., could correspond to the demands of morals.

23. I long considered titling this book "The Morals of Politics." On one hand, the relatively extensive discussion of general ethics, and on the other, the possible misunderstanding of this title, which seemed to suggest that there is only a moral politics, ultimately dissuaded me from doing so.

absurd the converse error of believing that a good state does not need intact families. For precisely that reason it is a mistake to think that political ethics deals with merely one field of applied ethics among many others. The concretization of the moral in the social and political is something that is not merely external to the moral and happens to it, so to speak; it is the moral itself that requires the social and the political. The concept of applied ethics wrongly supposes that abstract norms are the norms that truly matter and that the need to give them concrete form results only from actual developments. In reality, the point is to grasp these developments in their necessity.

Completely distinct from the preceding concepts are descriptive psychological and sociological concepts related to people's actual ideas of what should be valid. (Juristic concepts—unlike the concepts of the philosophy of law—should also be subsumed under this head, insofar as they are concerned only with norms that are actually recognized within a society, even if they cannot always be enforced.) This distinction is made more difficult by the misleading homonymy of the word "value." This word may refer either to what ought to determine individual or collective human behavior, according to a rational practical philosophy (as in Max Scheler's value ethics), or to the individually or socially recognized ideas that actually guide the behavior of an individual or a culture (as in Max Weber's sociology), no matter how much they might contradict values derived from ethics. In dealing with this and other similar concepts we can make use of the specifications "ideally valid," "individually valid," or "socially valid." Individually and socially valid values or preferences are the subject matter of empirical moral psychology and the sociology of mores; ontically, they are located in the world of experience. (The moral nature of individually or socially valid values consists in that element within them that corresponds to ideally valid values.) The psychology and sociology of mores consists of descriptive statements and as such they are ethically neutral; and from the process of philosophical justification it may emerge that not only the values of individual cultures but even generally widespread moral feelings and convictions have no claim to validity. It is even possible to distance oneself from one's own moral feelings; one can very well hold the view that one's own guilt feelings are the result of an unfortunate socialization and have no objective ground; and unlike an appeal to moral arguments, an attempt by someone to exploit these moral mechanisms to his own advantage may be considered deeply immoral. Only an extreme intuitionism will identify descriptive statements regarding one's own moral convictions with normative statements.[24] In European intellectual history it was the French moralists who first conceived the psychology of morals as a new discipline distinct from ethics. However, these early moralists still recognized absolute moral norms on the basis of which they criticized the mechanisms of moral psychology. This changed only with Nietzsche, who is best interpreted as a moralist without morals. Nonetheless, because of the distinction between genesis and validity even the most uncanny discoveries of moral psychopathology do

24. Cf. R. M. Hare (1952), 165 ff.

not help resolve the problem of validity. Even if it were possible to prove that certain moral convictions result from neuroses, this would not help us decide whether these convictions are right; one could still take the point of view that human nature is unfortunately so bad that it can approach truth only through neuroses.

The Hegelian concepts of "morality" (*Moralität*) and "mores" (*Sittlichkeit*) are also used in this book as descriptive concepts. What I understand by the "mores of a culture" is its ethos, that is, all its central, socially valid values, on one hand, and on the other the feeling of collective identity in particular; the latter springs from the general confidence that everyone recognizes these values. By "morality" I understand the isolation of the individual from the concrete values of his mores, on one hand, and on the other in particular from the collective identity that springs from mores. Because these terms are used purely descriptively, we can speak of the mores of Nazi Germany or of the morality of anarchistic terrorists. The "morals of morality and of mores" (in general, that is, independently of the concrete social values with which they are connected in a given historical situation) designates the distance from and proximity to the collective identity of one's own culture that a rational ethics requires a moral person to have.

It is obvious that the terminology proposed here deviates from general usage. The word "morals" is very often used descriptively: "the morals of the bourgeois epoch" is equivalent to what is here called "the mores of the bourgeois epoch"; the "genealogy of morals" is a meaningless expression in the language adopted in this book (because the moral is just as timeless as the objects of mathematics)—Nietzsche's stimulating book on the sociology of mores should be titled "On the Genealogy of Mores and of Moral Feeling." Since no homonymy is more dangerous than the one that leads to a confusion of the normative and descriptive levels (because if not detected it can lead to ethical nihilism), the philosopher's authorization to standardize linguistic usage is especially justified here. Yet one is simply following a maxim that will be justified later on (chapter 3.5) when after a critical standardization one inquires into the causes for reality's deviation from the standards set, thus in this case, for the homonymy of the word "morals." These causes are deeply grounded in metaphysics, and attempting to offer a full examination of them within the framework of this book would prevent us from turning to the issues with which we are primarily concerned here.[25] So I shall limit my remarks to the following. On one hand, the following implication is immediately plausible: If there were no ethical analysis of the morals of social phenomena, then the question of what one ought to do on moral grounds would be meaningless. Practical philosophy must be able to claim to evaluate and regulate individual and social phenomena if it does not want to abdicate its role. On the other hand, moral convictions are themselves psychic facts, and in an analogous way, ethical theories that are intersubjectively recognized or even merely debated belong to the social world as well. A sociology of ethics—an analysis of its status within social systems—is therefore an absolutely legitimate task; and it is clear that

---

25. On the following, see my remarks in (1990c), 215 ff., 234 ff.

while qua sociologist, a sociologist must understand the meaningful content of ethics in order to be able to relate it to other social systems, he may ignore (or, according to a certain understanding of sociology, must ignore) its claim to truth. In a certain sense what holds for ethics also holds for sociology itself: one can analyze the social context in which sociology (or specifically the sociology of ethics) emerges without thereby necessarily accepting this science's claim to truth. Only insofar as we constantly have to presuppose that our own activity may lead to the discovery of the truth, and that this activity coincides with the science that we are observing, do differences at the foundational level arise—admittedly, these are differences that do not strike a sociologist qua sociologist.

All this has to be acknowledged, and as we will see later, it is of greater relevance to ethics than most ethicists assume. But to deduce from this that ethical theories could be replaced by sociological theories would obviously be to commit a fallacy. It would be like describing a book simply as a physical object of a certain weight that has printer's ink sprinkled over its pages. It is incontestable that a book is this as well; and certainly there can be situations in which there might be a reasonable cognitive interest in perceiving it in this way and in no other. But that does not mean that the essence of a book is exhausted by such descriptions. Just as the dimension of meaning goes beyond that of physical being, the normative dimension transcends that of any mere meaning. In certain contexts it is possible to ignore the normative dimension, while in others it would be absurd to do so. To clarify what is at issue in this connection, we can use the Husserlian terms *noesis* and *noema,* independently, of course, of their background in the philosophy of consciousness. Noesis is the act of consciousness in which a subject grasps ("intends") something, and the noema is the object of this act, what is grasped ("intended"). Similarly, an ethical theory must be distinguished from what the theory is about. The theory itself belongs to the empirical social world, and can be investigated in terms of the latter's categories. On the other hand, the theory's noema belongs to a world of pure validities, and it is with this world that ethical theory is concerned. Only the theory itself, and not its noema, can be sociologically objectivized. Although sociology can make ethics its theme, it cannot therefore practice ethics itself, just as a historian of mathematics needs to be trained primarily in philology and thus is not in a position to make further advances in mathematics himself. The history of mathematics is a philological not a mathematical discipline, even though it can only be to the historian's advantage to know something about mathematics; and the sociology of ethics is a department of the social sciences, not of ethics. The comparison of ethics with mathematics is made advisedly, for even if, unlike mathematics, ethics refers to empirical entities, the principles in accord with which it evaluates these entities are located in a world of pure validities. Plato is absolutely right in saying that the method of mathematical thinking—its transcendence of empirical facticity—is essentially related to that of ethics. Anyone incapable of rising to the sphere of pure validities misses the essence of ethics.

The solution proposed here regarding the relationship between ethics and sociology has extensive analogies with Spinoza's parallelist solution to the mind-body problem. According to Spinoza interaction between the physical and the psychic does not occur; the physical can be causally explained only by the physical, and the psychic only by the psychic; however, it is incomplete to consider the world in terms of a single attribute. Similarly, the purely ethical and the purely sociological approaches are each incomplete, even though they both deal with closed systems. An ethical argument can be considered a social fact, especially as a weapon in a power struggle; but this does not allow us to decide either positively or negatively whether the argument is valid. Indeed, precisely because of the complementarity of the two approaches it will always be the case that interests of the most varied kinds are connected with a moral argument; and seeking to contradict moral positions by revealing such interests is a primitive form of "unmasking." Conversely, a theoretical analysis of the validity of arguments implies nothing regarding their effectiveness in the social world; for pure validities *justify* other validities, but they do not *cause* anything real. Whether a valid or invalid moral argument[26] will have an influence depends on the ability of the social environment to receive it, and this ability is oriented exclusively toward properties relevant to theoretical validity only in exceptional cases. Few people move about in the rarefied mountain air of pure validities; they must direct all their energies to knowledge and therefore seldom descend to action. More concrete psychic forces such as moral feelings, or at least a strong sense of self-respect, are indispensable if people are to act in accord with the principles of ethics. Whereas epistemology (including logic) and ethics are disciplines concerned with pure questions of validity, *rhetoric* is the science that—because of its knowledge of human behavior and its transformations through history—asks what linguistic structures produce which individual or social preferences (and thus also actions). For those who want to influence purely rational creatures, rhetoric would probably be superfluous; but since human beings are not purely rational creatures, rhetoric is indispensable as a link between ethics and politics. Whether it is morally permissible to use arguments that are not objectively rigorous, but have a stronger rhetorical effect than objectively conclusive ones, is of course once again an ethical question that cannot be answered by merely analyzing the social environment. In the work of Plato, Aristotle, and Cicero, ancient rhetoric very conscientiously asked this question, because rhetoric emerged from a moral interest. The emancipation of rhetoric from this bondage, which began with the Sophists and reached its conclusion in the moderns, explains but does not justify more recent philosophy's lack of interest in this key discipline.

From what has been said it follows that ethically neutral sociology commits an abstractive fallacy similar to that committed by behaviorism: whereas the latter ignores

---

26. The word "argument" is homonymous in a way similar to the word "sentence," which can refer both to a linguistic unit and to the proposition to which this unit refers. However, since in this book the context always makes clear how the word is being used, I have not taken the trouble to draw a terminological distinction between argument as expression (this alone can have an effect on other people—or rather, only in this way can one have an effect on other people) and argument as the meaning of an expression (this alone can be valid or invalid).

the psychic in its explanations of the physical world, the former neglects the normative dimension. Here we must repeat that one cannot prove that either has gaps in its area of research: ethical reasons can produce no changes in the world as experienced; at best it is real psychic insight into ethical reasons that causes something, and it is not implausible that events in the physical world (including movements of one's own body) are not caused by such psychic insights but rather by the brain states that accompany them.[27] But what is erroneous in these approaches is that they present partial areas of reality, which they plumb with great precision as if they were the whole. Archaic humans attributed souls to soulless beings and valued things that were morally neutral: these were errors that modern science and ethics have rightly corrected. But at least archaic man knew that there was something psychic and that the psychic element in humans had its center in the recognition of values that are more than psychic or social facts. The neurophysiologist, who has lost the ability to perceive his own interior dimension (*Innenseite*),[28] and the theoreticians of social systems who assess all moral arguments in relation to their social utility and can only shrug their shoulders when asked which of them are objectively valid, are surely far ahead of archaic man from a scientific point of view. In wisdom, however, and in an intuitive sense of the world as a whole, they are inferior to him, and if the loss of wisdom were necessarily the price to be paid for science, then it would be absolutely reasonable to ask whether this price were not too high. Fortunately there is philosophy, which seeks to combine wisdom and science; and only from a philosophy informed by the social sciences can we expect an answer regarding the morals of politics.

2.2. REJECTION OF CERTAIN OBJECTIONS TO A MORAL EVALUATION OF POLITICS

The preceding discussion presupposed that alongside the descriptive dimension there is also a normative dimension which is not reducible to the descriptive. The ideas actually held by people regarding values and norms can be reduced to the descriptive dimension, but as we have seen, this does not imply that ideally valid values and norms can themselves be subsumed under this dimension. Of course, this shows only that a normative perspective is possible, not that it is inevitable. A more complete demonstration of the inevitability of a normative perspective is the task of the metaphysics of morals, and without extensive discussion of the essence of foundations and the possibility of non-hypothetical knowledge we cannot achieve ultimate clarity in this domain.

---

27. See below, chap. 4.1.2. Naturally, the mind-body problem cannot be solved in this book.

28. The expression is dreadful, since it remains confined in the spatial sphere, to which subjectivity does not belong. However, since "subjectivity" designates very different things, I use it to refer to what Descartes called *res cogitans*.

This should not be surprising, for where else could we find ultimate clarity except in the ultimate and the unconditional, that is, in the absolute? But the problem of an ultimate foundation, which inevitably confronts anyone who wants to work out a theory of the normative, cannot be developed here.[29] I can only allude in a general way to the impossibility of circumventing the normative question: anyone who contests its legitimacy is himself making a normative validity claim. He has no choice but to acknowledge the existence of normative theories; what he means is that such theories are not legitimate—and this is obviously a normative proposition. The truth that every critic is obliged to claim for his own theory is itself a normative category, and any attempt to naturalize this category is hopeless, if only because any such theory must itself claim to be true. Truth is transcendental. It is a condition of the possibility of any theory, and can therefore not have the same status within the theory as do empirical objects. One can explain in terms of genetic or evolutionary epistemologies how someone comes to regard certain facts as true. But the question of whether these facts are really true cannot be resolved in this way; every genetic theory of this kind rather presupposes the solution of the problem of truth if it is to be taken seriously. The dimension of validity accessible to transcendental reflection not only cannot be subsumed under that of facticity, but precedes it. However, one could reply that truth may incontestably be a normative category, but it is only a *theoretical*-normative category. But practical-normative, that is, ethical, demands are much more closely connected with theoretical-normative categories than is commonly believed. Thus the fact that truth cannot be circumvented immediately implies the demand that we seek the truth. Indeed, in the first reflection on validity— which represents the beginning of philosophy—the theoretical-normative and the practical-normative dimensions coincide: the fact that one *should think* in a certain way grounds both logic and ethics. Moreover, the necessary communicability of theories opens up an intersubjective dimension: a person who formulates a theory has always already recognized a minimal ethics for intersubjective behavior. This becomes vividly clear with regard to the duty to be sincere: obviously someone who reserves for himself the right to lie without having any special justification for doing so can hardly say from the outset that he considers lying permissible; for lying works best when others consider the liar sincere.[30] The theory that lying is legitimate even without a special justification thus cannot be communicated—the logic of any theory that implies communicability necessarily entails the opposite ethical assumption, that is, the view that lying (except in possible exceptional cases) is not permissible. In general, we find in reflections of this kind the possibility of grounding universalism.

---

29. On this subject, see my more detailed discussion (1990c), 143 ff. I am aware particularly at this point how much I presuppose in this book that deviates from current opinions and that I have grounded partly elsewhere, partly not yet at all. However, I see no other way to proceed if this book is to be about political philosophy rather than about metaphysics.

30. Cf. Pascal's sixteenth *Provinciale* (1966; 343 f.), as well as Fichte (1971; 4:287).

Anyone who is not convinced by these admittedly very abstract arguments for the impossibility of going beyond the normative should consider that contesting the existence of a difference between normative and descriptive has the following consequence: If any actually existing set of mores were globally established, there would no longer be any point in opposing to it a moral sphere that transcended it; it would be as good as meaningless to describe it as "immoral." Had Hitler had atomic weapons available to him at the right time, he would certainly have made use of them without scruples and would probably have won the war. National Socialist mores would have likely determined world history for a long time. Any sober social science analysis must admit this, and ethics has nothing to oppose to the supposition. However, what is unacceptable for sociologism is that it is forced to make the much more far-reaching admission that under these circumstances Hitler would have been *morally* right—and this statement is significantly more important than the former assumption. If one does not want to capitulate to the normative power of the factual, one has no choice but to recognize that *the moral transcends the social.* Cratologists certainly understand why all totalitarian systems have a vital interest in denying that the moral is transcendent.[31] But it is philosophically clear that the recovery of the autonomy of the moral with regard to the factual social world is a task of the utmost importance—a task that modern European culture, even after overcoming National Socialism and communism, is still far from having fulfilled.

Yet even if one acknowledges the existence of an independent moral sphere, the question arises as to how this sphere is related to others. The reference to the subsystem of morals in systems theory suggests that although there is in fact something like morals, it should be concerned with itself, and not with other subsystems such as law, economics, or politics. To this we must reply emphatically that it is part of the essence of morals to claim the right to evaluate *every* kind of human action (and omission).[32] Economic practices, political decisions, and legal systems can be either moral or immoral; and an ethics that does not attempt to develop norms for them betrays the unconditional character of morals that is the latter's distinguishing feature. Whereas the hypothetical imperatives with which individual practical disciplines such as medicine, technology, and jurisprudence are concerned always teach only that "If you want to be healthy, control nature, or achieve certainty in law, you have to do this or that," the essence of ethics consists in laying down an unconditional, categorical imperative: "You should do this or that, quite independently of what you might want." To be sure, ethics must understand and—to a large extent, though not completely—justify the various subsystems' tendencies toward autonomy as being among the conditions of modernity. The

---

31. This interest is nowhere more clearly described than in Orwell's *1984.* The brilliance of his theory of totalitarianism lies far more in the acknowledgment of this central point than in his other observations.

32. This does not in any way exclude the existence of morally indifferent acts or omissions.

fact that economics is primarily concerned with being able to pay its debts might be morally approved, insofar as only the rationalization of economics makes it possible to prevent hunger and starvation, as morals demand; the fact that the military is primarily concerned with defeating the opponent is to be welcomed in the case of a just war. But what remains morally crucial is, first, that these tendencies to autonomy be related to legitimate goals, and second, that their implementation does not result in the sacrifice of goods and values higher than those that are the purpose of becoming autonomous. Anyone who is no longer willing to ask whether these two criteria have been met has abandoned the realm of morals.

In this context, it is of the utmost importance to understand that the moral is not a phenomenon that can be grasped in a purely descriptive way, but nor is it a normative subsystem *alongside* other normative subsystems. Thus it is misleading to oppose moral values to non-moral values, for instance, aesthetic, scientific, or contemplative values. The criteria for the aesthetic evaluation of works of art are certainly not the same as those for the moral evaluation of actions, but the production of a work of art, scientific activity, and even contemplation are actions that are as such subordinate to moral evaluation. On one hand, this means that it is a moral duty—*ceteris paribus*—to be concerned about the intrinsic value of the aesthetically beautiful: an aesthetically gifted person acts more morally when the development of his aesthetic talent plays a role in his plan of life than when he neglects it out of laziness. On the other hand, this means that aesthetic values have to be mediated with other values; and obviously this is possible only on the basis of some of the highest principles, which themselves are not particular. The moral is the ultimate legitimating authority that determines the relationship of different values to each other; and that would be impossible if it were merely a partial normative system among others rather than the most general normative system that stands above them. In the latter case one could appeal to non-moral values (aesthetic or religious, for example) and justify virtually any crime in their name.[33] However, this invocation of an opposition between moral values and other values contains a kernel of truth, even if it is poorly expressed. In this language, "moral norms" are those that are valid for intercourse among normal persons in common situations; and their violation in the name of generally irrelevant values—aesthetic values, for instance—is what people have in mind when they talk about a conflict between the moral and the aesthetic. Nonetheless, in the terminology used in this book it is clear that these other (e.g., aesthetic) goods must be morally relevant, too, when a serious moral conflict is presumed to be involved. For example, we often overlook in a highly gifted artist's or scientist's social behavior things that we would not forgive in others; thus it seems petty to reproach a great artist for having an unconventional love life. It may be possible to justify this by saying that a high degree of talent is almost necessarily connected with difficulties in finding one's identity,

---

33. Kierkegaard's Abraham in *Fear and Trembling* (*Frygt og Bæven*) is a terrifying example of where this kind of development necessarily leads. Cf. my discussion of *Fear and Trembling* (1992b).

and this gives erotic behavior, for instance, a character that deviates from what is morally demanded; this may provide an excuse. Perhaps one could even speak of justification when what has to be evaluated negatively from a moral point of view is counterbalanced by the higher value set upon scientific and artistic achievements that benefit the whole society, achievements that are presumably aided by these irregularities. However, this does not in any way mean that one should be prepared to accept everything—murder, for example—not even if it can be shown that it inspired splendid works of art by the murderer.[34] And it also does not mean that every average individual may apply to himself the exception reserved for genius, no matter how widespread the misuse of this argument in a time that has lost any sense of standards and in which anyone can therefore consider himself an exception on the model of Raskolnikov.

2.3. IDEAS ON AN ETHICS OF ETHICS

From the forgoing it follows that one cannot have too much moral conviction: the normative sphere cannot be got beyond, but only fallen below. However, something very important is probably addressed by the commonly heard complaint about what could be called "moralism." Yet it is only morals itself that can legitimately criticize this moralism; it is only a self-limitation of the moral that can be taken seriously, not a limitation of the moral by something external to it—for this something external would itself have to appear before the tribunal of moral judgment. Thus the demand for an *ethics of ethics* is meaningful,[35] no matter how abstruse it might at first sound; it necessarily arises from the theory of the complementarity of the social and ideal dimensions outlined above. Since ethics—despite the ideality of its object—is an individual or social performance, it can and must be subjected to moral norms as well. However, it is no accident that in the great ontogenetic and phylogenetic crises represented by adolescence and the Enlightenment the idea of an ethics of ethics is not understood; anyone who grasps the unique ontological status of the normative and thereby cuts himself off from socially accepted mores will be seized by a longing for developing norms that makes him blind to the possible negative side effects of his own activity. Whereas in traditional cultures, and still in early modernity,[36] awareness of the social peril involved in philosophical and especially ethical activity resulted in the adoption of esoteric forms of communication, this kind of awareness evaporated in the Enlightenment, which did

---

34. The contradiction between art and the moral norms that shape bourgeois life has played a major role since the nineteenth century, for instance, in the fiction of Thomas Mann. But whereas one feels sympathy for Tonio Kröger, Leverkühn oversteps the limits of tolerance allowed even the greatest artist.

35. It does not lead to an infinite regress because the principles of the ethics of ethics are identical with those of an ethics of the ethics of ethics.

36. Cf. Leibniz, *Nouveaux Essais* I 3 § 24.

not hesitate to popularize philosophy. The maturity of an individual and of a culture has much to do with the extent to which they have grasped the necessity of an ethically grounded self-limitation of ethics—an ethics of ethics.

The first principle of the ethics of ethics has to do with the relationship of the ethicist to his potential audience. It is often difficult to formulate norms for others insofar as the explicit formulation usually assumes that the ethicist's addresses are tempted to violate them, or would never have discovered these norms themselves;[37] and it requires extraordinary tact to avoid giving the impression[38] of this assumption implicit in the practice of imposing norms.[39] As a general rule, any teaching relationship sets up an asymmetry that is often unavoidable and morally acceptable only when the power it grants is not arrogantly exercised—especially when the contents of the ethics taught are universalistic in nature, for in the latter case a self-contradiction appears. Since ethical activity is not a goal in itself, but is directed toward action,[40] the ethicist must seek to act in accord with his own theory in every respect. It is certainly true that an ethical theory can never be refuted by the fact that its representatives do not conduct themselves in accord with it; but such ethicists must be subject to more severe moral judgment than other people who act in violation of moral commands, because the discrepancy between the former's teaching and their lives has an especially discouraging effect. Personal models

---

37. It does not require great psychological insight to see that certain people only begin to moralize because they sense a tendency *in themselves* to violate moral commands; thus it is a mistrust with regard not only to other people but also to themselves that can lead to the development of norms. Conversely, my dear friend Reiner Schürmann, for example, could afford to formulate a philosophy that was fatal to the principles of ethics—because he was one of the most candid people of our time.

38. Cf. Scheler's well-known criticism (1980; 211, esp. 220 ff.). Thus Socrates did not teach ethics, but rather limited himself to asking a few questions. However, one must also beware of false modesty, which can seem even more arrogant than explicit feelings of superiority; in any case this ironic modesty did not win Socrates any friends. The foregoing implies the important hermeneutic maxim that the lack of evaluation in an author's work does not allow us to conclude that his point of view is ethically neutral. Thucydides would have spoiled everything had he written at the end of book five, after the brief description of the killing and enslaving of the Melians, "How evil the Athenians were!" Instead, the great artist—for the founder of objective historiography was certainly also a great artist—placed in books six and seven immediately after this passage the description of the Sicilian expedition, which is the climax and turning point of his *History* that brings on the downfall of Athens. Thus Thucydides *expressed* (but did not explicitly say, as Tacitus would have) two different things: first, it is a historical law that a positivistic power politics makes no friends; and second, that Athens had no moral right to complain about its catastrophe, no matter how deeply the exiled Athenian might have empathized with his people. Cf. Hobbes's excellent remarks in the introduction to his translation of Thucydides: "Digressions for instruction's cause . . . he never useth; as having so clearly set before men's eyes the ways and events of good and evil counsels, that the narration itself doth secretly instruct the reader, and more effectually than can possibly be done by precept" (1839 ff. a; 8:xxii; cf. also viii).

39. Imposing norms does not consist merely in propositions, but is carried out through concrete *speech acts*. This also holds true for the activity of imposing epistemological norms; if we keep this in mind, many of the problems raised by Wittgenstein in *Über Gewißheit* (*On Certainty*) dissolve.

40. Cf. Aristotle, *Nicomachean Ethics* 1103b26 ff.

do not provide the justification for the validity of moral judgments, but they motivate people to act morally in a significantly deeper way than does the most complete rational grounding. For precisely this reason, Socrates is the ideal paradigm of the philosopher, because he combines two things that were unfortunately separated in later ethical systems. He lifted people out of traditional mores into the sphere of rigorous ethical arguments, and at the same time he *was* what he demanded. In contrast with this unity, the conception that ethics is concerned only with the analysis of propositions and personalism's abandonment of rational grounding in ethics are both unacceptably one-sided.

It is less grave but still unacceptable when the ethicist does not act in contradiction to what he teaches, but nevertheless refrains from any action that goes beyond his own ethical activity. For it would undermine the meaning of ethics if one spent one's whole life reflecting on what one should do before actually beginning to act. Here we confront a problem that is of immense significance for modern ethics in particular. The methodological doubt that has plagued and driven forward modern philosophy ever since Descartes forces the philosopher to distance himself from current mores and to seek a rational foundation for ethics. However, this search is partly so demanding, and partly so satisfying in itself, that it can lead to the mistaken impression (which no doubt constitutes a great temptation for discourse ethics) that the elaboration of an ethics (or, at a higher level, a very general meta-ethics) is the true moral duty. Indeed, in enlightened cultures in which the claim to rationality is itself a component of power, the latent, if not always manifest, function of ethical discourse may consist, not in encouraging action, but rather in discouraging it. Anyone without illusions will recognize that ethics today is constantly misused as a pretext for putting off necessary but painful and unpopular decisions. This happens in many ethics commissions charged with assessing the impact of technology. These are currently springing up everywhere and have essentially two functions: first, they have a pacifying effect on public opinion, without, however, causing what is required to be done; and second, they provide jobs for philosophers and social scientists and thus buy loyalty to the state in accord with the principles of what is in this case an exceptionally expensive welfare policy. For we should not deceive ourselves: many of the ecological problems of late industrial societies could be resolved by simply consuming less, and in this context the task of the numerous well-paid ethical discourses is solely to distract attention from this simple solution, whose very simplicity collides with the discursive needs of academics as well as with the interests of the defenders of the status quo.

It cannot be denied without self-contradiction that ethicists' activity is morally significant. But from that it does not follow that it is the highest or even the only such activity: to believe that would be to make the magic circle of reflection, which is fundamental but not everything, absolute. To be sure, the ideal person will possess ethical virtue in addition to all the moral virtues, that is, the ability to defend these virtues in the framework of an ethical theory—Plato's Socrates possesses both moral and ethical virtues. However, this does not mean, first, that ethical virtue—that is, the ability to conduct competent argumentation on moral issues—makes it unnecessary to have the usual moral virtues; or, second, that one cannot be a moral person without engaging in ethical reflection—an arrogant misconception found in some ethicists, but fortunately not in the most important ethicists. To contest St. Francis of Assisi's holiness on the basis of his inadequate argumentative competence would be highly inappropriate.

A moral person must not only do far more than engage in ethical reflection—he must also, for instance, act in accord with his own ethics. Even the most important ethicist will often obey moral commands with regard to which he does not yet have a fully worked-out ethical theory and perhaps never will have. It follows from the rational understanding of ethics that it must in principle be possible to systematize all our moral duties in the framework of an ethics. But the theoretical possibility of rationally reconstructing morals does not mean that it is already completely reconstructed or that it will be within the foreseeable future. For that very reason one of the first steps to be taken by the ethicist is to sketch out a "provisional ethics," to adapt Descartes's famous expression.[41] Despite its pathos, the refusal to recognize a provisional ethics at least for a certain time and to reflect further on it during one's own practical activities is immoral, because it suppresses the temporality and finitude that is our lot and within which all our actions take place.[42] It is ethics itself that requires that the demands of ethics and the demands of action be balanced; and the smile with which a practical man who has long exercised important responsibilities usually greets a professorial ethicist who has himself done nothing and would like to tell the practical man what he should do, is not always, but often, justified. Indeed, insofar as action presupposes a suspension of the objectivizing attitude that is possible with regard only to past actions, it can even be said that the ultimate meaning of ethical reflection lies in its own elimination—even though this can only be temporary.[43] It is obvious that during work on ethics important guidelines will be provided by moral common sense, by the traditions of one's own culture, by the ways of life of people felt to be models or admired for some of their actions on the basis of rational arguments, and by the classics of ethical thought. Certainly, these guidelines are not infallible—common sense may be mistaken, traditions are full of nonsense, great models also have moral failings, and classics may be wrong. But even

---

41. Descartes speaks of his "morale par provision" in the third part of the *Discours de la méthode* (1964 ff.; 6:22) and in his letter to Picot at the beginning of the French edition of the *Principes de la philosophie* (1964 ff.; 9/2:15). There we also read that a fully elaborated ethics is the final part of philosophy.

42. One needs a provisional ethics not only to be able to act morally before the conclusion of the work on ethics, but also for reasons purely internal to ethics. Science (and ethics is a science) can be pursued successfully only if one has an intellectual *goal* that guides one's work. A great mathematician must already believe what he wants to prove before he can set about proving it, and the idea of how to prove something is often a greater achievement than the technical work involved in carrying out this idea. In philosophy, anyone who refuses to live with temporary gaps in his line of argument and to think further about them will never write an important work.

43. This is how we should understand Goethe's famous maxim: "Der Handelnde ist immer gewissenlos, es hat niemand Gewissen als der Betrachtende" (1991; 758). ("The person engaged in action is always unconscionable; no one except the contemplative has a conscience." Trans. E. Stopp, 127.)

one's own ethical efforts are fallible; caution is just as appropriate with regard to them as with regard to the tradition, and so long as one is not really sure that one's own ethical theory is better than that of the tradition from which it deviates, one ought to follow the latter. However, it would be absurd to exclude the possibility that ethics can bring about a correction of current moral ideas; only in this way can ethics contribute to moral progress. But the ethicist should never forget that the ability of even enlightened cultures, and yet more so of traditional cultures, to deal with moral revolutions in a positive way is surprisingly limited. The ethicist should, wherever possible, connect his new moral demands with the actual mores and avoid leaving the impression that he does not recognize the partial moral value they always represent.[44]

In fact, the moral dangers of ethics cannot be reduced to the possible negative *consequence* that ethics may prevent people from acting and condemn a culture to Hamlet-like hesitation. Ethical reflection often has an even intrinsically negative value insofar as it displaces immediate moral feelings that have a positive value. The identification with one's own culture, the basic trust of our fellow human beings, the spontaneous wish to help when one thinks one sees a possibility to do something good, can irreparably dwindle away through a certain form of ethical reflection. Critics of ethical reflection from Hegel to Nietzsche rightly criticized this loss of graceful spontaneity that we find in highly reflective societies everywhere. In a superlatively absurd way, because here even the basic value of ethics is falsely determined, this problem arises for hedonistic utilitarianism. Pleasure is not the only or even the highest value. But whereas even the most rigorous moralist cannot deny all sympathy with the unreflective bon vivant (Falstaff, with all his vices, is such a rounded personality), there are few things sadder than the utilitarian who calculates the maximum pleasure, including the renunciations now and then required for its achievement. What is valuable in sensual pleasure is its vital spontaneity. To sacrifice this to something higher is morally commendable. But to give it up for the sake of a pleasure calculated through reflection is ludicrous, since this reflective pleasure is neither pleasure nor something qualitatively higher, but simply a repellent mixture of pleasure and renunciation—even if it seems to be the only pleasure accessible to the sense of values of many people in the bourgeois age.[45]

Nonetheless, we must emphasize that no truly great ethicist (not even Kant) lacked the spontaneity that is an indispensable mark of a great personality. It is only inadequate reflection that estranges us from emotional spontaneity. The great philosopher is one in whom reflection has become second nature and whose spontaneity is revealed precisely in

---

44. Thus it is morally questionable whenever ethicists are concerned primarily with exceptional situations and neglect the usual cases for which traditional mores always offer more or less reasonable norms. Since any such exception, no matter how well justified, may tempt us to apply it also to cases in which it is not appropriate, the sensitivity with which a culture fends off the attempt, for example, to "critically" discuss the most elementary moral prohibition—namely, killing innocent people—is, although not a sign of intellectual sovereignty, more positive than complete indifference to such attempts.

45. Cf. Scheler (1980), 257 ff.

the liveliness of his thought. Above all, because of the value of spontaneity, any reasonable ethicist will also have to acknowledge that countless actions are neither moral nor immoral, but simply morally indifferent.[46] Nothing escapes ethical judgment, but the latter may decide that a given action or omission is neither good nor bad, or that different alternatives are equally good. And even when a better alternative is conceivable, there may be two good reasons for abandoning the search for it: first, if the most that will be achieved by the alternative solution is a moral triviality that does not outweigh the loss of natural spontaneity that is the price to be paid; and second, if pursuing this alternative solution would leave one with too little moral energy remaining to pursue more important moral goals. Realistically, one has to assume that the moral (and especially altruistic) energies of any individual are limited—in varying degrees, of course, but nonetheless always limited. Concentrating on the essential and allowing oneself at least small sins of omission is therefore commanded by *moral* prudence. In any case, it is extremely important for everyone to find out how much moral energy he has, in order to make use of it as economically as possible.[47] Underestimating oneself means failing to do the best one can, while overestimating oneself easily leads to forms of self-deception and unwitting hypocrisy.

Finally, we should mention the following problem, which is actually the most important of the ideas nowadays opposed to the project of an ethics. Everyone who is concerned with morals in his own conduct confronts the question how he should behave with regard to people who do not have the same concern with morals. Without any doubt dangers loom in answering this question—dangers both individual and political in nature. The fact that we can secretly (or sometimes not so secretly) rejoice in other people's failings because by contrast they bring out our own moral excellence, very significantly diminishes this excellence. Even for non-Christians, this remains one of the most important and original insights in the moral message of Jesus of Nazareth, even though many Christians have succumbed to the temptation.[48] Irreconcilability and denigration of opponents during political conflicts about values, and especially after the victory of a party, are extremely dangerous for a state. But all this means only that this kind

---

46. The failure to recognize the existence of the morally indifferent is the mark of pietistic religiosity. No matter how important an increased attention to the moral dimension of one's own intentions has been, the concentration on one's own subjectivity, which avoids turning into overt narcissism only because of its theological justification, remains questionable.

47. Even though economics, like any human activity, is subject to ethical judgment, it is nonetheless possible to apply economic categories to ethics. Economic thinking becomes decisive when scarce resources are involved, and altruism is a scarce resource. On the ambivalence in the concept of the economic, see H. D. Lasswell and A. Kaplan (1969), 79.

48. It is particularly repulsive when this joy in one's own excellence is bound up with an objectively false position, and one has reason to suspect that the false and simplistic position was assumed only in order to appear morally better than the other party. This moralism becomes unbearable when the attacks on the moral self-respect of others become the sole means of maintaining one's own self-respect, and one has simultaneously persuaded oneself that there are no objective moral norms. The contradiction in this position is so blatant that it points to a high level of cultural decline in a state when many organs of public opinion can make a living—and obviously a good living—off this attitude.

of behavior is *not* moral, even if it considers itself moral; and it would be absurd to draw the conclusion from the criticism of false moral convictions that we have to go beyond the moral. The view that one *should* do away with morals is self-contradictory, for on what ground could this judgment be based except on that of morals, from which it wants at the same time to move away? One could argue meaningfully to that effect only by saying that morals itself commands caution in applying legal sanctions in particular, but also moral sanctions (such as a withdrawal of respect). It is clearly immoral to try to impose certain moral commands by force of law; and the use of moral sanctions as a public or private reproach is often morally unacceptable as well. A particularly instructive example of this is the moral condemnation of a person who has done something immoral in a very difficult situation (for instance, in an unjust state) when this judgment is made by another person who was not involved in such a situation and who has therefore enjoyed what has been aptly called "moral luck."[49] While the moral judgment that many people in totalitarian states have done things they should not have done is objectively correct, that does not mean that every person who has not made himself guilty of such an offense because he was never a citizen of a totalitarian state has the right to communicate this judgment to the guilty. From the norm that *a* should do *F* it does not follow that everyone has the right to say this to *a;* it does not even follow that there is anyone except *a* who can say it to him without being asked. The principle of autonomy requires that every person has to work out minor moral misdemeanors with himself, with the victim of his offense or with a person whom he himself seeks out or whom he trusts; and even in the case of more serious transgressions the critic should be qualified to judge in an official capacity, through a special relationship with the offender, or through a special moral authority. And even then *tact* is required, that is, the kind of restraint that allows the other to gain insight into certain things by himself.[50] This in no way suggests that the quality of a relationship between people such as a friendship is not shown precisely by

---

49. See B. Williams's article (now in 1981; 20–39), as well as Thomas Nagel's article with this title (now in 1979; 24–38; the Nazi example is on p. 34). My defense of a moderate intentionalism will show that I agree, albeit to a very limited extent, with Williams's and Nagel's articles, which raise an important problem.

50. Cf. a fine passage in Gadamer (1975; 13): "Daher gehört Unausdrücklichkeit und Unausdrückbarkeit dem Takt wesentlich zu. Man kann etwas taktvoll sagen. Aber das wird immer heißen, daß man etwas taktvoll übergeht und ungesagt läßt, und taktlos ist, das auszusprechen, was man nur übergehen kann. Übergehen heißt aber nicht: von etwas wegsehen, sondern es so im Auge haben, daß man nicht daran stößt, sondern daran vorbei kommt. Daher verhilft Takt dazu, Abstand zu halten, er vermeidet das Anstößige, das Zunahetreten und die Verletzung der Intimsphäre der Person." ("Hence an essential part of tact is that it is tacit and unformulable. One can say something tactfully; but that will always mean that one passes over something tactfully and leaves it unsaid, and it is tactless to express what one can only pass over. But to pass over something does not mean to avert one's gaze from it, but to keep an eye on it in such a way that rather than knock into it, one slips by it. Thus tact helps one to preserve distance. It avoids the offensive, the intrusive, the violation of the intimate sphere of the person." Trans. J. Weinsheimer and D. G. Marshall, 16.)

the possibility of talking about one another's weaknesses within it; but it remains crucial that the criticism takes place within a justifying framework. The offender's feeling of self-worth and self-respect, without which moral improvement is inconceivable, would otherwise be dreadfully wounded.[51] Finally, it goes without saying that a theory of moral sanctions that does not acknowledge the possibility of remorse and does not recognize the concept of forgiveness is radically incomplete.[52]

In general, it is not difficult to understand that all concrete arguments against moralizing politics themselves presuppose certain moral values. their persuasive force depends on these ideally valid values being recognized. Ethics must take very seriously the idea, which goes back to Machiavelli, according to which many of the usual norms of individual ethics are valid only when those to whom they are addressed live in the framework of an order guaranteed by state power. If we recognize that there is no general duty to take potentially fatal risks, and in particular that giving in to violence and trickery is not morally obligatory but is in general even forbidden, every reasonable person will acknowledge, that in a situation approaching the state of nature, duties are valid that are not valid within a state. For within a state one is protected by the state's coercive power, whereas in the state of nature good-willed trust can have lethal consequences. Since the existence of a state order is the precondition for the coming into effect of many individual ethical duties that are desirable in themselves, the foundation of states is a morally privileged goal; and because of the great moral importance of this goal the battle to achieve it may justify the use of means that should not be used for goals of less moral excellence. In any case it is clear that conduct that leads to the founding of states cannot be assessed in relation to norms whose validity already presupposes the existence of the state. Admittedly, it follows from the forgoing only that certain duties are not imposed upon the founder of a state, nor to some extent on any statesman, that are imposed on normal citizens—though this does not entail that the former are not bound by moral duties at all. Only the complete decoupling of politics from ethics is to be rejected as nihilistic. On the other hand, the idea that politicians are freed from some duties of individual ethics, when this is necessary in order to maintain some good higher than the one involved in these duties, must be seriously considered in any ethics. Politics may stand above individual ethics but it cannot escape ethics as such. However, a comprehensive ethics will oppose those who seek to detach politics from morals as

---

51. The young Hegel vividly expressed this point in the following way: "Jeder kann einem solchen (sc. moralischen Kritiker) antworten: die Tugend hat das Recht, dies an mich zu fordern, aber nicht Du" (1969 ff.; 1:438). ("Everyone can answer such a person (*sc.*, a moral critic): virtue has the right to ask that of me, but you do not."

52. What is disturbing about the self-righteousness with which many people who have had moral luck pass judgment on those who have committed offenses is not only that they would do better to leave this judgment to those who have been put to the same tests and have nonetheless proved themselves (which cannot be said of the former); they also generally fail to understand that guilt can cause one to mature in a way that remains unknown to those who were never tempted.

well as moralistic simplifiers who pass disparaging judgment on politicians who have lived under conditions more difficult than their own—politicians who have done what is morally right, even when it deviated from the average person's moral ideas.[53]

Much the same goes for Hobbes's arguments against moralizing politics. The fact that civil war is a dreadful evil means that it is a moral duty to prevent it (unless a still greater evil threatens, a possibility that cannot always be excluded). From this it follows that one must in fact deal very carefully with the right of resistance. Yet this does not mean that one should not ask oneself which laws in one's own state can be considered bad on moral grounds, or that one should not work to change these laws within the legal framework provided for doing so. However, even in the case of legal criticism one will try to avoid disturbing too greatly the mores of one's own time, if one agrees with Hegel that the morals of mores consist in preventing an absolutizing of morality that makes common action much more difficult in the long run, among other things because it leads to the aforementioned spiteful moral arrogance.

---

53. C. A. J. Coady mentions (1993) three ways of resolving the conflict between morals and politics: one can fully detach politics from morals; one can promote the view that morals is self-contradictory; or one can distinguish between lower and higher moral principles. It goes without saying that only the third path can be taken.

3

Principles of Ethics

Although it is impossible to work out a comprehensive ethics in this book, certain principles of ethics underlying our discussion must be formulated, even though they cannot be fully grounded.[1] I begin with a few metaethical considerations. First, I assume that ethics is a rational discipline, and thus that normative and value judgments can be true or false.[2] Ethical systems can be criticized only on this basis; and although it is undeniable that ethical statements also have expressive or evocative meaning-components, it would be erroneous to try to reduce them to these components.[3] "Oh, if only he would come!" does not have the same logical status as "It is his duty to come"; the former is a wish without any claim to validity, the latter an assertion that claims to be objectively true. Second, I assume that the ideal validity of a value cannot be deduced from any empirical facts (not even from social facts such as the recognition of socially valid values), but is instead grounded in an autonomous normative sphere: purely normative propositions do not follow from descriptive propositions.[4] This does not mean that nothing that is, is as it ought to be. Neither does it mean that there are no natural qualities (of actions, for example) that

---

1. On the terms used and the arguments presupposed in the following pages, see the outstanding book by my teacher F. von Kutschera (1982), to which I owe a great deal with regard to the criticism of non-cognitive and subjective theories of ethics. However, I see the problem of grounding ethics differently; I consider his theory of the experience of value as important in the area of the psychology of morals, but not in that of the theory of validity. Kutschera's *Einführung in die Logik der Normen, Werte und Entscheidungen* (1973) is a good introduction to the preliminaries to ethics that are formalizable (e.g., deontic logic).

2. Since normative and value judgments differ from descriptive judgments, other terms, such as "right" and "wrong," might be introduced, so long as the difference in truth value is not abandoned.

3. As A. J. Ayer (1936) and his followers tried to do.

4. As is well known, Hume was the first to formulate this point clearly (*A Treatise of Human Nature* III 1,1 [1977; 177 f.]). Thus the discontinuity between *Is* and *Ought* has become known as Hume's Law.

can be characterized normatively.[5] Such interpretations of the prohibition on the so-called naturalistic fallacy[6] are themselves fallacious; but the basic idea that underlies Hume's Law is correct. However, we must add one important qualification: what ought to be, ought to *be;* and that means that "ought" implies "can." There can be no obligation to do something that is in principle impossible. However, we can be obliged, for instance, to create a situation in which something becomes possible which at the moment is not feasible. We will return to the metaphysics of the relationship between *Is* and *Ought* in chapter 3.4.1. Here let us note only that the verbal pair "is-ought" is unfortunate insofar as it seems to presuppose that moral obligation is not part of being. In reality, however, it means only that moral obligation is not rooted in *real, empirical* being; its being as an *ideal* not posited by humans is thereby no more denied than is the possible function of being a principle with regard to empirical being.

Neither normative nor value judgments can be derived from descriptive judgments—but how are the first two related to each other? Non-naturalistic ethics can be divided into two groups, depending on what is considered more important and more fundamental: normative judgments, for instance, general imperatives, or value judgments that predicate value of specific contents. This marks the distinction between teleological and deontological ethics.[7] Philosophers commonly call deontological an ethics for which obligations, prohibitions, and permissions are the basic concepts,[8] and teleological an ethics for which goods and values are basic.[9] It seems to me—and this is my

---

5. If two actions, objects, etc., are differently valued, they must also have different descriptive qualities (cf. Hare [1952], 80 ff.). From this it follows that in ordinary language a word such as "good" has, in addition to its valuative meaning, a descriptive meaning as well. If one calls a person "good," one usually suggests that he has certain qualities. But this does not alter the fact that the two semantic elements can and must be distinguished. See Hare (1952), esp. 111 ff.

6. The term is taken from Moore, *Principia Ethica* (1903; 10 ff.). However, first, his argumentation is vague; second, the expression "fallacy" is misleading; third, not only naturalistic (in the narrower sense) but also social contents are impermissible as the sole foundation of normative propositions (for which reason people now speak of a descriptive fallacy); and fourth, Moore excludes more than does Hume—for example, a logical or metaphysical grounding of ethics. Since I consider the latter permissible, I recognize only Hume's Law, but continue to speak, following customary usage, of "naturalism," meaning by that term a violation of Hume's Law.

7. As a comprehensive concept including both "normative" and "evaluative," I sometimes use "axiological," and sometimes "normative" in the broader sense, whereas we could use "prescriptive" for "normative" in the stricter sense.

8. Prohibitions and permissions can be reduced to obligations: "It is forbidden that A"—formalizable as F(A)—means that it is obligatory that ~A (O(~A)); "it is permissible that A" (P(A)) means that it is not obligatory that ~A (~O (~A)).

One problem with the triadic division of the fundamental deontological concepts is that it classifies as "permissible" not only morally indifferent but also supererogatory actions—that is, actions that have a high moral value but go beyond what one can normally expect from people.

9. Another definition is found in Rawls: In teleological theories, "the good is defined independently from the right, and then the right is defined as that which maximizes good" (1971; 24). According

third point—that the priority of value judgments over normative judgments is obvious. On one hand, the existence of an objective order of values entails corresponding obligations, permissions, and prohibitions. It is forbidden to fall below a certain moral level, that is, to harm certain fundamental goods and values. To this extent, teleological concepts ground deontological concepts. On the other hand, we have already seen in discussing the principles of the ethics of ethics that the pragmatics of imposing norms and imperatives necessarily implies that the person to whom they are addressed feels an inclination to violate the norm. This premise cannot always be taken for granted; in any case, it is a descriptive assumption that should not enter into the foundations of ethics. Finally, it is disturbing that in normative ethics, human action receives too one-sided an emphasis. Nicolai Hartmann rightly pointed out that the commanding and forbidding of actions constitutes only one part of ethics. No less important is the recognition of reality's plenitude of value, which does not depend on human action to be good and meaningful.[10] Value judgments are thus more basic than normative judgments.

Fourth, ethics is a science insofar as it has to begin with general principles. From these and from other premises (which, as we will see, may include descriptive premises), it has to derive concrete norms.[11] From the point of view of moral psychology, it is certainly true that one first judges concrete, individual cases morally and then raises such judgments to general principles, but this is relevant only genetically, not in terms of the theory of validity. One ought to take moral intuitions very seriously and not sacrifice them to theory-building unless it is necessary to do so. But this can in fact become necessary, and it is extremely suspect when someone seeks out moral principles insofar as they ground the convictions he has already formed. Even Rawls's concept of reflective equilibrium[12] is not free from this circularity—at least, so long as Rawls cannot ground the claim that no radical errors can occur on either general or concrete levels. To do so, however, would unavoidably require reflection on the problem of the ultimate foundation.

Finally, I assume that the duty to be moral cannot be reduced to any subjective interest. We are concerned here with a categorical, not a hypothetical, imperative. One should not be moral because in the long run it is in one's enlightened self-interest; because

---

to Rawls, deontological theories are non-teleological (30). This definition is not equivalent to the first one, since in Aristotelian ethics the idea of maximization plays no role, even though it is a teleological ethics according to the above definition.

10. Cf. Hartmann (1935), 7 f. My revered colleague G. Scherer's impressive efforts to make the concept of "meaning" (*Sinn*) an alternative to abstract normativism should also be mentioned here. However, the phenomenological approach cannot do justice to the normative difference—in the specific case, to the fact that in subjectively honorable experiences of meaning the immoral can also be felt to be meaningful.

11. Thus I am proposing a "Cartesian" approach to moral philosophy (in Hare's sense [1952; 38 ff.]).

in that way one can become happy; because one will be rewarded for it in another life; and so forth. One would have to act morally even if none of these things were the case. (However, from the unconditional nature of this imperative springs a consciousness of one's own dignity that can compensate for the loss of all those things—though only if this sense of dignity is not what one had in view from the beginning.) What one ought to do is thus not grounded in volitions, in factual subjective preferences—but this does not mean that there can be no subjective preferences that coincide with what one ought to do. On the contrary, this coincidence is necessary if the moral is to *have an effect*.[13] But something is not moral because it can be reduced to subjective preferences. Rather, it is the other way around: a subjective preference is moral when it corresponds to the ideal order of values. This does not exclude the possibility of a moral obligation to work toward a compromise between factual human preferences. But first, this obligation would be valid independently of whether there is a corresponding meta-preference in all people; and second, such an obligation would concern merely the harmonizing of *legitimate* interests. And this means that preferences are subordinate to a moral judgment that transcends them.

With the exception of the third point, the foregoing corresponds to Kant's position, which is superior in its basic idea to all the subjectivist positions that are currently dominant in the English-speaking world.[14] No matter how impressive the precision achieved by decision theory, ethics remains irreducible to it, even if ethics can learn a great deal from it. Yet although Kant's arguments for an objective ethics remain convincing, it is necessary to deviate from him in the detailed formulation of ethics.[15] The following reflections start out from Kant's most important innovation—his radical intentionalist universalism—and seek to pursue it further in a critical manner. In the first section the question is *what* can be morally valued; the second section begins an analysis of the criteria of moral valuation. Observations regarding the role of empirical knowledge in ethics, the relationship between *Is* and *Ought* and between the descriptive and normative sciences, and the relationship of morals, history, and religion round out the chapter.

---

12. (1971), 46 ff.

13. From the approach defended here it does not follow that the problem of motivation cannot be resolved. Here, it is more difficult to resolve it than if one reduces moral obligation to volitions, but the ease of translating the normative sphere into reality cannot be the decisive argument for ethics—otherwise we would have to decide in favor of power positivism.

14. An exception is Rawls's theory, whose important relevant insights, however, should not mislead us regarding what is unsatisfactory in its foundational idea. It remains captive to the economic concept of rationality that it seeks to overcome; the original position is a construction introduced merely to show under what conditions even modern *homines oeconomici* would agree with Rawls's ideas of justice. If we presuppose the original position, moral and subjective preferences coincide—yet the thought experiment constituted by the original position is itself a counterfactual element that shows that this coincidence is a fiction. Cf. chap. 7.2.2.1.

15. Cf. my article on Kant's practical philosophy (1992a; 15–45).

3.1. On Intentionalism

It is well known that, according to Kant, only maxims that provide the foundation for free acts, that is, for volitions, are the subjects of moral predicates. Thus ethical valuation is a matter of answering two questions: first, whether these maxims embody principles that are general laws or can be willed to be general laws, and second, whether they are willed *because* they are in accord with the categorical imperative. The intentionalist position represents a significant advance in the history of moral consciousness: it alone enables us to distinguish between *wilfully negligent* acts and acts that are not objectionable even if they lead, through a series of unfortunate circumstances, to terrible catastrophes, because the persons involved have neither willed these catastrophes nor been guilty of any culpable negligence.[16] The fact that in Herodotus, Croesus does not punish Adrastus, who has accidentally killed Croesus's only healthy son,[17] and that in Sophocles' *Oedipus at Colonus*, Theseus receives Oedipus with respect, is a credit to both writers. Christianity represents the decisive breakthrough toward an intentionalist point of view—one has only to read the moral precepts in the Gospels or the *Ethica* of Abelard, whose intentionalism is nearly as well developed as Kant's. On the other hand, several utilitarian thinkers seem to fall far below the level of Kant's reflections on this question. Yet intentionalism requires many additions and corrections in order to become truly acceptable; only a qualified intentionalism, such as the one I am seeking to put forward here, can be convincing.

3.1.1. The Limits of Intentionalism

It is true that the moral respect we rightly grant or deny a given individual is chiefly determined by that individual's intentions, where by "intention" we mean an act of the will that is expressed, insofar as possible, in actions. Kant did not call mere good wishes "intentions."[18] It is also true that the moral value of an intention depends in part on

---

16. This does not exclude liability in *civil law:* when you drive a car, you assume risks for which you are responsible even if you have committed no offense, because no one obliges you to drive a car. However, there is no conceivable analogue of this in criminal law. A further consequence of intentionalism is that a failed attempt must not be judged in a very different way from a completed act. The fact that in modern systems of criminal law a failed attempt is usually less severely punished (cf. the German Penal Code § 23, Sect. 2) is not compatible with intentionalism without further arguments.

17. See Herodotus, *The Histories* I, 45. Trans. A. de Sélincourt, 18.

18. Cf. the following example in Scheler (1980, 134 f.): A paralyzed man who would willingly jump into the water to save a drowning man can hardly be seen as having such an act of *will*, for he knows very well that he cannot realize his wish. However, one can speak of a genuine intention in the case of someone who starts to jump into the water and is prevented from doing so by a stroke that occurs just at that moment.

how much one's own interests are injured by this intention. Normally, we consider a person who makes greater sacrifices in order to do what is morally obligatory to be acting more morally than one who can do the same thing without sacrificing his own interests to his duty. A person who saves the life of a small child by pulling him out of a fountain into which he has fallen arouses less admiration than if that person must jump into a swiftly running river at the risk of his own life.[19]

If one considers the postulate of universalizability insufficient to provide the basis for an ethics,[20] however, then in order to evaluate intentions it first becomes necessary to evaluate states of affairs. One intention is—*ceteris paribus*—better than another if it seeks to produce a state of affairs that is better than that sought by the second intention. There are, to be sure, certain intentions that by themselves represent what is morally relevant. If someone regrets his guilt, this act of consciousness already has an intrinsic value. In most cases, however, the intention must result in an action; and here we have to decide whether only the action itself or the action together with its consequences must be evaluated. If someone is professing the truth, then moving his lips in the right way is the only thing required to do something of intrinsic worth. But on one hand, in opposition to Kant, the foreseeable consequences of telling the truth have to be taken into account in the moral valuation of this action, while on the other hand, it is clear that most actions are not ends in themselves but are directed toward a state of affairs lying outside themselves. If one helps someone in serious difficulties, the overcoming of that person's difficulties, not one's own action of helping, is what a moral human being intends.[21] A disagreeable subjective inversion of the moral occurs when the ultimate motive for helping someone lies not in sympathizing with the latter's difficulties, but rather in the need to enjoy one's own excellence; and just as, *ceteris paribus*, a greater sacrifice of one's own interests is more moral, similarly it is immoral when someone undertakes great sacrifices that are not actually required and that may even be counterproductive, merely in order to appear moral to himself. (Ultimately this is not a genuine sacrifice at all.) Self-sacrifice is morally too sublime to be carried out in any but the most serious cases. Thus it is morally objectionable when someone misuses self-sacrifice—for example, in order to put an end to his life and in this way to resolve his own problems of identity. The infinite contrast between Sophocles' Antigone and Anouilh's Antigone, who is a caricature of existentialist intentionalism, clearly shows what is involved. It is a pity that modern writers, instead of producing characters like

---

19. See also Jesus' remarks regarding the widow's offering, Mark 12:41–44 and Luke 21:1–4. Here we must assume that the widow has no opportunity to make more money. An exceptionally hard-working person who helps many people hardly acts less morally, even if he need not make any important sacrifices himself, than a lazy man who helps someone on one occasion and as a result has to go hungry for a day.

20. See below, chap. 3.2.2.

21. Cf., however, chap. 3.3.2.3. But still, in the end, the means can be enjoyed as a goal in itself only if, at the beginning, it was seen exclusively as a means.

Sophocles' three-dimensional heroine, increasingly offer us creatures like Anouilh's imitation—a frustrated tyrant, who is concerned only about herself and who, through her unnecessary martyrdom that causes the downfall of others as well, does more violence to Creon than Sophocles' despot does to his opponent. Sophocles' Creon cannot harm Antigone's essence and, ultimately, cannot even harm her fame; in contrast, Anouilh's Antigone destroys Creon's moral credibility for outsiders.[22] In contrast, in *Murder in the Cathedral*, T. S. Eliot very rightly has Becket's fourth and last tempter entice him with the splendor of martyrdom. Only when he rejects martyrdom as the easiest path to fame is Becket ready to become a martyr for the sake of the issue involved.

In the framework of political philosophy, circumstances that are marked by the existence of certain *institutions* are clearly of special importance. To be sure, a meta-intention to make one's own intentions as moral as possible can exist, especially among moderns, and this should be seen as morally positive. From it arises, among other things, the effort to develop a rational ethics. But this meta-intention must not remain the sole moral intention.[23] Political philosophy is not conceivable without a normative doctrine of institutions, and the chief task of political ethics is to evaluate intentions and actions that are directed toward the realization of affirmative institutions. Granted, the degree of affirmativeness of a political institution or a set of institutions, i.e., a political system, must be assessed, among other things, in relation to the extent to which moral intentions are possible within it. One of the reasons a totalitarian system is immoral is that it encourages treachery and malice. To that extent, in political philosophy moral intentions can indeed aim, *mediately,* at moral intentions. But this criterion for evaluating political institutions is not the only one.

Certainly, intentionalism is right in maintaining that states of affairs, although they can be evaluated morally, cannot be described as moral or immoral in the same sense as a person's intentions, since only the latter can pose the moral question. One can speak of "objectively right" and "subjectively moral,"[24] and many ethical debates turn on the lack of differentiation between the two concepts.[25] There is no clear correlation between the two; one person can do for base motives what is objectively right,

---

22. Whether Lord Jim's self-sacrifice in Conrad's novel is in fact justified (e.g., because running away would definitively destroy the natives' faith in the white men), or is instead a mechanism of compensation and a case of moral self-gratification, is a question whose answer determines the interpretation of Jim's character and of the work as a whole.

23. The definition "a man M's action A is moral, if M has sought to make it moral" is not only unacceptable based on its content, because it opens the way to subjective arbitrariness, but also formally unacceptable, because it is circular or leads to an infinite regress.

24. It is striking that our languages make a sharp distinction between the negative predicates (*schlecht* vs. *böse*, bad vs. evil) but do not make an equivalent distinction in the case of the positive predicate (*gut*, good).

25. Consider the controversy between the Peripatetics and the Stoics and the introduction by the latter of the concepts of ἀξία (worth) and ἀπαξία (unworthiness) alongside those of ἀγαθόν (good) and κακόν (bad).

while another can do for the purest reasons what is objectively wrong. We must acknowledge that Kant is right in saying that everything subjectively moral has a high intrinsic value—but we must also maintain, against Kant, that this is not the only thing with intrinsic value. One of the most interesting problems of ethics arises from the fact that the highest form of a subjectively moral effort to realize a better world is possible only in a world that is not objectively optimal. In an optimal world, action would necessarily be reduced to the affirmation of what already exists. Any heroic intention to sacrifice one's own central interests, or even one's life, in the name of a higher state of affairs would be superfluous, and for that very reason an objectively optimal world is not optimal, insofar as the objectively right and the subjectively moral are both concerned. This fact is of great importance for understanding historical processes, and we will examine it later (see chapter 8).

Second, there is a moral danger for intentionalism in the fact that it can constantly suspect that the intentions underlying actions that incontestably produce good results, are not good (the intentions not being as manifest as the actions); the objectively right is thus assumed to have been produced only for self-interested motives.[26] It would certainly be naive to deny that someone can do something objectively good for base motives, or simply because it is convenient (in order not to lose the respect of others). Especially in the case of historical movements involving many people, it would be unrealistic to assume that these common actions arise solely out of moral interests: "Die geistigen Interessen müssen immer mit den materiellen Interessen eine Allianz schließen, um zu siegen. Aber der Teufel hatte die Karten so sonderbar gemischt, daß man über die Intentionen nichts Sicheres mehr sagen kann." ("In order to win, spiritual interests must always ally themselves with substantive interests. But the devil had so mixed up the cards that one could no longer be sure about intentions.") This remark of Heine's (1835; 188) about the Reformation holds for any major historical event, including those with the greatest moral pathos, and his caution with regard to intentions is just as appropriate. Let us recall, for example, the "Déclaration contre la traite des nègres" (Declaration against the Slave Trade) issued by the Congress of Vienna on August 2, 1815, which states that the slave trade is incompatible with the principles of humanity and of universal morality. This declaration was due to the intervention of Great Britain, which had already abolished the slave trade in 1807. However, humanitarian motives did not play the only role, or even the most important role, in this decision. As late as 1784, the British government had defended the slave trade in the House of Commons against the Quakers' abolitionism. The shift in opinion had to do with the fundamentally different economic situation resulting from the independence of the United States.[27] However, one cannot deny that moral unease regarding the slave trade, which grew in the course of the eighteenth century as a result of the universalist morality of the Enlightenment, in-

---

26. La Rochefoucauld was one of the first modern moralists to have represented this viewpoint, in a stylistically unparalleled form.

27. See W. G. Grewe (1988), 651 ff.

creased the perception of its economic inefficiency. Neither can it be maintained that all abolitionists who put forward economic arguments for their position thought solely in terms of these categories; some of them may have understood that this was the only way they would be able to persuade the majority to do something that was morally obligatory. In general, moral judgment is often made more difficult not only by the fact that selfish interests and moral principles may overlap for contingent reasons, but also by the fact that in politics there are cases in which moral reasons require making demands that are directly in one's own rational self-interest. A person who believes that it is his moral duty to help certain political ideas become accepted will seek political office; but a certain position of power is unavoidably associated with holding political office, and thus one can always say that the person concerned cares only about power. This is, of course, entirely possible. There are probably more people who seek political office for the sake of the associated feeling of power than people who seek power for the sake of a moral goal; it is more often the case that moral goals are a pretext for egoism than that a justifiable search for power is the result of a moral will. But what concerns us here is that in cases in which moral and selfish motives coincide, one can theoretically conclude, for want of further information, that either kind of motive is dominant. Precisely because *theoretically* there is a stalemate, one must and should turn to *practical* criteria. Without concrete proof, suspicion is not morally permissible, not because probability statements speak against it, but because suspicion undermines the trust without which common action, especially in the realm of politics, is not possible.[28] What is disagreeable about the school of suspicion that has dominated European thought since Marx, Nietzsche, and Freud is that it so commonly becomes a self-fulfilling prophecy. On one hand, when we assume that others are acting selfishly, we consider ourselves justified in acting just as selfishly (if only not to play the role of the fool); but vice versa, this provides even greater encouragement for others to act selfishly. On the other hand, positive assumptions regarding others often, though not always, have a positive effect; thus it is morally obligatory to try first to put a positive interpretation on the actions of others, and to show them that one is doing so. Anyone who has forgotten this is not a realist but a cynic.

In any event, the form of self-righteousness that seems to be justified by intentionalism must be completely rejected, even though it is no easier to refute than a solipsism that resists certain reflections: intentionalists consider actions, in which intentions are objectified, to be deficient in comparison with intentions, but since intentions, as belonging to interiority, always seem to be known with certainty only as one's *own* intentions, one can always take comfort in believing that one is better than anyone else. Confronted by the great deeds performed by other people, one can complacently gloat over one's own

---

28. Unless one has grounds, it is unjust to be skeptical regarding great actions. Moreover, if a person has never been put in a situation in which he might have risked his life, that does not mean that he would not have done so had it in fact become necessary. The latter suggestion is also impermissible if it cannot be explicitly grounded.

excellence, thanks to the simple thought that one never knows what immoral intentions underlay these actions.[29] The basic flaw in the web of this Pharaseeism consists in forgetting that one can be just as mistaken about the motives of one's own actions as about the motives of others—self-deception is paradoxically often easier than deceiving others. Moreover, since an intention is more than the wish to have a certain intention, because one can speak of intentions only with regard to real possibilities of action, one may be very mistaken in thinking, for instance, that if only one had more power, one *would* make better use of it than the person who currently has that power. The less seriously one takes the possibility of one's own failings because suspicion of others absorbs all one's energy, the more likely one is to succumb to temptation when one comes into the corresponding situation. But that does not mean that a person's first moral duty is self-distrust, which can express vanity as well as self-praise. In both cases one's own subjectivity is taken much too seriously; it can discover and develop itself only by fighting for objectively right situations, and requires a certain trust in itself and in others in order to become active at all.

Third, even if we arrive at the well-founded idea that a person acts exclusively or chiefly out of egoistic motives, the moral preference for a person who has not succeeded but is full of good intentions, compared to a person with bad intentions that in a given situation produce good results, does not exclude the possibility that one might support the latter more fully than the former—if supporting the latter is the only possible way of achieving the obligatory goal. This case is associated with complications arising from the fact that, first of all, no one willingly allows himself to be made an instrument, and second, any instrumentalization is questionable from a moral point of view; but this does not affect the validity of the argument. If it is morally obligatory that a certain condition be realized, we will support actions that are necessary in order to do so, and not the intentions connected with these actions, for the actions themselves are more direct means to the required end. Thus it is not contradictory to consider a politician morally inferior and at the same time the right one in a specific historical situation (for instance, because he alone can replace officeholders who are still more repulsive). Hence, even on the basis of an ethical theory that maintains that the phenomenon of the moral cannot be traced back to rational self-interest, it is not *eo ipso* inadmissible to support the rational egoism of modern capitalism, *if* it is the only way to overcome massive poverty, and *if* its negative side effects are not as bad as massive poverty. In general, every great statesman who does not want to fail in his attempts to achieve morally superior institutions must be able to recognize the economic interests that will be better satisfied by

---

29. This line of thought is often based on the following sophism, which is supposed to demonstrate a general psychological egoism: In every intentional action one is doing what one wants, and thus what one wishes; when one does something because one wishes it, one is acting egoistically. But apart from the fact that "egoistic" is not synonymous with "corresponding to one's own wishes," the fact that someone does something that corresponds to his own wishes does not imply that he does it *because* it corresponds to his own wishes. Cf. Hegel, *Enzyklopädie* § 475 (1969 ff.), 10:297 f., and F. von Kutschera (1982), 60 ff.

better institutions; otherwise, he will find it difficult to mobilize the forces he needs in order to have an effect on history.

Fourth, it is not wrong to take critical reservations into account in judging the personal worth of a person who fails, not occasionally but continually, in his attempts to realize his good intentions. In addition to good intentions, intellectual and practical abilities are also part of the worth of a person as a whole. It is not enough to want the good in general—we must also *recognize* it in its concrete specificity, and know how to *realize* it against all possible kinds of resistance. An individual intention underlying an action must always be interpreted in the context of the overall nature of the person who performs it. If we do not do so, intentionalism puts the more intelligent and conscientious person at a serious disadvantage. This can be shown by the following observation. It is well known that modern German criminal law distinguishes within intent between *dolus directus* and *dolus eventualis,* and within negligence, between conscious and unconscious negligence. The distinction between *dolus eventualis* and conscious negligence consists in the fact that the former tacitly accepts consequences in which it has no interest, for the sake of a goal with which it knows them to be associated, whereas the latter perceives the possibility of these consequences, but considers them unlikely to ensue. (In unconscious negligence, the possibility of such consequences has not even been weighed.)[30] If the probability that these consequences will accompany the action is very high, then if two persons commit the same act, one who is habitually more aware and more intelligent will be more severely punished than one whose superficiality and thoughtlessness are well established.[31] This should not be considered unjust—at least, with one important qualification. In the case just mentioned, the more intelligent and aware person may in fact be seen as morally inferior—but only if one considers him morally superior if he decides to do what is good and, because of his superior intelligence, also has greater success than a person with the same intentions but lesser intellectual and practical ability. Anyone who ascribes greater guilt but not greater merit to the more intelligent person is so obviously unjust that only his own envy can prevent him from seeing it.

3.1.2. What Is Morally Attributable?

The critique of intentionalism can be deepened, on the basis of a more comprehensive conception of personality, through arguments that employ the concept of the

---

30. An extreme intentionalist like M. Köhler (1982) considers unconscious negligence to be punishable only when in general, even if not in this specific case, the person involved has consciously decided to behave in a negligent manner. Apart from the fact that this kind of decision cannot be proven, in this extreme case the question arises as to whether in fact only individual conscious acts can be considered relevant in criminal law.

31. This is connected with the paradox Plato discusses in his *Hippias Minor,* and which he resolves within the framework of his intellectualist ethics.

unconscious. Even though the theoretical foundation of the corresponding ideas, as they were developed by Schopenhauer, Eduard von Hartmann, and Freud, is notoriously weak, the empirical evidence for such theories is strong. Thus it is completely plausible to assume that a person's gestures tell us more about the core of his personality than does the stream of consciousness that accompanies them, which may be controlled by a deeper authority—the unconscious. It may well be true that someone fails to achieve his intended goal because he *wanted* to fail, even if the person involved never realized that he wanted to fail, either before the fact or even after it. The will is more than the sum of volitions in the stream of consciousness; one's body can express it more truly than one's consciousness.[32] But concrete behavior that is not consciously willed—a sudden illness, an accident, losing a key, missing a train—is not the only example relevant here; acts of perception and thought result from a selection made by ratiomorphous mechanisms operating unconsciously. It has been proven that there are subliminal stimuli, and it is not implausible to assume that very different selection mechanisms are connected not only with the intellectual capacities but also with the moral preferences of different individuals, and tell us a great deal about the core of their personality.[33]

Yet even if one does not accept this more comprehensive conception, which leaves the Cartesian mind-body dualism behind, even an intentionalist will have to concede, at the least, that a person who cannot go beyond good intentions becomes morally guilty when the pleasure he takes in his own good intentions prevents him from ever letting himself be advised or even guided by those whose personality consists in more than just good intentions. Intellectual limitation in recognizing the concrete conditions for achieving the good does not provide a basis for any kind of unmediated moral guilt. But since we have a moral duty to correctly assess ourselves and to learn from the views of those who have the same good intentions as we do, but have greater intellectual and practical abilities, we become guilty if we do not do so. Here we encounter the problem of the right relationship between *autonomy* and *belief in authority.* On one hand, there is no doubt that Kant's discovery of the principle of autonomy, for which Christianity prepared the way, is one of the most important landmarks in the history of ethics. A norm is valid not because others think it is valid, whoever these others might be (ancestors, the church, the state). On the other hand, the principle of autonomy led to the notion that a norm is valid for someone only if he thinks it is valid for him—an idea that is not only

---

32. Presumably the relationship between the body and the stream of consciousness, as a way of expressing the will, changes in the course of cultural evolution. This is well illustrated by the well-known quip that the main difference between Americans and Russians consists in the fact that when they want to get out of an appointment, Americans claim they have fallen ill, whereas Russians actually fall ill. Conversion disorders are more common among people with low levels of education (P. G. Zimbardo [1988], 532).

33. Thus, for example, a politician's character is revealed by the possibilities of action that he considers. Even if he decides to pursue what is morally right, the very fact that he weighed certain other alternatives sheds light on him.

not superior, but even more dangerous, and characterized by a disagreeable vanity. The feeling of freedom of conscience that accompanies this position should not keep us from noticing that it destroys any system of morals and that its legal recognition would necessarily result in anarchy. It is true in a trivial way that one can follow a norm with conviction only if one is convinced that it is valid; but it is just as true that one cannot be legitimately convinced of its validity by the idea that one is in fact convinced that it is valid. Objective arguments are always necessary, and an objective argument based on a meta-level means that the ability to understand complex objective arguments in particular is not the same in all people. From this it follows that one has to develop in oneself the ability to recognize intellectual and moral authorities.[34] Inevitably, this act of recognition is always that of the person involved and to that extent refers to the inevitable dimension of autonomy. But this autonomy is ennobled if it is able to acknowledge superiority on its own. One of the most terrible consequences of the Enlightenment is that it destroyed any sense of moral authority.[35] Primarily to blame for this was the incompetence of traditional authorities, which were unable to cope either intellectually or morally with the process of modernization. However, the vices of overestimating oneself and of envy, which developed ever more freely in the course of the triumphal conquest of modern subjectivity, made their own contribution to the decline of respect for authorities.

A further amendment of intentionalism emerges from the position (exemplified, for example, by Max Scheler) that maintains that not only volitions but also *emotions* are the subjects of moral predicates. Whereas in Kant the only decision that counts morally is one made abstractly on the basis of the feeling of duty to help an innocent person in difficulty, the critics of Kant's rigorism from Schiller onward emphasize that immediate feelings of solidarity also have a subjectively moral value—one that is perhaps even greater than that of pure volition. By this they mean, first, that moral feelings are socially useful: if the moral is to have an effect in the world, it must be borne by real psychic forces.[36] There is much to be said for the assumption that the abstract intention to be good has less effect than direct moral feelings (whose moral value does not, however, follow from their factual existence, since moral feelings can deceive and therefore require judgment based on a rational standard). Second, these critics maintain that feelings corresponding to what the moral law demands also have an intrinsic value, because they bridge the gap in our being that would otherwise result between what is and what ought to be. On this view, a person who rejoices directly in the objectively right and in the moral intentions of others is

---

34. In a world in which a comprehensive moral decision always has to include empirical knowledge such as that produced by the individual sciences, a great statesman must also be able to recognize important scientists. Ideally, he will be a moral authority himself; in the modern world, he cannot also be a universal scientific authority, no matter how great his talent.

35. One of the major contributions made by Gadamer's hermeneutics was a rehabilitation of the sense of authority and tradition (1975; 261 ff.).

36. Kant acknowledged this; cf. *Metaphysik der Sitten, Einleitung zur Tugendlehre* XII (1976 f.; 8:530 ff.).

morally better than one who is annoyed by the latter (out of *Schadenfreude* or envy, for instance) but does not acknowledge that his annoyance determines his action. This position seems to me convincing, as long as it does not become just as one-sided as Kant's.[37] Obviously the most morally convincing person is one who has a great range of moral feelings, as well as the will not to allow his own behavior to be governed by these feelings if they contradict what is demanded by practical reason. The same goes for the concept of *virtue*. Virtue is to some extent the mechanism of the moral, the habit of being guided by henceforth unquestioned values and norms that makes concrete decisions of the will superfluous in individual cases. No matter how much this orientation may lead to morally aberrant behavior in exceptional situations, it also unburdens the moral person; indeed, without such relief the individual would probably not have the energy required to deviate from what is right in normal situations when it proves morally necessary to do so. This position intermediate between intellectualism and emotionalism can easily be given concrete form if we think of the example of patriotic feelings and patriotic virtues, which are particularly important for politics (cf. chapter 7.3.3.3.7).

A common objection to the singling out of feelings and virtues on a subjectively moral basis is that feelings and virtues, unlike actions, are not producible by an act of will. This is certainly true, but the idea that only volitions are morally significant is itself questionable. The reference to freedom as a condition of the possibility of an action being judged does not get us very far, if what we have in mind is not only freedom of action but also freedom of the will. Whether the latter exists is notoriously subject to dispute, and therefore strength of will can be regarded as a gift as much as can good subjective feelings. Modern people may find it extremely humbling that there is something that cannot be forced, especially something as crucial as feelings of happiness or love. But perhaps this humiliation is instructive: it can lead modern people to see that they themselves determine neither their factual existence nor much of their adult lives. The fact that a person who sets out to become happy will surely not succeed in doing so not only is an argument against eudaemonistic ethics—because it follows that the latter cannot be practiced (which has forced modern thinkers to give up the concept of happiness and replace it by that of utility)—but also contains a more fundamental objection to the self-empowerment of modern subjectivity, reminding it with deep irony that it can achieve full subjective satisfaction only if it does not intend it as such.

Still, over time we can certainly work on morally good feelings and virtues, at least to some extent. For instance, moral feelings can be cultivated through interaction with ap-

---

37. The Kantian position seems to have been produced as a result of a mistaken interpretation of the sacrifice that one has to make for the sake of the moral law. Certainly it is true that someone who forgoes more is acting more morally, *ceteris paribus,* than one who forgoes less; but that does not mean that someone would forgo less because he *likes* to forgo something. It is entirely possible that someone might gladly forgo something of whose value he is fully aware, even if, psychologically, mechanisms of compensation of the sour grapes type are a temptation. Nonetheless, we can grant that the human type singled out by Kant has an especially strong will—but the moral is not limited to volitions.

propriate persons, the enjoyment of morally inspiring works of art, and religious practices; and that our culture has lost any sense for this kind of cultivation says more against
our culture than against the possibility of such cultivation. To give a concrete example,
even thoroughly decent people have had aggressive thoughts (going even so far as murder) in dreams and even when awake. They are not responsible for these to the same degree that they are responsible for concrete aggressive intentions. But such thoughts must
disturb anyone who is plagued by them, and they can constitute an objection against
someone who regularly encourages their appearance through the enjoyment of literary or
cinematic trash that glorifies violence or even merely represents it to an excessive extent.

Whether one should evaluate morally not only volitions and feelings but also *persons
as a whole* is a particularly controversial issue. On one hand, we say we should evaluate
persons as a whole because one can hardly assume that volitions and emotive acts occur
without cause. Their cause is, in part, the core of the personality. It is realistic to assume
that a person who commonly and willingly lies will continue to do so; we interpret certain
actions as indices of corresponding volitions, and the latter as the expression of a certain
character. On the other hand, the reluctance we feel in our culture with regard to passing
moral judgment on a person is also understandable. First, the core of the personality is
only one factor in explaining an action—the situation is the other one. True, there are
people who do not behave immorally under any circumstances, and others who behave
immorally in every situation. But in most people the previously mentioned moral luck
plays a role; if all people found themselves in analogous situations, the moral differences
among them would seem much smaller than they normally appear to be. The so-called
fundamental attribution error consists in people's tendency, when explaining another
person's behavior, to give internal attribution priority over external, but to do the opposite when they explain their own behavior. The reason for this error is easy to explain; a
person who is himself acting first perceives his own environment, whereas when he observes another person acting, he usually focuses on him and not his environment. The failure to take moral luck into account has largely to do with this error. Second, the greatest
danger in a negative judgment of another person (and not only of his action) consists in
defining him negatively to some degree. However, one must never deny that a person's
character may change, and in any case, negative judgments must not become self-fulfilling
prophecies. Finally, we must take seriously the view that even the worst character—not
only its behavior—is a product of circumstances. While the person concerned cannot
himself adopt this point of view (for reasons that will be examined in chapter 4.2.2.1), it
is not inappropriate for others. The sublime thing about determinism is that it transfigures hatred of evil into a peculiar form of sympathy and teaches us to see our own merits chiefly as gifts of God that are the basis not for privileges but for responsibilities.

Finally, intentionalism is of special importance in determining the nature of *collective responsibility,* which is crucial for any political ethics. From the foregoing it follows that institutions such as state organs or societies can be more or less objectively
right, but not more or less subjectively moral: only persons and their acts (such as intentions and feelings) can be subjectively moral. A collective is never morally guilty, but only

individual members of the collective. In some cases, all of them may be guilty; but that has to be proven in each individual case. Nonetheless, the following qualifications are necessary. First, it is obvious that it can be blameworthy to want to remain in a collective that has made an extremely immoral decision, even if one has voted against it. However, in this case the individual can be morally reproached only for his willingness to continue to belong to the collective and not to resign, emigrate, and so forth, after the original immoral decision was made. He cannot be reproached for the decision itself, since he sought to prevent it. He might also be reproached for having made the morally right decision only for himself, without having done everything he could to change the voting behavior of others. Indifference to other people's guilt is itself blameworthy—particularly if one lives with these other persons in the special kind of relationship called a "community."[38] Second, this special relationship probably explains the collective shame we may feel with regard to actions of members of our own family or country. Since part of our own identity is produced by our identification with them, what dismays us is something that belongs to our selves. Germans who had the good luck to be born after 1930 bear no collective guilt for the Nazis' crimes, but they are right to be concerned about the element in the German soul that made these crimes possible and may still be operative. Third, it goes without saying that every heir can be made responsible in civil law for the debts associated with his inheritance, for he could refuse to accept the inheritance. Analogously, it is fair that the legal successors of a criminal state make reparations payments, and the refusal to do so would be immoral even when the person who refused to make them himself bore no blame for the crime concerned. In general, we can say that one should not profit from the guilty deeds of others; anyone who does so besmirches himself morally, even if he sincerely refused to be involved in those deeds. However, anyone who profits from an unjust system and, as he continues to profit from it, distances himself verbally from it in order to achieve the full enjoyment of his own morality, merely adds to this guilt that of hypocrisy and self-righteousness.[39]

A corollary in the psychology of morals to the above is that the feeling of responsibility for one's own contribution to a social process is declining, not only in the mass but also in large and anonymous groups.[40] This is one of the reasons for the ecological crisis; many people think their decisions will have no effect on the course of things as a whole. However, it is precisely at this point that a qualified intentionalism proves its

---

38. Cf. Scheler's discussion of the principle of solidarity (1980; 516 ff., 522 ff.). The more the relationship between action and omission is conceived as symmetrical, the more plausible this principle becomes. No work in world literature has plumbed this issue more deeply than Dostoyevsky *The Brothers Karamazov*. On the concept of community, see below, chap. 4.3.2.

39. Consider those critics of capitalism who want to keep on milking the capitalist cow right up to the moment of capitalism's collapse.

40. Since in any case an individual is generally the object of fewer reproaches if he acts as part of a group rather than alone, within a group, people are always more prepared to adopt a type of conduct that is likely to make enemies outside the group. For example, committees refuse requests more easily than does an isolated individual.

worth. Since forgoing objectively harmful behavior is subjectively moral, one is duty-bound to forgo this behavior, even if by doing so one cannot stop the destruction of nature; at least one has not contributed to it. Especially given that collective changes in behavior can start only with individuals, there is a realistic chance that one's own renunciation will objectively contribute to such a change. It may also be permissible to do something that is usually morally prohibited (prohibited because if it were universalized it would have negative consequences) if it has direct positive consequences in a given case. For instance, it is not necessarily self-contradictory to drive a car to a demonstration against the use of cars if, and only if, there is no other way of getting there to take part in the demonstration, and if participating might lead more people to give up driving cars than forgoing participation.

All these reflections on the possible meaning of talking about collective guilt, which is always awkward because it is misleading, should not keep us from recognizing one thing: On the basis of the unpredictability of certain consequences of social interaction—even that of global, socially caused catastrophes—we have to take into account the possibility that no individual person acted in a morally objectionable way, because no matter how hard they tried, none of them *could* have foreseen the consequences of the collective action. The underlying social fact that the result of the interaction of many individual actions often cannot be willed or foreseen by anyone is difficult to grasp, and it is one of the reasons for the growth of conspiracy theories that seek to find a clear intention behind the dreadful complexity of social events in order to satisfy the need for a simple world and unequivocal ascriptions of responsibility.

However, it is clear that there is a duty to inform oneself as much as possible regarding the possible consequences of one's own behavior, especially when this behavior is extremely innovative and therefore risky. It is also obvious that in most catastrophes of a political or ecological nature caused by collectivities, at least, this duty has not been fulfilled by the majority of the members. To put it very summarily, and in a form that might be misunderstood, in such a case we may say that we are confronted by a collective guilt. Moreover, the breach of duty is even greater if one not only has failed to inform oneself, but has ignored information that was offered, or even expressly rejected it. The hatred one feels for those who reveal the negative consequences of one's own actions has to do precisely with the fact that they transform one's negligence into an intent (in the sense of *dolus eventualis*). This hatred, felt by people with good intentions who find themselves deprived of the possibility of referring to these good intentions, is a crystal-clear proof that these intentions were not so good, even before their confrontation with reality.

3.2. ON UNIVERSALISM

One of the chief differences between ancient ethics and modern ethics (for which Christianity prepared the way) is the latter's *universalism.* In the modern age, ethical theories as various as those of Hobbes, Kant, and the utilitarians all share the principle that rights and duties are applicable universally and must be general, no matter in what these rights and duties consist[41] (whether in the rational pursuit of self-interest[42] or the greatest good for the greatest number, or in universalizable maxims). To be sure, every universalism must make room for exceptions to this principle; but these are precisely exceptions that need to be justified, whereas for pre-universalist ethics, general moral norms are really exceptions in a recognized system of norms that consists chiefly of special norms for individual groups. Indian mores, with their norms for the castes, are a striking example of this, but to a limited extent so is Aristotle's ethics.[43] The elaboration of a universalist ethics presumably involves a process that runs parallel to changes in humanity's theoretical consciousness. Modern science's higher degree of abstraction distinguishes it from ancient science, whose mathematics started out more from individual figures than from general categories.[44] In terms of the theory of foundations, universalism is connected with the generality that thought and language necessarily presuppose, and to that extent it is not implausible to say that universalism explains only what is presupposed in language.[45]

One important early adumbration of universalism, not to be confused with it, is the idea of justice, which is widespread even in pre-universalist cultures. This idea acknowledges that something is not valid because *I* happen to have a certain privilege, but rather because there is a ground for it that, while not unrestricted, is more general and does not concern me alone. Thus an absolute monarch who is totally convinced of his divine right can hardly be described as universalist, since universalism would not justify radical in-

---

41. Cf. the important § 23 in Rawls (1971; 130 ff.), which lists five criteria and sums them up as follows: "A conception of right is a set of principles, general in form and universal in application, that is to be publicly recognized as a final court of appeal for ordering the conflicting claims of moral persons" (135).

42. A universalist normative egoism, such as we find in Hobbes, is, of course, performatively inconsistent, since as a theoretician Hobbes grants every person a right to act in order to maximize his self-interest, but as a self-interest maximizing individual he should not do so (because it would be in his self-interest that some people not act in order to maximize their self-interest). Cf. Epictetes, *Discourses* II 20, as well as Fichte's reflections in *System der Sittenlehre* (1971), 4:319 f. (On the other hand, the assumption that it is best for each person to take care of himself would be compatible with a universalist ethics. See Moore, *Principia Ethica* 58 ff. [1903; 96 ff.]). Normative egoism will therefore not be further discussed in the following pages; utilitarianism and Kantianism remain the most important alternatives. No doubt the restrictive conditions for a possible ethics become more productive if we take into account not only the semantic but also the performative dimension of language, that is, if we consider, for instance, that ethical theories must be publicly communicated; this excludes some things as performatively self-contradictory.

43. See, for example, *Politics* 1259b22 ff.

44. M. Schramm, one of the most insightful contemporary historians of science, demonstrated this (1991) by using the example of the differences between ancient and modern theories of symmetry. Particularly illuminating are his reflections (26 f.) on Euclid's proof I 5.

45. This is the well-known theory of discourse ethics. It remains remarkable how language, at least since the development of the article, is able to transform even indexicals into something general: *I* does not refer solely to me; every rational being is *an* "I."

equalities among people by appealing to an accident of birth. However, if this monarch were prepared to abdicate immediately if someone proved to him that he was not in fact the legitimate heir to the throne, he could claim to possess an important aspect of morals, namely, an elementary form of justice.[46] What gave Montezuma II's fall a deeply moving moral dimension that could not escape even the Spaniards[47] was precisely this readiness to give up his power, because he thought he recognized in the Spanish invasion the return of Quetzalcoatl. For the religious consciousness of Aztec high culture, the divine was the unity of real power and moral validity, and thus the acquiescence before the alleged gods also sprang from fear of their power—but not only from that. Montezuma II was probably genuinely convinced that the gods to whom he owed his power had the right to demand that he give it back; and since he, at least, could not exclude the possibility that Quetzalcoatl might return in the form of a Spaniard, his ability to act was limited. His paralysis was one of the major causes of the decline of his people, who deserved a more sober or, failing that, even an unscrupulous ruler who was less just toward the gods. But in this paralysis we see, in an imposing if also melancholy form, how deeply elements central to the idea of justice were felt even by some of the most powerful representatives of pre-universalist cultures—including the emperor who took over Montezuma's kingdom. Although Charles V remained a prisoner of the Middle Ages in all his political convictions, he nonetheless represented their value with full justice. The human greatness in his abdication, the sublime words he uttered on handing the Netherlands over to Philip on 25 October 1555, and his last year spent in a monastery can fail to move only those in whom ideological prejudice has dried up all direct moral sensitivity. These figures are certainly superior[48] to those representatives of universalism who acknowledge it only because universalism is socially useful in the current form of society, and who would abandon it if it ceased to be useful in this way—even if universalism represents a moral advance over pre-universalist mores. I will return to this problem in chapter 3.5.1 and at that point examine the difference between pre-universalist and anti-universalist practices.

3.2.1. Universalism and the Postulate of Universalizability: Kantianism, Utilitarianism, and Discourse Ethics

The basic idea of universalism finds expression in the postulate of universalizability: A rational being is obligated, permitted, or forbidden to do something if and only if all

---

46. Even Rawls recognizes, in § 10 (1971; 54 ff.), that formal justice already consists in impartial and consistent, equal treatment of similar cases—no matter how erroneous the determination, on the level of the contents, of what similar cases are.

47. Cf. Cortés's second letter to Emperor Charles V: "Y certifico a vuestra sacra majestad, que no había tal de los españoles que oyese el razonamiento, que no hubiese mucha compasión" (1985; 129). ("And I assure your holy majesty that none of the Spaniards who heard his argument failed to feel great compassion." See also Díaz del Castillo's history, chap. 101 (1986; 187 f.).

48. This follows from the option for a qualified intentionalism.

rational beings are obligated, permitted, or forbidden to do it. This directly entails universalism's emphasis on symmetrical relationship; asymmetrical relationships are not universalizable, because in them not all *relata* can act in the same way. However, there are important differences between particular universalist positions. Thus, in the framework of his ethics, Kant distinguishes perfect and imperfect duties, depending on whether a general observance of one's own maxims is impossible or simply not desirable. The former occurs, for instance, in the case of lying, which would lose its meaning if everyone assumed that everyone reserved the right to lie.[49] However, the second criterion (by which Kant wants to justify the obligation to help others) leads to the question what condition one should want, and thus how one should evaluate conditions; in this way it points beyond strict intentionalism (even if Kant is more concerned with which moral condition one ought to wish for oneself than with which condition of the external world might be desirable).[50] The fundamental move beyond intentionalism was made by utilitarianism, for which the ultimate criterion of the moral is the greatest good for the greatest number.[51] Within utilitarianism we can distinguish between act utilitarianism and rule utilitarianism: whereas the former evaluates an individual act on the basis of its consequences, the latter determines the value of a behavior according to the value of the corresponding *type* of behavior and assesses this type of behavior, in a way somewhat similar to Kant's, by the result that would be produced if everyone pursued it.[52] The discourse ethics of Apel and Habermas also belongs among the universalist theories; it adds to the Kantian approach the procedural condition that a discourse comprehending an affected people must determine whether the value of the result of the general observance of a norm is superior to that of all possible alternatives.

The decisive difference between the Kantian position, on one hand, and especially the act-utilitarian position, on the other, is that Kant cannot justify making exceptions in the case of perfect duties, whereas for utilitarianism a greater general good justifies any behavior that harms individuals. It is not hard to see that both positions are one-sided and in any case cannot be easily combined with our moral intuitions. On one hand, a strength of the Kantian position lies in the fact that it grants every individual certain basic rights which may under no circumstances be sacrificed to the interests of others—something that can hardly be grounded in the framework of act-utilitarianism.

---

49. F. von Kutschera objects against Kant that while it is certainly "very implausible empirically" that one would continue to make and receive promises "if dishonest declarations of intention became a general practice," it is not precisely impossible (1982; 199). On the other hand, we should note that for Kant the issue is not the prediction of actual human behavior, but rather the dimension of meaning: the *meaning* of the institution of promising would be canceled out, no matter what individuals might continue to do out of habit.

50. Cf. *Metaphysik der Sitten, Tugendlehre* § 35 (1976 f.; 8:595).

51. To be more precise, this principle underlies only classical utilitarianism; later developments assume that the average utility should be maximized. It is obvious that the two approaches give very different answers to the question as to which population policy is morally best. See chap. 7.3.1.1.

52. On the different forms of rule utilitarianism, see D. Lyons (1965).

For the latter, killing a person would not only be unproblematic if another person were thereby brought into existence, but also morally obligatory if the damage to the murdered person would be compensated by the utility to the survivors (understood purely subjectively)—more or less as in Dürrenmatt's play *Der Besuch der alten Dame.*[53] On the other hand, one of utilitarianism's achievements is to have made it possible to move beyond Kant's rigid prohibition on lying. We still have to ask whether there is a third position besides the Kantian and the utilitarian, which would combine the advantages and diminish the disadvantages of both.

Although it may justify extremely unequal treatment, even act-utilitarianism is a universalist position. In the utilitarian preference-relation, the utility of every person enters in with the same weight; and the basic utilitarian command holds for every person to the same extent, no matter how much, on the basis of differing factual preferences and different circumstances, different kinds of behavior might be obligatory for individuals in order to maximize the total utility. Moreover, we should note that the distinction between act-utilitarianism and rule-utilitarianism is not airtight. To be sure, one can say that for a rule-utilitarian the prohibition on lying is generally valid, while for an act-utilitarian it is not always valid. But because of his universalism, even an act-utilitarian must assume that in the event of an analogous situation occurring again, in which the utility of lying might be greater than the harm it would do, then every other person would have the same right or the same duty to lie. (The likelihood that the situation would occur again plays no role here.) Thus an evaluation of modes of behavior is always involved; however, these modes of behavior may need to be so precisely defined by the surrounding circumstances that they might be instantiated only once in reality. The idea that it is permissible to lie in order to save an innocent human life is not in fact compatible with Kant's extreme deontological position, but it is compatible with universalism. A conception of this kind does not alter the objectivity of moral obligations, and thus in no way transforms ethics into a science of hypothetical imperatives. Hypothetical imperatives prescribe that if you will *a,* then you must do *b.* In contrast, conditional obligations (which determine, for instance, under what conditions lying is permitted) are valid completely independently of the possible goals of individuals, that is, objectively—not absolutely, however, but conditionally.[54]

Granted, every universalism must recognize exceptions to the postulate that when moral and legal obligations and prohibitions are binding on *one* rational being, they are binding on all rational beings; still, the way in which these exceptions are grounded is

---

53. Utilitarians have devoted a large part of their ingenuity to the avoidance of this consequence—for instance, by arguing that the right of the general population to kill an individual would lead to an increase in fear and dread and should be rejected *for that reason.* But completely apart from the fact that a *secret* murder of an innocent person would be compatible with this additional argument, the idea that only this additional argument could save the innocent person from his murderers is repulsive.

54. Conditional obligations may be formalized neither as $O(A \supset B)$ nor as $A \supset O(B)$; a dyadic deontic operator $O(B/A)$ is required. On the grounding of conditional obligations, see below, chap. 3.3.2.

important. A relatively trivial objection is that it would be nonsensical to assume, for example, that if *b*, who is married to *a*, has a duty to love *a*, then all people are obligated to love *a*. It is easy to reply that *b* has this duty only because he is married to *a*, and therefore the general obligation would be that everyone—*ceteris paribus*—has a duty to love his or her spouse if *b* has a duty to do so. A more serious objection is that there are also duties that are rightly valid only for certain groups, such as the duty to serve in the military. Here we should note that exceptions are compatible with universalism if doing one's duty is connected with factual conditions that are not met by all people. That children and elderly people are usually not physically able to withstand battle justifies exempting them from military service; in the case of women, such an exemption would depend on corresponding empirical assumptions, whose validity cannot be examined here. In any case, it is interesting that empirical assumptions are included in the application of the postulate of universalizability, because the previously mentioned condition that it must be possible to fulfill a duty moves from the sphere of moral obligation into that of being. The most important objection is that certain positively valued conditions could not be achieved at all if everyone had the same moral rights and duties— if everyone took up the same occupation, for instance. But here as well, we must reply that there is no norm requiring everyone to take up a given occupation; there is merely a significantly more general norm to take into account one's own talents and the needs of society in choosing an occupation. In general, the differentiation between state and society makes it necessary that a head of state or even a simple official have rights that an ordinary citizen does not have. From the elementary conditions for justice in the sense mentioned earlier, it follows that such an official must be prepared to treat others in an analogous way when they hold the same position. If a head of state claims rights that are granted him alone, he must also recognize them for his predecessors and successors. However, this has nothing to do with the point of a universalist ethics. The latter requires far more in order to be able to justify such a differentiation. In the utilitarian version, it requires that the introduction of differentiations increase the total utility. Since the utilitarian principle would justify brutally unequal treatment of individuals, however, the alternative demand—that inequalities be such that they are to everyone's advantage and are connected with positions and offices open to all—is indispensable. This corresponds to the second principle of justice in Rawls,[55] whose criticism of utili-

---

55. Cf. Rawls (1971), 60: "The first statement of the two principles reads as follows: First: each person is to have an equal right to the most extensive basic liberty compatible with a similar liberty for others. Second: social and economic inequalities are to be arranged so that they are both (a) reasonably expected to be to everyone's advantage, and (b) attached to positions and offices open to all." The two principles and the associated priority rules of precedence are further refined on several occasions, for example, 83, 250, 302. Particularly important is Rawls's more detailed interpretation of the second principle in § 12 f., and especially of the difference principle, which requires the greatest benefit of the least advantaged. Even though I agree with Rawls's difference principle with regard to politics, its unconditional validity in the economic domain is more questionable. Cf. chap. 7.3.1.2.

tarianism is one of the most impressive achievements of contemporary ethical theory. Certainly one cannot maintain that a differentiation on universalist bases would be better for everyone than any other conceivable situation. A hereditary monarch will usually be worse off after the abolition of his position; and in general it would be absurd to refuse to alter a situation merely because it is Pareto-optimal, that is, because some people would be worse off if this change were made. Morally repellent conditions may be Pareto-optimal.[56] However, what is crucial is that even a hereditary monarch would prefer that the highest state office be held in a non-hereditary way rather than return to the state of nature. Since a condition without state power would be worse for everyone than one with state power, and the latter inevitably involves different competencies for individual state officials, these inequalities are morally justified if they are in accord with the aforementioned principle of justice. Universalism does not lay down a single criterion for the choice of candidates for political offices. Choice by lot would be just as compatible with universalism as a general vote or appointment by a committee on the basis of competence in the subject, and additional arguments are required in order to give one criterion precedence over others. In contrast, holding offices on the basis of heredity would not be compatible with universalism. (However, one could probably describe as compatible with universalism a parliamentary monarchy in which the monarch's position is legitimated by the consensus of his people and he is prepared to abdicate at any time, should this consensus cease to exist. Even an enlightened absolute monarch like Frederick the Great could be seen as a universalist, if he himself no longer believed in the divine right of kings but considered this belief indispensable in order to guarantee civil peace in the historical moment in which he lived.)

The preceding remarks have already refuted one widespread objection to universalism, which is weaker than it at first appears to be, but which nonetheless points beyond pure formalism and therefore deserves further comment. Whereas in principle universalism grants all people equal rights, we start from the assumption that our duties with regard to a person also depend on our relationship to that person. If two children fall into the water, and one of them is the child of the only person who can save them, this person has first of all the duty to try to save both of them; but if he can save only one, then it is his duty to save his own child, not the other. Doesn't this contradict universalism? Against this, this is arguably not the case because, first of all, all parents have an analogous right to give their own children precedence, and second, it is grounded in the way people come into the world that there is a special relationship of trust and

---

56. The overestimation of Pareto-optimality (a pure principle of efficiency) by neoclassical political economy points to a remarkable moral blindness, even if it is correct that if possible, all conditions—including just conditions—should be Pareto-optimal. B. Barry has strikingly characterized the former peculiar interpretation of Pareto-optimality in the following way: "The definition requires that if some gain and some lose in a change from one situation to another nothing can be said about its desirability. But the principle is instead sometimes taken to entail that if some people will lose from a change that change should *not* be made" (1970; 50f.).

responsibility between these helpless creatures and those to whom they owe their existence. Analogously, special duties are grounded in contracts, as well as in legally non-binding relationships such as friendships, which are open to everyone to establish and which lead to normatively desirable results. In any case, universalism must be interpreted in such a way that it allows for limited communities and is even compatible with the assumption that such communities have their own intrinsic worth. The extreme individualism of most universalist positions and their tendency to be unable to justify institutions other than a universal state are lethal for political philosophy.

3.2.2. Formalism and Material Ethics: The Problem of Grounding Ethics

The position taken in this work is that of universalism; a non-universalist ethics is in my view necessarily false. This does not mean, however, that the postulate of universalizability is sufficient to elaborate an ethics. First of all, this postulate merely says that *if* a norm is valid for someone, it is valid for everyone. But it says nothing about the existence of such norms. Nonetheless, one can show, with Kant, that many norms are not universalizable. Kant's argument for a prohibition on lying remains strong even if one takes into account the possibility that there are certain well-defined exceptions to it. But his grounding of the prohibition on suicide already presumes a natural teleology that can be questioned; and his reflections on imperfect duties lead to the problem of what one should want. The universalist can always say that when one claims something, one must always grant others the same right, but that takes us no further than the Golden Rule (in either its negative or its positive version). That isn't much, for according to this rule, someone thinking of suicide who had come to believe that life is a torment might even have the right to kill as many people as possible before taking his own life (while hoping that others might kill him in the process).[57] The evaluation of certain circumstances is also inevitable if we want to move beyond very abstract minimal norms. This recognition is the enduring contribution of utilitarianism as a universalist but not formalist ethics, in which certain basic insights of ancient teleological ethics persist, even if in a very simplified form. But the basic error of utilitarianism consists in, first, guiding its valuations only by the factual subjective preferences of organisms capable of suffering, and second, lumping together in the concept of utility highly heterogeneous things. To begin with the first point: a utilitarian, whose ethics is more social than the Kantian ethics, would always inquire into the needs of others. However, should he come to the conclusion that although he did not hate life, other people did, he would not hesi-

---

57. Cf. the exceptionally cumbersome argumentation in Moore's *Principia Ethica* 95 (1903; 155 ff.). Moore believes that one cannot prove that the existence of human life is a good; yet since at the moment there is no possibility of wiping out the whole human race, and since if one were to begin to do so one would encounter resistance, it is better not to try.

tate to put them out of their misery by killing them (assuming for a moment that he did not consider the ensuing complications). So far as the second point is concerned, one of utilitarianism's crudest simplifications is that even if, like Mill, it assumes different qualities of pleasure, it must transform these into quantities in order to calculate their relative value—in complete agreement with the basic principle of both modern natural science and capitalism.[58] For utilitarianism the utility of an act of moral forgiveness ultimately differs only quantitatively from that of sexual pleasure, and the utility of a human life is only a multiple of the utility of gastronomic pleasure. If someone kills a child because his flesh tastes good, any normal utilitarian will be shocked, because the utility of life is greater than that of eating—but that does not mean that if the number of those taking part in the meal is great enough, this kind of behavior might be not only permissible but even morally obligatory.[59] This criticism is meant to show only that when one leaves Kantianism behind, classical utilitarianism is not a feasible alternative, not that one ought to stay with Kantianism. The mere universalizability of a maxim is compatible with the most morally reprehensible contents, and therefore cannot be the sole criterion for the morals of a maxim. The question of whether in war one should take prisoners is not determined by reference to the postulate of universalizability. What is determined is only that we may not morally demand of the opposing party that it take our soldiers prisoners, while we kill their soldiers after the battle is over; chivalry does not exclude holding human life cheap. In order to arrive at an answer to this question, one needs to assume that there are substantive goods. If human life is a good, then confronted by two equally universalizable maxims one can make a moral choice in favor of taking prisoners.[60]

Thus it seems indispensable to leave formalism behind and work out a universal material ethics in which goods and values play a role. (The distinction between goods and values is that goods are objects, and in some cases also actions and events, to which values are attributed as qualities; values are related to goods as colors are to colored objects.)[61] However, it must be admitted that Kant's universalist formalism is stronger than has thus far been shown. Kant was sensitive to this problem and formulated the

---

58. Cf. V. Hösle (1991), 55, 63.

59. And indeed, this duty would also hold *for the victim of the cannibalistic act.* For even if utilitarianism takes all factual preferences in earnest morally, it nonetheless strictly requires the sacrifice of an individual's most elementary interests for the sake of the whole; utilitarian ethics requires a far more sweeping altruism than do people's usual moral convictions. It is remarkable that the same theory first acknowledges the most repulsive need and then demands the sacrifice of the most legitimate!

60. The assumption that human life has value in no way implies the conception that murder is permissible if it is a necessary condition for engendering another person: there would be just as many living people if one refrained from doing either. This argument can be easily answered by pointing out that human life is not the only morally relevant good—and murder violates not only human life, but human life with an actual will to live and its own autonomy. Furthermore, not everything can be made mensurable; see below, chap. 3.2.3.

61. Cf. Scheler (1980), 35 ff.

categorical imperative not only as the postulate of universalizability, but also in the following form: *"So act that you use humanity, whether in your own person or in the person of any other, always at the same time as an end, never merely as a means."* [62] He himself considered this formulation to be equivalent to the postulate of universalizability, but this is clearly incorrect; the postulate of universalizability is compatible with all people being allowed to treat each other as instruments. And yet, with his assertion of equivalence, Kant had something in mind that he himself could not correctly reconstruct, but which was of great importance for the later development of logic and ethics. His assertion of equivalence is based on the following thought: The categorical imperative is unconditionally valid, and thus not a means for other interests; but also those who are in principle able to understand it and to subject themselves to its unconditional nature may not be considered means—they must also be respected as ends in themselves. Kant is reflecting on something that is a subjective condition of the possibility of the categorical imperative becoming effective—his concretization of the categorical imperative in terms of ends in themselves results from a kind of transcendental reflection. Furthermore, it is conceivable that Kant's conception of a realm of ends, that is, a community of rational beings considering each other ends in themselves, can be privileged by its formal characteristics. Symmetry is not the specific difference of affirmative relationships, for mutual instrumentalization is also a symmetrical relation. But whereas relationships of domination are transitive and asymmetrical, and friend-enemy relationships are symmetrical but intransitive, mutual recognition can claim to be both symmetrical and transitive. Since the transitivity and symmetry of a relation entail its reflexivity, this mutual respect also leads to a mediated form of the relationship to oneself: If I respect all those who are respected by those whom I respect, and if the latter also respect me too, then I can also respect myself.

Transcendental arguments play an explicit role in ethics in Fichte's *Sittenlehre*, in transcendental pragmatics, and in Alan Gewirth's work. [63] Thus one might try to develop an immanently formalist universalism into an ethics of goods and values by reflecting on the goods that constitute the condition of the possibility of ethical decisions, independently of whether the latter are made in isolation or through discourse. For instance, it can be argued that every person has a right to life, because life is a necessary condition for argumentation. Every ethical theory must morally justify its own possibility, and this implies that the life of arguing beings is a good; since, moreover, a rational ethics is universalist, it has to grant a right to life to *any* being capable of argument. It can hardly be denied that this approach is very fruitful and that such arguments

---

62. "Handle so, daß du die Menschheit sowohl in deiner Person, als in der Person eines jeden andern jederzeit zugleich als Zweck, niemals bloß als Mittel brauchest" (1976 f.), 7:61. Trans. M. Gregor (1998), 38.

63. Cf. Apel (1973), especially the final essay, as well as Gewirth (1978). However, because Apel's approach is oriented toward intersubjectivity, he is in danger, like the utilitarians and probably Jonas as well, of allowing violations of basic individual rights for the sake of the whole.

may be able to ground certain moral goods. But first of all, they cannot ground all moral goods, and second, the point of view from which the justified goods are observed is distorted. Thus formalist universalism, which seeks to ground itself through reflexive arguments, is in principle incapable of understanding the life of organisms that are not argumentative (or at least not capable of argumentation) as good. Kant's efforts to justify the prohibition on cruelty to animals are characteristic of this blind spot in formalism.[64] The utilitarian respect for all beings capable of suffering is not an alternative insofar as, first, it was never sufficiently grounded, and second, the utilitarian limitation to suffering does not do justice to the point that painlessly killing animals and, even more, painlessly exterminating an entire species are also morally problematic. In view of the ecological crisis, a theory of the intrinsic worth of natural and especially organic being is indispensable, and such a theory is not compatible with modern formalist positions. The recourse to a more comprehensive metaphysics of nature, such as Hans Jonas has elaborated, may be required.[65] Even in the above-mentioned grounding for the idea that the life of rational beings is a good, it is implausible to assume that it is a good *solely because* it is necessary for argumentation. It is true that the life of a human being has a higher value than that of an animal because it is the life of a being that is capable of moral feeling and even argumentation. But what is disturbing in the favoring of human life as a good in terms of the logic of argument is the transformation of all goods into means solely for the goal of ethical argumentation. More persuasive is the conception of pre-modern metaphysics and ethics according to which life has an intrinsic worth. Intellectual values are given priority over the value of life; but that does not mean that the value of life exists solely for the sake of the intellectual.[66]

---

64. Cf. the section "Amphibolie der moralischen Reflexionsbegriffe" (whose title is typical) in the *Metaphysik der Sitten* (1976 f.; 8:577 ff.). Kant argues in a purely anthropocentric way: tormenting animals is morally prohibited solely because it weakens our empathy with other humans. To this we must reply that empirically we might find the opposite: cruel behavior toward animals diverts aggressiveness that might otherwise take human beings as its victims.

65. It is remarkable that even Rawls, at the end of section 77, is willing to admit as much. "Certainly it is wrong to be cruel to animals and the destruction of a whole species can be a great evil. . . . I shall not attempt to explain these considered beliefs. They are outside the scope of the theory of justice. . . . A correct conception of our relations to animals and to nature would seem to depend upon a theory of the natural order and our place in it. One of the tasks of metaphysics is to work out a view of the world which is suited for this purpose" (1971; 512). In her book (1990), U. Wolf opts for a place for animals in morals based on an ethics of compassion, but she acknowledges that a metaphysical theory would be a possible alternative.

66. Naturally, for any teleological ethics that does not assume a *single* good with intrinsic worth, the problem arises as to what combination of the various goods should be given preference. What is tempting and at the same time absurd about utilitarianism consists in its offer of utility as a common currency (cf. Rawls [1971], 554 ff.). And if one maintains that there is a hierarchy of heterogeneous values, this leads to the temptation to strive to achieve the highest good in the maximum quantity possible. Here only an axiological principle that favors diversity can help us; see below, chap. 3.5.1.

Despite this choice of a non-utilitarian teleological ethics, we must make a few important restrictions. The ethics defended here includes in its values the universalist idea of justice as an indispensable element—thus it seeks to not negate formalism, but rather to "sublate" (*aufheben*) it in the Hegelian sense. Justice is the basic value, but not the only one, and therefore the reduction of political philosophy to a theory of political justice should be rejected, no matter how important this reduction may have been in the development of the modern constitutional state founded on the rule of law. Justice is not the only value that one can adopt from Kant's deontological approach. Sincerity and respect for contracts are certainly others. However, the latter have to be connected with other values; indeed, one may maintain, against Kant, that there are situations in which, unlike justice, they must even be sacrificed to other values. In fact, this seems to me one of the strongest arguments for proposing a goods-and-values ethics: it would not be possible otherwise to justify exceptions to the normally valid obligations, the so-called *prima facie obligations*.[67] Some of these moral obligations, such as "Thou shalt not kill," "Thou shalt not steal," and so forth, are also found in criminal law, and at least the more developed systems of criminal law acknowledge that the commission of a criminal offense is not sufficient to justify punishment. In any case, it follows from modern intentionalism that no grounds excluding guilt may exist; but even before one turns to this question, the problem of a state of emergency that justifies making exceptions arises. In German criminal law, taking someone else's property in order to save a human life is not excused, but justified: thus it is objectively not against the law. The general idea of law holds that lower legal goods, which criminal law otherwise protects, may be sacrificed to significantly higher goods if that is the only way to avert danger.[68] Whereas criminal law normally only permits, not commands, such actions, on the level of morals there may be a duty to perform them—at least when the difference in rank between the good endangered and the good to be sacrificed is great. In any case, the strict deontologism in Stanley Kubrick's film *Dr. Strangelove* seems exceptionally grotesque. The British executive officer Manbreak might be able to prevent the outbreak of an atomic war—which would probably annihilate most of humanity, and which has become very likely as a result of the mad General Jack D. Ripper's decision to launch a squadron of bombers—by communicating by telephone to the political headquarters the secret code urgently needed to recall the bombers. But he has a problem: he doesn't have enough change to use the only phone booth at his disposal. So he asks an American officer to fire his gun into a Coke machine in order to make it disgorge its coins. The first reaction of the officer (who does not fully understand the situation) is to refuse; the

---

67. Two kinds of exceptions to prima facie obligations may be distinguished. The first does not determine when one is exempted from the norm, and merely states that it should not be too often (consider, for instance, conventions of politeness). The other, more interesting kind, which is the only one that will be discussed in the following, characterizes certain situations in which prima facie obligations *should* not be observed. Cf. Hare (1952), 49 ff.

68. Cf. German Penal Code § 34.

Coke machine is private property, and he is not authorized to damage it. If Kant had thought that this case (or another analogous one, in which the world could be saved only by lying) was to be decided in accord with the principle *pereat mundus, fiat iustitia,* then one would have no choice but to consider the ethics of the most important moral philosopher of the modern age as a public menace, given its consequences.[69]

3.2.3. Comparative and Metrical Concepts in Ethics: The Tragic

Granted, there are certainly cases, precisely in politics, in which moral judgment is considerably more difficult than in the cases just mentioned—secret service activities are a famous example of this. That they can prevent wars and save lives is just as true as that they violate a great many prima facie obligations: Can they be justified? In any case, it is clear that the idea of justifiable exceptions is acceptable only if there is a hierarchy of goods and values. Otherwise, the door is wide open to arbitrariness.[70] We do not get far with classificatory value concepts such as "good" and "bad" when we are discussing an act that violates one value and realizes another one (which is usually the case); comparative value concepts such as "better," "worse," "a higher value than," and "a lower value than" are indispensable.[71] It would be ideal if the hierarchy of values represented a quasi-ordering: all values should be comparable in their dimension of value, and thus the corresponding relations should also be connected;[72] the latter should also be transitive. These demands alone can exclude the possibility of being constantly confronted by ethical dilemmas, although this does not mean that these demands can completely eliminate such dilemmas.

---

69. One has to recognize that Kant translated this principle—which Hegel (1969 ff.; 7:240) describes as "empty words"—in the following way: "Es herrsche Gerechtigkeit, die Schelme in der Welt mögen auch insgesamt darüber zu Grunde gehen (1976 f.; 11:241). ("Let justice rule, even if the rascals will all perish.") Yet what would we do if the downfall of the rascals also entailed that of all other people?

70. Consider Jesuit ethics. Here we should note an ambiguity in the word "relativism." The position defended here, which allows for exceptions to prima facie obligations, could be called "relativistic" insofar as, according to it, the validity of norms follows from the complex tangle of values that stand in a relation *to each other;* yet that does not mean that these values draw their respective validity from their relation *to various subjects with various interests.* In the following pages, only the latter position will be termed "relativism," and only for this position is there no general answer to the question as to what is morally commanded.

71. That does not mean that comparative concepts should replace classificatory concepts. Insofar as it evaluates alternatives, ethics needs only comparative concepts, but the question of whether the best possible action is itself good or bad is in no way trivial, as we will soon see. Comparative concepts are easier to define than classificatory concepts, and this holds for descriptive concepts (e.g., "longer") as well as for normative concepts. Cf. Hare (1952), 183 ff.

72. See the earlier discussion of the relationship between aesthetic and moral values (chap. 2.2), which is supposed to establish the connected character of the value relation.

We can discuss here only in a marginal way the question of whether it is possible or even desirable to transform these comparative value concepts into metrical ones.[73] Up to this point at least, this is not in view for ethics—except in the trivial case where the comparison of enumerable goods of equal value is concerned. But even in that case it is rightly questioned whether human lives can be weighed against one another. According to German criminal law, killing an innocent person is never justified except in situations of self-defense, even if it is the only way of saving the lives of any number of other people; however, the so-called supra-legal state of emergency (which is, however, interpreted only as excusing certain actions)[74] points to the fact that in relation to this principle, further discussion is needed. An attempt to transform qualitatively heterogeneous goods and values into metrical values would not be reasonable for the simple reason that if one accepts the Archimedean axiom,[75] a certain multiple of the lower good would always be of greater value than a single instance of the higher good; but that leads to the absurd consequences of utilitarianism that have already been criticized.[76] Even if there might be situations in which the killing of a person (especially a guilty person) is morally permissible in order to save the life of an innocent person, it goes without saying that this can never be allowed for the sake of economic advantages, no matter how great. Life has an unconditional priority over all economic goods because one can enjoy these goods only if one is alive; and if a person is not prepared to die for economic advantages, then in the framework of a universalist ethics he cannot demand the same of any other person. In this connection the concept of the lexical order is relevant. Certain values are related to each other in such a way that the $n + 1^{th}$ value comes into play only when various alternative actions respect the nth value to the same extent; the more basic values are without exception valid in relationship to the later ones, and their violation can under no circumstances be justified by reference to the later ones. In this conviction Kant and Rawls are far ahead of the utilitarians—no matter how inadequate it may be that Kant, because of his formalism, did not enumerate the goods that are prior to the rest, and no matter how much one may acknowledge that if cer-

---

73. In metaethics, the word "value" is used with differing meanings. On one hand, it has to do with qualitatively different ideal entities, and on the other, it can also mean the quantitative value that would be attributed to individual situations after a successful process of transforming value concepts into metrical ones.

74. Cf. A. Schönke and H. Schröder (1982), 415 ff. On the problem, see chap. 7.3.2.

75. This is, of course, not absolutely necessary—Euclid was already aware of non-Archimedean magnitudes (III 16), and in axiology the principle is even less indispensable than it is in mathematics. The famous scale of Critolaus (Cicero, *Tusc. Disp.* V 17, 50) already seems to deny it.

76 In his dystopia, J. Zamyatin has provided an unsurpassable caricature of the idea of a mathematicized morals. Cf. especially entries 3 (1976; 37 f.), 19 (142 f.), and 20 (152 f.) One can hardly imagine a greater contrast than that between, on one hand, Plato's and Kant's conviction that because of their a priori nature, ethics and mathematics are essentially related, and on the other, the ideas of Number D-503 regarding the reduction of morals to the four basic modes of calculation.

tain basic goods are generally guaranteed, utilitarian arguments for the distribution of less basic goods may be legitimate.[77]

Despite all these differentiations, any ethics that denies that there are such things as moral dilemmas—dilemmas that can even lead to tragic conflicts—is superficial. Even if there is a clear hierarchy of goods and values, many situations where decisions must be made involve conflicts between several goods, and this can easily lead to stalemates. (In addition, the rules for adding up differing goods are not simple. Apart from the problem of a lack of metrical concepts, we can take as our starting point that the value of the conjunction of two events is not always equal to the sum of the values of the events taken separately.)[78] A special case occurs when duties toward a certain person or institution arise from proximity. Thus someone toward whom we have a special responsibility may make demands on us that we can fulfill only by foregoing the achievement of a higher value for which we bear no comparable responsibility. The often cited Sartrean example is such a case.[79] If one's own country is occupied in an unjust war and there is a prima facie duty to join the resistance to the invader, then one may be confronted by a conflict if, at this same moment, one's seriously ill mother needs care. The political liberation of one's country is a greater good than the mother's health; but a person has a greater duty toward his mother than toward his country, for which—at least in most situations—his own efforts have a much smaller marginal utility than for his mother. Such conflicts play a role in most political tragedies. However, we should not forget that we can speak of tragic conflicts only when there is an objective order of values, and that the decline of tragedy in our time has much to do with a rampant relativism that is as unfavorable to the tragic as is the dogmatic narrow-mindedness that uncritically identifies with its own mores or assumes that there is a single basic value. The historical and cultural locus of the tragic is very limited—neither oriental nor late modern cultures are capable of the kind of differentiation of moral feelings from which the tragic springs.

Finally, we must note that even if certain actions, such as carrying on a just war, can be legitimated, they nonetheless harm goods, such as the lives of other people; and people can and even should suffer for this reason,[80] even if those who have made the decision to injure the lesser good cannot be considered guilty—guilt presupposes that one should have acted otherwise. But the fact that an action is better than any alternative does not mean that it is simply good. Anyone who considers justifiable acts as good without any further qualification will be exposed to two temptations: first, to engage in

---

77. Hegel's *Philosophy of Right* can be interpreted to represent a synthesis of Kantianism and utilitarianism: the abstract right that is grounded and interpreted in a Kantian way is followed by welfare, whose promotion is morally obligatory, but only insofar as it does not contradict right. The concept of the ethical life leads beyond both Kant and utilitarianism.

78. This follows from Moore's famous principle of organic wholes (*Principia Ethica* 18 ff. [1903; 27 ff.]). See also below, chap. 3.5.1.

79. Cf. Sartre (1966), 39 ff.

80. Cf. Augustine, *De civitate Dei* XIX 6 f.

good conscience in acts that cannot be justified;[81] and second, not to do all he can to avoid situations in which the lesser evil must be chosen. The political man (*Machtmensch*) can derive a peculiar enjoyment from the fact that he is allowed to do things that are forbidden for others; and this enjoyment is morally disgraceful, even if the corresponding action can be justified. Few things better show Lincoln's moral greatness than his sadness coupled with decisiveness in opposing the southern states' attempted secession. The fact that the manner in which he died has contributed to his mythical stature in American consciousness is explained precisely by the way his death made it clear that Lincoln himself took the risks that he imposed on others.

In this section we cannot yet attempt to circumscribe positively the problem of the hierarchy of goods and values—a problem that is one of the most difficult in ethics, and in dealing with which often only intuitive approximations are possible. At least, this is the case given the current state of ethics. This should not be taken to mean that the reconstruction of our intuitive judgments on the basis of principles is impossible or should not even be attempted. For reasons that will be discussed in section 3.4.1, it will be necessary concretely to demonstrate which goods and values could be realized in connection with individual real structures such as the human being, the state, and so on. Here we should note only that this problem cannot be resolved by taking as a foundation the factual moral valuations of those concerned and constructing from them an ideally valid valuation. Even when they coincide, individual preferences may be false; Sen's paradox convincingly shows that Pareto-inclusiveness does not provide a sufficient condition for the legitimacy of a collective preference.[82] But even independently of the fact that there are obviously illegitimate preferences, a political ethics that sought, for instance, to base itself on the aggregation of the factual preferences of the citizens (or those concerned) would be erroneous. Thus the various attempts of political economy to construct social preference functions out of individual ones[83] have shown how difficult, and to some extent hopeless, such a program is[84]—even if the problems of the interpersonal comparability and interdependence of subjective valu-

---

81. Cf. B. Williams's essay "Politics and Moral Character" (now in 1981; 54–70), especially 62: "The point . . . is that only those who are reluctant or disinclined to do the morally disagreeable when it is really necessary have much chance of not doing it when it is not necessary." I find interesting Williams's view that a politician need not himself be capable of carrying out the ugly things that he may occasionally have to order done—if that were required, only brutal people would be qualified for a political career (69 f.).

82. A. Sen's paradox can be better exemplified as follows: Imagine a wrongdoer and an extremely benevolent person, both of whom agree that if one of them has to die, it should be the benevolent one (who has a tendency to sacrifice himself). From this it does not follow that it is objectively better that the latter die.

83. The classic work on this problem is by K. J. Arrow (1951).

84. Because of Condorcet's or Arrow's paradox, the requirement of a majority, on which voting is usually based, leads from transitive individual preferences to an intransitive social preference.

ations could be resolved.[85] So far as this problem is concerned, the individualistic assumption that usually underlies the program mentioned is probably descriptively correct: many individual preferences emerge from a previous social preference of the culture to which one belongs. The theory advanced here does not exclude the possibility that—if the problem of an objective hierarchy of goods and values could be solved— the problem of the aggregation of factual individual preferences might arise again within a fully elaborated ethics (for example, within a normative theory of economic policy), and that the search for a social preference function would thereby gain a limited moral relevance. Respect for legitimate subjective preferences is certainly a moral duty, but it is not the only one. *If* certain basic goods are generally guaranteed, independently of the interests that may be invested in them, then the promotion of particular interests as well is meaningful. The latter should certainly be developed, but within a framework that as such is not reducible to them. Only the attempt to make the problem of aggregation the basis for ethics in general, and for political ethics in particular, is mistaken. It seems much more important to produce a normative theory that determines which preferences a moral person ought to have. Since these preferences should be generally valid, for such a theory the aggregation problem is solved. The disturbing withering away of the concept of the common good in contemporary political philosophy has much to do with the fact that fewer and fewer people understand the idea of a common good that is not simply cobbled together from individual preferences, and the decline of the concept of the common good characterizes the real politics of present-day states, no less than it does political theory. Without a revival of this concept, which will be more closely examined in chapter 7.3.3.3.4, politics cannot recover its dignity.

3.3. A Priori and Empirical Knowledge in Ethics

One of Kant's most important insights is that normative judgments (and in an analogous way, value judgments) are a priori synthetic judgments and thus cannot be either grounded or falsified by a posteriori judgments. The judgment "Thou shalt not kill" is not affected by reference to statistics about murders. No matter how much Kant's recognition of this makes him superior to all empiricists, his view that experiential knowledge plays no role in resolving moral problems is one-sided. This view has to do with his formalism. Yet an underestimate of experience is also found in Scheler, who assumes a substantive a priori. Both Kant and Scheler are no doubt right to think that the judgments "Thou shalt not lie" and "A spiritual being's (a person's) life has high value" are not a posteriori judgments. But that does not mean that experiential knowledge is not important in deriving more concrete norms from these propositions. This kind of knowledge is obviously necessary on two fundamentally different levels.

---

85. Cf. J. Nida-Rümelin (1987), 55 ff., 80 ff.

3.3.1. The Subsumption Problem

First we must mention the subsumption problem. The second of the two cases of normative judgements just mentioned involves the question, Is this concrete being a person? In the course of history this question has been repeatedly asked with regard to human beings. There is reason to believe that in discovering foreign cultures, some of the conquerors who disgracefully assaulted them were sincerely convinced that members of these cultures were not persons in the full sense of the word, and hence they did not consider that their conduct violated the principle that the life of a defenseless person should be spared.[86] The discussion of the rights of the Indians in the Spanish colonies dealt no less with the subsumption problem than with the working out of general principles of intercultural behavior; anthropological-historical discussions of the intelligence and the morals of the Indians were no less important than properly ethical discussions.[87] However, we have to take into account the possibility that someone who wants to free himself from a general principle—but does not dare to do so openly because it could come back to haunt him—might use the subsumption problem as a pretext for representing his inexcusable acts as socially acceptable. This strategy must be reckoned with, especially in enlightened societies. But even in the latter, problems of subsumption exist. Currently, the abortion issue is probably the most explosive one. Hardly anyone denies that persons may not be killed with impunity; but whether embryos are persons is precisely the problem. However, this problem occupies a peculiar intermediate position between a question of principle and a question of subsumption, insofar as there is also a consensus regarding the functions of embryos. It is clear that an embryo cannot survive on its own and has no self-consciousness (one could say the same of newborns), and at the same time it is equally clear that it is developing toward an autonomous and self-conscious being. Thus the real problem is whether such a potential being with self-consciousness should be seen as a person in the sense this term has in the philosophy of law.[88]

One reason the answer to the question whether an adult human being is a person is difficult is that the interior dimension of others is not immediately accessible to us. Whether someone has an interior dimension (obviously a necessary but not a sufficient condition for being a person) is not so easy to figure out as the question of whether an object has a specific length; without a theory of the experience of other minds this question cannot be fundamentally answered. In adult humans the acknowledgment that another is a person is usually connected with the process of recognition (*Anerkennung*), to

---

86. Analogously, for the pre-universalist slaveholder the slave was not a person.

87. One has only to read Ginés de Sepúlveda's and Las Casas's apologies (which were made easily accessible in 1975).

88. This intermediate position results from the fact that in ordinary language the word "person" is both a descriptive and a normative concept. If beings that are currently self-conscious are the only ones counted as persons, the argument will be over the normative question of whether beings with potential self-consciousness may be killed.

which we will return again in chapter 5.1.2.1. Physical and cultural alterity are barriers to this process of acknowledgment, and overcoming these barriers is a particularly affirmative achievement from a moral point of view.[89] The barriers would be at their highest if one encountered beings that belonged to another biological species or had issued from highly developed artifacts and sometimes, but not always, seemed to behave like persons—a possibility that cannot be excluded and that would pose the subsumption problem in a particularly difficult form. The example discussed up to this point allows us to distinguish two aspects of the subsumption problem that have differing status in epistemological theory. On one hand, we have to answer the general question as to what characteristics a spiritual being possesses, what allows us to recognize it, and so forth. This is possible only within the framework of a (non-normative) *theory*. On the other hand, it is obvious that the last subsumption—for example, whether such characteristics are available—is itself no longer a theoretical performance but involves only a simple application of *judgment*. It is the lack of such judgment that people call "stupidity," and it must be acknowledged that the most important theoretical achievements are compatible with stupidity.

3.3.2. Means and Ends

Experience plays a second important role in ethics. Even if one is convinced that certain beings are persons, how can we help protect their lives when they are in danger? It is not possible to protect or realize goods without knowing something about the necessary *means* to these ends. This kind of knowledge is empirical in nature, and to that extent a concrete ethics without experiential knowledge is impossible. Yet every action has *consequences* in addition to its intended goal; some of these consequences one cannot know, and others one can know, but in fact does not, and so far as possible should find out. Thus the administration of a medicine that is helpful for one person can have negative side effects for others, and since these side effects are morally relevant, they must be taken into account in deciding whether this medicine should be used. The consequences of a type of action are to be discovered empirically, just as are the means—that is, the presuppositions for the achievement of a goal. However, it is clear that here we quickly encounter limits. No matter how right it may be that without a given noble act certain terrible catastrophes would not have entered into the causal sequence of that

---

89. One of the most impressive works on this set of problems is David Lynch's film *The Elephant Man*, which is based on a historical case in the nineteenth century. In this film, the physician Frederick Treves succeeds in discovering in the completely misshapen John Merrick an intellectually and morally distinguished person. The scene in which Treves's superior first realizes, on a second encounter with Merrick, that he is not an idiot but a full human being, and understands what an objective injustice he would have committed through his error in subsumption, which would have resulted in Merrick's expulsion from the hospital, is one of the most moving in the history of cinema.

which exists, insofar as this causal sequence is not predictable, it is completely irrelevant to the moral evaluation of the act in question. Yet this does not alter the duty to foresee as many consequences as possible and to take them into account in making one's own decision.[90] It is precisely modern technology's spectacular expansion of the consequences of our action in space and time that makes this duty particularly urgent, and it fundamentally changes the overall ethical situation in comparison with the model proposed by Kant—who, because of his intentionalism, could still assume that common sense was sufficient to understand our duties.[91] The loss of the feeling that one's common sense suffices, together with insight into moral principles, in order to arrive at morally defensible decisions is perhaps the most demoralizing and humiliating trait of the age of technology—a trait that probably best explains the growth of ethical nihilism in an age that is least able to afford it.[92]

A special problem arises when our actions have negative side effects only because they increase the likelihood that other people for whom one bears no responsibility will make immoral decisions. The making of a new decision by another responsible person, who does something inherently negative that one has not only not encouraged him to do, but even warned him against, implies shifting most of the responsibility to this person. However, it would be one-sided to deny that if this behavior is very likely, one has to take it into account in one's own initial decision. To give a concrete example, an extortionist who kills a hostage because the person being extorted has not complied with his criminal demands is solely responsible in criminal law and bears the greatest moral responsibility for the killing of this person. There are many cases in which it is morally compulsory not to give in to the extortion, for instance, because it may lead to further cases of extortion. But one can come to this conclusion only if one has conscientiously considered all the relevant alternatives—such as only pretending to meet the extortionist's demands, and so on. If the action with negative consequences for which the first actor created the possibility presupposes only negligence (and not intentional offense) on the part of the second actor, the former's share of the responsibility is greater, since negligence is more frequent than intentional crimes. For instance, if one has not made an effort to prevent a dangerous discovery from being negligently misused, one has more to reproach oneself with than if the misuse occurred through intentional malice. One's own share of the responsibility is even greater if it was foreseeable that an irresponsible person would be tempted to make such a misuse, and yet one did not do everything one could to prevent this misuse; for the actions of irresponsible persons are almost to be regarded as natural events.

---

90. What is dangerous about the theological doctrine of double effect is that it completely underestimates the moral importance of side effects that are foreseeable and involuntary but have been accepted.

91. The differences between the current situation and the one described by Kant are examined in a particularly effective way by Jonas (1979).

92. On the other hand, the problem is complicated by the fact that the sheer magnitude of empirical knowledge leaves its champions less and less time to acquire rational knowledge of values.

Here we see an interesting limitation of the dualism of *Is* and *Ought*. Certainly it is true that normative and descriptive propositions do not follow from each other, but it is nonetheless possible to construct *mixed syllogisms* that deduce from a normative proposition and a descriptive proposition a further normative proposition.[93] From the normative proposition "You should realize value V" and the empirical proposition "Under conditions C, means M is necessary in order to realize V" follows the derived obligation, "You should use means M under conditions C"—at least when the use of means M is not prohibited on the ground that it violates other moral values. Descriptive and normative insights are two different sources of knowledge that are independent of each other, but that does not mean that they cannot work together. In a very similar way, every substantial descriptive theory combines logical and empirical elements. Even if we were to follow Kant in assuming that these two items of knowledge have no common origin, we would not be able to deny that knowledge in the full sense of the word first emerges from their collaboration. Analogously, every responsible decision presupposes a combination of normative and descriptive knowledge, and no social science that wants to provide a basis for such decisions can balk at this kind of combination—while being aware that the normative element has to be provided by philosophy.[94]

The concept of a mixed syllogism also clarifies the opposition between absolutism and relativism in ethics. The major premises of an ethical syllogism are valid, like mathematical truths, always and everywhere (naturally, this does not mean that they are acknowledged in every culture, and still less that people everywhere act in accord with them—though neither of these qualifications puts their validity in question). However, we can say that the *conclusions* of a mixed syllogism are neither always nor everywhere valid: their validity presupposes the truth not only of the normative major premise but also that of the descriptive minor premise, and the latter may very well depend on the circumstances. M is not a means to V always and everywhere; in different situations it may even be that opposite means are required to realize the same value. In order to

---

93. The practical syllogism of which Aristotle speaks is related (for example, *De anima* 434a16 ff., *De motu animalium* 701a7 ff., *Nicomachean Ethics* 1144a31 ff., 1146b36 ff.) to the previously mentioned case of the combination of a general moral principle with a concrete subsumption. Sometimes, however, reference is also made to means toward an end (*Metaphysics* 1032b6 f.). In any case, according to Aristotle the conclusion is not a proposition but an action. See also Thomas Aquinas, *Summa theologica* I/II, q.76 a.1 c, q.77 a.2 ad 4, q.90 a.1 ad 2. Aristotle's and Aquinas's application of this conception to weakness of will is interesting. In recent ethical literature it is Hare's special contribution to have reconstructed the logic of practical syllogisms (1952; 27 ff.). Cf. also the important essays by G. H. von Wright (now in 1977; 41–60; 61–81), who makes a sharp distinction between conclusions in the first and in the third person.

94. The fact that the minor premise is descriptive does not imply that it has to be a posteriori. There are also theoretical a priori synthetic propositions; for example, philosophical social science seeks to derive some characteristics of social systems and their developments from their concepts. See below, chap. 3.4.

maintain a suitable population density on Earth, a great number of children was a reasonable goal in historical periods with high infant mortality and smaller populations; in later times, with larger populations and lower death rates, the same goal demands a decline in the birth rate. Unfortunately, many people do not succeed in rising to the level of general moral *principles.* Concrete *norms,* which follow from the principles and the descriptive minor premises, are more comprehensible, and so people will stubbornly cling to them even after the situation has changed. This is one of the great dangers of abstract absolutism. However, the corresponding danger in abstract relativism is even greater, because for it both principles and norms change, so that people are left with nothing stable to which they can cling. Not only is abstract-absolutist behavior usually objectively less damaging than relativistic behavior, because it at least remains predictable, but so far as the subjectively moral element is concerned, abstract absolutism is also superior because it errs only with regard to the descriptive premise. It thus commits an exclusively intellectual mistake, whereas relativism misses the dimension of value that is the heart of the moral. Nonetheless, in defense of relativism, it sometimes represents a reaction of despair to the narrow-mindedness of abstract absolutism.

3.3.2.1. Technical, Strategic, and Communicative Rationality

From the foregoing it emerges that ethics requires not only knowledge about pure value judgments but also knowledge about the means to given ends. Obviously, within means-ends rationality one can distinguish between *technical* and *strategic* rationality: the former provides answers in the realm of subject-object relationships, the latter provides answers in the realm of subject-subject relationships; the former is grounded in the natural sciences, the latter in the social sciences. The engineering sciences are a classic example of technical means-ends rationality, and motivational psychology and, more generally, cratology are classic examples of strategic means-ends rationality. Medicine mediates between these two forms of rationality, since it is concerned with a natural object of a very special kind, the human body; and the transformation of medicine into a pure natural science at the expense of folk psychological knowledge does not do justice to this intermediate position. Between technical and strategic rationality there are two ethically relevant differences that must be briefly examined here.

First, theories in the social sciences differ in nature from those in the natural sciences insofar as they themselves are part of the realm of objects that they analyze. A theory in the social sciences is itself a social fact, whereas a theory in the natural sciences is not a natural fact.[95] For precisely that reason a theory in the social sciences not only describes but changes its field of objects, and changes it not only by adding a new

---

95. To be sure, the books in which the theory is laid out and the parts of the brain that are correlated with the intellectual activities involved in producing them are natural objects—but the theories as such are not.

fact to it, but also far more deeply because this new fact fundamentally alters the over-all structure of the previous facts. Consider the so-called Oedipus effect of predictions that can, depending on the circumstances, confirm or falsify themselves (the latter by leading to countermeasures).[96] Theories in the natural sciences are social facts, of course, and communicating them is subject—like any action—to certain moral duties, since the knowledge of causal mechanisms that they provide can be abused. However, the salient point is obvious. A person working out a theory in the natural sciences that can serve as the basis for new weapons does not necessarily trigger the construction of these weapons, even if his theory is taken seriously; the actual construction depends on social condi-tions that the theory itself does not produce. However, if, for example, a culture starts believing in a theory in the social sciences according to which this culture, because of the necessary evolution of human society, will bring new political institutions to all other parts of the world, then this belief is itself sufficient to trigger the corresponding actions. (Naturally, certain conditions must be met in order for such a theory to be be-lieved; but if it is believed, then this belief operates autocatalytically.) From this it fol-lows that the communication of theories in the social sciences is subject to even more moral restrictions than are those in the natural sciences. Thus it is misleading, in the current situation, when people complain only about the negative consequences of knowl-edge in the natural sciences while saying nothing about those of knowledge in the social sciences and in ethics. (We have already discussed the ethics of ethics.)

    This leads us to the second morally relevant difference between theories in the natu-ral and in the social sciences. Knowledge in the social sciences can certainly be used in terms of means-ends rationality, but it is closer to value-rationality than knowledge in the natural sciences. On one hand, we must not neglect the knowledge regarding actu-ally existing institutions, the factual values of other people, and so forth, since these are real power factors that we have to take into account because we need them as means for establishing our own ideas. Only someone who knows how a state functions can make a political career in it, even if his goal is a radical transformation on the basis of new moral principles. In this case, such social facts, just like natural contexts, enter into our decisions only as objective material, not as their normative principle. On the other hand, existing ideas regarding values that deviate from our own can and should con-tribute as much as possible to the correction of our own—although with reference to the arguments in their favor, not to the fact of their being widespread. The moral obli-gation to respect other people as ends in themselves forbids us to use someone's beliefs about values, in which he most fully expresses himself as a person, merely as a means to our own ends; the instrumentalization of another person has a completely different moral status from the instrumentalization of natural forces. When we ask each other about values and options for action (and this may also take place through reading works

---

96. Cf., for example, Popper's sixth chapter (1960). In addition to the myth of Oedipus, Shake-speare's treatment of Macbeth is the most famous example of this kind of self-fulfilling prophecy.

in the social sciences), this process can take place on either level, normally on both at the same time. In asking someone about his values, we want to find out both how he intends to act in order to know how to react, and what values of his we should adopt, if need be. In telling him about our own values we seek both to factually influence him to adopt them and to convince him that they are objectively better; and the degree to which the former or the latter is the case gives the exchange a primarily *strategic* or *communicative* character.[97] The lasting contribution of discourse ethics is its emphasis on the intrinsic value of communication regarding moral questions, no matter how much one may object that discourse ethics ignores many other aspects of the moral in a misleadingly one-sided way, leading to the absurd notion that morals are concerned solely with harmonizing factual needs in order to produce a consensus.

Despite the distinction between strategic and communicative behavior as ideal types, it is obvious that they are linked by a gray area, which will be further examined in chapter 5.1.2.2.5. Pure communication reaches its apex in argumentation concerned exclusively with the theory of validity, whereas pure strategy reaches its apex in calculating duplicity on the receptive side and in manipulation or threats on the active side. In reality, however, an intermediate form is usually practiced, and this is absolutely right for two reasons. First, we have already shown that insight into pure relationships of validity has an effect on only a few people; an appeal to moral feelings and other feelings analogous to moral ones is much more effective. If a recommendation is objectively right, one can increase its chances of being adopted by appealing to people's sense of honor, for instance, because this is a stronger impulse, even if one does not consider the sense of honor an infallible moral criterion. This is especially true when the other person identifies with this feeling and therefore does not easily get the impression that he is being instrumentalized. Secondly, this moderate form of strategic behavior also occurs with regard to ourselves. Anyone who has come to know himself will avoid situations that might turn his impulses in a direction that is morally wrong, but he will support his feelings when he believes they could strengthen an abstract moral decision. For example, a person who has seen that he has a duty to get involved in a battle will refrain from reading literature about world-weariness. The *I* can harness the self for its own goals, but to do so it must know the self very well, because otherwise the instrumentalized self may take its revenge, just like any one else's.[98]

---

97. As a theory of understanding, hermeneutics is neutral with regard to this distinction; therefore it is absurd to try to ground ethics on hermeneutics alone. Cortés was an outstanding interpreter of a foreign culture, and he used his hermeneutic expertise to destroy it. However, hermeneutic expertise is a *necessary*—not a sufficient—condition for moral action. On the relationship between the various forms of rationality, see V. Hösle (1992a), 62 ff., where Apel's ideas are critically elaborated.

98. It is clear that one can objectivize moral feelings only on the basis of moral insight. Situations that cause an individual to have pangs of conscience, for example, may be avoided by that individual only if he is convinced that these pangs of conscience are unjustified, at least in their intensity, but force themselves on him on the basis of some psychological ground.

To repeat: From the fact that a value is socially valid it does not follow—as Kant rightly saw—that it is ideally valid and that one is morally bound by it. However, it does follow that one must examine the value, if only out of respect for its representatives, until one is clear about its validity; it also follows that even if one reaches a negative conclusion, one must acknowledge this value to be a fact and even take it into consideration to a certain degree if one wants political success within the culture concerned. To what extent one must respect socially accepted values depends, among other things, on the conditions determining one's own success and the disparity between socially valid and ideally valid values; a more detailed examination of this problem will be attempted in chapter 8.1.3. Here I note only that the refusal to accept any compromise between ideally and socially valid values usually condemns one to failure, and is sometimes (but not always) an expression of the extreme intentionalism according to which only one's own good conscience, and not the achievement of the objectively right, matters. Conversely, complete adaptation to socially accepted values without being convinced of their morality is the mark of opportunism. The situation is no better if, at the end of the process of adaptation, one has gone so far as to believe in the values that have made one's own career possible—and in fact, believes in them *because* one has made one's career on the basis of them.

3.3.2.2. The Ideal and the Non-Ideal Part of Ethics

In general, we can easily see why descriptive assertions regarding the individual or socially valid values of other people or cultures are indispensable within ethics. Obviously, every ethics begins by outlining an ideal situation within which people behave in a morally privileged way. Kant's realm of ends is a classic example of such an ideal, and the presentation of such an ideal is the rational and indispensable core of utopianism. But the ideal behavior of the individual in the realm of ends is morally obligatory only because he can assume that all others behave correspondingly. If this assumption is not justified, he is not necessarily obligated to behave just as he would if it were. In any case, any complete ethics must take into account the possibility that some people will not act in accord with their moral obligations, and establish its own norms for moral actors in such a situation. Thus Rawls divides his theory of justice into two parts: the first or ideal part presupposes a general agreement with the demands of justice, while the second, non-ideal part inquires into norms under less favorable conditions, which can be partly reduced to natural or historical contingencies, and partly to factual injustices.[99] Obviously, only descriptive propositions regarding the situation in which one has to act can determine which norms are appropriate, and it is therefore indispensable to collect information about one's own time or the people with whom or against whom one must act. To give a simple but striking example: All other things being equal, peace is morally

---

99. (1971), 245 ff. Apel similarly introduced a supplementary moral principle (1988; 145 ff.).

preferable to war. But it is not always better to put off war for a year if in the meantime the aggressor can increase its power more than the victim of aggression can increase its own, for that would mean either the latter's defeat or a longer and bloodier war. Therefore in order to make the right moral decision it is important to find out whether the other side has aggressive intentions or not, and that is possible only on the basis of empirical (sociological and psychological) knowledge. Admittedly, according to the previous discussion, our own theoretical assumptions can influence the other's behavior; trusting the other can lead the other side to trust us, and thus become a self-fulfilling structure. But this holds only within certain limits, and therefore it could very well be the case that the absolutely good-natured person who prefers to act in accord with the ideal theory is precisely the person least suited to deal realistically with the possibility of evil on the other side; he would probably find it more difficult to make the right decision than someone who knows evil from first-hand experience but has overcome it in himself. Here we leave open the question whether a pure and good person unaffected by negativity is better than someone who has been exposed to all kinds of temptations and has resisted them. However, in times of political crisis the latter is the person to whom one should entrust the common welfare, for evil should be opposed, especially when one is responsible not only for oneself but for others. Someone who cannot look evil in the eye should not seek to become a politician, especially since he, too, can find a way of life that deserves the highest moral respect. But this does not hold when the inability to see reality as it is goes hand in hand with self-righteous complaining and slander concerning those who have this ability. Moralistic critics are right when they insist that a realistic assessment of the situation alone does not make one capable of moral action; a political criminal who wants to succeed will also try to assess reality as it is. But such critics err when they fail to understand that prudence, while not sufficient, is nonetheless a necessary virtue of a moral politician, and when they consider their own flight from reality a sign of moral superiority.

A great politician must look simultaneously toward the heaven of pure ideals and toward the earth, with its real inhabitants—even at the risk of beginning to squint, which means, to abandon the metaphor, that he loses the harmonious purity of his soul. If he wants to be moral and at the same time effective, the statesman's knowledge must range from sociobiology's insights into human behavior to pure moral philosophy. His goal will always be to bring the current situation with its factual values closer to ideal values, and the theory of the measures one has to use in following this path is the true core of politics.[100] Moral *Realpolitik* stands between abstract idealism, which fails to recognize the actual context, and the kind of pragmatism that operates within this context without trying to improve it. It is a sign of the poverty of a culture when those who are politically active within it consist exclusively of moralists blind to reality and crafty po-

---

100. Fichte divided the "closed commercial state" (*Der geschlossene Handelsstaat*) into three parts: politics mediates between the normative demands of philosophy and a descriptive assessment of the current age.

litical men; and this combination is not at all uncommon because the two groups, despite their opposition as contraries, are obviously complementary. Political men like it when their opponents do not know what is going on, while the patent wickedness of the former allows the latter to delight in their own excellence—which a responsible *Realpolitik* might put in question by showing them that there is something higher than joy in one's own morality.

3.3.2.3. Intrinsic and Extrinsic Value

In the systematics of ethics it is clearly important to distinguish between situations that are good in themselves, that is, that have a positive *intrinsic* worth, and those that have only a derived, *extrinsic* worth (are "useful") as means to something that is valuable in itself. However, for various reasons this fundamental distinction is too crude. There are not simply ultimate ends and means to these ends; the more complex a person's life-plan or the social structure of a society is, the more quickly means to means to ends, means to means to means to ends, and so on, become necessary. Thus higher-level means, even if they are without any intrinsic value, become ends for the actors.[101] Military service is not an end in itself, but instead serves political ends; however, since the top levels of the military are usually not involved in the determination of political goals, they have to be satisfied with fulfilling their military tasks, and farther down in the hierarchy a soldier's goal may consist in doing office work for his superior officer. In short, something that within a more complex whole is a very limited means may become for someone a goal in itself. Moreover, there are clearly entities that have both an intrinsic and an extrinsic positive value.[102] Without good health one cannot complete more complex tasks, yet health also has its own value as an expression of vitality. A constitutional state founded on the rule of law guarantees the achievement of many values, but it also has a high value of its own. In addition, carrying out the whole process from the lowest means to the highest goal is in a certain sense an end in itself, as is suggested by our reflections on the characteristic relationship between the subjectively moral and the objectively right. At the level of the organism it is already one-sided to interpret the movement of an animal as a mere means to the end of getting food and ultimately of self-preservation, since the self that is supposed to be preserved is one that moves itself.[103] Not all, but many of the

---

101. Cf. Thomas Aquinas, *Summa theologica* I/II, q.13 a.3 c: "Sicut in operatione medici, sanitas se habet ut finis . . . Sed sanitas corporis ordinatur ad bonum animae." ("Just as health is an end in medical treatment . . . But the health of the body is directed toward the good of the soul.")

102. Cf. Plato *Republic* 357b ff. The distinction between things that are good in themselves and those that are good because of their consequences was made particularly clear by Moore (*Principia Ethica* 15 ff. [1903; 21 ff.]).

103. Cf. Jonas (1966), 106: "It is one of the paradoxes of life that it employs means which modify the end and themselves become parts of it." ("Es ist eines der Paradoxe des Lebens, daß es Mittel benutzt, die den Zweck modifizieren und selbst Teile desselbe werden" [1966; 106]).

performances through which an individual and a social system of self-preservation are maintained, including the use of means without intrinsic worth, belong even more to the self. Since every moral action has a high subjectively moral intrinsic value, the use of means that are themselves without intrinsic worth is intrinsically valuable if it is determined by the morally obligatory orientation toward conditions with intrinsic worth. Here we see that the distinction between intrinsic and extrinsic values and the distinction between objectively right and subjectively moral are not orthogonal: first, everything subjectively moral has an intrinsic worth, and second, there are no means of realizing the subjectively moral in the same sense that there are means of realizing objective conditions with intrinsic value. Under certain conditions one can save a person's life solely by making use of one's own powers; but one cannot by oneself cause the good actions of others, precisely because then these actions would not be *their* actions.

In general, the distinction between means and ends can easily mislead us, because means very seldom lack additional consequences. In reality, almost every technical innovation triggers unintended results. For example, every new medium determines—quite independently of the ends it serves—the nature of further action, which the theory of the alleged neutrality of technology naively overlooks. It is not the case, for instance, that television is good or bad depending on whether what is broadcast is good or bad; television as a medium has to be evaluated because, independently of its content, it alters the structures of our consciousness. The relationship between means and ends becomes particularly problematic when the only available means to a good end is neither morally indifferent nor positively valued, but rather negatively valued. May it then be utilized? Does the goal justify the means? Or should one always choose actions that have a positive intrinsic value but negative side effects? The answer to these questions depends, among other things, on the relationship between the two values, that is, between the value of the means and the value of the end, and thus it refers back to the previously mentioned problem of the hierarchy of goods and values. In any case, from the moderate intentionalism and teleological approach of this book it follows that an action that produces something that is in itself negatively valued has to be measured against the goals for the sake of which it was made. Saying this does not exclude the possibility that there may be actions that cannot under any circumstances be justified by a higher goal; we have already discussed this issue. Furthermore, it is self-evident that the violation of normally valid moral obligations for the sake of allegedly higher values, which in reality are not higher at all, represents a temptation without which the totalitarian and terrorist crimes of our time could not be understood. Yet even the most disturbing abuse of an argument cannot disconfirm it. Thus we have to remember that the actions of politicians must be evaluated in the light of the *strategy* they are pursuing. It is a necessary (but certainly not a sufficient) mark of a great policy that it is based on a comprehensive strategy, and that many decisions that seem to be pure ends in themselves are in reality at the same time means to a greater end, which may become increasingly clear even to the actor in the course of its realization, but which from the outset guides political action as an ideal that is sometimes merely glimpsed, and sometimes clearly seen. Obviously in such strategies it is constantly a matter of answers to multi-stage decision problems (which can be graphically represented in decision trees); there are always new decisions to be made in which the alternatives available at any given point in time t_n depend on decisions that were made at earlier points t_1, t_m. Thus, just as a mature person develops a plan of life on the basis of which he makes individual decisions,[104] a statesman should have a long-term plan for political action. On one hand, this plan should go beyond his own life, at least in certain areas. On the other hand, everyone who conceives a political strategy has to take into account the possibility that he will be far less capable of carrying it out to the end than of carrying out his own life-plan, because he is threatened not only by the general mortality of human beings but also by specific perils—in democracies, failing to be re-elected, and in non-democratic states, a fall from power. Therefore not only should he put off certain decisions as long as possible in order to keep open certain options for himself and his successors, but also—when further delay is no longer possible and a decision must be made because in all likelihood no comparably favorable conditions will occur for a long time—he should take into account the consequences of failure halfway to the goal, which could be even worse than merely continuing with a less valuable status quo.

Striking examples of this kind of failure are connected with the names of Bismarck and Gorbachev. The former was allowed to establish German unity, but not to restore a long-term European balance of powers that might have been able to prevent the First World War; the latter was able to end Soviet totalitarianism, but not to transform the Soviet Union into a modern state by simultaneously preserving the territorial status quo and avoiding bloody conflicts among or within the individual republics. One can hardly hold it against politicians who have lost power halfway to their goals that they do not respect successors who transform their morally well-grounded political strategies into something objectively disastrous.

3.3.3. The Importance of Decision Theory and Game Theory for Ethics

The question of the legitimacy of using a given means becomes even more difficult when it is only *probable*—depending on the occurrence of other events—that this means will lead to negative consequences, while not making use of it will also result, with a certain degree of probability, in negative consequences, that is, when it is a matter of assessing *risks*.[105] Hence it is appropriate to examine briefly here the instruments

---

104. On the concept of a life plan, see Rawls, § 63 (1971; 407 ff.).

105. The modernity of Jesuit ethics is shown by the fact that it made the problem of the relationship between means and ends as well as probability central to its interests (by considering as probable ethical opinions, not—as in the following discussion—empirical states of affairs). It quickly succumbed, as Pascal splendidly showed, to the relativistic current that *may* emerge from this problem. But this does not alter the fact that these are serious problems that cannot be ignored, but rather must be solved if ethics is not to capitulate to reality.

that decision theory has made available for the solution of this problem. Even the mention of prescriptive decision theory in a book on the morals of politics may seem surprising, insofar as this discipline was initially developed without any relationship to ethics. It is completely amoral, but not immoral, and therefore it can be used in an ethical theory. Its basic interest is the search for criteria of rational decision. In decision theory, a decision is understood as "rational"—in complete opposition to Kant's conception of practical reason—if it selects among possible alternative actions (including the omission of any action) the one that is subjectively best for the person concerned. Decision theory presupposes that a person's preferences with regard to the possibilities open to him are consistent, and that they can be rank ordered (an order that may in some cases be expressed by metrical concepts). This order of preferences, which is supposed to be transitive, is a subjective fact and need not coincide with the ideally valid order. A plan is rational if it has the best possible chance of satisfying the largest possible number of and the most important wishes. In decision theory these wishes do not have to be moral wishes, but nothing prevents them from being moral; thus decision theory can be put in the service of the goals of ethics. Indeed, one could even say that decision theory not only may, but should be used in ethics. If someone has moral goals, he should seek to realize them rationally. If the goals should be achieved, then rationality should control the relationship between means and ends. Therefore the promotion of means-ends rationality is a conditional obligation.

How decisions should be made under conditions of certainty—that is, when it is clear which events will occur independently of my action—is a relatively trivial question. If I prefer to walk without an umbrella, I will leave it at home if I can be sure that it will not rain. More interesting are the cases in which a decision has to be made under conditions of uncertainty or risk. One speaks of "decision under uncertainty" when the person making the decision does not know what will happen and cannot assign a subjective probability to each of the possible outcomes; in decisions under risk, on the other hand, he assigns subjective probabilities to each of the possible outcomes. How one should behave in making decisions under uncertainty is debated within decision theory.[106] When what is at stake is not a decision made by an individual maximizing his self-interest, however, but rather a moral decision that can have negative consequences for people who will not benefit from the interests of others, then justice demands that it be guided only by the maximin principle, which requires the choice of one of the alternatives in which the minimal values are maximal. (Exceptions are conceivable, not only in cases in which all concerned are in agreement, but also when the differences between the minima are small and those between the maxima are very large, and the action indicated by the maximin principle has the significantly smaller maximum. Consider the following pay-off matrix:

---

106. See, for example, R. D. Luce and H. Raiffa (1957), 275–326.

o	n
1/n	1

When *n* is large, the first column will certainly be given priority.)

In making decisions under risk, one should act in accord with Bernoulli's principle, that is, the rule of maximizing the expected value.[107] The expected value of an action is determined as the sum of all values that one attributes to the result of the corresponding action when the various possible states of affairs are realized and when these values are multiplied by the subjective probability of the corresponding states of affairs.[108]

The situation becomes more complex in decision situations in which the occurrence of a possible event depends on my behavior, or at least on assumptions regarding my behavior. Whether I take my umbrella with me or leave it at home does not determine whether it will rain or not. However, in assessing the probabilities of actions, whether one's own or those of others, the structure of self-fulfilling or self-defeating expectations plays a role. A person who considers it highly probable that he will win a battle is more likely to win than one who considers it less probable that he will win. Either of these opposed assumptions can confirm themselves; to some extent like the proposition "This proposition is true," they can be either true or false, depending on whether they are considered true or false. Therefore, in this case it is moral, not theoretical, grounds should determine the decision—for example, the will to win that can be a result of the conviction that one has a moral duty to win.

The same goes for many (but not all) intersubjective relationships: our own behavior affects the probability of a specific behavior on the part of others. For example, if we have to decide whether to carry weapons in meeting with an opponent under conditions like those of the state of nature, we will form hypotheses regarding the behavior of the other party; but of course our own decision will also be the object of hypotheses or conclusions made by our opponent. Under certain circumstances, distrusting the other can cause the other to distrust us, and trusting him can cause him to trust us. Thus if here too both assessments of probability confirm themselves, then moral, not theoretical, grounds determine our choice, and naturally they indicate that we should choose trust. However, there are certainly also cases in which our own generosity would be shamelessly

---

107. This does not mean that one should always prefer a game with the expected value of a sum of money *M* to the certain payment of a smaller sum; for the subjective utility of a sum of money is not proportional to the size of the sum. That the subjective attitude toward risk differs from person to person is a fact of descriptive psychology. We also acknowledge that differing attitudes may be reasonable, depending on circumstances; being ready to take risks in investing money is more intelligent if one has a large fortune.

108. On the mathematical details, see F. von Kutschera (1973), 101 ff. One of the most useful works on decision theory is by R. C. Jeffrey (1965). His model deviates in many respects from the basic model described by Kutschera.

exploited by the other party, and in which we are thus forced to carry arms; therefore a theoretical judgment is still required to determine whether this is a situation in which theoretical reflection leads to a stalemate and hence a decision must be made in accord with moral concerns. To be sure, it is rightly pointed out that aggressors tend to subscribe to an ideology that one must either attack others or expect an attack from others, and that they almost always find this ideology confirmed by their experience because in each case the other party in fact tends to attack an opponent who shows that he thinks in this way; but this does not imply that displaying a naive trust à la Rousseau automatically disarms the various villains.

By taking into account the fact that the probability of the relevant events is influenced by one's own decision (or by assumptions regarding one's decision), decision theory is extended to *game theory*. It is obvious that the latter is indispensable for cratic and thus also for political decisions. However, game theory, which was first developed in the last century,[109] is not only mathematically much more complex than decision theory, but also, because of the difference between technical and strategic rationality, its application to ethics is far more complicated than that of a decision theory that does not include game theory.[110] It goes without saying that in assessing the behavior of other people, the descriptive assumption that they will act in accord with the principles of prescriptive decision theory and game theory may be false; to suggest this is often irrational. Morally more important is the fact that game theory generally, and not just in the case of zerosum games, assumes a situation of competition, whereas ethics demands respect for all legitimate interests, including those of the opponent, and strives to resolve conflict situations. Game theory and decision theory are morally neutral; the interests of the opposing players may be both moral and immoral in nature. But if both sides want the same condition, and know that they both want it, then the solution of the problem of how to behave becomes trivial. On the other hand, game theory proves its worth in situations in which people want different things or at least have to reckon with the possibility that the other party wants something different from what they themselves want.

3.3.3.1. Moral Preferences in Decision Theory and Game Theory

In general, four important restrictions must be made regarding the application of decision theory and game theory to ethics. First, it goes without saying that for ethics, only a *moral* assessment of the various circumstances is relevant. In a just war, for instance, it makes no moral difference whether the politicians who have to make the decision or the people who have elected them subjectively prefer a strategy in which, *ce-*

---

109. The fundamental work is that of J. von Neumann and O. Morgenstern (1944). A useful introduction is found in M. D. Davis (1983).

110. Cf. R. B. Braithwaite (1969). However, this work's discussion of game theory is stronger than its discussion of moral principles.

teris paribus, the expected casualty rate is minimal on each side. To recommend such a strategy morally, it is sufficient that human life represents a very great good.[111] The factual preferences of other people must be respected in any moral decision, but on two very different levels, as has already been seen above. If, on the basis of universalism, we come to the conclusion that future generations have the same rights as the present generation, then ignoring negative developments in the future simply because they will affect only future generations is morally impermissible. (Only the uncertainty of the future could be taken into account.)[112]

The following example reveals the importance and the limits of game theory for ethics. Interactive situations analogous to the so-called prisoner's dilemma are certainly not rare. The pay-off matrix is such that for each individual, considered egoistically, the best result occurs when he defects and the other cooperates; the second best when both cooperate; the third best, when both defect; and the worst, when he cooperates and the other defects. If both act on the basis of rational egoism, then both will defect—and this result is not even Pareto-optimal. It would be quite false to call this a paradox. Experience shows that it is not in a rational egoist's interest that all people think in a rational egoistic way, and this can only please those concerned with ethics. From a moral standpoint, maximizing one's own self-interest is not the goal. But this does not imply that one should cooperate under any conditions whatever—neither will a moral person want defectors to grow too strong as a result of his goodness. Rather, the moral evaluation of the four different outcomes is as follows: Most desirable is mutual cooperation, then comes mutual defection, and finally the asymmetrical situation in its two variants, which are roughly equally bad from a moral point of view.[113] This evaluation results from the fact that the first two cases are at least characterized by formal symmetry, and obviously the first is to be preferred over the second—we have already seen that symmetry is generally a necessary though not a sufficient condition of moral behavior. For moral persons, one-sided defection is a rupture of symmetry and thus in principle equally bad no matter from which side it proceeds. However, since we are far more responsible for our own behavior than for that of others, the moral person will prefer for once to push trust too far than to unjustly distrust the other. Not to have taken the first step toward the other when this could have been done without too great a risk is a moral evil more serious than the possible substantive disadvantages that might have resulted from trusting too much. If we know that our partner is moral (and even knows that we

---

111. In reality, the strategy that should be adopted is considerably more complex. First of all, the victory of the party conducting the just war may not be endangered, and second, one has a greater responsibility for one's own soldiers than for those on the other side. These considerations must be added to the principle mentioned, which, in the interest of simplicity, is the only one that can be considered here.

112. On the following, see D. Birnbacher (1988), 87 ff.; see also below, chap. 7.3.1.1.

113. Naturally, there are cases in which cooperation is not in the legitimate interest of a third party (think of cartels); but here we are not considering cases involving a third party.

ourselves are moral), then the solution is clear: we will cooperate. If, on the other hand, we know that the other intends to deceive us, then we will defect, for it is not moral to allow oneself to be exploited by others. In case of doubt, when no deadly risk is involved, we will try to cooperate with the other. However, we should strike back if our own cooperation is met with defection on the part of the other—not out of revenge, but in the hope that in this way the other will at least be induced to act more in conformity with duty, which, when based on egoism, is worse than acting out of duty itself but better than non-cooperative behavior. Changes in others' behavior should be honored—if the other begins to cooperate, we should return to cooperation ourselves. This provides a *purely moral* argument for the "tit for tat" strategy, which, because of the "combination of being nice, retaliatory, forgiving, and clear," is known to be the most successful in the evolution of cooperation under certain weak assumptions.[114]

Analogously, the moral assessment of so-called "chicken situations" differs from assessment based on self-interest. Chicken situations are distinguished from prisoner-dilemma situations in that the worst result (considered egoistically) occurs when both parties defect, and the third best when one cooperates oneself, and the other defects. Hence on the level of self-interest there is a tendency not to defect, if the other does so (insofar as one has not already beaten him to the punch)—at least so long as this does not set an example and there are no spectators who might draw lessons from one's own behavior. But even if the latter is not the case, in general morals require the restoration of symmetry, even if this involves disadvantages for oneself. Naturally, this rule is not absolutely valid; what is at stake is crucially important. No rational person will risk his own life or that of others in order to save face in some minor matter. But if the losses are reasonable, one must accept them—not for the sake of one's sense of self-worth, which would be satisfied by paying the other party back, but because it is probably the only way to teach others to behave justly.

3.3.3.2. The Status of Probabilities

A second point regarding the application of decision theory to ethics is that the concept of subjective probability is no less problematic than that of subjective preference. The concept of probability is notoriously one of the most difficult in all of philosophy, and it is not possible to analyze it in detail here. However, we must say this much: a great deal depends on the correct philosophical interpretation of the probability calculus. This calculus, as defined by the Kolmogorov axioms, for instance, is widely accepted by the various schools. For ethics, and especially for political ethics, it would be lethal to conceive probabilities as *exclusively* subjective.[115] Assessments of probability are subjective facts, and there are certainly many situations in which there

---

114. R. Axelrod (1984), 54. The term "tit for tat" in this context comes from Anatol Rapoport.
115. Here I must leave open the question to what extent neo-Bayesians really do this.

are good grounds for making different assessments of probability. Yet that is not always the case. However, if they are not to be completely arbitrary, and if one assessment of probability is to be more reasonable than another, then they must be grounded in something that transcends them—such as factual knowledge, for example. Otherwise it would be impossible to consider Churchill's assumption that Hitler was preparing a war of aggression as more rational than Chamberlain's contrary assumption. Anyone who reduces the rationality of assumptions regarding probability to their internal consistency commits an error analogous to that of an ethicist who limits himself to the postulate of universalizability or even to pre- or anti-universalist ideas of justice. To be sure, a Nazi who would kill himself if proven to have Jewish ancestry[116] is fulfilling certain minimal moral demands that would not be met by a Nazi who thought that he himself determined who was a Jew; but to maintain that the first sad fanatic is not only more moral than Göring (who claimed that it was he who determined who was a Jew), but also that one could really expect no more from him morally, is much too repellent an idea.[117] Much the same goes for the purely subjective interpretation of probabilities, which we can illustrate by the following example. It is well known that many communists were convinced that the great effort of world revolution would almost certainly lead to paradise on earth, and they were prepared to pay with their lives in order to bring it about. Now, if one does not accept the principle that human lives must not be weighed against each other, that is, if one believes that the killing of an innocent person is permissible if that is the only way to save a larger number of innocent people, then one cannot condemn Lenin or even Stalin, insofar as they really believed that their crimes would very probably lead to overcoming hunger, war, and exploitation. We can concede that someone who commits a crime on the basis of an absurd assessment of probabilities and puts himself at risk deserves greater respect than a person who suddenly changes his assessment of probabilities when it appears that acting on it would entail unpleasant consequences for himself. But we should note that this kind of consistency is far from being sufficient to make someone a moral person. Moreover, what is unacceptable in the subjectivist position is that it does not even allow us to say that on close inspection, Lenin's behavior is perhaps less immoral than it at first seems, although his theoretical assumptions are at the least irrational; or that, on even closer inspection, the fact that he considered these irrational assumptions beyond criticism is highly questionable morally—indeed, we are forced us to hypothesize that these crazy assumptions were developed after the fact in order to deceive himself and others regarding the pleasure taken in the criminal intention of smashing a world to pieces.

---

116. I take this example from Hare (1963; 157 ff.).

117. Schiller, who was a Kantian, put these words in the Countess Terzky's mouth: "Denn Recht hat jeder eigene Charakter, / der übereinstimmt mit sich selbst, es gibt / kein andres Unrecht, als den Widerspruch" (*Wallensteins Tod* act 1, sc. 7, vv.600 ff.). ("For each character, which coincides with itself, is right; there is no other crime than contradiction.")

In short, a satisfactory philosophical theory of probability must explain why certain assessments of probability (and consequently, certain decisions based on them) are more rational than others. Obviously, assumptions regarding probability (such as the assumption that in throwing a die, the probability of any given number coming up is 1/6) involve two different types of rational grounds. First, the rationality of this assumption proceeds, on one hand, from the *experience* that when a die is frequently thrown, each number comes up once every six times—assuming that one can master the problem of induction.[118] Second, *mathematical thought* plays a role here; in the case of the die, its symmetrical shape is crucial. Similarly, the social sciences seem partly to induce certain rules of human behavior empirically and partly to derive them from general principles.[119] Without such theories, rational assessments of the probability of social events are not possible—which does not mean, of course, that these theories are easy to develop. Especially crucial is the question of how to determine the probability of individual events by subsuming them under propositions regarding relative frequencies.

It goes without saying that there are quite a few cases in which lack of knowledge prevents us from making plausible assessments of probability, that is, cases in which decisions are made under conditions of uncertainty and the only permissible behavior is prescribed by the maximin rule. It can be assumed that such decision situations are very common. For example, in introducing risky technologies, the determination of specific probabilities may be undertaken only in order to present as legitimate the initially desired result—the introduction of the technology in question. Often enough, actual probability assessments are determined by choices one has already made and for which one is seeking secondary rationalizations. Since people's current superstitions about science lead them to be impressed by formulations that look complicated but are in reality trivial, it usually does not occur to them that the values for the variables are completely arbitrary, and that the decision is thus neither rational nor moral.[120] In this connection it is particularly important to note that in assessing the risks of nuclear energy, for instance, it is important to determine not only the probability of a natural event such as a maximum credible accident, but also the probability of its possible social consequences, which are far more difficult to predict than the consequences of the event itself.[121] Skepticism regarding the possibility of attributing probabilities to certain human

118. In my opinion, this is impossible without metaphysically grounded a priori synthetic propositions; even Popper's falsificationism presupposes them. Cf. Hösle (1990c), 78 f.

119. Think, for example, of the concept of mixed strategy in game theory.

120. To be sure, the transformation of a decision made under uncertainty into a decision under risk is desirable. But not everything that is desirable is possible, and if there were only subjective probabilities, then we would always have to reckon with decisions made under uncertainty when our own decisions affected people with correspondingly different assessments of probability.

121. In addition, defining the risk as the product of the probability of an event that causes damage multiplied by the extent of the damage does not take into account the infrastructure, whose construction is obligatory in relation to the worst possible scenario. A major technology with a risk of a maximum credible accident involving one million casualties at a probability of 1/10,000,000

behavior transforms decision situations into situations in which decisions must be made under uncertainty, and thus significantly decreases the readiness to undertake morally risky actions.[122] However, the development of riskier strategies of a technological or socio-technological nature is only one extreme that a responsible politics must avoid; no less dangerous is the opposite notion that in view of the hyper-complexity of the modern world, all actions are equally risky and therefore to be avoided.[123]

The foregoing should not be understood to mean that probabilities are objective properties of events. Since I do not exclude a thoroughgoing determinism, it may well be that how the die will fall is always predetermined. But so long as one cannot predict the relevant determinants in individual cases, and so long as counting up the results of individual throws has not led to a different assumption, it is rational to assign the probability of 1/6 to any possible throw. Assessments of probability are thus always related to the knowledge available in the case in question—but the relation between the two is not arbitrary. First of all, there is the duty to seek the relevant knowledge; and second, on the basis of a given state of knowledge, one probability assessment is normally more rational than the others.[124] After reading *Mein Kampf*, any reasonable person must consider

---

over a specific length of time requires quite different precautions in the form of ambulances, medical personnel, and so on, compared to those required by a technology with a risk of a maximum credible accident with one thousand casualties at a probability of 1/10,000 over the same length of time. Moreover, aversion to risk increases psychologically with the extent of the danger, even with a corresponding decrease in probability, and this can be justified ethically by the fact that in a greater accident, more people are usually harmed who are not in any way responsible for the accident and therefore are completely innocent. Cf. H. C. Binswanger's important article (1990).

122. This theoretical skepticism is the main reason for Guicciardini's greater caution, compared to Machiavelli, when risky political strategies are at stake. See *Ricordi*, Serie C, 51, 81, 114; Serie B, 171 f. (1977; 123, 144 f., 243 f.).

123. N. Luhmann sometimes argues in this way; however, he neglects, first, the fact that there is also a responsibility for not doing something, even if it is admittedly smaller, and second, the fact that dangers proceed not only from clumsy attempts at direction but also from the status quo. Friedrich Dürrenmatt commits neither of these errors. In his play *Die Physiker* (*The Physicists*), poor Möbius bears less responsibility for the wretched state of things than does the mad doctor, and his initial attempt to keep out of things is no less fatal than the killing of the nurse. The absurdity in Dürrenmatt's work consists in the complete impossibility of finding a moral way out, and it is considerably eerier than the convenient advice to let things float, precisely because even the option of omission is morally impermissible. (Here I do not explore the possibility that Möbius might have chosen to commit suicide rather than murder, which Dürrenmatt does not consider.) Since Luhmann can argue only sociologically and the sphere of pure validities remains closed to him, one is justified in recalling that his current success proceeds, in terms of the sociology of knowledge, from the fact that he gave profuse expression to the feeling that nothing could be done in any case, which became widespread after the collapse of chiliastic hopes. Frustrated world revolutionaries are among his most eager adepts. It goes without saying that this observation does not constitute a refutation of his approach.

124. Granted, in individual cases, depending on one's other assumptions, additional information may be interpreted as strengthening or weakening a given probability assessment. If someone believes that Hitler always says the opposite of what he thinks, he will interpret *Mein Kampf* differently from the way he would interpret it if he did not share this belief.

it likely that Hitler wanted a dictatorship and war; and since this work had been published, not only all Germans who were tempted to vote for him, but also the political decision makers in neighboring countries had a duty to read it, precisely because doing so was a good basis for a rational assessment of probabilities.

This brings us to the concept of *conditional* probability. Advances in knowledge change probability assessments and, to that extent, the foundations for morally responsible decisions. Different conditional probability assessments result in different conditional moral obligations. But insofar as at time t_1 the additional knowledge was not available no matter what efforts were made to obtain it, the decision made at that time is to be considered moral even if, on the basis of knowledge acquired later, one would have had to behave differently. Nothing is more unjust than to take factual success or failure as the ultimate criterion for the rationality or irrationality of a probability assessment; nothing is cheaper than the arrogance of those who can tell us all about the outcome after it has occurred.[125] The crucial point about a decision is that it must be made *before* success or failure occurs.[126] If unforeseeable (not unforeseen) events determine success or failure, then the successful decision may have been the wrong one and the failed decision the right one.[127] History can make no moral judgments, because norms do not follow from facts; but what history can do is create facts which it is important to take into account in a later moral decision. If all attempts to assassinate a tyrant fail, that does not make the tyrant right, and it does not even mean that the would-be assassins made an error; but the neighbors of the state concerned have to be prepared for the fact that the tyrant will probably remain in power even longer. Social psychology suggests, as a corollary to the above, that in public opinion even the most accidental success increases the authority of the power-holder.

To adduce a concrete example of a correct but disastrous decision: Even a person who considers dropping atomic bombs on Hiroshima and Nagasaki as deeply immoral cannot hold it against Leo Szilard that he urged Einstein to write his famous letter to

---

125. It is to the credit of Churchill—who was no less impressive as a historian and writer than as a statesman—that in his history of the Second World War he criticizes only those military and political measures concerning which he had previously made his opinion publicly known. "I have adhered to my rule of never criticizing any measure of war or policy after the event unless I had before expressed publicly or formally my opinion or warning about it" (1948 ff.; 1:v).

126. In *Fear and Trembling*, Kierkegaard mocked with unsurpassable irony those who think the criterion for the justice of an action is its success, with the compelling argument that the result has followed the action since the creation of the world, but the decision has to be made beforehand, and one would certainly arrive too late if one were to wait for the result of an action before beginning to act. Even the most fortunate result would be of little help to the hero—who is a hero already at the moment of the action—if he does not yet know about it (1963; 5:58 f.)

127. This was already clearly recognized by the Greeks. Herodotus (VII 10) attributes to Xerxes' uncle, the Persian Artabanus, the statement that the quality of a decision did not depend on the success of the enterprise: "Even if [a man's plans] go against him, and forces he cannot control bring his enterprise to nothing, he stil has the satisfaction of knowing that he was defeated by chance—the plans were all laid." Trans. A. de Sélincourt, 378.

Roosevelt that convinced the latter that it was necessary to build the atomic bomb. In view of the information then available to Szilard and available to him alone, there were rational grounds for the fear that Hitler might build an atomic bomb, and trying to beat him to it was urgent on moral grounds, even in accord with the maximin rule, that is, in the case of a decision under uncertainty. From this emerged the necessity of warning Roosevelt, even if the actual state of German physics probably did not in fact require the Americans to build atomic weapons. However, Szilard could not know that the latter was the case. His part in bringing about the dropping of the atomic bomb—which in my opinion cannot be morally justified, but at most can be excused—caused Szilard distress, and in fact in 1945 he did everything he could to prevent it. Yet if remorse reflects the acknowledgment of a subjective guilt, he could have *regretted* his earlier involvement, but not felt *remorse* regarding it.[128] Moreover, the feeling that one has acted in a subjectively moral way but had an objectively wrong effect can be more burdensome than repentance,[129] because it reminds us of the insurmountable finitude of consciousness that always and everywhere characterizes the human condition, even in cases of moral decisions, insofar as the latter involve empirical knowledge and assessments of probability. It is no doubt correct that the moral principle does not stem from this world and that insofar as we grasp it, we rise above the sphere of contingency; but by trying to introduce this principle into reality, we expose ourselves once again to its contingency. Acting in a way that is morally right but objectively wrong is perhaps the experience that existentially most profoundly opens humans to religion, as the sphere in which we must acknowledge that our moral will to shape the world has limits that we must respect.

---

128. I can agree with Williams (1981; 27 ff.) that in terms of psychology of morals, one must position between remorse and theoretical regret concerning past events for which one has no responsibility ("spectator's regret") what has been called "agent-regret," that is, the unpleasant feeling produced by the involuntary and unforeseeable negative consequences of something one has done that is in itself unobjectionable. But from this we can conclude only that this feeling has a merely moral-psychological significance, and not a truly moral one (even if it has an important moral function, namely to urge us to examine all the ways in which we might have become guilty of some moral offense), or rather that its true meaning is not moral but religious in nature.

129. In his drama *Das Eis von Cape Sabine* (1965; 49–123), J. Maass depicted the following moral situation (inspired by the Lady Franklin Bay Expedition led by A. W. Greenley at the beginning of the 1880s, on which chap. 38 of Fontane's novel *Der Stechlin* is also based). When his polar expedition got into difficulties, Commander Barrister recognized that Able Seaman Buck was constantly stealing from the extremely limited stores of food which, properly distributed, would have been barely adequate to allow all members of the expedition to live a few days longer. The thief had once saved the commander's life and was certainly not an evil man—just a hungry one. Nonetheless, the commander became convinced that he must have Buck executed, not because his crime was in itself a capital one, but because in that situation there was no other way of ensuring with high probability the survival of the other members of the expedition. Shortly after Buck's execution, the rescue ship arrived with a sufficient supply of food. The commander feels no remorse regarding his decision, since the probability that the ship would arrive in time had been minimal. His suffering is deeper. Maass has him say: "Reue wäre ein vergleichsweise komfortables Gefühl" (123). ("In comparison, remorse would be a comfortable feeling.")

3.3.3.3. Actions and Omissions

A third objection to the integration of a re-interpreted decision theory into ethics has to do with the relationship between acts and omissions. For decision theory, omission is only one form of action among others, whereas traditional ethics has always recommended that morally risky actions be avoided in case of doubt, even if the risk of not acting is greater than the risk involved in the action, because one is less responsible for the outcome when one does not do something than when one does it. Classically, this position has been represented by Catholic moral philosophy, which, on the basis of its pre-Kantian philosophy of nature, assigns—*ceteris paribus*—a positive status to natural events.[130] In contrast, utilitarianism, in opposition to Kant, tended toward giving action and omission the same status, and thus legitimated the transition from the liberal state to the welfare state. It is not easy to arrive at a balanced position here.[131] However, this is of crucial importance for political ethics, since the statesman is the perfect example of a person whose omissions are spurious omissions.

In order to explain what this means, let us glance once again at German criminal law, which makes significant ethical distinctions that go far beyond those made by many professional ethicists. On one hand, most criminal offenses consist of actions that violate prohibitions and not of failures to do something that is obligatory. There are good reasons for this. First, commands require far more than do prohibitions, and thus the same degree of obedience cannot be expected in the case of commands, which can easily lead to excessive moral demands. Second, commands necessarily remain indeterminate: it is always clear when one has harmed someone, but very unclear when one has sufficiently helped someone. Third, in most omissions, responsibility is shared—not only I but also another might have been able to help the person in need. Thus the failure to provide help to an accident victim when one's help was necessary and could be expected, is much less severely punished than directly causing a situation that one did not avert solely by failing to do something. This does not necessarily mean that the same can be said about morals, since natural law norms are a proper subset of moral ones; the demands made on a moral person are certainly higher than what can be reasonably coerced by force of law.[132] Thus, allowing an innocent person to starve is a serious moral sin, even if virtually all well-off people are guilty of it. (Here one presupposes that reasonable help is possible and not demoralizing or counterproductive.) But

---

130. Not only the normative favoring of natural events, but also the very distinction between natural and non-natural events, are major problems.

131. On this problematic—including the difficult question as to how action and omission can be precisely distinguished from each other on the descriptive level—see D. Birnbacher's fundamental study (1995).

132. Only uncle Nolte in Wilhelm Busch's *Die fromme Helene* reduces good to the evil that one does not do, and takes pleasure in his own moral excellence. The facial expression this great poet and graphic artist has given uncle Nolte says more about this position than any philosophical analysis could.

this example also shows that the asymmetry between action and omission must exist in morals as well: for it is immediately clear that however this omission is evaluated, murder is a significantly more serious crime. Moreover, the sheer number of starving people whom one does not know individually at all shows that the duty to provide help cannot be sufficiently fulfilled even by the most altruistic person, whereas the prohibition on murder is easy to obey. Finally, it must be conceded that the disorder in the world would significantly increase if everyone considered himself responsible for everything.

On the other hand, German criminal law recognizes so-called spurious (*unecht*) crimes of omission.[133] If someone fails to provide help that he has a particular duty to provide (for example, on the basis of a law, a contract, or interference), he can be punished as if he had intentionally performed the corresponding act. This is immediately plausible; anyone who has assumed special responsibility by agreement or by his behavior can be held to it. Whereas an accidental passerby has only a general moral responsibility for a drowning child, the father, the kindergarten teacher, or the person who negligently knocked him into the water have a very special responsibility that proceeds from their concrete relationship to the child. However, in the administration of justice there is an important exception that is difficult to reconcile with this principle from the point of view of the doctrine of criminal law. Physicians, whose relevant omissions are a classic example of serious crimes by omission, will not be punished if they do not make use of every artificial means to keep a terminally ill patient alive, but they will be punished if they directly bring about a patient's death. This asymmetry indicates that the principle of the equal status of action and omission when someone has a peculiar responsibility is sometimes exaggerated (or else it indicates that this exception is not reasonable). Yet this does not alter its rightness in principle. Still stronger demands ought to be made, at least morally if not legally, on a politician than on a physician, since the politician's omissions can result in far greater evil than those of the physician. It is clear that a statesman fails to meet his responsibilities if he washes his hands of the matter and claims to be innocent when he allows the rabble to lynch an innocent person, even if the alternative were to have the rabble dispersed by means of force. Indeed, a politician should be required to order actions that are intrinsically very negative in value (involving the secret service, for instance) if failing to do so entails a greater moral risk. If a person is not subjectively able to do this sort of thing, then he should not become a politician. And yet the hard-to-deny distinction between active and passive euthanasia[134] points to the fact that completely equal status for action and omission is unacceptable, not only for a physician but also, and especially, for a politician. Why? A politician normally has to deal with competent adults, and if the latter bring on their

---

133. See German Penal Code § 13, and A. Schönke and H. Schröder (1982), 159 ff.

134. This distinction can be justified, on one hand, by the social importance of a taboo on killing people that is as unqualified as possible, and on the other, by the fact that someone who has asked for a lethal injection could still change his mind when it was too late. This possibility is excluded in the case of someone who has indicated his wish not to be resuscitated.

own misfortune, it may in some circumstances be reasonable to let them pay the price for the consequences of their foolishness. In any case, this is not the same thing as directly producing these consequences. Particularly if this kind of omission under certain conditions has morally positive consequences, it may be justified, no matter how much under other conditions it would be a terrible violation of duty.[135] We might add here, as a descriptive corollary of moral psychology, that since most people easily excuse their own omissions and those of others, quite independently of whether they are objectively justified, false crimes by omission for purely egoistic reasons are common. A sin by omission stands at the beginning of many great political careers.[136]

3.3.3.4. The Finitude of Human Knowledge;
"Satisficing" and Maximizing; Political Genius and a "Political Topics"

The fourth critical point about decision theory is that it greatly overestimates human capabilities of calculation. In the question whether to take an umbrella along when going for a walk, the relevant number of conditions to be taken into account consist of only two—whether it will rain or not. Yet this is not the usual case. If one reflects in a vacuum, the possible alternatives for action are no less numerous than the events in

---

135. Had Roosevelt reckoned with Japan's attack without a prior declaration of war, then the death at Pearl Harbor of two thousand sailors, which he might have been able to prevent by giving the command for a higher level of alert, could perhaps be justified by the wish, only too justified from a moral point of view, to see the American people enter with grim determination into a war he considered just and inevitable. Presumably had Roosevelt really expected the attack, he would not have consciously decided not to give this command. Probably, in the inner hope that the Japanese would attack not only Great Britain but also the United States, he did not even consider the immediate consequences of not giving this command (that is, he repressed them).

136. A paradigmatic example: After much hesitation, Alexander I finally supported the conspiracy against his father, Czar Paul I, organized by Count Peter von Pahlen, but demanded assurance that not a hair of his father's head would be touched. Even if the initiative for the coup d'état (whose possible justification will not be examined here) did not proceed from him, he nonetheless failed—as did many others in the czar's immediate entourage who became suspicious—to do anything to stop it; indeed, he failed to even think about the fact that a tyrannical person such as his father would not simply agree to abdicate. Pahlen, who had given Alexander his word of honor that his father would not be harmed, failed to be present when the czar was murdered, and even failed to tell his fellow conspirators what *he* had committed himself not to do. (Something analogous might perhaps be true of the degree of Alexander the Great's participation in the conspiracy against his father.) In any case, it seems to be part of the accepted way of doing such things in systems of hereditary monarchy that the beneficiaries are not expected to take an active part in murdering their closest relatives, but only expected not to take countermeasures and to make a generic declaration that those who acted on their behalf will not be punished—a declaration that those concerned do not for the most part observe, however, since the presence of their benefactors evokes partly a feeling of dependency and partly pangs of conscience. Alexander I merely exiled Pahlen from St. Petersburg, but Caligula forced Macro, who was the murderer of Caligula's predecessor Tiberius and who had saved Caligula's life (if we can believe Tacitus, *Annals* VI 50) to commit suicide.

each of these alternatively possible actions, and merely tabulating all the possible combinations of actions and events would in most cases fill up not only the time within which the optimal action must be taken, but one's whole life. Therefore we are fortunate that certain actions are immediately prescribed by the pressure of events and the expectations of others and that we can always consider only a few alternatives—otherwise we would never act. This holds to an even greater extent for the ethical interpretation of decision theory. A moral evaluation of the various combinations of actions and events requires even more presuppositions than ordering one's own preferences, and in most cases it is possible to make that evaluation only approximately because very different values must be taken into account. Thus, if modern teleological theories of ethics posit as a fundamental obligation that one should act in such a way that the expected value of the result is maximal, they are saying something correct but empty. This imperative is empty not only so long as what counts as a positive value and how individual values are related to each other go unsaid, even if all objectively valid values could be grasped, it would be wrong to believe that a finite mind could take into account all the various actions along with all the various possible situations. In addition, it is not reasonable to command that one do what is optimal—which would mean that non-optimal actions were forbidden. It can be forbidden only to fall below a certain moral minimum, and however commendable and respectable it may be to approach the optimum, it is still unjust to view as moral failures those who are unable to reach it (which presumably includes all human beings). Heroic behavior is morally sublime, but it is not a duty in the usual sense of the word.

Empirical psychology has shown that most people who have to make a rational decision do not consider all the possible alternatives for action, but rather set for themselves a minimal value that they do not want to fall below; then they choose the alternative that in the series of considerations is the first to achieve this value or to go beyond it. H. A. Simon calls this procedure "satisficing" in contrast to "maximizing."[137] Much the same is certainly the case in most moral decisions as well, and rightly so. For since reflection itself is an action, it is also the object of a decision, and it is reasonable to consider right from the outset how much time one ought to devote to it. If there is a danger that one might reflect so long that one would no longer be able to put the outcome of one's reflection into practice, an abbreviation of the thinking process is called for on the basis of an elementary principle of the ethics of ethics already mentioned. Thus, for example, certain consequences should be acknowledged as inessential and ignored in further reflection. Precisely when life and death are involved (as is repeatedly the case in politics), it is often crucial that a first, still rather crude decision be made instead of hesitating for a long time, because before one has found the ideal plan one may already be dead. Even setting aside such extreme situations, it is obvious that only too often the better is the enemy of the good: the pursuit of goals that are in themselves very desirable

---

137. See H. A. Simon (1955).

but scarcely realizable can prevent one from devoting all one's energies to truly realizable goals, because one's own energies are limited. Finally, an especially problematic case is one in which someone who wants many good things, but has no comparative concepts and therefore cannot establish a list of priorities, devotes all his energies to an objectively less important project, even though in the given cratic situation it has hardly any chance of being realized, and as a result he fails to perform more urgent duties. To give a fairly recent example, it was politically unwise for President Clinton to devote so much time at the beginning of his term of office to an attempt to establish equal rights for homosexuals in the army. This judgment is based not on approval of discrimination against homosexuals, which is contrary to natural law. But the abolition of this kind of discrimination is less important than the solution of many other problems. Since in addition the resistance against this policy, which is right in principle, was foreseeable, President Clinton would have been wiser to work for it after he had acquired a certain authority by resolving more urgent issues.

However, there are people who have a remarkable instinct for nearly optimal alternatives, and immediately discern what others see only after much reflection. It goes without saying that every great statesman must possess this instinct for the politically right decision; laboriously sifting through all the possibilities is not only incompatible with the time pressures under which political decisions normally have to be made, but is rarely compatible with the will to achieve things that is required in a statesman. Even if a rationalistic philosophy rightly demands that decisions made on instinct be reconstructed on an argumentative basis, it should recognize that under the pressure of time it is reasonable to rely on the instincts of those who have proven themselves. As I have already said, that does not mean that success is a criterion for deciding whether someone has made the right decision; but if a person is repeatedly successful, it is rational to ascribe certain mental abilities to him even if he is incapable of explaining them in words.[138] Reason is more than what takes place in the consciousness. This insight, which we owe to the Platonic theory of art, should not be forgotten by a rationalist. Even if the mechanisms in accord with which intellectual instincts function remain murky,[139] it can be presumed that in such people the ratiomorphous apparatus eliminates, on the basis of experience, the alternatives that are not relevant, so that conscious thought then can concentrate on a few relevant ones. However, the possibility cannot be excluded that even in the greatest political geniuses the ratiomorphous ap-

---

138. Ultimately, this also holds for the person concerned, who can convince himself of the achievements of his instinct only through experience with himself. Therefore it is important that, if possible, he make decisions laden with consequences only after arriving at a better knowledge of himself through less risky decisions. Since politics is inevitably an intersubjective phenomenon, the problem of being one's own standard, which raises so many questions in art, science, and philosophy, cannot arise.

139. Poincaré's (1912; 53 ff.) account of the unconscious thought processes involved in mathematical work is still worth reading. Presumably something analogous could be said about a person who strives to make the morally right decision in politics.

paratus is calibrated in accord with certain social and political contexts; if these change—and they often do precisely because of his own successful activities—his instinct may suddenly fail him. Between the unconscious instinct of the political genius and the pedantic analysis of all formally possible alternatives we should place what one might call, following Aristotle, a *political topics,* that is, a handbook of questions to ask while making political decisions. This refers to the attempt to rank, not all, but rather the essential normatively relevant parameters that must be taken into account in making a morally correct political decision. This book is conceived, among other things, as an attempt to develop such a political handbook. The foregoing implies that such a political handbook neither can nor seeks to replace political genius. On one hand, it arises from the philosophical need to reconstruct ex post facto why certain decisions made by political geniuses are right, and on the other hand, it seeks to make possible a broader consensus for politically necessary decisions.

3.3.3.5. Criteria for Decisions That Are Morally Right

Let me sum up what must be included in a morally correct decision. First, it must be based on a universalist ethics. In cultures that have not yet achieved universalism, it is an indispensable minimum condition of morals that the members of this culture apply their pre-universalist ideas to themselves, even when this goes against their own interests. Second, a moral decision must be based on the right values: it must take into account the values of objective conditions—in politics, this means chiefly institutions—as well as the subjectively moral values of intentions, feelings, and the persons who have them. Third, it is indispensable to look into the means to, and the side effects of, the planned actions. This is not possible without drawing on the empirical knowledge of both the natural and the social sciences; after setting the morally right goals, one needs the most correct information possible regarding reality. In looking into the values of other persons, one should pursue not only a strategic but also a communicative interest; one should try to learn not only about but from the persons concerned. In judging the consequences, one should often begin with various possible outcomes and try to determine their probability, in accord with the current state of all available knowledge in the natural and social sciences. However, it is clear that, given the limitations of human theoretical and valuative knowledge, divergences regarding the morally right decision are inevitable even among those with great intelligence and earnest moral will. Indeed, stalemates can also result for oneself. We have already discussed conflicts between values of approximately the same rank, and following the brief introduction to decision theory, we can add the further case in which two alternative actions of very different intrinsic worth have the same expected value, because a probable event could cause the action that is intrinsically better to become a misfortune.

What should one do, then, if, for example, two persons advise two very different ways of acting in a given situation? Obviously the maxim that recommends choosing the middle path between two opposed counsels is not always appropriate. That it may be absurd is immediately shown by the following example. If one physician advises a patient to have an operation, and another advises him not to have it—assuming that in giving advice, neither physician is following his self-interest, but rather has to the best of his knowledge arrived at an assessment of the risks involved both in having the operation and in foregoing it—then a decision to have half the operation performed would be clearly unreasonable. In general, one can show that the notion that one ought to base one's decisions on either an arithmetical or a geometrical mean between different expert assessments of probability leads to absurd results. If one constructs an arithmetical mean, various events to which probabilities are attributed lose their independence of each other, even if they were independent when the original probability assessments were made.[140] Nonetheless, the idea of the middle way—that is, a compromise between different ideas—is very attractive to human nature, especially in democracies, and rightly so, insofar as compromises often satisfy everyone concerned and encourage common support for the strategy chosen. If three equally worthy alternatives can be ranked quantitatively in accord with a certain parameter, it is reasonable to give priority to the middle one over the two extremes. However, it often happens that it is impossible to decide with sufficient certainty which of the two extreme options is the right one, even though it is clear that the middle one is wrong. In his provisional ethics, Descartes included this counsel: if you are lost in a forest, you must in any case keep moving straight ahead, for if you constantly change directions just because you suspect you may be wrong you will probably turn in circles and never get out of the forest.[141] In Western tradition, the *locus classicus* for an analogous situation in political ethics is found in Livy 9.3, in a passage about the Second Samnite War,[142] whose extraordinary significance Machiavelli clearly recognized in his *Discorsi*.[143] After the Samnites had trapped a large number of Roman soldiers in a narrow canyon near Caudium (321 BC), they had to decide what to do with them. They asked Herennius Pontius, the elderly father of their general, who told them they should let the Romans retire with honor. The Samnites did not like

---

140. Cf. M. Nicholson (1990), 71–76.

141. (1964 ff.), 6:24 f.

142. In this context, it is completely irrelevant whether the events reported by Livy actually happened or not. The story is true in a deeper sense of the word, in the same way that a great work of fiction is true: it deals with a possibility through which we understand something essential more easily and more deeply than through factual reality. In the stories collected by Livy, so much political wisdom of the greatest state-building nation in history has been concentrated that the entire first decade of criticism of Livy's work since Niebuhr cannot really undermine his historical intelligence—the latter term being understood in a different way, of course, than it is in positivist historiography.

143. II 23.33 f (1984; 357 f.) and III 40.9 (1984; 562). Without concrete relation to this history, but entirely in the same vein, we read in I 26.5 (1984; 121) that people who can be neither entirely good nor entirely bad take extremely damaging middle ways: "Ma gli uomini pigliono certe vie del mezzo che sono dannosissime; perché non sanno essere né tutti cattivi né tutti buoni."

this advice and asked for another and, as they thought, better counsel. Then Herennius Pontius advised them to kill all the Romans.[144] The Samnites began to doubt his soundness of mind, and despite his thorough and fully convincing argumentation, they nonetheless chose a middle way. They let the Romans live, but humiliated them terribly by forcing them to pass under a yoke. In this way they made even more bitter enemies of the Romans without having significantly weakened them.[145] In following the other two options they would have either reconciled their opponents or annihilated them; thus both options would have been more in their rational interest.[146] Analogous cases from later history are not hard to find. Following the Bolshevist revolution the Western great powers should have either committed themselves to a serious war, with the goal of overthrowing the Soviet regime, or stayed out of the country altogether; the poorly coordinated partial intervention mounted by various countries necessarily resulted in generations-long hatred *and* contempt of the Western powers on the part of the Bolshevists (as well as an increase in terror tactics within the country).

Thus we can often have completely different views on very good grounds, especially in politics, without being able to arrive at a compromise. In such cases, opposition both on political and substantial issues, is compatible with great intellectual and moral respect for one's opponent. It is not infrequent that two persons seeking the adoption of very different courses of action will be very close to each other in basic values and worldview—much closer than to a third person whose option is located between theirs. Since a decision regarding a concrete action is the result of many different factors, including values, assumptions concerning means-ends relationships, and assessments of the probability of certain outcomes, it can easily happen that people with extremely different valuative and descriptive premises come through their mixed syllogisms to the same conclusion—just as, conversely, it is possible that on the basis of the same valuative premises, very slight differences in the descriptive premises may lead to completely different conclusions. To give a specific example: One could oppose NATO's deployment of the Pershing II missiles either because one was fundamentally a pacifist; or because one believed that in the era of atomic weapons, self-defense was not permissible; or because one believed that defensive wars were permissible in the nuclear era as well,

---

144. The normal situation in the real world is that people with opposed characters represent the two opposed options; Herennius Pontius's cool rationality, which allows him to pass calmly from one option to the other, indicates the legendary nature of the story. It is interesting that in Livy, Herennius Pontius is an old man who can hardly move about—and that seems to suggest that the usual emotional structures from which the various virtues draw sustenance have been extinguished in him.

145. "Ista quidem sententia," said Herennius Pontius regarding the decision ultimately adopted by the Samnites, "ea est, quae neque amicos parat nec inimicos tollit"(9.3.12). ("This is a decision that neither makes friends nor does away with enemies.")

146. This is not meant to suggest that acting on Herennius Pontius's second recommendation would have been of equal value from a moral standpoint.

but that the potential aggressor was NATO; or because one assumed that there was a right to self-defense in the nuclear area and that the Soviet Union had aggressive intentions, but considered deployment of the Pershings militarily superfluous and economically a waste of money. In all these examples, *grounds* play a role in a moral syllogism.[147] In addition, there are also people who support a political goal on the basis of *causes* not connected with the issue. Just as someone may have supported the deployment solely because doing so was useful for his career, so there were probably also people who opposed it because they had trusted friends who opposed it for reasons of which they were not aware, but in whose company they felt at home. Finally, for some people the deployment was only the spark that caused a long-smoldering rage against the "system" to explode—a spark that might have taken any number of other forms. There are many other conceivable combinations of premises and causes; what matters here is merely that a person can be much closer in basic values and assessment of the situation to someone who is his opponent in making a political decision, than to a political ally who in a specific situation is pursuing the same goal but for completely different reasons.[148]

One of the most disappointing illusions of a person's initial foray into politics is a vast overestimation of the moral commonalities among political allies and the consequent demonization of political opponents. The latter is often done in order to be more sure of one's own decision, which one instinctively senses is not objectively well grounded (especially with regard to its descriptive premises). Although the chief goal of this book is to recover a moral understanding of the political, it is also necessary to warn against the kind of political moralism[149] that is no longer capable of distinguishing between moral opponents and political opponents. There are both moral and political grounds for insisting on this distinction; one has no right to slander people whose moral values are no worse than one's own and whose theoretical assumptions are not obviously absurd,[150] and it is politically dangerous to do so because the only result of this kind of slander is to make col-

---

147. Here I abstract from the fact that on the meta-level the most varied positions can be taken with respect to valuative premises. Someone can be a pacifist because he thinks the New Testament prescribes this position, because he considers pacifism justifiable in discourse ethics, and so on.

148. It goes without saying that intellectual honesty demands that we first get clear about the premises and only then move toward a conclusion. However, in practice the direction is often reversed. We arrive at political convictions regarding a very complex phenomenon—we decide, for instance, that the deployment of the Pershings is bad—and then look for valuative and descriptive premises that could support these convictions. Sometimes even manifestly false descriptive premises are adopted solely in order to ground one's own thesis. Cf. below, chap. 4.2.2.2, on secondary rationalization.

149. On the criticism of political moralism, see H. Lübbe's essay (1987). No matter how right many of the observations of this stylistically outstanding and phenomenologically powerful study are, it nonetheless lumps too heterogeneous things under the concept "political moralism"; a clear categorization of the factors in a morally acceptable political decision is lacking; and partly as a result, Lübbe underestimates the guilt of contemporary political decision makers.

150. It is a sign of Churchill's nobility that in his history of the Second World War he criticizes Chamberlain's judgment but not his moral principles.

laboration in resolving outstanding problems more difficult. One of the deepest and sometimes also the most painful experiences in the process of political maturation consists in recognizing that one must often have more moral respect for one's political opponent than for one's allies, and sometimes even for oneself. We can sincerely believe we are defending the right position, without having any illusions regarding the fact that opportunistic interests were the most important motive in making our own decision, even before substantial arguments were formulated; and we may sense that our opponent has a greater moral purity without being convinced that he is objectively right. The Pontius Pilate of the Gospel according to St. John, and even more of Bach's *St. John Passion*—who is one of the most fascinating figures in the gallery of the forms of moral-political consciousness—stands on this level: he is both captivated by Jesus' moral authority and convinced that he has a greater political understanding of the issues than Jesus does.

3.4. Ontology, Science, and Ethics

3.4.1. On the Relation between Descriptive Analysis and Analysis of Values

It is clear that what is missing in this section on the principles of ethics is an explicit doctrine of goods and values. The difficulties involved in working out such a doctrine are only one reason for my reticence. A second reason is that it is possible to elaborate such a theory only if one defines the relation between *Is* and *Ought* more precisely than it has been defined in the preceding pages. Fundamentally, carrying the foregoing observations further, one can say, first, that Kant was right that moral obligations do not follow from ontological facts. Secondly, however, I agree with representatives of a metaphysically grounded ethics such as Hegel or Jonas, but also the Kant of the third *Critique*, that being is not indifferent with regard to moral obligations, that it is so structured (for whatever reasons) that values can be realized in it. The theological concept of creation offers one possible answer (whether it is the only possible answer, is another matter) to the question of why being can partly correspond to the demands of the ideal sphere, namely because the latter is its generating principle. A reasonable concept of creation does not suggest that the ideal intervenes in the real world. On the contrary, that is completely out of the question: real things are caused only by real things. Instead, it means that the system of laws in accord with which these causes operate is not ungrounded, but rather grounded in the ideal world. Such a conception implies a rehabilitation of teleological thinking that is compatible with modern natural science. Obviously, teleological arguments can never replace causal explanations. But even if we must seek for the causes of every event, the question of the grounds for the system of natural laws cannot be answered in this way. Teleological arguments that maintain that only in such a system could beings have developed that recognize these natural laws and are capable of moral action are absolutely legitimate as an answer to this question. The existence of such reasonable beings is obviously an ontological, not a moral fact. But without the existence of this ontological fact, the subjectively moral would have no chance. This does not mean that morally this fact is exclusively positive; only human beings are capable of evil, and their power over nature allows them to destroy far more species of plants and animals than is or was possible for other species. Yet this does not alter the fact that their existence is morally relevant and that ethics must acknowledge the existence and nature of human beings, just as political philosophy must acknowledge the existence and nature of the state. And they must be acknowledged not only as the rebellious material through which—for lack of something better—moral demands must unfortunately be realized, but as entities that are already valuable by virtue of their structure, however much they may decrease or increase their worth through certain actions. Human beings and the state have an intrinsic worth even before they assume any concrete form; through their emergence the world becomes more valuable, even if they are capable of diminishing the overall value of the world through destructive behavior. In the evolution of the universe, entities of ever greater worth therefore come into existence with the emergence of the organic, human beings, and their various institutions; the history of being is a history not only of facts, but also of the realization of values in the world. Let us note, however, that something is not more valuable because it developed later; it is more valuable because of its greater complexity, among other things, and as a rule—but not always—complex beings develop only after simpler ones. To that extent, there is a *certain* parallelism between ontic development and the development of value, but it does not automatically arise from a naturalistic definition of the good. Because of its more complex locomotion, sense perception, and feeling, an animal is more valuable, *ceteris paribus*, than a plant, and it would remain so even if it were biologically possible that it had evolved earlier than plants. On the other hand, parasites can only come into being if their hosts already exist, but they are usually less complex and therefore less valuable than the latter.

These few observations have an important consequence for the conception of philosophy that underlies this book. According to a minimalist understanding of philosophy, it can only deal with normative propositions, specifically in the context of epistemology, ethics, and aesthetics. It is certainly correct that philosophy must deal with such propositions, if only because there is no other discipline that could assume this task. But that does not mean that philosophy can be reduced to this alone. In the realm of theoretical philosophy, for instance, there is not only the theoretical-normative discipline of the philosophy of science, which determines when certain assertions can be taken seriously from a scientific point of view, but also the philosophy of nature, which inquires into the *essence* of nature and seeks to understand why nature is as it is. It goes without saying that the efforts of the latter must converge with those of the natural sciences, yet this does not mean that natural science could make it superfluous. Natural science demonstrates only that something is the case, for example, that certain laws prevail, and on this basis it can explain certain events and to some extent even predict them; in doing so, it takes as its starting point unproven and, in the framework of its theory, unprovable axioms and fundamental concepts whose clarification is not a specific task of natural science. In contrast, the task of the philosophy of nature consists in reflecting on the fundamental concepts and axioms of natural science and, so far as possible, grasping them in their necessity. Similarly, philosophical anthropology and social philosophy have as their goal a deeper understanding of the principles of the corresponding empirical sciences; and it is not outlandish to maintain that one of the possible foundational strategies of these descriptive philosophical disciplines consists in showing that moral decisions are made possible only by certain qualities of human beings, social institutions, and their historical development, which have been observed by the empirical sciences. Empirical anthropology notes that the human being is a deficient being; philosophical anthropology asks why it is important that a moral being be a deficient being. In an analogous way, political philosophy does not consist solely of normative propositions concerning what the state should be; in the context of political philosophy, the descriptive propositions of political science may acquire a more comprehensive grounding.

From this way of seeing things, a further argument follows for the previously grounded relativization of the distinction between means and ends. I am trying to clarify this point through the relationship between means-ends rationality and value-rationality, and here I want to concentrate on the strategic form of means-ends rationality. First, we should acknowledge that value-rationality is the true domain of philosophy, whereas the insights of strategic means-ends rationality are derived from the relevant empirical and formal disciplines. However, philosophy's contribution cannot be limited to the statement that the discoveries of strategic means-ends rationality should be taken into account in order to achieve goals favored by value-rationality. Philosophy can and must strive to do more. It must first attempt to understand why human beings are capable of strategic behavior at all, or how the nature of this kind of behavior is connected with human nature. Second, it must be able to ground, so far as possible, the concrete principles that underlie those empirical and formal sciences. Thus philosophy does not consist solely of normative disciplines. For every individual descriptive science there is a corresponding philosophical discipline that is concerned with its principles and seeks to understand their necessity.

Philosophy cannot limit itself to recognizing that the fundamental structures of reality are as they are. Its ambitious goal, which can be only partly realized, will always be to understand these basic structures by relating them to even more general principles, among which the principles of ethics have an important place.

3.4.2. Methodology of the Social Sciences

In the framework of a book on the morals of politics it is particularly important to clarify the relationship between social philosophy and the social sciences, because the political is a social phenomenon, and political science is a social science.[151] A few remarks on

---

151. On the various approaches in the social sciences, see R. J. Bernstein's impressive book (1976).

the methodology of the social sciences as well as on the ontology of the social are therefore appropriate here. They will no doubt appear too brief to some readers, and too long to others; yet it seems indispensable to justify why certain approaches in the social sciences are given priority over others in this book. First, I maintain that the social sciences are *theoretical* sciences that seek knowledge regarding social phenomena. Naturally, this knowledge can be made useful for practical purposes (whether these purposes are moral or not); the engineering sciences are related to the natural sciences in the same way that social technology is related to the social sciences. Whereas the *object* of knowledge is identical in the first two disciplines and is distinct from that of the latter two, the first and the third agree in their epistemological *interests,* as do the second and the fourth: in the first case the standpoint is manipulative, in the second it is contemplative.[152] Engineering and social technology make use of knowledge derived from the natural and social sciences to satisfy existing interests that are themselves presupposed and not evaluated; the manipulative disciplines are no more normative than are the contemplative disciplines. However, the mere collection of a series of hypothetical imperatives that might be useful for politicians is not enough to constitute a social *science.* For that, the object realm of the social has to be examined in all its complexity, completely independently of the cratic usability of the corresponding insights—even if there is much to say for the supposition that an observation thus freed from practical concerns would be even more useful cratically than the limited observations of social technology. Whereas the Indian Arthaśāstras belong to social technology, Hobbes's *De cive* can claim to have founded social science, because it lays out for the first time the program of deriving, in the most cogent way possible and from the smallest number of axioms possible, theorems regarding social behavior. However, from the point of view of the theory of science, *De cive*'s greatest defect is that it does not sufficiently distinguish between descriptive and normative propositions.

It follows from the previously mentioned fact that every theory not only claims to be valid, but is itself a social phenomenon, that every theory in the social sciences or historiography is related to power. It would be naive to deny that Mommsen's *History of Rome* had political effects and that its author wanted it to have political effects. But the crucial point is that Mommsen believed that, on the basis of a factual analysis of Roman history, he could provide grounds for making certain political choices in his own time; it would never have occurred to him that he had interpreted Roman history as he did only in order to justify those choices. It may be that Mommsen deceived himself in this regard. Similarly, the reader would be well advised not to forget that a work like Caesar's *De bello civili* not only reports on a power struggle, but was itself a weapon in this power struggle, which was not concluded, but merely continued by other means.[153] But in Caesar's case, and even more in Mommsen's, it still remains to be shown where

---

152. Cf. H. D. Lasswell and A. Kaplan (1969), xi f.

153. In the case of *De bello civili* this is obvious. It is less obvious in Sallust's two treatises, but according to Mommsen, this does not prove "that they are not partisan writings, but only that they are good partisan writings" (1976; 4:190, n. 6).

they committed errors. The fact that someone has an interest in a particular truth does not mean that it could not be a truth. Even the most undeniable mathematical truths have been proven only because someone sought to do so for a length of time and therefore over time had presumably developed an interest in not having his efforts be in vain. Anyone who denies, in the name of ideology criticism, that works in the social sciences and historiography can be true, solely because interests underlie them, destroys his own position's claim to be true, since it is linked to interests as well. Moreover, he can no longer appeal to the evidence for the absolutely correct thesis that interests can sometimes cloud the objectivity of work in the social sciences, because he must draw on other sources if he wants to show, for instance, that Caesar consciously or unconsciously represented things falsely; on his theory, these other sources would have to be subjected to the same skepticism.

No matter how much the theoretical character of the social sciences should be maintained and the generic postulate of a unity of theory and practice in the social sciences should be rejected, two qualifications are still in order. First, it is obvious that the social sciences, unlike the classical natural sciences, include cases in which the construction of a theory alters the object of the theory, since the object and the theory belong to the same ontological sphere. Atoms do not do atomic physics, but people constantly make assumptions regarding social matters, even if these are sometimes only pre-scientific assumptions, and a change in these assumptions brought about by science may also change human behavior. "The phenomenon of economy can not exist at all . . . unless at least some of the simplest elements of this science itself, in the form of insight into connections, are presupposed in its object (that is, in the individuals)."[154] This implies the possibility of self-fulfilling statements in the social sciences; and since, as we have already seen in chapter 3.3.3, there are even cases in which two mutually exclusive assertions are equally self-fulfilling assumptions, moral criteria may be required to select one in preference to the other. But this does not hold true generically; wishful thinking must be distinguished from scientific analysis. One is factually allowed, of course, to make a moral demand that contradicts social reality, but one is not allowed to behave as if social reality were fundamentally what one wants it to be. The mixed character of practical syllogisms demands—not only on grounds connected with the ethics of science, but also on general moral grounds—an effort to be objective in describing reality, and especially social reality. Two things are fatal for political ethics: on one hand, the denial of the possibility of normative knowledge, and on the other, questioning the possibility of knowledge about the factual social world. Whereas the former cripples any moral will, the latter makes it impossible to make one's own will effective in a responsible way. A second necessary qualification is that the method of the social sciences is different from that of the natural sciences—the former are essentially interpretive sciences based on understanding (*verstehende Wissenschaften*). To better grasp this distinction, a reflection on regional ontology is indispensable here.

---

154. O. Morgenstern (1935), 346.

3.4.2.1. Social Being as the Fourth Sphere of Being:
Explanation and Understanding in the Social Sciences.

First, what is the place of the social in the whole of being (and, correspondingly, the place of the social sciences in the cosmos of the sciences, and of social philosophy within the philosophical disciplines)? On the basis of the ontology that I have elsewhere developed as a critical elaboration of Popper's theory of the three worlds,[155] it can be said that *the social constitutes the fourth sphere of being.* The first sphere of being (which in Popper is conflated with the fourth) is the sphere of ideal meaning, to which belong both mathematical entities and ideally valid values.[156] The relevant sciences are the basic parts of theoretical and practical philosophy as well as of mathematics. The second sphere is that of physical being, which is accessible to external experience and is the subject of the natural sciences—physics, chemistry, biology. The third sphere is constituted by the so-called "interior dimension," which is grasped through introspection; it is an object of psychology. Social being, which constitutes the fourth sphere, emerges from the cooperation of several beings with interior dimensions, whose behavior is characterized by conscious relating to other beings with interior dimensions; it is the object of the social sciences (which include the humanities).[157] Ontologically, its attraction consists in the fact that it unites the external and the interior dimension in a unique way. Indeed, the synthesis it produces overcomes the divisions within empirical being. Since introspection always opens up only one's own interior dimension, another person can be accessible only through the *physical manifestation* of his interior dimension; nonetheless, it is the manifestation of an *interior dimension.* So what is the social? Its bases are all the physical manifestations of the interior dimension, which are related, in accord with their express intention, to another subject.[158] However, we will speak of a social *interaction* only if this type of manifestation is also understood by the other subject concerned, and if it sometimes happens to trigger a manifestation of the other's in-

---

155. (1990c), 214 ff. The ontologizing of the individual spheres will certainly not be welcomed by every reader. Nonetheless, one will probably acknowledge (as Ulrich Steinvorth points out) that the different realms I distinguish correspond to different claims to validity: to the first realm, the claim to be true conceptually and logically; to the three others, the claim to be true empirically. In addition, to the third realm corresponds the claim to veracity, and to the fourth, the claim to justice.

156. Plato is the founder of a theory of the first world. Within modern philosophy, Frege defended it; however, his "third realm" does not play a particularly foundational role in practical philosophy.

157. Thus interactions between conscious beings from different species—for example, between humans and dogs or between hunters and hares—fall under the concept of the social. But the concept can also be defined in such a way that it includes only interactions among intelligent, self-conscious beings. Generality is a quality of scientific theories, and hence a general sociology that included the sociology of plants and animals would be a major scientific achievement.

158. An action is social in the full sense of the word only if this intention is conscious; but the posture that a person unconsciously assumes and that conveys a disposition to certain social interactions may also be considered something social.

terior dimension that is related to the first subject. If you greet someone you know who does not see you, this can perhaps be called a "social event," but certainly not a "social interaction." On the other hand, if the person greeted intentionally ignores the greeting, then it is certainly an interaction, since keeping silent can be a form of communication, and omissions can be actions if they occur consciously. In order to be understood, the greeting must have a specific form; the social includes not only actors but also a *medium*, which on one hand is produced through interactions (not through individual social events), and by which, on the other hand, interactions are guided. From this definition it follows, first, that the social does not belong to the ideal world but rather to the empirical world; second, that the social is always to be attached to physical entities and events (such as symbols, actions, and so on); and third, that these physical entities and events are understandable as an *expression* of an interior dimension. Whereas ideal entities would continue to exist if humanity destroyed itself, this does not hold true for social phenomena. They presuppose the existence of beings with interior dimensions. However, in the form of institutions they can make themselves independent of particular instances of such beings. They are never completely independent of the existence of intelligent beings with bodies; a state can survive the death of all the people who constructed it at an earlier point in time, but only if other people have been born to take their place. But this relative independence is fascinating enough. It has inspired organicist models of the social, insofar as the form, just as in the organism, has acquired an independence from the individual material components, which are constantly being exchanged. At the same time, the organism can no more get along without a material basis than an institution can get along without the subjects that constitute it. In addition, institutions, like biological systems, seem to strive to preserve themselves and even to sacrifice individual persons to this goal. But whereas the organism is a physical object (although an animate one) to which one can point, words that indicate institutions refer to entities that exist behind the concrete things to which one directs attention, so to speak; however, unlike mathematical entities, they exist only in and through what is pointed to. This is the reason why the social and the political are so often described with metaphors, for metaphors create a transition between various realms, and the social consists in a synthesis of ontologically different things.

The intelligent beings that constitute the social must have bodies that belong to the physical world. Although I am not aware of a stringent a priori proof that excludes the possibility of bodiless rational beings, it is clear that the relations among such beings would have to be of a *fundamentally* different kind than those among beings that interact through the bodily manifestations of their interior dimensions. With regard to human beings, even the most sublime ideas of the greatest geniuses do not represent anything social unless they are communicated to someone else. Finally, it is obvious that interactions among machines (that is, beings without interior dimensions), however complex, do not constitute something social, unless they have been programmed by beings with an interior dimension and function as means of communication for these beings. However, in that case it is the programmers, not the machines themselves, that constitute a social phenomenon. One terminological problem is whether interactions among beings with interior dimensions that do not include in these interactions a reference to the existence of other beings with interior dimensions can be categorized as social phenomena. According to the previous definition, this question is answered in the negative. If one adopts a different definition, one will at least have to concede that such phenomena do not constitute the social in the full sense of the term. Nonetheless, they often represent a foundation on which the social is erected.[159]

The correct answer to the fundamental question of the methodology of the social sciences—whether they explain or interpret—is implicit in the essence of the definition of the social we have introduced. They are interpretive sciences because without understanding the *intentions* of intelligent beings and their *meaning*,[160] social science cannot be practiced. Anyone who denies the possibility of objective understanding therefore destroys as well the idea of social science. Here we must keep in mind that other people's intentions are more easily understood when one is acquainted with them from one's own experience. Hence, at first glance it seems completely plausible to argue for the unity of theory and practice in the social sciences by pointing out that one can only understand the social behavior of others—that is, practice social science—if one commits oneself socially. However, it can be objected that although the political scientist probably has certain intellectual advantages if he knows the logic of the desire for power from his own experience, this in no way proves that he has to have political ambitions himself if he wants to engage in political science. He may have renounced all political goals. Indeed, if one suspects that one's own interests distort—not necessarily, but regularly—the obligatory objective perspective, one would even have to believe that such a scientist would be much more likely to be a first-class political scientist or political historian than would a politically ambitious one. It is reasonable to maintain that Thucydides' wonderful work was only made possible by the combination of two factors: on one hand, his own previous political engagement, without which it would be difficult to explain certain of his insights into the mechanisms of power, and on the other hand, his complete renunciation of any further political activity and his retreat to a purely observational attitude, which made it possible for him to coolly objectivize even his own earlier activity. Thucydides writes about Athens as if he were a physician who had set out to describe with precision the course of an illness he had already diagnosed as incurable—though the insight that nothing more can be done in no way ex-

---

159. Cf. Weber (1980; 11): "Ein Zusammenprall zweier Radfahrer z. B. ist ein bloßes Ereignis wie ein Naturgeschehen. Wohl aber wären ihr Versuch, dem andern auszuweichen, und die auf den Zusammenprall folgende Schimpferei, Prügelei oder friedliche Erörterung 'soziales Handeln.'" ("For example, a mere collison of two cyclists may be compared to a natural event. On the other hand, their attempt to avoid hitting each other, or whatever insults, blows, or friendly discussion might follow the collision, would constitute 'social action.'" Trans. A. R. Henderson and T. Parsons, 113.)

160. Here the concept of meaning is purely formal. Even the notion that life has no meaning (that is, no value) is a construct with meaning, that is, it is understandable as an intention.

cludes the possibility that the physician may have a passionately empathetic, although not often openly expressed, affection for the sick person.[161] To be sure, it could be objected that even after making this renunciation, Thucydides must have sought out politically involved informants in order to write his work; and if by practice one means any intersubjective activity, then it is clear that a social scientist cannot give up practice in this sense. For the most part, the social scientist will interact not only with his colleagues but also with those who constitute the object of his research. But on one hand, this form of practice does not mean that one has to engage in the specific type of activity that interests one theoretically (whether this is of a political, economic, or some other nature). On the other hand, the example of the historian who is concerned with past times shows that understanding need not be mutual; social systems can be approached from the outside (in this case, even ex post facto). A second objection to the demand that the social scientist be socially engaged is that although personal experience may make it easier to understand the intentions of others, it is not an indispensable condition for doing so. We can no longer feel the fears felt by archaic humans, and yet modern culture (perhaps only modern culture) can carry out good anthropological research. Why shouldn't an asexual person become a major expert on sexual behavior, or an areligious person an innovative researcher in religious studies?

The objectivization of the interior dimension in external forms that are common to different subjects necessarily implies that the social follows a logic not fully reducible to that of the interior dimension of individuals. The social sciences therefore cannot be solely interpretive sciences. On one hand, the isolated individual's behavior is not necessarily transparent even to him. One can be mistaken regarding one's own motives, and to that extent, an understanding of the subjective intentions of others can miss the true causes that really explain their behavior. On the other hand, the social has its own dynamics, which is based, first of all, on the fact that the intentions of individual actors differ from one another and therefore can lead to a result no one wanted. The prisoner's dilemma, mentioned earlier, is a well-known example of how a result that is not Pareto-optimal can be produced precisely when everyone is thinking only about maximizing their own interests. Moreover, the special ontological status of the social as an innerness that is manifested *externally* should be mentioned: for example, a large crowd can have physical consequences, such as the collapse of a building, that were not foreseen by anyone. Finally, according to the theory of functionalism, the objective function of institutions is often concealed. The manifest function, which the people who keep the institution going attribute to it, can deviate from the objective function, even though only the latter can explain why this institution has a real utility and therefore, if one applies the

---

161. The relationship between theory and practice in the ancient historians and its effects on the emergence of a *science* of historiography would be worth investigating. These comments about Thucydides could also be applied to Sallust and Tacitus, albeit with significant modifications. The reason why neither Livy nor Caesar became truly first-class historians is that the former did not perform an autopsy of the political, and the latter did not renounce politics.

principles of Darwinism to cultural evolution, why it was created or continues to exist. The objective and subjective end, the teleonomy and the teleology, need not coincide. A familiar example is provided by rain dances, whose manifest function—causing rain— conceals the latent function, of which the community is not aware, but which really supports the institution, namely, the strengthening of the feeling of community. Yet, however much the manifest function may be an illusion, we must still note that one of the necessary aspects of institutions is that they can be reflected upon. In short, the possibility in principle of making social institutions an object of reflection by people who belong to these institutions is what makes them an anthropological phenomenon—no matter how different the level of reflection may be in myth, art, science, and philosophy.

3.4.2.2. Philosophical Interpretation and the Self-Interpretation of Social Structures: The Problem of Methodological Individualism

Here we encounter a fundamental problem for any social science, and especially for social philosophy: How are the scientific or philosophical interpretations of a social structure related to its self-interpretation?[162] On one hand, it is unlikely that the two would coincide, for then scientific and philosophical effort would be superfluous. It would be naive to deny that false self-interpretations of social structures constantly appear, indeed, that they are virtually inevitable. It can be in the interest of a small minority group to deceive others regarding the true power relationships, for example; and it can even be the case that everyone in a given culture makes false assumptions regarding that culture because the truth would not be compatible with their self-respect. Indeed, because of the remarkable fact that certain things cannot be intended as such, the correct interpretation of some social structures means their demise. The refusal to adopt such an interpretation arises from a reasonable instinct for self-preservation on the part of the corresponding social structure, which is in conflict with the interests of social scientists who want to learn about the structure by observing it from the outside.[163] If a culture thinks it understands that its religion is good solely because it is socially useful, then its religion will quickly dissolve, and along with it, its social utility. Wanting certain things means condemning oneself to not achieving them—they must just fall into one's lap as pleasant side effects. If the latter become the main focus of interest, they will be forfeited. A person who thinks too much about being in love and not enough about his beloved is no longer in love. In the same way, a culture can dissolve if its self-interpretation takes a new form, as, for instance, when a religiously determined culture interprets itself with scientific or philosophical categories. (Moreover, even phi-

---

162. Cf. Voegelin (1962), 27 ff, who speaks of self-illumination.

163. In exceptional cases, the penetration of ethnologists into archaic societies can destroy the latter. Even when the ethnologists exercise great discretion, this penetration sets in motion processes that subtly transform the society. Thus the ethnologist, who has no magic cap to make himself invisible, often finds that what he is looking for eludes him.

losophy, which thrives on reflexive structures, can be damaged by excessive reflexivity. For example, contemporary philosophy suffers from being too much concerned with itself and not enough with philosophical problems.)

On the other hand, the scientific-philosophical interpretation cannot exist without some connection with self-interpretation. This is not meant in the trivial sense that even a false self-interpretation is a social fact and thus has to be taken into account by a scientific interpretation. False self-interpretations are just as real as rain dances, and even if false interpretations say more about their subject than about their object, yet because of the coincidence of subject and object, self-interpretations always also shed light on the object interpreted. As I have indicated, we are not concerned with this argument here, for it still regards the social systems to be interpreted scientifically or philosophically as pure objects *about* which we may learn, but *from* which nothing can be learned. What concerns us far more here is that there must be a certain continuity between the self-interpretation of a social structure and the scientific or philosophical interpretation. Otherwise, the basis for the ability to know the truth, which the social scientist or social philosopher must necessarily claim, remains unclear. However, if the latter must believe they have this ability, they should not deny it completely to their objects, and if their prejudices prevent them from doing so, they must reckon with the possibility that their own pre-understanding is no less open to criticism than that of their objects. This argument (which is fatal for various theories that there are universal contexts of delusion [Verblendungszusammenhänge]) is convincing, at least when the scientific or philosophical interpreter himself belongs to the culture with which he deals. To give an example, Plato in the *Republic* calls for a radical break with the Greek polis's self-interpretation—a break that is connected with a turnaround in the soul. Nonetheless, not only does it strike us today, but also Plato himself had understood, that it was precisely Greek culture that had produced a thinker who had discovered a new world—the ideal world—and on this basis made possible a new approach to social phenomena. Plato's turn toward the world of pure validities would not have been possible in other cultures; there must consequently, have been many things in Greek culture and even in pre-philosophical culture before Plato that prepared the way for this break. In fact, it is not hard for a trained intellectual historian to find in Homer, and especially in the great tragedians, nuances in the way of viewing the world that are not found in earlier cultures, and that point toward Plato. In short, the great achievement of social philosophy that consisted in raising itself to the level of a world of timelessly valid ideas presupposes, in genetic terms, an exceptionally complex cultural background, and would not have been possible without a certain continuity between the pre-philosophical self-interpretation of a culture and the efforts of social philosophy. Generalizing the argument somewhat, even the most abstract interpretations of modern social science and social philosophy could not have developed had the human mind not possessed from the outset a certain capacity for truth—a capacity that we respect in seeking as much rationality as possible in the self-interpretations of human societies and in recognizing in the inevitable critical analysis of this self-interpretation that without these errors, we probably could not have arrived at our critical convictions at all. Thus, on formal grounds alone, a philosophical or sociological interpretation of religions would be better if it succeeded in showing that religions are not merely erroneous interpretations of societies, but that they involve, even if an inadequate form, something that cannot be neglected by even the most highly developed theory, whether this be the concept of the absolute or that of the moral. However, even if this kind of interpretation allows more continuity with the self-interpretations of traditional societies than do the interpretations current today, it is scarcely compatible with the self-interpretation of the *present*, which thinks it has found its identity in the liberation from all absolutes. But this is certainly more a social fact than a fact that is relevant to the theory of validity.

It is incontestable that a large portion of an individual's values, ideas, and feelings are induced by the community. The individual is in no relevant sense "complete" without the community to which he belongs. Insofar as methodological individualism denies this, it is erroneous. But it is right in maintaining that assertions regarding social phenomena are bad metaphysics if they cannot be anchored in the concrete consciousness, or at least in the behavior, of individual intelligent beings. Moreover, ethical grounds speak in favor of methodological individualism, since responsibility is first of all individual. It is no accident that a systems theory such as Luhmann's undermines the presuppositions of ethics. For example, if one says that a state is conducting a war, one must always refer to concrete persons who are participating in the battle or commanding it. But in fact it is possible that only a small minority are fighting with strong convictions; indeed, it is even conceivable that no individual does so. Yet the erroneous belief that others passionately support the war and would expect one to do the same can lead to the pursuit of a war even when no one wants to continue it any longer. This is a striking example of the partial autonomy of the social, which has freed itself from the concrete wishes of individuals, but nonetheless remains inseparable from concrete, individual acts of consciousness (such as wrongly believing that others want something they do not). However, one must keep in mind that this favoring of methodological individualism is located within an approach that recognizes an ideal world. This means, on one hand, that assertions regarding the ideology of a society have to be translated into assertions about the convictions of individuals; and on the other hand, that the convictions of the individuals themselves are not atomic facts, but are partly caused through contact with the convictions of other individuals and partly grounded through the relationship to the sphere of pure validities. This explains why the number of not only actual but also possible convictions is much smaller than it would be if the convictions held by reasonable beings were not determined and limited by objective demands. It also explains why reasonable beings can understand each other; a thought that they think in common—for instance, the Pythagorean theorem—is something different from the subjective acts of thinking it. The former is one and the same, the latter differ depending on the individual.

3.4.2.3. Social Sciences and Historical Sciences:
The Sources of Knowledge in the Social Sciences

Since the social is part of the empirical world, the social sciences are empirical sciences: assertions in the social sciences can be empirically verified, or, if they are statements of laws, they can at least be falsified. Theories that are in principle exempt from empirical verification or falsification belong to social philosophy, not to the social sciences. However, experiments play a role in the social sciences that is different from the role they play in the natural sciences, because they can be carried out only in a very limited way—partly for reasons of practicability and partly for moral reasons. Social behavior is often too complex to be repeatable under the same contextual conditions, and there are obvious moral reasons why social scientists cannot initiate revolutions, for example, in order to satisfy their curiosity.[164] In this connection it is important to draw attention to the relationship between the *social* and the *historical* sciences. It is clear that—unlike chemistry and psychology, for instance—the two disciplines do not really deal with two different fields of objects. For every special discipline within the social sciences, there is a corresponding historical discipline: economics and economic history, political science and political history, and so forth. By a very crude approximation, one could say that historical disciplines are related to systematic disciplines in a way similar to that in which protocols regarding experiments are related to theories in the natural sciences. Thus historical reports on the course of revolutions must be evaluated if one is interested in developing a general theory of revolutions; the historical sciences make available the material on the basis of which the social sciences construct their theories.[165] (Nonetheless, one must grant that a comparative sociology usually does not get as far as might be desirable, because the number of the societies to be compared is often much too small to allow meaningful generalizations.) This thesis corresponds neither to the self-understanding of the majority of modern social scientists nor to that of most contemporary historians—which is probably one of the reasons for the crisis in both disciplines. In any event, Michael Mann's great work, *The Sources of Social Power,* shows that a fruitful combination of historical and sociological thinking is still possible today. Naturally, it does not follow that the historical sciences cannot also be practiced as an end in themselves. On the contrary, there are very good grounds for doing so, such as

---

164. But only in Huxley's *Brave New World,* wide-ranging social experiments are carried out on the population even when they lead to thousands of casualties (cf. chap. 16 [1977; 221f.]). The communist experiment was at least carried out by people who identified with it and had something to lose if it collapsed.

165. Since, as we have mentioned, certain social experiments are not permissible, the *past* plays a role in the social sciences that it does not have in fields where experiments can always be repeated. However, we cannot examine here the problems connected with the special ontological status of the past.

their importance in the formation of collective identities, which is not possible without common memories. It was thus a mistake to replace instruction in history in the schools by instruction in the social sciences—but a mistake not on grounds belonging to the theory of science, with which we are solely concerned for the moment, but rather on political grounds.

The assertion that the social sciences are empirical sciences implies no endorsement of empiricism with regard to concepts or judgments; neither form of empiricism is a relevant theory of knowledge for either the natural or the social sciences. To begin with empiricism regarding judgments, it is obvious, first of all, that hardly any simple empirical propositions can be grounded solely through observation. Every observational statement (and a fortiori, every historical report) is impregnated with theory. Thus individual hypotheses can almost never be falsified. Only theoretical complexes can be falsified, and in such a case it remains unclear which part of the theoretical complex should be rejected. Second, it is completely out of the question to reduce all true empirical propositions to simple empirical propositions, if only because of the problem of induction, which remains impossible to resolve within the framework of empiricism, even logical empiricism. So far as empiricism regarding concepts is concerned, it is still more erroneous. Experience does not unequivocally indicate a single way of constructing concepts. However, not all conceptual systems are equally good. Different concepts should correspond to real—or even merely possible, objectively conceivable—differences. But not all differences are equally significant, and what is now scorned as "essentialism" has for the most part been nothing other than the attempt to work out a conceptual system that would be as fruitful as possible. One criterion for the quality of a conceptual system is whether it underlies a theory that explains as much as possible. In this book I am interested in developing concepts that can serve the goals of both ethics and the social sciences. Since, for instance, the difference between actions and omissions is ethically significant, in differentiating the concept of power I will distinguish between forms of power that are based on negative sanctions and those that are based on positive sanctions; this simplifies the moral evaluation of forms of power. In addition, in constructing my concepts I have made very restrained use of neologisms, and have even accepted the fact that some of my terms have more than one meaning. *Nominal definitions* will seldom be found in the following pages; I leave *semantic analyses* to specialists in linguistics. What I am usually aiming at is the *explication* of familiar terms, that is, I seek to specify their meaning with the goal of elaborating a theory that is as simple and at the same time as comprehensive as possible.

Given the previous discussion, it follows that an intelligent social scientist has to use not only empirical knowledge but also other components of knowledge; indeed, it is of the greatest importance to recognize that strictly empirical work in the social sciences can, under certain circumstances, be almost misleading. Not all true propositions are interesting, that is, general in scope or fraught with consequences; and the feeling that one is an objective scientist can lead one to stockpile huge amounts of quantitative data from which a more general theory can never be drawn. In actuality, we must keep in mind that the social sciences are ethically neutral insofar as they neither ground nor need normative propositions, but they need values insofar as they have to *select* from the social material what is important for them. (To this extent every change in values in a society leads to new branches of the social and historical sciences: think of women's studies or environmental history.) Yet this does not mean that social scientists must identify with the object they are analyzing. Someone can write a history of torture out of repugnance for that institution; but he must in any case have an interest in it. Whether this interest is meaningful is a question that cannot be answered empirically, just as general inquiries, unlike answers, cannot be justified empirically. How one arrives at interesting questions that open the way to new insights is one of the most neglected but important problems of the theory of science, for the quality of a science depends on the questions it asks no less than on the answers it provides.

So far as concept formation is concerned, every kind of empirical research presupposes *categories,* that is, the most general concepts; and it is not absurd to maintain that these categories that make experience possible in the first place cannot stem from themselves. Thus, *philosophical analysis of essences* is a fruitful complement to the empirical method, even if it leads out of the social sciences and into social philosophy. The analysis of essences can be practiced in two different ways. On one hand, the essence can be approached descriptively, as it were—the phenomenological school is the classical representative of this approach. The problem with phenomenology is that its reflections on methods are inadequate. However, the focus on an intuitive grasping of wholes is conceived precisely as an alternative to analytical thought, and one can hardly deny that the works of Heidegger and Sartre, for instance, have increased our understanding of the essence of some social phenomena more than many works of empirical social science. On the other hand, one can attempt to put the descriptively grasped essences in a conceptual context that grounds them and shows their development—Hegel's *Philosophy of Right* is a paradigmatic example of such an approach. Hegel's method of developing the individual categories out of one another is, of course, dialectics, but its extremely complex structure cannot be discussed in detail here.[166] What is essential is that Hegel elaborates referential relationships between concepts, that he works with contradictions between the form and the content of concepts, and that he thinks that these contradictions can be overcome only through synthetic concepts. In any case, Hegel wants not only to grasp the essence of ethical life but also to explain why there must be a phenomenon such as ethical life in the realm of the social. In post-Hegelian social philosophy, F. Tönnies's 1887 *Gemeinschaft und Gesellschaft* is the most impressive example of an attempt to introduce the basic categories of sociology on the basis of a purely conceptual development.

Let us note in this connection that in the descriptive disciplines, no less than in ethics, comparative concepts are more useful, because they are more differentiated, than

---

166. On this subject, see D. Wandschneider's extremely helpful book (1995).

classificatory concepts. We can leave open the question whether a social structure is a community or a society if we can only find out which of several social structures comes closest to being a community, and which come closest to being a society. Typologies should never deny that in reality there is a continuity among forms. In general, in the development of conceptual systems it is not decided in advance which real structures correspond to them, indeed, whether there are any such structures at all. The problem of subsumption must be distinguished from that of the development of concepts. Thus Max Weber's ideal types, which mediate between Tönnies's stronger a priorism and the empiricism of most of Anglo-American sociology, are justified partly because real phenomena can be subsumed under them, and partly because in the construction of ideal types a role is played by the demands of the logic of the subject that need not be fulfilled in all their instantiations. From the ideal type of totalitarianism, or from the logic immanent in this concept, certain phenomena can be deduced that need not be present in all totalitarian systems, and indeed may not be present all together in any single totalitarian system, because contingent contextual conditions have not made it possible for the ideal type of totalitarianism to be completely realized anywhere.[167] But that does not argue against the use of ideal types, as long as we acknowledge that concrete empirical analysis should be inspired by ideal types, but that each of the phenomena need not be subsumed under a single type. Here we can only mention the question whether ideal types (which in many respects can be compared with biological species) are a subjective construct or whether they have a special ontic dignity, in comparison with which their instantiations are deficient. On the basis of objective idealism one will choose the second answer, and in any case we should reject the error that consists in thinking that if categories and ideal types cannot be given a purely empirical ground, then they are mere constructions without any relation to reality. Radical constructivism cancels itself out, because the concept of a construct is also subject to the verdict that constructivism makes with regard to other categories: it is a construct produced by a group of intellectuals who have lost contact with reality and feel superior by blaming reality rather than themselves for this loss. How can one see through something as a *mere* construct if one cannot contrast it with reality?[168]

In addition to Weber's theory of categories, we will make repeated use here of the network of concepts that H. D. Lasswell and A. Kaplan proposed for social and political phenomena in their book *Power and Society*. This book, the result of the collaboration between a multifaceted political scientist and a philosopher, seems to me one of the most important works in the social sciences written in this century. However, the logical structure of the book is unsatisfactory. In addition to definitions, it introduces countless propo-

---

167. Even the average representative of a class—who must be distinguished from the ideal-typical representative—need not exist. It can very well happen that there is no one whose weight coincides precisely with the average weight.

168. Leibniz's criticism of Locke's subjectivization of concepts has lost nothing of its force.

sitions that are to be seen as mere hypotheses open to empirical testing. But the individual propositions are not independent of each other; if some of them are accepted (as axioms, so to speak), then the others follow from them purely logically, without requiring any further empirical verification. This is one of the reasons why the empiricism of Lasswell and Kaplan's book goes too far: it underestimates the logical connections between the various propositions. The other reason is that individual propositions in the social sciences are often *nearly* tautological, and hence empirical testing becomes almost superfluous. That bodies expand when they grow warmer is no doubt a synthetic proposition—there is no conceptual connection between subject and predicate. But the proposition that anyone who strives for power uses means that expand his power is not synthetic to the same degree. Between the motive and the action there is a logical connection that arises immediately from the intentional structure of human consciousness. Of course, the proposition is not a strict tautology. One does not always do what one wants, because one may be prevented from realizing what one wills or not know the means necessary to realize it. But understanding the logic of intentions spares one a great deal of empirical research into the connection among variables—research that could be conducted in good conscience only if one had no sense of the logic of intentions.

It remains to mention the use of *mathematical* aids in the social sciences. As a general science of structures, mathematics comprehends the various sciences of the empirical world, and therefore it should not be surprising that some mathematical theories can be applied to both biological and social processes. For example, the mathematical relationships investigated by cybernetics hold for all cybernetic systems, whether these involve artifacts, organisms, or social systems—that is, they hold independently of all ontological differences. Mathematical models are extremely useful in many social sciences, especially if one realizes that the stringency of the relationships derived from such models still does not imply that there is a part of reality that precisely corresponds to them. Mathematical models have proven themselves, in particular in political economy, but also in other fields, such as the theory of international relations. Thus it would be irresponsible to neglect mathematical models, though overestimating them is just as great a danger. Whereas game theory has proven useful in many social sciences, and Richardson's model of arms races, for example, has been fruitful in a certain area of the theory of international relations, skepticism is still appropriate with regard to other mathematical theories, at least up to this point. If one examines the application of catastrophe theory to certain problems in international politics,[169] one immediately sees how little has been achieved thus far. It is particularly irritating when half-educated people connect all discontinuities in social events with catastrophe theory. Not only are there no concrete reconstructions of such events using the tools of catastrophe theory, but in the case of many discontinuities it is clear from the outset that they could have nothing to do with catastrophes (in the mathematical sense of the term). The application

---

169. Cf. M. Nicholson (1990), 167 ff.

of basic concepts from catastrophe theory, chaos theory, and so forth, in the context of the social sciences often amounts, from the point of view of the sociology of knowledge, to a mere attempt to impress. Interdisciplinarity is important, but it should not be confused with charlatanry. It is obvious that the effort to mathematicize the social sciences at any cost springs from a slavish admiration of the natural sciences and a misunderstanding of the ontologically relevant differences between the physical and the social worlds. The transfer of a scientific method to a sphere in which it is inappropriate is not a scientific achievement that should impress us, but rather a misunderstanding of the first presupposition of scientific thought: a clear recognition that method depends on the object.[170]

A question sometimes raised is whether there are *laws* in social science; unless this question is answered in the affirmative, the social sciences are meaningless. Scientific knowledge is always knowledge of the universal, and sciences of the empirical world always involve laws. The concept of an idiographic science, that is, a science that describes only individuals,[171] is a contradiction in terms, and it becomes completely misleading when it is applied to the distinction between the natural and the human sciences (*Geisteswissenschaften*). First of all, there are idiographic propositions in the natural sciences as well. The forensic toxicologist, who determines the poison that has killed someone, seeks to produce an idiographic proposition. Second, such propositions in the natural and human sciences generally already take for granted a conceptual framework to which the assumption of certain laws also belongs. "Caesar's ambition made him cross the Rubicon" implies that ambition generally leads to risky behavior and that certain types of behavior, under which some of Caesar's previous actions might be subsumed, must be interpreted as expressions of ambition. Indeed, any application of the category of causality, of which the historical sciences make extensive use, ultimately presupposes the assertion of a law; singular causal explanations are, as Hume rightly recognized, meaningless. Hempel and Oppenheim's famous covering law model[172] is also relevant to explanations in the social sciences: real events (physical, psychic, or social) can be explained only on the basis of antecedent events and laws.[173] However, four qualifications are required. Because humans have a peculiar capacity to grasp relationships of meaning, a logical connection between cause and effect may exist in human actions; we have already discussed this possibility. But it is never the grounds themselves that cause something, but only the insight into the grounds (or its physiological correlate) that can, as a real cause, bring about a corresponding behavior. Second, it has to be acknowledged that social phenomena are the most complex things we know—incomparably more complex than any physical event. Thus idiographic discoveries regarding an in-

---

170. Voegelin (1952), 4 ff.
171. Cf. Windelband (1894).
172. Cf. Hempel (1965).
173. This leaves open the question of whether these laws are deterministic or statistical.

dividual social event have a higher intrinsic value than analogous discoveries regarding a physical event; and since humans can enter into a relationship to the universal, a biography of an important person is impregnated with the universal to quite a different extent than is the description of an individual physical object, even one so great as the Grand Canyon.

Third, it is in any case unrealistic to hope to find the laws that determine human behavior in the form of anything but the crudest approximations.[174] This is so because even most so-called natural laws are abstractions—they are valid if one can, under ideal conditions, exclude the influence of certain parameters. But this exclusion of disturbing contextual conditions is impossible in the realm of the social, and to that extent one will almost always find exceptions to the laws proposed, especially since in the sphere of the social far more parameters are relevant than in the physical world. But these exceptions do not prove, as is often believed, that in the social sciences there are no laws in the strict sense of the word; they prove only that the real laws are more complex than those known thus far and presumably those that will be known in the future. In actuality, one must concede that many of the so-called social laws are abstractions from modern European history and are valid not universally but only conditionally; by formulating them, European social science has often merely made it appear that there is no alternative to its own culture.[175] Much the same goes for so-called laws of historical development. The triad of the stone, bronze, and iron ages is abstracted from the prehistory of Europe and is in no way valid for the rest of the world. But something analogous is also sufficiently known from the history of the natural sciences. The Galilean transformations are not universally valid, but rather valid—as excellent approximations—only for certain classes of systems moving at a constant velocity relative to each other. Anyone who tries to express them universally will run up against the Lorentz transformations. Similarly, many of the laws formulated by the social sciences will certainly be revealed to be over-generalizations, which follow from more general propositions if one adds the relevant qualifying conditions.[176] From the quantity and complexity of social laws it immediately follows that monocausal explanations of social events are, for the most part, false. Ambition is not a sufficient cause for the crossing of the Rubicon— there must have been certain contextual conditions that made the ambitious Caesar decide to take that step. In *War and Peace* Tolstoy rightly mocks historians who offer as the cause of major historical events the whims of so-called great men or other accidents.

---

174. For that very reason the future remains *subjectively* open. Besides, there is Popper's well-known argument that even if it were determined which important discovery would be made in the year 2114, we could not know it today because then it would not be first made in 2114.

175. No less unscientific is the opposite procedure, which consists in projecting one's own utopian dreams onto archaic cultures and imagining that they overcame general human constants.

176. The way in which Machiavelli handles the cratological recommendations handed down to him already consists in distinguishing the conditions under which they are valid from the conditions under which they are not valid.

Thus it is obvious that the assassination in Sarajevo only *triggered* World War I; the *causes* were different and manifold, and without them this assassination would never have led to a war. The same causes might have looked for another triggering event, and found it, too, if that assassination had not taken place.[177] The triggering event must also be distinguished from a *pretext*. A pretext is what is presented as the cause for one's own behavior, even when in some circumstances it does not have even the limited causal effectiveness of a triggering event.

Fourth, we must once again recall that theories about the social realm—unlike theories about nature—belong to the sphere that they describe. They therefore alter the latter, even if they are false. This means, on one hand, that someone who wants to understand nature can ignore false theories in the natural sciences, but someone who wants to understand the social world must also carefully study influential but absurd theories in the social sciences. On the other hand, it has the following consequence: a theory in the social sciences can be successful if it is "falsified" by leading to countermeasures that prevent its predictions from being fulfilled. Naturally, this is not precisely a falsification, for the theory only maintained that certain things would happen *if* no countermeasures were taken. One can learn from history and free oneself from the power of *conditional* laws that are valid only so long as one has not grasped them as such.

The social sciences can both analyze the synchronously existing relationships between various individuals or social spheres and examine social transformations. Not only states but also changes are the subject matter of the social sciences—*states of equilibrium* as well as *developments.* Realistically, one must acknowledge that reality shows far fewer states of equilibrium than one might hope for the sake of theory; this holds for general social processes as well as for economic processes. Thus, for example, the often praised stability of archaic cultures is from one point of view a myth, since they were characterized by repeated power struggles. However, it is correct to say that archaic cultures had no history, insofar as "history" in these cultures is mainly a matter of oscillations around a point of equilibrium. Such cyclical changes are fundamentally different from *laws of development,* in which time becomes important in a quite different way: it becomes an *irreversible* magnitude, and thus a perspective on a unified development including all of human history opens up.[178] Obviously, laws of historical development and other social laws are connected in a special way. For example, the relationships between religion and politics change in the course of history, and how the behavior of each sphere changes may be based on the nature of laws of historical development. The concrete historical form taken by the relationship between politics and religion would thus—along with many other laws in social science and the given antecedent conditions—determine the course of individual actions that take place in the area of tension between politics and religion.

---

177. Thucydides already makes this categorial differentiation: see I 23.

178. Within the natural sciences there is a similar distinction between two concepts of time: on one hand in dynamics, and on the other in theories of cosmological and biological evolution.

3.4.2.4. Pre-Scientific Knowledge and Knowledge through Art

The project of the social sciences to explain social events on the basis of laws and antecedent conditions is no doubt reasonable. But we could not survive in the social world if we did not already have a *pre-scientific* knowledge of the social. It is precisely the extraordinary complexity of this sphere of being that shows the absurdity of the idea that one must first have discovered the system of its laws and developed it by moving forward analytically from simple to complex assumptions, before one can venture to act in the social world. In the social world, if anywhere, there is an intuition that grasps essential structures without being able to ground its assumptions. To repeat: The project of an analytical social science is reasonable; and there is no general objection to attempts to mathematize those areas of the social world that are accessible to that kind of approach. What should be rejected is merely the idea that one must give priority to the advice of a social scientist—that is, a person who has succeeded in understanding scientifically one tiny area of the social world—over that of another person who is familiar with the nature of this world through powerful intuition and lived experience. Anyone who has read the ancient historians has noted that they lack the analytical approach to the world that characterizes modern social scientists; but we can learn from them things that are found in no book in the social sciences. That is true even where the ancient historians report facts that are not correct, as we have already seen in discussing the anecdote about Herennius Pontius's advice as reported by Livy. One further example must suffice. Livy commits a crude anachronism when he has Lucius Valerius Flaccus, in his speech opposing Marcus Porcius Cato, quote the latter's *Origines* in connection with the controversy regarding the repeal of the *Lex Oppia* (195 BC); the *Origines* were in fact written much later.[179] But even if this speech cannot have been made as reported by Livy, it shows something important: that it is always a smart move in a political debate to quote something from one's opponent's writings that supports one's own position or at least seems to support it. Livy falsely represented an individual case, but he did so because he wanted to formulate a general truth about clever rhetorical behavior. It is a fundamental characteristic of ancient historians that they make use of the correct in order to attain the true—that is, they take individual truths of fact as an opportunity to discover truths about essences. Indeed, they often represent the truths of fact in accord with the truths about essences underlying them. In the discoverers of historically correct truths of fact such as Thucydides, this tendency is already obvious; one has only to think of the speeches he reports. Precisely for this reason his history of the Peloponnesian War is not only a historical masterpiece, but also a resource for every political scientist and, even more, one of the most perfect works of art ever created.

The essence of *art*—one of the most underestimated sources of knowledge in the age of science—consists in its relationship to truth. Art represents truth in something

---

179. 34.5.8: "tuas adversus te Origines revolvam."

concrete, in an attractive sensory form that is especially closely connected with the content. Art is a synthesis of historical science and philosophical social science: like the former, it deals with something concrete and individual, but like the latter, it aims at truths about essences. The fact that, unlike philosophy, it is based on something concrete explains its superior power over the hearts of human beings, who are always individuals; because this concrete element is fictive and situated in a possible world, it can approach the truths about essences that even ancient historiography could not approach. The *truth* with which art is concerned must be distinguished from mere *correctness*—the latter is neither a sufficient nor even a necessary condition for truth. The fact that on 28 November 1803 Hegel ordered from the Brothers Ramann "half a cask . . . of white French wine" is no doubt recorded and to that extent correct; but it is not "true" in a more comprehensive sense of the word, because nothing more general, no truth about essences, shines through it. Conversely, assertions regarding Don Carlos in Schiller's play are not correct, at least regarding the historical Don Carlos, and there never has been anyone of whom everything recounted in the play is correct. But the play says an enormous amount about the problem of power—it is full of moral truths as well as truths about the political world. Just as the status of a scientific theory depends on deducing the most possible from the fewest and simplest axioms possible, a great work of art, by concentrating on a few essential figures, makes the extraordinary complexity of human relationships visible in a far-reaching way.

Granted, this concentration inevitably entails abstraction, and presumably an abstraction not only from what is correct, but also from what is true. Thus it cannot be denied that many things that are correct but are skimmed over by artists (and philosophers) have more dignity than it seems to the latter; many correct things are certainly hidden truths. To that extent, careful research into what is correct, which is indispensable in any case for all sorts of reasons, will ultimately benefit truth. But in an era that can no longer understand the distinction between truth and correctness, it is urgent to recall that this distinction exists. It explains why reading the ancient historians often brings us more experience of truth than reading modern historians of ancient times, and why the study of Shakespeare's tragedies and histories sometimes provides a better understanding of political phenomena than reading academic journals in political science. In any case, only the combination of the two—of insights into truths about essences and detailed knowledge of factually correct things—can produce the necessary theoretical basis for a rational politics.

3.5. MORALS AND HISTORY

The preceding reflections on historical science lead us to the problem of how the objectivity of ethics defended here is related to the obvious diversity of moral ideas seen in various cultures, as well as in the historical development of individual cultures. The fact that Kant did not take a position on this problem, indeed, that he presumed with unquestioning naiveté that the basic idea of his intentionalist and formalist universalism was to be found in all cultures, has damaged his position in a lasting way, especially after the development of historicism. To defend the idea of the objectivity of ethics, we must first acknowledge that genesis and validity have little to do with each other. Even the image of nature has developed in the course of history, but this is not by itself a proof that the modern worldview based on the natural sciences is just as well or as poorly grounded as the mythical worldview. And a person who considers this "proof" as conclusive must deal with the argument that his relativistic serenity is also a very late result of human history, and can therefore make, according to the same argument, no claim to validity. The late appearance of a certain moral position such as universalism, for instance, proves only that it is intellectually complex and genetically presupposes a great deal—like all good theories. Moreover, the history of moral consciousness is not arbitrary; a logic of development can be found within it. Piaget's work on the development of moral judgment in children[180] was continued and refined by L. Kohlberg (1983), and has been applied to the phylogenesis of human moral consciousness in the work of Apel (1988) and of Habermas (1983), for instance. The successes of this application are remarkable, even if, in my opinion, the whole program goes astray by presupposing not only a universalist but also a formalist ethics as the goal of development. On the other hand, it is a considerably more difficult task to show, on the basis of a substantive value-ethics, when and why certain goods were first found valuable; and under some circumstances to show, as well, why this experiencing of value later disappeared from history. The presupposition that there has been only moral progress is not necessarily right—however inevitable it is that those who note the social decline in the experiencing of values consider themselves and others as capable *in principle* of once again recognizing these values, against the current of their own time.

In addition, it is also the fact that the unacceptable norms of many cultures become more comprehensible if we acknowledge that they can be only partly reduced to valuative assumptions that differ from our own; and it follows immediately from the moral obligation to communicate that one must do everything one can to understand why socially valid norms deviate from ideal norms. These norms are partly based on different subsumptions and different theoretical presuppositions. We have already noted that at least some Spaniards were not certain that the natives they found in the New World were truly human beings in the full sense of the term. On the other hand, some meso-American cultures justified the practice of human sacrifice by the notion that the sun needed a constantly renewed supply of human blood—otherwise it would not continue to rise.[181] If this mythical assumption were right, we would also have to accept human sacrifice in the sense that it can be excused by a state of emergency (if we abandon the principle that

---

180. Cf. J. Piaget (1932).
181. Cf. W. Krickeberg (1961), 50: "Not an innate tendency to cruelty, but rather a fanatical belief in the duty of humans to care for the continued existence of the sun, led to human sacrifice."

human lives cannot be weighed against each other, no matter what the emergency). However, one must concede that the fascination of archaic cultures with the idea of sacrifice was probably more original than this myth, which may have been thought up precisely in order to justify the practice. Nonetheless, it is not impossible that in archaic cultures, the recognition of the idea of sacrifice contains an element of reason that is alien to our culture, but is worth more fundamental examination. I will return to this problem in chapters 4.4.3.1 and 7.3.3.2.2. Finally, many norms that seem strange to us may also be theoretically rational conditional obligations, depending on contextual conditions different from our own. For example, in the case of extremely strong drives, whose control is a relatively late achievement in human culture, only the cruelest punishments could be a deterrent. This is not to deny that there has also been an evolution of genuinely valuative feelings and thought. Valuative and theoretical thought, as well as the corresponding institutional contextual conditions, have developed in parallel and have contributed to a transformation of the moral.

3.5.1. The Greatness and Limits of Moral Evolutionism

A common objection to moral evolutionism is that it absolutizes European moral ideas and legitimates their spread to other cultures. This objection touches on a very important problem which will be discussed later in detail (for example, in chapter 8.2.1.1). Here the following hints must suffice. Obviously, this objection presupposes that European colonialism was unjust, and it needs a moral justification for this judgment. Since colonialism is an intercultural phenomenon, the objection requires an interculturally valid ethics: anyone who maintains that ethics is valid only within one's own culture cannot propose norms governing encounters between differing cultures. An interculturally valid ethics is what is at issue in this book. If, on rational grounds, ideas first developed in the European Enlightenment are part of this ethic, that is no argument against these ideas—they had to appear somewhere for the first time. No reasonable person believes that moral ideas are valid because they emerged in Europe; I am claiming only that certain ideas are valid no matter where they were developed.

Moreover, every reasonable evolutionism must recognize five restrictions. First, it is a priori just as unlikely that the factual moral ideas of even the most highly developed culture coincide with the full concept of the moral, as that even the most archaic culture lacks any embryonic form of universalism. If universalism can be grounded transcendentally, it must be present in at least a rudimentary form in every human being; and, conversely, a material ethics that strives to move beyond formalism will assume that, of the various goods and values that must be recognized, some are more likely to be found in the mores of other cultures than in modern European mores. It is obvious that the Indian caste system is incompatible with a universalist ethics. But that does not mean that there is nothing to be learned from Indian mores. The values of organic nature, which modern civilization has become so completely incapable of feeling, are present to an astonishing degree in Indian culture. The modern European morally enriches himself not only by learning to feel these concrete values again, but also by approaching the foreign culture with the desire to learn from it morally, and thus by perceiving the intrinsic value of its valuative feelings.[182] It goes without saying that this morally fruitful encounter with another culture is no more possible on the basis of a dogmatic attitude of moral superiority than on the basis of a relativism that maintains that one cannot learn from other cultures, or even that there is nothing worth learning.

Second, we must point out that the moral value of a human being is in no way identical with the value of the mores of the culture to which he belongs. A person who has the good fortune to be born into a universalist culture is "morally lucky," but that does not justify moral arrogance. Indeed, the terrible experiences of the twentieth century show only too starkly how superficial an individual's incorporation of achievements in moral culture can be, and how easily—to put it metaphorically—the moral veneer peels off. The mores of one's own culture do not replace the arduous labor involved in their existential appropriation, which must inevitably take place through the individual subject; and this appropriation can be far deeper in a representative of a less developed set of mores than in a given representative of modern universalism. Zarathustra's attitude toward women was in all likelihood not so universalistic as that of the modern petit bourgeois, but it would be grotesque to hold that the latter is a greater moral figure than Zarathustra, to whom we owe a radical advance in the development of human moral consciousness—just as it would be absurd to consider each of us a more intelligent mathematician than Theaetetus because we know several theorems that he did not know.[183] Mohammed's authorization of polygamy is not morally defensible, but one should recognize that he *limited* to four wives the prevalent polygyny of his time, so that his ruling improved the status of women in comparison to what was then usual. A shallow representative of a more developed culture and of a superficial evolutionism who travels among foreign cultures in order to lecture them on his own moral superiority deserves contempt, especially that of people among whom a partial approach to universalist ideas is still connected with great personal risk, whereas for universalists in our own culture it is socially most convenient to profess universalist ideals. If the subjectively moral value of an attitude is also measured by the magnitude of one's own interests that one sacrifices to it and the degree of personal risk that one must take for its

---

182. My underestimation of its positive aspects is the most troublesome limitation of my essay on Indian ethical life (1986). At the time, Habermas generously made a stimulating oral criticism of this essay. Debates on the issue and personal discussions with Indian colleagues—with Wittgenstein's admirable student G. Shah, for instance—and a longer stay in India forced me to make extensive corrections in my point of view. However, it was important for my own development to have initially taken a clear stance against relativism, and then, on better foundations, to grant that its motives are partially right.

183. Having pointed this out, in opposition to Hegel, is one of Kierkegaard's greatest philosophical achievements.

sake, then a universalist culture is paradoxically the most unlikely place imaginable to encounter universalist convictions of great value.

The foregoing does not alter the fact that however much we may admire subjective commitment that goes so far as self-sacrifice, in seeking to make a balanced moral judgment it is no less important to ask *for what* one sacrifices oneself. For example, J. Burckhardt goes to the opposite extreme when he denies that there has been moral progress by remarking that "We may be sure that even among the lake-dwellers men gave their lives for each other."[184] Against this view we must maintain that the pre-universalist practices of pre-modern cultures are objectively wrong. But moderate intentionalism forces us to acknowledge that these practices are not culpable if those who act in accord with them cannot be aware of any alternative. The situation is fundamentally different in the case of an anti-universalist ethics such as that of the Nazis, in which long-acknowledged universalist ideas were consciously rejected. We have already noted that even an anti-universalist can observe minimal principles of justice. Nonetheless, the difference between the genocides that have occurred repeatedly in the course of human history and that perpetrated by the Nazis remains immense. We owe to historicism the important insight that it is not easy to arrive at universalist ideas, but that does not mean that one can evade them with good conscience once they are known. The artificial atavism of various anti-universalists, from Nietzsche onward, is not the expression of an unexamined identification with the mores of one's own culture, to which universalist ideas are alien. Instead, it arises from the absolutely modern idea that one could produce out of thin air a new set of mores, and thus it is a matter of putting archaic-smelling wine into brand new bottles. The deeply repulsive aspect of modern anti-universalism becomes clear in its connection with technology. I am not making the trivial point that the increase in power brought about by modern technology makes it possible to do more objective wrong than would have been possible without it. I am instead referring to an inner contradiction in this application of technology with anti-universalist intentions. However ethically neutral technical knowledge may be, modern technology remains dependent on a *forma mentis* whose high capacity for abstraction has also produced universalism. In the combination of modern technical (including sociotechnical) knowledge and formal-universal law with archaizing rituals, a contradiction is evident that was alien to even the most brutal archaic cultures. Political practices more immoral than those of modern anti-universalism are simply inconceivable.

Third, any reasonable evolutionist would in fact concede that moral evolution involves great moral risks of both a subjective and an objective nature. The complete destruction of humanity (which can be seen as objectively wrong even before the clarification of the problem of whether there is someone to whom it can be imputed) is only possible for technological civilizations, and the subjective affirmation of anti-

---

184. (1905; 66): "Aufopferung des Lebens für andere kam gewiß schon bei den Pfahlmenschen vor." Trans. J. H. Nichols, 132.

universalism, the most terrible form of evil, presupposes a distancing from the mores of one's own culture handed down from the past, a distancing that was also the presupposition for the discovery of universalist ideas. Collective moral nihilism, which no longer feels bound to anything, is a specifically modern phenomenon that has no parallel in traditional cultures. *Corruptio optimi pessima*—the corruption of the best is the worst. Indeed, even among people who realize universalist ideals in the best possible way, a decline in the moral feelings that characterize archaic and traditional societies is, while not inevitable, very probable.[185] The wealth of sympathetic feelings that we still encounter in so-called developing countries fills the more noble persons among us with a nostalgic longing for this lost ability to share in the sufferings and joys of others. This longing is itself a kind of pain, but one that is reflective, and that cannot compare in intrinsic worth with the immediate pain of sincere compassion (among other reasons, because it is directed toward oneself). Anyone who cannot share Max Weber's deep despair regarding the impoverishment of the human soul brought about by the advance of the process of rationalization only proves how justified this despair is. For the takeover of specialists without spirit and sensualists without heart is less depressing than that "this nullity imagines that it has attained a level of civilization never before achieved."[186] Rousseauian admiration for the noble savage is not a reasonable alternative; but it is a sign of the greatness of Tacitus, Leibniz, and Vico that as convinced representatives of the Roman Empire and modern science, respectively, they were able to recognize the superiority of the barbarians at those points where it truly existed.[187]

To sum up the current point: the progress of moral consciousness toward universalism, first, is accompanied by significant losses on other moral levels, and second, is always also a progress in the opportunities for evil. To deny this would be brashly impertinent, in view of the events of the twentieth century. But to deprive oneself, on the basis of the experience of these events, of the only ethical means that would allow a judgment of the crimes peculiar to that century is not an acceptable alternative. The problem of a determination of the current situation of humanity from the point of view of a philosophy of history will be discussed in detail later on; and it goes without saying, on the basis of the first chapter of this book, that the moral-political consciousness as

---

185. Cf. Scheler (1974), 42 f.

186. Weber (1965), 189: "dies Nichts . . . sich ein(bildet), eine nie vorher erreichte Stufe des Menschentums erstiegen zu haben." Trans. T. Parsons, p. 182. Both Zamyatin and Huxley represented in the wittiest way the arrogance of a dehumanized society with regard to its primitive predecessors as well as to members of so-called primitive cultures, whether those presumed to be living on other planets, or those tolerated in reserves maintained for research purposes. Like Weber, they discern in this arrogance, which makes self-criticism impossible, one of the most disgusting traits of the process of modernization.

187. Cf. Tacitus's *Germania*, Vico's *Scienza nuova*, and Leibniz's *Nouveaus essais* I 2 § 20: "Un méchant Européen est plus méchant qu'un sauvage: il rafine sur le mal." ("A vicious European is more vicious than a savage: he is vicious in a more refined way.")

well as the institutional reality of the present-day world is not something that cannot be surpassed. However, there is much to be said for the view that in both, there is something that is, in a certain sense of the word, unparalleled: namely, moral universalism and its institutional expression in the constitutional state founded on the rule of law. My greatest concern is that in the historical cataclysms that face us, we will abandon not the self-destructive aspects of modernity, but rather precisely its universalism. That Heidegger, the deepest and most inscrutable critic of modernity, confused Nazi anti-universalism with a positive surmounting of modernity—an inexcusable error—should serve as a warning even to those for whom the Enlightenment's shallow historical optimism has become suspect or even repugnant, in view of the dangers that face us.

Fourth, it in no way follows from the affirmation of the basic idea of evolutionism that the spread of universalist ideas at any price is morally obligatory or even permissible; and thus it does not follow that, in this spread, one may make use of even a fraction of the means that were used during colonization and that rightly arouse in any decent European a deep uneasiness about his own history. In discussing the ethics of ethics, we saw that from the fact that certain norms are valid for *a*, it does not follow that any random person has a right to establish these norms for *a:* the principle of autonomy urges restraint. Yet since this principle can be understood only on the basis of a universalist ethics, the latter should not be rejected if one wants to condemn the practices of European culture that contradict this principle. And one cannot say that the violent practices of archaic cultures are absolutely all right, and at the same time campaign against the violence of the colonizers. True, one could argue to the effect that the combination of violence and hypocritical appeals to a universalist morality of Christian origin is much more objectionable than mere violence alone, but it would not be difficult to counter this argument by asking whether colonialism would have been better if such appeals, which tempered many practices, had not existed. Hypocrisy is usually a very complex phenomenon (which we will examine in chapters 6.2.2.2.3 and 6.2.2.3.1); here, suffice it to say that it is necessarily connected with moral evolution.

However, does not every representative of a universalist ethics inevitably think that this would be a better world if all cultures adopted universalist principles? In a certain sense this question must be answered in the affirmative: certain fundamental violations of elementary human rights are categorically forbidden. In any case, it is hardly bearable when people who enjoy the blessings of universalism express, out of their boredom with our culture, sympathies with the circumcision of women in African countries or with the killing of *dalits* in India, and regard them as interesting practices that are not worse but only different than our own. But this does not mean that a single form of universalism should dominate the whole world, or in any case that it must be the European-American one. Universalism can be expressed in various different forms, and their multiplicity is no doubt a value.

In order to clarify this axiological idea, on which a great deal depends, let us first examine an analogous problem that arises in discussing, not cultures, but individual persons. In every teleological ethics a role is played by the concept of the ideal, that is, an ideal state of the world that is supposed to be the objective of all moral effort. In ancient ethics, and especially in Hellenistic ethics, the elaboration of this ideal is concentrated on the image of the ideal person, that is, the so-called wise man. If it were possible to formulate the ideal of such a person, who realizes all positive values in an optimal way, would it be desirable that all human beings were like him? In my opinion, the answer must be no, for the following reasons. Such an ideal person would unite in his person not only all the values relevant for intercourse among human beings; since aesthetic and philosophical qualities, for example, are also values, he would possess them too, in their fullest form. Now it is clear, first of all, that no individual person (not to mention everyone) can have all these qualities—not merely for factual reasons, which have no role in an inquiry of the kind we are making here, but also for more fundamental reasons. Certain qualities exclude others, at least in a finite being. To give an example that is of special importance for the subject of this book: The immediate goodness and capacity for love that Christianity has declared to be the highest value are usually helpless in battling the initial assaults of evil—not, however, in overcoming evil in the long run. Conversely, those who overcome evil immediately are necessarily political men who lack the virtues praised in the Gospels. It is of little help to praise the golden mean, for it is often (not always) something mediocre that lacks the admirable aspects of *both* virtues. In dealing with a bad person, one can take a consistently hard line or turn the other cheek in the hope of shaming him; but it is not advisable to alternate between the two strategies in accord with the principle of chance. In his essay on Machiavelli, the great historian of ideas Isaiah Berlin rightly pointed to the problem discussed here, but he did not draw the right conclusion from it. He seems to think that the system of ultimate values is not consistent in itself[188]—which is obviously absurd, since in such a system everything could be proven. In truth, one can mean only two things in talking about different, mutually incompatible values. On one hand, one can maintain that "the moral" demands only consistency. Thus it would be just as moral to base a society on the values of the ancients as to base it on Christian values; what one cannot do is mix those values. Which values one decides to adopt depends on every individual's subjective assessment. On the other hand, one can understand this statement to mean that in every morally rich society, some people are guided by ancient values and some by Christian values, but it would not be possible to cultivate all values at the same time and to the same extent in a single person. However, nothing would prevent a person from admiring in others virtues that he not only did not possess but which he knew very well he could not possess without losing the ones he had. One of the most striking literary examples of this is the description of the meeting of Myriel and Napoleon in the opening pages of Victor Hugo's *Les Misérables*. The just priest is waiting in Cardinal Fesch's antechamber when Napoleon happens to come in. Myriel keeps looking at him until the annoyed emperor asks why the *bonhomme* is staring at him that way. "Your

---

188. Cf. (1980), 71: "the uncomfortable truth which Machiavelli had, unintentionally, almost casually, uncovered; namely that not all ultimate values are necessarily compatible with each other."

majesty," Myriel replies, "you are looking at a good man, and I am looking at a great man. Both of us can benefit from it."[189] Napoleon is so impressed by this answer that he has Myriel named bishop (apparently in the belief that the power associated with this office is compatible with goodness of heart). The story does not merely point to the opposition between simple goodness and historical greatness, but also vividly shows that two very different people can coincide at *one* point: they may very possibly admire each other, even if they know that they have different virtues that are in some situations even opposed to each other. However, if contradictory moral demands are not to result, it is important that such persons also take the place in society that corresponds to their virtues. A statesman may, indeed must, have virtues different from those of a priest; but he should not attempt to play the role of a priest, nor should the priest try to play the role of a statesman. But not only is it psychologically impossible that one person possess all virtues; an a priori proof of this impossibility can even be given. If someone possessed all the virtues, then he would lack the lived virtue that consists in being able to recognize without envy virtues that one does not have; therefore he would not possess all virtues. If values that result from mutual processes of recognition have a special meaning, then the various virtues must be distributed among individual persons. Finally, if all humans corresponded to the ideal, they would be copies of each other; their plurality would not have the meaning that it has where human beings differ from one another.

Analogously, we must assume that only an irreducible plurality of cultures makes possible the intercultural relationships from which actions of special value can proceed. Although partial syntheses of different cultures are possible and fruitful, a *single* world culture would probably be reduced to the lowest common denominator of a hedonistic consumerism because there would no longer be any intellectual challenges outside it. Consequently, the ideal of a single culture is extremely questionable. More reasonable is the ideal of a cosmos of different cultures that would express with increasing effectiveness the values peculiar to them, seek to overcome the disvalues they have, and be prepared to learn from each other, and, where this is not possible, to respect each other and treat each other in accord with just principles. Moreover, it is worth mentioning here the axiological principle that a whole consisting of n different goods of differing values can have a higher overall value than a whole consisting of an n-fold repetition of the good with the highest value. This idea may seem surprising, but it can be made comprehensible on the basis of Moore's principle of organic wholes and grounded in greater detail by reference to the value of the relationships that exist between the individual elements in an organized whole. Setting aside the question of the concrete decision made by members of the culture concerned, it could very well be the case that the continued existence of a culture with cultural goods of a lower value, alongside one with cultural goods of a higher value, might be better in every respect than the adoption of the latter's values by the former.

---

189. "Sire, dit M. Muriel, vous regardez un bonhomme, et moi je regarde un grand homme. Chacun de nous peut profiter" (1963; 11).

3.5.2. Moral and Religious Consciousness

The considerations in this section have to do with the historical development of moral consciousness, and thus point beyond the sphere of ethics toward that of the philosophy of history. The latter has its place in the theory of being, of ontology or metaphyics. Thus the question of the relationship between *Is* and *Ought* arises again. Here we will repeat and carry further a few brief remarks on this subject. As already discussed, it is not possible to derive *Ought* from *Is*—at least not if one takes "being" to mean the being of empirical existents. But even a two-world theory, according to which a sphere of moral obligation and a sphere of being exist independently of each other, is unsatisfactory insofar as it remains unexplained how being can be sensitive to moral demands at all. This *possibility* at least ought to be comprehensible. A philosophical *guarantee* for the triumph of moral obligation within being, in the form of a metaphysical history of success in the Hegelian or especially the Marxist mode, is not possible—at least not if one takes the history of being to be *human* history. The possibility that our species might destroy itself should be taken seriously, and cannot be excluded a priori. But if the idea of ethics is to be meaningful, then being must be structured in a particular way; it must contain beings that are at least capable of recognizing moral obligation, and whose actions are influenced by this recognition, despite all the resistance from various interests. The assumption that presuppositions concerning reality follow from the validity of moral obligation is by no means a trivial one, and in my opinion it can be understood only in the framework of an objective idealism according to which factual being takes its principles, at least in part, from ideal structures. This is not the place to analyze objective idealism in detail. However, it is not difficult to see that objective idealism has an inner relationship with certain basic assumptions of religious consciousness, and in view of the immense historical importance of religions, we must briefly discuss those aspects of the religious attitude that are relevant to morals.

Religious consciousness is obviously not identical with moral consciousness, no matter how closely related their development may be. Kantian autonomous ethics is the classic example of an areligious—not irreligious—ethics, and one cannot understand the positive achievements of the modern constitutional state if one does not acknowledge the possibility of such an ethics. Indeed, the notion that the moral law would be valid even if there were nothing but itself and the empirical world provides the basis for a special moral pathos that a naive religious person is not in a position to feel.[190] And yet reflection on morals always leads back to the question of religion, and there is much to be said for the view that if a religious renewal of humanity is to occur under the conditions of modernity, it will be ignited by this reflection. To what extent does moral

---

190. In my opinion, the myths of the conflict between heroes and gods that we find in various cultures are the first expression of the separation of the moral from the religious. See V. Hösle (1984b), 163 f.

reflection lead to religion? Reflection on the ideal validity of the moral law does not yet achieve this. Its transcendence with regard to everything empirical points to a dimension beyond the factual world, but pure transcendence, if recognized by religion at all, is certainly not enough for religion, which necessarily assumes that the transcendent is related to the world, even if it is not absorbed into it; indeed, religion is actually the attempt to explain the world on the basis of its transcendent origin. In philosophical terms, religion is concerned (at least at a certain level of its development) with the relationship between *Is* and *Ought;* and its highest task is to make humans capable of dealing with the fact that being is not as it ought to be. The function of overcoming contingency that has been ascribed to it[191] is only part of religion's basic dimension. Certainly, every religion initially deals with the aspects of our existence that we cannot control, such as birth and death, which cannot be mastered by either magical or technological practices. But religion becomes deeper when it concentrates on what escapes the application not only of means-ends rationality but also of value-rationality. The partial but nevertheless insurmountable impenetrability of being with regard to all moral attempts is one of the most powerful sources of the religious. This impenetrability includes, on one hand, evil, whose power does not contradict the validity of the moral, but must inevitably dismay anyone who is convinced of its absoluteness. But subjective evil is not the only problem that worries the moral person. The leader of a polar expedition, mentioned earlier, who discovered after the fact that the execution of a friend was unnecessary, felt something worse than remorse—he felt that he had done something objectively wrong despite all his subjectively good intentions. No one who tries to have an effect on history is spared the experience that its impenetrable complexity repeatedly turns the results of our actions into something that contradicts all human intentions—including, especially, moral intentions. In this situation, in the absence of a certain religious orientation it is difficult not to despair and to preserve a basic trust in history as a *possible* place where the moral law might be realized.

Philosophy cannot restore this believing, basic trust where it has already broken down; deep emotions cannot be elicited by arguments alone. The only thing philosophy can do is to adduce the classic theodicy argument according to which higher, subjectively moral acts cannot exist without the objectively wrong, or the act of forgiveness without evil. This is not the place to analyze this argument in greater detail. If it can be made airtight, then it has the extremely positive consequence of allowing moral persons to meet the bad and ultimately even the evil not with hatred, but with a special form of sympathy. If the bad and the evil are necessarily part of the best of all possible worlds, then we must fight against them while at the same time acknowledging that they have a positive function in being as a whole, because they alone urge us to fight for the moral, and because through this battle we can learn to become more mature and to deepen our knowledge

---

191. Cf. for instance H. Lübbe (1986), 160 ff. It is clear that on this basis Lübbe can only misinterpret theodicy as an attempt to make religion superfluous (195 ff.)

of what is morally right. In any case, we must always first try to understand how certain moral-political errors must occur as a result of human nature and history's logic of development—not in order to learn to put up with them, but because this understanding can temper our hatred and thereby make reconciliation with our opponents more probable. Particularly after the end of a confrontation, it is noble if the winner—particularly one who knows that right was predominantly on his side—does not deny the defeated opponent that partial recognition which is morally possible, and is willing to come to terms with the tolerable end to which the unfortunate episode has come. On the other hand, the grouchy bitterness of the kind of moralism that, lacking patience or humility, never forgets that something has happened that should not have happened, and ultimately does not love being because it is not the way this moralism thinks it ought to be, is morally not very convincing. Indeed, actual religions often enough add to political battle a dimension of particularly passionate hatred, which is produced by the dualistic conviction that one's own side represents pure good and the other side pure evil. In contrast, a philosophically enlightened religiousness centers on the recognition that the truly good is never completely on one side, but first arises from the conflict between the two sides. The extraordinary beauty of Abraham Lincoln's second inaugural address (4 March 1865) results from this serenity; the demand that we not be too quick to judge, in order not to be judged ourselves, and the recognition that God has his own purposes that are not fully identical with those of either side, are expressions of a deep religiousness that is independent of any church. Lincoln first wrote down such thoughts in a lonely meditation on divine will in September 1862, after the Union had suffered grave defeats on the battlefield, and it is a sign of his greatness that he publicly reaffirmed them shortly before the Union victory. In this meditation, we read that "The will of God prevails. In great contests each party claims to act in accordance with the will of God. Both may be, and one must be, wrong. God cannot be for and against the same thing at the same time. In the present civil war it is quite possible that God's purpose is something different from the purpose of either party; and yet the human instrumentalities, working just as they do, are of the best adaptation to effect his purpose. I am almost ready to say that this is probably true; that God wills this contest, and wills that it shall not end yet" (1969; 655). Similar thoughts are found at the end of the Old Testament story of Joseph, perhaps its finest part: after the father's death, the brothers fear that Joseph will now take revenge on them for what they have done to him. But Joseph knows that without their act, his rise to power and the victory over famine would not have been possible. "You intended evil against me; but God intended it for good, to do as he has done today, namely, to save the lives of many people."[192] "So now am I . . . to make ill again what God has made good?"[193]

---

192. Genesis 50:20.
193. "Und nun soll ich . . . wieder böse machen, was Gott gut gemacht?" These words are added by Thomas Mann's Joseph at the end of *Joseph and His Brothers* (1975; 1362 f.). Trans. H. T. Lowe-Porter, 1207.

It is dreadful when fascination with the theodicy argument tempts people to want to help the good, either by doing evil themselves or by leading others into temptation, in the belief that evil is the presupposition for the development of the good, or at least that familiarity with evil produces a broadened horizon that is intellectually stimulating. A person who tries to play God in this way is guilty of the greatest conceivable offense. This is the point of Werner Bergengruen's novel *Der Großtyrann und das Gericht* (*A Matter of Conscience*). However, it would be superficial to overlook the fact that this idea is a real temptation at a certain level of intelligence and reflectiveness.[194] In the work of Thomas Mann (a more refined and spiritually rich writer than Bergengruen), the despicable nature of figures ranging from Joseph to Gregorius consists precisely in this: from the outset, their conscious-unconscious goal is to make others or themselves guilty, for only from this guilt can arise the wonderful good of overcoming it. Mann's Joseph provokes both his brothers and Potiphar's wife to commit their crimes, and at the end it is consequently Joseph himself who asks—not without a certain arrogance— his brothers' pardon. Nonetheless, his intelligence and his grace counterbalance his subtle wickedness; where these virtues are lacking, this structure—because it neglects the infinite difference between the finite mind and God—becomes diabolical.

---

194. For reasons that we cannot go into here, this fascination is particularly characteristic of German culture.

II

Foundations of a Theory of the Social World

4

Man

M an is by nature a political animal. Whereas Aristotle did not yet
see human beings' political nature—as such and without further qualification—as being their specific difference, and con-
sidered other animals to be political as well,[1] the concept of the political that underlies
the present book is applicable, among all entities known to us, only to human beings.
Other animals are also *social,* but if politics has to do with the determination and implementation of state goals, then it goes without saying that creatures that act only instinctively cannot be considered political: ant colonies can neither discuss nor change
their social order.[2] Only intellectual beings that can inquire into validity can lay claim
to the predicate "political."[3] Nonetheless, the opening sentence of this chapter deliberately states that man is a political *animal,* for without the organic (or, more precisely,
the animal) basis, even intellectual beings could not be political. Indeed, if there are
purely spiritual beings (whose existence or even possibility is neither affirmed nor denied here), we cannot exclude the possibility that they might be social, get involved in
struggles for power, and wound each other psychologically. However, only organisms

---

1. Only after making his famous statement that man is by nature a political animal (ὁ ἄνθρωπος
φύσει πολιτικὸν ζῷον, *Politics* 1253a2 f.) does Aristotle explain that human speech on one hand,
and the knowledge of the useful and the harmful, the just and the unjust, on the other, are peculiarities that make humans political to a higher degree than other animals. *Lebewesen* ("living creatures")
is an incorrect German translation of the Greek word ζῷον, since for Aristotle it refers not to plants,
but only to organisms with the ability to move about—that is, animals, including human beings.
Christian sensibility hesitates to count human beings among the animals, whereas it has no similar
hesitations regarding "living creatures"; hence the translation error. On the biological context of Aristotle's statement see, for example, W. Kullman (1980).

2. Cf. J.-W. Lapierre (1968), 207 ff., one of the few works on politics that deals with its biological underpinnings.

3. Here I cannot yet examine the difficult question of what a state is. In order for all human beings to be considered political beings, the concept of the state must be very broadly conceived. On
this subject, see chap. 6 and 6.2.2.1.

can suffer physical violence, especially lethal physical violence; and lethal violence is the *ultima ratio* of politics. Mortality and the ability to kill another member of one's species on one hand, and the comprehension of the dimension of moral validity on the other, are the two conditions that must be met by a political being, and only a moral animal fulfills both conditions simultaneously. Of the creatures known to us, only humans are moral animals.

The breadth of the horizon spanned by the phenomenon of the political is astonishing—uplifting and repulsive at the same time. Whereas economic activity, for example, lacks the moral feeling that can transfigure politics, philosophy lacks the earthiness that characterizes politics because the latter is rooted in the organic. Perhaps only the erotic has comparable intensity and breadth. For the erotic also involves phenomena that are based on the biologically grounded sex drive, but can be sublimated into purely spiritual forms of expression; and in the erotic as well human beings are animals and demigods at the same time. But the biological foundation of love has to do with humans' coming into the world, whereas the biological starting point for politics is that human beings must leave this world, that they must die, and indeed that there are other members of their species who can cause them to die. Although this lends the political, in contrast to the erotic, a darker character, it gives the political a bitter dignity that the erotic often lacks. Humans come into the world through eros, not only in the sense that they owe their physical entry into the world to the erotic activities of others, but also in the sense that erotic desire opens up a new world to the person who desires. In contrast, the political keeps its eye on the gate through which human beings leave the world; it points beyond the self through its relationship with death, but also through the foundation of a sphere of the general. In fact, the second difference between the erotic and the political consists in the number of subjects who can participate in the corresponding interaction: in a happy erotic relationship that number is two; in politics, it is unlimited and potentially includes all human beings. On one hand, the intensity of the dual erotic relationship permits a closeness that politics, by its very nature, cannot offer; on the other, the responsibility one can assume with regard to other people in whom one has not the slightest reason to expect an echo of one's own soul is morally no less fascinating than erotically based action on behalf of the beloved. Finally, the enemy relationship normally associated with the political opens up a new quality of the intersubjective that is opposed to that of the erotic and requires moral regulation to a very different degree. Love can usually take care of itself and is destructive only in its aberrant forms, whereas hatred calls for moral constraint if it is not to end in annihilation and self-destruction.

The following reflections are divided into four very distinct sections—so distinct that they may even seem incompatible. The first is concerned with those aspects of the human being that have a biological basis and presents many ideas and much information drawn from sociobiology and ethology. The second section deals with the specific problem of human identity, which arises from the fact that humans are beings with self-consciousness. In a short third section, various aspects of the social anchoring of humans are discussed, which will be further examined in chapter 6. Finally, the fourth section draws a few consequences for ethics. Whereas the basic categories of the first section go back to Darwin, the second operates in the framework of a conceptual world that was decisively shaped by German idealism; the third section uses the categories of modern cultural studies and philosophy of culture, while the fourth section returns to the ethical discourse of chapter 3. Certainly there is a great tension among the three descriptive sections, which are structured according to the meta-categories of objectivity, subjectivity, and intersubjectivity. But I am convinced that this tension arises less from a weakness in the theoretical construction than from human nature itself, that peculiar intermediate nature that stands between animal and God and is a constant source of astonishment.[4] The human being is the animal that has become a problem for itself—the creature in whom the miracle of life blushes before the still greater miracle of the spirit—and much of this second miracle consists precisely in this blushing, which is to that extent a blushing at the ability to blush. It is an error to see human beings only as intellectual animals, but it is just as great an error to forget that human self-consciousness is the self-consciousness of an organism. Analogously, it is a mistake to dissolve human beings into society, but it is no less a mistake to fail to recognize that human self-consciousness could have first emerged only in society, and that even the most autonomous self-consciousness presses toward community. These tensions can in fact be rending, and not only for theoreticians of the human, but also for their object—and it is no accident that the two coincide. Human beings can thus be far greater threats than animals: aggressive persons with a pathological need for recognition are much more dangerous than even the most bloodthirsty animal. Stein, the disillusioned melancholic in Joseph Conrad's *Lord Jim*, who calls man "amazing" but denies him the predicate "masterpiece" he so willingly accords butterflies, is not without profundity.[5] But Stein is nonetheless himself a man, and since the tensions he has overcome within himself are greater than those of mere nature, in which he glimpses "the balance of colossal forces," he can be considered a masterpiece still more impressive than even the most perfect butterfly. In fact, a human being *can* arrive at a plenitude of value that is denied any animal; the unity of life and spirit, of individual and community, is not fundamentally closed to him. However, this unity is possible because on one hand life itself is closer to spirit than it seems to biologism, and on the other the spirit represents a more continuous development of life than spiritualism has assumed.

---

4. Think of Renaissance anthropology, especially Pico's *On the Dignity of Man* (*De hominis dignitate*). However, no one more deeply understood the greatness and misery of human beings in their inner relationship than did Pascal, who was as great an anthropologist as he was a poor philosopher of religion. He rightly asks: "Tant de contradictions se trouveraient-elles dans un sujet simple?" ("Could it be that so many contradictions are found in such a simple subject?"). And he states: "L'homme n'est ni ange ni bête, et le malheur veut que qui veut faire l'ange fait la bête" (1982; 226 f.) ("Man is neither angel nor animal, and unfortunately a person who tries to act like an angel ends up acting like an animal.")

5. J. Conrad (1988), 133 f.

4.1. The Human and the Organic

Long before ethology and sociobiology, humanity knew that politics had an animal basis. The fable is the literary genre in which the relationship between the political and the animal was expressed early in human history. The fables of the *Pañcatantra,* for example, produced, according to the frame story, a quick and salubrious effect on unfit princes, and European fable literature, too, constantly alludes to the basic problems of politics. "In fact, a clear and plausible theory of politics and international law can be drawn from one of the classical fable books of Aesop and La Fontaine."[6] The various animal epics and romances about Reynard the Fox from the Middle Ages up to Goethe provide a further example of this relationship perceived long ago; George Orwell's *Animal Farm* is a prominent twentieth-century example. In almost every period metaphors drawn from the world of animals have been among those most favored in political discourses.[7] The behavior of animals is constantly proposed as a model for statesmen,[8] and political phenomena are represented in the form of mythical beasts such as Leviathan and Behemoth. It is particularly remarkable that half-human, half-animal creatures like the Centaur or the Minotaur again and again symbolize something political.[9]

The popularity of political fables also proceeds from the fact that they offer a way of criticizing without directly wounding. But it would be insufficient to refer to this formal ground alone; clearly something basically animal-like was always perceived in the way human beings exercise power, and especially in their use of force.[10] Nonetheless, there is a fundamental difference between the political fable and modern ethology: fables are primarily concerned with attributing human traits to animals and only secondarily with using animal behavior to comment on human behavior; whereas ethology's goal is to interpret as objectively as possible organic, and especially animal, behavior, which may then shed some light on human behavior. Ethology clearly has an advantage on purely formal grounds: it avoids the vicious circle that is basic to the fable, since the latter really

---

6. See Schmitt (1938), 77: "Man kann in der Tat an der Hand eines der klassischen Fabelbücher von Aesop und Lafontaine eine klare und einleuchtende Theorie der Politik und des Völkerrechts entwickeln."

7. See F. Rigotti (1992), 117 ff. The same author refers to Churchill's witty "disarmament fable" of 24 October 1928 (1974; 4520–4522).

8. See Sun-tzu (1988), 63; (1989), 83.

9. See Machiavelli, *Principe* 18.2 (1986; 155 f.); B. de Jouvenel (1945), 11 ff.

10. See Machiavelli, loc. cit.: "Dovete adunque sapere come sono dua generazione di combattere: l'uno con le leggi, l'altro con la forza: quel primo è proprio dello uomo, quel secondo è delle bestie: ma, perché el primo molte volte non basta, conviene ricorrere al secondo. Pertanto, a uno principe è necessario sapere bene usare la bestia e l'uomo." ("You must know, then, that there are two methods of fighting, the one by law, the other by force: the first method is that of men, the second of beasts; but as the first method is often insufficient, one must have recourse to the second. It is therefore necessary for a prince to know well how to use both the beast and the man." Trans. L. Ricci and E. R. P., Vincent, 64.)

does not leave the sphere of the human. It is true, however, that this circle points to an insight that in ethology, notwithstanding all its achievements, is often virtually forgotten, namely, that human behavior, despite its animal basis, has certain peculiarities that are not found in any other animal, and that transform the nature of the characteristics that human beings share with other animals. The sex drive is not known to human beings alone; but the fact that a human being is a person among other persons, and that he can ask moral questions, also transforms the immediate feeling of the sex drive in a subtle and momentous way. The human being is by no means the only animal that kills other members of its species, but cruelty, that is, the imperiling, harming, and ultimately killing of others in connection with a battle for recognition, is just as specifically human as is the capacity for forgiveness. To this extent, Hobbes's famous sentence, *homo homini lupus*,[11] is, depending on the circumstances, both an expression of excessive pessimism and a way of playing down the situation (or a slandering of wolves).[12] More profound are the metaphors that find statesmen or state power a composite of animal and human— the decisive difference between the Centaur and the Minotaur consisting in the fact that in the former a human head rises over an animal body, whereas in the latter the human organism is put in the service of an animal command center. The image of the Centaur is realistic: that the spirit cannot fully free itself from its animal basis will be recognized by anyone who is concerned with political anthropology. On the other hand, the image of the Minotaur is terrifying; it may symbolize the modern totalitarian state, in which specifically human achievements such as modern technology and modern law are subordinated to the most brutal instincts.

In order to answer the question "What is a human being?" we must first determine more precisely the place of humans in the whole realm of the organic. This already follows from the fact that the true is indeed the whole, and that the essence of a thing can be grasped completely only by considering its relation to the whole. It is true, however, that the finite nature of human knowledge constantly forces us to violate this principle; without abstracting from the whole, local advances in knowledge cannot be achieved. Thus in the framework of this book the particular nature of ideal being must be ignored as well as that of inorganic being. We cannot, however, completely disregard organic being: first, because without a knowledge of certain general organic types of behavior much of human political behavior must remain unexplained, and second, because the intellectual dimension of human beings, which cannot be reduced to the vital, must be wrung from the organic through constantly renewed efforts. In addition, the ecological problem is one of the most urgent problems of present-day politics, and since it is probable that our current practical deficits have to do with the abstract opposition between human beings and nature that began in the seventeenth century, a re-situation

---

11. (1839 ff. b), 2.135.

12. Hobbes knew this, of course. See *De homine* chap. 10.3 (1839 ff. b; 2:91). A similar observation is found in Augustine *De civitate Dei* XII 23.

of human beings in their natural surroundings would be helpful in resolving this problem, even if many people find it objectionable. The fact that humanity must not fall short in undertaking this is proven by the great example of Herder's *Ideen zur Philosophie der Geschichte der Menschheit.*[13]

4.1.1. The Nature of the Organic

What is an organism? Unlike numbers, concepts, or ideally valid values, organisms are first of all *real* entities. Real being is characterized by certain properties that cannot be attributed to ideal being, of which spatiality and temporality are the most fundamental. Whereas the question "Where is it now?" makes no sense when asked about the number five, it is completely appropriate to ask it about most real entities—for example, about an elementary particle, a cat, or an artifact. Not about all real entities, however, because mental states (which constitute the third world, and in any case do not belong to the ideal world) are determined only temporally, and not spatially; only the body, which is correlated with the mind, is determined spatially. Thus it is not meaningful to ask "Where are A's phantom pains?" (though one can ask "Where are the parts of the brain that are responsible for phantom pains?"), but the question "When did these phantom pains occur?" remains a legitimate one. To this extent, in the real world temporality has an even more important status than spatiality, and the most significant differences between individual structures in the real world arise from their differing relationships to time. The deep ontological meaning of time, its inner relationship with the concept of being, has paradoxically to do with the fact that time endangers the property that traditional metaphysics was most prone to associate with being: duration. Ideal entities are what they are, without any possible dissolution; real entities are time-bound and transitory,[14] and the various modes of this transitoriness constitute the various strata of being. However, it would be one-sided to view real being as determined solely by its spatiality and temporality, that is, by its transitoriness. Even though every natural *thing* is transitory, it passes away in accord with certain *laws,* and the most general natural laws are themselves neither temporal nor spatial.[15] In the shape of these laws, something general appears in nature that is more than the sum of the individual things. As we will see later, in the course of development temporality penetrates being ever more deeply, while on the other hand real being displays the ability to bring forth

---

13. Among more recent works interpreting the philosophy of history as a continuation of natural philosophy, L. A. White's (1959) is particularly impressive.

14. The "alwaysness" (*Immerigkeit*) of space, time, and energy cannot be discussed here.

15. There are in addition laws that come into effect only at a specific point in the development of the cosmos. For example, Kepler's laws were not valid before the planets existed, but they follow from the law of gravity and antecedent conditions, and if the idea of explanation is to remain meaningful, there must have been laws from the beginning.

concrete structures, such as human thought, that are general in nature: this twofold tendency produces new modes of being.

Even more important than duration is another category, which is endangered by time as well, but is also first constituted by it in many of the forms in which it appears: identity. We will need to discuss this category in detail, along with that of the identity crisis. Admittedly, the category of identity crisis is paradoxical, for one of the basic axioms of metaphysics holds that each being is self-identical. How then can identity enter into a crisis? Clearly we cannot speak of an identity crisis in the case of ideal objects; their formal identity with themselves is a tautology. However, the real identity of real objects is no longer so obvious, precisely because it is endangered by time. By real identity we mean here first of all the preservation of a certain form realized in matter over a certain span of time. Real objects of the second world are always a unity of form and matter— such that the specific unity they represent at any given moment can be dissolved under the impact of outside influences and be transformed into another.

What is ontologically new in the organic mode of being[16] consists in the fact that an organism on one hand governs its self-preservation as such (but does not necessarily *will* this self-preservation, since it is still not clear that an interior dimension exists); on the other hand, this has become significantly more difficult than in the case of the inorganic. The organism does not leave to the environment alone attacks on the specific unity of matter and form it represents, but in a certain sense undertakes them itself: its extraordinarily complex form, which is distinguished by a particularly purposeful relationship between whole and parts, can survive only through metabolism, that is, through the exchange of matter. The exceptional improbability of the organism's organization can only be explained by assuming that it increases entropy around itself and constantly transforms new matter into its form. This means that on one hand the organism, as an open system in a steady state, is constantly changing the corporeal substance of which it consists—after a certain point one can hardly continue to speak of an identity of matter, but the form remains the same.[17] On the other hand, form's independence of matter in this case is only partial, for even if matter is rejected, other matter must be taken on—form has freed itself from this specific matter, not from matter itself. Indeed, in a certain sense the organism is even more dependent on matter than is the inorganic, since it constantly needs new matter; it not only *can* but *must* exchange its matter. Thus its self-preservation is not something obvious, but rather a task that it can carry out only if it is affected by its environment and acts upon it. The desired states that control its behavior cannot be determined, as in the case of a thermostat, without taking into account what is essential for its survival; rather, they are directly related to the latter. To this extent, every organism is a self-referential system that represents in itself

---

16. Here I am basically following Jonas (1966), who does not take reproduction seriously into account, however. I am also indebted to many stimulating discussions with D. Wandschneider and to his articles.

17. Here I am ignoring processes of growth and especially metamorphoses.

its own peculiar conditions, such as lack of food. The relationship between the organism's form and its self-preservation and exchange of matter is detailed: the organism and its organs take the form that is most useful to them in carrying out their task of exchanging their matter and thus ensuring their survival. Each organ serves the survival of the whole and at the same time its own survival; through a kind of feedback causality, each organ produces effects on itself. This is the foundation of the teleonomy that characterizes the organic world.

Because of its dependency on finding additional food, organic being is transitory in a sense completely different from that in which the inorganic is transitory. Its transitoriness is not only the possible result of outside attacks, but can also be a consequence of the outside world's refusal: the organism can die of hunger. Its mode of existence is essentially precarious, because it has detached itself from the homogeneity of inorganic being and yet remains dependent upon its environment. It is no longer a question of the indifference of inorganic being with regard to its environment, with which it belongs to *a single* world; the matter-exchanging organism is a self that must distinguish itself from an environment and yet can only survive in this environment. With mortality, transitoriness enters a new dimension: insofar as the organism itself has made an effort to preserve its form, the latter's destruction is incomparably harder than the disintegration of an inorganic molecule. In more highly developed organisms, temporality and even death are internalized; the organism ages, and death no longer comes only as a result of outside attacks or a lack of food. Because of its unavoidable mortality, the organic mode of being is dependent on reproduction; without reproduction, this mode of being could not have been maintained. Substances that replicate themselves need material, of course, in order to produce copies of themselves. Replication radicalizes the emancipation of form from matter and its simultaneous dependency on matter, which characterizes organic being. On one hand, the self-replicating substance frees itself not only from individual bits of matter that are exchanged in the process of metabolism, but also from the individuals that are its bearers at any given time: it is general, like natural laws, but unlike them it is simultaneously real in something individual. It is no longer a question of an individual organism, but rather of copies of the self-replicating substance in as many organisms as possible. On the other hand, this also means a further increase in the organism's dependency on matter: there are now many organisms that must be nourished. In this way, purposeful form, metabolism, reproduction, and mortality constitute the mutually inseparable essential characteristics of living beings.

Self-replicating substance is one of the most fascinating structures of reality. Not only does the adventure of living depend upon it, but completely independently of later developments, the first replicators, the predecessors of the present DNA molecules, have a very special ontological status. They repeat themselves—they represent in reality the reflexivity that enjoys a favored status in foundational terms, and that plays the central role within the ideal world. Precisely because they reflect a particularly remarkable ideal structure, replicators are axiologically superior to molecules that do not reproduce themselves. But they are also ontologically superior; because they replicate themselves, they have, when they find sufficient food, a tendency to spread. This proposition is tautological, and so is the further observation that the success of a replicator in spreading depends upon its longevity, the speed of its reproduction, and how accurately it copies itself. After a certain time, a replicator possessing these characteristics will be more numerous than one that lacks them. Of course, imprecise replication—that is, copying errors that slip into the process—may lead to the development of a molecule that has these characteristics in an even higher degree. Competition then arises between different replicators, in particular for the material they need in order to reproduce themselves. This competition necessarily leads to the dying out of the less fit replicators, that is, those that are less adapted to the conditions of their environment. For instance, it favored the replicators that succeeded in developing a protein wall that protected them from other replicators, so that the latter could not break them up in order to construct out of them copies of themselves. To be sure, it is not easy to recognize as an objective fact this brutal competition—which ultimately becomes a competition among higher organisms of the same species. But it is easy to see that it necessarily results from the success of life: because the replication of these molecules is so successful, they ultimately compete with each other; since the productivity of life has no internal limit, other lives inevitably must limit life.

4.1.2. Ethics and Sociobiology

The preceding line of thought applies the basics of the Darwinian theory of evolution to the first replicators. In my presentation, I have followed chiefly the second chapter of R. Dawkins's book *The Selfish Gene* (1976), which not only discusses the discoveries and insights of sociobiology in a knowledgeable and penetrating way, but also deals with the general mechanisms of evolution, which according to the author determine the development of the world from the first replicators, through the organic "survival machines" programmed by the genes, and on to the highest forms of culture. It is precisely this comprehensive perspective that makes his book interesting for theoretical philosophy. Sociobiology is of special interest for ethics, however, because it offers a causal explanation for genetically determined behavior in all organisms, and thus in human beings as well; Dawkins's book deals with the biology of selfishness and altruism. This explanation sheds light on many social phenomena observed by animal sociologists and anthropologists and also has a more fundamental significance that is already implicit in the foregoing remarks on replicators. The crucial point of sociobiology—a discipline that has been systematically outlined by E. O. Wilson, for example—consists in a rejection of the assumption of classical ethology, which we find in K. Lorenz and I. Eibl-Eibesfeldt, that in evolution a certain behavior may be selected because it is for the good of the species. This thesis is countered by the insistence that there is no group selection, and that the gene is the fundamental unit of selection. This objection is founded on the following simple and effective argument: It is true that a group whose members sacrifice themselves for each other[18] in an emergency may have advantages over other groups in which this kind of behavior is unknown. However, the problem is that the members of such a group would have no survival advantage over other members of their own group whose genes determine their behavior in such a way that they take advantage of the others' self-sacrifice without sacrificing themselves when their turn comes. In short, genes for selfish behavior would necessarily prevail over genes for undifferentiated altruistic behavior—where "altruistic" designates a type of behavior that is useful to other organisms, even though it decreases the chances of reproducing the organism's own genes in the largest possible number. A gene that programs a type of behavior that leads to the greatest possible replication of this gene no matter what the cost has an undeniable advantage in terms of natural selection over genes that do not: this is the *tautology* behind the sociobiological criticism of classical ethology, which cannot be rejected precisely because it is an analytical truth. However, the tautological character of this proposition should make us skeptical regarding the wide-ranging consequences drawn from it: tautologies cannot be falsified, but neither can they provide the foundation for radically new orientations.

To be sure, sociobiologists do not deny that there is animal behavior that seems altruistic and may even include self-sacrifice for another member of the species—the extreme form of altruism. Their explanation for this kind of behavior, in its most general form, was first given by W. D. Hamilton. It goes like this: For each level of relatedness, there is a specific degree of probability that a gene found in a given individual will also be found it one of its relatives. Between parent and child, for example, this probability, the so-called "coefficient of relationship" is one-half, while between first cousins it is one-eighth, and so on. From this it follows, *ceteris paribus,* that a gene that programs a parent to sacrifice himself for three of his children has a good chance of prevailing, for even if the gene is lost once in this way, it is still preserved on average 1.5 times. In the case of a parent's sacrificing himself for his child, as a rule the gene has a greater probability of surviving than in the opposite case—at least when the children have a greater life expectancy and a greater likelihood of reproducing than do their parents; this must be taken into account in addition to the coefficient of relationship and provides the basis for an advantage of the future over the past. Indeed, there can be no doubt that most altruistic behavior in the animal world occurs among family members. Thus it is hardly an accident that with the exception of termites, all social insects, which are usually considered the model of self-sacrifice for the sake of the community, belong to the order of hymenoptera. As is well known, the males are haploid, so that the coefficient of relationship between sisters is three-fourth: the latter are more closely related to each other than the mother is to her children, so that in the sense of genetic selfishness it is much more rational for "workers" to care for sisters than to reproduce themselves. The

---

18. Naturally, classical ethologists also called this kind of behavior only "analogous to human morality," not "moral." For morals presuppose a behavior that is independent of purely genetic determination.

second possible explanation for altruistic behavior is connected with the advantages of mutual altruism in terms of natural selection. Mutual altruism may occur between individuals of the same species as well as between individuals of different species (in the form of symbiosis). When the utility an individual receives from others is larger than the expenditure he makes for it, then cooperative behavior can develop—only, however, when there are sanctions against freeloaders who take advantage of others' altruism without practicing altruism themselves.

The necessity of sanctions leads us to a very important concept in sociobiology, which we owe to J. Maynard Smith: the concept of "evolutionarily stable strategies." Maynard Smith applies ideas borrowed from game theory to the evolution of behavioral strategies, showing that certain strategies, precisely those that are evolutionarily stable, cannot in principle be bettered by any other strategy. Which strategy is evolutionarily stable depends on the possible strategies of others; it cannot be determined without taking them into account. Two examples may clarify the basic idea.[19] We already mentioned the development of mutual altruism. Suppose a population of a species of bird consists of individuals who remove parasites from each others' heads that cannot be reached with their own bills. Then, through chance mutation, an individual emerges that allows others to preen it, but does not preen others. Obviously, such an individual has advantages over the others—he expends less time and energy. His payoff, that is, his chance of leaving genes in the gene pool, is larger. (The precise metrical determination of this payoff would depend on numerous surrounding conditions; it is not important that it be precisely determined here, since we are concerned only with the basic idea.) Therefore, genes of this type, which we may call the "cheat," will inevitably spread at the expense of those of the other type, which we may call the "sucker," especially since the payoff of the cheat will always be larger than that of the sucker, whatever the ratio—which continuously increases to the advantage of the cheat—between the two types. From this it follows that the cheats will finally prevail completely at the expense of the sucker, and of course this will mean their end, if we presuppose that this act of mutual altruism is necessary for survival. This sad fate can be prevented only if a third strategy develops, which we will call that of the grudger. By this term we refer to individuals who, like the sucker, preen other members of the species—with the exception of those who have acted as cheats with regard to them. This kind of strategy is formally more complex than the two others, because it does not prescribe a single type of action, but rather makes the individual's own behavior dependent upon that on the opposite side; it is called a "conditional strategy." In addition, this kind of strategy can only develop in a species in which individuals have the ability to recognize each other as specific individuals. The strategy of the grudgers will then prove, at least when the individuals adopting it constitute a certain percentage of the population, to be superior to that of the cheats, whose percentage will inevitably decline. Moreover, this strategy is

---

19. See R. Dawkins (1976), 198 ff., 74 ff., and, for the second example, J. Maynard Smith (1982), 11 ff.

evolutionarily stable insofar as strategies such as those of the suckers and the cheats are unable to infiltrate it once it is established. However, the cheat's strategy is also evolutionarily stable, for if a population consists chiefly of cheats, then neither the sucker nor the grudger have any chance of penetrating it: the success of the grudgers depends upon their meeting a sufficient number of others who are grudgers. Thus there can be several evolutionarily stable strategies, and the evolutionary stability of a strategy in the sense defined above does not in any way exclude the possibility that those who follow it will destroy themselves. What is essential is that even if the payoff for cheats is very small, in a population in which they are dominant this payoff is higher than that for the grudgers and the suckers. Finally, it is very interesting what must happen in a population with a large number of suckers, a minority of grudgers that exceeds the critical frequency, and a similarly large minority of cheats. Obviously, the cheats must increase very much at the expense of the sucker; the latter will soon become extinct. But at the same time this sets off the revenge of the grudgers: the latter slowly but steadily increase in number until they alone remain. It is important to note here that the large number of suckers at first imperils the chances of survival of the grudgers, because it favors the increase of cheats.

The second example is related to differing strategies, not with respect to altruistic behavior, but rather to aggressive behavior. We will call "hawks" those members of a population who fight hard in conflicts and retreat only if they are seriously wounded, and we will call "doves" those who only threaten but never wound. The number of points that may be scored by the various possible outcomes—victory, defeat with serious wounds, defeat without wounds (whose cost consists only in a loss of time)—could be +50, −100, and −10, respectively; these payoffs are largely arbitrary, but clarify our thinking when we use them in our calculations. Which strategy is evolutionarily stable, that of the hawks or that of the doves? As can be easily seen, neither is evolutionarily stable: on one hand, hawks could immediately force their way into a population consisting of doves. The net payoff of the doves is the average of the two possible results, (50 − 10 = 40 and −10, for an average of 15) , whereas the hawks will always achieve a payoff of 50. However, if hawks spread, difficulties arise for them: if a hawk encounters a dove, he immediately wins out over it; but if he encounters another hawk, one of them will always be seriously wounded. In a population consisting solely of hawks, on the other hand, a hawk's payoff will be the average of 50 and −100, that is, −25, and that is smaller than the payoff of a dove in the same population, which is 0. So what will happen? There might be oscillations, but more likely is the development of a stable ratio of hawks and doves in which the average payoff for each is the same. (In terms of the point system given above, the ratio would be 7:5.) Alongside this kind of stable polymorphism in the population's gene pool, it would also be conceivable—strictly mathematically speaking—that each individual uses both strategies in the same ratio of 7:5, that is, out of twelve cases, he would use the hawk strategy seven times and the dove strategy five times. Obviously it would be important that the shift from one strategy to another be governed by a random mechanism; in any case the opponent must not know in advance which strategy one intends to use; otherwise, it would be rational for him to use the hawk strategy only when the other had decided to use the dove strategy. However, there is also another, considerably simpler strategy, which is almost evolutionarily stable: this is the one that might be called the "retaliator" strategy. An individual who uses this strategy is one who acts like a hawk when he is attacked, but like a dove when he encounters a dove or another individual using the retaliator strategy. This is also a conditional strategy.

If we accept the basic principles of the synthetic theory that combines genetics with Darwinism, we have to acknowledge that the sociobiological criticism of earlier ethology is compelling; and the reference to the connection between two characteristics so rare as haplodiploidy and the extreme sociality of hymenoptera will fail to please only someone for whom prejudices are more important than intellectual curiosity. The status of the Darwinian theory of evolution from the point of view of the theory of science cannot be examined here.[20] Even if the theory is a magnificent scientific achievement, which managed to *explain* many facts that pre-Darwinian biology could only *describe*, and whose importance moreover goes far beyond biology, two problem areas must be mentioned that require further reflection. First of all, the relationship between genotype and phenotype must be conceived neither so atomistically nor so one-sidedly as some sociobiologists suppose.[21] The genes not only fix the phenotype (many genes having polyphenic effects, and most characteristics being polygenetically determined); in addition, the already existing phenotype influences which gene manifests itself and in what form. In this connection we should refer to the opposition between gradualists and punctualists among theorists of evolution: it is not immediately clear how trans-species evolution is supposed to have occurred solely on the basis of gradual changes (no doubt numerous)—what good would a proto-wing or *one* wing have done a reptile? Individual gene complexes might be responsible for meta-characteristics such as symmetry and even for whole construction plans, so that sudden leaps could have led to the emergence of new forms. In addition, the phenomenon of gene coupling indicates that the atomistic model should give way to a more holistic one.[22] This could have consequences for sociobiology, which always considers individual strategies of behavior in isolation and compares their advantages for survival, although it is well aware that selection always takes place in the phenotype of the genome. Since the individual organism is a unity in a deeper ontological way than the gene, it could be that genes that program a particularly brutal way of pursuing an individual's own interest are usually coupled with others that give the corresponding organism disadvantages. At the moment there is no

---

20. Cf. V. Hösle (1988), 356 ff., especially on the unjustly criticized tautological elements in the theory of evolution. (These elements correspond in large measure to Spinoza's theory of science.)

21. Here I am setting aside the not inconsiderable difficulties involved in defining the concept of "gene."

22. The demand for a fundamental holism has also become stronger in physics, especially because of the empirically proven Einstein-Podolsky-Rosen correlations. See H. Primas (1992).

evidence for this assumption, but the possibility cannot be excluded. There may be less chance than Darwin thought, and natural laws may still be discovered that limit chance more than we now suppose.

The second objection is significantly more important. Not only the success of modern cybernetics, but also theoretical arguments speak against an interactionist solution of the mind-body problem. By this we mean that propositions such as "Because the animal was hungry, it looked for prey" should either be interpreted in such a way that the word "hungry" denotes a physiological, not a psychological condition, or else be translated into the corresponding physiological propositions. For it is not clear how, without violating the basic conservation laws of physics, something psychic can cause something physical. However, the rejection of interactionism leads to a major problem for the theory of evolution: since survival advantages are related solely to physical behavior, and since the latter can be caused only by physical, and not psychic, processes, how can we explain the evolution of the psychic, which we are unlikely to contest in the way Descartes did? If we acknowledge that part of evolution cannot be explained by Darwin's principles, we will perhaps also be inclined to consider whether some so-called expressive behavior— such as the singing of birds, in which a subjective state seems to be expressed—belongs to that excess of evolution that Darwinian principles cannot explain.[23] But here we are only alluding to problem areas that cannot be discussed in greater detail. In the following pages I will therefore proceed as if the assumptions of sociobiology were beyond doubt.

After this exposition of some of sociobiology's basic ideas, the question arises: What does all this have to do with a book on ethics? Since there is no doubt that normative propositions do not follow from descriptive propositions, and since in my view not even propositions concerning the general social recognition of certain norms can ground their ideal validity, it is superfluous to emphasize that it cannot be a question, for instance, of pleading for social Darwinism on the basis of sociobiology. Such "arguments" are ridiculous even from a formal point of view: the fact that a certain behavior is widespread among organisms has no significance for the norms that ought to govern human action; and, from the point of view of content, such ideologies tend to degrade human beings to the level of other animals and to play down the achievement of cultural evolution. Nevertheless, ethics can certainly learn from sociobiology, on two sharply distinguished levels. First, we have already seen that descriptive premises also enter into a practical syllogism. Knowledge about human behavior is also indispensable

---

23. It is Popper's special merit to have drawn attention to the incompatibility of Darwinism and epiphenomenalism (Popper and Eccles [1977], 72 ff.). But whereas he derives a form of interactionism from this observation, I would rather abandon Darwinism's claim to explain everything. To be precise, one must say that a non-interactionalist Darwinism cannot explain how interiority comes about, although it does not exclude this possibility. But in any case Darwinism can no longer claim to explain the most important characteristics of the organic. It is obvious that materialistic epiphenomenalism does not do justice to the inner logic of the psychic; my criticism of interactionism should therefore not be interpreted as a commitment to epiphenomenalism. *Tertium datur*, as Leibniz, for instance, shows in his criticism of Descartes.

if one believes that this behavior is immoral and therefore should be changed as much as possible, for at least we know in this way what we should oppose. Even on the descriptive level it is obvious that human behavior is by no means determined genetically in every respect; a simple transfer of sociobiological insights into anthropology is therefore absurd. However, it should be considered proven that human behavior is partly determined by genetic programs—though the precise determination of this part is a matter of controversy. (Even if a very large part of human behavior is genetically determined, we should not forget that the environment to which human beings had to adapt was an environment shaped by culture.) Even if one is inclined to think that in theory reason gives every human being the ability to act against his genetic programming, it is unquestionably true that this requires a conscious effort; it is therefore important to discover which genetic mechanisms predispose us, *ceteris paribus,* toward which kinds of behavior. It has to be conceded that no altruistic behavior that disadvantages an individual's own genes can result from evolution in a Darwinian sense, and that therefore altruistic behavior can have a *genetic* basis only if it is limited to relatives or is strictly mutual. This may be disappointing, but this assertion has to be qualified in three ways. First, the expression "selfish gene" is misleading insofar as genes cannot, of course, have intentions—they only behave *as if* they had an intention (namely, to maximize their chances of reproducing themselves). An interior dimension, which is a necessary condition for the emergence of intentions, can be attributed only to organisms as a whole (at which level of the organic remains an open question); only they can be described as subjects.[24] These subjects may in fact sacrifice themselves, as we have seen, if only for their relatives, but the overcoming of the immediate drive to self-preservation that the genes require of the individual organism remains a sacrifice, even if this strategy must be beneficial for the reproduction of the genes in order to be preserved in the evolutionary process. In fact, the opposition between the classical thesis, which maintains that animal behavior serves to preserve the species (and which is indefensible in this form) and the basic thesis of sociobiology is less crude than is often thought, since according to both theses the organism serves something general that transcends it—for the older theory, this is the species, while for sociobiology it is the individual's own genes. Even if these genes are less general than the species, they are still more general than the individual organism. According to sociobiology, only genes are selfish, not organisms—the selfishness of the former can promote altruism on the part of the latter, even if this altruism is necessarily limited.[25] (This is a crucial point, to which I will

---

24. Seeing organisms as machines that are moved by genes according to their own interests is a strange form of animism, which ascribes intentions to entities that most certainly do not have them, and which follows from the atomistic error that the original and primitive, not the complex and developed, are ontologically decisive.

25. See K. Bayertz's introduction to the volume of essays he edited (1993): "*Phenotypical altruism* can be interpreted as a *genotypical selfishness.* Altruism and selfishness are not mutually exclusive; they coincide in certain ways."

return later.) Second, it is therefore entirely comprehensible that among human beings cultural evolution was ultimately able to lead to the idea of a universal altruism: an inclination to limited altruism, and even to heroic self-sacrifice for one's closest relatives, is genetically given, and nothing prevents us from assuming that there is a genetic disposition to act on behalf of others if doing so does not limit one's own chances of reproducing. Nevertheless, the universalistic extension of altruism is undoubtedly a *cultural* achievement indebted to the horizon of the general that reveals itself within the human mind, though it can still be connected with something genetically given. In fact, another phenomenon proves that human behavior is not bound by the guidelines of genetic selfishness: the phenomenon of malice. If we take the latter to be a type of behavior that harms others but is not advantageous to oneself, and may even be disadvantageous, then, third, it becomes immediately clear that malice cannot be the result of genetic evolution: it is as much a human peculiarity as is universal brotherly love. On one hand, the lack of such a genetic legacy is comforting; on the other, the (always only partial) excuse that a bad person might offer by referring to the power of natural evolution ceases to be available.[26]

In view of the genetic predispositions that can be overcome only slowly and through an enormously laborious cultural evolution, it is hardly surprising that the mores (*Sittlichkeit*) of most cultures, even if they recognize in abstract form norms arising from the moral principle, are also determined by social norms whose evolution can be explained in sociobiological terms.[27] On one hand, this holds true for nepotism in the broader sense, that is, for the privileging of relatives, which in most cases goes far beyond what can be justified also on universalist grounds (see chapter 3.2.1). For relationships within a (usually genetically related) group, norms are recognized that differ from those recognized for relationships with the out-group—this fundamental principle of various tribal mores is probably based, though not exclusively, on biology. On the other hand, we must take into consideration the sexual ethics that in so many cultures treat the two sexes quite differently. After the loss of isogamy (one of those breaks of symmetry that are responsible for the complexity and beauty of the world), males, because of their numerous small and motile gametes, can have significantly more offspring than females. Their reproductive strategies will thus be different from those of females, who cannot increase the success of their genes by frequently changing their sexual partners, and therefore generally have a stronger desire for long-term relationships. Moreover, since the male cannot be sure that he is the father of the children born of the female,

---

26. Since the phenotypical manifestation of genes also depends on the corresponding environmental conditions, we cannot exclude the possibility that genes that in primeval times determined something quite different ended up predisposing individuals to adopt malicious types of behavior. Moreover, we have to concede that dysteleological elements can establish themselves in genes—but because of accidents, not because of a selection pressure in this direction.

27. On this subject, see C. Vogel's remarkable book (1989), on which I have drawn again and again (see especially 34 ff.).

biological evolution favors the male's control over his female partner's sexual behavior. It is easy to recognize the continuing effects of these strategies in human societies as well. Once again: principles of justice undoubtedly demand that the double standard employed in evaluating male and female sexual behavior be overcome; but sociobiology can help us understand why it is so difficult to do so and why it has been overcome only in a few parts of the world.[28]

But the contribution of sociobiology to ethics is not limited to such descriptive propositions. On the contrary, the concept of evolutionarily stable strategies has, second, a fundamental significance at the *normative* level of ethical theory as well. After all the criticism of the naturalistic fallacy, this may be surprising, but it follows from the postulate of universalizability, from the principle that what ought be ought to *be,* and also from the fact that the concept of evolutionarily stable strategies is in no way specific to biology, but plays a role in every kind of evolution, including cultural evolution.[29] To take the last point first, it is obvious that there are certain analogies between biological and cultural evolution.[30] Cultural innovations (which may of course be voluntary) correspond to mutations, and the tendency of cultural artifacts to spread corresponds to biological replication—in fact, this sort of tendency is still more important in them than in genes. As entities of the second world, genes have their own being, whereas the being of the entities of the fourth world is dependent upon subjects who understand them. When the last representative of a given theory or norm dies, the underlying theory or norm dies with him; it can survive only if it has already been internalized by other subjects.[31] Since the receptive ability of any human being is limited, and since certain theories may even be incompatible and thus cannot be simultaneously considered as true, it is inevitable that they will also be in competition, even though the fourth world, because of its peculiar ontological status, inevitably manifests itself as competition between different human beings trying to establish their theories. When differing entities are competing for resources that are scarce but crucial for survival—whether these are matter or attention— then only those who can prevail over their competitors can survive, and this tautology holds for both biological and cultural evolution. Thus, for instance, one of the elements

---

28. At the most, sociobiological arguments can lead us to consider a diminution of guilt, though even this is questionable in view of human freedom with regard to genetic programming.

29. To be sure, the concept of stable strategies can be differentiated according to whether it relates to a genetic basis, to individual learning, or to cultural traditions. Since my use of the word "evolution" is not limited to the biological, here the notion of an "evolutionarily stable strategy" includes all three kinds.

30. The differences are no less obvious: cultural evolution advances more quickly than does biological evolution, because acquired insights can become the subject of a tradition, and a synthesis of unrelated lines of development is possible. However, in the following pages these differences will be ignored.

31. Of course, I am speaking here of theories and norms as objects of the fourth, not the first, world. See chap. 3.4.2.1. We could refer here to a "hibernation" of a theory when the latter is available at least in written form and thus remains revivable.

of every moral theory will be a precept to the effect that the theory should be communicated to other people; in any case, theories that forgo such a command have a hard time surviving and at the very least do not prevail when involved in conflict with other theories. (Here I assume that not every person can develop by himself the theory involved.) In short, if a form of moral behavior is to be universalizable and establish itself in reality, it cannot be evolutionarily unstable.

To come back to the example of altruism, sociobiological arguments based on game theory allow us to see that if an altruist not only wants to be an altruist himself, but also, because he is convinced that altruistic behavior is normatively required, legitimately wishes this behavior to become widespread and to go on existing after his death, then he will necessarily prefer to offer his help to those who accept the same moral principle— at least in cases in which he must choose between various objects of his altruism because his altruistic energies and his means are not unlimited. It is precisely when the altruist wants not merely to preserve life, but is also convinced of the value of the subjectively moral, that he will prefer to show his altruism with regard to others who are altruists or at least potential altruists: in any case, this is a moral program that has a better chance of becoming generally established than the strategy of helping both selfish people and altruists without distinction.[32] Someone who acts in the second way may seem to be more altruistic than someone who acts in the first way; however, the result of the former's behavior would be that sooner or later altruism would die out, for this strategy is not evolutionarily stable in the face of possible infiltration by uninhibited selfish people who exploit others. Since at least in certain situations sucker individuals inevitably help the cheats flourish, we can see why the grudgers not only detest the latter but also dislike the former—for their behavior makes it more difficult to realize a grudger strategy that is evolutionarily stable. In an analogous way, a moral program consisting in yielding to all aggressions cannot generally prevail: anyone who does not adhere to this type of behavior will be victorious.

These considerations are of great significance for ethics, even if a number of qualifications are necessary. First, it is clear that evolutionary stability is only a necessary condition for the morality of a strategy, not a sufficient condition. As the cheat's strategy shows, there can be several evolutionarily stable strategies, one of which may even lead the population involved to die out and it is important to repeat again that this result in no way puts in question the evolutionary stability of this strategy. (Here we see to what extent the intuition that lies behind the unsatisfactory concept of group selection can also be reconstructed in a certain sense on the basis of sociobiology: given two populations that *both* adopt evolutionarily stable strategies, the one in which the individual sacrifices himself for the community is more likely to survive than the one in which that is not the case—if, and only if, the corresponding altruistic strategy is able to defend

---

32. Naturally, helping people who can no longer help others, for example the dying, is morally very commendable; indeed, if the latter have themselves led an altruistic life, it is a duty. But even Mother Teresa was able to continue her noble work only because she also trained nuns to help her.

itself against parasitism.) However, the conjunction of evolutionary stability and the ability to survive also remains only a necessary, not a sufficient, condition for morality. Thus evolutionarily stable and survival-enhancing strategies may be morally abominable, but a well-intentioned strategy that is not evolutionarily stable and survival-enhancing will not endure for long, and if what ought to be ought to be, then this kind of strategy is less moral than one that is concerned about its evolutionary stability and its ability to survive. Second, in discussing moral strategies, consideration of their genetic foundations and limitations is naturally irrelevant. The inevitable limiting of altruism to altruists when resources are in short supply is also reasonable for human beings, because it alone can prevail; yet it would be wrong for a reasonable person to gauge the likelihood that another person is an altruist by how closely related to him he is—for human virtues are determined genetically only in a very limited degree. All the same, we have to acknowledge that before more complex cognitive abilities developed, there was scarcely any alternative to altruistic behavior being limited to close relatives, precisely because in that case alone was there a sufficiently great probability that one's own altruistic stake would not be lost in the great game of evolution.

If we understand this, the result is a more cheering perspective on the gloomy statements of the sociobiologists. According to the latter, selfishness is the underlying, dominant chord of life; altruism is only an epiphenomenon that always remains bound to genetic selfishness. In contrast, according to the view being presented here, life is from the outset a splendid mixture of selfishness and altruism, of self-preservation and self-transcendence. This mixture results from the nature of the replicators, which by multiplying, on one hand, repeat *themselves* and, on the other, in *repeating* themselves strive to rise above themselves. If we consider once again an organism's self-sacrifice for the sake of its offspring, it appears at first glance to be altruistic; this naive interpretation constitutes the thesis. Yet sociobiology teaches us the antithesis, that behind that type of behavior the selfish gene is hidden. However, if we look more deeply and think synthetically, we are struck by the fact that this selfishness is the sole way to help altruism triumph: only because the animal is willing to sacrifice itself for its own offspring can it make it possible for the strategy of self-sacrifice to be continued in the future as well; the probability of this would be much smaller if it sacrificed itself for the offspring of others. An organism that sacrifices itself acts as if it were thinking about its genes—that much we can concede to the sociobiologists. But the decisive point is *that it thinks about genes that program self-sacrifice,* that it is selfishly concerned about genes that determine altruistic behavior. In culture, which is communicated not through genes, but rather through intellectual acts such as teaching, role models, etc., altruism need not be limited to relatives, no matter how strong the genetic mechanisms that are tending in that direction. Yet if we have to choose between two different recipients of our good deeds, then, on a higher level, but for the same reasons as those that hold in the case of selfish-altruistic genes, we must—and may with good conscience—give priority to the persons most likely to continue the tradition of altruism. In sum, sociobiology interprets the peculiar linkage between selfishness and altruism just as one-sidedly, though in a different direction, as does the traditional conception, which is more inclined to emphasize harmony; both schools misunderstand the dialectical logic of selfishness and altruism that precedes all the concrete forms in which they appear. Thus, for one thing, altruism is necessarily secondary with regard to selfishness, and this follows not only from the fact that the altruist rightly considers his behavior valuable and wishes it to be continued, but also, in a more fundamental way, from the fact that the altruist can become active only when there is someone who needs something himself; a society of complete altruists without any needs of their own is not possible, because there would be no one in such a society whom these altruists could help. Metabolism is the basis of the elementary neediness of every organism, and the natality and mortality of living things point necessarily to other people—to the predecessors who brought us into the world, and to the offspring that continue us after our deaths. Therein lies the germ of altruism. In the evolution of living things altruism is extended from the closest relatives to those who are useful to oneself in the framework of reciprocal altruism; in human beings it ultimately includes those who, although they themselves recognize the principle of altruism, nevertheless do not necessarily observe it with regard to the first benefactor, who need not be interested in his own physical survival or in that of his genes, but must inevitably care about the ongoing effects of his principle. In short, what appears to be the triumph of selfishness can also be interpreted as the sole way in which altruism can prevail in the course of evolution. Both interpretations are compatible with the facts, and the grounds for drawing one or the other conclusion are philosophical in nature. The suspicion that Dawkins's interpretation may have been influenced by an unconscious fascination with the modern glorification of selfishness (in business, for instance) is not unfounded. However, anyone who wants to understand the world as a system that makes the implementation of the moral law hard enough, to be sure, but nonetheless gives it a certain chance, will prefer the other interpretation. We have to look at the world in a reasonable way in order for it to look back at us in a reasonable way.[33]

It seems to me that this new interpretation of the biology of altruism and selfishness in particular illuminates the essence of objective idealism. To elaborate it into a metaphysics and natural philosophy would exceed the limits of this book, but this is nonetheless the place to mention a few fundamental ideas in order to clarify the real point of this approach. There are essentially four ways of reacting to Darwinian sociobiology, namely, the moralistic, the cynical, the dualistic, and the objective-idealist. The moralistic way of reacting consists in indignation and a refusal to recognize the facts, even in defaming as social Darwinists the biologists who have written the respective studies, and so on. This position is not only shamefully deficient from an intellectual point of view, but also profoundly immoral, because first of all no one has a right to slander others (it is always easier to accuse than to confute), and second, there is a duty to acknowledge facts, no matter how hard they are—that is, no matter how much they conflict with the obligations of morality. The refusal to do so often indicates a lack of

---

33. Cf. Hegel (1969 ff.), 12:23.

self-discipline that reflects a lack of confidence in one's capacity to wage war on the morally questionable, and an unwillingness to adhere to the moral law when there is much in oneself that must be overcome in order to do so.[34] The second, still more repulsive, reaction is the cynical one, which maintains that there is and can be nothing, but selfishness everywhere in the world. This position does not follow from the previously mentioned biological discoveries, but solely from a philosophical interpretation of them; as a result, it is more widespread among philosophers than among natural scientists. It is even more immoral than the moralistic reaction. The third, dualistic reaction emphasizes the impossibility of deriving normative propositions from descriptive ones. It holds fast, in a Kantian way,[35] to the purity of the moral law, which is opposed to a nature that is without any morality whatever. For this position, as for Gnosticism, nature is deprived of God; to be sure, it is no longer a realm of evil that still elicits an affective reaction, even if it is negative, but rather a sphere in which one must not search for values or primitive manifestations of the moral. Naturally, one wonders why, on such a view, a moral being could emerge at all in such a nature, and how it can have any chance of doing justice to its own destiny. The answer can consist only in reference to the power of culture—or else in the recognition that morality has in fact scarcely any chance of being realized, which nevertheless in no way limits its validity. Certainly this "nevertheless" cannot be denied a peculiar sublimity resembling that of polar lights on the frozen wastes. But the beautiful surpasses the sublime, and so we find more satisfactory the fourth, objective-idealist position, which recognizes that the moral law is also at work in nature, and that the principle of altruism is already present, in a rudimentary form, in the first replicators, and eventually frees itself in a process lasting billions of years, moving toward the form it first assumes in universalist ethics: *Tantae molis erat moralem condere gentem.* The history of nature thus becomes the prehistory of ethics. It cannot be said that nature is simply good; and it is utterly absurd to say that it is the source of the good, which has its ground in an order other than that of the real. But since nature participates in this ground, we can still maintain that nature is as good as it can be at the respective levels of development leading to the mind. Of course, this interpretation of natural existence from a moral point of view is permissible only because we have acknowledged that an apparently merely biological concept, that of the evolutionarily stable strategy, also belongs to ethics, and it belongs to ethics because the basic idea of Darwinism is not specifically biological but rather ultimately a tautology, if we presuppose the existence of competing entities. Two things are gained by looking at matters in this way. On one hand, the proposed interpretation permits us to ascribe to life an intrinsic value. Not only is life distinguished by its reflexive structure, but also by the dialectic of selfishness and altruism that is manifested in it: the objectively valuable

---

34. Naturally, this form of moralism is connected with a decline in one's sense of one's own sinfulness. See chap. 1.6.3.

35. Here I am simplifying and am ignoring Kant's search for a way of overcoming the dualism of nature and freedom in the *Critique of Judgment.*

and the analogous to human morality are combined in it. On the other hand, we can acknowledge with a certain calmness the organic basis of human nature, which does not necessarily predispose us toward evil, even if life itself develops toward higher forms of altruism. Indeed, the assumption is entirely well founded that only the conflict between differing intellectual beings with an organic basis *and* the conflict between vital and intellectual natures in individual human beings has allowed morality to evolve into the extremely complex—yet, in its very complexity, fascinating—subject that it is.

4.1.3. The Evolution of the Organic: Forms of Animal Behavior

The basic idea of sociobiology is in theory valid for all organisms. However, the differences between individual organic species are enormous, and it is important to determine more precisely the place of human beings within this manifold spectrum. In particular, the question arises as to whether evolution has a direction. Initially, the answer to this latter question has to be "no"; the organisms that prevail are those that are able to adapt to a sufficient (though never complete) degree to their environment. This does not always involve a bloody competition among the various organisms; an organism that has found a new ecological niche may be spared the battle, at least temporarily. Whereas selection diminishes biodiversity, not only mutability but also ecological isolation are particularly important evolutionary factors creating biodiversity.[36] The discovery of new habitats is at least as important in evolution as displacing other organisms from already existing habitats; in it we see the tendency of life to extend its own valuable structure wherever it can exist. Moreover, it is crucial that each organism not only seek to adapt itself to its environment, but also in some degree create its environment and, in doing so, alter the physical world in a profound, often irreversible way; here we have only to think of photosynthesis in green plants. The concept of autopoiesis correctly draws attention to the organisms' creative, not merely reactive, character. Indeed, organisms themselves become the environment for other organisms, and therein lies a *possibility* of higher development (alongside which occur constant involutions as well). It is important to repeat this central point: an organism is not higher than another because it developed later; the criterion of higher development is instead the quantity and the differentiation of its performances and the complexity of its interior dimension (which often go hand in hand with increased vulnerability). Higher organisms in this sense *can* emerge precisely because less developed ones become their environment. This is not necessarily the case, but the basic division of living beings into the kingdom of plants and the kingdom of animals indicates the point involved.

It is well known that plants are autotrophic, that is, they feed on inorganic matter; animals are heterotrophic and thus need organic nourishment. What is interesting about

---

36. I thank E.-U. von Weizsäcker for several suggestions on this subject.

heterotrophy is that, through it, the reflexivity that characterizes replication is to some extent carried over into metabolism: even if the animal naturally cannot feed on itself, in it the living feeds on the living. It is obvious that a heterotrophic metabolism is possible over the long term only on the basis of autotrophic organisms—autotrophy is the more basic form of metabolism. But precisely the ultimately parasitic aspect of heterotrophs, which live off other organisms, has forced them to do things that result in the realization of new values. First, there is *locomotion,* which plants do not need, but which is indispensable for animals, at least those who live on land, because they have to find their food.[37] In crossing spatial distance, there is a tendency to overcome the particularization characteristic of the natural realm; because the animal lives in different places, it realizes a form of the general that is denied to plants. Between the animal and its food a certain distance must be bridged; paradoxically, it is precisely this lack, this mediacy and distance, in which Jonas saw the secret of the animal mode of existence,[38] which opens up to the animal a kind of world quite different from that possible for the plant. Only this loss of unity with the environment makes possible the development of a self that does more than take in food; alongside the physiological functions of plants, actions now emerge. Thus the animal must, in order for locomotion to fulfill its goal, *perceive* its food. The sensory apparatus that ideally bridges this distance and culminates in the more abstract ways of sensing at a distance represented by hearing and seeing evolves along with motor functions: receptors and effectors, *Merkwelt* (the world as sensed) and *Wirkwelt* (the world of action), to use Uexküll's terms, correspond to each other. In *perception,* the outside world is *modeled* in the subject; it mirrors itself in the subject in its *variable* appearance, just as in the *organs* of plants and animals, *assumptions regarding stable structures in the external world* have taken shape. The concept of perception still does not imply an interior dimension. When and how this interior dimension emerged remains obscure, at least for an objectifying natural science, since only its physical correlate, and not this interior dimension itself, can cause behavior. Nonetheless, it cannot be reasonably denied that at least higher animals have developed interior dimensions. Thereby they double and even triple their temporality: Time passes not only in their bodies, but also in their interior dimensions, which overcome the tension between drive and fulfillment; moreover, through memory they can reproduce temporal relationships in their interiority. Thanks to their interior dimensions, animals become self-enclosed centers. Whereas plants are ultimately not individuals, since morphologically their open form already shows an inadequate closure, and since in them growth and reproduction are somehow continuous, animals fundamentally distance themselves from the rest of the world. Hence animals deepen the developmental tendency that already underlay the emergence of the first organisms and is continued in

---

37. Mushrooms, which are heterotrophic, are an exception.

38. See especially (1966), 99 ff., which are among the most important pages ever written in the history of natural philosophy.

the ongoing process that leads to the higher animals and finally to human beings—thus the ability to maintain an almost constant body temperature increases animals' independence from their environment. On one hand, animals are mortal in a much more definitive way than are plants, which vegetative division makes potentially immortal, and they are also more fundamentally endangered by their constant dependency on organic nourishment; on the other hand, for these very reasons animals have an identity with themselves that is not merely attributed to them by human beings, but that they themselves feel. It is worth noting that not only autotrophic but also heterotrophic organisms have become basic food sources for other heterotrophic organisms: In the case of carnivores of the first and second orders not only mortality but also the ability to kill takes on a new dimension, because it is no longer plants, but rather individual creatures capable of feeling that are destroyed. However cruel this basic structure of higher organic being may be, it has obviously accelerated further development: a higher degree of mobility, more acute sense perception, and the emotional ability to deal with greater tensions are required to hunt moving prey than to eat grass. Of course, many herbivores have also had to acquire analogous abilities in order to escape predators and thus survive: a clear co-evolution links predators and their prey. It is no accident that human beings developed from animals that were both hunters and hunted, and that the hunting behavior of our closest recent relatives, the chimpanzees, differs conspicuously from that of specialized carnivores.

Since *Homo sapiens sapiens* is the result of a biological evolution, there is a priori a good case to be made for the hypothesis that much of our behavior is genetically determined. Only ideological prejudices can oppose scientific investigation of this hypothesis—prejudices that may be based on very different world views, such as the Christian overemphasis on the special status of human beings on one hand and, on the other, the modernist *verum-factum* principle, which would like to subject humans without restriction to its own social experiments and desires for change. A sober analysis yields three results: first, not only human anatomy and physiology but also many characteristics of human behavior have a genetic basis; second, in humans, areas of freedom with regard to genetically determined behavior programs have opened up that are completely unique in the organic world, but which themselves almost certainly have a genetic basis; third, at a certain point in hominization cultural evolution became as important as biological evolution, and ultimately became far more important. To begin with the first point:[39] fixed action patterns, innate releasing mechanisms, releasing stimuli, internal motivating mechanisms, and innate dispositions to learn exist in human beings, as has been shown by experiments with infants (including deaf-blind infants), comparison of the expressive behavior of members of various cultures, and finally the comparison of human behavior with that of animals to which they are closely related. The genital displays found in many human cultures are also found in many primates,[40] and since it

---

39. Here I follow I. Eibl-Eibesfeldt, "Zur Ethologie des Menschen" (1980), 547–656.
40. Op. cit., 595 ff.

might prove difficult to explain this kind of behavior on the basis of the intellectual nature of human beings, a biological basis is likely. Nonetheless, this behavior could be explained functionally, even without a common genetic origin; but what is the purpose of the contraction of the hair erectors on the shoulders and back when a person is threatening? The origin of this behavior becomes clear when we observe that among chimpanzees this mechanism raises the fur in order to make the animal seem larger. In humans, since we no longer have fur on our shoulders and backs, this behavior lacks any function and thus can be explained only as a phylogenetic relict. Finally, sexual and aggressive behavior is found in so many animals that by studying it we may be able to learn something about the structure of human behavior even if it is only a matter of analogies and not homologies. In this way we can perhaps discover the inner logic of a specific form of behavior.

It follows from the nature of living beings that animal behavior must first of all serve the two fundamental goals of food intake and reproduction; and because of the plurality of living beings we must add to these protection against other organisms' search for food. To what extent do these goals lead to social behavior? According to the previously proposed definition, this can happen only among beings with interior dimensions. The distinction between behavior involving members of the same species and behavior involving members of different species is fundamental: a higher degree of empathy is more likely among animals of the same species. Whereas among the higher animals mating and caring for the young represent in themselves intraspecific social events,[41] this holds for food intake only in the (not very common) case of cannibalism. However, like the search for a sexual partner, the search for food—in which the animal may be either the subject or the object of this search—can become an *occasion* for intraspecific social events in which both competitive and cooperative situations may emerge. The theory of the selfish gene suggests that competitive situations are likely when resources that are important for survival are in short supply; altruistic cooperation will develop only toward relatives or when it is mutual. So far as intraspecific aggression is concerned, it is notoriously difficult to define it: it does not necessarily end with either the wounding or even the killing of the opponent, as is shown by the frequent occurrence of socalled tournaments, with their inhibiting mechanisms to prevent competitors from really hurting one another. But even a purely functional definition of aggression, which supposedly leads to spatial and social distancing,[42] is not sufficient, because this would include every corresponding form of communication. Obviously the essence of intraspecific aggression is the use or threat of physical force with the goal of resisting a behavior on the part of another member of one's species that is incompatible with the satisfaction of one's own drives. Together with defense and submission, intraspecific aggression constitutes a unit that is in most species clearly distinct

---

41. One criterion of the higher development of animals consists precisely in the extent to which reproduction leads to more complex social events.

42. Op. cit., 423. The subsequent information comes from the pages following p. 423.

from interspecific fighting behavior. It can be considered proven that many animal species have a genetically based drive toward intraspecific aggression, and that among animals the degree of aggressivity is also influenced by experiences with other members of the same species. Of course, among animals aggression always serves biological functions; it is never an end in itself. This also holds for biting as a fear-response, in which aggressivity arises from the individual's own fear.

As we have seen, it is in the interest of every organism to limit aggression as much as possible; we also mentioned that the retaliator strategy is evolutionarily stable, whereas the hawk strategy is not. It is interesting that an evolutionarily stable strategy also results when the originally assumed symmetry between the adversaries is abandoned in favor of an asymmetrical initial situation.[43] When one of the adversaries differs from the other in some respect, a great deal of energy can be saved by granting priority to the one marked by the relevant characteristic. The latter can be objectively relevant—for instance, it is a reasonable strategy to yield to the stronger. But this is not necessarily the case: A break with symmetry is advantageous as such, no matter in what the asymmetry consists, because it reduces conflicts or at least quickly resolves them. An important example is territoriality: the strategy according to which intruders withdraw and residents defend their territory is evolutionarily stable and plays a major role in the animal world.[44] In addition, among certain social predators and among chimpanzees, the priority of the first possessor is recognized: the prey of lower-ranking animals is respected even by higher-ranking animals. This rule avoids many conflicts, as does, for example, the inhibition among hamadryas baboons against stealing another male's female.[45]

A strategy that also throws light on human behavior is the xenophobic expulsion of those alien to the group, which is not necessarily connected with the principle of territoriality. The rejection of members of one's own group whose behavior deviates from the norm is a reaction that also belongs to this context. Space-related intolerance, that is, the expulsion of all conspecific intruders, seems also to be a basis for some human behavior, such as war.[46] Note that this does not mean, first, that only a behavior homologous or analogous to animal territoriality underlies wars, because the causes of all human behavior, and especially a behavior as complex as warfare, are extremely diverse. Second, the observation that in many animal species and human cultures the violation of one's own territory triggers aggression in no way implies that this ought to be so; on the contrary. Yet one can surmount immoral behavioral tendencies only if one becomes aware of them. However, evolutionarily stable strategies—which, as we have said, are not necessarily moral—can be overcome only with moral strategies that are themselves

43. Cf. R. Dawkins (1976), 83 ff.; J. Maynard Smith (1982), 94 ff.

44. This strategy is not wholly arbitrary, because its reversal would result in animals having constantly to abandon their habitat, which would be a great waste of energy. But what really matters is that it would be evolutionarily stable, even if the asymmetry were completely arbitrary.

45. See I. Eibl-Eibesfeldt (1980), 489 ff., especially 483 ff., on rank order.

46. On this subject see I. Eibl-Eibesfeldt's own investigation (1975).

evolutionarily stable. To elucidate further this very important idea by using another example: few kinds of human behavior are more repulsive than the teasing or even mistreating of marginalized people such as the bodily handicapped. This judgment is in no way affected by the fact that analogous behavior occurs in many animal species: the sight of such things can easily dispel the illusion that nature is the source of everything that is good. Of course, it is not hard to see the basis for xenophobia and reactions against conspecifics with deviant behavior among animals. Those who act differently or those about whose behavior nothing is yet known can be a danger; and since animals do not have the intelligence necessary to distinguish between deviant characteristics that present a real danger and those that do not, the emergence of generic rejection reactions is not hard to explain in terms of evolutionary biology. Human intelligence and morals allow us, and in fact obligate us, to distinguish between those deviant behaviors that sometimes demand the greatest admiration (genius and saintliness, for example, always represent deviant behavior) and for the most part tolerance, understanding, and support, and behaviors that must be opposed because the social order of the group and thus also its ability to be open would be destroyed by them (criminal behavior, for instance). A mirror image of animals' lack of differentiation results when well-meaning universalists fail to grasp the necessity of occasional rejection reactions, because they consider each form of alterity to be good in itself. However, it is not hard to see that this view would quickly disappear if it were not protected by the differentiating strategy: unlimited openness with regard to the other can lead to the other's triumph over the principle of openness with regard to the other.

Alongside aggressive behavior, many species of animals also engage in cooperative behavior and even form temporary or permanent groups whose size varies from a couple to extensive clans; these are divided into *anonymous* groups, in which the members do not know each other individually, and *individualized* groups. *Closed* anonymous groups occupy a position between *open* anonymous and individualized groups, since their members can find out whether someone belongs to the group or is an invader; the latter will be rejected. The essence of the respective social relationships thus depends among other things on cognitive abilities—an important indication of the interdependency of the various achievements of organisms. The advantage of living in groups is obvious: protection from extremes of weather and from predators, cooperation in hunting and caring for the young, division of labor. Group bonding presupposes an exchange of *signals* that function as releasers and that must have two properties in order to be noticeable: they must be simple and improbable. They include not only communication about the external environment (think of the language of bees) but also signals that function as the glue holding the group together, for example, by attenuating aggression, such as gestures of greeting, submission, and appeasement.[47] A similar strengthening of group bonding is produced

---

47. I. Eibl-Eibesfeldt (1980), 191 ff. What is interesting about these signals is that some of them are themselves already what they mean—a greeting is and signifies a proof of respect for another.

by actions such as social grooming or sharing food: even if this kind of behavior first emerged only as a means of ensuring the survival of the individual's own genes, the stability of the group is such an important and fundamental means that these behaviors very quickly became ways of serving this goal rather than serving primarily to remove parasites or get food. What seems to be a means has itself became a goal: just as the first animals already move about in order to feed themselves, but feed themselves in order to survive as self-moving organisms, so social animals live in groups for the sake of all the previously mentioned advantages, but these advantages serve the survival of social beings. We have to suppose that even the evolution of an interior dimension goes hand in hand with its interpretation by conspecifics on the basis of expressive behavior; otherwise its emergence would be even more difficult to explain than it already is. At any rate, this has the important consequence that one cannot assume that there is first an interior dimension that is accessible only to the individual in question, which would then have to be laboriously deciphered; only that interior dimension emerges from the outset that can be intersubjectively understood because it develops in several individuals. The real question is therefore not how one can explain animal intersubjectivity on the basis of private interior dimensions, but rather the reverse: how in the course of evolution interior dimensions that are closed to each other developed out of intersubjectively shared interior dimensions. The answer will point to the advantages of deception in terms of natural selection.

Genealogically, the roots of group bonding are manifold. Care for the young and sexual bonding are primary, but bonding through fear—flight toward other members of the species—and joining together in defense or attack communities have also played a role. Obviously, these two sources of animal intersubjectivity are fundamentally different. In sexual bonding and care for the young it is a matter of passing on life, while defense or attack communities seek to avoid their own destruction or to destroy alien life; in the former the social quality of the group is grounded in itself, whereas in the latter reference to organisms alien to the group is constitutive. Defense or attack can certainly increase the social cohesion of the groups they threaten or by which they are threatened because, for one thing, aggressivity is contagious. To be sure, both sources of group bonding are connected insofar as it is ultimately the mortality of the organic that makes reproduction necessary; but this does not alter the fact that it definitely matters whether it is based on bonding through threatening others or being threatened by others or through the need to pass on life. Here the categorial difference between love and politics among human beings finds its biological basis.

The essential difference between caring for the young and sexual behavior consists in the greater symmetry that characterizes the latter. Since Freud mating has often been seen as the original social act, so here I will add only that in the ontogenesis of animals who care for their young the mother-child relationship precedes mating. Therefore it is not plausible to interpret the behavioral repertory of this relationship in sexual terms; on the contrary, behavioral modes drawn from it have been made secondarily useful in sexual bonding: simply consider kissing, which probably started as mouth-to-mouth feeding. In any case, it can be said that many other social types of behavior are derived from the repertory of sexual activities; this holds for both appeasing and threatening behavior. Yet conversely it can also be said that originally aggressive behavior, which many animals have to learn even before arriving at sexual maturity, has influenced the program for sexual behavior; after all, mating is commonly preceded by the elimination of competitors, and even mating itself can be a kind of battle. Given the high degree of differentiation of the human interior dimension, the will to power and the sex drive nonetheless have phenomenologically very different qualities, and Adler was right to criticize the early Freud by arguing that it is not possible to reduce the striving for power and recognition to the sex drive.[48] However, the two drives may sometimes overlap—in the quality of feeling no less than in expressive behavior. Sadism is the best-known but not the sole example of this kind of overlapping.[49]

Furthermore, human social hierarchies also have one—and again, by no means the only—source in the realm of animals. Individualized groups include mostly sociogenic rank orders, which, unlike biogenic rank orders, are based on the members' becoming acquainted with each other as individuals. For the most part, this acquaintance takes place in the form of battles for privilege in mating, feeding, etc. Success in such battles determines the individual's place in the hierarchy, since the members of the group re-member who is superior to them and who is inferior; when necessary, a little threatening as a "reminder" is sufficient. This leads to less frequent fighting and stabilizes social relationships, but small changes are constantly occurring, and battles are always flaring up, for example, when old members are leaving or new ones join the group. The new members include the young: mortality and natality are inevitable, natural mechanisms for the partial revision of the hierarchy. Aggressivity is often very great between animals that stand close to each other in the hierarchy. Thus, among jackdaws, the alpha birds are particularly friendly to the omega birds, and in conflicts between subordinates they always intervene on behalf of the lower-ranking bird—presumably because they are less threatened by the latter. From the outset, certain characteristics can be considered as in-dices of standing in the hierarchy and help avoid battles: red deer fight each other only if they have antlers of approximately equal size; dropping antlers means a decline in rank. What is particularly remarkable about this is that attacks by the lower-ranking animals always occur immediately after the shedding of antlers, even though osteolysis deprived them some time earlier of any usefulness in fighting.[50] This suggests the symbolic value of antlers in this phase. Moreover, it is interesting that among hens the pecking order

---

48. By recognizing an autonomous death drive, Freud tried to take the more complex reality into account, even if his subsumption of aggression toward others and toward oneself under a single drive remains unsatisfactory.

49. The chapter "Dûdu's Klage" ("Dudu's Complaint") in Thomas Mann's *Joseph in Ägypten* (1975; 2:881 ff.) is a masterpiece of comedy. It becomes increasingly clear that the feeling of superiority felt by the potent dwarf with regard to the eunuch, and his will to take revenge on Joseph, are mixed with sexual desires.

50. I. Eibl-Eibesfeldt (1980), 486.

is not necessarily transitive, so complex triangular relationships can develop, and that among baboons older males can join together to dominate all others in the group even though in isolation they would be subdued by single individuals. A female's standing can be raised by mating with a higher-ranking male, and that of lower-ranking males can be raised by helping a higher-ranking male in his battles. The advantages of high rank, and especially alpha status, are particularly important with respect to reproduction: alpha animals have priority in reproducing themselves and may even prevent other males in the group from reproducing.[51] Among certain species of fish, the mere existence of alpha animals, to which the attention of the others is primarily directed, can even determine the sex of the lower-ranking individuals. In the presence of higher-ranking individuals, pigeons learn less well than when they are away from them. By giving lower-ranking pigeons success experiences in fighting pigeon models, E. Diebschlag has nonetheless succeeded in getting them afterward to win in battles with higher ranking pigeons—a fine example of how one's success experiences influence one's expectations of success and thereby one's success. On the other hand, among higher mammals alpha status is no longer based merely on using pure force in dealing with other members of the group: the ability to drive off enemies, to protect the weak and to resolve conflicts within the group, general organizational abilities, intelligence, and the ability to assert oneself are increasingly important. Since these abilities are often correlated with age, among baboons, for instance, elderly males enjoy high status even after the waning of their physical strength, the latter being compensated for by the splendid fur of old age. As Eibl-Eibesfeldt puts it, *dominance relationships,* which are based on the use of force against conspecifics, are replaced by *leadership relationships.*

4.1.4. The Biological Bases of the Human Sense of the Moral

Excursions into the natural prehistory of politics are useful for improving our understanding of some aspects of human behavior: the continuity leading from threatening behavior among animals through primitive war dances to military parades before state visitors is simultaneously astonishing, frightening, and reassuring. It is astonishing because the differences between animals and modern states are very great; frightening, because one wonders how highly complex industrialized societies can prevent the misuse of their power if their politicians' behavioral models are partly determined by mechanisms that were selected under environmental conditions fundamentally different from today's. It is reassuring, however, to consider that the lowest common denominator of a type of behavior found among so many different creatures is very probably grounded in

---

51. This has eugenic advantages for the whole species. Naturally, we cannot say that this kind of behavior evolved because of these advantages for the species; it results from the selfish genes' struggle to replicate themselves. But it is no accident that in this case their struggle leads to a result that is useful for the further development of the species.

an objective necessity—that of self-preservation in an inimical milieu. Nothing can be done about this necessity, and so the real question may be not how one should overcome it, but rather how one can do justice to it without neglecting the demands of morals. But where do morals come from? We have already explained why the moral world transcends the empirical world and why any attempt at a naturalistic grounding of ethics is doomed to fail. Yet this does not mean that *the sense of the moral* is not part of the empirical world. Even if the slow opening-up with regard to that transcendent dimension is the result of cultural evolution, there are biological conditions that made this opening up *possible* and even *necessary*.[52] Such conditions can be cited in theoretical, technical-poietic, and practical behavior, depending on whether knowledge of the extraspecific environment, its shaping, or interaction with conspecifics is considered primary.[53] This distinction is helpful, even though the close relationship linking these three spheres is obvious: even in shaping an object—a non-social act—humans are determined by a feeling for the appropriate and the beautiful that they owe to their socialization.

So far as the first group of biological conditions is concerned, we must first mention the trivial point that responsible moral action presupposes a *survey of the consequences of the action*. Animals already have goals, but only humans can foresee long-term consequences even when the latter exceed a certain level of complexity. The central representation of space among primates was a significant step toward the development of this ability; primates can already try out operations in their imaginations, but the evolution of the human brain has increased this ability to an extraordinary extent. This development has made humans *creatures of possibility:* in our imagination, we not only mirror reality, but also anticipate possible outcomes. Thanks to our capacity for representation, these outcomes become reality in the third world, but not in the second or fourth, because we finally discard them. We can, as has been pointed out, let our ideas die for our own sake. In order to eliminate lethal behavioral models, we do not need to test them in reality; instead, we can anticipate the outcome in our imagination, and thus survive. (Herein also lies one of the roots of *art.*) In addition, our lifelong *curiosity behavior*, which makes the discovery of new connections possible, is essential. In most animals this kind of behavior is limited to the young, whereas in humans, as a result of their partial neoteny, it is retained throughout almost the whole life span. Animals' encounter with the world is closed off structurally after a certain age; in order for the world to be experienced anew, new individuals have to be born. This is true in a fundamental sense for humans as well, but humans retain at least in part the ability to discover new aspects of the world through knowledge, and thereby constantly to conceive *new alternative actions.*

---

52. I am indebted to A. Portmann (1956) and to conversations with my friend Professor Dr. Wilhelm Schüle for many suggestions regarding this subject.

53. The homonymy of the word "praxis," which refers both to interventions in the extrahuman world and to social interactions, should be avoided—Aristotle's well known differentiation should not be undercut.

The *use of tools* belongs to the second group of conditions for the sense of the moral. The use of tools was promoted on one hand by the development of prehensile hands and the erect gait that makes prehensile hands free for use, and on the other by what has been called somewhat misleadingly the "deficient nature" of human beings.[54] Since most of our organs are significantly less specialized than those of most animals,[55] this weakness makes the use of weapons and an upright gait a necessity. Even though individual tools are also used by animals, a specifically human achievement consists in the fact that the form, function, and mode of production of these tools no longer needs to be already provided in nature; indeed, humans were able to make even fire, which inspires fear in almost every living being, useful for their own ends. This has important consequences for ethics. One is that this has contributed to a broadening of our scope of action, both with regard to nature, whose ecological balance early humans already affected, and to members of our own species. Another important consequence is that along with objectivizing behavior toward nature, we have also developed the ability to objectivize our fellow human beings—another extension of human power that is based on a change in mentality, not on the availability of tools. The communicative culture of whales is admirably graceful, and it is not irrational to suspect that these intelligent marine mammals are happier than humans. But if they are, it is because of a lack: they do not have a technical behavior toward the world, which could not develop in water because the fluid state is not malleable, and thus neither have they learned to instrumentalize other members of their species in the way humans can. Closing oneself up in oneself, conceiving the world (including the social world) as an object that can be known as it is in itself and in which one can intervene as one wills—that could be achieved only by a being with technical skills; and such a being needs ethics much more urgently than does the dolphin. It is plausible that in the course of hominization the bridge between technical and social skills was built through hunting. Not only did hunting demand cooperation as well as good tools; the primatologist C. Vogel, who believes that the development of social intelligence preceded that of technical intelligence, proposes the interesting notion that the translation of the acquired social abilities to the subject-object dimension took place through hunting because the prey can be the object of partial empathy and mediates between a conspecific and a dead object.[56] The importance of hunting during hominization and in the prehistory of human beings, who were, after all, hunters during 99 percent of their history, gives cause for concern, because at least among chimpanzees it is almost certainly connected with intraspecific aggression—an exception

---

54. Cf. Gehlen (1966): "*Mängelwesennatur.*"

55. To be sure, the brain and the hand are highly specialized organs, but they are organs that are not specialized with respect to any specific environment. They provide the basis for being specialized in not being a specialist (K. Lorenz [1977], 190). Man's ability to survive in different ecological environments is also promoted by his cooling system.

56. C. Vogel (1989), 69 ff.

in the animal kingdom, which leads us to expect that human beings would be especially dangerous.[57]

We have already listed humans' practical, social abilities, the third type of behavior and the most important for the development of the moral sense. What is particularly fascinating about this is that humans are simultaneously more social and more asocial than other animals.[58] Their greater sociality is shown first of all by *long-term spousal bonds*, which are found among many birds but only a few mammals. These bonds were favored by the female's continuous readiness for sexual activity and by concealed ovulation, which require an ongoing relationship and, together with the long juvenile life of offspring, favor the development of the family. The dissociation of sexuality from well-defined rutting seasons led to an increased sexualization of the whole of human life. At the same time, however, it resulted in a weakening of the sexual drive, which was distributed over the whole year, and thus this most powerful of all drives became controllable; only in this way could an *I* develop that is more than the self's drives. Second, we must mention *parental care*, which goes on longer in humans than in any other animal species; humans are secondary altricial animals with significant opportunities for *individual learning*. Presumably humans' differentiated *sympathetic functions* developed in the framework of the family. In order to coordinate social activities, the miracle of human language developed; its precision with reference to the external world as well as in expressing our own feelings constantly astounds us. But its real achievement is to have made learning independent of one's own experience (and, a fortiori, independent of genetic programming); it makes *traditions* possible. The latter occur in the animal world as well, but there they are dependent on the presence of the object with which they are concerned. In contrast, language makes available even what is not present, what one cannot point to—thus immeasurably broadening human power not only over nature but also over other humans, to whom precise commands can be communicated. Individual learning and cultural evolution increasingly limit the power of the instincts, which are replaced by cultural entities, that is, institutions. The replacement of rigid types of behavior by individual reactions that are no longer determined by genetic programs, but can be guided by cultural norms, is what people usually mean when they speak of *freedom*. To be sure, the reduction of instincts led to entirely new developmental possibilities for social life: in humans the releasers produce mere affects; they do not directly produce motor behavior as in other animals. In addition, however, the residues of instincts can "dedifferentiate" and neutralize themselves in peculiar ways. But this reduction also enabled humans to act not only independently of genetic programming, but also contrary to the norms of their own mores. Only among humans is there biologically senseless

---

57. As a being that thinks abstractly, the human being can put all his biological drives in the service of any ends he chooses.

58. Augustine already puts this succinctly: "Nihil enim est quam hoc genus tam discordiosum vitio, tam sociale natura" (*De civitate Dei* XII 28). ("For there is nothing so social by nature, so unsocial by its corruption, as this race." Trans. M. Dodds, 410.)

cruelty, which always presupposes empathy, as well as the idea of universal justice: As a paradoxical result of the exceptional social care we enjoy in our youth, we acquire the ability to distance ourselves from all other members of our species. Such a being, which no longer must do anything, but can do a great deal, is in urgent need of morals if it is not to undermine what pre-human evolution has already achieved that is objectively right. The loss of inhibitions against killing conspecifics, which exist among many animals, must frighten us: "The weakness of human nature, which is no longer protected against itself by strict forms, is murderous in kind."[59]

4.2. The Human Identity Problem

4.2.1. Life and Spirit

As we have said, despite all the biological roots of human behavior, the decisive aspects of human beings cannot be explained biologically. In order to understand this, we must go back to the specific difference of humans as compared with animals. The relationship between humans and organisms can be formulated most concisely as follows: the human being is the life form that completes life's trajectory in that it is capable of negating life. This sounds mysterious and requires explication. This explication has two stages. First, we must correctly interpret the assertion that humans can negate life; second, we must grasp the extent to which this negation represents the completion of life's trajectory.

If we search for the essence of man, there are two reasons for rejecting as unsatisfactory any attempt to answer this question by listing those qualities that only he seems to possess. First, one can argue that almost all such qualities are found, at least in a rudimentary form, in other higher animals as well; the distinction is only gradual. Second, it is always awkward to cobble together the essence of a thing from all kinds of unconnected qualities; rather, it is the other way around: individual qualities should be understood on the basis of the essence. However, one can begin by reviewing the properties that seem attributable only to humans[60] and move from there to the determination of the essence. Obviously one can distinguish two entirely different types of such characteristics. On one hand there are the specifically human achievements that are grounded in the extension of human thinking as against all pre-human thought, such as the use of language and tools. This point was discussed at the end of the preceding section. The thinking in which they are rooted was emphasized by ancient philosophy when it called

---

59. Gehlen (1975), 135: "Die Schwäche der menschlichen Natur, die durch strenge Formen nicht vor sich selbst geschützt ist, ist von einer mörderischen Art."

60. I say "seem" because it is not a priori impossible that there might be other beings on this planet or other planets that have the same normatively relevant properties as humans have, even if they belong to another species. See chapter 4.4.2 on speciesism.

man *animal rationale,* a "rational animal." On the other hand, there are characteristic traits that at least on first inspection cannot be traced back to abstract thought but are not known to exist in almost any other animal, such as laughing and weeping, feelings of guilt, and the ability to commit suicide. To be sure, both groups of qualities belong to humans; in addition, they are more closely connected to each other than one might first think. But if one were to find oneself in the impossible situation of having to choose between the two groups, the latter is clearly the more important. A thinking machine that could neither laugh nor weep would be less human than an intellectually limited being that could laugh and weep.

However, it is not these acts as such that are crucial; they are significant as expressions of a structure that is still more fundamental than man's supreme intellectual achievements, even if they were not properly grasped until the advent of modern philosophical anthropology. We are talking about man's ability to distance himself from reality and from himself, that is, his *eccentric position,* as Plessner called it.[61] A person who laughs rises above reality; he deprives it of its earthly gravity, reflects himself out of it—illegitimate authorities are brought down by laughter. A person who weeps expresses his pain at his impotence, of which he has suddenly become aware; he thereby supposes that this impotence ultimately contradicts his dignity. A cry of pain involves taking no distance from reality; on the contrary, the person who cries out in pain is trapped within reality. But anyone who weeps over the death of someone close to him, over a friend's betrayal, or over his own guilt protests against what has occurred, even if he is externally resigned to it and no longer fights against it. In his programmatic, and not always argumentatively satisfactory but nonetheless brilliant, work, *Die Stellung des Menschen im Kosmos,* Max Scheler makes the essential point: "Man is the kind of being who, by means of the spirit, can take an ascetic attitude toward life. . . . Compared with the animals . . . man is the being who can say 'No,' the 'ascetic of life', the protestant par excellence against mere reality."[62] However, the crucial fact is that man can protest not only against external reality but also against the reality that he is himself: man is not fully contained by what he is at a given moment. This holds first of all for his body: man not only *is* body, he also *has* his body as an object. Man can also distance himself from his drives, even in the very act of satisfying them, indeed he can distance himself from even the highest intellectual talents insofar as he recognizes that they are a gift that has been given him and do not constitute the core of his personality. The fact that he can objectivize himself, that he can place himself at a distance from himself, is what is peculiarly human. By becoming an object for himself, man splits into two elements, namely,

---

61. Cf. Plessner (1961), from whom I have borrowed many ideas.

62. (1988); 55: "Der Mensch ist das Lebewesen, das kraft seines Geistes sich zu seinem Leben, das heftig es durchschauet, prinzipiell *asketisch* . . . verhalten kann. Mit dem Tiere verglichen . . . ist *der Mensch der 'Neinsagenkönner',* der *'Asket des Lebens',* der ewige Protestant gegen alle Wirklichkeit." Trans. H. Meyerhoff, 54 f. Cf. already Nietzsche (1980), 4:134: "Geist ist das Leben, das selber in's Leben schneidet." ("Spirit is life that itself cuts into life.")

the objectivized *I*, henceforth called the "self," and the objectifying *I*-subject, the *I* par excellence. This structure is implicit in what Kant called the "original-synthetic unity of apperception": I can consider every state of consciousness as mine; in principle I can extend every idea (for example, "it's raining") to the express consciousness that I am the one who states that it is raining. This is the ultimate root of the performative-propositional double character of human speech, which has been emphasized by modern speech-act theory, and especially by transcendental pragmatics. The languages of other animals also refer to external reality, but only man can thematize the character of this relation to the world. Bees can communicate to each other that in a certain meadow at a certain distance a certain source of food is located; but a proposition with this kind of information (we may call it *p*) can be formulated in the speech act, "I hereby assert that it is true that *p* . . . ," by no animal other than man.

This ability becomes particularly interesting when humans refer to ideas about themselves (for instance, "I know that I am not in good shape"), for then subject and object coincide. This is true to a still greater degree when the act of consciousness extends not just to a single condition but to the whole person (for instance, "I know who I am"). However, self-consciousness becomes most interesting and most mysterious when it relates negatively to itself, as in self-hatred. Hatred is a relationship of opposition, and yet in self-hatred the hater and the hated are identical—which perfectly explains why this hatred is so irreconcilable. In fact, the double nature of *self-consciousness* is at the same time a unity to a quite different extent than the organism, for even if the organism does not survive certain divisions, the parts still exist as physical objects (not as organs) even after the division: a self without an *I*, however, is just as inconceivable as an *I* without a self. The well-known problems of the reflection theory of self-consciousness have to do with the fact that the *I* cannot be understood as reflection on an already existing self, since *before* reflection this self is not the self of the *I* and therefore cannot be a self at all, for the *I* is the always already existing unity of the *I* and the self. If the *I* were only accessorially added to the self, there could be no unity of self-consciousness. One must at least keep in mind that the addition of this reflection fundamentally alters the pre-reflective center. It is important to grasp that the difference between *I* and self is relative: the *I* is the observing element, the self the observed element. However, this does not determine the content of the performances of the *I* and the self. To be sure, the self is first of all a structure whose qualities arise from the vital sphere, and the *I* is something that leads beyond the organic; but if the *I* observes its own tendency to observe, then what was *I* becomes self; if the *I* identifies completely with the strivings of the self, what was self becomes *I*. The problem of human identity is that of the identification of *I* and self.[63]

The twofold unity of self-consciousness constitutes the essence of man; from it springs that second group of characteristics that appear in no other animal. The ability to distance oneself from one's own self is a necessary condition of having spirit, which

---

63. On identity as a psychological category, cf. esp. the fundamental works of E. H. Erikson (for example, 1959).

is something fundamentally different from intelligence. Intelligence without spirit is certainly not unusual; in modernity, it seems to be becoming the rule. And yet the social sciences influenced by Hobbes err when they maintain that man merely satisfies his drives as do other animals, even though he is able to think up particularly ingenious means for doing so that have no equivalent in the animal world. According to this view man is nothing but a particularly crafty rat,[64] and even if the fact that he was able to develop such a self-image says a great deal about man and about a certain period in his history, it is nonetheless wrong. Certainly man has interests, and surely human behavior is to a large extent determined by the attempt to realize his own interests. But any man, even the most ethically stunted, ultimately cannot escape the question—no matter how energetically he may repress it—whether his interests are *legitimate,* whether they are compatible with his self-respect, whether they spring from his own true self—or whether he must be ashamed of them. It is true that so far as its concrete content is concerned, shame is a feeling that cannot always stand up to rational examination; but the formal structure of this feeling is deeply reasonable, no matter how unreasonable its content may be. The ability to measure one's own interests against rational values has its ultimate root in this shame—no matter how indispensable the contribution of reflective moral intelligence may be. Anyone who views man as a utility-maximizing being overlooks the fact that this utility can be problematized; and it can be problematized because the self to which this utility belongs is no brute fact, but rather a task for the *I.* Interests are always *someone's* interests; and *who* this someone is, is a question that is prior to the question as to what his interests are. Not all power struggles, for instance, are based on the pursuit of interests; rather, questions of identity are usually combined with the problem of interests. This does not make life any easier; on the contrary, conflicts connected with the problem of identity are generally more violent and more difficult to resolve. But such conflicts have to be acknowledged in the social sciences; in addition, one may suspect that without the question of identity, human existence would be easier, but significantly less fascinating. Even among people who devote themselves exclusively to the satisfaction of their own interests, there is reason to believe that behind the refusal to concern themselves with the question of identity often lurks the naked fear of questioning or even taking a look at their own selves, and that a large part of their hectic activism serves the purpose of avoiding the specifically human encounter with their own selves.[65] The most extreme expression of the ability to have an identity crisis is suicide, considered as a radical negation of one's own vital basis and even of one's own self: one can commit suicide to escape not only physical pain, but also the torment that one is for oneself. (However, in the latter case the true problem is not resolved: the fact that one was despicable is not undone by suicide.)

---

64. This is not meant to imply a negative judgment on rats, whose intelligence we should sincerely admire, but rather on those who can conceive themselves and their fellow humans only in the image of these clever animals.

65. Cf. Pascal (1982), 192 ff.

The claim that human negation of life completes the trajectory of life sounds truly self-contradictory, even if it is easy to see why much depends on whether one can make it clear or not. The interest in its justification has to do with the fact that it asserts that between life and intellect there is both continuity and discontinuity, and that, paradoxically, the continuity consists precisely in the breakdown of continuity. We have already seen why only the connection between the two does justice to the phenomena: man is an animal, but he is a very special animal, and his special character is shown precisely by the fact that he radicalizes the principle of animality. Jonas's reflections on the difference between plants and animals were mentioned above: An animal is characterized by a certain mediacy of its existence that opposes it to its environment in a way entirely different from that of a plant; the unity of plant and environment bursts apart with the formation of individualized subjectivity in animals. Man merely intensifies this development, first by reflecting himself out of nature by using his spirit in a way unknown to animals, and second by setting himself as a self-conscious being in opposition not only to the environment but also to his own self. "True men emerge when the painter of the bull and even of its hunter, turns to concerning himself with the unpaintable image of his own conduct and the state of his self. Over the distance of this wondering, searching and comparing perception there is constituted the new entity 'I.' This is of all the greatest venture in mediacy and objectivization."[66] It seems to me that this is not only the greatest, but also the greatest possible venture in the history of being: if real being in its opposition to the ideal is determined by spatiotemporal isolation, if in the evolution of real being subjective centers develop that increasingly distance themselves from their environment, then with the double structure of self-consciousness something ontologically insurpassable has been achieved—for here the subject sets itself against itself. Certainly subsequent biological evolution can bring about changes and even progress: we can imagine self-conscious organisms whose bodily structure differs considerably from ours, whose drives have a structure profoundly different from ours, who think faster and better than we do. But an organism that surpasses the structure of human self-consciousness in a way similar to that in which the latter surpasses the animal mind is not possible. The differences between individual beings with self-consciousness are no doubt enormous, and the differentiation within the human species is more extensive than in any other precisely because man can free himself from his environment in manifold ways; there are probably turning points in the history of human self-consciousness that constitute entirely new human types—whereby the direction of the evolution of human history deepens being's tendency toward subjectivization: But these beings that differ from one another always have in common their possession of self-consciousness. Stubborn battles for recognition can therefore always flare up between genius and fool, between the representatives of late industrial societies and those of archaic cultures, but never between a man and a dog.

---

66. Jonas (1966), 185.

4.2.2. Elements of Self-Consciousness

In the following I will attempt to clarify somewhat the nature of human self-consciousness, its presuppositions as well as its consequences. Three preliminary remarks are necessary here. First, it goes without saying that I must concentrate chiefly on those aspects of man that are important in the context of this book, that is, on those without which political behavior cannot be understood; in these the concept of action plays an incomparably greater role than the concepts of thinking and feeling, which can therefore only be touched upon. Second, genetic questions will have to be almost entirely neglected. How self-consciousness evolved phylogenetically and constantly re-emerges ontogenetically, or even which parts of the brain are responsible for this—these are surely questions that neither philosophy nor, in the current state of knowledge, probably any other individual branch of knowledge can answer in more than a preliminary way.[67] We can only attempt to describe phenomena as they represent themselves to us, even if we do not know what causes these phenomena. Thus we will deal with phenomena of fully developed self-consciousness, not with its early forms. It is obvious that today in normal cases, or at least in ideal cases, man first thinks and then acts—even if it is entirely probable that in the slow process of hominization action preceded speech and speech preceded silent thinking. Third, when possible I will direct my attention to necessary relationships between individual phenomena—necessary in the sense that there is a conceptual connection, not an empirically existing correlation. Thus it will be surprising that the problem of self-consciousness is first introduced in abstraction from the social dimension. To be sure, no one will deny that *Homo sapiens sapiens* can develop his self-consciousness only through socialization—but that is simply a genetic assertion, which does not concern the essence of self-consciousness. In addition, and especially to understand human history better (and not only that of possible other rational beings), it is of crucial importance to grasp that man's ability to make claims to validity can in principle emerge even in an individual, isolated self-consciousness.

The first necessary, but not yet sufficient, condition of self-consciousness is the *existence of consciousness,* that is, of states that belong to the mysterious third world, which is not immediately accessible to outside observation, but only to introspection.[68] Even if it follows from this that it is not easy to determine whether another being has consciousness, we must note two things: First, such mental states are not identical with the *brain states* with which they are correlated. If we could—to borrow a famous reflection of Leibniz's[69]—wander about in another person's brain, we would learn many interesting things and perhaps even find the *causes* of mental states—but we surely could not

---

67. One of the most impressive scientific theories of consciousness, which transfers Darwinian principles to the brain's modes of functioning, is provided by G. Edelman. See especially his book published in 1989.

68. Cf. chap. 3.4.2.1.

69. Cf. *Monadologie* 17.

find these mental states themselves. Certainly, many of the human intellect's functions take place unconsciously; indeed, it is not an exaggeration to think that compared with the ocean of the ratiomorphous apparatus, consciousness in all organisms, even in humans, is a tiny island. It is an error to deny that the artificial intelligence of computers throws light on the way the brain works—that is, on those of its functions that take place unconsciously. We can even agree that this island can exist only in this ocean—without driving certain intellectual and volitional processes out of consciousness into the unconscious, consciousness could not focus on what is essential to it; *relief* is crucial particularly for the survival of a being that has the ability to have an identity crisis. But however tiny this island of consciousness may be, it exists, and it cannot be understood on the model of computers, to which we have not the slightest reason—at least up to this point—to attribute consciousness. And not only does this island exist, but it alone makes the search for the mode of functioning of the ocean of the ratiomorphous apparatus interesting—because it alone can feel something like interest. Second, we must note that mental states cannot be identical with physical states that are intersubjectively accessible, that is, they cannot be identical with the corporeal and, in particular, with *facial expressions*—a position toward which the later Wittgenstein tends. This position is destroyed by the simple fact that humans can pretend, and that a one-to-one correlation between a mental state and an expression does not exist. (If it did, it would still be only a necessary, not a sufficient, condition for the identity thesis.) A broad spectrum of interactions among humans, which is vital for politics in particular, could not develop at all if Wittgenstein were right.

Nonetheless, we have to admit four points. First, it is correct that *the other* usually recognizes my identity by the constancy of my body, and especially of my face: precisely because my *I*-perspective is by definition inaccessible to others, my body has to function as a factor of identity; for others I exist only in the body that expresses itself. My countenance in particular, and especially the look in my eyes, are for others the expression of a sphere that they must not violate, which participates in something absolute, something holy—by the look in my eyes I am identifiable as a person. In the Moluccas, for example, a headhunter could attack only from behind: if he saw the face of his victim, he had to abandon the attempt; otherwise his act, which was respected in itself, would have been considered murder.[70] As so often happens, pathology teaches us the meaning of normal functions we do not notice when we are in good health: the serious deficiency known as prosopagnosia, in which a patient can no longer recognize other faces, is a powerful indication of the extraordinary importance of this function in social intercourse among human beings. No less important is the sense for gestures and mimicry, which usually reveal emotional changes in fellow human beings, but which can also be deceptive. Yet, on one hand, the case of mummified corpses shows that the continued existence of the body is not a sufficient condition for personal identity, and on

---

70. Cf. C. Vogel (1989), 124.

the other hand the intellectual possibilities of metempsychosis and metamorphosis suggest that it is not a necessary condition either: it is not logically self-contradictory to assume a continuity of one's own *I* despite changes in the body.[71] The unfortunate Gregor Samsa's problems of identity in Kafka's *Metamorphosis* have more to do with the reactions of others than with the transformation of his body.

Second, it goes without saying that the *body* belongs to a conscious or even a self-conscious being in an entirely different way from that in which even the property about which we care most belongs to us. This holds true insofar as the body is both the real condition of the possibility of one's own self-consciousness and an immediate presupposition for intersubjectivity. At least in this finite world, consciousness is to be found only in the physical, or, more precisely, in the organic.

Third, there are acts of consciousness in which the corporeal is concerned, even if they are not themselves physical: the inflammation of an organ is physical, but not the pain that it causes; for as phantom pains show, pains can exist without organs; the *content* of consciousness nonetheless refers to something physical.

Fourth, we can assert the following: The expressive behavior of the body can sometimes manifest levels of the self that are deeper than the accompanying processes of consciousness. I have already referred to the psychoanalytic theory according to which certain actions are not mediated by conscious acts of the will, but neither can they be categorized simply as purely physical processes: they satisfy certain wishes of the self, even if, at least during the action, the corresponding acts of consciousness have not occurred at all. But that does not mean that these wishes did not exist; they are *unconscious* and are not allowed to cross the threshold of consciousness. The organic basis of human beings sufficiently explains how such teleonomic behavior can occur and remain, even if to a lesser extent than conscious action, morally absolutely attributable.[72] Such behavior remains attributable because it cannot be explained in purely physical terms; semantic relationships are discernible in it that stand in an obvious relation to the conscious self. To be sure, several aspects of Freudian psychology are erroneous, for example, the overestimation of the sex drive in explaining complex human behavior, the concentration on childhood experiences at the expense of later life development (moreover, these experiences are not described so much on the basis of direct observation of children as on that of later reports made by adults), the underestimation of the importance of socialization for babies, and finally the complete lack of the autonomy of the moral. Some antagonistic feelings toward Freud are certainly understandable because the previously mentioned assumptions have harmed the science of psychology as well as society. Nonetheless, the theory of the unconscious is a brilliant achievement

---

71. Cf. the famous chap. 2, 27, in Locke's *Essay*.

72. This kind of teleonomy also exists with relation to the highest goals that the most intellectual person can set for himself; the growth of a genius cannot be explained without it. D. Emmet (1972) has rightly introduced the concept of vocation, alongside objective function and subjective purpose, as the structure through which significant subjective achievements affect social reality.

that ensures Freud an enduring place among the great innovators. So much in human behavior that before him seemed to be without cause (for example, slips of the tongue) is now partly explainable, partly understandable, and if no science can forgo a thorough causal explanation, at least as a regulative principle, then Freud can claim to have brought the theory of man closer to having the status of a science.

For political psychology in particular, the importance of the category of the unconscious is obvious. For instance, the political man does not always think about the extension of his own power; indeed, it may even be that he seldom thinks about it, because it is important for the stability of his self-consciousness to make his desire for power taboo and to believe that he is concerned only with matters of substance. But if he always acts in accord with the logic of the extension of power as it is known to him, if he indignantly rejects tips about strategies that are objectively more helpful but threaten his position of power, and if he passionately enjoys the moments when his drive to power is satisfied, as at least his facial expression will indicate, then we can say that such a man is obsessed with power—even if we have no reason to doubt his assertion that the idea that he wants power only seldom enters his consciousness. Indeed, in a certain sense such a man is significantly more dangerous than one who openly avows his drives, for unlike the latter, he can hardly control them. This implies the duty to achieve as much clarity as possible regarding what goes on in one's own self, for the self is more than the current stream of consciousness—it is the principle that generates this stream, as well as unconscious behavior. Nonetheless it must be fundamentally possible to raise this unconscious stratum of the self into consciousness—the unconscious cannot in principle escape introspection. Helping other human beings to shed light on their unconscious should for the most part be seen as morally positive. However, interest in another person's unconscious can be purely manipulative if one does not want to help him achieve a better knowledge of himself, but simply to use for one's own ends those of the other's drives that he does not perceive at all and therefore cannot control. The most dangerous kind of political man is one who knows the unconscious drives of others and uses them, but is unable to subject his own drives to critical analysis. Hitler is the first and up to now unsurpassed example of this combination of highly developed analytical abilities, so far as the masses' unconscious desires are concerned, with a complete lack of the ability for critical self-perception. He is the first of a whole series of modern despots and demagogues in whom a thorough knowledge of the possibilities of manipulation discovered by empirical psychology is combined with complete blindness with regard to themselves.

4.2.2.1. Memory, Thinking, Feelings

Mental states are not the only necessary condition for self-consciousness. Since they are temporal and not spatial, their continuation is subject to peculiar problems: whereas the real identity of a physical object implies its continued existence in space, this solution is not available for entities of the third world. Time's mode of being is fundamentally different from that of space, since the being of time is its passing, its constant passing over from a not-yet-being, the future, into a no-longer-being, the past; genuine being is attributable only to the present, which can hardly be conceived as extended. Therefore only retention and protention give acts of consciousness the ability to grasp contents that transcend the minimal points in time—for instance, one could scarcely perceive a melody as such if one lived only in the present. Thus past acts of consciousness must continue to exist in the present act of consciousness. To this extent *memory* is an extremely important factor of identity: organisms that have consciousness but to do not have the ability to imagine past acts of consciousness lack an elementary condition of the possibility of self-consciousness.[73] Moreover, human memory has been favored by the reduction of instincts. Whereas the consciousness of even higher animals is more or less exhausted by their behaviors at a given moment, human consciousness has a fluidity thanks to which everything can in principle be recollected at any time. However, memory is still not identical with self-consciousness.[74] Even if I knew everything about the past consciousness of another person, I would still not be identical with him. Conversely, while the ability to relate to oneself could never develop in a being without memory, yet it need not come to an end in the case of a temporary loss of memory; on the contrary, the question "Who am I really?" can be the starting point for a recovery of memory. Of course, memory is no more a mere category of consciousness than is thinking. Earlier experiences can also be stored in a data-processing system and determine the latter's subsequent behavior; no doubt much of this structure is also effective in human memory. Past acts of consciousness are not always remembered, and during the time that they are not in consciousness, they must subsist somewhere—precisely in their physical substrate, the brain. Hence they gain influence on behavior as well as on conscious experience, even if they are not present in consciousness: the specific quality of every act of consciousness is also shaped by the past history of consciousness, even if the latter is not concretely remembered. Thus the specific quality of an experience of a new injustice will be determined by an analogous earlier experience even if at the moment of this second experience one does not think about the first one: one would experience it in a different way if this first experience had not preceded it. Memory is based on series of associations of which a person is by no means always conscious; a certain man's face may arouse fear in me because long ago a man with a similar face did something harmful to me, even if I can no longer explain to myself where my current feelings of fear come from. Familiarity with another person's series of associations makes it easier to manipulate him.

It goes without saying that rational identity involves more than the formal element of memory. No less important is *what* is remembered—and what is forgotten. Memory is highly selective, indeed, reconstructive; identity is shaped only through the rejection of the inessential and concentration on the essential. Certain events are of special

---

73. However, I would not go so far as Popper, for whom not only self-consciousness but also consciousness presuppose memory (Popper and Eccles [1977], 69 ff.).

74. Cf. Leibniz, *Nouveaux Essais* II 27, and J. Butler's well-known criticism of Locke.

importance in the formation of the identity of the self; their constantly renewed memory is a central factor in identity. These include especially those experiences in which the *I* recognized which elements belong only accidentally to its self and which on the contrary belong to it essentially and cannot be altered by any distancing of the *I*. However much the *I* may be able to play with its self, however much in the self can be considered external with respect to the *I*, there is an ultimate core of the personality without which the concept of the external would have no meaning. This core is concealed not only from others but often even from the *I*; it is, as it were,[75] the substance in which all determinations inhere, that which, together with external contextual conditions, causes an individual's behavior throughout his life and distinguishes it from that of others. Even if this core may be completely determined by genes, early education, and so on, no one can complain about it as if it were something alien, something forced upon him, for there is nothing upon which the self could have been forced. In addition, the complaint would inevitably be a complaint made by an *I*, and the latter as such must necessarily attribute to itself a self of its own—in our case, precisely the self about which it is complaining. However, the *I* can and should modify the self, and in those aspects of the self that it recognizes as a result of its own influence it may see a product of freedom and therefore set a particularly high value on them.

In all changes in the self that are in part determined by the *I* a certain *continuity* of development must be clear; even ruptures must be teleologically comprehensible if the *I* is not to have the impression that its history is the history not of *one* self but of two or more selves. Conversely, a self that does not change at all is not a product of freedom; the true achievement lies in the combination of change and continuity, in the duration recognizable in the process of alteration. Naturally, the teleological context of development, without which one's own life easily comes to seem meaningless, is not always simply apparent, and occasionally subjective reconstructions can be very far removed from what the development actually has been. In any case, these reconstructions constitute one of the *I*'s most important tasks. Certainly the *I* does not constantly think about the inner unity of its life, but one can occasionally already deduce from the first gestures of an unknown person whether or not the *I* from which they flow has succeeded in finding a rational unity in the development of its self.

No less important than the relationship to the past is the *orientation toward the future*, the anticipation of what will come to pass. Between past and future there is an obvious asymmetry, since the past no longer can be undone, whereas the future is open to being shaped.[76] A being that intervenes in the world is necessarily oriented toward the future, and the belief in one's own freedom (whether it be rational or illusory) takes its nourishment from the openness of the future, whose course in the best of cases seems

---

75. The "as it were" is important, for the unity of the *I* and the self is dynamic and cannot be grasped with categories of substance metaphysics.

76. Therefore in *Sein und Zeit* § 65 (1979; 323 ff.) Heidegger rightly distinguished the future among the three temporal modes.

to be explainable only after the fact. The specificity of man's relationship to the future proceeds from his ability to think, which lends a double, even contrary, character to the future. On one hand, man can range over broad temporal spaces of the future and thereby give himself up to a thrill of freedom that is denied all other animals, who remain bound to the present moment. On the other hand, this ability to think about the future also entails a burden—it increases anxiety (*Sorge*). Hobbes aptly named man "*fame futura famelicus*"[77]—man already suffers from tomorrow's hunger—and a significant part of his activities, including, and especially, political activities, can be explained only on the basis of this anticipation of future hunger. Unlike animals, man has not only a need for nourishment so long as he is not satisfied, but also afterward a need to feel secure regarding tomorrow's nourishment; A. Gehlen speaks of a "need for the maintenance of the situation in which needs are met."[78] If this need is fulfilled by stored-up supplies, clothing, and shelter, it is no longer felt as such; it retreats into the background of consciousness. How important this background feeling of the need being fulfilled remains is indicated by even the slightest dangers to future security, which lead to insecurity and irritation even when they are not consciously perceived.

However, still eerier than anxiety is the following insight, which arises from excursions into the future: That there will be a time in which I will no longer exist. The future itself may never come to an end, but in comparison with its openness my own finiteness is even more negatively clear. Moving beyond the present and thus the most immediate temporal mode is paradoxically the condition for discovering one's own temporality and mortality. With the *consciousness of one's own mortality* this temporality, whose unfolding influences the development of being, reaches its apogee, and no doubt the emergence of self-consciousness is linked to that of the consciousness of death—even if in a peculiarly circular way, since an elementary self-consciousness must already exist in order to conceive death as one's own death. To be sure, the consciousness of death is initially conveyed by the experience of another person's death: the final cessation of communication with a beloved person throws the survivor back on himself. But the transfer of death to one's own future signifies a still more extensive deepening of the developing self-consciousness—however paradoxical it may be that *I* can imagine that I will someday no longer exist. For I cannot abstract from my own idea that abstracts from my existence; somewhere I am concealed, observing, when I imagine others gathered around my grave. On one hand the consciousness of death makes it easier to objectivize one's own self: the insight that this self is not simply there, but will someday be annihilated, allows the *I* to break out of the self in sheer horror and constitute itself as something relatively autonomous with regard to the self.[79] On the other hand, the self acknowledged to be finite now takes on a new meaning: the time that still remains must

---

77. *De homine* chap. 10.3 (1839 ff. b; 2:91).

78. (1975), 51: "Bedürfnis nach Beibehaltung der Bedürfnisdeckungslage." Cf. in general 50–54.

79. On a very high and complex level, the contribution of the consciousness of death to self-consciousness can be investigated in the *Epic of Gilgamesh*.

be correctly used; the self must not let itself be driven, but must be shaped by the *I*. The irreversibility of time is consciously recognized for the first time; the knowledge of the uniqueness and finiteness of one's own existence flashes across the emerging self-consciousness. Art, which eternalizes the dead in architecture, sculpture, painting, and words, is an expression of an elementary protest against death.[80]

With insight into death a general animal ability also appears in a peculiar light: *the ability to kill.* Anyone who has grasped the irreversible nature of death and at the same time knows that he can kill—can even kill another being just as aware of the irreversibility of death as he is—must in his innermost core tremble at this ability of his to cause something that he can never undo. Perhaps even more than the fear of one's own death, shuddering and pleasure in one's own ability to kill have promoted the emancipation of the *I*.[81] Since in the course of life the relation between the past that has already been lived and the remaining future changes, the consciousness of death becomes correspondingly more acute; indeed, because of the knowledge of inevitable death, the process of aging acquires a meaning for the aging being that a being without consciousness of death could not have. Naturally the consciousness of a higher animal, for example a dog, also changes in the process of aging; but this change takes place only *in* consciousness, not *for* it. The connection between self-consciousness and consciousness of death is so fascinating because paradoxically only the consciousness of death makes death into a metaphysical affront. I am not referring to the trivial point that only a being with a consciousness of death can feel a horror regarding death that is unknown to other animals. Rather, I am pointing out that a being with self-consciousness can be seen as an image of the absolute insofar as it instantiates in the most complete form within the real world the reflexive relation that inevitably belongs to the concept of the absolute. The unconditional dignity of man results from the fact that he is the bearer of something that mirrors the absolute. For this reason the death of a self-conscious being is incomparably more horrible than the demise of an animal with mere consciousness. That even the being that comes closest to the absolute is not spared the inevitable fate of everything organic may clearly be felt to be absurd. And yet what makes this death so disturbing is a quality—self-consciousness—that can develop only in a being with a consciousness of death; but there can be no consciousness of death without death. In short, death is terrrible because it isolates something that could not exist witihout death. With a still greater right than in the case of all other organisms, in the case of self-consciousness death only takes back what belongs to it anyway because it owes its existence to death. Perhaps that is why self-consciousness not only fears death but is also fascinated by it in a peculiar way and in any case likes to provoke it.

---

80. It is in accord with history's tendency toward subjectivization that the work of art is originally meant to eternalize its object, and only much later its creator.

81. The success of the opening scene in Stanley Kubrick's *2001: A Space Odyssey* is due not only to the accompaniment of Strauss's music but also to the cinematic perfection with which it represents the connections just outlined.

Complementary to the consciousness of death is the human knowledge that life is not only extinguished but also comes into being anew—without this knowledge there could be no consciousness of the continuity of living being and its constant new beginning. Because of the anisotropy of time, however, one's own birth is not something that one can anticipate; and since any given age in life can be experienced as such only in contrast to another, adulthood (or, at the earliest, youth) is the first age one experiences as a distinct age, whereas a child does not feel that he is a child—one can long for childhood only long after it is past. It is the youth of others, which one does not simply remember as youth but immediately experiences as such, and the birth of others, that make it possible for us to consciously experience the natality of the organic. At least this is true of the male. The female has a more immediate relationship to the sphere of birth because her connection to the fetus is not a connection between two autonomous beings, and it is hardly an accident that the significance of natality, alongside that of mortality, was emphasized by a *female* student of Heidegger's—Hannah Arendt.

Self-consciousness is shaped only through *consciousness of the world,* for the *I* is first of all only the formal function of self-attribution; and even if the exclusion of the other is grounded in this function, the formality of this function, which is found in all other beings with self-consciousness, nonetheless in no way allows us to see in it solely the *principium individuationis:* all such beings are equally *I*'s. Beings with self-consciousness differ from each other through the concrete determinations of their selves; this is the *principium individuationis,* which can certainly also qualify and distinguish from other ways the specific way in which the *I* concerned fulfills the task of self-attribution. The self precedes the *I,* even if, as I said, the *I* can fashion it. In this labor lies freedom's chance, but it is always a matter of freedom, which did not arise ex nihilo but has to attach itself to something already existing: the *I* does not choose its self, but can at most transform it, and no *I* can attach itself to a self without a world.[82] What the self is, is decisively determined by its experiences with the world, and above all with other human beings. Of special importance is the fact that we can learn from other people's mistakes; we do not need to experience defeats ourselves in order to learn how they can be avoided: we need only observe others.[83] Even the moral dimension, that is, virtues and vices, of the self is usually strongly influenced in the first years of life; genetic structures determine a range of dispositions, a few of which are realized through these early experiences.[84] The specific way in which man relates to the world is connected with the capacity for relating to himself to a far greater extent than was apparent up to this point. Ultimately we can say that

---

82. I leave open here the question of whether the *I*'s work of transformation is not itself determined by the self.

83. Cf. A. Bandura on "vicarious motivations" (1986; 283 ff.).

84. So far as aggressivity and altruism are concerned, research on twins seems to have proven that genetic factors play a significant role. Cf. P. G. Zimbardo (1988), 645 f., with additional bibliography. I have drawn much of the information scattered over the following pages from this rightly famous textbook.

only man has a world, precisely because he alone has the ability to set himself over against it; other animals have only a limited environment, into which they are absorbed.

Man's relationship to the world is twofold in nature, both *theoretical* and *practical:* man is a *thinking* and *acting* being. Certainly, the poietic self of every organism, and thus also of man, is first of all a vital drive center, whose first encounters with the world arise from the satisfaction of elementary drives such as the drive to nourish itself. However, even a small child does not react merely passively to the stimuli of the external world; on the contrary, a baby already actively seeks stimuli. Sensory and motor faculties develop in parallel; the child's receptive capacity is heavily dependent on his movements, in which he experiences the world and his own body simultaneously. In addition, the socialization that makes him more than a being with drives begins very early in man's ontogenetic development; a baby already develops a special interest precisely in social phenomena.[85] Through socialization man learns to control his vital functions, and in his relation to the world he is very soon no longer concerned solely with what in the latter serves his organic functions; the world as sensed and the world of action are no longer correlated in him. It is true that there are connections between the theoretical and the poietic relation to the world: individual technical and scientific discoveries presuppose each other, and not only on the highest level of abstraction; systematic poietic intervention in the world and the elaboration of a theoretical relation to the world are equally expressions of man's consciousness that he stands, as it were, outside the world. The dialectics of technology consists in the fact that early man already achieved a more comprehensive satisfaction of his needs only by forbearing to quench them immediately. The oldest tools already presuppose a playful testing out of possibilities: through such testing the laws of form were grasped, and man understood that the world is more than a releaser for his drives, indeed, that it has its own being and structures. Gehlen aptly speaks of a "*transcendence in the here and now,*"[86] which opens up to man and ultimately leads to the recognition of objects having a value of their own. As Marx rightly saw, that is why *labor* is such a central anthropological category: through labor man discerns his power over nature, his ability to actively shape it and to subject it to his own ends—on the condition, however, of taking an objective stance toward reality. Since in order to master nature he must also have control over his own body and its fine motor skills, labor is the phenomenon through which man learns no longer to be his body but to have it; labor mediates the body techniques that are so characteristic of human beings.[87] In addition, labor demands that man forgo the immediate satisfaction of his drives. In this respect as well it is an important factor in the formation of self-consciousness. But that does not alter the fact that early in human history theoretical speculations were already freed from any connection with practice. A person pondering the beginning of the world is not satisfying any economic interests; instead, his reflection has for him the character of *an end in itself.*

---

85. Cf. D. Stern (1977).
86. (1975), 16: "*Transzendenz ins Diesseits.*"
87. Cf. M. Mauss (1973), 363 ff.

What is *thinking?* Primitive forms of consciousness already presuppose the ability to *make distinctions,* and as a thinking being man can also *compare* the distinguished elements with regard to something common. Thus man orders all his experiences in a *categorial network;* each individual sense impression is subsumed under *general concepts* that are only partly influenced by experience. Therefore different people can interpret the same experience in different ways. Only through these general concepts and the most general of them, the categories, can man deal with the plenitude of reality pressing in upon him and reduce its complexity; they are points of crystallization that structure our experience of the world and even determine the mode of perception. The selection that they carry out relieves us and, as it were, creates intellectual environments in which we can feel at home and that we also need as retreats when we make intellectual breakthroughs. The most innovative genius is often extremely conservative in certain areas of his worldview. Naturally, the particular individually and socially realized systems of general concepts differ. Indeed, the great historical thresholds result in discontinuous changes in the categorial system that since Kuhn have often been called "paradigm shifts." Not everything that people call a "paradigm shift" is equally crucial: the paradigm shift from classical mechanics to quantum mechanics leaves much unaltered; it is almost harmless compared with the break that divides the magical thinking of so-called primitive peoples from the scientific thought of the Greeks. The existence of these differences between the conceptual systems of individual persons and cultures can certainly be granted to perspectivism, and one can also concede to pragmatism and evolutionary epistemology that the different necessities for survival in various cultures can partly explain why diverse systems of categories have developed: if they are to survive, Eskimos have to be able to perceive more differences in snow and to name them than do people who live in deserts.

However, we must make two qualifications. First, one must not fail to recognize that despite all differences commonalities exist. Thus a few concepts are common to all humans, such as the category of causality, from which magic as well as science spring. Even if they interpret them very differently, both magicians and scientists are looking for the *causes* of an event. Second, criticism of another person's one-sided perspective always already presupposes that it is in principle possible to raise oneself above such one-sidedness—and that means that there is an ideally valid system of general concepts against which these real systems can be measured. Just as we distinguish between mores and morals, we must distinguish between the countless factual epistemic systems and the one ideally valid epistemic system, and it is obvious that all ontogenetic and phylogenetic investigations concern only the genesis of the factual systems and make no contribution to a theory of the ideally valid system. In actuality, all concepts (that is, not only normative, but also descriptive, concepts) are idealizations of empirical reality. It remains incomprehensible how legitimate idealizations should be distinguished from illegitimate ones if there is no autonomous ideal world. Philosophy's primary task is to reconstruct this ideal system. However, anyone who wants to try to predict how a given person will behave must deal with both his descriptive and his normative system of categories, for the latter, and not the one that is reasonable in itself, will determine his behavior. Together with concrete experiences, this system of categories explains in large part which image of the world people develop. For every normal person a minimal condition for the appropriateness of this image is its *consistency*. The latter is absolutely compatible with the fact that categories are developed as opposed pairs: one can only conceive unity if one has access to the category of plurality.

To be sure, the ability to think has promoted the genesis of self-consciousness and has been promoted by it. If one can free himself from concrete sense data—initially in imagination, which does not remain bound to the concrete sense impression, but does remain bound to the sphere of sensibilia, and then in thinking—he finds it easier to distance himself from his own self, which then appears just as much as an instantiation of something general as, for example, a particular cat appears as an example of a species. The *ability to count* has also often been interpreted as specifically human, for two reasons. Not only did processes of abstraction whose complexity we can now hardly imagine contribute to the concept of number, but it is characteristic of counting that it never comes to an end: in the domain of intellectual operations, the concept of the infinite corresponds to the self-transcendence of self-consciousness.[88] But man's greatest achievement does not consist in being able to form the concept of an animal or the number five. Rather, his knowledge culminates in his ability to pose the *question of validity*. He can distance himself from his own ideas as well as from his wishes by asking himself whether the former are *true*, and whether the latter are *morally right*. In other words, he can *judge*, represent stimuli as propositions, and affirm or deny the latter. The ideas of the true and the good are the greatest and most consequential discoveries of the human intellect. Once one has grasped them, one can no longer evade them. Anyone who thinks he has seen that all truths are illusions has to consider this conviction of his to be true. These ideas have a generality that is attributable neither to my interior dimension nor to events in the external world: This flower may wither tomorrow, or I may forget it; but that it existed at such and such a time in such and such a place remains forever and everywhere true—and if there are other people, it is true for all of them to the same extent. These ideas open up a horizon of *freedom* that leads beyond the mere negative freedom from constraint: man can investigate the *reasons* for theoretical or practical assumptions and thereby free himself from the blind *causes* that would otherwise drive him on. Indeed, man can rise to the observation of the first world. Early man, who painted on the walls of his cave what was for him simply threatening, the animal, thereby already raised himself above all individual animals to the essence of the animal; and the spirits he glimpsed in the world were his way of grasping the beings of the ideal world. Knowledge of eidetic connections and the capacity to passionately distance oneself from one's own self constitute what we call "spirit." Without the former this capacity becomes a torment, since

---

88. However, not all human cultures have many counting words; in the language of the Bushmen, for instance, "three" is already "many."

the problem of identity cannot be resolved if there is not an authority that is not part of the empirical world, but nonetheless *is* in the highest degree; without the latter that knowledge remains cold and does not give life to the principle, which it alone can make its own. Both intelligence and feelings nourish the intellect that seeks *order* in the world because it is itself structured in accord with principles of order.

Naturally, attaining a solid grasp, based on arguments, of the pure dimension of validity is an extremely lengthy process and as such cannot be placed at the beginning of human history. But that it nonetheless involves something basically human is shown by the *phenomenon of religious life*, which underlies both art and philosophy. In religious life there occurs a reference to that which can ground claims to validity, and however crude this reference may be, however great the distance between the most primitive superstition and pure reflection on validity, the conviction that the world is more than what is the case nonetheless reaches from those beginnings to this reflection. Certainly religion can be explained psychologically as the projection of a normative self-image of man onto the heavens. But the crucial point is that this normative self-image has a meaning only if there actually is a normative sphere that was not made by men. Man may have created his gods, but in this act of creation a dim recognition of an ideal world that is not his own creation is manifested. In metaphysics and ethics man finally achieves his greatest possible proximity to the ideal world—and he grasps that without a being like him, being would not be complete, because without such a being the structures that determine real being could not be within real being.

Only to a very limited extent can the specifically human in *feelings* be mentioned here. Unfortunately, although learning how to deal with feelings is one of the crucial tasks of a human and intellectual existence, they are one of the most neglected sides of human consciousness, and this judgment holds for both empirical psychology and philosophy. So far as the latter is concerned, not much that is innovative has been achieved since Scheler's trail-blazing studies. The two types of feelings that he analyzed in *Wesen und Formen der Sympathie* (*The Nature of Sympathy*)—that is, feelings of sympathy on one hand, and love and hate on the other—are certainly not the only ones that in their elaborated form can be attributed to man alone, but they are certainly the most important. So far as the feeling of sympathy goes, Scheler rightly distinguishes fellow feeling (*eigentliches Mitgefühl*) from immediate community of feeling (*unmittelbares Mitgefühl*), on one hand, and, on the other, from emotional infection (*Gefühlsansteckung*) and emotional identification (*Einsfühlung*).[89] In emotional identification, as it occurs for example in sexual intercourse or in a great mass of people, the consciousness of an independent individuality is extinguished; everyone feels something similar, but without realizing that it is different persons who feel something similar. In emotional infection, moods are transferred; here there is no emotional identification, yet the melancholy of the second person, who is infected by the gloom of the first, is in no way intentionally directed

89. See Scheler (1974), 23 ff.

toward the cause that made the first sad, but rather toward his own worries. Only in genuine sympathy do I feel the other's joy or suffering, even if it is not my own—I can mourn with a friend the death of his father, whom I did not know at all. An example of the immediate community of feeling with one and the same anguish, on the other hand, would be the common pain of two parents over the loss of their equally beloved child. Genuine sympathy is an exceptionally complex intentional act because in contrast to other feelings it is directed not toward the cause of the pain, but rather toward the pain felt by another person; it is to some extent a meta-feeling. It is based on the *I*'s uncanny capacity for abstraction, by virtue of which the *I* considers any other self as being in principle of equal value with itself. Yet feeling is more than mere recognizing; abstractly understanding that the other person deserves sympathy does not mean that one feels sympathy. Feeling has mental qualities of an intensity for which thinking vainly longs. The same holds for love, which Scheler analyzed in a way that is still unsurpassed. It is absurd to maintain, like Spinoza, that what one considers a cause of joy is an object of love. First, love can cause the most painful torment known to man and, second, we will not love a rascal even if on a whim he makes us his heirs. Rather, love is the feeling of a value. A person who loves not only acknowledges theoretically his beloved's plenitude of values, rather, the latter becomes emotionally present for him. Even if value judgments must in principle be accessible to rational analysis, this does not mean that the values asserted in them cannot also be emotionally present. Love is the sense for the value dimension of existents, wherefrom it follows that a culture that has convinced itself that there are no objective values will necessarily be loveless. Not only objects but also, and especially, persons can be valuable, and that includes oneself, so that the idea of self-love is in no way false. On the contrary, a person who does not love himself will also mistrust his own feelings of value and may therefore hardly love anything or anyone else.

4.2.2.2. Principles of the Theory of Action

Human *action*, the causation or prevention of a change in the world that is directed by the will and is normally oriented toward a goal, should have a central place in any anthropological theory, for it mediates in a concrete way between the biological and intellectual sides of man. A merely thinking being is not necessarily by virtue of its essence an organism, and not every behaving organism is an intellectual being; on the other hand, only an intellectual organism can act. Even if it remains mysterious how the psychic should be able to affect the physical,[90] action seems to represent a fascinating unity of the corporeal and the mental. Moreover, intentions to perform actions constitute the most important class of the subjects of moral predicates—one is *responsible* for actions because they spring from one's own *I* (by whatever the latter may itself be mediated).

---

90. Even if it is appropriate to have serious doubts regarding interactionism, it cannot be denied that from a first-person perspective on action, a thought precedes a physical event.

Action has its origin in animal behavior, which is directed first of all toward nourishment and reproduction. Without *needs,* whose satisfaction often promises *pleasure* and whose non-satisfaction sometimes results in *pain,* even human action would be difficult to explain.[91] But first of all, because of the human ability to control drives, most, but not all, needs lose the urgency that characterizes them in animals: they become *interests,* between whose appearance and satisfaction many means may be interposed. Second, this is the reason that human needs are incomparably more differentiated than those of other animals—over and above biological needs arise culturally mediated needs such as cognitive, aesthetic, and religious ones.[92] A. Gehlen aptly speaks of "a need for needs that extend beyond the basics of existence."[93] On one hand, this meta-need springs from man's relative independence with regard to nature; on the other hand, the extension of the sphere of needs may once again restrict freedom. The plurality of human needs and the decoupling from the instincts threaten any human interior dimension with chaos, which can be overcome only by a *stabilization* of the structure of needs. It is in particular important to hierarchize by means of an *order of preference* the various needs and interests, since they can never be satisfied all at once. It is clear that more complex needs can develop only when the primary needs are satisfied, indeed, only when the background feeling that they are being fulfilled produces a sensation of security; but this is not possible without institutions. Moreover, the satisfaction of elementary needs can be made to serve the expression of higher ones; a meal eaten in common can set the seal on a friendship. Thirdly, among men even more than among other higher animals, many actions that originally served organic ends have become goals in themselves: consider only sexuality. However its realization may be evaluated, the *possibility* of masturbation and homosexuality is a privilege of higher animals, and indeed a criterion of more advanced evolution. But even in working toward freely set, and as such desired, goals it can very well happen that the means employed ultimately become a goal in themselves: that is how the fine arts developed out of technology.

Needs and interests are determined by external factors, by inner predispositions, or by individual choice. However, determinants underlie this choice itself that do not cease to operate because they do not appear in consciousness; reference to them may humble any conception of freedom that sees in the possibility of satisfying all one's own interests the highest goal of man. Thus neoclassical theory errs when it makes the factual preferences of isolated individuals an absolute and tries to reconstruct social interactions on the basis of these preferences—in truth many interests are themselves the

---

91. This does not mean that man strives directly for pleasure. The normal person strives first for food and not immediately for the pleasure that eating may produce; only in times of decadence can someone—through the use of drugs, for instance—want to avoid the detour through the thing itself and aim directly at pleasure. Cf. Scheler (1980), 56 f. On the other hand, whenever he can, man directly avoids pain, even if he cannot get rid of the causes of pain.

92. Consider A. Maslow's well-known hierarchy of needs.

93. Gehlen (1966), 331: "[ein] Bedürfnis nach Bedürfnissen . . . , die über diese Existenzminima überhaupt hinausgehen." Trans. C. McMillan and K. Pillemer, 325.

result of social interaction. Nevertheless, it will be conceded that some needs, such as that for nourishment, are common to everything organic, while others, such as the need for a stable identity, are common to all men; and while many needs differ from one individual to another, they are based on real personal differences. In our time a steadily increasing number of needs are nonetheless produced by the wish to distance oneself from others and to surpass them by creating one's own identity. Methodologically, it must be admitted that discussing actions before developing a theory of the social is misleading insofar as the most important determinants of action—needs as well as the values in relation to which they are assessed—are for the most part social in origin: Actions generally occur against the background of a social system, and many interests are explicitly altruistic. However, even castaways on desert islands can act, and *privati* (solitary individuals using a private language) are conceivable.

Needs trigger drives that in turn release the energy for action, but they cause only the general wish to act, not the concrete action itself: if one is hungry, one will do something, but what one will do depends on the concrete situation and on one's own character. An important variable is the *intensity* of the need; this is gauged in accord with the strength of the pressure that exists in the direction of an action that could reduce the tension. It not uncommonly happens that mutually opposed drives are activated simultaneously; among animals this can result in many different reactions, as we know from ethology: distinctions are drawn between superposition, averaging, alternation, cancellation, transformation, repression, and prevention of the corresponding types of behavior. Of special interest are so-called *displacement activities:* "Deer engage in sham feeding when the pressure to stay conflicts with a slight pressure to flee."[94] The explanation for this phenomenon is disputed; according to Tinbergen, an energy surplus that is prevented by a conflicting behavioral program from being discharged into its normal channel flows over into another path in order to find some kind of discharge, no matter how senseless the behavior in question may be in a given situation.

Displacement activities have been shown to exist among human beings as well: behavioral programs from the realms of body care, food intake, and sleeping can occur in the presence of antagonistic drives. What Gehlen calls "stabilized tension" is specific to humans. With regard to powerful persons, for instance, one may feel simultaneously the wish to submit and to be aggressive, and this can lead to a new arrangement of feeling that results in certain types of behavior that represent a middle distance.[95] So-called redirected behavior also throws light on human beings: animals that are attacked by higher-ranking individuals do not defend themselves, but take out their aggression on lower-ranking individuals. To be sure, there is a great difference between the behavior of other animals and that of man: for instance, the example of redirected behavior just mentioned occurs among humans against the background of struggles for recognition, which shape identities; moral judgment of the corresponding impulse can certainly in-

94. I. Eibl-Eibesfeldt (1980), 262. Cf. in general 259–264, "Konfliktverhalten."
95. Cf. Gehlen (1975), 78 ff.

hibit its eruption. Very generally, among humans there is not only a conflict between different biologically based drives, but also between drive and moral judgment; the latter can arise from an autonomous moral insight, but is mostly adopted from others. One of Freud's most convincing theses is that in such a conflict (in his terminology, between the id and the superego) *defense mechanisms* go into effect. The number and diversity of these mechanisms are great;[96] since their place in the structure of the human intellect varies, a few of them will be discussed later in this chapter. In the language of psychoanalysis the previously mentioned example of redirected behavior would be called "displacement"; one speaks of "repression" when the corresponding drive is expelled from consciousness (but under certain circumstances continues to determine behavior). Moreover, in reaction formation an overemphasis on all intentions that are opposed to the repressed drive occurs. The flight from conflict into passivity is called "emotional isolation," while the separation of incompatible strivings so that they no longer appear simultaneously in consciousness is called "compartmentalization."

If an individual is prevented from engaging in drive-satisfying behavior, one speaks of frustration, and there are good reasons for hypothesizing that although frustrations can be differently elaborated and do not always determine aggressive behavior, they do elicit a tendency to aggression. In humans, a reduction of the intensity of tension can also take place through fantasy, through actions that do not affect the actually intended object (substitute actions), or through a cathartic expression of emotions: sometimes it is more important to do *something* than do the right thing, just in order to escape internal pressure.[97] If the need is immoral, it is reasonable to shift over to catharsis or to substitute actions that are less repugnant; openly expressing feelings of antipathy or reducing internal motor pressure by shifting aggression to things is certainly better than coming to blows with someone, and in certain situations it may even be better than bottling up one's aggression within oneself and thereby building up a fund of hatred. In actuality, modernity, which is based on the cult of opinions, overestimates the power of mere ideas in an almost touching way; the discovery that certain drives such as the aggressive and sexual drives can trigger morally disturbing actions is hardly enough to control them. As an organism, man must carry out bodily processes in order to master his drives; mere talk cannot replace actions. The recommendation to use substitute actions as an escape is not valid if the need is objectively justified, for then the corresponding action to be replaced by a substitute is permissible and indeed in some cases even obligatory. This is particularly true in politics, in which controlled collective use of substitute actions in times of irrational excitement may be the only way of avoiding greater

---

96. Cf., for instance, the summary chart in P. G. Zimbardo (1988), 434.

97. While substitute actions perform a function similar to that of displacement activities, they nonetheless differ from them in that they are actions, and thus willed. A person who scratches his head in a perplexing situation does so involuntarily; a person who goes to a boxing club to take out his aggressions knows what he is doing; moreover, his action is objectively related to the one originally intended.

damage, but in which substitute actions can also distract attention from the fact that one is unable and unwilling to resolve urgent problems.

Among actions, one can distinguish the following types, which together play a great role in the human behavioral repertoire: In addition to *impulse actions*, which are closely related to reflexes—such as digging into a bowl of candies that is at hand without having really felt a need for them—and actions that are not *goal-directed*—such as strolling through grocery stores in order to buy something or other—there is action in the full sense of the word, which is characterized essentially by the conscious anticipation of results: it has a concrete goal that is subjectively intended. Thus the teleonomy of the organic becomes a *teleology*. The desired condition is represented in consciousness before it is produced in the external world. A still higher level is achieved when the action is carried out as an instantiation of a *scheme of action*, which can be elaborated by man as a thinking being that knows that every performance springs from a more general competence.

In the case of *actions performed under the influence of passion*, the immediate result of action is willed, but neither are the consequences of one's own action considered, nor is the actor in a position to reflect for a long time about the choice of the most appropriate means. In actions that are determined by *habit*, if asked the actor *can* explain what he is doing and what its consequences will be, but as a rule they take place unnoticed. A very large part of human behavior is determined by habits that have become mechanical, and even the most conscious actions can become habitual after many repetitions—in fact, must become habitual if they are to take place with a certain reliability. This holds at least for the motor aspect of actions: one can write only if one no longer needs to pay attention to each individual letter or even to moving his fingers in the ways necessary to produce it. But even in the case of thinking habitualization is inevitable: a great mathematician can concentrate on new questions only because he instinctively masters simpler operations without paying attention to them. The habitualization of moral thought and action is called "virtue." In times of intellectual and moral paralysis it is the most deeply automatic, and therefore usually oldest, mechanisms of action that keep people on track. A liturgy that has become habitual, for instance, can survive for centuries after the breakdown of the corresponding body of dogma. Moreover, this is the reason why precisely in times of crisis in which a relatively complex level of consciousness has become questionable there occurs a regression to earlier, and often more primitive, forms of reaction that should themselves be much more questionable.

In the case of *carefully considered actions* questions of both the consequences and the means are weighed; the list of means considered may be very long, and entirely new means may even be devised that previously did not exist at all.[98] Sometimes the goal can be achieved with relatively little difficulty; sometimes it is necessary to overcome resistance, which is particularly strong, naturally, when the center of resistance is itself a per-

---

98. The first means were probably not employed *as means*, but after it was learned that certain objects or types of behavior onto which people had stumbled by accident had certain consequences, they consciously resorted to them when they wanted to produce those consequences.

son or even oneself; for often one has to sacrifice immediate interests of one's own in order to do justice to long-term interests. *Willpower* consists in not deviating from one's goals even if the resistance is great, and persistently working for their realization; *flexibility* (which in this sense is completely compatible with willpower) is defined as the ability to deviate from the originally adopted means-ends sequence when negative feedback is encountered, without for that reason giving up the goals themselves. The contrary concepts are *weakness of will* and *stubbornness,* which are likewise not mutually exclusive: someone may prefer to give up his goal rather than the means that he at first chose for achieving this goal, because he does not grasp the difference in generality and importance between means and end. Naturally, in addition to general knowledge regarding means-ends relationships, judgment—that is, the subsumption of situations under a general concept—is also required in order to act successfully. A *stupid* person acts against his long-term interests because he does not see that the steps he is taking will produce a result opposite to the one he intends; a *clever* person knows the right means and how to subsume situations under rules. The satisfaction of one's own interests, including long-term interests, does not necessarily lead to *happiness,* since certain interests necessarily make a person unhappy, whether they are satisfied or remain unfulfilled. Yet happiness (including one's own) is not the highest value. What is truly human is rather, as we have already seen, the evaluation of one's own desires and needs on the basis of general criteria. In making this evaluation, the individual and social values are not necessarily really moral; they must only transcend subjective needs and interests. Even if some values may have been adopted only because they legitimated already existing interests, recognizing them leads to specific actions that can no longer be described as oriented toward interests, but must be described as oriented toward values, precisely because under certain circumstances the individual's own interests are sacrificed to them. To be sure, one can use the word "interest" in such an undifferentiated way that even the most ascetic action appears to be interested, for of course every action must be the result of a motive. However, the crucial question is what kind of motive it is—whether it is experienced as pre-moral or moral. In any case, it cannot be denied that man has the ability to set aside pre-moral motives for the sake of what he regards as moral, and to alter his goals. This ability differs from one individual to another; in the following, we will speak of *moral willpower* or *weakness of moral will.*[99] Against Socrates' view it must be objected that there is clearly such a thing as weakness of moral will, and that it is even compatible with great moral intelligence. However, the contradiction between the values recognized and one's own behavior is painful—even more painful than purely theoretical *cognitive dissonances.*[100] The mechanisms that cause dissonances to disappear are manifold and in part known since the French moralists. If a change in one's own behavior does not succeed, one may challenge the evident descriptive

---

99. This is an unfortunate choice of words because here "moral willpower" means only the ability to sacrifice interests to one's own norms, independently of whether these norms are really moral.

100. This concept is derived from L. Festinger.

propositions that alone, as the minor premise of a practical syllogism, manifest the contradiction between the values and one's own behavior, or one may distance oneself from the values. Psychoanalysis speaks of the defense mechanism known as "denial of reality" when one simply does not perceive the facts standing in the way of one's own wishes, and of "rationalization" when some more or less rational ground for one's own behavior is adduced, although the behavior is determined exclusively by drives and one would hold fast to it even if all such pseudo-rational grounds were irrefutably disconfirmed. Examples are legion, especially in the realm of political psychology. Presumably the majority of Germans really did not consciously perceive the signs (which were numerous) indicating that Jews and gypsies were being murdered, because perceiving them would have made it a duty to perform dangerous actions. However, what was said in chapter 3.1.2 implies that these major collective acts of repression are morally attributable. Analogously, most sadistic war criminals probably calmed any qualms by reflecting that their acts were "military necessities." Nonetheless, not all individual and social values can be described merely as *secondary rationalizations* of needs (and even if they were, that does not suffice to determine their validity). Certainly such processes play a major role in history: normative and descriptive theories are often developed in order to legitimate a habit that arose for quite different reasons; rites are generally older than myths. But the fact that man does not simply satisfy his needs as do other animals, but rather seeks to justify them, remains worthy of attention and respect, even if the legitimation itself is absurd. Satisfaction could have been had more easily, and the detour that it has taken cannot be explained solely by the need, but must also involve man's tendency to transcend himself, which is grounded in his nature.

In brief, human behavior is clearly determined by various parameters. Normally, one must *want* something, *be able* to have it, and *be permitted* to have it (that is, believe that one is permitted to have it). First, we must mention every individual's needs and interests, which are partly produced by the core of his personality, partly mediated by other people, and partly induced by the situation. Presumably it is correct that without interests there would be no action; a pure intellect would simply observe. But they are only necessary, not sufficient, conditions for actions. Second, one must also have the ability to realize what one wants; that is, one must be aware of the necessary means and be able to put them into practice. Third, one's own actions are measured against values; depending on the values, some needs and interests prove to be incompatible with them; and some are in fact compatible with them, but in such a way that they need certain means for their satisfaction that themselves cannot withstand examination. How far this theoretical insight has practical consequences depends on the degree of moral willpower and on the intensity of the needs. Finally, we should not underestimate the power of habits that conflict with the achievement of the goal, which often win out. Even if most people can *forgo* actions that they consider immoral, it is much more difficult to *do* what one is inclined to forgo. Impulses to commit immoral actions are much easier to master than those to commit immoral omissions, because moral judgment is a controlling authority, but not does not itself provide the psychic energy necessary for every kind of action. What the *I* can do is shift energies to moral ends by forgoing the satisfaction of drives; what it cannot do is create these energies. Drives are therefore neither to be demonized nor to be immediately lived out, but instead correctly channeled; great deeds for either good or ill cannot be accomplished without strong drives. The sex drive can pervert man, yet he can also sublimate it into the most refined forms of love; aggressive drives are required by both villains and heroes. It is certainly wiser to know one's own drives and acknowledge them—insofar as one seeks to achieve with and from them the moral optimum that one is granted—than to repress them and thereby give them an opportunity to take a terrible revenge.

In order to explain human behavior, theoretical expectations must also be taken into account: the same goals can lead to very different actions if there are different assumptions regarding the appropriate means. These differences are partly conditioned by deviating experiences, because there is a universal human tendency to generalize certain personally momentous experiences, though this is of course not always permissible.[101] In part, a role is played by different systems of categories and *frames of attention* that first determine which events will be perceived at all. The whole environment is not perceived; the part to which attention is directed is called a "milieu." The political importance of collective attention frames is obvious: whoever controls them controls a great portion of a group's theoretical assumptions and therefore its behavior. To be sure, attention frames are never sufficient, but rather necessary conditions for actions: they determine what one can grasp, and the evaluation of what is grasped then leads to actions.[102] The stabilization of a person's interests, values, and theoretical assumptions makes his behavior more or less predictable, because it fixes attitudes, that is, predispositions, to react in a particular way in specific situations.

4.2.2.3. Descriptive and Normative Self-Images: The "Me"

"To be created in the image of God means to have to live with the image of man."[103] The relationship to the dimension of the morally right changes the identity problem in a dramatic way. Without this relationship man would have only a *descriptive self-image;* but because he looks toward something greater than he, a *normative self-image* is necessarily produced. The *I* not only entertains assumptions regarding what it is, but also regarding what it ought to become. The *I* can only accept its self if the descriptive self-image corresponds to the normative self-image; however, this harmony is justified only if both self-images are also truly rational, that is, if the *I* really knows its self and if its normative self-image is appropriate. The normative self-image of himself that man

---

101. S. Marx (1994) has aptly shown how the genre of moral narrative dissolves in Kleist's work because it no longer contains repeatable patterns of reality, and therefore his heroes misunderstand all apparently familiar situations.

102. Cf. H. D. Lasswell and A. Kaplan (1969), 26 f., 112 f.

103. Jonas (1966), 186.

constructs results in a practical syllogism: on one hand, the *I* must recognize certain values that are general or at least transcend it; on the other hand, the recognition of general values in no way resolves the question of what normative self-image I should have of myself. I may well recognize that I should become a useful member of society, but what line of work I should go into remains undetermined. For that, I need information about myself—whether it be about the standing of my parents (in a traditional society), or about my talents and needs, my possibilities and necessities (in a modern society). Since of course every human being is more than what he is at the moment, an exaggerated descriptive self-image, an overestimation of one's own abilities, may be justified and even be necessary in order to achieve perhaps less than one would like to achieve, but more than one would have achieved without that exaggerated self-image. Even the idealization of other persons that is peculiar to love may sometimes be more fair to them than a sober description of their being—which often forgets what others could be and would be if one reminded them of what they could be. What has been called "self-efficacy,"[104] that is, the confidence that one can do certain things, is an important element in the descriptive self-image and will understandably be defended against threats—even if not all means used in its defense are rational.[105] *Self-actualization* consists in fully exploiting one's own possibilities and bringing the descriptive self-image closer to the normative self-image; for this it is necessary, of course, neither to fall short of what one could do, nor to go beyond one's limits. The *I* requires a good deal of experience with its self in order to discover the value peculiar to it; especially when these limits imply creative achievements, there are only a few other people who can help one to define them. No doubt the actualization of one's own talents is one of the most pleasurable activities granted to human beings. On one hand, working on something that is complex in itself and requires skilful effort and, on the other, the feeling that through this work one can finally do justice to one's own self, contribute to this satisfaction. However, the difference between descriptive and normative self-images also carries the risk of failure. As the "undetermined animal," man must shape and educate himself; and since he does not necessarily carry out this task in a satisfactory way, "he is an endangered being, facing a real chance of perishing."[106] Even if the pleasure of self-actualization infinitely exceeds the kinds of pleasure granted to other animals, man pays a high price for it with the torment of failure. Inner dissatisfaction with oneself can have an important impact on one's behavior, even if it is not consciously acknowledged because acknowledging it would be too humiliating; it is externalized in all kinds of hectic activism or, worse yet, in an aggressive attitude toward others. The suffering is deepest when one has committed an act that blatantly contradicts the norms he rec-

---

104. Cf. "Self-Efficacy," in the impressive work by A. Bandura (1986), 390 ff.

105. I am thinking in particular of so-called self-handicapping, in which someone limits his own abilities in order to be able to comfort himself with the explanation that his failure was due only to this disadvantage.

106. Cf. Gehlen (1966), 32: "er [ist] das gefährdete oder 'riskierte' Wesen, mit einer konstitutionellen Chance, zu verunglücken." Trans. C. McMillan and K. Pillemer, 25.

ognizes, that is, when he has become *guilty*, and when he must even acknowledge that the way he has conducted his life up to that point has been determined by values he has since understood to be immoral. Nonetheless, the recognition of one's own guilt can indicate a step toward truth and therefore toward the recovery of one's dignity, which is not possible for a person who resorts to denial of reality and other defense mechanisms.

However, it is of the utmost importance that the guilty *I* know how it must deal with its own guilt, and that forms of *atonement* are available. Sometimes the injustice that one has committed can be reversed; of course, because of the irreversibility of certain events such as death, this is not always possible, even if the wish to reverse one's own unjust act is virtually unquenchable in any guilty, but moral, person. For a society's psychological health a great deal depends on possibilities of atonement being recognized in such cases as well. Only in this way can *projection*, the most morally repugnant of all defense mechanisms, be avoided. If a person feels that something has happened that ought not to have happened, but does not have the courage to confront directly the fact that it happened through *him*, because he does not know how to deal with this conclusion, he will look for scapegoats;[107] and the hatred he feels for them will depend not solely on the disvalue of the act about which he senses an urgent need to be indignant, but also on the degree of contempt that he unconsciously feels for his own act of denial. Projections easily become autocatalytic structures. In chapter 6.2.2.3.1 we will see why in modernity the mechanism of projection arises even from mere inclinations that one dares not admit to oneself, and becomes a political issue of the first rank. Even if it is true that a great deal of pointless suffering can be avoided by not making exaggerated moral demands, the more far-reaching demand to get rid of all normative self-images is not entirely the solution of the problem that man inevitably represents for himself and for others. For even if this eradication could overcome all suffering, it would have the drawback that what would then come about could no longer be regarded as a *human* society.

Our descriptive and normative self-images are crucially shaped by the *images that others have of us*—or by the assumptions that we harbor regarding the images others have of us. George Mead called these assumptions "Me,"[108] an expression that in my view refers to the third element of identity, along with the *I* and the self. Whereas traditional philosophy of consciousness concentrated primarily on the categories of *I* and self, and conceived self-consciousness as pre-social, most philosophers and empirical psychologists of the past century have more closely examined the social aspect of

---

107. The mechanism of projection is well described in the second scene of Max Frisch's *Andorra:* "Das ist das Böse. Alle haben es in sich, keiner will es haben, und wo soll das hin? In die Luft? Es ist in der Luft; aber da bleibt's nicht lang, es muß in einen Menschen hinein; damit sie's eines Tages packen und töten können" (1975; 28). "That's evil. Everyone has it in him, no one wants to have it, and where should it go? Up into the air? It's in the air; but it doesn't stay there long, it has to go into a person, so that they can someday seize it and kill it."

108. Cf. (1967), esp. 173 ff.

I-identity, and rightly so.[109] They have significantly broadened our knowledge of the empirical phenomena that are correlated with human self-consciousness, though in doing so they have not attained the level of some of the insights of classical philosophy of consciousness. For example, as a social behaviorist Mead observes human behavior primarily from an outside perspective and thereby misses precisely what distinguishes consciousness and self-consciousness from the second world. It is part of the essence of *I*-ness that it can objectivize its self and can speak of it in the third person; but there is always a remainder that is left over, an excess of the first person that goes beyond all these acts of objectivization, which are inevitably the acts of an *I*. I can talk in the third person about the man I was yesterday as if the latter were a stranger; but I always can and must keep in mind: "I am the one who asserts that this person who bears my name, but with whom I no longer identify myself, has done this and that." Transcendental pragmatics, as one of the most ambitious attempts to transform philosophy of consciousness into a philosophy of intersubjectivity, has acknowledged the irreducible doubleness of the first- and third-person perspectives,[110] but even it assumes that a private self-consciousness could not make any claims to validity. If it refers to the *genesis* of the corresponding human ability, it is surely right. But how an ability comes into being is one thing, and what its concept presupposes is another; only the assumption that even an isolated individual's self-consciousness can function normally can support the thesis that in a society that has fallen victim to collective insanity an absolute loner can be right in opposing this society.[111] This should not be construed as a denial that even in the case of sense perception—and, in any case, in memory—social confirmation is important; any rational person will at least feel insecure if others do not share his perceptions; and any direct memory will be disturbed if others who were present at the time cannot confirm it: direct memory and socially mediated memory of facts are not supposed to contradict each other. Moreover, in all usual cases the *Me* is an important factor of identity. Certainly the *Me* is a selection made from the images that others have of me; not all images others have of me interest me, indeed, my selection will be influenced by my self. But the images that finally go into the *Me*—for instance, because they come from people I care about—are relevant to identity. It is not only the will to succeed in my social milieu that forces me to take other people's images seriously; the very fact that

---

109. Pascal also made an important contribution in this area. "Nous ne nous contentons pas de la vie que nous avons en nous et en notre propre être: nous voulons vivre dans l'idée des autres d'une vie imaginaire" (1982; 203). ("We are not content with the life we have in ourselves and in our own being: we want to live an imaginary life in the minds of others.")

110. See A. Øfsti's admirable essay (1988).

111. Cf. my criticism of various reconstructions of Wittgenstein's private-language argument (1990c; 181 ff.). It would be worth making a careful investigation to discover why the insistence on a *privatus*'s ability to know has met with so much denial in our century. From the point of view of the sociology of knowledge, I would hypothesize that two of the factors are a justified interest in intersubjective structures, on one hand, and the mass-democratic resentment of aristocratic, exceptional personalities on the other.

others do not share the privilege of the first-person perspective on me (which, like every privilege, is also a limitation) can enable them to have insights regarding me that remain closed to myself. Indeed, in a certain sense it can be said that experience of the other forms the bridge between experience of the self and experience of the world, and that the use of the second person achieves a mediation between the abilities to use the first or the third person. The unity and the distinction between *I* and self could scarcely have come about had I not experienced how I can reify others and especially how others can reify me. The *you* is itself a synthesis of the *I* and the *he;* and I experience myself through the other as such a synthesis.

Because the other develops a certain image of me, he forces me to compare myself with this image—and thereby promotes the division between *I* and self. Indeed, one can even say that under some circumstances I must present myself as others want me to be.[112] I can evade the threat to my identity posed by the other's image only by integrating into myself what is external to me: *introjection* is the defense mechanism that complements projection. The result is, first, that I have to shape my self and that in doing so the *I* experiences itself as an active principle; second, that during these attempts at shaping my self I discover that there is something in my self that resists all these attempts, however strong the pressure of others may be. This pressure is always powerful, and not only in the form of external sanctions, which can remain external to my own self: if I violate the introjected norms and the other catches me doing it, as a rule I feel *shame*—a feeling that should be strictly distinguished from that of guilt, in which the *Me* is not present.[113] The following human abilities have their basis in the experience of the *Me.* Thus man can assume *roles,* that is, correspond to others' expectations that are directed to him as the bearer of a general quality. Role-specific behavior is not innate; however, we must make a strict distinction between the fundamental roles that one can evade only with great difficulty, because they very early represent a part of one's own self, and peripheral roles that one can exchange for others. Gender roles are—or at least have been until recently—a good example of the first case, whereas professional roles are a good example of the second case, at least in the upper stratum of differentiated societies. On one hand, it is an error to speak of self-alienation in the case of the first type of roles, for the self first constitutes itself through a socially recognized, stable relationship to the world; it is their social role that gives many people their identity. But even if the relationship between fundamental and peripheral roles may turn out to be very different in particular cultures and, within them, in particular strata and particular individuals, we must recognize that any human can assume a role into which he is not completely absorbed but that he just tries out and plays with, even if it is not necessarily his profession. This follows from the difference between *I* and self; and children's role-playing as well as the widespread representation of another person in drama,

---

112. This is the subject of many of Pirandello's works.

113. Modern anthropology rightly distinguishes between shame and guilt cultures; the latter developed later.

dance, song, and recitation prove this empirically. Archaic totemism already presupposes the ability to put oneself in the place of another being—even a non-human being—and to identify with it; and even if identification with an *animal* shows that here man has not yet completely come into himself, the *act of identification* with something or someone that is not oneself is specifically human. The desire to be someone else is peculiar to beings with self-consciousness. Therefore it is too simplistic to interpret disguise and deception only as means to another end; they are often an end in themselves, insofar as the disguiser and deceiver experiences through them an extension of his personality by seeming to be more than he is. On one hand, the *I* enjoys the plurality of selves that it can assume; on the other, it can be the concrete position of the played self, which may be that of a powerful individual, that increases the feeling of self-worth.[114] To be sure, it is a symptom of a serious illness when someone becomes a multiple personality; but even this psychological illness and even that vice are only possible on the basis of the fascinating double structure of human self-consciousness. Moreover, it is possible for someone not only to play another person, but also to *represent* something general, such as an institution; and he may very well learn to distinguish between acts that he performs as a private individual and those that he performs as a representative of another person or an institution. Political phenomena cannot be understood without reference to this capacity for representation.

However much others ease the shaping of one's own identity, the *Me* can also trigger the most terrible identity crises. *Identity crises*—the *I*'s rejection of the self—have many different causes. They correspond to particular identity factors. Different kinds of identity crises can result from the inability to identify with one's own body (for instance, after it changes in puberty), the failure of memory (which can itself be caused by an identity crisis, however), the refusal to come to terms with one's own finiteness and mortality, and inappropriate descriptive or normative self-images. But in almost any identity crisis the *Me* plays an essential role. Only a few people preserve their identity intact when they encounter the contempt of their fellow humans, especially of those they care about, no matter whether this contempt is objectively justified or not. In general it is truly frightening to see how quickly a person's self-image adapts to the image that his environment forms of him: flattery is believed just as sincerely as conduct is regretted when reproached by others, even when the most inadequate arguments are used in the reproach.[115] However, one criterion of a person's greatness consists precisely in whether, even if isolated from the community, he continues on his path, not out of obstinacy, but rather on the basis of objective arguments and an unshakable feeling for the rightness

---

114. The *Odyssey* is the greatest example of this tendency, which has surely become stronger in the course of human intellectual history.

115. The influence of others on the formation of opinion does not concern the self-image alone. Salomon Asch's famous experiment (1951) shows that even obvious errors are made by more than a third of the research subjects when only a relatively small number of others have unanimously given a wrong answer to the question asked.

of his own position. This sense of superiority derives its dignity from the fact that it appeals to something that transcends the individual, who may suffer far more from the burden of this demand than his environment suffers from his irreconcilability: think of the Old Testament prophets. Moreover, a negative *Me* is not the only cause of a socially induced identity crisis: contrasting images that others have of one are no less dangerous. When these images are connected with different people's differing expectations of one, role conflicts can result that are conceived as tragic. I say *conceived* as tragic, for it may well be that the conflicts are not in themselves tragic, but have a simple moral solution. But since the person concerned is not aware of this solution, since the moral first of all appears to him in the form of demands that other people make on him, he can feel himself to be in a moral dilemma from which he cannot escape. The hierarchizing of roles is therefore still more important than that of needs.

Yet, others are not relevant to me only through the images they have of me. I can be identical with myself only if I am an individual, that is, if I *am different from others.* At the same time, I want to be recognized by others as different from them, and this is possible only with common categories and values. Too much commonality threatens individual identity no less than too much foreignness. No matter whether I assume that others know about me and have an image of me, their mere existence can threaten my identity. The idea of *doubles* already expresses the first aspect of this threat early in history. It is superficial to reduce the dangerous element in a double simply to the fact that, because of his behavior, other people could attribute to me acts for which I have no responsibility at all. What is truly uncanny about a double is that he makes me *superfluous,* for I already exist.[116] In reality this kind of threat results from the presence of a superior person who seems to have already realized one's own normative self-image in an exemplary way that one could not achieve, not to mention surpass. What is crucial is not that another person is hopelessly superior to me; if that were all, it would be no problem for me. A brilliant poet in no way puts in question the identity of an excellent physician who has ambitions only in the area of medicine. What is far more important is that the other is precisely what I myself want to be, but cannot be. If general shortcomings that one recognizes in oneself lead to inferiority feelings, and these trigger the defense mechanism of *compensation,*[117] then superior people, by providing opportunities for comparison with themselves, can set in motion myriad attempts at compensation. In general, the importance of compensation mechanisms in people's psychic reality can hardly be overestimated; they play a role even in the loftiest intellectual performances. For example, political men typically fascinate German intellectuals, who, unlike their British and French counterparts, seldom have political responsibilities. Nonetheless, one can discern in these mechanisms, which have many deplorable results, something formally rational, insofar as they are grounded in man's striving for wholeness, for what he himself has not become.

---

116. The various versions of the Amphitryon material show how the first problem, which can still be treated comically, increasingly passes over into the second, which requires a tragic treatment.

117. Cf. A. Adler (1947), 53 ff.

The other may be no less disturbing for me if he is *completely different* from what I am or would like to be. The fact that the other pays little attention to the values that one seeks to realize and regards something completely different as true must make one feel unsure of oneself because claims to validity are necessarily general. Although something is not true just because other people acknowledge it, if something is true, it must in principle be considered true by other people as well. If it is not possible to find an explanation for the difference between one's own convictions and those of others, the suspicion inevitably arises that one might be wrong—and this suspicion is all the more tormenting if the deviation takes place within one's own group (or in a society that believes in universalism and therefore cannot simply distinguish between "we" and "the others"). Since man is a social being, others communicate values to him; those who introduce one to culture and whose lives are seen as *exemplary* contribute to the strengthening of moral convictions considerably more than the argumentative acknowledgment of this normative dimension. A breakdown of trust in those whom one has seen as models generally shakes belief in the values that one has recognized; but this also endangers the normative self-image. Disappointments—or, worse yet, betrayals—by an admired or beloved person almost necessarily trigger an identity crisis. On one hand, one has so long identified with the other person that one cannot rid oneself of the suspicion that his behavior may be justified; one is not only the injured one but at the same time partly adopts the standpoint of the person who caused the injury, and this increases the pain involved. On the other hand, if one finally comes to the conclusion that one has made a mistake about the other person, one must distance oneself from the earlier identification, which represents an important part of one's own self; one begins to doubt one's ability to judge other people, and this affects very generally the relationship to others and the stability of the *Me*. The most intensive relationship to the other, the one in which one's own personality is communicated the most, is dual in nature: love (in the narrower sense) and friendship. This relationship is a particularly fascinating way of solving the identity problem: the *I* learns to identify with its self because it experiences it as accepted by another person; it broadens itself, because it takes on responsibility for another self. The failure of this solution can therefore result in the most wrenching of all forms of the identity crisis.

4.3. MAN AND CULTURE

We have come increasingly closer to the social dimension, which must finally become a subject of its own. In an ontogenetic approach, one would have had to begin with it, for self-consciousness develops in children only through interaction with other people that already have self-consciousness. The dreadful condition of most so-called wolf children can hardly be explained by saying that they were abandoned because of their intellectual defects; rather, the latter (which may certainly have become partly irreversible) are a result of their abandonment. In phylogenesis the problem is more complicated. If one wants to avoid an infinite regress, it must be supposed that the thunderbolt of self-consciousness struck somewhere for the first time. Interpersonality can be constituted only when there are already persons. However, it is plausible to assume that early forms of self-consciousness in subhuman hominids that lived in social groups supported each other. It can be supposed that the *I*'s emergence out of the self took place at the same time in several individuals; in any case, only such a simultaneous emergence can have prevented earlier achievements that may have occurred among individuals from collapsing because of a lack of opportunities for development. But however these beginnings of self-consciousness that are lost in the obscurity of human prehistory may have occurred, it holds for all history that man has always already come into being in a social whole. Eduard Meyer does not exaggerate when he writes: "Therefore organization in such groups (hordes, tribes), which we encounter empirically everywhere we encounter human beings, is not only as old, but much older than human beings: it is the indispensable presupposition of the emergence of humanity" (1981; 1:1, 8). Man is a cultural being from his ontogenetic and phylogenetic beginnings, but culture is—according to a good definition—"*a historically derived system of explicit and implicit designs for living, which tends to be shared by all or specially designated members of a group.*"[118] Language and mores are the two fundamental elements of culture, of the bonds of any human society. However, our reflections on the differing roles that man can assume point to the fact that societies are less closed than they were long believed to be. To be sure, societies can be distinguished from one another; but first of all any culture can be divided into subcultures, and second, there are always many people who are at home in several cultures. This holds as well, and especially, for the pre-modern world, in which certain individuals frequently performed religious functions in the context of a society, and even in a language, different from the ones in which they performed their political functions.[119]

4.3.1. Man as a Symbolic Being: Language

Nothing points more clearly to the social dimension of the human intellect than *language.* No doubt there is a pre-linguistic stream of consciousness, but even the most intimate needs and feelings differ according to the degree to which they can be articulated in language; and using the same language has a unifying effect on the world of feelings.[120] The gratitude that so many cultures feel for their poets, and that culminates in the almost sacred standing attributed to them, especially in archaic cultures, is based on the fact that poets have broadened the interior dimension of their linguistic communities

---

118. Cf. C. Kluckhohn and W. H. Kelly (1945), 98. This article is one of the most interesting on the concept of culture.

119. Cf. M. Mann (1986 ff.), 1:13, who defines a society as "a network of social interaction at the boundaries of which is a certain level of interaction cleavage between it and its environment," and who denies that societies are unified and closed in a thoroughgoing way.

120. Cf. Gehlen (1975), 75, on the linguistic character of human motivation.

and at the same time standardized its expression. What are the functions of language?[121] For one thing, language *objectivizes* ideas in something external—first of all in symbols[122] whose shape reminds one of the thing represented, and then in signs, whose physical being has become completely independent of the object represented, but which signify the latter nonetheless. Therein lies an achievement in abstraction that is closely connected with the basic structure of self-consciousness, which opposes the *I* to the self: When I name my pain, it is, so to speak, outside me; I can relate to it in an objectivizing way, and I am not so hopelessly given over to it as when it remains unarticulated. In this way language first *represents* external objects, and second, it *expresses* the wealth of the interior dimension. In addition, the speaking subject *communicates* his thoughts to others, and thereby constitutes intersubjectivity. The fact that man inserts signs or symbols between his stream of consciousness and the world is of fundamental importance not only for anthropology but also for ontology. Language is the paradigmatic image of the fourth world, it is the basis of any culture whose rise, apogee, and decline can always be gauged by the condition of its language.[123] Language is a structure that transcends subjective consciousness; on one hand, it makes it accessible to other consciousnesses and, on the other, it integrates it back into the physical world; without a material basis language cannot exist, even if it only uses this material basis in order to refer to something else. A spoken word is no mere *flatus vocis;* its meaning is what makes it into a word in the first place. What it means, not what it immediately is, is its true being. Because language interposes itself between man and his environment, man can be more immediately at home in the symbol system than in the natural universe—which can lead to mastery over the world as well as to the loss of the world. Therefore E. Cassirer was not wrong in calling man the *animal symbolicum*, the "symbolic animal."[124] Myth, religion, art, science, philosophy, as we know them from human history, are possible only on the basis of a linguistic system of symbols. They are particularly indebted to the fascinating ability of human language to make itself its own subject, indeed, to correct itself and productively extend itself: within language one can speak of one's own language and its defects in comparison to other languages, for instance. Even if any language is necessarily an individual

---

121. Here I set aside the complex connections between motor functions and language. On this issue, see, e.g., Gehlen (1966), 193 ff.

122. One can define the concept of symbol in such a way that it includes signs as well (symbol in the wider sense), or else coordinate symbols and signs as two species of a common genus. My terminology is not uniform.

123. Cf. D. Sternberger's apt words: "How many languages and which languages a person speaks determines how much and which thing, world, or nature is opened up to him. And every word that he utters changes the world in which he moves, changes him and his place in this world. Therefore nothing is indifferent in language, and nothing is so essential as the way of speaking. The corruption of language is the corruption of man" (D. Sternberger, G. Storz, and W. E. Süskind [1968], 7). No less impressive than Sternberger's analysis of the connections between language and politics is V. Klemperer's study on the language of the Third Reich (1969).

124. (1960), 40.

language, any speaker has access to a general linguistic competence (*langage*) that allows him to learn other languages as well and thereby to transcend the limits of his own. Any individual speech act already seeks to open up intersubjectivity, yet an utterance (*parole*) is primarily the act of an individual. First, because only insofar as a language is constituted as a system with its own logic (*langue*) do we get at something that is independent from the individual acts; it is now the latter that have to comply with this logic of language. We see here in a paradigmatic way a fundamental characteristic of all media of the social: on one hand, they are constituted only through the interactions of real people; on the other, all interactions take place only through these media. This is the circle that makes the origin of language so obscure, for it seems that language has to be already presupposed in order to introduce language.[125] This circle can be broken only if one assumes with Vico that the first language was the language of the body; in human beings body posture, gestures, and mimicry have in fact attained a level of differentiation that we find in no other animal. The relationship between these expressions and their meanings cannot have been arbitrary: a gesture of humility, for instance, is related to what it means. This thesis presupposes that there are common predicates for the interior and exterior dimensions, and thus that it is not merely a convenience of language when we call a well, a pain, or a voice "deep"; this leads beyond a certain interpretation of the body-mind dualism and has implications that cannot be analyzed here. However, early man cannot have used only facial expressions as releasers—other animals do that as well. What is specifically human is *representative behavior,* which goes beyond genetic programs, which makes the absent present, and which purges a person's own needs and fears. Gehlen rightly discerns in the representative rites of early men—for example, the ritual representation of hunting—the beginnings of language, which is itself an act, even if its materiality is reduced to a minimum.[126] In any case, the first successful speech acts must by definition have been comprehensible to at least two human beings at the same time; otherwise they would have fallen back into nothingness and would not have contributed to the constitution of *langue.* Moreover, the concept of language can be generalized so that it includes not only the expression of ideas through sounds, but any means of communication or any system of rules for social action. In this sense ritual representation is not an early form of language, but rather language itself; therefore one can say for instance that Hindus from Kerala and Bihar speak the same language, even though their languages (in the narrower sense) are radically different. Finally, what is important is the medium in which language is exchanged. We will return to the differences between oral and written culture in chapter 6.2.2.2.

By learning language, the child grows into a world of meanings that are already intersubjectively shared: they are the basis on which the individual consciousness raises itself up until it finally reaches in some cases the ability for genuine innovation, indeed,

---

125. On the characteristics that distinguish human language from animal languages see C. Hockett's fine essay (1973).

126. (1975), 150 f.

is able to reflect itself out of the whole world of the intersubjective spirit. In this sense, the *We* is still more original than the *I:* before the child recognizes that he has his own opinions, he becomes acquainted with the views of the smallest group, especially the family; indeed, the expression "become acquainted" is misleading insofar as it wrongly presupposes that there is already a self-assured center that encounters others qua others. The *difference between tradition and conscious communication* is precisely that in the former only the communicated content is given, whereas the awareness that *another person* has this opinion is an indispensable part of conscious communication. "This is what gives tradition its binding power, that we take traditional reactions to be our own, and to be entirely derived from the subject-matter to which they refer. It is a corollary of this that the content of tradition does not appear as something past, like a memory, but as a thing present. . . . Here we are living *in* the past—without being aware of the act of remembering which brought us thither, and hence *without realizing that it is the past* in which we are living."[127] In this sense Scheler can rightly hold that man lives at first more in others than in himself; only by learning to objectivize that *in* which he lives, and by achieving distance from it, does the child begin to grasp the difference between his own experience and that of others.[128] However, the power of tradition does not consist solely in the fact that it instills certain views in us that we do not perceive as alien. Still more uncanny is the power of tradition in shaping the implicit knowledge that only a few people can raise into consciousness, and even then never completely. The morphological and syntactical structure of language, for instance, which one for the most part masters without being able to make it explicit, determines much of a person's worldview; it constitutes a cognitive background to which a person who cannot reflect on it remains captive. Thus it must have consequences for the structure of social relationships when, for instance, in Korean even in sentences in the third person the verb must indicate whether one is speaking to a person with a higher or a lower social status.

Certainly connected with the appropriation of tradition, its theories, its values, and its implicit knowledge is the danger of adopting errors—errors that will be all the more difficult to shed insofar as what is meant by them cannot be simply given the status of an object (which is a necessary condition for objective criticism). Enlightenment thought, anchored in the philosophy of consciousness, was certainly right in making this sober observation. But the crucial point that it overlooked is that, apart from this path paved with errors, man has no other access to truth. Conversely, the sociologism and historicism of the nineteenth and twentieth centuries were right to point out that traditions are

---

127. Scheler (1974), 49: "Darin besteht die bindende Macht der Tradition, daß wir tradierte Reaktionen für unsere eigenen, auf der Sache, gegen die sie sich richten, allein beruhende halten. Und damit verbunden ist uns der tradierte Inhalt nicht wie der erinnerte 'als vergangen', sondern 'als gegenwärtig' gegeben. . . . Wir leben hier in der Vergangenheit—ohne daß uns der Akt des Erinnerns mitgegeben ist, der uns in die Vergangenheit führte; und eben darum, *ohne es zu wissen, es sei die Vergangenheit,* in der wir leben." Trans. T. Heath, 38.

128. Op. cit., 241.

indispensable for participating in the intellectual world. But because they absorbed the *I* into the *We*, they were not able to explain how it is possible for the *I* to repeatedly free itself from tradition's errors—indeed, in some very few cases, even the most fundamental ones. This is explicable only if one attributes to the individual a capacity for insight into truth, a capacity whose claim to validity is *not* by the grace of society—even if its genesis may take place only within society. Just as the child learns to walk only if adults take his hand and lead him for a while—of course, with a view to his learning thereby to walk by himself—so man develops the ability for independent thinking only within a community, whose value can nonetheless be measured by the extent to which it allows or even promotes the objectively justified transcendence of its own traditions.

From what has been said it follows that language is the *instrument of both truth and error* (the latter including deception and self-deception). On one hand, it is a tool that extraordinarily expands the intellect's grasp on truth; on the other, signs develop an autonomy with regard to the objective sphere they represent, and also with regard to the ideas for which they stand, whereby they make *pretense* possible. The concept of the slogan indicates what I mean: symbols have their own logic, they can release collective behavior—indeed quite independently of whether their referent exists or is appropriately represented and even independently of whether the person who uses the symbol believes in the existence of the referent. A word such as "freedom" has not only an objective meaning, whose clarification is one of the primary tasks of philosophy; it is at the same time an entity of the fourth world that partly expresses and partly elicits certain feelings and can determine human behavior in a way that has nothing to do with its proper meaning: Quinctius Flaminius, the "liberator" of Greece, knew this very well. It is shown among other things by one of the most important properties of language, namely, that it has words for general concepts. This property alone makes possible the development of science and is itself an expression of the tendency of the human intellect to transcend particular sense experiences; but it holds within itself the risk of overgeneralization: as in science, sweeping assertions are based on the use of words for general concepts; thus, through language, assertions about experiences with a particular foreigner easily become assertions about foreigners in general. On one hand, if one wants to know the world, the task is made easier by the fact that one has access to logograms that stand for a whole series of characteristics; someone who uses the word "state" assumes the presence of several characteristics that he no longer needs to list specifically. On the other hand, therein precisely lies the danger: a person who sees a necessary but in no way sufficient condition of statehood present may feel tempted to use the more general word "state," which elicits in his hearer certain theoretical expectations that are not objectively covered in every case; the hearer may think that the corresponding structure not only has a flag and and an international personality, but also a factual monopoly on power, and may thus be terribly deceived.

This danger increases when the general concept is simultaneously used normatively. Because of the exceptional difficulty of grasping the autonomy of the normative, the great majority of people considers certain descriptive concepts as by definition good or bad—the fact that there can be good and bad democracies, that the word "democracy" used as a general term in political science in no way presumes that this form of government is the morally right one in a given situation, for example, is in our culture something that cannot be made intelligible to everyone.[129] The power of normative concepts shows itself in noun compounds as well. It is well known that it is more blessed to give than to receive; therefore, words such as *Arbeitgeber* (employer; literally "work giver") and *Arbeitnehmer* (employee; literally "work taker") presuppose a great deal. An interruption merely postpones the conclusion of something without preventing it; therefore the connotations of the word *Schwangerschaftsunterbrechung* (termination of pregnancy; literally, "interruption of pregnancy") are entirely different from those of *Abtreibung* (abortion). The word *Freitod* (suicide; literally "free death") suggests an act of freedom, not murder. Naturally, it is not exclusively the case that language creates thoughts; in principle, thought can definitely elude the power of language, indeed, it can even transform language. But in general it can be said that words determine attention frames, and, moreover, normatively used concepts motivate actions. In such situations language becomes a first-rate instrument of power; whoever can control it can reduce resistance. This was discovered at the latest by Thucydides; we may refer to his famous analysis of the change in language during the civil war in Corcyra (Corfu) (III 82). In his description of "Newspeak" Orwell sketched out the nightmare of an artificial language that limits a speaker's possible thoughts to those desired by the power-holder.[130] Yet despite all the discussions of the general phenomenon and the strongest factual evidence, all that a band of rogues seeking wealth and power has to do is describe itself as a "liberation movement" in order to trigger sympathies, even, or perhaps especially, among an educated audience, since educated people are obviously often more at home in the world of words than in that of their own experience of life.[131] This phenomenon is not surprising: meanings belong to the ideal world and as such do not intervene in the world of the social. For the latter to occur, processes of anchoring certain insights in the motivational apparatus of real persons and groups of persons are indispensable. In any case, a comprehensive philosophy of language has to take into account both sides of language—its reference to the first world as well as the fact that it is a social phenomenon.

4.3.2. Custom, Social Orders, Social Subsystems

Just as language is an intersubjective medium against which the individual may develop his thoughts, but even then only with its help, so *mores* are the intersubjective hori-

---

129. Cf. H. D. Lasswell and A. Kaplan (1969), xx, 22, who call such concepts and propositions "normatively ambiguous."

130. Cf. Orwell (1984), 417–428.

131. It is this kind of person who recently allowed himself to be convinced that reality could be reduced to signs. However, it is self-evident that the concept of a sign has no meaning if there is nothing other than signs.

zon that makes individual action into something meaningful. The child rises above vital performances because he (partly unconsciously) *imitates* adults' actions and *adopts roles;* often these become habitual before he becomes aware of their real goals. Just as important as one's own needs is the experience of the needs of others and how they satisfy them; Gehlen has aptly termed the abstract content of a society's institutions the "grammar of their needs."[132] Not only the common language, but also, and especially, the common actions through which man opens up the world satisfactorily explain why customs that are objectively as absurd as magic persist for such a long time; nothing is more self-evident than what others do, and nothing is more real than others' belief in reality. What requires explanation is more how a child can call out that the king has no clothes than why he does not admire the new clothes like everyone else. Every particular action is first of all oriented toward types of action that are practiced generally, and only when one has been trained in the corresponding type of action is there perhaps a chance for an innovative action that may then itself become the model for a new type of action that will be adopted by others. The orientation toward a general type of action is tautologically valid for all interactions; for instance, a certain behavior would not count as a greeting if in principle it could not be understood as such by both parties involved. But even technical-poietic behavior is usually guided by already existing models: tools are no less symptomatic of a culture than ways of dealing with each other; indeed, the historian of past cultures without writing will be able to begin only with a culture's tools in order to gain access to its ways of dealing with each other, because objects of the second world defy time in an entirely different way from entities of the third or fourth worlds. The concept of *usage*, a broader concept, subsuming that of *custom*, does not involve a specification of the reason why it is generally observed: it may very well be that a usage exists only because the corresponding action is the most appropriate for achieving each individual's goals, without his having considered the others. However, it can also be that a usage has spread because one has been guided by what others do; in that case, we speak of "custom." One can further distinguish between mere usual manners of conduct (*Üblichkeiten*), whose violation is surprising but not alienating,[133] and *ethical life* or mores (*Sittlichkeit*), whose violation elicits sanctions that are considered legitimate. Mores imply a normative claim (which the external observer of mores states descriptively without having to share it): there is a consensus that the mores concerned should exist; compliance with it is part of every individual's normative self-image. There is, as in the determination of the correct use of language, a certain circular relation between facticity and normativity: a given ethical behavior should exist because most people practice it; and it is generally practiced because people believe that it should exist. Sanctions regarding violations of public life can be of various kinds; in more developed public life a

---

132. (1975), 78: "Grammatik ihrer Bedürfnisse." Even if social pressure may prevent certain needs not only from seeking satisfaction but even from venturing into consciousness, they can nonetheless determine human behavior; thus they are not first produced by society.

133. *Fashions* are usual manners of conduct that are ephemeral.

distinction is drawn between decorum, whose violation may not be punished by force, and law, which must in some cases be protected by force.[134] Moreover, the use of force is not the only effective sanction—being shunned, or becoming an object of contempt or ridicule, may be feared more than legal punishment, because a negative *Me* imperils one's own identity. (I presuppose that there are cases in which a violation of the law does not entail any loss of honor—for instance, because the law is not grounded in one's own mores, as in the case of domination by foreigners.)

As a concrete type of action, a custom is not the most general determination of a group acting in common: customs receive their meaning from a comprehensive *social order* that, on one hand, consists of a complex web of usages and, on the other, is the unifying principle within which usages become compatible with each other, work together, and serve the preservation of social order. The same type of behavior can have very different meanings in different social orders; it must be interpreted in relation to the whole. Customs are related to social orders as organs are to organisms: by supporting the social order, customs support themselves, since they can exist only within social orders. Many customs can promote the survival of man, and thereby their own survival, only in connection with other customs, as interdependent parts of a system. Naturally, survival is not the highest value for all societies; indeed, if survival were the only value, we could be sure that we were not dealing with a human society, of which an ascetic transcendence of the vital and an adaptation to the first world is no less a part than is an adaptation to the external environment. And yet it remains tautologically correct that if a group of human beings decided to commit collective suicide (the ability to commit suicide is after all peculiar to humans), their social order would not survive.

Social orders are themselves a result of evolution, albeit even more of cultural than of biological evolution; in both, selection mechanisms are at work. Cultural selection occurs both *between* the various social orders competing with each other and *within* them, between alternative types of action: if customs are to emerge, other possible types of action have to be repressed. As in organisms, a social order's adaptation to its environment is always only partial: just as the history of the organic is responsible for the numerous manifestations of purposelessness displayed by individual organisms, so earlier historical processes are the reason why there exist in every social order elements that make its adaptation to the environment more difficult or at least no longer have any use. Gehlen has coined the concept of non-binding authority[135] and used it to describe cultural relics that are continued and enjoy formal respect, but are no longer fed by a living identification. In any case, *non-simultaneity* is characteristic of *all* social orders, which on closer examination always prove to be less coherent than they at first seem: In a famous metaphor, Vico compared customs from earlier epochs of a social order with a stream of fresh water that continues on unmixed with the surrounding salt water

---

134. Cf. Weber (1980), 15, whose terminology I adopt only in part.
135. (1975), 215f.

long after the river that bore it has entered the sea.[136] In modernity, this non-simultaneity has been increased in an entirely new way by the extraordinary acceleration of development. Like biological evolution, social evolution is an ongoing process. In the individual realization of a general type of action, as in the actualization of *langue* through *parole,* deviations are just as inevitable as in the replication of a genetic program. However, the great majority of deviations fail to establish themselves; indeed, one can distinguish cultures by how open they are to changes. One thing is certain: even the most open culture cannot survive if it does not have ways of reproducing its social order; the pressure to adopt its customs must be considerable in any social structure that wants to endure. In terms of individual psychology, this pressure is maintained by people's unconditional desire to perpetuate their respective convictions and habits, and inertia is not the only factor operative in this: In a being that wants and ought to be identical with itself in the sense explained above, the wish for continuity is even more tenacious than the tendency of DNA to replicate itself.

Only in rare cases do people willingly alter their social order; the latter's transformation is due only partly to internal developments such as technological or moral progress; humans owe this possibility to their ability to think and to evaluate their own action in moral terms. Exogenous factors play a larger role. These include on one hand changes in the natural environment in which human society has its place, and on the other interferences with other societies; we have already seen that most people belong simultaneously to several societies. Interactions sidestepping a society's existing institutions constantly occur. Mann uses the splendid term "interstitial emergence," and he is correct in writing that "societies have never been sufficiently institutionalized to prevent interstitial emergence."[137] These interactions between societies can be limited to intellectual exchanges or trade; their most dramatic form is military subjugation of one culture by another. If one wants to apply the different types of equilibrium to cultures, one can say that archaic cultures are either *stable* or *unstable:* deviations from the initial state of equilibrium lead either to a quick return to the starting point or, if the deviation becomes too great, to a rapid distancing from this starting point and the breakdown of the order; the choice is between persistence or decline. In contrast, the social order of modernity seems *ultra-stable,* that is, it can carry out by itself constant adaptations to changes in the environment.

Within social phenomena we can distinguish two classes, those that are guided by a unified will and those that do without this kind of will.[138] Whereas macroeconomic phenomena are at first based on no common will (apart from governmental economic policy, which belongs to the political, not the economic, sphere), the action of a business firm that is analyzed by microeconomics is guided by a common set of goals, however these may have come into being. Unlike the market, a firm is a *corporate group,* that

---

136. Cf. *Scienza nuova* sec. 412, 629.
137. (1986 ff.), 1:16.
138. M. Mann (1986 ff.; 1:8) distinguishes between diffused and authoritative power.

is, "a social relationship which is either closed or limits the admission of outsiders by rules," in which "its order is enforced by the action of specific individuals whose regular function this is, of a chief or 'head,' (*Leiter*) and usually also an *administrative staff*. These functionaries will normally also have representative authority."[139] Without the existence of corporate groups, it is difficult to explain the persistence of social orders and their subsystems by reference only to mechanisms of self-regulation, even if the efficiency of these mechanisms should not be underestimated. Since corporate groups *act*, that is, since they achieve or prevent in a goal-directed way changes in reality, one can attribute to them responsibility for certain acts.

In order to survive, social orders must fulfill various tasks: In history, social orders are differentiated, like organisms in their evolution, into different *subsystems* with differing *functions*. To the subsystem of the economy, for instance, correspond particular corporate groups that perform economic functions. However, it is of great importance to note that the correlation between functions and corporate groups is not one-to-one: an army, for example, performs not only military but also economic and ideological functions, even though it is centered around the military function; a church must organize itself, pursue economic tasks, and so on, and thus cannot limit itself to religious functions. Moreover, there are interactions between the individual functions; for instance, the reproduction rate of a society depends on economic conditions, and these depend on the political framework, and this in turn depends on the religion that legitimates it, and so on. What are the central functions and types of corporate groups in any society? Mann speaks of four sources of social power—ideological, economic, political, and military. This approach covers a large part of social phenomena, but it has three shortcomings. First, Mann deals with these four sources only empirically; no attempt is made to deduce them. Second, he overlooks one of the most important functions of the social—biological reproduction. Finally, it is obvious that political and military functions are closely connected—politics is not absorbed into the military, but it can hardly exercise its directive function if it does not control the military.

How would a deduction of the basic functions of the social be conceivable? Clearly it is necessary to go back to human nature; but man is the intellectual animal. Above we listed three basic goals of animal behavior: reproduction, metabolism, and defense and attack. What is specifically human is the posing of the question of validity. This entails the following basic social functions. The sphere of the social, at whose center stands biological reproduction, is the *family*.[140] However, the social order must think not only

---

139. Weber (1980), 26: "eine nach außen regulierend beschränkte oder geschlossene soziale Beziehung[, bei der] die Innehaltung ihrer Ordnung garantiert wird durch das eigens auf deren Durchführung eingestellte Verhalten bestimmter Menschen: eines *Leiters* und, eventuell, eines *Verwaltungsstabes*, der gegebenenfalls normalerweise zugleich Vertretungsgewalt hat." Trans. A. R. Henderson and T. Parsons, 133.

140. At the risk of coining a neologism, one could speak of *familyness* (*Familialität*) in order to distinguish the subsystem from the particular instantiation (as "economics" is distinguished from "business").

about its biological but also its cultural reproduction: this occurs in *education*, on which man, who is by nature a cultural being, is absolutely dependent and which at the beginning of historical development occurs within the family. *Economics* is concerned with the organized satisfaction of needs, which have their ultimate source in organic metabolism. To be sure, man very soon rises above mere biological needs; and thus there can also be an economic treatment of aesthetic or religious goods. But the crucial point is that the sphere of economics first opens up when goods become scarce—and only goods that have a material basis, however ethereal, can be scarce. The *military* deals with violent conflicts, usually with those who stand outside one's own social order, whether for aggressive or for defensive ends. However, force must also be used within and with regard to those who endanger the social order and are not prepared to settle conflicts amicably. In general, a social order cannot concern itself only with the tasks that arise from the organic nature of its members; it must also be concerned about *itself*. A corporate group that sets as its goal the preservation of the social order as a whole against attempts to dissolve it proceeding from within or without is called a *political corporate group*, whose highest form is the *state*. Since the latter's conduct includes the use of force on people, it is in great need of *legitimation;* for that reason usages that seek to preserve the social order and usages that serve to justify this preservation are both part of any social order. These are the origins of the *political* and the *religious*, which differ by their integrative functions from other subsystems and therefore are not to be located on the same level.

The religious, as it has been introduced here in the context of social philosophy, is a very broad concept: it includes all attempts at legitimation and interpretation of the world and the elaboration of fundamental theoretical systems of categories, as well as the statement of basic norms and their illustration in works of art. It goes without saying that in this sense Marxism-Leninism is a religion (the term "surrogate religion" ought to be avoided in a descriptive context); even the conception that there are no binding norms and that *therefore* (?) everyone has the right to do whatever he wants so long as he does not hinder anyone else is a religion, and, indeed, precisely the civil religion of modern liberal states. The concept of legitimation, as it is used here, is purely sociological: it can be both objectively absurd and extremely subtle. Sometimes the legitimating factor (for example, the divine order) is a construct that looks so much like what is to be legitimated (one's own social order) that it could easily be confused with it; but even so humble a difference is indispensable if man is not to betray the self-transcendence that makes him human. Certainly systems of legitimation seek to *legitimate,* that is, to justify the factual order; but with the recognition that a legitimation is needed at all, a step is taken that can never be taken back and that contains within itself the potential for both stabilization and endangerment. Systems of legitimation always have their own logic. If one analyzes the oldest systems of legitimation, rites and myths, one can emphasize their psychological presuppositions and their social functions as well as the immanent logic of the corresponding sign systems. Thinking through the logic of systems of legitimation can lead to demands for changes in the social order, for the latter not only adapts itself to its environment, but also transforms it on the basis of new theoretical and practical insights—if it wants to; the substantive constraints on every social order are always also determined by itself or by the preferences of its members. Therefore, in every developed social order, *morality* is the part characterized by its distancing itself from its own mores in the name of norms that transcend the latter. Moreover, a moralistic attitude can become part of the mores of certain social orders: in some Western societies, for instance, a person is hardly acceptable in society if he does not show that he is able to think "critically," that is, to complain about the government and drag traditional religion through the mud. However, the power of the social, even and especially over later-period subjectivists, is manifested in the form of a streamlined orientation of the profuse developments of their interior life toward the current mores of violating older mores, in the form of the mediocrity of their most private and rebellious feelings, and in the form of an irritable hostility to all those who harbor doubts as to whether this morality turned into mores is actually the highest expression of morals—that is, those that in such a situation paradoxically have a far better claim to be the representative of morality (and morals).

To be sure, the development of the social order must lead to a further increase of its subsystems, to a differentiation of functions—consider for instance art, philosophy, and science, which differentiate themselves from religion. Of particular interest is the technological function, which runs through all subsystems because it does not have a goal of its own, but is concerned only with making it easier for other subsystems to attain their goals. Technological innovations are therefore often enough equally important for the family, economics, the military, politics, and religion. Electronic data processing has changed in an analogous manner production, warfare, administration, science, and the way we find partners—whether for the better is not yet clear. Although the number of social functions can be increased, no social order that wants to be autarkic can consist of less than the five subsystems of family, economics, military, politics, and religion. A monastic order can forgo biological reproduction and economic activities, but only so long as there are other people who bring children into the world that it can recruit, and so long as there are economic subjects who provide food. No less dangerous than falling short of the necessary minimum number of basic social functions is the autonomization of social subsystems in modernity: if the economic subsystem promotes childlessness to a great extent, in the long run this will harm economics as well.

Why does a social structure want to exist—or, more precisely, why does a sufficient number of the people who cooperate in this social structure want it to exist? This can be attributed to the sheer fact that human beings can physically survive and develop their intellectual beings only within social structures. It is in no way sufficient that one somehow interacts; the forms of interaction must be defined if individual actions are not to hinder each other but mesh. This definition is compatible with the greatest inequalities among men; what is important is only that, for instance, the Brahman and the Sudra know how they are to treat each other, no matter how asymmetrical their interaction may be. If in every case we had to debate who was to do what, we would never act at all; indeed, the conflicts that would arise from such debates would soon destroy people. Only because most things are already established and decided in advance can concrete differences of opinion and power struggles be settled in such a way that the community benefits from them and does not destroy itself. If stable, mutual expectations did not bind people together, the centrifugal force of selfishness would rapidly dissolve any social structure; without a common medium, whether it be language or mores, interactions are doomed to fail. This follows directly from man's reduction of instincts, which—as the differences among cultures show—is compatible with an incredible number of different types of behavior. The regulation of the latter within a society is the task of institutions, "Only through institutions does social action become effective, enduring, standardized, quasi-automatic, and predictable."[141] Institutions are stable models for interactions, and though they do limit freedom, freedom could not develop at all without them. This shows why groups with other mores, and even more often people from one's own group with a developed morality, are perceived as threats. It also explains why many societies of the past tended to be closed, that is, those who did not initially belong to the group were forbidden to participate in common social actions, or at least allowed to do so only in exceptional cases. Still today, even the most educated foreigner living in another culture feels a strong inclination to seek contact with people from his own country. There are at least two reasons for this: first, there is hardly anything more stressful than seeing that one's own expectations are not fulfilled and at the same time feeling that one has not fulfilled the expectations of others. Second, a person will encounter the moral first of all in the form of the mores of his own culture, thus questioning one's own mores all too easily triggers existential insecurity regarding what ought really to be valid. An individual confirms his belief that he is right by being together with people who behave in exactly the way he himself does. For we consider the norms of our own group to be the right ones and those of others to be wrong, and, all the more so, the more they deviate from our own—and there is truly no lack of radical differences between human cultures.

This is the place to mention the famous distinction between *community* and *society*.[142] We speak of community when in the individual's consciousness what is common to the group is the ground of his own thinking and willing;[143] we speak of society when conversely it is individual thinking and desiring that grounds the group according to one's own self-understanding.[144] Both community and society presuppose that the persons who constitute them are conscious of their individual independence; only in the *mass* is

---

141. Gehlen (1975), 42: "Alles gesellschaftliche Handeln wird nur durch Institutionen hindurch effektiv, auf Dauer gestellt, normierbar, quasi-automatisch und voraussehbar."

142. Cf. Tönnies (1887).

143. Perhaps the most impressive literary figure who incarnates this kind of man is Platon Karatayev in Tolstoy's *War and Peace*.

144. Naturally, people can be deceived in this regard: a club of relativistic dandies can consider itself a society, even if in reality the identity of the members depends on their belonging to the club; a community of joint heirs can see itself as a community, even if in truth it is only (repressed) interests that hold them together.

the latter extinguished by an elementary emotional identification. Of course, archaic cultures were already acquainted with the phenomenon of society: once a contract is made, even primitive peoples inevitably enter this sphere. Of course, not even the dullest schoolboy in a late culture is unacquainted with experiences of community: a child's relationship to his parents and siblings (if he is fortunate enough to have any) is always of a community nature, and the nature of this relationship determines to a large extent the structure of his personality. Nevertheless, it can be said that the ability to understand groups as societies has increased through history (reaching a high point in Hobbes);[145] archaic man sees even in the contract more a form with its own right and its own dignity, in which the contracting parties participate, than a means for imposing his own will. Thus the most primitive community already has a consciousness of the fact that the social order *is* in a particularly intensive sense. It is encountered with gratitude and reverence; many gods are hypostatizations of the mores that ensure one's own survival and that are felt to be valuable: consider, for instance, Aryaman, Mitra, and Bhaga, the Aryan gods of hospitality, contract, and sharing. Myths and rites celebrate the social order, which is also seen as divine because it stands in a mysterious relation of correspondence to the natural order: early on, order is already felt to be the basic category that encompasses both the natural and the social. Both orders are considered connections between different, indeed, even opposed things; and therefore archaic man already knows about the dangers that threaten any order. Social orders in particular can collapse—which would mean a descent back into chaos that can be prevented only by acting it out in rites and driving it away through acts of renewal. The admission of young people into the community—initiation—is precisely the occasion for recalling the emergence of the social order and thereby giving the group new strength, making it young again. Even burials are an occasion for renewing the bond with ancestors. It is of great importance that the reference to the common order be not only theoretical but also objectify itself in community actions—on one hand, more elementary social binding powers are thereby released than in mere talk and, on the other, potential conflicts are defused.[146] Bloody sacrifices succeed in channeling the aggressivity that threatens the group in such a way that it strengthens the community; and they succeed even better if a—more or less voluntary—self-sacrifice takes place. In fact, to pre-Hobbesian man the idea that one should protect the social order *only* because it is in one's own interest is extremely alien. The political may have emerged in order to defend family and economics against threats, but as in the case of locomotion and of animal sociality, the initial means quickly becomes an end in itself and alters the end it was originally supposed only to serve. The protection of the social order can demand the

---

145. At the same time, the longing for community has naturally grown stronger; archaic man did not long for either nature or community, because longing presupposes an experience of difference. Schiller's concepts of the naive and the sentimental can easily be transferred from the relationship to nature to the relationship to community.

146. I follow, among others, G. Balandier (1967), 128 ff.

life of an individual, whose worth is measured against something greater than himself. Indeed, man is prepared to sacrifice himself for the social order precisely because he sees in it something that can approach the quality that is denied him: immortality. Perhaps the first man endured his horror at his own mortality only because he simultaneously saw something that survived the individual—the social order itself. But the social order has not only an ontological quality that is denied the individual; it is also valuable, not only because it protects life, but also because it demands life: self-sacrifice serves not only to protect others but also to protect an order of which self-sacrifice is periodically a part. Only this property explains why one can be so proud to be a member of an order of this kind. In the social order, far earlier than in the individual person, man was able to recognize something sacred. However, this very fact proves the ultimate superiority of the individual over any institution—for it is always the individual who recognizes the sacredness of the social order and sacrifices himself to it, whereas the order can only motivate individuals to moral actions, while remaining incapable of carrying out such actions itself. The ontological difference between the social order and the human beings that constitute it is essentially dependent on the fact that humans are born and die. This is another reason why birth and death are phenomena that no culture can simply accept as natural events but that are always subjected to acts of conferring meaning, no matter how different the forms they may take. Yet even independently of their social function, birth and death are necessarily a problem for humans. A being with a consciousness of death and the ability to commit suicide must inevitably ask himself the question where we come from, where we are going, and indeed what the point of the whole extravaganza of life is; primitive forms of belief in even a very minimal existence after death, in the presence of the spirits of ancestors, must have signaled a decisive step forward in the process of hominization.

Archaic man's sense of community should not conceal the fact that particular interactions were in many cases based on a selfish motive. If one recalls the results of sociobiology, it was virtually inevitable that even, and especially, early men were driven by a basic selfish tendency that was moderated only within the more immediate family circle. This explains, on one hand, the importance of kinship systems in archaic cultures: one should not deny their biological basis, even if their cultural transformation necessarily follows from the nature of man. Thus clans define themselves through common ancestry, but the latter often is often traced back to a mythical being. On the other hand, the mechanisms that have promoted the evolution of cooperation among people who are not closely related are fascinating.[147] Crucial in this must have been the strong

---

147. On this subject, see R. Axelrod's fine book (1984). As we have already said, in iterated prisoner's dilemma situations the "tit-for-tat" strategy has proved to be successful in a broad variety of situations, that is, it proves robust. Naturally, tit for tat is better than alternative strategies only if the value of mutual cooperation is larger than half the sum of the values to be achieved by one's own and by the other's defection; otherwise alternating defection would be the ideal solution. The stability of the strategy depends on the value of the discount parameter (59).

symmetry in economic and military cooperation, which was protected from the violation of reciprocity. The more recent anthropology of Malinowski, Mauss, and Lévi-Strauss has drawn penetrating attention to the importance of this category among so-called primitive peoples. Exchange—whether of goods or of women—is the central social act; the social order, even if it did not emerge solely through exchange, developed further through an exceptionally complex network of reciprocal relationships.[148] Originally, the strategy of not providing any service in return when the other had already performed a service for one must have been evolutionarily stable; cooperation could come into being only if several people *simultaneously* changed their strategies in favor of cooperation and transacted a significant part of their interactions with each other; otherwise the strategy would not have been initially viable. Symmetrical cooperation was promoted both by long-term relationships and by the increase in the ability to remember, for in brief interactions the temptation not to abide by reciprocity must have been great. From this temptation and from the indispensability of reciprocity follow the dreadful punishments incurred by those who do not behave symmetrically, and the irreconcilable hatred against those who once acknowledged the higher principle, but later became renegades—"traitors."[149] Only the strict distinction between those who behave in accord with the new strategy and those who do not, as well as their unequal treatment, gives the evolution of cooperation a means of preventing backsliding. However, the retaliator strategy, with which we are already acquainted from the animal world, probably established itself among human beings not only because it is evolutionarily stable, but also because humans early on found symmetrical cooperation to be morally desirable and a breach of symmetry to be a violation of their own dignity. Indeed, already in the *do ut des* ("I give in order that you give") it is not simply a matter of acquiring desired goods; exchange has the character of an end in itself insofar as it constitutes symmetrical relationships; what ultimately matters is these relationships, and not the goods exchanged. In general, a Darwinian theory of cultural evolution can explain only how certain strategies—of cooperation, for instance—have been developed; it still cannot answer the question how this kind of customs was sanctioned by

---

148. Cf. Gehlen (1975), 45 ff.: "Man kann die archaischen Sozialstrukturen auf diese beiden Schwerpunktsmotive zurückführen: das der stabilen Kontinuität und das der Gegenseitigkeit." ("One can trace archaic social structures back to these two primary themes: that of stable continuity and that of mutuality.") See also 197. Moreover, not only the exploitation of the other but also gifts threaten the symmetry—or they oblige one to do certain things in return. Archaic man is therefore well aware of the ambivalence of gifts, which may be poisonous (cf. the German for poison is *Gift*). Cf. M. Mauss (1973), 143 ff. On the importance of reciprocity, see also B. Malinowski (1926), 24 ff., and L. A. White (1959), 79 f.

149. I mention here only the report regarding Tullus Hostilius's terrible punishment of Mettius Fufetius for breaking his word. Only an already civilized period can allow itself disapproval such as Livy's (I.28.11). More realistically, Virgil wishes only that this betrayal, not the punishment, had not taken place: "At tu dictis, Albane, maneres!" (*Aeneid* VIII, 643). ("But then, you should have kept your word, / O man of Alba!" Trans. A. Mandelbaum [1981] VIII, 834–835).

a specifically *moral* feeling, especially if this feeling repeatedly demands actions that turn against one's own survival and even the power of one's own social order. In human beings, mechanisms of the formation of customs are combined with the moral insight that one must treat others as one would like to be treated oneself—and not only because this is in one's long-term interest, but for its own sake and without any other goal. This insight has its ultimate ground in man's ability to distance himself from himself and to consider himself from the other's point of view; and only this ability, together with the previously mentioned mechanisms and man's growing into an intersubjectively shared intellectual world, can make comprehensible the miracle that the moral belongs to another order than the real, and yet can finally gain a footing in the material world as well.

4.3.3. Collective Identities

The way in which human beings are introduced to the intellectual world implies that alongside individual identities there are also *collective identities*—indeed, that each person first has a collective identity before he discovers his individual identity. It follows from the principles of the social sciences developed above that any discourse on collective identity must be translated into assertions regarding the behavior of particular individuals: it is always concrete human beings who identify with a collective. But the fact that such *acts of identification* occur—partly consciously, partly unconsciously, and in sufficient number to allow the corresponding structure to emerge—is obvious and justifies the formulation of a theory of collective identities. Even an initial glance at social phenomena already shows the irrefutable necessity of this category. If a group of people feels itself to be a *We* from which another group is marked off as a *They* (the others), this inevitably has far-reaching consequences for politics.[150] This *We* can be extremely multifarious: we Americans, we women, we employers, we socialists, we blacks; and in order to understand a specific social situation it is of the utmost importance to find out precisely how these *We*'s are determined. Someone can simultaneously claim membership in several *We*'s; the *We* that in case of conflict has priority over the others may be called the *We par excellence.* The emergence of the modern state has much to do with the fact that the political *We* has become the *We par excellence.* The lack of the category of the *We* explains some of the descriptive errors in Hobbes's and Locke's political theories.

What necessarily belongs to a collective identity?[151] Since by virtue of their nature, the previously mentioned elements of individual identity are part of the identity of intellectual beings, collective identity can be analyzed in strict parallel with individual

---

150. Cf. H. G. Lasswell and A. Kaplan (1969), 11 f.: "Identification serves as the mechanism for the creation of the political 'we.' It is this 'we' which lies at the center of political phenomena."

151. In the following I disregard the specific differences that distinguish the individual types of collective identity from each other (for instance, by their degree of generality).

identity. Human beings with collective identity must first of all have *common contents of consciousness;* second, they must *know that they have common contents of consciousness;* third, they must even *know that all know that they have common contents of consciousness:* only this raising of reflectivity to the third power constitutes collective identity. Naturally, not all the relevant contents of consciousness can be known to everyone, but at least everyone must know (and know that everyone else knows) who knows them. Most collective identities include the restriction of the highest knowledge (for instance, religious knowledge) to a group of initiates; yet every layperson knows it is the priests who know the secrets. In addition to homogeneity in content, we must also mention agreements in form that, as it were, constitute a collective *style* of thinking. It is plausible to assume that there is not only a common consciousness, but also a *collective unconscious.* Alongside certain repressed drives and ideas that characterize people in all cultures, it is not improbable that specific types of behavior are peculiar to individual cultures that are not determined by consciousness, for instance, because the culture does not allow the corresponding area to enter consciousness.

It is less easy to say what corresponds to the individual's *body* at the social level. Insofar as the body is the basis of action, the *institutions* whose collective identity is concerned in each case correspond to it. Institutions become truly capable of action only when they develop into corporate groups. However, to the extent that the body is not only the physical basis of consciousness but also its expression, collective objectivizations of acts of consciousness, that is, *symbols* in the broader sense of the word, are the counterpart we are looking for. Just as it is facial expression by which we recognize other people and from which we deduce their current moods, so symbols are of special importance in identifying a structure with collective identity. Under certain circumstances, someone who knows an institution from within because of his own activity can forgo its symbols; from the outside, the institution appears as an entity of its own only through symbols, and for large groups this also holds for the inside point of view. Symbols correspond to a higher level of biological releasers, yet they are cultural constructs.[152] Hardly any comprehensive collective identity can forgo symbols in the narrower sense, that is, symbols that are not arbitrary signs but are instead similar to what they mean—from the cross to the hammer and sickle, such symbols have a far greater power to bond through recognition and emotional identification than do mere words. Even the common language is not a negligible factor of collective identity: Identities are created not only by what one thinks, but also by how one formulates

---

152. Cf. Gehlen (1975), 26: "Der Sinn eines 'Denkmals' z. B. ist ursprünglich keineswegs der, daß dieser oder jener eine subjektive Erinnerung produzieren soll. Das sichtbare Denkmal ist vielmehr die urtümliche Form, wie gemeinsame Handlungen oder Entscheidungen im Zustande des Vollzugsansatzes auf Dauer gestellt werden." ("The meaning of a 'monument,' for instance, is not originally that it is supposed to trigger a subjective memory in this or that person. The visible monument is rather the primitive form in which common actions or decisions that are just beginning to be carried out are made permanent.")

one's thoughts. For instance, youth groups that are looking for a new common identity will seek to distinguish themselves from adults not only by the way they dress but also by the way they talk.[153] Symbols, which are themselves objects of the second world, stand for a complex structure of the fourth world;[154] attacks on symbols (for example, a flag) are therefore attacks on the feeling of collective identity and are often more passionately repulsed than aggressions against an individual member of the group, precisely because they are potentially directed against all members.[155] Naturally, an individual person can also acquire a symbolic meaning; then an attack on him need not necessarily be intended as an attack on the institution he represents (the aggressor may not be aware of his symbolic function or not have thought about it), but as a rule it will be felt as such. Anyone who boxes the ears of an ambassador provokes the state he represents. No less important is *collective memory,* whether it be constituted by mythical or historical *traditions.*[156] In this memory, a special role is played by events through which the collective self-attribution of common theoretical and practical convictions first took place and basic aspects of the collective self entered the collective consciousness. As a social phenomenon, a collective memory can be articulated only in intersubjective media; common narratives and even more their conversion into common actions are central to the preservation of collective identity. It is essential that a *continuity* remain discernible to the collective self during its development. The *orientation toward the future* also plays a fundamental role: A group's belief that it has a common future, indeed, that it can face the future only together, contributes to the strengthening of collective identities no less than does the belief in a common origin. The particular convictions that one shares must be objectively connected with each other: a group of people who happen to share the notions that Gottsched is the greatest German dramatist, that Goldbach's conjecture is false, and that Freemasons rule the world can hardly develop a common identity, precisely because nothing connects these three notions. This could change only if a theory could make people believe that there was an inner connection among these notions. Since as a result of the ontological dependency of collective identities on the behavior of individuals, these identities are threatened with collapse in an entirely different way from individual identities, it is important for their survival that such connections be found: only the latter can prevent the abandonment of particular elements of identity and thus the collapse of the collective identity. However, far more important than common theoretical convictions are *common interests* and, still more, *common values* (which are promoted by a common

---

153. Sometimes groups use special languages for a more far-reaching end, namely, to be able to communicate with each other in a way that outsiders cannot understand.

154. Cf. chap. 3.4.2.1.

155. Cf. K. Lorenz (1977), 286.

156. The concept comes from the French sociologist Maurice Halbwachs. A concrete analysis of the transformations of the structure of cultural memory in various early advanced cultures is presented by J. Assmann (1992).

language) that require *common actions.* The course of the latter decides how capable of survival a collective identity is; either it falls apart when it encounters the first difficulties or, on the contrary, troubles and sacrifices weld the group together and strengthen its collective identity. A collective identity is also constituted by *descriptive* and *normative self-images:* an institution, for instance, not only has assumptions about the world but is also aware that it has these assumptions and several other characteristics; and it also knows that it is not entirely as it really believes it ought to be. No doubt there is also a counterpart of the *Me* in collective identities, which should analogously be called *Us;* what an institution is, is significantly influenced by the image that it has of the images that other institutions and individuals have of it. Indeed, even if the latter ignore it, their mere existence can be relevant to an institution's identity. An encounter with very similar as well as with very different cultures *can* unsettle collective identities. Acute competition can easily arise between similar cultures: Islamic fundamentalism may be more radical than the many other fundamentalisms precisely because Islamic culture and Western European culture are very closely related, and the superiority that the latter has gained in the modern period is particularly hard for the former to accept. But even the discovery of something that is culturally entirely different in kind, in the form of the Mesoamerican advanced cultures, was a shock for early modern Europe. Here the following distinction between individual and collective identities has to be taken into account. One individual's success may trigger an identity crisis in another; as a rule, the latter is not destroyed altogether, since his organic basis at least continues to exist. The success of an institution, in contrast, may destroy another in that its members may transfer their loyalties to the more successful one. This holds only when the institutions compete with each other, which even *coordinated* institutions do not always do: consider the difference between national religions (i.e., those that are limited to a specific people) and universal religions. In the case of *subordinated institutions* such as the state and social groups, there is no relationship of exclusion, but they may also very well fight for a transfer to themselves of a share of participation, loyalty, etc. Naturally, alongside the conflict between different collective identities there is also the conflict between an individual and a collective identity: in the form of the adolescent crisis, this kind of conflict shapes the life of most people. Actually, a reflected identity is first formed in the course of such a crisis; and the collective identities to which the individual adapts after this crisis are fundamentally different from the earlier ones: it is, so to speak, a second intersubjectivity that is founded through autonomous subjects, or, when a preceding community already exists, that consciously acknowledges the latter as such. The adolescent crisis does not necessarily dissolve communities, but it changes their nature—even in archaic cultures, whose initiation rites symbolize this transformation.

The decrease of individuals' identification with the collective of which they have previously considered themselves members can be termed a "collective identity crisis." The causes of such a crisis correspond in part to those of individual identity crises: the decline of common convictions, interests, and values; the neglect of symbols; the collapse of the collective memory represented in traditions; the loss of belief in a common future; the perception of discontinuities in one's own history; the feeling that there is a contradiction between descriptive and normative self-images; the tensions between one's own self-image and the image that others have of one; feelings of inferiority as compared to another collective identity; incomprehension when confronted with something that remains too foreign. Because of their differing ontological status, collective identities are frailer than individual identities; they need constantly to recall their reasons for being. One such reason is the threats posed by others: enemies are therefore exceptionally important in strengthening collective identities, and sometimes a victory over enemies leads to a serious crisis.[157] Nonetheless, we should keep in mind that a collective identity that is not opposed to any other is conceivable. This thesis is obviously of great importance in order to refute a popular objection to the possibility of a universal state; in retrospect it also makes it clear why it was so important to insist that self-consciousness was possible in a *privatus* as well. For, given the extensive parallelism between theories of individual and collective identity, only the assumption that a stable identity is possible even without contrast to others can save the notion that a universal *We* is not an absurdity. If an individual can understand himself primarily on the basis of himself and not in distinction from others, then a *We* ought also to be able to acquire its own identity positively by reference to common values rather than by excluding others. Indeed, a collective identity that defined itself primarily negatively—"we are what the others are not"—might be inferior to one that defines itself positively, because it does not know concretely what to do with itself. But that does not mean that it is in reality the less frequent form. One result of identity crises is a decrease in the predictability of the actions of the person or institution concerned. The previously acknowledged values have become questionable; but since after a phase of disorientation the necessity of action inevitably imposes itself, the actors will resort to older levels of their selves. Objectively, the latter are even more problematic, but they are all that remains, the only thing a collective in particular can count upon. Regressive or reactionary tendencies are therefore extremely likely in times of crisis. An immediate consequence of collective identity crises is the dissolution of the various *We*'s and thus shifts in the distribution of power that go much farther than those that might result from a group's military defeat, if the latter's collective identity remains intact (as did that of the Jews after the catastrophe of 587 B.C., for instance). In general, without a theory of individual and collective identity we cannot understand the phenomenon of power, which will be the subject of the next chapter.

---

157. The first historian who clearly saw this was Sallust, who in the proem to his *Historiae* dates the crisis in the Roman state from the victory over Carthage. However, it is still a long way from him to Orwell's *1984*, with the totalitarian state's artificial invention of enemies in order to dominate the masses.

4.4. The Moral Element in Man

4.4.1. Intrinsic Values in Pre-Human Nature

Even if value judgments do not follow from descriptive judgments, only that is evaluated that either is or at least should *be* and therefore can be; and Hume's Law certainly does not exclude the possibility that entities are valuable. What is valuable in the entities mentioned thus far? It is perfectly meaningful to suppose that already in inorganic nature much—perhaps even everything—is valuable; insofar as it gives expression to logically excellent structures such as symmetries, it can claim to have value.[158] The feeling for the beauty of nature in its sensible appearance as well as for the mathematical "beauty" of certain natural laws instinctively recognizes such an intrinsic value in nature; and anyone who shudders to think that by manipulating the brain a feeling for the "beauty" of opposed structures could be achieved, should not too quickly resign himself to the idea that this beauty exists only in the eye of the beholder. In actuality, ordinary language already distinguishes the sense of beauty from that of the pleasant; "pleasant" is a two-place predicate: something is always pleasant only for someone. In contrast, something is beautiful in and for itself; and the value of the beautiful is not reducible to that of the enjoyment of the beautiful. On the contrary, it contributes to the value of nature (in the narrower sense) in that, unlike artifacts, it is not made by humans, but rather reflects through its own being, as it were, something absolute. Therefore it would be very odd if, although the being of nature is not mediated through the subject, its value was. For example, landscapes certainly have an extrinsic value as biotopes for the survival of species and as relaxing retreats for human beings; yet even relaxation affects deeper levels of the personality if the encounter with nature leads to a recognition of its intrinsic value. As a rule, it is better for the subject as well if it does not relate everything to itself—and one destroys this fact if one interprets it in such a way that on the meta-level the subjective is nonetheless the ultimate criterion. It is compatible with what has been said that, *taken together,* an intellectual being's enjoyment of a beautiful landscape and the landscape's existence are significantly more valuable than the latter alone.

Apart from all the intrinsic values already possessed by inorganic nature, the emergence of the organic marks a qualitative leap forward in the development of value. The special relationship of the whole to its parts, the metabolically determined organic mode of being that must take care of *itself,* as well as the reflexivity of replication, mirror structures of the ideal world and anticipate elements of moral action; from this follows the value of the organic, and especially of sensitive organic being, which is the first structure *for which* values exist. The landscape cannot enjoy or even value itself, whereas the organism is precious enough to itself to guide its own self-preservation, and even to desire it. So

---

158. The limitation of intrinsic value to human beings in modern ethics is thus an error, which can, however, be understood in terms of historical teleology: without it the idea of human dignity would probably not have been so clearly grasped.

far as the value of the organic goes, it differs depending on the organism, and the appearance of the interior dimension is an important turning point: the value of a blade of grass is much less than that of an elephant. Obviously, assertions about the intrinsic value of an organism, if they are not to be completely subjective, can be based neither on its utility for man nor on its kinship with him. Assertions about utility are morally relevant, to be sure, but only insofar as they have consequences for human beings; it is certainly legitimate to raise a plant that feeds many humans rather than protect a highly developed animal that harms humans; but with such reflections we are moving into the sphere of extrinsic values. The degree of kinship with man proves nothing. Dolphins, because of the complexity of their achievements, such as the differentiation of their forms of communication and their intelligence, have a larger intrinsic value than many of our direct ancestors, whose behavior is more primitive than that of whales. Nothing indicates that evolution does not arrive at complexity and even personality by different paths.

The value of the organism sets limits to human action. On one hand, the killing of organisms is almost inevitable if there are to be more than plants (indeed, without heterotrophs, a number of plants could no longer exist and compete with each other); therefore, a person who loves life cannot in principle be against the destruction of life: if one radically rejects the latter with horror, one is ultimately defending the ideal that there should be no life, which is just as paradoxical as committing suicide out of fear of death. But, on the other hand, limiting killing to what is necessary is absolutely reasonable. This means that man has the right to intervene in nature in order to make it more beautiful and richer, for not everything that has established itself in nature is more valuable—*that* assumption would in fact amount to a crude naturalism. Killing animals in order to protect ecosystems is legitimate; animal rights activists who deny this are acting irresponsibly.[159] Not only may one sacrifice lower animals for the sake of the life of higher ones (including humans), but one may also kill higher animals for the sake of preserving biodiversity, because a differentiated whole is more valuable than one that consists exclusively of higher entitites, as was explained in chapter 3.5.1. But the killing of a higher animal always requires justification and thus is not morally indifferent; although it is permissible in order to save a human life, for instance, it is questionable whether it is also permissible in order to satisfy an appetite that can be satisfied in other ways. Arguments for vegetarianism are to be taken very seriously when they are not made absolute (naturally also because of the problem of providing food for the world's population). It is interesting to ask why torturing an animal is commonly considered morally more problematic than killing it, whereas in the case of human beings we take the opposite view. In this connection we must note that, as a thinking being, man sees his future lying before him and wants it, while an animal, living in the present, seeks first of all to avoid pain; therefore torturing an animal requires a more serious justifying ground—for example,

---

159. The respect for animals in recent ethical life and ethics is commendable, but it must also be lamented that irrational feelings often cloud the debate: action on behalf of individual frogs combined with complete indifference to the lot of laying hens is neither intellectually nor morally persuasive.

saving a human life—than does killing an animal. For this reason, current practices of mass livestock raising, even if they were not connected with killing, are far more immoral than traditional livestock raising with slaughter at the end of a life appropriate to the species. Finally, we must emphasize that an organism without its own self-consciousness is significantly less individualized than is man; the importance of the individual pales before that of the species. Species protection is a morally more urgent task than protecting animals, even independently of the possible utility of individual species for human beings.[160] However, even the annihilation of a particular species, such as a parasite, is moral if it is the only way to save many human lives.

4.4.2. Human Dignity, Personality, and Basic Goods

Still greater than the axiological turning point between the inorganic and the organic is that between organisms without self-consciousness and those with self-consciousness. Only the latter can experience values *and* analyze them conceptually; even if conceiving a value is far from being the sole value (otherwise the conception of values could only conceive itself), it is itself valuable in a high degree. It is clear that *all* such organisms participate in a *dignity* that raises them above other animals, no matter what species they belong to. But the notion, which must be empirically grounded, that of the beings known to us only man has self-consciousness, is not unreasonable; should we arrive at another conclusion, human dignity would have to be extended (and then called "personal dignity"). For example, were we to find an animal that commits suicide out of shame, it would have the same claim to respect as does man. For it is not membership in a species that determines a being's dignity, but rather whether it is a *person.* However, any being that has self-consciousness and is able (at least potentially) to recognize moral duties with regard to other beings with self-consciousness is a person—that is, a being that can say "I" and can at the same time transform this indexical into a noun and thereby see others as *I*'s. Even if "speciesism"—the theory that, notwithstanding any possible future discoveries, *only* humans and *all* humans have special rights—is untenable,[161] the second part of this assertion is especially worthy of consideration: the idea that *any* example of the species *Homo sapiens* has certain basic rights. In any case, one will not regard the actual possession of self-consciousness as a necessary condition of personal dignity—

---

160. It is no accident that the protection of individual organisms is generally limited to protecting animals, which follows from the fact that the individual plant is an individual to a much smaller degree than is an animal.

161. Locke was one of the first critics of speciesism, long before Kant: "For were there a monkey or any other creature to be found that had the use of reason to such a degree as to be able to understand general signs and to deduce consequences about general *ideas,* he would no doubt be subject to law and, in that sense, be a *man,* how much soever he differed in shape from others of that name" (*Essay* III, 11, 16; cf. also IV, 4, 15 f.).

its potential possession is sufficient. Anyone who denies this will have to deny personal dignity not only to human embryos but also to fetuses and infants (and perhaps even to people who are only temporarily in a coma or sleeping dreamlessly). To be sure, potentiality arguments require clarification, but it is significant that anyone who attributes rights to infants [162] cannot avoid such arguments. It seems to me crucial that the potentiality involved is that of a developing organism; in fact, one goes astray if one uses a more general concept of possibility, because then one must also attribute rights to non-procreated beings.[163] But even in relation to human beings who will never, or (for example, being in an irreversible coma) will never again, have an actual self-consciousness, the second part of that assertion seems to me reasonable. It goes without saying that the truly human is not based on a certain IQ, but rather on the ability to relate to oneself. No intellectual handicap, no matter how extensive, that does not fully destroy this ability can make human dignity (as a special case of personal dignity) in any way problematic: a child with Down's syndrome, who can laugh and cry and feel guilt, is far more *human* than the utilitarian wondering how one might be able to increase the total or average utility by means of general eugenic abortion, or the homeowner who is enraged by the loss in his property's "value" caused by the establishment of a home for the handicapped in his immediate neighborhood. Moreover, even in the case of handicaps that remove the organic basis for self-consciousness (for example, anencephaly), reference to possible abuses remains a strong counterargument against so-called euthanasia. What was customary in most archaic societies, which had to deal with extreme scarcity, should not be allowed in a culture that is declining far more because of its abundance and its lovelessness than the fact that a few resources are spent on seriously handicapped people and are thus not available for the luxury of others. In short, all humans and all possible other persons have a dignity that cannot be weighed against other goods, and that thus can only be respected, but whose value cannot be assessed. In them appears a structure that must be respected even if they themselves disregard its value—as is possible for any such being by definition.

Human dignity establishes not only rights, but also duties with regard to oneself. Even if suicide may be morally acceptable in extreme cases, under no circumstances is the collective suicide of the species morally acceptable, even if it were decided upon unanimously. Indeed, this unanimity would in a certain sense only increase the disvalue of the corresponding decision because it would indicate that no one any longer had an

---

162. This also holds for A. Leist (1990), whose discussion compels great respect for the clarity and seriousness of its argumentation, even if I cannot agree with his pleas regarding abortion during the first three months of pregnancy. Because he attributes an actual interest in life to fetuses (but not to embryos) on account of their ability to feel, he remains dependent on potentiality arguments—for it can be asserted that human fetuses are to be treated differently from dog fetuses only in relation to the *result* of the development, that is, in relation to what is not yet actually there.

163. It is significant that Aristotle's concept of potentiality is deeply rooted in his philosophy of the organic, even though it goes beyond it—but the idea of a possible world that in no way participates in reality would have been incomprehensible to him.

awareness of the duties we have not only toward individual human beings, but also toward the idea of humanity. The preservation of humanity means not only the continuation of its physical existence, but also the protection of human nature, of the dignity of the species (with which the creation of certain animal-human chimeras is not compatible).[164] Using genetic engineering and brain surgery to do away with the elements of the personality that are part of the essence of an organism with self-consciousness would remain a crime even if those able to agree were to give their permission, and even if it were to result in an enormous increase in pleasure. Any reasonable person would, all other things being equal, give pleasure priority over pain. But that does not mean that one may do away with the pain that makes man the being whose sufferings represent a moral problem in an entirely different way from those of an animal. We may feel sorry for someone who is suffering from the death of a family member or from guilt, but in a certain sense a person who no longer suffers from this is still more worthy of pity, even if the feeling one has for him lacks the emotional participation involved in the first kind of sympathy. A transformation of human society into one on the model of Huxley's *Brave New World* is to be preferred to a physical extermination of humanity chiefly because the latter might find its way back to the human; but one ought not to call "human" those conditioned pleasure automatons who have done away with the sufferings of love and death. Their satisfaction with themselves would not decrease the guilt of those who constructed this new world; on the contrary. "Thus, it could be that we would rather have to accuse ourselves of the fact that *no* accusation against us issues hence. The absence of protest would then itself be the gravest accusation; but the accuser in that case would *not* be the future injured party, but rather we ourselves."[165]

Life is the basis of personality, and a person's life is the most elementary good: if it is destroyed, the person can enjoy no other goods. But although life is the *basic* good, it is not the *highest*. It counts for so much because only through it can develop what really makes a human being human, that is, more than a mere organism. From this follows an important consequence that we will deal with in chapter 7.2.2.2, in discussing the distinction between law and morals: Even if *for others* attacks on my life are the greatest crime, I may, indeed should, risk my life in order to become worthy of it in the highest

---

164. This does not mean that possible descendents of chimpanzees and humans, for instance, would have no rights. Arguments for the dignity of the species cannot be reduced to arguments for individual rights any more than the latter can be reduced to the former.

165. Jonas (1979), 88 f.: "Es könnte also sein, daß wir uns veilmehr dessen zu verklagen haben, daß von dort *keine* Anklage gegen uns kommt: die Abwesenheit von Beschwerde wäre dann selbst die größte Anklage, aber der Kläger wäre gerade *nicht* der künftige Geschädigte, sondern—wir selbst." Trans. H. Jonas and D. Herr, 41. My whole paragraph is influenced by Jonas's ideas; we owe him the great service of having elaborated the independence of the *Ought* (*Sollen*) from any volitive act (*Wollen*) as the basis of any ethics of the future. I find compelling his notion that not all moral assertions can be conditional obligations (to the effect that they would be valid only so long as there were human beings)—for then a world with human beings could not be better than one without them. This entails a moral realism—in their validity, moral assertions are not related to subjects.

sense. In law, all other goods are subordinate to life; they include, first, the *inviolability of the body* and *formal self-determination;* second, *property and fortune* as the objective entities through which alone a person can carry out his more complex plans; third, *personal honor* as the medium within which a person must operate socially. In one's relationship to oneself, on the other hand, life is considered fulfilled only if through it the *I* is able to realize its self. To be sure, in one's relationship to oneself life also has a great extrinsic value, because it remains the condition for all activities with a higher intrinsic value; but it itself does not have the highest intrinsic value. The *spirit* is what first gives *life*—the basis of the spirit—its true meaning. In ethics, the complex relationship between life and intellect—which is so complex because life is the *real* presupposition of intellect, and the intellect the *ideal* presupposition of life—results in many difficulties that would not arise if we had a one-dimensional hierarchy of values; however, this mutuality, which is grounded in the dialectic of the ideal and the real, contributes a lot to the intellectually fascinating beauty of the moral. Even if not every person is asked to risk his life, relinquishing for the sake of intellectual values some of one's own vital values, which are bound up with the self-enjoyment of the living being qua living being, is profoundly human. Scheler[166] is right in asserting that vital values cannot be reduced to the value of the pleasant. Precisely those who avoid anything unpleasant and hedonistically take advantage of every opportunity to enjoy some pleasure will seldom consciously feel their own life processes, which make themselves noticeable only to those who strive against difficulty. Presumably early phases of human culture have a greater sense for vital values than later ones, which concentrate partly on the value of the pleasant (and what serves to achieve it, that is, utility), and partly on intellectual values. Sophisticated hedonists are just as much products of the dissociation resulting from the loss of the sense for vital values as are thoroughly spiritual ascetics.

4.4.3. The System of Virtues

Even though each person has an inalienable dignity, this dignity consists precisely in the fact that he must make himself what he ought to be, and that he can either fail or succeed in doing so. Great vices as well as great virtues are the prerogatives of humans. What are the most important virtues, what are the most important vices, and how do they follow from human nature?[167] From my discussions of the nature of self-consciousness it follows that there are also pre-social virtues; the moral is not exclusively a group phenomenon. Admittedly, the term "pre-social" is misleading insofar as all pre-social virtues

---

166. (1980), 122 ff.

167. It may be found surprising that in the following I sketch out a theory of virtue: even those who complain of the loss of virtues do not usually try to do that. But if the lack of a theory of virtues is one of the most dreadful deficiencies of our culture, then one should not only complain but seek to remedy it—no matter how awkward the first renewed attempts in this direction may be.

are also important for the community and can develop within it. Thus the precedence of intellectual over vital values is a central norm for any individual person. Yet the priority of intellectual values can be rendered intelligible for the social realm as well. For a scientific insight can be shared by several people, without being thereby diminished; in contrast, a cake cannot be eaten whole by several people; indeed, even a book in which this insight is written down cannot be used by several people at the same time and to that extent belongs in the sphere of economics. The noema of Beethoven's Ninth Symphony rises above the circle of economics, but the individual concert performances of it, which cannot be heard by everyone, do not.[168] The intellectual person is thus, *ceteris paribus,* more social than one who pursues material pleasures: if two people are interested in the same intellectual insight, the latter constitutes a kind of bond; if, on the other hand, two people would like to have the same piece of land, conflicts are quite likely to arise. And yet the term "pre-social virtue" is meaningful: it is intended to suggest that, in contrast to social virtues, these virtues could exist even if only a single person survived.

Man's first task is to set himself in order, to bring self and *I* into agreement. From Fichte and Kierkegaard to Nietzsche and Heidegger, this has rightly been emphasized as the first moral act.[169] Certainly the will to self-perfection is far from exhausting all moral duties; anyone who tends in this direction, as does Kierkegaard, loses sight of half— indeed, the more important half—of the moral. But no less one-sided is the theory that asks only how one can satisfy others' needs, without discussing the more fundamental problem of which needs are appropriate for an intellectual being and which of one's duties to oneself may not be violated through respect for the opinions and wishes of others. Social virtues that are not connected with this care for oneself lead inevitably to a society of mediocre and conformist phantoms who live not in themselves but only through others; conversely, seriousness in seeking one's own identity need not necessarily lead to selfishness: The difference between the two qualities is the point of Ibsen's *Peer Gynt.*[170] To know oneself, to assess correctly one's possibilities, and to develop those of one's talents that best serve moral ends is one of the primary duties, because most of the others depend on it. If a high self-assessment is objectively justified, then it is more moral than a

---

168. Cf. Scheler (1980), 110 ff., and already Spinoza, *Ethica* IV 36 f.

169. In the present, it is especially H. Krämer's achievement (1992) to have drawn attention to the importance of the relationship to oneself for a comprehensive ethics. However, Krämer misses the impossibility of moving beyond the normative dimension or reducing it to another—and this is regrettable in such a first-rate scholar to whom we owe so much for the correct understanding of Plato. Against him and with Kant (1976 f.; 8:549 f.), I strongly insist that there are duties to oneself. The possibility of these duties follows from what was said earlier about the relationship between *I* and self and about the normative self-image. For Krämer (and Habermas), on the other hand, a theory of the relationship to oneself can be reduced to mere rules of prudence (which, deviating from the terminology used here, he calls "ethics," and not "moral philosophy").

170. Among people, it is a question of being oneself; among trolls, a matter of being concerned only with oneself: "Der ute, under det skinnende hvelv, / mellem men det heter: 'Mann, vær deg selv!' / Her inne hos oss mellem trollenes flokk / det heter: 'Troll, vær deg selv—nok!'" (1978; 2:153).

humility that fails to exhaust all of one's possibilities. Indeed, every person may and should be proud that he is a human being and that he has the privilege of acting morally—a privilege that ennobles him precisely because it obligates him categorically. This pride is absolutely compatible with the consciousness of one's own mortality and finitude, on one hand, and with the feeling of gratitude for what one is and has not made, but has rather received, on the other; and finally, it is compatible with an unpretentious modesty in dealing with others: True pride has its measure within itself and does not need others' homage. Conversely, haughty arrogance, repression of the fear of death, and the lack of genuine self-esteem frequently appear together. Since there are no special duties to God— beyond fulfilling the general moral duties—we can say that genuine religious life consists in a feeling of one's creatureliness, and in the knowledge that one's own moral autonomy is not based on finiteness, but rather springs from a higher principle.

4.4.3.1. The Pre-Social Virtues

The first of the pre-social virtues that distinguishes human beings from other animals is *temperance* in the broadest sense. This refers to the ability to forgo immediate satisfaction of needs, whether these are of a general biological nature or specifically human: in the first case, we can speak of moderation; in the second, of temperance in the narrower sense. In both an act of self-abnegation is involved through which *I*-ness is first constituted. Notwithstanding all the differences between individual cultures, there is no society that did not in some way transform metabolism and especially reproduction. Among humans, eating and drinking are not mere biological processes, and hence in German even their names differ from those of the corresponding processes among animals. Hunger is not the only thing that may determine when we will eat; for instance, sacrifice before eating is an expression of a forbearance whose manifest function is a propitiation of the divinity, but it is in reality an end in itself, to be precise, a confirmation of the partial autonomy of humans with regard to their drives—a confirmation that is also served, for instance, by periodic fasts. Much the same holds for the sex drive. Certainly, the dangers to individuals posed by sexually transmitted diseases, and the dangers to the stability of society posed by unplanned pregnancies, have played an important role in determining the corresponding norms. But in both respects steps can be taken, at least today, that make rather modest demands on intelligence and willpower. Promiscuity must have an intrinsic disvalue if it is supposed to be morally questionable under present conditions—one of the achievements of modern means of contraception is to have promoted this insight. Does promiscuity have an *intrinsic* disvalue, then? Three moral arguments can be given in favor of this claim—even without any further utility, controlling the sex drive is deeply bound up with human dignity, a fact that was first recognized by Vico. Thus, first of all, as we have already said, controlling drives in general has an intrinsic value, because it increases the power of personhood. Second, however, the sex drive, unlike the drive to eat, is a social drive; but the reduction of another person to an object of pleasure represents an instrumentalization that does not disappear because this instrumentalization is mutual and voluntary. Third, it must be emphasized that in promiscuity there occurs a major devaluation of sexuality, because the latter ceases to be the privileged expression of the inner attitude that is called "dual" or "erotic love." Just as a word is abused when it is used to refer to the most disparate things (for example, the word "reactionary" in current discourse), promiscuity inflates sexual intercourse as a means for expressing love. In actuality, therein lies its true moral significance, which is also misjudged when it is interpreted solely as a means of repro-duction. The union of the bodies should express a spiritual union.[171] Moreover, the longing for physical union is an interesting anomaly in the social world; there is some-thing fascinating about the fact that people who draw back when someone touches them on the arm want under some circumstances to be physically very near someone else.[172] Since, moral reservations about promiscuity notwithstanding, the sex drive is strong and vital for the continuation of society, one widespread solution to the dilemma is a double moral standard with regard to male and female sexuality—a solution that de-spite its biological roots is not compatible with a universalist principle of justice. Even if moderation can be expected of everyone, it rises to *asceticism* in only a few—although admiration for these few is general. Even an ascetic can be intemperate in the narrower sense of the word: if ascetic behavior becomes compulsive, if the ascetic is not able to limit his habits when the circumstances demand that he do so, a loss of autonomy oc-curs. Obsession is never a virtue, even if it drives someone toward the highest goals. Happiness is not the ground of the validity of the moral, but to make happiness, one's own or especially that of others, a secondary goal is permissible and even obligatory when doing so does not contradict moral obligations. To torment oneself pointlessly is in any case contrary to duty. Asceticism is most meaningful when vital values are sacri-ficed to intellectual values.

In general, the systematic training of thought, that is, *temperance* in the broader sense, is an important virtue. This does not mean solely that temperance is required in order to perform certain other tasks that are morally obligatory; an effort to be objec-tive in order to grasp the structures underlying reality definitely also has an intrinsic value. Here we must distinguish between the ability to know the universal, that is, for example, the laws, and the ability of concrete subsumption; the latter is temperance in the narrower sense. The value of temperance depends also, but not solely, on the value of the thing known; thus it is particularly valuable when the prudent person not only examines empirical reality, but also rises to the first world, that is, when he devotes himself to *contemplation*. What is crucial is that in doing so he grasps the intrinsic value of his activity and that his reflection has for him the character of an end in itself. To seek to acquire mathematical knowledge for its own sake is more noble, *ceteris paribus,* than to seek it only in order to increase the sphere of utilities. *Wisdom* consists in the ability to

---

171. On this subject see Scheler (1974), 117 ff.
172. Cf. Felix Krull's speech with which he overcomes Zouzou's aloofness in chap. 10 of the third book of Thomas Mann's novel *Die Bekenntnisse des Hochstaplers Felix Krull.*

interpret the individual on the basis of the whole; it is particularly commendable when this interpretation is also related to one's own misfortunes, which are understood and accepted in their necessity. Whereas prudence first allows man to become unhappy, because it makes him familiar with the dark side of existence, which the superficial person easily overlooks, there is no purer and more unconquerable source of happiness, that is, of reconciliation with the world, than wisdom. Early in the history of ethical life ascesis and contemplation, from whose connection the spirit arises, were presumably associated, and people who stood out because they possessed these two virtues to a certain degree assumed positions of leadership within the religious subsystem. The differentiation of prudence into the subsystem of science, which completely emancipated itself from religion, belongs to a later stage of development.

I call *"poietic virtues"* those that have to do with the realization of goals in reality. Not only knowledge, but also action ennobles man; imposing one's own goals on nature is a sign of the elevation of the intellect over nature and should be considered positive if the values of nature mentioned earlier are not violated. The latter is in no way necessarily the case; traditional agriculture even increased the diversity of species. Although intellectual values rank higher than vital values, the intellectual man must also live in actual reality: satisfying moderate needs through one's own industrious labor, bringing production and consumption into balance, making the most out of the least, being sparing with resources and at the same time operating without meanness in this subordinate sphere are all elements of *economic* virtue. The essence of *technological* virtue is disciplining oneself in such a way that one deals appropriately with the demands of the object and succeeds in becoming adequate to it, even creating new structures that did not previously exist and increasing the stock of reality by adding artifacts to it. If at the same time a sense for beauty is not lacking and the artifacts are given a form that is not merely useful but also refers through the sensible to ideal relationships, one speaks of *aesthetic virtue.* The three kinds of poietic virtues were once united in craftsmanship and were only later differentiated into science, technology, and art. In its inner value, art approaches contemplation, because like contemplation it rises to the first world, yet at the same time makes the latter accessible to the senses.

The temperate person forgoes the satisfaction of a few vital needs, but he does not put life itself at stake. The readiness to do so constitutes the third of the classical cardinal virtues, *courage,* which is related to temperance in a peculiar way. On one hand, temperance and courage both involve an overcoming of immediate vital instincts; on the other, the instincts that are overcome are very different: In the case of temperance it is a matter of pleasure, and in that of courage it is a matter of fear—in its early forms, the fear of disadvantages in general and, in its most advanced form, fear of death; courage is the actual advancing toward death.[173] The active energy needed by the courageous person often makes

---

173. For this reason we cannot attribute courage to other animals, at least so long as they are not aware of death; we can attribute to them only a kind of behavior analogous to courage.

him take delight in life, whereas the ascetic does not easily have access to the vital impulse that the actions of courageous people demand; temperance inhibits, courage sets in motion. Nonetheless, the Socratic thesis that in their highest form the cardinal virtues mutually presuppose each other is absolutely right. A person who risks his life but is not prepared to forgo the pleasures of the senses is not very prudent; a person who renounces vital instincts but, being full of fear, clings to life has obviously not achieved this renunciation out of strength, but rather out of weakness, and is thus not truly temperate. Analogously, the truly courageous person must be aware of the dangers that he is running and therefore needs prudence; conversely, the love of truth requires courage, because some truths are frightening: ignorance frequently results from cowardice. The moral problem of courage consists in the following: on one hand, human life is more valuable than animal life because it is capable of virtues, including courage; on the other hand, only a living person can exercise virtues, including courage. Therefore it is irresponsible to risk one's life pointlessly; however, fearfully preserving one's life for the sake of the mere continuation of this fearful preservation is miserable. Certainly a person who does not learn early on to take risks will not develop the *habit* of courage; but if he does it too often, he may not survive to risk his life when it really matters, by saving a number of people's lives.

We should distinguish between several forms of courage, depending on whether they are directed against natural forces, enemies of the group, or one's own group. The battle against nature demands, given similar risks, less self-renunciation than does conflict with foreign conspecifics; but the most difficult thing is to oppose those to whom one is bound by collective identity, even when doing so is not connected with any risk to body and life, but only with social isolation. It is this form of courage that is called *"the courage of one's convictions,"* and neither is it possessed by every person who does not shy away from death at the hands of an enemy, nor need a person who is endowed with it be able to look death in the eye without blinking. A more passive form of courage consists in accepting all the blows of fate—poverty, illness, loss of friends—with composure, and drawing from the reduction to oneself a strength that cannot be broken by any external event. However, the danger of this stoic form of courage is that everything external (including the social) may become indifferent, that one is neither upset by the bad nor takes pleasure in the good. Knowing up to what point to fight and when to reconcile oneself to the inevitable is the task of prudence, and often of wisdom, which is foremost in determining the right borderlines between active and passive courage. Viewed sociologically and historically, courage is the virtue of those who first shaped the subsystem of the political.

Prudence, wisdom, the aesthetic virtue, and courage ought not to be devalued as merely *secondary virtues*. To be sure, this depreciative concept does correspond to something essential. There are actions that are useful exclusively as means to something else; the intention to carry them out has intrinsic value only after one has arrived at the sincere conviction that they are necessary in order to achieve something that is good in itself. If this testing is omitted, the ability to follow commands precisely can be dreadfully abused; in a few situations it would be far better if this ability did not exist. The differences between the behavior of the German and Italian civil populations with regard to the Jews during the Second World War, which are morally so important, find their deepest ground in the greater kindness of the Italians and the greater coolness of the Germans; but in addition we have to keep in mind that the Italians did not possess certain secondary virtues that the Germans had, which under tyranny had become in reality secondary vices. Nonetheless, we must insist that without secondary virtues, such as organizational abilities, morally obligatory demands that they have a certain complexity (such as those of justice) cannot be fulfilled either. The implicit assumption that one could basically get along well even without secondary virtues is therefore false. But that is not the reason why the subsumption of the pre-social cardinal virtues under the concept of secondary virtues is misleading. To be sure, a skinflint can be relatively temperate, a cheat can be relatively prudent, and a robber can be relatively courageous. After the terrible abuse of courage, for instance, in unjust wars, we must emphasize that still more important than the formal virtue of courage is what one is fearlessly fighting for. But all this does not alter the fact that the previously mentioned virtues have an intrinsic, and not a merely extrinsic, value. If certain commands that are objectively in line with what is right were carried out by machines, there would be no objection; only so long as this possibility does not exist, their precise implementation by human beings is morally obligatory because of its extrinsic value. But courage is not a virtue solely because it is repeatedly needed, for instance, in order to ward off injustices; if these injustices could be overcome without courage, the moral universe would be the poorer, because risking one's own life is something honorable that cannot be replaced by something else. Similarly, one ought to be temperate not only because it facilitates fair allocation; refraining from consumption would also be morally obligatory in a land of plenty, because it would uphold a principle of the human. Let there be no mistake: a society in which everyone could have what he wanted without having to ask himself whether he *is permitted* to want what he wants would not be very attractive; one would find no personalities in it. In interactions among the members of such a society, who in losing labor would have lost one of the most elementary forms of their relationship to the world, it would be difficult to express love as well; for it is not easy to separate the concept of love from that of renunciation. However, since man is denied happiness if he is not the object and, even more, the subject of love, there would be much irritable malice to compensate for the lost love. The transformation of traditional virtues into secondary virtues in the current debate has much to do with modernity's absurd monism, which always wants to reduce everything to either equality or to maximizing total utility; it is refuted by the simple reflection that even a *privatus* could have those virtues, which in him could not possibly be subordinated to social values.

4.4.3.2. Social Virtues

This does not deny that without social virtues a theory of virtues would seem very meager. The smallest common denominator of social virtues consists in the transcendence of natural selfishness, in breaking the bounds of the obsession with oneself, which already happens in acts of sympathy, and for which hermeneutic abilities can be useful. To this extent, all social virtues involve altruism. However, it is clear that this self-transcendence is at the same time a deepening, broadening, and enriching of one's own self; when the latter is concerned only with itself, it is necessarily small and misshapen. People with the ability to take into account the cares and problems of others usually profit themselves most from this ability; their virtue is its own reward.[174] In addition, we have already seen in discussing sociobiology that morally affirmative structures may, and indeed ought to, strive to stabilize and extend themselves; to that extent it is absolutely moral when one supports primarily those who share one's moral convictions. It is not permissible to sacrifice oneself for the sake of a rogue, unless sacrificing oneself could lead to the rogue's moral reform; and not every person may believe he has this ability, which Jesus obviously possessed to an exemplary degree. In general, one ought to evaluate not only one's own needs, but also those of others; however fine virtues such as *generosity*—that is, the wish to share what one possesses—and the corresponding *gratitude* may be, it can be genuinely immoral to renounce the satisfaction of one's own needs for the sake of the other if one comes to the conclusion that one's own needs are more moral than those of the other. In any case, it is a mistake to want to base the moral on an asymmetrical act, as Levinas does. It is true that we must emphasize that man's natality and mortality result in asymmetrical relationships, whose regulation is an important task. But the wish to always be the giver can be an expression of vanity; in any case, it cannot be universalized and can violate the autonomy of the other.[175] Finally, we must note that a social interest in others can sometimes arise from a flight from oneself, that is, from the fact that one is not able to set oneself meaningful tasks.[176]

The moral person will take seriously not only others' needs, but also and especially their ideas of what is valuable. *Shame* is such an interesting phenomenon because it makes the social roots of moral sensibility clear: I am ashamed when the other perceives my transgressions or even my naturalness (e.g., my nakedness)[177] and dependency that are not in accord with my spiritual vocation.[178] But the deepening of the feeling of shame to the feeling of guilt indicates that in making a moral judgment about myself I am not dependent on judgment by others: even if others know nothing about my transgressions, or even if they know about my acts but condone them, I can judge myself negatively; conversely, natural feelings of shame can also develop when not I but

---

174. Cf. G. Huber's fine observations (1995), 285 ff.

175. In Lessing's *Minna von Barnhelm* Tellheim exemplifies this idea in an insurpassably comic way.

176. Cf. Nietzsche (1980), 4:77, 242.

177. To this extent the covering of the genitals, which is widespread among most archaic cultures, is deeply human and in no way serves only practical needs of protection. With deep insight the Yahwist made this act, as the original human act, as it were, follow the eating from the tree of the knowledge of good and evil (Genesis 3:7).

178. Sympathetic people can also feel shame for a third person, as Leibniz already pointed out (*Nouveaux Essais* II 20 § 17).

rather the other, who exploits my dependency, for instance, is the one who becomes morally guilty. Whenever possible, one should seek not to harm others' self-respect and moral sensibility (even when one does not share the latter); politeness arising from a sense of tact is a virtue that should not be underestimated. Social skill has first of all an extrinsic value, because as a rule it is a necessary condition for being able to assume mediation and leadership positions; intrinsic value can be assigned to it if it springs from a systematized sense for the needs and values of others as well as for the right degree of distance from them. The desire for recognition by others must not lead to the denial of the morally obligatory; but being effective socially, trying to communicate what is right to others, considering their judgment not as infallible but still to be taken seriously is better than being indifferent—understood in this way, ambition is a virtue,[179] though only so long as it remains subordinate to other virtues. If, on the contrary, ambition becomes the decisive motive for seeking to acquire other virtues, it has only an extrinsic value: if it intensifies into self-denial out of lust for power, it is a vice.[180] The prudent and just person may, indeed should, feel joy at social success; on the other hand, anyone who seeks primarily recognition, and sees the solution of objective problems only as a way of gaining it, is not worthy of respect. Ambition must be distinguished from the desire for fame, since the latter can be content with knowing that it will gain recognition only after death; and no matter how far it goes beyond ambition because of its broader temporal horizon, it likewise fails to grasp the moral as an end in itself. It is usually the last weakness from which very great persons free themselves.

4.4.3.2.1. Justice

The most fundamental of all social virtues is justice. Yet the essence of justice is missed if its place in the system of virtues is not grasped. Justice is surrounded on both sides by other virtues—on one side by the pre-social virtues, and on the other by the social virtues that transcend justice: friendship and love.[181] Abbreviations and distortions of a society's mores are inevitable if the latter are reduced to justice, or even justice within a society—even if justice is developed to an extent unknown to any earlier age. For formal equality is absolutely compatible with generally tolerated vices; it is not justice itself that can decide in which direction a change should take place if, for instance, a privileged group practices special vices—whether in the direction of overcoming these vices or spreading them to everyone. Since we have already discussed the principles of justice, it will suffice here to mention their anthropological origin. The enormous power of abstraction, thanks to which the *I* can objectivize its own self and see it as only *one*

---

179. Cf. in this sense Aristotle, *Nicomachean Ethics* 1125b1 ff.

180. See Augustine's apposite observations, *De civitate Dei* V 19 f. and those of Thomas Aquinas, *De regimine principum* I 7.

181. It will be noticed that the order of the *Nicomachean Ethics* has been taken as the model for the order used here. However, it is supplemented by love as a virtue, to which only Christianity has risen.

instantiation of *I*-ness, is the ultimate ground of justice; and with the increase of this power in modern subjectivity, the idea of justice necessarily becomes universalistic. The original position Rawls invents is only a metaphor for this power of modern thinking, which is able to abstract from all contingent differences except from the power of abstraction—in which I, like any other *I*, participate. When it is related to human things, the metaphysical standpoint that views the world *sub specie aeternitatis* produces the universalistic concept of justice.[182] Similarly, Kant's distinction between the phenomenal and the noumenal *I* can be given an empirical meaning if one relates it to that between the self and the *I*. However, it is not possible to reconstruct the noumenal in purely empirical terms; and since reference to the values of the first world is constitutive for any *I*, the noumenal is still more appropriately interpreted in terms of ideal values.

Justice consists in the recognition that the rights one ascribes to oneself must be respected in all other equal persons. However, in the first part of this book we have seen that the precise determination of equality, on one hand, and of rights, on the other, are not provided by the concept of justice itself; additional reflections are necessary. We listed above the basic goods that should be granted every person and that should be protected by the state, if necessary. However, justice is not the property of legal norms alone; justice in the full sense of the term also includes what cannot be coerced. Thus the just person has a lively sense of the rights of others, just as if they were his own; indeed, he can comprehend even his opponent's standpoint, insofar as it is not wholly absurd. The priority of justice over other virtues is shown by the fact that one may be rightly proud of one's temperance, courage, etc., but only when one acknowledges the comparable achievements of others and one does not prevent anyone else from developing such virtues. Indeed, according to the broadest principle of justice, there may even be a duty to help others develop similar virtues, for instance, in the framework of a system of education organized by the welfare state. Of course, one cannot simply drum virtues into another person, but there are no doubt real conditions of the possibility of these virtues. How far the establishment of equality must go, and how far it may go, will be discussed in detail in chapter 7.3.1.2. The autonomy of the individual implies limits in both directions.

The concept of justice is connected with that of symmetry; and thus just as it is unjust to take something away from someone else, it is also unjust to allow something to be unlawfully taken away from oneself.[183] Insofar as good-naturedness is grounded in inertia, it is not really a virtue; such a good-natured person is not truly good.[184] A person

---

182. Cf. the fine passage at the end of Rawls's *Theory of Justice* (1971; 587).

183. Cf. Cicero, *De officiis* I 23 f.

184. Cf. La Rochefoucauld's maxim 237 (in the 1678 edition): "Nul ne mérite d'être loué de bonté, s'il n'a pas la force d'être méchant: toute autre bonté n'est le plus souvent qu'une paresse ou une impuissance de la volonté" (1967; 61). ("No one deserves to be praised for his goodness if he does not have the strength to be wicked: any other kind of goodness is usually no more than indolence or impotence of will.") See also Nietzsche (1980), 6:122 f: "Meine Furcht ist gross, dass der moderne Mensch für einige Laster einfach zu bequem ist: so dass diese geradezu aussterben. Alles Böse, das

who is just in the full sense of the word is prepared to fight injustices, and therefore he needs courage; and if the social order is unjust, one cannot be truly just without the courage of one's convictions. Conversely, courage becomes complete only when formal fearlessness is put in the service of the battle against injustice. Indignation at injustice need not be accompanied by anger; rather, *composure* in form is quite compatible with relentlessness in the cause. Resolute resistance to evil impies still less the kind of revenge that is not concerned with avoiding future evil but rummages about in the past. Especially when defeat has led the opponent to see the truth, *being conciliatory* is one of the noblest virtues. It is connected with wisdom insofar as it is able to draw even from the bad, from what ought not to be, a meaning in the whole of being; and it springs from the knowledge of one's own weaknesses, which also long for the forgiveness that the just person must not deny if he himself seeks it.

Alongside natural duties of justice, there are also special *obligations* that result from agreements. Here the crucial moral principle requires that one abide by the agreements one has made. Indeed, a formal agreement is not even necessary in order to ground an obligation; behavior implying a specific intention suffices—if one benefits from the advantages of just institutions, one ought to make an appropriate contribution to their survival; for who else would have an obligation to do so, if not the beneficiaries? What one promises to do, one ought to do; analogously, what one says should be true to the best of his knowledge and belief. The duty to be *sincere* is a special form of obligation: a person who communicates has thereby conclusively, through the implications of his behavior, promised to be sincere, because that is a presupposition of any communication. Of course, in certain situations one can also refuse to communicate: not everything that is considered true must or even may be said (the sense of tact, for instance, forbids this), but everything said should be true. This does not follow solely from obligations to others; truthfulness is also valuable if one considers it from pre-social points of view, because it represents a unity of the inner and the outer. Absolutely compatible with this is the fact that in exceptional cases lying and even breaking a promise is permissible and even obligatory—for instance, if it is necessary to break it in order to save the life of an innocent person.

4.4.3.2.2. *Friendship and Love*

What are the limits of justice? Justice declares that *if* one wants to cooperate with others, one must cooperate in a certain way; it does not say that one ought to cooperate. Cooperation that is guided by justice is usually motivated by rational self-interest—even if the latter is limited by justice, which cannot itself be reduced to rational self-interest. In addition, however, there are also forms of cooperation that serve no goal

---

vom starken Willen bedingt ist . . . entartet, in unsrer lauen Luft, zur Tugend." ("I greatly fear that modern man is simply too lazy for certain vices, so that the latter are almost dying out. Everything evil, which is determined by a strong will . . . degenerates, in our tepid atmosphere, into virtue.")

beyond themselves, but are ends in themselves: one cooperates out of joy in cooperation and for no other reason. Relationships that are ends in themselves we call "friendships," and no doubt the ability to form friendships is one of the finest human virtues. Naturally, cooperation between friends also never lacks an external goal either; one must have common goals in order to experience the world together, and one must experience the world together in order for friendships to develop. Self-consciousness already presupposes consciousness of the world—and how much more does this hold for relationships with other people! Even in the most intensive dual erotic relationship a lack of the world and concentration on selfishness *à deux* quickly becomes negatively evident; without an objective material "any relationship becomes pathological, parasitical, cannibalistic—and one has not even swallowed anything real."[185] Yet this does not change the fact that in friendship the common experience of the world is so important precisely because only through it can one get to know a friend; it is not that the friend helps one gain mastery over the world, but rather that the world helps one understand the friend. To be sure, many interactions, especially among young people, are neutral in the sense that although they begin for the sake of some external goal, they are open to deepening into friendship; in the course of time, however, it gradually becomes clear whether working together is an end in itself or not, whether one wants to continue it after the achievement of the external goal or not. On the basis of the enigmatic phenomenon of sympathy, which presumably has to do with the ratiomorphous apparatus's physiognomic-mimetic insights, during the first seconds of making contact with another person important preliminary decisions are made regarding whether a friendship is possible or not, and these preliminary decisions can remain influential even if reason perceives that they were irrational—for example, that they were based on completely external similarities to people with whom one has had positive or negative experiences. It is well known that Aristotle classified friendships depending on whether they were directed toward the pleasant, the useful, or the valuable. Friendships that are based merely on common utility, for instance, business friendships or political alliances, should not be called "friendships" at all, because the relationship is not an end in itself. Nonetheless, such relationships can sometimes deepen into true friendships; and it is not without significance that even if one remains in the realm of the useful, one acts as if more were involved: the social climate, and thus also business, is thereby improved. It is important, however, that both sides be aware of the formality of the affirmation, because otherwise disappointments are inevitable, just as in intercultural relationships they commonly arise from the fact that one has not correctly understood the other's rhetoric. Friendships that are based on the pleasant, that is, on immediate feelings of sympathy, are enjoyed as ends in themselves, but they are seldom enduring, because the motive is too shallow: it is attached to the other's surface, to his outward appear-

---

185. Jonas (1979), 369: "[ohne einen objektiven Stoff] wird jede Beziehung pathologisch, parasitär, kannabalisch—und man hat nicht einmal etwas Wirkliches verschluckt." This passage is not included in the abridged English translation of this work.

ance. The full concept of friendship presupposes that common *values* are recognized. Of course, values are not merely external to a person; a person himself is also more or less valuable, depending on the extent to which he grasps the right values, feels them, and makes them the guiding principle of his conduct. Moving from the common recognition of values to the personal value of the other is the foundation of the most enduring and best friendships. Indeed, since criticism by those who have no right to criticize is unwelcome, friendship is the appropriate medium for moral improvement. Being able to talk about one's own weaknesses with someone without having to fear that this information might be used against oneself, indeed, in the well-founded trust that one will be able to work on overcoming them together, is the mark of true friendship. The more masks social life forces one to wear, the more urgent the corrective of friendship is in order to preserve one's own identity. Certainly symmetry is part of the concept of friendship, as it is of that of justice. But the difference between the two is obvious: in a business relationship that is a business relationship and nothing else, what the other does in return is what counts; in a friendship, what the other does in return is important only as an expression of an attitude. A person who gives without receiving anything in return will wonder whether his friend feels the same way about him, and it is this, not the substantive loss, that will worry him. However, admiration can be asymmetrical. The value of another person can definitely be felt, even if one knows that one is oneself less valuable than the admired person. The morally positive aspect of the feudal order cannot be understood if one does not acknowledge this possibility. Of course, the recognition of superiority is an achievement that is morally respectable in itself and therefore ensures the admirer the superior person's respect, if he is truly superior. *Fidelity*, the ability to stand by someone admired or loved even if the relationship is no longer in one's own interest, and even if this person has changed in unpleasant ways, is one of the most noble virtues and the mark of true friendship. If the ability to cling to the right values despite all resistance is the ability that confers dignity on a person, and if the person who recognizes the right values is valuable to a particularly high degree, then a world without fidelity would lack dignity even if it had all other virtues. Fidelity to the dead is called *piety*, and it is the finest victory over death that man can achieve.

The expense connected with true friendship makes it impossible to be a friend to many people. The positive orientation toward the other that characterizes friendship, and its connection with the universality of justice, is the achievement of the virtue that Christianity has placed at the center of the moral: love, in the sense of *charity*. Obviously one cannot love everyone, if loving means helping others in a specific way; this shows the finitude of the material world, manifested in the fact that it inevitably becomes smaller through division. Even time is divisible, and it is neither possible nor desirable to devote the same amount of time to everyone. However, it is in principle possible, even if it is extraordinarily difficult, to approach each person with an attitude that seeks to discover and feel his own personal values. Charity is the combination of respect and benevolence, of the distance demanded by the other person's autonomy and the nearness demanded by solidarity with him. This does not mean that one should consider everyone to be good; there is no doubt that there are bad and evil people, and it is definitely a duty to oppose them. One is far from the spirit of true charity if one wants to satisfy everyone—a wish whose roots are indolence and a lack of the courage of one's convictions. Thus it follows from the duty to be objective that one should acknowledge one's own faults as well as those of one's neighbor, and if a lack of charity is necessary to do this, then, so long as it is required, it is absolutely justified. "Only those who do not love discern shortcomings; therefore, to put them in their proper place, one must not love, but only to the extent that this is necessary."[186] This does not alter the fact that the highest human virtue consists in sincerely recognizing, even in battle, the virtues of the other, if there are any, and in being aware of the positive no less than the negative traits of the other. And if there were a person who lacked any personal values, then, first, one would still have to respect his dignity as a human being (which does not allow us to deny conclusively the possibility of change), and second, one would feel sympathy rather than hatred. In general, the capacity for love consists in a developed sense for the plenitude of value in the world, both human and non-human. Feeling the objectively right and the subjectively moral with gratitude and understanding the bad and the evil on the basis of their causes constitute the essence of the love that one can have for another person, and even for the totality of being. It is this capacity for love that makes human beings worthy of love in the highest degree, and it is this sense for being's plenitude of value that crowns and completes this plenitude.

The virtues described above are universal insofar as they are found in every culture, however fragmented and limited their manifestation may be. However, the specific form they take is absolutely dependent on culture and period, and since they constitute a system, changing one of them means a transformation of the rest. The Christian deepening of the concept of love and the modern extension of the demands of justice have profoundly transformed the structure of friendship; along with the specifically capitalistic shaping of the economic virtue and the new assessment of technological virtue one of the most consequential changes in humanity's system of virtues has taken place. Social and political contextual conditions make certain virtues more urgent, and others less necessary or even superfluous; virtues that are not regularly practiced wither away, because habitualization is part of the concept of virtue. Thus courage is the most important virtue in heroic ages; if a universal state with a true monopoly on force is one day established, physical courage will become rarer, whereas the need to have the courage of one's convictions will increase. The affluent society no longer produces the need for temperance; and however respectable the form of temperance that springs from no external pressure may be, one has to assume that the number of temperate people in wealthy societies is small. Whereas differences in customs are disturbing, but cease to seem strange at a certain level of intelligence and abstraction, it is differences in the system of values

---

186. Goethe (1991), 815: "Die Mängel erkennt nur der Lieblose; deshalb, um sie einzuordnen, muß man auch lieblos werden, aber nicht mehr als hiezu nötig ist."

and virtues that ultimately distinguish individual cultures from each other. It is these latter differences that make intercultural relations so fascinating and at the same time so difficult. It is comforting, however, that cultures are differentiated more by their interpretations and emphasis than by a sheer denial that temperance, courage, or justice are virtues; and it is also comforting that in principle any culture can produce people who have the capacity to love—that is, to recognize the value of another culture's virtues. May the monism of one virtue—the triumph of justice over the other virtues in modernity— not completely destroy this capacity!

4.4.4. The System of the Vices

Before we turn to vices, it is appropriate to reflect on the relationship between virtues and vices. On one hand, virtues and vices are opposed—and for some virtues it is still true, as Plato and Aristotle taught, that they must be distinguished from two vices, insufficiency and excess, as courage must be distinguished from cowardice and from recklessness. On the other hand, however, in a certain sense virtues presuppose the possibility and even the reality of vices. This is true first of all insofar as a few virtues are possible only if there are people who are not virtuous. To the extent that courage is directed primarily against people rather than against nature, it would be superfluous in a world where everyone was just; in a world composed of angels, there would be no need to have the courage of one's convictions.[187] However, here vice is a purely external condition of the possibility for virtue. In the case of prudence, the relationship is more complex, for at least if we make the empirical assumption that there are vices, we will have to require that a person who is prudent in the comprehensive sense of the term also know about vice. But knowing about something is a more intimate relationship than fighting it, because the thing known occupies the knower in a very different sense than does the thing fought against (qua thing fought against, I set aside here the fact that one must also know this thing, in order to successfully fight it). One must enter into the inner logic of the vice in order truly to grasp it, and one must certainly reckon with the danger that in the process this inner logic may take possession of oneself as well. Indeed, more than one person who really knows vice more deeply has concerned himself with it only because it is familiar to him from an inner point of view. This is the third and most intimate reason why virtues presuppose vices. A person seems to be truly temperate only if he has overcome an opposing impulse within himself; an asexual creature would hardly be considered chaste. A person who, for whatever reason, has had enough of life and seeks death in battle may be doing something objectively right and be considered admirable because he wants his death to serve some objectively just cause; but a person is courageous in the

---

187. From this Aristotle deduces the precedence of temperance and justice over courage: *Topics* 117a35 ff.

full sense of the word only if he loves life and therefore is not fully without fear of death. Socrates already referred to this peculiar dialectic of virtue and vice; and indeed it is not easy to say which is the morally better: the pure person, who knows no temptation, or one who has overcome temptation through the power of his will. A weakling who has not been confronted by evil only for contingent reasons is not pure; that person is pure who, on one hand, never has evil thoughts even when severely tempted and, on the other, is unable to accuse another person of being wicked.

Grace (*Anmut*) is based on this double structure: with dancelike ease grace moves within the demands of the moral and knows nothing of the dangers that threaten it. It is appropriate to childhood, and if it endures in adulthood, it cannot but be moving. In contrast, *dignity* (*Würde*) characterizes a person who knows what is negative about himself and others and is able to combat it resolutely without dwelling on it any longer than is absolutely necessary.[188] In any case, it is inadmissible to concern oneself with evil either because one is secretly attracted by it or because one cuts a better figure when compared with the misdeeds of others; and even if the dignified person has no illusions regarding the moral poverty of human beings, does not expect too much from life, and for the same reason is on familiar terms with death, he never wallows in the depths of the immoral. Which is better, grace or dignity? The answer can only be: How good that there are both. On one hand, grace is not evolutionarily stable; only a person who knows vice can defend himself against it. On the other hand, the finest reward the dignified person can receive is a vision of grace: that is what gives the dignified person strength in his battle and prevents him from being defeated at the very moment of his victory over the negative, whose means he must in part adopt. It certainly was unjust when in earlier cultures the roles of grace and dignity were distributed according to innate characteristics (for instance, sex); but without the ideal of grace a culture inevitably becomes dreadfully impoverished, and indeed soon loses its dignity as well.

4.4.4.1. Pre-Social Vices

Some vices are no less peculiar to humans than the virtues. This does not simply mean that the concept of vice presupposes a moral order that is accessible only to human beings; in a very concrete way, certain vicious types of behavior are possible only for a being that has reflected itself outside the laws of the merely living.[189] Thus, to begin with

---

188. I define the concept somewhat differently than does Schiller in his immortal essay, "Über Anmut und Würde," because I combine his concepts of the naive and the graceful.

189. The reader will have noticed that in the following system of the vices I have adopted the Christian tradition's classification of the seven deadly sins, just as in my arrangement, which is based on intensification, I have inverted, with slight variations, the sequence of Dante's *Purgatorio.* There is a correspondence to the system of virtues, but not a one-to-one correspondence. On one hand, phenomenological richness is more important than a strict parallelism, and, on the other, the negation of love, for instance, has different forms and degrees.

the negation of temperance, only man can eat or drink, or indulge in sexual activities, beyond any appetite or biological necessity, with the goal of maximizing pleasure—just as he alone can forgo the satisfaction of an urgent drive. Whereas any *addiction* is especially reprehensible if it is not only the expression of a lack of temperance but also results in a destruction of self-mastery in other domains, it is not easy to decide whether *gluttony* or *lust* has the larger disvalue. On one hand, the social dimension and even a vague memory of love elevate lust over gluttony, which is completely mindless; on the other hand the instrumentalization of a person (which, as we have said, remains an instrumentalization even if it is mutual and voluntary) is more morally oppressive than consuming things, and only the most extreme brutishness could think of comparing sexual needs to those for food and drink. For that very reason pure lust is rare: Don Giovanni's problem is not an insatiable sex drive but rather an unstable identity. Yet even renunciation is threatened by moral dangers. If it arises not from inner conviction but from social pressure, for instance, there is a temptation to depreciate what one has to give up. A reasonable renunciation, in contrast, consists in recognizing the value of the pleasant while knowing that there are higher values. Only a person who does not feel these higher values will console himself for having to give up something he would like to have had by slandering it.[190] The feeling from which this renunciation arises is called "ressentiment," and it has no doubt played a role in shaping individually as well as socially valid values. In his *Genealogy of Morals,* Nietzsche rightly pointed this out, but Scheler was the first to integrate this insight of moral psychology and moral sociology into a consistent system of morals, and on this basis he also grasped the factual historical development far better than Nietzsche did.

In addition, the loss of reality can go considerably farther among human beings than among other organisms, which must be in some way adapted to their environments if they are to survive. Cared for by society, however, man can afford to indulge over long periods in abysmal stupidity and even mad systems unknown to other animals. The uncanny and dangerous thing about these is that they can be combined with sectorial intelligence, and therefore can do more damage than would otherwise be the case. "I fear

---

190. The classical example is given by Scheler in his famous book on ressentiment: "Das zur Einstellung vieler alter Jungfern gewordene Immerwiederaufsuchen sexuell bedeutsamer Vorgänge in der Umgebung, um harte negative Werturteile über sie zu fällen, ist hierbei nur die in die Ressentimentbefriedigung umgewandelte letzte Form der geschlechtlichen Befriedigung selbst. Die Kritik *vollzieht* also hier *selbst,* was sie der Scheinintention nach verwirft" (1978; 19). ("The constant searching for sexually significant events in one's environment in order to make severe negative judgments about them, which has become characteristic of many old maids, is only the final form of sexual satisfaction transformed thereby into the satisfaction of ressentiment. Such criticism thus *itself carries out* what it apparently reproaches.") In the Catholic world, the priest in the confessional who seeks an especially detailed account of offenses against the Sixth Commandment provides a further example, which enjoys great popularity in literature and film. However, there is also ressentiment against the higher values that one oneself lacks—think of the man of the world's irony with regard to naive persons, whom he actually admires.

that animals regard man as a being of their own kind that has lost the healthy animal sense in a highly dangerous way—as the mad animal, the laughing animal, the weeping animal, the unhappy animal."[191] Moreover, intellect can misunderstand itself instrumentally and not enjoy its own insights as ends in themselves, but debase them as means to the end of satisfying needs. A lack of wisdom, that is, an inability to assume the standpoint of the whole, is widespread even among highly intelligent people.

Man's poietic capacities allow him to exploit natural resources and violate economic virtues as no other animal can; man can put artifacts into the world that no longer fit into nature. The unlimitedness of his possibilities can deprive him of any sense of measure, without which beauty cannot be enjoyed. The economic virtue is threatened by the vices of *extravagant expenditure* and *avarice*. Whereas the former contradicts temperance, the latter is another morally negative form of renunciation. It is true that the miser forgoes immediate enjoyment, but not for the sake of intellectual values, not in order to help others, but rather for the sake of leaving untouched the possibility of future private enjoyment. However, since this future possibility is sacrificed to other future possibilities, the only thing that could justify this kind of behavior is never attained: therefore the behavior is illogical. But it is, like its active variant, greed, specifically human: only a person who is *fame futura famelicus* can relapse into avarice and greed; and only avarice and greed could ultimately produce in a few human cultures economic systems in which renunciation is no longer required by external scarcity.

Cowardice takes many different forms, and since courage is a virtue that presupposes a great deal and cannot be expected from everyone, not all the modes in which cowardice appears make a person contemptible. Worse than the fear of mortal dangers is the refusal to acknowledge one's own mortality, the denial of death; from this often arises a lack of piety. A lack of the courage of one's convictions can be so great as to become complete dependency on other people's opinions, and since, like one's own, these opinions have themselves often been formed in dependent ways, the process of forming opinions in such groups can become wholly unpredictable. The supposition that enough other people will adopt a given opinion is ultimately the deciding factor. After an initial hesitation, because no one wants to run the risk of being isolated, once the process of consensus is underway, there is an acceleration, since it would be no less embarrassing to be the last one to join the others. The fear of one's own self is what underlies this tendency to seek refuge in what "people" believe.[192]

Within the Christian system of the cardinal sins, *acedia*—a concept that is not easy to translate—rightly plays an important role. Thus *acedia* has to do with sluggishness; yet

191. Nietzsche (1980), 3:510: "Ich fürchte, die Thiere betrachten den Menschen als ein Wesen Ihresgleichen, das in höchst gefährlicher weise den gesunden Thierverstand verloren hat,—als das wahnwitzige Thier, als das lachende Thier, als das weinende Thier, als das unglückselige Thier." A concrete dramatization of this aphorism can be found in the fourth part of Swift's *Gulliver's Travels*.

192. Cf. Heidegger, *Sein und Zeit* § 27 (1979; 126 ff.).

the ultimate ground of this sluggishness is a melancholy attitude in which the world as well as one's own life seem to have lost any meaning. Whereas in gluttony, lust, greed, and cowardice it is false values toward which one's striving is directed, *acedia* slows and even extinguishes any striving;[193] a sad indifference remains that can no longer recognize any true differences in value. To this extent Thomas Aquinas, who goes far beyond Aristotle in the analysis of vices because Christianity has a sense of evil completely different from antiquity's, rightly opposes *acedia* to the joy that arises from love for the highest divine good.[194] And yet it has to be admitted that temptation to *acedia* must be known to everyone who keeps a critical distance from his culture's activities. A certain disgust at false values, one's own as well as those of others, is a necessary condition for rising to higher values and identifying collective illusions as such. Of course, what matters is that *acedia* should determine only a transitional phase of one's existence, not one's whole life.

4.4.4.2. Social Vices

The whole nastiness of which man is capable is first shown in the social vices. *Selfishness* is, as we know, not specific to man; but in human beings it can, on one hand, free itself even from responsibility for one's own offspring and, on the other, grow, on the basis of the capacity for foresight, into something monstrous, and violate the most elementary obligations of justice. *Deceptions* occur throughout the organic world; but even among higher animals they are hardly consciously willed as deceptions. In contrast, a being in which the *I* distinguishes itself from the self and can play different roles has almost boundless possibilities of deception (both as a means and as an end in itself)— possibilities that are especially repulsive when they make use of the most affirmative forms of intersubjective relationships, friendship and love, that is, when they grow into the *betrayal* that Dante has rightly punished in the deepest circle of hell. It is usually easy to deceive, because the other is willingly deluded into believing in a more pleasant reality. "One is never deceived, one deceives oneself"[195]—unless one is exceptionally stupid. But the converse also holds: One never deceives only other people, one always deceives oneself as well—unless one is exceptionally prudent. There are few false people who are not also false with regard to themselves, hardly a con man or hypocrite who is not ultimately taken in by himself.[196] In fact, injustice is specifically human only insofar as the perpetrator's violation of the inextinguishable consciousness of justice sets in motion all sorts of secondary rationalizations.

---

193. Cf. Dante, *Purgatorio* XVII 127 ff.
194. Cf. *Summa theologica* II/II, q. 35.
195. Goethe (1991), 842: "Man wird nie betrogen, man betrügt sich selbst."
196. Tolstoy attributes to Napoleon а искренность лжи, a frankness in lying (epilogue, *War and Peace*, 1:3 [1971; 637]). Similarly, Nietzsche writes that the Christian is "false *to the point of innocence*" ("falsch *bis zur Unschuld*," *Der Antichrist* 39 [1980; 6:213]). Trans. J. Hollingdale, 164.

The motive for most unjust actions, selfishness, is common to all organic beings. What is specifically human is this: Just as the relationship to the other person in friendship can be enjoyed as an end in itself, harming another person can become an end in itself. Naturally, this does not happen without a cause, but the latter is identity-related, not biological. In chapter 4.2.2.3 we have already seen how important the *Me* and even the existence of the other are for the stability or instability of one's own identity, and therefore it should not be surprising that this existential question constitutes the background of so many human interactions and relationships. Even the enjoyment of presocial values can be limited by the fact that there are other people who do the same thing. A person who has solved a mathematical problem ought to draw a pure joy from the corresponding experience of truth, but this joy can be decreased if another person has solved the problem more quickly. Indeed, there is a type of person to whom values become accessible only when he compares his own experience of value with that of other people. Such a person may be able to enjoy a concert, for instance, only if he reflects that others are not hearing it or, if they are hearing it, cannot analyze it as well as he can. Scheler aptly calls this type of person—dominant in the present-day industries of culture and science—"mean": "The noble person experiences values *before* making comparisons; the mean person experiences them only *in* and *through* comparison. The relationship between one's own and other people's values thus becomes in the 'mean person' the selective condition of his experience of values in general."[197]

This attitude produces *envy* and *malice,* uneasiness with regard to the values and goods of other people and joy in witnessing their suffering and their vices. The latter is particularly repulsive, and it does not speak well for Germans that they have a special word for this feeling—*Schadenfreude*—which several other languages have had to borrow. What is interesting about envy is that, unlike jealousy,[198] it cannot always be reduced to injured self-interests.[199] Someone who is angry when a less qualified person gets a position he had hoped to get for himself is certainly not superior and has at least not yet understood how the social world inevitably functions; but here we cannot speak of envy in the proper sense of the word. Indeed, even if it rankles someone that a person better than he receives something good, this can be explained by his interest in the latter, and is not yet envy in the full sense. It is a matter of envy only when we begrudge someone the possession of something not because we ourselves thereby lose it or are denied it, but because other people's possessions bother us even if we thereby gain ad-

---

197. (1978), 13: "Der Vornehme erlebt die Werte *vor* dem Vergleich; der Gemeine erst *im* und *durch* den Vergleich. Die Struktur: 'Beziehung von Eigen- und Fremdwert' wird also im 'Gemeinen' zur selektiven Bedingung seiner Werterfassung überhaupt."

198. Jealousy usually presupposes a triadic relationship: I am jealous of A because I am concerned to have B's exclusive love or recognition: B, not A, is the person I am interested in.

199. Cf. the twelfth chapter of Melville's *Billy Budd, Sailor,* the most consummate literary treatment of envy, which, as Melville rightly remarks, is less often confessed to than any other felony (1986; 326 ff.).

vantages that we would otherwise not have had. Envy of a superior benefactor is not at all rare: the benefaction's violation of symmetry is sometimes more humiliating than indifference, and for this reason gratitude is not common among human beings.[200] To be sure, it is not yet envy when someone opts for a more just distribution of property; but if someone does not even accept Rawls's second principle, this can be explained only on the basis of envy—for things will go worse for him as well. Envy becomes greatest and at the same time most hopeless when it is directed not toward external goods but toward personal values.[201] Thus it is wrong to relate the uneasiness often triggered by greater persons solely to the privileges that are sometimes associated with greatness; and it is entirely erroneous to believe that power struggles are always solely about the fact that someone wants to have the position that another holds, and that it is unfortunately not possible to satisfy this wish unless the other person is dismissed. It is not what the other *has*, but what he *is* that is disturbing in a great person; and what he is, is almost inaccessible to outside influences.[202] External possessions and even bodily beauty can be lost, but the core of the personality remains unharmed. Certainly, one can destroy another person, but one cannot undo the fact that he existed. Indeed, after death a great person shines even more brightly, and while one may act in such a way as to inherit his position of power, in doing so one moves further away from his essence than one already was.

Two things can save us from envy. First, it is important to learn to feel values purely, without regard to the relationship between one's own values and those of others; second, to return to the first example, not only the elegance of a mathematical solution but also the value of the other person's mathematical intelligence should be recognized and even loved. "Against another person's great qualities there is no remedy other than love."[203] Nevertheless, it must be conceded that one can envy a greater person only if one has recognized his superiority, even if one has made every effort to dispute it; and however contradictory and therefore tormenting this envy may be,[204] this

---

200.   La Rochefoucauld does not exaggerate when he writes in his maxim 238: "Il n'est pas si dangereux de faire du mal à la plupart des hommes que de leur faire trop de bien" (1967; 62). ("It is less dangerous to harm most people than to do too much for them.") Cf. Nietzsche (1980), 4:114.

201.   In discussing Cain's fratricide, Augustine speaks of "invidentia illa diabolica, qua invident bonis mali, nulla alia causa, nisi quia illi boni sunt, illi mali," that is, of evil people's envy of the good (*De civitate Dei* XV 5).

202.   If the envious Iago succeeds in destroying Othello not physically but morally, it is only because Othello is not immune to temptations, because he is not great in every respect. If one betrays Christ, one can only hang oneself.

203.   Goethe (1991), 724: "Gegen große Vorzüge eines Anderen gibt es kein Rettungsmittel als die Liebe."

204.   In *Don Quixote*, Cervantes aptly writes: "Todos los vicios, Sancho, traen un no sé qué de deleite consigo; pero el de la envidia no trae sino disgustos, rancores y rabias" (1994; 2:83). ("All vices, Sancho, are accompanied by some kind of pleasure; but the vice of envy is accompanied only by disgust, rancor, and rage").

recognition remains a cognitive achievement that may under some circumstances raise the envious person above his contemporaries who are not envious only because they are too dumb to recognize this superiority. May the historical Salieri rest in peace. But the poetic figure of Mozart's envious rival, who has occupied European art ever since Pushkin's short and brilliant play *Mozart and Salieri* (1831), is so fascinating because he is basically the only one who grasps Mozart's genius, and the only one, including Mozart himself, who—at least in Pushkin—never reflects on himself, because of his humble naiveté.[205]

Haughtiness has its root mainly in frustrating interactions. A person who considers himself a better mathematician than he really is, and *therefore* looks down on others, is not truly haughty; a person who is haughty would like to raise himself above others and for that reason begins, in whatever way, to overestimate himself. For pleasure in one's own achievementgives no one a reason to humiliate others; on the contrary, people with exaggerated feelings of self-worth can be extremely generous in their dealings with others, because they do not feel in the least threatened by them. Rather, it is repressed internal insecurity that is compensated by haughtiness. Whereas a vain person seeks only a confirmation—which he cannot receive from his internal judge—that he has done this or that brilliantly, this is not enough for a haughty person: he must also show the other person that he considers him inferior. The envious person strives only for a wrongly understood equality, which cannot be denied a spark of rationality. The haughty person, in contrast, seeks inequality to his own advantage—and this makes haughtiness a vice even more dreadful than envy. It is particularly horrible when the attempts at compensation cannot be based on one's own achievements, but console themselves with the real or imaginary achievements of a collective to which one belongs. Fascism and National Socialism owed part of their success to the fact that they offered members of the petite bourgeoisie who had become humiliated and disoriented this kind of compensatory identification with a strong *We*.[206] Consequently, even underestimating oneself is morally dangerous—one must at least keep in mind one's own human dignity, and that forbids, for instance, *groveling* not only before more powerful persons, but also before greater persons. Completely unbearable is the false, sometimes pseudo-religiously motivated, humility that in a contradictory way thinks very highly of itself while whining *via negationis* for recognition by others.

As a rule, envy and haughtiness are not sufficient to motivate someone to commit acts of violence against others. A person must convince himself that he has a right to commit such acts, and that requires at least the appearance that he has been attacked. *Anger* over an injustice suffered and the desire that the offender atone for his of-

---

205. In Pushkin, the central sentence is: "Ты, Моцарт недостоин сам себя." ("You, Mozart, are not worthy of yourself.")

206. Cf. "Der Riese Agoag," in Robert Musil's *Geschichten, die keine sind* (1989; 103–107). Musil tells how a weak, often humiliated, little man escapes in a bus in order to enjoy seeing how everyone else has to get out of his (that is, actually the bus's) way.

fense are certainly understandable, indeed—insofar as they remain within appropriate bounds—are to be preferred to their lack, for we have already seen that the defense
of the law is part of the essence of justice. The thirst for vengeance obviously has a
biological root; even where retaliation is objectively justified, emotional qualities are
mixed with the desire for revenge that do not stem from man's intellectual nature
and even frighten an intellectual person. Nonetheless, something human is mixed with
this drive, an outcry at the violation of one's own dignity—and it is this outcry that, together with the biological ground, can sometimes make human revenge something far
more dreadful than anything we find in the animal world. If revenge is only a pretext for
giving full expression to one's own envy and haughtiness, then man is capable of doing
things whose moral disvalue can only be horrifying. Cruelty, that is, tormenting others
with no goal other than that of satisfying one's own need for recognition, is specifically
human;[207] and one can certainly concede that to this extent it is more complex than
mere mutual instrumentalization, that it is an end in itself—like love. As a rule, cruelty
is motivated by the wish to inflict on others injuries one has oneself suffered, and if the
first offender is not available, then any other person who resembles him through the
same collective identity or some external characteristic can serve as a substitute victim.
However, not only the objective injustice, but also the superiority of another person,
or the mere fact that he witnessed one's own weaknesses and one had to feel ashamed
around him, or even his formal otherness can put one's own identity in question and
trigger cruelty. Thus it is clear to anyone who has an eye for the phenomena that the incredible cruelties that people inflict on each other in order to achieve a homogenization
of opinions do not spring solely from the interest in better controlling a body social.
Much deeper levels are involved in such cases: here as well it is not a question of *having*
but of *being*. It may be that the deviant opinion held by another does not harm anyone;
but completely independently of any consequences it may have, it is relevant to others'
identities. Indeed, one can even hate another person because one has done him an injustice and his mere existence reminds one of something that puts one's self-respect in
question—perhaps especially if he has borne this injustice with nobility.[208] Cruelty is
an especially common result of disappointed love; in hatred as in love, the other occupies one as a person, not because of his possible harmfulness or utility. In addition, hatred may be the only way to overcome the latent self-hatred characteristic of all identity

---

207. Naturally, animals can kill other animals, and even conspecifics, in the most agonizing
ways; but they do not do this for the sake of this agony, but rather, for instance, because they are hungry, and hunger can be more quickly quenched by tearing parts from an animal and immediately eating them than by taking the time to kill it before eating it.

208. "Proprium humani ingenii est odisse quem laeseris" ("It is characteristic of the human
mind to hate the person you harm") we read in Tacitus (*Agricola* 42, 3), whose deep insight into the
abysses of human wickedness was matched by no earlier writer. In the delirium tremens of the *Patna*'s
engineer in Conrad's *Lord Jim*, the Islamic pilgrims he has shamefully left in the lurch are transformed
into pink toads, all of which he would like to smash.

crises and especially of the most wrenching one—by projecting it outwardly. But the most terrible hatred is the one that arises from a disappointed love of God, the whole of being, or however it may be called. The objectivity of the order of values, which is not made by humans, can profoundly humble the will to freedom; indeed, transgressions of an ethical order felt to be heteronomous are almost necessarily part of the process of maturation. But if the adolescent crisis persists, a type of person can develop for whom transgressions against the moral are the only way to confirm his own freedom and to take revenge on the fact that it is not he himself who has determined the moral. Thus it can happen that someone kills a person not because this is useful for him, and not even because the person threatens his identity, but because he wants through this action to express his freedom and his contempt, not for the murdered person, but for the moral order. Readers of Dostoyevsky, at least, will have already encountered this type of person, without whom the politics and history of the twentieth century would be difficult to understand. To be sure, hatred and cruelty contain their own punishment within themselves; the contradiction involved in forcing others to acknowledge that one stands infinitely higher than they and therefore does not need their recognition is wrenching and self-destructive. Yet, before destroying himself, such a person can reduce whole worlds to rubble and ashes, especially if he acquires extensive *power*.

5

Power[1]

One might say about power what Augustine said about time: So long as one does not ask what power is, one knows what it is; but as soon as one tries to explain it, one no longer knows what it is. Nevertheless, since the end of the nineteenth century philosophy and the social sciences have expended an extraordinary amount of intellectual energy on efforts to clarify this concept. In any case, there is something obsessive about the modern interest in the concept of power (which had not yet found a place in Hegel's *Encyclopedia of the Philosophical Sciences*). The question of power plays an enormous role in modern culture, comparable to that played by the question of God in early modern metaphysics; it is well known that Heidegger interpreted Nietzsche's theory of power as a legacy of early modern metaphysics.[2] The broadening of the concept of power in the course of recent decades is almost frightening. Not only are so many and so heterogeneous phenomena lumped together under the rubric of power that it can hardly be imagined that they share a lowest common denominator; in addition, the true point of this broadening consists in understanding even our knowledge and our moral ideas as forms of power. Whereas traditional political philosophy subordinated power to judgments of morals and of truth, the modern social scientist views what he calls morals and truth *sub specie potestatis.* The history of the word "ideology" is characteristic of the change in perspective I have in mind. Destutt de Tracy's *Éléments d'idéologie,* published in the first years of the nineteenth century, was concerned with epistemology and the philosophy of language, and even if the Hegelian K. Rosenkranz's concept of the idea was very different from that of the French sensationalist, he was still far from connecting it with the

---

1. This chapter includes my article (1995); many of the critiques of it were helpful, and I am grateful to the critics for making them, as well as to Dr. H. Griepentrog for his critical reading of this chapter.

2. More precisely, the concept of power is the counterpart in the social sciences of the concept of force in the natural sciences, to which God is reduced if he is considered only omnipotent but no longer omniscient and perfectly good.

concept of power when he titled the third part of his *Wissenschaft der logischen Idee* (1859) "Ideologie"—for by that term he meant merely "theory of ideas." In the period between Destutt de Tracy and Rosenkranz, a new discipline arose that fundamentally changed the meaning of the term "ideology,"namely, the sociology of knowledge. Since Comte and Marx, and still more radically since Sorel, Pareto, and Mannheim, we no longer see ideologies as being epistemological or metaphysical theories whose claims to validity have to be taken seriously, but rather as social constructs with a specific function in a social system. Sometimes the word is used only when the existing order is legitimated by the construct, and sometimes also when it urges a new order.

In chapter 2 I already showed why the two approaches based on the theory of validity and on sociology are mutually compatible and even complementary: if one wants an overview of the whole of the social, one must combine both of these approaches. The application of this to the concept of power is obvious. Thus two opposite errors must be avoided.

On one hand, the abstract moral theoretician deals with moral and political theories only immanently, without ever asking whom they benefit. In so doing, he deprives himself of an instrument that could help him answer the question why obviously false, refutable, and even self-contradictory theories stubbornly persist through history (of course, their refutation cannot consist in pointing to the interests they serve); even in the case of good theories it would be naive to overlook the fact that power interests are useful in ensuring their success. Locke's *Two Treatises of Government* had a real political result, and even a real political goal: in the short term, justifying the overthrow of the Stuarts and, in the long term, the establishment of a new understanding of the relationship between the economy and the state. The widespread effect of even metaphysical theories is also influenced by external factors, and not solely by their objective qualities. For instance, Heidegger is a first-class thinker, but it would be naive not to see that his influence in the German Federal Republic of the 1950s had something to do with the fact that his explanation of National Socialism played down its criminal nature. Much the same can be said about the success of critical theory and the theories of Habermas and Luhmann—they all encountered such a widespread response in their decade only because they provided a legitimation of widely felt needs (for revolution, for a critical morality remaining within the bounds of discourse, for adaptation)—but this observation does not in the least prejudge their scientific value. Even if propositions belong to a sphere of pure validities, sentences and speech acts are social phenomena; therefore, any sentence that formulates a true moral proposition can exercise a social function and become a power factor. That the mass murders carried out by the National Socialists are the greatest crimes of this century is a dreadful moral truth. But that the corresponding sentence can also be a weapon that can be used, for example, to ward off criticism of the policies of the state of Israel, would be too obvious to need emphasis—were it not in the absolutely comprehensible interest of certain politicians to divert attention from this truth. Can anything other than power interests in moral sentences explain why the genocide of the Romany has not been incorporated into public consciousness in the same way as that of the Jews?[3] Who would want to ignore the fact that in Western democracies, where violence seems to be under control, power struggles are fought chiefly over positive incentives and over moralizing scandals in which facts are revealed that sometimes involve not a single specific violation of political duties, but are used to distract public attention from more important problems? However, the abstract moralist is not only naive, he is often also dishonest, for he conceals from himself and from others the fact that he, too, usually wants to have an effect, and that he is therefore also striving for a certain form of power. Carl Schmitt was not an important ethicist, and even less a morally impressive person, but he was certainly a first-rate expert in constitutional law and political science. The moralistic polemic against what may now again be an excessively intensive study of his works is therefore partly justified, but only partly; in any case, the boundary lines between intellectual friends and foes that this polemic undeniably draws confirm the irrevocable correctness of his insight into the meaning of friend-foe relationships in interactions among human beings. To raise into consciousness what one aims at, indeed must inevitably aim at, is an elementary moral duty, and therefore the refusal to recognize a few painful, but unfortunately apposite, truths about human striving for power is not a moral achievement—any more than is the Victorian prudishness that made any discussion of sexuality taboo while not only failing to surmount sexuality, but allowing it to express itself in the most uncontrolled way. Finally, the one-sided moralist usually lacks a sense for the necessity of the ethics of ethics.

On the other hand, the complementary standpoint is no less one-sided: it considers theories, especially moral and political theories, to be *nothing but* weapons in a power struggle. Even if we concede that theories, as social constructs, are that too, there is first of all on the purely descriptive level a significant difference between these particular weapons and the others: theories may not be *perceived* as weapons; they work only so long as it is not known that they were developed for this purpose. Nothing damages the credibility of a theory more than the obvious wish to use it as a power factor.[4] For the point of a moral theory is to provide a basis for an action that transcends particular interests; if from the outset it is conceded that a moral theory is nothing more than an expression of power interests, its effect necessarily fizzles. Second, we must once again recall that no one, not even the pure theoretician of power, can move beyond the dimension of validity: Pareto considers his sociology to be *scientific,* and as such not merely a secondary rationalization of the wish for success; similarly, Nietzsche understands his own analyses as an expression of intellectual *honesty,* and he would be deeply outraged if someone were to see in them only a way in which a psychopath in need of recognition hoped to attract attention and exercise power. If one means by "refutation" not an activity in the area of the theory of validity but rather an activity that attains

---

3. It goes without saying that Jews are completely justified in putting their own sufferings in the foreground; but historians concerned with objectivity ought also to report on genocides that are more apt to be forgotten because their victims have less power and are less able to express themselves.

4. Cf. J. Elster (1983), 44 ff.: "Willing what cannot be willed."

subjective convictions, one must certainly concede that the pure theoretician of power is irrefutable. For such a theoretician would refuse to study the content of any objections, considering exclusively their function in the social whole and seeking to discover how they serve the opponent's search for power; and because of the inevitability of the will to produce an effect, he would find what he was looking for. Yet this does not mean that one should doubt the impossibility of moving beyond the normative; it only means that one has to explain to such an opponent that, according to his own principles, it is pointless to discuss matters with him further, and that he should look for someone else to talk to. Certainly, even if one has grasped the complementarity of the two approaches, the pure theoretician of power remains interesting for two reasons. First, his concrete insights must be taken into consideration, even if one declines to absolutize them. Second, one can not only learn from, but also learn about, the theoretician of power—anyone who rejects his position must explain how he could have arrived at it. This task was already undertaken in the first and second chapters of this book, and it will occupy us again in this chapter and in the sixth chapter. In the following pages I will first delineate more precisely the concept of power and the forms and ways in which it appears; second, I will sketch out the principles that guide the purely political man (*Machtmensch*); and, third, I will attempt to make a moral assessment of the phenomena described.[5] Here my approach is still phenomenological and sociopsychological; the social contextual conditions and the historical development of power will be discussed later on.

5.1. The Essence and Appearance of Power

5.1.1. On the Concept of Power

What is power? The word "power," which is central in all the social sciences and especially in political science, not only has different meanings in different authors, but even the same author often uses it in different senses. This is connected among other things with the fact that the corresponding concept belongs to a family of concepts that also includes the concepts of influence, authority, domination, and force, and despite many attempts, their relationship to each other has never been so precisely defined as to make it possible to establish a unified usage. Even this book does not lay great store by a unified terminology. It is more important to learn to distinguish between power in a broader and a narrower sense, and to understand what is meant in each case, than to use neologisms to create a rigid terminological framework. Problems of fact should be distinguished from problems of words.

One can begin to approach power by naming a few characteristics of the corresponding predicate. First of all, we should note that "power" is not a one-place predicate, but

---

5. Moral sentences (or propositions) in the first section usually refer to the level of consciousness held by the actors under investigation, and are only occasionally my own judgments.

is always (at least) a two-place predicate. One never simply has power, but always has power over something or someone. Perhaps one can also exercise power over oneself: then power would not necessarily be alio-relative, but its relational character remains untouched. This is certainly less trivial than it at first appears to be, for it shows that the existence of something else that always potentially *limits* power is the condition of the possibility of power. Absolute power could be attributed only to an infinite creator God; in every other case this is not possible on grounds of conceptual analysis. From the relational character of power it follows further that the power relationship can change even if one of the relata has not changed at all.[6] After World War I, the French army was the most powerful in the world; but it lost its superior power, despite the absolute increase in its strength from 1919 to 1939 owing to the armament of the Third Reich.[7] Here we can already discern the difference between power and bases of power—whether one has bases of power depends solely on him, but whether he has power does not.[8] Second, as a rule "power" is understood as a dispositional predicate, and power is distinguished from the concrete exercise of power. The German word *Macht*, like the English word "power," is homonymous; only French differentiates between the disposition (*puissance*) and its actualization (*pouvoir*).[9] A person who is granted a single exercise of power will not yet be called "powerful"; indeed, as we will see, the expectation that someone can exercise power in the future increases the consequences of an individual exercise of power. Third, the concept of power is related to the concept of *physical force* insofar as power is responsible for changes in reality that would not have occurred without it, or for the absence of changes in reality that would have occurred without it. However, power differs from physical force in that its effect has to be willed: the concept of power generally implies, fourth, an intentional or more precisely a volitional *act* on the part of the power-holder,[10] or at least an unconscious wish. The wind, or even a rapacious animal, are not powerful, even if they can cause the most extensive destruction—and thus changes—because they do not *will* these effects. Indeed, the people who unknowingly brought the plague from the Crimea to the West in the fourteenth century did not exercise any power either, even if they changed more than did the most powerful despots. The proximity of the concept of power to the concept of action is obvious: power can be predicated only of a creature capable of action, and only the powerful person who knows how to translate his will into a change in reality is capable of action in an extensive sense. But the concept of power does not have to do with all possible changes; fifth, it is usually limited to processes in

---

6. Cf. Montesquieu, *Esprit des lois* 9.9.

7. Cf. H. J. Morgenthau and K. W. Thompson (1985), 174 ff.

8. The use of the verb "have" in connection with power is to this extent misleading—in the strict sense one can have only bases of power (P. Bachrach and M. S. Baratz [1970], 19). Nonetheless, in the following I will not deviate from common usage and will speak, for instance, of *Machthaber* ("power-holders").

9. Cf. R. Aron (1972), 174.

10. Cf. D. H. Wrong (1979), 3 ff. I am greatly indebted to this outstanding book.

the social world. This does not hold for all known definitions of power. In Hobbes, for instance, in whose rudimentary definition the element of intention does not even play a role, power is not necessarily social in nature.[11] In colloquial usage, the word "power" is replaced in non-social contexts by "mastery" or "control"; we are more likely to speak of mastery over nature than of power over nature, and of self-control rather than of power over oneself. I will follow the colloquial model by generally using "power" as a predicate indicating a relationship between subjects or groups. At the same time, we must distinguish between two forms of sociality. Someone may want to make a piece of pottery, and his power may consist only in knowing how to keep others from getting their hands on his clay. The relation between him and the clay is not social, but the exclusion of others is, and one can speak of "power" here insofar as he is the cause of other people's refraining from doing certain things. Or someone may want to set up a social organization; in this case, he will cause other people to act; here we have sociality in the full sense of the word. Naturally, by limiting the concept of power to social phenomena I am not denying that the extension of human mastery over nature has consequences for the exercise of power as well; on the contrary, the developments of technology and social technology clearly mutually influence each other.

Sixth, the power relationship is *asymmetrical.* We will see later that the power relationship puts severe restraints on the more powerful party as well—costs are connected with the exercise of power, but that does not alter the fact that in a true power relationship, the power-holder must normally be distinguished from the power-subject. If two princes are described as being equally powerful, our first thought is that they have an equal amount of power over their subjects—that is, we think first of an asymmetrical relationship, and only second that they can influence each other's decisions to the same degree.[12] The seventh conceptual characteristic concerns the *amorality* of the concept of power. Whether or not the content of the will of the power-holder is moral, and even whether or not it is in his rational interest, is irrelevant: if someone wants to destroy his own means of existence and is able to force other people to do likewise, one will speak of "power" even if the end of the process is the self-destruction of the power-holder.

If we try to sum up the aforementioned elements of the concept of power, we come very close to the famous definition given by Max Weber: "*Power* is the potentiality that one actor within a social relationship will be in a position to carry out his own will, [even] despite resistance, and regardless of the basis on which this potentiality rests."[13] However, there are two problems with this definition.

---

11. "THE POWER *of a Man* . . . is his present means, to obtain some future apparent Good" (*Leviathan* chap. 10 [1651; 150]).

12. Of course, it is conceivable that two persons might exercise power over each other in differing domains. D. H. Wrong (1994; 63 f.) speaks of "intercursive" in contrast to "integral" power.

13. (1980), 28: "*Macht* bedeutet jede Chance, innerhalb einer sozialen Beziehung den eigenen Willen auch gegen Widerstreben durchzusetzen, gleichviel worauf diese Chance beruht." Trans. A. R. Henderson and T. Parsons, 139; translation modified.

First, "regardless of the basis on which this potentiality rests" includes extremely different ways of imposing one's will; therefore, other social scientists have more narrowly defined the concept of power and use the term "influence" for what Weber calls "power," considering power a special case of influence, which we will discuss later. (Terminologically, one can also distinguish between "power in the broader sense" and "power in the narrower sense.") Of course, the word "influence" is also ambiguous. First of all, it can be used to refer both to a concrete attempt to influence and to a general disposition. But more importantly, when one says to someone that, for example, he has influenced a decision, one may think either that a different decision would have been made had one not thought of that person,[14] or else that in making the decision this person's wishes with regard to the issue were taken into account. Clearly these two meanings are not the same: in the first case, someone exercises influence even if he himself has not the slightest interest in the decision concerned, and even if decisions are made with the intention of harming him; in the second case he must have preferred one of the possible decisions over the others, and the decision makers must have tried, for whatever reason, to satisfy him. In both cases, however, the person who exercises influence in different ways is taken into account by those involved in the decision-making process. I will term the first case "social effect" and restrict the word "influence" to the second case.

The second objection to Weber's definition of power has to do with the expression "even despite resistance." It is not completely clear whether Weber means that resistance is a necessary part of the definition of power; the "even" (*auch*) seems to speak against this interpretation. In any case, situations are conceivable in which there is no resistance because the position of the power-holder is completely unchallenged;[15] even if as a rule a position of power results from struggles and almost always remains potentially threatened, one has to reckon with the possibility that no one thinks of resisting—even if there would be a good chance of succeeding. Power can be especially far-reaching and subtle precisely when the power-subjects no longer have any autonomous will: I refer to certain sects. Power can always inhibit the formation even of intentions; its causality then consists "in the neutralization of the will, not necessarily in overcoming the will, of the power-subject."[16] At the same time, it is easy to see why Weber used the expression "even despite opposition." If, for example, two persons have completely identical values and opinions, then it is hardly likely that their interactions will involve conflicts, and they will be able to impose their respective wills in these interactions; but one would scarcely call their relationship a "power relationship," because it lacks the element of asymmetry. One is no more likely to speak of power when someone has only a few humble wishes that do not conflict with those of any other person, and when he can completely realize

---

14. A more general idea of influence might conceive this condition still more broadly: had this person not existed.

15. Here Weber could interpret his definition in the sense of a counterfactual conditional sentence ("even if there were resistance"). The problematics of such sentences cannot be discussed here.

16. N. Luhmann (1975), 11 f.

them; however, one probably would speak of power if someone is able to realize only part of his intentions, but these intentions are connected with extensive changes in the behavior of other people. It is certainly meaningful to consider the first person happier and freer than the second; but in common linguistic usage he could hardly be called "powerful," even if he has perhaps already achieved what the powerful person vainly seeks to achieve through his desire for power. "Even despite resistance" is thus not a dispensable part of the definiens of power; however, the definition will have to be supplemented if the case of voluntary servitude is to be included within the category of power.

Weber's definition presupposes that the power-holder has a will—therefore, we cannot call "powerful" a person who could force another to act in a particular way, but for whom others' conduct is in principle, for whatever reasons, a matter of indifference: the possession of bases of power is not yet power; the latter always involves the fundamental will to exercise power; without it one cannot even speak of a disposition.[17] Insofar as others do not know that someone does not want to make use of the bases of power at his disposal because he does not care what others do, he may very well have a social effect; but we cannot call this "influence," or, a fortiori, "power." A more interesting, but always unstable, limiting case of power exists when someone wants to impose a change because he has access to the corresponding bases of power, but does not know that he can do what he wants to do, and for that very reason ultimately cannot do it. The reason why, despite his unbearable coarseness, the Siegfried of Richard Wagner's *Der Ring des Nibelungen* moves us again and again is that he does not know the power of the ring that he has acquired; the carelessness with which he plays with this basis of power has, compared with the obsession with power characterizing the Nibelungs Alberich and Mime, and with the dignity of Wotan's abdication of power, something graceful about it. It is no accident that in an era suffering from its reflectiveness such heroes have gained popularity—several of Hitchcock's films deal with people who have bases of power such as information whose importance is unknown to them but not to their environment. Naturally, such a person has a social effect; indeed, this effect can even grow to be an influence or even power if others fear that he is aware of his bases of power; but since his power remains unknown to him, he will not make use of it—which would diminish others' fear of it until finally they would openly seek to take control of his bases of power.

We have now turned our attention away from the intentional states of the power-holder, and toward those of the power-subjects. In fact, certain intentions on both sides are part of the normal case of a power relationship. The power-subject must be as aware of the bases of power at the disposal of the power-holder as he is himself; indeed, certain forms of power are essentially based on the power-subject believing in the power

---

17. At most, one could follow D. H. Wrong (1994; 68 f.) in speaking of "possible power," which he distinguishes as "potential for power" from "power as potential" (*puissance*) and even more from "actual power" (*pouvoir*).

of the power-holder.[18] This belief is not without foundation; it has been preceded by assessments (possibly mistaken) of the other's bases of power and often by concrete *struggles* in which the power-holder has shown that he is able to overcome the will of others. Stable power is often first constituted as a result of such struggles; it involves a mutually accepted *view of the power situation* that determines the ultimate distribution of power just as it itself consists in assumptions about the distribution of power. For power is never solely a function of the bases of power; it is just as much a function of the mutual assessment of the bases of power (the assessment itself being a basis of power at a higher level, of the assessment of the other's assessments, and so on). Opposing wills, bases of power, their demonstration and assessment, real confrontations, a theoretical assimilation of these confrontations, and finally, on the basis of this assimilation, a mode of behavior corresponding to the expectations of the other—these are the decisive steps in the constitution of power. In sum, Weber's definition may be modified in the following way: Influence (power in the broader sense) is the probability that a person or a corporate group—the influence-holder—will be in a position to carry out his or its will despite the resistance of another person or corporate group—the object influenced—or to prevent the latter from resisting it.

5.1.2. Phenomenology of the Genesis of Power

After this preliminary discussion of the concept of power, we will now turn to the real genesis of power from the anthropological elements we have examined up to this point. Power, we said, is generally constituted through conflicts. But how do conflicts arise among people? Obviously the concept of conflict presupposes a plurality of wills that do not want the same thing. More precisely, we should say that they do not want the same *state of affairs,* for they may both want the same *object* without this tending to produce peace—quite the contrary. "In this way a harmony may result resembling that depicted in a certain satirical poem as existing between a married couple going to ruin: 'O marvelous harmony, what he wants is what she wants,' or like the pledge which is said to have been given by Francis I to the Emperor Charles V: 'Whatever my brother wants (Milan), that I want too."[19] In fact, wanting the same object is a necessary condition

---

18. Hobbes rightly emphasized the constitutive importance of belief on the part of the power subject: "For the power of the mighty hath no foundation but in the opinion and belief of the people" (1682; 16).

19. Kant, *Kritik der praktischen Vernunft* § 4, remark (1976 f.; 7:137): "Es kommt auf diese Art eine Harmonie heraus, die derjenigen ähnlich ist, welche ein gewisses Spottgedicht auf die Seeleneintracht zweier sich zu Grunde richtenden Eheleute schildert: *O wundervolle Harmonie, was er will, will auch sie* etc. oder was von der Anheischigmachung König *Franz* des Ersten gegen Kaiser *Karl* den Fünften erzählt wird: was mein Bruder *Karl* haben will, (Mailand) das will ich auch haben." Trans. L. W. Beck, 27 f.

for strife, for the mere difference in the contents of the will is not enough—the wills involved have to want *mutually exclusive conditions;* for instance, that an object belong to A, and that the same object belong to B (and therefore not A). Now, autonomous wills are not the first starting point for the social; we have already seen that the differentiation of autonomous desires takes place against the background of a community. The child shapes his will by first learning to want what his immediate environment wants; the marking off of his own will and opinions from those of the immediate family circle is a long process. To be sure, the infant already strives to get food without worrying about its mother's needs; but this striving is not yet willing, since the latter involves a clear setting of goals, and therefore as a rule it also requires an ability to use language. Usually, the first goals the child makes his own are collective goals, family goals, in which his own welfare is taken into account. This takes place not only in an abstract, rational way, but also in an emotional, sympathetic way: one wants to do something together, to eat together, etc.[20] The conviction that one lives in a world of common theoretical views and practical goals is always only partially justified; the differences are overlooked rather than absent. But that does not alter the fact that the conscious experience of difference is one of the most important steps in the ontogenesis of human beings. On one hand, only through this experience can one become an autonomous individual; learning to say "no" is the child's first step on the path toward adulthood. On the other hand, this experience is painful. It is painful, on one hand, because the child understands that the imposition of his will can be frustrated not only by natural but also, and even more so, by social impediments; on the other hand, quite independently of this consequence, the loss of "being at home" in what others think and will is threatening in itself. A general death drive is certainly alien to the organic. But the enormous loneliness to which humans are condemned—through the structure of self-consciousness, in which being's tendency toward individualization culminates, and especially through the previously mentioned loss of being-at-home—can actually move them to long for a condition that relieves them of the burden of personal decision making, and that condition can be a relapse into the inorganic, or an absorption into the mass.[21] In almost every conflict one senses, alongside the concrete reason for the conflict, a subliminal outrage that it could come to a conflict at all, that this splitting of the *I*'s could happen. The cleft between wills is felt to be more threatening than that between mere theoretical opinions. For opinions can remain in the sphere of the interior dimension; the will, in contrast, presses toward the outside, toward the physical world equally accessible to all subjects. This constitutes both its dignity and its danger: it bridges the interior and exterior dimensions and thereby produces intersubjectivity, but in its destructive forms as well. In willing, man's self-consciousness and his animality are united in a characteristic way. Every interaction presupposes a substantive foundation, although in the case

---

20. This lack of an experience of collective goals is one of the results of hospitalism.

21. In the terminology employed by Nietzsche in the *Geburt der Tragödie aus dem Geiste der Musik,* one should speak of a longing for the Dionysian and a flight from the Apollonian.

of language, for instance, it is, as it were, ethereal. On the other hand, the will can lead to massive changes in one's own body and then in external reality—changes that can menace the organic basis of others.

Human willing certainly does not serve only external goals such as the satisfaction of needs. The *formal* structure of willing has its own dignity in itself, even independently of the *contents* of the willing. This transformation of external reality in accord with man's ideas is an expression of his sovereignty over nature. *In the will, man's axiological superiority becomes ontological,* for the will recreates nature in the image of man. By overcoming what is something other in relation to him, man appears to become truly *free* for the first time. Certainly this conception found its highest explication only in German idealism. But when they had killed game, the early hunters must have already felt not simply joy at not having to worry about food for a while; in addition, there must have also been a note of pride in their achievement, even if it was only after the introduction of livestock raising and agriculture that it could have risen to become the self-esteem that we find in the first *stasimon* of Sophocles' *Antigone*—not to mention the age of technology's fantasies of omnipotence. Successes in imposing one's own will are enjoyed by a being with self-consciousness not only because of their consequences, but also as ends in themselves. Thus man experiences the magnitude of his achievement, and at the same time of his true self, in relation to the magnitude of the opposition that he has overcome—in the case of hunting, for instance, in relation to the dangerousness of the animal killed.[22] Indeed, because of the dignity of man it also seems just that he can force nature to conform to his will; and in self-perception success seems to confirm the right: that the hunter was so clever and so bold as to kill a predatory animal concretely demonstrates the superiority that could have been assumed only abstractly before this success. What is decisive is that even a coarse, violent person never argues that he is right *because* he was able to impose his will; he will always refer to certain more general characteristics that underlie the concrete success, such as strength, courage, endurance, intelligence. Merely accidental successes that one cannot explain even to oneself do not enhance self-esteem; instead, they have something humiliating about them, because they do not arise from oneself.

5.1.2.1. Struggles over Interests, Recognition, and Values

We started out from an analysis of the imposition of the will on something natural. In order to approach the phenomenon of power, we must now examine the case in which someone imposes his will on another person. As we have already said, there are significant differences between the mere marking off of wills and binding them together in

---

22. Dangerousness—a relational concept—depends for instance upon the medium in which the hunt takes place; and since man lives first of all on land, the greatest hunting novel has a whale as its hero: not only the latter's strength, but also the medium that protects him must be overcome by the *Pequod*'s crew.

cooperation; I begin with the first case. Suppose an animal with self-consciousness sees an object in which it is interested and which it would like to possess; then another animal of the same kind appears and acts as though it wants to do the same thing. I presuppose that the two creatures do not know each other and recognize no common principles of justice such as the *ius primi possidentis,* for instance, which would only result from conflict. This presupposition reminds us of Hobbes's state of nature, but here, in contradistinction to Hobbes, and in accord with what was said earlier, we will start from the assumption that these creatures are striving for identity and that they have been socialized and therefore have memories of the possibility of setting common goals that are felt to be morally binding. Their wishes with regard to the object cannot be simultaneously fulfilled. What will happen? If the superiority of one of them is obvious, the other one may immediately give up satisfying his will; if fighting would be dangerous for both of them, they may arrive at a compromise, which as a rule presupposes common principles. If, on the other hand, both think they can win, each will try to keep the other from gaining possession of the thing he wants, in order to impose his own will. This conflict, which was at first about opposed interests, will very quickly take on a new quality and become an end in itself. Thus we already saw that the value of an object can increase with the difficulties that have to be overcome in order to possess it.[23] However, humans are even more dangerous opponents than ferocious animals, and thus conquering them is an even more important occasion for feelings of self-worth. Moreover, finding one's own will restricted by another human being is a greater challenge than finding it impeded by unruly nature. Nature cannot perceive my dignity, but another person should kindly understand that my will must be respected. Finally, in chapter 4.2, we have seen how far the other, through his mere existence and especially through the image he forms of me, can both endanger and constitute my identity. To allow him to form an image of me according to which he can bend me to his will is relevant to my identity; indeed, even the other's look that turns me into an object in the world at his disposal already deprives me of my dignity.[24] Only man can objectivize, and he can do so precisely because he is the being that, thanks to its self-consciousness, is not absorbed into the world; thus at the same time he frees himself from any objectivization. But man's objectivizing tendency can also be directed toward another human being, and thus necessarily poses a serious threat to his identity with himself. This holds to an even greater extent for another person's victory over me. Even if he were to die immediately thereafter and no third person were to learn of my defeat, that is, if there could be no question of a loss of prestige, a bitter aftertaste would remain. It is not just that the future disadvantages that arise from the defeat are depressing—the defeat itself has given me information about myself that is pro-

---

23. In the theory of prices, this mechanism finds expression in Veblen goods: one does not accept a high price because the commodity is considered valuable, but rather considers a commodity valuable because it is expensive.

24. Cf. Sartre's well-known analyses (1943; 310 ff.).

foundly humiliating. At the very least, I do not have in a sufficient degree the abilities to which I had laid claim by entering the conflict; to that extent the other's victory is absolutely justified.

With this step in our reflection, the *struggle for interests* has surreptitiously become a *struggle for recognition* in which what is at stake is the determination of one's own abilities in relation to those of others.[25] Let us have no illusions: Not only do struggles for interests very often turn into struggles for recognition, but sometimes it is the latter type of struggle that was intended from the outset, because it alone can allow a person to find out about himself. The object one wanted was in fact a matter of little interest; it was only a pretext for this contest at a higher level, which can absolutely have the character of an end in itself and in which play can turn into deadly earnest, depending on the circumstances.[26] Only conflict with others may resolve inner conflict between competing self-assessments; in addition, there are also structural inner conflicts that make constant strife with others inevitable. This is commonly the case precisely in the adolescent crisis, in which the individual has to break out of the unity of the family through power struggles that are extremely painful because they are in part directed against one's own self,[27] and one does a young person no favor when one yields on every issue and thereby fails to provide what really matters: an opportunity to measure his own strengths against those of someone who has already grown up. It is this refusal that has been called, using an apt oxymoron, "repressive tolerance," and it can be even more humiliating than brutal resistance to the adolescent's demands. For if there is a great initial inequality between the opponents, even a defeat can be a partial triumph for the weaker of the two, because the victory has cost the winner effort and because the winner has at least acknowledged the existence of the defeated opponent. Ignoring can be even more painful than opposing and hating, since the latter ensures the challenger at least a social effect, and thus an extension of his being by virtue of the fact that the other is thinking about him. In addition, the very fact of being taken into account to some extent produces the symmetry that is violated in a striking way by being ignored by a person about whom one is constantly thinking, whether one's thoughts are good or bad. Certainly one often includes under the rubric of ignoring a conscious decision not to notice the other, to whom a social effect, however modest, cannot be denied. Therefore it is infinitely harsher when one does not even show the other that one is not thinking of

---

25. Cf. A. Honneth (1992).

26. Consider the kind of situation that is called "chicken" in game theory. If one thinks only of one's own interests, then one will always give in to the violation of symmetry (especially if doing so does not become a precedent); but both rigorously moral grounds and the wish to show the other that he cannot lord it over me—that is, the problematics of recognition—can lead to one's accepting great disadvantages, solely in order to cancel the violation of symmetry.

27. They are nonetheless necessary. A person who has not developed the ability to deal with conflicts in the family will easily fail in the world or hate his opponent more than he would have had he learned to handle conflicts.

him—because one really is not thinking of him.[28] In any case, the basis for many struggles for recognition is not the Cartesian *cogito, ergo sum,* but rather a kind of *cogita me, ut fiam* (think about me, so that I may become). Especially when the person whose attention one seeks is felt to be exceptionally superior, whether because of his age or outstanding abilities, such a penetration of his sphere of attention, no matter how fleeting, can be extraordinarily important for the stabilization of one's own identity.

However, struggles do not occur solely about interests and recognition, about the imposition of one's own will, and the extension of one's own being through the response in other people's consciousness. First we said that it was unbearable when another person did not take into account my will, of whose dignity he, as a rational being, had to be aware. But a human being would not be a human being if he were unable to add to this reflection another one (in fact, it is not always added): that the other, precisely because he is a rational being, must expect another person to respect *his* will. The struggle that began as a *means* of gaining control over a *thing,* has become, as a struggle for mutual *recognition,* an *end in itself,* because it deepens the identities of the persons involved in the struggle through greater acquaintance with themselves, and broadens them through their *being-for-each-other.* However, now it appears that this struggle does indeed have an *intrinsic* value, but it is a *negative* value, in that it simply should not exist, because it injures the dignity of rational beings. To be sure, a victory over another person, even more than a victory over nature, can manifest the victor's freedom in the highest degree. But archaic man already knew something that modern man tends to forget: Any concept of freedom that implies that freedom consists solely in being able to impose one's will is inadequate. Still more important than being able to do what one wants is to want what is right, and therefore to be able to determine at least in part the contents of one's own will and to bring them into line with what is normatively obligatory. Only the moral person is truly free; for this reason the restrictions prescribed by morals are not impediments, but rather the conditions of the possibility of his freedom. These restrictions already concern the sphere of nature, but they concern still more other human beings. For striving to impose one's will is valuable only because it is the will of a being with unconditional dignity; and beings with unconditional dignity are other people as well as myself. If I force another person to bend to my will, this requires justification in an entirely different way than when I plow the earth; and it is well known that even this was a problem for earlier cultures. Therefore, in almost any struggle between human beings, alongside different interests and mutual recognition, different *values* come into play, that is, different legitimations of different interests. In a struggle I am concerned neither solely with an external object, nor solely about the other's recognition of my person; I am also about the recognition of a moral principle that goes beyond the present point at issue. Moral principles are universally valid; they are binding not only on myself, but also on others; they ought to be ob-

---

28. "You despise me, don't you?" Ugarte asks Rick in *Casablanca.* "If I gave you any thought, I probably would," Rick replies—an answer that is more brutal than a simple "yes."

served by the greatest possible number of people; and thus this *Ought* can allow or even imperatively obligate me to overcome the other's will which is not in accord with this *Ought.* Struggles about values can therefore be considerably more bitter than those about interests. There is no contradiction between this and the hope that if as a result of the struggle a common moral principle is acknowledged, further struggles would become unnecessary; for the moral principle would explain which wills one ought to have, and would dissipate the insecurity regarding what is mine and what is thine, from which the struggles arose: it is precisely this hope that seems to justify the use of any means. However much the struggle for recognition, which concerns me as a whole, may in its moral significance transcend the struggle for particular interests, and however much the struggle for recognition itself may be transcended by the struggle over values that are valid for a community—and, in the ideal case, for the whole of humanity—this increase in meaning can also go hand in hand with an increase in hatred. In a struggle for recognition, the *opponent* with whom I am fighting over interests can become a personal *enemy,* and in a struggle over *values* he can ultimately become the *bearer of evil,* against whom anything is permissible. Since it is presupposed that the beings struggling against each other not only have interests but have also experienced socialization, value-consciousness accompanies most struggles: socialized beings must have, along with their own wills, ideas regarding what is right between human beings; and the outrage at finding that one's own normative ideas or those of one's own group are not recognized by others is usually mixed with annoyance at the fact that one cannot simply impose one's own will on the object. Even in cases in which one has oneself violated the norms of the accepted mores, it will still be difficult to admit this to oneself; almost any struggle over interests is played out in the interior perspective as a struggle over values. One will at least outwardly act as if one were concerned solely with principles, and not with particular interests or one's own sense of self-worth. For my interest as such is not binding on anyone else; however, the appeal to values may partly impress the other and partly help me find allies. A person who wants to impose his will at any cost will not forgo the use of any weapon, not even an appeal to moral principles, which then becomes purely instrumental.

What has been said implies that it is exceptionally difficult to discover which kind of struggle is involved in an individual case, especially since in most cases all three levels are present—though in differing degrees. As a thinking being, man has to relate his interests to general principles; conversely, it follows from general principles that certain interests are legitimate, that certain objects are due to this or that person. To that extent, interests and values are inevitably mixed together. Analogously, a person who acts on behalf of a moral principle draws his identity from the latter; and one who questions the principle can indirectly damage the stability of his personality. Conversely, no one can expect to be taken seriously if he does not appeal to something that is more general, but stands in a special relation to his personality: it is precisely the most pathologically vain persons who see themselves as being concerned solely with the point at issue. Nonetheless, despite all the difficulties we must keep in mind that we can distinguish in principle among three ideal types: the representative of interests, the psychopath in need of recognition, and the person inspired by values. In the course of a lengthy struggle, the real sacrifices each party is willing to make usually show who belongs primarily to which type. The psychopath in search of recognition may well sacrifice his own interests, and even his own life; he may even be more likely to do so than a person inspired by values, who knows that he must survive in order to impose the values he promotes; but if someone accepts the misunderstandings and contempt of others in a masterly way, he must belong to the third group.[29] Fanatics also belong to this group; the values I have in mind need not be morally right. But even a fanatic like Lenin is to be clearly distinguished from psychopaths in need of recognition; Lenin's vices included brutal injustice, but not vain self-contemplation. Conversely, a vain or interested person can certainly act on behalf of the right cause—but not *because* it is the right cause.

One could object to the conception that struggles involve moral ideas by saying that the latter are themselves the result of struggles. The *moral* is certainly not a result of history, but *moral ideas,* as a part of the empirical world, can be explained causally, and it is no doubt correct that what has factually established itself has been recognized again and again as moral. Pascal developed this point in a famous passage of his *Pensées.* That power imposes itself, he writes, is necessary (more precisely, it is an analytic proposition); that the moral (Pascal is speaking of justice) imposes itself is just, that is, it is a moral demand that is as unconditionally valid as that descriptive proposition. Thus, what is needed is the union of power and morals; only such a union can fulfill both the descriptive and the normative requirements. After Pascal has equated morals and mores—wrongly, but with an ironic awareness of the illegitimacy of this step— he explains that the union of power and morals is possible in two ways: either the just becomes powerful, or the powerful becomes just. Which of these two possibilities is more likely? "Justice is subject to dispute, while power is easily recognizable and indisputable. Thus we have not been able to lend power to justice, because power has contradicted justice and declared that it was unjust, and has declared that it was itself just. And thus, not being able to make that which is just powerful, we have made that which is powerful just."[30] Certainly, Pascal grasps a large part of real human history. But only a part. However much moral ideas owe to the balance of power that is established on the basis of struggles, these struggles also have been motivated, as we have shown, by moral ideas—a spiral of power and morals that constitutes history. First, insofar as struggle is not ontogenetically the earliest interaction between human beings, it occurs against the background of community values, by which the ruthless promotion of one's

---

29. Here I disregard the exceptional case in which a psychopath in search of recognition may take pride in imagining that no one can understand him—but he probably at least wants this to be recognized by others.

30. "La justice est sujette à dispute, la force est très reconnaissable et sans dispute. Ainsi on n'a pu donner la force à la justice, parce que la force a contredit la justice et a dit qu'elle était injuste, et a dit que c'était elle qui était juste. Et ainsi ne pouvant faire que ce qui est juste fût fort, on a fait que ce qui est fort fût juste" (Pascal [1982], 165).

own interests is always already tempered. Second, it must be recognized that victory over others is generally not a mere brute fact; it is an expression not only of physical strength, but also of greater self-discipline and greater willingness to risk one's life, that is, it is an expression of the virtue of courage. It is this virtue that underlies the struggles from which ideas of justice emerge: through struggle, one virtue grounds other virtues. In actuality, Plato was completely right in seeing the roots of the phenomenon of power not in intersubjective but in intrasubjective structures.[31] The twofold nature of man as a being with drives and with reason produces the virtues of temperance and courage: in both, man wins a struggle over himself; and it is this victory that, on one hand, qualifies a person for struggle with others, and on the other hand reaches its apex in such a struggle. He who has never struggled against himself, against his own desire or fear, will scarcely know how to struggle against others—that is, neither the weak-willed nor the graceful person will be able to do so.

5.1.2.2. Means of Struggle

5.1.2.2.1. Force and Ruse: Enslavement

Why does a struggle presuppose the courage to look death in the eye? Are there not also struggles that do not go to extremes? Certainly there are; yet only against the background of *physical force*, especially *deadly physical force* as the *ultima ratio* of any struggle. All three dimensions of struggle indicate that recourse is repeatedly had to this means; indeed, anyone who is intellectually honest will have to admit that, given the biological and intellectual nature of man, what really requires explanation in human history is not the abundant bloodshed that characterizes it, but rather the fact that even more people have not been killed and murdered. So far as the three dimensions go, we may say first that the other can be prevented from possessing the object one is interested in only by being physically repelled if all other possibilities of arriving at an agreement have been exhausted. Yet if I deprive the other only of the physical means he needs in order to impose his will, he may make another attempt; if I repel only the body, in which for me the will solely exists, the other, once he has licked his wounds, may attack again; in short, the simplest and most conclusive means of getting rid of the threat to my will represented by the other is to kill him. *For death is irreversible.* However, since the other will think just as I do, this means that I myself have to reckon with the possibility of dying if the other survives—another reason for killing him. Second, I should in any case reckon with the possibility of my own death if I am

---

31. Augustine said much the same in his discussion of the virtues of the Christian prince: "si luxuria tanto est eis castigatior, quanto posset esse liberior; si malunt cupiditatibus pravis quam quibuslibet gentibus imperare . . ." (*De civitate Dei* V 24). ("If their luxury is as much restrained as it might have been unrestrained; if they prefer to govern depraved desires rather than any nation whatever. . . ." Trans. M. Dodds, 178.)

set on winning recognition.[32] We have already seen how much the awareness of death has contributed to self-consciousness: man shows that he is more than a living being by overcoming the fear of death and putting his life at risk. However, I show my self-consciousness most clearly to another person by manifesting my courage in interaction with *him*—precisely in the struggle for life and death. If I struggle against nature, the other may not be aware of it; if I struggle against him, he is well advised to give me his full attention; the coolness of the objectivizing glance will melt away in the fear of death, and he will understand that I am entitled to a dignity that he cannot heedlessly ignore. Indeed, I may believe that I can preserve the absoluteness of my will only by reducing to the inorganic anyone who fails to respect it. Third, the moral manifests its highest validity by demanding, under certain circumstances, the sacrifice of my own life. I can meet this demand only if I am not afraid to let the struggle become one of life and death, if this proves necessary. Not the mere desire for recognition by the other, but rather the moral issue itself demands that one put one's life at risk, so that one may be get it back—should one survive—with a new and higher moral quality.

Since for the other the will is only in the body, a struggle between wills is necessarily a struggle between bodies. But this struggle may not necessarily involve a clash between bodies; external objects can mediate between bodies, objects that have the function of wounding or killing the alien body, that is, *weapons* (in the narrower sense). Superiority in weapons can compensate for the lack of physical strength: early in human history, the spear allowed man to kill mammals much larger than himself, and innovations in the development of weapons have often decided the outcome of wars. Mastery over nature and power have in the development of weapons their first great intersection. Insofar as weapons extend the ability to kill—the invention of atomic weapons extended this ability to a great part of the biosphere—one can certainly see nothing positive in them. And yet something formal in weapons is captivating—the fact that they are a product of theoretical and poietic intelligence. Through weapons the physically weaker party gains an opportunity to win out over the stronger; and even if the former is not necessarily in the right any more than the latter, the breaking-up of physical strength's monopoly on power is a significant change in the history of power that has made this phenomenon more complex and more fascinating. At any rate, weapons also belong to the second world—they shift the focus of force out of one's own body but remain in the sphere of corporeality; indeed, they must ultimately also have an effect on bodies: the view that technological development could ultimately lead to virtual wars on computers is absurd. It is possible to make do in some situations with symbolic conflicts, as one could also do in earlier times, but if the conflict is taken seriously, it will lead to the use of force against bodies. A detachment from the sphere of corporeality is represented by the *information* that is necessary to make the most efficient possible use of force, for the will needs accurate assumptions about the external world in order to be

---

32. No one has grasped this point more profoundly than Hegel. See (1969 ff.), 3:145 ff.

able to intervene in it. Having certain information regarding unprotected weaknesses of the opponent, his aggressive intentions, and his weapons can mean victory or the avoidance of a defeat; on them may depend the decision whether one attacks or defends oneself. Weapons and information have one thing in common: they can and must be transported if the conflict extends over large areas. The transportation of men, things, and information in space is an important basis of power.

In general, it is important to be able to make in advance a realistic assessment of each side's probability of winning. If the situation is favorable to oneself, one will seek physical conflict; if not, one will seek to avoid a decision. What matters in both cases is determining *by oneself* what should happen, forcing the opponent to accept the principle of either acting or withdrawing, and not letting oneself be put in the same position. Therefore, a sense for the development of the relative balance of power is of special importance. Even if I am now stronger than the other, it can nonetheless happen that tomorrow I will be even stronger, whether because I have gained new strength, or because the other's strength has decreased,[33] so that it may be completely sensible to wait until the following day before joining battle. Conversely, I may feel myself to be inferior today, but know that tomorrow the opponent will be hopelessly superior to me, so that it is better not to put off the battle. A sense for the *kairos,* the right point in time for the conflict, is of vital importance in every power struggle, and not only in those based on force: Quintus Fabius Maximus Verrucosus, the Cunctator, saved his country by his delaying tactics because he understood that time was on the side of Rome and against Hannibal, who was campaigning on foreign territory; Hannibal lost the Second Punic War because he was not able to exploit his victory at Cannae.[34] Time is not only on the side of the local population—it is also on the side of conservative forces, whereas the powers of change, which must move against the background of mores that are alien to their principle, are dependent on a quick victory. Thus Schiller's Wallenstein is defeated because he hesitates too long and does not tremble "before the slow, silent power of time" that favors the forces already in place.[35] Machiavelli is certainly right when he says that most people tend, depending on their characters, *either* to delay *or* to engage in rash action: the ability to alternate between both modes of action in accord with the situation is not widespread.[36] Nonetheless, the possibility that this ability exists cannot be excluded, and one should in any case try to develop it in oneself.

Using dependency on information, *ruse* becomes one of the most interesting structures in the fabric of power. Ruse is involved when I thwart the other's will by making use

---

33. Even if my strength decreases, but to a lesser extent than that of the other, it is sensible to wait: Cf. *Kauṭilīya-Arthaśāstra* 7.1.26.

34. Cf. what Maharbal says to Hannibal in Livy, 22.51.4: "Vincere scis, Hannibal; victoria uti nescis." ("You know how to win victories, Hannibal, but you don't know how to use victories.")

35. *Wallensteins Tod* act 1, sc. 3, vv. 83 f.: "vor der langsamen, der stillen Macht der Zeit."

36. *Principe* 25.5 ff. (1986; 188 ff.); cf. 3.8 (93 f.) against fundamental hesitation as a matter of principle.

of the other's errors or even see to it that he gets false information, that is, when I subject him to *disinformation*. Moreover, one should not oppose ruse to force. To be sure, it can be a goal of ruse to escape the opponent and not to let matters come to a use of force at all. But that is not entailed by the concept: ruse can certainly aim at physically neutralizing the opponent; I can try to lure the opponent into an ambush in order to destroy him. However, the means used by ruse are neither an unmediated nor, like weapons, a mediated form of physical strength: as a concept, ruse is the opposite of the latter, not of force. Of course, only in exceptional cases can ruse destroy the other entirely without the use of direct or indirect physical strength (for instance, by making him fall into the trap that he himself has laid); as a rule, in its own interest it will restrict itself to limiting as much as possible the physical struggle required to impose its own will. Insofar as ruse intellectualizes the means of struggle even more than weapons do, it is to be assigned a positive value; and Odysseus's pride in having duped Polyphemus is a very important step in the development of the human mind's self-awareness. Yet two moral problems are connected with it. First, it generally (though not necessarily) leads to lies and thereby harms the most elementary foundation of intersubjectivity. Second, ruse can harm the symmetry of the struggle to the extent that the opponent does not always reckon with it, whereas in an open battle the means used are known to both sides. (An unexpected attack is already a kind of ruse, because it takes advantage of the other's ignorance.)

However much the struggle for life or death may be an obvious possibility, there are arguments on all three levels of the conflict against letting things go to extremes. It may be in my interest to kill the other; but it is still more in my interest not to be killed myself. If I kill the other who disputes my right to an object, I am sure of the desired object, at least so far as the danger posed by the other is concerned; if I am killed, I lose not only this object, but all actual and possible objects that I otherwise enjoy in the present and could enjoy in the future. The way the dying person looks at me may provide the elation of recognition; but, first of all, the dead man cannot revive this feeling in me, and, second, his look may refuse any recognition and be shot through with feelings ranging from hatred to contempt to pity.[37] The fact that I have won does not guarantee that I am right; and in view of the dignity of human life the fact that I have risked my own life cannot simply compensate, morally, for putting an end to another life. For that very reason people seek to limit conflict so that it no longer is a matter of life and death; and it is these attempts at limitation that really first produce the phenomenon of power: one cannot exercise power over a dead man. In fact, when wills conflict, a deadly physical struggle is by no means the only way of imposing one's own will. One party may immediately yield in view of the superiority of the other; and even if it comes to battle, in its course one of the parties can *surrender*. Of course, the one who is defeated but not killed will have to pay the costs of the conflict. In this particular case, the van-

---

37. Think of Major von Crampas's death after the duel with von Innstetten in Fontane's *Effi Briest*. Innstetten cannot forget Crampas's last glance with its undertone of "Was that really necessary?" See chaps. 29 and 35 (1974; 243, 285).

quished cannot satisfy the victor by simply giving up what he wanted; the victor has after all risked his life and does not want to do so again. Therefore, the victor will render the vanquished incapable of fighting and will at least *disarm* him. Indeed, in a situation without official authority he will even demand the loss of the autonomy of the vanquished party's will. The loss of freedom means *slavery*, which has one of its sources in such conflicts, that is, the one that gives it the most convincing appearance of legitimacy in pre-modern cultures and, moreover, often in the eyes of the slaves themselves, so that this way of exercising power in fact presupposes a further element, which will be discussed later.

The slave is marked by his absolute *obedience* to *commands*. As Hobbes correctly saw, a command is characterized by two traits: first, for the one obeying it, a command is valid without citing any grounds; second, its content is as a rule in the interest of the person commanding, not in that of the one obeying.[38] However, the dialectic of obedience consists in the fact that over time the person who obeys can, through the temperance learned from work, gain the mastery over himself that the victor had shown by his courage; and therein lies, as Hegel showed, a possible revenge. In general, one should keep in mind that the person obeying is closer to reality than the one commanding: the latter decides, but it is the former who translates the decisions into realities.[39]

Enslaving the other signifies a greater power than killing him—indeed, only enslaving him, not killing him, constitutes power *over* another person. For if a dead man can no longer harm me, he can also be of no use to me; in this way, I can achieve only exclusion, not cooperation. The dead man neither promotes my interests nor recognizes me, nor does he give me, as in the case in which he prefers living on as a slave to dying, a partial moral confirmation of my power. If power ultimately consists in the ability to impose my will extensively, then my power is increased when I have another will at my disposal: the more activities the latter carries out in accord with my own will, the more powerful I am. Moreover, if I kill the other, I do away with the physical basis of his will, which is thus no longer there, at least for me; but I cannot undo the fact that the other did not recognize my will. This is possible, however, if I *coerce* the other—that is, if I exercise force not against his body, but against his will. By coercion the other can be brought, not to wish and to strive, but to want and to do what I want—and not only not to do what I do not want: I become master not only over what he does not do, but also over what he does. If I slay an opponent who wants something for himself that I also desire, I have only prevented him from *imposing* his will, I have not changed his *will itself*. If on the contrary I want to get a secret out of him, more is required, because the other will not speak if he himself does not want to—no matter what the pressure is that may finally lead him to yield. But the application of physical pain is not the only, or even the primary, way of coercing the will of the other. Far more crucial is the *destruction of the*

---

38. *Leviathan* chap. 25 (1651; 303).
39. Cf. Freund (1965), 155, and a general discussion of commanding and obeying, 101 ff.

other's self-respect. Only in that way can I *break* the will of the other—a considerably more elaborate task than simply killing him, and one known to no animal other than man. In torture as it is usually practiced the will of the other is only partly snatched away, and the coercion of the will takes place through the detour of the body, that is, through something external. In order to dissolve the other's will, a rapid *alternation* of opposed feelings—of pain and delectation, for instance, or fear and trust—is important: they tear the will apart and deprive it of its center of gravity. Nonetheless, a person who is subjected to this kind of thing, or even one who is drugged and brainwashed, can afterward comfort himself with the thought that only the physical basis of his personality has been attacked.

The apex of breaking the will is attained, on the other hand, when torture is used to bring someone to do something on his own for which he has the deepest moral contempt. In Room 101 in Orwell's *1984*, O'Brien gets Winston Smith to betray Julia; without having received any incitement to do so, in his panic he suggests that the horror that threatens him should be visited upon her instead. At this point his will is finally broken, because he can no longer love either her or himself; henceforth he can love only Big Brother.[40] In criminal and terroristic groups (for instance, of the kind found in Dostoyevsky's *Demons*), one is considered a member of the group when one has committed one's first crime—for thereby the moral bond that connected one with the external world is dissolved, and a regenerating self-respect is virtually impossible from that point on. However much the destruction of the intellectual basis of the other's will, of his self-respect, concerns something mental, it is usually communicated by means of physical force, as in Room 101. However, there is also the case of purely psychological coercion. To be sure, since it is an intersubjective act, it must be mediated by language, and thus it cannot be completely without materiality; but it is the meanings that count. One can wound a person more deeply with words than with acts; and the foundation of self-respect, which can remain intact in a person fatally wounded in a duel, may be dreadfully shaken by an offense to his honor. Particularly in love relationships, which are the basis for a special kind of dependency, a sudden withdrawal of love can cause the most terrible agony. In Ibsen's *Rosmersholm*, Rebecca's insinuations drive Beate to her death, without any acts of violence being required.[41] I will come back to this purely psychological form of force.

---

40. The recognition of Orwell's insight into the essence of physical and psychological coercion does not imply the concession that a state such as the one he has constructed could exist in reality. For reasons that will become clear later on, this possibility should instead be denied.

41. Think also of Jean and Julie in Strindberg's *Miss Julie,* or Johannes and Cordelia in Kierkegaard's *Either/Or,* as well as the characters in several of Bergman's films. Presumably it is no accident that Scandanavian culture in particular has a special sense for mental coercion—the more perfectly the constitutional state based on law functions, the fewer outlets there are for human aggressivity other than purely mental cruelty.

5.1.2.2.2. *Threats*

However, not only limited physical struggle or the infliction of pain, but also *threatening* someone with the former, or more generally with negative sanctions such as bodily injury or deprivation of freedom, property, or honor, may suffice to force the other to adopt a specific behavior. Threats may not only be directed against one's own goods, but also endanger the goods of those close to one, of whom one is fond or with whom one is connected in a collective *We*—and in this case the latter become *hostages*. (A special case is threatening with an exclusively moral mischief, where physical mischief affects the threatener himself, as in blocking a street by means of a sit-down strike.) As we know, many other animals engage in tournaments as well as in damaging fights: not only the weaker party, but also the stronger is normally interested in avoiding an actual battle, for the outcome can always be predicted only with a certain degree of probability, and even a victory requires an expenditure of strength. To be sure, the intellectual element that is peculiar to threatening in contradistinction to force means a certain diminution of power, for threats evoke merely the prospect of force. But precisely this intellectuality of threatening simultaneously means the expansion of power, for it is *general*. Between organisms without memory every power struggle has to be repeated in order to impose one's will in each case; in contrast, threatening includes many future cases. The expansion of power represented by threats depends crucially on how long I can threaten. If an end to my ability to threaten is foreseeable, I can already demand less than if this end is pushed far into the future, because in the first case I can no longer threaten, for instance, that I will inflict damages ten years hence: a president at the end of his non-renewable term of office or a mortally ill or aged monarch is, *ceteris paribus*, less powerful than someone at the beginning of his term or in his youth.[42] Conversely, an heir to the throne can threaten even if he does not yet have any power to command; and that it is unwise to awaken the mortal hatred of a crown prince, even if one is acting on the instruction of the king, was learned in a particularly dreadful way, for instance, by Álvaro Gonçalves and Pero Coelho, the murderers of Inés de Castro.

However much threatening involves reference to the *future*, it becomes truly effective only when it is plausible; belief in it is usually guided partly by certain characteristics of the threatener (such as physical strength, for example), and partly by previous experiences with the threatener, whether on the part of the person threatened or on that of others. What is crucial, in any event, is the subjective assessment of the threat made by the person to whom it is addressed: what he believes is more important than what will actually happen, if it is a question of avoiding battle. If the stronger party can harm the

---

42. Remarking that the rising sun enjoys more honor than the setting one, in the year 79 B.C. the twenty-six-year-old Pompey obtained by sheer defiance from the aged Sulla a victory that was denied him by constitutional law (Plutarch, *Pompey* 14). However, an old despot can also use the time he has left to commit particularly atrocious acts.

weaker, but the latter does not believe he can, the latter will not be willing to do the former's bidding without a fight. Certainly one can say in a certain sense that one has power over another even when the former can, for instance, annihilate the latter although the latter does not believe this to be so. For by simply getting rid of him he could impose his will on things or other people if the latter got in his way. But he could only get him out of his way, not force him to cooperate; therefore the threatener, who can "only" annihilate the other, paradoxically has less power over the latter when the latter does not believe in his power than when the threatener can only injure him, for instance: only in the latter case could he bring the other to obey him. For the threat to be effective, not only the subjective convictions of the person threatened with regard to the threatener's abilities are important; no less important is, on one hand, whether the person threatened really does not want what the threatener threatens to do to him and, on the other hand, the degree of his *fear* of what he is being threatened with. A person who is weary of life will not be frightened when threatened with death; and even someone who clings to life and is convinced that the other person can kill him, may feel less fear of death than of violating his duty. For as we have seen, the person coerced must himself want to do the thing involved, and even if he wants to do it only because he is trying to avoid a greater evil, he still has to will it. He can therefore always remain steadfast if he considers guilt worse than death and pain.[43] However, his situation becomes more difficult if his refusal makes him responsible for not only his own death but also that of others who cannot console themselves with a comparable consciousness of having made their own heroic decision; hostages are therefore a particularly subtle basis of power for intimidating even the courageous. Nonetheless, the courage of the person threatened can unsettle the threatener, because it makes it clear to him that he has to reckon with significant resistance; indeed, it might even compel more respect than giving in to his threat.

How important the intentions of the person threatened are for the power relationship is shown in the occasional success of *bluffing:* the threatened person's belief that the other possesses bases of power is ultimately more important than the latter's real possession of them, or even the belief on the part of the power-holder that he has them (assuming, of course, that he is able to feign); what is decisive is only that the threatener know or consider likely that the other believes that he has bases of power at his disposal. One of the reasons for Cortés's victory over the Aztecs was probably that he understood early on that Montezuma thought he was Quetzalcoatl—what counted was not that he had the latter's divine power, but rather that Montezuma reckoned seriously with the possibility that he did, and that Cortés, because of his superior hermeneutic abilities, understood this. The talented bluffer must in any case have an infallible instinct for which kind of person will fall for a bluff, or which situations produce a general inclination to believe a bluff. These include situations in which the bluffer has plausible cratic or psychological grounds for not revealing his bases of power before the actual conflict. Anyone

---

43. The Stoic thinkers, and especially Epictetus, drew special attention to this fact: He who is without fear and desire is not subject to alien power.

who is fearful and who lets his fear be clearly seen is usually easy prey for a bluffer (who will not necessarily show that he has noticed the other's fear, so that the latter does not suspect that his opponent knows that conditions are favorable for a bluff). In the twentieth century, the classical examples of successful bluffs are Mussolini's march on Rome and Hitler's foreign policy in the first years of the Third Reich. However, Hitler's cratic genius (unlike Mussolini's) understood early on that one could not get far with bluffs alone—they can make an impression only in an initial phase, while the real bases of power have to be built up. Successes with threats have something autocatalytic about them—the more people believe my threats, the more my power increases, and the more I can threaten others. Therefore references to one's own power are one of the favorite techniques of increasing power. However, the collapse of a power that is not combined with the ability to carry out all the threats it has made can be just as rapid as its rise. Here lies a fundamental problem for the form of power based on threats. On one hand, what is threatened must always be carried out; otherwise the credibility of the threat melts away. To that extent the power-holder may even wish that the other would give him an excuse for showing that he is capable of carrying out what he has threatened; for that reason, he may even provoke a violation of his command. On the other hand, the necessity of carrying out the threat indicates an acknowledgment that the threat did not suffice, and thus that one has been less powerful than one had thought, or at least hoped that the other thought one was. Therefore, even if one is victorious in the battle itself, this victory is a defeat—not to mention the costs and the risks connected with carrying out the threat. In addition, the threatened party's fear may paradoxically be less after the punishment than it was before—a person who has to endure negative sanctions sometimes finds that they are not as bad as he had imagined.

Indeed, the ambivalence described is basically applicable to the threat as well, and not only to its carrying out. On one hand, only explicit threats with sanctions can move the other to determine precisely the cost of his resistance; on the other hand, they irrevocably commit the threatener—on pain of loss of face, that is, of the future credibility of his threats. It therefore deprives him, as well as the power-subject, of freedom; and even if the threat produces an immediate effect, that is, even if it is successful without any real use of force, one's use of it has made an enemy who could later take revenge, which one might have been able to avoid had the threat been indeterminate. At least in situations in which one is not completely sure of one's superiority and is not prepared to fight, threats therefore become vague: "We will do what our own interests oblige us to do."[44] The exercise of power through threats thus includes the *art of indirect communication.* It is no accident that so-called diplomatic language lives off this art, for in international relations, the mode of power is normally implicit threats. Speaking softly and carrying a big stick is not only obviously better than shouting without weapons, it is also—on purely cratic grounds—better than shouting and brandishing a stick. However, the weaker party who

---

44. This was Viviani's famous answer to the German ambassador, Schoen, on 1 August 1914.

does not understand this language must reckon with physical sanctions: "Whoever re-fuses to listen will have to feel"; however, a stronger party who does not make use of this language unnecessarily makes enemies. An explicit refusal is already wounding; therefore, it is fitting not to let things come to an express request, but rather to signal in advance that it will be turned down. This holds all the more for threats, which (like slander) oper-ate whenever possible through allusions. For force reveals the pudenda of power, which people unwillingly point out or even expressly notice; they shame people, at least at a certain level of civilization. But people know those pudenda exist, and that they are no less important for stabilizing inter-human relationships than their physiological counter-parts are for the continuation of life. In addition to allusions, paralinguistic means such as posture, gestures, mimicry, and tone level are also crucial; in fact, they are often far more important than what is actually said. If Henry VIII was really the way Holbein painted him, then he hardly needed to open his mouth at all; the man's posture and fa-cial expression are already a threat. The following passage from the sixth chapter of Man-zoni's *I promessi sposi*, which is one of the most perfect works in world literature and bril-liantly clarifies problems related to morals and power aspects, vividly illustrates what is meant here: Don Rodrigo receives Father Cristoforo, who he has reason to think might reproach him morally. "'What can I do for you?' he asks him, planting his feet squarely in the middle of the room. The words," Manzoni continues, "were these, but the way in which they were pronounced clearly meant: 'Beware of the one before whom you are standing, weigh your words, and be quick about it.'"[45] Indeed, precisely the contradiction between the form and the content can be especially intimidating, since it blatantly mani-fests the meaninglessness of the content of what is said. If the real contextual framework of a situation is objectively threatening, the power-holder can even allow himself to appear especially affable, for he does not need to fear that the other will take advan-tage of his apparent friendliness: reality compensates for the efforts of the paralinguistic means.[46] And should the other misunderstand the situation, he only shows his stupidity; any contradiction between the real background and formal communication can therefore be a means of obtaining information regarding the social intelligence of the threatened person. Presumably this contradiction is also enjoyed by many power-holders as an end in itself: if wearing a mask extends one's identity, then so does occasionally concealing

---

45. "'In che cosa posso ubbidirla,' disse don Rodrigo, piantandosi in piedi nel mezzo della sala. Il suono parole era tale; ma il modo con cui eran proferite, voleva dir chiaramente: bada a chi sei da-vanti, pesa le parole, e sbrigati" (1977; 991).

46. R. Bolt gives a good example in his fine play about St. Thomas More, when he has the king, before his decisive conversation with his Lord Chancellor, say in a particularly jovial way, "No court-ship, no ceremony, Thomas. Be seated. You *are* my friend are you not?" (1970; 30). The political man Thomas Cromwell ironically imitates the king's turn of phrase when he speaks with his collaborator Rich (42)—partly in order to show that he, as a good Machiavellian, sees through power's ambiva-lence, partly to make fun of the king by imitating the cliché the latter used and to take revenge for the humiliations that every ambitious aspirant to power has to suffer at the hands of his superior, and partly to create an atmosphere of chumminess between himself and Rich.

one's own power, with which one has identified oneself. On the other hand, by masking itself, power also shows its consideration for the pride and sensitivity of others; and if it does not become too obvious that this consideration has purely strategic grounds, it can definitely produce a consensus and thereby provide another power factor, which we will examine later. Augustus, unlike Caesar, understood how to conceal his power properly and leave the formal structure of the old constitution virtually untouched; and only on his deathbed did he ask for applause for this extraordinary piece of acting.[47]

The vagueness of threats includes not only leaving open the sanctions that will be imposed in the case of disobedience, but also sometimes leaving open one's expectations of others: this latter form of vagueness explains the phenomenon of obedience in advance, of which Kafka offered an unsurpassable psychological analysis in *The Trial*. On one hand, because of the unpredictability of individual circumstances, as well as because of the indeterminacy of language, every command is dependent upon the power of judgment, and even the imagination, of the person who is to carry it out: a complete refusal (conscious, of course) to make use of this kind of power of judgment and imagination underlies most of Till Eulenspiegel's funny pranks. On the other hand, the expectations can remain so vague that in principle more can always be done, and the threatener therefore constantly has the possibility of being dissatisfied and imposing his sanctions. In the ideal type of the totalitarian state a twofold vagueness reigns: one can be arrested *at any time*, because one has *always* somehow failed, and *everything* can be done to one; force becomes *terror*, and fear, which always has a clear object, gives way to *dread*. The societies depicted by Orwell and, in an entirely different way, by Kafka are good examples of the omnipresence of vague threats. It is important that the threat, even if vague, be known; otherwise it would have no effect. Winston Smith encounters Room 101 early in his sufferings; he does not know exactly what happens there, but he quickly understands that in that place the mysteries of force may be revealed in his body and his soul.[48] Both are crucial: the fear of the room wears down the victims long before they enter it; the fact that they do not know what will be done to them there does not allow them to prepare themselves, to build up forces of resistance, and possibly to bring themselves to commit an act of despair that could be dangerous even to the power-holder.[49]

5.1.2.2.3. *The Third Party*

The struggles and threats we have described up to this point change qualitatively if there are not only two human beings involved in the conflict, but a *third* as well. In

---

47. Suetonius, *Augustus* 99.

48. See Orwell (1984), 355, 362 ff.

49. From this it follows that the National Socialist system must have had an interest in seeing to it that everyone knew about the concentration camps—if not about everything that happened in them. This does not imply, however, that through special apathy or a highly developed selectivity in their own perception some people may not have succeeded in not even being aware of the concentration camps' existence.

actuality, the appearance of a third party means a fundamental alteration of the relationship between the two competitors with which we began.[50] Some languages rightly distinguish the dual from the plural; and Latin rightly differentiates between *alter*, the other in a dual relationship, and *alius*, the other in a plural relationship; the logic of these relationships is fundamentally different. Thus it is no accident that all stable and happy erotic relationships are dual in nature; and even if the converse is obviously not true, one can nonetheless say that in a relationship between two isolated men—Robinson Crusoe and Friday, for instance, or even in a duel between two lone knights—an erotic element is almost always involved. Why? The essence of the erotic (which *can* find expression in the repertory of sexual relationships, but need not do so)[51] consists in two people behaving toward each other *as wholes* in a positive and identity-expanding manner. The relationship to totality is an indispensable part of the erotic; and that means that an erotic relationship between three people is inconceivable because each one would have to *divide* his *undivided* attention between the two others, and this is an obvious contradiction.[52] Conversely, there are forms of struggle and hatred that demand that all one's attention be focused on the essence of the other and, to that extent, have a identity-founding effect.[53] Between these forms of struggle and hatred and the erotic, there are certainly striking analogies: one may risk one's life either to save one's beloved or to win recognition from one's opponent; and erotic courtship can itself be a kind of struggle. Kleist's *Penthesilea* offers the most impressive representation of the connection between these two forms of intersubjectivity.

But no matter how fascinating this connection may be, it is not our subject here. Instead, we are concerned to determine to what extent *alter*'s threat has a different nature when there is an *alius*. Since my power depends in part on the perception of this power by others, the struggle between me and *alter* can actually take place because of *alius*, whom I actually have in mind and threaten when I fight against *alter*, and even independently of whether *alter* is an ally of *alius*. To that extent even the annihilation of *alter*, which was earlier described as being under certain circumstances counterproductive, may be a completely rational way of achieving the goal, if it is really a matter of *alius*. Conversely, before a battle, I will inform *alter* of all those I have already de-

---

50. On the alteration of the logic of intersubjective relationships by the appearance of a third person (which G. Simmel was one of the first to analyze), cf. Sartre (1943), 486 ff. The third in politics is the subject of P. P. Portinaro's book (1986).

51. The distinction between the erotic and sexuality is obvious. Mythical friendships between heroes (Gilgamesh and Enkidu, for instance) almost always have an erotic aspect, but not necessarily a sexual character; the sexual relationship between man and woman first took on an erotic character only as a result of a long process.

52. Certainly the lover is still interested in other people, but in case of conflict the beloved's claims have precedence; time and again, the beloved enjoys total attention, and this privileged relation is the defining feature of the erotic.

53. One may even die when one has finally achieved the death of the hated person, because one no longer has any purpose. I am thinking of Hofmannsthal's *Elektra*, for instance.

feated or that might be my allies in a battle: not only those I have subjugated but also my powerful friends contribute to my own power. To illustrate this idea we can turn back to Manzoni. After Father Cristoforo has succeeded in thwarting Don Rodrigo's heinous desire, the latter is intent on revenge and turns, through his cousin, to a powerful aristocratic uncle. Even if the narrator does not conceal his ironic pity for this poor pompous ass, the latter is revered by his nephews as the very model of Machiavellian politics; in fact, he is capable of doing more than planting himself in a room and letting his tone of voice become threatening—which did not particularly impress Father Cristoforo. His uncle the count decides to have Father Cristoforo transferred out of the village in which he has successfully opposed Don Rodrigo, and to this end he invites the Franciscan provincial responsible for him to come to dinner at his house. Chapter 19, in which the count succeeds in forcing the provincial to do his will, contains deep insights into the essence of power struggles—insights that have lost little validity despite all the changes that have occurred since the feudal age. The setting of the great dinner already demonstrates power: the provincial is seated among powerful relatives who manifest superiority by their mere appearance, their natural self-assurance, and the uninhibited way in which they speak about important matters,[54] on one side, and, on the other, subservient clients whose facial expressions already show that under their patron's tutelage they have forgotten how to say "no." Against this cleverly selected background the count begins to speak about his connection with the Spanish court, until his guest (who must at least by now have understood that the intent is to put pressure on him) succeeds in suddenly changing the subject of the conversation to the Holy Father, whose brother is a Franciscan and a cardinal. . . . However, the count does not allow himself to be thrown off the track, and after the meal he pursues his request in a private apartment. He immediately expresses his hope that they will agree to resolve a common problem, emphasizes his long-standing friendship with the Capuchins, and makes vague threats in the event that the tensions between Father Cristoforo and his nephew cannot be settled. It is his sad duty, the count says, to have to get involved in this affair, which could easily culminate in a conflict between his household and the order—the provincial knows how the world works: "Everything becomes a corporate affair."[55] The reassignment that he eventually recommends could, moreover, even be advantageous for Father Cristoforo himself. The provincial quickly recognizes that he will have to give in if a scandal is to be avoided. He emphasizes that he himself had already considered, on quite different grounds, transferring the priest; the noble house will be expected to do something in return for the order, and the prospect of this is held out. Finally, the victor insists that the provincial precede him in leaving the room.

---

54. "qualche parente . . . che, col solo contegno, con una certa sicurezza nativa, con una sprezzatura signorile, parlando di cose grandi con termini famigliari, riuscivano, anche senza farlo apposta, a imprimere e rinfrescare, ogni momento, l'idea della superiorità e della potenza" (1973; 1106).

55. (1973), 1108: "Tutto diviene affar di corpo."

This episode has been described in detail because it reveals further elements of power that have up to now been ignored. Many things distinguish this scene from life-and-death struggles over an object; among other things, there are numerous third parties. Thus it will be noted that for the first time in this section the expression "power struggle" (*Machtkampf*) has been used here. This may seem surprising; did the struggles described previously not lead to power? Were they not also power struggles? In fact, the expression is ambivalent. If we take "power struggle" to mean a struggle that has consequences for the distribution of power, nearly every struggle is a power struggle. But we will not use the expression in this sense here. A power struggle is a struggle that is being consciously fought *for power*—and that is not the case in all struggles that result in power. Someone who is fighting for an object is fighting first of all for the latter, and perhaps for recognition and for values, but not necessarily for power. A struggle becomes a power struggle only if the possession of the object is decisive for the future distribution of power and *that is why* it is being fought over. Power thereby entitles one to further possibilities of imposing one's will, and to that extent it is comparable to money. In actuality, since T. Parsons (1969), this has been a favorite comparison; rightly, insofar as in both cases it is a question not of individual things, but of *general possibilities* of acquiring individual things, and in both an important role is played by the intentions of the persons who hold this entitlement and those of the persons who do not hold it. Finally, the intentions that constitute money and power must be translatable into physical reality if *inflation* is to be prevented: the latter inevitably occurs if more money is printed without production increasing correspondingly, and if there are more threatens without any increase in the real bases of power. Analogously, *deflation* occurs if the symbolic images—money and threats—decrease, but not the real entities that they signify. Thus one can certainly speak of "inflationary" and "deflationary" styles of exercising power. On one hand, the fact that man strives for something general and not only for individual things is entailed by his nature as a thinking being that is *fame futura famelicus;* on the other, the striving for power, like that for money, can become almost an end in itself. In capitalism, money no longer serves to buy goods; instead, buying goods serves to increase money. Similarly, the political man (*Machtmensch*) no longer strives for power because it makes it easier for him to possess things and people; instead, the possession of things and people is evaluated by how much they increase his power. Making the striving for money and power reflexive is certainly specific to modernity, yet because the others' power is more dangerous than their money, and because life-and-death struggles are rooted in questions of identity, striving for power for power's sake is certainly more primal than striving for money for money's sake. Of course, it is clear that, like other conflicts, a power struggle must be ignited by something concrete, for abstractions are accessible to beings with sense perception only through the concrete. Thus, for example, a power struggle can take place over an object whose possession is crucial for determining what other opportunities for power are available. Think of the ring of the Nibelungs or, in the real world, of particularly lethal weapons, strategically important fortifications, and so on. After the foundation of law and the state, leadership in parliament, the administration, or the constitutional court may be particularly desirable because it offers opportunities to exercise domination—a form of power that we will examine later and that seems, because of its stability, particularly worth striving for. However, the struggle for an object that is in itself a matter of indifference can also be important for future opportunities to gain power—and not because of the object in question, but rather because of a third party's perception of the struggle. It is this connection that is called "prestige" (or "reputation"), in reference to the assessment of one's own power by another person.[56] For my power depends in part on how great others consider my power to be; for that reason a defeat can diminish power even if the object lost is trivial: it is not the object, but rather the process of loss, that matters.[57] Whereas certain of my qualities are inalterable indices of my power, my prestige can change depending on what happens to me,[58] and therefore I must defend it. Others determine what produces prestige—even the most objectively senseless custom may be interpreted by others as a sign of power, and not observing it may lead to a loss of prestige. From ancient times to the present, the formalities of diplomacy show the importance of prestige. However, there are forms of power that are so firmly anchored in other structures, such as the real ability to exercise force, that they can calmly accept a temporary loss of prestige, even if it almost always leads to attempts on the part of others to extend their power—attempts that must fail, however, if it is only prestige that has diminished, and not what it signifies.

To come back to Manzoni's story, the count actually cares little about his nephew or Father Cristoforo, whom he has never met; but his prestige is at stake—the "riputazione del potere che gli stava tanto a cuore" (1105) ("reputation for power that was so dear to his heart"). But why would his nephew's defeat endanger his prestige? Here we must recall first the concept of collective identity developed above; the nephew is part of the family's *We*, on the basis of which the uncle thinks and feels, and on the basis of which he presumes that others believe he thinks and feels. Even if the family's honor were indifferent to him, in a world that bases collective identities essentially on kinship, this indifference would be interpreted as a sign of weakness and of his inability to defend his own interests. On the other hand, the nephew is a very concrete power factor—the uncle's power depends on his ability to command others, and in particular on his ability to rely upon the loyalty of his relatives. What is crucial is that thinking in terms of prestige

---

56. One could even speak of prestige in dual relationships, because defeating an opponent increases the winner's courage and therefore prejudges the later relationship; but a person who has taken part in a power struggle usually knows more about the real bases of power than does a spectator who is not personally involved. A Pyrrhic victory is interpreted only by the latter as a manifestation of power and thus increases prestige—the word "prestige" is derived from the Latin word for illusion. On the importance of prestige in international politics, see H. J. Morgenthau and K. W. Thompson (1985), 86 ff.

57. Cf. Montesquieu (1734), 49.

58. R. Axelrod (1984; 145 ff.) distinguishes between labels and reputation: the former are inalterable characteristics, the latter can change.

leaves the uncle little choice and virtually *forces* him to do what he does; even if the uncle's reference to the obligations of his position is supposed to make it easier for the provincial to yield (because he can comfort himself with the thought that the symmetry between them is not really violated, since both of them have to do something they really don't want to do), it is not merely a rhetorical maneuver, but concerns something essential: defending one's own prestige is an expensive and demanding process that significantly reduces the freedom of action of the power-holder. Moreover, the provincial has to think of his own prestige; therefore he emphasizes, in order not to seem to yield too easily, that he himself had already considered the possibility that the count suggests; and the count makes it easier for him to do so by saying that a reassignment would also be in Father Cristoforo's own interest. After his victory on the essential point, the count can allow the provincial a small comfort in formalities—he willingly grants the provincial the prestige of passing through the doorway first, because on one hand he hopes that this will soften the defeat, and on the other because he is well aware that he loses nothing by making this small gesture, but rather strengthens his reputation as an exceptionally clever strategist, for the other guests who see the provincial precede the count will presumably be capable of interpreting this as a sign of the former's defeat. In fact, under some circumstances it can be a sign of mastery to show that one does not take the formalities of prestige too seriously. For instance, what Livy tells us about the meeting between Quintus Marcius Philippus and Perseus after the declaration of war is characteristic. As we still do today, both sides argued for a while about on which side of the river the two delegations should meet—for obviously the one who moves toward the other loses prestige; indeed, giving ground on a detail regarding the contextual conditions under which the negotiations will take place seems to be tantamount to prejudging the outcome. After futile exchanges between the two parties, Marcius decides the issue for Rome—with a joke (42.39.5). Thus he saves Rome's prestige and also shows that real power does not depend on these formalities, which he at least can joke about.

The third party changes the relationship between ego and *alter* because by simply observing it he tends to universalize the originally dual relationship. If the count were to give in to the provincial, he would have lost nothing essential, but he would have encouraged third parties to turn against him in other situations in which his vital interests were definitely at stake. Anyone who has had to deal privately with power-holders and could do so in a relatively open way has perceived how their behavior, even with regard to oneself, changes strikingly as soon as a third party appears: the way in which one deals with one person must not prejudice anything in the relationship to a third. Aristotle goes so far as to recommend that in the presence of slaves one should not laugh, nor, it goes without saying, embrace a woman.[59] As comedy never tires of pointing out, the servant who witnesses his master's confidences or even dependencies in fact loses respect for his master. Through his more or less omnipresent testimony, the third party

---

59. Cf., frag. 183, in V. Rose's edition of the fragments.

forces the power-holder to wear a *mask* in all his relationships: he may not behave as the nature of the current relationship would actually demand, but must always think of the third party—just as a good actor, at least at the beginning of his career, must keep in mind not only his counterpart on stage, but also the audience. In a decisive passage, Manzoni has emphasized the playacting element in the conversation mentioned above. At one point in their discussion, in which what is really at issue—the count's fear that he will lose prestige—is concealed behind a mountain of pretexts such as concern about the relationships between his household and the order, the count drops his mask, so to speak. In one of his marvelous comparisons, Manzoni refers to the situation in the theater when a curtain is mistakenly lifted earlier than planned and reveals a singer who is talking casually with a companion, and *at the moment is not thinking that there is an audience anywhere on earth.*[60] In attempting to persuade the provincial, the count has emphasized that it is up to them, the elders, to settle the dispute between the young people, thereby constructing a fictive alliance between himself and his opponent, and opposing the two other parties to this short-lived *We.* But as he is speaking of his own advanced age, he slips in an "alas!"—the only sincere word in the whole dialogue. This is because, the narrator tells us, the count is actually concerned about his age, because it puts in doubt whether he will finally attain the position that he seeks. It is this small ambition that constitutes the content of the old man's life.

The third party does not alter the dual power struggle solely because he observes it and thus makes the other parties wish to influence his observations and conclusions. The third party can also act—for instance, he can take part in the struggle himself and perhaps even decide its outcome by allying himself with one side. Which side will he take? Will he be one's *friend* or *foe,* or will he be *neutral?* This question arises because as a rule a human being is a more efficient weapon than many physical objects. To be sure, he is also a more autonomous weapon—what he offers in the way of additional strength he can take away again through the independence of his will. To that extent one must concede that the third (or fourth) party lends an interest to power struggles that an opposition between two parties lacks; and the mathematical analysis of n-person games is, in fact, of a fundamentally different kind from that of two-player games, precisely because in the former case coalitions are possible. But the third party is not only a potential weapon, whether for oneself or for the other. The third party can also represent the solution of the antinomy that consists in the fact that both sides appeal to values. Both cannot be right, and since through their struggle they have lost the ability to judge each other's values in an unprejudiced way, a possible way out for both parties may be to turn to a third party as *judge:* The *tertius inter partes* becomes a *tertius super pártes.*

---

60. "Chi fosse stato lì a vedere, in quel punto, fu come quando, nel mezzo d'un'opera seria, s'alza, per isbaglio, uno scenario, prima del tempo, e si vede un cantante che, non pensando, in quel momento, che ci sia un pubblico al mondo, discorre alla buona con un suo compagno" (1973; 1108).

But whether the third party is an ally or a judge when he appears on the scene, force and the threat of force on the side of the person having power, and hatred and fear on that of the power subject, are no longer sufficient as bases of power. Indeed, even in a dual struggle that does not end in death, the fact that the victor *has to sleep* is already a problem. He can tie up his slave, but bonds can be undone. He can mutilate him, but a mutilated slave is not as capable of working as the victor would want him to be in broad daylight, and he may be particularly thirsty for revenge. In short, even in a dual relationship stable power cannot be founded on force and the threat of force alone; somehow it must be recognized by the subject, as it usually was in the case of slavery. This holds a fortiori for plural relationships—how could an individual become the master of more than one person? To be sure, thanks to superior weapons, better organizational abilities, and a convincing ideology, a small number of people can dominate a significantly larger number; but there must always be a number of people who rule, even if they are very few. Someone who wants to extend his power must therefore be able to share it; and he can do that only if he knows how to use bases of power other than force and threats.

What does extending power mean? How can the extent of power be determined? At least the following three parameters are relevant: Power is *extensive* depending on the number of people who are subject to it; it is *comprehensive* depending on the number of spheres of activity that it controls; and it is *intensive* depending on the degree of self-denial it can demand with a chance of success.[61] In particular, extensive power, and most comprehensive power as well, cannot be founded on force alone, because the power-holder needs certain collaborators to carry out his orders if he wants to force a larger number of people to bend to his will. In fact, the ability to use force, as we saw, is not connected solely with one's own physical strength. Since the emergence of a technologically applicable natural science, even so abstract a scientific discovery as how to split an atom can decide the outcome of violent conflicts. But such knowledge is no more important than knowledge of social technology: without the ability to *organize* human activities, an extensive use of force is not conceivable. What is the essence of organization? Organization consists first of all in the *differentiation* and autonomizing of those activities that can be made more efficient through the division of labor. Second, their *integration* is no less important if the process of differentiation is to be put in the service of a unified goal: For this purpose a *hierarchical* structuring of functions is indispensable. The top level of the organization must be able to do two things: it must *delegate* as much as possible if it seeks extensive power, and *retain* as much as is necessary to avoid losing this power. Intermediate positions' obvious tendencies toward autonomy must be forestalled; to that end, it is necessary to *control* them—a function that no organiza-

---

61. M. Mann (1968 f., 1:7 ff.) differentiates only between extensive and intensive power, and in fact the boundary between comprehensive and intensive power is not razor-sharp. Nonetheless, there is a difference between the two forms: unlike a military officer, a father confessor cannot command someone to risk his life, and thus has less intensive power. But his power is more comprehensive—he can monitor most of the penitent's spheres of life, from his sexual life to voting.

tion should lack, and onto which the focus of power easily shifts if it is not itself controlled. Thus by way of the third party, further elements of power have crept into force itself. In more complex societies the power-holder is not the one who uses force; rather, he orders force to be used; and he has power only if his orders are carried out. But why are they carried out? A possible answer would be that the obedience that makes the organized use of force possible in the first place is itself based on the fear of violent negative sanctions. But this answer is hardly adequate. First, the quality of this kind of obedience is significantly lower than when obedience follows from free agreement. The deeper the cooperation among the power-subjects is supposed to be, the more force has to be transcended as a means. Secondly, the circle between collective force and obedience is easy to see through; and if those who carry out the command to use force understand that power ultimately lies in their obedience, the temptation is great to mutiny and seize power for themselves—at least so long as they have, as is assumed here, no other motive for their obedience.[62] Certainly mutineers also need to be organized in order to have a collective operation; and the inability to organize themselves is the main cause why in the course of history small minorities have so often been able to dominate great masses of people. But in principle an organizer could appear relatively spontaneously, even if he will seldom last long, because those who now have to obey him can follow the same line of thought—so long as another reason for obedience has not yet been found. The late Roman period, in which power oscillated between the emperor, who ordered the use of force, and the Praetorian Guard, which had to carry out the order, is a striking illustration of this type of situation. In such a situation, a certain stability can be sought on the basis of force and threats only if each individual is afraid to band together with a comrade against the commander because he sees in his comrade a potential *agent provocateur*—and it is naturally even more important that the existence of a secret police be known and that its efficiency be perhaps overestimated than that it really be as omniscient and powerful as it is feared to be. The situation of those immediately surrounding Stalin must have been of this kind, although not that of the people, whose obedience was motivated *economically* and *ideologically*.[63]

---

62. The psychology and sociology of mutiny was developed in an aesthetically unsurpassable way by Eisenstein in his film *The Battleship Potemkin*. It is obvious that the closed society of a ship's crew allows certain structures of power to appear in a paradigmatic fashion. Nowhere else is it more important that the authority of the officers be upheld, because it is not easy to bring in reinforcements, and nothing is more dangerous than for officers to show fear and therefore weakness. "If possible, not to let the men so much as surmise that their officers anticipate aught amiss from them is the tacit rule in a military ship. And the more that some sort of trouble should really be apprehended, the more do the officers keep that apprehension to themselves, though not the less unostentatious vigilance may be augmented" (H. Melville [1986], 369). Cf. Tolstoy, *War and Peace*, 3:2, 9, end.

63. To that extent Arendt (1970) is quite correct in saying that power is always more than force (or violence). But she errs when she denies any relationship between power and force—force, or at least the threat of force, remains the *ultima ratio* of power (in the narrower sense). E. Canetti (1960, 2:7) aptly writes: "Der Unterschied zwischen Gewalt und Macht läßt sich auf sehr einfache Weise

5.1.2.2.4. Positive Sanctions

We have now come to the two other main bases of power or influence, which can already be of great importance in dual relationships, and are as a rule indispensable in plural relationships. For there are only three fundamental ways of imposing one's own will in a conflict: One can threaten the other with harm if he resists; one can offer him advantages if he cooperates; or one can persuade or convince him that the desired behavior is also right for him—stick, carrot, and belief.[64] This trichotomy is classical; it can be found embedded in the famous doctrine of the four *upāyas* in the *Kauṭilīya-Arthaśāstra*,[65] and it also underlies, for instance, Galbraith's theory of power.[66] Only Parsons has a four-part classification: he divides up the possible sanctions depending on whether they are positive or negative and, on the other hand and orthogonally thereto, whether the channel through which they have an effect concerns the situation or the intention.[67] The difference between the classical trichotomy and Parson's classification is that the latter makes a further distinction, within what Mann calls "ideological power," between positive and negative sanctions. Certainly we can concede that positive convincing and threatening with a withdrawal of recognition are not the same thing; the loss of a collective identity can be extremely painful. But usually it is so painful because one senses that recognition is rightly withdrawn, that it is a punishment for something one has done in violation of one's own duty. Therefore, the difference between these two subtypes of ideological power does not seem to me to be as consequential as that between military and economic power. The triadic division is rooted, for one thing, in the fact that human actions can be either ends in themselves or means of achieving a good or avoiding an evil and, for another,

---

darstellen, nämlich am Verhältnis zwischen *Katze* und *Maus*. Die Maus, einmal gefangen, ist in der Gewalt der Katze. . . . Aber sobald sie mit ihr zu *spielen* beginnt, kommt etwas Neues dazu. Sie läßt sie los und erlaubt ihr, ein Stück weiterzulaufen. Kaum hat die Maus ihr den Rücken gekehrt und läuft, ist sie nicht mehr in ihrer Gewalt. Wohl aber steht es in der *Macht* der Katze, sie sich zurückzuholen." ("The difference between force and power can be illustrated in a very simple way, namely by the relationship between *cat* and *mouse*. The mouse, once caught, is in the cat's power. . . . But as soon as the cat begins to *play* with it, a new element arises. The cat lets the mouse go and allows it to run a little further. As soon as the mouse has turned its back and run away, it is outside the cat's force. However, it is still within the cat's *power* to get it back.")

64. Applied to sexual behavior, these forms become (if one respects the differentiation between persuading and convincing) rape, paying a prostitute, seduction, and verbal, loving courtship.

65. Cf. 7.16.3 ff., where *sāman, dāna, bheda,* and *daṇḍa* are mentioned. *Dāna* (gift) corresponds to positive sanctions, and *daṇḍa* (stick) to the negative sanctions based on force. *Sāman* (reconciliation) comes close to convincing. *Bheda* is something special, the splitting of the opponents; in my ordering it is to be placed among the negative sanctions after the appearance of a third party.

66. See J. K. Galbraith (1984), who distinguishes among condign, compensatory, and conditioned power; similarly, E. Gellner, already in the title of his 1988 work. See also K. E. Boulding (1973).

67. Cf., for instance, the matrix on (1969; 412).

in the fact that there is a certain correspondence between it and three of the subsystems of the social.[68]

Attacks on the body, the property, or the honor of the other or those close to him are *negative sanctions*—they inflict something undesired. *Positive sanctions,* on the other hand, offer something that the other wants: *threatening* with something *feared* corresponds to *promising* something *hoped for.* If I want the other to let me have an object, I may offer him another that is more important to him than the one he is supposed to let me have and which matters more to me than the one I am willing to give up. At first, promises and threats seem to follow the same logic. Just as the threatener extends his sphere of action when he threatens in a vague way, if the promiser is greatly superior, vague promises may suffice: one will show one's appreciation, one will help to advance the other's career, etc., etc. Similarly, the future prospects of imposing negative or positive sanctions significantly extend power or influence. A suggestion of power based on positive economic sanctions may take place, for instance, through clothing or conspicuous consumption and leisure. One's power increases with the other's fear and neediness, and decreases with the latter's courage and prudence. The counterpart of weapons is *production techniques* that constantly create new positive sanctions—and this is the second great intersection between power and mastery over nature. Economic organization takes the place of military organization. The destruction of the other's self-respect has as its counterpart *blandishments,* to which even great persons are not immune (especially when what is praised is not so much what they obviously are but what they want to be). However, despite their partial parallelism, there are also crucial differences between positive and negative sanctions. Thus making possible negative sanctions explicit is wounding, while making positive sanctions explicit is almost always in the interest of the person to whom this prospect is held out. Only when the donor would like to appear generous in his own eyes or, more often, in those of a third person, may it be better for the receiver to leave his reward undetermined until the end: the donor may consider advance negotiations so burdensome and so degrading for both sides that he rewards the receiver correspondingly if he is spared them. Indeed, the donor may prove his superiority to common practice by providing surprising rewards that go far beyond what was expected. However, he will find it easiest to show this kind of generosity to persons with whom he has little to do—in order to avoid creating expectations that would restrict his freedom, of which he is so proud.

But the crucial difference between positive and negative sanctions lies deeper. Thus one may wonder whether offering positive sanctions does not amount to a simple exchange that cannot have anything to do with power or influence because it is *symmetrical,* and is in the interest of both parties because it overcomes a situation that is not Pareto-optimal. In fact, one could not subsume under this category an exchange between two

---

68. Since the bases of power for convincing include love, the latter can be assigned to the subsystems of reproduction and religion, between which the economic and the military mediate as the sphere of difference.

equally rich persons. However, the situation changes radically if there are great initial inequalities. Because of the decreasing marginal utility of all goods, the rich person who offers a hungry person bread can demand significantly more of him than he himself gives—possibly all his labor, which can produce far more than the dependent receives in return. In this case, a formally *voluntary* agreement is certainly involved that does not concern force. Of course, this exchange is in the interest of both parties, and insofar as it is an element of the power relationship, it goes without saying that the hotly debated question of whether power is a zero-sum game[69] must be answered in the negative. (Indeed, even the form of power that is based on negative sanctions need not be a zero-sum game: if the power-subject receives more in return by participating in the power of the power-holder—for instance, by serving as a simple soldier in a colonial army—than he gives up qua power-subject, we are dealing with collective, not distributive power.) Nonetheless, if the poor person has no alternative way of satisfying his needs, he must accept this exchange, and it is not completely inappropriate to speak of coercion.[70] This does not in any way deny the qualitative difference between power based on negative sanctions and power based on positive sanctions. For the power-subject the first form of power represents a far more extensive infringement on his autonomy, and for the power-holder the asymmetry of negative and positive sanctions is manifested in the fact that the costs of exercising power are differently distributed: in the case of positive sanctions, these costs have to be paid if the desired behavior is achieved, whereas in the case of negative sanctions they have to be paid if there is resistance to what is required.[71]

It is thus certainly reasonable for authors such as Parsons to speak of "power" only in the case of negative sanctions, and describe reliance on positive sanctions as "influence." However, it must be conceded that sometimes refusing positive sanctions can be worse than threatening with negative sanctions. A robber who demands my money at gunpoint is threatening me with physical violence; a businessman who threatens to fire a worker is not. And yet the second threat may be, depending on the labor market, far more significant; it can provide the basis for a more extensive and more comprehensive power than the merely punctual threat of instant death. Lasswell and Kaplan's definition of power is therefore not guided by the criterion of whether positive or negative sanctions are applied; for them, power is "participation in the making of decisions," and they define "decision" as "a policy involving severe sanctions."[72] However, either a negative sanction or the withdrawal of a positive sanction can have far-reaching effects. What is unsatisfac-

---

69. Cf. T. Parsons (1969), 383 ff.

70. In *Federalist* 79, Hamilton writes aptly: "In the general course of human nature, *a power over a man's subsistence amounts to a power over his will*" (1787 f.; 400; cf. 371).

71. Cf. D. A. Baldwin (1971/72), esp. 28. R. Paris refers to the fact that praise is cheap in the case of success as well as in that of failure of the intentions connected with it; and the same holds for censure (1995; 93). This is a further argument for putting the forms of power based on opinion under one rubric.

72. (1969), 75, 74.

tory in this definition is that the concept "severe" is not sharply defined, and, depending on the implied target, the same measure may or may not be a "decision." Of course, one has to concede that the distinction between positive and negative sanctions from a subjective perspective is not always razor-sharp either (quite apart from the fact that one can both threaten negative sanctions and promise positive sanctions when the other resists or cooperates, respectively). If people have become used to certain goods—depending on the social conditions that alone make the correct interpretation of the corresponding behavior possible—halting their delivery may be perceived as a negative sanction even more than taking away something people already have but consider less important; therefore, bringing them to a halt can trigger a reaction that may be comparable in severity to that of a victim of an attack, and even become dangerous for the influence-holder. In addition, since man is an organism dependent on food intake, depriving him and those for whom he is responsible of food can be just as lethal as inflicting an injury on him. In any case, one must distinguish between positive sanctions that are *pleasing* to another person and positive sanctions on which another person is *dependent.* With the first kind of positive sanctions, one makes *allies* who are of more or less the same rank; with the second kind one creates a *power base* or, in an extreme case, founds the notorious *societas leonina* (at least so long as, in order to survive, one is not just as dependent upon the cooperation of the other as the other is dependent on oneself). Only in this configuration does the asymmetry that is part of the concept of power exist.

In a second case, positive and negative sanctions are closely connected, that is, in the case of threats made by a third party. If A is threatened by C, B can promise to protect A if A submits to his wishes; and to the extent that protection is a positive performance, it can be termed a positive sanction. But first of all the failure to provide this defense may be just as fatal for A as denying him food, and, second, protecting A may take the form of a threat addressed not, of course, to A, but to C; the positive sanction then consists in a negative sanction with regard to a third party. Just as the rich man who wants to continue to exercise power over the poor has to perpetuate their poverty, so a person who wants to extort protection money will want to make sure that the threat posed by the enemy is maintained—and will even, in an extreme case such as the Mafia, play the role of enemy himself. For the form of power that thinks in terms of force, presenting oneself as the enemy of the enemy is the best way to avoid the hatred that results from sheer violence—and there is no doubt that both Mussolini and Hitler were masters of this tactic. They would not have succeeded had they not convinced a large portion of the traditional elites both within their countries and abroad that they, and they alone, could ward off the communist threat. In such a situation it is paradoxically the bitterest enemies who are useful; and no one is more dangerous to those whose power is based on such a relationship than those among the enemies and dependent allies who try to make peace among themselves.

5.1.2.2.4.1. *Diplomatic Abilities*

Both the ability to offer positive sanctions and the ability to inflict negative sanctions depend, among other things, on the number of people that obey one or with whom one can ally oneself. Even if an alliance is usually a symmetrical relationship and therefore cannot be subsumed under the concept of power, a talent for creating alliances is still one of the most important power factors in a world with more than two independent actors: power is exercised not over allies, but through allies. To be sure, the ability to form alliances depends in part on the positive sanctions one can offer and on the negative sanctions that one can threaten to impose; but not everyone who can offer positive sanctions is automatically a skillful ally. For that requires a sense for the way people talk among equals, the ability to make compromises, and an appearance that elicits good will—a person who can share power may be better able to extend it than one who is not capable of sharing power. On the other hand, a person who cannot put together alliances, that is, who cannot cooperate as one among equals, will, no matter what his individual superiority, be able to exercise far-reaching power only in exceptional cases, as long as those who are individually inferior but together superior do not unite against him; and only if they are incapable of doing so does he have a chance at world power: Rome's rise to power would not have been possible had its many opponents been able to work together during the crucial third century B.C. In fact, this is the basis for what can be called the "nemesis of power": it explains why so few states were able to arrive at imperial standing, and why their rise almost always took place without others being aware of it—indeed, as a rule, *without their being aware of it themselves.* The more powerful someone is, the more disagreeable it is to cooperate with him, because by the very nature of the thing less can be achieved through this kind of cooperation than through cooperation among those who are equal in power; the alliance easily degenerates into forms of dependency. Excessive power is generally perceived as a threat, and therefore increasing one's power beyond a certain limit is usually a warning sign for others and often counterproductive for the power-holder himself.

If the ability to form alliances is a positive factor in power, the complementary negative factor consists in the ability to weaken foreign coalitions, to foment divisions within others' alliances. Together, these abilities constitute the core of the *diplomatic* talent, which often has the greatest significance in power struggles between more than two actors. So far as the foundation of alliances is concerned, it is obvious that they are stronger if based on common values and not merely on common interests.[73] A person who succeeds in convincing the other that cooperation is based on an underlying collective identity, will achieve more than if he can offer only the prospect of mutual advantages. Therefore, for example, alliances between similar political systems are usually more durable than those based solely on interests, which fall apart when the interests situation changes—as may be the case precisely when the alliance has achieved its goal: after the victory over Hitler there was no longer any raison d'être for the continuation of the cooperation between the Soviet Union and the United States that had been made necessary by their common enemy. "And when the common enemy lies prostrate on the

---

73. Cf. Thucydides III 10.

ground, who then binds the new friendship together?" Wrangel rightly asks Wallenstein in Schiller's drama.[74] We should distinguish between common interests that are
identical and those that are complementary: in the first case, both parties want the same
thing (on egoistic grounds); in the second, they are interested in different things that
cannot, however, be attained without a certain event, which is therefore sought by both,
even though for different reasons. In the fourth partition of Poland, the Third Reich and
the Soviet Union pursued complementary, but never identical, interests.

The ability to divide one's opponents is a matter of creating opposed interests and
mutual mistrust between the opponents. One way of doing this can be insincere praise
of one opponent at the expense of the other. Making communication between opponents
more difficult or even preventing it is also helpful, if the goal is to halt their cooperation.
On higher levels, ruse manifests itself when it is possible to deceive the opponent about
his own power base and friends. *Traitors* in the opponent's ranks are even more likely
to bring him down than deceptions regarding the physical world. The closer they stand to
the opponent, and the more deeply they have gained his trust, the more important traitors' services become. There are traitors who from the outset seek proximity to the opponent with the intention of bringing him down; others, in contrast, are already allied
with him before they make the decision to betray him. Treachery can consist in passing on
confidential information, in stalling production by passive resistance, in sabotaging important installations, or in undermining the organizational efforts of the person betrayed.
It culminates in the traitor's instrumentalization of the person betrayed, that is, making
him work for his own ends, whereas the person betrayed believes he is pursuing his own
goals. What is paradoxical about this situation is that, because of the changed conditions,
the betrayed person's successes contribute to his own downfall.

5.1.2.2.4.2. Supply and Demand: The Relationship between Positive and Negative Sanctions

The form of influence or power based on positive sanctions depends, in accord
with the law of supply and demand, on four factors. First, it depends on the opportunities for the person with influence to offer positive sanctions, in relationship to others'
possibilities—if I have nothing, this form of power is denied me, and it is also significantly limited if I am only one among many who are making similar offers; it is increased if we are bound together in a cartel or if I have a monopoly. Second, no less important are my own needs for the other's service, its marginal utility for me. The less I
need the other's service, the more I can demand in exchange for my positive sanctions.
Third, the more potential buyers I have, the less dependent I am upon any individual
client—at least so far as my customers compete with each other. In the latter case their
number decreases the individual client's bargaining strength, whereas the power of a

---

74. "Und liegt zu Boden der gemeine Feind, wer knüpft die neue Freundschaft dann zusammen?"
(Schiller, *Wallensteins Tod* act I, sc. 5, vv. 377 f.).

monopsony is great. Fourth, the other's needs for my positive sanctions should be mentioned. Even in the case of negative sanctions the other cannot be forced to adopt a certain behavior if he can just overcome his fear, and this is even more true for positive sanctions. A person who needs nothing cannot be enticed by anything; and even if no one can be wholly without needs, personal differences with regard to the quantity and quality of the needs remain large. It is obviously in the interest of the rich man that what he has to offer be desired—otherwise his power quickly melts away. It is also obvious that the power of Western countries depends very crucially on the propagation of the Western style of consumption throughout the world—at least so long as the other form of power that has to do with force does not come into play.

My discussion of these four factors has been imprecise insofar as what really matters is the other's perception of one's own position. I may not be the only supplier of positive sanctions, but that weakens my position only if the potential client knows this. I may be completely dependent upon the other's services, but if he does not perceive this, his demands will not be so great as they would be if he did. Here as well we see that information is a major power factor that is no less important for the system of positive sanctions than for that of negative sanctions. Still more important than access to individual bits of information is the general ability to process information, that is, education. Not infrequently, economic dependencies can be diminished solely through education. Moreover, what we have said holds not only for economic relationships in the narrower sense, but to some degree also for diplomatic relationships, since even alliances are sought-after services. Here too, subjective marginal utility is what counts— Italy, which was never a major military power, could determine the outcome of World War I when it entered the conflict in 1915, and was therefore able to demand a great deal. It should not be surprising, however, that when the crisis was over the allies evaluated Italy's contribution more objectively—that is, no longer in accord with its marginal utility in 1915.

Which form of power is more fundamental, the military or the economic? On one hand, force is always superior *in the short run*. Only if there is a general unwillingness to risk one's life can economic power become decisive—otherwise in a conflict steel will win out over gold. Machiavelli rightly notes that good soldiers can acquire the necessary money, but money cannot so easily acquire the necessary soldiers.[75] Crassus was wrong when he thought that to become *princeps* one had to accumulate enough money to pay an army[76]—it was the person who could lead an army and win battles who became *princeps*. In any case, nothing is more ridiculous than what Galba, who was hated because of his miserliness, is supposed to have said to the mutinous soldiers pressing around him with murderous intent—he asked them to allow him a few more days to pay them the

75. Cf. *Discorsi* II 10.18 and 26 (1984; 318 f.).
76. Cf. Cicero, *De officiis* I 25.

donative [77]—for someone who can kill the other no longer needs gifts from him. Someone who gives without receiving anything in return must always make it seem that he gives willingly—for if he gives unwillingly, people will think he is afraid and soon ask more of him; eventually, a power relationship based on positive sanctions will be transformed into one based on negative sanctions.[78] In all times of crisis in which the more complex forms of power crumble away, the first and most original form, that is, force, clearly emerges.[79] Perhaps the fact that force is the ultimate ground of power explains a phenomenon that is in great need of explanation. I am referring to the importance, even in the age of telecommunications, of the physical presence of the power-holder. It is hardly surprising that in earlier times coups d'état often took place when the ruler was absent,[80] for it is on the latter's ability to take quickly the cratically correct decision that putting down a coup depends. But why wouldn't a decision communicated by telephone suffice—assuming, naturally, that the telephone lines are not cut? To cite a more general and less dramatic case, why are personal meetings between decision makers still necessary today? Of course, one might reply that the telephone does not transmit the exceptionally important elements of mimicry and gesture; being able to look someone in the eye is a far better antidote for deception than merely hearing a voice. But since the development of television, this argument also seems inadequate. In my opinion, the only correct answer is that physical presence—that is, the possibility of exercising immediate, bodily resistance—has an entirely different reality content than a face on a screen. The will of a person who is bodily present has an intensity very different from that of a person of whom we perceive only the voice or the image—for it creates the impression that in the worst-case scenario he might impose his will by force.

On the other hand, we have already seen that power based on force alone is short-lived—and not only because the use of force involves a high risk of violent death. At least the dread of a third party, whose force is still more feared, is required in order to

---

77. Tacitus, to whom we owe the anecdote (*Historiae* I 41), nonetheless reports that there was an alternative tradition, according to which Galba presented his throat to his assassins, saying they should make haste and strike, if that seemed to them in the interest of the state. One would like to believe that the worthy old man died thinking of the general welfare and with heroic indifference to his own fate.

78. Marx aptly writes about the national assembly's granting a one-time allowance to the president of the republic: "Sie machte sich so der doppelten Schwäche schuldig, das Geld zu bewilligen und zugleich durch ihren Ärger zu zeigen, daß sie es nur widerwillig bewillige" (*Der achtzehnte Brumaire des Louis Bonaparte*, 8:160). ("They thereby became guilty of the double weakness of granting the money and at the same time showing by their vexation that they did so only against their will.") See also Machiavelli, *Discorsi* I 32 (1984; 130f.).

79. Pascal (1982, 182) refers to such a situation: "Quand la force attaque la grimace, quand un simple soldat prend le bonnet carré d'un premier président, et le fait voler par la fenêtre. . . ." ("When force attacks posturing, when a simple soldier takes a chief magistrate's cap and throws it out the window. . . .")

80. Cf. also Machiavelli, *Principe* 3.4 (1986; 90).

lend it durability; indeed, without a system of positive sanctions that go beyond it, it can hardly endure for long. For only positive sanctions can motivate the responsible actions of executive organs without which power is incapable of adaptation, especially in times of crisis. Unlike Machiavelli, Kauṭilya believes that money is a more important basis of power than troops, because it is constantly needed and universally utilizable.[81] In normal situations, people resort to force unwillingly; they grow tired of it more easily than of shaping human relationships by exchanging positive sanctions. To be sure, one can appropriate all sorts of things by force, but when it has used up what it has appropriated, force is not capable of producing anything new. Therefore, if *We*-feelings are weak, the strong army of a beleagured king may very well kill him and go over to employers who pay better wages, even if they could kill them too—that is, if they arrive at the conviction that killing them would not improve their lot in the long term. For force is destructive and parasitical; the construction of something new is for other forms of power. Indeed, even in times of crisis what counts is not naked power, but rather its *organization;* it is not the strongest fighter, but rather the most capable general who will be able to take power in such a situation, and in his organizational and motivational performance lies the key to overcoming *anarchy*, which is not a condition of a general vacuum of power (for the nature of the political abhors a vacuum even more than does physical nature in traditional philosophy), but rather the rule of force.

5.1.2.2.5. Power and Opinion

What was said regarding the relationship between force and the power of positive sanctions holds to an even greater degree for the relationship between force and the third form of power or influence, which consists in changing convictions. On one hand, the power of opinions seems the most ephemeral of the forms of power, defenseless against economic sanctions, not to mention against force. Only so long as neither force nor economic need has to be reckoned with can opinion imagine that it is the true power factor—a superstition into which intellectuals periodically fall in the modern media world with its secondhand experiences, although reality has often mercilessly contradicted them.[82] On the other hand, it is certainly not false to say that the form of power that operates in the medium of opinions is superior to the others. For if I can motivate the

---

81. 7.9.26 ff. Cf. also the debate with Kauṇapadanta, who represents a point of view similar to Machiavelli's, 8.1.41 ff. However, it is strange that while Kauṭilya ranks a store of money higher than soldiers, he ranks fortifications even higher—even though the latter count only if they can be defended by force.

82. See Livy's comment—which is typical of Roman scorn—regarding the legislative rhetoric the Athenians used to compensate for their actual powerlessness to resist Philip V: "Athenienses quidem litteris verbisque, quibis solis valent, bellum adversus Philippum gerebant" (31.44.9). ("The Athenians waged the war against Philip with letters and words, in which alone they are strong.") They could play out their verbal aggressivity only under the protection of Rome, for which, as we know, they would eventually have to pay.

other to adopt a certain behavior only by threatening him with negative sanctions or by promising him positive sanctions, then I have to reckon with the fact that this behavior will cease the moment the sanctions stop; if, on the contrary, I have convinced or persuaded the other that a certain behavior is good for him or good in itself, he will do what is desired by himself, without any external pressure. The power-holder may feel superior to the one who has to carry out the work of persuading because he does not need to wait for the subjective insight of the power-subject; he may enjoy the asymmetry that no longer obtains in a collective conviction—but the price he pays is that he knows (or can know) very well that without his ongoing effort, which will end with his death, if not before, what he wants would not occur. On the other hand, convictions inspire the other's innermost heart, and can survive for centuries the death of the person who brought them into the world. Nothing shows this more impressively than the triumph of Christianity. Hardly any of the soldiers of the Roman Empire who witnessed the Crucifixion would have considered as more than mad stammering the prediction that the man who was dying on the Cross would communicate his will (in whatever form) to more humans than would the empire they represented. And yet this prediction would have been correct—compared with the power of ideas, that of the lances proved ultimately inferior.[83]

The apparent contradiction between the two assertions can be easily resolved by distinguishing between opinion and idea. If we understand an opinion as a subjective representation *that we have,* then it is obvious that it will yield to more severe means of pressure. Ideas, on the other hand, are convictions *that have us.* Certainly we can imagine a situation in which it would be possible to destroy everyone who clings to an idea or is just attracted to it; and certainly even ideas have to be institutionalized, that is, they have to be connected with a system of positive or even negative sanctions, if they are to last for long, as the history of Christianity shows. Ideas qua ideas cannot overcome physical force.[84] But the converse also holds: without ideas no power is stable. The Red Army's divisions were not equal to the ideological superiority of the West and, in Poland, to that of the Holy See. Enormous empires, if based on mere force, crumble nearly as fast as they were conquered—think of the Mongolian empire. Even power that is based on positive sanctions only awakes the desire for more and more, and is therefore necessarily unstable if people are not convinced that only certain things can be legitimately demanded and expected. It is possible to kill someone who wants to change such convictions if he has no access to weapons; but if he has been able to have an effect for a long enough time before his death, the change in consciousness he has brought about will change reality more than force or money could. Indeed, even his death may contribute to the triumph of his ideas—for one's way of life is even more convincing than arguments, and how one dies is part of this way of life. More quickly than anything else, the blood of martyrdom may cause ideas to flourish, and force may thus produce the exact opposite of what it intended.

---

83. Cf. the fine observations in Mill (1972), 183 f.
84. To that extent, Machiavelli is surely right in *Il Principe* 6.6 f. (1986; 106).

Within the forms of influence based on changing opinions, different distinctions are to be made, in at least two dimensions. On one hand, one must determine whether the convictions that are to be changed concern *values* or *means to an end*. One can explain to someone that he can more effectively attain his goals with certain means rather than with those he has previously employed, and thus attain a change in his behavior: the power of science is of this kind. Or one can try to change someone's goals by proving, for instance, that they are not moral. In human history, art, religion, and philosophy have repeatedly succeeded in changing the way goals are set, even though this is very hard to do—much harder, in any case, than changing convictions regarding the means for given ends. For values belong to the innermost core of the self; the recognition that one has heretofore had false values almost always elicits a painful identity crisis, and people usually resist it with all their strength. On the other hand, one can distinguish the means used in trying to change the other's views according to whether they concern means to given ends or values. Thus, as ideal types, priests have authority regarding values, elders have an authority regarding means to given ends, philosophers have the ability to convince others in matters concerning values, whereas scientists have the ability to convince others regarding means to given ends.

5.1.2.2.5.1. *Manipulation*

First, one can *manipulate* other people. The concept of manipulation is not easy to define; in my view, the crucial characteristic is that the person exercising influence affects the thinking and emotional life of another person in such a way that the latter scarcely notices it. This does not exclude the possibility that someone might be manipulated to adopt a view that is objectively right and is best for him: indeed, in manipulation the autonomy of the influence-subject is infringed upon, but not necessarily his welfare. Nonetheless, more than any other form of influence, manipulation is distinguished by an especially insidious characteristic: it is not perceived as a form of influence by the influence subject. If someone complains about being manipulated, he can always speak only about the past; for it is in general self-contradictory to say "I am now being manipulated." As a rule, only the sentence "Someone is now trying to manipulate me" is meaningful, insofar as it suggests that the attempt has failed. In any case, manipulation should be considered a form of power (in the broader sense); indeed, one can even concede that it is one of the most extensive and comprehensive forms of power, precisely because it is so difficult to defend oneself against it. If manipulation is successful, conflicts do not arise; the idea of resistance cannot be formed at all.[85] Debates do not occur because alternatives do not even enter people's consciousnesses.[86] However, it is crucial that the person exercising influence intends to produce an effect; otherwise we can speak at most of a social effect. Indeed, if certain convictions are part of what is taken for granted by a

---

85. This is the point of S. Lukes's study (1974).

86. The concept of "decisionless decision" elaborated by P. Bachrach and M. S. Baratz (1970), 42 f., belongs in this context.

culture, one can certainly acknowledge that they limit the scope of thought and action; but one can only speak of "power" if there are people who are aware of a possible alternative and who are consciously working to see to it that others do not become aware of it. The social effect of a person who works out a system of categories that sets its stamp on a whole period is enormous, because he thereby determines what counts as a meaningful question; thus at the same time he determines which problems require efforts to persuade people, and which critical questions can be set aside. But only if he at least realizes that he is shaping attention frames and at the same time influencing what is experienced as a milieu, can we speak of influence or power in the broader sense—for example, in the case of an overt battle to influence opinion, in which certain slogans are created and used by which thought is supposed to be guided. On the other hand, the generic extension of the concept of power to traditions, for instance, contradicts the intentional element that must be attributed to at least one of the two sides involved in a power relationship. It is not an impressive critical intellectual achievement, but rather a sign of the vagueness of concept formation in the social sciences when "power" is spoken of in dealing with all social interactions, meaning only that some forms of social causality exist—which is no doubt correct, but tautological.

Manipulations can encourage the emergence of certain convictions, as is proven, for instance, by commercial advertising and political propaganda. The subliminal character of part of our perception makes it particularly difficult to defend oneself against suggestions of this kind, and therefore permits us to speak of manipulation. Hypnosis is manipulation in a pure form, but can only seldom be used as a basis of power, even if the arts have repeatedly played with this idea—think of the German expressionist films of the 1920s (which adumbrated Hitler's abilities to manipulate the masses through suggestion) and Huxley's *Brave New World,* where it is broadened and systematized in hypnopaedia. Possible interventions in human genes responsible for intellectual and moral capabilities would bring manipulation to an apex and represent the third intersection between mastery over nature and power. One of the subtlest forms of manipulation consists in making the other believe something by giving him the impression that one does not want to tell him something or possibly even wants to hide something from him. If the other believes that he has succeeded in getting information out of me that I did not intend for him, he will not be inclined to suspect that I am manipulating him. Possessing the art of steering a conversation and making casual allusions in such a way that it does not occur to one's interlocutor that they are its true goal is what constitutes a successful manipulator. It is true that Othello is not particularly intelligent, but the procedure used by Iago to drive him to murder Desdemona is, although rather clumsy given its target, classical from a formal point of view: Iago exploits Othello's dominant passion, jealousy, and Iago's initial insinuations in the third act leave Othello with the feeling that it was *he* who had forced Iago to express his suspicion against his own will.

Whereas the manipulative character of positive insinuations is not so easy to conceal, it is considerably easier to influence others' opinions by not allowing certain facts to come to their attention. State censorship is an important means of manipulation of this second kind, but so is concentrating the mass media in a few private hands. In a peculiar dialectic, moreover, not only *limiting the flow of information* is a form of manipulation, but also *increasing* it. For since the human intellect can process only a limited amount, overloading it with stimuli can significantly diminish its ability to recognize fundamental information as such. It is obvious that the difficulties present-day politics experiences in trying to respond appropriately to the demands of our time have to do with the current information glut—even if this does not mean that these difficulties were all created by an explicit will to manipulation on the part of the various power-holders. But in a few cases such a will can be proven: if, for instance, one cannot conceal a scandal that endangers one's own position, then surely the second best maxim is to shift attention from it to other scandals, for public opinion cannot process too many scandals at once.

5.1.2.2.5.2.   *Persuading and Convincing: Weakness as a Power Factor*

Second, we should distinguish from manipulation those forms of influence that are openly directed toward changing other people's views. Whereas the Romance languages use words such as *persuasione, persuasion, persuasión,* and *persuasâo* to designate both the act of *convincing* and that of *persuading,* German and English are justified in making a distinction between the two; indeed, even Latin does this, insofar as *persuadere* in the sense of "convince" takes the accusative and an infinitive, whereas in the sense of "persuade" it requires the use of an *ut*-clause. This differing construction makes sense: convincing is first of all directed toward the recognition of a state of affairs existing independently from me (whether it is theoretical or valuative in nature), while persuading demands immediate action. One could say that persuasion is primarily directed toward the psychic elements in the other that are suitable for triggering actions, whereas convincing seeks to reveal relationships of descriptive and valuative validity, that is, it *argues* (which does not lead to immediate action). Persuading and convincing cannot be distinguished in terms of whether they have short- or long-term effects; cheap tricks can succeed for generations, and the best arguments are very soon forgotten. It is also not part of my concept of convincing that the convincer be right; but he must himself be convinced, in a subjectively sincere way, of what he is trying to communicate to others. An example will show what I mean: someone who points out to another, on objective grounds, that the latter's behavior has dangerous consequences for his health is trying to convince. On the other hand, someone who tries to awaken fear, chiefly through vague insinuations, and perhaps even through deception, cannot himself be considered a threatener, because he does not generate fear of his own negative sanctions, but here one is dealing with a case of persuading, not convincing. This example also shows how difficult it is to distinguish between persuading and convincing. A person who urges someone to give up a certain behavior, or recommends that he do so, will, when searching for means to given ends, base his advice on the damage or utility for the person concerned, that is, on negative and positive sanctions; and since there is a natural fear of the former and a natural interest in the latter, this form of influence even has similarities with the forms of power discussed earlier. Certainly the advisor does not himself threaten or demand, but rather argues in the advisee's interest. But it is sometimes wise for him to make it clear that he is not pursuing any interest of his own on this occasion, so that the advisee does not misunderstand his *warnings* as *threats* and feel called upon to defy him.[87]

But to what extent does a person who argues only with regard to values make use of the psychic mechanisms of the other? Even someone who believes that moral behavior is irreducible to self-interest must concede that it is very important for one's own self-respect to be able to consider oneself in good conscience to be moral. One can in fact exercise mental coercion on a moral person that endangers his identity by giving him to understand that he is immoral; in particular, one can make use of the moral-psychological mechanisms that arise from his own life history. Thus someone may feel guilty and try to compensate for this by going to the other extreme. Someone who comprehends such psychological structures can exercise a significant degree of power. Thus a nation that has waged an unjust war tends to consider all wars reprehensible (while a nation that is proud of the moral achievement represented by its last war, will tend to justify all its wars; just compare the current attitudes in Germany and in the United States with regard to war); and even having imposed an unjust peace treaty after a war can weigh heavily upon a noble actor. Thus many representatives of the British elite felt a certain shame because of the Versailles peace treaty—something Hitler understood early on, and which allowed him to build up his power position. Naturally, from the fact that Germany was unfairly treated in 1919 it does not follow that in the 1930s everything should be accepted; but the laws of moral psychology are not guided by those of logic. A good part of the *power of the so-called weaker sex* consists, or at least consisted before women's liberation, in having mastered this situation. The phrase "power of the weaker sex" is not self-contradictory, because physical strength is only one power factor among others. Thus in love the weaker is often the stronger: "L'amor è un agile / Torneo, sua corte / Vuol che il più fragile / Vinca il più forte," sings Nannetta in Boito's *Falstaff* libretto (act 1, sc. 2). ("Love is an agile / Contest, its court / Desires that the weaker / Triumph over the stronger.") Here we see a fundamental dialectic of power: since it is humiliating to be dominated by a foreign power, and since the will to power is human, most power-subjects will try to make use of the forms of power that allow them to regain a partial superiority. Since Hellenistic and Roman New Comedy, the techniques of manipulation used by clever slaves or servants on their legally or economically superior masters have been a favorite theme; women, who are almost always the weaker members of the family, can make use of not only ruse (and their erotic attractiveness) but also their weakness. "The sick wife in particular: no one can outdo her in the subtlety

---

87. A masterwork in this vein is Churchill's letter of 4 February 1941 to the Japanese foreign minister, Matsuoka. He neither threatens nor requests nor moralizes; like a well-intentioned advisor he merely asks questions concerning the means to given ends, whose answers, which he leaves Matsuoka to determine, he urges him to take into account in future decisions. Even if the letter had no effect, Churchill was still rightly proud of it in 1950.

with which she dominates, pressures, tyrannizes."[88] Anyone who has even a little sense of honor would begin a fight only with someone who is as strong or stronger than himself; therefore, under certain circumstances not only women but also children and the aged can draw power from their weakness.[89] What decent person would not find it easier to challenge a Goliath than a venerable old man? Not only the life experience and continuity of time that age represents but also its weakness contribute to the inviolability of the elderly, who, if they behave prudently, can be more secure in their power position than strong young men who provoke resistance.[90] In this same context we can also place the tactic used by the early Boris Yeltsin when he was rising to power: his sentimental tearfulness played on the image of the humiliated victim of the system with which millions of Soviet citizens who had been the oppressed by the Communist Party could sympathize; he thereby quickly won a position of power that was in no way inferior to that of his predecessors.

Persuasion bearing on values is mixed with persuasion bearing on the means to given ends if it is based, as in the case of religion, on reference to punishment after death. This is a form of power only so long as the power subject believes in the assertions of the religion; even more one-sidedly than in the case of threats backed by real force, here it is the believer who creates power. We can see from this example that, depending on the context, the same behavior can constitute either persuading or convincing. A fat provost who obtains privileges by defiantly claiming that he has connnections to divine powers is persuading; on the other hand, when at the end of his conversation with Don Rodrigo, in the course of which he has emphatically pointed out the injustice of the latter's intention, Father Cristoforo appeals to the Last Judgment, this is definitely part of his attempt to convince Don Rodrigo, because he considers it to be true and reasonable that anyone who torments a weaker fellow human being will be held to account for his actions in another world. In addition, Father Cristoforo's conduct as a whole shows that he is fully convinced of the truth of what he preaches to others.

---

88. Nietzsche (1980), 5:370: "Das kranke Weib in Sonderheit: Niemand übertrifft es in Raffinements, zu herrschen, zu drücken, zu tyrannisiren."

89. However, this holds mainly when the weaker person does not have, or show, too clear an awareness of the power to be gained from his weakness; paradoxically, his power exists only so long as he does not make use of it as such. Cf. Schiller's related reflections on Hadrian VI in *Über naive und sentimentalische Dichtung:* "Es ist übrigens gar nicht so leicht, die kindische Unschuld von der kindlichen immer richtig zu unterscheiden, indem es Handlungen gibt, welche auf der äußersten Grenze zwischen beiden schweben und bei denen wir schlechterdings im Zweifel gelassen werden, ob wir die Einfältigkeit belachen oder die edle Einfalt hochschätzen sollen" (1959, 5:702). ("It is moreover not so easy always correctly to distinguish childlike innocence from childish innocence, since there are actions that hover on the extreme border between the two and simply leave us in doubt as to whether we should laugh at their naiveté or prize their noble simplicity).

90. From this, as well as from other things, follows in the private sphere the irreplaceable importance of grandparents in bringing up children.

Despite all the difficulties of marking the borderline, there is also a sufficient number of cases in which persuading can be clearly distinguished from convincing—namely, when the argumentative content is minimal but irrational psychic mechanisms are exploited with virtuosity. This occurs, for instance, in the part of advertising and propaganda that operates consciously, shamelessly exaggerating certain assertions that may be basically true, ceaselessly repeating them, and using, for example, symbols to connect them with elementary drives and fears.[91] Propagandistic tricks usually work better if they are not perceived as such, yet there are certainly people who feel flattered when they notice that someone has targeted their most primitive instincts. And even if the arts of persuasion are in principle recognized and rejected, only a few people retain this alert awareness for a long time and continue to regard with a critical eye not only the behavior of others but also their own weaknesses. Well-known tricks of persuasion consist in emphasizing only the good aspects of the position one has chosen and concealing the bad aspects or, in order to anticipate this type of objection, acknowledging one of the less relevant negative effects, discussing it at length, and showing that it cannot compete with the advantages; in this way one seems oneself to be critical. If there is not much to be said for one's own position, it is advisable to engage in a polemic against a still more absurd position, and to do so as if there were no third (or fourth) position, thus providing, as it were, a negative "proof" of one's own view. Here it can certainly be effective, if the interlocutor does not fall below a certain intellectual level, to act initially as if one were well aware of and appreciated the advantages of the opposing position; in this way one seems more objective. For the persuader, it is always crucial to know what the audience wants to hear; with the help of the audience's favorite cliches, he will move along as if supporting himself on a handrail. A person who is primarily concerned with people's mechanisms of agreement, because for him the question of truth is in comparison a matter of indifference, is what we call a "demagogue" or "agitator."[92] Here we can distinguish *demagogues* who merely express in a striking way convictions that already exist from those who strengthen these convictions, and from those who create new ones. It is obvious that from a formal point of view—that is, independently of their content—the third kind of demagoguery represents a greater achievement than the second, and the second than the first. However, it is clear that a creation *ex nihilo* is not possible; even the most innovative proponent of change must connect his views with already existing convictions, in order to be able, for instance, to astonish people by proving that something follows from these convictions that contradicts other convictions that had been held just as strongly. Whereas the *agitator* seeks a rapid and unmediated success, the *doctrinaire* is a person who shapes his views into a more or less

---

91. On political symbols, see the outstanding analyses in H. D. Lasswell and A. Kaplan (1969), 103 ff.

92. Because of the impossibility of going beyond the normative, the demagogue will not only hardly ever openly acknowledge that he is not concerned with the truth, but seldom admit it even to himself.

closed system. His impact is never so quick as that of the agitator, but his influence can last for generations. Both the agitator and the doctrinaire strive primarily to get the other to act in a certain way, and secondarily to produce justifications for it; the *theoretician*, in contrast, starts out from general principles and deduces from them which action is desirable. Since this distinction is formal, it does not exclude the possibility that the doctrinaire, or even the agitator, might happen to be right, and that some theoreticians, despite their superior method, are mistaken. Whether the doctrinaire wants to preserve the status quo or change it plays no role in defining him; the former might be called an "ideological" and the latter a "utopian" doctrinaire.

Despite the distinction between persuading and convincing as ideal types, in reality they are, as we have seen, mixed, although in differing degrees. Even the philosopher who wants to convince must use a language that others understand if he is to have an effect, and he must simplify his arguments;[93] had he not considered the intellectual patterns of his interlocutor, no communication would take place.[94] This consideration need not be conscious; it can occur automatically, as it were, if the two communicating parties share the same background in traditions. Conversely, persuading that does not seem—to the person persuaded, at least—to assume that the emotional structures it employs are objectively justified will be counterproductive; it can easily be interpreted as an attempt at manipulation. As Aristotle already showed in the second book of his *Rhetoric*, the credibility of a discourse intended to convince depends on factors that concern the speaker (more generally, the communicator), the listener (the receiver) and the structure of the discourse itself. Not only *what* is said but also *who* is speaking is perceived; in particular, the intellectual and moral virtues of the speaker as well as his interest in the listener's welfare get special attention. Moreover, the collective identity that binds the speaker to his listeners is crucial. If one speaks from the point of view of the *We*, he can, *ceteris paribus*, count on far greater interest than if he is one of "the others." This is especially true if the speaker shares the fate of the community he is addressing, for then it is clear that he is also speaking in his own interest.[95] Within a group characterized by a collective identity, a person is particularly well qualified as a speaker if he possesses certain rhetorical and intellectual abilities that others do not have (otherwise it would not be very tempting to listen to him), and yet the latter nonetheless ultimately recognize themselves in him: if the communicator comes across as too superior, he may easily arouse envy or fear. It is almost always effective when someone to whom conservative opinions are ascribed enters a decisive debate on the side of the progressive

---

93. Aristotle designates the example as the rhetorical equivalent of induction, and the enthymeme as the rhetorical equivalent of the syllogism (*Rhetoric* 1356a35 ff.).

94. This holds even more for the efforts of philosophers to have a political effect. Cf. P. L. Oesterreich's remarkable book (1994).

95. This is the reason why the comparison of the statesman and the captain of a ship is rhetorically more effective than that between the statesman and the physician. Nothing much happens to the physician if the patient dies; the captain perishes with his crew.

view—for in that case the undecided will take this change of opinion very seriously even if it is not objectively well-grounded, whereas people seldom pay close attention to those who repeat what they have long said. This is true not only when a real change of opinion has occurred, but also when the earlier opinion was only simulated. Among the factors on the side of the receiver, his ability to concentrate and his emotional condition during the communication are crucial: one must speak differently to someone who is angry (if one cannot put off the conversation) than to someone who is frightened. Reference to things that are already known must be made again and again, so that the listener has the impression that he is moving on familiar ground; allusions that create in him the feeling that he is particularly well-informed or intelligent are always welcome. The speech must know how to bring out the essential point; everything else must be made subordinate to the latter. As we already know from animal communication, this kind of attention can be attracted by simplicity and conspicuousness.

The goal of manipulating, persuading, and convincing is *consensus*. Since consensus is a symmetrical relationship, one might think that with it, even more than with positive sanctions, we have left the field of power and influence. However, the asymmetry consists in the fact that the *production* of consensus does not proceed from all concerned to the same extent: the propagandistic, rhetorical, and intellectual abilities of individual human beings are decidedly different. Nonetheless, there can be no doubt that convincing, unlike manipulating and persuading, does not violate the other's autonomy, but often actually constitutes it, *for outside reason there is no freedom*. In a certain sense, the rational consensus goes back to the original unity that precedes any conflict; indeed, since this unity is no longer a given, but is rather achieved through one's own insight, the process of convincing combines the independence of the wills that emerged in the struggle and the original collective identity within which alone man can develop. Praise of rational consensus can therefore never be great enough, and one of the good things about discourse ethics is that it has made consensus the central focus of its analysis. Yet already on the descriptive level, the following shortcoming of this theory must be pointed out. It is obvious that convincing is not the only form of social interaction. It occurs only in contexts that are protected from other forms of conflict (and not protected by consensus alone), and it remains constitutionally endangered: if a consensus is not formed, other forms of delimitation and coordination of wills become inevitable, going as far as the use of force. In general, people know this; for that reason, even the most relaxed discourse is sustained by the consciousness that it *must* succeed if worse things are to be avoided. In general, no discourse is free of domination, because in the state of nature it is not so easy to talk; but even in a dialogue protected by strong institutions one can—or at least, should—never forget that resort to force is the price to be paid for its failure.

5.1.2.2.5.3. *Authority*

A complete taxonomy of the forms of power has to acknowledge that in traditional cultures certainly, but in modern ones as well, the phenomenon of *authority* plays a major role. Like persuasion, authority may achieve a *voluntary* change of opinion on the part of the influence-subject, with the influence occurring *openly:* this distinguishes it from manipulation, with which it is often confused in the present, but to whose ideology it is not adapted and which would prefer to limit it to the parent-child relationship. Other than in the case of convincing, in authority the influence-subject forgoes critical examination of what is communicated to him; he takes it in without question, in the sincere belief that it is true. Naturally, the recognition of the other's authority is not unfounded: age and experience of life, previous objective successes, expert knowledge, general recognition by others, and the office held are factors that provide a basis for authority. To give a vivid example: between the first two scenes from *I Promessi sposi,* cited above, Lucia's flight from her native village has taken place, and Don Rodrigo is pursuing her with violent means. Father Cristoforo helps her flee, and he takes the threatened girl and her mother into his church. It is night, and since he fears an attack by Don Rodrigo, Father Cristoforo orders the sexton, Brother Fazio, to lock the church door. The latter at first refuses to do so, for it seems to him improper for a Franciscan priest to spend the night with women in a locked room. The conflict is resolved when Father Cristoforo suddenly turns to him with the words: "Omnia munda mundis," forgetting that Brother Fazio does not understand Latin. But that is just what settles the matter. Had the father begun arguing, Manzoni writes, Brother Fazio would have given several counterarguments, and heaven knows when and how the situation would have ended. But when he hears these words heavy with mysterious meaning uttered so resolutely, they seem to him to contain the answer to all his doubts. He calms down and says, "Enough! You know better than I."[96] Two things characterize this passage: on one hand, Brother Fazio gives in when faced with something that he does not concretely understand, still trusting in the superior knowledge of the Latin-speaking father; on the other hand, Father Cristoforo, in uttering these words, is not at all thinking about the fact that Brother Fazio does not understand him. Father Cristoforo does not make use of his authority intentionally, and that is precisely what makes it effective.

A person's authority can depend on its representing something general, such as a tradition; but it may also be grounded in *individual* qualities. A physician can exercise his authority through his white coat and his diploma—or because one has already seen that he can help in a competent way and with personal efforts. Statesmen who have achieved something important in difficult situations retain their authority for the rest of their lives if they make no errors. From these we must distinguish the form of individual authority that operates directly, even if it has not yet been proven. There are people who radiate something to which others willingly respond—a superiority that can

---

96. (1973), 1016: "Se il padre si fosse messo a questionare con ragioni, a fra Fazio non sarebber mancate altre ragioni da opporre, e sa il cielo quando e come la cosa sarebbe finita. Ma, al sentir quelle parole gravide d'un senso misterioso, e proferite così risolutamente, gli parve che in quelle dovesse contenersi la soluzione di tutti i suoi dubbi. S'aquietò, et disse: 'basta! lei ne sa più di me."

be manifold in nature.[97] On first meeting someone, feeling may tell us that this is a person whom we can trust, and whom we may even be willing to accept as our guide. A pleasing appearance, a natural self-assurance in manner, clear indications of prudence, strength of will, organizational abilities, courage, and moral earnestness may cast a much stronger spell on us than the best arguments set forth by colorless persons. If in times of radical change one has no clear idea as to how one should behave, one will be attracted less by people with well-established and obvious virtues than by individuals who seem to have something mysterious about them and who seem to be more than they at first appear to be. To the extent that the slow penetration into surmised, but not yet clearly manifest, strata of personality is part of the essence of the erotic, it is not absurd to connect this form of authority with erotic attraction.[98] This seems to me a plausible explanation for part of David's success, and perhaps also Caesar's.

This brings us to the concept of charisma, the most enigmatic form of authority. Whereas the previously mentioned forms of individual authority are connected with abilities dealing with means to given ends, pure charisma has to do with demands related to values: the ideal type of charismatic does not so much show the way to an already acknowledged goal, but rather reveals the goal itself, which can be sensed rather than be defined.[99] The lapidary story about Matthew's vocation,[100] which Caravaggio represented in one of the most perfect paintings in European art, stands paradigmatically for this kind of influence: someone obeys unconditionally the mere command, "Follow me," issued by a person whom he has never met before, even if he must thereby give up his position and radically alter his whole way of life. Jesus neither argues nor makes use of rhetorical devices: he lets the magic of his personality produce its effect. But perhaps it is misleading to say that he "lets it produce its effect," for the charismatic often produces such a strong effect precisely because he is not concerned with producing an effect, and because he simply is what others long to be. In actuality, in borderline cases charismatic authority can transcend the sphere of power and influence, because it is completely unaware of itself. This lends it its own attraction, even

---

97. Kent wants to continue serving Lear on the basis of his feeling of feudal loyalty, but he aptly makes the point at issue here when he disguises himself and once again offers Lear his service: "Dost thou know me, fellow?" Lear asks. "No, sir," Kent replies, "but you have that in your countenance which I would fain call master" (*King Lear* act 1, sc. 4).

98. Thus this is a form of power, if it has an asymmetrical effect and is consciously used, whether to attain specific goals or simply to enjoy the dependency of the other; and since true love is opposed to power, few things are more immoral than merely playing with the person, male or female, who feels this erotic attraction, knowing that the relationship will never become symmetrical.

99. Thus what Freund (1965), 146, says about the usual leader does not apply to the charismatic: "Le guide conduit ses compagnons là où ceux-ci ont choisi et décidé d'aller; ils ne se fient à lui que parce qu'il connait le chemin." ("The guide leads his companions where they have chosen and decided to go; they entrust themselves to him only because he knows the way").

100. Matthew 9:9.

if it is unlikely, of course, that the charismatic will go for a long time without noticing his own special abilities. Charisma challenges the old order; by its very nature, it is connected with new moral demands. Naturally, the sense for charisma may not be wholly groundless; but in any event it is not, as in non-charismatic forms of authority, the fact of having been tested by the past that legitimates charisma. To that extent one can certainly say that charisma is ultimately grounded in the mystery of personality. Through certain ways of acting, words, and gestures the charismatic convinces those who believe in him that he has access to a spiritual world for which they, dissatisfied with their own time, have long yearned in a vague way without being able to find it. Even if the charismatic is characterized by the fact that he sets his own standard, which, although adopted by others, is not derived from others, it goes without saying that his subjectivity expresses something still more general than the norms handed down by tradition. Something divine seems to be at work within him, even if this feeling was only once in all history expressed in the assertion that the charismatic was the one God become man. Whether the charismatic is a moral genius, a charlatan whose authority collapses like a house of cards the first time he is defeated, or even a criminal grotesquely transfigured by the need for role models, only history—or, more precisely, the rational reconstructability of his demands in a later period—will show. However important this test is, it would be naive to believe that moral revolutions have been set in motion by rational arguments alone: as a rule, the latter limp along behind charismatic leaders. Socrates' charisma, though, seems to have been based on the impression that the pleasure and strength of arguing were embodied, so to speak, in this man; but this kind of charisma is conceivable only in Greek culture, and even there it was accessible only to an elite circle. Nonetheless, even this charisma is not completely comprehensible without the sacrifice of the charismatic's life, which was the price of that pleasure.

It is self-evident that the charismatic can exercise a terrible power by granting and refusing recognition; the withdrawal of his recognition can be more feared than death. Nevertheless, here we are not concerned with positive and negative sanctions in the sense defined above. For pleasure and pain affect only my outer self; the judgment of a great person affects me because I know he is right. If I notice that the charismatic makes use of his authority in an immoral way, I am freed from his influence; on the other hand, when he himself suffers because he must reject me, his judgment is all the more terrible, because it is more objective. In such cases the dependency of the influence-subject can result in a will to annihilate, whose consequences the greatest moral charismatics often have to bear. The humiliation signified by an asymmetrical love (in which power and its overcoming are bound together in a dreadful manner, and which can give rise to the most ambivalent feelings of which humans are capable), the feeling of shame which the superiority of the other elicits, and the destruction of autonomy that results from any great admiration can sometimes be overcome only through a violent emancipation, perhaps through betrayal. These dark connections are already adumbrated in Alcibiades' speech in Plato's *Symposium*.[101] The honest Thomas More's inability to share Henry VIII's notorious "scruples of conscience" cost him his head.[102] It seems arguable to me that Judas betrayed Jesus because he was deeply humiliated by his moral perfection; and Jesus probably understood this betrayal and felt deep compassion for Judas. Dostoyevsky's transformation of the person kissed into the person kissing has a profound meaning.

The discussion of the manifold forms of power and influence is now complete. We will still see how in *domination* they combine in complex ways—only their mixture can achieve the stability that political domination requires. Since one of the greatest works of art ever devoted to the problem of politics summarizes and orders in a penetrating scene the previously mentioned shapes taken by power, let us conclude this section by describing it. The tensest scene in John Ford's *Young Mr. Lincoln* is the one in which the young lawyer, who has already played the role of the third party between two rival groups on several occasions, prevents the lynching of the two brothers who seem to be responsible for a murder and have just been taken to prison. The excited mob tries to storm the building, in front of which Lincoln stands alone to protect it. The overcoming of the form of sociality called "the mob" is the first act of the political—only if this regression to an animal, pre-rational condition is warded off and a plurality of responsible individuals emerges, can we speak meaningfully of politics.[103] Breaking this spell requires first of all courage. Thus Lincoln has first to use all his physical strength to fend off the aggressive mob. This force (or rather counterforce), which cannot be successful for long, is followed by speaking to the crowd, that is, threatening it. Thus Lincoln first challenges one of the mob, whose weakness he knows, to fight him one-on-one. On one hand, he thereby moves beyond the level of acts of violence and, on the other, by using individualization, that of the mob. Then he restrains the populace by a speech that conceals his own design; force and threat are followed by ruse. His speech does not lack humor and thereby suggests a collective identity that includes both himself and his opponents. Only after their murderous frenzy has ebbed does he begin to argue rationally: he shows the calmed crowd that it would hardly be in their interest to lynch men who have not yet been sentenced by a court; the same thing could happen to them someday. This part of his speech is partially an appeal to rational self-interest and partially a genuinely moral argument. Finally, he calls one man out of the crowd and reminds him of

---

101. Cf. esp. 215e–216c.

102. In his play, R. Bolt aptly showed how it was precisely More's moral incorruptibility that led insecure characters (especially Rich) to beg for his recognition and—when it was refused them on good grounds and in a polite manner—to become his deadly enemies.

103. Cf. also the thirteenth chapter of Manzoni's *I Promessi sposi* (1973; 1057 ff.), where Ferrer saves the vicar from the wild crowd, which he calms down through a ruse. He gets the vicar away from the crowd, which is eager to lynch him, by saying that he wants to take him to prison and punish him there—adding softly and in Spanish, "*si es culpable*" (1061, 1064). On the phenomenology of the forms of the mass, which are partly a result of basic organic functions, see Canetti's classic work (1960).

the biblical commandments that he appeals to on Sundays. Force, threat, ruse, manipulation, persuading, convincing—all these would produce no effect if Lincoln's personality did not stand behind them all, his fearless putting his own life on the line for what he considers right. No other work of art has shown more succinctly what makes a political hero than has this scene in Ford's film.

5.2. POLITICAL MAN AND HIS MAXIMS[104]

The expression "political man" (*Machtmensch*) will be used in at least two senses. First, we can reserve the predicate for those who seek power for its own sake, and indeed for those for whom the achievement of power is the highest or even the only good; in the following pages such persons will be called "power-obsessed."[105] Second, we may also call "political men" those who manifest a mode of behavior that favors the attainment of positions of power—partly because they have an instinctive feeling for it, and partly because they consciously observe the necessary rules of behavior. Obviously, even if they intersect to a large degree, the range of the two concepts is not coextensive: one may be consumed by a desire for a position of power without succeeding in attaining it, or one may have a natural talent for acquiring such a position but may either be interested in doing so only insofar as it is necessary in order to achieve certain goals, or may even reject the whole sphere of power. The latter is not common, since as a rule one likes that in which one has experienced success, but it is neither conceptually nor empirically impossible that a person with cratic talent might prefer to develop other abilities. The opposite disposition—that is, an unconditional striving to acquire power—is not the best for acquiring positions of power either, because the lust for power often has a negative effect on others and triggers countermeasures. In normal situations, the person most likely to attain power is presumably one who possesses the necessary cratic abilities but neither seeks power for its own sake (or at least does not do so too obviously) nor appropriates cratic knowledge through theoretical efforts, but rather has taken it in, as it were, with his mother's milk—that is, one who has not himself dealt with the problem of power intensively and consciously.[106] When Caesar's death cata-

---

104. Since the highest form of power is political power, the political man (*Machtmensch*) is usually interested in political power. Many of the following observations therefore presuppose categories that will be developed only in later chapters; but what is of interest here is the pure power aspect, which is more abstract and more general than the categories of the political.

105. This corresponds to the human type A. Spranger calls "Machtmensch," and that H. D. Lasswell and A. Kaplan (1969; 78) call "homo politicus": "The *political man* (homo politicus) is one who demands the maximization of his power in relation to all his values, who expects power to determine power, and who identifies with others as a means of enhancing power position and potential." This is supposed to be an idealization comparable to that of the homo oeconomicus.

106. I hypothesize that certain cratic skills are instilled in early childhood; the children of princes often acquire them by unreflectively observing their parents' dealings with subordinates.

pulted the nineteen-year-old Octavian into an enormous responsibility and position of power, he could manage only because, like a tightrope walker, he was able to act in a way appropriate to the situation without too much reflection—we could even speak of a cratic grace had it not been connected with bloodshed and executions. And yet, from a purely formal point of view, one is struck by Octavian's laconic use of the one terrible word, "moriendum," in refusing his opponents' pleas for mercy[107] and by the quick decisiveness with which it was pronounced, impressively deviating from the wordy rhetoric of Cicero—who, foolishly overestimating himself, imagined that he could use and then get rid of Octavian, whose instinct for power was vastly superior. Cicero's pun on the different meanings of "tollere" (to elevate; to get rid of) in the phrase "laudandum adulescentem, ornandum, tollendum" was a rhetorical, not a cratic, performance, if only because Cicero made his maxim known, apparently out of joy in his own linguistic ability, even though doing so made it harder to translate it into actual politics. Octavian immediately let him know that he was quite capable of seeing to it that he was not gotten rid of. And he kept his word.[108]

5.2.1. On the Psychology of the Striving for Power

Why do people strive to gain power (and in any case to retain the power they have)? The simplest case is that in which someone is interested in a position of power only because it is connected with a handsome salary, job security, and a certain social prestige. Had this combination been available in another, similarly accessible social sphere, the person involved might just as well have become a leading employee in a department store as the assistant head of a government department. The so-called "apparatchiks" are recruited among such people, who may occasionally derive additional motivation from being able to obey and not needing to make any decisions for which they themselves bear responsibility. For them, it is deeply satisfying to carry out commands, and if as a result of promotions they themselves are put in a situation where they have to give commands, then they always do as was usually done before. Moreover, power can be a means of achieving certain goals. A far-reaching position of political power is often indispensable, especially if goals are involved that affect many people, independently of whether these goals are moral or criminal. Under the conditions of a modern state founded on the rule of law, a bloodthirsty private individual has to be content with killing a few dozen of his fellow men; then an end will be put to his activities. In order to carry out a genocide, he must seek political power, because only the latter allows the legal use of force. Much the same holds for noble goals. A private individual may emancipate

---

107. Cf. Suetonius, *Augustus* 15: "orare venium vel excusare se conantibus una voce occurens moriendum esse."

108. Cf. Cicero, *Ad fam.* XI 20, 1 (from a letter of D. Brutus).

his slaves and perhaps, if he is wealthy, buy the freedom of a few more; but as a private individual, he cannot abolish slavery in his country. To do that, he must hold an influential position in his country's legislature. However, in some cases the goal that motivates the striving for supreme power is elementary—pure self-preservation, for instance. It is precisely the person who has used power in a violent way who must fear that the injustice that he has committed will be avenged if he gives up power;[109] and there are certainly situations in which not the preservation but the attainment of the supreme power is absolutely necessary if one wants to survive. Even if Octavian had remained in private life in 44 B.C., his situation would probably have been dangerous; the aura attributed to him as Caesar's heir would have imperiled his opponents even if he had been a cratic zero, because he could have been used by third parties, and his heirs at least might have been capable of exercising power. Thus someone may fight for very extensive, comprehensive, and intensive power in order to achieve ambitious goals, but in some cases just to avoid being killed. Indeed, others' fear that a certain person might seek the supreme power can certainly frighten that person himself and force him, as it were, to try to seize power in order to defend himself against the dreaded fear reactions of others—that is, this kind of fear can become a self-fulfilling prophecy.[110] Since hardly anyone challenges the right to self-preservation, it is not surprising that those in power often appeal not only to noble goals, but also to the peril to their lives, even if there is no such peril or if they themselves bear the responsibility for the fact that their lives are no longer secure. Indeed, perhaps it is precisely the desire to spur oneself to the greatest achievements that gets the political man into a situation from which there is no way out. Presumably Caesar breathed more easily when, after he had crossed the Rubicon, the die was cast and there were finally no alternatives other than sole dominion or death: the temptation to wait and to hesitate had been overcome once and for all.

However, precisely the example of someone who gets himself into a situation in which he needs a position of far-reaching power in order to defend his own life suggests the hypothesis that power is not being sought solely as a means. We have already said that power, like money, can become a general title to wish fulfillment. Certainly, in such a case power is no longer a concrete means to a concrete end; indeed, perhaps no one knows any longer what it should be used for, but it is still a means. And even in a case in which the striving for power continues to drive someone even after he has attained all his goals, it can sometimes be said that he is concerned not so much with power as with the continuation of an activity that has become second nature, so to speak, and whose cessation would result, because of a lack of contemplative abilities, in a terrible emptiness— a phenomenon that is known to us from other activities, and that is not peculiar to the

---

109. According to Suetonius (28), this was one of the two reasons why Augustus, on both occasions when he toyed with the idea of giving up power, decided not to do so. (The other reason had to do with his concern for the state.) In Thucydides (II 63), the same argument does not allow Pericles to see any alternative to pursuing further Athenian power politics.

110. Cf. Machiavelli, *Discorsi* III 33 (1984; 131 ff.).

striving for power. Much the same occurs when someone seeks positions of power merely out of vanity. Just as someone may become a minister in a corrupt government because it offers an opportunity to enrich himself, so may someone want to become an ambassador because it pleases him to be addressed as "Your Excellency." And yet even in this case the power position is not an end in itself—it serves to satisfy vanity, or perhaps the fulfillment of wishes that the public recognition of one's position makes easier; what matters is the perception of the splendor of one's own standing in the reactions of others. Insofar as prestige is a source of power in the broader sense, it is also of interest to the truly power-obsessed, yet always only as a means; the thirst for prestige, which harms no one, so long as nobody disturbs the self-enjoyment connected with it, must therefore be sharply distinguished from genuine striving for power. A person who seeks prestige will always prefer a position that is higher from the point of view of protocol to one that is lower, but the power-obsessed will do so only if it is connected with greater responsibility and decision-making authority. Where this is not the case—as in many political systems in which, for instance, the head of state is only a figurehead—the power-obsessed person will on the contrary tend to leave positions that involve merely formal standing to others, and concentrate on the real positions of power.[111] Indeed, under certain circumstances, through the force of his personality he will even succeed in making a second-rate position (such as the general secretaryship of a political party's central committee) into a decisive one.

It is characteristic of the power-obsessed person that he enjoys imposing his own will against that of another person or many other persons as an end in itself and quite independently of the issues involved. It goes without saying that he conceals this enjoyment from others, and often from himself; but the unprejudiced observation of people forces us to recognize that it exists, no matter how painful the duty to be intellectually honest may be in this case. In the importance of the *Me* for a stable identity lies the deeper ground for this enjoyment, and in analyzing struggles we have already seen that, in addition to imposing interests and values, the desire to be recognized as an individual is a driving force. Yet the usual struggle for recognition, as it is commonly conducted by young people or as it is sometimes triggered by an encounter with a stranger, is always also about gaining knowledge of oneself or others; and this curiosity is as a rule intertwined with the wish that the other recognize the values with which one identifies or the interests that one has. Yet, there are certainly cases in which this kind of wish is only a pretext, and the point is simply to subordinate the other's will to one's own, even in the

---

111. Naturally, this kind of decision may be made not only by the power-obsessed, but also by goal-oriented politicians. In his political testament of 1752, for instance, Frederick the Great speaks only condescendingly about the possibility of attaining the title of emperor: "Un roi de Prusse doit plutôt s'efforcer d'acquérir une province que se décorer d'un vain titre; . . . il ne vous est permis de sacrifier à la vanité qu'après avoir solidement établi votre puissance." ("A king of Prussia should seek to acquire a province rather than to adorn himself with an empty title; . . . you are allowed to sacrifice to vanity only after having firmly established your power.")

tiniest details, without any information for oneself, the other, or third parties resulting from this struggle—that is, cases in which the driving concern is to feel the inferiority, dependency, and fear of others. Caligula, for example, once began laughing during a banquet, and when the consuls sitting next to him asked why he was deigning to laugh, he answered, "For what reason other than the fact that all I have to do is wave my hand in order to have your heads cut off?"[112] It is this attitude that we call "tyrannical," and which is to be found, even if provided with fewer bases of power, no less in private than in public contexts. It is also tyrannical when one does something for another person to which the latter has a right, but represents it as if it were an act of kindness or a favor; for not only individual misdeeds are tyrannical, but also the attitude that sees in the rights of others not a moral limitation on one's own arbitrary will, but rather only a concession one makes.[113]

The observation of tyrannical ways of behaving in dual relationships, in which both partners sometimes sink their teeth into each other, so to speak, suggests the hypothesis that one source of tyrannical behavior is that the person involved is not worthy of being loved and is incapable of loving. For instance, a person who in his childhood was denied the experience of being unconditionally accepted, or who has never been loved by another, or who was never allowed to experience his own private will as an accident of a deeper common will may seek to compensate for this and other frustrating experiences of his own inferiority by trying to impose his will—to which no one has ever voluntarily and willingly responded—on other people, and especially on those who elicit his ressentiment. Precisely because he cannot love, that is, cannot recognize values in reality, the latter seems to him a mere object that he can treat arbitrarily, in the firm belief that he is allowed to do whatever he wishes, and even finally destroy it. Conversely, the fulfillment of all a person's wishes because of the weakness of those around him also predisposes him to tyrannical tendencies, and there is much to be said for the hypothesis that the alternation of spoiling, weakness, and loveless coldness in childhood is the ideal seedbed for tyranny. So far as the previously mentioned compensatory mechanism is concerned, Shakespeare, with deep psychological insight, makes the obsession with power on the part of his greatest villain, Richard III, arise from his disappointment that his crippled nature does not allow any woman to fall in love with him: "And am I then a man to be beloved? / O monstrous fault, to harbour such a thought! / Then, since this earth affords no joy to me / But to command, to check, to o'erbear such / As are of better person than myself, / I'll make my heaven to dream upon the crown, / And, whiles I live, t'account this world but hell, / Until my misshaped trunk that bears this head / Be round impaled with a glorious crown."[114] Similarly, Richard Wagner connects the possession of the ring of the Nibelungs with the refusal of love:

---

112. Suetonius, *Caligula* 32. Whether or not the anecdote is a later invention does not matter here; in any case, Suetonius's Caligula is the ideal type of the tyrant.

113. Cf. also Montesquieu (1734), 116.

114. *Henry VI,* Part 3, act 3, sc. 2, vv. 163 ff.

"Nur Einen sah ich, / der sagte der Liebe ab; / um rotes Gold / entriet er des Weibes Gunst," Loge sings,[115] adding as an explanation that Alberich's renunciation of love springs from his vain effort to win the Rhine maidens. It is hardly an accident that of the two most successful of the power-obsessed men of the twentieth century, one was still unmarried shortly before his death, and the other was left alone when his wife committed suicide; Stalin's second wife Nadezhda Allilueva took her own life in 1932 after a political conflict with her husband over the situation in the country, which nonetheless had the result that Stalin, for the last time before his death, offered to resign at one of the next Politburo meetings. However repellent any tyrant is, one thing is clear: this kind of person is never happy, even and especially when his life is crowned only with successes.[116] Generous souls will not withhold pity even from him.

Certainly, frustrating experiences with love (and not only with erotic love, but also with parental love and love among siblings) are not the only cause for the will to power. The striving for power is certainly incompatible with that finer form of dependency that we call "love"; indeed, we can even say that the will to power and love are two mutually exclusive basic types of intersubjective relationships, because power is characterized by asymmetry, whereas fulfilled love is characterized by symmetry. But this striving need not always be caused by a lack of the ability to love, but can instead have the latter as its result, and be itself rooted in a wrongly understood concept of freedom. Thus there is hardly any doubt that the "Eritis sicut Deus" with which the serpent awakens the desire to know can also be satisfied by possessing positions of power.[117] Precisely the Judeo-Christian God, who does not, like Aristotle's god, merely dedicate himself to *theoria*, but is the creator of the world, might best be imitated by a single person undertaking to control the social world, and perhaps to transform it or even create it anew. If the world is a stage and God is its director, then the characters in these dramas (which might be called "directors' dramas") who hold in their hands the strings that control the other characters' movements, may well feel similar to God. Vincentio in Shakespeare's *Measure for Measure* and Prospero in *The Tempest* fulfill a quasi-divine function; and the fact that they enjoy this even independently of the restoration of law they achieve thanks to their roles cannot escape the attentive reader. (Nevertheless, the duke remains human through his love for Isabella, and Prospero through his fatherly inclination toward Miranda and his final renunciation of power. The great tyrant in Werner Bergengruen's novel, on the other hand, no longer has anything human about him—and he is, typically, unmarried.) To be sure, the wish for absolute power can emerge especially in a situation in which the only alternative seems to be to become dependent on others; the person who was an anvil will want to become a hammer, if that is the only way to overcome his fate, or to satisfy his thirst for revenge. But, more generally, the will to power, as an expression of the

115. R. Wagner (1978), 544.

116. Plato saw this better than anyone else (*Republic* 577c ff.).

117. In Augustine's *De civitate Dei* XIX 12 we read, "Sic enim superbia perverse imitatur Deum." ("Thus pride imitates God in a perverse way.") See also *De vera religione* 45, 84.

striving for unconditional autonomy, is grounded in the special position of man and in his characteristic relationship to the absolute. Certainly it is illusory to hope that as power-holder one will have unlimited freedom: the objective constraints to which one is exposed if one wants to remain in power, and the counterreactions of others, sharply restrict one's scope of action. When power-holders nostalgically evoke the quiet happiness of ordinary people,[118] this is not a mere cliché, but can be felt very deeply, even if they themselves may have smiled at this topos at the beginning of their career. In any case, the will to be exclusively active and not passive, self-determined and not determined by others, is in itself something that ennobles human beings—but striving for power is hardly the right way to do justice to the demand for autonomy. Even in the case of the mastery over nature that modern natural science and technology have achieved in such an eerie way, the question arises: What is the source of the content of human desire? If it is set by natural drives, then the victory over nature is in reality a victory of nature over man, since then it has programmed him to deal with nature in a certain way. Freedom in the full sense of the term exists more in a situation in which man rises above the tyranny of causes to contemplate reasons in the pure sphere of validities than in one in which he succeeds in satisfying heteronomously induced desires. Indeed, out of shame at the mere naturalness of his own drives man can strive toward the highest success in satisfying them, in order to compensate for the substantively inferior through a triumph in the formal. The power-obsessed person's claim to freedom may analogously arise from the feeling of not being free in his needs, but rather dependent on various psychic and social contingencies—of being dominated by the drive to power.[119] Therefore, a nearly omnipotent tyrant would never be able to become like God, whereas the ascetic, who determines his wishes autonomously and limits them to what is morally permissible, can make a far greater claim to be the image of God.[120] For striving to be an image of God is absolutely legitimate—but not the striving for that quality of God—his omnipotence—which can be beneficent only when it is combined with omniscience and perfect goodness, which are fundamentally denied to man.

The difference between the usual tyrant and the power-obsessed person of the second type, who wants to be like God, can be discerned in the fact that for the former it is extraordinarily important that his power be recognized by inferiors, whereas the latter (who likes to play the role of the *éminence grise*) has no objection to power subjects imagining that they are independent, if he himself sees through their illusion. On the contrary: because of his autistic traits and his incapacity for communal behavior, he may

---

118. One may think of the second beginning of Euripides' *Iphigenia in Aulis*, Shakespeare's *Henry IV*, Part 2, act 3, sc. 1, and *Henry VI*, Part 3, act 2, sc. 5, or Schiller's *Die Braut von Messina*, vv. 2561 ff.

119. Cf. Augustine, *De civitate Dei*, end of the preface to the first book: "de terrena civitate, quae cum dominari adpetit, . . . ipsa ei dominandi libido dominatur." ("of the earthly city, which, though seeking to rule . . . is ruled by its lust to rule itself.") Cf. XIX 15.

120. It goes without saying that the voluntarist concept of God, which makes of God an omnipotent tyrant, is intellectually untenable and morally repellent.

get special enjoyment out of the fact that people are unaware of his power. The popularity of the genre of the spy novel and the sometimes almost grotesque overestimation of the power of the secret services in the modern world indicate that the second type of power-obsessed person has a special attraction for our age. Presumably because the latter has become, on account of its extreme individualism, increasingly incapable of experiences of community, the mysterious person who pulls the strings has become a fascinating ideal: as a secularized god, he guarantees the social order. Nevertheless, it will have to be admitted that he is less ordinary than the first type—if he could exist in pure form. In reality, it is highly unlikely that he would not reveal the truth at least to a person close to him (who would, however, have to be at the same time a subordinate if the power-holder were himself almost omnipotent): for the longing for intersubjectivity is ineradicable in human beings.[121] Typically, many of these spy novels—including, and especially, the literarily demanding ones such as those of Le Carré—derive their life from the tension between the hero's isolation and his erotic entanglements, between the burden of his secret and the pressure to reveal it. Someone who would be content with his own knowledge of his power would have to be virtually a god himself—and indeed a god different from the triune God of Christian tradition.

In fact, we discern here a fundamental tension, even a contradiction, within the essence of the power-obsessed person. On one hand, it is counterproductive if the latter acknowledges from the outset that he is concerned only with power. The ideological expense involved in justifying one's own use of power is always considerable and can never be reduced to the indication that the power-holder simply enjoys exercising power. (It would be conceivable at most that the power-holder enjoys exercising power as a representative for all those on whom his power depends and who symbolically participate in the increase in power that the concentration of power in the hands of a single person entails.) Indeed, the drive to justify one's power in the eyes of others and, depending on one's character, also in one's own eyes produces the most absurd theories; and however much the need for legitimation may sometimes set limits to the will to power, ideology in the service of the power-holder is seldom overtaxed when it is a question of finding some reason for committing crimes. Indeed, since not everyone has the courage and energy to be openly cynical, the power-holder and his ideologues may succeed in persuading themselves and each other that their ideological pretexts are objectively justified: Henry VIII may have finally felt genuine scruples because of his marriage with Catherine of Aragon, because feeling them was required to retain his self-respect— even if his hatred for More indicates that at the bottom of his soul he did not believe that these scruples were sincere.[122] The fact that Papinian paid with his life for his refusal

---

121. The need to talk about one's own guilt, even if doing so puts one in danger, was unsurpassably represented in Dostoyevsky's *Crime and Punishment*.

122. In Shakespeare's *Henry VIII* it remains an open question of whether the king is consciously or only unconsciously hypocritical—presumably the latter, since otherwise his shamelessness would be too great. However, even a hypocrisy that is not a function of conscious deception but

to justify the murder of Geta by his brother and co-emperor Caracalla[123] is remembered because it is an exception to the rule; in general, Kant's statement is valid: "You can expect anything from a rationalizing animal."[124] And yet, on the other hand, the more intelligent power-holder who is also more honest with himself sees the arbitrariness of his ideology—since he thinks *sub specie potestatis,* he can scarcely help but reject claims to truth that seek to be more than functions of power interests. Indeed, if what drives him is the pure will to power, then he can only reject the idea of truth in itself and has to regard truth as something he has posited, as a product of his freedom. If moreover he is edified by the perception of the dependency of others on himself, he will not be able to avoid dropping the veil occasionally; he will derive a special enjoyment from the fact that the victim has to acknowledge that his tormentor himself does not believe in his own ideology, does not feel bound to it, but is merely playing with it. At the end of all three of the great dystopias of our century there is an encounter between the power-holder—the so-called benefactor, Mustapha Mond, and O'Brien—and those who revolt against the system, and even if only O'Brien openly acknowledges the drive to power as an end in itself, all three power-holders enjoy talking with people who are capable of questioning the state ideology. They ultimately prefer them to the masses, who do not question the ideology because of sheer stupidity.

5.2.2. The Ambivalence of Cratology

However, it is precisely this problem area that presents a fundamental paradox. On one hand, the logic of the obsession with power requires that one's own ideology be interpreted as a mere means and its claim to truth be rejected. Anyone who is not prepared to do this is to that extent not obsessed with power in the strict sense of the word, since he recognizes the existence of other values—for instance, truth—alongside that of power. On the other hand, the final step taken by the person obsessed with power—liberating himself not only from any respect for his fellow men but also from his own ideology— is playing with fire, for his power absolutely depends upon the ideology being believed by others, and their belief is deeply influenced by their perception of the power-holder's attitude toward it. Just as a child subliminally notices whether his parents, with whom he attends church service, are internally present or are merely carrying out a conventional act, so a population senses whether the ideology that justifies domination is taken

---

rather of hormones remains repellent; in any case, one can only find it funny when this man obsessed by the sex drive and the drive to power appeals to his conscience: "Would it not grieve an able man to leave / So sweet a bedfellow? But conscience, conscience! / O, 'tis a tender place, and I must leave her" (act 2, sc. 2, vv. 141 ff.); cf. act 2, sc. 4, vv. 165 ff.

123. Cf. *Historia Augusta,* "Caracalla" 8, where this description is, however, only one of various versions of the background of Papinian's execution.

124. Reflection no. 1521: "Von einem Thier, das Vernünftelt, kan man alles besorgen" (1923; 891).

seriously by the power-holders. In the long run, the smiling wink with which the high priests of ideology greet each other cannot escape the dominated, and even if they do not notice it, the emptiness of declamations that are not backed by belief inevitably becomes obvious in time. Therefore, one can say that as a rule the person who is obsessed with power will not be cratically more successful than one who believes in the ideology on which his power is based, even if he achieves this only through mechanisms of self-deception and of the *sacrificium intellectus*. Here we are touching on the secret of the power of the Catholic church, which extends over centuries and continents, whereas those ideologies that sought power and only power in the *intentio recta*, as it were, have never lasted long, even if they had the most terrible bases of power. Franco did not have the almost animalistic will to power of a Mussolini or a Hitler; his ideology was much more closely related to the traditional mores of his people than the far more innovative ideology of the other two dictators, and set limits to the more unrestrained use of cratic techniques; that was one of the reasons he was able to remain in power longer than they did. Anyone who wants to exercise a position of power within a given social system is cratologically well-advised to be guided by the factual mores—and even to believe in them. To be sure, in the will to power it is precisely the element vying with the divine power to create that so easily transforms the amorality of the cratic standpoint into a conscious violation of the moral—breaking free from traditional mores, and indeed from the moral and from truth as such, is seen as the loftiest expression of the unbridled freedom the power-obsessed person longs for, even if in so doing he is digging his own grave.

The paradox in the striving for power just described is based on the contradiction between the asymmetry of the power relationship and the impossibility of going beyond communication, between the instrumentalization of everything that can bind people together and the inextinguishable wish to be recognized by others as the person that one is. This contradiction results in a peculiar characteristic of the discipline that investigates the maxims of the successful use of power, that is, cratology: its rules, if made public, are double-edged, so that they would ultimately have to be kept secret by those obsessed with power. For instance, Machiavelli's famous discussion of conspiracies can be useful to both camps—both to the conspirators and to those who want to protect themselves from conspiracies;[125] the cratologist is the classical servant of two masters. Hence it is thoroughly comprehensible that *Il Principe* has also been interpreted as a work that was intended to warn the people against the wickedness of tyrants.[126] However historically false this interpretation is, it is an essential truth that the revelation of

---

125. Cf. *Discorsi* III 6 (1984; 471 ff.). See also the express observation in I 40.2 (1984; 147). It is typical that the same ambivalence holds for the *Kauṭilīya-Arthaśāstra:* At the end of the eleventh book, which deals with the king's policy with regard to oligarchies, we read that the king should use the previously mentioned tactics against oligarchies, and that the oligarchies should protect themselves against them (11.1.54 f.); cf. also 1.20.3.

126. Among many other others, see Spinoza, *Tractatus politicus* 5.7, and Rousseau, *Contrat social* III 6 (1975; 284).

certain maxims constitutes a horizon of symmetry that is not incompatible with taking sides in a power struggle; and it is also correct that most of the tactics Machiavelli discusses were already known to rulers before his treatise; at least they were better known to them than to the ruled. To this extent one can certainly concede that Machiavelli strengthened de facto the side of the dominated; and Carl Schmitt's witticism makes an important point, namely, that if Machiavelli had been really Machiavellian, he would have written, instead of *Il Principe,* a book full of moving and edifying precepts[127]—if one wanted to be malicious, one could add: like Frederick II's *Antimachiavel.*[128] Conversely, such a resolutely liberal work as Maurice Joly's *Dialogue aux enfers entre Machiavel et Montesquieu*—which reveals with great literary wit and political acuity the strategies of Napoleon III's plebiscitary dictatorship—ended up providing the basis for one of the most infamous forgeries of all time, the *Protocols of the Learned Elders of Zion.* In this text, Machiavelli's recommendations in Joly's work are frequently reproduced verbatim and presented as the means of an alleged Jewish plan for establishing world domination— the shamelessness of the anti-Semitic forgers being manifest in their attributing to their opponents tactics such as deception that they use themselves. It is possible that the people who produced this concoction even believed in part what they wrote—we have already discussed the importance of mechanisms of projection. In actuality, almost every person obsessed with power, in order to justify his own behavior, is convinced that his fellow men are also concerned only with power, and that he must protect himself against them—if he cannot subjugate them, they will subjugate him. A pessimistic anthropology, which becomes a partly self-fulfilling prophecy, is part of the standard ideology of every person obsessed with power—though this does not mean that a Rousseauistic anthropology would come any closer to the truth.

However, the ambivalence of cratological techniques lies even deeper. Not only can both sides reckon with them; one side can also know that the other side counts on a certain trick being used: on the basis of the familiarity of a given trick one can make use of a meta-trick and exploit the naive wiliness, so to speak, of the other, who thinks he has seen through one's own trick.[129] Murders camouflaged as suicides are common; but psy-

---

127. (1927), 65.

128. This is not meant to suggest that Frederick was a conscious hypocrite. But as crown prince he did not sufficiently consider the objective constraints of politics and the questionable sides of his own personality.

129. Cf. Gracián, *Oráculo manual,* 13. Therefore, Machiavelli advises the assumption that an obvious mistake (for instance, in using a ruse) conceals another (higher-level) ruse: *Discorsi* III 48 (1984; 570 f.). In philology, this ambivalence has the consequence that many arguments for considering a text to be a forgery are double-edged: for instance, to mention one of the most famous problems in Latin studies, if someone discovers prominent characteristics of Sallust's style in the two letters to Caesar attributed to Sallust, it is objected that "the more they look like Sallust, the less authentic they are"; on the other hand, if one points out the problematic passages—for instance, the "liberis" in II, 7, 3— the supporters of authenticity will reply that this is too foolish an error to be committed by an otherwise so talented rhetorician; the passage must be interpreted differently than it usually is; indeed, it proves that the letter is authentic.

chopaths in search of recognition are also capable of presenting suicides as murders. A particularly clever murder would thus be one that was disguised as a suicide that wanted to seem to be a murder—that would, like a picture puzzle, confuse the public for years, especially if the intrigue of the deceased, whose discovery might have led the person to commit suicide, may have been instigated by an *agent provocateur* working for the other side. The choice of ruse or meta-ruse cannot follow simple rules if it is to be unfathomable. Game theory has shown us that in such cases the use of a chance device, that is, playing a so-called mixed strategy, can be most effective.[130] Sometimes the greatest subtlety consists precisely in proceeding in an exceptionally simple and open way, because that is the last thing the other expects. In Poe's masterpiece, *The Purloined Letter,* the minister proves superior to the prefect because he places the letter so diligently sought precisely where it is the easiest to find and where it is least expected. Only Dupin, who is familiar with the enigmatic and ambiguous nature of the minister, who is no less a poet than a mathematician, is able to see through him. Whereas Poe's minister is particularly subtle, the hero of Grillparzer's play *Weh dem, der lügt* (*Woe to Him Who Lies*) succeeds because he constantly tells the truth—simply, and thus without any ulterior intention—even when it is not in his own interest to do so. Yet, precisely because it is clear that this is not in his own interest, other people find it impossible to believe him.[131]

Finally, the multi-leveled nature of strategies is described in an unsurpassable way in Le Carré's *The Spy Who Came In from the Cold.* The British agent Leamas defects to the Eastern bloc, but in reality his superior—"Control"—has ordered him to defect, and it is only a trick intended to incriminate an extremely dangerous East German agent, Mundt, and to bring about his downfall. But in the course of the this agent's trial, which takes place in East Germany, the judges recognize, on the basis of various discrepancies, that Leamas is a false defector—while Leamas understands that his boss wanted to produce precisely this view. Mundt is rehabilitated, and this is just what London headquarters wanted, because this East German agent has long been working for the British, and it has now become possible to eliminate the faithful Communist Fiedler, who had begun to suspect him. Since the plan involves bloodshed and a terrible instrumentalization of one's own agents (not only Fiedler, but also Leamas's Communist lover, Elizabeth Gold, who had been brought into the affair in a revolting way, are shot), the reader has no doubt that it is morally impermissible. But the shifting from one level to another is intellectually stimulating: on the first level, Leamas appears to be a traitor who uncovers a double agent on the other side. On the second level, both he and Mundt appear to be faithful servants of their respective states. On the third level, finally, Mundt proves to be the traitor he already seemed to be on the first level, but Leamas himself turns out

---

130. Intuitively, that was understood early on; cf. Frederick the Great (1920), 51.

131. Cf. La Rochefoucauld, Maxims 127 and 129 (1967; 34): "Le vrai moyen d'être trompé, c'est de se croire plus fin que les autres." ("The best way to be deceived is to think oneself more clever than others.") "Il suffit quelquefois d'être grossier pour n'être pas trompé par un habile homme." ("To avoid being deceived by a clever man, it sometimes suffices to be crude.")

to be betrayed. The most expressive image of the labyrinth constituted by such a shifting of levels is the endless reflections in two mirrors that face each other, which make it impossible to tell reality from mirror image; in fact, in Orson Welles's classic film *The Lady from Shanghai,* the complicated, Chinese-boxes story of intrigue and love ends in a mirrored room, in which only shooting out the various mirrors produces ultimate clarity.[132]

5.2.3. The Logic of Power

If in the following pages certain cratological rules are developed that are in large part connected with the more general discussions in chapter 5.1, it is clear on the basis of what has been said that, first of all, they are guided by a purely theoretical interest, and not the intention to offer advice to any side in a power struggle, and therefore, second, that they do not promote the view that striving for power for power's sake is morally respectable—quite the contrary. Anyone who sees reality exclusively through cratological categories is thoroughly contemptible. However, the political man (unlike the power-obsessed) is not necessarily morally bad: there can be situations in which it is legitimate to seek power, and since in such situations the person who knows the relevant rules has advantages over one who does not know them, a discussion of these rules is morally permissible.[133] To be sure, we want wicked people to be cratically incapable, because then they are less dangerous, and I would be dismayed were the following overview to prove useful to them. But since in our time it is not exactly the powers of evil that suffer from cratic naiveté, such a risk is minimal. Let us once again emphasize that cratic success does not really depend on the theoretical study of cratological textbooks. A political man instinctively follows the relevant rules; a theoretician who has laboriously learned them, but does not know how to apply them, will necessarily fail. Indeed, it is commonly the case that the person best suited to understand cratology theoretically is precisely one who has no ambitions of his own—political men prefer to repress the ugly side of cratology, since being aware of it might restrain their will to power; power struggles can be analyzed in a far more unprejudiced way by melancholy ascetics like Gracián, for instance. Moreover, it is clear that there are few rules that are independent of context: the access to positions of power in a dictatorship requires tactics different from those used in a democracy, and depending on the character of the dictator whose

---

132. The point of the Morgenstern paradox is that perfect foresight on both sides would make strategic action impossible (and that it therefore cannot be a condition of economic equilibrium). O. Morgenstern illustrates this by giving the example of Conan Doyle's story about Sherlock Holmes and his near equal, the master criminal Moriarty (whom Holmes ultimately admires) (1935; 343 f.).

133. It will hardly be found surprising that in this discussion considerable attention will be paid not only to Kauṭilya, Thucydides, Machiavelli, Gracián, Frederick the Great, but also to Shakespeare (although I have tried to systematize them a bit).

support the aspirant to power needs, in different dictatorships very different behaviors may prove necessary. Still greater are the differences depending on the forms of power concerned: only in military and political conflicts, and not in economic and ideological ones that take place within the framework of a state monopoly on force, can overcoming the opponent involve killing him. Nonetheless, there are a few generally valid rules on the observation of which success or failure depends, and a few qualities that any power-holder must have. These rules extend to all forms of power; they find their application in a physical power struggle between two commanders as well as in an economic power struggle between two entrepreneurs and in an intellectual power struggle between two thinkers who are fighting to gain a dominant influence over public opinion. Finally, we should note that peculiarities of character usually prevent a person from acting in a cratically optimal way—a brilliant plotter seldom succeeds in resolving conflicts in a way that inspires confidence. In reality, there are also various types of political men, whereas in the following we will be concerned with the ideal crat.

How does one rise to positions of power, and how does one retain them? Even if *attaining* and *retaining* power differ conceptually,[134] in reality they usually merge, so that many maxims are valid for both phases. A minister who wants to become prime minister has to retain his position as minister if he wants to rise higher; and sometimes even one who has the highest power has to try to expand it if he wants to keep it, because stagnation would mean decline—a problem that is familiar to apparently omnipotent dictators, and that often causes their downfall.[135] Nevertheless, it may be useful to deal with the maxims of the aspirant to power[136] and those of the power-holder one after the other—if only because the behavior of most people who have achieved the position of power they sought differs from their behavior before achieving it: power is not always the drug that transforms a decent Dr. Jekyll into the monstrous Mr. Hyde, because many a person grows morally because of the responsibility that he must assume, but it almost always changes the person who exercises it.[137] This is partly self-evident: the power-holder has certain duties and responsibilities that he would fail to meet if after

---

134. This differentiation is already found in the *Kauṭilīya-Arthaśāstra* 1.1.1. It is worth noting that in 1.4.3 the increase of power and its bestowal on others are also described as objects of political science.

135. Cf. Hobbes, *Leviathan* chap. 11 (1651; 161): "So that in the first place, I put for a generall inclination of all mankind, a perpetuall and restlesse desire of Power after power, that ceaseth only in Death. And the cause of this, is not alwayes that a man hopes for a more intensive delight, than he has already attained to; or that he cannot be content with a moderate power: but because he cannot assure the power and means to live well, which he hath present, without the acquisition of more." Joly's Montesquieu says something similar to Machiavelli: "Ce qui ne cesse de m'inquiéter pour vous, c'est que je vous vois toujours obligé de réussir en toutes choses, sous peine d'un désastre" (15th dialogue [1864; 153]). ("What constantly worries me in your case is that you are courting disaster if you do not always succeed in everything.")

136. I use the word *Aufsteiger*, which has a negative connotation in German, purely descriptively here.

137. Cf. already *Kauṭilīya-Arthaśāstra* 7.5.47 and 7.14.2.

taking power he treated others as he did before. Falstaff and his men have to learn that, as king, Henry V adopts a tone different from the one he took as Prince Hal, and Falstaff is dreaming when he hopes the abrupt change in Henry's behavior concerns only public encounters.[138] There is no doubt that Shakespeare also saw in Henry V an ideal monarch because he has his old drinking buddy Bardolph hanged for a church robbery, unmoved by common memories.[139] Machiavelli rightly emphasizes that, before taking power, an ambitious man may be generous, but afterward he usually is not, indeed, should not be, because he is then drawing on public property.[140] Before taking power, it is often counter-productive to show certain character traits or convictions that can certainly be developed after attaining the desired position. Not all promises that are made before rising to power are kept after power is achieved.

It is common for a power-holder suddenly to change the way he treats those who have brought him to power. Shortly before his death, Richard II prophetically tells Northumberland, who has helped the usurper Henry IV seize power, that the time is nigh when he will fall out with the new king: "Northumberland, thou ladder where-withal / The mounting Bolingbroke ascends my throne, / The time shall not be many hours of age / More than it is ere foul sin, gathering head, / Shall break into corruption. Thou shalt think, / Though he divide the realm and give thee half, / It is too little, helping him to all; / He shall think that thou, which knowest the way / To plant unrightful kings, wilt know again, / Being ne'er so little urged, another way / To pluck him headlong from the usurpèd throne. / The love of wicked men converts to fear, / That fear to hate, and hate turns one or both / To worthy danger and deservèd death."[141] Conflicts between king and king-maker[142] are in fact common, especially since under certain circumstances the basis of the king-maker's power can represent a great danger to the king. The king-maker's unjustified expectations of the king or the latter's ingratitude may result in bloody conflicts, although it is often difficult to tell which of the two is the cause. What is most difficult is the case in which the king-maker and the king think in terms of different categories and values, as in the terrible story of Henry II's

---

138. *Henry IV,* Part 2, act 5, sc. 5.

139. *Henry V* act 3, sc. 6, vv. 100 ff.

140. *Principe* 16.3 f. (1986, 150 f.).

141. *Richard II* act 5, sc. 1, vv. 55 ff. Consider also Edward IV and Warwick in *Henry VI,* as well as Machiavelli, *Principe* 3.14 (1986; 97 ff.): "Di che si cava una regola generale, la quale mai o raro falla: che chi è cagione che uno diventi potente, rovina; perché quella potenzia è causata da colui o con industria o con forza, e l'una e l'altra di queste due è sospetta a chi è diventato potente." ("From which may be drawn a general rule, which never or very rarely fails, that whoever is the cause of another becoming powerful is ruined himself; for that power is produced by him either through craft or force; and both of these are suspected by the one who has been raised to power." Trans. Ricci and Vincent, 14.)

142. "King" and "king-maker" stand here for general cratic relationships—thus the "king-maker" (in the figurative sense) may himself be the king, and the "king" may be an archbishop appointed by him.

consuming hatred for his former friend and lord chancellor, who as archbishop of Canterbury no longer observed the fidelity that his liege lord expected of him and that the archbishop now believed he owed to God alone—a hatred that ended in the murder in the cathedral.[143]

5.2.3.1. Maxims of the Aspirant to Power

Obviously, rising to power is more demanding than retaining a position of power because, all other things being equal, a social law of inertia always makes changes harder than continuing the status quo to which people are used and in which they have proven interests, whereas changes seem to make everything uncertain.[144] Still more difficult than replacing a person in office is a rise to power that involves changing an entire constitution. Rising to power is easiest when it occurs through hereditary succession, for then the change in an office, which even in the most stable social system must be repeatedly made because of death, takes place in accord with laws handed down since time immemorial, whose latent function consists precisely in making grueling and dangerous power struggles unnecessary or even impossible.[145] Only if the heir first in line cannot be unambiguously determined, or if he is obviously unsuited and several pretenders exist, do tenacious power struggles become likely. Yet, filling positions of power through heredity has become rare in the modern world, because it is incompatible with universalism (however, it still plays an important role in the transmission of economic bases of power, and family relationships can be useful in politics and academia as well). As a rule, people do not rise suddenly to elevated positions of power; they must work up to them and for a long time deal with the power-holders in office. In an already developed state, the aspirant to power usually cannot make use of force, because the state monopoly on force is not yet in his hands; threatening with force one does not yet have is ridiculous and will have as its sole result that one will be denied access to all still existing avenues to the monopoly on power.[146] Thus he cannot build his career on others' fear (though occasional, casual hints to the likelihood that he will some day hold power may be useful, especially if they come from a third party); people must feel respect or sympathy for him, or he must prove himself useful—ideally, indispensable— to the power-holders in office. Wherein this utility consists depends on the needs of the power-holder; objective abilities that serve the common good may be required, but not

---

143. It is not a point in favor of C. F. Meyer's novella *Der Heilige* that it seeks to explain Thomas Becket's turn toward God by the killing of his daughter, that is, by something completely external, and not an internal religious conversion.

144. Cf. *Principe* 6.5 (1986; 105 f.).

145. In the second chapter of *Il Principe* (1986; 86 f.), Machiavelli rightly discusses hereditary monarchies in a cursory manner, because they give rise to few cratological insights.

146. Cf. *Discorsi* I 44 (1984; 154 f.).

necessarily. Especially before the development of a constitutional state based on the rule of law, private services—for instance, sexual favors[147] or flattery—may also be rewarded with positions of power. (Flattery may easily be interpreted by the power-holder as an objective achievement, since he may in fact be sincerely convinced that the person who praises him must be very clever.) Even in a democracy the abilities that are honored are extremely varied and depend on the level of the electorate—objective achievements may be involved as well as demagogic talents. Obviously there are only a few universally desired abilities, but it is a generally valid cratic maxim that one must discover which abilities are desired by those who have to decide regarding one's own rise to positions of power.[148] There may nonetheless be power-holders who react to nothing with more irritation than when they sense that someone is speaking and acting not out of his own convictions, but rather in order to please those on whom his advancement depends—in such cases the pure crat will pretend to be intellectually autonomous and sometimes even contradict his superior, namely, when he has the impression that the latter ultimately appreciates being contradicted. There is no simple rule of thumb for finding out whether someone is honest—if there were, and if it were known, the other would only need to behave as this rule says an honest man behaves.

However, there are a few formal abilities that almost any successful aspirant to power must possess. He must show that he can carry out the tasks that are essential for the maintenance or expansion of his superior's power—whether directly, or indirectly through the fact that the subordinate's proven objective competence increases the reputation of the power-holder. He must *make* decisions and be able to *implement* them, against all resistance, but with the necessary flexibility. A person who always merely gives in, or who endeavors only to satisfy the wishes of the other without having any of his own, is not a political man; he will rise to power only if he is useful as a puppet for someone who pulls the strings in the background, or if he inherits or marries into his position.[149] Similarly, Hamlet is not a potential political man, because he reflects too long; indeed, even Schiller's Wallenstein ultimately fails because he feels an almost religious horror at the emergence of intentions from the inner into an outer world that is never completely controllable. To be sure, hasty decisions can also cause someone's sudden downfall—it is not advisable to tilt against windmills; Don Quixote, in whom Tur-

147. Mark Antony claimed that Octavian, while still a virgin, had prostituted himself in exchange for his adoption by Caesar (Suetonius, *Augustus* 68). However that may be, it is clear that Octavian could not have maintained himself for long if his abilities had been solely sexual in nature. On the contrary, his friends justified on cratological grounds his various adulterous relationships with the wives of his enemies: in this way, they said, he gained information regarding the plans of his opponents (Suetonius, *Augustus* 69).

148. Cf. *Principe* 19.12 (1986; 164f.).

149. Consider the ludicrous character of Lepidus in Shakespeare's *Julius Caesar* and *Antony and Cleopatra*; he does nothing but advise peaceableness and let himself be drunk under the table. Cf. the harsh words of Antony (*Julius Caesar* act 4, sc. 1, vv. 18ff.) and of the servant (*Antony and Cleopatra* act 2, sc. 7, vv. 14ff.).

geniev rightly recognized Hamlet's countertype, is just as unsuited as the latter for a career as a political man. But the inability to make decisions or to take any risks is still more fundamentally incompatible with being a political man than is hastiness. Although any plan and any decision can be improved if one thinks about it longer, one must have a sense for the decreasing marginal utility of further reflection and the price to be paid for temporizing. What is ideal is to carefully consider the decision and then carry it out vigorously and quickly once it has been made.[150] Where the realization of a major goal is not possible, one must have the staying power to keep it at the back of one's head and to jump on the opportunity when circumstances suddenly change, even if this requires that the plan be modified. In any case, an abrupt cancellation of decisions generally decreases one's prestige—just as do promises and threats that are not carried out.[151] Formally, the presence and even the recognition of alternatives is part of the concept of decision; and since only one alternative can be chosen, the decision maker must *be able to say "no."* In particular, he must never allow an opponent who exploits his inexperience, distraction, lack of time, or his disinclination to engage in a debate because he doesn't feel well at the moment to take him by surprise and get him to make promises he will later regret. However, his "no" must be said with as much grace as possible so that it does not seem injurious and shows that the rejected request has been considered and carefully weighed.[152] Granting trivial favors and maintaining hope, so that the rejected person remains dependent,[153] are especially recommended; for in general it is better to rely on the hopes of others (though one must not make fools of them) than on their gratitude.[154] It is always good for a negative decision to be made by a group because then it cannot be attributed to any one individual.[155] Conversely, the political man must have no fear of being rejected; refusals, conflicts, and even enmities must not frighten him. Verbal aggressions should almost never get under his skin, even if he has to reckon with the possibility that insults may lead others to a hatred that no longer allows them to perceive their own interest.[156]

---

150. Cf. Guicciardini, Ricordi C 191 (1977; 171f.).

151. Cf. *Principe* 19.1 (1986; 158f.).

152. In one of his famous letters to his son (18 November 1748), which are characterized by a noble way of life as well as by cratological cynicism, Chesterfield praised Marlborough because he was able to turn people down in a more pleasing way than others granted their requests; even a person whose request he actually rejected was won over by him (1963; 86).

153. In some cases conditional promises in case something happens that one considers unlikely, but which the other does not, may be recommended; they appear to prove one's good will and cost little. However, one has to reckon with the fact that one will be taken at one's word if, contrary to expectations, the unlikely events finally come to pass.

154. Cf. Guicciardini, Ricordi C 24, 36 (1977; 113, 118). Gracián, *Oráculo manual*, 5 and 70.

155. Cf. Hegel (1969ff.), 11.567: "Korporationen, Kollegien sind viel strenger im Abschlagen als Individuen." ("Corporative bodies and collegial organs are much more severe in rejecting than are individuals.")

156. Cf. Guicciardini, Ricordi C 150 (1977; 157).

In order to make the right decision, it is less necessary to know a great deal oneself than to have access to those who can provide the necessary information; thus one must have good advisors. They should be able to criticize one, even if respectfully; to allow oneself to be flattered is unwise;[157] anyone who fears criticism because he sees it as imperiling his authority should at least employ a court jester. Recourse to qualified advisors is cratologically disadvantageous only if it constitutes a dependency on people who themselves seek power. Since most decisions involve assessments of probability, one should always take the various possible outcomes into account; still more important than the attribution of probability values is to have *further options for action* and *reserves*, in case the expected event does not occur. The ability to draw up *lists of priorities*, to distinguish the urgent from the less urgent or the purely secondary, is also essential. In addition, it is clear that the political man must have a definite *sense for the feasible*, as well as be prepared to accept the lesser evil in certain situations, and be able to quickly recognize—in game theory terms—equilibrium points. The philosopher is characterized by his tendency to revel in abstract ideals, and although even the great, innovative politician cannot get along without a bit of philosophy or a *vision*, he always has an instinct for which gearwheel of reality could best engage the demands of the idea, how to unite the particular and the general. Nothing is less characteristic of the political man than getting lost in the general, than digressing from the concrete power struggles that have to be waged toward mere words that may be right in themselves but in reality only distract from the questions of detail that have to be resolved. If someone can be disarmed by satisfying him with rhetorical declamations in response to a concrete demand, he lacks the most elementary requisite of a political man: the love of details (in which, depending on the case, the devil or God lies). However, a person who is able to deal only with questions of detail will usually remain a mere apparatchik; without an important idea, political changes of great scope cannot be made.[158] Obsession with the purified ideals of the French Revolution as well as his enormous capacity for work (and his military genius) made Napoleon's rise to power possible.

The aspirant to power will soon have people working for him to whom he must *delegate* as much as possible, in order to gain time for his own achievements, but for whom he remains *responsible*. A person who cannot delegate anything because he is profoundly distrustful will never be able to build a position of power; conversely, a person who does not care whether his commands are precisely executed will soon lose his power. In choosing collaborators, that is, in personal politics, there are, from a cratological point of view, two points to be taken into account: on one hand, collaborators should be competent to carry out the tasks assigned to them; on the other, exces-

---

157. *Principe* 23 (1986; 182 ff.).
158. Even a sober realist like Frederick the Great indulged, in his political testament, in political reveries (1920; 59 ff., 219 ff.).

sive competence on their part could result in one's being displaced by them, especially if they have no other way of rising in the hierarchy. Their weaknesses—of which one must be aware—can become dangerous; but they also keep them dependent. Fearful mediocrities will always choose other mediocrities; on the other hand, first-rate collaborators prove the sovereign nature of the person who has sought them out. Yet the latter must be careful if he cannot count on their loyalty, which must be tested from time to time.[159] In a mirror image of his behavior toward subordinates, the aspirant to power will seek to convince his superior of his loyalty (naturally not through direct professions of fidelity which, particularly if repeated, only arouse suspicion, because one does not say what goes without saying),[160] and he will always avoid winning an overt victory over him. If he gives him advice, he will do so in such a way as to create the impression that he is merely reminding him of something that he was not thinking of at the moment.[161] He may conceal an unusual talent, in order not to arouse fear; he will worry more about being overestimated than underestimated; he will not achieve certain feats in order to avoid arousing suspicion—especially in the military realm. "Better to leave undone than by our deed / Acquire too high a fame when him we serve's away. / . . . Who does i' the wars more than his captain can / Becomes his captain's captain; and ambition, / The soldier's virtue, rather makes choice of loss / Than gain which darkens him."[162] In a passage of his interpretation of Livy that moves beyond the text, Machiavelli praises Brutus for having hidden his intelligence in order to liberate his fatherland under more favorable circumstances; he extols this feigned stupidity as the expression of the greatest acuity.[163] In fact, sometimes there is no smarter way to act than to pretend to be dumb.[164] It can even be advisable to have and to show moral defects, because being flawless can easily be unsettling and, when compared with one's own weaknesses, humiliating.[165] If no common virtues are shared, then at least common vices can provide a bond.[166]

---

159. Cf. *Kauṭilīya-Arthaśāstra* 1.10.17 ff., which nonetheless warns that such testing may put into dependents' heads ideas that would otherwise never have occurred to them.

160. Cf. Marcus Aurelius, XI.15.

161. Cf. Gracián, *Oráculo manual* 7.

162. Shakespeare, *Antony and Cleopatra* act 3, sc. 2, vv. 14 ff. Cf. Montesquieu (1734), 108.

163. *Discorsi* III 2 (1984; 465 ff.). Cf. also Sun-tzu (1988), 80.

164. It is no accident that two successful politicians of the 1980s, Reagan and Kohl, were underestimated by their opponents—which speaks against the latter, not the former.

165. Cf. Gracián, *Oráculo manual*, 83.

166. Cf. Joly, 24th dialogue (1864; 243): "La passion des femmes sert un souverain bien plus que vous ne pouvez le penser. Henri IV a dû à son incontinence une partie de sa popularité . . . le résultat le plus réel de la galanterie du prince, est de lui concilier la sympathie de la plus belle moitié de ses sujets." ("A passion for women serves a ruler far more than you can imagine. Henry IV owed part of his popularity to his lack of chastity . . . the most genuine result of the prince's philandering is to win him the sympathy of the more beautiful half of his subjects.")

5.2.3.2. Maxims for Fighting Enemies

Intellectual or volitional gifts do not always win friends. On the contrary: "The evil we do causes us less persecution and hatred than do our good qualities."[167] Fear of too great a concentration of power, concern about a competitor, and disinterested envy are strong enough motives to oppose the aspirant to power. In an egalitarian society, things are harder for the very talented than for the mediocre, and usually it is only historic crisis situations that bring them to power.[168] Churchill would never have become prime minister had it not been necessary for the survival of Great Britain—his intellectual independence (consider his repeated changes in party membership) had made him too unpopular. In general, we may note that as one rises to power, one's enemies increase in number. One would not want as a colleague, not to mention a superior, everyone that one would like to have as an effective subordinate. For the aspirant to power, the most dangerous moment arrives when he begins to emerge from the spacious antechamber of power but has not yet reached the point at which he has become almost invincible— for whereas at the outset it is not necessary to harm him, later on it is almost impossible to do so, and therefore the intermediate phase is the stormiest. At the beginning of his rise, references to his own power, or even occasional bluffing, may be useful;[169] in the critical phase, on the other hand, a deflationary style of power is urgently recommended, in order not to attract other people's attention.[170] Indeed, for this reason it can even be prudent to maintain spurious opponents and represent occasional small defeats as if they were great ones, in order to keep others' fear and mistrust within limits.[171] In any case, it is of the utmost importance *to distinguish friends from foes.* These concepts attain their greatest cratic significance in war. But even in bloodless power struggles their importance is obvious: an enemy tries to thwart one's will, whereas a friend furthers it; in this sense there are no fewer enemies within one's own institution than outside it. Since the problem of power first arises from a conflict between different people, one

---

167. La Rochefoucauld, Maxim 29 (1967; 13). "Le mal que nous faisons ne nous attire pas tant de persécution et de haine que nos bonnes qualités."

168. Cf. *Discorsi* III 30.12. The other possibility mentioned by Machiavelli is that the persons who envy one die out. For even if new competitors are constantly born, the original ones, and especially the older ones, are the bitterest adversaries.

169. Cf. La Rochefoucauld, Maxim 56 (1967; 19): "Pour s'établir dans le monde, on fait tout ce que l'on peut pour y paraître établi." ("To establish oneself in the world, one does everything one can to seem established there.") This includes references to one's encounters with the powerful, and sometimes also confidential (often only seemingly confidential) information from which others can conclude that one has direct access to the power-holder.

170. Cf. Montesquieu (1734), 104.

171. In a remarkable dialectic, one's own power—or, more precisely, other people's perception of one's power—can be a factor of weakness. Cf. Thucydides VI 33.4. Joly's Machiavelli repeatedly advises the modern despot to create spurious enemies in order to calm public opinion: 12th, 15th, and 17th dialogues (1864; 115 ff., 154, 168 ff.). Sympathy with the weak for no other reason than that they are weak is a general human phenomenon—they are less threatening than the strong. Cf. Livy, 42.63.2.

can discern in the opposition of friend and foe the basic cratologic category par excellence. Carl Schmitt's analysis remains an important contribution: after reading *Der Begriff des Politischen,* one sees power struggles differently.[172] It is true that Schmitt's achievement is diminished by his confusion of the concept of the cratic with that of the political, but regarding power struggles, and especially political power struggles, it remains absolutely true that one must have a sense for those with whom one can cooperate as friends or allies and those whom one must battle as enemies or at least keep an eye on, because they will oppose one's own intentions, if necessary with every means at their command. A person who has no sense for this will fail, even if he has a great deal of knowledge. Conversely, a person who can distinguish friends from foes, soberly assess their power, discern their weaknesses and insecurities, and store up experiences with them in a good memory, and who reckons with every weakness and malice on the basis of a realistic anthropology, can remain in power for a long time—even if he has few abilities other than these. Goethe's Egmont falls into a trap because as a result of his magnanimity he is not able to put himself in the place of a man like Alba; on the other hand, William of Orange sees through the opponent whose moves he has carefully observed as in a game of chess, and to whom he attributes no nobility of mind—perhaps because he himself is less generous than Egmont. Not being careful in dealing with secret enemies can be dangerous; conversely, a person who has no sense for possible coalitions that would be useful to him (and which, rightly or wrongly, the other party regards as useful as well) will fail to take advantage of opportunities for rising higher.

Naturally, in power struggles one must not let one's own options be known; discretion (but not petty secretiveness, which would be noticed) is an elementary cratic requirement.[173] A "leaky spot" that allows secrets to seep out can be just as dangerous as a leak in a ship.[174] Because of the same finitude of the human intellect that necessitates "satisficing" rather than maximizing, it is impossible to take into account all the possible strategies that might be employed by the opposing side, but one can always attempt to surprise the other—the German Wehrmacht's breakthrough via the Ardennes north of the Maginot line had not been foreseen by the Allies. In the short run, outright lies, if they are expressed in a tone of heartfelt conviction or accompanied by a review of all the arguments in favor of the feigned behavior,[175] are cratically advisable. In the long run, however, among other reasons because it is difficult to be consistent in lying over an extended period of time, lies almost always diminish the appearance of reliability, which can be essential in other situations. A mixture of mendacious explanations of good

---

172. Using an expression of André Gide's, Freund (1965; 442) rightly attributes to Schmitt's friend-foe theory a "banalité supérieur" because it is so convincing.

173. Obviously, the converse situation may also exist, in which a certain person should receive information that the official concerned is not authorized to pass on; in this case recourse to a third party is usual, whether he is aware of his function or is simply used.

174. Cf. *Kauṭilīya-Arthaśāstra* 7.13.44.

175. Cf. Guicciardini, Ricordi C 37 and 199 (1977; 118 and 175).

intentions (which were willingly believed, because it was more comfortable to believe them) and a politics of *fait accompli* served Hitler well. Conversely, it is useful to anticipate the other's plans and to worm his secrets out of him (doing one's best to keep him from seeing that one has seen through him, of course, because otherwise he will change his plans.)[176] In addition to positive sanctions, one can use an old trick in dealing with inexperienced opponents: one asks about things they want to talk about but that, while they are of no interest to oneself, are connected with what one wants to know; one behaves as though one does not believe them or contradicts them, so that the opponents find themselves forced to reveal what they know in order to impress one with it. "Affected doubt is the best skeleton key that curiosity can use to get to know what it wants."[177] Sometimes a weak-willed opponent can even be forced to comply with one's own will by giving him the impression that one has allowed oneself to be led on by him.[178] The political man will generally observe not only his environment, but especially others' observations (and also their observations of his observations); this can give him an edge in knowledge. Thus—to refer to a favorite theme of comedy—of two men who do not yet know each other and for that reason fear each other or believe the other to be of higher rank, he who first perceives the other's fear has won. A problem drawn from folk mathematics throws a great deal of light on a central cratic ability: a king plans to choose a prime minister from among three candidates, and he wants the smartest one. He has them blindfolded and tells them that each of them will have a white or a black hat put on their heads, but not more than one of them will get a black hat. The first one to figure out the color of his own hat (which he cannot see) will become prime minister. The blindfolds are removed; for a short time no one speaks. Then one of the candidates calls out that he has a white hat. How did he arrive at this conclusion? Had one of them had a black hat, the others, who would have seen this hat, would have been able to conclude at once that theirs were white. But since they did not see a black hat, they could not immediately exclude the possibility that they themselves had the black hat. Only the recognition that in this case the others would have immediately called out that they had white hats leads to the right result—what had to be observed was not the hats, but the observations of the hats, and this involved a shift to higher level.[179]

An instinctive feeling for how others think about oneself is as important cratically as the ability to avoid letting more powerful opponents see one's own enmity or even annoyance. Since sphinx-like taciturnity is a quality that only power-holders can allow

---

176. In Poe's *The Purloined Letter*, Dupin wears dark glasses while visiting the minister, so that the latter does not see what he is observing.

177. Gracián, *Oráculo manual*, 213. In Spanish, the passage reads as follows: "Una duda afectada es la más sutil ganzúa de la curiosidad para saber quanto quisiere" (1946; 75).

178. Cf. Frederick the Great (1920), 53.

179. There is another version of the story, in which a candidate gives the right answer already before the blindfolds are removed; for, he argues, the king is just, and if he had had a black hat put on someone's head, he would have put this individual at a disadvantage. Here the candidate does not observe the observations of his competitors, but the function of the king's plan.

themselves, because it can prevent the growth of the trust an aspirant to power needs, the simulation of good will would be advisable if it did not also lack credibility when employed with regard to everyone, and therefore strike a false note. General politeness, which is able to differentiate, is a more sensible compromise.[180] Nonetheless, it remains remarkable how surely political men recognize falsity, or even a slight decrease in loyalty: as a rule, their hermeneutic competence is first-rate. A false note, a twitch in a facial muscle, a thoughtless gesture, or a glance exchanged with a third party can betray more than long explanations.[181] Exaggerated politeness, resort to commonplaces, and ceremonious stiffness among friends are all signs that the warmth of convictions has decreased.[182] However, since the other may have himself completely under control, surprising news or encounters that trigger, like a reflex, a determinate facial expression betraying his innermost feelings are useful in order to perceive his designs.[183] It is commonly an overestimation of oneself that leads even distinguished personalities to underestimate the number of their opponents—they cannot imagine that people do not like them. To be sure, at a higher level the task of discovering opponents' designs can and indeed must be delegated to others. But it cannot be completely transferred to others—one must at least know whether one can trust those who assume this task. And since the freedom they require to carry out the task necessarily makes it possible for them to engage in intrigues, it is particularly difficult to acquire a clear proof of infidelity if one has no instinct for it. Callippus was able to beguile Dion because the latter had assigned him to find out how loyal his soldiers were—and Dion interpreted all warnings by third parties that Callippus was conspiring with the soldiers as signs that his agent was conscientiously doing his duty, until Callippus murdered him with the help of the soldiers.[184]

Friendships based on feelings of sympathy or, better yet, on common values, are, from a strictly cratological point of view, definitely preferable to alliances based on interests alone.[185] Only in exceptional historical situations is it possible to retain power for long without sincere friends or at least selflessly loyal subordinates. Between peers, friendships can be strengthened by marriages; particularly in traditional societies, marriages have been a tried and true political means, especially in foreign policy: *Bella gerant*

---

180. "Be thou familiar, but by no means vulgar," is part of Polonius's advice to the departing Hamlet (*Hamlet* act 1, sc. 3, v. 61).

181. Cf. *Kauṭilīya-Arthaśāstra* 5.5.5 ff.

182. Cf. Shakespeare, *Julius Caesar* act 4, sc. 2, vv. 19 ff.: "Ever note, Lucilius, / When love begins to sicken and decay / It useth an enforced ceremony."

183. Cf. Livy, 37.7.10, where Africanus advises his brother to have a completely unexpected visit made to Philip to discover the latter's attitude with regard to the Romans.

184. Plutarch, *Dion* 54 ff.

185. An interesting intermediate possibility is a friendship that arises out of a common rejection of previously shared values. Catholics who have become atheists and Marxists who have gone over to post-modernism are often thick as thieves, because they can exchange jokes that relieve for a while the loneliness that is the inevitable punishment of cynicism.

alii, tu, felix Austria, nube ("Others may wage war; you, happy Austria, marry").[186] The power-holder produces loyalty by establishing collective identities and mobilizing *We*-feelings. His subordinates must be able to see that he himself is guided by certain moral principles. Friendships are to be carefully cultivated. This implies not only doing favors for others (favors that are the more prized the more they presuppose a detailed acquaintance with the individuality of the person to whom they are granted); no less important is the readiness to accept other people's good deeds, especially if they are not requested (which one should not do too often), but freely offered.[187] A person who does not allow himself to be given anything seems to want to avoid being obligated; moreover, it is humiliating to be always only the receiver. However, it is usually also necessary to overcome antipathies and to form alliances that are based on interests alone; indeed, a major power factor consists in knowing how to mediate as a third between two parties that do not trust each other and in bringing together people who have little sympathy with each other and can only communicate through one's mediation.[188]

An important common basis for alliances is a battle against a third party;[189] in fact, the saying that the enemy of your enemy is your (natural) friend, that is, your ally, is an elementary cratological truth. Because border conflicts are frequent, this saying is used in foreign politics to mean that the neighbor of your neighbor (who is not at the same time your own neighbor) is a traditional ally.[190] However, it often happens that ideologically opposed parties find it easier to cooperate with each other than with those in the middle of the spectrum, with whom there are more points of friction and whom the other two parties see as competitors and may even—after the breakup of a common identity—detest as traitors. Since, however, the observation of one's own friends and foes by a third party has important consequences for one's prestige, this kind of cooperation usually takes place covertly. Here we encounter the reason why conservative parties were often able to have more uncomplicated dealings with the Soviet regime than could the social democratic parties.[191] On one hand, the Soviet Communist Party regarded the social democrats as more dangerous competitors; on the other, conservative regimes did not need to fear that their voters would consider them too accommodating in their negotiations, because they were seen as bitter enemies of the Soviet Union. Despite the fact that there can be many autonomous centers from which everyone competes with every-

---

186. Perhaps Roman history would have taken a different course had Julia, Caesar's daughter and Pompey's wife, lived longer.

187. Cf. *Principe* 10.3 (1986; 128).

188. A increase in the third party's power is the point of the saying that one must resolve conflicts between warring parties in the following order: facilitate, mediate, arbitrate, assassinate. Cf. F. V. Kratochwil (1989; 183 ff.) on implicit and explicit third parties.

189. The ambassadors from Korkyra call this the surest guarantee (Thucydides I 35.5).

190. Cf. already *Kauṭilīya-Arthaśāstra* 6.2.15.

191. An exception was Willy Brandt, who nonetheless inevitably had to resign after his close aide and associate Gunther Guillaume was unmasked as an East German spy—a step a conservative head of government would probably not have had to take.

one else, when a conflict comes to a head and open confrontations result, there is a tendency to form two sides, and secondary conflicts are normally subordinated to the primary opposition.[192] However, we can sometimes be surprised by what proves to be the main conflict in a specific situation and which coalition-building operations are set in motion. In an opposition between two institutions, it can occasionally happen that those on both sides who want to continue the conflict temporarily join forces in order to battle internal enemies working to put an end to it: their alliance is paradoxically based on the common desire to continue their enmity. It not infrequently happens that internal enemies are hated more than external ones, because it is the disappointment of expectations, the fracture of collective identities, and particularly the breakup of friendships and apostasy that produce the most irreconcilable hatreds.[193] As is well known, if "deadly enemy" is the comparative of "enemy," then "fellow party-member" is the superlative.

Overcoming problems together may result in an enduring and substantial friendship, but as a rule alliances based on interests are not stable and may even turn into enmities. So far as their size is concerned, the following principle is valid: since an alliance must distribute its winnings among its members if it does not want to give rise to the next conflict, it will usually be only as large as is necessary in order to attain the intended goal.[194] But falling short of this threshold is even more dangerous than going beyond it; in order to attain the optimal size, one will have to convince some possible allies that others have also decided to join the coalition.[195] The ally must not be too weak, because then he would be a burden; and few things are more dangerous than to allow oneself to be drawn into risky conflicts by trusting in a weak ally.[196] However, except in emergencies,

---

192. Mao Tse-Tung's reflections on the primary and nonprimary sides of contradiction (1977; 51 ff.) combine such old cratological insights with a crude understanding of dialectics.

193. For example, the leaders of Megara feared the Athenians, with whom they were at war, less than their exiled compatriots (Thucydides IV 66). Cf. also Aristotle, *Politics* 1328a1 ff. Even emigrants are often considered traitors.

194. This is W. H. Riker's (1962) well-known thesis. Frederick the Great even believed that too many alliances were more of a hindrance than a help (1920; 75).

195. A risky trick consists in telling each of two hesitating candidates that the other has decided to join the coalition, in order to produce what one has already declared to be a fact. But this can work only if there is no communication between the two candidates. "In solchen Fällen tut das Beispiel alles. Der Mensch ist ein nachahmendes Geschöpf, / Und wer der Vorderste ist, führt die Herde. / Die Prager Truppen wissen es nicht anders, / Als daß die Pilsner Völker uns gehuldigt, / Und hier in Pilsen sollen sie uns schwören, / Weil man zu Prag das Beispiel hat gegeben" (Schiller, *Wallensteins Tod* act 3, sc. 4, vv. 1433 ff.). ("In such cases example is everything. / Man is an imitating creature, / And whoever is in front leads the herd. / Prague's troops assume / That the people of Pilsen have paid us tribute, / And here in Pilsen they should swear fidelity to us, / Because in Prague the example has been set.")

196. Cf. Thucydides VI 13 and Machiavelli, *Discorsi* II 11 (1984; 320); also Frederick the Great (1920), 45: "La Suède est un allié à charge, qui peut se trouver dans le cas de demander des secours, mais qui ne saurait en rendre." ("Sweden is a burdensome ally that may need to ask for help, but cannot itself provide any.")

alliances with a stronger partner are also to be avoided.[197] One either becomes dependent on him, or one's own contribution will be obscured by his fame;[198] and nothing is more foolish than to assume risks without any prospect of gain.[199] Therefore a limitation of an ally's power by the common enemy is sometimes quite desirable.[200] Finally, neutrality in a conflict that will eventuate in one's being handed over to the victor, no matter who he is, is not a smart option; it condemns one to play the role of the weeping third party.[201] This is a reasonable choice only if the conflict will lead to a diminution of the power of both opponents, and the victory, no matter which side wins it, will not endanger oneself, and if one's own intervention might even unite the opponents;[202] then it can even be sensible to look on, as did William the Conqueror, or even to instrumentalize a secret enemy so that he assumes the burden of a battle against another, and then step in as the laughing third party when he is exhausted by his victory. Even if it is occasionally useful to increase one's own prestige by defeating an opponent, who can be created if one is not available,[203] nothing is more foolish than the principle "The more enemies, the more honor." Essential for survival are a sober assessment of how many enemies one can fight, given one's own strength, and dividing the enemies, playing them off against each other in accord with the principle "divide and rule." For not only defeats, but also Pyrrhic victories that weaken one for further conflicts, are to be avoided; if further conflicts are on the horizon, one should not invest much more energy in a victory than is required to realize one's goal, and one should exhaust oneself only when it is absolutely necessary. The limitation of the number of enemies is obligatory in both personal and military conflicts: Hitler's infamous attack on the Soviet Union before defeating Great Britain was cratically as insane as Great Britain's noble offer to come to Finland's aid in the Finnish-Russian War, which fortunately proved impossible to carry out because of Sweden's not exactly heroic policy of neutrality. On the other hand, one of the ways Churchill showed his political genius was by quickly understanding, despite his deep dislike for the Soviet Union, that the Third Reich was the more dangerous enemy, and that fighting it had absolute priority. In order to successfully wage this fight to the end, he was capable and willing to engage in reliable and loyal cooperation with the Soviet Union, without, however, ever indulging in the illusion that the brotherhood in arms could be transmuted into a real and enduring friendship after the defeat of the unifying opponent. Because Stalin also had no such illusions, he wanted to maintain the common enemy as long as possible: in 1943 he forbade the carrying out of an assassination attempt on Hitler planned by Pavel Sudoplatov because he anticipated that after

---

197. Cf. *Principe*, 21.6 (1986; 179).
198. Cf. Gracián, *Oráculo manual*, 152.
199. Cf. Frederick the Great (1920), 43, on Saxony's foreign policy.
200. Cf. *Kauṭilīya-Arthaśāstra* 7.18.12 f., 34.
201. Cf. Thucydides VI 80, *Principe* 21.3 ff. (1986; 177 ff.); and Montesquieu (1734), 52, 88.
202. Cf. Guicciardini, Ricordi C 221 (1977; 183).
203. Cf. *Principe* 20.6 (1986; 173).

Hitler's death the United States and Great Britain would sign a peace treaty with Germany and thus the basis for their alliance with the Soviet Union would disappear—considerably earlier than Stalin wanted it to. Even a tyrant like Stalin was able to limit the number of his enemies: only internally, where he felt secure, did he eliminate his opponents; before World War II, he largely forwent exporting the revolution because this might have endangered the buildup of his position of power in the Soviet Union. However, Stalin risked a great deal in the purges, and they turned out successfully for him only because of the peculiar state of the soul of the Russian people at that time, whereas Hitler ran no great risks, cratologically speaking, in carrying out the genocide of the Jews and Gypsies: If enemies are strictly limited and the pillars of one's own power need not fear that they will someday themselves be counted among them, indifference (if not worse) with regard to the greatest crimes is to be expected.

The ability to postpone unnecessary conflicts until one has strengthened one's own position is cratically central. Sometimes in order to keep an impatient opponent or a dangerous ally at arm's length, and perhaps even irritate and weaken them, it is sufficient to avoid the decisive confrontation, not to say "no" to their demands, but rather to say "yes, but," or to ask for time to consider: Franco was able in this way to make a fool of even Hitler. One should never allow oneself to be put under pressure and always avoid situations one cannot get out of without losing face and from which one cannot proceed without great danger.[204] However, it is also indispensable to actually avoid and resolve conflicts. Pugnacity is alien to the political man, for whom conflicts always serve a goal and do not become a goal in themselves; nothing seems to him more ludicrous than fighting losing battles. To avoid hostilities it is necessary, on one hand, not to do anything that might elicit fear in the other party, for wars not rarely, perhaps even often, arise from the fear of war: distrust on one side produces distrust on the other.[205] Readiness to compromise, and even the credible will to create trust, for example, by offering guarantees, even in cases where one cannot count on mutual good will, is crucial. However, it is important to distinguish between actual compromises on issues and mere dilatory compromises that do not resolve any issue but only serve to put off an unavoidable decision: seeing this kind of postponement—which may be necessary for survival in some situations—as a genuine resolution of the conflict is illusory.[206]

As a rule, it is a disadvantage to gain the reputation of having a diabolical cratologic intelligence. An important cratic maxim is that one should not allow one's cratic and cratological abilities to become too clear[207]—someone who writes a *Principe* seldom inspires trust. On the other hand, it is a fatal error to imagine that being accomodating can resolve all problems. Oppositions arising from fear can usually be disposed of, but enmities based on hatred, envy, or thirst for power can seldom be eradicated. If only a conflict

---

204. Cf. H. J. Morgenthau and K. W. Thompson (1985), 589.
205. Cf. Guicciardini, Ricordi C 120 (1977; 146).
206. On the distinction between genuine and apparent compromises, cf. Schmitt (1928), 31 f.
207. Cf. Gracián, *Oráculo manual*, 45, 219.

of interests is involved, a compromise can often be found—insofar as the parties share common principles of justice. In contrast, in cases where the two parties to the conflict have completely different values, the result is usually profound distrust or even hatred. In any case, there are enemies who interpret any kind of friendliness as a sign of contemptible weakness and an opportunity to make further demands. Even potential allies feel no admiration for someone who is neither willing nor able to defend himself. (Hence one should not complain, except to real friends, about the injustices one has suffered.) It is always unwise to show oneself to be fearful, and Machiavelli is generally right in saying that it is better to allow oneself to be deprived of something by force than by the fear of force.[208] In particular, nothing is more laughable than a threat that simultaneously makes it clear that the threat is not seriously meant—in this way one loses any future credibility. Concerning the behavior of the British government after the Italian attack on Ethiopia, Churchill writes sarcastically that "the Prime Minister had declared that Sanctions were war; secondly, he was resolved there must be no war; and, thirdly, he decided upon Sanctions."[209] To be sure, a mutual refusal to give in can have disastrous consequences, but for that very reason it is better to have a reputation for intransigence than for always giving in—sometimes even in advance. Anyhow, the weaker party also has the possibility of withstanding a conflict by concentrating on defending himself or avoiding contact with the stronger party and thereby wearing him down.[210] This cratic maxim holds for personal as well as for military conflicts: telling one's secretary not to put through any calls from one's opponent or going underground and pursuing guerrilla warfare are two concrete applications of the same principle.

Before open conflict breaks out, there is usually a phase of latent ill will in which the goal is to put the other party at a disadvantage—for example, by using malicious gossip and slander (to the effect that he is seeking absolute power, and so on) to denigrate him. The extraordinary difficulty of assigning to a single individual the responsibility for rumors, and the significant damage they can very quickly produce, make them a dangerous weapon in power struggles; Fama is truly the horrendous monster Virgil describes.[211] On the other hand, clearly attributable and basically innocuous direct insults are counterproductive; indeed, the opponent's strength may increase with his wrath.[212] Their cratic utility may consist solely in provoking the other to attack—and this can be of great importance when in a given political situation the aggressor will be blamed and support allotted accordingly (which is why there must be a cratic maxim not to allow oneself to be provoked). To attain this goal, it may be useful to employ *agents provocateurs*, to simulate attacks on oneself[213] or one's collaborators, or to make

---

208. *Discorsi* II 14.7 (1984; 327). See the whole chapter.
209. (1948 ff.), 1:153.
210. Cf. the vivid simile in Frederick the Great (1920), 95.
211. *Aeneid* IV 173 ff.
212. Cf. *Discorsi* II 26 (1984; 366 f.).
213. This was how Peisistratus first rose to tyranny. Cf. Herodotus I 59.

attacks on third parties that result in aggression on the part of one's real enemy, who was ultimately the target in attacking the third party.[214] If the opponent belongs to one's own camp, one way to damage him may consist in assigning him to carry out with honor a task that he will very probably not be able to fulfill or that will necessarily make him unpopular;[215] or one can so strongly support his recommendations that by being exaggerated they turn into their opposite and are counterproductive. It is ideal if one can even get two opponents to oppose each other and remain as the laughing third in the background as they wear each other down. It was a cratic masterstroke when in 1980 Helmut Kohl was able, by withdrawing his hopeless candidacy for chancellor, to eliminate with one blow two opponents within his own party and at the same time ensure that he would once again be a candidate for chancellor at a later time more favorable to him. In difficult situations, in which the top position is imperiled, it may be better to be the second man, waiting in the background.[216]

If it has finally come to open conflict, it is indispensable to withstand it until a mediation, a lenient compromise on the basis of mutual exhaustion or the intervention of a third party, or a defeat of one of the two parties to the conflict has occurred. In any case, after the outbreak of hostilities, one can reconcile the enemy even less than before by means of concessions, which will be attributed to mere fear—nothing is more ludicrous than withdrawing from battles as quickly as one has allowed oneself to be drawn into them. During the conflict, one must show no weakness, which would only strengthen the other side's will to hold out: how many sieges have been abandoned because the besieged deceived the enemy by pretending to have stocks of supplies that suggested that it would be a long time before they could be starved into submission![217] Some battles that resulted in heavy losses on both sides have been considered as ending in the victory of one side only because it left the field after the other one—victory and defeat are partly constructions on the part of the onlookers, who may be more impressed by endurance and courage than by external superiority. It is particularly important to overcome or at least to conceal any internal tension during the struggle. As a consul, Gaius Terentius Varro was no stroke of luck for Rome, but when the Roman senators went to meet him at the gates of the city on his return from the catastrophe at Cannae and

---

214. Cf. *Discorsi* II 9 (1984; 315 f.)

215. Cf. *Kauṭilīya-Arthaśāstra* 1.13.19 f.

216. Cf. Shakespeare, *Coriolanus*, act 1, sc. 1, vv. 264 ff.: "Fame, at which he aims, / In whom already he's well graced, cannot / Better be held nor more attained than by / A place below the first; for what miscarries / Shall be the general's fault, though he perform / To th'utmost of a man, and giddy censure / Will then cry out of Marcius, 'O, if he / Had borne the business!'"

217. Cf. Guicciardini, Ricordi C 102 (1977; 140): "Uno assediato che aspetta soccorso, publica sempre le necessità sue molto maggiore che non sono; quello che non lo aspetta, non gli restando altro disegno che straccare lo inimico e a questo effetto torgli ogni speranza, le cuopre sempre e publica minore." ("Anyone who is besieged and is expecting help will always proclaim his need to be greater than it is. But someone who does not expect help, having no alternative but to tire the enemy and make him lose hope, will hide his needs and minimize them publicly." Trans. M. Domandi, 66 f.)

thanked him for not having despaired of saving the fatherland, it was the only right thing to do.[218] Similarly, after being appointed prime minister, Churchill forwent a witch hunt for those responsible for the Munich agreement, and did so despite heavy pressure, particularly from the Labour Party. Churchill would have had more right to do so than anyone else, but he understood that the present would lose the future if it sat in judgment on the past[219]—which did not prevent him from removing supporters of appeasement from crucial offices and moving them to less important, if also sometimes externally impressive, posts. So long as one can and must continue to fight, one should give no sign that one is thinking about surrender—Alexander I's rejection of all Napoleon's attempts to contact him and Stalin's refusal to abandon Moscow were important factors in Russia's two victories. Conversely, when on 15 June 1940 Chautemps proposed asking the Germans what conditions they would set for an armistice, it was tantamount, in the situation of France at that time, to already accepting these conditions.[220]

In contrast, if one is interested in putting an end to a conflict, it is advisable to enable opponents to retreat without losing face, and not to block the only way out if this might increase the forces of despair.[221] (However, it may be wise to do this only in regard to one's own soldiers.)[222] Few things have contributed more to the mythical image of Caesar than his reputation for leniency, which—as he himself noted—bore much fruit in the civil war.[223] However, the crat is interested in leniency only as an instrument: when a Roman legate took a city in Illyria, he at first forwent plundering it, in order to encourage a neighboring city to surrender; but when the hoped-for result did not occur, he had the first city plundered after all, in order not too greatly to frustrate the soldiers, who now had to prepare for a second siege.[224] Generosity can also be cratically wise after a victory, partly because it helps placate the hatred of the defeated through symbolic concessions, and partly because it may establish lasting friendships.[225] Hardly any of Bismarck's decisions is more impressive than his unconditional commitment to a generous peace settlement with Austria after its defeat in the Austro-Prussian War.[226] Precisely when the opponent can feel respect (for the virtues manifested during the conflict), and when he allows himself to be taught otherwise but does not change his mind rashly,

---

218. Cf. T. Mommsen (1976), 2:134 ff.

219. Cf. Churchill (1948 ff.), 3:7 f.

220. Cf. Churchill (1948 ff.), 3:181 f.

221. Cf. above, chap. 2, nn. 7–11, as well as Thucydides I 82 and Gracián, *Oráculo manual*, 172.

222. Cf. Sun-tzu (1988), 61, 65; (1989), 80, 85; *Discorsi* III 12 (1984; 502 ff.). It is well known that Cortés had his ships scuttled (not, as one often reads, burned) in Veracruz on the pretext that they were not seaworthy, in order to deprive his men of any hope of retreating.

223. *De bello civili* I 74.7: "magnumque fructum suae pristinae lenitatis omnium iudicio Caesar ferebat consiliumque eius a cunctis probabatur."

224. Livy 43.1.1 ff.

225. Cf. *Kauṭilīya-Arthaśāstra* 9.4.8 and *Principe* 20.7 (1986, 173 f.).

226. Bismarck even reports that he had played with the idea of committing suicide when King William initially rejected his proposal (1898 ff.; 2:47).

after being defeated he can become a truer friend than allies whose support is based on interests, or than traitors, who generally inspire little sympathy even in those for whose benefit they committed their treachery, if only because the suspicion arises that they might betray their new ally as well. Schiller's Wallenstein anticipates the Swedish emissary Wrangel's objection when he remarks, "I see the chancellor still does not really trust me. Yes, I admit it—the situation is not entirely to my advantage—Your Excellency thinks that if I can treat the emperor, who is my lord, this way, I could do the same to my enemy, and that the latter would be more forgivable than the former."[227]

5.2.3.3. Maxims of the Power-Holder

After achieving an elevated position of power, many of the previously mentioned maxims must continue to be followed, for power struggles never end. Not only does every president remain dependent on the support of the people if he is to be re-elected, but even a president elected for life or a dictator can be overthrown. Thus a leader's popularity requires, especially in nontraditional societies, to be constantly renewed. It is important that he not be constantly in the public eye; if he is constantly present, he will become worn out. Occasionally surprising public opinion can mobilize support; however, there is nothing more counterproductive than creating expectations that then remain unfulfilled. Even if no new achievements can be made, a periodic reminder of old ones can take their place.[228] In any case, the art of self-presentation is one of the keys to retaining power. At the same time, a certain distance and inapproachability, the impression that one is holding something in reserve and has access to bases of power of which others are unaware and therefore cannot factor into their calculations, increase the aura.[229] Exaggerated affability can lead to the evaporation of the respect that a power-holder needs.[230] However, it is no less dangerous when the power-holder no longer communicates directly with those over whom he rules and on whom his power ultimately depends, for then power passes de facto to those who inform him and monitor his exchanges with others.[231] (In traditional societies,

---

227. *Wallensteins Tod* act 1, sc. 5, vv. 258 ff.: "Der Kanzler, merk ich, traut mir noch nicht recht. / Ja ich gestehs—Es liegt das Spiel nicht ganz / Zu meinem Vorteil—Seine Würden meint, / Wenn ich dem Kaiser, der mein Herr ist, so / Mitspielen kann, ich könn das gleiche tun / Am Feinde, und das eine wäre mir / Noch eher zu verzeihen, als das andre." Cf. also Thucydides III 9 and Livy I 11.

228. Gracián, *Oráculo manual*, 81, recommends phases of absence, so that one is missed; this does not hold for the power-holder, but only for intellectuals hungry for fame, among others.

229. The power-holder does not have to really have secrets; he can, as Hegel says about the eponymous hero of Schiller's *Wallenstein*, also be "secretive" because he "has no secret" (1969 ff.; 1:618).

230. Cf. Gracián, *Oráculo manual*, 177.

231. In an eerie way, this holds for the eponymous hero of Melville's superb story "Benito Cereno." However, we must also put under this head the isolation of some modern despots (for example, that of Honecker or Ceauçescu) from their people, whom they knew only through the heads of their secret police and other lackeys, who flattered them and swept any problems under the carpet. See the interesting report by E. Naraghi on the last Shah of Iran (1991; 15 ff.).

an exaggerated[232] sacralization of the king was a favorite means of disempowering him.)[233] Harun ar-Rashid in *The Arabian Nights* and Shakespeare's Henry V[234] make important discoveries by mixing incognito with the common people, where they hear many things they would never be told, partly because their interlocutors would be understandably intimidated if they knew whom they were talking with. In democracies, the power-holder can inspire trust precisely by openly seeking out his subordinates and asking them their opinion concerning problems in their area of competence. This desire for knowledge ennobles him, especially if his superiority in other ways is incontestable and the person asked does not know whether the power-holder wants to learn only from him or also about him. Indeed, even admitting one's own weaknesses and errors (which cannot always be hushed up) can win liking and even respect for the power-holder—but only if his achievements are unquestionable. Thus in 1990, after having overcome Soviet resistance to the reunification of Germany, Helmut Kohl could indulge in sovereign self-criticism by acknowledging that his earlier comments on Gorbachev had been unjustified. Otherwise the power-holder will act as if he had not heard criticism: anyone who begins to justify himself has already put himself under pressure.

Regarding the old question of whether the power-holder should rely more on fear or on love, Machiavelli is right in claiming that the combination of the two is ideal, that hatred should be avoided, but that under no circumstances should the fear of negative sanctions be renounced.[235] Fear as such does not produce hatred if the person who is afraid recognizes, first, that the fear is necessary in order to avoid worse things, such as anarchy, and second, if it is allied with personal respect. The power-holder must not become contemptible, because his despicableness, even more than his mere hatefulness, encourages the violation of the norms represented by him, since following the commands of a contemptible individual is incompatible with self-respect. A ruler who is hated can remain in power for a long time, because fear is generally a stronger motive than hatred,[236] but he will find it difficult to survive crisis situations,[237] because he will lose at least those of his supporters whom he has not made accomplices in his crimes and who must therefore fear heavy punishment if deprived of his protection[238] (unless they have been prom-

---

232. On the other hand, a moderate sacralization can increase the king's authority and thus one of his instruments of power.

233. Cf. Frederick the Great (1920), 102.

234. I am referring to the first scene of act 4.

235. Cf. *Principe* 17 (1986, 151 ff.). Machiavelli's concept of love naturally does not imply the kind of thoroughgoing symmetry that I have attributed to it above.

236. Cf. Montesquieu (1734), 182.

237. Cf. Shakespeare, *Richard III* act 5, sc. 2, vv. 20 f.: "He hath no friends but what are friends for fear, / Which in his dearest need will fly from him."

238. "Quant aux principales dignités, aux principaux démembrements du pouvoir, on doit s'arranger pour les donner à des hommes dont les antécédents et le caractère mettent un abîme entre eux et les autres hommes, dont chacun n'ait à attendre que la mort ou l'exil en cas de changement de gouvernement et soit dans la nécessité de défendre jusqu'au dernier souffle tout ce qui est" (Joly,

ised amnesty); but a ruler who is no longer feared or is even regarded with contempt will probably be displaced after a short time and in most cases, even before a crisis—even if perhaps, unlike a hated ruler, in a non-violent way. Yet only someone whom people like and whom they willingly obey will be able not only to get them to stop doing certain things, but also to spur them on to the greatest efforts. For this, it is indispensable that the power-holder recognize the achievements and the successes of the power-subjects, and even inconspicuously seek them out himself where they commonly occur. He should often and publicly praise, but restrict his reproaches as much as possible to private conversations (and never make them in front of the criticized person's subordinates) or show his disappointment only by withdrawing his recognition, so that the persons he rules find out by themselves what they have done wrong.[239] He should avoid the arrogance that people are likely to attribute to him even if there is no real justification for doing so, because the asymmetry of the situation has something embarrassing about it; a condescending nature can make more enemies for the power-holder than the real damage he inflicts on other people.[240] Humor and self-irony can be effective antidotes against the temptation to be arrogant usually coupled with a position of power. With a reasonable system of positive sanctions (such as good wages and the prospect of future promotion), that is, a system correlated with performance, something can be achieved; but is important not to give too much too soon, because this only creates unfulfillable expectations; there must be a long series of graduated opportunities for advancement,[241] and the aspirant to power should never be too sure that he will receive a specific position. Not only because economic means are always limited, but also because nothing is more willingly done than what one feels to be an end in itself, it can be said that great cratic changes have never been possible without

---

7th dialogue [1864], 62; cf. 8th dialogue, 70). ("As for the chief offices, the main divisions of power, one must be sure to give them to men whose antecedents and character put an abyss between them and other men, each of them being able to expect nothing but death or exile in the event of a change of government, and being forced to defend the status quo until their last breath.")

239. A particularly noble form of reproach is self-criticism that is in fact directed toward subordinates. P. Lenz-Medoc once said that he had been with Pope John XXIII when a newly created cardinal came in and in an unbearably vain way complained about the burden of his new office. The pope listened to him for a while and finally replied, "I can well understand your feelings, for when I became a cardinal, I felt just as you do—until my guardian angel appeared in a dream and said: 'Angelo, please, don't take yourself so seriously.'"

240. Cf. Frederick the Great (1920), 106: "Le manque d'attentions fait plus d'ennemis aux princes que le mal réel qu'il font." Even great persons are constantly suspected of being arrogant; a certain jovial affability is the usual way out of this situation.

241. Cf. Frederick the Great (1920), 35: "Comme tous les hommes, par un effet de leur inquiétude naturelle, tendent sans cesse à améliorer leur état, il faut de l'économie jusque dans la distribution des récompenses, afin d'avoir toujours quelque faveur en réserve qui serve à tranquilliser les plus avides. Donner peu et souvent: c'est un moyen infaillible de rendre les hommes heureux." ("Since all men, as a result of their natural discontent, constantly strive to improve their condition, economy is required even in the distribution of rewards, in order to always keep in reserve some favor that will serve to quiet the most avid. Giving little and often: that is an infallible way to make men happy.")

arousing enthusiasm, no matter whether these changes were for the better or for the worse: Hitler and Stalin were able to drive people to sacrifice themselves because they were devoted to the cause. However, subordinates can be prepared only step by step for projects that demand great sacrifices—Guicciardini advises "getting men to swallow bitter pills in several gulps."[242] Rhetorical abilities are crucial for motivating people, but it is still more indispensable, in order to impose a certain behavior, that the power-holder himself live, or at least seem to live, in accord with the established norms, and thus perform his *function as a model*.[243] "For princes are the glass, the school, the book, / Where subjects' eyes do learn, do read, do look."[244] So that he may be recognized as the highest authority when conflicts arise, the power-holder must *seem* to be impartial and knowledgeable. I say "seem" because, from a cratic point of view, what counts is primarily seeming and not being,[245] even if in the long run seeming without being is difficult to maintain—which does not mean, however, that being without seeming is critically relevant. It is critically ideal, because it costs nothing and does not obligate one in any way, if other people can be employed for one's own ends, while they believe that they are only carrying out their own intentions—that is, when one can make use of "useful idiots," of whom there are always an astonishing number. But one must take care that one is not oneself being instrumentalized while thinking that one is using others.

Although overestimating oneself can be disastrous, an appropriate self-assessment is indispensable: if he is the best of the competitors, the power-holder should know it, because he will be able to derive strength from this knowledge. A person who does not really want his position of power will soon lose it, and few things are more ridiculous than the false coyness about oneself involved in acting as if one did not really want the offered authority, but has accepted it only under coercion. However, it can be cratically wise to let others approach one first, because in that way they commit themselves to support one's own power, and this has a more convincing effect on third parties—even Shakespeare's Richard III lets himself be asked to accept the crown.[246] Since it is impossible to rule without at least a partial consensus, occasional threats to resign may be useful, especially in a system with a separation of powers. Yet this weapon must be used sparingly, because it quickly loses its edge and because one may be taken at one's word. Not only may self-respect obligate one to resign if one can no longer carry out what one believes in, but it can also be cratically wise, because one's absence can more easily remind people of who one was than continued presence, and because it is not inconceivable that one may ultimately be called back and then have the possibility of doing what one really wants to do. De Gaulle's calculation in 1946 succeeded, though considerably later than he had hoped,

242. (1977), 174 (Ricordi C 197): ". . . di far inghiottire le vivande amare, quando si può, in più di uno boccone." Trans. M. Domandi, 92.

243. Cf. *Discorsi* III 22.12 (1984, 524).

244. Shakespeare, *The Rape of Lucrece*, 615 f.

245. Cf. the witty book by T. Meyer (1992).

246. *Richard III* act 3, sc. 7.

and therefore under very different historical conditions. However, one should always realistically assess the results that might be produced by one's withdrawal; Italian deputies taking part in the Aventine secession who believed boycotting legislative work would result in anything more than a further extension of Mussolini's power were naïve.

Because of human ambition, the power-holder must always reckon with the fact that there are people who want to take over his position. For the most part, they can be found next to the top,[247] and since they themselves generally have enemies, the power-holder will ally himself with the latter. Thus some monarchs have resisted the aristocracy by allying themselves with forces from the bourgeoisie, and many Greek tyrants did the same by allying themselves with the people. An opportunity to deprive opponents of their power may consist in bringing them into one's own leadership structure, which they must therefore acknowledge, and burdening them with concrete responsibility; it may be easier to control them if they are operating in proximity to one and under one's own supervision than if they construct opposing positions of power at a great distance. It was crucial for the success of French absolutism, for instance, to attract the nobility to the court and to entrust it with splendid, but cratically insignificant, positions. However, it can also be that offering positions to opponents gives them a chance and even helps them to achieve precisely what should be prevented. On no account should one bring in weak opponents, because this only enhances their status; and with strong opponents, one must be careful that they do not shift the focus of power in a way that is to their advantage. (It was a sign of enormous cratic naiveté when the nationalist conservative establishment in Italy and Germany found it possible to believe that after they had brought Fascists and Nazis into the government they would be able to use them for their own ends—it soon became evident who was stronger.) Unlike dealing with external enemies, in dealing with internal competitors the maxim "divide and conquer" is seldom appropriate. It can be pleasant if external enemies are fighting with each other; if on the other hand one's own ministers or people are fighting against one another, that may get competitors off one's back for a moment, but the government or the state will soon no longer be able to act.[248] On the contrary, the ability to unite one's subordinates is very crucial for the success of the power-holder. Therefore, for example, a head of government should try to put an end to squabbles among ministers and not create them himself by openly preferring the advice of one of them to that of the others.[249] Doing the latter can produce only short-term advantages.

---

247. Cf. *Principe* 3.6 (1986; 92) and 9.2 (122); also Montesquieu (1734), 74.

248. Cf. *Principe* 20.4 f. (1986; 172 f.); *Discorsi* III 27 (1984; 533 ff.); *Kauṭilīya-Arthaśāstra* 7.11.19 (which otherwise recommends the "divide and conquer" strategy; see, for example, 1.13.18; 5.1.14). Cf. also Shakespeare, *Henry VI*, Part 1, act 4, sc. 3 f.

249. Cf. Frederick the Great (1920), 39: "Il peut être bon dans des cas embarassants de consulter un ministre qu'on croira le plus sage et le plus expérimenté; si on en veut consulter un autre, que ce soit séparément, pour ne point jeter . . . des semences d'animosité qui ne finissent jamais." ("It can be a good idea, in difficult cases, to consult the minister one thinks the wisest and the most experienced; if one wants to consult another, let it be separately, in order not to sow . . . the seeds of animosity that never cease."

The power-holder must defend himself against those who try to rob him of his position—and he must do so with special energy at the beginning, because more attacks will be made on a person who is new in power than on one who has already shown himself to be unyielding.[250] At the beginning of a rule, especially one that is not secure, negative sanctions are commonly imposed,[251] and there are certainly rulers who have governed magnanimously after an initial phase of brutality—Aśoka and Augustus are well-known examples, whereas Hitler's and Stalin's lust for blood only increased with time.[252] In any case, the use of strength where it is cratically necessary should be distinguished from cruelty: the pure crat is not inclined toward crimes that contribute nothing to his maintenance of power. Brilliantly, Marguerite Yourcenar has her Hadrian, who considers deception and murder justified in connection with his mysterious adoption by Trajan, say, regarding the rumor that he had his wife murdered, that he had never been tempted to commit so superfluous a crime;[253] one can hardly avoid having the impression that the emperor is more annoyed at being accused of doing something superfluous than at being accused of committing a crime. Concerning ruthless action, Machiavelli offers the following cratological advice: If limited to specific and predictable occasions (particularly at the beginning of a rule), it produces less hatred than if it is continued indefinitely;[254] the number of enemies against whom one proceeds should not be too great and undetermined; harsh punishment is more advisable than a lighter one that does not break the will but only produces a thirst for revenge.[255]

The power-holder can allow himself to proceed against his internal enemies particularly when external enemies pose a threat—for the common enemy welds together

---

250. "Res dura et regni novitas me talia cogunt / moliri et late finis custode tueri," complains Dido in Virgil's famous verses (*Aeneid* I 563 f.) ("My kingdom is new; hard circumstances have forced me to such measures for our safety, to post guards far and wide along our boundaries." Trans. A. Mandelbaum (1981), 20. Cf. *Principe* 17.1 (1986; 152).

251. Which negative sanctions are threatened and used depends on the contextual framework. In constitutional states, in which citizens' life and property are protected, a favorite method is blackmailing with information regarding violations of the law, of which most politicians are guilty.

252. Even if it had been cratically necessary to eliminate Ernst Röhm, Hitler's abominable thirst for revenge, which went far beyond what could have been considered—if only subjectively—to be cratically required, was shown by the way he used the opportunity to settle old accounts and to murder opponents (for instance, Gustav Kahr) who could no longer have posed any conceivable danger to him. After this, it should have been impossible not to see what kind of man Hitler was.

253. (1974), 279: "Il va sans dire qu'un crime si superflu ne m'avait jamais tenté."

254. *Principe* 8.7 f. (1986; 120 f).

255. *Principe* 3.5 (1986; 91): "Per il che si ha a notare che gli uomini si debbano o vezzeggiare o spegnere; perché si vendicano delle leggieri offese, delle gravi non possono." ("For it must be noted, that men must be either coddled or destroyed, because they will revenge themselves for small injuries, but cannot do so for great ones." Trans. Ricci, 9.) See also 17.3 (153): "perché gli uomini sdimenticano più presto la morte del padre che la perdita del patrimonio." ("for men forget more easily the death of their father than the loss of their patrimony." Trans. Ricci, 62.) Cf. also *Discorsi* I 26 f. and, on human vindictiveness, II 28 (1984; 121 f., 370 ff.).

the collective he confronts. In such a situation, the power-holder can hardly be replaced, and a conspiracy against him is regarded as unpardonable treason.[256] In fact, there is an interesting dialectic between internal and external enemies. An attack by or on the latter can distract from internal problems[257] and can therefore be much desired. In Shakespeare's play, the dying Henry IV advises his son to distract his subjects' attention from his own questionable legitimacy by launching into a foreign adventure.[258] However, the hoped-for effect is generally achieved only when one is successful in the foreign enterprise— many a tyrant has been overthrown as a result of failed attempts at expansion. However, the reason that Saddam Hussein, for instance, was able to retain power after the First Gulf War is that, on one hand, his external opponents did not want to divide up his country, because they feared strengthening Iran, and, on the other hand, there were apparently no realistic alternatives within Iraq. Indeed, if one is already not liked or even hated, it can strengthen one's own power both inside and outside the country to be less hated and feared than the most likely alternative.[259] In certain situations the anger over a long suffered wrong can be so great that one wants to be freed of it even if this might result in a still greater wrong, which at least has not yet been experienced to the point that one is tired of it; yet, as a rule it is cratically advisable to allow only alternatives that are worse than one's own government. Civil war may be such an alternative; especially after a long phase of such conflicts that produce exhaustion, the power of even a tyrant has often been strengthened, and a Caligula can contemplate the idea of putting a whinnying Consul in charge even of Roman senators, the descendants of the founders of a world empire.[260] Another possibility is a terrible successor: if the opponents of the power-holder know that they will be tyrannized even more dreadfully after his downfall, they will do nothing to bring him down. Indeed, even after his death he may at least be remembered fondly because he was better than his successor[261]—one of the reasons why a mediocrity, on one hand, favors bad up-and-coming younger people and, on the

---

256. Wars are already seen by the *Kauṭilīya-Arthaśāstra* (7.13.34 f.) as opportunities to conduct purges.

257. Cf. *Principe* 21.1 (1986; 176 f.). Cf. already Plato, *Republic* 566 d ff.

258. *Henry IV,* Part 2, act 4, sc. 5, vv. 212 ff.: "Therefore, my Harry, / Be it thy course to busy giddy minds / With foreign quarrels, that action, hence borne out, / May waste the memory of the former days."

259. Cf. Joly, 23rd dialogue (1864; 234): "Le trait essentiel de ma politique comme vous avez pu le voir, a été de me rendre indispensable; j'ai détruit autant de forces organisées qu'il l'a fallu pour que rien ne pût plus marcher sans moi, pour que les ennemis mêmes de mon pouvoir tremblassent de le renverser." ("The essential feature of my policy, as you have seen, was to make myself indispensable; I destroyed as many of the organized forces as was necessary to make it so that nothing could continue to operate without me, so that even the enemies of my power feared to overthrow it.")

260. Cf. Suetonius, *Caligula* 55 (if reliable).

261. Cf. the famous anecdote—related by Thomas Aquinas (*De regimine principium* I 6), among others) according to which a tyrant hated by everyone is astonished to learn that an old woman sincerely wishes him long life—and hears her explain that he was even worse than his predecessor, who was worse than *his* predecessor, and she fears that things will go on in the same way.

other, fears few things more than succeeding an important man, who set the standard by which he will be judged. For hardly anyone obeys a mediocrity more unwillingly than someone who has served a great person.[262]

One of the most important maxims for the political man has to do with the delegation of authority where exercising it oneself is risky. The power-holder will do well not to make unpopular decisions by himself (in any case, not alone), or at least not seem to do so, but all the more will he reserve for himself decisions that will make him popular or maintain his popularity[263]—just as he will take credit for successful enterprises and blame unsuccessful ones on a scapegoat.[264] To decrease anxiety regarding his power, the power-holder will repeatedly have to give the impression that he is not the one that makes all the decisions; and sometimes, in making a decision that corresponds to his innermost wish, he will act as though he had unwillingly yielded to external pressure or objective necessity.[265] If things are to be done that are morally questionable, the power-holder will protect himself by means of the opinions of others, and refuse ultimate responsibility himself. Even Henry V, whom Shakespeare certainly sees positively, is a master of delegating to others the responsibility for morally dubious enterprises such as the war against France.[266] Sometimes the power-holder will merely hint at what he wants and in some cases ultimately make a point of distancing himself from what has happened. "For when the powerful man is weary of the conflict, / He adroitly throws onto the little man, / Who has innocently served him, the bloody mantle / Of blame, and stands there easily purified."[267] In the third scene of the third act of *King John*, Shakespeare describes in a striking way how the king leads Hubert de Burgh, a man in his service, to believe that the mere presence of his little nephew Arthur, the son of his elder brother, endangers him. After introductory declarations regarding the fondness he feels for Hubert and that Hubert feels for him, the king says that Arthur "is a very serpent in my way," and asks, "Dost thou understand me? / Thou art his keeper." Hubert understands what is being asked of him and replies, "And I'll keep him so, / That he shall not offend Your Majesty." Then King John utters two nouns—"death" and "grave"— that are not elaborated into a sentence, and certainly not into an explicit command; and when Hubert finally says, "He shall not live," the king interrupts him, saying, "Enough,"

---

262. What Camões says about kings—that no kingdom obeys them that is used to sovereign princes if they are not better than the predecessors—also holds for any power-holder: "Mas o Reino, de altivo e costumado / A senhores em tudo soveranos, / A Rei não obedece nem consente / Que não for mais que todos excelente" (*Os Lusíadas*, 3:93).

263. Cf. *Principe* 19.7 (1986; 162): "li principi debbano le cose di carico fare sumministrare ad altri, quelle di grazia a loro medesimi."

264. Cf. Gracián, *Oráculo manual*, 149.

265. Cf. Joly, 7th and 9th dialogues (1864; 61, 87).

266. *Henry V* act 1, sc. 2, vv. 96 f.; act 4, sc. 1, vv. 134 ff.

267. Schiller, *Die Braut von Messina* vv. 1781 ff.: "Denn wenn der Mächtige des Streits ermüdet, / Wirft er behend auf den geringen Mann, / Der arglos ihm gedient, den blutgen Mantel / Der Schuld und leicht gereinigt steht er da."

and adding, "Hubert, I love thee," but remaining in the framework of indeterminate promises—the king will not say what he will do for Hubert. After he has spoken with the charming little boy, Hubert decides to spare him (he realizes that he should not have spoken with him, if he wanted to commit the murder);[268] but when the news of the boy's death (resulting from an accident) becomes known and causes great difficulties for the king, Hubert is not received with gratitude by the king.[269] On the contrary, John calls *him* a murderer and goes on to say that "It is the curse of kings to be attended / By slaves that take their humors for a warrant / To break within the bloody house of life, / And on the winking of authority / To understand a law, to know the meaning / Of dangerous majesty, when perchance it frowns / More upon humor than advised respect."[270] Only the presence of the means—Hubert—put the idea into his head at that time, the king claims; had Hubert shaken his head or even, doubting, asked him to say explicitly what was to be done, he would have come to his senses. It has to be granted John that had Hubert put his hints into effect, he would also bear a heavy guilt, perhaps even heavier than that of the king, because the latter, as he says, may have had a reason for wanting Arthur dead, whereas Hubert had no comparably urgent motive to kill him; yet of course John's own guilt remains great.[271] Nonetheless, John does not have Hubert killed—whereas one of the most terrible stories in *Il Principe* deals with how Cesare Borgia first sent Ramiro de Lorqua into the Romagna in order to pacify it by brutal violence and then, when he had carried out his assignment in accord with Borgia's wishes and had thus made himself, for obvious reasons, both superfluous and unpopular, had him killed and displayed, cut into two pieces, in Cesena, in order to show the people that he did not identify with what Ramiro had done, and that he himself certainly knew how to make use of force when he considered it necessary to do so.[272]

5.2.4. The Loneliness of the Power-Holder

It goes without saying that the structure just described condemns most people in power—and not just the power-obsessed—to loneliness.[273] Hardly any work expresses

---

268. Act 4, sc. 1, vv. 25 f.

269. Much the same goes for Exton, who murders Richard II on a hint from the usurper Bolingbroke (*Richard II* act 5, sc. 4, and act 5, sc. 6).

270. Act 4, sc. 2, vv. 209 ff.

271. This also holds, though in a limited way, for Faust, who surely never wanted Philemon and Baucis to be killed; but one does not give Mephistopheles and the three mighty men orders.

272. 7.8 (1986; 112 f.).

273. Nonetheless, it is possible, though difficult, to keep sincere friends not only while rising to power, but also after the highest position of power has been attained—if they are able to respect the distance that the power-holder as such requires. Presumably this was easier in feudal times, when people were still familiar with the concept of an asymmetrical friendship. Einhard confirmed that Charlemagne had a great capacity for friendship: "Erat enim in amicitiis optime temperatus, ut eas

this more poignantly than Schiller's *Maria Stuart*. Even there, the queen declines to accept responsibility for executing her opponent, and she punishes Burleigh and Davison, who have interpreted her intention absolutely correctly. However, she hopes in vain to win in this way the friendship of Talbot, who had opposed the execution of Mary Stuart. He sees through the queen's maneuver and advises her not to exile the truest friends "who have acted on your behalf, and who now keep silent for your sake,"[274] whereas he himself resigns every office. Since Leicester has also gone over to France, at the end of the play Elizabeth stands on the stage alone and without friends. However, even without such a reason, many things condemn the power-holder to loneliness. In a monarchy, even the king's most personal choice, that of a bride, is subject to the strongest restrictions—think of Titus and Berenice.[275] Generally speaking, too close a relationship with a person can limit the power-holder's freedom of decision and threaten his impartiality. He must keep his distance, even with regard to his own family: officials' executions of their own sons in the early Roman republic may be legendary, but it is certain that in extreme cases this kind of thing was expected of Roman statesmen.[276] The account, in the second book of Samuel, of David's grief over the death of his son Absalom after a battle is very true to life and therefore presumably historical. The rebellious Absalom was an enemy of the state, yet he was also David's son, and David's mourning is absolutely comprehensible from a human point of view. But it disturbs his soldiers, who have fought for him and risked their lives, and the general, Joab, who killed Absalom in violation of David's order, shouts at him: "Thou hast shamed this day the faces of all thy servants that have saved thy life . . . Thou lovest them that hate thee, and thou hatest them who love thee . . . Now therefore arise, and go out, and speak to the satisfaction of thy servants, for I swear to thee by the Lord, that if thou wilt not go forth, there will not tarry with thee so much as one this night."[277] There is nothing left for David to do but to overcome his private pain and do what Joab advises. Sigmund Freud is surely right in seeing in the restriction of the king's freedom of action by courtly protocol a sublime form of the revenge of the underlings. "In exactly the same way, the ceremonial taboo of kings is *ostensibly* the highest honour and protection for them, while *actually* it is a punishment for their exaltation, a revenge taken on them by their subjects. The experiences of Sancho Panza (as described by Cervantes) when he was governor of his island convinced him that this view of court ceremonials was the only one that met the case. If we could hear the views

---

et facile admitteret et constantissime retineret, colebatque sanctissime quoscumque hac adfinitate sibi coniunxerat" (*Vita Karoli Magni* 19). ("For he was perfectly moderate in friendships, so that he easily formed them and kept them faithfully, and he treated in the most sacred way whoever had become friends with him.")

274. Act 5, sc. 15, vv. 4017 ff.: "die für dich / Gehandelt haben, die jetzt für dich schweigen."

275. This is only one case among many, but one that was made immortal by Racine's treatment of it.

276. Cf. Livy 2.5 and Virgil, *Aeneid* VI 819 ff.

277. 19:5–7.

of modern kings and rulers on the subject, we might find that there were many others who agreed with him."[278]

Even when the power-holder can give full expression to his feelings, he will seldom be able to avoid suspecting that other people's love for him is interested and not sincere. Xenophon has the tyrant Hieron complain to Simonides that he can indulge in all the pleasures—for instance, the beautiful Dailochos is willing to submit to his wishes—but he feels like a robber to whom no one gives anything willingly, but who takes everything himself.[279] Even a despot who can, for whatever reason, feel secure will be pained by the suspicion that everything is done only out of fear and interest, never out of love; and it is tautologically true that an omnipotent ruler cannot know another person's freely given love.[280] This suspicion is one of the reasons for Tiberius's distrust and misanthropy; and one can hardly hold it against him that the servility and calculation of those around him did not exactly fill him with respect for his fellow men.[281] One of the few passages in which the reader cannot deny his sympathy even to Tacitus's Tiberius is the one in which the physician Charicles, as he is leaving Tiberius, surreptitiously takes the old, sick man's pulse; this does not escape the aged observer of men, and, enraged that someone is trying to predict his imminent demise, he returns to the banquet table to show himself and others that he is still alive.[282] Indeed, for no one is death more terrible than for the hated power-holder, who is well aware that nothing will survive him, that the end of all his fantasies of omnipotence will be followed by an explosion of hatred, and later, worse yet, enter into the dark night of oblivion—no other person falls into death from a higher point. For that very reason, Tiberius became for a time steadily more dependent on Sejanus, because the latter had saved him from falling stones—and this was presumably one of the very few times in Tiberius's life when he could feel that someone was really thinking about him and not, despite all subservience primarily about his own interests.[283] But it is dangerous when the power-holder, in order to escape his dreadful loneliness, occasionally confides his secrets to a subordinate[284] or even begins to desire his friendship.

---

278. (1913), 60 f. Trans. J. Strachey, 51.

279. *Hieron* 1.31 ff. Cf. especially sections 1, 3, and 4.

280. By "freely given," I mean here not "substantively reasonable," but "uncoerced and unpredictable."

281. However, he bore part of the responsibility for this, and therefore his hatred for his fellow men included self-hatred. Cf. Montesquieu (1734), 113.

282. *Annals* VI 50.

283. *Annals* IV 59: "Maior ex eo, et quamquam exitiosa suaderet, ut non sui anxius, cum fide audiebatur." ("After this he was greater than ever, and though his counsels were ruinous, he was listened to with confidence, as a man who had no care for himself." Trans. A. J. Church and W. J. Brodribb, 141.)

284. Cf. Shakespeare, *Pericles* act 1, sc. 3, vv. 3 ff.: "Well, I perceive he was a wise fellow and had good discretion that, being bid to ask what he would of the King, desired he might know none of his secrets." See also Gracián, *Oráculo manual*, 237.

Probably he will soon regret this, and the atmosphere of familiarity and friendliness will at best be replaced by the icy distance that helps preserve power. For anyone, there is "on one hand a fundamentally paradoxical relation . . . between dependency on love and on recognition, and the wish to be a winner on the other"; but this paradox, which "proves the insurmountable crookedness" of our nature,[285] is usually particularly marked in a power-holder. Caligula, who seems to have sincerely loved only one person, his wife, Caesonia, is said to have remarked characteristically that he wanted to get out of her, by torture if necessary, why he loved her so much[286]—obviously in order to compensate for the loss of autonomy that is represented by any love and that must especially torment a power-obsessed person. Caligula was a psychopath, but in other, subtler forms this problem is found in most power-holders. Philip, in Schiller's *Don Carlos,* suffers like King Midas from the fact that everything he touches turns to gold—but into the gold of the asymmetrical relationship that the king's power represents. "King! Only king / And king again!—No better answer / Than an empty, hollow echo? I strike / this rock and want water, water / For my raging, feverish thirst— and it gives / Me red-hot gold."[287] Therefore he is fascinated by Posa, whom he sees as the "einzge[n] Mensch, der meiner nicht bedarf" (the only man who doesn't need me) and who could thus provide him with the truth.[288] For him, only Posa's recognition would have any value, whereas the subordination of lower individuals would merely disgrace them, but not bring him any honor.[289] However, the feeling that he has been exploited and even betrayed even by Posa, who felt true friendship only for Carlos, leads Philip to completely renounce the human and political opening he had considered to make, and hardens him once and for all and to the highest degree. It is a point in the mature Schiller's favor that he, whose earlier plays merely scourged the wickedness of the power-holder, learned, while working on *Don Carlos,* to see the dignity and the misery of the opposing side. Philip is a despot, but he definitely feels responsibility, and when he errs, he is a victim no less than an executioner. He may never get water to drink, but he finally produces it himself—his tears are genuine and truly human.[290]

---

285. The passages quoted are taken from M. Hennen (1995), 403.

286. Suetonius, *Caligula* 33.

287. Act 3, sc. 2, vv. 2511 ff.: "König! König nur / Und wieder König!—Keine beßre Antwort / Als leeren, hohlen Widerhall? Ich schlage / An diesen Felsen und will Wasser, Wasser / Für meinen heißen Fieberdurst—er gibt / Mir glühend Gold."

288. Act 3, sc. 5, v. 2845.

289. I allude to Polybius's well-known statement in Livy 45.44.20 regarding the disgusting servility of Prusias.

290. However, it is possible that because of his suffering the power-holder may begin to see himself as the one truly subjected to power, and begin to derive from this a special kind of legitimation of his power. See Robespierre at the end of act 1 of G. Büchner's *Dantons Tod.*

5.3. POWER AND MORALS

How are the forms of power and the maxims of political men to be evaluated morally? Obviously a serious answer to this question must take two things into account: on one hand, the forms of power have an intrinsic—positive or negative—value; all other things being equal, force is always more questionable morally than is persuasion. On the other hand, one cannot resolve the moral problem posed by power if one does not consider the goals that power seeks to achieve in each case. Whether someone seeks power in order to construct or overthrow a constitutional state based on the rule of law, in order to protect or destroy human life, for the sake of reasonable values or particular interests clearly makes a difference morally. Generic demonizations of power like that in Schlosser's and Burckhardt's well-known dictum that power is inherently evil, no matter who exercises it,[291] are false because they overlook the fact that the evil that certain forms of power undeniably represent can be controlled only by other manifestations of power. In addition, it is unfortunate that, for the most part, not just any form of power is sufficient to overcome the force of evil. Usually, if it wants to win, it must be the same kind of power as the evil power: violence can seldom be deterred by economic sanctions alone.

In view of the impossibility of avoiding the exercise of power, condemning it in principle leads to a pessimistic worldview that is, moreover, self-contradictory, because it inevitably makes a claim to power itself. Even theoreticians who fundamentally reject power want to have an effect; the power of the radical "critics of power" has sometimes been considerable in the culture industry of enlightened countries; and distrust is appropriate with regard to those who strive to overcome power, because for the most part they simply want it for themselves. At most, it would be reasonable to wish that the distribution of power among people were nearly equal—but even that implies that this distribution must be defended against those who are not in agreement with it; and it is not easy to see how this is supposed to take place without power struggles, or at least a readiness to engage in power struggles, and without the establishment of institutions with a monopoly on the use of force.

From this it does not follow, of course, that the opposite conception of Nietzsche—who was obsessed with the theoretical problem of power—is correct, namely, that power is to be affirmed as such; and Machiavelli's reduction of *virtù* to the ability to impose one's will must also be rejected, although this ability is at least a secondary virtue. In any case, only a differentiated evaluation of the forms of power as well as of the ends it serves can be convincing. Just as the theoretical social sciences are not helped by statements such as "everything is power," so sweeping assertions regarding power do not advance ethics.

---

291. Cf. Burckhardt (1905), 36, 97, 139.

5.3.1. The Impossibility of Doing without Power

First, the moral quality of the wish to impose one's own will depends on the content of this will. Since what is morally obligatory should not be merely wished, but be translated into reality—because what is right should become might and moral maxims should be evolutionarily stable—it is permissible, indeed sometimes even obligatory, to try to impose a moral intention against resistance—and even against social resistance. To be sure, it would be desirable not to encounter resistance on the part of others; and it is certainly a moral service to work for a world in which, because of a broad consensus, power struggles would become rarer, or at least less serious. But on several grounds it is impossible to imagine a complete end to power struggles: first of all, because of the finite nature of human reason, even assuming good will on all sides (which is an assumption not many would share), conflicts over what is moral are inevitable, and in good conscience one can hardly yield on a point concerning something one considers morally obligatory.[292] Second, competition, as a milder (because legally regulated) form of power struggle, contributes to the common good; precisely when, on the basis of a universalist ethics, one rejects filling offices by hereditary succession, seniority, and so on, competition becomes indispensable. Third, it is self-evident that even institutions that make power struggles less frequent cannot be established without debate and conflict—at least, not everyone will conceive these institutions in the same way; someone who works for consensus as the ultimate authority for conflict resolution will have to fight (ideally, only by means of better arguments) those who do not believe in this authority. And even after it has been agreed that rational arguments are the final criteria for decision, it is obvious that individuals' different argumentative competencies will lead to an unequal distribution of power. Fourth, it can hardly be denied that certain virtues such as the courage of one's convictions are first shown in power struggles—hence it would be regrettable if the latter disappeared altogether.

To be sure, it is reasonable to avoid superfluous conflicts: a wise man, when he found his way blocked by a fool whom he had made morally insecure, and who said, "I don't step aside for rogues," was right to respond in a friendly tone, "But I do," as he turned off into a side street. Nonetheless, the saying "The smarter man yields" is not always correct—world domination by fools is not an ideal. Moreover, this statement cannot be universalized, and it is surely contrary to duty to call for capitulation to injustice. (Indeed, even most pacifists do not deny that resistance is allowed—they merely think it should not be violent, or at least not include violence toward people.) Constant surrendering does

---

292. To that extent even the friend-foe difference, which is necessarily part of the concept of power, is a necessary consequence of the moral difference between good and evil. But that does not mean than every friend-foe relationship is moral in nature; and therefore Schmitt's adherence to the friend-foe difference in "the age of neutralizations," although intended to be an act of resistance against the current tendency not to make differentiations, is in reality itself a contribution to the leveling-out of moral differences and thus to nihilism.

not get power out of the world—on the contrary, it increases the obsession with power on the other side: It is sheep that first create the wolf.[293] That yielding can be immoral is particularly clear if one thinks about the exercise of power delegated by others. As a rule, it is already contrary to duty to allow oneself to be abused; for in that way one accepts a violation of one's own dignity, which no one, not even oneself, has a right to do—quite apart from the fact that one thereby encourages the aggressor to behave in a similar way toward other people. In addition, those who do not acknowledge duties to themselves can hardly assume that a surrendering on principle is permissible when one has responsibilities for others. One may, indeed should, sometimes turn the other cheek, but one has no right to offer up the cheeks of other people. Frederick the Great rightly held that a ruler who fails to punish a crime shares the responsibility for it,[294] and Fichte, in his splendid essay on Machiavelli, which seeks to provide a justification of *Il Principe* in terms of moral philosophy, writes with great clarity: "People are not the property of the prince, so that he can regard their welfare, their independence, their dignity, and their determination within the whole of the human race as his private affair, and can err as much as he wants and when it goes badly, say: Well, I made a mistake, but so what? The injury is mine and I'll bear it—in the same way that the owner of a flock of sheep through whose negligence part of the flock has died might console himself."[295] Conrad's Lord Jim may have put his own life on the line, but his guilt is based on the fact that because of his naive trust in Brown his friends and protégés were killed.

Whoever the figure at the entrance to Hell is, of whom Dante says that he made the great refusal through cowardice,[296] Celestine V in any case exemplifies what Dante must have had in mind: that it is not always commendable to resign a responsibility one has accepted, especially if doing so makes it possible for a rogue to ascend to power. The piety of the noble hermit is unquestioned, but he should never have become pope in the first place, or, after he had become pope, he should not have resigned in a situation in which a Boniface VIII was the most likely successor. The opposition in character between the unworldly recluse and the jurist obsessed with power could hardly be greater; but since by a peculiar dialectic the former paved the way for the latter, he bears part of the responsibility for the perversion of the papacy in the lust for worldly power. Whereas Dante places Boniface in hell,[297] Celestine (if it is he) is not granted even this

---

293. Cf. Shakespeare, *Julius Caesar* act 1, sc. 3 vv. 104 ff.

294. (1920), 2. One already finds something similar in Nizam al-Mulk (1960), 66, at the beginning of chap. 10.

295. (1971), 11:426. "Die Völker sind ja nicht ein Eigenthum des Fürsten, so daß er deren Wohl, deren Selbständigkeit, deren Würde, deren Bestimmung in einem Ganzen des Menschengeschlechts, als seine Privatsache betrachten, und fehlen könne nach Belieben, und wenn es schlecht geht, sagen könne: nun, ich habe geirrt, aber was ist's denn weiter? der Schade ist mein und ich will ihn tragen; so wie etwa der Besitzer einer Heerde, durch dessen Nachlässigkeit ein Theil derselben zu Grunde gegangen wäre, sich trösten könnte."

296. *Inferno* III 59 f.: "vidi e conobbi l'ombra di colui / che fece per viltate il gran rifiuto."

297. *Inferno* XIX 52 ff.

clear sentence: divine justice and divine mercy despise both cowards and irresponsible people who have not committed themselves to anything and thus displease both God and the devil; the pilgrim walks past them in silence.[298] It is obvious that Dante has in view a frequently recurring, general type of person who fails, especially in historically exceptional situations, because he does not have the willpower that is required to exercise responsibly the office he holds: in the twentieth century, we should recall Prince Georgi Yevgenyevich Lvov, the first prime minister of the provisional government after the Russian February Revolution. Tolstoy's doctrine that evil should not be resisted may be discussed in cloisters; but one should not go into politics if one flirts with it.

Shakespeare would not be the great analyst of the problem of power had he not also created characters that correspond to this type: Richard II and Henry VI, who bring immeasurable suffering on their countries through their inability to reign.[299] Both ruler figures are all the more fascinating because they are in no way contemptible but rather, in their own ways, magnificent personalities—one a sensitive esthete, and the other a saint who touches us by his sheer goodness. But neither of them is a political man. Richard II, who enchants us through the unheard-of splendor of his speech and the richness of his feelings, especially his capacity for suffering, and at the same time repels us by his tendency to narcissism and his weakness of will, recognizes his own guilt, since he does not resist his deposition.[300] Only against his murderers does Richard defend himself; and he is able to knock down two of them and wish them to hell before he falls—an act of self-assertion that ennobles the dying king. In contrast, stabbed by Gloucester, Henry VI dies addressing words of forgiveness to his murderer: "O, God forgive my sins, and pardon thee!"[301] Naturally, these words remind us of those of Christ, and Henry VI is such a disturbing figure precisely because, on one hand, his failure to act is responsible for the dreadful disaster of the War of the Roses and because, on the other hand, like the hero of Dostoyevsky's *The Idiot,* he shares many characteristics with Christ: only a few women in Shakespeare's work are comparably selfless. Already as a child, Henry VI could not bear conflicts and thus could not really settle them; by urging reconciliation he is not able to resolve a single conflict, but rather merely postpones them and thereby makes them even more dangerous.[302] The war with France seems wicked to him, and even though he considers himself not suited for marriage, he accepts the recommendation that he marry a French prince's daughter in order to make peace. Unable to stand by the decision once it has been made (in truth, it was rather forced on him than independently made), he breaks this engagement for the sake of an-

---

298. *Inferno* III 50, 63.

299. In this connection one should also mention Grillparzer's Rudolf in *Ein Bruderzwist in Habsburg.*

300. Act 4, sc. 1, vv. 248 ff. "Nay, if I turn mine eyes upon myself, / I find myself a traitor with the rest; / for I have given here my soul's consent / T'undeck the pompous body of a king, / Made glory base and sovereignty a slave, / Proud majesty a subject, state a peasant."

301. *Henry VI,* Part 3, act 5, sc. 6, v. 60.

302. *Henry VI,* Part 1, act 3, sc. 1; act 4, sc. 1.

other Frenchwoman, Margaret, whom Suffolk recommends to him—with the intention of dominating the king by making himself Margaret's master.[303] With his bookish learning and naive piety, Henry only earns the contempt of the aristocracy[304] and of his wife[305]; the power vacuum that he allows to emerge around him results in the most serious strife between competing aristocrats, each of whom is trying to instrumentalize the king for his own ends and ultimately seeking direct rule. Incapable of protecting blameless friends, unwilling to investigate an only too justified suspicion, the melancholy king witnesses the downfall of an order, a downfall that he accepts as God's will, without wanting to judge his opponents. Even on the occasion of the death of Cardinal Beaufort, who was tormented by guilt, Henry prays for mercy on the soul of his enemy and says, in awareness of his own guilt, "Forbear to judge, for we are sinners all."[306] To put down Cade's rebellion, he wants to send not the army but a pious bishop; like Christ on the Cross, he deplores that the people do not know what they do.[307] Fully aware of his cratic incompetence, he would gladly be a subordinate, and he certainly realizes that not only is he unhappy, but he has brought disaster upon England, and the country must curse his rule.[308] After Richard of York's rebellion, he is prepared to recognize him as his successor, thus disinheriting his own son. But, under pressure from his wife, the king is forced to retract this decision as well, and he sees with deep pain how his country is falling ever more deeply into civil war and chaos. Plagued by doubts regarding his legitimacy,[309] he feels himself responsible for the suffering of countless innocent people, and urgently asks God to let him die; he feels more guilty than a father who has killed his son, more guilty than a son who has killed his father.[310] Henry's suffering is heartbreaking because he has no illusions about himself and has a great ability to get outside himself and to empathize with the unhappiness of others. One cannot reproach him, because he has not chosen his kingship.[311] Even after he has been dethroned, Henry VI remains, in accord with the legitimist ideas of his time, a pawn in the hands of the true power-holders; the king-maker Warwick puts him back on the throne after he has fallen out with his successor, Edward IV, whom he had previously helped take power. After being deprived of the throne a second time, Henry is murdered, so that similar problems will not arise again. Henry, who would have made a good scholar or priest, is himself a victim of the legitimist system, which has catapulted him into a position for which his character is not suitable.

---

303. *Henry VI*, Part 1, act 5, sc. 1; act 5, sc. 5.

304. *Henry VI*, Part 2, act 1, sc. 1, vv. 242 ff.; act 5, sc. 1, vv. 93 ff.

305. *Henry VI*, Part 2, act 1, sc. 3, 53 ff.

306. *Henry VI*, Part 2, act 3, sc. 3, v. 31; cf. act 3, sc. 2, v. 140.

307. *Henry VI*, Part 2, act 4, sc. 4, vv. 9 ff., 38.

308. *Henry VI*, Part 2, act 4, sc. 9, vv. 1 ff., 18 f., 49.

309. *Henry VI*, Part 3, act 2, sc. 2, vv. 43 ff.

310. *Henry VI*, Part 3, act 2, sc. 5, vv. 1 ff.

311. Much the same goes for the sultans of the declining Ottoman Empire, who had been brought up in the harem and nostalgically longed for their gilded cage.

Henry's fate shows two things: on one hand, it is not reasonable to put someone who is not a political man into such an office, and since there is a moral duty to do all one can to prevent a disaster like the one Henry triggers, it can certainly be said that being a political man can be morally justified. On the other hand, Henry radiates an aura unlike that of any of Shakespeare's other kings (with the exception of Lear), which helps us see why in a legitimist system the monarch is considered the representative of the divine—he utters hardly a sentence that does not shame us by its guilelessness and trust in God. In a world of cratic calculation, he reminds us of a possible social order in which force, threats, and ruse could be superfluous; and we can certainly say that someone who has never felt the longing for such an order can never become a great statesman. It is true that while in office one may not yield to the temptation of fatigue and sadness that arises from the necessity of defending oneself and maintaining fear. But it is no less true that the noble power-holder must have felt this temptation—anyone who has never felt it is crude and brutal.[312] A person can exercise power with a clear conscience only if he sees as one of his main tasks to create through his activity spaces in which people like Henry VI can live in security and free from fear and guilt. Indeed, Shakespeare never deified power or celebrated it as an end in itself: Lear, Hamlet, and Romeo are not political men, and doubtless they are deeper and more fascinating than even Henry V. But they bring suffering and confusion into the social world, and the tragedies devoted to them end with capable ruler figures restoring the framework of power within which alone people can live peacefully. On one hand, the conclusions of these works, especially that of *Hamlet*, recognize the impossibility of doing without power and the impossibility of a long enduring vacuum of power—in agreement with Machiavelli. However, unlike Machiavelli, Shakespeare has these ruler figures feel the human value of those heroes who created chaos—their tragic greatness does not alter the necessity of the prose of power, but it points to the instrumental value of power, above which rises the intrinsic value of the great sufferers and lovers.

5.3.2. The Conditions of Moral Striving for Power

The fact that there are circumstances in which striving to preserve or attain a position of far-reaching power may be morally permissible or even obligatory does not, of course, mean that this striving is always to be evaluated positively in moral terms. Instead, four conditions must be fulfilled (and they seldom are): the position of power that

---

312. However, only in exceptional historical situations will so noble a figure as Václav Havel rise to the highest offices of state—that is, someone who attributes his success to an existential sense of guilt suggestive of Kafka. "I would even venture to say that everything worthwhile I've ever accomplished has been done to conceal my almost metaphysical feeling of guilt. The real reason I am always creating something, organizing something, it would seem, is to defend my permanently questionable right to exist" (1997; 30 f.).

one seeks must be limited; it must be solely a means; one must be personally qualified for it; and one must not consider anything to be permissible in seeking to attain it.

First of all, the position of power sought must be objectively necessary, that is, serve the common good, and be compatible with principles of justice that actually demand the most egalitarian sharing of power possible. Since, as we will show later, an institution with a monopoly on the use of force is generally acceptable only if it is connected with a system of the separation of powers, this implies that striving for a position of power can be approved only within such a system. Someone who seeks more power than this kind of system allows is acting immorally, and the more his wishes deviate from the historically already recognized and institutionally realized forms of the separation of powers, the greater his guilt.

Second, not only the position striven for must be reasonable, but one must also be the right candidate for it. One can hardly abolish the office of head of government, but that does not mean that everyone should seek to become president. Such an office requires certain qualities, and not only cratic ones—otherwise, almost anyone who succeeded in rising to that office would be by definition the right person. However, it goes without saying that cratic abilities are also indispensable for the common good, if only because it is desirable for the sake of continuity that certain offices be held for a longer period of time. Anyone who lacks such abilities will never be able to become a successful politician, and it is a mistake to think that if one has occupied oneself for years with the theoretical knowledge of the common good one can also quickly acquire an instinct for power necessary to put this knowledge into effect; volitional abilities are different in kind from intellectual ones. But it is no less a mistake to believe that it all comes down to cratic abilities alone: the mere possession of such abilities is far from being enough to show that one has a moral right to exercise power. Indeed, the frenzy of one cratic success after another is frequently nothing other than an attempt to repress the persistent inner doubt as to whether one really has all the necessary qualities—a vain attempt because every success shows only that one has cratic abilities, and not that one has the additional qualifications that legitimate the exercise of power. In order to silence this doubt, the power-holder may surround himself with intellectually and morally superior people to whom he constantly demonstrates his superior power partly by doing things for them in a condescending way, and partly by humiliating them—although this does not prove, either, that he is superior in the things that matter.

In any case, all efforts to attain a position of power should be preceded by a sober and precise assessment of one's own abilities and, more exactly, a comparison of one's own abilities with those of the leading candidates. Whereas the pure crat, who would like to avoid defeat as much as possible, will ask primarily whether his chances are good, the morally obligatory question is whether one is the most appropriate person for the position of power, or whether one might instead do more for the common good in a subordinate position. It is true that a person may grow during the power struggle, and that one often does not know in advance precisely to what extent one is suited for an office. It is also true that it is psychologically difficult to withdraw after one has entered the race. But that does not change the fact that the number of power struggles can be limited only if people avoid overestimating themselves and if the contemptible kind of person who can neither accept a subordinate role nor lead[313] does not get out of hand. It is deplorable how seldom leaders—out of insight into the ability of other successors, not out of cratic calculation—make way for others. Haydn's generous recognition of Mozart's superiority has few counterparts in politics; and it does no credit to Chamberlain that it took the defeats in Norway and the German attack on Belgium and the Netherlands to force him to resign. Conversely, the uninhibited way in which Churchill declared that his appointment as prime minister neither excited not alarmed him, but rather seemed to him "by far the best plan," is a sign of greatness, and the sound sleep into which he fell with relief on the night after making the first decisions in his new office should not be begrudged him.[314] For years, Churchill had, without worrying about his increasing isolation and without getting involved in party intrigues, openly said what he believed he knew and what now turned out to be right, and he could rightly think he was the person who, on the basis of his intelligence, his will power, and his confidence-inspiring integrity, was best able to bring the war to a good end. In this situation, Churchill had not only a right but a duty to want to be at the head of the government. Plato's view that the ideal power-holder must allow himself to be forced to exercise power[315] is not realistic—the aspirant to power must already want power himself; otherwise the person who attains power will be the one who is in a position to force him to exercise it.

Third, it is clear that seeking a position of power is moral only if it is not enjoyed as an end in itself. A person obsessed with power is never moral, because his will is not bound to a normative authority; on the contrary, he wants the position of power in order to rise above the norms that equality with others entails. The political man, in contrast, can be moral—if his will to power is limited in accord with the two previously mentioned conditions and if it springs from dedication to a moral cause, from a feeling of responsibility. This means that his own subordination to this cause must be even more resolute than the subordination to his own will that he demands from others. Only a person who controls himself and has learned to obey can demand obedience from others; and he may do this only if this obedience is ultimately in their own—rational or moral—interest. Whether someone seeks power as an end in itself or in order to resolve an objective problem is usually shown by his readiness to renounce power when he has fulfilled his task. There may be cases in which it is morally not possible to renounce power—for instance, for a monarch in a legitimist system, or when it is associated with terrible risks, or when there is not yet an equally well qualified successor. But in principle it should be emphasized that the moral power-holder must have the ability to let go of power once he has done what he intended to do.

---

313. I allude to Plutarch's famous judgment of Perperna: μήτε ἄρχειν μήτε ἄρχεσθαι πεφυκώς (*Sertorius* 27, 1). (". . . by nature unable either to rule or to be ruled.")

314. Cf. Churchill (1948 ff.), 2:234: "I thought it would be by far the best plan," and 238 f.

315. *Republic* 519c ff. Cf. Augustine, *De civitate Dei* XIX 19.

This demand is not to be made solely because of the principle of sharing power—it is also valid on grounds that have to do with individual ethics alone. Marcus Aurelius's fine remark that one ought to accept without arrogance and let go easily[316] holds for all things, but especially for power. Even if to prove himself in the social world a person must usually be prepared to get involved in power struggles and to emerge from the sphere of interiority into the social world, responsibility to himself remains the ultimate controlling moral authority. Cratic successes easily drown out the voice of conscience, and, surrounded by flatterers and other interested people and under the pressure of rapidly changing tasks, the power-holder can all too quickly become untrue to himself.[317] Seeing that his will can be so easily imposed can make him forget the human condition, partly leading him to a ludicrous overestimation of his capabilities, and partly depriving him of the possibility of acting in a natural, non-strategic way. For we should not deceive ourselves: the power-holder himself is often the most wretched victim of power, whose logic forces him at every moment to adopt a certain way of behaving and even thinking and feeling, whereas power subjects only occasionally feel the impact of power. Often the power-holder loses the inner autonomy that is in principle granted every person and becomes completely heteronomous, dependent upon the demands of the moment, which can be very extensive if it is a question of maintaining oneself in power.[318] Often he will be no less instrumentalized by others than he instrumentalizes them for his own ends, and he enjoys immediate goodness even more rarely than they do. Perhaps the most moving scene in Melville's *Moby Dick* is the one in which the revenge-obsessed Ahab, whose will to power persecutes his subordinates even in their dreams,[319] sees through his madness for a moment and experiences Starbuck's admiration and compassion.[320] The encounter between the two souls lasts only a moment, and is immediately followed by the catastrophe; but in reading these pages the reader feels that even more than the crew their tyrant Ahab is infinitely unhappy.

On the other hand, Sophocles' last two plays, *Philoctetes* and *Oedipus at Colonos*, have such a perfect reconciliatory power because in both cases a person with magical powers that symbolize the strength of his personality encounters not only figures such as Odysseus and Creon, who want to make use of him, but also fellow human beings such as Neoptolemus and Theseus, who respect him in his greatness. Neoptolemus in particular recognizes, in addition to the bow, which is the only thing that interests Odysseus, Philoctetes' wound—behind the attribute of power he discerns the vulnerable and wounded human being whose instrumentalization is not morally better because it was committed by lesser and ultimately weaker men. For the noble man, power is

---

316. 8.33.

317. Cf. Pascal (1982), 196.

318. The witches in *Macbeth* are the aesthetic expression of this heteronomy of the power-holder, which is also repeatedly emphasized in Tolstoy's *War and Peace*.

319. Chap. 31 (1992; 131 ff.).

320. Chap. 132 (1992; 548 ff.).

usually a burden that he cannot always share (especially when it is essentially rooted in his nature), but whose recognition by others as a burden nonetheless makes it easier for him to bear.

Against the power-holder's emotional atrophy and tension the only thing that helps is the antidote of occasional failures, and perhaps of a partial defeat. Woe to the power-holder whose ring the gods refuse! The downfall for which the power-holder must always be internally prepared can be all the more dreadful and sudden. If he mentally anticipates what can be forced on him by the never completely controllable social world, the loss of power may physically destroy him, but cannot shatter his essence. It is all the better if he is able to make autonomously the decision that removes him from power[321] and offers him the opportunity to spend his remaining years in the serenity of an old age that knows that it no longer has to make any decisions, but to which people like to turn, because through experience and contemplation it has gained insights from which the new power-holder is still far away. Because they resigned from office, even persons as bloodthirsty as Sulla and Diocletian deserve a certain respect, because this shows that they were at least not obsessed with power. Not every power-holder will spend the evening of his life in a monastery, like Boris I or Charles V; and not everyone will, like Churchill, be able to react to his failure to be reelected to office by writing one of humanity's great historical works. But every power-holder ought to take time in the evening of his life to give an account of the consequential decisions that he made at the zenith of power, and move from the phase in which he shaped reality into that of tranquil contemplation in which he no longer misunderstands himself as the maker, but learns to see himself as the expression and the tool of forces that go far beyond him.[322]

Whether Wolsley's final speech in *Henry VIII* was written by Shakespeare or by Fletcher, only a specialist in English literature, and not a humble philosopher, can decide. But every reader senses that it is great poetry, because it sets forth in a masterly fashion how the lord chancellor, who shortly before was almost omnipotent but is now deprived of all his privileges, appears, as it were, naked before his God and acquires a dignity that the plotting political man never attained. His acknowledgment of a series of elementary rules of decency seems all the more credible because it comes from the mouth of a Machiavellian, who had earlier completely ignored them. There is something moving in his advice to Cromwell, which clearly expresses his own regrets: "Let all the ends thou aim'st at be thy country's, / Thy God's, and truth's; then if thou fall'st, O Cromwell, / Thou fall'st a blessed martyr!" No less moving is his sober observation that

---

321. On cratic grounds, the power-holder will not make the decision known far in advance, because he would thereby significantly diminish his power base for the remaining period of time. Hans-Dietrich Genscher, the long serving foreign minister of the Federal Republic of Germany, handled his withdrawal from the political scene in an ideal manner.

322. Given the opposition between contemplation and lust for power, there are few things more grotesque than the obsession with power on the part of academic philosophers who compensate for their lack of ideas and their inability to observe existence by engaging in busy scheming. Their lives as professors emeriti will be bitter.

not even his fame will outlive him: "My robe / And my integrity to heaven, is all / I dare now call mine own. O Cromwell, Cromwell! / Had I but served my God with half the zeal / I served my king, he would not in mine age / Have left me naked to mine enemies."[323] The heteronomy of Wolsey's downfall stands in sharp contrast to Prospero's voluntary renunciation of power at the end of *The Tempest*, which was written shortly before *Henry VIII*. Whatever has been said against this interpretation, it is almost impossible not to interpret Prospero's last words as Shakespeare's farewell to the stage— the directorlike character in the work of art and the real director merge in a fascinating way. Prospero disposes of all the magical power by means of which he was able to coerce and deceive, and now turns to the audience with a request whose fulfillment is no longer guaranteed but rather depends on the audience's voluntary agreement—the request to pray to divine mercy to grant him pardon for the offenses he has committed. Without this help through prayer, the end of the life of the almost omnipotent magician and director, who has now himself become dependent on others—in fact, has made himself dependent on them—would be despair. "Now I want / Spirits to enforce, art to enchant, / And my ending is despair / Unless I be relieved by prayer, / Which pierces so that it assaults / Mercy itself, and frees all faults. / As you from crimes would pardoned be, / Let your indulgence set me free."[324] However, one can hardly assume that the audience at the first performance of *The Tempest* truly had a choice—Prospero may have laid aside his magical power, but the force of the language of the man who is the greatest poet not merely of power but also of love remains unimpaired even at the end and cannot have failed to move the audience to enthusiastic applause.[325]

The fourth condition that must be fulfilled in order that one may seek a position of power in a moral way concerns the acts that are required as means to that end. For one thing is clear: as a rule a position of power does not fall into one's lap, and unless one observes at least a few of the previously mentioned cratic maxims, and even and especially a few that have a negative intrinsic value, the achievement or even the retention of positions of power is inconceivable. Naturally, the moral price that has to be paid in individual political systems in order to attain power differs greatly; and it goes without saying that there is a moral duty to work on behalf of institutions in which one can rise without making moral sacrifices that are too great, in which power and morals have become as compatible as possible. But this general rule is of little help to a person who lives in an unjust state, because he can only work on behalf of such institutions if he already has a

---

323. Act 3, sc. 2, vv. 447 ff., vv. 453 ff.

324. Epilogue, vv. 13 ff.

325. Here, of course, a serious problem is concealed. On one hand, nothing is more moving than when a person who has become guilty of an offense submits himself to the mercy of his fellow men or God; on the other hand, this submission loses its value if it is combined with the knowledge that it will succeed. But how is this knowledge to be avoided within a Christian theology that teaches that God is good and merciful? After reading the Gospel, how can a prodigal son return home without ulterior motives and secret hopes? The repellent nature of Thomas Mann's Gregorius in *Der Erwählte* is rooted in his extreme reflectiveness.

position of power; he will hardly be able to acquire such a position without at least initially violating certain moral obligations. Indeed, even in a democratic constitutional state the human sacrifices required for a political career are considerable—and all the greater the more degenerate the people and the power-holders are whom one must please. Should these sacrifices be made? Since the political is indispensable, no one is served by giving a generic negative answer, especially since the consequence would be that only the most unscrupulous individuals would go into politics. (On the other hand, little is more repellent than rogues' attempts to justify themselves by declaring that all the unworthy acts or moral crimes of which they have become guilty on the road to power were committed only in order to attain a position that would have allowed them to do what is best—a position that they unfortunately only just failed to achieve.)

Obviously, in answering the question as to whether such sacrifices should be made, various parameters are relevant. First, we must of course consider the alternatives that are open to one on the basis of one's talents. Someone who can write *The Tempest* should in no case go into politics, at least if he is not destined to do something historically great in that area: a suitable prime minister is easier to find than a great poet, and in the long run the poet may even exercise a greater political influence than the head of government, because he may contribute to a change in values that can set the course for a new understanding of politics. Human will is an amorphous and at the same time refractory material; a sculptor who can give marble, or a philosopher who can give concepts, a vivid form is more likely to do something of lasting value. Second, the sacrifices that one must make have to be weighed—in an unjust state decent people will more seldom develop political ambitions than in a state founded on the rule of law, and even in the latter it can under certain circumstances be morally better and personally more satisfactory to be a good father than a minister.[326] Even to gain the whole world, one ought not to forfeit one's soul; but no one is more contemptible than a person who betrays the moral law for the sake of a little position that does not even allow him to do much.[327] Third, the likelihood that one can attain a position that will allow one to do some great good has to be taken into account. Fourth, one has to consider what might happen if one does not oneself assume a certain position: in a conflict that threatens the whole of humanity, such as World War II, even the most important intellectual should serve his country if it is conducting a just war, in whatever way might be required. From the point

---

326. It not rarely happens that at the very moment in which he attains his goal, an elevated position of power, the nobler person becomes painfully aware how much that is essential has been sacrificed along the way—for example, a woman's love. His victory leaves a bad aftertaste. Instetten (in chap. 35 of *Effi Briest*) cannot really enjoy his appointment as head of a government department; indeed, it makes him aware that his existence is ultimately a failure. The uneducated, good-hearted servant, Roswitha, seems to him more intact in her nature than he is; it seems to him that he has made a mess of his life.

327. Cf. Pascal's criticism of the Jesuits: "Les jésuites ont voulu joindre Dieu au monde, et n'ont gagné que le mépris de Dieu et du monde" (1982; 501). ("The Jesuits have tried to join God to the world, and they have only earned the scorn of God and the world.")

of view of decision theory, the problem should be approached in such a way as to compare the expected (moral) value of one's own entry into politics—which includes both the value of one's own success and the disvalue of one's failure, multiplied by the respective probabilities—with the expected (moral) value of alternative activities that one might undertake (including the consequences of not getting involved in politics oneself, such as the probable takeover of power by a less capable person or one obsessed with power). Only in this way can we answer the ancient question of whether the *vita activa* or the *vita contemplativa* should be preferred—there is no general answer. Gorbachev did well to enter politics, and Kant not to do so; Boethius was morally right to take on political responsibility in the historical situation in which he lived, even if in another period he could have devoted himself in good conscience totally to philosophy, and even if he had to pay a high price for his decision. Since it is not realistic to assume that a precise evaluation of the various states of affairs and a clear assessment of probabilities can be made, it goes without saying that inclination will play a role in one's own decision—which is, moreover, objectively justified, since the inclination to engage in an activity makes success in it more likely.

5.3.3. On the Moral Evaluation of the Political Man's Maxims

How are the political man's maxims to be evaluated in detail, and how can they be brought closer to the demands of morals? In order to prove the claim made in this chapter—namely, that power is not necessarily bad—it is important to show that a few of these maxims are morally neutral, and others even promote the development of virtues, even if nothing can be done about the bitter truth that some of them have an intrinsically negative value, which may, however, be compensated for by their indispensability in achieving an objective good.

Thus, to begin with the maxims of the aspirant to power, adaptation to the wishes of the power-holder is not necessarily bad; if the latter has in view what is generally best, it is morally reasonable to carry out his commands and to learn as much from him as possible. What is crucial is the sincere will to serve the common good through the power-holder—one should neither do his bidding out of servility nor instrumentalize him in the interests of one's own career. If his person does not command respect, his office may—a respect, however, that requires that one resign or even resist when the power-holder commands things he has no right to command. On the other hand, to the extent that he only has unpleasant traits that are objectively harmless, it can be instructive to obey him. For learning to get along with people whom one does not much like is part of the process of maturation—anyone who cannot do so will never achieve the integration that humanity needs if it is not to wear itself out. Also, the norms of factual mores, if they do not too sharply contradict what is morally obligatory, should be treated with respect—if not for their intrinsic worth, then for their utility in making other people's behavior predictable and thereby reducing conflicts. To be sure, falsity is repellent, but one has a false understanding of honesty—which is misinterpreted as the expression of one's contingent emotions rather than as a duty to a higher self-image— if one denies that every person should be dealt with politely—not because he might still become useful, but out of respect for the human dignity he possesses. Since there is no duty always to say what one thinks, a certain reserve with regard to pouring out one's heart is permissible, and perhaps even obligatory, because it increases the value of openness toward those people who deserve it. Also, it is morally better not to show off one's own talents; not only with the power-holder but with anyone, it is often more ad-visable to allow them to stumble upon the truth than to communicate it from outside. Not only in conflicts with enemies, but also in dealing with subordinates and voters, it may be morally permissible not to reveal more complex plans and to slowly prepare the public for one's own intentions, if one can be certain that they are the right ones, but could not yet be recognized as such. In chapter 8.1.4 we will discuss a famous case of not revealing a political strategy during an election campaign. However, it is also much more intelligent cratically to appeal openly to subordinates' willingness to make sacrifices if one can count on it: otherwise they will feel that they are being used.

There is a duty to try to achieve what is recognized as right; and to this end it is in-dispensable to establish priorities, to take lesser evils into account, and to distinguish the feasible from the utopian. This does not mean that the quality of a society is not also measured by the quality of its utopias; but the moral power-holder, too, must have, in addition to a moral vision, the most precise knowledge about the factual interests of others. However, it goes without saying that one cannot satisfy everybody's interests. A person who, as in Hebel's well-known calendar story, says that both parties are right, and then also agrees with his subordinate, who tells him that both parties cannot be equally right, is not acting morally, because he is violating elementary obligations to be consistent. If one is sure that it is not one's own particular interests that one has set over other interests, but rather what is morally required, then one may, indeed one must, be able to say "no." In order to convince oneself and others that one has violated their in-terests not out of a lust for power but out of insight into what is objectively obligatory, it is advisable, on one hand, to give up overtly the satisfaction of one's own analogous interests. On the other hand, one must be able to listen, one must be willing to under-stand others' interests, and one must try not only to learn about them but from them. The moral power-holder is capable of sympathy—he is not concerned to enjoy his own position of power, but rather, on the contrary, seeks a feeling of collective identity with power subjects. All must repeatedly feel at the same time that they have a common task, which they can fulfill only in a system of the division of labor that necessarily includes a different distribution of power. If the power-holder is capable of recognizing the achieve-ments of others, he may also make demands on power-subjects—making too few de-mands can be just as bad as making too many, and usually people are grateful when one is able to motivate them to make great efforts: boredom and inner emptiness are a source of unhappiness, while the consciousness of being able to do things and having achieved something is a source of happiness. One should not hesitate to reverse wrong decisions; generally, it often takes more courage to change one's opinion than to stick to it, and this is true in particular for the power-holder. In order not to appear inconsistant, it is advisable to mention new information that has caused one to change one's mind and in no case to yield without offering a justification for doing so. It is a virtue not to be afraid of someone saying "no," or of the rivalry of others: someone who is injured in the core of his personality by a refusal is not at ease with himself. Others' slanders ought to disturb one because, on one hand, they prevent the fulfillment of one's own tasks, and, on the other hand, they represent a testimony to the opponent's moral poverty; however, anyone who allows them to call his personal integrity into question is not sovereign. In choosing collaborators, one must take into account their objective qualifications as well as their moral integrity, which includes the subordination of one's own ambition to the common good. The moral maxim must be to protect not primarily oneself but rather the common good from ambitious people; and that one has really followed this maxim is proven by one's readiness to yield to more capable people if they present themselves. A power-holder must be deeply distrustful of servile individuals; they are often obsessed with power, and just as they will one day exert their own power without regard for the common good, so they revere already at the beginning of their ascent the power of the power-holder simply because it is power or because it is a necessary means for seizing power themselves.[328]

Dealing with enemies is morally most problematic. Nonetheless, it is part of the virtue of justice not to give in to injustice, and it is certainly more respectable to assume the labors and risks of conflict not out of a lust for strife, but rather for the sake of what is right, than constantly to yield to infringements. It is crucial that one always reckon with the possibility that one might be wrong—just as the cratically clever man must be able to think himself into his opponent's plans, so the moral person must try to understand what is reasonable in his enemy's position. Moreover, it is essential that one keep oneself as free as possible from hate for the opponent as a person. One should combat the opponent's vices, but one should first recognize the virtues that he may also have; second, one should never exclude the possibility that he might change. Disregard for oneself on the part of the other should be borne calmly—the truly great man will not be affected by the refusal of recognition by inferior persons, and it is a sign of weakness when he is incensed by such things. In conflicts that are morally desirable for the sake of the common good (for instance, economic or scientific competition), objective debate ought to be conducted without personal animosity; and it remains an achievement of the limited warfare of the eighteenth century that in that era even military conflicts could evidently be conducted without hatred and demonization of the opponent—even if it is certainly cratically sensible that moral attacks on the opponent be more violent the more the war seems to be in need of justification. The fact that in conflicts people try to limit the number of enemies

---

328. In *Der Untertan,* Heinrich Mann has provided a brilliant literary representation of the psychological connections between servility and the obsession with power—connections already understood by Plato (*Republic* 575c f.). See also Montesquieu (1734), 116.

is morally sensible even if there are many villains worth fighting; for one's own defeat would in no way help the forces of good. Indeed, sometimes one must be satisfied with bringing down a smaller rogue and leaving the greater one untouched, because a war against him would be beyond one's own powers[329]—which is not just but it is better than letting the smaller rogues escape as well.

Friendships are to be cultivated at all events, and even the building of alliances based on mutual interests is unproblematic so long as the ally's values are not still further from one's own than those of the opponent. Alliances of the latter type are greatly in need of justification; one should not be the first to enter into them, and they should be accepted only when absolutely vital interests are at stake. From a cratic point of view there is also much to be said against them, precisely because one cannot rely upon them: the Russian people had to pay a high price for Stalin's non-aggression pact with Hitler and for his trust in his German partner. If alliances formed in accord with the motto "My enemy's enemy is my friend" become the usual practice in politics, a weakening of the structure of values on which politics is based is inevitable; ultimately, only cynicism remains. New alliances are morally permissible when with the formation of new insights old value oppositions prove to be outmoded, but even then one must take into account the demoralizing effect that such alliances may have on subordinates who do not yet share these new insights.

Also, morals require that one make it possible for an opponent who is not absolutely evil and dangerous to withdraw with honor. The same holds for generosity after a victory. *Parcere subiectis et debellare superbos*[330] is one of the maxims that are equally valid cratically and morally. Thus there is no clearer shibboleth to find out whether one is dealing with a noble or a vulgar person than the way in which he behaves after a success. The inferior man regards victory as a criterion for determining which side is right, and therefore when he is defeated he grovels, and when he wins he is supercilious, whereas the moral person—to paraphrase the motto of Churchill's history of World War II—is resolute in war, defiant in defeat, magnanimous in victory, of good will in peace. Indeed, especially after an overwhelming success it is wise to remember how easily things might have turned out differently. The joy over a victory should always be mixed with a certain melancholy over the fact, first, that the battle was necessary at all and, second, that in this world the correlation between right and power cannot, and never will, be absolute, and that therefore one's own triumph always represents in part an undeserved stroke of luck. Particularly after internal tensions it is of the utmost importance to be able to achieve reconciliation with the opponent—the ability to forgive

---

329. An example is the fearful refusal of the Roman senate to consider as officially true the information provided by L. Tarquinius to the effect that Crassus was behind the Catiline conspiracy: "pars tametsi verum existumabant, tamen, quia in tali tempore tanta vis hominis magis leniunda quam exagitanda videbatur, . . . conclamant indicem falsum esse" (Sallust, *Catilinae coniuratio*, 48.5). ("Even if some of them regarded it as true, they nevertheless declared the informer to be false, because it seemed that in such a time a person with such great power should be soothed rather than provoked.")

330. Virgil, *Aeneid* VI 853: "Spare the submissive and vanquish the insolent."

is not only politically useful but also has a great intrinsic value. Nelson Mandela's ability to remain free from hatred, despite the unjust imprisonment that robbed him of the enjoyment of the best years of his life, was a necessary presupposition for South Africa's ability to maintain internal peace, at least up to now, and it also ennobles him as a person. However, since it is easier to give than to receive, we must also respect a person who calmly accepts a final defeat—as conversely Cato would deserve reproach if he killed himself solely to prevent Caesar from having a chance to prove generous toward him as well.[331] It can even be the case that the leaders of two opposed groups are ultimately closer to each other than they are to their subordinates, because they sense only in each other the formal greatness of which they are proud in themselves: herein culminates the chivalry that was perhaps more widespread in pre-universalistic mores than it is in modernity with its resentment of aristocracies. Viśākhadatta's "Mudrârâkṣasa" ends in such a noble way because after his triumph over the opposing minister, Rakṣasa, Cāṇakya introduces him to the king as his successor and resigns his own post: no one seems to him so well suited to succeed him as the man whose qualities he has learned to prize in the course of their long power struggle.

Conflicts should for the most part be conducted openly; and it is often people who are afraid of conflicts who are inclined to insidiousness and conspiracy. A moral person will never slander others; he must be satisfied with telling the truth about wicked opponents. Secretiveness is permissible, as is mutual playing with mixed strategies.[332] So far as breaking one's word goes, one must distinguish between occasional assents that are not really taken seriously by anyone, yet should be avoided as much as possible, and contracts. Machiavelli famously justifies breaking contracts by arguing that in doing so one only anticipates the other's breaking of his own word.[333] It can hardly be denied that there may be situations in which this argument cannot be rejected out of hand, that is, those in which the other plans to gain important advantages by being the first to break a promise. But first of all, there must be the clearest evidence that the other will break his promise, and, second, even in such a case any other precaution is better than doing what one is afraid the other will do—that is, break a promise. Only if life itself is at stake—one's own life and, even more, that of others for whom one is responsible— can an exception to this rule be justified. In general, it is not only moral but also cratically more rational to be prepared to ward off the other's attack than to attack first—at least when the latter is contrary to existing mores. Provoking the other side may lead to the desired success, that is, to a sudden, irrational reaction on the part of the opponent, and thus also to a third party's endorsement of one's own position, but it is morally despicable insofar as there was a realistic possibility of preventing the conflict from breaking out. However, the one who allows himself to be provoked bears part of the blame.

---

331. Cf. Plutarch, *Cato the Younger* 72.

332. On the moral difference between secretiveness on one hand and lying and deception on the other, see Thomas Aquinas, *Summa theologica* II/II, q.40 a.3.

333. *Principe* 18.3 (1986; 156).

We have already seen that even after the achievement of power one must continue to fight. If the power-holder is rightly convinced that he himself is the best choice, he may, indeed he should, fend off those who try to make his position insecure—they would do the same if they held his position, which would lose its dignity if its possessors were changed in quick succession. At the same time, he should seek out the most competent successor he can find and be prepared to hand the power over to him when the right time comes. If this successor outshines him, then it should redound to his greater glory that he has put the common good before his own luster: one of the greatest achievements of Nerva's brief rule was the adoption of Trajan, whereas Commodus's brutal rule casts a shadow over his father Marcus Aurelius's gentle one, since the latter was not forced to appoint his son as his successor. So far as the relationship to the king-maker is concerned, it is, on one hand, reasonable for the king to remind the latter that according to the constitution certain decisions are to be made by the king, and not by the king-maker; it is self-contradictory when the gratitude that the king-maker demands for his favor consists in allowing him to take over the position he has provided for the king—thus he takes back his favor, so to speak, for which he nonetheless demands gratitude. On the other hand, it is often the structure analyzed above, according to which one does not like benefactors because one finds the former dependency on them humiliating—that is, despicable ingratitude—that underlies changed behavior toward those who have helped one gain one's position of power and that is often met by terrible hatred on the part of king-makers.[334] Gratitude as a private person and authority as a person holding public office determine the proper attitude toward the king-maker. It goes without saying that the moral power-holder commands nothing criminal. However, if certain measures are morally legitimate but risky because failure is possible, and if the public is not convinced that engaging in this kind of action is better than avoiding it, even if it might lead to undesired consequences, then it may be permissible, for the sake of the stability of the organs of leadership, to have a subordinate bear the responsibility for this undertaking. But two conditions must be fulfilled: first, public opinion must be convinced in the medium term that right decisions make a good statesman and that a decision under risk does not become wrong simply because one has no luck; second, one has the duty to take care of those whose career has been sacrificed to the superstition of the masses, or at least been interrupted.

The central moral obligation for a person who has attained the apex of power is that he set an example for what he demands of others. The moral problem faced by someone who leads a public existence consists in the fact that he must present himself to the public, whereas it is rightly considered better not to boast about one's own moral achievements. But certainly the moral being must also shine forth, because only in this way can it have an effect on others,[335] and a person who holds such a position can hardly forgo

---

334. The ingratitude reaches its fullest possible extent if the king-maker himself was a king, indeed, is one's own father: one thinks of *King Lear*.

335. Cf. also the tension between Matthew 5:16 and 6:1 in the Sermon on the Mount, and Augustine's clarification in *De civitate Dei* V 14.

making himself visible. Nonetheless, he should make known only those virtues that he actually possesses; being without appearance may be imperfect, but appearance without being is repulsive. And he ought to be free from vanity—that is, he ought to consider this self-presentation inevitable but not enjoy it, and, in dealing with himself and thus with others, he ought to retain the naturalness that characterizes a person who is thinking about the issue at hand and not about himself. The power-holder should acknowledge in a general way some of his own faults, but it cannot be his task to incriminate himself. He may, indeed must, defend his private sphere—it is precisely the dignity of the public realm that demands this. Not only is the power-holder forbidden to mix private and public affairs (if he does so, he is called corrupt), but power-subjects should also know the difference between them. Just as it is unacceptable when the power-holder uses, for instance, public means for his own family, so it is grotesque when subordinates make their judgment of his performance dependent upon information about his sex life.[336]

5.3.4. On the Moral Evaluation of the Forms of Power

5.3.4.1. The Morals of Consensus

The real question that arises in connection with the moral justification of power concerns not so much the maxims, which are more or less invariant with regard to the individual forms of power, as these forms themselves. It is not hard to see that the later forms are in general easier to legitimate: persuading is less problematic than offering positive sanctions, and the latter less than force. However, this holds only *ceteris paribus:* using force to defend oneself is morally better than persuading others to attack innocent people. Because of the greater moral complexity of the earlier forms of power, I will begin with the later ones.

Agreement through consensus as an expression of the autonomy of all parties concerned is the ideal way to demarcate wills and especially to produce cooperation, and it is entirely understandable that modern ethics since the formulation of contract theories seeks in consensus the ultimate normative foundation of morals. The special status of consensus consists in the fact that it is the only form of power (in the broadest sense of the word) that can at the same time be one of the reasons for the legitimacy of power.[337] This does not hold for any other form of power; yet this does not mean that consensus is the only ground for the legitimacy of power. In fact, it is obvious that people may do everything they want within the broad sphere of the morally permissible (but only within it); at those points within this sphere where their acts concern others, their factual

---

336. This holds except in a case in which the sexual transgression sheds light on other vices of the power-holder (such as dishonesty) that endanger his ability to carry out his task.

337. To be exact, one would have to say that consensus itself is grounded in the good of autonomy; it is its immediate expression.

agreement suffices to legitimate them. But it is clear that factual consensus as such does not constitute the sphere of the morally permissible. Since there are duties to oneself, an action can be immoral even if it is mutually desired—killing someone who asks to be killed may be justifiable in some cases, but it is certainly not unproblematic in general. It was not at all rare that oppressed people such as slaves, for instance (and probably also some of the accused in Stalin's show trials) approved of the way they were dealt with—which makes their oppression worse, not better. Therefore, it is extremely important to find arguments regarding what is to be left to the consensual choice of individuals and what must be considered normative limits on factual consensuses.

To be sure, a moral consensus to determine what binding values are is also to be sought. However, a great deal depends on grasping the difference between this kind of consensus and the kind that can emerge within the framework that the former establishes. One kind of consensus creates new agreements on its own; the other, on the contrary, does not *make* this framework—it recognizes something that exists independently of it, and is therefore bound to something that precedes it. Transcendental pragmatics certainly seems to recognize this, but it is to be reproached for its formalism. It is ridiculous to urge a search for a better argument if one has no theory of what would constitute a better argument. If one reduces arguments to formal deductive relationships, then anything can be proven; for by positing different premises one can ground even opposed conclusions. Without an ultimate foundation of *material* ethical principles—and that inevitably means: without a theory of the absolute—conflicts cannot be resolved in an argumentative way; without them, an appeal to discourse only privileges greater staying power on committees or greater rhetorical skill. Surely everyone is familiar with parties in a conflict chatting about things that have nothing to do with the debate before they come to the subject at issue. The function of this is obvious: it decreases the latent aggressivity and increases the readiness to arrive at a consensus, and therefore it is strongly to be recommended. But, however positive this warming-up talk may be, it precedes the real work, and it is disastrous to confuse it with the latter. Aeschylus could still believe that speech, discourse, solved political problems; and certainly the pacification of the Furies by Athena's eloquence at the end of his *Oresteia* is a moving breakthrough into a new style of politics, to which the gloomy silence of Bia, force incarnate, stands in stark contrast at the beginning of *Prometheus Bound.* But the fifth century B.C. already had terrible experiences with the dangerous nature of speech; and after the rise of the demagogues even Plato could no longer have the trust in Peitho (the goddess of persuasion) that Aeschylus still had and to which discourse ethics seems to return.

However, it is not enough that values remain in their being in themselves (*Ansichsein*), and it is just as insufficient if they are recognized by a single individual only—they must gain a footing in the social world. To that extent, one must work for a consensus regarding the right values, and the deep feeling of happiness that arises where a community is conscious of values that are accepted by everyone is the finest reward for a common recognition of moral truths. Since without a consensus social structures collapse, it may sometimes be sensible to lend external agreement to systems of value from which one has internally distanced oneself—at least if one recognizes in them at least a partial truth and if their extrinsic value in avoiding anarchy is greater than their partial untruth. Against the one-sided rationalism of most moderns, we must recall what was said earlier regarding the power of opinion and conviction, as well as the observations on the ethics of ethics. The compelling nature of a moral argument depends on properties having to do with the theory of validity, but its real credibility has to do with how it is exemplified. An exemplary life does not solve the problem of validity, because normative principles are required in order to determine whether a life is exemplary; but it strengthens the argument in a way that is not available to the argument itself. Only a life that has been lived, not an argument, elicits imitation.

From what has been said it follows that factual consensus—no matter how desirable it may be—cannot be the sole reason for the legitimacy of power. At least two additional justifications of power should be recognized. The control of parents over children is a classical example of a legitimate use of power, which does not always have in view the factual, but often the rational, interest of power-subjects. On this alone can the justification of parental power be based—not, for instance, on the fact that parents are the cause of the children's existence. Forms of paternalism may also be permissible with regard to adults, especially if their capacity for judgment is limited—someone who pulls an unhappy lover out of the water in which he wants to drown himself is exercising power, and even force, but not an immoral power or force. Although not without reservations, one can point to certain forms of domination by civilized peoples over less civilized ones. The reservations are based on the fact that every adult, even from a less civilized culture, can naturally make a claim to a certain degree of maturity that is denied a child. This kind of power is justified only if it proceeds from a feeling of responsibility for those over which the power is exercised, out of the insight that one can do and grasp something that they cannot do and recognize, but which they need. Moreover, this kind of power must work toward making itself dispensable—its goal must be to produce autonomy. To this end, it must also ultimately respect a sphere of autonomy, however limited, in which it does not intervene and whose growth it promotes. Hans Jonas has been reproached for conceiving political power primarily in accord with this asymmetrical model of responsibility, and for having neglected consensus among equals; and this reproach is justified. But no less one-sided is the notion that morally permissible power can be reduced to consensus alone.

However, neither consensus nor one-sided responsibility exhaust the grounds for the legitimacy of power. In addition to *factual* and *rational* interests, *moral* interests must be taken into account. By "moral interests" we mean that forms of the exercise of power may be legitimate that may very well violate the factual and even the enlightened rational self-interest of power-subjects. The criminal, for instance, need not actually agree with his punishment for the latter to be considered just. In a certain sense, one can say that he has already given his consent by committing a criminal act, because as a rational and moral person he presupposes that he may be treated in the same way as he has treated others. But in any case, this agreement is only implicit; it is grounded in his ability to think morally: he has to recognize that harming a fundamental good and symmetry may be prevented, if necessary, by force. The same goes for military conflicts. During a war, both parties are already making use of force, and therefore of a form of power, against each other; after the victory a state will sometimes become an occupying power. Of course, the great majority of wars is not just, and not all occupying powers are morally legitimate; but that does not mean that on principle there might not be just wars and legitimate powers of this kind. A right to defend oneself and to defend others from attack should not be denied, and the forms of power based on the use of this right may be entirely legitimate, even if they are not based on consensus. Of course, it is desirable that such a consensus develop later on, but since this is only a possibility that at the outset could not be predicted with certainty, the proleptic anticipation of such a consensus cannot be the true justification of the use of force. Had Germans never learned in all of history to see how much good their defeat in World War II did them, the British and French declarations of war would be no less legitimate, but on the contrary still more necessary. It is not consensus that legitimates the appeal to the right to defend oneself and others; on the contrary, it is the legitimacy of this appeal that makes the production of a post facto consensus desirable.

5.3.4.2. The Morals of Forms of Power Based on Opinion

Since we have already discussed authority in chapter 3.1.2, a few further remarks will suffice here. On one hand, it is self-evident that subjection to authorities should not lead to blind obedience. There is a duty to do one's best to test repeatedly the credibility of the authority, and it is a sign of inertia and intellectual cowardice to avoid this duty. In distinguishing between false and true authorities, there is one important criterion: their consistency. Just as a scientist who contradicts himself loses his credibility, so one can no longer obey a moral authority when the latter's life contradicts his teaching. He may still be right, but one has to concentrate on testing his arguments and free oneself from any personal influence. To be sure, hardly anything is more painful than being deceived, whether through negligence or even intentionally, by the authority that one has heretofore trusted; and it may be excusable to be afraid of the loss of a security that has up to that point sheltered one from certain responsibilities. But self-incurred minority (*selbstverschuldete Unmündigkeit*) is blamable and a serious violation of duty. On the other hand, authorities are indispensable. The more complex the world becomes, the less one can master all the information one needs in order to act morally—one must learn, as it were, to operate on the meta-level, and to develop a sense for those whom one can and should trust. This holds, anyway, for the realm of means-ends rationality. But even in the realm of value rationality, a sincere admiration for morally superior persons ennobles those who lack the ability possessed by charismatics to set their own standards: If you cannot be a Socrates, try to be a Crito. If one lacks knowledge, one ought not to conclude, out of envy and simply because one does not have it oneself, that there could not possibly be anyone else who has that knowledge. Love for superior persons is the expression of a substantively conceived freedom, and it is mere spitefulness to consider this a particularly wicked form of power in cases in which even the superior person does not abuse this love.

Nonetheless, a person who achieves consensus, whether through the strength of his personality or through arguments, is well advised to use his intellectual superiority with moderation. There is something irritating, especially in post-Enlightenment times, about being brought to see reason by others. The genius of Socratic maieutics consists in respecting the autonomy of others by allowing them to draw the right conclusions by themselves, and directing them only through questions. In rhetoric, irony has the same function: when Mark Antony repeatedly praises Brutus as an "honorable man," the audience is more likely to gain the impression that they have themselves come to the conclusion that the murderers of Caesar are rogues.[338] Traditional cultures diminished the asymmetry between teacher and pupil in that the former saw himself only as an interpreter of earlier wisdom or simply as a tool of the gods—and this was felt to be a task that was not at all pleasant, but a terrible burden. It was the obvious suffering involved in this task that made obedience easier for the others. Of course, masochism is not rare; and one must warn against the kind of inverted power positivism that claims that if things are going badly for you, it proves that you are right. Yet one should think, for instance, of Jeremiah, who curses the day he was born because he can no longer bear the hatred with which his fellow men meet him, and yet cannot escape his mission, because when he tries not to think about God it is as if a fire were burning in his heart.[339] Here even the modern reader who does not believe in verbal inspiration has the impression of an unconditional moral authority, because Jeremiah expects far more of himself than of others.

Certainly it is worth striving to convince others as much as possible through arguments that are rigorous with regard to the theory of validity. However, there can be situations in which this is not possible because of the public's limited ability to understand, and in such situations it is morally obligatory to speak the language people can understand. The crucial factor is to tell the truth, but one may, and indeed should, express it in the most effective way, if necessary. It is inherently desirable that the true also be beautiful; and even a simplification of the truth and especially of one's arguments may be permissible if it is the only way to communicate it to others. The public eloquence of the ancients is one of the things that moderns should envy them; the dissatisfied conceit of most intellectuals in the mass democracies of our century has much to do with the fact that they have lost the ability to use, in addition to their specialized language, the language that is accessible to the majority of their fellow citizens. If the idea of a philosophically grounded rhetoric is decaying, the pure reflections on validity of a highly abstract philosophy and the techniques of manipulation of empirical psychology survive it as its *membra disjecta,* and with regard to this disastrous dualism it must be maintained

---

338. Shakespeare, *Julius Caesar* act 3, sc. 2, vv. 75 ff.
339. Jeremiah 20:7 ff.

that it is morally important to present good arguments in such a way that they really have an effect, and that means bringing the level of the theory of validity and the level of the social together. In his masterly essay on the revolution in Naples, Vincenzo Cuoco has analyzed the academic rhetoric of the intellectual Jacobins who ruled the city for a few months, and who, instead of speaking in the language of their people and thus attracting them to their side, got carried away by the abstractions of the eighteenth-century French *philosophes* and drew on examples from Roman history. Neither the one nor the other could move the people; indeed, they must have rightly gotten the impression that the new leaders could hardly be interested in the people's welfare, if they did not even try to make themselves understood.[340] Just as even the subtlest philosopher should be able to write exoteric as well as esoteric works, so the ability to speak in several languages is indispensable for a moral political man—provided that he does not use them to say things that contradict each other. To be sure, demagogues who say what others want to hear are contemptible; but one only strengthens them if one is not willing to formulate what needs to be said in a way best understood by one's respective audience.

In fact, someone who later learns that a certain conviction has been transmitted to him through a rhetorical trick should be angry only if he feels that he has been deceived; if on the contrary he has the impression that it was at that time the only way to make him understand a certain truth, he should be grateful. Much the same can be said of the use of the mechanisms of moral psychology. It is not wrong to motivate someone to do something morally right by trying, for example, to elicit his compassion; it is not permissible, however, to make use moral feelings to achieve goals that are morally wrong. The Grand Inquisitor in Dostoyevsky's *The Brothers Karamazov* even uses morally weak people's need for forgiveness to cement the position of power of the church, which provides absolution if sinners are prepared to obey it blindly. A weak person can be forgiven if he resorts to this source of power as the only one available to him; on the other hand, there is not always a duty to give in to him. Even the demands of a weaker person can be illegitimate; for instance, the Third World elites that manipulate the guilt feelings of young people from the former colonial powers in order to pursue their corruption undisturbed should be resisted. Indeed, there is something nefarious about playing with something that in the human soul comes closest to moral insight and therefore to the divine in humans. Anyone who counts on others' sympathy in order to gain more at the expense of a third party than he deserves in accord with the principles of justice

---

340. "Che sperare da quel linguaggio, che si teneva in tutt'i proclami diretti al nostro popolo? *Finalmente siete liberi.* . . . Il popolo non sapeva ancora cosa fosse libertà: essa è un sentimento e non un' idea; si fa provare coi fatti, non si dimostra colle parole. . . . *Il vostro Claudio è fuggito, Messalina trema.* . . . Era obbligato il popolo a saper la storia romana per conoscere la sua felicità?" (1975; 179). ("What can one hope to achieve with the language they spoke in all their proclamations directed to our people? *Finally you are free.* . . . The people still didn't know what freedom was: it is a feeling and not an idea; it is proven by deeds, not by words. . . . *Your Claudius has run away, Messalina is trembling.* . . . Were people obliged to know Roman history in order to recognize their happiness?")

is in a sense acting even worse than someone who steals it illegally, because he tries to burden others' generosity with guilt, and because he makes people mistrust a source that, although not the ultimate ground of the validity of the moral, nevertheless supports its reality in the empirical world. Nietzsche's rage at the weepy moral sentimentality of the weaker, which he rightly diagnoses as a power factor, would be on target if it were combined with a consistent theory of justice that made it possible to determine to what point the demands of the weaker are legitimate, and at what point they are to be rejected. In any case, the moralizing of the weak becomes entirely unbearable if they have not themselves met the obligations they set for others—when, for instance, small human birds of prey start complaining about hunting attacks only after they themselves have been the victims of larger birds of prey.[341]

Even though manipulations belong to the sphere of opinions, they are still characterized by a peculiar quality that distinguishes them not only from other kinds of opinion, but also from all other forms of power: they operate virtually unseen and for that very reason are particularly effective. They abolish the symmetry that characterizes an open duel and are therefore in great need of justification. They are not categorically forbidden—unlike consensus, they have a negative intrinsic value, but they are legitimate if they are the only way to protect a fundamental good such as human life. Even in the case of less elementary goods, manipulations are permissible if they benefit the person who is manipulated; in this case the latter will even be grateful for them later on. Thus manipulations play a certain role in upbringing, in order to protect a child from harm; sometimes they are even necessary in order to bring a person to form his own autonomous opinion. However, there is a great danger in the fact that the manipulator—unlike a person seeking to convince—is not confronted by objections; before deciding to manipulate, he must be very sure, first, that what he wants to communicate is right and, second, that manipulation is the only possible way of communicating it. An examination of his decision by a third party is indispensable. Manipulations are also permissible if they constitute a self-defense reaction to an opponent's attempts at manipulation. One may first decide to engage in manipulation if one has vainly tried to convince a third party who is being manipulated by the opponent that he is in fact being manipulated; but there can certainly be cases in which a unilateral renunciation of manipulation would result in an unacceptable advantage for the opponent. The previously mentioned grounds for justifying manipulation do not mean that manipulation is a trifling offense. On the contrary, the deep demoralization of contemporary industrial societies is connected in part with the fact that, thanks to advertising, manipulation has become the form of communication in which the most energy is invested. Since the goals for which this kind of manipulation is undertaken can in no way justify it, a crippling feeling of the loss of autonomy is inevitably spreading.

---

341. I borrow the metaphor form Machiavelli, *Discorsi* I 40 (1984; 152).

5.3.4.3. The Morals of Positive Sanctions

Offering positive sanctions is analogous to consensus insofar as it too involves an agreement (regarding an exchange). And yet the distinction between the two is obvious: in principle, consensus includes everything; in contrast, an exchange based on offering positive sanctions takes place *within* a situation that is itself assumed as a brute fact. The contextual framework may therefore be unjust, and its injustice does not disappear because the parties involved in the exchange seek in it their mutual advantages (which, in order to be morally permissible, should not be at the expense of a third party). Indeed, it can certainly be the case that in such a situation a voluntary exchange merely increases the inequality between the two partners—and thus possibly the injustice of the contextual framework as well. Therefore, despite the symmetry of the exchange situation, the dependency of one side can be oppressive and thus morally questionable, the more so if the superiority of the other side cannot be justified by its own achievements. Under certain circumstances, great differences in economic power can serve the common good, but this is not always the case. In any event, the wealthier party has a moral duty to help overcome the most blatant forms of dependency, and the poorer one should contribute to this by limiting his needs. In doing so, he must be supported—which means concretely that the incitement of needs by advertising that suggests that human dignity begins when one has reached a certain income level, is deeply immoral; and measuring one's own recognition by the economic performance of others is no less so.

Furthermore, it is clear that economic superiority never gives one a right to what cannot be bought because it is incommensurable with other goods, that is, the other's convictions, his love, his dignity. A person who changes his views because he has been promised certain advantages sacrifices the autonomy of reason that alone makes it possible to limit power. Therefore he is acting immorally—and all the more immorally the farther he is from the necessities of survival. However, someone who uses his superiority to get something that is ultimately not to be bought is acting still more immorally—although a prostitute who is not forced into prostitution by bitter poverty may also be guilty, the man who takes advantage of her services is far more contemptible. Venality and bribery are worse than a public official's acceptance of a benefit for doing his legal duty and its active counterpart: in these cases one's own legal duties are violated for the sake of getting something in return. Likewise, one should not try, by offering positive sanctions, to get something that the other has in any case the legal duty to do or omit (possible emergency situations excluded), for then the other is confirmed in the belief that he is bound by the law only if he receives additional rewards. A power-holder who acts in this way harms not only himself but also the majesty of the concept of law, and therefore betrays those for whom he is responsible.[342]

---

342. Cf. Cicero, *De officiis* II 53.

5.3.4.4. The Morals of Negative Sanctions

Force and the deprivation of freedom contradict the autonomy of human beings in the most decisive way. In addition, force endangers the basic good of life; one of the morally urgent tasks consists therefore in limiting its use to a minimum. But we have already seen that this cannot be accomplished by one party unilaterally renouncing force. If someone attacks me in order to kill me, I am allowed to defend myself, even if doing so puts the other's life at risk. Otherwise, a life will obviously be destroyed, and it is not clear why the life of the person who acts immorally should have more value than that of the victim of his aggression. The same argument can be used to justify not only self-defense but also defense of others from attack; a moral distinction between the two can hardly be justified on the basis of a universalistic ethics. At most we could say that a person who does not do everything he can to help himself does not deserve the help of others; and surely not every kind of defense of others can reasonably be expected from third parties. Especially if both opponents bear a certain blame for the conflict, one may postpone pacifying attempts until both parties have exhausted each other and are ready for peace—at least so long as innocent people do not have to suffer from this conflict. One not only may, but must, defend oneself against deadly force—the strategy of not doing so is not evolutionarily stable. However, the situation becomes more difficult if the other threatens not my life but my freedom—then do I also have a right or even a duty to defend myself? By fighting I may endanger my own life and that of the other, which would otherwise remain secure. Obviously there is no general answer to this question, if only because threats to freedom can be very different in nature—they can range from slavery to integration into a superior country. One strategy for answering in the affirmative would be to argue that a person who risks my freedom today might demand my life tomorrow, and that today I can fight him with a greater chance of victory than after I have lost my freedom. However, this depends, of course, on the circumstances; there may very well be cases in which a temporary surrender to force increases the likelihood of survival and even the probability of one day recovering one's freedom: a surrender can save strength that will later be needed for revenge; and especially when one is confronted by a non-diabolical opponent, passive resistance may achieve more, and with fewer sacrifices, than the use of countervailing force. Gentle mockery of power in the manner of Hašek's good soldier Schweik can be more subversive in the long run than heroism doomed to failure. On the other hand, it should be pointed out that human life is human only when it is not understood as an end in itself, but is rather in the service of freedom. For its sake, I may, indeed must, put my life and that of the other at risk. However, it is too abstract simply to oppose freedom and life, for the dead cannot enjoy their freedom. Nonetheless, one's own death can protect the freedom of the members of one's group, and even in the case of a complete defeat it can be remembered as exemplary. Someone in the state of nature who protects only himself finds it easier to surrender than one who is defending a legal order that has already been wrested from nature; resistance to a politically superior culture is more difficult to justify in both cratic and moral terms. When defending oneself can bring about nothing real but only something symbolic, endangering anyone but the aggressor is hard to justify— the sacrifice made by all those who are fighting to the last drop of blood should be voluntary. The fact that in the battle of the Alamo in 1836 the only man who did not want to die with his comrades was given the opportunity to escape significantly increases the dignity of the heroism of those who remained.

It goes without saying that force must be the *ultima ratio*. Negotiations must have preceded its use—however, only so long as the continuation of the negotiations does not too greatly favor the opponent's preparations for aggression. Clear threats are advisable if one is prepared to impose negative sanctions, because they can sometimes prevent the use of force without using countervailing force. Thus Great Britain's failure to make its position clearer in July 1914, as well as its failure to couple the reduction of its military presence in the South Atlantic in the early 1980s with an unambiguous declaration of its continued interest in the Falklands, were serious mistakes.[343] Such threats must be credible, and that is why not only on cratic, but also on moral, grounds it is generally inadvisable to engage in bluffing, which might undermine one's credibility and thereby increase the risk of an explosion of violence (quite apart from the fact that lying needs special justification). It is hard to say whether deception is permissible in conflicts with the enemy. The fulfillment of two conditions is morally decisive in justifying it: first, each side should assume that the other might use deception; this avoids a violation of symmetry. Second, the use of deception should diminish the casualties on both sides. Thus it can hardly be denied that the maintenance of a secret service, for instance, makes peace more secure and often increases mutual trust, because it may become clear that the opposing side has fewer aggressive intentions than one had assumed. Insofar as secret services can hardly function without making attempts at disinformation and constantly exposing them, the latter kind of deception is justified. Indeed, even betrayal can be justifiable under certain circumstances, no matter how great its intrinsic disvalue is. However, it is permissible and even obligatory to break faith with an ally and even with a superior if one comes to the conclusion that he is a criminal. There is certainly a doubt, even if not regarding the objective rightness of this step, at least regarding its subjectively moral quality, if it is taken only shortly before a defeat. Nonetheless, distrust of traitors is inappropriate if they run significant personal risks and if they are moved not by opportunism but by the painful discovery that the other side is morally superior. The allies' refusal to have anything to do with the German resistance to Hitler could at most be justified by the argument that a complete defeat of Germany was objectively indispensable.

Against the justification of counterforce we may cite two highly respectable authorities—Jesus' Sermon on the Mount and Gandhi's doctrine of non-violent resis-

---

343. Since in democracies public opinion does not permit open threats, in such cases diplomatic channels have to be used.

tance. One would have to be callous not to be intimidated by these authorities. Yet, I can reasonably interpret both views only in the sense that they correctly point out that countervailing force is not the first moral option in dealing with force. Neither Jesus nor Gandhi urges us to surrender to evil. On the contrary, both put their lives at stake in battling against evil and made countless enemies for themselves. Moreover, they have one thing in common: both refer not to conflicts in the state of nature (between private individuals or states), but rather to conflicts within a relatively just state, which already has a monopoly on force. Within such a framework, it does not endanger the lives of innocent people when I turn the other cheek to someone who has struck me. Indeed, I may achieve more than by striking back: that depends on me and on the aggressor. In his representation of the encounter between Myriel and Valjean, who has been arrested by the police for robbing his kindly host, Victor Hugo makes it clear what the issue really is: Myriel does not let his silver be taken away from him out of weakness; rather, in following the Gospel's command, he brings about an inner transformation in Valjean. "Do not forget, never forget, that you have promised me to use this money to become an honest man."[344] These words, uttered after Valjean has been pardoned for his crime, have a greater effect than any punishment—especially since Valjean had not actually promised anything. Finally, Gandhi can be interpreted as rightly sensing that he could achieve his goal within the British Empire even with non-violent resistance, and where this is possible, it is naturally preferable to force. But to advise the Jews in the Warsaw ghetto to allow themselves to be deported without making any attempt to resist by force would have been simply too shameless.[345]

Four qualifications should close these observations on force. First, it goes without saying that not all that is moral can, and may, be realized through force; that which has to do with inner conviction can be neither bought nor coerced. Jesus, for instance, rightly recognized that the spiritual power he sought was not to be based on force. In the area of conviction, renunciation of force is an unconditional duty, and anyone who uses armed force in trying to make others recognize the highest moral duties is acting in a deeply immoral way, and only proves that he himself is not doing justice to these duties. But an elementary part of morals that still needs to be defined may not be merely left to the good intentions of others—and that includes in particular the prohibition of force. It is permissible to force people to renounce force, and that is not possible without force. Naturally, the use of force is easier to justify if it

---

344. "N'oubliez pas, n'oubliez jamais que vous m'avez promis d'employer cet argent à devenir honnête homme" (V. Hugo [1963], 51).

345. Whereas the first Warsaw uprising certainly represents a great moral performance, one cannot say quite the same about the second: Was endangering so many human lives that would otherwise have had a good chance of surviving, really wise, especially since the chances of success were slim and the worst had to be reckoned with, given the Nazis' murderous intentions and Stalin's will to power? On the moral distinctions between the two uprisings see the first part of T. Todorov's prologue (1991).

is directed against those who have personally violated elementary commands—the punishment of a criminal is morally less problematic than a defensive war in which in all likelihood people who are innocent, and probably also civilians, will die. Second, it hardly needs to be mentioned that force is permissible only as a means (of defense against injustice or as deterrence) and that it should be limited to the minimum required. Any use of force—even against the biggest criminals—that goes beyond these bounds is barbaric and never permissible. In particular, torture as an end in itself, even when used to break the will of the most evil people, is abominable. Whether the threat of torture and, if this does not work, torture itself is allowed as a means to acquire by force information indispensable for saving human lives is an extremely difficult question, and one can only sympathize with those ethicists who categorically deny it,[346] especially since the overwhelming majority of cases of torture in history and in the present are certainly not only unjustifiable, but even have to be counted among the worst of mankind's crimes. However, one can imagine situations (which every decent person must fervently hope never to encounter) in which the survival of countless innocent people depends on getting a mad terrorist who will respond only to torture to reveal where he has hidden an atom bomb set to go off in the near future, and if one assumes that one (as the police commissioner in charge, for instance) is also responsible for the consequences of one's own (perhaps spurious) omissions, one will probably be able to provide a justification for torture in such situations. (Far more difficult to answer is the question of what should be done if the terrorist will respond only to the torture of his children. The answer is somewhat easier if the children are *themselves* endangered by the atom bomb.) Third, care must be taken not to become like the evil one is fighting against. If one destroys it but by the end of the process of escalation has oneself become what it was, evil has won out—for the question is not who instantiates it. It is well known that it is a matter of debate who represents evil in *Moby Dick*—whether it is the white whale defending its life or Ahab. The right answer can only be that the hatred against the whale, who represents the amorality of nature, dehumanizes Ahab—his pathological and irresponsible thirst for revenge is ultimately worse than the brutality of nature. Only those who have freed themselves from hatred will emerge from battle morally unimpaired.[347] Fourth, there is a duty to prevent the emergence of situations in which force may be used. Indeed, it is simply not true that the use of force arises solely from human wickedness. Thus it is not always easy to distinguish the aggressor from the victim. World War II is a classic example of such a case; yet even here the Allies can be faulted for having encouraged Hitler's aggression

---

346. As does, for instance, R. Spaemann (1982), 71, and, more generally, 61 ff., although I can agree with his reflections only in part.

347. The almost sublime impression that emerges from J. Le Carré's character George Smiley is based on the goodness, vulnerability, and melancholy he maintains in his battle against Karla.

by an inappropriate foreign policy. In the case of World War I it is harder to decide who was to blame. Since human beings are oriented toward the future, not only the concrete use of force, but also the threat of force is a matter of concern, and this concern can lead to a first strike that understands itself in a subjectively entirely sincere way as an anticipatory countervailing force. How to get out of this vicious circle of mutually anticipated force is one of the most difficult questions facing humanity—and it is the crucial origin of the *state*.

6

The State and Its History

L ike man, the state is a structure dealt with by many disciplines. On one hand, the state is a social entity, and as such an object of the descriptive social sciences (including the historical sciences). As a result of its central place within the world of the social, which was always recognized in historiography, as the sciences have divided into different disciplines, a social science that deals specifically with the state has developed—namely, political science. Yet precisely because of its centrality the state also remains within the purview of the other social sciences, which partly cannot pursue their own investigations without taking it into account, and are partly able to contribute, through their specific results, to a deeper understanding of the state itself: I am thinking, for instance, of economics. Even if as a corporate group the state achieves a certain independence with respect to the actions of individuals, it remains, of course, dependent on them; the complex web that connects the state back to the behavior of individuals is the object of political psychology. Political anthropology deals with the question of whether one can speak of a state with regard to all human societies, and especially with regard to societies that are very different from those of modern Western Europe. It is clear that the modern state, characterized by a monopoly on force and territoriality, is anything but an anthropological constant. Even the existence of stateless societies must be admitted if one defines the state as a society's enduring, institutionally and personally differentiated center of action. In every human society, however, there is an *organized collective use of force,* always directed toward the outside and for the most part toward the inside as well, whose goal is the preservation of the social order, *which is experienced as legitimate.* If one sees in this the core of the political and an embryonic form of statehood, then one can confidently assert that all human societies are political. However, the road from these uses of force to the modern state is very long.

On the other hand, the state cannot be observed solely from without.[1] In contradistinction to nature, it owes its being to human efforts, and just as the individual can-

---

1. Here I am building on Hart's distinction between internal and external points of view (1961; 99).

not exist without a normative self-image, so the state cannot survive if a collective does not share a common conception of how it should be. The existence of the state depends upon the recognition and imposition of certain norms. Indeed, since the state is a corporate group that makes use of the highest form of power in order to regulate relationships among individuals, it is of the utmost importance that it also regulate precisely those relationships to which it owes its own being; the state must therefore be not only a regulative but also an administrative group.[2] If it is not, it endangers not only itself, but also the whole of social reality, which depends on its ability to function. The essence of law is the regulation of human relationships under the threat of coercive measures felt to be legitimate in the event of violations, and all law has an internal relationship to the state as it guarantor. However, only in constitutional law is the state not only the executor and subject, but also the theme and object of law. From this follows the great importance of constitutional law for almost any social order, as well as for every legal system, at the center of which it stands. Far from all cultures have been able to deal with their constitutional law in accord with scientific principles, but where this has been the case, as in modernity, the theory of constitutional law is one of the most important disciplines for understanding the state. It goes without saying that it is not identical with the theory of the state; in his *Allgemeine Staatslehre* Georg Jellinek rightly divided this discipline into a general social theory of the state (what we would now call political science) and a general theory of constitutional law.[3] Some works are clearly to be attributed to only one of the two parts of this discipline: thus Hermann Heller's *Staatslehre* is exclusively a work of political science, whereas Carl Schmitt's *Verfassungslehre* is, at least so it claims, a work on constitutional law. Hans Kelsen's famous polemic against Jellinek's twofold conception of the state and his defense of the identity of state and law (1928) therefore miss the point—they lead to a dissolution of the reality of the state, to which more belongs than can be predicated of it by constitutional law. For instance, the influence of kings' mistresses on their policies is not primarily a problem for constitutional law, but rather for political science. On the other hand, Kelsen is right that the existence of law and that of the state are equivalent: there is no law without a state, and no state without law. But that only means that law is a crucial structural feature of the state, not that the two are identical. It is also correct that it would be a mistake to describe the state as the power of the law; for the state is always a power of the law organized *in accord with the law,* and the elimination of areas not subject to the law is a very important goal. But that still does not justify Kellner's identification. For even if every complete legal system must thematize its own realization, and thus have a constitutional law component, the state normatively constructed by constitutional law

---

2. I refer to Weber's well-known distinction (1980; 27 f.).

3. (1922), 11. In addition, there is politics as "the theory of the achievement of certain state goals" (13). Even if Jellinek considers "value judgments" to be the domain of politics so conceived, it is important to emphasize that this involves only hypothetical imperatives. Positivism did not rise to the sphere of a categorical moral imperative.

is not to be identified with the real state—just as there is more to every real person than his normative self-image, with which he never completely coincides. One can further acknowledge that the influence of mistresses on monarchs might be discussed in a treatise on constitutional law, but simply as something that contradicts the norms of constitutional law, and thus ought not to exist. What is crucial is that it is not so much the objects as the cognitive interests of experts in constitutional law and of political scientists that differ from each other: the latter describe the political part of social reality, and the former answer a normative question on the basis of a legal system that is presupposed to be valid. Thus, for instance, in certain contexts the political scientist will develop the broadest possible conception of the state, whereas experts in constitutional and international law will be far more cautious, since the subsumption of a social corporate group under the concept "state" entails important legal consequences. In other contexts, the political scientist will deny the status of true states to states recognized by international law. However, the political scientist will resort to the juristic concept of the state in order to explain why, for instance, weak states that no longer have any real monopoly on force are still recognized as states at all, and do not completely collapse.[4] In actuality, law may also be described from without; the sociology of law founded by Vico and Montesquieu, which analyzes the function of both positive law and jurisprudence within human societies, is part of the social sciences (indeed, part of political science) and not of jurisprudence, even if some of its insights may again prove important for the work of legal scholars.

Also to be considered in this connection is the remarkable status of jurisprudence in the system of the sciences. In various respects, jurisprudence, which Jellinek mistakenly describes as a normative science,[5] is a structure intermediate between the descriptive social sciences and the normative disciplines of legal and political philosophy. In this, it is the twin of systematic theology, which mediates in an analogous way between religious studies and rational theology (or philosophy of religion). As in the case of theology, one can therefore entertain doubts as to jurisprudence's scientific character. No reasonable person denies that both disciplines make brilliant use of scientific methods when interpreting mores or texts relevant to their fields—whether these are religions and sacred books, on one hand, or constitutions and laws on the other.[6] And yet the scientific character of jurisprudence is diminished by the fact that it neither merely describes, like the history of law or the sociology of law, nor argues purely normatively, like the philosophy of law. It is true that jurisprudence transcends the descriptive level, for its goal is to regulate actions; but first of all, this regulation has its ultimate foundation in something positively given, which is itself no longer normatively grounded,

---

4. Cf. R. H. Jackson and C. G. Rosenberg (1994), 281: "Juridical statehood is more important than empirical statehood in accounting for the persistence of states in Black Africa."

5. (1922), 20.

6. However, this interpretive achievement differs from that of the historian of religion or law, who pursues another line of questioning.

but only described,[7] and second, it is dependent on law being somehow considered socially valid as well—even if not forever and for everyone. Just as it is indispensable to conceive the validity of morals independently of all social facts, so it is wrong to cling to the existence of a legal order when it has been illegally abolished without any prospect of being reinstated.[8] This is not meant to deny that from the point of view of the sociology of knowledge there is no alternative to the normativism of jurisprudence: the importance of jurisprudence for the survival of states and therefore of human society is far greater than that of philosophy and still more than that of the social sciences. However, this practical precedence does not necessarily entail an epistemological precedence, and only the ultimate level is concerned in this preliminary observation. Political philosophy goes beyond the half-normativism of jurisprudence, since it does not set norms for action on the basis of the law in force, but rather applies the normative question to the law in force itself. Thus, like the purely descriptive social sciences, it distances itself from the law's positive validity—not, however, in order to withdraw into a value-free sphere, but rather to give the validity of the law a deeper legitimation.

The following remarks will be concerned, first, with the essence and forms of the state; second, with a few of the stages in the historical development of the state; and third, extremely briefly, with the main characteristics of the modern state system as the result of the development up to this point. In so doing we will draw on political science and the historical sciences. The modes of thought peculiar to constitutional and international law are of interest here only as they are refracted in political science, that is, insofar as they are also part of the describable reality of states. Juristic-normative statements are not examined in this book (and fall outside the competence of its author); moral-normative statements will be avoided as much as possible, since they will be the subject of later chapters that seek to provide a justification of the state. In the first section (6.1), I will investigate a few of the many intermediate links between simpler social relationships and those that are articulated in the state, and also analyze the most important elements of statehood. The homonymy of the word "political," which can characterize both cratic and state structures, suggests that the concepts of power and the state are closely connected—even if they are, of course, no more identical than are the concepts of law and the state. State domination is a specific form of power—and indeed, as a rule, the highest one. It is essential to understand, on the basis of human nature and the logic of power, why everywhere we find human beings, we also find, if not

---

7. This is not to deny that there are jurists who deal with specific questions in the philosophy of law and the philosophy of the state without noticing that they have left the juristic level behind. What makes Carl Schmitt's works so fascinating and at the same time so irritating is precisely that he constantly moves from constitutional law toward political science and philosophy without realizing what he is doing.

8. This holds a fortiori for legal changes in the law; and herein lies, in fact, an important difference between theology and jurisprudence: the normative basis of the former changes much more slowly than that of the latter, even in the case of constitutions.

a state, at least forms of political domination. Since this book seeks to outline a moral politics in the current world-historical situation, in the third section (6.3) the most important characteristic traits of this situation will be sketched. The current world-historical situation is crucially influenced by the remarkable structure of the modern state, which since the early modern period has spread over ever greater areas of the world, and is today the form in which political power is most powerfully expressed. First, however, we must explain why states and their politics change at all, as well as why the modern state has been able to impose itself so powerfully in comparison with pre-modern political structures.

6.1. From the Power Relationship to the State

In Max Weber's theory of the categories of the social, the concept of domination (*Herrschaft*) is one of those that mediate between the concept of power and the concept of the state. Domination is defined as "the probability that a command with a given specific content will be obeyed by a given group of persons."[9] In contrast to the more amorphous concept of power, here two points are crucial: first, the stabilization of the power relationship between given individuals, and second, the power-subject's recognition of the power-holder's will, a recognition that is manifested in obedience to commands. These two elements are not equivalent, but as a rule they are closely connected. The power-holder's will is much more easily acknowledged as legitimate if contact with him occurs more than once; conversely, a stabilization of the power relationship can be achieved only with difficulty if power-subjects do not recognize the power-holder. In colloquial speech, the use of the word "domination" already presupposes a certain recognition of the power-holder's right to issue commands, as the following example of a very intensive but absolutely ephemeral power relationship proves. A robber who puts a knife to one's throat and whom one hopes never to meet again can successfully demand that one hand over one's money, but one would hardly call this demand "an exercise of domination," for although one takes notice of this demand and acts in accord with it, this cannot be called recognition. At most, if the robber has enslaved his victim and makes him work for him, for instance, then we might speak of "domination." Yet one can speak of domination whenever the power-subject has an opportunity to escape from the power relationship but does not, for whatever reason, do so. In this case the psychological causes that underlie the recognition of power may be of very different kinds, but for the most part a bundle of heterogeneous motives will be involved.

How does power extend to domination, and why are power relationships established over the long term and recognized? Simplifying somewhat, we can distinguish four forms of social relationships that may lead to domination and ultimately to the

---

9. (1980), 28: "die Chance, für einen Befehl bestimmten Inhalts bei angebbaren Personen Gehorsam zu finden." See also 541 ff. Trans. A. R. Henderson and T. Parsons, 152.

state: collective identity in the family, habituation to the power of the stronger arising from a defeat, a contract proceeding from one's own interests, and a fascination with the authority of a leader (chapter 6.1.1).[10] The distinction is one among ideal types insofar as almost every form of domination draws on all four sources.[11] And yet it is not hard to discern the important qualitative distinctions between the domination of the pater-familias over his children, the domination of a master over his slaves, the union of peers into a group with sovereign authorities in which the chairmanship rotates, and finally, the domination arising from the authority of a strong personality. The system of negative sanctions underlies the master-slave relationship; the system of positive sanctions underlies the union of peers, and the power of ideas underlies authority. Collective identity transcends these forms of power, and can nonetheless be an important component of domination—at least if one defines the concept of collective identity in such a way that it does not necessarily imply complete symmetry between those united in this way. The preceding remarks on power would be misunderstood if they were interpreted to mean that all human interactions are determined by power. It is possible to define the concept of power so broadly that it includes influence and social effect as well, but as it is used in this book the concept of power implies a plurality of wills that experience themselves as different. But this is certainly not man's earliest experience. On the contrary, in chapter 4.3 it was shown that the experience of common meanings and common goals precedes the experience of a specific world of one's own. In comparison to that experience, power struggles are, as it were, a fall from grace, disruptions of an original unity, without which the adversaries could ultimately not understand each other at all.[12] What is crucial here is that in the genesis of human society and therefore also of the state, lethal struggles for power were involved as well as this sense of community and security. Only if the analysis of power is combined with the reflections on the bases of culture can one approach intellectually the state, which is, so to speak, a synthesis of the feeling of unity and struggles to subjugate, of centripetal and centrifugal forces.

Anyone who—like most modern philosophers of the state—tries to base the state exclusively on the relationship among autonomous individuals (and even solely on the relationship among rationally egoistic individuals), whether this relationship manifests itself in the form of a struggle or a contract, overlooks the other foundation of the social, the family. It is true that as it develops, the state increasingly detaches itself from the family, but without the family it cannot be understood either in its own genesis or as

---

10. Cf. R. Zippelius (1991), 103 ff., who discusses theories of patriarchy, genetic contract theories, and theories of power as for the emergence of the state (there is in addition the patrimonial theory, which is, however, less general, because it presupposes a settled way of life). I owe much to Zippelius's book.

11. According to Hobbes's model, for instance, domination is based on a combination of the second and the third elements.

12. To that extent one can say, from the point of view of the history of development, that the individual forms of power are a product of the differentiation of an original experience of domination, even if they necessarily precede it in conceptual development.

a modern state. For the reproduction of its citizens constantly takes place within such an institution, which not only consists of autonomous adults, but also brings up helpless and defenseless individuals and makes them into autonomous adults. Filmer's *Patriarcha* cannot provide a point of departure for a justification of the state. And yet Locke's sharp distinction between family and state is connected with the danger that one might no longer understand how much social behavior, even that of adults, is determined by an element that precedes the separation of individuals. Even the modern individualist understands himself in terms of concepts that were made available to him through a language that is not his own creation; even the crudest egoist has needs that are not set by himself, but communicated to him by his culture; even the most narcissistic egomaniac begs for others' recognition or even love. Even if the medium of social interactions itself proceeded from concrete relationships, it still shapes and structures later interactions that acquire their fluency and comprehensibility from the fact that they are guided by reference to the same medium. It is certainly possible to make a basic classification of social interactions by asking whether they take place within a *single* culture or between members of different cultures—in the first case there is, in addition to all personal oppositions, an atmosphere that is lacking in the other type of relationships. To be sure, one of the tasks of human history—indeed, its primary task—is to alleviate the radical difference between the two forms of relationship; but this has become possible only because in addition to relationships among independent individuals there has also been this other type of relationship, which is entitled to claim absolute priority ontogenetically as well as phylogenetically. Only Hegel's interpretation of the state as a synthesis of forms of relationship realized in the family and in civil society seems adequate to the facts.

However, this still does not suffice to determine the specificity of *political* domination. This is possible only if the indispensability of the political function is recognized alongside the other basic social functions, and if at the same time it becomes clear why this function can best be fulfilled through a domination with coercive force (chapter 6.1.2). On this basis the elements of which a state necessarily consists can be examined more closely (chapter 6.1.3).

6.1.1. Forms of Pre-Political Domination

6.1.1.1. Domination in the Family

Why do children obey their parents? One answer to this question is suggested if one thinks of the way in which human beings come into the world. Every person's first relationship is with the mother. As an ideal type this relationship is opposed to the interaction of a power struggle. The fetus has no will of its own, but participates in both the organic and the psychological life of its mother. This original unity is dissolved at birth—the child faces an outside world in which it must now cry for its food. But so far as intellectual assimilation goes, the child remains for a long time in a condition that is comparable to that of its food intake when it was in the mother's body—it takes in information without being aware that it is encountering something alien. The same things must be done for the child for many years, and in the process he gives joy to himself and to those who care for him through the freshness with which he recognizes new things and does new things, in accord with the laws of the development of the body and the soul, in a world that is as yet unknown to him. At the same time, his natural will must be adapted—by force, if necessary—to the demands of the culture in which he is growing up. The first-time experiences that shape him explain why he develops particularly close relationships with the people with whom he experiences these things. The emotional intensity of the relationships to siblings and to early friends finds hardly any later parallel—just as falling in love for the first time can never be repeated, because later on, falling in love no longer provides the special thrill of opening up new dimensions to the soul.

The admiring way a child looks up to those who are already adults, and especially to the adult who is the most powerful in his immediate environment and to whom he therefore thinks he owes the most, explains why the parent-child (and especially the father-child) relationship becomes a paradigm of domination. The parents are not only stronger than the child; since they have given him life and take care of him for a long time, their power is naturally *felt* to be legitimate. From interaction with them emerge later on more reflected ideas of legitimacy; his own feeling of self-worth feeds on the affective identification with them; he feels a deep gratitude to them. Their superior knowledge and their advantage of greater life experience provide the foundation for their authority. Breaking free from one's parents to a certain extent in the course of one's life is indispensable in order to gain autonomy. In archaic times there may well have been bloody rebellions against fathers felt to be tyrannical; one thinks of the myths in Hesiod's *Theogony,* which allow us to suppose that analogous experiences between human beings may have preceded them. But Hesiod's Zeus also justifies his domination by extended procreations; and one should not forget that even today, in a modern constitutional state such as Germany, the head of state can be called a *Landesvater,* and the director of a doctoral dissertation is known as a *Doktorvater.*[13] In any case, the larger social units that first developed had their roots in biological kinship: tribes, clans, and smaller kinship groups were humanity's organizational forms at the beginning of its development. The respect felt for the father is transferred to the council of elders; an exceptional position of power is justified by the fact that the person in question belongs to the lineage installed to rule by the common tribal father.

---

13. The state can also be represented as feminine, as is sometimes done in English, or in an expression such as "Mother Russia"; in any case, it is seldom neuter.

6.1.1.2. Obedience on the Part of Those Subjected by Force

Children's obedience to the father is not based solely on a feeling of collective identity—fear of his physical superiority also plays a role. This element is the most crucial in explaining the domination over those who, according to Aristotle, belong, in addition to wife and children, to a complete household: slaves.[14] With slaves, the structure of a household is fundamentally altered.[15] Whereas in the ideal case the relationship between children and parents is determined by gratitude, that between spouses by love, and that of more distant relatives to each other by a feeling of collective identity, the relationship between slave and master cannot be explained except by earlier struggles for power, whether military or economic in nature. These struggles need not necessarily have been waged by those who currently hold the roles of master and slave. We will examine this relationship in greater detail because it clarifies an element of political domination. In the emergence of most political corporate groups, processes of subjugation were probably involved, a bloody victory of one group over another (whether within the same tribe or over a foreign tribe). The feeling of greater distance that distinguishes relationships within a state from relationships within a family results not only from the impersonality that characterizes exchange relationships among persons who do not share a collective identity; in the past, it also often resulted from the hatred that had earlier been discharged in bloody conflicts. Nonetheless, only this feeling of distance made possible higher forms of freedom.

Why does a slave obey even if he could free himself from his master? It is generally in the interest of the power-holder that long-term power relationships be established—partly because he welcomes either the exercise of power in itself or its consequences, and partly because he has to fear revenge if he loses power. But such a stabilization can be convenient even for the power-subject. If he cannot achieve power himself, it may be far better for him to prepare himself for a power-holder whose will he knows and to which he has gradually become accustomed, than to get involved in one exhausting and possibly even life-threatening power struggle after another. Indeed, independently from that, obedience may have become almost second nature for him, so that he would find it troublesome to free himself from it. It can be convenient not to have to make decisions entailing great responsibilities, but rather to rely on others' directions. A drive to serve is no less common than a drive to dominate. Block, the merchant in Kafka's *The Trial*, is certainly a grotesque caricature, but a caricature of servile tendencies that are present in most people and that can erupt again in disturbing ways even in the post-Enlightenment period. Through identification with the power-holder the power-subject may even feel a secret pleasure in being mistreated. That he may

---

14. Kant still regarded the right of the head of the household over servants as the third title of the right of domestic society: *Metaphysik der Sitten* I § 30 (1976 f.; 8:395 ff.).

15. Cf. Vico's distinction between the "famiglie de' figliuoli" and the "famiglie de' famoli" in the "Iconomica poetica" of the *Scienza nuova*.

associate with someone so powerful can fill him with pride, especially when he learns that others also tremble before his master, and that they feel insecure even with himself, because they are not sure whether he might, for instance, exercise some influence on his master.[16] The cratically clever power-holder will repeatedly give his power-subject opportunities to oppress others, in order that he might find it easier to humble himself before his superior. "The feelings opposing domination undergo a deformation in which they are not directed toward the main founders and beneficiaries of the organization of domination, but against the lower-level recipients of orders—not the judge, but the executioner is despised—and against the members of other groups in the service of domination, above all if they are not part of the basic stratum from an ethnic point of view."[17] And very special satisfactions are granted even to the executioner at the bottom of the social ladder when he goes about his work, especially when he may be allowed to deal with fallen masters. In addition, in occasional festivals the fiction of a world upside down may be indulged—the Saturnalia, for instance, functioned as a social safety valve.

In any case, over time the superiority of the master is acknowledged in most long-term power relationships. The master no longer finds it necessary to force his power-subjects to carry out his commands each time; instead, obedience becomes almost automatic. But that does not mean that negative sanctions are no longer threatened if the power-subject does not obey in the expected way, or that the power-subject is not aware of that possibility. But this threat is not constantly present in the power-subject's consciousness. D. Claessens, drawing on Weber, defines domination as "the condition in which the expectations of those on whom power was or is exercised have adapted to this condition; or, it is the condition in which both role-relationships have become so intertwined that 'power' is experienced only in a 'flatter' way—the relations between the two parties are taken for granted."[18] On one hand, we have already seen that without displacing the contents of consciousness a constant concentration on new demands would hardly be possible—to that extent nothing special is involved here. On the other hand, in our case there is an additional reason for forcing the relevant contents of consciousness into the background: it is humiliating to know that one is threatened by negative sanctions. A cratically clever power-holder can only be pleased by this displacement; for a power-subject who feels humiliated is more dangerous than one who has resigned himself to his lot.

---

16. Consider the psychogram of the troika driver Balaga sketched by Tolstoy in *War and Peace* (2:4, 16). He is beaten by his masters, risks his health and his life for them, and loses more money through their escapades than he receives from them. But when, urged by them to drive at ever greater speeds, he runs down a peasant and nearly kills him or strikes him with his whip, his heart swells with joy and he is proud of his masters. Conversely, the suffering power-holder may also identify with his power-subjects: Cf. above, chap. 5, n. 290.

17. C. Sigrist (1979), 262.

18. (1974), 18.

To this extent it is less difficult than it might seem to bring a power-subject to respect the power exercised on him and thereby to constitute domination. On one hand, negative sanctions are usually combined with positive ones—the working slave must, for instance, be fed if he is not to starve to death. But the power-holder offers above all protection—and if the latter is initially only protection against his own negative sanctions, when there is a general threat to existence it can nonetheless easily appear to provide protection against third parties, for which obedience is not too high a price to pay. On the other hand, it is easy to give moral reasons for one's subordination to the will of the power-holder. From the earliest times, it might be argued, some people have always obeyed others; a glance at nature confirms that the stronger dominate the weaker. The stories about the gods show that in their sphere as well, relationships of domination based on dreadful power struggles also prevail. Finally, if one had been victorious oneself, one would have treated the defeated side just as one is being treated. In short, the power relationship is said to be as it ought to be; it corresponds to the order of the world and is in accord with what is right. By means of this conviction on the part of the power-holder and his power-subjects, power becomes domination. Naturally, in a descriptive approach to the phenomenon of domination the question is not whether the convictions of power-subjects regarding the legality and legitimacy of the power relationship are objectively reasonable. They may be absurd without this altering in any way the stability of the power relationship and thus its character as domination. The transformation of a power relationship into domination is, however, not irreversible. The slave may recognize that his enslavement is unjust, and only be waiting for the most propitious moment to throw it off. In this case, domination may turn into force, and only new power struggles will be able to stabilize it. Moreover, domination also collapses when the power-holders doubt its legitimacy; and it not seldom happens that they come to doubt it even before the power-subjects, simply because they usually have more time for reflection. But since power struggles are exhausting, the stabilization of power in forms of domination is one of humanity's most important tasks. Domination provides relief—without this achievement, higher forms of culture cannot develop at all. This does not mean that all forms of domination are *morally* legitimate—the moral differences between slavery and the rule of law created by equals are outrageous. But insofar as both systems are considered legitimate by those involved and are therefore *socially* legitimated, they are both systems of domination.

6.1.1.3. Domination by Contract: The Aporias of the Genetic Contract Theory

At the end of chapter 4.3.2, we mentioned the importance of exchange in the development of cooperation. This suggests that this institution may play a role in producing domination as well, for not only an exchange of goods but the constitution of domination can be in the interest of two or more parties—for example, when it puts an end to the mutual threat of force that exists in the state of nature. Consider, for instance, an economic corporate group in which people participate to achieve a certain goal. The individuals are ultimately indifferent to each other, but they need each other's help as a means to their ends. At the same time, it is important that every alternative for action need not be constantly negotiated anew, but that the corporate group pursue a more or less continuous strategy. The latter is capable of functioning only if it is possible to issue commands within it, that is, if there is a form of domination that threatens to impose negative sanctions on deviant behavior. Therefore people agree on a leadership position, and agree all the more readily the more easily and more regularly its occupant can be changed. Through the *alternation* of dominating and being dominated, or through a periodic reconfirmation of domination, is produced the *symmetry* whose violation makes domination problematic. The indispensable advantages of domination, without which the corporate group would have no will of its own over and above that of the individuals who compose it, are connected with the preservation of equality. Neither love nor direct fear, but rather calculation underlies obedience to domination, which is terminated when cooperation in the corporate group is no longer in one's own interest. Many associations are constituted on this principle, and this suggests that political domination could also have emerged in accord with this model. The spread of the contract theory in modernity—in theory and in practice[19]—shows how natural this idea is. The line of thought goes like this: contracts are made in one's own interest, but are useful only if they are also observed—thus people make a meta-contract regarding the foundation of an institution that guarantees that contracts will be observed.

However, the fact that this idea first became dominant in the modern age is already suspicious. To be sure, one can find ancient predecessors, especially in the Jewish world, in which the idea of alliance was crucial, and not solely for the relationship between God and man. David made a covenant with the elders of Israel before he was anointed as king.[20] But it would be a mistake to absolutize this special form of the emergence of the state. First of all, history shows that the least political ruling groups came into being through contracts—loyalty to older relatives on one hand, and subjection to foreigners by force on the other are the normal forms of archaic domination. Certainly, coming together voluntarily in political ruling groups probably also occurred in early times, but as a rare exception, for instance under pressure of extreme difficulties on both sides, and *as a combination of already existing corporate groups* that owed their existence to other principles of order, but not as a coming together of isolated individuals. As a general descriptive theory of the emergence of the state, the contract theory is untenable, although its normative content remains unaffected.[21] Second, not only the facts, but also a simple thought experiment suffices to refute the theory of political domination as based on the contract model. Economic corporate groups founded on a contract, discussed above, are

---

19. Think of the social contracts that the Puritans who emigrated to America made in founding their communities.

20. 2 Samuel 5:3.

21. In "Of the Original Contract," Hume already clearly showed that the theory of the social contract, understood descriptively, was untenable (1987; 465–487).

such efficient institutions because they function *within* a state and can call upon its power to sanction if one of the parties breaks the contract. It is for the most part an invalid argument by analogy when one tries to use what takes place within a framework to explain the framework itself. In most contracts in civil law, there is a guarantee that the contract will not be broken—a guarantee provided by the state. But despite all the mechanisms of the separation of powers, which are in part a late achievement of political intelligence and can hardly be used to explain the first states, a comparably strong guarantee for contracts in public law is not possible. For who would supervise the supervisors? How can an infinite regress be avoided? Different state organs might conceivably supervise each other, but since their cooperation for evil ends cannot be excluded, one would consequently have to give every individual an equally large share of state power, and thereby dissolve the state that one set out to constitute. Among the Puritans who founded communities there was at least a common belief that those who violated the contract would be punished in the other world—the strains and risks that the emigrants had to face were a sufficient guarantee for this belief. But if someone subjects himself—through a contract limited in time or content—to the rule of an unknown person with a monopoly on force over a corporate group, what protects him against the violation of the contract by a ruler who cannot as such be forced to fulfill his commitments? The more the state is not itself an association that one can leave whenever one wants to, the more this question arises—for one is entirely at its mercy.

It does not help to point out that it would be in everyone's interest to establish a bearable form of domination instead of continuing the war of all against all. Even if a legal form of domination is preferred by all to the state of nature, even though it is less pleasant than arbitrarily exercising one's own power, this does not mean that it actually comes about, for every person finds himself in a prisoners' dilemma situation with regard to this transition. To be sure, the state of nature is not Pareto-optimal, but Hobbes is wrong when he claims that it suffices to see this in order to surmount it. In prisoners' dilemma situations, both parties' assessment of their rational self-interest always leads to both of them defecting and to a failure to achieve Pareto-optimality. If the other does not keep his commitments, it would be foolish to remain true to the contract oneself, and if he does keep them, one gains advantages by breaking the contract oneself.[22] In general, there is a solution to the dilemma only if the two people involved, first, are not thinking primarily about their own self-interest, but are willing to observe the principle of fidelity to contracts even independently of their advantage; second, trust that this also holds for their contractual partner; and third, can assume that the other also trusts them. The second and third conditions are essential, for as we have already seen in chapter 3.3.3.1, a moral person rightly wants to prevent the other from violating

---

22. For a position of reflective self-interest the iteration of prisoners' dilemma situations does not provide a solution either. If a defection in the last instance of a series is instrumentally rational for both sides, then the next-to-last instance really becomes the last one to be considered, and the same holds for it—all the way back to the first instance.

symmetry—and not for selfish reasons, but out of a sense of justice. In such a crucial question as subjection by another through force, even the strategy of "tit for tat" can be too risky for it might very well be that one will not have a chance to react.

In short, if people were truly the kind of self-interest maximizing, atomic individuals that Hobbes conceives, a state would hardly have been founded—they would have either destroyed or enslaved each other. That this is not the case is due to the fact that people are acquainted with principles that go beyond self-interest. Within the family the identification with the welfare of one's own relatives; outside the family the recognition of fundamental norms of justice—especially the one that specifies that contracts are to be fulfilled, a norm that cannot be reduced to rational self-interest. But we have already seen that one's own recognition of this norm does not suffice; there must also be a mutual trust with respect to its recognition by the other. From this follows the irreplaceable importance of the category of mores for a genetic theory of the state. The social function of mores is precisely to produce the trust in generally observed norms without which contracts cannot be made. This holds especially for contracts in the realm of public law, which are the only ones that ensure that violations of other contracts are punished by sanctions. Mores are required to support the state, and no matter how much the form of the state and law may influence mores, the state cannot create mores *ex nihilo*. By nature, they precede it. All contracts presuppose a legal order, but the legal order presupposes shared ideas about value. For instance, a monarch's electoral contract is meaningful as an institution only if the monarch and the estates are united by a common belief that is not itself the result of a contract. Absolutizing contract-theory thought is based on a repression of what is always already presupposed by relationships between autonomous individuals. Common interests and common theoretical attitudes hold a group together only for a short time if there are not also common values. Without feelings of solidarity, long-term cooperation can hardly exist.[23] Therefore one can maintain that at the beginning of the construction of the state only a common collective identity (on the basis of kinship or respect for authority) or force were possible bonds uniting people and not a contract, which belongs to later levels of development. Only political men or confidence-inspiring authorities—ideally, people who are both at once—can lead the way out of paralyzing prisoners' dilemma situations.

6.1.1.4. Domination on the Basis of Authority That Is Not Based on Kinship

Max Weber's triadic typology of legitimate domination (or "authority") is justly famous. The distinction among traditional, rational (or legal), and charismatic domination structures a broad spectrum of forms of domination. Traditional domination corresponds to a peculiar combination of the first two forms of domination discussed

---

23. Cf. H. D. Lasswell and A. Kaplan (1969), 30 ff., which elaborates a significant alternative to methodological individualism.

here, while rational domination basically corresponds to the third form. However, what is disturbing about Weber's classification is that according to it the difference between traditional and rational domination can be connected with a historical process of development in the course of which the former is replaced by the latter, whereas charismatic domination can develop both in eras of traditional domination and in those of rational domination. In actuality, the three types of domination are not of equal value, if only because charismatic domination can always appear only temporarily, whereas the two other types of domination shape their respective eras. They are both "normal" forms of domination, whereas charismatic domination has an innovative character.[24]

In chapter 5.1.2.2.5.3 above, charisma was discussed as a special form of authority, the one of the forms of power based on opinion most likely to lead to domination. Manipulation can always only be joined to other forms, because domination is necessarily public and cannot be completely concealed; convincing and persuading, on the other hand, are individual activities that have to be repeated over and over and do not suffice to provide a foundation for domination. However, on the basis of his authority a person can become a leading figure, obeyed even without the pressure of negative sanctions, and without any prospect of an exchange between his position and one's own. Older family members may also possess an authority based on kinship, but since this form of domination has already been discussed, here we are concerned solely with the authority of people to whom those subject to domination are not closely related. If such people have superior instrumental knowledge, it is in one's own interest to follow them. However, this constitutes subjection to domination rather than a consultancy contract only if the people with superior knowledge are also granted the power to command. People will be prepared to make this concession only for the sake of very important goals, the most important of which is one's own survival. If someone knows how to save people from famine, to lead people through a desert, or to defeat enemies in battle, he will not be denied general obedience when he asks for it—especially if he is irreplaceable. Moreover, domination based on military authority often contains an implicit threat: someone who has defeated external enemies will also know how to deal with internal enemies. The domination of those who first explain what goals one should have—for instance, priests in traditional societies—is more subtle and often more enduring. Moses' domination over Israel, for example, was based more on the superiority of his insights into value than on the superiority of his insights into the means to ends. He represented a concept of God that most people found, even if half-unconsciously, more elevated, and which entailed a higher concept of law that was resisted, but ultimately had to be acknowledged. Much the same can be said about Mohammed. Domination derived from the authority of value rationality is, as it were, a synthesis of domination in the family and the forms of domination based on differences. As in the latter, a person who exer-

_____

24. It might seem possible to distinguish between charismatic domination in the traditional world and in the modern world. Thus D. E. Willer (1967) has proposed a fourth type of domination, that of ideological authority.

cises domination on the basis of the authority of his value rationality is not connected with those subject to domination in an immediate collective identity; indeed, one is seldom a prophet in one's own land. On the other hand, the person who has superior value rationality seems only to want what one has always oneself wanted or thought one wanted, at the bottom of one's heart, at a deeper level of one's self; he combines foreignness and closeness in a fascinating way. However, his domination will be lasting only if he does not rely wholly on his charisma, but has access to means of physical pressure in case charisma does not produce its effect on everyone.

The importance of charismatic—that is, innovative, authority-founding—domination for the course of history can hardly be overestimated. We have seen that without a basic social trust that certain principles are generally acknowledged, contracts are not even conceivable. Every society therefore jealously defends its own mores. At the same time, however, societies must change—whether because their environment changes; or because the principles of their mores contradict moral obligations, which are gradually discerned; or because young people demand a renewal of the society. This process is accompanied by great risks, and it is an achievement of good charismatic domination when it can be directed along lines that are not destructive for the society and when a rational collective identity is created by making possible new experiences of meaning. However, the concept of charismatic domination is full of tensions, not to say a *contradictio in adjecto,* insofar as the innovative element that is by nature connected with the charismatic endangers domination that strives to be enduring. The latter can endure only if the contents that the charismatic figure represents remain, while at the same time the formal element of the charismatic fades away.[25]

6.1.2. The Basic Social Functions and Political Domination

6.1.2.1. Reproduction

Reproduction, nourishment, and defense are general organic functions that among human beings become different social subsystems. Here it must be repeated that most corporate groups do not fulfill only a *single* basic function, and that some functions—in particular, the political function—may be assumed by different corporate groups. The state is a late product of history; political functions were, however, exercised early on, for example by the tribe. Not only can human beings not reproduce alone, but economic and military needs also make indispensable life in groups in which there must be not only a demarcation of wills, but cooperation as well. Although the military is probably the most important source of the political, reproduction and economic life also depend on the political, because they cannot get along without a legal order.

---

25. Cf. Weber (1980), 142 ff., "Die Veralltäglichung des Charisma" ("The Routinization of Charisma").

The elementary human corporate group is the family. On one hand, its essence includes reproduction; on the other, the personal quality of the relationships within the family must be distinguished in kind from those in, for example, economic corporate groups. The connection between these two aspects, which is in no way analytic, follows from earlier remarks on the way in which human beings enter the world. The infant's long period of helplessness, both corporeal and mental, sufficiently explains why in every human society an institution concerned with bringing up children had to develop—in the human infant's extreme need for protection and the long duration of this condition lie the key to explaining man's high level of intellectuality on one hand, and a significant part of human institutions on the other.[26] It is natural that the same human beings who brought the child into the world also devote themselves to bringing him up; only in exceptional cases is this task taken over by others. However, the father has no immediate, biologically given drive to care for his children; and since in most archaic cultures fathers have no legal duties toward their children, the human race would be in a bad way if the father's co-responsibility for his children were not anchored in mores. Presumably the latent function of such a peculiar institution as that of the *couvade* (in which the father goes to bed at the birth of his child and simulates the symptoms of labor and childbirth) consists precisely in involving the father emotionally in the welfare of his child. However, we should mention especially the stabilization of the relationship between husband and wife in marriage, which is preceded by a formal public bonding, the marriage ceremony. In every culture there are probably also sexual interactions that remain fleeting and produce no lasting bond; but in addition to these the embedding of sexual *interactions* in *relationships* of significant stability is indispensable if the time-consuming process of bringing up a child—which is difficult for one person to manage—is to be successful. Marriage has incontestably been one of the most important factors in humanization no matter how different its forms are, which range from rare polyandry and common polygyny to monogamy. Even where extensive promiscuity is ethnologically proven, it is found only within certain well-defined groups.

Living together for a long time enables a man and woman to develop a more differentiated perception of each other's needs, along with an increasing ability to articulate and communicate their own interior dimensions. The background feeling that the need

---

26. Cf. the beautiful comparison in Augustine's *De civitate Dei* XIII 3: "infantes infirmiores etiam cernimus in usu motuque membrorum et sensu adpetendi atque vitandi, quam sunt aliorum tenerrimi fetus animalium; tamquam se tanto adtollat excellentius supra cetera animantia vis humana, quanto magis impetum suum, velut sagitta cum arcus extenditur, retrorsus reducta distulerit." ("[I]nfants, we see, are even feebler in the use and movement of their limbs, and more infirm to choose and refuse, than the most tender offspring of other animals; as if the force that dwells in human nature were destined to surpass all other living things so much the more eminently, as its energy has been longer restrained, and the time of its exercise delayed; just as an arrow flies the higher the further back it has been drawn." Trans. M. Dodds, 414.)

for sex is being fulfilled allows the development of higher forms of inclination: Vico aptly calls marriage the first friendship in the world.[27] The positive thing about marriage is that within it a relationship which, unlike that between parents and children, has no genetic foundation and is mediated by the partners' own agreement, can become an end in itself. One is not at home in marriage; a home has first to be made. Feelings of community are gradually developed, they are not simply already there. Certainly the free choice of one's partner became a general right only late in human history, and the sex drive and the desire for children play a crucial role in the development of marriage—a desire that emerges in a human being (as an animal that plans) in part from concern about his own future, since in old age he may be just as helpless and in need of care as he was as an infant. Cultures react to this fact in extremely different ways: where food is scarce, mores call for old people who are unable to work to be killed, and sometimes even eaten. In part, the desire for children springs from the striving for immortality. Some religious conceptions (whose genesis is easy to explain in terms of the theory of evolution) connect life after death with sacrifices for the dead made by their descendants. Naturally, economic factors have also favored marriage—in particular the obvious utility of a division of labor: the man can hunt, the woman can gather plants. But despite all the ways in which marriage is connected with goals, and despite the fact that the erotic as the quintessence of a dual relationship enjoyed as an *absolute* end in itself is a very late product of human cultural development, even marriage in early times can probably be interpreted as a synthesis of a power struggle and the parent-child relationship. On one hand, as an encounter between two adults with differing interests, it is a struggle (and even a clearly physical struggle, as in the case of marriage based on abduction of the bride). The male's bodily superiority and the specific characteristics of his sexuality have often enough allowed physical force, as a form of power, to determine marriage, against which women only gradually acquired the ability to defend themselves. Not before the twentieth century did the battle of the sexes become a political issue of the first importance. (Thus women's economic achievements have always been great, often much greater than those of men, but for a long time women were prevented from entering the labor market.) On the other hand, the common desire for carnal possession, especially when a lengthy courtship precedes it and the uncovering of the body follows that of the souls of the people involved, as well as the duration of the relationship and of common responsibility and care, could lead at an early date to forms of symbiosis in which the difference between *I* and *Thou* is temporarily forgotten in a *We*-consciousness.

However, the nuclear family, which has existed as an institution of its own only for a relatively short time, is not sufficient for the survival of humankind. Already at the beginning of history, not only did economic and military constraints lead to living in larger groups determined by kinship, but it was precisely the concept of kinship itself

---

27. *Scienza nuova* sect. 554.

that caused tribal pressure on the family—and thus the beginnings of the political. Why? In chapter 4.3.2 it was emphasized that the purely biological foundation of the kinship system was already transcended in early times. Thus the kinship bonds that connected the elements of the highest corporate group might be very loose; ultimately, only a mythical ancestor, perhaps a totemic animal, guaranteed the blood relationship in which the group certainly believes, but which in reality hardly exists any more. The common belief in unity, the feeling of collective identity, is more essential than the real genetic connection. Moreover, it is well known that one of the most important differences between cultures depends on whether they are patrilineal or matrilineal, that is, on whether the child is considered to be related to the father or to the mother. It is unlikely that a true matriarchy can have existed, but there were probably cultures in which the mother's brother, and not the biological father (who has no legal connection with his offspring), was considered the child's closest male relative. Evidently, the decision to adopt a matrilineal or patrilineal system in determining kinship relations is based not on biology but on culture, for the child is equally related genetically to the father and the mother, to the father's brother and the mother's brother, to cross-cousins and parallel cousins—but not in the group's self-understanding, for which the child belongs to only one side. The importance this precedence granted to one side of the family, no matter which one it is, can hardly be overestimated. Like the development of anisogamy, it is another of the violations of symmetry that make the world more complex. It was through the sharp division of the environment into relatives and non-relatives that the prohibition on incest and especially the requirement of exogamy in many cultures acquired a precise meaning. It is well known that biologists and anthropologists disagree as to whether the human taboo on incest has a biological foundation. Nevertheless, an aversion to certain forms of incest has been proven to exist among some higher mammals, and it is hypothesized that this kind of behavior has the genetic advantage of preventing the negative influence of certain recessive genes and broadening the gene pool. On the other hand, the fact that relatives are not defined in genetic terms alone is evidence for the cultural foundation of the human prohibition on incest. The social importance of the requirement of exogamy is obvious: through the exchange of women between different groups new bonds of solidarity are constructed and strengthened. It is the whole complicated algebra of kinship relations that first makes the stability of archaic societies comprehensible. Through a cultural act that detaches itself from the symmetry of nature, clear assignments emerge, producing a web of graspable structures that can be further developed. It was modern anthropology (especially that of Lévi-Strauss) that first offered a precise understanding of these connections, but it remains noteworthy that Augustine had already basically grasped the social importance of the prohibition on incest. In his interpretation of Genesis he dealt with the fact that initially, incest among siblings was widespread—the second human generation had hardly any alternative. Yet with the growth of the human race, incest was forbidden; in this way, Augustine says, each individual was able to develop a larger multiplicity of family relationships. If father and father-in-law are not identical, as they are in incestuous marriage among siblings, one is related to more people—the bond of love is multiplied.[28]

Precisely because the system of kinship relations is not primarily natural-biological, but rather a cultural creation, it can be maintained only through social supervision. For that reason one can certainly say, no matter how paradoxical it sounds, that the tribe, from which the state proceeds, is more original than the family.[29] This assertion seems absurd insofar as the tribe is larger than the families that compose it and presupposes a plurality of families as the condition of its possibility. The multiplicity of forms in which families can appear in the most diverse cultures shows, however, that the one chosen by a particular culture is not self-evident and hence must be defended against possible deviations. Consequently behind the institution of the family stands a force that is ultimately felt by all concerned to be legitimate and is therefore the germ of statehood. However much the tribe first transcends the families, the families were able to develop only within the tribe. Power needs love to reproduce itself, but love achieves stability only through the pressure exercised by power. However, it is no accident that the tribe is felt to be a kind of larger family—in this way its power ultimately appears to be the expression of a collective will that includes everyone, even wrongdoers.

Consequently, for all phases of human history we can take as the starting point a co-evolution of the institutions of the family and the state (or its early forms). This does not imply that the tribe is the only corporate group that is allowed to exercise a force acknowledged to be legitimate—on the contrary, the elaboration of a state monopoly on force is an extremely late product of history. In early times, as much of the use of coercive force as possible remained with the smaller social units. It was the head of the household who was supposed to punish his wife, his children,[30] and his servants when they did wrong within the household; even vendettas were for the most part reserved for near relatives. Only when strife between smaller kinship groups erupts does the tribe intervene. The tribe is the highest corporate group that is allowed to use legitimate force, but certainly not the only one.

---

28. *De civitate Dei* XV 16: "Habita est enim ratio rectissima caritatis, ut homines, quibus esset utilis atque honesta concordia, diversarum necessitudinum vinculis necterentur, nec unus in uno multas haberet, sed singulae spargerentur in singulos ac sic ad socialem vitam diligentius conligandam plurimae plurimos obtinerent." ("For it is very reasonable and just that men, among whom concord is honorable and useful, should be bound together by various relationships; and that one man should not himself sustain many relationships, but that the various relationships should be distributed among several, and should thus serve to bind together the greatest number in the same social interests." Trans. M. Dodds, 500.)

29. This is the thesis of E. Meyer (1981; 15 ff.), which in many ways reminds us of Aristotle's statement that the polis is by nature earlier than the household: *Politics* 1253a19.

30. In any case, so long as they had not attained majority. The lifelong Roman *patria potestas* was not the normal case.

6.1.2.2. Economic Life

Economic necessities, such as hunting big game, also required social units larger than the nuclear family. Not only does the partially defective nature of man result in his needing clothing and shelter in addition to food, but, as we have seen in chapter 4.2.2.2, the structure of his needs differs fundamentally from those of other animals. For that very reason, among human beings the subsystem of economics extends much further and deeper than metabolism alone requires—high fashion no longer has much to do with protection from the weather. Indeed, the interlinking of our planet in the modern world economy is only the endpoint of a development that is based on the peculiarity of the structure of human needs. On one hand, physical needs force human beings to be social; on the other, the *Me* leads people to consider themselves of less value if they cannot satisfy the needs that others of the same standing can satisfy. Conspicuous consumption emerges. Life in society makes it easier to satisfy needs, but this is in part offset by the pressure to satisfy needs that the isolated individual would never have felt at all. The dependency of a person's feeling of his own value on a comparison of his consumption with that of others is unworthy of a wise man, but obviously only a few people surmount this dependency. However much the wish to match or surpass others in satisfying needs has brought humanity today to the edge of the abyss, it has nonetheless been an important moving force in the development of culture, because it has motivated people to work in a manner that has an intrinsic worth and is ultimately felt to be an end in itself.

Population growth has also greatly increased needs. In addition to the level of the needs of individuals, the number of those who have needs has to be taken into account. Even if the mathematical ratios that Malthus (1798) believed he had discovered are not accurate, he was right on one point: man can reproduce himself to a greater extent than he can increase the production of food. Animals also tend to multiply too greatly in relation to the food sources available to them. On socio-biological grounds it is easy to explain why programs for maximizing one's own reproduction will be found in greater numbers in the following generation. It follows from the logic of these programs, which have in view their own replication and not the welfare of the individual organism, that it is better to surpass the maximal value—and that means to be brought down under it again by the inevitable deaths that would ensue—than to fall beneath it. However, if going beyond this maximal value leads to catastrophes that in the middle and long term decrease one's own offspring more than falling beneath this threshold would, programs for limiting one's own reproduction have a chance. Such programs—that is, not only programs for limiting the reproduction of conspecifics, which are easy to explain— already exist in the animal world.[31] In the case of human beings, on one hand such a latent function is inherent in various mores that have an entirely different motivation,

---

31. Consider the Bruce-effect among mice, which may be in the interest not only of the males, but also of the mother. See Dawkins (1976), 174.

and, on the other, the problem was early on raised to the level of an object of reflection and planning behavior.[32]

The economic process is articulated in three steps: production, distribution, and consumption. A person's own needs are satisfied either by his own or another's labor, and labor's efficiency is increased by the development of technology. In the narrower sense, technology is the goal-directed procedure of transforming natural materials and energies and producing tools, apparatuses, or machines; in the wider sense, the term refers not only to poiesis, but also to praxis, and therefore includes social technologies as well. However, it is essential to note that even the most perfect technologies always only transform materials, and cannot create them *ex nihilo,* and that this transformation cannot go beyond certain limits. Economic and technical processes always take place within nature, which is the first source of all prosperity; its laws—for instance, the laws of conservation—are generally valid, and it is an illusion to believe that one can escape them. Man can wrest nothing from nature, because he does not stand outside it; only by changing antecedent conditions can he achieve results that would not have occurred without his intervention. If one wants to develop technologies, all the goods produced cannot be immediately *consumed;* some must be *invested* in means of production, in the hope that forgoing some consumption in the present will make it possible to produce more in the future. The classical division of the total economy into three sectors makes sense insofar as the primary sector, to which agriculture, forestry, and the fishing industry belong, on one hand arises from a heterotrophic organism's immediate need for food, and on the other is directly concerned with living nature, whereas the secondary sector, of which the mining and processing industries are a particularly important part, deals with inert nature. If life is conceived as a particularly intensive manifestation of nature, we can say that in the secondary sector there is an alienation from nature. The tertiary sector is constituted by services, and it is therefore concerned not with poiesis but with praxis.

Since through the *division of labor* significantly more can be produced than without it, higher cultures cannot forgo it, even if its differentiation and perfection was achieved only in the course of history. It leads to the formation of *ranks* and *classes,* whose members develop (on the basis of their similar ways of life, modes of labor, supply of goods, education, or economic power) common interests (in material and immaterial goods such as prestige) as well as common values, and may organize themselves into corporate groups that mediate between the family and the state.[33] Such corporate groups can be

---

32. Cf., for instance, Plato, *Republic* 372b f. and Aristotle, *Politics* 1335b19 ff.

33. Ranks can also be formed by groups of people who exercise no specific economic function, but rather a military, political, or religious one—see, for instance, Aristotle's well-known six-part division (*Politics* 1328b ff.) Even if in some human societies reproduction was made impossible even for large groups (among other reasons, because one could then give them more political and religious power without anxiety about doing so), the express limitation of reproduction to a single social group is known only in animal societies.

open or closed depending on the ease with which people can be accepted into them. An extreme case of closedness is represented by castes, into which one is placed on the basis of birth alone; a society of estates is characterized by fewer opportunities to rise and fall beyond the limits of the social strata—for example, because of marriage prohibitions—than is a class society. Great openness makes adaptation to new demands easier, but it may also weaken feelings of solidarity within the group. Class membership is so important because it decisively influences which interests one has. In actuality, there are not only general organic and general human interests, as well as individual interests, but also interests specific to social classes. Interests are usually strengthened by developing realistic expectations that they can be satisfied; and that is the case if one sees that people whom one feels to be like oneself have the same interests, and if one can work together with them to satisfy these interests. For this reason hardly anything contributes so much to the satisfaction of needs as the consciousness of one's own membership in a class.

Unless people are coerced or threatened, they can usually be motivated to work only if they can themselves at least share in the consumption of what is produced by their labor, or if it or an equivalent belongs to them independently of its present use. Animals defend their territory or what they are presently eating, but the category of *property* is specifically human because it constitutes a relationship between a human being (or a corporate group) and a thing (which may also include other people, namely slaves) that goes beyond immediate use or possession. This act cannot be denied a formal intellectual character, since it is grounded in man's ability to transcend the current situation of his needs. Without a clear regulation of the order of property an efficient, long-term planned economy is difficult to achieve. It must also be clear who has a claim to the property of the deceased, if conflicts are to be avoided. Inheritance law—and thus also family law—is an important part of any economic order. In archaic times the law of inheritance could strengthen the notion that not the individual but rather the family was the true property owner. Property that survives the individual, such as land, must be attributed to a corporate group that is just as enduring as the property is and thus more long-lived than the individual. The economic order is determined partly by unwritten norms and partly by the legally defined economic system.

If no force or ruse is to be employed, one can normally expect the help of others in fulfilling one's own needs only if one provides something in return. *Exchange* is the institution that supports the subsystem of the economy if theft and robbery are not permitted. At higher levels of civilization, exchange is preceded by a verbal statement of the union of several wills, that is, a contract (which generally, but not necessarily, establishes mutual obligations). What one can exchange for something is determined partly by mores and partly by haggling. Archaic economies serve primarily to provide subsistence for producers, and exchange occurs only occasionally. The importance of exchange increases in the course of history, in that commerce becomes an economic activity of its own, and reaches a culmination in the modern market economy. In the latter, the organization of exchange, which presupposes developed trade, is no less important than the forms of production. Just as human language vastly simplified communication by making the physical presence of the object referred to superfluous, processes of exchange are enormously facilitated when a good is no longer directly exchanged for another (barter), but instead an appropriate medium of exchange is used. Such mediums of exchange must be generally recognized, of course, if one does not want to exchange something valuable against something worthless. In the history of such mediums of exchange we can see an increasing abstraction. Natural mediums of exchange such as cattle are followed by artifacts that are divisible almost at will; the latter are at first valued also because of their material worth (coins made of metal) but ultimately acquire a purely symbolic function (paper money): the fourth world becomes independent of the second. The introduction of *money* fulfills at least three functions: first, money is, as we already said, a medium of exchange; second, it becomes an instrument for evaluating all goods and services—it makes everything commensurable;[34] third, it serves to preserve value (so long as inflation can be avoided). For that very reason money can lead to an increase in the striving for property that would have been unimaginable in earlier times. The need for natural products is always limited, but the need for money is not, precisely because it is not a question of a concrete object of need, but rather of a title to all possible objects of need.[35]

Whereas exchange in the marketplace presupposes a plurality of autonomous actors, a central planning and direction of the economy is conceivable. The opposition between these two latter types is not to be resolved in terms of a historical logic of development; instead, the two types have been realized again and again in history. The Incan state, for instance, had a centrally planned economy. The question of whether planning is centralized or decentralized should be distinguished from that of whether the dominant form of property is private, social, or state. Even in a decentralized economy planning on the part of independent units is indispensable, and in addition to competition between these units a collective identity must also be built up within them. The work climate inside an enterprise is crucial for success; it can even take on the quality of intensity that characterizes a community. The feeling of belonging to an enterprise can be—even if Marxist theory and politics has not grasped this—much stronger than class solidarity.

6.1.2.3. The Military Function

In addition to the specifically human modes of reproduction and metabolism, there is a third factor that condemns this animal to sociality: the necessity of defending itself against natural forces such as wild animals, including the most murderous of all, human beings. It is obvious that humans who joined together in stable larger units had advantages in conflicts with fellow humans who belonged to significantly smaller groups; life in the nuclear family was not evolutionarily stable. Common military undertakings

---

34. Cf. Aristotle, *Nicomachean Ethics* 1133a20 ff.
35. Locke recognized this very clearly: *Second Treatise* § 37 (1690; 294 f.).

involving men from different families were an important source of the emergence of political corporate groups. Which factors allow us to distinguish among military conflicts?

First, we must mention the people who take part in the conflict. Their level of education and their warlike spirit are far more important than their number. People's warlike spirit depends on whether they are fighting as volunteers or on the basis of a universal conscription, whether for their own country or as mercenaries for the highest bidder, etc. Moreover, the quality of military leadership is important. In the American Civil War, one of the reasons that the South managed to hold on so long was the superiority of its officers, who were able for four years to balance out the North's crushing superiority in troops and resources. In addition, the method of fighting is of great significance—innovations in tactics and strategy (which is, however, more a task for politics) can determine the outcome of a war.

Second, after the persons involved, the location of the conflict is an essential factor. Thus we must differentiate between wars of defense and wars of aggression. All other things being equal, the aggressor's forces need to be several times as large as those of the people who are defending themselves against him. The precise ratio depends on historical contextual conditions such as the state of the technology of fortification and weapons. In the era of modern artillery, systems of fortification have lost much of their importance. In addition, the element in which the conflict takes place must be taken into account: whether on land, on water, or in the air. Thus, for instance, with the development of air power, domination of the air has proven decisive. Among individual elements, topographical and meteorological conditions have to be considered.

Third, the tools for fighting should be mentioned—weapons, for instance. Antiquity already knew cutting weapons and thrusting weapons as well as weapons that are hurled, the former being usable in close combat, the latter in distant combat; later on, firearms were used, and in the twentieth century, atomic, biological, and chemical weapons. As weapons became more transportable, the definition of what constitutes weapons of close and of distant combat has undeniably changed. Weapons can be distinguished not only according to the distance over which they are used, but also according to the damage—short-term or long-term—they cause. Moreover, the quality of logistics plays a major role; it includes among other things the supply of materiel and food as well as the transportation of persons, things, and information. For control over large territories, the importance of good supply and rapid transport is obvious.

Changes in weapons, logistics, and modes of combat often decide the outcome of battle, so that it is crucial for a state that is following an evolutionarily stable strategy to adopt successful changes as quickly as possible—I refer, for instance, to the battle wagon with spoked wheels, or the saddle and stirrup. In addition, these changes often also had extensive organizational consequences for the political structure of a society. Thus, particularly in earlier periods of history, the distinction between individual combat and formation-based warfare was essential. Formation-based warfare makes subordination and discipline indispensable, whereas single combat depends more on individual courage; the latter corresponds more to oligarchic, the former more to monocratic or democratic principles. Modern firearms, for instance, are suited to a "democratic" tendency in that they are relatively inexpensive to acquire and easy to learn to use. With such weapons, the traditional distinction between infantry and cavalry dissolved. The appearance of new forms of combat and weapons had much to do with the decline of the feudal order in Europe in the fifteenth century: Charles the Bold was not the Swiss confederates' equal in the technology of weapons and battle.

Since military matters concern physical survival, on one hand, and since arming people can lead to a threat to members of one's own group, severe punishments for violations of discipline are nearly unavoidable—no form of power is so intensive as the military. Consider, for instance, Roman decimation. As a rule, people kill the enemy with even fewer hesitations if they have had to execute one of their own comrades. In such an act every feeling of individual responsibility fades, because a person who refuses is often himself threatened with death. "The military form represents the most precise and most practicable way of organizing power, because it represents the highest degree of both precision in command and of the certainty that the behavior commanded will follow with factual regularity."[36] All other things being equal, societies with a tight military organization have great advantages over those that lack such an organization. It goes without saying that the quality of the relationship between warriors is of a nature entirely different and even opposed to that within the family. In the former, there is the strictest impersonal obedience, in the latter individual inclination; in the former, constant confrontations with death, in the latter, common responsibility for bringing up new human beings. And yet most military orders also develop a strong feeling of collective identity that promotes trust in the group and thereby strengthens courage. In actuality, not only marriage, but also comradeship in arms is an origin of friendship, and, by way of homosexuality, of the erotic. Being dependent on each other in extreme situations that, so to speak, strip them bare, as well as risking their lives together, welds people to one another no less than does the transmitting of life together. For instance, the essence of the Dorian state cannot be grasped if one does not see in this fact the strongest source of its power of social bonding.

Of course, wars may be not only defensive, but also aggressive. However, we have already seen that it is not always easy to distinguish between aggression and preventive defense—at least some of those concerned can appeal with subjective sincerity to this difficulty. Precisely because "the others" have their own language and their own mores that differ from one's own, trusting them often amounts to negligence. If they observe among themselves norms that contradict those one acknowledges oneself, they can hardly be trusted in foreign relations. Yet the foreigner is not always only an enemy, he is also a guest—*hospes* derives from *hostis.* Thus most peoples have granted the right to hospitality to a defenseless foreigner without rights who follows certain formalities in approaching them—for instance, after he has touched the hearth he is inviolable. The

---

36. H. Heller (1934), 299.

idea of hospitality is one of the finest testimonies to the universalistic determination of man, his ability, already in archaic eras, to transcend in principle thinking in terms of the opposition between *We* and *They*. This opposition results in sharply deviating norms in internal and foreign relations, but as a being with a unified self-consciousness every human being, even the archaic, has in principle the ability to question this rigid distinction. Through reflection on the bonds of one's own community, the force used against persons belonging to foreign groups can be not only increased but also moderated. The perfect beauty of the *Iliad* consists precisely in the fact that it ends with the bravest warrior being able to see his own father in the father of his opponent and feel toward the latter as he feels toward the former. In this transfer of sympathetic feelings from a community relation to the enemy the principle of humanity is contained.

6.1.2.4. The Legal Order and Political Domination

Even more than reproduction, economic life requires legal regulation and cannot rely on mere mechanisms of self-regulation. The relationship between autonomous individuals mediated by things is full of conflicts to a far higher degree than is the erotic relationship. At least in the former case conflicts are in principle avoidable through the threat of coercion, whereas with regard to the whole sphere of the affects coercive measures are virtually helpless. Contracts are meaningful only if what they mean is clear, and if someone who wants to break them can be made to observe them. Not only rogues will try to disregard contractual obligations; even a decent person who has reason to suspect that the other party to the contract will not observe it, may see in the restoration of symmetry a moral ground for breaking the contract himself. Threats therefore strengthen the normal person's readiness to observe the law—especially since even most good people have moments of moral weakness, and wish, when they are in a normal situation, that they had motives for dutiful behavior that had a stronger psychological effect than does pure moral insight. To that extent, threats stabilize the social order. However, both sides must ultimately consider the use of force legitimate if it is not to lead to resistance on the part of the person affected and those responsible for his protection. What was just said is even more true of the military function. In this case, it is still more important to legally regulate social relationships within the group if the conflict is not to end in a bloodbath. A military association already organized for a collective use of force may have been the first to turn that coercion inward, and thus to mark off a special form within the web of mores—namely, law. The separation of the military function from the civil political function is not self-evident, because, as Aristotle aptly says, it is impossible that those who have the opportunity to use force and to resist will always let themselves be ruled.[37] A devaluation of the

---

37. *Politics* 1329a10 f.: ἦ δὲ τῶν ἀδυνάτων ἐστὶ τοὺς δυναμένους βιάζεσθαι καὶ κωλύειν, τούτους ὑπομένειν ἀρχομένους ἀεί. Aristotle suggests, then, that the military and political functions should be exercised by the same persons, but not at the same time. In the *Republic*, Plato also makes the political rulers a proper subset of the Guardians (412b ff.)

military, an increase in the importance of the economic, which also needs political control, and finally the insight that violence-free conflict resolution helps to maintain the stability of the social order, on one hand, and requires special legal competence, on the other, are the presuppositions for this process of differentiation. The economic is always imperiled when threats of force from outside or inside become the major concern. Presumably military leaders whose authority was based on family relationships or individual abilities initially saw to it, by turning the power given them inward, that the transgression of certain mores such as the violent imposition of private interests in the future, was punished by the collective with coercive force. Since most people in the group understood that the functions of the community would be thereby improved, a recognition of these regulations and of the procedure for implementing them for the future as well probably took place. We can hardly imagine how primitive the first laying down of laws was. When Romulus strikes Remus dead and cries "This is what will happen to anyone else who jumps over my wall,"[38] his statement contains both the crucial elements of law—a certain behavior is *generally* forbidden, and a *negative* sanction is envisaged for any transgression of the prohibition. However, if Romulus was not struck dead at the next favorable opportunity, that would probably have been only because the witnesses to the deed ultimately arrived at a consensus that Romulus had *acted rightly* in doing what he did—whether because jumping over city walls was already forbidden by the mores, or because of the self-evidence of this prohibition, or because of trust in his charisma. But even this charisma can have been felt only on the basis of certain common mores that are for the most part the result of being brought up within the framework of the same culture, and the sole basis on which a legal system can gradually be built.

The legal system is, at least at the outset, a proper subset of the mores of a society. It is a *subset,* because in order to be able to speak of law at all, there must be general agreement that one should behave in accord with the law. However, this agreement does not yet constitute a factual obedience to law. But the obedience must also exist to at least some degree if there is to be law in the full sense of the word. In any case, only if there is law in the full sense of the word can a society allow itself the luxury of regulations that no one obeys, but which jurists nonetheless love to comment on as valid law. The original form of all law is customary law—that is, factual practice that over time has been enriched by a legal consciousness that this practice corresponds to law. Where there is no central authority that lays down the law, customary law remains one of the most important sources of law. This holds for international law as well as for the constitutional law of states without a written constitution.[39] However, the normative character of law always implies something in addition to factual mores; law can sometimes contradict them, but it must always have as its goal to bring them into line with its own demands. Law represents a *proper* subset of mores because the expense connected with the use of coercion (which is

---

38. Livy, 1.7.2.

39. British constitutional law, for instance, consists of customary law, conventions, and written statutes.

pointless in certain spheres anyway) is too great for it to be applied to all violations of mores—and this holds even for the totalitarian state. Since the concept of law implies that of the coercion through which the law maintains its social effectiveness, the development of law goes hand in hand with that of political ruling corporate groups. The application of the law itself was soon legally organized; civil and public law developed in parallel. Indeed, in a certain sense public law is more original. One can imagine a society in which only who is to rule is determined; civil law without procedural law, on the other hand, can exist only so long as there are no breaches of the law and so long as the parties to a conflict voluntarily submit to arbitration. Habermas aptly speaks of a "*co-original constitution of binding law and political power.*" If the peculiar function of the law consists in stabilizing expectations regarding behavior, and that of political power consists in realizing collective goals (especially of a military nature), then both have the following functions for one another: law legitimates political domination and becomes one of its means of organization; political domination guarantees the coercive character of law.[40]

Law can stabilize expectations regarding behavior only if it does not consist wholly of individual norms (e.g., court judgments), but rather includes general norms as well (such as universal laws). The latter's extent varies greatly in different legal orders, but no social order can get along entirely without them, for then the person to whom the norm is addressed would not be able to determine his behavior in advance so as to make it correspond to the intention of the norm-giver. In addition, universal norms also provide an enormous relief for the norm-giver, since he does not constantly have to make new decisions.[41] Further, "law must be *socially effective*—and for that purpose a practicable method of coercion that is itself in accord with the law, if possible, should be available. Moreover, the *certainty of the law* presupposes that the legal order of norms is clear, perspicuous, and comprehensible. The law's public character is crucial for its validity. It must be known, and one must know that it is known to all other people subject to it. The precise determination of the law may be the province of experts; however, its fundamental principles, which emerge from those of one's own culture, must be familiar to every person subject to it. An elementary condition for the certainty of the law is that law be consistent with itself—individual norms, for instance, may not both permit (or even command) and prohibit the same behavior. At the very least, there must be a recognized procedure for resolving contradictions in the law when they arise, which may happen at various levels.[42] Indeed, because of the heterogeneity of the sources of

---

40. Cf. Habermas (1992), 176 ff.: "*[eine] gleichursprüngliche Konstitution von staatlichem Recht und politischer Macht.*" Trans. W. Rehg, 137 ff.

41. Cf. R. Herzog (1971), 303 ff. Herzog's work, from which I have drawn a good deal, is important partly because of its reception of Gehlen's anthropology, which he usefully applies to the theory of the state.

42. Cf. the typology in K. Engisch's masterly essay (1935), 43 ff., which distinguishes innocuous technical (i.e., terminological) contradictions from contradictions regarding norms, goals, values, and principles.

the law and their emergence over long periods of time, it is almost inevitable that such contradictions actually exist, and an important task of jurisprudence, where it exists, is to resolve them. Also desirable, but even more difficult to achieve than the unity of the legal order, is its closed or gap-free character—that is, its ability to resolve, in principle, all conceivable conflicts.[43] Since this goal can never be completely achieved, the judge, as the doctrine of free law has rightly emphasized, often has to do more than merely subsume an individual case under a general law; his activity inevitably has an element of creativity with regard to the law given to it. Yet it is not enough for the law to be consistent with itself; it should also not contradict what is vital for the social order. To what extent the law does justice to this latter demand cannot be determined by juristic means alone—a legal system can be absolutely unified and closed, and socially effective as well, but still not achieve the rational collective goals that it has set itself. On the contrary, it may even be counterproductive. Thus if it is not immediately to collapse, any society has to include a few fundamental norms that are imposed by coercion. But the differences between what goes beyond this minimal domain are very great. Both mores and laws can prescribe norms, not only regarding crucial issues, but also the most insignificant details, whose concrete determination will clearly result in major differences among the various legal systems. It is Montesquieu's achievement to have recognized that between the different areas of law there is not only a juristic but also a sociological connection. The constitutional law of a republic requires—not on logical grounds, but rather in order to preserve the citizens' political power—a business law different from what would be needed in a despotic regime.

However, no legal system can answer all open questions—even if it is ideally applicable to all individual cases, it cannot settle all of them directly. Legal conflicts are therefore inevitable. Like all power struggles, they can be based on concrete interests, on the wish to see one's own view confirmed, or on real, objective differences in interpretation, which arise, for instance, from different convictions about values. If legal conflicts are not to lead to an outbreak of violence, there must at least be a consensus about how to proceed—for example, who should be appealed to as a judge in order to determine the law in a specific case. In addition to specific forms of behavior every social order thus needs various norms of competence and organization that determine who can set norms and thus establish obligations, and what procedure is to be followed in doing so. Higher legal norms must regulate the production of laws.[44] The more variable the legal order is, the more important norms of competence become. The latter must be brought into a hierarchical relationship if the legal system is to remain consistent. Archaic societies still need no regulations concerning laws changing the constitution, because they have no written constitution and because they do not even consider changing the constitution in

---

43. Unity and closure correspond to the consistency and completeness of formal systems.

44. Cf. Hart's famous distinction between "primary" and "secondary rules" (1961; 77 ff.). Schmitt overlooks the existence of norms of competence when, in his polemic against abstract normativism, he claims that the idea of law cannot say who should apply it (1922; 37).

the material sense, but they do need regulations concerning who may make judgments. The judge must have formal privileges. He must stand above the parties to the conflict, he must give each side a legal hearing, and he must not be biased. Moreover, it is assumed that he also knows what is objectively right—whether on the basis of his wisdom or by asking the gods. Even when the decision is left to chance or to physical strength, as in trials by ordeal, it is presupposed that the outcome will manifest the divine will—that is, something objectively right. The latent function of such decision procedures is clear: they prevent the explosion of violence and thus the collapse of the social order. Even if the trial by ordeal consists in a use of force, for instance in a duel, only individual force is involved—an individual force that will kill one or perhaps several people, but at least does not endanger the community as a whole. To be sure, one of the functions of law is to reduce conflicts by determining which of a multiplicity of possible regulations is authoritative in a given case. In chapter 4.1.3 above, reference was made to the emergence of certain behavioral strategies in the animal world that limit conflicts—the similarity between them and certain basic principles of human law is striking however this similarity is to be interpreted (as homologous or analogous). However, at least in early times it is also part of the essence of human law that it is also materially right—in other words, that it determines the *just* solution. Something is not considered right because it may be coerced; it may be coerced because it is right. From the objective law arise the subjective rights of the individual. It is generally acknowledged that he may do certain things. The individual's rights always correspond to duties of others—his right to property, for instance, corresponds to others' duty not to attempt to seize it. However, as a rule the symmetry of rights and duties also holds for the individual. To his right to property corresponds his own duty to respect the property of others. Only universalism was able to grasp this idea in its full generality, but the importance of reciprocity is already great in archaic legal orders.

The validity of the law occupies a peculiar intermediate position between the ideal validity of value and the social validity of a custom. On one hand it goes without saying that the validity of law is a special form of social validity; whether a law is valid or not can be determined only empirically. If there is no longer anyone who considers a regulation as law, we can no longer say that it is legally valid. Thus a law can become obsolete without having been expressly repealed. On the other hand, a law can lose its regulative force with regard to facticity without for that reason ceasing to be a law, but only so long as there are groups that recognize it and seek to bring social reality into line with its demands. Governments in exile that no longer exercise de facto governmental functions may be legally recognized by other states or a group within their own population as the only legitimate government, but only insofar as there is still some prospect of restoring the earlier situation. The German Federal Republic's refusal to recognize East Germany as a separate country could hardly have been maintained into the twenty-second century, but it proved extremely useful politically in accelerating the collapse of the East German dictatorship, which was triggered by other, more real factors. In such a case there are usually two social structures that claim to represent the law. Indeed, because of social change, an opposition between mores and law or between a new level of the development of morality and the law may arise. Then something would be formally recognized as law that was constantly violated or felt to be immoral. However, it is self-evident that such conditions endanger social peace. Since the existence of individual legal norms that are generally violated imperils the prestige of the law as a whole, prudence requires action to prevent such a situation. As a rule, the legal order must in the long run be adapted to new social conditions or moral demands. However, since in archaic times law was not considered a human creation, the path to changing the law through legislative amendment was blocked—statutes are much later than the law. In ancient times, an adaptation of the law to new social demands took place in exceptional situations partly through prophets, and partly through the rediscovery of allegedly old, divinely inspired law; in normal situations, it took place first through legal fictions and second through the concept of equity, which allowed deviations from abstract law (consider especially Anglo-Saxon law).[45] One of the most important turning points in the history of law is the emergence of jurisprudence as a separate discipline that must always be distinguished from the law in force, but which acquires a major influence on the application of the law and on legal policy.

6.1.2.5. Religion

Why is law not considered a human creation? The answer is simple: because if it were it could not be binding on human wills. Pre-modern consciousness can explain the fact that neither the individual nor even the whole society can change the law at will only by maintaining that the law is owed to beings stronger and better than those now living, whether these be gods or founding heroes, or by interpreting law as an image of the cosmic order. To that extent any legal order, at least in pre-modern societies, is grounded in religion, and we will see later that even in modern states a question arises in discussing the possible limits of constitutional amendments that stands in objective continuity with the archaic belief in the eternity and divinity of the law. The legitimation of the order of law and domination may be cosmological, theological, metaphysical, or anthropological, but no social order can do without a justification of political power, because a system that lacks such convictions and consists solely of negative and positive sanctions cannot survive crises. If "political theology" refers to the connections between religion (in the broadest sense, including philosophy as well) and legally structured power, then analyzing it is an indispensable part of any sociology of domination. However, as we have already said, theological categories (in the narrower sense) are only one of various possible ways of justifying a social order—a way that was, however, of special importance in the Western world and influenced the development of juristic concepts, especially those concerned with public law.[46] This should not be surprising, given the essential affinity between the status of theology as a branch of knowledge and

---

45. Cf. H. S. Maine (1861), 22.
46. This is Schmitt's well-known thesis (1922; 1970).

that of jurisprudence. Finally, the fact that violent power struggles can be fought even in the sphere of religion results directly from the impossibility of moving beyond power relationships—and that also holds for religions that demand that the whole sphere of the state be transcended.

Naturally, it does not follow from what has been said that religious convictions always precede the law factually in force—often enough the relationship is the other way around. But far less often than the Enlightenment thought, there is an explicit and conscious instrumentalization of religion to the end of legitimating the social order, and precisely because its legitimating power dissipates when it is perceived that religion in actuality arises out of what it is supposed to justify. To that extent, in most societies the subsystems of the political and the religious are distinguished, even if a sharp separation or even an opposition of the two is rare, and was first systematically carried out by modernity. To be sure, this distinction almost inevitably leads to tensions, but the apparently ideal way of surmounting them—a direct identification of the political with the religious—is a fallacy. If the political is absorbed by religion as it is when priests rule as individuals or through their office, for the most part the sense of objective political constraints is lost. It is no accident that conquerors often support theocracies in other countries, because such rulers present little resistance to the extension of the conquering nation's power.[47] (However, it is also conceivable that religion might fanaticize politics, but that can become dangerous only if the political does not lose its autonomy.) On the other hand, if religion is made subordinate to politics, as it was in Caesaropapism, as a rule the legitimating effect of religion (in the broader sense) sooner or later evaporates—as became clear in Soviet Caesaropapism, for instance. Paradoxically, it can be said that the less religion thinks about its legitimating effect, and the more it follows its own objective logic (at least when its objective logic has implications for the legitimation of the social order), the stronger that legitimating effect is.

Wherein does the objective logic of religion consist? Any examination of religion has to distinguish between two questions: on one hand, a question from the point of view of religious studies and phenomenology of religion concerning the organizing principles of the manifold forms taken by religious phenomena, and on the other, a question from the point of view of the philosophy of religion concerning religion's theoretical and practical claims to validity. After the Enlightenment brought the second question into the foreground and, so far as it was well disposed toward religion, discussed the latter essentially as an early form of the moral, it was the special contribution of Rudolf Otto's masterful book *Das Heilige* (*The Idea of the Holy*) to have pointed out with the utmost vigor that religion cannot be reduced to morals. Its point of departure is the experience of the numinous. From a descriptive point of view, there is nothing objectionable about this proposition. However, Otto also recognizes that religious history is determined by a progressive rationalization and ethicization of the numinous, on the basis of which the

---

47. Cf. Weber (1980), 689f.

numinous becomes the sacred, which is to that extent a category composed of religious and moral determinations.[48] But in terms of the theory of validity, this does not yet mean that the fundamental concept of a rational philosophy of religion could not free itself completely from the numinous, that the numinous must have its place among legitimate concepts. It could be that the experience of the numinous was the only way in which archaic man could approach the concept of the moral and thus domesticate himself, so to speak. It is true that for archaic men the gods were primarily powerful rather than good, but the sociology of religion could in principle explain this by noting that it made consent to the factual social world easier. By deriving the gods partly from factual power relationships, man legitimated the latter and thus contributed to social peace. Nonetheless, in the interest of a possible justification of the elements of almost all religions that go beyond the moral, we should consider that even a rational philosophy is confronted by the question of how the being of factual reality is to be explained in its permeability with regard to the demands of the moral law. Thus the fact that religion deifies natural and social being can also be interpreted as an early form of this completely rational questioning that does not capitulate to facticity.

In any case, in the history of religions we must distinguish between gods that represent primarily idealizations of conspicuous, intensive, or enduring acting forces, and those that make contrafactual demands. The latter come later, and they reach their high point in the representation of the one god over all peoples. Only for the former is the thesis developed by Durkheim defensible, namely, that in religion a society transfigures itself. The second group of gods transcends the real social order in a fundamental sense, even though peculiarities of the society concerned inevitably make their way into the image of these gods as well. An intellectual development can likewise be observed in the history of the first group of gods—it is a long way from Usener's momentary gods to the later anthropomorphic gods equipped with individual personalities. Along the way, man learned to understand himself, and to attribute a special worth to himself. If, for instance, the gods are no longer in the shape of animals but of humans, then man will be ranked above animals. Insofar as in dealing with the gods certain principles must be respected that also play a role in behavior among human beings, worshipping them can contribute to the moral development of mores. Relieved of the constraints of social existence, man can try out in his relationship to the gods virtues such as gratitude. However, where there is a mechanical procedure for realizing one's own wishes, where one no longer has to reckon with the possibility that the divinity might make a free decision (that is, in the case of sorcery and magic, which are to be sharply distinguished from religion[49]), we are dealing with early (rudimentarily instrumental) forms of technology, and not morals. The second group of gods belongs especially to the pre-history of morals. The relationship to the first group of

---

48. (1971), 134 ff.
49. This also holds in cases where they themselves serve religious ends, as in theurgy.

gods is managed by a special *priestly rank* that is part of the social order and, as a rule, has an interest in preserving it. This priestly rank can form a ruling corporate group that is called "hierocratic" if it uses psychic but not physical coercion in order to impose its own order; if it claims a monopoly on legitimate hierocratic coercion, we speak of a "church."[50] In contrast, the new gods that challenge the factual order are manifested in the testimony of *prophets*, who for the most part do not belong to the priesthood, and who have religious needs but no religious office. Inner moral constraints drive them to announce new doctrines that usually encounter the fiercest resistance on the part of the priestly rank. Often they are defeated, and their ideas disappear; sometimes they are killed, but their teaching is adopted after their death; sometimes they succeed in founding a new, victorious religion that is institutionalized and then deals with deviationists just as the earlier religion dealt with the founder of this one. However, for even the most radical innovators, a partial connection with the factually existing reality and a legitimation of at least part of the existing mores are indispensable if they are to be successful. Thus the gods that make new demands may appear under the names of the old, traditional gods. But this does not alter the fact that the Yahweh of the Yahwist is essentially different from the Yahweh of the prophets, even if the prophets were subjectively convinced sincerely of the continuity of their god. Often innovators describe their own innovations as a reformation, as a return to an earlier condition, or like Aeschylus in the *Prometheus*, resort to the idea that the divinity itself has developed— both ways of avoiding a radical break. The latter mode of thought also plays a role when systems of legitimation based on argument have taken over the function of earlier religions. Hegel's philosophy of history and philosophy of religion constitute the most important attempt to discern in the development of systems of legitimation an evolution of the absolute itself.

Within religions a distinction is drawn between national religions (that is, those peculiar to a specific people) and universal religions. In the former, people and religion coincide—the idea of converting members of other peoples to one's own religion seems absurd. In contrast, universal religions strive in principle to win all people over to their own standpoint; they transcend the political order within which they develop, and feel responsible for all of humanity, not solely for the people of the founder of the religion. As a rule, they engage in missionary work, sometimes, but by no means always, in an aggressive way. Islam increased the readiness to fight holy wars, whereas Lamaist Buddhism transformed the Mongols from a scourge of humanity into a peaceful people. Even if universal religions, according to their vocation, claim to embrace more people than do national religions, they are not necessarily successful. Jainism is a small universal religion, whereas Hinduism is ultimately only a national religion, although, because of population growth in India, a very large one.

---

50. I follow Weber's definitions (1980; 29).

As I said in chapter 4.3.2, I am using the concept "religion" in such a broad sense that it includes non-theistic ideas of legitimation in traditional societies such as Confucianism, as well as modern—or post-modern—systems of legitimation that would never describe themselves as "religious." As a rule, I avoid the word "ideology," not only because its use usually implies a distancing from the systems of legitimation so designated, and thus is certainly not value-neutral, but also and especially because "ideological" (in the narrower sense) is supposed to designate systems of legitimation that legitimate the status quo, whereas systems of legitimation that demand instead a social order that deviates from the existing one are called "utopian." However, we have already seen that there can be no purely ideological or purely utopian systems of legitimation. If it is to be comprehensible, every system of legitimation must coincide in part with the social order from which it stems, and deviate from it in part if it is to have legitimating force. In addition, through historical changes a utopia can become an ideology—that is what happened to Marxism-Leninism in Russia in 1917. Moreover, not only traditional religions but also secular utopias usually immunize themselves against criticism. Although this contradicts the emotional commitment to freedom from prejudice in modern, post-Enlightenment ideologies and utopias, an exceptional talent for observation is not required to see that criticism of certain basic assumptions of enlightened societies is not always welcome in the latter—and all the more unwelcome the more justified it is. Granted, force is not used to protect the civil religion, but isolating unpopular views and refusing positive sanctions are favorite procedures. There is a deeper social necessity that certain suppositions be put beyond criticism—if there is no ultimate foundation, then one can argue only on the basis of certain unchallenged principles whose questioning would endanger the performance of the system of legitimation. However, the principles of a system of legitimation are questioned not only by the mad, but also by geniuses, among others; and if success is not to be the sole criterion that allows us to distinguish between the two, then there must be a standard that transcends the various systems of legitimation. Ever since the emergence of Greek philosophy, people have been searching for such a general standard, and even if this search according to an objectivizing contemplation is only another system of legitimation among others, it has perhaps a special status—at least a higher status than the post-moderns' system of legitimation, which puts, without further examination, all systems of legitimation on the same level, but thereby surreptitiously excepts itself.

6.1.3. Elements of the State

The preceding remarks have clarified the genesis and function of the state. Certainly, there are human societies in which the power of mores is so great that violations of them seldom occur, and the punishment of those violations can be left to those immediately affected; however, for every society it remains true that "independence of external control and cooperation in internal affairs are the essential characteristics of the community."[51] The development of the political is characterized by the following traits: the community tends to become larger; through immigration or enslavement the bonds of kinship are weakened; at the same time, the specific social-psychological feeling that distinguishes political from family relationships increases. The functions of the highest corporate group are thereby inevitably made more complex. The clash of differing mores, along with differentiation in ranks, for instance, make a more frequent and more extensive jurisdiction necessary;[52] the integration of the various groups of the society becomes a central task. The increase of public activities leads to funding them economically, that is, to taxing the population (for instance, in the form of arbitrary demands for tribute). The administrative staff of the leader of the political ruling corporate group becomes larger and is differentiated in accord with differing functions, for instance, the civilian and the military. Political offices are no longer inherited, that is, awarded on the basis of kinship; personal achievements are taken into account. This goes hand in hand with an increase in the political leader's power, which may have been very slight in simple societies; he is granted the right to punish and even to impose capital punishment. However, as a rule this process is accompanied by efforts somehow to control the newly established power. At the same time, this power is more and more desired. In order to limit power struggles whose goal is to acquire this power in illegal ways, further institutions become necessary.

On one hand, the structure that slowly emerges from all this—the state, with whose later forms the following remarks are primarily concerned—leads to an enormous increase in human domination over humans. Only in the state can power be simultaneously so extensive, comprehensive, and intensive. Precisely through legalization, the ruler's will is extended beyond the moment—according to its claims, extended to all eternity, or at least long after his death. The human need to transcend one's own mortality is served not only by the founding of a family or the creation of an enduring work—already in antiquity, the foundation of a state or of a constitution was considered one of the most perfect ways of eternalizing oneself. Whoever lays down the laws determines the rules that regulate all legal power struggles; this means the achievement of a second-level power (even if illegal power struggles may constantly break out). On the other hand, the legalization of power in the state also implies its limitation. Even where the ruler is not formally bound by his own laws, if he fails to respect them he undermines his own authority, and thereby also the laws' claim to be obeyed. To that extent, the expression "the rule of law"[53] is certainly not only ideological, as it is constantly said to be. It

---

51. I. Schapera (1967), 218. I am indebted in the following remarks to Schapera's contrast between the hunting and gathering culture of the Bushmen and the farming and shepherding culture of the Bantus.

52. Cf. J.-W. Lapierre (1968; 525), who traces a "politification" of social groups to processes of differentiation and an increase in heterogeneity.

53. The idea is already defended by Aristotle, *Politics* 1287a1 ff.

is trivially correct that it is always human beings who lay down and apply the law; a rule of law that is not mediated through human beings is a pipe-dream that may be moving, but remains childlike. However, what is crucial is whether the power that humans exercise over humans is structured in accord with law or not. If it is, it may (but by no means must) lead to a significant improvement of the *conditio humana*. Love for positive law as such is certainly a rare motive (primarily to be found among positivist jurists), and hardly a rational one that could support a state. Far more important are the insight that law is the foundation of a social order with which one identifies and the conviction that it is just.[54] In any case, the state is potentially both the horrible Minotaur that, in the form of totalitarianism, tries to abolish to a large extent a society's autonomy and commits in the concentration and death camps of the twentieth century the greatest crimes in history, and the power that frees people from the constant threat of force they represent for each other and that limits human domination to the minimum required to guarantee a just and good life.

6.1.3.1. State Population (*Staatsvolk*)

Since Jellinek, the state has been seen as consisting of three elements: a state territory (*Staatsgebiet*), a state population or citzenry (*Staatsvolk*), and state power (*Staatsgewalt*).[55] This classification requires two qualifications.[56] First, it is clear that the three elements are not independent of one another, but are essentially interconnected. A state citizenry is not a mere collection of human beings, but rather a group subject to state power; a state's territory is conceptually related to its territorial supremacy. Second, the first element is not necessary; political corporate groups and even states without a stable state territory are possible, and there have in fact been political groups, at least, without such a territory. If one considers a stable state territory to be one of the necessary elements of the state, one is thinking of the modern state, or else one works within a conceptual framework of international law that thematizes only states that exist and are recognized as such today. Both the qualifications just mentioned become equally clear if one thinks of Cicero's famous definition, according to which the state is a matter of the people (*res populi*), but the people (*populus*) is defined as body bound together by a legal consensus and a common interest.[57] Here there is no mention of a state territory;[58] the citizenry is understood politically from the outset.

---

54. As is well known, Schmitt (1934) considered abstract normativism, decisionism, and thinking in terms of a concrete social order to be the three basic types of juristic thought. Characteristically, he does not mention thinking inspired by natural law.

55. (1922), 394 ff.

56. Cf. M. Kriele (1975), 85, on which I have drawn heavily.

57. "Res publica res populi, populus autem non omnis hominum coetus quoquo modo congregatus, sed coetus multitudinis iuris consensu et utilitatis communione sociatus" (*De re publica* I 25).

58. Nor is there any mention of state territory in Kant's and Hegel's definitions of the state (*Metaphysik der Sitten* I § 45 [1976 f.; 8:431]; *Grundlinien* § 257 [1969 ff.; 7:398]). An early exception is

The first element that necessarily belongs to a state is a certain number of human beings. This number can vary greatly, as both history and the present show—Liechtenstein and China are both states with a citizenry. However, it may not fall short of a certain magnitude. Thus it is obvious that the solitary king in Saint-Exupéry's *Le petit prince* is a witty *contradictio in adjecto,* because "king" is a multi-place predicate. But even two human beings can hardly constitute a minimal citizenry, because dual relationships are distinguished qualitatively and not only quantitatively from plural relationships. In particular, they lack the objectification produced by a third party, who alone can play the role of judge. In addition, a state implies a long-term future as well—it must be able to continue from generation to generation and transcend individual mortality. It is true that there have been states that have existed less than a generation, and that most states have ceased to exist, whether because they were vanquished in war, collapsed in civil wars and secessions, came to an end through the rules of hereditary succession, or voluntarily merged with a neighbor; but one can certainly assert that in general states exist longer than do business enterprises, even if they have very seldom reached the record age of the longest-lived churches. In any case, states generally seek to survive for the longest possible time.

There is in principle no more a top limit for the size of a citizenry than for the duration of a state. Certainly we speak of a citizenry only if it is actually dominated by a common state power—and at a certain level of the development of the technologies of communication and traffic, populations of a certain size can no longer be dominated. Many a state is not strengthened but weakened by expansion, or even dissolved or at least transformed in its legal structure. Hence the profundity of Aristotle's insight, which draws on biological morphology, that certain structures cannot be arbitrarily expanded quantitatively without transforming or even destroying their essence.[59] But what is decisive is that technological-administrative progress in structures can also extend, together with the structures, the possible limits of a state as well. Already in Aristotle's time, which had mastered the transition from orality to scripturality, it was naive to make the loudness of the human voice the criterion for the upper limit of a population by arguing that heralds had to be able to be heard by everyone. Thus there were intercontinental empires even before the technological revolution of modernity. (There may be natural law-based, fundamentally untransgressable limits only to intergalactic empires—because of the limit value represented by the speed of light, and because of the length of human

---

the Stoic definition of the state in Arnim, *Stoicorum veterum fragmenta,* 3:329, which introduces the spatial function.

59. *Politics* 1326a30 ff. Cf. also Montesquieu, *Esprit des lois* 8.20, as well as Hegel (1969 ff.), 5:441: "So erhalten auch Staaten durch ihren Größenunterschied, wenn das Übrige als gleich angenommen wird, einen verschiedenen qualitativen Charakter. Gesetze und Verfassung werden zu etwas anderem, wenn der Umfang des Staats und die Anzahl der Bürger sich erweitern." ("Thus states acquire, through their difference in size, all other things assumed to be equal, a different qualitative character. Laws and constitutions become something different when the area of the state and the number of its citizens grow.")

life, which consists of only a few decades, in such empires communication would be too slow.) Neither is it conceptually impossible that a state might include the whole population of the earth. It is trivially correct that such a state could no longer implement a foreign policy, but a capacity for foreign policy is not a necessary conceptual characteristic of the state.[60] Otherwise, one would have to deny the status of statehood to island or mountain states that were difficult of access and that could sometimes do without any foreign policy for long periods of time. Furthermore, we will see that the arguments for the justification of the state point in the direction of a universal state. To be sure, anxiety with regard to "others" is one of the causes of the socially binding forces without which no state can exist, but that does not prove that a universal state could emerge on earth only out of fear of extra-terrestrial aggressors, even if that kind of fear would admittedly make its establishment easier (cf. chapter 4.3.3).

The concept of a citizenry does not presuppose quantitative aspects alone. To begin with a relatively simple negative condition, a group that consisted of an extremely potent patriarch, his harem, and a large number of offspring would still not represent a state in the full sense of the term, even if it were larger than the population of a diminutive state. Since Aristotle, it has been clear that the state must not be conceived of as a large family. The relationships between the components of the two structures are qualitatively different. In a state, the feeling of collective identity always also results from surmounting a sense of alterity; wherever such a surmounting is not necessary, one ought not to speak of statehood. However, we must maintain, in opposition to Jellinek,[61] that a group composed of a slaveholder and slaves could constitute a state at least so long as the slaves acknowledged the slaveholder's power, that is, so long as a relationship of domination exists, and the slaveholder uses or at least threatens to use force. In a descriptive context it cannot be a matter of calling illegitimate forms of domination "unpolitical"; thus it must be possible to call "states" structures whose citizens have hardly any subjective public rights, or any subjective rights at all. Nonetheless, *citizens,* who as a whole constitute the citizenry,[62] always have certain specific rights and duties—for instance, a right to residence and to a qualified protection—that are not granted to everyone subject to state power. The latter include transients as well as aliens with a residence in the state territory, and are considered part of the *population,* but not part of the citizenry. Slaves are also part of the population, even if they are not recognized as persons. Naturally, a state can determine citizenship only with regard to its own citizens; a state that allowed others to decide this central question would quickly lose its sovereignty.

---

60. Only in the context of international law might the "capacity to enter into relations with other states" be named as a fourth element of statehood—as it is, for instance, in the Pan-American Treaty of 26 December 1933 on the Rights and Duties of States, Art. I; cf. A. Verdross and B. Simma (1984), 224.

61. (1922), 407 f., 424.

62. This concept of the citzenry must be distinguished from that according to which the *Staatsvolk* is the nation that constitutes the majority in a state or from which enfranchised citizens are recruited.

However, contemporary international law does not recognize every acquisition of state-hood; there must be a genuine point of connection between the new citizen and his state, for example, descent from or marriage to a citizen, or his birth or long-standing residence in the country concerned.[63] Plural citizenship can lead to a series of collisions (particularly with regard to compulsory military service) and is therefore limited as much as possible, for instance through laws stipulating that one loses his citizenship if he acquires citizenship in another state. Since statelessness also has negative consequences—especially a lack of protection for the person concerned—it is regarded as desirable that everyone have one and only one citizenship.

From the citizens we must distinguish the *enfranchised citizenry* of the state, who even in a democracy are a proper subset of the citizenry, and consist of those who have a right to participate in politics.[64] Minors in every state belong to the complement (*Differenz-menge*) of citizens and enfranchised citizens; however, this complement may be considerably larger, and in the limit case it may include all citizens except for the head of state. Even where citizens and enfranchised citizens nearly coincide in terms of persons, two aspects are still involved whose difference follows directly from the concept of domination: the enfranchised citizens are the *subject*, and the citizens are the—privileged—*object* of state power. On the other hand, the notion that enfranchised citizens have only (subjective-public) *rights*, whereas the citizenry has only *duties*, is misleading. First, for the most part the citizenry also has certain rights (but not subjective-public ones), and second, there are sometimes also duties that only and precisely enfranchised citizens have—consider the duty to vote or the duty to serve on juries. In the second case we are concerned with the duty to collaborate as a subject in the exercise of state power. These latter duties provide the basis for the *status passivus*, whereas the subjective-public rights provide the basis for the *status activus*. The *status negativus*, on the other hand, concerns the claim that the state refrain from certain actions, whereas the *status positivus* concerns the claim to positive state performances in the individual's interest. The concept of human rights presupposes that there are certain basic rights that not only the citizens of one's own state but all humans have, and these are mainly, though not necessarily, concerned with the claim that the state refrain from certain actions.

Not all combinations of people are capable of constituting a citizenry (*Staatsvolk*). Given that the community of laws is part of the concept of the state, a minimum of common customs, for instance, is indispensable for the existence of a state. However, this does not mean that a citizenry must form a *people* (*Volk*)—otherwise the concept of the "multi-ethnic state" (*Vielvölkerstaat*) would be a contradiction in terms, and moreover a people could not live in different states. Everyone knows how hard it is to define a people. As criteria one might mention here biological aspects such as common ancestry—

---

63. Cf. A. Verdross and B. Simma (1984), 789 f., on the International Court of Justice's decision of 6 April 1955 in the Nottebohm case.

64. Limited voting rights—the right to vote on the municipal level, for instance—might conceivably be granted to those who are not citizens.

which by its nature vanishes as history moves on—and still more important, a common cultural heritage—for instance, a common language or religion, common values, a peculiar *Volksgeist,* or common historical experiences, for instance in coping with fateful threats—and finally the subjective element that the group in question regards itself as a people, that it has a *We*-feeling[65] and believes it has a common future.[66] But almost never do all elements occur at the same time, and basically none of them is truly necessary—not even the last one. It may happen that an ethnologist coming from the outside observes that two groups of people who live far away from another and know nothing at all about one another, nonetheless form a single people, insofar as they are related to each other and have a very similar culture. In general, the peculiar features of a people are sometimes better preserved when they are practiced unreflectively, and excessive emphasis on those features is often a sign of the decline of such traditions, indeed, even contributes to their decline, because reflection may diminish their vitality, and explicit turning toward the past may result in a loss of the ability to adapt. In any case, it is clear that the concept of a people, in contrast to that of a citizenry, is pre-political. Between these two concepts mediates that of the *nation*—the nation is a people (and sometimes also a citizenry) that has a common matter of political concern and therefore generally strives to become or to remain a citizenry.[67] One indispensable *definiens* of this concept is the group's consciousness of its own collective identity—a group that does not consider itself a nation can never be a nation. Naturally, not every people is a nation. On the contrary, before the nineteenth century almost no people constituted a nation. Nationalism was the first to formulate, in connection with the transformation of traditional societies into modern industrial states, the normative thesis that a people ought to be the basis for citizenry; its triumph certainly did not everywhere make peoples into citizenries, but often enough it made them into nations. Because of the normative connotations of the concept "people," since then groups of people who have all the descriptive pre-political characteristics that otherwise define a people, but whose political unification is not desired, have often no longer been designated as "peoples," just as conversely a citizenry is simply called a "people" even if it consists of ethnically different groups. Nevertheless, we should note that although today Germans and Austrians, on the basis of their common language, among other things, could

---

65. The circular nature of this element has often been emphasized; cf. R. Herzog (1971), 42 f.

66. Cf. Ortega y Gasset (1930), 188: "Con los pueblos de Centro y Sudamérica tiene España un pasado común, raza común, lengua común, y, sin embargo, no forma con ellos una nación. ¿Por qué? Falta sólo una cosa, que, por lo visto, es la esencial: el futuro común." (Spain shares a common past with the countries of Central and South America, a common racial background, a common language, and yet, it does not constitute a nation with them. Why not? There is one element lacking, the essential one: a common future." Trans. A. Kerrigan, 160.)

67. Cf. H. Heller (1934), 261: "Zu einer Nation wird das Kulturvolk, das an sich politisch amorph ist, dadurch, daß es sein Zusammengehörigkeitsbewußtsein zu einem politischen Willenszusammenhang entwickelt." ("A cultural group which is in itself politically amorphous becomes a nation by developing its consciousness of belonging together into a common political will.")

probably be correctly regarded as a single people, they constitute neither a citizenry nor a nation. (In such a situation, efforts to distinguish themselves from one another in order to defend their own identity are particularly likely.) They were *one* citizenry only from 1938 to 1945, and *one* nation from the rise of pan-German ideas in the nineteenth century to their final collapse in 1945. Conversely, there was both a Soviet citizenry and a Soviet nation, but never a Soviet people.

Later we will discuss in greater detail the normative problem connected with ideas of nationalism. Here we are concerned only with descriptive propositions. Thus it must be repeated that no state can survive unless its citizenry has certain things in common—no matter how much it may itself create commonalties, unless it counts completely on force as a means of power, it can never create them *ex nihilo*, but only on the basis of already existing common traits. Any domination, and a fortiori any state domination, requires communication, for instance. This in no way means that a citizenry must have a national native language—many languages can be spoken in a state. If there is a lingua franca, being bilingual is completely sufficient to make it possible for everyone to communicate directly with everyone else. Since most people can become bilingual if they have been raised that way from childhood, this direct communication is easy to attain. In addition, translators always make it possible to communicate with those who have mastered only one language. Moreover, precisely in the case of language we see how what seems to be a condition for the state is in reality often its result. The political unification of France did not spring from the linguistic homogeneity of the country; to a large extent, political unification produced linguistic homogeneity. Furthermore, differences in the real language and in linguistic analysis often first arise on political grounds. After Moldova was split off from Romania, the Moldavian language was, for obvious reasons, elevated by Soviet Romance scholars into a distinct language, and this was made easier by the shift from the Roman to the Cyrillic alphabet. Something similar occurred with the disintegration of Yugoslavia, when even translators between Serbian and Croatian suddenly appeared. (Compared with that, the renaming of Serbo-Croatian in Zagreb as "Croatian-Serbian" was entirely comprehensible.) In exactly the same way, political, not linguistic, motives are generally involved when in India, for instance, the question of whether Hindi and Urdu are a single language or two different ones is debated. Indeed, even in one and the same language, such as Hindi, with its rich vocabulary that draws on Sanskrit and Persian, a political choice may underlie the decision to favor one half of the lexicon—a Hindu fundamentalist will avoid whenever possible words derived from Persian. In short, even language (not to mention the other characteristics of a people) can become a function of the political, even if the latter conversely seeks to present itself as the expression of a linguistic unit.

Since the goal of political discourse is action, common mores that underlie law are even more important than language.[68] It is not necessary that the mores of all population

---

68. Cf. already Machiavelli, *Principe* 3.3 (1986; 90).

groups be determined by the same principles as the law in force; within the limits of the legally permissible a great variety of mores are conceivable. But the existing mores must include respect for the law in force, even if only just because it is law, and even if it deviates in its content from one's own mores. Therefore mores may not stand in direct opposition to the law; otherwise conflicts endangering the unity of the citizenry will inevitably result. In multi-ethnic states, different laws may conceivably be valid for different parts of the population, as in many German kingdoms after the migration of peoples—under Theodoric, Ostrogoths were subject to German law, and Romans were subject to Roman law. Today in India, for instance, the inheritance laws are still different for Hindus and Moslems. But first of all such regulations almost always lead to social and legal frictions when it does not prove possible to separate the population groups from each other (thus in India the conversion of one of the marriage partners raises serious problems with regard to inheritance law).[69] Second, such states, too, must adopt a common law, insofar as there must at least be a consensus regarding who is subject to what law. Even so peculiar a legal system as that of the Ptolemies—whose legal pluralism was not governed by the principle of personality, since for instance private individuals could choose at will between Egyptian and Greek contract forms—had to have at least a unified rule regarding which court was to apply which law, and who had the right to decide this question. Certainly, it is desirable that the citizenry have a feeling of belonging together that goes beyond a common legal consciousness and mutual trust, and its absence will make itself painfully evident in crisis situations. But this is not absolutely indispensable, as is shown by the willingness, in dynastic times, of a region's population to align itself with another state under certain circumstances. If it felt itself equally well protected within the framework of the new state, it was just as loyal to it as to the earlier one.

However, it goes without saying that a consciousness of belonging to a certain state is indispensable. This is the first of four levels of political awareness, and the one that small children already attain. The second level is marked by the ability to conceptualize, the third by subjective involvement, and the fourth by active participation.[70] Even the second level is reached by most, but not all, adults; the third is primarily accessible to enfranchised citizens; the fourth is accessible to only a minority of enfranchised citizens. The identification with one's own citizenry, genuine patriotism, should be distinguished from identification with the current government and even from identification with the constitution in force. One can hate the current government, and even reject the constitution, but still not want to live among another people. This holds even when if one does not have the rights of an enfranchised citizen—patriotism is not found solely among enfranchised citizens. Even after the Nazi *Reichsbürgergesetz* (the law concerning

---

69. The Ostrogoths in Italy and the Visigoths in Spain made it hard for Romans to convert to their own Arianism, in order to keep the populations distinct: "Germanic Arianism was neither fortuitous nor aggressive: it was a badge of apartness, within a certain accepted unity" (P. Anderson [1978)], 118).

70. I follow R. D. Hess and J. V. Torney (1968), 19.

citizenship), the patriotism of many German Jews continued unabated. Constitutional patriotism is to that extent—in a *descriptive* context—only a special form, not the normal form of patriotism. Sometimes what seems to be patriotism can ultimately be only affection for a certain area, a certain landscape, quite independently of the people that live there. There are people who would seek to remain in an area even if, except for them, the whole population were to change. In 149 BC, the preservation of the citizenry and state power was not enough for the Carthaginians, who risked the loss of both solely in order not to give up their city, which the Romans had ordered destroyed. (However, they had good reasons to suppose that the destruction of the city would be followed by the destruction of their state power and an immediate economic decline.) Corresponding to the three elements of the state, one could speak of patriotism related to the citizenry, to state power, and to the state territory—three forms that are, of course, usually mixed with one another.

An enfranchised citizenry must have significantly more things in common than a citizenry. The enfranchised citizenry not only obeys but also directs the state's destiny, and common action and direction presuppose far more than common omission from breaking, and common execution of, the law—the required homogeneity is greater, because conscious decisions have to be added to mores. Therefore it is no accident that practically all multi-ethnic states known up to now were either non-democratic or else granted basic democratic rights only to a small minority of the citizens. Tendencies toward democratization often lead to the collapse of multi-ethnic states or to overruling majority votes; conversely, the construction of multi-ethnic states endangers democracy. Consider, on one hand, the breakdown of the Ottoman Empire, Austria-Hungary, and not long ago, the Soviet Union; and on the other hand, for instance, the collapse of the republican form of government after Rome's successful expansion. Empirical evidence only confirms the conceptually plausible connection. Because of the widespread positive evaluation of both multicultural societies and democracy, this conclusion may be painful. But first of all, that does not make it false, and second, one cannot maintain that a multicultural society is incompatible with democracy, but they are considerably harder to unite than monarchy and a multicultural society, for instance.[71]

6.1.3.2. State Territory

We have already seen that only in the modern age is the state necessarily a territorial entity.[72] Previously, there were also states of nomadic tribes; indeed, Grotius still ac-

---

71. Cf. R. Zippelius (1991), 78.

72. Cf. Rousseau's subtle observation: "avantage qui ne paroît pas avoir été bien senti des anciens monarques, qui, ne s'appelant que rois des Perses, des Scythes, des Macédoniens, sembloient se regarder comme les chefs des hommes plutôt que comme les maîtres du pays. Ceux d'aujourd'hui s'appellent plus habilement rois de France, d'Espagne, d'Angleterre, etc.; en tenant ainsi le terrain, ils sont bien sûrs d'en tenir les habitants" (*Contrat social* I 9 [1975; 248 f.]); ("an advantage that does not

knowledges the existence of nomadic states,[73] whereas today we can speak only of "nomadic" governments, that is, of internationally recognized governments in exile. In any case, the origin of the state is to be found in a corporate group consisting of persons, but it is not hard to see that territoriality is almost necessarily characteristic of a developed state. All human interactions require legal regulation, and interactions are almost inevitable where people share the same living space (*Lebensraum*). Those who are overrun by a nomadic people also come into contact with its members and are subject to their coercion, even if they are not part of the citizenry—like transient foreigners in a modern territorial state. In the latter case it is the transients, and in the former the citizenry, that is in movement. To that extent, of course, the nomadic state also occupies a space (even if it is a changing one), for the simple reason that human beings are creatures with bodies that take up space.[74] But human beings need not only some kind of physical space; as organisms, they live in a specific *living space* that is better able to satisfy their needs than other spaces and to which they may develop deep emotional bonds. Finally, as cultural beings, when they have reached a certain level of cultural development they want to be sedentary: thereby some social relationships are stabilized, marriage and private property are strengthened, and land ownership is first made possible. From the sedentariness of the citizenry follows the sedentariness of the state itself, that is, the necessity of a state territory. But most citizenries not only want to live in a sedentary manner, today they can hardly live any other way. Original occupation has always been rare in modern history; in most cases people have acted as if less densely settled territories with a population that had only more primitive forms of organization were unpopulated. But today, after the dividing up and settling of the whole earth, there are scarcely any stateless territories left, and so it is no longer possible for a citizenry to move into an unpopulated territory not subject to any state power—if we exclude the colonization of outer space. Thus today it is difficult to imagine a peaceful change of state territory. It is compatible with this that the destruction of the living space through environmental damage may set in motion migrations of people of unimaginable magnitude, and could thus again create political units that consist of a citizenry and state power, but no longer of a stable state territory. It may be that international law would not recognize them as states; their power would be felt, however, and it would be a conceptual confusion to exclude them from research in political science on the ground that they were not recognized states. A collective force would surely emanate

---

seem to have been much appreciated by ancient monarchs, who, calling themselves only the kings of the Persians, of the Scythians, or the Macedonians, seemed to regard themselves as the leaders of men rather than as the masters of the country. Today's monarchs more cleverly call themselves the kings of France, of Spain, of England, etc.; by thus holding the territory, they are very sure to hold the inhabitants as well").

73. *De jure belli ac pacis* II 9, § 7 (quoted in A. Verdross and B. Simma [1984], 230).

74. Cf. H. Heller (1934), 405, who speaks of the "territorial function even in the case of nomadic states."

from them which, even if it were illegal in terms of international law, would be felt to be legitimate—and would perhaps be legitimate, if there is a right to self-preservation. Moreover, it is an indication of the great importance of state territory for the modern state that many modern states allow the emigration of even a large part of the population, but not the secession of a part of the state territory.

No doubt the development of states with a large and contiguous territory increased the efficiency of state power, which was then able to extend itself unimpeded over a unified area. State power was thereby both strengthened within and better protected against attacks from without. Since what counted was no longer personal relationships but rather space-mediated relationships, law became more objective and more abstract. A foreigner living in the territory did not become a citizen, but he gradually ceased to be a person without rights and became an equal with regard to civil law. Furthermore, the principle of territoriality can lead to a lessening of conflicts, at least if the boundaries between states are clearly defined.[75] However, the theory of so-called natural borders has led to several wars. Like the view that a state must seek to include the whole nation within its citizenry, the idea that there is a natural state territory endangers peace, particularly since the criteria for determining what constitutes a natural state territory are even less clear than those for defining a people. In connection with this point, as well, it should also be noted that it is often the state itself that first succeeds in deriving a political meaning from natural facts, or in devaluing them, through the development of technology, which is a result, among other things, of state policies.[76] Thus being an island offers special protection against attacks only if the state concerned has a strong naval fleet. Nonetheless, it must be conceded that the geographical framework is not without great significance for the life of a state. Climatic factors influence the character of a people—the fact that Nordic peoples had to prepare for winter and could not, like the Greeks and Romans, gather in public places year round, favored the development of certain economic virtues as well as a more individualistic spirit. Furthermore, even if great technological advances are made, certain soils cannot produce more than a certain quantity of food, and this sets limits to population growth. Moreover, however much technology decreases certain kinds of dependency on nature, it also creates others and makes the goal of economic autarky seem illusory for most states— consider the increasing importance of certain minerals and energy sources, especially for military reasons. In addition, it does not require much imagination to see that in the future ecological catastrophes will occur particularly in countries with certain natural environments—the rise of the level of the oceans will affect coastal states in a very different way from states located in the mountains. Finally, we must mention the importance of the form of borders in conflicts between states. All other things being equal, borders should ideally be as short as possible in relation to the state's surface area, i.e.,

---

75. However, the precise determination of all boundaries was first attained later on—and in the high mountain areas of Bavaria, not until the twentieth century.

76. On the following, cf. H. Heller (1934), 239 ff.

the territory should be circle-shaped, the militarily and economically important areas should be centrally located, and the country's border should be protected by geographical obstacles. Access to the sea—preferably via ice-free harbors—significantly broadens a state's scope for action.[77] On the other hand, exclaves often give rise to conflicts because they can be reached only by passing through foreign territory.

Borders cannot be determined unilaterally, but must be acknowledged by all states concerned. A large part of international law has to do with the delimitation of state territories.[78] This is easier to do on dry land than on water; there is a host of regulations regarding inland, internal, and archipelagic waters, and especially the territorial sea. Individual states were increasingly granted rights to the sea outside coastal areas, which was long considered free; consider the institution of the exclusive economic zone. Only the high seas and outer space are still beyond the reach of state territory—for how long, remains to be seen; the latter will depend on the development of weapons in outer space, among other things. Light is shed on the essence of the state by the fact that the old principle of the three-mile zone for territorial sea goes back to the range of cannons at the time, for it is necessarily part of the concept of a state territory that it can be controlled by the state.[79] Unlike airspace, which is part of the three-dimensional state territory, "radio" space is for the same reason not a part of state territory, because it cannot be dominated. The freedom of broadcast transmission is thus acknowledged in customary international law, even if there was no consensus between the West and the former East Bloc states regarding the limits on its content. In fact, one must concede that technological innovations exploded the complete impermeability of state territory that the modern theory of sovereignty so vigorously defended. To be sure, today as well no one is supposed to enter a state's territory against its will—but ideas can do so, thanks to the mastery of electromagnetic waves, and ideas are a factor of power and influence whose importance must not be underestimated, as the collapse of the East Bloc has shown. The freedom of broadcast transmission could be a harbinger of the end of the sovereignty of states.

Every state has territorial sovereignty over its state territory. That is the basis for its exercise of territorial supremacy. It can also transfer this supremacy partly or wholly to other states, without thereby abandoning territorial sovereignty—consider lease agreements. Territorial supremacy has two implications: the state territory is both the basis (the body, as it were) of domination and the stage on which it is displayed, and it thus belongs to the state as both subject and object. The first determination entails the exclusion of any other sovereign control not derived from the state itself (exceptions such as military occupation granted). To be sure, states can, for instance, grant the diplomats

---

77. A few of the points just discussed are already found in Aristotle, *Politics* 1326b 26 ff.

78. In A. Verdross and B. Simma's classical textbook, no other chapter is as long as the one on "Die völkerrechtliche Abgrenzung der staatlichen Souveränitätsbereiche in räumlicher Hinsicht."

79. "Imperium terrae finitur, ubi finitur armorum potestas" ("Control over land ends where the power of arms ends"), reads Bynkershoek's classic principle (quoted in A. Verdross and B. Simma [1984], 682). The idea is still found in Kant, *Metaphysik der Sitten* I § 15 (1976 f.; 8:375 f.).

of other states extraterritorial status, as it used unclearly to be termed, but it is the territorial sovereign himself that freely grants it. The second determination implies the domination of the state over all persons who are in the state's territory, that is, over foreigners as well. A difficult, but partly merely terminological question is whether one can also attribute to the state direct domination over things, which Jellinek denied, as is well known (1922; 398 ff.), but Kriele affirms (1975; 97). In any case, it is clear that an *imperium* under public law must be distinguished from a *dominium*, even if the two concepts were differentiated only later on, and even if this distinction runs counter, for example, to feudalism's conception of the state. In the latter, the vassal obeyed his feudal lord because the land belonged to the lord; in the modern age, the state exercises sovereign power over the territory because it has to dominate people.

The principle of territoriality does not imply that the scope of application of all norms must be limited to the state territory. For instance, German criminal law generally takes as its starting point the place where the crime was committed, but it also recognizes other starting points. Among others, the active personality principle, according to which the citizenship of the offender counts, and which carries further the old conception of the state as a corporate group consisting of persons; the protection principle, which defends certain domestic goods from all attacks, no matter where they might take place; and finally, the universality principle, which generally threatens certain acts with punishment, no matter where, by whom, or against whom they are committed.[80] However, acts of state can only be undertaken in one's own territory, in which alone judgments on the basis of these principles can be rendered and carried out.

6.1.3.3.   State Power: Inner Sovereignty

State power is the form of domination peculiar to a political ruling corporate group, and more precisely to a state. In Weber's terminology, a ruling corporate group is called "political" to the extent that "the enforcement of its order is carried out continually within a given *territorial* area by the use and threat of physical force on the part of the administrative staff." The state, which according to Weber exists in this form only in modernity, is a special kind of political corporate group, namely, the one whose "administrative staff successfully upholds a claim to the *monopoly* of the *legitimate* use of physical force in the enforcement of its order."[81] Furthermore, the state is described as a compulsory association with continuous organization, a compulsory association being defined in contrast to a voluntary association as a corporate group "the established order of which has, within a given specific sphere of activity, been successfully imposed on

---

80. Cf. A. Schönke and H. Schröder (1982), 54 f.

81. Weber (1980), 29: "... als sein Bestand und die Geltung seiner Ordnungen innerhalb eines angebbaren geographischen *Gebiets* kontinuierlich durch Anwendung und Androhung *physischen* Zwangs seitens des Verwaltungsstabes garantiert wedern." Trans. A. R. Henderson and T. Parsons, 154.

every individual who conforms with certain specific criteria."[82] Setting aside the conceptual element of the territory, Weber's definitions make the crucial point: physical force that is felt to be legitimate and a monopoly on physical force are the essence of the political corporate group and the (modern) state.[83] Because of its use of physical force as a means of power and because of the compulsory character of the state association, state power is the highest power of a corporate group, a power no one can now escape. One can flee a state, but if one is not prepared to put up with living in the polar regions, one can flee only to an area that is subject to another state power. In contrast, a church cannot, at least today, impose any physical punishment, and if there are voluntary associations whose members submit to the penal authority of the association's leadership, this submission is voluntary. One can leave the association if one is no longer interested in being a member of it. Exclusion is usually the most serious punishment a non-political ruling corporate group can impose; and even if this punishment is sometimes felt to be more dreadful than death itself (think of excommunication), yet it is qualitatively different from the punishments that are at the state's disposal. If, in discussing the forms of power in chapter 5.1.2.2.2, force was described as the pudenda of power, it can be said that in the state these pudenda can and may often be openly displayed. "Ultima ratio regum": like the sword, which is part of the imperial regalia, this inscription on old cannons discloses to citizens the ultimate ground of state power.

However, this ultimate foundation can be disclosed only because the exercise of force by the state, as a ruling corporate group, is *acknowledged* as legitimate—as an indispensable means for making law a social reality. State power serves to implement the law. That does not mean that physical force and the threat of it (whose purpose is to make the use of force unnecessary) are the only means of power available to a political corporate group; if they were, the corporate group could not long survive, because punishments could not replace the common mores that must provide the basis for a state.[84] Therefore it can and will use all other means of power: further negative sanctions, positive sanctions, manipulations, consensus-building. Public honors such as the awarding of medals mediate between positive sanctions and convincing. In economic policy, the

---

82. Ibid., 28: "... Verwaltungsstab erfolgreich das *Monopol legitimen* physischen Zwanges für die Durchführung der Ordnungen in Anspruch nimmt." It is odd that Weber does not also define political corporate groups as compulsory associations with continuous organization. Trans. A. R. Henderson and T. Parsons, 151.

83. However, I use the word "state," for the most part in order to designate what Weber calls a "political corporate group," and distinguish the *modern* state from it.

84. Cf. Montesquieu, *Esprit des lois* 19.17 (1748; 1:470): "Les princes qui ... gouvernèrent par la force des supplices, voulurent faire faire aux supplices ce qui n'est pas dans leur pouvoir, qui est de donner des moeurs. Les supplices retrancheront bien de la société un citoyen qui, ayant perdu ses moeurs, viole les lois: mais si tout le monde a perdu ses moeurs, les rétabliront-ils?" ("Rulers who ... governed by imposing punishments wanted to make punishments do something that it is not in their power to do, which is to produce mores. Punishments will exclude from society a citizen who, having lost his mores, violates the laws: but if everyone has lost his mores, will they re-establish them?")

spectrum of possibilities for state influence includes, for example, legal prohibitions on certain types of action, taxes that steer economic development, financial incentives to engage in a certain behavior—for instance, in the form of subventions, but also on the basis of decisions made by the state as a major entrepreneur—and finally, what is called "moral suasion." Indeed, often enough the statesman, even if the use of force is legally open to him, will expressly declare that he wants only to appeal to his public authority, and wants to forgo the *ultima ratio*. But this does not change the fact that physical force remains an outstanding means. The state is capable of granting positive sanctions primarily because it has the power to tax, which it can implement by coercion; and it is even the case that its appeals often have such a rapid effect because people know that if they are not effective, negative sanctions might follow. In addition, the state is far from using coercion to impose everything it seeks to communicate as political values, but the phenomenon of compulsory school attendance indicates that it can at least force people to listen to certain appeals. On the other hand, it must also be emphasized that even the state's penal authority draws its power from, for instance, the fact that the punishment is considered just and as shaming the person punished. Where this is no longer the case and punishment is seen as pure external coercion, punishment falls "wholly under the common concept of one specific thing contrasted with another, or as an item with which something else—the crime—can be purchased. The state as judicial power trades in specific wares, called crimes, for sale in exchange for other specific wares [punishments], and the legal code is its price-list."[85]

There are two grounds for the claim made by the modern state—unlike pre-state political corporate groups and pre-modern states—that it also has a *monopoly* on legal physical force, which becomes its defining feature. First, the use of state power is endangered when extra-state use of force is permitted for under certain circumstances the latter might be directed also against the state itself, and in fact was in the age of medieval polyarchy. Second, in modernity force is increasingly seen as problematic; its use ought to be limited to the indispensable minimum, and this must be the one exercised by the state itself. While the state deprives individuals of the power of resorting to extreme negative sanctions, at the same time it guarantees them the other sources of power as rights—property and honor. Closely connected with the state monopoly on force, as a monopoly on enforcing the law, is the monopoly on legislation, which the modern state also holds. However, these two monopolies do not exclude the possibility that in certain exceptional situations the individual may be justified in making a private use of force—for instance, in situations involving self-defense or defense of others against imminent attack, or with regard to his own children. But first of all, these are al-

---

85. Hegel, in his essay on natural law (1969 ff.; 2:480): "[die Strafe fällt] ganz unter den gemeinen Begriff eines bestimmten Dinges, gegen ein Anderes, oder einer Ware, für die etwas anderes, nämlich das Verbrechen zu erkaufen ist; der Staat hält als richterliche Gewalt einen Markt mit Bestimmtheiten, die Verbrechen heißen und die ihm gegen andere Bestimmtheiten feil sind, und das Gesetzbuch ist der Preiskourant." Trans. T. M. Knox (1975), 92.

ways exceptional situations in which the state cannot intervene; and second, it is the state itself that allows these exceptions. Analogously, sovereign rights, for instance, which municipalities and other public law corporations have, are delegated to them by the state—a derived, not an original power is involved.[86] Against this theory of Jellinek's, it has been objected that the state does not delegate power, for instance, to the organs subordinate to it, but rather acknowledges the latter as preceding it.[87] However, in dealing with this question we must distinguish three different levels. If we are thinking historically, it goes without saying that these powers subordinate to the state already existed before the development of the state monopoly on force. If we argue ethically, it turns out, as we will see later, that every right, and thus also the right of the state, is grounded in a moral sphere that transcends the social world. If we view the problem from a constitutional point of view, on the other hand, we will largely follow Jellinek in attributing to the state at least a prerogative in making and enforcing laws. If the state may also acknowledge already existing law, it is still on one hand its (possibly tacit) recognition that first guarantees the validity of this law. On the other hand, for the same reason the state can in principle withdraw its recognition—but if the latter is expressed in the constitution, it can do so only on the basis of a constitutional amendment. In any case the following holds: "What distinguishes state power from the power of the subordinate corporate groups is the *priority of state power*."[88]

In modernity, law thus exists only insofar as it is legislated or recognized by the state. This holds not only for civil law, but also for constitutional law itself. The state is a self-organizing structure. In this self-organization it is crucial that state power be unified for only thanks to this property can the state be an organized unit making decisions and able to act. Since state power is itself legally organized, but is at the same time also the guarantee of the laws, the homogeneity of the norms of constitutional law, which are in large measure norms of competence, is more important than the homogeneity of the other legal norms. If there are contradictions in civil law, one can turn to the judge or the legislator; but contradictions or even mere loopholes[89] in constitutional law can lead to civil war, because it is no longer clear by whom one should be guided. The unity and indivisibility of state power cannot be a matter of discussion, because this means only that the system of legal norms, and especially of the norms of competence, should be self-consistent. Also compatible with this would be precise determinations regarding the procedure of the division of a state that would challenge the indivisibility of the state, but not that of state power. On the other hand, state power's ability to enforce the law depends on the involvement of those subject to that force, which grows greater in

---

86. Cf. G. Jellinek (1922), 430.

87. Cf. R. Herzog (1971), 88 f.

88. M. Kriele (1975), 88.

89. In the United States Constitution, the right of secession for individual states was such a case; this right was neither guaranteed nor expressly denied. Calhoun definitely had arguments for his interpretation.

proportion to the number of opportunities at their disposal to collaborate in various organs. In addition, a guarantee of basic rights is not conceivable without a separation of powers. However, no mechanism of differentiating state power may put in question its unity, if conflicts are not to break out that can no longer be resolved and whose resolution can no longer be enforced using recognized means of coercion. Therefore the central question of every theory of the state is this: "How is the state to be understood as produced in a plural way and yet operating in a unified way?"[90] The separation of powers may not contradict the indivisibility of state power; and in fact the two concepts are absolutely compatible if, and only if, a clear delimitation of the competencies of the various state organs and their hierarchical order can be produced. Thus in a constitutional state founded on the rule of law, the executive and the judicial branches are bound by the laws, and the laws may themselves not contradict the constitution. In a federal state, federal law takes precedence over state law. Since the connection between the separation of powers and the indivisibility of state power is not easy either theoretically or practically, it is historically entirely understandable that early modern theory of the state believed it could ground the unity of state power only by postulating a single individual or a single state organ as its holder, as in Hobbes's absolutism and in Rousseau's radical democracy. The liberal idea of the separation of powers on both the horizontal and the vertical axes does not endanger the unity of the state only if, first, it is generally recognized when a decision has to be considered final and legally binding, and second, the constitution's content is construed in such a way that the state can make vital decisions in a timely way. These two requirements must be distinguished from one another—the first, which is more or less that of the constitutional certainty of the law, can also be fulfilled in states that are incapable of action. The *liberum veto* of every individual delegate in the Polish Diet was an extremely clear constitutional institution—but it is no less clear that the state thus represented a unit of decision, but not a unit able to act.

Here we are approaching the concept of sovereignty, the most difficult and complex in constitutional law. The word is often used homonymously. Thus "sovereignty" can sometimes mean only "the highest deciding authority": the decision of state power must be final and beyond legal appeal, no matter in which state organs it is articulated. This is a necessary condition for the unity of the legal system, and it is met in all modern states capable of functioning, even in modern constitutional states with the separation of powers. In the latter case, the decision-making power is distributed among different authorities. In the German Federal Republic, a law has an incontestable validity if it has been passed by the lower house of parliament (and in some cases the upper house of the parliament as well), signed by the president of the republic, published in the Federal Law Gazette, and confirmed by the Federal Constitutional Court as being in conformity with the constitution. The state organs as a whole are in this sense sovereign with respect to the society. More far-reaching is the statement that the term "sover-

---

90. H. Heller (1934), 340. "E pluribus unum," as it is aptly put on United States coins.

eignty" means *legal omnipotence*. The latter does not exist for most state organs insofar as they are bound by the constitution. However, within the framework of their constitutions almost all states have the possibility of changing their own competencies (and thereby for the most part also the constitution)[91] and thus they have a competence of defining competencies or an authority over competencies. The organ that exercises this authority has a special power (several organs may be involved); in this case, one speaks of an organ that has sovereignty over the constitution. However, several constitutions impose limits on the authority over competencies. State organs that have sovereignty over the constitution do not always have legal omnipotence as well. But these limits— setting aside for the moment their possible moral foundation—are precisely *legal* limits, and are formulated in constitutional law. It is still state law that limits *itself,* even in cases where, as in Article 20 IV of the German Basic Law, it establishes a right of resistance. If the "sovereignty" of state power means that while the latter is not omnipotent, it sets its own limits, then one can, indeed must, speak of a sovereignty of state power— which coincides, however, with the sovereignty of the constitution and may not be identified with the sovereignty of a state organ.[92] To be sure, a good constitution will ensure that it cannot be repealed by legal means, by determining the limits of legally possible amendments to the constitution, for instance, or by limiting the state of emergency in terms of both content and duration. But all these reasonable demands should be anchored legally as much as possible—the autonomy of the law cannot be escaped by constitutional means, and it is precisely this autonomy that leads to the concept of sovereignty as the final decision-making authority provided for by the law.[93] In short, from everything that has been said it does not follow that there is no sovereign, but on the contrary that the concept of law implies the concept of sovereignty.

The two concepts of sovereignty discussed thus far suggest, third, a synthesis. Even if it is conceded that every reasonable constitutional law includes implicit or explicit limits to constitutional amendment, it remains indispensable that there be an organ that has final authority in deciding when these limits of legal omnipotence have been transgressed. The people asserting itself through referenda, the parliament, the head of state, or the constitutional court can assume this role of the protector of the constitution; to that extent, they could be called "sovereign" (in a restricted sense). The concept would be particularly worthy of consideration if the same organ that can amend the constitution also decides the legal limits of constitutional amendment, as is the case in some parliaments. Since enforceability is part of the full concept of law, the law cannot be content with being valid only for itself, so to speak. The organ that implements the decisions made by the protector of the constitution by threatening negative sanctions

---

91. Where this is not the case, G. Jellinek (1922; 534 f.) and Schmitt (1928; 17) speak of rigid constitutions.

92. To that extent we must certainly agree with M. Kriele (1975), 111 ff.

93. Therefore this concept, as Schmitt rightly saw, is the counterpart in constitutional law of the theological concept of God or the metaphysical concept of the Absolute.

(and which is not necessarily identical with it) can therefore also claim to be sovereign in a fourth, still more restricted sense of the word.[94] A glance at the real existence of the state that supports the law explains, fifth, Carl Schmitt's well-known definition: whoever decides with regard to states of emergency is sovereign.[95] Insofar as the goal of a state of emergency is usually to ensure the survival of the state, and it restricts to that end the mechanisms of the separation of powers that endanger the state's capacity to act as a unit, it manifests in an especially intensive way the final goal of all constitutional law. However, the organ to which special authority is granted ultimately has greater responsibility than the one that decides on granting this authority; therefore the former could be considered as sovereign rather than the latter. In a good constitution,[96] the two organs are not identical. The Roman consul or consular tribune, who had to follow the Senate's recommendations, could not appoint himself dictator; the *senatus consultum ultimum* empowered the magistrate, not the senate itself, to take emergency measures. In any case, what is crucial is that the declaration of a state of emergency must have a constitutional basis if it is to be a topic in constitutional law; to that extent it refers back to the sovereignty of the constitution.

The protector of the constitution, the person who has command over the army and/or police, the organ that decides regarding states of emergency, and the one to whom special authority is transferred in states of emergency are in a privileged position to commit violations of the constitution. Because of the self-control of the highest level of public law, it is fundamentally possible that it may materially violate the constitution, even if because of the same constitution its decisions cannot be appealed. Even the mechanisms of the separation of powers can do no more than decrease the likelihood of a violation of the constitution—they cannot eliminate its possibility, because the corresponding organs could always work together toward this end. Only the requirement of the unanimity of the whole citizenry could constitutionally exclude the possibility of an abuse of state power (and even this only so long as, for example, the constitution did not call for the protection of future generations), but then the sphere of domination as such would be eliminated. The higher ranking the law is, the less it can guarantee its own enforcement, because an absolute self-grounding in the sphere of the real is not possible. Whether experts in constitutional law rank decisions that are materially unlawful, but are made by the relevant organs in a formally correct way, as violations of the constitution or as legal developments of the constitution depends on whether they have a primarily material or primarily procedural concept of law—and on whether they and the population that may accept or prevent these violations have sufficient

---

94. This concept of sovereignty approaches the concept of "supremacy" developed below, which can, however, also be granted to persons or groups (generals, for instance) who exercise no constitutional function at all.

95. (1922), 13.

96. Unlike the case of the president of the republic in the Weimar Constitution (Art. 48, Sect. 2), to which Schmitt was naturally referring.

courage. To be sure, someone who, in a dead-end situation, violates the constitution, seizes power, and keeps the state capable of action can be a savior of the state and become a *pouvoir constituant* for a new and better constitution. But the question of whether he is justified in doing so is not a problem in constitutional law (for as Anschütz's well-known remark puts it, constitutional law stops here, or can only answer the question in the negative), but rather a moral and political one. Experts in constitutional law may draw up constructions after the fact in order to legitimate the violation of the constitution—think of the adoption of the theory (defended by Bismarck, among others) that there was a "gap in the constitution" after the Prussian constitutional conflict of 1862–1866—but sincerity obliges us to acknowledge that these constructions are based on a comprehensible political desire for social peace, and not really on constitutional arguments.

In actuality, it is obvious that the constitution is constitutionally but neither socially nor ethically autonomous and sovereign. On one hand, it presupposes human beings who support it on the basis of factual mores, and on the other hand, it can receive an ultimate legitimation only through ethics, not through jurisprudence.[97] Thus ethics can determine that a law that was correctly passed through a process involving several state organs is nonetheless immoral. Certainly it is desirable that only moral laws be given the force of law, and it is worth the honorable person's effort to consider how this can become still more probable than it is in the modern constitutional state with a separation of powers. But all such reflections might make state power even more complex—they could not do away with its sovereignty if they were not prepared to risk legal peace as well. Conversely, ethics can certainly come to the conclusion that a flagrant violation of the constitution by a coup d'état or revolution, whether successful or not, was morally permissible and even obligatory—for instance, because it was the only way of avoiding civil war or massive injustice on the part of the state. The complete inability to deal with this possibility marks the limit of purely juristic thought, for which any revolution is *ex ante* repellent because prohibited by the constitution, but which will, if it is successful, become *ex post* the unquestioned basis of juristic thought's own activity. The expert in constitutional law becomes not only morally but socially blind when he reassures himself with the belief that violations of the constitution are not only unacceptable but could for that very reason finally not occur at all.

On the other hand, sovereignty does not necessarily mean factual power, and is thus not a sociological concept. Hence Lasswell and Kaplan conceive sovereignty as "the highest degree of authority"; by "authority" they mean only *formal* power.[98] The highest degree of *effective* power they call "supremacy"; and on the basis of both concepts they distinguish between "state," "government," and "governors" on one hand and the "body

---

97. H. Kelsen's basic norm is a desperate attempt to provide ultimate legitimation through a concept that is supposed to be purely juristic, but it cannot be this; instead it represents the empty husk of the problem of moral validity.

98. (1969), 177 ff.

politic," "rule," and "rulers" on the other, the two sets of terms corresponding to formal and effective power, respectively.[99] The distinction is undoubtedly essential. The decision-making officers foreseen by the constitution can be dependent on non-state or foreign state powers, the state organs with sovereignty over the constitution may be well aware that a legal constitutional amendment would not be accepted by the society, and thus either could not be actually implemented or might even lead to their assassination, a coup d'état, a putsch, or a revolution—this in no way alters their sovereignty on the basis of the constitution in force. A political scientist, however, will always try to discover (even if in order to do so he needs more than familiarity with constitutional law) where the real centers of power in a society are, and where the socially established limits of legal state power are located; he will want to know not only what is legally, but also what is politically possible. Thus, for example, objective economic pressures significantly limit even the most sovereign ruler's room for maneuver. In modern democracy, the parties are not state organs, but their effective power may be greater than that of the formal state organs. Even constitutional counterparts to Benito Cereno are not rare in history—namely, heads of state who can constitutionally decide everything, but in reality are marionettes in the hands of gray eminences (think, for instance, of the late Merovingian kings and their mayors of the palace). A personal cratic incapacity can condemn a head of state to this role—he may be completely dependent upon his mistress, an advisor, or other favorites, although because of the jealousy of the constitutionally subordinate ranks, which feel that they are ignored, the influence of the various Madame de Pompadours and Rasputins is often overestimated. Sometimes the devaluation of the formally highest office is the result of long historical processes that force this role even on people who would have been in themselves willing and able to rule, and suffer dreadfully under their factual impotence. However, it is also true that a political scientist who wants to be more than an expert on constitutional law must seek to understand why those who have the real power do not appear directly as such, but rather follow the detour through the legal possessor of state power. This detour indicates that the law is always a form of power, even if it is sometimes an inferior one—namely, when it has only authority and no longer the ability to impose negative sanctions. The fact that the true power-holders use the law as a pretext is usually a sign that they do not feel sure of themselves and that they do not want, and are not able, to give up the social legitimation that the law signifies. Sometimes it is foreign policy concerns and sometimes internal political concerns that make it necessary to maintain a façade of legality; and sometimes the true power-holder may have thoroughly convinced himself that he is a faithful advisor of the head of state and nothing more. But so long as the factual new power relationships are not legalized—which sooner or later must be the goal of every power-holder who wants to

---

99. A synthesis of both conceptual types is expressed by the concept of "polity," which is defined as "the regime and the rule" (214). ("Regime" is one of the formal concepts; see 130).

rule for a long time—the legal head of state holds with his authority at least a potential power[100] which, in the case of a blow to the status of the true power-holder, often becomes the obvious basis for a new construction of power. By the twelfth century at the latest, the Tenno was no longer the true power center of Japan. But with the resignation of the last shogun in 1867, power returned to him, because he had preserved his authority over the intervening centuries, even if he had lost true power.[101]

6.1.3.4. The Legal Forms of Relationships between States: External Sovereignty

The concept of sovereignty applies not only to relationships between state and society, but also to relationships among states, and thus means that in making decisions a political corporate group is not bound to follow the instructions of foreign powers, that it has the capacity for exclusive legal self-determination, that it is independent. From this arises, in modernity, the international personality of such political corporate groups, and at first (though this is no longer true today) only sovereign states, which alone could be relied upon to fulfill international obligations, were granted international personality. Although it has been shown that in the early advanced cultures of the Near East individual relationships between states were already shaped by law, the idea of a comprehensive order of international law presupposes a universalistic ethics such as hardly existed before Christianity, but also and especially the modern state, with whose development international law significantly accelerated. Internal and external sovereignty stand in a tense relationship to each other. On one hand, external sovereignty seems to be a logical consequence of inner sovereignty: if the state is not bound by its society, why should it be bound by external powers? Inner sovereignty without external sovereignty seems incomplete and inconsequential. On the other hand, external sovereignty endangers precisely what has been achieved by inner sovereignty: namely, peace through the hierarchizing of decision-making structures. External sovereignty implies a plurality of states, and the fact that they have no common arbiter—at least none with the power to impose sanctions—means that conflicts between states can often be resolved only with the means that the state, thanks to its monopoly on force, seeks to ban: physical force. Organized power struggles in which force is used and whose goal is to change acknowledged law are called "wars"; they often take a heavy toll of lives, on one hand because they are waged by well-organized corporate groups, and on the other because in them something is at stake that is considered of exceptional importance.

---

100. Cf. above, chap. 5, n.17.

101. It goes without saying that the pair of concepts "real power"–"legal authority" does not coincide with the *potestas-auctoritas* pair of Roman constitutional law; for first, the person who had *potestas* was recognized constitutionally, and second, the Senate held real power. However, it can be said that the concepts of *auctoritas* and legal authority both imply particular respect based on tradition that remains more or less immune to factual shifts in power.

In the case of external sovereignty, we are dealing with a legal concept, not a concept in political science. In order to survive, a diminutive state can allow a powerful neighboring state to restrict its freedom of decision in the most flagrant way without any effect on its sovereignty.[102] However, there are also legal restrictions on sovereignty, and there arises a terminological question, which various authors answer in different ways: What degree of sovereignty must exist for us to be able to speak of a state? Thus the diverse types of associations between states[103] involve very different degrees of restriction on state power, ranging from international regulation of individual relationships to administrative unions, alliances, confederations, protectorates, and federal states.[104] Thus, to begin with one extreme, in a federal state, which can emerge from a federation agreement or through an act of the people establishing a constitution, the member states exercise state power and under some circumstances may even enjoy international personality, but they are not sovereign, because the nation as a whole can immediately obligate their citizens, and as a rule it can apply federal compulsory action. Well into the twentieth century, protectorates and quasi-states played a major role. They can freely decide their internal affairs, but leave the direction of their foreign policy to a foreign power who is their protector or suzerain. They are sometimes called "half-sovereign," because they do not enjoy external sovereignty.[105] Finally, on the other end of the spectrum stand associations between states in the wider sense—when states regulate individual relationships through treaties or join administrative unions, they are still considered sovereign, although they have assumed international obligations. Mixed forms of such associations are also conceivable—for instance, the European Community occupies a peculiar position intermediate between a federal state and an administrative union. On one hand, the member states have their own sovereign power, and can, for example, levy immediate financial obligations on their citizens; on the other hand, their jurisdictions are limited—there is no question of federal compulsory action—and they do not have the competence of defining competencies. Since in addition the sovereign governmental functions

---

102. Sometimes the term "political sovereignty" is used to refer to real—military or economic—independence.

103. A comprehensive classification is found in G. Jellinek (1922), 737 ff., a critical elaboration in Schmitt (1928), 361 ff. and R. Herzog (1971), 396 ff. With the decline of monarchies, connections between states that consisted solely in a common head of state, and that in the case of a so-called personal union could be dissolved again on the basis of different orders of succession to the throne, have become less common.

104. Nonetheless, citizens of the member states are also citizens of the nation as a whole, in contrast to the relationship between protectorate and protector, which *for that reason* can be seen as a more thoroughgoing restriction of sovereignty.

105. In G. Jellinek's system of the associations between states, the two are distinguished by the fact that the protectorate is founded in terms of international law, and the empire dominating the quasi-states (*Staatenstaat,* as in the Ottoman Empire) is founded in terms of constitutional law (1922; 744 ff.).

are presumed to be with the individual European states, the European Community and the European Union should be described not as a state, but as a supranational organization—which does not exclude the possibility that there might some day be a European federal state. The closer the association between states, the greater is the required constitutional homogeneity of the cooperating states, since without the latter, mutual trust and a feeling of collective identity can hardly come about.[106] For example, a federal state whose member states had a partly monocratic, partly republican form of government would be difficult to imagine, because the central state would have to opt for one of the two forms and thus expect some of its citizens to identify with two different forms of government at the same time.[107] Moreover, in a federal state the power of the member states should not be too different—the special status of Prussia in the German Reich and of Russia in the Soviet Union endangered the federal structure.[108]

We have already seen that sovereignty within the state does not mean legal omnipotence. Much the same goes for external sovereignty. States are just as bound legally to international obligations as state organs are to the constitution. Indeed, just as the constitution cannot be abolished by the organ with sovereignty over the constitution, so there are a few fundamental norms of international law that do not go back to agreements and that cannot be abolished by agreements, because they constitute the conditions of the latter's possibility, that is, the norms regarding the creation of positive international law and those regarding international personality. They hold for all states. But the validity of international law is a difficult matter. Precisely because of the sovereignty of states in matters of foreign policy, there is no guarantee for international law comparable with that for internal state law, and it is therefore less effective than even constitutional law. Only if it were possible to create a universal institution with its own means of coercion could the social effectiveness of international law become like that of other law, but then the plurality of states would disappear at the same time. Thus the execution of international law, when it comes to that, is decentralized, because it remains dependent on the legal orders of the states. Still today, no organ of international law can act without decisions by individual states that enable it to do so. A further peculiarity of international law is that the great majority of it comes into being in a decentralized manner, through voluntary agreements among states, not through legislation passed by a central authority. Coordination, not subordination characterizes international law relationships. Submission to the jurisdiction of an international court is always voluntary. The fact that the effectiveness of international law is nonetheless greater than most lay persons think is attributable to the motivating force of the fear of

---

106. Cf. Montesquieu, *Esprit des lois* 9.2.

107. The German Reich of 1871 was a constitutional monarchy, not a monocracy, and the three republican city-states Lübeck, Bremen, and Hamburg represented only a small minority in comparison with the other member states.

108. Cf. Mill (1972), 367 f.

economic sanctions, loss of prestige, and isolation, among other things.[109] Just as law is generally based on mores, the efficacy of international law also depends on the spread of an international set of mores and its formulation in international public opinion.

As for the question regarding the relationship between state law and international law, there are essentially three possible answers, which are all also represented: the primacy of international law, the primacy of state law, and finally a dualism of the two laws. They make sense at the moral, sociological, and juristic levels, respectively. It is right that the meaning of international law is eliminated when its validity falls within the purview of the individual state—therefore international agreements are to be kept (setting aside for a moment the possible grounds that might justify breaking them). From a sociological point of view, however, it is true that state law has a stronger form of validity than does international law—indeed, the latter is possible only because of the existence of this form of validity with a greater power to impose itself. From a juristic point of view, finally, most states presuppose that they must first transform international obligations into national legal norms—if necessary, through a general constitutional norm. So long as this does not take place, national law does not become invalid simply because it contradicts international obligations; but the obligations continue to exist even if they imply a change in internal state law. Whether a state finally opts to transform its own law or to break the international agreement depends only on the state itself—for instance, on its will to create supranational organizations.

In actuality, the sovereignty of states in no way excludes the possibility that they may cede to such supranational communities individual sovereign rights. Even the complete surrender of the state's own sovereignty is conceivable (for instance, through the creation of a federal state or even a unitary state), insofar as only the new structure itself is sovereign. But where is the dividing line to be drawn? Why is the member of an administrative union considered sovereign, whereas a member state of a federal state is not? Is the dividing line fluid? It is obvious that the latter question must be answered in the negative: the category of sovereignty is sharply defined. We are concerned with a sovereign state only so long as it retains the ability to decide whether it renews its obligations (which is the case only so long as it does not delegate the competence of defining competencies). What marks the loss of external sovereignty is therefore the moment at which the state can no longer repeal its cession of sovereign rights. But the word "can" is ambiguous, as it is in the discussion of internal state sovereignty, for it may refer to either a legal permissibility or a physical ability. The latter is what counts in social reality. So long as a state can decide to withdraw from an association that claims to be irrevocable, and the latter does not have the power to force it to keep its agreement, it has remained independent. If this is no longer the case, the association itself has become a state in the

---

109. To that extent there are certain analogies between modern international law and primitive law—even if the former is rational and not based on taboos, and also presupposes the distinction between private and public and a class of experts that applies it, as F. V. Kratochwil (1989), 252 f. rightly points out.

fullest sense of the word. The right of secession is the shibboleth that distinguishes between a confederation and a federal state,[110] and we must emphatically maintain that between the two there is a qualitative difference. However, there can be situations in which it is legally disputed and cratically undecided whether a withdrawal from the association is possible. In such cases there is confusion as to the level on which the state is to be located. It is only a slight exaggeration to say that the American Civil War first made it clear that the United States, and not the member states, was the real state. Moreover, confederations are seldom stable—either they develop into federal states, as in North America, Switzerland, or Germany, or they fall apart.

To be sure, the member states of a federal state also have statehood, and even in differing degrees in different federal states. Thus the American member states have more legislative competence than do the German, and also insofar as in the United States every state has the same number of votes in the Senate, the federal principle is more pronounced than it is in Germany. But they are not states in the full sense. Therefore it is misleading when it is said that in the federal state sovereignty is divided between the central state and the member states. For what was said earlier about state power—namely, that its unity presupposes an ultimate decision-making authority—also holds for the federal state.[111] The number of state organs is increased, certainly, by the federal principle of organization; and in a federal state, in contrast to a decentralized but unitary state, the federal organs do not have exclusive control over the competence of defining competencies.[112] Indeed, the federal constitution can, like the Basic Law of the German Federal Republic, consider the division of the federation into states to be one of its inalterable components. But if conflicts between the nation as a whole and the member states are not to become insoluble, there must be an authority that can resolve them; and only if this is a federal organ are we dealing with a genuine federal state. In case of doubt, the federal court must have the right to decide whether a legal dispute must come before it or before a court of a member state; otherwise the latter could legally escape the central authority.[113]

---

110. However, the Soviet Constitution of 1977 recognized, in the famous Article 72, the Soviet republics' right of secession. But this was not meant seriously, and so long as the communist party, as the sole party allowed, kept the state in its grip, the risk of the article being taken seriously was slim, especially since there were no determinations regarding the way in which secession was to take place. Nonetheless, the article played a role in the dissolution of the Soviet Union, even if this dissolution ultimately was not achieved by legal means.

111. Cf. the annihilating criticism of the idea of the division of sovereignty in H. J. Morgenthau and K. W. Thompson (1985), 341 ff. In *The Federalist Papers*, Hamilton and Madison defended, against their better judgment, elements of this idea, in order to make it psychologically easier to accept the federal constitution.

112. Sometimes they share this competence with the federal organ that represents the member states, and sometimes with the member states themselves.

113. Cf. Tocqueville (1835 ff.), 1:217: "La cour suprême des États-Unis fut donc revêtue du droit de décider de toutes les questions de compétence. Ce fut là le coup le plus dangereux porté à la souveraineté des États." ("The United States Supreme Court was thus endowed with the right to decide all questions of competence. That was the most dangerous blow struck against the sovereignty of the states.")

The uniformity of the legal order does not allow any division of sovereignty, and the disputed issue regarding the relationship between national law and international law results precisely from the fact that there is no sovereign universal state that alone could guarantee the uniformity of the law. Without such a universal state, it is constantly left to individual states to determine to what extent they transform international obligations into national law, and the dualism of the two remains insurmountable.

6.1.3.5.   State Apparatus and State Organs[114]

We have already seen that on one hand the state consists in the domination that a few real—that is, living—people exercise over others, but on the other hand it claims to last for generations and to survive the individuals exercising domination. This tense relationship is rooted in the complex ontology of the social, which has as one of its most difficult tasks to determine the ontological status of the state, because most other corporate groups presuppose the existence of the state in order to be able to exist themselves. Here we are concerned also with a juristic and not solely a sociological problem. At least the present-day state is not only a corporate group, but also a juristic person (under public law) with rights and duties (which can, of course, act under some circumstances in private law forms as well). The construction of this concept, which was alien to the whole of Roman law, for instance, obviously presupposes an objective clarification of the sociological problem. On the basis of the principles developed in chapter 3.4.2.1, only a compromise between extreme individualism and the organic model can be acceptable. The state exists as a social as well as legal structure only so long as certain people perform certain acts—although they perform these acts with the consciousness that they are contributing to an order that in accord with its ultimate meaning points beyond their own existence and that is legally structured. Juristic persons may be conceived neither as fictions nor as really existing entities independent of the human beings who support them—they are schemata of imputation that as such can be actualized through the concrete behavior of real individuals on one hand, and on the other make it possible to evaluate precisely this behavior. The fact that the state has certain rights always means that certain persons have corresponding rights, not as private persons, however, but as persons exercising a certain office.

Historically, one must imagine the emergence of new political corporate groups in such a way that the physical and personal resources that constitute the basis of a corporate group were first laid for a concrete end, such as defense against enemies. Tribes, for instance, were originally often politically united only to such ends and for a short time. But humans' ability to foresee future potential threats easily leads to such organizations outliving their concrete occasion, not to mention the striving for power on the part of the ruler and his administrative staff. Indeed, the ruler will often, if not always successfully,

---

114. The following remarks are in part valid not only for the theory of the state, but also for a general theory of corporate groups.

seek to ensure that the political organizational structure outlives him, whether out of concern about his own offspring or about his own posthumous reputation, or out of a feeling of responsibility; and only in this way can a people become a state. Certainly the original rulers tailored their power position to the peculiarities of their own persons. But the hope that their position could be maintained over time probably soon forced them to distance themselves from their immediate feelings, and not to directly identify with their own person the position they assumed. Thus were the foundations of the office laid as the set of certain rights and duties distinct from the person occupying it and enduring beyond him. Certainly not every political corporate group in history is familiar with the concept of an office—an institution such as paying homage to the new ruler presupposes that the duties of loyalty between subordinates and ruler are due to their feudal origin, of a personal nature, and not automatically transferred to the ruler's successor. But Roman constitutional law, at least from the Republic on, already distinguished between the office and the office-holder.[115] Even in traditional monarchies, in which the king may have considered himself to be the state, the cry "Le roi est mort, vive le roi!" points to the fundamental difference between the concrete king and the office of the king. A sharp distinction between private and public emerges where the office is seen primarily as the quintessence not of rights, but rather of obligations. Public funds in the strict sense are involved only when people become aware that one can be lavish with one's own money, but not with public money. However, it does not suffice that a single office-holder thinks this way; instead, this attitude must be expected from everyone in order for an office as such to be constituted. The difference between private and public is not found in all cultures and in order to be legally ensured, it presupposes scrutiny of the office-holders. But in order to be socially legitimated, primitive rulers must already have based their position of power on something more general that raised it above its empirical contingency, so to speak. Just as the medicine man who puts on a mask feels that he has been transformed into another being, the ruler who has been ceremoniously installed in office, and who now differs from others by his special clothing, insignia, etc., will have been animated by the feeling that he has, as it were, become a new man. He may also feel that this authorizes him to express his lowest instincts, but it is just as possible that he will now conscientiously play a role that demands self-restraint. Indeed, since one often has to conceal one's most fundamental beliefs in order to rise to power, the power-holder has usually already learned not to let himself go, and to distinguish between his innermost feelings and his public appearances. To be sure, this can be based on purely strategic considerations, and still does not imply the readiness to think about something like the common good, but it is nonetheless a necessary condition for the latter.

When the power-holder is considered the occupant of an office, the concept of the state also changes. It becomes a *system of offices or state organs,*[116] and it is not to be

---

115. Cf. T. Mommsen (1974), 66.

116. The second concept is—at least in Germany—more general than the first, under which the legislative organ, for instance, is not subsumed.

identified in any way with the people who occupy these various offices. The persons who exercise the ruling functions represent something that points beyond them as private individuals—they act "in the name of" the state. From a constitutional point of view, three requirements must be met. First, there must be general organizational statutes in order to constitute state organs capable of action, statutes that determine the modes of functioning of the individual state organs, the most important, but certainly not the only one of which is a state's constitution. Second, there must be concrete organizational acts that establish, abolish, or change the individual governmental agencies and types of agencies. Third, because of the ontological dependency of state organs on concrete human beings, individuals must be installed in the various offices. The latter may happen as a result of a law, as in hereditary monarchies, for instance, through regulations regarding succession to the throne, or through concrete acts of nomination, as when a new head of state is appointed by his predecessor or by a vote of the people or of representative organs. The appointing organs must themselves be determinate state organs, and in German they are called *Kreationsorgane* (organs entitled to constitute other organs). Already in absolutism the principle of individual appointment to offices took on a far greater importance than it had in feudalism, because nobles were no longer born into offices. Only in this way does staff policy become possible, and since the activity of shaping is inconceivable without people on whom one can rely and whom one chooses, the modern state, unlike its medieval counterpart, is no longer "exclusively an element of *order,* but rather, at least in addition, but also generally primarily, an *instrument of shaping* in the hands of human beings who have become mature."[117]

Of the many categorizations that can be used to divide up the various state organs,[118] the most important is the one that distinguishes between *independent* and *dependent* organs. Unlike the latter, the former are not subordinate to the command of other organs, but independent. A plurality of independent organs is conceivable—indeed, it is the mark of states with a separation of powers—but avoids leading to complications only when the spheres of responsibility are clearly delineated. The latter need not always be determined by the constitution, but may, as it were, get going in accord with customary constitutional law, often after exhausting power struggles whose factual conclusion acquires normative force. It is also conceivable that state organs may only make decisions in concert, that is, have *incomplete* jurisdiction. For a law to go into effect, for instance, the approval of the parliament and the head of state are usually required in a modern state; moreover, in a bicameral system in the narrower sense of the word, approval by both houses is required. From positive cooperation on an equal footing by two (or more) state organs, we must conceptually (but not always practically) distinguish the mere right of veto—and even more the mere suspensive veto—that may be granted to an organ. We are dealing with an *ex officio* organ (as opposed to a *simple* organ) when the

---

117. R. Herzog (1971), 211.
118. Cf. G. Jellinek (1922), 544 ff., which I follow to a large extent.

quality of being an organ presupposes the possession of the quality of being another organ—for example, the German emperor of the Second Reich was emperor as the King of Prussia. *Extraordinary* organs, such as the Roman dictator in contrast to the consul, exist, unlike *normal* organs, only exceptionally. However, the competence of the Roman dictatorship was fundamentally regulated. In addition, in Roman history there were also organs created by special legislation for a specific function, such as the *Decemviri*.[119] Organs that represent other, *primary* organs, without being bound to instructions, are called *secondary* (for instance, as the parliament represents the people), and to that extent they also belong to the category of immediate organs. Dependent state organs, on the other hand, are subordinated to independent organs and responsible to them. However, only a few of them are *optional;* if they are *necessary,* the superior organs must appoint to them and cannot dissolve them at their own discretion. However, dependent organs are subject—like agencies without juristic personality, and also certain juristic persons under public law such as municipalities—to the supervision of superior organs, or at least to their legal and sometimes also to their substantive supervisory power. The first case involves only the supervision of the administration's conformity to the law; the second case involves the supervision of its appropriateness as well.

In the organization of the state apparatus two principles must be distinguished. First, the problem arises as to whether the organs are to be conducted *monocratically* or *collegially,* that is, whether decisions are to be made by one person or more than one. In a monocratic organ, the head of the department can certainly also delegate decision-making authority, but he can take it back whenever he wants to. In contrast, collegial organs—such as parliaments, for instance—are dependent on the collaboration of a number of people in making decisions. A certain number of the members of the organ (the quorum) must usually be present in order for it to be capable of making decisions at all; a decision will then be made either on the basis of unanimity or on that of a qualified, absolute, or relative majority. If some members have a veto right, then an objection made by one of them suffices to block a decision. The principle of collegiality has many forms[120]—in addition to the participation of all members in all questions, there are also limitations in subject-matter or time (for instance, rotation of the power of decision). Between the monocratic and collegial principles there are also intermediate forms. A collegial organ may have only an advisory function, but must be listened to by the person making decisions monocratically; indeed, its recommendations may even have de facto binding force. Conversely, it may be that decisions are made only by a collegial organ, but as a rule in accord with the recommendations of the relevant expert. The advantages of monocratic organs lie in the consistency, precision, and rapidity of decision making, in a better guarantee of secrecy as well as in clear responsibilities. On the other hand, collegial organs can advise more thoroughly and more

---

119. T. Mommsen (1974; 68) calls only the latter "extraordinary" magistrates.
120. Cf. Weber (1980), 158 ff.

easily surmount the inevitable particularity of each individual's viewpoint; they remain capable of action even in the case of loss of members. Each individual's participation in the decision-making process can lead to a stronger self-esteem and a greater involvement, but only so long as the number of the members is not too large. In actuality, the number of people of which a group is composed can be distinguished not only quantitatively but also qualitatively, and a sense for the right number in setting up collegial organs can be crucial for the success or failure of their work.[121] An organ with two or three members easily leads to polarizations and stalemates or to a situation in which the minority is constantly overruled by the majority; if it has more than twenty members, contingent alliances are often relied upon for consensus-building, and not everyone will succeed in presenting his view.

Second, the state apparatus may be determined by more or less *centralization* or *concentration*. "Centralization" means here the extensive elimination of dependent state organs with juristic personality and transferring their functions to the superior state organ, whereas "concentration" means the unification of various functions in a single agency. Eliminating municipalities would be an act of centralization; merging two ministries or the abolishment of a subordinate agency would be horizontal and vertical concentration, respectively. Even in extensive decentralization the state must not be endangered as a unit making decisions and able to act. If one wants to avoid what has been aptly called "polyarchy" and is characteristic of some pre-modern political corporate groups, thorough hierarchizations must not be neglected, which ensure the transitivity, as it were, of the power relationship. The effectiveness of the state depends on the subordinate organs being legally bound, in certain questions, to follow the directions of the superior organs; for instance, the bureaucracy must obey the administration. (To be precise, since in a constitutional state, law has priority, the bureaucracy is bound not only by the government's directives, but also by the laws.) Moreover, in order to impose their own ideas the heads of each agency must have at their disposal all the instruments of personnel policy—instruments that are, however, significantly limited by the fact that in most modern countries public officials are usually employed by the state for life. What has just been said is not a plea for the widest possible centralization and concentration—rather, the latter should be limited to what is necessary. In reality, an extremely tight centralization is usually counterproductive, for two reasons. First, people on the site are much better able to make a competent decision than people who are far away. The fact that Italy's regions had no real financial autonomy was one of the reasons for its decline. Second, areas where free, responsible decisions can be made lead to greater motivation. Tocqueville makes this point very well: "It is true that the centralization of administration succeeds in uniting all the nation's available forces at a certain moment and in a certain place, but it makes their reproduction more difficult. It makes

---

121. Cf. Kauṭilīya-Arthaśāstra 1.15.34 ff.

the nation victorious on the day of battle, and in the long run decreases its power."[122] He rightly stresses that centralization can prevent abuses that might occur without it, but that it can hardly set in motion any positive changes in society. Gorbachev was able to transform his country's foreign policy, yet any positive internal political renewal had been made impossible by Soviet centralism. In general, the threat of negative sanctions, which are easier for a distant center to use than the other means of power, can for the most part only prevent people from doing something, whereas with positive sanctions, such as economic rewards, people can be moved to action; but important actions spring from a feeling of self-esteem that is easily destroyed by excessively strong hierarchization. The ideal solution is to provide areas in which subordinate departments are able to act freely, but can be taken away in exceptional cases. It is noteworthy that in the passage just cited, Tocqueville spoke of a decrease in a nation's "puissance" resulting from centralization. According to a naive conception of power, this is nonsense, for decentralization increases the number of decision makers. However, power, as we have seen, is not necessarily distributive—there is also collective power. The latter can increase when more people participate in decisions.

6.1.3.6. The Tasks of the State

In the theory of state functions, two very different questions are dealt with.[123] On one hand, there is the question of which tasks the state is to fulfill—for instance, tasks of internal and foreign policy. Naturally, the precise determination of these tasks depends on the final goals that the state acknowledges—questions of economic policy or religious policy increase in importance when the state counts among its goals care for the physical well-being or the spiritual welfare of its citizens. However, a few tasks must be fulfilled by all states. On the other hand, the concept of state functions is used to refer to the types of behavior through which the state can fulfill its tasks—the classical triad of legislative, executive, and judicial (to which can be added the constitution as the foundation of the three powers) is orthogonal to the state's tasks insofar as the legislative, executive, and judicial branches can each be conceived as dealing with tasks concerning internal and foreign policy. In the following pages, the state's tasks will be discussed first, and then the types of state conduct.

Historically, the oldest state functions are the military and the judicial. Since the first and elementary goal of the state is the protection of human life, especially against intraspecific aggression, keeping the peace, both within the state and outside it, is the

---

122. "La centralisation administrative parvient, il est vrai, à réunir à une époque donnée, et dans un certain lieu, toutes les forces disponibles de la nation, mais elle nuit à la reproduction des forces. Elle la fait triompher le jour du combat et diminue à la longue sa puissance" (1835 ff.; 1:154 f.).

123. Cf. R. Herzog (1971), 109 ff., 300 ff.

key problem of politics. We already mentioned that the creation of military organs may have first made possible the institutionalization of legal coercion by law within the state; yet the distinction between military and civil offices quickly became one of the most fundamental structural characteristics of the state. The character of a state depends crucially on whether the military is subordinate to civilian authorities or controls the latter. The first division of state functions is between the internal policy and foreign policy. However, the two are closely connected, since certain internal policy structures are a necessary condition for conducting a successful foreign policy, and since conversely the realization of foreign policy goals can be a precondition for reforms in internal policy. Indeed, even the perception of internal politics abroad or of foreign policy at home are significant for foreign and internal policy—internal policy defeats weaken a politician who is dealing with a foreign power, just as failures in foreign policy weaken him domestically. Questions of internal policy, such as protecting minorities, can be an object of foreign policy, and even of international treaties. If a state has committed itself under international law to take certain steps, they are no longer a matter of internal affairs, and the accusation of meddling in internal affairs is false, even if the matters criticized are of an internal nature.

Although the development of modern international law has radically changed the nature of *foreign policy*, we must emphasize that today *security policy* is still a central, key area of the foreign policy of every state that wants to pursue an evolutionarily stable strategy—indeed, in the era of weapons of mass destruction it has even increased in importance. Because of the state of nature in which states remain in relation to one another, we must constantly reckon with the use of force, the most elementary form of power, to resolve conflicts between states. However, avoiding or limiting explosions of violence is the original and most important function of the state. Thus every state must be prepared for the possibility of a war, i.e., if the war ought to be just, the state must be prepared to defend itself and build up military forces for this purpose. (However, these military forces are sometimes also used internally.) The borderline between aggression and defense is not always easy to draw, as is shown by the concept of preventive war, which has no doubt very often been misused, but behind which a problem is concealed. Military enterprises arise both from an insatiable striving for power and from a need for security, without it always being possible to draw a clear distinction between the two; for even the striving for world domination can present itself as an attempt to overcome international anarchy. Often the fear of the other's possible plans for aggression plays a role—plans that themselves result only from fear; many a war was not really desired by anyone.

We must reject the thesis maintained by a few theoreticians of international relations that a state will attack its neighbors precisely when a cost-benefit analysis (which can, of course, be mistaken) recommends such a step. Even if politicians' responsibility differs in nature from that of individuals, there are moral constraints on statesmen and the public opinion that supports them, and at a certain level of civilization, a groundless attack on a weaker state, or even the destruction of a state, especially if it belongs to one's own culture area, are not clearly compatible with one's own values. Moreover, human behavior is not always rational in declarations of war—passions that have risen to fever. pitch on both sides can play a greater role than cool reflections; a supposed threat or insult on the part of others can lead to a relapse to the level of the mere masses. In addition, this thesis does not exclude the possibility that there is a significant number of situations in which peaceful interdependence is in the general interest, for the costs of wars, as well as of domination over a large area, are great. Even the surrender of one's own territory is conceivable, if this would facilitate an internal constitutional change or if control over the area costs more than it brings in.[124]

However, it is correct that one must always reckon with the *possibility* that a neighboring state (not necessarily its current head) may in the future act in accord with a mere cost-benefit analysis, especially if war was usual in history up to that point. Both success, which wants to repeat itself, and defeat, which produces a desire for revenge (which can be even stronger in a collective than in an individual), are possible causes for the next war. Seeking first to produce by peaceful means and then to preserve a *balance of power* that makes any war very risky is one of the strategies that can prevent the outbreak of a new war. Nevertheless, the effectiveness of this strategy must not be overestimated, for since it is not easy to tell when two states or alliances are really equal in power, all parties will try to gain a margin of security, and since there are hardly any clear criteria for determining when this margin is sufficient, the effort to produce a balance of power easily leads to an effort to maximize power and thus to an arms race, for example.[125] States that because of their military potential exercise a significant influence on other states and the community of nations as a whole are called "great powers." If there are two great powers in the international system, it is called "bipolar"; if there are more than two, "multipolar." Multipolar systems are distinguished from bipolar systems by the possibilities of alliances, among other things, and are therefore less clear. If one assumes a division of the state system into two groups, then the number of possible alliance formations with n states is $(2^n/2) - 1$; and even if the mathematically possible alliances include many that are politically impossible, the number remains alarmingly large.[126] It becomes far greater if the system is divided into three parts (two opposing sides and a neutral side); a further differentiation is unlikely, since the enemy of the enemy is generally a friend. States in a bipolar system can more easily rely on informal arrangements than in a multipolar system, since the lack of possibilities for

---

124. Cf., in R. Gilpin's impressive book (1981), the chapter "Limitations on Change and Expansion" (146 ff.), which mentions geographical borders, opposing military forces, and the fact that there are optimal sizes for political systems. See also Montesquieu, *Esprit des lois* 9.6 and 9.10, on the utility of buffer states, whose incorporation is not in one's own interest.

125. Cf. H. J. Morgenthau and K. W. Thompson (1985), 227 f.: "To that effect, all nations actively engaged in the struggle for power must actually aim not at a balance—that is, equality—of power, but at superiority of power in their own behalf. And since no nation can foresee how large its miscalculations will turn out to be, all nations must ultimately seek the maximum of power obtainable under the circumstances."

126. On alliances, see M. Nicholson (1990), 116 ff.

forming alliances means that they do not have to deal with constant shifts in power.[127] Outbreaks of war can also be discouraged by one state's *hegemonic* position, which nonetheless easily arouses hatred and envy, which may be stronger than caution with regard to it. A hegemonic power exercises a strong influence on the foreign policy of other states, although the latter remain—unlike a universal state, which has not yet existed—independent in their internal policy. When a state directly dominates many peoples, one speaks of an "empire." Domination can also be informal, if for example the true head of government of a dependent country is the empire's ambassador. Not every hegemonic power is an empire (the United States is not, for instance); empires are usually great powers (but not necessarily, and sometimes only in the fictions of diplomatic intercourse, like the Ottoman Empire after the Crimean War, for instance), and only rarely hegemonic powers (like the Roman Empire, for instance).

There are always states that repeatedly seek a change in the status quo, by force, if necessary. This kind of change is commonly (but not conceptually necessary) desired in one's own self-interest—here self-interest can refer not only to the welfare of the state concerned, but also to the particular interests of the rulers or of the classes that support them. Naturally, wishing does not suffice to realize this goal; if one is prudent, in making such a decision one takes into account as factors the weakness of the opponent and the situation of the international system. The insights of victimology, a subdiscipline of criminology, can also be applied to the theory of international relations, so long as they are not misunderstood as a justification of the aggressor. Yet it can hardly be denied that the shameful first three partitions of Poland would not have been so easy to make had the constitutional structure of the kingdom been different. Foreign policy directed toward change can be called "imperialistic"—this at least is Morgenthau's terminology.[128] However, this has the remarkable consequence that a policy intended to preserve an empire cannot be called "imperialistic"; according to this view, in 1990 it was the Lithuanians, not the Soviets, who were an imperialistic power. This is a peculiar way of using words, but if the concepts are clearly defined, one can accept this use, especially since the difference between preserving and changing is also fundamental for internal policy.[129] On the other hand, we cannot accept Morgenthau's trichotomy distinguishing among the policy of the status quo, imperialism, and the policy of prestige. The latter is not a third type of policy on an equal footing, because it can serve to preserve the status quo as well as to promote expansion. Instead, one might designate as a third type the goal of a conjoint change; the construction of international organizations cannot be subsumed under either the category of the policy of the status quo or that of imperialism.

Even for imperialists, war is seldom a goal in itself. Augustine rightly maintains that even those who disturb the peace only want another kind of peace, and are not in any

---

127. Cf. M. W. Doyle (1986), 136.

128. (1985), 52 ff.

129. In M. W. Doyle (1986; 19), on the other hand, "imperialism [is] the process of establishing and maintaining an empire."

way against peace in itself: "Nam et illi qui pacem, in qua sunt, perturbari volunt, non pacem oderunt, sed eam pro arbitrio suo cupiunt commutari. Non ergo ut sit pax nolunt, sed ut ea sit quam volunt."[130] The wish to change the status quo can arise from simple greed, but it can also be based on a subjectively sincere and sometimes even legitimate striving to surmount a deeply unjust situation. War goals can be classified in accord with the elements of the state. Sometimes a state territory should be gained, possibly with the population living on it; yet one can also desire to drive out this population if it is not a matter of dominating people, but rather only of dominating land. Conversely, in earlier times there were also military campaigns in which the goal was the enslavement of the population, not control over an area. Such goals can also include the overthrow of a foreign government without encroachment on the territory of the foreign state and without subjugating its population, or the dividing up of a multi-ethnic state in order to ensure the various peoples' right of self-determination. Expansion may be economically motivated (for example, by a country's resources, the market that it represents, or one's own population growth), and it can also have military causes—an area may be strategically significant and control over it a favorable starting point for the next war; crushing a country may re-establish the balance of power. The overthrow of a state power felt to be contemptuous of human dignity can be desired as an end in itself. But in a war it may only be a question of one collective gaining the respect of another that the latter had previously denied it. Wars of revenge belong to this type, if what is involved in them is more overcoming a feeling of subjective insult than winning back a territory that is important only for psychic reasons having to do with identity, rather than for economic or strategic reasons. Behind a declaration of war there may also be the wish to distract attention from internal problems or to be able more easily to suppress internal opponents—yet for the most part this strategy backfires if one does not win. Finally, it cannot be denied that in addition to the desire for fame and the desire to prove one's courage, and mixed with them in some murky way, sheer lust for death and robbery, as well as the anticipation of being able to rape with impunity, can be powerful motives for going to war.

Certainly, the goal of legitimate security policy is to make the use of the armed forces superfluous. Therefore, precisely when this policy has been successful, the military force can easily be considered superfluous—a fallacy in which moralistic intellectuals sometimes indulge. But the build-up of an army is only one of several possible means for achieving foreign policy goals. Confidence-building measures such as disarmament treaties can mean more security—however, only if it is guaranteed that the all parties to the treaty will keep their commitments. Likewise, the task of collecting information about foreign states is part of security politics, especially information regarding secret activities and preventing analogous activities in one's own country. Great powers began engaging in espionage and counter-espionage very early in history, as any reader of Sun-tzu and

---

130. *De civitate Dei* XIX 12. ("For even they who intentionally interrupt the peace in which they are living have no hatred of peace, but only wish it changed into a peace that suits them better. They do not, therefore, wish to have no peace, but only one more to their mind." Trans. M. Dodds, 687.)

Kauṭilya knows, and the emergence of modern diplomatic missions has given these activities unanticipated opportunities for development. Because of the secrecy with which the activity of these services is necessarily connected, they often escape public supervision and may become a special power factor. There is more to foreign policy than security policy—if only because every state has not only military, but also, for example, economic and cultural interests with respect to other states. Often a strengthening of foreign trade is desired by one or both sides, and sometimes cultural exchange is seen as enrichment, or the expansion of one's own culture (especially religion) is seen as a sacred duty. But even where ultimately security policy goals are concerned, such as the avoidance of armed conflict or the annexation of a state, economic and ideological measures can be given precedence over military ones. The Cold War was not conducted solely through proxy wars and armament; no less important was the attempt to attract neutral countries to one's own side by using positive sanctions or an ideology felt to be true and appropriate to the time. (To that end attempts were made to gain influence over governments and also the opposition, and even to provide financial support for rebels and putschists). The so-called politics of development also had roots in this need, as is shown by the crisis into which it fell after the end of the Cold War. Even if the concept "development aid" presupposes the category of development, which was first produced by modernity, it can still be said that the effort to achieve economic and especially cultural homogeneity was early on seen as a task of foreign policy, because it was seen as increasing the likelihood of peaceful relationships or as augmenting one's own power.

Achieving foreign policy goals in a peaceful way is the task of *diplomacy*.[131] In particular, diplomacy is concerned with the settlement of disputes to which one need not oneself be party, but in which one can offer one's good offices to the opponents as a third party. This represents at least a gain in prestige, but it can also be connected with more tangible advantages. In order to operate effectively, diplomats must first rank in importance the goals of their own states, and also ascertain, clearly and with a realistic assessment of the distribution of power, the means for achieving them. Second, they must determine, in a lucid and unprejudiced way, the goals of the other side, its means of power, and its theoretical and practical categories. Third, they must examine how far these goals are compatible with each other or could be made compatible in the common interest. A state's means of power that are military in nature have already been discussed in chapter 6.1.2.3—geographical peculiarities and the availability of resources relevant to waging war, the quantity and quality of the armed forces, the state of weapon technology and battle technology, as well as of logistics. No less important are political factors in the narrower sense, such as the size of the population and its will to persist, the quality of its government and its diplomacy.[132] The fulfillment of the tasks of diplomacy is eased by the modern system of mutual diplomatic missions that not only pres-

---

131. On the following, see H. J. Morgenthau and K. W. Thompson (1985), 563 ff.
132. Cf. H. J. Morgenthau and K. W. Thompson (1985), 127 ff.

ent their governments internationally, but also perform symbolic and cratic functions of representation: they represent their own state abroad, and they attempt to awaken sympathy for its goals. An important goal of foreign policy is to increase the prestige of one's own state, which is not to be underestimated as a power factor; this can take place only through public measures. At the same time, however, we must insist that diplomacy depends on keeping negotiations secret. One can suggest compromises only if one need not fear a loss of prestige in the event that they are rejected, and if third parties that are somehow affected cannot immediately take countermeasures. Therefore few things are more ludicrous than the modern mass media's demand that diplomacy be completely open to the public.

The second function of every state is the *maintenance of internal peace.* We have already shown that without the administration of justice no human society can survive—periodic outbreaks of violence are inevitable if, first, conflicts of interest are not mediated by an impartial third party, and if, second, the latter's decisions are not implemented even against those who resist them. However, these two elements are not identical. Even late in the history of the state, justice was dependent for the imposition of its judgments on the private involvement of the parties concerned. So far as the first point goes, the *construction of a judicial system* is the original task of internal policy. With the increase in social change and the development of new moral ideas, however, the law had to be modified; a special *legal policy* became necessary. Legislation became an important function of the state, and is still becoming more and more important as the social dynamics grow. The state cannot deal solely with the task of maintaining public order; it must also concern itself with the shaping of society, and thus of the law. Paradoxically, the necessity of state intervention increases as the subsystems of the society become more autonomous, for the latter's autonomy means more room for maneuver, to which the state must react. On one hand, the state can seek to shape society in order to counter a danger to the order of society that has arisen; on the other hand, it is also conceivable that it wants to impose material ideas of justice, and to this end is even prepared to imperil the existing order, although it thereby usually imperils itself as well. Just as in the sphere of foreign policy, the fundamental distinction is between the politics of the status quo and the politics of imperialism, so in internal politics the basic alternative is that between preservation and change. Thoroughgoing power *within* the existing institutions does not yet mean power *over* these institutions; someone who wants to change them often enough risks having the situation slip out of his control.

Unlike the systems of justice and administration, legislation is not a conceptually necessary state function. By far not all states, and not even all modern states, have achieved a systematic codification of law. The latter is almost always preceded by a long process of judicial updating of the law that is in some cases inspired by individual laws—think of the history of Roman law. But even today, labor law in Germany, for instance, is still partly pure judge-made law. The advantages of codification are obvious: the legal system acquires greater clarity and determinacy; the demands of the separation of powers can be better taken into account; crucial changes are easier to make than in judge-made law,

which by its very nature tends to be conservative. However, the chief danger of codification lies in the fact that it can result in the law being disconnected from the mores that
must support it if it is to be more than a declaration of good intentions. That only a
small part of British constitutional law is formulated in individual laws, and especially
that British constitutional law provides no basic rights, seems a matter for concern—
but we must take into account the fact that hardly any modern state has recorded fewer
violations of basic rights than Great Britain. *In case of doubt, mores are a better guarantee
than even the most complete codification.*[133] The settlement of conflicts between private individuals is the task of civil law, which today covers (according to the German systematization that guides this whole paragraph), for example, civil law, commercial law, and
copyright law. However, we have already seen that public law is more fundamental than
private law because the former alone can guarantee the execution of private law. Thus
the judicial system must be legally organized—it needs, in addition to substantive law,
a law governing the constitution of courts and procedural law. Moreover, in the case of
developed statehood, judgments must be enforced, not only in private law, but also in
criminal law. In actuality, every state also has *punishments,* that is, negative sanctions
that are attached, in order to protect certain legal goods, to certain acts as their legal
consequences. On one hand, breaking the law must not be worthwhile if the state is
not to dissolve as a legal order. On the other hand, overcoming private revenge and making punishment a state affair is one of the state's most important achievements, which,
for one thing, protects it from explosions of violence that could shake its foundations,
because revenge tends to become an infinite process, and for another, can lead to a humanization of the application of negative sanctions, because they are not carried out
by those affected. In more developed states as well, the prosecution of crimes, and not
only the verdict, proceeds from the states themselves, but justice obviously demands
that the prosecutor not be identical with the judge (although inquisitional trials continued to be held in Germany into the nineteenth century). In modern constitutional
states the public prosecutor's office is partly an administrative department, and partly
belongs to the third, judiciary power, which determines various respective forms of
dependency. Together with procedural law, one can subsume criminal law under the law
relating to the administration of justice. The execution of judgments requires an internal administration that must itself be legally organized: administrative law is based on
this necessity. Finally, it must be made clear, for example, who can enact laws. This leads
us to constitutional law, which together with the law relating to the administration of
justice and administrative law constitutes public law. The precise borderline between
public and private law is debated in jurisprudence, especially because important legal
consequences are connected with it. But wherever the borderline runs, there is no doubt
about the qualitative difference between the two. In public law (according to *Subjektions-
theorie,* the theory of subordination), a representative of public power is opposed to citi-

---

133. Plato even goes so far as to designate, not only codification, but a large number of judges
as an index of the decline of mores: *Republic* 405a ff.

zens and juristic persons in a relationship of precedence, whereas private law regulates relationships between parties on an equal footing.

Legislation regarding administration is meaningful only if there is *an administration*—the other great area of domestic policy alongside the judicial system. The heart of internal administration has been the *police system*. The history of the conception of *Polizei* in Germany reveals an increasing restriction: whereas under absolutism it included the largest part of state power, at the end of the eighteenth century it was limited to the administrative and enforcement police, whose functions are on one hand to maintain the public peace, security, and order, and on the other to avert dangers. Today, the police force (in the institutional sense) has only the latter function. Because constitutional law plays a central role in every legal order, special security precautions are often taken against political crimes, that is, attempts to overthrow the government. Especially in states that are supported by a slender social consensus, the political police plays a major role.

The administration, the judges, and at least the leaders of the military forces cannot be obligated to perform their functions solely by negative sanctions, because a system consisting of mere negative sanctions cannot support itself. Therefore every state must have an income and construct a *fiscal administration*. However, fiscal policy does not serve solely to cover state expenditures. On the assumption that the citizens like to avoid taxes, but also like to participate in state services, through its revenue and its expenditure aspects, that is, through the management of the budget, fiscal policy can also become an important way of steering economic events. Because almost all state action is dependent on financial means, the drawing up of the budget amounts to a predetermination of the whole policy, even if budget priorities are not always an indication of the priority of the corresponding political domains. Social policy is for instance more expensive than diplomacy, even if the latter is pursued with the greatest commitment. Since private as well as state economics is made much easier by a stable currency, monetary policy is one of the chief tasks of modern financial policy. On one hand, a monetary order must be constituted; on the other, the value of the currency must, whenever possible, be defended as long as other economic policy goals and particular interests do not require this aim to be neglected.

Like police administration and the administration concerned with ordinances regulating business, fiscal administration is now considered an *interfering administration* (*Eingriffsverwaltung*), insofar as it is authorized to intrude upon the freedom and property of those subject to the law. However, administration also includes what is called "administration offering services" (*leistende Verwaltung*)—one of the state functions that cannot be attributed to all states, and that was first juristically conceptualized in the twentieth century.[134] To be sure, it is already found in early states—the construction and maintenance of roads and navigable waterways or the erection of public buildings

---

134. This is one of the abiding achievements of Ernst Forsthoff's treatise of 1938. See E. Forsthoff (1959).

are well-known examples. But classical liberalism, which wanted to limit state functions essentially to defense against external and internal threats and to the judicial system, could do little with the administration of community services. In the twentieth century, the latter increased in an incredible way, and indeed in connection with a fundamental new definition of state functions that is designated by the phrase "the transition from the state based on the rule law to the welfare state." On one hand, the administration of community services often benefits indirectly other state tasks; by increasing the country's economic power, it also increases tax income, so that the army can be made larger and better equipped technologically, etc. On the other hand, it is absolutely an end in itself. With the expansion of human power over nature and society, caring for basic needs (*Daseinsvorsorge*) becomes steadily more difficult for individuals; without state help they would often be unable to do so. Forsthoff has aptly pointed out the dissociation of effective and dominated space among moderns. Whereas the pre-modern farmer seldom left his farm, but dominated the latter and had in it the basis of his life, the modern tourist has an incomparably greater effective space, but may have only a one-room apartment as his dominated space.[135] The dynamics of the Industrial Revolution on one hand and capitalism on the other have forced the state to undertake tasks that were earlier alien to it and that have made it in part like a private business—I refer, for instance, to the postal and telephone systems, energy supply, refuse and sewage disposal, government aid for residential construction, social security and public welfare, the health-care system, and environmental protection.

Alongside the five classical departments (war, foreign policy, internal policy, justice, finance), in the twentieth century an abundance of new ministries emerged, not all of which serve exclusively to provide a living wage for those who work in them, but occasionally perform tasks that are absolutely indispensable. The ministries for economic affairs and social services are key ministries in every modern state, and the research and technology ministry will presumably also become a key ministry. The objects of economic policy can be both the economic system and the concrete economic process. Here distinctions are drawn between policy regarding the system and policy regarding the process. Economic policy in the first sense is indispensable, whereas in the second sense it is frequently useful, and sometimes—because it triggers countermeasures— counterproductive. Among the concrete goals of economic policy, which is closely connected with budgetary and monetary policy, are stability of the economic situation (stability of price levels, full employment, balance of payments—three goals that are, however, not necessarily compatible with each other) and, especially in modern times, economic growth. In addition to production, distribution is also part of state policy, of both economic and social policy. Redistribution measures can result from certain ideals of justice, but also from the necessity of keeping the supporters of one's own power happy by means of positive sanctions. The more numerous and greedy these support-

---

135. (1959), 25f.

ers are, the more comprehensive distribution policy becomes. The greatest advantage of redistributions backed by a policy of growth is that some people can be made richer without necessarily having to make others poorer. An elementary component of caring for basic needs is the maintenance of the state territory and the citizenry, because without the latter the state cannot exist. In many historical situations, this may be a trivial function; however, today it is no longer trivial, but rather requires a special policy regarding the environment and population or the family. Depending on the density of a state's population and the economic and ecological situation, the goal of population policy may be to increase the population, or at least its politically leading part (early examples are the *lex Iulia de maritandis ordinibus* and the *lex Papia Poppaea* under Augustus), or to prevent further population growth. The increase of state tasks can endanger the separation of state and society. Whereas the politics of constitutional law is a form of politics internal to the state, family and economic policy encroach on pre-political subsystems. However, it may certainly be the case that only this state intervention ensures the survival of these subsystems.

The administration of community services is not the only state task that was rejected by extreme liberalism. Much the same goes for the educational and cultural system. One can consider the latter as part of the administration of community services, but the one presupposes that by this is meant only *training* to meet economic needs. *Education of the whole personality* (*Bildung*), on the other hand, can hardly be subsumed under the administration of community services—for it is the medium that creates collective identity, which every corporate group needs if it wants to endure. Thus the state must *represent itself to itself* in order to strengthen citizens' feelings of belonging together, their patriotism; it can hardly do without common symbols such as flags, coats of arms, national anthems, inscriptions on coins, and regular celebrations on national holidays of certain politically important events.

In addition to these external matters, numerous states have tried to produce common beliefs about values, partly in order to give that feeling of unity a deeper validation, partly to overcome contrasts within the state, and partly to serve goals recognized as transcending the state. Thus the manifest function of the public worship of the ancient state may have been to provide for its people's basic needs, but its latent function was to strengthen the citizenry's feeling of belonging to a community of values. Whereas most ancient Greek statesmen pursued religious activities only in the framework of maintaining the status quo, it was basically with the emergence of universal religions that the possibility of using religion as a means of transforming society arose. Aśoka, Constantine the Great, and Charlemagne are paradigmatic examples of this kind of attempt,[136] which sprang partly from a concern to preserve their political empire, and partly from sincere identification with the new religious ideas. Not only religion but also art can be a means

---

136. The first, unsuccessful attempt can probably be attributed to Akhenaton. Aśoka's patronage of Buddhism ultimately failed to achieve its goal.

of the state's self-representation. Thus the *Ara Pacis* (altar of peace) and Virgil's *Aeneid* are expressions of Augustus's program of cultural politics (which in no way necessarily diminishes their aesthetic value). Public buildings certainly do not serve solely to create space for the activities of politicians and government officials; Nietzsche once aptly called architecture "eine Art Macht-Beredsamkeit in Formen" ([1980; 6:118] "a kind of oratory of power in forms"). From the first states in history to modern industrial states, the politics of construction projects has always been a major political issue—Procopius extolled Justinian's buildings as well as his wars. Naturally, celebrating a state's politics through works of historiography (and analogously, the *damnatio memoriae* of political opponents) is one of the most favored options for self-representation—at least so long as the study of history has not yet become a wholly ethically neutral undertaking. Not much foresight is needed to predict that in the future philosophical politics will be a central part of cultural politics. Since every more complex power is dependent on an obedience on the part of its subjects that does not arise solely from fear, every political corporate group has to legitimate its own power, whether in more emotional or more rational ways. However, the state must also try to convince its citizens that the concrete decisions it has made are reasonable, if it wants to produce positive commitment. Public relations— which is always in danger of lapsing into pure propaganda—is a crucial state function, especially but not solely in democracies.

6.1.3.7. Constitution, Legislative, Executive, Judiciary [137]

With what means can the state fulfill the functions outlined above? The goal of state action ought always to be the production of certain conditions, which naturally include the maintenance of its own ability to act; but a perversion of the state, which one can find in both despotic regimes and democracies, is involved when its activity becomes a goal in itself and is no longer directed toward specific tasks. In order to achieve certain conditions, *individual acts* are indispensable. Plato even expressed the view that in the ideal state the rulers ought to rule without laws, which would only prevent them from implementing new ideas in a way suited to the situation; but he conceded that the second-best, realistic solution would include laws. [138] In actuality, individual acts are not sufficient, on grounds of both practicability and justice. A rational being that can construct general concepts demands *general norms.* Power might be able to construct itself out of individual acts alone, but this is not possible for a legally structured power. General norms that include a larger number of cases—ideally, even an unlimited number of cases—are indispensable. Yet not a single structure could consist of general norms alone. Individuality is part of empirical reality, and it cannot be controlled by general norms alone. The distinction between general norms and in-

---

137. This section benefited from many discussions with Prof. Dr. Gottfried Mahrenholz and with Burghard and Waltraut Kreft.

138. *Statesman* 293c ff. and 297e ff.

dividual acts is relative, since between a norm such as "Human dignity is inviolable" and the command to stand at attention, there are many intermediate levels (for instance, general directives); nonetheless, the distinction is essential in order to understand the difference between legislative and executive. Even the concept of the judiciary can be connected with the conceptual pair "general"-"particular" insofar as the judiciary, despite the great differences in the tasks it has to cope with today, usually consists in an express judgment that puts an end to a conflict by determining that an individual case corresponds to a general norm. Here as well the levels of generality differ—laws or administrative acts may be involved that are evaluated in relation to the constitution or to a law; but there is always a difference in generality between the standard by which the evaluation is made and what is evaluated by it.

The most general norms determining state activity are laid down in the *constitution*. "Constitution" has several meanings, but this concept always refers to the core of the state. If one conceives the state as a system of real separation of powers, then a constitution will be the principles in accord with which power is distributed in the corporate group concerned, that is, what is sometimes called a "polity." If one takes as one's basis a juristic conception of the state, the "constitution in the material sense" means the basic norms of public law. Since the eighteenth century, these basic norms have been commonly laid down in writing in one or more individual laws—the constitution in the formal sense, which usually cannot be changed in the same way as normal laws. Ideally, the constitution in the formal and in the material senses ought to coincide, but never do so completely. Every constitutional document grants constitutional status to quite inessential determinations, such as the nature of the flag, for instance; conversely, there are a few basic determinations of public law that are not included, for whatever reason, in the constitutional document, although they are of great importance (consider simple election laws). The constitution in the material and in the formal senses can be disregarded; the priority of mores over laws also holds for constitutional law. The Mexican Constitution of 1824, for instance, resembles that of the United States; the two polities were divided by an abyss. Nonetheless, precisely because of the fundamental importance of the constitution, the theory of the constituent power is one of the most difficult parts of constitutional law. Indeed, it is actually no longer a juristic problem, for jurisprudence is by definition dependent on preceding law, and therefore the concept of the *pouvoir constituant* belongs to political philosophy or political science, but not to constitutional law, because it is the condition of the possibility of the existence of constitutional law. Every constitutional law presupposes a constitution; it can no more say with its means what legitimates the constitution than mathematics can mathematically justify its axioms. It can only note that a people regards a system of norms as its constitution. The fact that the constituent power (the power that creates constitutional law) that has worked out the constitution resulted from a general vote can perhaps provide a moral legitimation for its work, and it can provide a social legitimacy for its results, but it is irrelevant for a juristic doctrine of the constitution. Only if the constitution itself determines under what conditions it goes into effect (as does, for example, Article 144 f. of the German Basic Law) can constitutional law determine whether this condition was fulfilled; however, whether the corresponding determinations are legitimate or not is no longer a juristic problem. The fact that the Federal Republic of Germany's Basic Law declared that it needed to be adopted by only two thirds of the German states in order to go into effect, and thereby assumed that it would also be valid in those in which it was rejected, may deviate from the usual procedure of socially legitimating a constitution. Legally, this is as little a matter for concern as the imposing of a constitution by a monarch, because jurisprudence lacks all criteria for deciding this issue—only the constitution itself makes the relevant criteria available. All constitutional constructions that base the legitimacy of Article 144 of the Bonn Basic Law on, for instance, the supremacy of the occupying powers, seek in vain to move beyond the sphere of law by juristic means. The "legitimacy of a constitution does not mean that a constitution came into existence in accord with earlier valid constitutional laws."[139] In view of the existentially crucial significance of a constitution as the foundation of state power, even a poor constitution is better than none, because without it a state moves in a legal vacuum. After Yeltsin had broken the old Russian constitution in October 1993, there was no alternative but to adopt the new one as soon as possible, and even if there were irregularities in the vote counting, the latter were more easily forgivable than the irresponsibility of those who voted no.

There are two requirements that a modern constitution (in the formal sense) must fulfill. First, it must contain the basic norms concerning the various competencies; second, it must determine the principles that underlie law (private as well as public) and politics. This includes, on one hand, the recognition of basic rights, and on the other the setting of state goals. However, this can be done in such general and vague phrasing that the concrete legal content of the corresponding norms is nearly nil. The delimitation of the competencies of state organs may also be "brief and obscure"—though this might be welcomed only by would-be monocrats. The importance of the constitution increases when its norms are actionable, that is, when there is a constitutional court. It is still more important that every citizen be aware of basic rights as limits on state power. The constitution's shaping of the citizens' legal consciousness is no less significant than its juristic function.

Among the most important norms regulating competencies in the constitution are those that concern its amendment. As a rule, this is more difficult than changing a law—for example, a qualified majority may be required. Does this mean that with a qualified majority any article of the constitution can be repealed? As is well known, that was the dominant view of experts on constitutional law in the Weimar Republic, and thus the Enabling Act passed by a two-thirds majority on 24 March 1933, which allowed Hitler to assume dictatorial powers, was considered a legal abolition of the constitution. It remains one of Carl Schmitt's great achievements to have been a very early opponent of this position, arguing that the organ with sovereignty over the constitution

---

139. Schmitt (1928), 88 (original in italics): "[Die] Legitimität einer Verfassung bedeutet nicht, daß eine Verfassung nach früher geltenden Verfassungsgesetzen zustandegekommen ist."

operates on the basis of the constitution, and is thus a *pouvoir constitué*, not a *pouvoir constituant*, and hence could not repeal the constitution as a whole.[140] Schmitt's conception deviated from contemporary positivistic constitutional law theory; in it persists the archaic conviction of the inalterability of the basic law. Thus Attic law punished the γραφὴ παρανόμων, that is, the proposal of laws that violate the *nomoi* or basic norms. Because of the historical experience of the end of the Weimar Republic, among other things, the Federal Republic of Germany's Basic Law expressly forbids certain changes in the constitution (Article 79 III).[141] But even where the constitution is silent regarding this problem, the logic of constitutional law demands a prohibition on complete self-cancellation. However, there are two objections to an "eternity clause" (*Ewigkeitsklausel*) such as that in the Bonn Basic Law. The more technical of the two is the objection that Article 79 III wrongly includes provisions that it would be better not to have given such a strong guarantee, such as the federal nature of the state, and that this kind of article suggests that everything not specifically spelled out in it may be changed. More fundamental is the complaint that the creators of a constitution ought not to impose their ideas on future generations, or to force them to choose between adherence to these ideas and illegality. We will have to deal with this objection in greater detail in the normative part of the book (chapter 7.3.3.3.2).

Producing general norms is the main task of the *legislative* branch of the state. The legislative function need not be exercised by the assembled people or by a parliament— a priest-king or a council of elders can assume the legislative function. We must distinguish between the forms in which state domination is exercised and the organs entrusted with it, just as we distinguish between social functions and social corporate groups. Locke does not yet attribute the different functions he distinguishes to different state organs;[142] only after Montesquieu demanded that particular functions be exercised by different organs did the confusion of the two occur easily. The difference in modern parliamentary states between a law in the formal and in the material senses has to do with the aforementioned difference. A law in the formal sense must come into being with the participation of the representatives of the people; in contrast, executive orders and charters, too, are also laws in the material sense; indeed, even a few decisions of the German Federal Constitutional Court have the force of law in the Federal Republic of Germany, insofar as they regulate an undetermined multiplicity of cases. However, the greater generality of the laws in the formal sense arises from the fact that in Germany executive orders may be issued only on the basis of an authorization in a formal law. That the

---

140. (1928), 26 f., 102 ff. The political threat to the Weimar Constitution posed by the constitutional view he was opposing was particularly clearly formulated in Schmitt's "Legalität und Legitimität" (1958; 263–345). On this subject, see V. Hösle (1987b).

141. The provision must be understood reflexively, that is, as including itself, if it is not to become meaningless. The Athenian coup d'état of 411 began by abolishing the provision prohibiting γραφὴ παρανόμων: Thucydides VIII 67.

142. Cf. *Second Treatise* chaps. XII and XIV (1690; 364 ff., 374 ff.).

equivalence between parliament and the enactment of general norms is not unlimited becomes clear when we see also the reverse relation: parliaments repeatedly make decisions that are not of a general nature. This is true, of course, for all acts of supervising the administration of the bureaucracy (for example, through ombudspersons employed by the parliament, such as parliamentary commissioners for the armed forces), to the extent that the parliament has the corresponding rights; a few parliaments exercise judicial functions as well, for instance when members of the executive branch are put on trial for high treason. But even laws themselves are not necessarily and always general. Up until the advent of liberalism, classical philosophy of the state assumed as its starting point that laws should regulate an indeterminate number of individual cases for an indeterminate time; and it further assumed that laws were an expression of reason. For example, Aristotle distinguishes between ψηφίσματα, decisions made by the popular assembly, and νόμοι, laws; the latter are supposed to be just, whereas the former are supposed to have come into being through the efforts of demagogues.[143] But with the loss of belief in natural law, the concept of law was separated from the demands of reason, and the procedure involved in drafting the law became crucial. However, Carl Schmitt, for example, insists that generality at least is a necessary component of the concept of law—this extremely formal element, the last relic of natural law, could not be replaced by the procedural element of the way in which the law comes into being. It easy to understand why a procedural concept of the law was propagated in the nineteenth century—a parliament in conflict with the Crown could use it to broaden its own decision-making authority by demanding that all politically important acts have the form of laws, that is, may not occur without the consent of parliament (think only of budget laws, which are in fact one of the most important means of power available to parliaments). But the ultimate consequence of this new determination of the concept of law would be the abolition of the separation of powers, since then the parliament could also render judgments or carry out administrative actions, without thereby leaving the legislative sphere, because everything it did would fall by definition within its purview. "If constitutional law determines who ought to legislate, that obviously does not mean that the legislature ought to use the legislative procedure to decide court cases or to carry out bureaucratic and administrative actions.... A merely formal concept of law—law is what the legislative authorities order in the way of legislative procedures— would make the rule of law into an absolutism of legislative authorities, and eliminate any distinction among legislative, administrative, and judicial functions."[144] Despite the

---

143. *Politics* 1292a6 ff. Νόμοι could be changed only with difficulty, for instance by a special *nomothetes;* ψηφίσματα were not supposed to contradict them.

144. Schmitt (1928), 151: "Wenn durch Verfassungsgesetz bestimmt ist, wer Gesetze geben soll, so bedeutet das offenbar nicht, daß dieser Gesetzgeber das Verfahren der Gesetzgebung benutzen soll, um Prozesse zu entscheiden oder Verwaltungsakte und Regierungshandlungen vorzunehmen.... Ein bloß formeller Gesetzesbegriff: Gesetz ist das, was die gesetzgebenden Stellen im Wege des Gesetzgebungsverfahrens anordnen, würde aus der Herrschaft des Gesetzes einen Absolutismus

great importance of this observation, we must nevertheless maintain that no modern state is conceivable without what in German are called *Maßnahmegesetze,* that is, laws that serve to deal with a specific task and that make available the legal means necessary for doing so. Nonetheless, such laws are also subject to the scrutiny of the constitutional court, if there is one; for instance, they may not violate the principle of equality before the law. This kind of scrutiny eliminates the threat of a new absolutism Schmitt evokes.

The enactment of a law is usually preceded by a long process. In the latter, who has the right to introduce bills and who concretely drafts them is of special political importance. Since this is often the government and the administration, their dependency on the legislative is for this reason alone less than the formal relationship of subordination suggests. On one hand, the parliament itself conducts debates on general political goals (debates that may under some circumstances have great influence on the formation of opinion in the society), and on the other, the true work on specific bills is done in committees. Today, members of parliament and parliamentary committees with a right to make decisions increasingly have to be *advised,* partly by experts in the various areas of state activity (economics, environment, etc.), and partly by jurists. The importance of advisors for all state organs increases on three presuppositions: first, when the information indispensable for a more or less reasonable decision is available only to specialists; second, if rising in the state organs concerned requires particularly time-consuming power struggles that make it no longer possible to train oneself in the field with sufficient thoroughness; and third, if there is rapid turnover in the people holding offices and parliamentary seats.

Since the state sets norms in order to exercise an influence on reality, the function with which it intervenes directly in social reality is its true center—that is, the *executive,* which one can subdivide into administration and bureaucracy (whereby the corresponding state organs are also sometimes meant). This holds in any case for the archaic state. General norms are distilled from concrete commands only through a long process; the office of king and commander-in-chief of the military forces precedes that of the legislator and judge. Laws are not constantly enacted, legal judgments are not constantly rendered, "but administration . . . must always be exercised. Without it the state could not exist for a minute. Despots without law and judges are at least conceivable, but a state without an administration would be anarchy."[145] There may be, as in Switzerland, part-time, unpaid parliaments; judgments may be handed down only on certain days when the court is in session. But were the executive to go on leave without arranging for a stand-in, that would be the end of the state. Even in modern constitutional states with the priority of law and constitutional requirement of a specific enactment of laws, it is one-sided, and almost false, when the state organs entrusted with executive power are

---

der Gesetzgebungsstellen machen und jede Unterscheidung von Gesetzgebung, Verwaltung und Justiz beseitigen."

145. G. Jellinek (1922), 612.

assigned only the task of carrying out the laws, for they also enact general norms.[146] Thus many material decisions are made in the form of administrative acts, and the importance of the principle of discretion in administrative law indicates how much of the performance of executive state organs depends on their own guidelines. These organs are most strongly bound to the legislative in so-called "conditional programs," which under certain conditions prescribe a specific action for them. However, a general norm can hardly comprehend completely reality's wealth of detail. For that reason, in the application of the law even subordinate departments almost always retain a certain scope of discretion: their activity is not completely bound, either. The administration's activity is largely free, even though not to the same extent as the legislature's.[147] But it could probably be said that executive organs more than any other are entrusted with the execution of general norms, even if this is not their sole task.[148] Because of its special closeness to reality, political men strive more for posts in the administration than in the legislature or especially in the judiciary, and for the people, "politicians" include especially members of the administration and the next candidates for such positions. However, it is a disturbing sign of politically dangerous conceptual confusion when the administration is confused with the state, which it can at most represent, but with which it can never be identified.

So far as the relationship between administration and bureaucracy goes, despite the legal dependency of the latter on the former, it is clear that bureaucracy has essentially more power than the analysis of the legal relationship suggests. Just as the administration does not merely carry out laws, so the bureaucracy does not merely follow the administration's orders. First of all, it is closer to things. It is only the bureaucracy that implements the administration's orders, and no matter how much manifest violations of the law on the part of the bureaucracy may be punished by the administration, battling slackness or even obstruction remains difficult.[149] Second, the development of a modern bureaucracy is accompanied by an advantage over the administration in knowledge and experience, which, in a technologized world determined by legal categories, it acquires through the continuity of its work. In dealing with a bureaucrat trained in the work peculiar to his office, a member of the administration constantly finds himself "in the position of a dilettante confronting an expert." Every bureaucracy seeks to increase this superiority of the professional insider still further by *keeping secret* its knowledge and intentions.[150] Third, the more the bureaucracy's tasks increase—for example, with the development toward the welfare state—the more unthinkable becomes a change in even a considerable part of the bureaucracy when the administration changes. In a phase of

---

146. Cf. R. Herzog (1971), 330 ff.

147. I refer here to G. Jellinek's distinction between free and bound activities (1922; 616 ff.).

148. However, they are not the only organs with executive tasks that can also be carried out by courts—consider non-contentious litigation.

149. Cf. Mill (1972), 166, 247. See also 232.

150. Weber (1980), 572. Cf. especially 551–579: "Essence, Presuppositions, and Development of Bureaucratic Domination."

limited state functions Andrew Jackson could still introduce the "spoils system," according to which most public offices were filled with new appointees when a new president came in; but what was conceived as a service to democracy necessarily degenerated into an increase in the power of corrupt party machines, and with the increase in government functions a bureaucratic "civil service" became inevitable (the "Pendleton Act" of 1883). Fourth, since the outlook for the further exercise of power is a decisive power factor, precisely in a democracy with a regular change in administrations, the bureaucratic apparatus that persists through that change inevitably acquires a significant power advantage. What constitutes the crown's greatest advantage in the classical monarchist conception— namely that it remains, whereas administrations pass away—is true in the modern, democratic state for the bureaucracy. However, it goes without saying that in the modern state as well, every new administration must attempt to gain influence over the bureaucracy. The German institution of the political official (*politischer Beamter*) is such an attempt to increase a department head's control over his department, for political officials can be appointed without their having completed the usual career and can be dismissed without any special justification. However, such exceptional regulations contradict the concept of the public official; therefore the British system, in which the government consists of significantly more than the members of the cabinet and includes all the leadership positions in the ministries that may be refilled in case of a change of government, is more reasonable.

We have already seen that the *judicial*, as compared to the legislative, is the more original state function, and that the legislative ultimately developed out of the judicial and the executive. Only from decisions made in particular cases could general norms emerge. Nonetheless, even the oldest judges in history exercised a function that was more judicial than executive—or legislative, insofar as law as based on precedents—in that they saw themselves as making their decisions on the basis of a standard of superpositive justice, not posited by themselves, but pre-existing them. With the development of an independent legislative branch the judicial branch diminishes in importance, even if it retained the task of creating new law. The weight of its judgments depends on their not being overturned at the first opportunity; only an invariable practice in the dispensation of justice can guarantee the certainty of the law. The power of the law is strengthened when there are several levels of appeal, for in this way human failure can be more easily avoided. Because it is bound to predetermined standards, on one hand, and because of its weaker relationship to existing reality, on the other, the judiciary has less real power than the legislative and the executive; no doubt for that reason among others Montesquieu writes that it is "en quelque façon, nulle" ("in a way, null").[151] However, its decisions are the last and therefore the final; moreover, precisely because of its greater distance from political power struggles and their neutrality, it can acquire significant authority. The latter is grounded in the personal and material independence of the judges

---

151. *Esprit des lois* 9.6 (1748; 1:298).

(i.e., their independence both with regard to their personal situation and with regard to their interpretation of the law), which in the modern constitutional state is the flip-side of their being bound by the law. Certainly influence may play a role in the appointment of judges, an influence that is usually extensively exerted by the appointing institutions in the case of appointments to the highest courts; but once appointed, a person remains in his position until his death, retirement, or the end of a non-renewable term of office, and thus cannot be removed or transferred. Judges must also be guaranteed a set salary. Because it basically, though not in every individual case, endangers the independence of the office of judge, it is a matter for concern when high judges develop ambitions with regard to other state offices, whereas it shows a deep sense for the relationship among the three classical powers that a former United States president, W. H. Taft, could become Chief Justice of the Supreme Court, but it is inconceivable, that a Chief Justice could become president of the United States. Moreover, partly because of the possibility of disguise, and partly because of the possibility of intellectual development, the judges appointed may surprise us—for instance, Earl Warren was appointed Chief Justice as a conservative, but then unexpectedly supported basic rights. If the form of power primarily at the disposal of the executive is the system of negative sanctions, and if modern parliaments, through their right to decide on the budget, have control over the means of positive sanctions, the authority already associated with the office, which in some cases may be increased through individual personality, is the form of power peculiar to the judiciary. For this reason the latter may easily seem the weakest in comparison with the two others.[152] However, as we have seen in chapter 5.1.2.2.5.2, in certain situations weakness can become a power factor; and thus the authority of the judiciary can make itself particularly noticeable in times of crisis—think of Italy in the 1990s. When the other state powers mutually cripple each other, it can, even if always only temporarily, become the decisive third element.

Moreover, against Montesquieu's dictum it must be objected that it was valid at most for his own time, when the judiciary had jurisdiction only over civil and criminal matters, and thus essentially regulated relationships among citizens. In contrast, jurisdiction over administrative and constitutional issues are "more political" forms of the judiciary because they also subject the two other powers to their scrutiny. Because of the

---

152. Hamilton rightly observes that "Whoever attentively considers the different departments of power must perceive, that in a government in which they are separated from each other, the judiciary, from the nature of its functions, will always be the least dangerous to the political rights of the constitution; because it will be least in a capacity to annoy or injure them. The executive not only dispenses the honors, but holds the sword of the community. The legislature not only commands the purse, but prescribes the rules by which the duties and rights of every citizen are to be regulated. The judiciary on the contrary has no influence over either the sword or the purse, no direction either of the strength or the wealth of the society, and can take no active resolution whatever. It may truly be said to have neither Force nor Will, but merely judgment; and must ultimately depend upon the aid of the executive arm even for the efficacy of its judgments . . . the judiciary is beyond comparison the weakest of the three departments of power" (1982; 393 f.).

priority of law, in the modern constitutional state the executive is also bound by the law, and since the full concept of the law includes its institutional guarantee, one can see in the possibility of going to court against administrative acts the absolute apex of the development toward the constitutional state. Whether this possibility exists in regular courts or in special administrative, financial, and social insurance courts, as in Germany, is secondary. No less important is constitutional courts' scrutiny of legislation. The right of scrutiny was first claimed by the Supreme Court of the United States, without an explicit basis in the constitution,[153] under Chief Justice John Marshall in 1803, in *Marbury vs. Madison.* Since in this exceptionally momentous decision brilliant legal innovation, re-evaluation of the political power of the Supreme Court, and cratic ingenuity are combined in the most marvelous way, let us examine this case briefly here.

Marshall was appointed Chief Justice by John Adams shortly before the end of the latter's term of office, because Marshall shared his "federalist" views. In order to extend his influence over the next term of office, Adams named, after his defeat at the polls, a few justices of the peace as well. As a result of an error, however, the latter did not receive their commissions of appointment in time, and the new president, Thomas Jefferson, refused to have the commissions delivered to these persons appointed by his predecessor. A few of those who were denied office went to the Supreme Court on the basis of the Judiciary Act passed by Congress, which gave the Supreme Court the right to issue writs of mandamus, and thus put Marshall in a very difficult situation. For the new administration made it clear that it would ignore a verdict in favor of the plaintiffs, and would thus damage the prestige of the new court. On the other hand, a rejection of the plaintiff's suit would also have been interpreted as a sign of weakness. What should be done? Marshall denied the request—arguing that the court lacked jurisdiction because the relevant provision of the Judiciary Act was unconstitutional. Since in so doing Marshall rejected the suit against the Secretary of State, on one hand, and on the other censured the Judiciary Act for attributing a jurisdiction to the Supreme Court broader than the constitution allowed, he seemed to be bowing to the two other powers; but behind this partial accommodation was concealed one of the greatest extensions of power in the history of the judiciary, namely the claim to judicial review of laws.

Whereas in the United States the Supreme Court is primarily the highest ordinary court, many current constitutional states have special constitutional courts. The goal of constitutional jurisdiction is on one hand to protect the individual, and on the other to delimit the competencies of the various state organs, which is particularly important in a federal state. However, constitutional jurisdiction presupposes first of all a written

---

153. However, the question was discussed in the *Federalist Papers.* The clearest argument is Hamilton's plea, in the previously cited *Federalist* 78, for court scrutiny of the laws to determine their constitutionality, and precisely on the basis of his argument regarding the weakness of the judicial branch (1982; 394 ff.). Already in 1610, in "Bonham's Case," England's Chief Justice Edward Coke had already declared an act of parliament null and void. On the judicial branch in the United States, see H. Wasser (1984), 194 ff., from whom I take the following information.

constitution, and second the priority of constitutional norms over ordinary laws. Even an extremely democratic ideology is not unqualifiedly compatible with a constitutional judicature—in a direct democracy, for instance, should even the results of referenda be subject to being declared unconstitutional by a constitutional court? Significantly, in the United States the decision concerns the individual case; an abstract judicial review does not occur there, as it does in Germany. Because of the connection with precedents, the laws concerned become inapplicable in the future as well, but they are not formally repealed; the German procedure, in contrast, represents de facto a disapproval of the parliament and the federal president who signed the law.

No matter how much subjective rights remain mere wishes unless there is a guarantee of the possibility of recourse to legal action to ensure that they are respected, and no matter how much the constitutional state must necessarily always be a state in which such recourse to legal action is possible, it is nonetheless lamentable when the judiciary becomes the dominant state power. Because of its connection with the *lex lata*, the judiciary is by definition a conservative power,[154] and radical social change can as a rule be initiated only by the legislative and the executive, which alone can alter law and society. If courts with jurisdiction in constitutional matters balk at necessary adaptations of the law (as, for example, from 1890 to 1932 the Supreme Court resisted the slow development of the welfare state), they endanger their authority. Nonetheless, it has to be conceded that the Supreme Court has on a whole exercised judicial restraint, for example by refusing to hear cases involving hard-to-define political questions. This happened as a result of the correct political instinct that a rejection of majority decisions will be accepted only in exceptional cases, but such cases can also be very important in order to protect the individual from suffering from the tyranny of the majority. However, in a dead-end situation, the courts may provide the solution for a political problem, but this is always a sign of the poverty of the other two powers. For instance, the increasing tendency in Germany to hand over unsolved political problems to the Federal Constitutional Court is an alarming sign of the inability of the parliament and the government to produce a comprehensive social consensus. Moreover, it is obvious that the decisions of a constitutional court are often more than interpretations in the strict sense of the term, that is, they are not limited to determining the *mens auctoris* of the authors of the constitution. The law-making element is always particularly large in the constitutional jurisdiction, and can be more than mere arbitrariness only if in addition to the rationality peculiar to hermeneutics and constitutional law the principles of ethical rationality are also taken into account.

It is sometimes maintained that *representing* the unity of the state not only in international relations, but also in internal matters is one of the state's peculiar functions. In actuality, this function must be distinguished from the three previously mentioned ones, but it can be assumed by the organ entrusted with administration. Thus most political

---

154. Cf. H. J. Morgenthau and K. W. Thompson (1985), 463 ff.

systems in the past, as well as many in the present, have only one state organ, which is simultaneously the head of state and the head of the administration. In parliamentary
democracies and monarchies, however, a special state organ is commonly entrusted with
this function, namely the head of state without any executive power, who is ironically
called the "state notary." The actual powerlessness of the highest representative can invite ridicule, especially if the office is misused as a way of getting failed politicians out
of the way. But the moral authority of the person holding this office can be considerable,
and he can do a great deal to promote the social consensus vital for politics in a democracy. One must not underestimate the function of the symbolic in spiritual structures.[155]
A distance from power struggles can lend the merely representative head of state, like the
judiciary, a credibility that can be a decisive political asset in times of crisis. One of the
causes of the breakdown of the Italian parties—though not the sole or primary one—
was Cossiga's awkward and constitutionally questionable behavior (which was nonetheless interpreted as an expression of sincere despair) in denying the legitimacy of the
political elites—behavior that was justifiable in the situation at the time, although it remains true that the head of state's normal task is to represent the unity of the state, not
its conflicts. No other state organ has such an exclusive and at the same time intensive
symbolic meaning that points beyond the being of the individual as the state notary.
When, as in hereditary monarchies, a person's future function is already determined at
birth, this kind of purely symbolic existence can be accompanied by considerable torment, particularly under the conditions of the modern public sphere. One day, Albrecht,
the nominal head of state in Mann's "Royal Highness," compares himself with a small
pensioner who has gone mad. "Every child knows him and shouts 'Hi!' when he sees him;
he is called 'the Hatter,' for he is not quite all there; his surname he has lost long ago. He
is always on the spot when there is anything going on, although his half-wittedness keeps
him from playing any serious part in anything. . . . Twice a day, about the time when a
train starts, he goes to the station, taps the wheels, examines the luggage, and fusses
about. Then when the guard blows his whistle, 'the Hatter' waves to the engine-driver,
and the train starts. But 'the Hatter' deludes himself into thinking that his waving sends
the train off. That's like me."[156] On the other hand, his brother Klaus Heinrich is prepared
to take over his representational duties, because he enjoys his popularity and remains
convinced of the indispensability of symbolic representation, which Albrecht ultimately
renounces out of love for humanity. "Human Highness is a pitiable thing, and I'm convinced that mankind ought to see that everyone behaves like a man, and a good man, to
his neighbor and does not humiliate him or cause him shame. A man must have a thick
skin to be able to carry off all the flummery of Highness without any feeling of shame.
I am naturally rather sensitive, I cannot cope with the absurdity of my situation. Every
lackey who plants himself at the door, and expects me to pass him without noticing,

---

155. Cf. Ortega y Gasset (1930), 40.
156. Thomas Mann (1982; 105). Trans. C. Curtis, 132.

without heeding him more than the door posts fills me with embarrassment, that's the way I feel towards the people. . . . "[157] However, Klaus Heinrich seems to sense that the man who puts on the mask of a lackey as the head of state impassively walks past him ultimately enjoys this role-playing himself, because he thereby participates in a being that transcends his own particular, private existence. Albrecht loves human beings as they ought to be, Klaus Heinrich loves them as they are.

6.1.3.8. The Forms of the State

Every state has a state power, state organs, a citizenry, and usually a stable state territory, and it fulfills certain functions; yet the differences among particular states are considerable. The size of the state territory and of its population are not very relevant for moral judgment, but how its power is organized is. Already in antiquity we find the classification of the forms of the state into monarchy, oligarchy, and democracy, depending on the number of those participating in domination: whether one, a few, or all. However, this classification is misleading for several reasons.[158] First of all, today very different structures are lumped together under the rubric of monarchy; their common dominator is only a non-deposable head of state. This head of state can come into his office by hereditary succession or by election, and thus there are hereditary and elective monarchies respectively. However, between an absolute (elective) monarchy such as the Vatican City and a parliamentary (hereditary) monarchy such as Great Britain, there are more basic differences than between a parliamentary monarchy and a republic, for both these can be called "democracies." Instead, what is decisive is whether the *organ with the competence of defining competencies* (if there is a single organ of this kind) is composed monocratically or collegially.

In the following we shall speak of "monocracies"; they include only absolute monarchies, not parliamentary or constitutional monarchies with the estates taking part in ruling. Even if such an organ is set up only temporarily, we are still dealing with a monocracy insofar as it can prolong its own term of office if it deems this advisable. The Roman dictator in the old republic was not a monocrat, since his maximum term of office was six months, and could terminate even earlier, if he completed the task assigned to him; for example, Cincinnatus resigned his office as dictator after his victory over the Aequi, only sixteen days after he was appointed to it. This type of dictatorship, which Carl Schmitt called "commissarial" (*kommissarisch*) is objectively very different from the "sovereign" dictatorship in which the dictator himself can decide the extent of his competence.[159] However, it is clear that most sovereign dictators initially

---

157. Ibid., 107.

158. Cf. Hegel's criticism: *Rechtsphilosophie* § 273, note (1969 ff.; 7:436 ff.).

159. This important differentiation is found long before Schmitt in Machiavelli, *Discorsi* I 34 (1984; 134 ff.).

recommend themselves as commissarial—the Enabling Act passed on 23 March 1933 by the German Reichstag was initially valid for only four years, and gave power not to Hitler personally but to the national government as a whole, leaving the rights of the president of Germany untouched. But on the basis of this act Hitler was able to put people he trusted in the crucial power positions in the state, to combine the office of president with that of chancellor after Hindenburg's death, and ultimately simply to extend the Enabling Act himself. Similarly, the communist dictatorships presented themselves as merely temporary, that is, until the emergence of the classless society, and even if this was not exactly a short-term historical goal, the sovereign dictatorship was nonetheless disguised as commissarial.

The monocrat has the greatest power when he can determine his own successor. Because of the legitimist ideology, that was almost never the case in medieval and modern European monarchies (only Peter the Great arrogated this right, but not long afterward Paul I issued regulations regarding succession to the throne). On the other hand, a few Roman emperors[160] selected their successors by adoption, and Hadrian even stipulated, in the same law by which he adopted Antoninus, whom the latter should adopt, and thus exercised a posthumous power almost unparalleled in history (and at the same time disempowered his successor). Otherwise, the Roman principate had no clear, unambivalent regulations concerning succession, and this was a source of countless problems.

Only if a monocrat has won his position of power by himself—for instance, through a revolution, a putsch, or a coup d'état, which may have been legitimated by plebiscite after the fact—should he be called an "autocrat," and not when his monocratic position has been conferred on him by the constitution. According to this terminology, Napoleon was an autocrat, but Commodus was not—a determination that does not, of course, say anything about the quality of their conduct in office.[161] On the other hand, Hitler can be called an autocrat, because in seizing power he carried out a legal revolution. The concept of a legal revolution may seem paradoxical, but it makes sense on the basis of what was said earlier about the constitution. Whereas "coup d'état" and "putsch" imply a personal but not a structural change in power through a violation of the constitution (in the case of a coup d'état, state organs take part in this violation), "revolution" refers to radical political changes, and "revolution in the emphatic sense" refers to revolutions that are also accompanied by profound social transformations (which are seldom made through legal reforms alone). Such changes usually result from a violation of the constitution, but can also come about by legal means in the case of

---

160. However, these were not monocrats in the strict sense of the term during the principate because of the very limited, but nonetheless continuing power of the Senate. T. Mommsen, exaggerating somewhat, famously called the principate constitution a "dyarchy."

161. The concept of autocracy used here coincides with that of the *tyrannis ex defectu tituli*, which is to be distinguished from the *tyrannis quoad exercitium*.

constitutions that provide no limits to constitutional amendment.[162] (The fact that the Nazi seizure of power was accompanied by such changes, that it was a revolution in the emphatic sense—perhaps even the only one in modern German history—can be denied only by someone who assumes that a revolution is by definition something positive.) For the power-holder, legal revolutions have the advantage of guaranteeing that he has—at least when a certain *Volksgeist* holds sway—the loyalty of the bureaucracy, on which he is dependent in a modern welfare state. Since he was not able to win them over, Kapp (a reactionary politician who led a putsch against the Weimar Republic in 1920) was doomed to fail. The current meaning of the word "monarchy" shows how much concept-formation, at least in everyday language, is guided by the appearance of historical continuity and mere names. Because in Great Britain, unlike France, there has continuously been someone bearing the title of "king" or "queen" since 1660, the form of the state in 1670 and that in 1990 are designated by the same term, even though in the interim the function of this office has been radically altered.

Second, the distinction between oligarchy and democracy is awkward insofar as all the democracies known to us are in some sense oligarchies. It has never been the case that "everyone" ruled, that is, participated in the administration, for instance. This fact, which Gaetano Mosca, Vilfredo Pareto, and Robert Michels elaborated with especial clarity, is unchallengeable; functional elites, at least, are indispensable in any complex society. In every group there are a few people who occupy leadership positions, at least for a certain time, and the larger the group, the more inevitable this is, because spontaneous coordination is no longer possible and not everyone can communicate with every other individual. These leadership positions may, but need not necessarily, be formally recognized.[163] The more indispensable a leader or boss is for the achievement of a group's goals—for instance, because of his organizational abilities—the more permanent is his position, even if he must be periodically re-elected. Neither are the rights of enfranchised citizens, the political rights, granted to everyone in any state. Athenian democracy, for example, guaranteed such rights only to a minority of the population. Men without property and especially women won the right to vote very late in history, and children

---

162. Enabling acts are a useful lever for such legal revolutions. Even before Hitler and Pilsudski (on 23 and 24 March), Dollfuss had (on 4 March 1933) dismissed the Nationalrat (the Austrian national parliament) on the basis of the wartime economy Enabling Act of 1917, which had been carried over into the Constitution of 1920—the same law on the basis of which Seyss-Inquart was able to implement the Anschluss law of 1938 and was thereby able to achieve what Dollfuss had tried to prevent at the cost of his own life. Since empowering the executive to issue executive orders can hardly be avoided, clearly determining the content, goal, and extent of such powers is the most important means for preventing such developments.

163. H. D. Lasswell and A. Kaplan distinguish in this regard between "leaders" and "bosses" (1969; 152 ff.) Pilsudski was a classical "boss." From 1928 to 1935 he exercised the real power in Poland, even though he was now only minister of war and general inspector of the armed forces (and in 1930 prime minister again for some months), whereas the president, who had the most extensive rights, especially after 1933, was a politically inexperienced chemistry professor who was Pilsudski's willing tool.

still do not have it. And even where an (almost) universal right to vote exists, it does not concern all state functions. Even the most elementary separation of powers would be incompatible with absolute democracy, for setting up different organs leads to a differentiation of decision-making authorities, and this means that the same group of people—even if it were "all"—cannot be the decision maker. Indeed, even if everyone actually participated in all political decisions (which is hard to imagine, and not only in the case of large states, because for one thing there are probably people everywhere who are not interested in politics), the outvoted minority would be dominated by the majority, and the majority would be organized by a tiny minority. It is entirely legitimate for political science to seek to discover whether certain groups do not have a better chance of building a majority, and certain people a better chance of leading it, for it is not the case that in every democracy all citizens belong alternately to the minority and the majority. A certain homogeneity of the population or a multiplicity of opportunities to form coalitions is most likely to lead to this kind of alternation of those who are dominant and those who are dominated, and thus usually to a greater kindness in dealing with each other, whereas a division of the population into two unequal groups establishes the dominance of the larger, if the state form in question is determined by the principle of majority rule. In that case, the dominance of the majority can be particularly ruthless, because under certain conditions it can exercise a real power of which many monocrats can only dream, their constitutional omnipotence often being strictly limited by political pressures.[164] The most dreadful monocracies are for the most part those that can at the same time count on the support of the majority of the population.

Nonetheless, the distinction between democracy and oligarchy makes sense. Thus one can distinguish between non-monocratic systems in which all or most adults participate in a few important political decisions, and those in which only a small group has any political rights, and term only the latter "oligarchies in the strict sense." The Republic of Venice is a good example of such a political system. In oligarchies recruitment takes place either on the basis of rules of heredity—in which case one can speak of oligarchies of birth—or on the basis of co-optation, whether the latter is limited to a particular class determined by birth or also brings in people from outside—in which case one can speak of open elites. Sometimes a quite advanced age is a condition for joining the oligarchy, as the names of institutions such as the gerousia or senate already indicate. Moreover, there can be a plurality of immediate state organs; however, it may also be that the oligarchs are all united in a single collegial organ with sovereignty over the constitution. If the number of those with political rights is quite large in absolute terms—as it is, for instance, in class oligarchies—voting will play a role in forming the government, which consists of a committee of the oligarchs. Autocratic oligarchic governments are also conceivable: consider a military junta that comes to power through a putsch, and which under certain circumstances complements itself through co-optation. On the

---

164. Cf. B. de Jouvenel, "La démocratie totalitaire" (1945), 379–415, esp. 383.

other hand, military dictators and military juntas, who legitimate themselves by means of plebiscites (something the Venetian aristocracy never even dreamed of doing), recognize a minimal element of democracy, which nonetheless remains merely apparent if there is no real alternative and the voting is, for instance, neither free nor secret. Because of the party organs' control of the state organs and the real decision-making authority of the politburo and general secretariat, most communist one-party states are or were, despite their soviet-democratic rhetorics, open oligarchies, which easily became monocracies if the general secretary could de facto no longer be dismissed. Not at all rarely, monocratic state forms have turned out to be intermediate between oligarchies supported by birth-elites and more democratic structures. The ancient tyrannies, and in a more limited form early modern absolutism and plebiscitarian Bonapartism as well, are examples of this, for in the eyes of a monocrat, all his subjects are equal.[165]

A democracy in the full sense of the term exists only when the first and basic appointing organ consists of the enfranchised citizens themselves, and nearly all citizens are enfranchised, when it is possible in reality for representatives of all groups in the society to rise to positions of domination, and especially when there is a universal right to be a candidate for elected office—after a certain age. (This does not mean, of course, that every character type has the same chance for political success.) In particular, the legislative, as the basic state power, needs democratic legitimation. At a minimum, either a large part[166] of the legislative function is exercised directly by the people, at least optionally, and the people has initiative rights, or the legislative power is completely delegated to representatives of the people who are elected by the people for a legislative session that is limited in time. The modes of voting in this case can be very different. In a democracy in the full sense, suffrage is universal (for adults), equal, free, secret, and direct; property qualifications, as well as systems in which voters are divided into different classes or plural vote systems, are incompatible with the first two requirements. However, plurality and majority vote systems in which individuals are elected at the local level, proportional representation in which the voter chooses among party lists at the national level, as well as mixed voting systems, are compatible with the previously mentioned requirements. The way electoral districts are drawn up in a plurality or majority vote system can have a significant influence on the outcome of the vote. It goes without saying that in a representative democracy the voter has many fewer opportunities to differentiate than in a direct democracy, at least so long as the representatives have no mandate. In proportional representation and in constituencies with multiple representatives, the list system with the right to cumulative vote and the right to mix candidates from several party lists represents a certain expansion of the room for decision making. On the other hand, we cannot speak of opportunities for differentiation if only a single party is permitted. However, the election of the head of state, the head of

---

165. Cf. Mill (1972), 221f.

166. Pure, direct democracies like Attic democracy no longer exist today; even in Switzerland, and even in Appenzell there is a parliament.

government, or judges by direct popular vote is not usually considered a necessary element of democracy in the full sense. Residues of the power of old oligarchies of birth, and also a basic choice of mechanisms of the separation of powers can lead to a system in which the parliament is divided into two chambers; the powers of the chamber not immediately legitimated by the people of the state as a whole may be different, and sometimes only advisory in nature. The second chamber can represent the nobility, as in Great Britain until 1999, where it was, however, largely deprived of power in 1911; in a federal state (and analogously in a unitary state such as France or Italy as well), it can be a chamber representing states or regions;[167] it may, as in Bavaria or Ireland, be structured in accord with the ideas of corporativism; and it may also include citizens who have distinguished and proven themselves by their special expertise.

Even if no absolute democracy exists, there can nonetheless be more or less democracy, and the degree of democratization can be measured in relation to different parameters. The (relative) number of equal participants in decision making, the number of the decisions to be made democratically, and the opportunities for differentiation in voting (for instance, the possibility of run-offs) are probably the most important. A greater degree of democratization by one parameter implies neither logically nor really a corresponding increase by another. Therefore the question of whether Switzerland before 1971 or the German Federal Republic was the more democratic country remains unanswerable, at least so long as the various parameters have not been weighted. Because of the people's direct participation in legislation, Switzerland was the more democratic country, but because of the lack of female suffrage at the federal level it was the less democratic country. Because of the normative evaluation of the word "democracy" at the present time, there is a tendency to consider structures of the separation of powers as characteristic of the concept of democracy. Thus in using the phrase "democracy in the full sense" I have referred to a political system with a separation of powers. But one could just as well say that the democratic principle in its pure form is not compatible with a separation of powers, and that anyone who argues for the separation of powers is *correcting* the basic democratic idea,[168] using arguments that may be good or bad, but in any case cannot be described as "democratic." That is an absolutely plausible terminological determination. Thus there is no objection to be made to seeing in radical Rousseauistic democracy the true democracy—so far as there is agreement regarding the far more important fact that this state form must be rejected—among other reasons, because dreadful abuses of power are possible in it.[169]

---

167. The members of this kind of second chamber can be elected directly by the people of the regions, by electoral colleges, or by independent regional parliaments, or they may consist of members of the state administrations.

168. Cf. Montesquieu's warning against confusing "le pouvoir du peuple," the power of the people, with "la liberté du peuple," the freedom of the people (*Esprit des lois* 2.2 [1748; 1:292]).

169. A good criticism of the ideologicization of the word "democracy" is found in G. Sartori (1992).

As I have already said, the chief of the executive branch in a democracy need not be elected by the people, but may be elected by the parliament (or appointed by the head of state, who has to consider who has the majority in parliament). On the other hand, we can no longer speak of democracy if, as in constitutional monarchies, the government depends neither on the people nor on the parliament. When a president with executive powers is elected by direct vote of the people, we refer to a presidential democracy; when the head of government is elected by the parliament, we refer to a parliamentary democracy. There is also a presidential democracy if the president, as in some federal states, is elected not directly but indirectly—through an electoral college, in some cases with mandates, and if, as in the United States, in case an absolute majority is not achieved, there is no run-off election by the people, but it is rather the parliament that decides. Between presidential and parliamentary democracy is the system currently used in France and in Portugal, in which there is a directly elected head of state with significant competencies (for instance, he is the commander in chief of the armed forces) as well as a government that is appointed by the head of state and is at the same time dependent on the confidence of the parliament. The center of power in such a system will lie more with the head of state, who enjoys the greater authority because he is directly elected. Having a mere state notary elected by the people does not make much sense. Nonetheless, the merely representative president also often has rights whose importance should not be underestimated, such as that of dissolving the parliament under certain conditions. On one hand, direct election by the people indicates an increase in democratic elements, but on the other it also indicates an increase in the monocratic power of the elected official with regard to the more oligarchic system of parliamentary democracy. An official elected directly by the people can usually be removed from office only by the people, if at all,[170] whereas the parliament can normally replace a head of government it has elected.[171] (In Great Britain, a head of government can nonetheless— even if he has lost the confidence of parliament—dissolve the parliament by appealing to the Crown, and thus appeal directly to the people.) But even in a presidential democracy with separation of powers the head of state remains dependent upon the cooperation of parliament, as is clear when the time comes to pass the budget bill, if not before. But the dependencies differ in nature in the two systems. The president can appeal directly to the people and undertake national leadership tasks without this guaranteeing his party's allegiance; the parliamentary head of government must remain in close con-

---

170. The impeachment process in the United States may be set in motion only if the president is suspected of having violated the law, and is thus to be sharply distinguished from a vote of no confidence with regard to his policies, even if the impeachment of Andrew Johnson was motivated more politically than legally.

171. An exception is Switzerland, where the government has no responsibility to parliament, even though it is elected by the parliament. This is explained on one hand by the direct-democratic structure of Switzerland, within which the parliament plays a limited role, and on the other by the idea of cooperative or consociational democracy (*Konkordanzdemokratie*), according to which all the major parties participate in the government.

tact with his party inside and outside the parliament.[172] In parliamentary democracy, the real relationships of dependency between members of parliament and the head of government are twofold. The head of government is not necessarily everywhere the leader of the majority party of the lower house, as in Great Britain, but he will seek to gain influence over the work of the parliament if he wants to remain in power—in Germany, for instance, by being the party leader; a chancellor who does not hold this office is significantly weaker. But he can retain his influence only if he does not move too far away from what his supporters in parliament want.

In some parliamentary democracies the government is entirely oriented toward the head of government, in others it is more collegially structured. Thus, as in Germany, the premier can have the authority to determine the general policy guidelines for the individual members of the cabinet, although the latter are responsible for their own portfolios, for in the German ministerial system the individual minister, not the government as a whole, is the highest administrative authority. But the whole cabinet may also have a collegial responsibility for governmental policy as a whole, in which case the head of government plays only the role of a *primus inter pares,* as in the Swiss departmental system, for example. The prime minister was also a mere *primus inter pares* according to the Prussian Constitution of 1850, but precisely this example shows that the personality of the person holding the office is even more important than the—often vague—rule in constitutional law. Bismarck gave the Prussian government a monocratic character more than did many a chancellor with extensive authority to determine the general policy, and it is possible that had Adenauer ended his political career as president of the Federal Republic of Germany, even without any change in the written constitution, the president, and no longer the chancellor, would have determined German policy. By becoming his own defense minister, Churchill succeeded in taking full control over the conduct of the war without any change in the constitution or the laws.[173]

Third, it should be pointed out that the degree of the state's penetration of the society has nothing to do with the aforementioned tripartite division. A monocracy can largely refrain from infringing on the private sphere of individuals, while a democracy in the full sense can interfere in every detail, and even disregard basic rights—this may not be likely, but it is not incompatible with the definition. The type of state that leaves the society as much alone as possible, should be called "liberal,"[174] whereas one that cancels the distinction between state and society is called "totalitarian." The latter requires

---

172. Cf. K. N. Waltz (1979), 85: "The typical Prime Minister is a weak national leader but an expert party manager." See especially 83 ff. on the differences between the United States and Great Britain.

173. Cf. Churchill (1948 ff.), 3:13: "In calling myself, with the King's approval, Minister of Defence I had made no legal or constitutional change. I had been careful not to define my rights and duties."

174. This presupposes that the state has at its disposal the (socio-)technological possibility thoroughly to dominate society, but deliberately refrains from doing so. One would not want to call a weak feudal state "liberal."

the instrument of a party as the decisive interface between state and society. A totalitarian state presupposes, in addition to the rulers' obsession with power, certain technological achievements and the will to recreate social reality as they like, and thus cannot have existed before the Industrial Revolution. Small steps in the direction of totalitarianism are found in the absolutist police states of the eighteenth century; Rousseau provided the basic building blocks for the totalitarian ideology on which the Jacobins relied. But truly totalitarian states did not appear until the twentieth century, even though they could not completely disassociate themselves from the mores of their people, which had to support their power.[175] When the ruler arbitrarily interferes in the private sphere of the citizens, but only on certain occasions, this should be called "despotic." Ivan the Terrible was a despot in this sense, not a totalitarian ruler. We can speak of "paternalism" when rulers are sincerely convinced that their interference is in the interests of those over whom subjectively they rule. Since power is not based solely on negative sanctions, a liberal state can be much more powerful than a despotic one if it can count on the few things that it demands being willingly and well done. If the protection of basic rights is not to be merely at the monocrat's pleasure, but instead guaranteed, then the monocrat cannot change the basic rights as he wishes; and that means that he must not have control over the competence of defining competencies. However, then he is no longer a monocrat. Liberalism in the full sense of the word is therefore not compatible with a monocracy. But neither is it compatible with a state form that assigns absolute power to the people or to the parliament. Liberalism's central demand is that freedom be protected through the *separation of powers,* which usually means that the offices separated must not be exercised by the same person. The separation of powers finds its clearest expression in judicial scrutiny of the executive and legislative, but can also be complemented by federal state elements. If this requirement is fulfilled, liberalism can get along well with a hereditary monarch as head of state, whereas the latter is usually incompatible with a totalitarian system. During the fascist period in Italy, the monarchy and the church were not up dealing with the situation, but they did prevent Mussolini from acquiring power as extensive as that Hitler acquired in Germany.[176]

An interesting question is how the modern welfare state is to be situated in the spectrum on which extreme liberalism and totalitarianism are the extremes. On one hand, it seems to lie in the middle, for the welfare state intervenes in society more than does the liberal state. However, it can also be argued that only the welfare state guarantees basic rights—depending on how one defines "basic rights" and "guarantees." But then one could even say that the welfare state is the true liberal state—just as it also can

---

175. Cf. Montesquieu (1734), 178: "Il y a, dans chaque nation, un esprit général sur lequel la puissance même est fondée. Quand elle choque cet esprit, elle se choque elle-même, et elle s'arrête nécessairement." ("In every nation there is a general way of thinking on which power itself is based. When power collides with that way of thinking, it collides with itself, and necessarily ceases.")

176. Even an oligarchic liberalism is conceivable. Montesquieu has rightly been called an "aristocratic liberal."

be seen as the real condition of the possibility of modern democracies, which presuppose a certain standard of education, and thus a right to certain positive benefits, in order to be able to function well.[177]

The mechanisms of the separation of powers are more complex than monocratic or purely democratic political structures. In order for a state to flourish on the basis of these mechanisms, various conditions must be met. First of all, the competencies of the different organs must be clearly distinguished from one another. In the worst-case scenario, obscurities in the constitution regarding this question can lead to civil war, particularly if no authoritative interpreter of the constitution is recognized by the quarreling parties. In few questions is legal precision so important as in this one, as conflicts between parliament and the crown in constitutional monarchies prove. Second, the construction of the constitution must be such that state organs are prevented as much as possible from crippling each other. This is far from guaranteed by a clear delimitation, which can lead to a stalemate. Since the parliament and the government are mutually interdependent, a great deal of acumen should be invested in resolving the problem of how stable parliamentary governments are possible. In order to achieve this, measures such as electoral thresholds, which within certain limits conflict with liberal and democratic principles, with freedom and equality, are not too high a price to pay. But third, all institutional acumen is in vain if the people are not prepared to compromise and cooperate also with political opponents. Livy (40.45 f.) describes very vividly how two bitter enemies were elected to the office of censor, and how, in a splendid speech after this election, a respected senator urged them to forget their old enmity in the interest of the common good. The two men were finally able to shake hands. To be sure, in this case it was not a matter of the relationship between two different state organs, but collegiality can also be interpreted as a mechanism of the separation of power (in the broader sense). In addition, these mechanisms include the prohibition or limitation of re-election and the strategies that serve to weaken the political power-holders socially. In pre-modern states, eunuchs, celibates, foreigners, or slaves could without great fear be entrusted with positions of power, since they did not have the entourage of relatives that in traditional cultures is always a decisive power factor.[178] In modern states, an analogous strategy of the separation of powers consists in entrusting key positions to people who have weak characters or lack many of the connections necessary for political activity. The necessity of the separation of powers was understood early in human history, even if no people before the Romans developed a system of the separation of powers as complex as that of the Roman republic (which can be described rather as an open oligarchy with weak democratic elements).

---

177. A. Touraine analyzes (1994; 37 ff.) three dimensions of modern democracy—separation of powers, general citizenship, and the social "representativeness" of those in power, which he sees as being realized mainly in the British, United States, and French democracies, respectively.

178. Cf. E. Gellner's concept of "gelding" (1983; 15).

Fourth, in classifying state forms we should consider, in addition to the constitutional question, the political-science question of who exercises the real power in the state. The dependency of the state on social forces must not be neglected in answering this question, because the state must be rooted in the society in order to exercise power over it. Furthermore, a state's free activity cannot be determined by law, but rather only by other, pre-state factors. Which foreign policy a monocracy or a democracy pursues, and which laws they will enact, results not from the state form as such, but rather from the economic, military, and religious interests and values of the monocrat or the democratic elites (which may be located also outside the parliament, for instance in the bureaucracy or in the political parties) as well as from those of the supporters of their power. Thus a monocrat can be convinced that he has to account for all his acts before the highest judge, or he can be an adherent to the religion of power—his behavior will be correspondingly different. Moreover, a certain economic class can hold the state firmly in its grip; or a religious leader can exercise such an influence that the state president and the head of government are well advised to follow his recommendations, even if the competencies of such a "spiritual leader of the nation," as in Iran, are only partly laid down in the constitution. In a democracy in the full sense, the trend of public opinion is a political element of the first importance, and those who can influence it exercise a significant power. The properties that qualify someone for leading positions in a state mark its politics in subtle ways. Correspondingly, democracies can be distinguished depending on whether voters elect the best candidates or demagogues as their representatives. If the former is the case, we can speak of an "aristocratic democracy," for the concept of aristocracy in no way presupposes, at least by its etymology, a birth-elite. If mediocre individuals have the best chances of rising to power, I will refer to "mediocratic democracy."

6.1.3.9. State and Society

We have now touched upon the difficult question of the relationship between social and state forces. First of all, it is obvious that there is a mutual relationship between the two, for two reasons. On one hand, political decision makers are human beings who participate in the other functions of the society; therefore we must assume that their experiences in the various subsystems of the society, the interests and values they have as a result of their belonging to a certain gender, a certain class, a certain religion, will influence their decisions. Conversely, experiences in politics in a mobile society can also play a role in determining which profession one pursues on leaving office, or to which religion one converts. On the other hand, the state also shapes society through the law, that is, for instance, it shapes the way families are structured and how the economy is managed (and even more how wars are waged). Conversely, precisely because of this legally based power of the state over society, social actors will seek to exercise influence on the state. This will be all the more likely the more the state intervenes in society.

Thus the modern welfare state has perhaps increased state power over society, but certainly in it society's efforts to influence the state have become more numerous. In democracies and oligarchies, this influence may consist in the constitutional act of voting; but even in democracies, and in any case in all other state forms, it is not limited to such constitutional acts. Because of the state monopoly on force in modern states, recourse to negative sanctions is less common in modernity; but because violations of law can occur, the possibility of the assassination of politicians, coups d'etat, putsches, and even the outbreak of civil war can never be excluded, no matter how unlikely it may be in certain situations. On the other hand, forms of power based on positive sanctions and on opinion are constantly used in order to influence the state; this necessarily means exerting influence on current or potential office-holders and seeking the most direct possible access to them. Those who can offer stronger positive sanctions—that is, the classes that have greater economic power—thus have, *ceteris paribus,* more political influence than the poorer classes, if individual office-holders or a large part of the electorate is interested in positive sanctions or even needs them. In many states there are laws prohibiting social forces from offering positive sanctions, but these laws are often not enforced, and a great deal of ingenuity is expended in getting around them. Moreover, the state is frequently dependent on loans, and even where it can tax as it sees fit, it has to take a special interest in persons with a greater economic ability. In certain situations, however, the power of those who can convince, persuade, or manipulate (these abilities often correlating with a certain economic status) may be greater.

One's own influence can be increased if one allies oneself with others; interest groups that are formed for purely social reasons generally also seek to gain political influence. In corporative systems, interest groups can dispatch delegates to a distinct state organ—a chamber. In party democracies, on the other hand, the parties, whose status and tasks are not even mentioned in many constitutions, are the point of articulation between state and society. They are distinguished from interest groups in that they explicitly seek to take over state offices and nominate candidates for elections. The greater the electorate, the less can the candidates personally introduce themselves to all the voters; their general political orientation is what counts, and their membership in a political party offers an important indication of this orientation. In contrast to political parties that overtly seek to satisfy particular interests, the so-called mass-based parties claim to represent all the interests of the society. The distinctions among such parties have more to do with the principles of justice that are assumed with regard to the mediation of various interests. In a federal state, for example, divergences may emerge in connection with the precise definition of the competencies of the federal government and the member states; similarly, the identity of a party may be shaped by the determination of the relationship between church and state, between preservation and change, and between the individual and state power. But every party will offer a political package that has to be accepted or rejected as a whole. In order to reduce the expense associated with the acquisition of political information for the average citizen, all parties pursue a strategy of information reduction that limits a party platform to slogans and faces—campaign posters graphically illustrate this tendency. Naturally, abstract principles can also be a pretext for pursuing particular interests of a collective or even a purely individual kind—for instance, the wish to take over political offices; parties are sometimes mere electoral clubs. The more general the platform, the more heterogeneous a party can be (especially if, as in the United States, the parties are open, that is, party membership is not formally defined). Battles among the various interest groups within a party can be more vehement than those between the different parties, even though prudence suggests that these battles not be fought in public, since voters seldom appreciate them.

From what has been said, it follows that the Marxist theory that the state represents the interests of the propertied class cannot be correct in this general form. Thus the relationships between classes and the state are different depending on the form of the state. Oligarchies have existed in which only the members of the propertied class enjoyed political rights, and for these the Marxist theory is generally true, even if a paternalist concern for the interests of the classes without political rights has certainly occurred, and indeed out of the most diverse motives. Moreover, it must be stressed that the wealth of the propertied classes often had a military base. Because of its greater military power, a group of people created economic and political privileges for itself. A religious basis for the power of oligarchies is also conceivable, as we see in hierocracies. In general, people can define their primary interests more on the basis of their gender or their military or religious position than on that of their economic status. In modernity, however, class identity often takes precedence over other identities (except for national identity), because relationships within the same class are more easily shaped symmetrically. Friendships between rich and poor are, if there is no longer a paternalistic worldview, more difficult than between people of the same economic level. It is obvious that some areas of politics are more open to the influence of certain social interests than to that of others. Thus in determining security policy the military and the arms industry have more influence than the banks, which for their part will seek to influence monetary policy, or than women's groups, which will try to have their say in matters concerning women. So far as modern democracies are concerned, the poorer classes obviously can achieve political power on the basis of the principle of majority rule, if only they are able to organize themselves, as the history of social democracy shows. If they do not then proceed to expropriate the wealth of the richer classes, that is partly because there are constitutional obstacles to doing so, and partly because they recognize that it would not be in their own interests even in the middle term, and perhaps would not be just, either—and this conviction could be interpreted as a product of the power of the propertied classes only if it were first refuted by rational arguments.

Classes can become political actors only if they are conscious of themselves and distinguish themselves from others, that is, if they cease to be classes in themselves and become classes for themselves, but especially if they are able to organize themselves. This necessarily involves the construction of elites. To that extent, the class theory of the state and the elite theory of the state are not mutually incompatible, even if they put the emphasis on different things. Classes capable of action need elites, and elites need the backing of groups that are often, but not necessarily, held together by class interests. Even if the previous head of an employer's association or of a labor union becomes a head of government, he will never be able fully to impose the respective group's interests— the point of a system with separation of powers is precisely to prevent this from happening (and even in a monocratic system the bureaucracy is always able to obstruct). The pluralist theory of the state has thus defended the view that in a modern, democratic-liberal state all the interests of the society are represented. In this connection we must first emphasize that it is not (competitive or majoritarian) democracy as such that guarantees this, since the principle of majority rule is clearly compatible with the repression of the interests of minorities. In general, it is almost impossible for the state, as a unit making decisions and able to act, to satisfy all interests, for a decision implies the choice of one alternative to the disadvantage of others. But the state's decision can represent a compromise between various interests, and a significant contribution to this is made by the mechanisms of the separation of powers and even more by a consociational democracy.

The stronger the institutional guarantees promoting compromise, the more immobile the policy of a state can become—to the point that it completely loses its autonomy with respect to the society. An alternative to immobility is the zigzagging state policy that occurs when slight majorities, which are constitutionally sufficient to conduct a policy, succeed each other in rapid succession. In such situations it may even seem that there is no longer any state, but only a multiplicity of state organs fighting with each other, each organ sometimes falling apart into a group of people mutually obstructing each other.[179] Even in normal situations one has to concede that the bureaucracy of a state is significantly less monolithic than Weber, for example, still believed. Thus the officials in the German *Bundeswirtschaftministerium* (Federal Ministry of Economics) are seldom in tune with those in the federal or even the state ministries of the environment; the shaping of foreign policy is influenced by military men, diplomats, and other officials. Like the Marxist theory, the pluralist and especially the "cock-up" theory tends to challenge the autonomy of the state. On the other hand, first of all we should remember that the political system remains a legal unity. If, after ever so many internal conflicts, the responsible organ arrives at a decision, for instance when it has declared a war, then the whole state acts accordingly; even a personal change in that organ changes nothing with regard to international obligations that have been incurred. Second, the political has its own logic, which cannot be reduced to that of social subsystems. In no area is this more clear than in foreign policy. The self-preservation of the political system often makes it necessary to take steps that sharply deviate from the society's short-term interests. This does

---

179. M. Mann speaks of a "cock-up theory" of the state in addition to class, pluralist, and elitist theories (1986 ff.; 2:44 ff.); the latter is further subdivided.

not hold solely for objective external pressures. The state is always basically in danger of falling apart internally, and this can be exactly what happens if an uncontrolled multiplicity of particular interests collide without there being any possibility of integrating them. A hot civil war, or even a cold civil war of mutual distrust, or even the decay of statehood are definitely to be avoided, because, among other reasons, such conditions frequently precede monocracies. This task guarantees the political a partial autonomy with regard to society. However, fear of an internal or external enemy can also be stirred up merely with the goal of covering up internal tensions.

How far the inertia of constitutional institutions or the political elites' will to shape policy influences the fulfillment of objective political demands depends on the structure of the constitution as well as on the personalities of the individuals in office. The former may prescribe more bound activities or leave room for more free activities, while the latter may or may not make use of the room to maneuver afforded them. In addition, the historical situation plays a role. Montesquieu is probably right in suggesting that when societies are born, the leading individuals shape the institutions, and afterward the institutions shape the leading individuals: "Dans la naissance des sociétés, ce sont les chefs des républiques qui font l'institution, et c'est ensuite l'institution qui forme les chefs des républiques."[180] A greater sense for the autonomy of the political is to be expected among those officials who devote themselves for an extended period to the service of the state. Whereas parliamentarians are generally likely to remain bound to their social role, the members of the administration, and especially of the bureaucracy, may consider themselves as constituting a class of their own. For the emergence of the modern state it was important for jurists to develop, with the support of monarchs (in France, for instance, through the development of the *noblesse de robe* or nobility of officials), their own class consciousness, which isolated them from the interests of the classes from which they originally came. This, along with the existence of a legal method peculiar to them, enabled them to be more impartial in dealing with conflicts among the other classes.

The category of integration has been used particularly by R. Smend to understand the state's mode of operation.[181] In fact, it is obvious that despite all the different interests and conflicts, at least with law the state makes available a common structure on the basis of which interests should be reconciled. If this basis is no longer accepted by a significant part of the population, the state ceases to exist. However, the state cannot merely preserve the law; it must also adapt it to changed conditions and pursue its policy in the realm of free activity. Since the status quo is always favored by the fact that one has gotten used to it and that it is precisely determined, resistance to change is usually significant, particularly since there is always a multiplicity of possible changes. Certainly there are, especially in modernity, a large number of people who want change for change's sake, but because of the desire for conflict associated with this attitude, this does not mean

---

180. Montesquieu (1734), 26.

181. See (1928), 136 ff. See, however, H. Heller's criticism of R. Smend (1934; 300), which should be accepted.

that they can agree about which direction the change should take. On this point a certain consensus is necessary with regard to basic values and basic theoretical assumptions; *public opinion* is a special form of this consensus. The concept of public opinion is misleading insofar as such a consensus is always only partial. Thus from a methodological-individualistic standpoint it has been rightly emphasized that in the public sphere, there are only individual opinions, whose intersection may be larger or smaller, and is often empty. The public sphere is a sphere which—like parties, but not organized as a corporate group—mediates between society and state. The public sphere transcends the private dimension, but is not a state organ. A public sphere can emerge on only two conditions. First, politics must be communicated to society. The public sphere of parliamentary negotiations, for instance, is important for this purpose, since not only the law, but also crucial reflections regarding a further development of the law, as well as the persons representing them, are made known to all interested persons. Second, the society must be concerned with political questions. Public parliamentary debates still do not lead to a public sphere if no one from the society is listening to them. If there is complete indifference to the state, which is experienced as a foreign power, there is no public sphere. Democracy favors the emergence of a public sphere and is promoted by it, for how are people to participate in political decisions if they are not informed? And how are politically informed people to be satisfied for long with being excluded from decision making? The functions of public opinion are to legitimate policies and to refuse to legitimate them, and thus also to scrutinize and control them. However, it cannot be denied that *arcana imperii* remain even in the democratic state—partly for security reasons, and partly out of respect for the human dignity that politicians have as well.

Public opinion is only *one* type of consensus that supports a state. The concept of public opinion includes not only its public nature, but also opinion; the latter is what we call the kind of conviction that considers itself fallible. In a hierocracy in which the ruled willingly accept their situation completely because they believe their rulers participate in divine wisdom, there is certainly a consensus (though unfounded), but no public opinion, because alternatives are not discussed or even considered. F. Tönnies defined "states (of matter) of opinion" as the extent to which one "is in agreement with oneself."[182] However, the word "opinion" usually suggests a liquid or gaseous state. To be sure, there can also be solid, well-founded opinions, but then they are no longer really *mere* opinions. In any case, one must acknowledge that in public opinion, alongside reasonable principles of practical and theoretical reason, the most absurd notions circulate.[183] Thus in public opinion is almost always lived out the wish, born from ressentiment, to prove oneself superior, at least in the sphere of opinion, to those who exercise actual power. The malice that accompanies jokes about the power-holders and the discovery of scandals is a classic mechanism of compensation. Because opinions are

---

182. See (1922), 23 ff., 137 ff.

183. On this, cf. the so far unsurpassed observations in Hegel's *Rechtsphilosophie* §§ 315 ff. (1969 ff.; 7:482 ff.).

amorphous and at the same time have great potential political weight, they are exposed to a large degree to manipulation, and indeed all the more so the more complex the political reality is with which public opinion has to cope. State and societal forces exercise a great influence on it, even when they do so only as if they were reflecting it (for instance, in the evaluation of opinion polls). Precisely because one is not sure of one's own opinion, one tends to be guided by what is considered public opinion, which is sometimes no more than the opinion of a loud minority seeking to compensate, through mere loquacity, for the lack of concrete experiences and substantial insights. In modern democracies, the opinion-shapers who are most successful are those who reach the largest audience and are able to move them especially deeply, and that is always only a small minority of the population.[184] The political importance of changes in the media that influence public opinion can hardly be overestimated; so far as mastery over them is based on special economic conditions, it is permissible to speak of an interconnection of the power of opinion and economic power. However, holding a majority of the shares in a television company does not make one telegenic, and this property can be decisive for a political career in a telecracy. Nonetheless, manipulation, if it is perceived as such, can become counterproductive, and the power of the manipulator of public opinion can collapse as suddenly as a house of cards. But a group can also succeed in achieving cultural hegemony in a society, for example, by making public laughingstocks of those who do not share certain new assumptions, or by hushing up their views.[185]

6.2. On the History of the State

The variety of forms social institutions and states have taken over time and space is astonishing, and invites respect for the richness of being and human imagination. On one hand, humanity is not realized solely in numerous individuals, but rather in a multiplicity of peoples and cultures that often differ sharply from one another, and with which individuals identify much more strongly than with humanity in general. On the other hand, cultures change in ways that are often fundamental, not all of them in the same direction; and even where the change is in the same direction, it will not be with the same rapidity, hence cultures that are contemporaneous with each other nonetheless often live in different times. It is not easy to say where one culture stops and the next begins—one can speak of a Bavarian, a German, or a Western European culture, depending on the level at which one seeks commonalties. When there are relatively few commonalties, for example when there are different languages, one can speak of a "culture area"

---

184. Cf. H. Heller (1934), 282, and generally the outstanding observations on p. 276 ff.

185. In the 1970s, the Italian left succeeded in gaining cultural hegemony, among other reasons, because the entrepreneurs offered no intellectual resistance to them and organized no counteroffensive in the educational system. The result is that today it is not easy to find an Italian intellectual who can correctly formulate the arguments in favor of a market economy.

(*Kulturkreis*) such as the East Asian or the Western European culture area. In view of the great importance of religion for every society, the world religions are *one* meaningful criterion of classification for culture areas. However, it must be kept in mind that the religious penetration of a society can be superficial. A tribal mentality will not be immediately overcome by Christianization, and therefore the differences between Spain and a black African country with a majority of Catholics are enormous; it would be misleading to assign them to the same culture area. In any case, without a precise definition of "culture," the question of how many cultures there are is meaningless. Drawing boundaries between cultures depends in large part on the members of the cultures themselves; the perception of completely different cultures can contribute to relatively more similar cultures gradually feeling themselves to be one—and the feeling of belonging together promotes further alignment with each other.

At present, the multiplicity of cultures seems to be decreasing in the same way as that of biological species (even if this process is partly balanced by the emergence of numerous subcultures). Why? Obviously the strategy of political self-assertion represented by the modern state is evolutionarily stable, but this does not exclude the possibility that it could be self-destructive. It is surely false to say that all cultures have an inner developmental tendency toward the modern state; we will see later that many peoples have even successfully fought against the transition to statehood in general. But ever since the organizational form of the modern state has existed, those states that are not able to make this form their own have hardly any chance in the event of a conflict with states who have succeeded in doing so. To that extent one can say that, as in biological evolution, the accidents of variation are limited by the necessity of selection. In the following I will attempt a short sketch of the history of the emergence of the modern state and its triumph, but first I want to discuss very briefly a few basic issues in the philosophy of history.

6.2.1. Basic Problems of the Philosophy of History

Discussions of the roles of accident and necessity in history are frequently unsatisfying, insofar as the concepts are seldom precisely defined; think of Tolstoy's remarks on this subject in *War and Peace*. Thus there are different conceptions of what "necessity" means. We can consider necessary what follows from a given system of natural laws and certain antecedent conditions; then all events are necessary in a deterministic universe. Or we can consider necessary the facts whose negation is not compatible with known natural laws, or those whose negation is logically contradictory. In addition to these classical concepts of necessity—the deterministic, the physicalistic, and the logical—the following *transcendental* concept of necessity is surely also meaningful: Necessary is whatever is a condition of the possibility of proposing a theory with a claim to validity (regarding any given object, for instance, regarding the concept of necessity). On the basis of this latter concept of necessity, we can say that only those worlds are possible in which at some point in evolution rational beings emerge and organize themselves in such a way that they can use arguments in dealing with each other. Indeed, since, as we have seen in chapter 3.4.1, there is much to be said for the view that *ought* helps determine what *is*, we can also say that the realization of central *morally obligatory* institutions, such as the constitutional state founded on the rule of law, is necessary in the world. (If one defends the freedom of the will, one will have to say that the world is necessarily so structured that free decisions for the constitutional state can be successful.) Obviously, the transcendentally and morally possible worlds are a proper subset of the logically possible worlds, but it is circular reasoning to deny, on the basis of formal logical concepts of modalities, the legitimacy of the transcendental and moral variants, and to view as erroneous the search for a necessity that goes beyond formal logical necessity, and yet does not relate merely hypothetically to valid natural laws or factual antecedent conditions. Kant's, Fichte's, and Hegel's philosophies of history presuppose partly the transcendental concept of necessity, and partly the moral concept of necessity; their contribution was to have combined the Enlightenment's interest in the philosophies of history with the insights of transcendental philosophy. However, none of these philosophers of history claims that there must have been a single path to the constitutional state; to that extent, according to them there is no (more than hypothetical) sufficient reason for all the particulars of historical development. For Leibniz, on the other hand, there is a sufficient reason for the selection of the one real world out of all the logically possible ones—the consideration of the simplest possible system of natural laws and the realization of the greatest possible plenitude of values. In his view, an a priori philosophy of history would have to ask itself how, given the structure of human nature, rational autonomy (that is, philosophy, science, and institutions that correspond to the principles of universalist ethics) could be realized in the simplest possible way. However, even in a Leibnizian universe with its thoroughgoing ontological determinism, because of the finitude of human reason there would be room for an epistemic indeterminism, so that even on this presupposition, future development would for us remain open and accidental *in this sense.*

Moreover, even someone who rejects the transcendental idea will have to concede that on the basis of the system of natural laws and perhaps even of logical laws, certain entities have a tendency to establish themselves, *if* they have once emerged—I refer once again to the concept of evolutionary stability. *That* they emerge may be physically accidental, i.e., not necessary, and it may depend on antecedent conditions that are just as accidental; but the dependency of one event on another does not mean that the former could have happened *only* in this way. The fact that the genesis of the modern constitutional state is based on the interconnection of a whole series of events that seem improbable when considered in isolation, does not logically exclude the possibility that had not this particular accident come about, others might have occurred that would have led to the same result. The fact that George I did not speak English contributed to the British royal house's declining involvement in governmental policy, but the madness of George III could have led to it as well. Indeed, at a certain stage in the development of

British society, because of human nature it was inevitable that Parliament would display political desires and seize any favorable opportunity to increase its power; and although this stage of development may itself have been dependent on accidents, it still has greater significance for later history than the dying out of the House of Stuart and its connections with the House of Hanover. Not all the different factors that lead to an event are equally significant; and people sometimes call "accidental" those on which it ultimately does not depend, because it found another triggering event, and which alone would never have caused anything essential. Thus, to remain with the same example, had the time for that development not come, George I would probably have learned English or provided himself with a translator for meetings of the cabinet. Similarly, the importance of battles, which are commonly seen as the paradigm of accidental events in the course of history, is for the most part overestimated. On one hand, victories and defeats in battle often result from superior political organization, and are thus less accidental than they might at seem at first glance; on the other hand, a victory in battle does not necessarily mean much. Hannibal's victory at Cannae or that of the Mongols at Liegnitz did not suffice to win domination over Italy or Europe. However, it is not always easy to distinguish unimportant triggering events from the true causes. For instance, Ernest Gellner writes (1981; 7) with brilliant sarcasm that had the Arabs been victorious at Tours and Poitiers and conquered Europe, we would all now admire the great Islamic sociologist Ibn Weber, who would have proved beyond a doubt that the modern process of rationalization could have been initiated only through a northern European Islamic sect of the sixteenth century. Gellner may be right, but there is still something to be said for the view that belief in the incarnation of God was decisive for European development. Should that be so, then one can naturally interpret this result in two ways—on one hand, to the effect that the genesis of the modern world depended on extremely improbable events that could not have been replaced by others, and on the other that if the creation of the modern constitutional state is one of the moral duties whose fulfillability is a limiting condition for being, then Christianity, as the shortest path to this goal, given human nature, was a historical necessity. Hegel seems to have thought so, and therefore attributed to Christianity a necessity that sharply deviates from the latter's conception of its role in salvation history, but nevertheless represents an important way of providing a secularizing "salvation" of precisely this conception.

Since the number of social events is incalculable, every reasonable historiography must choose among them. The criteria for selection are guided by the goal that the historiography serves. First of all, as a result of the importance of history for the constitution of individual and collective identities, attention is commonly focused on the stages on the way to what one currently is. In this perspective, historiography serves self-reconstruction. If it is a question of the self-reconstruction of the reason of the philosopher of history, we can speak of a transcendental self-reconstruction in history. However, if the selves involved are different, the histories will turn out to be different. For example, even if in the ideal case two good historical works on Germany in the nineteenth century contain no contradictory descriptive assertions, insofar as they are written by a German and a Frenchman, for instance, they will show different evaluations, and if they seek to be value-neutral, they will always differ in that one of them refers to events that the other neglects. Thus a French audience will be more interested in the details of the relationship between Germany and France than in matters internal to German intellectual history, which for German readers constitute part of their own value system. What is important to one of them may seem inessential to the other. However, the concept of importance should not be related solely to contemporary interests. Second, for that reason, historiography can also concentrate on events that were not consequential for anyone living today, but had crucial consequences for people who lived at the time. The decline of a culture whose endowment of life with meaning is now forever lost is for us today primarily a matter of indifference—but for those involved it certainly was not. Histories written from the viewpoint of the defeated are desirable on moral grounds, because ignoring the defeated may easily reflect consent to their fate. In opposition to a triumphalist historiography and philosophy of history, it is necessary to mention the annihilation of those who are no longer able to write histories.[186] Third, this may suggest which important values lost through this kind of decline a chance to more comprehensively determine social being. For the ideal value of a social value naturally does not depend on whether it established itself historically, and for the constitution of one's own identity it may be important to go back to alternatives to what one has been up to now, but no longer wants to be. Fourth, an event that has neither made history, nor in its own time was felt to be important, nor serves as a model today, may seem noteworthy in later times because it clarifies in an exemplary way certain basic structures of man and the social world. In this perspective, historiography becomes a science auxiliary to the social sciences.

The historical examples introduced up to this point served primarily the fourth goal. In contrast, the following extremely brief discussion seeks better to understand the present situation. Therefore its chief subject will be the main stages that have led to this situation. Here I am concerned with the *political* situation; changes in the other spheres of human society will be mentioned only insofar as they have political consequences, such as, for instance, technological or religious revolutions. Since the diverse social subsystems mutually influence each other, it is false to reduce history to changes in a single subsystem, such as the economic. An *internal* history of political philosophy that follows the logic of the development of political ideas was laid out in the first chapter, and will not be repeated; here, I am concerned essentially with the *external* development of real institutions, with the most important innovations and the mechanisms that have led to them. Changes take place partly *because of conscious processes of goal-*

---

186. Having done this is the contribution made by W. Benjamin's powerfully eloquent essay "Über den Begriff der Geschichte." Cf. also—in opposition to Hegel's attempt at a theodicy through philosophy of history—Burckhardt (1905), 36 f., 164; Jonas (1988), 52 f.; and G. Huber (1995), 333 ff.

setting that are occasionally influenced by ideas drawn from political philosophy.[187] For the most part, however, history develops as a natural process; that is, as in biological evolution, results repeatedly occur that were not willed or foreseen by any finite mind. The Marxist philosophy of history awakened the hope that the later evolution of humanity might erase this blindness, but it cannot be understood how this is supposed to happen so long as human beings have differing intentions and their struggle, in which no one ultimately gains the upper hand, is the motor of history. Since it is impossible and also not interesting to write the history of each individual person, societies and their cultures or their political organization into states are generally taken as the substrate of history. On one hand, this is useful; on the other, however, many changes take place across the boundaries of societies and especially their subsystems. This holds particularly for religious movements, which do not stop at state borders, and also to a lesser degree for changes in economic processes.

As we saw in chapter 4.3.2, Mann coined the term "interstitial emergence," thereby referring to the fact that in the intermediate space between the numerous already existing networks of social interaction, new networks are constantly being constructed, or at least the old ones are being extended.[188] Especially in this type of development, individuals play a major role. To be sure, institutions have their own dynamics, and certainly the greatest genius must fail if he grows up in an environment inimical to him—this deep truth is the point of Robert Schneider's important novel *Schlafes Bruder* (*Brother of Sleep*). But again and again, history also includes the process of transcending the existing institutions. For example, we have already seen that charisma can be a form of power that equals organized access to positive and negative sanctions. However, there are structural grounds that explain why in certain periods great individuals have special opportunities to do things. Above all, if institutions no longer correspond to the moral expectations of a culture, they necessarily lose power, and people begin to seek alternatives to the existing institutions. Figures such as Alexander, Caesar, Napoleon, Hitler, and Stalin are conceivable only in periods of historical crisis, after great political and social upheavals; in the sixth century AD, the second century BC, or the early eighteenth century, analogous figures would have had to be content with a lesser position of power in their cultures, or they would have been destroyed.

---

187. It goes without saying that if interactionism is rejected, one cannot speak of such an influence in the literal sense of the term; everyday language must be interpreted as an abbreviated form of a more complex solution of the mind-body problem.

188. The passage cited in chap. 4, n. 137 continues as follows: "Human beings do not create unitary societies but a diversity of intersecting networks of social interaction. The most important of these networks form relatively stably around the four power sources in any given social space. But underneath, human beings are tunneling ahead to achieve their goals, forming new networks, extending old ones, and emerging most clearly into our view with rival configurations of one or more of the principal power networks" (1986 ff.; 1:16).

I just mentioned historical crises. In actuality, in the course of the history one can distinguish periods according to how quickly and in what direction changes proceed. Changes take place in all societies—even in plant societies. Metabolism, reproduction, and death are processes that proceed from the temporality of the organic; in human beings they are also accompanied by the ontogenetic evolution of the capacity for thought, of emotions, and of identity-formation. Thus the ontogenetic change connected with puberty often leads in the direction of social changes. In generational conflict Plato already discerned (in the eighth and ninth books of the *Republic*) an important motor of history. Nonetheless, it can also prove possible to integrate the younger generation into the existing institutions, which thus gain considerably in stability. Historical change is then reduced essentially to the normal processes of individual aging and the replacement of one generation by the next. Even if a despot is assassinated by someone who as a result becomes his successor, this is far from meaning that a change in institutions has taken place. The successor may be the same kind of despot who will meet the same end. On the other hand, there are times in which institutions are changing, but slowly and imperceptibly; in such cases, one can speak of evolution. Usually this term implies a cumulative development, but oscillations around a state of equilibrium are also conceivable. In contrast, in times of crisis an unusual acceleration of the normal changes occurs, whose consequence is quite often the breakdown of state power, which can no longer control social changes, resulting in civil war or anarchy. Such crises can raise humanity to a higher level; however, the ultimate consequence of a great crisis can also be the destruction of a culture or its relapse into a condition surmounted centuries earlier. In each case, in the course of a crisis abrupt changes that would otherwise take centuries occur in a few years. This results from the fact that the general explosion of violence leads to privileges being rapidly abandoned that would otherwise be defended tooth and nail. Not all cultures are equally open to change of this kind: Lévi-Strauss's famous distinction between cold and hot cultures rightly points to the fact that the hunger for historical change varies greatly in different cultures. No culture is hotter than modern culture.

Crises in a society can be exogenously determined by changes in the natural environment such as ecological catastrophes or by interventions on the part of other states, especially through great wars. More interesting, because more complex, are endogenously caused crises.[189] Scientific and technological revolutions may be followed by massive social changes: the Neolithic[190] and Industrial Revolutions fundamentally altered human societies.[191] But intelligent political institutions are able to deal with change of

---

189. For the distinction between endogenous and exogenous decline, the *locus classicus* is Polybius VI 57. Naturally, the two kinds of crises overlap as well.

190. I always use the concept "Neolithic" in the economic, not in the archaeological sense.

191. C. Lévi-Strauss correctly compares the two revolutions in their importance for a cumulative historical evolution: "Deux fois dans son histoire . . . l'humanité a su accumuler une multiplicité d'inventions orientées dans le même sens" (1961; 63). ("Two times in its history . . . humanity has been able to accumulate a multiplicity of discoveries oriented in the same direction.")

this kind. Doing so becomes more difficult when a revolution in mores is involved, that is, when the basic values that support a society become questionable. Just as Kuhn transferred the concept of revolution from political history to the history of science, it can also be applied to the history of moral consciousness, and phases of normal moral development can be distinguished from those in which a paradigm change takes place. In such phases not only are individual actions morally evaluated in a different way, but even the principles on the basis of which this evaluation has been made are open to discussion. Kuhn's concept of the paradigm supposes an absolute discontinuity and incommensurability, and therefore ultimately the abandonment of the concept of a unified reason, but this is not intended in my borrowing of this concept—nothing can escape the standard of reason. However, the people involved in this kind of historical situation may have the impression that they are no longer speaking the same language and in principle can no longer understand each other. Presumably many a pagan Roman patrician felt that way when confronted by the moral revolution of Christianity.[192] After the triumph of Christianity, however, its representatives found themselves in the situation of being uncomprehending witnesses to changes that were borne by an elevated moral feeling, but must have seemed to them the quintessence of the unethical. Political revolutions and civil wars tend to follow religious revolutions. To be sure, not every culture has gone through a phase in which its fundamental convictions were exposed to the attacks of a morality that could no longer identify with them, but this can be said about many cultures. Fichte even claimed, on the ground of a priori reflections, to recognize the basic force of history in the battle between the naive, authority-based belief in one's own mores and criticism of them in the name of the reason.[193] In actuality, it is not hard to see that this kind of tense relationship has to occur if there is to be a place in history for progress in morals. Without factual mores, people would have destroyed each other; but without a critical distance from them, there could hardly have been progress toward rational insight into the morally obligatory. The moral and immoral aspects of morality are closely connected, and often difficult to separate. The refusal to bend to the opinions of the majority, to the dictates of the customary—for which one often has to pay a high personal price—is just as praiseworthy as the self-righteousness and vanity that often accompany morality are repulsive. Unfortunately, morality is no less frequently self-destructive in the form of sectarian conflicts than it contributes to a new and higher form of ethical life.

Despite all the differences between individual historical crises, they are "akin in many isolated details which have their root in human nature as a whole."[194] There are striking parallels even and especially between the crises that arise from a conflict between

---

192. Cf. H. E. Nossack's masterly novel *Das Testament des Lucius Eurinus*.

193. (1971), 4:460 ff.

194. Burckhardt (1905), 159: "... eine befremdliche, auf dem allgemein Menschlichen beruhende Verwandtschaft in vielen einzelnen Zügen." Trans. J. H. Nichols, 257. See also the whole fourth chapter of *Weltgeschichtliche Betrachtungen*, "Die geschichtlichen Krisen."

mores and morality, and we cannot dismiss the more far-reaching thesis that cultures that have to survive such a conflict age, in a certain sense of the word. Aging is not determined purely biologically among humans either; a decline in the freshness of access to the world necessarily accompanies, on one hand, the constant repetition of certain experiences that has a deadening effect, and on the other, the struggle with oneself and self-doubt, which are fatiguing. In order to be worth discussing, theories of cultural cycles must be cleansed of all crude biologism, but then they should not be denied a certain grain of truth. The greatest of them, Vico's, remains one of the most important achievements in the realm of the philosophy of history. Human beings' animal ancestry makes it obvious that the path to the rationalization of a culture, if it was ever achieved, was long and stony; at the beginning of every culture stands a form of thought and feeling very different from the later one. The domination of affects, the development of logical thought, and the substitution of law for force first appear late in human history. At the same time, there is some evidence that suggests that the few cultures in which extensive rationalization has been achieved are threatened by processes of dissolution. The more completely the different subsystems are developed, the more they are able to dissociate themselves from one another and become autonomous. If efforts are not made to maintain communication between subsystems, the unity of the culture is imperiled. The more widespread the ability to distance oneself from one's own mores becomes, the greater the increase in a selfish individualism that no longer recognizes reasonable duties and dissolves institutions. The more reason controls the passions, the more irrevocable is the decline of the emotional driving and binding forces that move human beings to action, both individual and collective, more strongly than does pure thought. (Sometimes, however, this decline takes place only after a phase of raging passions that are made subservient to reason, or what is taken for reason—consider the French Revolution.)

A culture's collective system of categories and values cannot continue to develop in an unlimited way; and just as scientific paradigm changes proceed from young people, so it may very well be that new moral ideas can proceed more easily from cultures that are fresh and unburdened by traditions that contradict those ideas. In art, religion, and politics, some eras are immediately recognizable as late periods—in reading Tacitus or Thomas Mann, one instantly sees that their styles are the end results of centuries of stylistic development. Hindu temples and Christian hymns of the twentieth century usually differ from their predecessors in the Indian Middle Ages and the early modern period by a false note that identifies them as aesthetic kitsch. Similarly, the luxury of moral reasoning can be afforded only by a culture that has resolved certain political problems, which it would not have succeeded in doing, however, had this reasoning existed from the beginning. But the possibility that a culture might succeed in regenerating itself cannot be excluded. Encounters with other peoples and returns to a culture's own past, that is, renaissances, are means of rejuvenation that have proven themselves in the history of European culture. One cannot speak of a general lifespan of cultures, and theories of cultural cycles go astray if they regard cultures as closed units. Cultures depend ontologically on individuals, and the latter can go back and forth between cultures—unlike cells, which cannot go back and forth between organisms. However, the clash of cultures can be fatal to one of them even if the conflict is peaceful in nature. The individuals may survive, but their culture will be absorbed by the other culture. Or a culture can lose its internal coherence and henceforth be determined by unsimultaneity, an asynchrony of its various elements—its technology may be modern, its legal system archaic. In the same way, however, the encounter between two cultures can give rise to a third culture more important than either of them.

Despite all the analogies between individual cultures, and despite the periodic decline of cultures whose achievements cannot always be adopted by others, and in any case never completely, we cannot ignore the fact that there has been progress in world history up to this point.[195] This progress is not continuous; rather, in the course of history, we can note, with regard to a few parameters, a series of values that are never abandoned for earlier ones.[196] A few insights of the theories of cultural cycles can be integrated into this model of progress, which are thereby carried further in a spiral-shaped model of history. This thesis of progress has an empirical content only if the parameters by reference to which progress can be observed are defined. Thus two sets of parameters can be named. On one hand, there is the extension of human power over nature and society. This includes, for instance, not only an increase of human life expectancy and a rise in agricultural productivity, but also a rise in the range of weapons.[197] To be sure, in the early Middle Ages there was a great scientific regression, and a partial technological regression, with regard to the achievements of the ancients; but there was no relapse below the level of the Neolithic Revolution, and perhaps a few factors that were partly responsible for the temporary scientific regression even played an important role in the genesis of the new science in the seventeenth century. On the other hand, we can speak of progress in the realization of the idea of law. It is obvious that the moral ideas of Homer's time were less universalistic than those of the Middle Ages and modernity, even if this does not mean that human beings used to be worse from a subjectively moral point of view. All this was already discussed in chapter 3.5.1; here I am concerned only to acknowledge the fact that a few—not all—

---

195. I say "up to now" because an enormous catastrophe in the next century is not impossible, or even, as we shall see, unlikely. In his provocative, often superficial, but readable book (1996), M. Wöhlcke transfers the idea of decline from individual cultures to the whole of world history, and more precisely after the completion of the process of modernization in some states.

196. I adopt the definition given in Leibniz's short text "De progressu in infinitum": "Dico igitur verum esse ascensum, si assumi nunc possit punctum infra quod non amplius descenderetur, et post aliquod tempus utcunque longum rursus perveniretur ad punctum altius infra quod non amplius descenderetur" (1965; 368). Cf. also the further clarifications and alternatives in "An mundus perfectione crescat" (368 ff.).

197. L. A. White refers to the "amount of energy harnessed and expended per capita per year" (1959; 41).

modern institutions in economics and the state correspond more closely to the principles of universalism than any of the institutions known to us from earlier periods. Moreover, respect for moral principles such as the separation of powers, which means a diminution of the state's despotic power, can lead to an increase in its infrastructural power. Jouvenel (1945) too one-sidedly spoke only of an increase in state power in human history, whereas J. A. Hall and G. J. Ikenberry (1989; 13) rightly note, on the basis of Mann's distinction between despotic and infrastructural power, that Western states have become so powerful precisely because they limited despotism and developed forms of collective, not distributive, power. The eighteenth-century French monarch had more despotic power than the British monarch, but only the latter could tax the nobility, and for building a world empire, this proved to be far more important than the satisfaction of despotic whims.[198]

Scientific-technological and legal progress seem to culminate in modern industrial society and the modern state, whose emergence will be the subject of the following pages.[199] Since such structures are a result of Western European culture, my remarks are Eurocentric in a certain sense of the word. In the term "Eurocentric," the concept "Europe" is not used geographically, for the former West European colonies such as the United States, Canada, and Australia are included, whereas the Eastern European region belongs to a culture area different from the one usually described as "European." This is not altered by Eastern Europe's repeated efforts to become more like Western Europe and even to interpret itself as the latter's heir—from the ideological view of Moscow as the third Rome to the Soviet conception of socialism as bringing capitalism to an end. At the same time, my interest is universal-historical, since I favor Europe not because I am a European, but rather, first, because Europe has become the fate of the whole planet, and, second, because universalist ideas give other cultures more opportunities than do any non-universalist mores. Precisely when one wishes that a few non-European values would become more dominant in the future, must one study the contextual conditions within which alone this could happen. Furthermore, it is no accident that the linear (or dialectical) view of progress in universal history has its world-historical place precisely where a single culture succeeded in dominating almost the whole world. Certainly, linear theological-historical models have played a role since early Christianity, and they may have favored European expansion in the early modern age, but a universal conception in the philosophy of history first emerged in the eighteenth century, when Europe's triumphal march over the globe was already far

---

198. See also the important essay by D. Knights and J. Roberts (1994), esp. 181 f.

199. Even before the Industrial Revolution, Montesquieu could write in *Esprit des lois* 21.21: "L'Europe est parvenue à un si haut degré de puissance, que l'histoire n'a rien à comparer là-dessus" (1748; 2:68). ("Europe has arrived at such a high degree of power that history has nothing to compare with it.")

advanced. Previously, cyclical models of history were predominant, and it is easy to explain why in the twentieth century, after Burckhardt's deep pessimism, they are gaining ground again. For the twentieth century was the first to be confronted with the question of whether the continuation of European expansion is possible or even desirable. This doubt leads on one hand to a search for buried alternatives that are not simply incorporated as elements of so-called progress, and on the other hand to a reckoning with the possibility of a breakdown of our contemporary civilization. In accord with this doubt, in the following pages I will constantly emphasize the values and virtues that were possible in pre-modern cultures. How strongly I have been influenced by Vico, Montesquieu, and Tocqueville, the greatest evaluative sociologists, will be obvious.

Despite the great differences between individual periods in human history I reject the basic thesis of radical historicism, namely that there is no common human nature that remains unchanged over time. First of all, the ultimate consequence of this conception could only be that the concept of human rights would lose its meaning. It could not be explained why so heterogeneous beings as the different human types realized through history could be subsumed under a *single* normatively relevant concept. Second, historicism (which is a special case of the nominalism that is always detrimental to science) destroys a good part of the significance of the historical sciences. Machiavelli could learn so much from Livy because he was not a historicist, because he assumed in particular that there are certain basic constants in human beings, power, and the state. There is nothing objectionable about this thesis even if one concedes that there are significant differences between the states of advanced cultures and modern states—for the political function is generally human and will be repeatedly exercised even in societies that still have no state as a independent corporate group of their own. Differences presuppose common features—thus modern man has his peculiarities, but at the same time he has much in common with all human beings, because he would otherwise not be describable as a human being. Indeed, common traits also connect him with other animals, with other organisms, with other entities, in correspondingly decreasing degrees. If modern man were incommensurable with ancient man, why should one so thoroughly study the latter at all? Classical philology's loss of its special status among the humanities, and even among philologies, is due to its all-too-rapid subjection to the dictates of historicism. Moreover, it is only fair and reasonable—because we are merely applying its own principles to itself—to note that historicism is the ideology of a specific historical epoch, and will disappear with it. Modernity began by distinguishing itself from all earlier periods, and historicism is the ultimate consequence of modernity's over-estimation of itself. At least, the classical modern period was an important one—the megalomania of the late modern period, which devalues itself with its constantly changing fashions, which is able to define itself only with the help of compounds involving "post" and "beyond," and which deconstructs a tradition incomparably greater than itself, can only be pitied.

6.2.2. Stages in World History[200]

The most important linear philosophy of history derives from Hegel. According to it, there is a continuous progress from the oriental world through the Greek and Roman worlds to the Germanic world, which for him includes the whole of Western Europe. "World history moves from East to West, for Europe is the end of world history, and Asia the beginning."[201] At first glance, this thesis seems primitive. In particular, the fact that it supposes no real, universalistic endpoint cannot be accepted, for other cultures remain unaffected by the realization of reason in the German world, which according to Hegel does not spread over the whole planet. Nonetheless, so far as technological and legal innovations are concerned, it can hardly be denied that up to this point in human history a leading position with regard to them has repeatedly been passed on to a (north)western neighbor. Mann, a social scientist and historian averse to metaphysical speculations, whose great sketch of universal history I largely follow in this chapter, speaks of a westward-northwestward movement.[202] To be sure, this thesis is connected with his book's interest in changes in power structures; it therefore neglects cultures that have made no contribution to the genesis of the modern world. But it remains striking that Mesopotamia, Phoenicia, Greece, Rome, Western Europe, and the United States follow each other geographically in the same direction. The causes of this development are obvious. When one culture has to be replaced by others, or at least has to clash with others in order for great innovations to occur, then the direction in which an expansion can take place also becomes that of world-historical progress. But expansion to the south, at least after a certain shift toward the west, was blocked by the desert, and expansion to the east was blocked by the existence of powerful kingdoms. (Alexander the Great, however, reversed the usual direction of development.)[203] In contrast, expansion toward the west was eased by two geographical particularities—on one hand, the deeper, moister, and more fertile soil; on the other, the possibility of traveling by sea.

If an intelligent historian from another planet received the first photos of Earth, he could probably immediately say that the Mediterranean area must be of special importance for the development of rational inhabitants of this planet, for ship travel had to develop earlier on this large, island-filled sea than on the oceans.[204] In actuality, gaining access to the seas was a qualitative step forward in human history, because it promoted

---

200. I would not have been able to write the following section without many conversations with my friend Prof. Dr. Paul Münch.

201. (1969 ff.), 12:134: "Die Weltgeschichte geht von Osten nach Westen, denn Europa ist schlechthin das Ende der Weltgeschichte, Asien der Anfang."

202. "*Westward* and *northwestward* drift of the leading edge of power" (1986 ff.; 1:539).

203. Cf. M. Mann (1986 ff.), 1:509.

204. Cf. P. Anderson (1978), 21. I base myself repeatedly on Anderson's critical-Marxist conception of universal history; after that of M. Mann, it is the most impressive I know of that has been written in recent decades, even if I do not share many of its premises. Nonetheless, Marxism has inherited some of Hegel's leading ideas, and this inheritance compensates for many of its errors.

and presupposed virtues that must remain alien to landsmen—just as rivers were earlier an important presupposition for the emergence of advanced cultures. The heirs of a culture that had learned to sail the Mediterranean were most likely to sail systematically the oceans;[205] and in this resides an important presupposition for the corresponding culture's expansion over the whole planet. In order to explain why the wonder of the modern state occurred in Europe rather than in Asia, E. L. Jones mentions, in addition to the Atlantic, the following geographical reasons: the lack of steppe nomads, fewer natural catastrophes, and the multitude of resources favoring trade (1987; 225 ff.). Geographical impediments can certainly be overcome once modern societies have emerged, but the latter must first of all be able to emerge, and I find plausible the more general thesis that too difficult as well as too favorable climatic conditions are detrimental to the development of more advanced cultural achievements.[206]

6.2.2.1. Hunters and Gatherers

The greatest turning points in human history are the Neolithic and Industrial Revolutions, at least so far as the extension of human power over nature is concerned. Thus Gellner (1988) divides history into three main stages, hunter-gatherers, agrarian society, and industrial society. On the other hand, if changes in moral consciousness are taken as the starting point, first, the emergence of universal religions, and second, the emergence of Protestantism and of a secular religion, will appear as the most important turning points. So far as the history of the state is concerned, its establishment and its transformation into the modern state are the most important turning points. Even if the state emerged after the Neolithic Revolution, and even if universal religions emerged after the state, the state is possible only after the Neolithic Revolution, and universal religions are possible only after the state. On the other hand, the modern state, Protestantism, and the Industrial Revolution emerged at roughly the same time, and are internally interconnected, which increased their historical power. Although in each case the earlier stage lasted much longer than the later one, the changes that took place in the later ones were more numerous and more wide ranging—the pace of development quickened, history accelerated. Concerning the first stage we know relatively little, because humans invented writing only in the agrarian stage, and hunter-gatherers in our own time have been influenced by the interference of later stages. In the framework of this book, a few hints must suffice. Even if according to the most recent research, Neanderthal man and *Homo sapiens sapiens* may belong to different and competing species, no further speciation has occurred for a long time. Most of the development of man is thus cultural in nature, and because of the common biological basis, some of the technological and

---

205. The Phoenicians' circumnavigation of Africa, sponsored by the Egyptian pharaoh, Necho II, was still a matter of just sailing along the coast. Cheng Ho's sea expedition to East Africa remained an episode.

206. Cf. Toynbee (1965), 1:170 ff.

institutional discoveries and inventions may have been made more than once, independently of one another, or easily adopted from another ethnic group.

Naive evolutionism assumes a general development from egalitarian societies through those with rank orders to the state, to status groups, and to advanced cultures. In some cases, a further distinction between relative and absolute rank orders is made; the former is not necessarily transitive and has no highest point in the social hierarchy, that is, no chieftain, a figure central for state-building.[207] Mann has formulated two convincing objections to this model (1986; 1:34 ff.). First, far from all ethnic groups have arrived at the form of an advanced culture, or even a permanent position of chieftain; probably at most six of the advanced cultures known to us evolved independently: in China, India, Mesopotamia, Egypt, Central America, and the Andes. Perhaps a few of these cultures were not formed completely independently, but were rather influenced by another, and certainly they influenced other peoples, but not all. Second, there is much to be said for the view that the emergence of elementary forms of statehood was not irreversible, and that instead, early states repeatedly collapsed, because a restriction on freedom was connected with them. Socially and territorially, states are relatively closed units, cages, so to speak. In any case, this assumption is suggested by modern examples of archaic peoples—Geronimo could unite several Apache tribes to go on the warpath, but he could not stabilize the corporate group established for this purpose. The fear of concentrating power in his hands was apparently greater than the fear of the whites. This sounds paradoxical, but it is deeply rooted in human nature. Thucydides rightly avers (I 76) that people would rather suffer violence than accept insults, for in the exercise of force the superiority of the stronger is evident, while insult offends the feeling of equality. Indeed, the refusal to establish leadership organs is usually based on a strong consciousness of equality;[208] reciprocity and self-help are supposed to take the place of central organs of government. Societies with such organs are formally more complex than those without them; Durkheim aptly calls them "organic" and "mechanical," respectively. However, the example of the Apaches also shows that at least when confronted by the modern state, societies without states had no chance, and even though the premodern state possessed no comparable power to impose itself, and even after conquering more primitive peoples, left their inner structure for the most part unaffected, it must have radiated a certain seductiveness. Even if there were cycles of centralization and decentralization, in the process of stabilizing state organizations a few power-holders must have succeeded in reaching a point beyond which there was no longer any going back, because too many interests depended on them.

The transition to the raising of crops and livestock, and frequently to sedentariness, which dissolved the hunters and gatherers' way of life, was made by many peoples, but represents only a necessary, not a sufficient condition for the emergence of state-

---

207. This is particularly E. Service's thesis (1975).
208. Cf. C. Sigrist (1979), 185 ff.

hood. Today one can hardly conceive what massive changes in human consciousness were necessary in order to prevent people from immediately killing animals. To be sure, in raising their animals, the livestock raisers were also guided by the goal of providing a food supply, which turns out to be even greater if it is deferred; but the inhibition of the immediate drive to eat, and indeed the effort to find out what animals need and take it into account, as is required in keeping and especially breeding livestock, are not natural. The natural is rather to appropriate what nature produces, without thinking about increasing it or even about preserving it as a long-term store. Gehlen, the philosopher who, after Vico, has most deeply penetrated the mentality of archaic man, is probably right in assuming in this context (1975) religious factors that alone could have had the power to control the drive to eat. According to Gehlen, the sanctification of animals in totemism made keeping them a religious duty, and thereby was created a presupposition for the domestication of animals, keeping and breeding them. With the success of this process the animal was banalized, and anthropomorphic gods replaced the theriomorphic ones in which the horror of wild animals had crystallized. Intelligence and the process of trial and error must have played a role in raising plants and animals. However, what is fascinating about Gehlen's theory is that it makes it plausible that already this fundamental cultural achievement was hardly willed as such, but resulted from a detour: an example of the heterogony of ends in which Vico thought he recognized the activity of divine Providence—and in this case, a particularly plausible thesis, since the detour was religious in nature.

The lives of hunters, gatherers, and fishers and the first, pre-state agrarian societies should not be idealized. Nonetheless, these oldest cultures had two properties that have to be evaluated positively. First, the level of needs was significantly lower than in the more civilized stages. M. Sahlins went so far as to speak of the original affluent society; and even if that is an exaggeration, it is one that provides food for thought. Sahlins's argument for his thesis is plausible: "There are two possible courses to affluence. Wants may be 'easily satisfied' either by producing much or by desiring little."[209] People worked relatively little, but enough to survive—at least so long as the size of the population was kept under control by all possible means, even the most brutal. The unity of man and nature was strongly felt, the sense for ecological balances (which were, however, repeatedly disturbed) was articulated in religion and in myths and rites, which may include more reason than the program of a unbridled, instrumental rationality. Burial rites and the worship of the dead indicate a strong piety with regard to the deceased. The relationship between the sexes was somewhat more symmetrical than in later times, because women's economic activity was obviously at least as important as that of men. Second, wars were less bloody than after the foundation of states. The claim that military enterprises were alien to archaic societies is false; it is almost only under conditions where survival is extremely difficult, as in the Arctic regions that can one find peoples

---

209. M. Sahlins (1972), 1f.

who have nearly entirely given up war, because it would have been suicidal. (Among Eskimos, even internal conflicts were overcome, for instance through singing contests.) But war was less frequent, and since the forms of organization were simpler, the casualties were fewer. In view of these positive characteristics of the societies of foragers of wild food, it is certainly conceivable that a few of these cultures even made a conscious decision not to adopt agriculture and the state.

6.2.2.2. Agrarian Societies

The transition to agriculture and livestock raising was probably favored on one hand by demographic pressure, and on the other by the greater productivity of the new economic form. However, the new form invited attacks, and defense against enemies thus became more urgent. Sedentary farmers were more exposed to attacks than were the often nomadic livestock raisers. Around 7000 BC, Jericho, the oldest *city* in the world, already had fortifications. New discoveries such as the wooden plow, the wagon, the potter's wheel, mining, and metalworking led to further social differentiations; special *ranks of craftsmen* developed that preserved and handed on technological achievements. *Foreign trade* emerged; after the stage of pure subsistence economy, markets formed that required legal regulation. Economic *overproduction* liberated a small group from having to provide its own food supply. The beginnings of *science* occurred at this cultural level, especially in the domains of medicine and astronomy. The sky fascinated people with its combination of order and movement, and it was considered the home of most of the gods, with the worship of which the oldest science was closely connected. *Art* attained a high stylization and refinement (even if art is the sphere of human culture in which it is most difficult to speak of progress: already the Magdalenian culture, and earlier, Upper Paleolithic cultural levels, produced brilliant achievements in art history). *Monumental edifices*, most of them with a religious function, expressed a new self-confidence, great architectonic ability, and significant organizational capacities. In Egypt, for instance, almost the whole economic power of the country was directed to the construction of the pyramids. Of special importance was the development of *writing* and numerical counting systems. Writing is one of the most consequential steps in the history of power, because on one hand it makes possible a simply unimaginable extension of communication in space and especially in time, and on the other hand it represents an objectivization and depersonalization of the speaking subjectivity. "The detachability of language from speaking derives from the fact that it can be written. In the form of writing, all tradition is contemporaneous with each present time. Moreover, it involves a unique co-existence of past and present."[210] The speech of archaic men proceeded from body language, as

---

210. Gadamer (1975), 367: "In der Schriftlichkeit entspringt die Abgelöstheit der Sprache von ihrem Vollzug. In der Form der Schrift ist alles Überlieferte für jede Gegenwart gleichzeitig. In ihr besteht mithin eine einzigartige Koexistenz von Vergangenheit und Gegenwart." Trans. J. Weinsheimer and D. G. Marshall, 390.

the numerous legal symbols in the Middle Ages still showed; on the other hand, cuneiform texts are strangely cold and impersonal, the paralinguistic elements having disappeared. An objective administration independent of the deceptions of memory became possible; laws, contracts, and diplomatic exchange took on a new, more enduring form; and new standards of precision were developed for communication. Furthermore, like architecture, writing serves the self-representation of power. This first great media revolution had to alter in a fundamental way the relationships among people, even if at first only a small, specialized group of servants of the power-holder were able to write, and several millennia passed before a larger portion of the population mastered writing.

All these structures favored the *state,* and were favored by it in return. A good deal of evidence suggests that military conflicts played a role in the state's emergence—the distinction between power-holders and power-subjects points to this origin. Other factors were probably new religious ideas, which legitimized this form of domination, as well as the form of economy that underlies irrigated agriculture. It cannot be an accident that all six of the early advanced cultures, whose characteristics I have just listed (a few of them, however, were already found earlier, while others are lacking in recognized advanced cultures), emerged along rivers. On one hand, the artificial irrigation of fields that in Mesopotamia preceded the foundation of cities by about two thousand years made possible greater population growth. On the other hand, people became bound to these particularly fertile soils—the possibility of moving on, which threatened every earlier attempt to found a state,[211] was thereby considerably diminished. People became dependent on cooperation with their neighbors, and organizational tasks became necessary that were best carried out by a central authority that established the corvee, distributed what had been produced in common, and protected the emerging differences in property. Territory, community, and hierarchy, the three elements of the state, were brought into particularly close connection by artificial irrigation.[212]

In the following, we cannot examine in detail the different agrarian advanced cultures before the emergence of the modern state. They varied considerably—the political and social structures in China were entirely unlike those in India, and the differences between them are still influential today. Thus the Indian subcontinent was first completely united by the English; earlier attempts to found an empire were few and short-lived, whereas in China the idea of empire was a recognized, if not always realized, norm, from the Ch'in dynasty on. Presumably the caste system, which implied a sharp distinction between religious and political power, made state-building more difficult. For the most part, Indian kings ruled for a short time and over limited territories, and they simply stole what they needed. Nevertheless, a few ideal-typical characteristics of most agrarian societies may be emphasized, especially in distinction to modern industrial

---

211. Cf. Montesquieu, *Esprit des lois* 18.14.

212. Cf. M. Mann (1986 ff.), 1:80: "Territory, community, and hierarchy were coinciding in irrigation more than they did in either rain-watered agriculture or herding."

societies.[213] Striking are first of all the greater inequalities, and second the incomparably less extensive social mobility. Only a small minority of people enjoyed a life that was not primarily determined by concern about their own subsistence, since the most important source of energy was human and animal muscle-power. The majority of people had to work hard, partly without personal freedom, that is, as slaves, or in other forms of dependency. Their mistreatment was hardly ever considered a moral problem; there was no respect for the dignity and the life of the individual person. There were significant differences between classes with respect to economic and political power, as well as to prestige. Within the family, women were usually sharply subordinated to men, and women's life expectancy was less than that of men.[214] However, feminist historians, too, should acknowledge that the lot of a male slave was considerably harder than that of an upper-class woman (even if presumably better than that of a female slave); the exploitation of the mother of one's own children is usually limited by considerations that are lacking in dealing with slaves. Nonetheless, even in their relationships with slaves who lived in their own household, as well as with members of the lower classes, people could develop a feeling of (often condescending) vertical responsibility that was as distant from the recognition that everyone is in principle equal as from the complete indifference to those who do not share their own way of life that sometimes accompanies such recognition. One's later role in life was determined by birth to a much greater extent than it is in modernity—most fully in cultures with a caste system. Thus chances for social innovations were lost, because talented individuals were not allowed to rise in society. Instead, power struggles were fewer, though no less violent, in oligarchies of birth, because fewer competitors for an office were available. People more commonly imposed their own goals with merciless determination, but there was less petty ambition. The horizon of possibilities was much more restricted, and since happiness has much to do with the harmony between what one is and what one wants to be, it is entirely possible that there was more happiness at that time than there is today—even if at the price of the violation of elementary universalist principles of justice.

Birth and death rates were both very high; therefore, despite important oscillations in the net reproduction rate, after the end of the hunting and gathering phase and the introduction of agrarian society, no significant population growth could take place. Although the basic tendency may be somewhat exaggerated, David Riesman (1950) rightly pointed out that demographic structures decisively shape the character of a society. Thus in agrarian societies birth and death were taken for granted. Infant mortality was high, and because of the short life-expectancy, every young person had to reckon with early death, whether as a result of violence, illness, or famine, which frequently occurred. There were many young people, and generations succeeded one another more rapidly than in a time with a very long life expectancy. It is obvious that in

---

213. Cf. E. Gellner (1983) and (1988).
214. M. Mann (1986 ff.), 2:16.

such a culture, the relationship to life, to death, to age, to sexuality, and to the other sex must have been entirely different from what it is today. On one hand the individual was more ephemeral than in modernity, since in the middle of life he was surrounded in a very real sense by death; he was more inclined to understand himself as part of a comprehensive generational context, to which he had clear duties. Dreadful institutions such as punishing a whole family for the crimes of one of its members show that the idea of strictly individual responsibility did not yet exist. Furthermore, the individual more easily fitted into traditions, which are more likely to be examined if the new generation does not enter into positions of responsibility until an advanced age. On the other hand, the permanent awareness of death could also lend the most uneducated person a depth that one seeks in vain in large segments of modern societies—vivid figures like the Shakespearian porters and gravediggers hardly exist any more. Sexuality's close connection with reproduction and birth lent it a sacredness in which—despite all the injustices and acts of violence, which are not in the least to be glossed over—at least a few women participated in agrarian societies as well.

The religion of agrarian societies sees a stable order as the fundamental determination of the world, as well as the highest norm. Within this order, everything has its place— the human being within nature, every rank within the society, every individual within his rank. The ordering of society corresponds to that of nature, which is seen as divine and full of meaning, and is thereby legitimated. Even those who are located at the bottom of the social ladder are capable of experiencing meaning; individuals with deviant character structures can often find a place in the religious subsystem. The literary genre that most perfectly corresponds to this social order is the epic.[215] Only a small part of the population can read and write; it thereby gains a monopoly on education, since there is no general public educational system. Education usually takes place within the family or other small social units (if one is educated at a foreign court, then that is for the most part because one is a hostage). Access to the world of the intellectual elites is—at least in theory—connected even more with matters of character than with intellectual presuppositions, because even specialized scientific activity serves the higher goal of gaining knowledge about the order of the world. Science is part of a religiously, and later on, philosophically grounded wisdom, into which one is initiated through personal relationships between teacher and disciple. In addition to the high religion practiced by the elites in ceremonial centers, usually in a language incomprehensible to the people, there is a multiplicity of local cults, which the high religion benevolently tolerates, at least before the emergence of monotheism. The disadvantages of agrarian religion and education are obvious. First, they exclude the majority of people from initiation into the higher orders of knowledge (and even from elementary human rights); second, in them criticism is not institutionalized. On the other hand, they have two advantages. Knowledge does not become independent of the personality in which it is grounded; indeed, even the uneducated can identify existentially with what they learn. They can

---

215. Cf. the impressive beginning of G. Lukács (1920).

wholly believe the little that is communicated to them instead of half-believing many more things. Second, agrarian cultures far exceed the last heir of monotheism, secular relativism, in tolerance and openness. Make no mistake, the ideology of pluralism and multiculturalism is not very open-minded, if one chooses a religion or culture that clings to a clear order of values. In contrast, many old advanced cultures were really multicultural to a high degree. Naturally, there were tensions, and even rebellions; yet periodic executions of ringleaders usually sufficed to restore internal peace.

The state in agrarian societies also differed significantly from the later one. Although it sometimes had a horrible despotic power (as in the Assyrian empire, but not, for instance, in the feudal monarchies of the European Middle Ages), its infrastructural power was always limited. Communication and transportation were so slow and so expensive that areas far from the center enjoyed extensive autonomy, so long as they did not revolt militarily and paid their tributes. Collecting taxes was expensive, associated with a great deal of corruption, and never general; even in China—despite a special class of state officials who had, however, very little relationship with the population as a whole—in the year 754 only 7.6 million of the 52.8 million inhabitants were taxed.[216] There was a lack of any ideology that would have demanded a unified legal system throughout the state. Traditional relationships of dependency (whether based on kinship or between lords and their personal dependents), guilds, religious groups, and village structure were the foundation of the social system, in which the state was only *one* power among others. With the exception of Egypt before the Roman Empire and Han-dynasty China there were no clear boundaries between individual states—cross-border social relationships were numerous. Often a common culture existed that included and bound together many states. However, one main difference among the political structures of agrarian states can be observed: there were both loose connections between cities, which sometimes had a common cultural center, and empires of great extent. The first of the two political structures was decentralized; in it, monocrats or oligarchies of birth exercised state power. The second structure was much more strongly centralized; the state form was for the most part a monocracy.[217] The increasing importance of military enterprises, for instance, in making trade routes secure or in providing protection against the marcher peoples and nomads who constantly threatened the great empires, was the crucial factor in the emergence of the first empires—for instance, in Sargon of Akkad's subjection of the Sumerian city-states in the twenty-fourth century BC. However, it is important to understand that even the empires of that time were much less centralistic and monocratic than is commonly thought. The monocrat was dependent on the cooperation of a military elite composed mainly of an oligarchy of birth, which could always revolt against him—Egypt and China were shaken by regional potentates' periodic attempts to liberate themselves. In addition, a role was played by the threat from foreign peoples, who were sometimes able to seize control of the empire, though

---

216. J. A. Hall and G. K. Ikenberry (1989), 25.
217. In this connection, Weber speaks of forms of "patrimonial domination."

the latter's administrative structure continued on as before—as did the Hyksos in Egypt during the Second Intermediate Period, or the Manchus (who quickly became sinicized) during the last Chinese dynasty. Popular uprisings, such as those of the Red Eyebrows and the Yellow Turbans in China, were another divisive factor. Therefore, if the empire was to be stable, the means of coercion had to be complemented by the construction of a collective identity of the ruling class.

Unlike the Assyrians, whose power was based primarily on their armies, the Persians succeeded in integrating even the elites of the subjugated peoples into their system of domination. Still today, the religious and political tolerance of this great state composed of many different peoples remains as remarkable as the cosmopolitan spirit of its administration, whose inscriptions were trilingual and whose correspondence was conducted in a language that was not in the least related to Persian, namely Imperial Aramaic. When Cyrus built a temple[218] to the god of the little nation of the Jews, whom he had allowed to return to Jerusalem after his conquest of the Neo-Babylonian Empire, he surely did not imagine that he was thereby giving a chance for regeneration to a religion that was to be of enormous importance for world history. Monotheism, which evolved in the religion of the Jews after a long period of monolatry (that is, the prohibition on worshipping other gods—who are, however, acknowledged to exist—in addition to one's own), was to give human history a new direction, especially after the idea of a chosen people, in which the origins of monotheism in monolatry remained operative, was surmounted by Christianity and Islam. Iranian culture can also pride itself on having produced one of the greatest religious geniuses of all time. The dualism of Zarathustra's religious conception can much more easily deal with the problem of the existence of evil; on the other hand, it lacks the inner conclusiveness of monotheism's concept of God. The fact that the monistic and dualistic approaches to philosophy have pursued these two alternative ways of thinking up until the present day shows to what awareness of the problem religions had risen in these centuries, the so-called axial age. Despite all the differences in doctrine, Zarathustra, the Old Testament Prophets, Buddha, Mahavira, Confucius, and Lao-tzu have one thing in common: they are all individuals who turned against the religious mores of their time and whose conceptions touched on philosophy, because their doctrine of God or the impersonal world order emphasized general principles. But this amounts, at least potentially, to moving beyond the personal and territorial limitation of national religions. Individuality and universality—that is the lowest common denominator that connects these figures. What is specific to Judaism is that it institutionalized the exception, as it were, in the form of the regularly appearing prophets (and thus it also institutionalized moral progress).[219]

The Persian empire collapsed when it was attacked by Alexander the Great (who thus conquered an already existing world empire, but did not create one himself), but

---

218. On Cyrus's edict, cf. Ezra 1:2 ff.

219. Cf. Mill (1972), 200 f. We can already see what prophecy means for politics in Nathan and his overt criticism of David (2 Samuel 12:1 ff.)

it had already been weakened by internal problems such as rebellions on the part of satraps and dynastic struggles, which its monocratic structure provoked. Only the Roman Empire—which was comparably open and tolerant, and which in addition succeeded, through brilliant innovations in the mechanisms of the separation of powers, in motivating the whole upper class and, through its legal system, a large part of the population, to support its own imperial ambitions—can claim to have achieved within the ancient world something even more important politically than the Persian Empire.

6.2.2.2.1. Phoenicians and Greeks

Before the rise of the Roman Empire, two cultures provided an enduring impetus for history. Neither of them succeeded in building an empire, but they were able cleverly to exploit and further develop the civilizing achievements of the great empires, such as writing. The most important achievements of the Phoenicians were in the area of economics. Maritime trade immeasurably increased the processes of exchange, since sea transportation was much less expensive than transportation by land,[220] made possible encounters between cultures that lived far apart, and could lead to a broadening of the intellectual horizon. The increase in trade promoted *coinage* as well as the emergence of an *alphabet*, which led to the spread of the previously mentioned revolution in media. It was now considerably easier to learn to write than with the original writing systems based on pictures, words, and syllables, because a few signs sufficed to express the wealth of what could be formulated linguistically; the alphabet facilitated the democratization of culture and the state. However, what is systematically the simplest is genetically the most difficult; the feats of abstraction that made minting coins and the alphabet possible are extremely complex. In a phonetic script, the sign does not resemble the thing to which it refers, whereas pictorial writing immediately reflects reality (bypassing language) and while logographic writing systems also fulfill phonetic functions, that is, they can be "read," they do so only on the basis of pictorial writing (ideographs can also stand for homophonic words or parts of words). Since sounds are normally expressed only in syllables, isolating the sounds from the syllables is unnatural and at the same time deeply related to the spirit of analysis, which breaks up a whole into its elements.

It is in this spirit of analysis that Greek culture accomplished the greatest breakthrough. If one asks what were the Greeks' greatest achievements, we can name two things: *science* and the *polis* (in addition to which there were also more tribal units, so-called *ethne*). While rather primitive from the point of view of the centralization of political power[221] and—even if they could repel the onslaught of a great empire—ultimately

---

220. Cf. P. Anderson (1978), 20: In Diocletian's time, it was cheaper to transport grain from Syria to Spain by ship than to transport it seventy-five miles overland.

221. Alliances and federations repeatedly appeared, but they seldom lasted long. The development of a constitutional autonomy of cities within a more tribal unit (*ethnos*) is called a pseudo-federation.

subjugated with amazing rapidity by a neighboring people they considered barbarian, the Greeks advanced the self-unfolding of reason more than any other people. If we define science as the deduction of theorems from axioms, then it can be said that the Greeks were the first to produce science, and indeed already in its full perfection. It is true that in antiquity science was not connected with technology (Archimedes was an exception), and it therefore never became a political issue. But this concept of science could be taken up again later on, and it proved indispensable for a systematic mastery over nature. To that extent, the Greeks are responsible for one of those shifts that made it possible for modern industrial society to emerge from a very special agrarian society— namely, that of the Christian West. One sees the importance of the Greek concept of science if one compares Europe with China. The technological achievements of the Chinese were first-rate, but it never occurred to this culture to put its own technology on a scientific basis; and for that very reason the project of modernity did not evolve in China. In Greece, as in other agrarian societies, the individual sciences were part of a comprehensive, normatively governed project of opening up the world. What is new in relation to all other advanced cultures is nonetheless that this project sought to overcome all pre-rational, mythical elements and relied on the *logos* with an exclusiveness unique in world history. Thus *philosophy* emerged as *a religion of reason*. Its development was favored by the agonistic spirit of the Greeks, their position between different cultures and the openness of their religion, which had neither dogmas nor a church. Greek reason stopped at nothing—as *Enlightenment* it also turned against the mores of its own time. Despite all the differences with the later Enlightenment in Europe, one can say that the sophists were the first enlighteners of humanity, and that they represent a phenomenon found in no other advanced culture. India, the culture whose philosophical tradition comes closest to that of the Greeks, has first-rate metaphysics, but no movement of enlightenment. However, Plato already understood that the power of morality, which the sophists strengthened, was partly responsible for the decline of Greek culture—a decline without which his own philosophy would scarcely have come about. Just as in China the age of the Warring States was one of the most productive culturally, so the age in which Greece tore itself apart politically was also that of its most perfect cultural flowering.

Greek rationalism is closely connected with *the democratic form of the state*, which the Greeks created. If reason is what counts, then political power cannot be put in the hands of a few aristocrats on the basis of their birth, but must be exercised by all free citizens. Respect for human beings is in fact expressed in Greek sculpture more powerfully than in any earlier art. Naturally, the democratic state form we find in a few Greek city-states was not founded on ideas alone. It has its social presuppositions in the development of a rank of free, property-owning farmers, working a soil that produced relatively high yields (which were owed to the use of iron plows, among other things), in the importance of trade for the world of the Greek cities, and in the hoplite phalanx, whose strength lay in the cohesion of the soldiers. Agrarian and political reforms became necessary in Athens, in order to enable the farmers to acquire armor and weapons, and in order to pay them for their service. Direct democracy was possible only on a small territory; the Greeks' most important political units were therefore the cities with their surrounding areas; they were connected by economic, diplomatic, and religious relationships, but regularly fought with each other. Athens developed a state form that can be described, in relation to one parameter by which democracy can be gauged, as the most democratic in history— in no modern democracy does so great a proportion of the enfranchised citizenry participate directly in the legislative, executive, and judicial functions. Since Pericles, there had even been compensation for service in a state office, in order to give all citizens an opportunity to take part in political activity. However, in his famous lecture "De la liberté des anciens comparée à celle des modernes,"[222] Benjamin Constant rightly points out that among the Greeks, the concept of freedom implied solely the enjoyment of political rights—freedom from the state was not one of their values.

Public service, *leitourgia,* was an honor; assigning public tasks to wealthy citizens and metics was a functional equivalent of taxation. The polis was also a religious community—the performances of tragedies in Athens were public events; the *theorika* ("spectacle money") enabled poorer citizens to go to the theater, as the state in general provided for their welfare. For political decisions, oracles were repeatedly sought, because the individual still did not trust himself to decide by himself. Moreover, the wonder of Athenian culture was possible only on the basis of countless people, then unnoticed and today forgotten, who led a miserable existence as slaves in the mines. Indeed, it has even been suggested that it was through the Greek polis that slavery first became an institution so widespread and so absolute in form, and that Greek liberty and slavery were two sides of the same coin.[223] Most slaves were barbarians, who the Greeks thought did not fully possess reason. It is hardly an accident that precisely those cultures that make important steps toward a more universalistic concept of reason and morals distinguish themselves especially strongly from those that have not made any comparable achievements. The Greeks were far more arrogant with regard to other peoples than were the Persians, among whom Themistocles was able to spend his last years in honor.

Generally speaking, the contradiction between democratic ideals in internal politics and a brutal foreign policy, even toward Greek "confederates," is particularly striking in the case of Athens. The claim that democracies are not inclined to go to war is surely false so far as Greek history is concerned. The Athenians cleverly exploited the fear of the Persians in order to create, in the Delian League, an instrument that they increasingly used for their own ends, for democracies with brilliant self-representations are expensive. Many Greek intellectuals, and above all Plato, regarded Attic democracy with a very critical eye, whereas the republican state form, especially after it was lost, was celebrated

---

222. (1872), 2:537–560.
223. Cf. P. Anderson (1978), 23: "Hellenic liberty and slavery were indivisible: each was the structural condition of the other, in a dyadic system which had no precedent or equivalent in the social hierarchies of the Near Eastern Empires. . . ." Hegel had already made somewhat the same point; see (1969 ff.), 12:311.

by the Romans. However, the Romans never meant by this a true democracy like the Athenian one, but rather the form of their own state before the establishment of the principate.[224] The Peloponnesian war was won not by Athens, but by Sparta; as a land power as well as an oligarchic state closed to the outside, Sparta represented Athens' ideal countertype, not least because of its superior political leadership. Athenian egalitarianism repeatedly threatened with banishment or death those who had contributed most to this commonwealth; envy of important statesmen was accompanied by seduceability by demagogues. Still, we owe to this war humanity's greatest historical work, which grounded realism in the theory of foreign policy (even if Thucydides' conception is significantly more complex than that of modern realists and should not be interpreted as amoral). The Oedipus effect of theories in the social sciences can be seen in the fact that "realistic" convictions, such as those the sophists had made widespread among the Athenian elites, became self-fulfilling expectations in the Peloponnesian war—because a few leading Athenians expected Sparta to launch a preventive war, they provoked the war themselves. But their fear was probably not justified, for the Spartans were less intellectual, and were not familiar with the "realistic" logic of the sophists. Sparta's hegemony after its victory did not last long. Like the First World War, the Peloponnesian war meant the political self-destruction of a whole culture, which then easily fell as prey into the hands of a new power.

The victory of the Macedonians was owed to military peculiarities such as the greater mobility of their infantry, their flexible use of cavalry, and organizational innovations. In addition, a role was played by the fact that their political system was more primitive, that is, it was more monocratic. At the same time, Macedonia claimed to belong to Greek culture. The Greeks' feeling of cultural superiority and the Macedonians' political strategy of reconciling internal contradictions by attacking an external enemy were expressed in Alexander's great military campaign. The encounter between Eastern and Western cultural forms, which had long since begun, was thereby further strengthened. Alexander pushed as far as India; the art and philosophy of the Indo-Greek kingdoms show to what degree cultural syntheses succeeded. It is true that Alexander sought in vain to connect the Greek and Persian elites, but the Hellenistic territorial states that emerged after his death necessarily mixed Greek and oriental structures. Cities were more Greek, while the surrounding areas remained oriental; the forms of political organization and legitimation can be described as syncretic. We should emphasize the construction of a state bureaucracy, which was lacking in the Greek *polis*. In Athens, there was a police force that carried out security tasks, but elsewhere citizens had to take care of themselves. Naturally, however, we still cannot speak of a law-governed administration. What is most fascinating about Hellenism is the construction of a Eurasian cultural *koine;* this aspect certainly connects this time with our own, in which something analogous is taking place on the planetary level.

---

224. Cf. P. Anderson (1978), 73: "The narrower the circle that enjoyed the characteristic municipal freedom of Antiquity, the purer was the vindication of liberty it bequeathed to posterity. . . ."

6.2.2.2.2. The Roman Empire

The Hellenistic kingdoms fell victim to the greatest empire of antiquity, the Roman Empire. Among the factors that favored the rise of this state was first of all a wholly new dialectic between unity and tension. Tribal units and city states were closely interwoven in the Roman *res publica;* in connection with them there was a dualism of democratic and oligarchic elements that was strikingly expressed in the famous formula, SPQR. Unlike the situation in Athens, in Rome power was in the hands of a small oligarchy of birth, but one which remained dependent on certain constitutional acts on the part of the population as a whole in the assembly (the method of voting by group in the *comitia* prevented the votes from being equal), and which increasingly opened itself up to capable persons rising from lower ranks. The most important part of the Roman Republic's internal policy was the *Struggle of the Orders,* at the end of which the plebeians also gained access to offices in the state and in the priesthood. Machiavelli, Vico, and Montesquieu saw in the conflicts between patricians and plebeians the true motor of Roman history— in no earlier people had class struggle played this kind of role. Certainly, the opposition between rich and poor was important in Greek politics as well, but the class opposition was not yet interwoven with the constitutional structure. In Rome, moreover, the conflict of the orders was attenuated by the fact that there were relationships of personal dependency between individual patricians and plebeians. Clients were usually more loyal to their patron than to their own class. Montesquieu rightly maintains that class tensions with a simultaneous feeling of the unity of the state were a central cause of Rome's greatness, just as dissonances contribute to harmony in music.[225] The fact that it was possible, though very difficult, to rise in society spurred Roman plebeians to great achievements, to which they would have been motivated in neither a closed oligarchy nor a democracy of the Athenian type, as Vico rightly recognized.[226] In addition to the generous competitiveness of the plebeians and the patricians' energetic defense of their own privileges, Vico mentions the acumen of the jurists as the Romans' third virtue. Probably no other people has used the law as systematically to defuse conflicts as did the Romans. This holds in particular for private law, in which they made even informally concluded contracts actionable—a legal idea full of consequences, and which one finds neither among the Greeks nor the Germans, for the original law is extremely formalistic.

---

225. "Ce qu'on appelle *union* dans un corps politique est une chose très équivoque: la vraie est une union d'harmonie, qui fait que toutes les parties, quelque opposées qu'elles nous paraissent, concourent au bien général de la Société, comme des dissonances dans la musique concourent à l'accord total" (1734; 82).

226. Cf. *Scienza nuova* sect. 280: "Le gare, ch'esercitano gli ordini nelle città, d'uguagliarsi con giustizia sono lo più potente mezzo d'ingrandir le repubbliche" (1953; 1:104). ("The contests waged by the orders in the cities for equality of rights are the most powerful means of making the commonwealths great." Trans. T. G. Bergin and M. H. Fisch, 42.)

If democratic freedom is the world-historical achievement of the Greeks, then *full pri-vate property, protected by the state, and an extremely differentiated system of contractual dis-posal of it* are the Romans' greatest legal creation. Slaves were also considered property, of course, and their importance for the economic system was enormous. Like every agrarian empire, Rome experienced social unrest among the lower strata, even if popu-lation growth suggests that on the whole more people could be fed.

The breakdown of the social and political balance in the Roman constitution was paradoxically a consequence of Rome's success in the realm of foreign policy. First, this success increased economic inequalities within, because the conquered wealth was not distributed equitably, and the long wars impoverished large segments of the population, whose years of dedication were not in the least rewarded by the Senate. All attempts at a solution of the social question failed; the Gracchi were killed. Yet the success in foreign policy led, second, to an independence of the army, which Marius's reform converted from a citizens' army into a mercenary force. Thus the generals had to try to provide for military veterans, who therefore became particularly devoted to them. Whereas Marius was a brilliant general, but lacked any comparable political abilities, another outstand-ing general with eminent political capacities, Caesar, resolved some of the social prob-lems caused by the expansion of Rome and its later development into what would prove to be the most stable multicultural empire in history. Third, since these successes had re-vealed the senatorial regime's inability to govern appropriately such an enormous em-pire, after long civil wars the old oligarchy was prepared to accept an almost monocratic state form, especially since Augustus, more gifted in this regard than Caesar, left to the Senate what appeared from the outside to be a magnificent position.

Rome's rise in foreign politics was owed to military and diplomatic achievements. Thus the Roman army was initially interwoven in a special way with the economic and political structure of the society, with the result that soldiers were exceptionally moti-vated. A considerable effort was made to justify the wars. The conviction that he was morally in the right was very important to the Roman, and for him this conviction was confirmed by his victories. However, the way in which the Romans dealt with their allies is particularly noteworthy. Reduced forms of Roman citizenship, and then, in the first century BC, citizenship itself, were granted to all Italics; in 212 AD, under Antoninus Caracalla, citizenship was extended to all free subjects of the Empire (with the excep-tion of the *dediticii*), even if only shortly before the great crisis of the Empire. The elites in the conquered areas, the provinces, were, with the exception of the hereditary enemy Carthage, integrated into the political system—the Roman emperors were recruited from many different peoples. A hundred years later the foreign elites had generally al-ready become Romanized; at the same time, the mores and religions of the subject peoples were always tolerated, provided they did not resist Roman rule. In the eastern, culturally more developed half of the empire, the local legal systems remained in force, even after the *constitituo Antoniniana*. The spread of Roman culture usually raised the standard of living for the conquered peoples; trade was significantly enhanced by the pacification of such a large area. Through their own labor, the legionaries made major improvements to the infrastructure of the conquered lands, and their demand stimulated economic activity: scholars have even spoken of a military Keynsianism.[227] However, one culture resisted Roman culture intellectually: Greek culture. Even if the Greeks were inferior to the Romans politically, they not only succeeded in preserving their own culture—Greek remained the *lingua franca* of the eastern half of the empire—but exercised a shaping influence on Roman culture: "Graecia capta ferum victorem cepit . . . ," conquered Greece subjugated the savage victor.[228] The Romans recognized the intellectual superiority of the people that was politically inferior to them, even if Cato the Elder not incorrectly sensed that Greek culture endangered old Roman mores. In addition, since the Romans had won control of the whole Mediterranean world, all kinds of eastern cults had moved toward Rome. Indeed, the infrastructure of the empire created the contextual conditions for the rapid expansion of Christianity. The empire and the program of a universal religion corresponded to each other, even if Christianity's reference to the transcendent endangered the Roman sense of the state.

E. N. Luttwak (1976) analyzed in great detail the strategies used to maintain the Roman empire. In the older system, the empire is surrounded by a series of client states, which are themselves surrounded by barbarian tribes. The legions are very mobile and are used where they are urgently needed. Temporary concentration of half the army in a single province does not imperil the system, because the legions' capacity to threaten is sufficiently great to hold most of the neighbors in check. Power is based on the prestige of the Roman name. The second strategy, pursued from the Flavians up to the crisis of the Empire, is characterized by territorialization. The legions are stationed on the borders, which are fortified, but they can also pass beyond them into enemy territory in order to increase the deterrent effect; the system of client states loses its importance.

However, all this could not prevent the collapse of the Roman Empire, which had both internal and external causes. Among the internal causes were surely the signs of degeneration among the elites—for neither the first nor the last time in history, the luxury that had made political and military virtues possible also contributed to its decay. Retrogressions in the arts and in legal technique can be observed in the second and third centuries. The rise of Christianity was a symptom of the decrease of identification with imperial ideology (which the Stoic emperors tried to revive), but also favored it. The most important external cause was the threat posed by the barbarians. The latter were attracted by Rome's wealth, and at the same time the spread of Roman innovations in technology and organization strengthened their own structures. Nonetheless, after the great crisis of the Empire of the third century, a partial recovery was made, which was accompanied by major constitutional reforms. The dominate of Diocletian was an important step toward an efficient *administrative state*. The bureaucratic apparatus

---

227. Cf. M. Mann (1986 f.), 1:297.
228. Horace, *Epistulae* II, 1, 156.

was enlarged, civilian administration was separated from military administration, the provinces were made smaller, the army strengthened, taxes were set on the basis of an estimate of the state's needs—probably the first budget in the history of the state. The new measures, especially the last one, were brutally implemented, and Christianity and Manicheanism, in which Diocletian saw enemies of the old Roman value system, were fought with special severity. Diocletian and Constantine, who viewed Christianity as the most suitable instrument for pursuing Diocletian's program of political renewal, were able to put off the fall of Rome, but not to prevent it. The pressure exerted by the barbarians grew steadily greater, and it was no longer possible to subjugate them, no attempt was made to integrate them, and instead an imperial German like Stilicho, to whom Rome was heavily indebted, was executed. Finally, the western Roman empire collapsed, and a phase of unprecedented retrogression of state power ensued. Under the Merovingians there was no longer any public taxation, administrative and diplomatic services shrank, and coins ceased to be minted. This was accompanied by a demographic decline and for many centuries by a loss of scientific and technological knowledge unique in world history. And yet it was Western Europe from which the project of modernity ultimately proceeded, not from the eastern half of the empire, which survived into the fifteenth century. The collision of humanity's greatest civilization, the Greco-Roman, with the barbarians proved in the long run to be incomparably more productive culturally than the Byzantine empire.

6.2.2.2.3. *The Western Middle Ages*

The assimilation of Romans and barbarians, especially the Celts and Germans, was favored by *Christianity*. For on one hand, Christianity was a universalist religion and on the other it combined elements of Greek speculation, which had already in the first century begun to penetrate Jesus' teaching, with powerful, existentially moving ideas that spoke to the imagination of illiterates and also satisfied the intellectual needs of the surviving intellectual elites who sought refuge in monasteries. The adaptation of ancient culture to the barbarian masses meant both destroying it and saving it. The ancient feeling of life was lost for centuries, but texts remained extant that made it possible to bring it back. The demand for a synthesis of philosophical conceptions with a deep need for salvation is also evident in other religions of salvation in late antiquity, especially in Manicheanism, which agrees with Christianity in a high regard for scripturality that would have been inconceivable at the beginning of antiquity. Both are book religions, even though Christianity leaves all other book religions behind by assuming that revelation occurred less in a text than in the person of Jesus—in this way it could repeatedly look beyond the holy text.[229] Its monotheistic structure gave Christianity a greater intellectual attractiveness than Manicheanism, especially since Christianity

---

229. Georg Scherer drew my attention to this point.

succeeded, through the doctrine of the Trinity, in surmounting abstract monism, and through Christology, in connecting up with a concrete historical event. It is true that these dogmas of Christianity seem to contradict reason, but in any case they have stimulated it in fertile ways, and they have made possible a perspective on history that differs from those of all other cultures. Thereby Christianity triggered an enormous change in human history, which depends, among other things, on the perspective that humans have on it.[230] On the other hand, *Islam,* the last major universal book religion that has thus far emerged in history, is purely monotheistic. More rational and simpler than Christianity in its structure, it achieved a comprehensive reception of ancient science and philosophy earlier than did medieval Christianity, but also entered a phase of intellectual stagnation earlier, and was not able to produce modern science, which presupposes a conception of human beings that was at least favored by the doctrine of the Incarnation of God in a man. Islamic universalism was combined from the outset with traditional, patriarchal tribal structures, which is probably why Mohammed succeeded in improving the status of women in his own time, but a more thorough emancipation of women nonetheless finally proceeded from the context of the Christian culture area. The expansion of Islam from Arabia toward the West and East destroyed the cultural unity of the Mediterranean world that Rome had produced, and it explains the differing developments in the individual regions of this area. Moreover, it should be mentioned that Christianity, in its explicit statements (but not necessarily in its real behavior; consider the crusades and the Inquisition), is less aggressive than Islam—the universal obligation of charity suggests greater leniency than unconditional obedience to the Divine will. Therefore it certainly appears paradoxical that it was precisely Christian civilization that was able to rise to a world domination that has been denied Islam, at least so far. For that reason, again and again Christianity seems hypocritical, not only to those who stand outside it, but also and especially to those who have been raised in the faith; but sensitivity to moral contradictions is fostered precisely by Christianity. A more important difference between Christianity and Islam has to do finally with the hierarchical organization of the Catholic church. In the Dark Ages it remained the most comprehensive and best-organized European corporate group; in the long term it made an emancipation of the political more difficult, but prepared the way for the latter in the realm of the technology of domination and administration.

Outside the Catholic church, social relationships initially crystallized in accord particularly with the feudal model. This had its roots in personal relationships of dependency in the Germanic tribes as well as in the colonate, mandatory hereditary land leases with which flight from the land in late antiquity was supposed to be halted. Thus it was a synthesis of Roman and Germanic legal institutions, just as Christianity is a

---

230. Cf. Hegel's dictum: "Weil die Inder keine Geschichte als Historie haben, um deswillen haben sie keine Geschichte als Taten (*res gestae*), d.i. keine Herausbildung zu einem wahrhaft politischen Zustande" (1969 ff.; 12:204). ("Because the peoples of India have no history as narrative, they have no history as deeds (*res gestae*), that is, no development toward a truly political condition.")

specific synthesis of Judaic religion and Greek philosophy. Vassalage, obedience and service in exchange for protection by a more powerful individual, was combined with a grant of land for life, through which the lord fulfilled his duty to support his vassal, in *feudal institutions.* These institutions were no doubt a step backward with regard to the sphere of statehood as represented by the Roman Empire, although Roman dependencies also existed—patrons and clients were discussed earlier. But in the Roman Empire these dependencies existed only alongside the state, whereas the feudal state, including even the Holy Roman Empire of the Middle Ages, was merely a network of such relationships and consisted of the hierarchy of fragmented landed property rights and mutual dependencies. The state played an almost marginal role in the life of most Europeans.[231] In such a system, the king could not command, but was instead dependent upon the voluntary cooperation of his vassals. If one were to apply to phylogeny L. Kohlberg's ontogenetic theory of the evolution of moral consciousness, one could say that the fourth stage of moral development, characterized by the law-and-order orientation of conventional morals, was replaced by a strong reciprocity, characteristic of the second stage of pre-conventional morals.

However, we must emphasize three points. Even if feudal relationships lacked the universality of statehood, they were not, first, family relationships. The establishment of lord-vassal relationships was initially voluntary on both sides—and therefore they possessed an element of individual freedom and responsibility that is alien to tribal societies (even if there was a tendency to hereditary fiefs). Second, the relationship between lord and vassal was not symmetrical, insofar as the services that they undertook to provide were of different kinds. But both parties obligated themselves; either party might commit a "felony," that is, a violation of these obligations, and the personal fidelity of the vassal to his lord, as well as that of the lord to the vassal, was one of the most important feudal values. To that extent, the feudal ethos was different from both the feeling of equality characteristic of the enfranchised citizens of classical antiquity and blind subjection to an oriental despot's will.[232] Third, Western feudalism developed on the foundation of a universalistic religion, which legitimated the system and contributed to a certain degree of internal peace in the Occident (although at the same time it encouraged enterprises such as the crusades). The economic system was based on farmers who were often only partly free, stood in manifold relations of dependency,

---

231. Cf. M. Mann (1994), 350: "In the twelfth century even the strongest [sc. states] absorbed less than 2 percent of GNP (if we could measure it), they called out highly decentralized military levies of at most 10 to 20,000 men sometimes only for 30 days in the campaigning system, they couldn't tax in any regular way, they regulated only a small proportion of total social disputes—they were, in fact, marginal to the social lives of most Europeans."

232. Cf. P. Anderson (1974), 409: "The composite ethos of the feudal nobility thus held 'honour' and 'loyalty' together in a dynamic tension foreign to either the citizenry of classical Antiquity, which in Greece or Rome had known only the first, or the servitors of a despotic authority like the Sultanism of Turkey, who knew only the second. Contractual mutuality and positional equality were merged in the full device of the fief."

and were for the most part subject to the justice (at this time the decisive state power) of the lord who owned their bodies or their land (*Leibherr, Grundherr*), in exchange for whose protection they had to pay taxes and provide corvée labor. Conflicts between the two classes increased from the thirteenth century on. There were still slaves in the Christian Middle Ages, but considerably fewer than in antiquity, because the enslavement of Christians became morally problematic. The high value put on work by the Western church was decisive for later development. Medieval agriculture made great progress (thanks to the further technological development of the plow, among other things), production and trade were promoted by the protection of property rights that feudalism recognized, and cities became centers for technological, economic, political, and cultural development. In addition to relationships under feudal law (to which the monastic communities already represented an alternative), from the high Middle Ages onward there increasingly developed corporative organizations that were not feudal in nature, but were based instead on free contracts and the mediation of individual interests— the universities are a good example of this. The transition from feudalism to capitalism is more continuous than it at first appears—Gellner wittily calls feudalism "a curious free market in loyalty."[233] The high and late Middle Ages can no longer be described as exclusively feudal: commercial capitalism emerged in the late Middle Ages. Probably a long phase of reduced statehood was required to produce the modern individualism that proved to be the strongest source of energy for the modern state.

The importance of law and jurisprudence for Western culture is shown by the *development and scholarly elaboration of canon law*, one of the greatest achievements of the human mind. Even the church, which had a monopoly on the sacraments, was bound by legal forms.[234] The celibacy of priests, which prevented the priesthood from becoming hereditary, fostered the development of an abstract concept of the office.

Early in the Middle Ages, the break between the Eastern churches and Catholicism was already beginning. Eastern Christianity has nothing to compare with scholasticism, the intellectual penetration of belief, or the science of canon law. The small dogmatic difference between the Orthodox and Catholic churches, the *Filioque*, is characteristic insofar as the Orthodox church has remained true to the older version of the Credo— if antiquity were the decisive criterion, it would be superior. But on the other hand, the formal fact that the Credo was further developed in the West already points to a more dynamic culture—as does the content of the change in the Credo. If the third Person proceeds from God the Father and from God the Son, then the relation between Father and Son, between the absolute and its manifestation in history, becomes more symmetrical; thus finite man also gains new value. Obviously this does not mean that the dogmatic difference explains the further differences between Eastern and Western Europe; differing developments in law and economics have also had at least as strong an

---

233. (1988), 158.

234. On the importance of canon law for the development of Western law and the state, see H. J. Berman (1983).

influence on religion. Very generally, Christianity is perhaps a necessary, but never a sufficient condition for the endogenous emergence of the modern constitutional state; endogenously, Ethiopia, for instance, would never have become a modern state. The slower development of Eastern Europe is also demonstrated in relation to serfdom. Whereas in Western Europe serfdom began to wane as early as the fifteenth century, it first became the foundation of economic life in the East at about the same time (and in Russia even in the sixteenth century). Moreover, serfs had considerably fewer rights than in Western Europe. In Russia they could be given away as presents, sold, or pledged; only the lack of the right to kill them distinguished them from slaves.

The fragmentation of state power in feudalism explains why this system made it difficult for the modern state to develop; indeed, in Germany it even made it impossible to establish a nation-state. Things were different, however, in France and England, the first two modern European states. In England, feudalism was in the service of the monarchy, among other reasons because the sub-vassals were directly obliged to the king. "William the Conqueror imposed on all free men occupying a tenement an oath of fealty or 'allegiance' to the King (Oath of Salisbury). . . . In the reign of Henry I, the crown insisted that a reservation of fealty to the King should form part of the ordinary oath of vassalage."[235] Thus was the transitivity of the power relationship ensured; the institution of liegancy was monopolized by the king. The jurisdiction of local feudal authorities waned in importance as that of the king increased; the office of sheriff was not hereditary. By replacing the vassal's duty to provide military service with a tax, the *scutagium,* the king was able to maintain his own salaried army, and thus his ability to strike militarily became independent of the vassals' readiness to serve. In France, the king, whose power was originally founded purely on feudal law, was able to make himself the overlord of the kingdom. Supported by jurists and the courts, the king exploited his feudal rights to deprive powerful territorial lords of their fiefs and to make them his subjects. As often happens in history, a legal system was used in order to create a social and political order whose principles were opposed to it. More or less regular tax revenues from various sources developed, and made it possible to develop a salaried bureaucracy, although the interests of local potentates had constantly to be respected and although the employment of commoners as counselors aroused resistance.[236] Political domination began to be defined in territorial terms. In the new political order, Charles the Bold had to try to unite his scattered possessions into a kingdom or watch his power evaporate. The conflict between the emerging European states, which put their neighbors under strong pressure to adopt the new evolutionarily stable political strategy, led to something like a national consciousness (for instance, in the Hundred Years' War). The organization of war was a crucial motor for state-building; for many centuries, 70–90 percent of the state's financial resources were devoted to military goals.[237] In the fourteenth century, the

---

235. F. L. Ganshof (1964), 165 f.
236. Cf. J. Strayer (1970).
237. Cf. M. Mann (1986 ff), 1:511.

Black Death killed a third of the population of Europe, not only shaking the dominant worldview, but also increasing the power of the state, which had to assume responsibility for matters of public health. Since the late Middle Ages, the monarchs' power had stood in opposition to the power of the estates that was not derived from the king's power—once again, a form of dyarchy, yet one considerably more radical than that of the Roman principate, since the monarch often could exercise his power only indirectly through regional rights of domination of the estates, and there was a multitude of competing claims to domination.

From what has been said it seems to follow, first of all, that Western feudalism represented a very complex form of society, and second that it was interwoven with peculiarities of European history that did not exist elsewhere in the same form. Certainly there were other societies that had a warring aristocracy, personal relationships of dependency, and land grants. However, one cannot speak of a feudal phase in all cultures—certainly not among hunters and gatherers, but even to call India a feudal state is conceptually absurd. Moreover, there are important differences even between the Western Middle Ages and cultures whose social orders are related to those of the Western Middle Ages. To that extent, Montesquieu was not mistaken when he called the system of European feudal rights, which produced a rule with a tendency toward anarchy and an anarchy with a tendency toward order and harmony, an event that had occurred only once in the history of the world, and would perhaps never occur again.[238] But one can probably say of any event that it has characteristics that will not be repeated. At the same time, however, every event and every social system also have general characteristics—and how many societies may be called "feudal" depends on the definition adopted. O. Hintze (1929) mentioned, in addition to the Carolingian empire's successor states, Russia, a few Islamic states, and Japan, and indeed he even suggested that the emergence of feudalism could be reduced to a general historical configuration, namely the deflection of the normal development from tribe to state by a premature imperialism. However important Hintze's limited expansion of the concept of feudalism may have been, only medieval Japan can be described as a truly feudal state if we assume a definition such as P. Anderson's: "Feudalism typically involves the juridical serfdom and military protection of the peasantry by a social class of nobles, enjoying individual authority and property, and exercising an exclusive monopoly of the law and private rights of justice, within a political framework of fragmented sovereignty and subordinate fiscality, and an aristocratic ideology exalting rural life."[239] Furthermore, the causes that led to structurally similar systems are different in the two cases. Even if in both, feudalism was the result of an encounter between two cultures (the Roman and the Germanic, the Chinese and the Japanese, of which in each case only one had already constructed a state), Japanese feudalism represents a gradual retreat from a higher form of statehood, whereas the feudal

---

238. *Esprit des lois* 30.1 (1748; 2:309): "un événement arrivé une fois dans le monde, et qui n'arrivera peut-être jamais."

239. P. Anderson's detailed definition is found in (1974), 407.

order of the Carolingian empire represented a—limited—reconstruction of statehood. However, it is hardly an accident that Japan was the non-Western state that modernized itself the most rapidly and efficiently.[240] This confirms what was said earlier concerning the relative proximity of feudalism and capitalism—namely, that immense difficulties in constructing a stable capitalism are experienced by cultures in which what is produced by an individual's own labor is not protected as property, but instead regularly expropriated by the powerful of the land. Yet this does not mean that Japan would have modernized itself even without Western influence. Many considerations suggest otherwise. First, because of its corporative and not merely feudal structures, the European city was a unique structure, to which the old Japanese cities can hardly be compared.[241] Second, medieval Europe was an international and intercultural web that demanded important hermeneutic, diplomatic, and military achievements that favored the construction of the modern state, and with which there is nothing comparable in Japan. Third, in Japan feudal relationships were more extensively asymmetrical—representation of the estates never evolved there. Fourth, we have to take into account the influence of the Christian religion, and especially Protestantism, without which modern science would scarcely have developed. Fifth, Europeans' travels and expeditions of discovery should be mentioned. Marco Polo's report on the extraordinary wealth at Kubla Khan's court made Europe seem poor in comparison. But it was Europeans who made their way to China, whereas at that time there were no Chinese working for European courts. However, curiosity is a stronger historical force than piling up treasures in a court. Sixth, the extension of the spatial horizon was accompanied by an extension of the temporal horizon. The Renaissance made possible a recovery of intellectual and political achievements that had not been pursued further in the Middle Ages.

6.2.2.3. Modernity

The elements whose combination determines the project of modernity (which begins in the late Middle Ages) have already been essentially listed, partly in the first chapter. Changes in religion, in the natural and human sciences, in technology, economics, the state, and the structure of international relations have produced what we call modern Europe. In the second half of the fifteenth century, *printing* with moveable type, the three-masted *caravel,* and cast bronze *cannons* emerged—three achievements that hastened the end of the medieval world. Printing led to literacy of an undreamed-of extent, and especially to an extremely rapid spread of written information—and thus also to both a democratization and an acceleration of the historical process. It is true that the transition to print culture is not comparable in importance to the transitions to writing and to electronic media, if we are considering the change in the relation to reality; but it can be said that printing made possible entirely new ways of organizing the economy

---

240. On Japan and the West, cf. J. P. Arnason (1993).
241. Cf. P. Anderson (1974), 422 ff.

and the state. The caravel allowed people to travel over the oceans, especially because the compass had also existed in the West since the twelfth or thirteenth centuries, and cartography had made great progress. The fall of Constantinople in 1453 and the almost complete domination of the eastern Mediterranean by the Ottomans increased the pressure to expand toward the west. Finally, cannons could destroy castles—thereby dissolving the ideological, geographic, and military borders of the Middle Ages. Nonetheless, it should be emphasized that technological achievements alone could never trigger social changes, as is shown by the example of China, which had discovered printing, the compass, and gunpowder before the West did. Still more important than brilliant technological innovations is the will on the part of a good portion of the society to use them—where this will is present, it usually also produces the necessary discoveries;[242] where it is lacking, even the most important inventions, such as the Roman waterwheel, which did not come into general use until the Middle Ages, remain isolated.[243] It goes without saying that in the following we will be concerned only with the common traits of the process of Europe's modernization, and not with the specific differences between individual European states, which are undeniable, but cannot be discussed in the framework of this book.[244]

6.2.2.3.1. Non-Political Changes

The change in man's self-conception is clearly shown in *Renaissance humanism.* However much humanism understands itself as a Christian movement, it also tends toward a new evaluation of man. The art of the Renaissance vividly expresses this and like Greek art, is a highpoint in the history of art. At first glance the Italian city-states may seem repetitions of the Greek polis, but the differences are considerable. The relationship between land and city is different; monocracy, which was in Greece a transitional state form, is in Italy the endpoint of the constitutional development; manual labor is differently valued; and Christianity's universalism paves the way for modernity. Simplifying to the maximum admissible degree, we could say that in the Renaissance man is preparing himself to take over God's role as master of the world, even if this process continued over many centuries and arrived at its conclusion only in our own time. If ancient man still saw himself as bound within the cosmos, the relationship to transcendence characteristic of the Middle Ages, which the vertical aspiration of the Gothic cathedrals perfectly expresses, emancipated him from the legitimating power of nature, which he increasingly subjects to his own control as God becomes more distant

---

242. Cf. Hegel (1969 ff.), 12:491: "Das Technische findet sich ein, wenn das Bedürfnis vorhanden ist." ("The technology is discovered when the need is present.")

243. Cf. P. Anderson (1978), 80.

244. It is obvious that the special constitutional law structure of the Holy Roman Empire of the German Nation marked in a special way the construction of modern states on its territory; cf. P. Münch (1996).

in his consciousness. Furthermore, the return to antiquity is crucial. Certainly there were also "renaissances" in other cultures,[245] and even in the West one can speak of various renaissances—for instance, the Carolingian or that of the twelfth century. But there is only one Renaissance *par excellence;* it begins in the fourteenth century, and from it emerged, after numerous processes of transformation, the modern humanities and the historical sciences, which represent a turning point in human history no less fateful than the modern natural sciences. The Renaissance *par excellence* prepares the way for modernity insofar as the study of one's own culture's past, independent of its contents, makes it possible to assume a critical distance from the present. But it was also a matter of the specific contents of antiquity to which people returned: reason freed itself from faith; the ancient sciences could develop further; the reception of Roman law on the continent facilitated the gradual surmounting of feudal law, and on one hand restored the Roman concept of full property, which could now develop its dynamics on a more universalistic basis than in the ancient slave-holding society, and with a different evaluation of labor, while in constitutional law, on the other hand, it enabled the new monocracies to move beyond feudal domination. (Not accidentally, the first monocracy of the Middle Ages was the papacy, which had never broken its connection with the Roman law tradition.) To be sure, Renaissance students of the ancients originally sought to apply their insights to their own age, but the distance between their own time and that of the ancients led the intellectual operation of philological understanding to become independent. It was recognized that certain things that people thought they had read out of authoritative texts they had merely read into them—and thus a terrible dilemma arose. Either one had to reject any further development of tradition, because such an elaboration contradicted the correct philological interpretation of the text, or one had to concede that the author of the text had made a mistake, and therefore had to undermine his authority. These were the two possible reactions to the emergence of modern hermeneutics: fundamentalism and a break with tradition, which the new means could reveal as partly a forgery.

This can be seen, for instance, in the development of *Protestantism,* which is doubtless one of the greatest turning points in human history. Through Protestantism, individualism gained in the course of time an absolute religious foundation. Every Christian is directly related to God, and is, as it were, his own priest; this suggests democratic consequences. The vernacular becomes the religious language, and the liturgy no longer puts so much emphasis on the special status of priests. The salvation of a person's soul, for the sake of which God was incarnated in man, is no longer the responsibility of the church, but rather of the individual himself. With this consciousness, the spheres of economics and the state can be dissociated from religion. No human type in history has ever been allowed and obliged to take himself so seriously as the Protestant. The Calvinistic doctrine of predestination increases even further internal pressure in a way that one can

---

245. See the tenth part of Toynbee (1965).

today hardly still imagine, because all means of influencing divine will through masses, the intervention of the saints, etc., drop out and the individual must discover by himself whether he is among the elect. The greatest moral seriousness as well as a permanent, excessive moral demand are both outcomes of Protestantism. Such a demand almost inevitably *also* expresses itself in neuroses, hypocrisy, and mechanisms of projection. We have already spoken of *hypocrisy* in connection with Christianity, and it is in fact not hard to see that this phenomenon necessarily accompanies progress in moral consciousness. It is a grotesque error to assume that mere ideas alone will change behavior; but if one does not abide by that which one has learned to see as one's duty, then it is tempting to deceive others and oneself about it. To be sure, hypocrisy is repulsive, but it can be a productive force that eventually allows the emergence of the virtue to which it ultimately pays homage,[246] for it upholds a standard to which the victim of one's own injustice can no longer appeal when one indecently assaults him without feeling guilt. Moreover, Protestantism's hypocrisy is particularly fascinating because it represents, as it were, a meta-hypocrisy—for the commitment to sincerity (for instance, in criticizing the hypocrisy of celibacy) is one of the most valuable Protestant virtues.

Far more dangerous than hypocrisy are the *mechanisms of projection*. Superstitious persecution of witches, which is not a medieval but an early modern phenomenon that has its geographical center in Central Europe, is perhaps best interpreted as an expression of a fear of the evil that people feel in themselves, but look for elsewhere, because they no longer enjoy the security of participating in morally valid mores.[247] Naturally, this also holds for the Catholic church, whose inner feeling of insecurity began in the fourteenth century. Through the denominational schism, the Catholic church lost its self-evident character and increasingly had to adapt to Protestantism in order to survive.[248] This interpretation is strengthened by the fact that phenomena comparable to witch-hunts in various respects, particularly in their cratic irrationality and the quality of their moral excitement, such as the Reign of Terror during the French Revolution, Stalin's "Great Purge," and Mao Tse-Tung's "Cultural Revolution," also accompanied ideologically justified attempts at modernization. In these cases as well, it was tempting to turn the feeling of people's own inadequacy with regard to the norms of the republic of reason or the socialistic society into hatred and suspicion of alleged counterrevolutionaries.[249]

---

246. Cf. La Rochefoucauld, Maxime 218 (1967; 56): "L'hypocrisie est un hommage que le vice rend à la vertu."

247. Cf. Hegel (1969 ff.), 12:506 ff., but of course still without the concept of projection.

248. A few formally Catholic thinkers also adopt much of the Protestant *forma mentis,* such as Pascal, in whom the loss of the idea of order in the conception of nature and the plumbing of new depths in his own subjectivity go hand in hand.

249. National Socialism is characterized by a different and even more repulsive structure, although in it excessive "moral" demands in connection with modernization play a role as well. But its explicit nihilism is unparalleled.

The disassociation from the intellectual power of the church is accompanied by a close association with Scripture and with the faith communicated through it—early Protestantism is far removed from the idea of the autonomy of reason. Indeed, in this respect it even represents a step backward with respect to humanism and Catholicism, because on account of its greater connection with Scripture, it has a tendency to regard critically the Hellenization of Christianity and to reject the rational theology of the Scholastics.[250] The doctrine of verbal inspiration and the historicist depreciation of any absolute claim to truth are both products of Protestantism, and it is therefore entirely possible that Protestantism, without which modernity would have been completely inconceivable, will at the end of this era lose far more in intellectual plausibility, and therefore in historical power, than will Catholicism. The decisive breakthrough to modernity is not represented by Luther, but rather by Zwingli. With the symbolic interpretation of the Last Supper the empirical world loses its sacred character—it remains only what it immediately is, and is no longer the context of meaning to which it refers. The latter appears to be a subjective creation, and thus the subject and no longer the world is felt to be the source of the conferral of meaning. A disenchanted nature, in which the gods of Greece no longer exist, is precisely what *modern natural science* needs.[251]

Modern science differs from ancient science in that it is, for instance, dependent on experiments. But since the set-up for experiments represents *in nuce* a machine, in modernity the relation of science to technology is given from the beginning. Conversely, modern technology acquires, in contrast to Chinese technology, a foundation in mathematics and the natural sciences. Unlike ancient, teleological science, modern science is interested in causal connections that can be mastered. Qualities are to be replaced by quantities. As in the social world, so in modern science abstract equality is the decisive category. The infinite is also positively evaluated, in astronomy as well as in mathematics. Faust and Don Juan, the greatest literary figures of modernity, both fall victim to infinite regress. Mathematical entities, and increasingly the qualities of nature as well, are interpreted idealistically by modern science as human creations: what is true is what we can make. Nature becomes a soulless *res extensa;* animals become things. Presumably the moral devaluation of extra-human nature in modern Europe—which stands in such marked contrast to Indian culture, for instance, with its belief in the transmigration of souls—was a presupposition for the development of the idea of human rights. In India, a few animals were treated as if they were humans, but many people were also treated as if they were animals, whereas the European Enlightenment made the latter at least problematic. The connection between science and technology would not have become so effective had philosophy not at the same time become convinced that there is

---

250. However, the Protestant tradition from Melanchthon to Leibniz represents a countermovement with regard to Luther; only with Pietism was the continuity with Catholicism finally lost. Dialectical theology is the position absolutely opposite that of rational theology.

251. On the relationships between Zwingli and modern natural science, see J. P. S. Uberoi (1978), 25 ff.

a moral duty to broaden mastery over nature, in order to make it possible for all human beings to achieve happiness in this world, and had it not sought, in the form of the Enlightenment, to help this conviction gain social effectiveness. The seventeenth century begins to replace religion by the project of a rational metaphysics, from which a new moral conception emancipates itself in the eighteenth and nineteenth centuries. *Modern ethics* seeks to limit conflicts by first almost completely abstracting from the religious foundation, and then from the contents, and thus becoming formal and even increasingly procedural. It is universalist, individualist, and activist. The Christian roots of modern ethics are obvious, even if it represents an attempt to deny its theological and metaphysical foundations.[252]

Capitalism is the economic form best suited to the spirit of the new age. It is based on the moral ideas of formal equality and of the voluntary nature of cooperation, and on the intellectual demand for rationalization, which is expressed, for example, in double-entry bookkeeping. Acts of charity are also subjected to the pressure to rationalize—begging is forbidden. In Protestantism, innocent paupers are cared for systematically, not on the basis of spontaneous sympathy. Non-economic sanctions, which had determined economic events in pre-modern societies, such as those based on kinship connections, religious or legal traditions, and naked force, became less important. Labor, not robbery, was supposed to justify private property rights, which were to be as unlimited as possible.[253] If the *verum-factum* principle is the essence of modern science, the self-made man corresponds to the modern economic ideal: a person is defined by what he achieves. The transformation of qualities into quantities also characterizes modern capitalism. Mass production emerges (initially, partly in response to the demands of the court and the military, and later, to those of its own workers); the exchange value of commodities becomes more important than their use value. The exchange relationships of the market are perfected, and especially one's own labor becomes a commodity; the logic of this idea undermines feudal allegiances and slavery. Agriculture is also increasingly practiced from the point of view of the market. Greater agricultural productivity frees up more labor, trade flourishes, and a more efficient allocation of resources results. Commodities, but also people, are transported more and more quickly, in order to further increase efficiency—no other society has ever known comparable mobility (including and especially social mobility). A *world economy* emerges whose mechanisms extend across the borders of sovereign states. It becomes possible to coordinate simultaneous events in separate places,[254] partly because the measurement of time becomes more unified and more precise (think of the mechanical clock),[255] and partly because new structures of trust

---

252. On the deep structure of modern ethics and morality, see Charles Taylor's penetrating analyses (1989).

253. In contrast, for a long time "Wars remained the greatest potential source of profit" for Islam (J. A. Hall and G. J. Ikenberry [1989], 34).

254. Cf. A. Giddens (1990).

255. Cf. P. Münch (1992), 172 ff.

are formed that are more reliable than those we know from earlier societies—although, or rather because, they are based on rational self-interest. Maximizing profit becomes an economic goal, which has no immanent limits. Modern man's structure of needs is markedly different from that of all earlier people, and agrees with science in its positive evaluation of the infinite.

Capitalism presupposes a dynamic *entrepreneurial type* who periodically transforms modes of production through technological, but also organizational, innovations, and partly discovers, partly creates new needs. Without such people, there would be hardly any economic progress, but they are also the people who constantly upset the economic equilibria and thereby help cause business cycles with periodically recurring unemployment. In the long term, the dynamic entrepreneur can only succeed if the political-legal structural conditions are stable and there is general reliability and high labor morale. Adventurers who want to make a lot of money quickly have always existed, but what was lacking were bourgeois virtues such as cleanliness, order, hard work, thrift, and fidelity to contracts, which would have provided the moral infrastructure for enterprises that were planned to exist over a long period. In the connection of the spirit of the entrepreneur and that of the bourgeois, Werner Sombart saw the essence of the capitalist spirit, a relation that is so fascinating because the two elements are opposed in nature: "If the entrepreneurial spirit wants to conquer, to acquire, the bourgeois spirit wants to impose order, preserve."[256] This-worldly asceticism in work and luxury in consumption play an equal role in the genesis of capitalism. The increase in thriftiness and the development of the credit system were promoted by the abolition of the prohibition on lending at interest, which had an important consequence—the pressure for economic growth.[257] In addition, the capital accumulation necessary for investments was achieved by expropriations within modern societies (consider the way small farmers were driven off their land) as well as by plundering in the wake of colonialism.

The original *commercial capitalism* was followed, from the eighteenth century onward, by *industrial capitalism,* which succeed in making the seventeenth-century scientific revolution technologically and economically useful. With industrialization, the second sector grew at the expense of the first; the values connected with the agricultural way of life, especially the bond with nature, declined in importance. "Agriculture was the economic foundation of humanity from the early Stone Age to the beginning of modernity, and what now interests us is how this was reflected in mores: Cultivating plants and keeping animals involves mutual service. Just as they are there for us, so we are there for them. . . . Man also most effectively reacts to the drastic dependency on unpredictable natural events by adopting an attitude that does not fundamentally exclude being prepared to give up, and he is far from finally rejecting the idea that he is a creature—but at least the superstitious belief in human omnipotence, which dominates

---

256. (1987), 1:329.

257. On the relation between interest and the principle of growth, see H.C. Binswanger (1991). An alternative to growth would be inflation.

the metropolises, is alien to him."[258] While the energy used by humans previously consisted largely of muscle power, inorganic forces and artificially produced or dead materials are now increasingly substituted for organic forces and organically grown materials—and this initially represented a way of relieving the burden on the animal world. With the systematic exploitation of fossil fuels, energy consumption no longer had to be limited to what was reproduced annually: "So long as wood was the standard material and domesticated animals were the most important source of energy, there was a non-technological *limit*—given in advance by the slow tempo of organic growth and the modest dimensions of organic reproduction—to the pace and growth of material culture, and thus ultimately to the increase in population as well."[259] In Great Britain, the country in which the Industrial Revolution first prevailed, 100 million tons of coal were already consumed in 1870. With the 800 million calories thereby produced, the energy needs of an agrarian society of 20 million adults could be met (the British population was then 31 million), although this coal was provided by only 400,000 miners.[260] Because of advances in food production, transportation, and medicine, life expectancy rapidly increased. The acceleration of exchange and communication fundamentally changed the relationship to space, time, and other people, who became more or less easily replaceable. The modern metropolis—which is qualitatively as different from the city as the latter is from the village—is an expression of the new anonymity of human relationships.

The rationalization of relationships between people from an economic point of view produces as its complement a *longing for love experienced fully as an end in itself.* If there have always been sexual relationships outside marriage, modernity brought forth, after medieval forerunners, the idea of an erotics that could in theory be realized only outside the family, because concern about a common management of property and progeny would poison the unconditional nature of the dual interpersonal relationship. Certainly, economic constraints or interests impose themselves with astounding brutality in bourgeois love relationships as well—just read Flaubert's *Madame Bovary.* But the ideology of free love persists with surprising tenacity, despite all the excessive de-

---

258. Gehlen (1957), 71f.: "Das ökonomische Fundament der Menschheit von der jüngeren Steinzeit bis zum Beginn der Moderne war die Landwirtschaft, und an dieser Tatsache interessiert uns jetzt der moralische Reflex: Die Hege und Kultur der Tiere und Pflanzen besteht nämlich in einem wechselseitigen Dienst. So wie sie für den Menschen da sind, so ist er für sie da. . . . Auch reagiert der Mensch auf die drastische Abhängigkeit von unberechenbaren Naturereignissen am wirksamsten mit einer Einstellung, die grundsätzliche Verzichtsbereitschaft nicht ausschließt, und eine letzte Auflehnung gegen die Vorstellung, Kreatur zu sein, wird ihm fernliegen—zum mindesten aber wird ihm der Aberglaube an die Allmacht des Menschen fehlen, der die Großstädte beherrscht."

259. Ibid., 10: "Solange Holz der maßgebende Werkstoff und die Leistung des gezähmten Tieres die wichtigste Kraftquelle waren, bestand eine nichttechnische, vorgegebene, in dem langsamen Tempo des organischen Wachstums und dem bescheidenen Ausmaß der organischen Vermehrung liegende *Schranke* für Tempo und Wachstum der materiellen Kultur, und damit in letzter Instanz auch für die Vermehrung der Volkszahlen."

260. I take these figures from M. Mann (1986ff.; 2:13).

mands and disappointments, until love declines into cynicism. The erotic becomes autonomous, as do economics and other subsystems of modernity, such as art, which breaks away from the true and the good and finds in aesthetes its gourmets. Like the later incorporation of women into the work force, which was grounded in the logic of capitalist development, making the erotic independent helps make relationships between the sexes more symmetrical. Whereas the Industrial Revolution made possible an enormous increase in the world population that is still continuing, *giving men and women equal sexual and economic rights* is one of the factors that have most strongly limited population growth—especially since the development of extremely effective means of contraception that do away with the burden of undesired pregnancy and at the same time make mutual sexual instrumentalization easier.

The virtues that are demanded during a time of population increase have to do with thriftiness and increasing production, whereas in an era of population decrease consumption and sales are more important than production.[261] The *rationalization* of the process of production in Taylorism and the *automatization* of production on the basis of new technologies that no longer take over only motor capacities but sensory and increasingly thinking capacities as well, cause the second sector to shrink to the advantage of the third, which is constantly extending itself. Services, the influencing of humans and symbols, become more important than the processing of materials. Marketing surpasses production in importance, and the creations of new needs through advertising that is not informative but manipulative becomes a central task of an economy that is oriented toward constant growth. As a complement to marketing specialists, a further basic figure of late modernity emerges in the psychoanalyst, who seeks to help individuals freed from the burden of poverty to compensate for their lack of meaning through a value-neutral activity that encourages them to be concerned with themselves.

So far as the religious presuppositions of capitalism go, they are no less important than the legal-political ones. Protestantism (along with Judaism) promoted capitalism, and in particular took care that the dynamics it unleashed did not become self-destructive. In any case, in the bourgeois, capitalism produced a type of person who conceives of himself essentially through his property rights. The whole feeling of Christianity is more or less dissolved in the absoluteness of private property—one's own as well as that of others. Economic activity is pursued with religious zeal, which immunizes it against deceptions just as in the long run it devalues the religious. An exceptional sense for symmetrical relationships, an aversion to parasitism, a high opinion of work, and strict control over the emotions, are the new virtues of the early bourgeois, which are developed in the "civilizing process." This may be accompanied by the loss of any ability to think beyond one's own rational interest—generosity, hospitality, spontaneous cordiality, selfless fidelity to persons one sees as models, a sovereign indifference to the economic sphere, heroic readiness to sacrifice oneself, and sympathetic responsibility

---

261. Cf. D. Riesman (1950).

with regard to weaker people belonging to one's own household are not among the virtues of modernity. Don Quixote is the great loser of modernity, but we have more sympathy for him than for the puritanical managers of commercial enclaves who in every contact with other human beings calculate what is economically profitable for them. Modern man is hardly happier than traditional man. Since modern man must make himself what he wants to be, and since the mobility of the system always permits further opportunities to rise in society, he is seldom content with what he has achieved. Society seems to him to be a human creation, therefore for the most part changeable and without intrinsic value. His feeling of self-worth is much stronger than that of earlier men, and often unduly exaggerated, but it is also more fragile, because at any time he can lose the prestige he has won, and because even stable social recognition cannot replace the relationship to transcendence. In the phase of population decline, even the virtues of the early bourgeois fade away; a human type spreads that honors only rights but no longer any duties, and never feels so threatened as by outstanding persons.

6.2.2.3.2. *Changes in Internal Policy*

The first absolutist states surprise us by their peculiar mixture of ancient and modern elements. They are shaped by modern ideas, but at the same time, seen in relation to the watershed of the French Revolution, they belong to the *ancien régime.* Not until the nineteenth century, and ultimately only in the fascist and totalitarian states after the First World War, were the last remainders of medieval influence overcome— but only thanks to the absolutist phase in the history of states. Even after royal and princely prerogatives were set above the rights of the estates and a state monopoly on force was established in opposition to the system of feuds in the Middle Ages, the power of the head of state remained far more limited by mores and religion, as well as by a plenitude of autochthonous regional rights and structures of domination, than in modern monocracies (think of rights as different as those of the nobility, the French *parlements,* or guilds). To that extent the term "absolutism" is misleading, since it would be more appropriately applied to the contemporaneous oriental despotisms whose infrastructural power, however, was not as great.

Although in modernity the monarch gradually came to be conceived as a representative, the dynasty of the rulers, not the people, was considered the final point of reference. For that reason, political conflicts could be resolved or at least alleviated by marriages between dynasties, even if their political fruits appeared only a generation or more later. Wars were often about hereditary succession. Even if the establishment of a standing army and an efficient bureaucracy was continued, offices were widely bought and sold, the largest part of the standing army often consisted of foreigners (it was considered risky to arm one's own peasants),[262] and the idea that citizens had a duty to pay

---

262. Cf. Bodin (1576), 766 and Mill (1972), 362.

taxes did not yet exist. Anderson aptly describes early modern taxes as "centralized feudal rent" in contrast to the "local feudal rent" of the Middle Ages.[263] The economic policy of mercantilism was concerned with the prosperity of the people and the state as well as with increasing the population, but it saw the international economic system as a zero-sum game. Law was unified—few things are more important for the long-term enterprises of capitalism than the certainty of the law—but special privileges still remained. With the state church, the state dissolved its connection to a supra-national church (this also holds to a limited degree for modern Catholic states), but assumed religious functions itself, and this made a recognition of religious freedom more difficult.

The monarch based his power partly on the nobility and the clergy, and partly on the *haute bourgeoisie*. Struggles with the nobility, such as those in Sweden that resulted in the focus of power repeatedly shifting back and forth between crown and the estates, should not conceal the fact that the king himself belonged to the nobility, even if he consciously promoted other classes. Political leadership positions were still for the most part filled by the aristocracy. In the development of modern states a role is frequently played by cooperation between a brilliant statesman and his monarch, and their mutual dependency is extremely interesting from a psychological point of view—consider the relationships between Richelieu and Louis XIII, and between Bismarck and William I. At the same time, absolutism also involves the destruction of the belief in a fundamental inequality among human beings. Politically disempowered aristocrats (who had to acquire new abilities) and bourgeois used the new economic system to construct an economic power that was beneficial for the principles of the modern state and further increased social mobility. Whereas a few states used force to impose the centralization of power, in others the system of positive sanctions or a mixture of the latter and coercion played the leading role. It was inevitable that in time the new bourgeois class would demand a share of political power.

Bourgeois revolutions broke the power of absolutism in the Spanish Netherlands in the sixteenth century, in England in the seventeenth century, in France in the eighteenth century, and tried to do so in Prussia in the nineteenth century and in Russia in the twentieth century. Everywhere in Europe, they ultimately led to the connection between sovereignty and the separation of powers typical of the modern state, and especially to the shift of most of the legislative power to the parliament.[264] The nobility was increasingly deprived of power, and monarchy was finally abolished everywhere where it was not content with a representative function. Thus many vices disappeared, but so did many great virtues, which sprang from the consciousness of playing a special role in society. Only where monarchs succeeded in avoiding major errors did the possession of the highest state office remain based on birth, as an exception to the egalitarian

---

263. (1974), 35.
264. I use the concept of "bourgeois revolution" with respect to the setting of political goals, not to the classes that carried out the revolution.

tendencies of modernity. To be sure, all these revolutions have common traits. In the fifth book of his *Politics*, Aristotle had already developed a theory of revolution, and modern social and historical sciences have subjected revolutionary situations and results to a comparative analysis.[265] Thus revolutions presuppose first of all a feeling on the part of a number of the citizens capable of organizing themselves that their basic rights have been violated, and second, an increasingly apparent impotence on the part of the government to find a remedy for the problem, on one hand, and to defend itself, on the other. For a revolution to succeed, weakness in the government is far more relevant than the strength of the revolutionaries, who often have no precise ideas when they rise up. The more manifold the dissatisfactions with which the government is confronted, and thus the less there is a simple strategy for resolving them, the more difficult it is to avoid an uprising of this kind. (Even if there is a such a simple strategy, the government may reject it out of stupidity or pig-headedness.) A prolonged phase of economic progress followed by a sudden collapse can particularly easily trigger aggressiveness aroused by the frustration of awakened expectations, and the sudden weakness of a hated system can stimulate the courage to resist it.[266] A weakness often becomes evident precisely through the will to reform, and therefore Tocqueville is right in maintaining that the most dangerous moment for a bad government usually comes when it begins to reform itself,[267] as the fate of *perestroika* showed. The revolutions mentioned at the outset were, moreover, all directed against a monocrat in the name of bourgeois values. And yet one of them is of singular importance: the French Revolution.

The French Revolution made national and social problems the crucial political issues that they remained throughout the nineteenth and twentieth centuries. No less important is the French Revolution's almost religious rhetorics, the claim to have begun a new era—Tocqueville aptly called this revolution a "révolution politique qui a procédé à la manière des révolutions religieuses" ("a political revolution that proceeded in the manner of religious revolutions"). By this Tocqueville means that the traditional revolutions were limited to their own countries, whereas the French Revolution aspired, like the universal religions, to renew the whole world;[268] it was the general revolution that Leibniz foresaw.[269] Wars thereby assumed the character of civil wars, and the ideologi-

---

265. Cf., for example, C. Brinton (1965) and C. Tilly (1993).

266. Cf. M. Mann (1986 ff.), 2:531 f., 724.

267. (1856), 266: "le moment le plus dangereux pour un mauvais gouvernement est d'ordinaire celui où il commence à se réformer."

268. "Une révolution politique qui inspire le prosélytisme; qu'on prêche aussi ardemment aux étrangers qu'on l'accomplit avec passion chez soi; considérez quel nouveau spectacle! Parmi toutes les choses inconnues que la révolution française a montrées au monde, celle-ci est assurément la plus nouvelle" (1856; 106 f.). ("A political revolution that inspires proselytism; that is preached as ardently to foreigners as it is carried out at home; just think what a new sight this is! Among all the unknown things the French Revolution showed the world, this one is surely the newest.")

269. See the famous passage in *Nouveaux Essais* IV 16 § 4, which most acutely analyzed, in the early years of the eighteenth century, the psychic structure of later revolutionaries.

cal justification of wars reached an intensity that had not existed since the confessional wars. Two characteristics distinguish the new ideology from the universal religions of agrarian societies: first, since the invention of printing and the Industrial Revolution, it has had a quite different infrastructural power; second, the secular worldview's loss of transcendence and the absolutizing of man is connected with special dangers. The decline of faith in God and in a future life in no way leads to a diminution of fanaticism and the readiness to become a martyr, but only to an abolition of the moral constraints that traditional fanaticism often still acknowledged.[270] The moral rhetorics of the new universalist ethics, which grasps the ideas of the rights of man and of the citizen and promotes to the highest degree the horizontal, intersubjective dimension of the moral, is connected with the will to make history oneself (*bonum factum*) and the desire to destroy characteristic of a subjectivity freed from God and all traditions, and produces events that are in no way bloodier than those previously known, but are so repellent because the actors involved have absolutely clear consciences. The hypocrisy of Christianity, even in its Protestant form, is not so bad as that of the Jacobins and their modern heirs, who are sincerely convinced that they are building paradise on earth while they are making earth a hell. The more universalist ethics becomes, the more hypocrisy and projection mechanisms increase. There is no contradiction between the objective and subjective originality of the French Revolution and the fact that the revolutionaries appealed to long-past historical events, interpreted in their own way, in order to create models and legitimacy for themselves.

However, it was inevitable that the Revolution would eat its own children and come to an end through a popular general, as Burke already foresaw in 1790.[271] Like Augustus, Napoleon combined new ideas with the *ancien régime*'s forms of legitimation, and thereby contributed to the principles of the modern state being spread all over Europe. The registration of citizens, general military duty, the introduction of passports, the intervention of state power on the local level, comprehensive codes of laws—all this was partly created and partly consolidated in the wake of the French Revolution. The new strategy was evolutionarily stable: Prussia was able to shake off the French yoke only because it carried out reforms. In fact, all the criticism of the French Revolution cannot deny that it represented the central step forward on the way to the modern state. In 1989, an attempt was made to establish the ideas of 1789 in Eastern Europe as well.

---

270. Cf. Tocqueville (1856), 108: "Elle est devenue elle-même une sorte de religion nouvelle, religion imparfaite, il est vrai, sans Dieu, sans culte et sans autre vie, mais qui, néanmoins, comme l'islamisme, a inondé toute la terre de ses soldats, de ses apôtres et de ses martyrs." ("It has itself become a kind of new religion, an imperfect religion, to be sure, without God, without worship, and without another life, but which nonetheless, like Islam, has flooded the world with its soldiers, its apostles, and its martyrs.")

271. "In the weakness of one kind of authority, and in the fluctuation of all, the officers of an army will remain for some time mutinous and full of faction, until some popular general, who understands the art of conciliating the soldiery, and who possesses the true spirit of command, shall draw the eyes of all men upon himself" (236 f.).

Anyone who seeks, as Hannah Arendt did, to oppose the American Revolution to the French, praising the former as a purely political revolution that did not concern itself with social questions, should not forget that the limitation of the revolution was easier in a new continent (not empty, but soon to be emptied by genocide[272]) for two reasons: first, because foreign entanglements could be limited, and second, because expansion toward the west offered the poorer classes opportunities for rising in society that did not exist in France (not to mention the institution of slavery in the states of the American south). Anyone who opposes the French Revolution to the Glorious Revolution and Great Britain's prudent policy of reform should remember that the Glorious Revolution took place without bloodshed because English absolutism had already been broken in the middle of the seventeenth century; a king was beheaded earlier in England than in France. And yet it remains that the fanaticism of the Jacobins is qualitatively different from that of Cromwell, who never wanted to make the whole world happy, and in any case from the aristocratic attitude of the American elites. The political system of Great Britain since 1688 and that of the United States have always been shaped by the idea of the separation of powers.

The French Revolution gave *nationalism* an immense boost. Obviously, various factors played a role in nationalism's rise to become the dominant political ideology. First, like the French Revolution, it is the result of a process of secularization and individualization. The church and, after industrialization, the old sociality became less and less able to meet the inextinguishable need for community: the nation had to help out (as did erotic love). Nationalism is an immanentist religion in which the self-apotheosis of a society, which according to Durkheim's one-sided theory constitutes the secret essence of religion, is explicitly carried out.[273] Second, the nation has the right size in order to promote the Industrial Revolution. Modern industrial capitalism presupposes a high degree of mobility, for nothing is more important than the allocation of labor to the right place. This increased mobility causes regional differences to disappear; a national culture and a common language become necessary in order to ease interactions between the individual regions. Furthermore, industrial societies presuppose a certain level of education—educating *all citizens* becomes one of the state's most important tasks. Children are no longer educated in the family, but in schools: one can speak of an "exo-training." The mastery of writing is no longer a special achievement, but rather the presupposition for all further specializations. Churches, universities, bureaucracy, commerce, the military, and newspapers contribute to a "revolution in discursive literacy."[274] The dissolution of traditional religions leads to the legitimation function being increas-

---

272. To be sure, North Americans did not deal with the Indians so cruelly as did the Spaniards; but Tocqueville's sarcastic remark that "On ne saurait détruire les hommes en respectant mieux les lois de l'humanité" (1835 ff.; 1:452 f.). ("People could hardly be destroyed with more respect for the laws of humanity.") hits home.

273. See E. Gellner's classic work (1983), 56.

274. M. Mann (1986 ff.), 2:36.

ingly taken over in modern societies by the intellectual—a new type in world history distinguished from that of the cleric by the fact that he lacks a firm connection with a way of life and belief in an objective order. For that reason he bears a great deal of responsibility for the outbreak of the French Revolution[275] as well as for the spread of nationalism, and later on, Marxism. The science whose banner he bears is sociology, through which society carries out a process of self-portrayal and which increasingly seeks to influence society. Gellner rightly emphasizes that nationalism is not merely *communicated* via modern media—modern print media *are themselves* the message of nationalism, since they are general but written in a specific language (127). The intellectual superiority of a minority whose nationality is perceived as different from one's own is the greatest humiliation of nationalism, and can, especially if this minority lacks political power, trigger hate reactions that can overshadow all earlier known genocides. Consider the Armenians in the Ottoman Empire or the Jews in the Third Reich. Third, nationalism corresponds to the egalitarian, rudimentarily democratic convictions of the modern age: in the eyes of the nation, everyone is equal. The borders between nations become more important than those between ranks within the same nation, and because as many people as possible are supposed to participate in political decisions, the construction of cultural homogeneity becomes a major task, especially since differences between single cultures and individuals are no longer considered God-given. It is precisely democracy that deals the death-blow to the old multicultural societies.[276] Fourth, nationalism allowed a wistful conjuring up of one's own past, whereas at the same time, under the brutal power of the industrialization without which it would not have existed, ways of life, languages, mores, religions, and regional and rank differences disappeared at a rate unique in world history.[277] But it is not solely this contradiction between its real essence and its self-image that makes nationalism, which heavily determined the politics of the nineteenth and twentieth centuries, one of the most alarming political ideologies in history—no less obvious is the contradiction with the principles of universalism which it simultaneously presupposes and slaps in the face.

In addition to nations, *classes* are the other great actor in recent history. In no earlier age have they had a comparable power, because in no other age were economic

---

275. Cf. Tocqueville (1856), 229 ff. The French intellectual was particularly dangerous, because unlike the German intellectual he was interested in politics, and unlike the English intellectual, he never exercised concrete political responsibility.

276. Cf. C. Calhoun (1994), 2: "They [sc. the citizens of the cosmopolitan cities] could coexist in large part because they were not called upon to join in very many collective projects. They were not called upon to join together in democratic self-government. . . . It was democracy . . . that transformed relations among the different groups of citizens."

277. E. Gellner aptly writes: "Nationalism . . . preaches and defends continuity, but owes everything to a decisive and unutterably profound break in human history. It preaches and defends cultural diversity, when in fact it imposes homogeneity both inside and, to a lesser degree, between political units. Its self-image and its true nature are inversely related, with an ironic neatness seldom equalled even by other successful ideologies" (1983; 125).

issues so important, or had broken away to such an extent from other subsystems. Unlike classes, ranks cannot be defined in purely economic terms. We understand why the nineteenth century could produce a sociological theory that made classes the center of history. Nevertheless, even for the past two centuries that theory is one-sided. Industrial capitalism produced two new classes, capitalists and workers. The often mechanical activity of the latter led to a loss of the sense of the meaning of one's own labor that farmers and craftsmen could still enjoy, and at the same time to the feeling that reality could be *made* to a large extent. In addition, the other classes continued to exist: the old elites of the *ancien régime,* the peasantry, the middle class, and the petite bourgeoisie. What was crucial was that class solidarity was hindered by various factors—by the economic sector and the firm in which the individual worked, by political and religious oppositions, and especially by national differences. A transnational proletariat never existed any more than a transnational bourgeoisie, even if transnational tendencies are noticeable, especially in the current capitalist class.[278] In addition to the conflict between owners and workers, there were also conflicts between agriculture and industry, state and church, center and regions. The latter two conflicts could intersect and strengthen each other if a region's religion differed from the center's—think of Ireland and Poland, which are not accidentally the two remaining most Catholic countries in Europe, even if the 1995 Polish presidential elections and the 1995 Irish referendum on divorce show that a weakening of Catholicism followed the dissolution of the Warsaw Pact and the beginnings of a British-Irish rapprochement.

But even if classes were not the sole and perhaps not even the most important actors in recent history, the distribution of the prosperity produced by the Industrial Revolution among the various classes was one of the greatest problems faced by recent politics. In the long run, the universalist ethics of modernity was no more able than traditional Christian ethics to accept an increase in the opposition between rich and poor. Although at the beginning of the era of capital accumulation an impoverishment of a large strata was probably inevitable in order to concentrate in a few hands the capital necessary for industrialization and to find salaried workers, industrial capitalism nonetheless set in motion an economic growth that made possible—at least so long as demographic growth does not outstrip economic growth—something that was denied agrarian societies: giving to the poor without taking from the rich (which the latter seldom allow). If, as in early liberalism, universal civil rights are virtually limited to the rights to freedom from interference, over the long term an inequality between classes is established or at least probable. As a result, the political struggle of the class that seemed likely to lose the most through the Industrial Revolution, namely the working class, had to do with guaranteeing collective rights to freedom from interference (which included freedom of association), rights to positive benefits, and political rights. So far as the latter are concerned, the abolition of property qualifications for voting rights and the in-

---

278. As M. Mann (1986 ff.; 2:29) rightly points out.

troduction of universal voting rights was the crucial demand; in some European states (especially so far as female suffrage was involved) it was not met until after the First World War. Rights to positive benefits can be classified, following M. Mann,[279] depending on whether they are cultural or economic in nature; the former include the right to education, the latter include the right to public welfare assistance. The more the state promoted the further development of the Industrial Revolution, which could not be supported by private capital alone and that was essential for the state on military grounds as well, the more it intervened in economic events, the less it could avoid co-responsibility for the social condition of the society. Nonetheless, the development to a modern *welfare state* was a very long and difficult process, on one hand because the propertied classes resisted (partly for purely selfish reasons, and partly with principled arguments), and on the other hand because in the meantime the ideology of the dictatorship of the proletariat had emerged, which considered itself an alternative to a capitalist-immanent solution to the social question, and was willing to abandon the achievements of modern liberalism, in particular the separation of powers. A revolution in this sense was all the more likely the more the working class experienced the state as a hostile power. In the United States, where there was no state to fight and whose population was recruited from people for whom self-reliance was one of the greatest virtues, socialist ideas had no attraction (however, during the New Deal welfare state conceptions were finally established in the United States as well); in Great Britain, liberal principles had taken deep root, and labor unionists, not intellectuals, ran the Labour Party; Germany, on the other hand, wavered, and in Russia these ideas became dominant. Where the modern welfare state was ultimately established, it achieved an infrastructural power that no other political structure had ever known—with the exception, of course, of the totalitarian state. This is all the more the case when it makes the transition from a "residual" to a "institutional" welfare state that no longer intervenes solely on behalf of marginal groups, but rather proceeds to an overall redistribution of wealth. Not mere social equality, but rather increasing prosperity thus becomes the main task of politics, which cannot otherwise realize its redistribution plans. At the same time, this means that greed, and thus the influences of the society on the state, steadily increase, and that the state loses its coherence and capacity for action. "Ironically, the 'strong' state over time may become enfeebled by its own action and thereby begin to look quite 'weak'."[280]

Hegel's apotheosis of the modern liberal constitutional state celebrates a structure that still lacked two of the characteristics that have emerged in the interim: it was neither democratic nor social. Since one can consider the (relatively rapid) establishment of universal political and social rights as the fulfillment of universalist ideas, it would be tempting to continue Hegel's philosophy of history into the twentieth century. In fact, in the Greek philosophy of the *logos* and democracy, in Roman private law and the

279. (1986 ff.), 2:19.
280. J. A. Hall and G. J. Ikenberry (1989), 13.

Roman Empire, in medieval Christianity and feudalism, in modern Protestantism and absolutism, and finally in the liberal state after the French Revolution, one can recognize the stages on the way to the type of state currently realized in the West, which most nearly corresponds to the demands of an universalist ethics. The path thereto is certainly not linear, but winding and accompanied by terrible relapses, but it seems nonetheless to lead to a result that could justify the thesis that there is reason in history. However, it is not only the dangers that threaten humanity in the new century that may still make us hesitate to accept an interpretation like the one proposed by Fukuyama. The experiences of the twentieth century are already sufficiently dreadful to discredit belief in progress—particularly since a crucial part of the justification of one of the horrors of that century, Soviet totalitarianism, was a philosophy of history based on progress. In actuality, any philosophy of history that overlooks the phenomenon of *totalitarianism*, which is the essence of the wicked twentieth century, is not trustworthy. The two totalitarian states are only two eruptions of a volcano that is still bubbling and may erupt again at any time.

Totalitarianism involves the self-idolatry of the masses unleashed by the Industrial Revolution, who have abandoned any relationship to a divine order, and who at the same time long for community. This need is satisfied by abandoning any personal responsibility and by participating in a group whose size means power. It is hardly an accident that from the late nineteenth century onward, the titles of several important works refer to the masses—think of G. Le Bon's *La psychologie des foules* (1895), J. Ortega y Gasset's *La rebelión de las masas* (1930), D. Riesman's *The Lonely Crowd* (1950), and E. Canetti's *Masse und Macht* (1960).[281] The terrible collective identity crisis that follows the loss of any relationship to transcendence, the vertical dimension of ethics, seeks compensation in a new feeling of belonging that liberalism is not able to provide. The masses thus become a new subject—or rather, an object of history, for nothing is more manipulable than the masses, and nothing more welcome to those obsessed by power. From the outset, the print media have had a broader audience than personal conversation or manuscripts; but the book is a source of conceptual knowledge, and even the newspaper is a presupposition for the emergence of a solid political public opinion, even if it draws too much attention to the ephemeral. On the other hand, radio, television, film—the new media of the twentieth century—tend to lead to illiteracy and have made possible an excitement of emotions that is denied the written word. It is no accident that the cratic genius Hitler immediately understood and exploited the possibilities of radio, and that film was vigorously promoted by totalitarian states—it is after all the total art that can be both abused politically and made the vehicle of the greatest aesthetic achievements of humanity; the twentieth century can be as proud of few things as some of its films.

---

281. See also the famous sixth chapter of the fourth part of the second volume of Tocqueville's *De la démocratie en Amérique:* "Quelle espèce de despotisme les nations démocratiques ont à craindre" (1835 ff.; 2:383 ff.).

The first totalitarian state in Europe was the *Soviet Union*. Liberalism had no chance in the easternmost country of Europe, where absolutism continued longest, and had even contributed to a stabilization of serfdom, where a civil society had never developed, and where there had been neither Renaissance, Reformation, nor Enlightenment. Certainly, the Western threat had forced the East to modernize as well—Sweden, which played the role of a European great power for a century, was, so to speak, the hammer of the East; Poland finally collapsed, whereas Prussia and Russia managed to adapt to the new structural conditions. However, Russia's adaptation had more to do with foreign than with internal policy. The February Revolution of 1917 overthrew an absolute monarchy, and even if we assume an especially rapid pace of development, it is not very plausible that between February and October Russia had already turned into a bourgeois state. Even apart from the fact that the philosophy of history thesis of a socialist final phase of history is unfounded, indeed refutable, even Marxists would have had to admit that the October Revolution could not introduce a phase that led beyond the state created by the bourgeois revolutions[282]—rather, it destroyed any chance of that kind of development and signified a relapse into despotism. Yet to interpret Soviet totalitarianism as merely a relapse is to play it down outrageously, for it was far more dreadful than traditional Czarism, which represented only one of its sources. On one hand, the state's increased infrastructural power, and on the other, the break with traditional ethics, made it something considerably more terrible than anything that Russia had previously suffered. In its mad desire to completely reshape history, Soviet totalitarianism is a completely modern product, the Jacobinism, as it were, of a relatively primitive society that was industrialized under extreme pressure. In it is expressed a form of the obsession with power that rejects any idea of an objective moral order and an individual conscience, and presupposes historically the crisis of monotheistic religions. Religions' claim to exclusive authority was adopted, but their relationship to transcendence jettisoned. Naturally, it is no accident that Russia, the European late-developer, became intoxicated by an ideology that led it to believe that it was historically more advanced than the rest of the world.

Soviet Marxism was a remarkable synthesis of the ideas of nineteenth-century Westernizers and Slavophiles, which were so typical of this Eurasian empire's desperate search for identity.[283] Even if certain stages of development cannot be skipped, interferences between the various cultures lead to a situation in which a normal development is felt to be humiliating if others have already completed such a development. In contrast, the Marxist philosophy of history gave communist states the feeling that they

---

282. P. Anderson also acknowledges this (1974; 259).

283. To that extent, even the most acute analyst of the intellectual depths of the human type from which the Bolshevist revolutionaries were to be recruited, Dostoevsky, cannot be exonerated of a certain share in the blame for the Russian catastrophe, for he strengthened the messianic expectations related to the Russian "soul," and therefore did not exactly make it easier to move closer to the Western constitutional state. Pan-Slavism is a forerunner of the current fundamentalisms.

were on a higher level—a feeling that strengthened their self-esteem and also had an incredible attraction for the intellectuals of countries outside Europe. Harder to explain is its power of attraction for the left-wing intellectuals of Europe, who would have been the first ones shot had they come within Stalin's area of domination. In addition to the common motive of helping to reshape history, their suffering from the self-contradictions of the bourgeois world also played a role.[284] It was not easy to see how the Marxist philosophy of history's assertion of the equality of all human beings as the highest value was compatible with reality, and the self-contempt that was determined by the perception of these contradictions and the narrowness of the bourgeois character could lead to complete blindness to the true reality of the Soviet Union, especially since its successes, for instance in the area of industrialization, were undeniable. At least there was a spark of reason in socialist ideas—the goal of social justice is justified, even if the means used in the attempt to achieve it were extremely inappropriate. Certainly there were some people who subscribed to these ideals only in order to allow themselves every sort of crime on the way to their achievement. Certainly there were enough Western intellectuals whose sympathy with the Soviet Union made it possible for them to participate in all the good things about capitalism, while at the same time taking a critical distance from it and, moreover, dispensing themselves from all the—allegedly petit bourgeois—charitable efforts that can relieve hardship where it can be relieved. These were intellectuals who, unlike minor KGB agents in the Soviet Union, enjoyed both a good lifestyle and a good conscience, and were not formally evil, to be sure, but were nonetheless among the most dismal persons the twentieth century produced (and who have not become any better since they have now transformed themselves into postmodernists). But there were also people with big hearts (even if often with little understanding), with a sense of sacrifice and unfulfilled religious needs, who identified with the Soviet Union and who were morally better than the representatives of liberalism whose sole motive was their own self-interest. The nightmare of the Soviet experiment exploded, and despite all external efforts this explosion was ultimately endogenous, because there still remained, in addition to blind dogmatists and cynics, a few people who naively believed in the values that the system's ideology preached—and thus the system's hypocrisy became productive.[285] Gorbachev underestimated the rottenness of the system, but probably this mistaken assessment was necessary in order for him to work toward reforming his country and international relations.

In contrast, the other totalitarianism of the twentieth century—*National Socialism*, which connected the national and the social questions—did not dissolve en-

---

284. On this subject, see F. Furet (1995).

285. W. H. McNeill (1963; 801) already wrote: "It is perhaps a Communist misfortune that Marxist-Leninist scriptures include rather more than their share of ardent denunciation of oppression, together with magnificently utopian anticipations of a free, leisured, and abundant material future. . . . An aging and prospering revolution cannot indefinitely justify failures to attain the promised land of communism by pointing to the dangers of capitalist encirclement."

dogenously.[286] Even if it exercised through this connection a greater influence on modern states, as is generally acknowledged,[287] its ideology represents the most infamous destruction of the universalist ideals that humanity had been elaborating since the emergence of the oldest advanced religions. A racial delusion based on pseudoscience annihilated the idea of universal human rights. The elimination of any normative restraint on the human will, which Marxism-Leninism's metaphysics of history still acknowledged at least formally, leads to a worship of power for power's sake, which is inevitable wherever nihilism has devoured the idea of an objective order of values—there is no longer any *ought* or concrete goals, only a blind desire to impose one's own will. From one viewpoint, National Socialism connected with the various fascist movements that had emerged after the dreadful crisis of the First World War, whose meaningless slaughter had radically shaken the belief in the reason of the inherited political order, and professed a nationalism and militarism that were often compensatory and, in nations whose development had lagged behind, especially aggressive. The fear of a possible social revolution on the Soviet model was combined with an aversion to individualistic liberalism that destroyed traditional beliefs in a strange mixture that on one hand protected the interests of the propertied classes, and on the other often represented progress on the way toward the welfare state; on one hand professed faith in traditional values, and on the other pushed through modernization in archaic forms. From another viewpoint, the opposition between Austrian fascism and National Socialism shows clearly that the two movements were entirely different in spirit. The former wanted to save tradition, while the latter shared with Bolshevism an emotional desire to crush the past. Despite their ideological enmity, National Socialism is far more related to Bolshevism than to Spanish fascism, for instance—think of the ideology that controls even the inner connections, the central control over the economy, the monopoly on means of communication, the omnipresence of the party, the dynamic character of the "movement," the idolatry of technology, and finally the use of terror. Even the number of victims is similarly elevated—but with a characteristic difference. Stalin raged against the supporters of his own power, and only the psychotic structure of the form of universalism at that time can explain how he could survive this without it backfiring on him. In contrast, Hitler murdered "ethnic aliens" (*Volksfremde*) in accordance with the anti-universalist structure of his ideology. To be sure, genocides have unfortunately occurred in the course of history, but a first-rate constitutional and cultured state being transformed in the course of a few years into a perfect, *formal* universal killing machine aspiring to completeness—*that* was unprecedented. In nineteenth-century Western Europe, torture had almost ceased to occur, but about a hundred years after Goethe's death, the Buchenwald concentration

---

286. We cannot discuss here the East Asian and Southeast Asian variants of totalitarianism, whose similarities with and difference from the two European forms have not been sufficiently investigated in the literature on totalitarianism to date.

287. Cf. H.-D. Klein (1989).

camp was built only a few kilometers from his home, a center for Western humanity. This will be, must be, remembered until the end of history. There is reason to think that a Hitler could have seized power only in Germany, and that is certainly no compliment to Germany. But it is a terrible mistake to believe that the crimes of the death camps could be carried out only by Germans. Foreigners collaborated in these crimes, and post-war history has shown that from Cambodia to Rwanda, people are capable of such things. Auschwitz expresses a horrible anthropological truth, perhaps regarding only modern people,[288] whose technological power and moral nihilism make them capable of dimensions of evil that are quantitatively and qualitatively entirely new, but certainly not, as many Rousseauists would like to believe, a truth regarding Germans alone. Unfortunately, one must add; for it would be wonderful if it could be said of only one people that in its case the civilizing process was merely a superficial varnishing that can flake off at any time. The truth is more depressing.

6.2.2.3.3. Changes in Foreign Policy

From a foreign policy point of view, the European system of states in the modern age is characterized by a limited number of territorial states that compete with each other and are at the same time bound together by a common system of values. From 1500 to 1900, the number of sovereign states in Europe sharply decreased (from about 200 to about 20, if one considers the states within the Holy Roman Empire as sovereign, which they were to a large extent factually, though not legally—they had "supremacy"). Dynastic interests, but especially the idea of the nation diminished the number of states, even if the idea of the nation was also responsible for the creation of a few new states. The destruction of the Ottoman Empire and the Austro-Hungarian Empire in the First World War, as well as the disintegration of the Soviet Union, Czechoslovakia, and Yugoslavia, have increased the number of states. Nevertheless, in recent European history up to 1945, no one state ever achieved hegemony. For a time, Great Britain was the only state present on all the world's continents, but it never had more than command of the seas, although this should not be underestimated with the globalization of politics and economics in modernity and with the increased importance of naval warfare. Nonetheless, even if the British Empire was far more extensive than the Roman Empire, its neighbors were incomparably stronger than Rome's neighbors. Much the same can be said of Russia, which for a time was also present on three continents. On the other hand, *attempts* to establish hegemony can be attributed to three other European great powers—Spain under Philip II, France under Louis XIV and Napoleon, and Germany under Hitler. However, the European states always managed to ward off

---

288. In one of the most impressive texts on the Holocaust, Z. Kolitz's *Yossel Rakover*, we read: "Beasts of the field seem so lovable and dear that I feel deep pain whenever the evil fiends that dominate Europe are referred to as beasts. It is not true that there is something beastly in Hitler. He is, I am deeply convinced, a typical child of modern man" (1995; 14).

these attempts, and to restore the *balance of power* within Europe—although the last time, only with the help of the United States.[289]

Even if a balance was maintained within Europe, this is not the case for Europe's relationship to the other cultures of the world. On the contrary, starting in the fifteenth century, European states—initially, Spain and Portugal—conquered areas outside Europe and finally eliminated the last blank spots on the map. Only a few states were spared European occupation or intervention, which were inflicted upon even the oldest advanced cultures. *Colonialism* was based on a variety of motives. Intellectual curiosity and the desire, necessarily anchored in a universal religion, to convert and civilize other peoples were combined with demographic pressure and brutal economic interests in raw materials, slaves, and markets. The competition between the individual European states added motives related to strategy and prestige as well. In 1936, Italy still thought it had a claim to a place in the sun. European expansion was possible only thanks to the military revolution[290] of the sixteenth and seventeenth centuries, which introduced firearms, improved fortifications, more efficient logistics, and superior seafaring. After the Industrial Revolution, the West, equipped with rapid-fire guns and armored ships, was almost unbeatable—at least so long as other states did not adopt Western technology. In addition to military innovations, we should mention the superior hermeneutic performance of Europe. Cortés would not have been able to subjugate the Aztecs, had he not cleverly won their Native American opponents over to his side. Again and again, anthropologists and ethnologists helped the colonial powers achieve domination. Finally, the increased infrastructural power of the modern state played a role generally.

A few European colonies on other continents became independent states, such as the United States, which are part of Europe culturally, however, and in a certain sense represent the project of modernity in a pure ideal-typical form. The emancipation of a colony from the mother country did not always mean that power was returned to the natives, some of whom had become a minority, and some of whom, as for a time in South Africa, were deprived of political rights. In the second half of the nineteenth century, just *one* non-European culture—characteristically, one with a feudal background that was oriented toward new goals, and had a long-standing ability to imitate other societies—was able, after the forced opening to the West, to adopt the technology, economics, and legal order of the West in half a century, and shortly afterward to defeat in battle a Western great power.[291] Since then, Japan has been an economic great power, and for a time also a military great power with a colonial empire. However, far from all non-European cultures have proven to be comparably "compatible with modernity." Even after the decolonization that took place, partly peacefully and partly violently following

---

289. Cf. L. Dehio (1948).

290. Cf. G. Parker (1988).

291. Ethiopia's victory over Italy at Adua in 1896 remains important, but could not prevent its subjugation forty years later.

the Second World War—as a result of the defeats suffered by most European countries and by Japan, the rise of nationalism in the former colonies, and the breakdown of colonialist ideology—and that extraordinarily increased the number of sovereign states,[292] many countries still found it impossible to attain the blessings of modernity. Political independence was accompanied by a persistent economic dependency. The burdens inherited from colonialism—irrationally drawn national borders, monocultures, disintegration of the old culture's internal coherence and self-respect—play an important role;[293] but apart from that it should be acknowledged that the project of modernity is full of cultural presuppositions. It is possible that only Western Europe could produce it, even if it is certain that it can be imitated by other cultures—although whether it can be imitated by all must remain an open question.

Since few things permit deeper insights into a culture than the motives for which their members are prepared to die and to kill each other, it is worthwhile to analyze why wars have been waged in the modern age. Most of the major wars and civil wars of the sixteenth century revolved around the confessional conflict that had destroyed the unity of the Christian world. Through the new power of states, wars became significantly bloodier than they had formerly been, especially since religious fanaticism legitimated a great deal. It took the catastrophe of the Thirty Years' War to recognize that Christianity did not require that murderous wars be waged against Christians of the other confession, and eventually, that Christians of different denominations could live together in the same state with equal rights. Since then in Western Europe religion has almost ceased to be a reason for going to war. During the war new alliances, such as that between Sweden and France, were already being formed that anticipated the replacement of confessional conflict by the reason of state. From the seventeenth century onward, there existed a *jus publicum Europaeum* that limited war into the twentieth century (with the exception of the wars against revolutionary France and the Napoleonic wars). This was connected with, among other things, the fact that the nobility saw itself as an international elite and that the royal houses were related to each other through marriage. It was not surprising to find Eugene of Savoy, the son of a French prince of the blood in the service of Austria; and there was no question of treason when, as a field marshal of that foreign power, he helped prevent the rise of his home country to hegemonic power. Until the end of 1808 Stein was the leading minister of Prussia; at the Congress of Vienna he was part of the Russian delegation. In 1862, the year he was appointed prime minister and foreign minister of Prussia, Bismarck still received an offer

---

292. This was not the case only where colonial domination was abolished by the former colony becoming a part of the colonial power with equal rights, as in Hawaii, for instance. Unfortunately this strategy was possible for only a few states.

293. These inherited burdens differ depending on the colonial power. France tried harder than Great Britain to share the blessings of its own culture with the peoples of its colonies, and for that reason respected the latter's own culture less.

from Czar Alexander II to join his service, an offer he seriously considered, and which he still mentioned with pride at the end of the century.[294]

The era of *limited warfare* in the eighteenth century was followed by one of national *wars*, therefore involving a very different internal participation. This was in turn followed by the *world civil war* of the twentieth century, fought between competing conceptions of economic and political order. According to C. Schmitt (1927), religion, nation, and economic system are the central political themes of the modern state-world, which mutually replace each other. Schmitt's thesis is more plausible than that of Lenin, which interprets imperialism as the highest stage of capitalism. First of all, there were imperialist wars long before capitalism, and second, the avoidance of war is usually in the interest of large segments of the modern economy. However, it must be acknowledged that control over non-European areas gained in importance, because of the development of commercial and industrial capitalism as well as the modern welfare state, and that after the end of the process of colonization, the conflicts between European powers led back to the old continent again, with greater violence. It is possible to see in the First World War a nemesis, a revenge for colonial expansion. Nationalist ideologies, as well as the desire to distract attention from internal problems and to overcome a widespread feeling of emptiness that was translated into an almost universal enthusiasm for war, led to the breakdown of the Concert of Europe.

The Industrial Revolution increased the destructive power of war in a completely unimaginable way—first in the American Civil War and then in the First World War. The attempt to reach a solution to international problems through the League of Nations failed, partly because of the political heterogeneity of the great powers of the period between the two world wars. A Holy Alliance was no longer possible, because the states were liberal, fascist, national socialist, or communist, and even the liberal states did not work together with mutual trust. Already before the war, an alliance was formed between Germany and Italy, and after the German attack on the Soviet Union, the latter joined a short-lived alliance with the liberal states that ended immediately after the defeat of Germany and Japan. This turned out to be very advantageous for the losers of the war, because they had to be incorporated into the Western community quickly, wherever they were. The Second World War was a total war between two totalitarian states, among others. A war can be defined as a total war if a very large proportion of the people identifies with it, takes part in it, is affected by its outcome, and if the goal is to establish domination over the whole planet and the most thorough penetration of society by the state.[295] Modern guerrilla warfare, which, interestingly enough, also typically has its origin in nationalistic ideas (first in the Spaniards' rebellion against foreign domination by the French), like modern nuclear, biological, and chemical weapons,

---

294. (1898 ff.), 1:308 f.
295. Cf. H. J. Morgenthau and K. W. Thompson (1985), 392 ff.

increasingly abolishes the distinction between combatants and non-combatants, and thus also helps undermine the regulation of war that was achieved after the Peace of Westphalia.[296] Even the Cold War, during which weapons remained silent in Europe, had—within the genre of cold wars, of course—characteristics of a total war: the violence of the propaganda was unprecedented. In any case, the Second World War put a definitive end to the era in which Europe had become the center of the world; but at least Western European countries' unification efforts have prevented a further European war. The military and ideological (but not the economic) leadership passed to the United States and the Soviet Union, around which a bipolar system of foreign policy was formed that was completed and stabilized by the United Nations. This system broke down with the dissolution of the last empire in 1991.[297]

6.3. The Current World Political Situation

If 1914, 1917, 1933, and 1939 each represent further stages in the collapse of the rationally oriented phase of European politics that had begun in the seventeenth century, 1945 and 1989 seem to represent a slow return to the principles of political rationality. It is no accident that the United States, which owes its establishment to the ideas of modernity, shared in the triumph over the two totalitarianisms. Nonetheless, it would be hasty to interpret the current situation as an expression of the victory of reason in history. On the contrary, no other era in human history is so imperiled as the present one, and even the collapse of the Soviet Union is probably only a foreshadowing of a *general* crisis of modernity, to which Soviet totalitarianism undoubtedly belongs. For *one* insight is becoming increasingly widespread—that the standard of living attained in Western countries is not universalizable, if numerous ecosystems on the planet are not to break down with consequences that would be disastrous for human beings and other species. If the history we have discussed in this chapter is the history of only a tiny part of nature that has, starting at a certain point in evolution, become increasingly distant from the rest of nature, then in the present, nature is catching up with man—or rather, it is striking back at him. It is no longer possible to understand humanity's future history without knowledge about ecological contexts. To be sure, human history was always interwoven with that of the environment, but now, for the first time, anthropogenic alterations of nature are putting the survival of the species in question. Ecological catastrophes are threatening in themselves. Moreover, they could lead to bat-

---

296. Cf. Schmitt (1963).

297. Despite the expansion toward Siberia and in the Caucasus, Czarist Russia was already an atypical colonial power, for since Russians themselves did not enjoy political rights in the narrower sense, the difference between them and other peoples was less oppressive than the analogous difference in the British colonies, for example. The Soviet Union can hardly be called a colonial power, because non-Russians could also rise to the highest party offices.

tles regarding distribution in which the whole arsenal of modern weapons of mass destruction might be used—which is all the more likely, the less culturally homogenous the various states are, the more immoral the mores of the various peoples, and the more irrational the mechanisms of selection that put political elites in power. What can be said about these factors?

6.3.1. The Structural Conditions of Foreign Policy

The current foreign policy situation is characterized by the fact that the United States is now *the only superpower.* Where it intervenes, conflicts like the one in the former Yugoslavia can be resolved fairly quickly. Militarily, economically, and with regard to the capacity for political action, the United States is the most powerful state on earth. Paradoxically, it can be said that the United States, the country where democracy was born, is today a more aristocratic country than the Western European states, in which the welfare state is far more fully developed. In the United States, more attention is paid to differences in performance. Indeed, the emphasis placed on individual self-reliance promotes a class of dynamic entrepreneurs who can be regarded as heroes of the market societies, so to speak, and yet leads, by way of the political selection process, especially in the Senate, to a meritocratic aristocracy that sometimes reminds us of the Roman aristocracy in its sense of the practical. However, it is clear that the United States alone cannot solve any of the great problems of the world. A conflict among expenditures relating to the military, investment, and consumption always exists; and since the masses want to share in the luxury of the elites, there is a general tendency to shift expenditures in the direction of consumption.[298] This tendency is especially strong in a welfare state, and because after the end of the Cold War the threat is considerably more diffuse than it was earlier, there is a great temptation to relapse into an isolationist policy such as was pursued after the First World War—with fateful consequences for the world.

The United States cannot be the world's policeman, and does not want to, quite apart from the hostile attitude of others toward its playing such a role. In addition, the United States is not the only country with nuclear weapons; therefore the risks are very great for the hegemonic power as well. Even a state in dissolution, such as Russia, remains a threat because of its possession of nuclear weapons, although otherwise its room to maneuver in the realm of foreign policy is at the moment limited. "In opposition to Carl Schmitt's conception, politics cannot always be understood on the basis of the state of emergency—in this case, the use of nuclear weapons; instead, power develops precisely in the normal situation. With nuclear weapons neither the usual day-to-day politics nor a short- or long-term economic policy can be pursued. Nonetheless, we cannot and must not fail to recognize that nuclear weapons

---

298. Cf. R. Gilpin (1981), 159 ff.

are of the greatest importance."[299] It can be pointedly said that nuclear weapons are too blunt an instrument for the resolution of the subtler political problems, but nonetheless only states that have them are sovereign in the full sense of the term—and this explains the widespread interest in having them, especially since the Nuclear Non-Proliferation Treaty only perpetuates the current inequalities and is therefore easily regarded as unjust.

What might still be the second economic power in the world, *Japan,* has been, for historical and constitutional reasons, extremely restrained militarily. The economic rivalry with the United States and European countries is considerable, however, and until several years ago, a rise of Japan to the leading position seemed entirely possible, among other reasons, because of its good educational system—which does not, however, foster individual creativity to the necessary degree. We cannot exclude, either, the possibility that the juxtaposition of modernization and an ancient culture might yet end in a serious collective identity crisis. *Europe* is still far from being a federal state, and there is absolutely no guarantee that it will ever become one. At least so far, one cannot speak of a common foreign policy for the member states of the European Union, as the Yugoslavian debacle has recently shown. However, expansion to the east and a deepening of Brussels' power are possible developments. Already before and especially after its reunification, Germany was the economic leader within Europe. Its internal stability is impressive, but the Federal Republic is only now beginning to extend its international responsibility to the military realm as well. Western Europe's only two permanent members of the United Nations Security Council, France and Great Britain, have, in part as former colonial powers, considerable influence in matters of foreign policy, although the latter has greatly decreased since 1945. Italy remains, despite its immense national debt, economically strong, but its internal political situation is quite unstable. Only its inclusion in international institutions ensures that it will not desert the ranks of liberal democracies, as it did after the First World War. The recent movements toward a plebiscitarian state form based on the mass media and relying not on bread, but primarily on circuses to keep the masses happy, have been very disturbing.

The collapse of the *Soviet Union* brought an end to its pacifying role, in the Balkans as well as in its former territory. On the enormous Eurasian land mass there will continue to be unrest, wars and civil wars are likely, as well as the proliferation of nuclear weapons to those who want them all over the world. Whereas the westernmost East Bloc states, which had already been ruled by Austria-Hungary and Prussia, could attach themselves to the Western mentality, this was more difficult for states with a primarily Orthodox population. The fate of Russia will be of the greatest importance for the fate of humanity. No country has ever fallen so far so quickly—from one of the two superpowers to a lower-level developing country. This necessarily triggers attempts at compensation, such as one saw in Germany after the defeat in the First World War, although

299. M. Hartwig (1995), 198.

then the distance fallen was much less. How a people that until recently claimed to assume the highest level of development of mankind and to show the rest of the world the path to be followed, is to deal with its current misery, is not easy to foresee. A civil society cannot be constructed in a short length of time; the state, which even in the Soviet Union was in a certain sense never autonomous because it depended on the party, is now reduced to residual functions. The real power is exercised by the Mafia-like structures that are developing every place where the chances of getting rich that modern capitalism offers are exploited without the corresponding legal and moral infrastructure. No country offers more cause for concern than Russia, because the disparity between the remaining military power, the broken-down ideological power, and economic impotence cannot be stable.

The *Third World* has in any case never existed as a unified structure, but the dissolution of the second world offers a further ground for avoiding this term. Today, the differences among the states that were once called "developing countries" are enormous.[300] First of all, there is a group of states that have mastered the process of modernization, and have even become important competitors for the West. East Asia and increasingly Southeast Asia are the regions whose cultures are most compatible with modernity. Most of these states have passed through developing dictatorships. The largest and most powerful of them, China, is still ruled by a nominally communist party, which began by introducing economic reforms—not without good reason, and unlike Gorbachev, whose internal political reforms were not exactly successful without economic validation (however, the Chinese alternative was not open to him, for various reasons). The tensions within China are considerable, and the transition to a more democratic form of government will not necessarily be smooth, but there is hardly any doubt that in the twenty-first century China, because of the size of its population and its culture, will be a military and economic great power whose influence on world politics will be substantial, partly because of its permanent seat on the Security Council. To be sure, the West has repeatedly frowned on states that have not attained its standard of living, but those that manage to attain that standard disturb it still more. On one hand, they endanger its economic leadership, and on the other, they increasingly threaten the environment, although the West, which they are only imitating in this regard, can hardly scold them for doing so. Other former developing countries can boast of high rates of growth, but we cannot speak of fair distribution. Internal polarizations are great; they diminish their internal political stability. India and many a Latin American country can be named as examples of this. A third group has rapidly gained wealth through oil exports, in which, as in Saudi Arabia for instance, the whole population sometimes participates. But the money that has flowed into these countries has not always been put into long-term investments, and a new impoverishment, when the oil reserves are exhausted, must therefore be reckoned with. Thus a few states that were once relatively rich (for instance,

---

300. Cf. U. Menzel (1992), 27 ff.

Argentina and Romania), have already grown poor over the past forty to sixty years, because their prosperity was based primarily on the export of the natural resources. Finally, there are, particularly in Africa, countries (we cannot call them states) whose poverty is inconceivable, and is increased still further by periodic wars that are considerably bloodier than traditional tribal feuds because they are conducted with modern weapons and means of communication. It is completely dilettantish to describe these countries, whose real decision-making entities are tribal structures, as "feudal." Feudalism is a very high level of development, and Africa could be considered lucky if it had had a feudal period. Nonetheless, the population growth of even the poorest lands constitutes a certain power factor, at least of a moral nature, if not of a military or economic one. The pressure of immigration on rich states with shrinking populations is already strong on the side of the inhabitants of these countries, and will increase.

The differences in state forms are no less great than the economic differences. Even where the legal forms are similar, the real political differences can be immense. It is meaningless to call Russia a presidential democracy, because Russia is no longer a state in the full sense of the term. It is of little use to call South Korea under Park Chung Hee, Saudi Arabia under King Fahd, or Zaire under Mobuto monocracies—the first laid the foundations for the economic miracle of his home country, which has become a modern capitalist state; the second governed a welfare state based on tribal structures; and, like many another African kleptocrat, the third has ruined his country for a long time. Despite the fact that modernity's ways of life are spreading over the planet like an oil slick, the differences among individual cultures and world religions remain large. It should be emphasized that the already-mentioned factor of compatibility with modernity alienates from one another cultures that are more or less closely related genetically, and brings closer together others that have entirely different origins. For a Western European, life today in Korea is sufficiently demanding, but less demanding than in Russia. One thing is clear: compatibility with modernity has nothing to do with the degree of proximity to the Western culture area. Indeed, it would be in principle conceivable that the self-destructive elements of modernity in the East Asian culture area, which is less determined, could more easily be overcome by individualism than could Eastern Europe; perhaps this culture area has the greatest potential for a further development of modernity. The western movement of history would thus return to one of its starting points—for the earth is round.

After the collapse of Marxist-Leninist ideology, a new ideology can be seen as the greatest challenge to the project of modernity: *fundamentalism.* The singular is misleading, however, insofar as there is in reality a whole spectrum of fundamentalisms—there are, for instance, Islamic, Hindu, Jewish, Christian, and Sikh fundamentalisms.[301] These fundamentalisms are fighting each other at least as violently as they are fighting against the West. Nonetheless, they have a lowest common denominator: they are all attempts, on one hand, to return to their own culture, which is endangered by the triumphal ad-

301. Cf. M. E. Marty and R. S. Appleby (1991).

vance of modernity, and on the other hand, as a rule they recognize the necessity of adopting those elements of modernity that are evolutionarily stable, that is, that provide the foundation for its current advantage in power, such as technological and especially military achievements. Their supporters are recruited from the strata that are among the economic losers in the process of modernization and are so dangerous because they have nothing to lose. Yet they also have a clientele among intellectuals, and especially among those who have been humiliated by the West or who at least feel humiliated. Their attractive power for young people is great. In these movements, sheer envy and occasionally even an instrumentalization of religion for political ends are sometimes combined with lucid insight into modernity's shortcomings and into the dangers of the asynchrony of their own countries, as well as with a justified pride in their own cultures, which must not unreflectively fall victim to Mickey Mouse and Coca-Cola. For no matter how many of them want to participate existentially in the Western lifestyle, it is obvious that the decision in favor of it is often based on manipulation and economic pressures.[302]

Since the end of the Cold War, the many states and cultures have been connected through a *world economy* whose laws can be escaped by hardly any state, especially since most states have joined the World Trade Organization. However, one can also say about states what was said earlier in criticizing liberalism for individuals: that treaties based on merely formal equality between unequals generally perpetuate this inequality. Since there is no central authority that determines the structural conditions of the global economic process (the World Bank and the International Monetary Fund have far more limited tasks), and since material duties to produce greater material equality are rejected in current international law (but not in the internal law of welfare states), it is illusory to suppose that with time an equalization of living conditions and an overcoming of the most unpleasant aspects of the international division of labor will come about by themselves. As the successes of a few former developing countries show, liberation from dependency is certainly possible, given the proper mentality and good governance, which are far more important than wealth in natural resources, for instance—but precisely only under special conditions. The existence of already developed countries can make it easier for developing countries, for then a model for the direction of development is available, foreign capital can be used to develop one's own country, etc. But it also makes things more difficult, as is shown by the phenomena of the flight of capital, the brain drain, and corruption, which has as one of its causes the wish to imitate the life of people in the West. The fact that one increasingly arrives at the conclusion that not all states are going to be granted the opportunity to attain the Western standard of living may be reassuring, given the ecological dangers of economic success, but this conclusion is not compatible with modern universalism's principles of justice.

---

302. In fact, C. Lévi-Strauss is not incorrect when he writes that the Westernization of the planet "résulte moins d'une décision libre que d'une absence de choix" (1961; 53) (". . . results less from a free decision than from an absence of choice.")

In addition to the global economy, *supranational organizations* frame the plurality of states. The most important of these organizations is the United Nations. Its most significant organs are the General Assembly, the Security Council, and the International Court of Justice; among the numerous specialized UN agencies UNESCO should be mentioned, because a fundamental importance is sometimes attributed to its pedagogical, scientific, and cultural tasks. In stark contradiction to the sovereign equality of all nations proclaimed in Article 2 (1) of the UN charter, a few states are more equal than the others—the five permanent members of the Security Council with veto rights. These are the victorious powers of the Second World War. Only one country not belonging to the European tradition is a member of this group, whereas since decolonization the non-European countries have become an ever clearer majority in the General Assembly. The Cold War led to the United States and the Soviet Union blocking each other for a long time; only under Gorbachev did the Security Council become capable of working, as was shown, for instance, in the 1991 war against Iraq. How long it will remain capable of working depends on developments in China and especially in Russia. As a whole, the Security Council has been able to prevent or end only a few wars. Local wars in areas irrelevant to world politics arouse little interest, even when they are extremely bloody; conflicts that endanger strategically crucial areas or that might escalate into a nuclear war, such as the conflict in the Near East, are taken more seriously. We said earlier that the collapse of the Soviet Union resulted in wars, but we should also recognize that the end of the Cold War made it easier to end decades-old conflicts because they could be limited and dissociated from their relationship to the world civil war. Global hopes and fears both disappeared. Finally, Italy should be particularly thankful to Gorbachev, because the end of the communist threat was a central reason why the corruption of Italy's anti-communist parties was no longer accepted nationally or internationally.

The current system of states is comprehended, alongside the world economy and the supranational organizations, by a third element, *nature*, within which human beings, of which states consist, have to survive. In addition to questions of security policy and economic policy, questions concerning global environmental politics are increasingly gaining a place in the forum of the world public sphere, and becoming a subject of international conferences and international treaties. Whereas at the beginning of the environmental debate the *consumption of non-renewable resources* was in the forefront of the discussion, today the problem of *environmental pollution* is moving into the center of attention. The threatening of the world climate by the clearing of rain forests and CO_2 emissions, the thinning of the ozone layer, the disappearance of plant and animal species, the pollution of drinking water, soil erosion, the effects of acid rain on forests—any one of these problems is serious enough, and is daily increased by population growth, and even more by the growth of each individual's needs. Whether international efforts to resolve these problems will be successful depends, naturally, on the structural conditions of internal policy that determine politicians' room to maneuver in making decisions. For however much the modern nation-state may no longer be able to deal with the tasks that now face us, and to that extent is obsolete, it is just as true that there is no alternative to it.[303] The great multinational enterprises and universal religions — especially the best organized one, the Catholic church — exercise considerable power, from which a corresponding responsibility flows; but the problems mentioned can be resolved only on the state level.

6.3.2. The Structural Conditions of Internal Policy

In the following we can outline only the essential features and main problems of the internal politics of states in the Western European culture area at the present time in the late modern period. This can be justified by pointing out that these states are among the most powerful in the world, that their way of life and their political institutions are seen as models, and that the earlier survey from the point of view of the philosophy of history concentrated especially on this culture area; in addition, my competence allowed no other choice. Since the institutional structures were already described in chapter 6.1, here I will discuss the mechanisms of the concrete political decision-making process. I emphasize in particular the weaknesses of the system, because criticizing them leads to the normative reflections of the third part of this book, not because I fail to see the strengths. That, at the moment, there is no better system is unfortunately undeniable.

First, we can note that the impulse that lies behind the project of modernity has weakened in some respects. This holds especially for the Old World — the United States still has an essentially unbroken relationship to modernity, partly because it has wagered very one-sidedly on this card, partly because the religious sources of modernity in the United States flow much more powerfully than they do in Europe, and partly because its culture is younger and less reflective. On the other hand, in Europe and especially in Germany, as the most intellectual country, the conviction that the developmental tendencies of the last centuries cannot be continued is becoming increasingly widespread. The limits to growth are evident everywhere, not only in the ecological realm. At the same time, the alternative major ideology of modernity, Marxism, has finally disintegrated in recent years, and the utopian upswing it inspired has evaporated. The depression it has left behind in its adherents is great. Whereas those who believe in a transcendental world can obviously not be refuted by empirical setbacks, the disappointment of eschatological immanentism, which had bet on the card of history, is definitive.[304]

---

303. This is also the thesis of P. Kennedy (1993), on whose book I have drawn extensively.

304. This was predicted by G. Le Bon more than a hundred years ago in relation to socialist ideologies: "Leur véritable infériorité par rapport à toutes les croyances religieuses tient uniquement à ceci: l'idéal de bonheur promis par ces dernières ne devant être réalisé que dans une vie future, personne ne pouvait contester cette réalisation. L'idéal de bonheur socialiste devant se réaliser sur terre,

The essence of the politics of Western European states over the last two decades can be most vividly expressed through the idea that the modern state has increasingly limited its means of power to the system of positive sanctions. A self-representation of the state as a morally legitimated power hardly ever takes place any more.[305] The public educational system limits itself to transferring the information that is required to survive in industrial society—and even this task is inadequately fulfilled, because for instance ecological knowledge is still not sufficiently communicated. The schools have abandoned the attempt to communicate value rationality, which is almost systematically undermined in higher education. There is one thing of which a professor can be absolutely certain: almost every student who enters the university believes or claims to believe that truth is relative—thus A. Bloom began his famous criticism of the American system of higher education, which still lags behind the European one in destructive tendencies.[306] The modern scientific system is nihilistic in its ultimate consequences, and the twentieth century made increasingly explicit the consequences of a value-neutral science whose increasing specialization furthermore dims the outlook for comprehensive connections. The decline of the churches' legitimacy as the traditional representatives of value rationality continues; we will discuss it later.

At the same time, the humanization of criminal law has limited the deterrent force of the system of negative sanctions, and the reference to negative sanctions in another world elicits derision in a society that has largely lost the belief in individual immortality. One of the sources of the effectiveness of punishments is that they represent a negative value judgment; therefore where punishment no longer shames the person punished, but is interpreted only as the expression of a failure of society, it cannot have its full effect. If the civil law consequences of strict liability are feared more than the criminal law consequences of committing a serious misdemeanor, the social mechanisms are fundamentally altered. If more political energy is invested in protecting a criminal from unjust prosecution than in protecting law-abiding citizens from crimes, the state is endangered in its very foundations—the social validity of the legal order. Openness to multiculturality becomes a matter for concern if it is willing to allow areas outside the

---

la vanité des promesses apparaîtra dès les premières tentatives de réalisation, et la croyance nouvelle perdra du même coup tout prestige. Sa puissance ne grandira donc que jusqu'au jour de la réalisation. Et c'est pourquoi si la religion nouvelle exerce d'abord, comme toutes celles que l'on précédée, une action destructive, elle ne pourra exercer ensuite un rôle créateur" (1934; 124). ("Their true inferiority in relation to all religious beliefs consists solely in this: Since the ideal of happiness promised by the latter is supposed to be realized only in a future life, no one could contest this realization. Since the socialist ideal of happiness is supposed to be realized on earth, the emptiness of its promises will appear as soon as the first attempts to realize it are made, and the new belief will at the same time lose all its prestige. Its power will therefore grow only until the day it is realized. And that is why if the new religion at first exercises, like all those that have preceded it, a destructive action, it will not be able to play a creative role later on.")

305. Cf. E. Forsthoff (1971), 56.

306. (1987), 25.

law, and leads us to consider people from other cultures to be not really bound by Western legal norms. It is a great error to believe that organized crime gangs would be impressed by the perfected development of the constitutional state. They are interested in quick gains, and the values on which they feed have to do with a cult of violence that mistakenly considers itself heroic, and that despises nothing so much as modernity's ban on violence. Since only the maintenance of internal security can justify the state's monopoly on the use of force, the formation of vigilante groups becomes more likely if citizens feel that the state has left them in the lurch. The fortunately long era of peace has ended up making obsolete the idea that there may be situations in which the state can demand that one sacrifice one's life.

All the more exclusively has the present-day state relied on positive sanctions. The distribution of bonuses to various clienteles, especially before elections, has always been an important way of winning votes, but in modern industrial society, the state has access to an unprecedented number of positive sanctions, while the decline of other means of power is something new. The modern welfare state is repeatedly exposed to the misunderstanding that it is buying the loyalty owed to itself; and the less it has a clear theory of justice that provides a moral justification for its redistributions, the more this happens. One thing is obvious: the people who get the most are those who cry loudest and exercise the strongest political pressure—not those who are the neediest. (Thus in Germany the lion's share of the redistributed wealth goes to the lower middle class.) It also remains unclear how the national limitation of the welfare state principle and the violation of the duties of intergenerational justice can be justified. The new political economy[307] errs when it sells its own descriptive assertions as normative ones, or believes that there are no normative statements, but it is largely right, when it uses economic categories to describe current politics. The action of bureaucrats and politicians is determined often enough not by an orientation toward the common good (which many of them regard as a purely ideological category), but rather by their own interests. Sincerity obliges us to recognize this, even if absolutizing only the descriptive theory easily becomes a self-fulfilling expectation. In any case, there are not only market failures, but also political failures. A special political business cycle has been constructed, according to which shortly before elections a government usually embarks upon an expansionary policy that accepts an increase in inflation in order to reduce the number of unemployed, and after the elections pursues a restrictive policy in order to be in a position to expand again before the next election. Naturally, this model presupposes that the voters do not learn anything from their observation of this cycle—a presupposition that is not always, but often fulfilled in democracies based on pleasing the voters.

In a democracy, politicians compete with one another; to that extent moral politicians, too, must fight for votes. This inevitably creates a market-like situation, even if votes and not goods are being fought for, and a simple majority can be sufficient for a

---

307. See B. S. Frey's good introduction (1978).

politician, a maximization thus not being required. In a two-party system, this leads, under certain conditions, to an approximation of the various party programs—just as one is well advised to open a business on a main street, if one wants to have many customers. (In multi-party systems, the situation is different, because of the possibility of forming coalitions.) As a rule, political candidates are guided by the voters' preferences, but just as there are innovative entrepreneurs who create new preferences, there may also be innovative political candidates. The surest path, however, is to be guided by factual ideas, and therefore there is a temptation to reduce politics to opinion polls. This holds all the more when many politicians have no time to form well-founded views of their own. The professional politician's early start on a political career seldom allows long reflection on the common good; and once he is in office, there is no longer time for a more fundamental further education. The demands of modern administration and the very heavy load of committee work, the cratic necessity of keeping ahead of the numerous possible competitors and opposing their intrigues, and finally the showbiz aspects of modern media democracy[308] lead to a situation in which the politician races from one engagement to the next. If he finally begins to exercise authority, he has to draw on a system of categories that he developed in his youth, or at least decades earlier. With the increasing acceleration of historical changes, this means that politicians are seldom up to date—the fifty-year-old of today has hardly any real grip on ecological issues, but he has been thoroughly taught that promoting economic growth is the state's first duty. To be sure, in the meantime he has heard about the new dangers, but he has not internalized the ecological point of view. The rapid technological development that creates new facts long before they have been ethically evaluated or legally regulated (consider genetic engineering), as well as the globalization of the economy on the basis of new information technologies, for instance, make the state increasingly a reactive structure. Since the Second World War, important innovations in administration have taken place, first in business and then in the state. The excessive intellectual demands connected with the complexity of the late modern period even endanger democracy and make an increase in the influence of experts unavoidable, even if the latter's knowledge, no matter how precise, seldom extends beyond their limited field.

The degree of the state bureaucracy's efficiency also leaves much to be desired; and no exceptional acumen is required to observe that the quantitative increase of tenured positions does not necessarily make them more useful to the public. Bureaucracies grow, according to Parkinson's "law," quite independently of the tasks they have to perform, and they often last longer than those tasks, because in this way new possibilities for rising in the hierarchy (not always for the most capable) and greater scope for decision making are created. Bureaucracies are thus increasingly concerned with themselves. They are often an answer to problems that they themselves produce, and their over-expansion serves exclusively the interests of those employed in them, or of those

---

308. Plato already coined the apt expression θεατροκρατία (*Laws* 701a).

who decide whether to hire them and thus have in their hands a means of awarding sine-cures. In actuality, the demand for a "lean" state expresses a clear awareness of these connections, especially since the financial room to maneuver in present-day states is shrinking.

Even financial policy is increasingly approaching its limits. If colonial expansion over the planet reached its limits in the first half of the twentieth century, the subsequent economic expansion continued down to the present—indeed, it will continue for a while longer: the collapse of the East Bloc and the opening of China have made new markets available. However, as we have already said, a few of the former developing countries have grown into modern industrial states—it is certainly no longer possible to view them as the periphery of the European-American center. Indeed, precisely the fact that they are less developed than the West gives them important competitive advantages, since labor is cheaper in them, and the ecological restrictions fewer; and it is part of the logic of capitalism that capital, an impersonal and highly mobile power, pours into these regions when profits are to be made there.

The economic structural conditions are changing to the disadvantage of the West, and it is becoming steadily clearer that neither the state bureaucracy nor the welfare state can be maintained at its current level, and that the goal of full employment is no longer viable. This is not necessarily a bad thing, insofar as limited cuts in Europe's social safety-net still will not let anyone fall through it, insofar as a new leisure culture must be discovered, and insofar as the modern welfare state has favored the growth of forms of general parasitism the continuation of which is not guaranteed by any human right. Nothing is more dangerous than when people think they have rights, but no duties, and the government is to be pitied whose task consists in satisfying unlimited needs with limited means.[309] In any case, the reduction of the European welfare state will not be easy, and will consume a great deal of political energy, for an ideal of limitation is generally not easy to communicate, and modern states have increasingly seen their chief task as being to increase economic growth, or have in any event drawn their social legitimacy from doing so. In addition, it is certainly not impossible that the necessary cuts will be made in a way that cannot be described as just and that will lead to major economic and political polarizations.

The necessary reduction of the welfare state will naturally make the construction of an ecologically sustainable society more difficult, for a government that is dependent

---

309. Cf. Tocqueville (1835 ff.), 2:308: "Lors donc que l'ambition n'a d'issue que vers l'administration seule, le gouvernement finit nécessairement par rencontrer une opposition permanente; car sa tâche est de satisfaire avec des moyens limités des désirs qui se multiplient sans limites. Il faut se bien convaincre que, de tous les peuples du monde, le plus difficile à contenir et à diriger, c'est un peuple de solliciteurs." ("Thus when ambition has no outlet other than administration, government necessarily ends up encountering permanent opposition; for its task is to satisfy with limited means desires that multiply without limits. We have to recognize that of all the peoples in the world, the most difficult to restrain and direct is one composed of individuals who want things.")

on being periodically re-elected cannot ask its citizens to make too many sacrifices; at least it thinks it cannot do so. In actuality, we must acknowledge that hardly any society has based its system of prestige so clearly on the money someone has as does modern society. Money is the value that has remained as the lowest common denominator. Ascetic ideals, such as the mendicant orders upheld, play scarcely any role in modern culture's system of values, and even honor is a value that has almost no authority compared with its status in the Middle Ages and the early modern period. The classical sources of personal strength and self-respect have dried up. The feeling that one stands at the center of divine attention has disappeared, and even the pride in humanity in one's own person is no longer great; all the greater are one's own needs and narcissism. Narcissism has its place as a mass phenomenon in the late modern period. Taking oneself as seriously as every petit bourgeois does today, is possible only in a culture that was once Protestant. But in Protestantism something absolute was involved, whereas the late modern period deflates, as it were, modern subjectivity, but attributes to the empty shell of the individual particularity an importance that no pre-modern culture can comprehend. The lost *I* continues to make the claim that it is the center of the world, but it alone still revolves around itself. From the self-responsible individualist of the early modern period has emerged, to use Riesman's (1950) categories, the other-directed person who no longer finds within himself the criterion for determining what is true and what is false, and for judging whether needs are legitimate, but is instead like a radar constantly focused on the opinions of others, who are themselves, however, also such radars. The cult of sincerity develops because no objective truth is any longer recognized; truth is only a question of sincerity, though it is deliberately overlooked that where there is no longer any truth or important personalities, sincerity also ceases to be a great value. The late modern individual experiences reality largely only at second or third hand—through the media. A hostage-taking incident becomes a media event, and the beguiling of the public's boredom and the career and profit opportunities for the journalists accompanying and interviewing criminals become more important than protecting the life of the innocent hostage.

For the modern possibilist (*Möglichkeitsmensch*), who neither wants nor is able to take a definitive stance, relationships, jobs, and the newspapers he reads replace marriage, profession, and real education. Thirsting for affection and intimacy, which are no longer experienced in the traditional institutions, but incapable of lasting love, which cannot exist without a sense for values and a capacity for renunciation, he bounces from one relationship to another; at least the relative brevity of his family life ensures that he does not reproduce himself to an excessive degree. This results, however, as does the lack of any awareness of belonging to currents of tradition enduring over time, in a reduction of the sense of responsibility for coming generations. In traditional societies, this sense of responsibility was very strong among both aristocrats and peasants—a peasant who bore exactly the same name as his father and the son who would inherit his property, saw himself as the occupant of an office, not as an individual. The shorter and shorter half-life of knowledge leads to a decrease in the authority of age, which, in addition to the spatial isolation of elderly people, is a further factor in the decline of traditions and the concentration of life on the temporal mode of the present. Much the same goes for intellectual and political achievements. Rapid success, which is denied most substantial works because one needs time to sound their depths, is more important to most intellectuals and statesmen than their posthumous reputation or the consciousness of belonging to a great tradition; the intrinsic value of solid work is hardly felt any longer.[310] Work is felt less and less to be an end in itself, as a vocation, or takes on the character of an addiction; and even if the increasing importance of leisure reminds us of traditional cultures, it is a kind of leisure that is no longer shaped by meaningful common experiences. In the late modern period, there is no functional equivalent of the festivals of ancient cultures because such festivals presuppose a strong sense of forms that has disintegrated under the hammer blows of an individualism that has become irresponsible. Leisure paradoxically attempts to recover—but now as something freely chosen—what in ancient cultures was coerced. Physical effort, which is becoming increasingly superfluous in the world of work, is now sought in leisure, and even in life-imperiling sports that make it possible to feel once again the thrill of the fear of death, although now without any moral background. Tourism sends Westerners all over the globe, where they can voyeuristically observe ways of life to which they feel infinitely superior, but for which they secretly long, and which they are at the same time destroying, just like the supporting environment, through their absurd travels.[311]

Since rising in politics is difficult and even a somewhat deeper understanding of the quite complex structures of the contemporary world cannot be had without hard intellectual labor, a type is emerging who converses about everything and thinks he has seen through everything—including, for example, that it is not worthwhile to commit oneself—whereby he compensates for his lack of power. For the "inside-dopester," as Riesman calls him, politics has become a pure consumer good. He draws a heteronomous feeling of self-worth from the fact that "those people up there" are concerned only about power, that they are just as mean as he is, and, as he observes with schadenfreude, that they are repeatedly ousted from office as a result of mutual intrigues and all kinds of scandals. The usual tone of political magazines—which combine an appearance of omnipotence regarding the psychological condition of the elites with know-it-all objective incompetence, great malice, and fantasies of omniscience, because yellow journalism rightly perceives that contacts with the media are a crucial power factor in mass democracy—is typical of the political psychology of the late modern period. Moralistic indignation regarding evil machinations alternates with the overt profession of a cynicism that is terrific at judging those who judge others, because it lacks

---

310. Cf. Tocqueville (1835 ff.), 2:304.

311. No one has grasped the madness of modern tourism more acutely than Tolstoy in *Anna Karenina* (IV, 1). However, there this luxury is possible only for a prince, whereas today every ordinary Westerner can indulge in it.

any sense of performative contradictions. Since scandals satisfy needs for both indignation and amusement, their discovery, and occasionally also their organization, is a
main occupation of the present time. Because of a peccadillo and with the help of the
media, sometimes complete rogues succeed in bringing down a political opponent who
is incomparably superior to them morally, for it is easier to discover, understand, and
describe small irregularities than the crimes that really matter. The egalitarianism of
modernity requires the adoption of an uninhibited tone in dealing with political and intellectual authorities, which the latter must allow themselves to be drawn into, because
paradoxically only this allows them to increase their power advantage. Out of the necessity of bitter power struggles within the individual parties, which are inevitable wherever
there are neither coherent party programs or important personalities, or at least no clear
criteria for recognizing such personalities, people make the virtue of a "strong" party
poster that shows a candidate for chancellor, behind whose back two grinning faces of
party-members suggest that their chief preoccupation is how quickly they can throw
their leader out of office.

Poor late modernity! Despite all the rhetorics of progress that force late modernity
to present itself as the apex of human development, at the bottom of its soul it is well
aware that this claim is a joke (more precisely, that it has the character of a madhouse
joke), that it is not moving beyond modernity, and that it is not a post-modern period, but
rather only its declining phase, a late-modern period. However, unlike the epochs of decadence in earlier cultures, this declining phase threatens for the first time the whole planet,
and might leave no people behind with whom a regeneration could start. Since universalizability is the principle of modern ethics, the idea that our way of life is not universalizable means, according to modernity's own standards, nothing less than this: it is
immoral. We all know very well that things can't go on this way, that we can be expected
to sacrifice luxury goods without which people have lived happily for millennia, and that
those who refuse to make this sacrifice, if in all likelihood this refusal will result in natural
catastrophes of the first order, becomes guilty of a moral offense that coming generations,
and even the next generation and perhaps the moral judge as well, will not forgive. The
incapacity of developed societies and states to do what is recognized to be necessary leads
to an increasing crisis in public trust in their policy, which is for the most part only a projection of their disgust with themselves. It is well known that the economic and political
elites in democratic market societies usually implement what the majority wants them to
implement, or at least what they think it wants them to implement; and it is certainly
not the case that politicians who propose to do what is necessary can always expect to be
elected, or that entrepreneurs who produce commodities in an environment-friendly way
will always find their products selling like hotcakes. But the hatred of others is always all
the stronger the more it is supposed to distract attention from self-hatred, and thus it is
very possible that demons made of hatred and thirst for revenge may channel this kind of
mood for their own particular political ends. The time is favorable for demagogues.

On the positive side, it should be emphasized that in a few countries the ecological problem has become the main theme of a specific party, even if thus far it has suc-

ceeded in becoming politically crucial only in Germany. Since the social question seems to be largely solved within wealthy states, it is possible that the social-democratic parties may lose influence worldwide, and that the main opposition will henceforth be between conservatives and "greens," as the example of Germany might suggest. But it is also possible that the necessary remodeling of the welfare state will strengthen the social-democratic parties (even if only ideologues could escape perceiving the necessity of this remodeling), while the conservative and green parties will work together. The preservation of creation is in itself a conservative topic, and as a rule only alliances of morality with mores that are rooted in unchallenged traditions are historically powerful. However, the differences in political style between conservatives and greens are considerable; and the feeling of belonging together is often founded more on common past experiences and on sympathies based on external symbols than on objective commonalties. It will be crucial for the green parties to surmount the infantile disorders of morality and to find leaders who have a natural authority. In any case, internal political borderlines will soon shift to a large extent. The right and left are increasingly splitting into different groups that correspond symmetrically to each other: those who continue the project of modernity without restriction, those who restrict it on the basis of a universalist ethics, and those who want to give up universalism altogether.[312] This process of disintegration causes the overestimation of the importance of membership in a given political party—an overestimation that in itself is inimical to the common good—to become completely grotesque in the judicial and administrative branches.

Poor late modernity! It is entirely possible that a synthesis of conservatism and ecologism will not be achieved, and that the moral paradigm change will lead to a schism in Western societies. This is all the more likely, the more the morally innovative side insists on the standpoint of moralism—that is, on the rejection of the existing mores at any price, while fully refusing to recognize the historical reason present in it. It is obvious that this kind of aggressive moralism is spreading, and that it is more concerned to emphasize its own special status and excellence, more concerned with satisfying itself morally and with getting the social environment morally whipped up, than with resolving objective problems. It should be morally rejected. It is also a danger to ethics, for as a rule it does not shy away from the most manifest self-contradictions—it approves abortion and rejects experiments on embryos, supports brutal guerrillas without ideas, but rejects protection for innocents by the United Nations, etc. Indeed, sometimes current moralism denies that there is an objective morals at all, and thereby it openly acknowledges that it is not interested in the subject itself. If it is only material values that it is rejecting, then a flight into the procedural is programmed in advance. Commissions will be set up

---

312. Cf. my more detailed discussions (1991), 37 ff. Already in 1930 Ortega y Gasset wrote: "Ser de la izquierda es, como ser de la derecha, una de las infinitas maneras que el hombre puede elegir para ser un imbécil; ambas, en efecto, son formas de hemiplejía moral" (1930; 32). ("Being on the left is, like being on the right, one of the infinite number of ways that a person can choose to be an imbecile: both of them, in fact, are forms of moral hemiplegia.")

from which little is to be expected other than the vacuity of confessions of good intentions and the concealment of particular interests under empty rhetoric. Moralism's power of judgment is for the most part cloudy, its concrete motivational potential very small—especially since the inconspicuousness of ecological threats unfortunately overtaxes the usual motivational apparatus. Compensatory actions, and even displacement activities are increasing in order to deal with our bad ecological conscience; these could still lead to explosions of violence that would overshadow all previous ones.

If the predicted ecological catastrophes actually occur and therefore convince even the last skeptics, who up to that point will play them down because absolute certainty is not to be had in empirical questions and because they would like to continue their lifestyle, it is first of all unlikely that dealing rationally with these catastrophes will still be of much avail, since it takes a long time to stop the effects of industrial societies. But second, even if the worst can be avoided, in all probability the way will be paved for an insatiable need for revenge. The generation that considers itself betrayed and deprived of its future may well, in an unprecedented intensification of the normal generational conflict that might revive the old myths of killing and emasculating the father, fall upon those whom they consider responsible (and who, in such settlings of accounts, are almost always the most innocent) and take the bloodiest revenge. Since a major problem in current constitutional law is that in it the interests of future generations are not represented through a state organ, these revengeful spirits will probably make their judgments "in the name of future generations," and no longer in the name of the people. Natural catastrophes could easily lead to wars, perhaps world wars, since ecological questions are global in nature—wars to protect the last resources, in which ecological destruction represents a means of fighting and exercising pressure. What will then remain of humanity—if anything remains—will be organized in political structures very different from those usual today; they may have certain similarities to those of feudalism. Its science and technology will be primitive; its systems of legitimation will differ markedly from current ones. Its historical accounts will be dominated by a simple narrative structure: how human beings presumed to desire to live without God and without measure, and how they, after a world-historical minute of mendacious arrogance, were terribly punished for it. This account will be incommensurate with the ingenuities of current historiography, but it will be very deeply rooted existentially, and perhaps it will contain more truth than the learned historical tomes of our own time. Poor late modernity! The humiliation that may await it will be terrible—far more terrible than that of the former Soviet Union. May it not be denied the grace of recognizing, in the collapse of its project, a deeper meaning and the power of a reason that goes beyond its intellect!

6.3.3. Religious Structural Conditions

The problem of intergenerational justice overtaxes late modernity, insofar as the crucial idea of modernity is that of a balance of rational selfishness. According to this balance, it suffices for a political system if all people think only of themselves, because taking into account the natural selfishness of others inevitably leads to a limitation of selfishness. According to this theory, rational selfishness is sufficient for the construction of a just system, but it is ultimately also necessary: more would be an evil. Reference to the dangers to the state posed by religious fanaticism was supposed to justify the second part of the thesis. The neutralization of theology, metaphysics, and increasingly, ethics in the program of quantitative economic growth, whose cornucopia could provide for everyone, was supposed to eliminate all conflicts. But this program is now reaching its limits and intergenerational justice cannot be based on rational selfishness because future generations will not be able to avenge themselves for the injustice done them by those who will be dead when the former could strike back.

To be sure, the Hobbesian position is not the only one in modern ethics. An extreme altruism is demanded by utilitarianism, which thereby goes beyond even Christian ethics, which continued to have an effect in the Enlightenment. But the fundamental problem of these areligious ethics is, first of all, that their foundation is not convincing, and second, that they have far less motivational power than religious mores that also provide a culture of emotions. Apart from exceptions who are all the more respectable, secular ethicists' willingness to sacrifice their interests is seldom striking, and the contradiction between what they demand and their own lives is often embarrassing. No one has expressed this problem of foundations so clearly as Nietzsche: "Wenn man den christlichen Glauben aufgiebt, zieht man sich damit das *Recht* zur christlichen Moral unter den Füssen weg. Diese versteht sich schlechterdings *nicht* von selbst: man muss diesen Punkt . . . immer wieder an's Licht stellen. Das Christenthum ist ein System, eine zusammengedachte und *ganze* Ansicht der Dinge. Bricht man aus ihm einen Hauptbegriff, den Glaube an Gott, heraus, so zerbricht man damit auch das Ganze: man hat nichts Nothwendiges mehr zwischen den Fingern."[313] In actuality, the belief in the self-evidence of the ideals of the Enlightenment, and indeed, in an objective reason, dissolved at the end of the nineteenth century as a result of the spread of historicism, among other things. The collapse of Marxism can be interpreted as the last consequence of this dissolution, because it represents an attempt at an ethics grounded in historicism. Since 1900, there has been a crisis in classical modernity that manifests itself in the arts as well. In the eighteenth century, physics was already rejecting teleological concepts; in the nineteenth century, with Darwin, biology followed; since the beginning of the twentieth century, with Durkheim, Weber, and Pareto, the social sciences also conceived themselves as value-neutral, and philosophy declared itself incapable of providing insights into values or moral truths. At the end of modernity stands a gigantic knowledge of

---

313. (1980), 6:113 f. "If you abandon the Christian faith, at the same time you are pulling the right to Christian morality out from under your feet. This morality is *very* far from self-evident: this point needs highlighting time and again. . . . Christianity is a system, a synoptic and *complete* view of things. If you break off one of its principal concepts, the belief in God, then you shatter the whole thing: you have nothing necessary left between your fingers." Trans. D. Large (1998), 45 ff.

mathematical structures, nature, and society, accompanied by enormous power, which is at the same time incapable of answering or even understanding the questions of what we ought to do or why science is a meaningful activity.[314]

Also, the classical forms of religious legitimation are not adequate to deal with the triumph of scientific-technological thinking, to which they have not been able to adapt themselves, but rather have opposed with a foolish overestimation of their own competencies. The churches clearly have trouble, partly in understanding the logic of modernity, and partly in resisting the current proceeding from relativism. Therefore the civic religion of states that have successfully mastered the process of modernization is increasingly the theory of rational selfishness or historical relativism. We have already seen, however, that these theories cannot motivate people to make the efforts that are necessary if there is to be a result of human history other than the one sketched out above. "Blood, toil, tears, and sweat" can no longer be proposed as a political program in a late modern culture, even in very bad times. Without a substantial religious taming, modernity will therefore not survive. Three ways out of this dilemma suggest themselves, but they are unacceptable. The first would be a return to the fundamentally religious basic structure of agrarian societies, but this is no longer possible, at least for the elites of the late modern period. The methodological naiveté of agrarian science, religion, and philosophy were partly untenable, and partly distracted attention from the ideological function of the corresponding systems of legitimation. In addition, the experience of the crusades and confessional wars in Europe showed that universal religions, of which there is more than one, do not always predispose people to quietism, but also to terrible aggression between religions. But this criticism does not mean that the current condition is theoretically and practically better. Second, we should reject still more firmly the attempt to create a new religion as a substitute for the traditional ones. Robespierre, Comte, and Lenin can be interpreted as the founders of modern Esperanto religions, and not only their well-deserved historical fate, but also simple reflection shows that all such attempts are doomed to fail. The absolute cannot be constructed. Third, there is the wicked idea of using genetic technology to alter human nature in order to create an ideologically controllable automaton, of the kind that is anticipated, for instance, in Huxley's *Brave New World* (further "progress" in communication technologies might already be described as steps taken in this direction).

So what should we do? Not much. The human being must learn to leave many things undone, to be patient, and to be on the lookout for any signs of the construction of a new ethos, as universalist as possible, in which most of the traditional mores, including, I hope, that of modernity, can rediscover themselves. Philosophy can critically accompany this ethos, but it can never produce it. Nonetheless, despite all the dangers, it can certainly discover a hidden meaning in the present situation. Modern subjectivity is not the highest stage of world history, but it is a necessary transitional point, for it completes the tendency of natural evolution. Animals are distinguished from plants by

---

314. Cf. the magnificent analysis in Jonas (1979), 57 f. Trans. H. Jonas and D. Herr, 22 ff.

their greater independence with regard to the environment; man is the liberated animal; modern man, who with Descartes opposes his own consciousness to the whole *res extensa,* and with Kierkegaard opposes the peak of the *I* to the self, merely continues this tendency, in which a marvelous logic prevails. For that very reason, modern atheism can be interpreted, within the framework of a philosophy of history that seeks to recognize in history the rule of the absolute, as a stage in the unfolding of the absolute. Left-wing Hegelianism interpreted the belief in a transcendent god as a necessary transitional stage on the way to the self-comprehension of the human spirit. But one can also interpret modern atheism as the mode of the absolute's presence that consists in its absence.[315] In the loss of rational autonomy—that is, the self-alienation of the intellect in the Middle Ages and the self-overestimation of the finite intellect in modernity—are (one can hope) two stages on the way toward a more rational relationship between God and the finite intellect. This relationship is the ultimate meaning of history. Certainly, it is not given to man to know whether its achievement is to be granted to *our* species, but we can in principle know what we have a duty to do and not to do. And that is enough.

---

315. The first who developed this conception—before Heidegger—was A. Huxley. See (1977), 231 ff.

III

Political Ethics

The reader who has come thus far will be weary. The author is no less weary and feels paralyzed by the feeling that the demands he confronts are too great. The normative and descriptive disciplines, already enormously complex in themselves, must now be related to each other again if an answer to the questions of our time is to be given. Moreover, he is burdened by the feeling that his efforts are futile so far as practice is concerned, even if they should turn out to be theoretically successful. Is it not presumptuous of philosophy to claim to show modernity the way out of the dead end at which it has arrived? Are powers of a quite different kind not needed here, ones that are more suited to move people to change than is abstract thought? This is surely true. But even these powers need the critical accompaniment of philosophy if they are not to wreak havoc. To that extent, there is no alternative other than to continue, putting our trust in reason.

In such a situation, learned people in earlier cultures turned to higher powers in order to draw strength for their undertakings. Even if the muses are among the powers that have fallen victim to the modern destruction of the gods, a moment of quiet reflection may still be allowed, however one may imagine the functional equivalent of the muses, which our own time cannot and must not renounce.

7

The Just State

Justifying the state means showing that it is better, on grounds of moral principles, that it exist than that it not exist. However, this kind of justification is harder than it initially seems. Our survey of the various forms of political organization that have been realized in history has shown that one cannot speak of *the* state, but only of a multitude of states that differ greatly from each other in their ordering principles, and indeed that many of these states have striven, and still strive, to incorporate other states or at least to force them to adopt their particular form. The task of legitimation therefore cannot be reduced to legitimating statehood in general, but rather includes outlining a normative theory of political institutions. This kind of outline is itself a political matter, however, and it is reasonable to fear that it might be used as a weapon in the power struggles between states and within them. Therefore we must immediately say that the philosophy of the ideal state has to be accompanied by a political ethics—that is, it must be explained which political measures are permissible in order to establish the ideal state. From the fact that a certain state form is better than another it does not follow that all means are allowed in realizing it. If these means are very likely to lead to civil war, using them runs the risk, for the sake of a higher state form, of falling below the level of statehood as such. Therefore it is important to explain why a state, completely apart from its form, usually represents a morally important achievement, and why for that reason the mores that support it are to be respected prima facie.

The previously discussed correlation between law and state implies that the evaluation of a specific state is not possible without the evaluation of the legal order that it protects and that supports it. Since constitutional law is also a part of the law, the philosophy of the state seems to be a part of the philosophy of law. However, we have already seen that coercion is not the sole means the state can or even must use; to that extent, political philosophy cannot be reduced to the philosophy of law. The theory of natural law is the center of political philosophy. But first of all, a good politician ought also to have access to the reservoir of other means that are not equipped with coercion, that is, he ought to be capable of making credible moral appeals. In politics, the system of positive sanctions has a peculiar character, for on one hand the state's financial support for a project is evidently a far weaker—and therefore easier to justify—means than, for instance, the use of criminal law; on the other hand, that support, insofar as it makes use of tax money, is still based on coercive means. Second, it would be naive to assume that ideal conditions ever obtain in reality. The positive law of a time is always only an approximation to natural law, and sometimes even manifestly unjust, but it produces expectations whose violation can certainly run counter to a principle of justice, even if the violation paves the way for a higher kind of justice. Indeed, the real life of the state also includes events that have nothing to do with law, or may even be partly illegal, and that also require moral regulation. Conversely, not all questions in the philosophy of law are part of political philosophy. The latter will discuss in detail the normative principles of constitutional law, but it will discuss those of private, criminal, procedural, and administrative law only insofar as they might find their way into a written constitution. Whereas this chapter will be concerned with a normative theory of institutions and the principles of political ethics in the ideal state, the next chapter will deal with the principles of political ethics in non-ideal situations, and especially in exceptional situations.

The philosophy of the state can proceed in various ways. First of all, it can start, as does Martin Kriele's (1975), from the real historical development, and deal, for instance, with the morally relevant steps in the realization of the present state, that is, state sovereignty, liberalism and the separation of powers, democracy, the welfare state, and—as a task for the future—the ecological state.[1] Second, it could largely dissociate itself from the historical development and practice a purely normative discourse. This strategy can be further subdivided into two alternative modes of proceeding. The great philosophies of law of the natural law tradition, especially that of German idealism, discuss first the principles of rational private and criminal law, and only then those of constitutional law, on the basis of the conviction that the state must be bound by a law that precedes the state in order to be legitimate. In contrast, Hobbes also assumes a few natural laws, but he discusses the principles of private and criminal law after those of constitutional law, on the basis of his belief that only the state can lay down the law. There is much to be said for all three ways of proceeding. Someone who is guided by historical development honors reason in reality and resists the temptation to reject wholesale all states that are not the way they should ideally be. However, he does not exhaust the possibilities of normative reason; he will hardly be in a position to anticipate future developments. In this respect, a purely normative procedure achieves a great deal; but it sometimes is no longer able to build a bridge to historical reality and thereby itself become effective (unless it does so by pretending to demonstrate the conceptual necessity of contingent things, as Hegel's philosophy of right repeatedly does, and in so doing it makes the unacceptable

---

1. Alternative denominations for the type of state meant here, which demands intergenerational justice and adaptation to nature, among other things, are *Naturstaat* ("nature-state"), for example, in K. M. Meyer-Abich (1990), 118 ff., and *Umweltstaat* ("environmental state"), for example, in C. F. Gethmann and M. Kloepfer (1993).

claim to grasp something supratemporal). Among the normative approaches, that based on natural law is closer to the moral principles set forth in chapter 3: a system of family law is not just because it is made by the state, but rather because it corresponds to the relevant moral principles by which the state is bound. And yet Hobbes is right on one point. The legitimacy of the state is not based solely on the fact that it makes just law. The state's peace-making function is a morally relevant achievement even if the law that it protects is unjust. Protecting states from dissolution can be a morally far more urgent task than, for instance, establishing a more rational family law. The value of the state is not derived solely from the ideas of justice and freedom, which it only sometimes—not always—realizes, even if it ought always to realize them; its value already arises from the idea of peace, which most states (at least, modern states) achieve domestically. Having seen this is Hobbes's enduring achievement, and even someone who clings to a natural law should not underestimate this discovery. The better ought not to be the enemy of the good; in this case, the just state ought not be the enemy of the state as such. In fact, historical development shows that the state's more complex achievements occur later than the sphere of statehood as such; they can be constructed only within the latter sphere, no matter how crude it may initially be. Had people waited to found the state until all the demands of natural law had been fulfilled, they would never have advanced to the sphere of statehood, and the most elementary moral principles would not have been respected. The normative circularity between natural law and the state consists in that the natural law legitimates the state in a special way, but is at the same time first realized through it, and indeed can ultimately be recognized only within it. This circumstance is to be accounted for by first offering a rough and preliminary sketch of why in general a state should be, and only then turning to the elaboration of the concrete principles of natural law by which the state is bound; in conclusion I will discuss the principles of natural law on which constitutional law is to be based.

7.1. The Justification of Statehood in General

Someone seeking to legitimate the sphere of statehood as such, and especially the modern state, can learn a great deal from Hobbes, but he will have to deviate from Hobbes in several respects. Thus it should be conceded that the formation of a monopoly on force and on law making diminishes the risk of violent conflicts. In view of human nature's aggressiveness and self-righteousness, the recognition of an authority that settles conflicts—no matter how just or unjust the settlement may be—is a blessing not to be underestimated. Even in choosing between the alternatives "unjust state or civil war," the former is not necessarily always to be given precedence—it depends on the extent of the injustice and the kind of civil war; the quiet of the graveyard in an unjust state is by no means always the lesser evil. But no reasonable person will deny that in general, civil wars are to be avoided. However, a justification of the state must prove more than that the state is better than civil war. For these two situations do not form a complete disjunction;

there was also the pre-state condition of human history. Hobbes conceived the condition of statelessness essentially on the basis of his experience of civil war, which he projected exponentially, as it were; but his description of the so-called state of nature is only partly correct, and since this misrepresentation favored his further procedure, he certainly had an interest in it. Thus one must draw a sharp distinction between a condition of civil war and a condition preceding the state. Civil wars presuppose a state, which loses only its unity: During the English Civil War, Cromwell could rely on the parliament's army, and he remained capable of exercising political functions. At that period, there was no war "of every man, against every man";[2] and the civil war was so bloody precisely because the two sides fought as units against each other.

Still less was there, as Hobbes supposes, a war of all against all in the historical condition that preceded the construction of states, and that must also be examined when comparing statehood with a conceivable alternative. For several hundred thousand years, humanity lived in corporate groups that repeatedly exercised political functions, that is, had to use force that was considered legitimate; but because of this allegedly legitimate force these groups did not become states in the narrower sense of the term. Since it is obviously impossible to return to these forms of organization, the following question may seem academic, but it is nonetheless philosophically legitimate: Would it not have been better to have remained at the stage that preceded statehood? There was certainly resistance to the construction of states, and this indicates that the transition to statehood cannot have been made by universal consent. The better to appreciate the greatness and limits of the pre-state condition, we must begin by asking what factors made possible, first, its stability, and second, the triumph of the world of the state in general and finally of the modern world of the state.

Why did people not behave as Hobbes imagined they did in the time before the emergence of states, but were rather able to live in the corresponding organizational forms (and quite peacefully, to boot) for an incomparably greater length of time than in states and even more than in modern states? Three factors should be mentioned. First, the human population was much smaller, so that frictions among wandering tribes were less frequent. Second, the possible interactions were considerably less complex than they were in even the first states in which irrigation was used in agriculture. Third, the power of mores and familial authority, the feeling of belonging together, was so great within the tribe that many conflicts did not appear at all or could be nipped in the bud. The calculating selfishness and the insatiable striving for power assumed by Hobbes are late products of historical development, and for that reason the original communities were much more stable than he imagines. On the aforementioned presuppositions, statelessness was entirely possible, indeed even sensible—but only on these presuppositions. The peculiar thing about modern anarchism, which is an offspring of extreme modern individualism, is that it opts for a form of political organization diametrically opposed to its

---

2. *Leviathan* chap. 13 (1651; 185).

spirit. Stable statelessness—which must, and here Hobbes's critics are correct, be strictly distinguished from modern civil war—can exist only when mores are extremely powerful. If mores dissolve, law must step in. And for that, the state is necessary.

The arguments in favor of the state can consist merely in saying that the overcoming of the historical presuppositions on which only pre-state groups could exist is morally desirable. If a world with more people pursuing more complex activities in greater freedom from traditional mores is preferable, then one must approve of the state, and ultimately even the modern state. Why a world with more people in it is—*ceteris paribus*—better than one with fewer people will be discussed in chapter 7.3.1.1. On transcendental grounds, it is furthermore obvious that a culture capable of philosophical reflection is—again, *ceteris paribus*—preferable to a less reflective one. But only more complex activities and greater freedom make possible more significant intellectual achievements, at least in science and philosophy—though not necessarily in art, in which (with the exception of architecture) great works were already accomplished in the pre-state era. The ancient Greek thinkers already realized that philosophy could truly develop only within a structure with the social qualities of a state; law fosters intellectual efforts of a entirely different extent than do mores. In addition, the lengthening of the human life span and the attenuation of poverty and illness are promoted by cooperation, just as cooperation presupposes a state. Furthermore, one can hardly deny that even the subjection carried out by the ancient oriental states resulted in an increase in coercion in comparison with the pre-state groups, but was nonetheless a necessary step on the way to freer polities; indeed, the opening up of possibilities for development outside the clan could then feel like a form of freedom, since dependency on the pharaoh, for instance, was more mediated than dependency on the patriarch. Analogous arguments hold for the transition from the pre-modern to the modern state, without which the industrial revolution and thus contemporary natural science would not have been possible, and which was able to feed far more people and allow them still greater freedom. Finally, only the modern state, in accord with universalist principles, was capable of guaranteeing all people in the society certain basic rights.

The price for these achievements consisting in the construction of a stable domination was not in general too high, even if this domination was accompanied by the risk of an abuse of power that was not previously possible, and even if many of the means employed in founding the state were not legitimate. Nevertheless, the state and the modern state can in principle be organized in such a way that the risk of abuse of power is limited. However, the reasons for a positive evaluation of the state are not valid for all state forms—the modern totalitarian state is surely a far greater evil than the pre-state condition. But the response to that threat can only be the democratic constitutional state, not a return to archaic forms of organization. In none of the arguments cited is it assumed that people in pre-state corporate groups were less happy than people in the state and especially in the modern state, since comparisons of happiness are notoriously difficult; if one indulges in them, then there are certainly grounds, as we have seen in chapter 6.2, for supposing that people might have been happier in the pre-modern age. But justice is a higher value than happiness, and the modern state can claim to have realized a universalist concept of justice to far greater extent than did earlier forms of political organization. Naturally, in these arguments in favor of statehood we are concerned with our evaluation after the fact, not with the judgment of those concerned. Of the latter, many who were subjected by force to the state's domination would certainly not have been prepared to pay that price, had they not been compelled to do so. Historically speaking, an original contract is in any case out of the question, and even normative contract theory incorrectly presupposes that the preference structure of all people is such that they would prefer the maintenance of internal peace to the threat of death connected with a lack of domination. That this is not so is proven, for instance, by those Apaches whose resistance to Geronimo has already been mentioned (chapter 6.2.2.1). To that extent, Hobbes is also in error on the normative level. If one posits contract-theory premises, one can justify the state only on very special assumptions, most of which are not fulfilled; for in general, statelessness is not a non-Pareto-optimal condition. Furthermore, it must be pointed out that the foundation of a state usually results in greater internal protection (setting aside for a moment the possibility that the state might abuse its power), but so long as there is a plurality of states, the risk of violent death in the course of a war between states remains great. In 1916, the statistical probability of dying a violent death was hardly less for a twenty-year-old German man than for an Amazon Indian of the same age.

However, the futility of the Apaches' battle also proves that once the strategy of statehood (not necessarily the strategy of pre-modern statehood, but that of modern statehood) has emerged, there is henceforth hardly any evolutionarily stable alternative to it. If modern states attack pre-state political corporate groups, the latter can choose among only three possibilities: being subjugated, constructing their own state, or perishing.[3] Insofar as there is an obligation to pursue evolutionarily stable strategies, this provides a further argument for adopting the strategy of statehood—even if this sometimes means betraying the innermost essence of one's own culture in order to allow it to survive externally. Of course, situations can arise in which an individual's heroic decision to die in order not to be unfaithful to his own culture deserves every respect; certainly in a just, modern state indigenous peoples who have lived in pre-political corporate groups should be given the opportunity to continue to practice their own culture (which because of the seductive attraction of modernity is for the most part possible only by separating them geographically), for these cultures realize values from which industrial societies in crisis can and should learn a great deal. Finally, we should recall that even an evolutionarily stable strategy can destroy itself—the state developed by industrial society may very well come to an end in a terrible catastrophe. But all that does not change the fact

---

3. Against this view it cannot be objected that modern guerrilla warfare has revealed the impotence of the world of the state, for guerrilla warfare is successful only when it has weapons that derive from modern technological development, which presupposes the state; furthermore, support by other states is an important factor in its success. If successful, a guerrilla movement usually seeks to construct a statehood even if it differs in content or in personnel.

that the truly moral task consists in making the state better, and not in leaving its sphere behind. A good state is a state that realizes natural law; and as we will see, natural law can find a guarantee of its existence only in the state. But what is natural law?

7.2. The Concept of Natural Law

The expression "natural law" is extremely inappropriate, since nature cannot provide grounds for the validity of norms.[4] In the literal sense, natural law would be the so-called law of the stronger (the larger fish eat the smaller, as they say in India)[5] or, since this is not a law in the legal or moral sense, the set of legal norms that have a biological basis. Probably there are such norms (for instance, in chapter 4.1.3 we discussed space-related intolerance in animals and humans), but their existence is irrelevant for the theory of validity. Neither are all such norms necessarily morally justified, nor can the morally important legal norms be reduced to these norms that can be explained biologically. Even if one relates the concept of "nature" in "natural law" to human nature, one misses the meaning of the concept. There may well be a smallest common denominator of all human cultures that can be called "human nature," but even this is neither a necessary nor a sufficient condition for what will be called "natural law" in the following pages. For instance, the incest taboo is common to most peoples, although it involves very different definitions of what counts as incest; but from this fact it does not follow that the state has a right (and even less a duty) to punish incest. Nonetheless, it is easy to see that the state is at least not well advised to prohibit things for which human nature possesses a proclivity, because that kind of norm is very likely not to be respected, and in the long run that would undermine respect for the whole legal system; the Catholic church's experience with celibacy and that of the United States with prohibition are not very encouraging. However, there are certainly also widespread human proclivities—such as that to revenge—against which one must fight, even if resistance has to be expected. The abolition of blood revenge was (and still is, in some states) a long and laborious process, but it is nevertheless an important task of the state. Would it therefore not be better to completely forgo the use of this misleading word, and speak instead of "the law of reason,"[6] since the relevant ground of validity is practical reason

---

4. One can give a normative value to the concept of nature, as was done in the pre-modern age, but this only postpones the problem, for the normative value is justified only if one has access to a normative standard that transcends nature and makes it possible to emphasize some natural events at the expense of others and to present them as the "true" nature.

5. Cf. Hegel, *Enzyklopädie* § 502, n. (1969 ff.; 10:311 f.). Spinoza is so consistent that he bases his concept of natural law on his power-oriented concept of nature. See *Tractatus theologico-politicus* chap. 16; *Tractatus politicus* chap. 2.

6. Cf., for instance, Fichte (1971), 10:498. Speaking of "political justice" rather than of "natural law" is a less satisfactory alternative, since not everything that can rightly be imposed by force can be reduced to the virtue of justice, and convictions that are incoercible are also part of justice.

and not nature? The answer would be "yes," were it not that neologisms are not easily accepted, and that there is much to be said for maintaining continuity with the tradition that has long spoken of "natural law."[7] In any case, not only Catholicism, but also thinkers such as Locke, Leibniz, Fichte, and Hegel have spoken of "natural law," and indeed the two latter philosophers did so in the framework of a practical philosophy based on the autonomy of reason.[8]

7.2.1. Natural Law and Positive Law

In the following pages, the term "natural law" will mean the set of the norms that on moral grounds may or even ought to be imposed by means of force, insofar as doing so is not inexpedient. Thus natural law is a standard for the judgment of the moral nature of positive law, a standard based on the principles of general ethics. If one rejects it, there is no possibility of making well-founded judgments concerning the injustice of a legal system; one deprives oneself of the possibility of an objective critique of positive law on the level of value rationality—and that ought to concern a society that considers itself enlightened and critical.[9] It is ridiculous to claim, in the spirit of the jurisprudence of interests, that it suffices to reconcile interests in order to produce law that is just. To be sure, interests are an important object of law, and it was irresponsible of a certain kind of conceptual jurisprudence to refuse them appropriate consideration. But interests often contradict one another, and this contradiction can usually be resolved without force only if there is a standard that transcends factual interests in order to evaluate individual interests. However, this kind of standard cannot itself be reduced to interests, because the same problem would arise again at the level of the conflicting meta-interests.

Natural law principles, at least according to the conception to be developed here, allow the judgment of both primary and secondary rules in Hart's sense. A minimalist conception of natural law could be conceived, in which solely constitutional law norms are to be evaluated. In this case natural law would, for instance, demand only a far-reaching democratic principle, and what individual laws democratic societies decided upon would be left to them alone. This reduction of natural law to procedures—such as discourse ethics, for instance, tends to defend—seems to open up a greater area of freedom. Furthermore, it avoids a problem that arises for a multi-leveled conception of natural law. Within such a conception, on one hand constitutional structures are to be judged on their intrinsic worth, and on the other one must ask with what degree of probability substantive–natural law norms can be realized within them; nothing guar-

---

7. An impressive attempt to revive the natural law tradition has been made by J. Finnis (1980).

8. Catholic natural law theory occasionally suffers from the fact that it confuses norms that may be imposed on all rational beings with those that a religious community may prescribe for its members with the threat of negative spiritual sanctions.

9. Cf. Cicero, De legibus I 15, 42.

antees that the two evaluative criteria will always converge. It may be that democracy is inherently better than non-democratic state forms, but that under certain conditions the introduction of a far-reaching democracy makes it impossible to achieve a more just property order or a just criminal law. This problem is by definition avoided in that minimalist position, since according to the latter all law made within a just state is itself just. But even if simplicity is certainly, *ceteris paribus,* an advantage, it is an advantage only *ceteris paribus,* and the other aspects of the two conceptions are by no means the same. For quite apart from the fact that a freedom people don't know how to use in a reasonable way is not necessarily a blessing, it is obvious that compared with the substantive conception, the proceduralist conception of natural law also represents a threat to freedom. For according it, basic rights are not binding on procedure, but rather exist only by the grace of procedure, which can abrogate them whenever it wants to. On the other hand, adopting substantive natural law principles means limiting the norm-maker's freedom of decision. But this limitation need not be an evil for those subject to state power even when the norm-giver is not a monocrat but a majority.

However, a convincing conception of natural law must take various things into account. Thus natural law cannot replace positive law; instead, it is itself an elementary obligation of natural law to allow law to achieve that certainty—which mere reason cannot produce—that alone can avoid conflicts. Moral law cannot be satisfied to be just; it must also lead to *the certainty of the law.* Only a state that combines justice and certainty of the law can be termed a "state governed by law." For the maintenance of the certainty of the law, the existence of a rule of recognition for positive law in Hart's sense is surely welcome, as long as it does not claim to be the true ground of the law's validity. One can call norms such as the obligation to make criminal laws clear and definite (*nulla poena sine lege certa*) and the prohibition on analogical extension in criminal law "formal" natural law principles;[10] in them, natural law transcends itself, so to speak, because it recognizes the necessity of its positivization. For example, there can be no rational arguments for having the statutory period of limitation on a certain crime begin after five rather than after six years, but there are rational arguments for an unambiguous determination of the period concerned. Whether one drives on the left-hand or the right-hand side of the road is a matter of indifference so far as reason is concerned; but that traffic must adhere to a single rule follows from the normative sentence that human lives are an important object of legal protection, and from the descriptive sentence that unregulated traffic endangers human lives. (On the same ground, in laying down a rule regarding traffic it is also unreasonable to upset factually existing habits without some special justification). There can be natural law principles concerning who has the right to determine the regulation of road traffic, but it goes without saying that even in the case of norms in positive law regarding the various competencies, a surplus exceeding what is demanded by natural

---

10. A list of such principles can be found, for instance, in Montesquieu's *Esprit des lois* 29.16 (1748; 2:302 ff.).

law is inevitable. To that extent there will always be a plurality of legal systems that are compatible with natural law—the system of its axioms is not complete.

Even if natural law cannot make superfluous the efforts of positive law and the legal scholarship accompanying it, natural law remains a *controlling authority of positive law*. Some norms of a positive legal system can contradict those demanded by natural law: The Nuremberg race laws, for instance, were contrary to natural law. There is legal murder (think of Stalin's terroristic justice), legal rape (for instance, the rape of a female slave by her master), legal theft (as, for instance, in the case of taxing the poorest and hardest-working in order to maintain their rulers' luxurious way of life). It has already been emphasized that from a negative judgment regarding a positive legal system alone it does not follow that one has no moral duty to obey the corresponding legal norms; in order to decide in such a case, additional principles drawn from political ethics are required. Fundamentally, the problem of the right to resist does not really belong to natural law theory, which only provides a standard for just legal norms, and cannot decide on the basis of this standard alone what should be done in the case of a positive law that is contrary to natural law. However, without such a standard the question of when resistance is permissible, and in some circumstances even obligatory, also cannot be answered. Indeed, even for the legislator the recognition that a legal system is contrary to natural law is far from implying that he is morally obligated under all circumstances to change it. For it goes without saying that the best legal system cannot take hold socially unless it is rooted in mores, and that the attempt to introduce it without them would be suicidal; and it is not always morally obligatory to risk one's own life, especially if its sacrifice would probably be meaningless. But the fact that the acceptance of an unjust legal order by rulers or their subjects is sometimes morally justified is far from making that legal order a just one, and in no way presupposes a denial of the idea of natural law. Such a denial would only lead to the extinction of even the guiding star for long-term changes and for a moral legal policy.

The theory of natural law was rejected by historicism because it overlooked *the historicity of law*. In fact, in the nineteenth century the history of law and the sociology of law defined themselves by turning away from the ideals of the natural law tradition. But Vico and Montesquieu show that the two approaches are not necessarily opposed to each other, and on the merits of the issue it is easy to see that even the discovery of the greatest plenitude of the most various legal systems does not contradict the basic idea of natural law theory. The history of law deals with the history of positive law, and sometimes also with the history of ideas about natural law; but as a subject of the moral, natural law is as atemporal as its discovery and realization by human beings is temporal. What was said in chapter 3.5 about the relationship between the moral and history also holds, analogously, for the relationship between natural law and history. Indeed, just as some arguments speak for a (limited) moral evolutionism, so it can be said that human history represents positive law's gradual and by no means continuous approximation to the demands of the idea of law. It is easy to explain why there is a connection between the development of moral ideas and that of the positive legal systems.

Since moral ideas are supposed to determine all our actions, the legal system cannot remain uninfluenced by them. Thus the intellectual connection between the ethical universalism of modernity and the idea of human rights is obvious.

Furthermore, we must recall that general ethics, and a fortiori natural law theory, includes *conditional obligations.* A law does not have only an intrinsic value; for the most part it also sets for itself a *goal*[11] that must be achieved under different conditions in different ways. Thus differing legal norms in individual cultures can be reduced partly to different structural conditions. For instance, it is entirely comprehensible that among different peoples the same crimes are punished with differing degrees of severity—they can have wholly different consequences because of different ecological presuppositions, different historical experiences, or a different national character; in addition, the same punishments may be experienced differently or imposed to differing degrees by the state. The punishment should be just, but it should also be a deterrent; the same kind of punishment does not achieve this goal to the same extent everywhere. But in this case only an inequality is an expression of an essential equality—namely, an equality with respect to the normative premises that lead, because of different descriptive minor premises, to different conclusions. To give two examples: the scarcer an environmental good, the stricter the regulations regarding its waste can justly be; the more threatened a state is by violent internal conflicts, the sooner emergency measures are justifiable. However, between these two cases there is an essential difference: the state is considerably less responsible for structural conditions of the first kind than for those of the second kind. It has a categorical duty to avoid, through a policy of limiting conflicts, the emergence of situations in which conditional obligations (or conditional permissions) of the second kind exist. One can say that some of the conditions that are relevant for the foundation of conditional obligations are morally indifferent, while others are bad in themselves, and that one must therefore work to overcome them, even if they have morally relevant consequences so long as they exist. Thus one can concede that the accumulation of capital in a few hands was probably a necessary presupposition for setting the process of industrialization in motion, and therefore it can be justified for the beginning of the industrial revolution—if, and only if, it is added that it must be considered a moral goal of this process of industrialization to surmount the inequality that made it possible.

Moreover, it is a formal natural law obligation that the system of positive law be *as consistent as possible.* It is true that the demands of natural law cannot be reduced to this obligation, but the latter implies that sometimes natural law principles force us to acknowledge certain obligations of positive law that contradict natural law, but nevertheless follow from fundamental positive law norms that cannot be altered at a particular point in time. Certainly there remains a duty to work in the long term toward the repeal of these fundamental norms. But natural law itself recognizes that one cannot always

---

11. Cf. Radbruch's well-known triad of justice, expediency, and certainty of the law (1973; 164 ff.).

begin by changing the subordinate norms if the legal system is to maintain a certain coherence without which it can hardly function. The spirit of a state's laws is usually based on a generative principle, and one must have first understood it before one undertakes to supplement the laws through individual demands based in natural law that contradict those norms.[12] An integrated legal order can sometimes be preferable to an inconsistent patchwork of reasonable and unreasonable legal norms, even if it is still farther removed from the demands of substantive natural law. For the coherence of the legal system is an elementary formal–natural law principle. However, inconsistencies in the legal system can sometimes be the starting point for a development toward a coherence that also satisfies substantive–natural law demands; to that extent, they are to be welcomed. Thus Hegel praises "the illogicality of the Roman jurists and pretors . . . as one of their chief virtues, for by dint of being illogical they evaded unjust and detestable laws."[13] Substantive progress has to be weighed against the loss of internal coherence. For example, even if capital punishment is considered contrary to natural law, one will hesitate to welcome a law that abolishes it as a punishment for murder, but retains it as a punishment for theft, for one would add to the absolute injustice of this punishment of the thief the relative injustice that his crime would be considered more serious than murder. Thus the German rule according to which an attempt to do bodily harm is not punishable, but an attempt to damage property is, contradicts the relative order of the corresponding objects of legal protection, which is much easier to determine than whether an attempted crime is punishable at all. For crimes against property are a lesser injustice than direct injury to persons.

From another formal natural law principle follows an additional correction to the kind of abstract thinking about justice that lacks a sense for social reality. This deficient thinking is wrongly held to be a necessary consequence of all natural law theories, whereas it is actually the result of a one-sided concept of natural law. Thus a reasonable theory of natural law obviously acknowledges that every legislation that ought to protect freedoms at the same time limits them, and that therefore the costs of making laws and enforcing them should not be excessively high. For instance, fair taxation is an important natural law principle; but beyond a certain point, increased fairness in taxation is connected with an overblown tax bureaucracy, which makes the costs shoot up even for those who would profit from a refinement of the tax system. In this case natural law demands that one be content with an approximate justice.

---

12. Cf. the holistic interpretive maxim in Montesquieu, *Esprit des lois* 29.11 (1748; 2:298): "Ainsi, pour juger lesquelles de ces lois sont les plus conformes à la raison, il ne faut pas comparer chacune de ces lois à chacune; il faut les prendre toutes ensemble, et les comparer toutes ensemble." ("Thus, in order to judge which of these laws are the most in conformity with reason, one must not compare these laws with each other singly; they must be taken all together, and compared all together.")

13. *Rechtsphilosophie* § 3, n.: ". . . die Inkonsequenz der römischen Rechtsgelehrten und der Prätoren als eine ihrer größten Tugenden . . . , als durch welche sie von ungerechten und abscheulichen Institutionen abwichen" (1969 ff. 7:41). Trans. T. M. Knox (1942), 20.

7.2.2. Natural Law and Morals

One of the most popular objections to the conception of natural law argues that it overloads positive law with moral demands that endanger its peacemaking function. The objection is significant; the precise determination of the relationship between morals and natural law is in fact one of the central tasks of the philosophy of law. To this objection it can be replied, first, that the superiority of theories of natural law to a certain form of legal positivism consists precisely in the fact that the former, in contrast to the latter, are able to explain why the state may not demand anything immoral or prohibit anything that is morally obligatory. In the interest of freedom, the state should fundamentally not demand even something that is morally indifferent. A decision for driving on the right rather than the left side of the road is not a counter-example: if the state orders traffic regulations, the specific determinations are not derived from morals, but one can derive from morals the conclusion that the regulations ought to be unified, if this is required in order, for example, not to endanger human lives. To that extent, the objection that the demand that law be bound by morals leads to totalitarianism is simply absurd.

Second, natural law is a proper subset of moral norms. Not everything that is morally obligatory may be imposed by force—it is the moral itself that forbids this. Against this view, legal positivism can only observe that a few states have legally ordered the use of terror to control people's beliefs, without being able to offer any further criticism of this practice; for that, it would need a standard that transcended positive law. According to the natural law conception, the law ought not to be a moral minimum (for that is the empty set of all moral norms), but certainly less than the full demands of morals. Obviously, the plausibility of a natural law theory depends crucially on whether it succeeds in drawing the dividing line between the obligations of individual ethics and those of natural law. Where is this line to be drawn, and why is it precisely a moral obligation to forgo the complete imposition of the morally obligatory by force, even if it were cratically possible to do so? To begin with the second question, the key to the right answer is to be sought in our reflections on intentionalism. Since it is hardly possible to discover another person's convictions or to compel him to have certain convictions, all coercive means have to remain outside the sphere of convictions, although the latter are the primary subject of moral predicates, and although for a state, the way its citizens think cannot be a matter of indifference. The freedom of thought from all legal pressure does not follow solely from the incapacity of the corresponding attempts to exert influence.[14] Even if it were possible to inject a moral idea into another person—by hypnosis, for example—one would destroy what constitutes the presupposition of morality: that the decision to be moral arises from

---

14. For example, Spinoza argues this way in the twentieth chapter of the *Tractatus theologico-politicus*.

the sources of an individual's own personality. Such forced moral ideas would therefore be, in a deeper sense of the word, not moral at all. Much the same goes for actions that can have value only as an expression of a corresponding conviction. Coerced sexual relations are horrifying, and therefore only an absurd matrimonial law can assume that there is a legal obligation to carry out this so-called conjugal duty. For instance, participating in a religious ceremony without the corresponding inner attitude is a sacrilege; a legal system can seek to make such participation a duty only if it is indifferent to religion in the normative sense. Similarly, coerced gratitude has something offensive about it, and it is far better to have to deal with the possibility—which is at least not restricted by criminal law—of the most despicable ingratitude than to be able to rely on coerced gratitude. Indeed, even if all the moral *actions* that are not the expression of a corresponding conviction were legally obligatory, it would be impossible to know, at least about others, and perhaps even about oneself, whether something good was done out of fear of sanctions or out of love for the moral law. However, a stronger morality can evolve only if the individual can be certain that his moral actions spring from his own choice. To that extent, it is the moral itself that demands a distinction between natural law and the moral in the narrower sense (that is, less the natural law norms). But even natural law will never be fully realizable. Thus it has already been hinted that one always has to respect the existing mores, which

always allow only a proprer subset of natural law to be metamorphosed into positive law. However, natural law as a whole at least indicates the direction to be taken by the gradual transformation of positive law, and also, so far as possible, of mores.

7.2.2.1. The Basic Idea, Forms, and Limits of Liberalism

Drawing a precise borderline between moral (in the narrower sense) and natural law norms is very difficult. Among the philosophers of modernity, only two things are not subject to controversy: First, convictions can never be a topic of natural law; indeed, after subtraction of the norms concerning convictions, there must still remain a large complement between the set of moral norms in the broader sense and that of natural law norms, and thus the set of moral norms in the narrower sense must not be empty. Second, on the basis of a universalist ethics it is clear that the principle of equal treatment, at least of all adult citizens, is one of the minimal demands of natural law that are indispensable. An equality in far-ranging basic freedoms, which must include the right to fail morally and to err, is the heart of natural law. This conception of natural law largely corresponds to the substantive ideas of liberal legal philosophy. The latter is compatible with political liberalism, and also with other constitutional positions, for example with one that gives precedence to democracy over the idea of the separation of powers. Indeed, in a certain sense one can consider all legal philosophies based on the contract theory as belonging to the great family of liberal theories, because even Hobbes assumes an equality of all in *the state of nature*, however much he also claims that it is in the interest of all to overcome this equality and freedom by subjecting themselves to the sovereign. Furthermore, Hobbes presupposes that a foundation of law must fall back on the rational self-interest of the atomic individual, and occasionally the essence of liberal legal philosophy is seen in this foundational idea. It is clear, however, that the former substantive conception of natural law and the latter foundational idea do not necessarily go hand in hand. Hegel, for instance, is a liberal in the former but not in the latter sense;[15] Hobbes is a liberal in the latter sense but not in the former so far as constitutional law is concerned.

Although in the following pages a position will be proposed that in some ways recalls those of Aquinas and Hegel, and in any case cannot be seen as a position based on contract theory, it must first be conceded that the foundational idea is certainly attractive—it would be wonderful if intelligent devils, that is, prudent egoists, satisfied the demands of natural law on the basis of rational self-interest alone. (I presuppose here that natural law would not be simply defined in relation to these intelligent devils, in such a way that the sentence becomes analytically true.) Particularly after the terrors of the wars of religion that were based on the mad notion that denominational homogeneity was a necessary condition of living together in a state, the attempt to find the lowest possible common denominator was certainly comprehensible. But on this basis not much can be achieved. For on the foundation of pure selfishness, it cannot be explained, for instance, why a terminally ill and intelligent sadist should not satisfy all his lusts—since he has to die anyway, and one can hardly threaten him with more than death. There would also be no reason why a still healthy but risk-loving warrior should subject himself to a state (not to mention the stupid devils who would not be able to understand Hobbes's arguments).[16] To be sure, if the state already exists, a return to the state of nature is hardly possible, but a justification of the state must seek to show why it is *better* (whatever may be meant thereby, depending on the context of the justification) that states exist, not that at the time there is cratically no alternative to them. A band of devils could not found a state, because they would first wear themselves out with their mutual distrust—which is not necessarily to be deplored. Conversely, it is a pleasure to be able to say that there must obviously have been a sufficiently large number of non-devils, since states in fact exist. States can certainly tolerate a limited number of devils, and the real question is more with what right one can force the latter to limit their devilry to a tolerable extent than with how one can persuade them to obey the norms of natural law voluntarily. Naturally, the rejection of the Satanological conception of the state does not imply that all or even the majority of human beings are angels. James Madison is right: "If men were angels, no government would be necessary,"[17] for then the threat of coercion would be

---

15. As was shown in chap. 1.6.2, Locke occupies a strange position intermediate between Hobbes's foundational approach and Hegel's.

16. Aristotle already observes that people prepared to commit suicide are the most dangerous (*Politics* 1315a24 ff.).

17. Hamilton, Madison, and Jay, *Federalist* 51 (1787 f.; 262).

superfluous. The *conditio humana* lies between the two extremes; and a species that is capable of the most astounding vices and virtues is precisely one that needs politics and is capable of it.[18]

This line of thought is so plausible that the contract theoreticians who wanted to base natural law on rational self-interest soon conceived the fictitious state of nature in which that contract was made in such a way that it had to lead to a result that corresponded as far as possible to their natural law institutions. Thus like Hobbes, Fichte wants to base natural law on a universal, symmetrical selfishness; but unlike Hobbes, he wants to derive from this starting point far-reaching substantive legal principles. Whereas for Hobbes the state has only to free people from fear of a violent death, Fichte demands more from a just state, namely a far-reaching symmetry in the relationships between legal subjects. However, since in certain specific historical situations this kind of symmetricization is not in everyone's interest, being guided by natural law obligations can certainly mean surmounting one's own selfishness. Fichte's natural law must transcend the factual selfishness of the individual, because it respects the selfishness of others; but it is not clear how this transcending can come about with an unequal distribution of power, if selfishness is assumed to be the foundation of natural law, or why this transcendence, if it must take place, is supposed to occur only toward a sphere that is determined by symmetrical selfishness.

This problem is most craftily solved by Rawls, who seeks, through the fiction of a contract in the original position to reduce his idea of natural law to the rational egoism of abstract individuals not yet equipped with concrete preferences. This abstraction from one's own *I* is the moral achievement that someone wanting to be guided by the norms of natural law must fulfill; but instead of expecting it from the individual, the theoretician Rawls fulfills this achievement in his construction and allows his constructs to be guided by their rational self-interest. However, the result of the decision in the original position will depend on how concrete or abstract the constructed individuals are. Beings that are aware of their economic capabilities and are in addition egoists will, depending on the individual case, partly refuse redistributions, and partly demand them; if they are not aware of their economic capacities, their decision will depend on their readiness to take risks. On the other hand, the alternative principle of average utility is the result of a decision in the original position, if one assumes so-called minimal persons, as Rawls has to admit, even if he rejects the principle (1971; 161 ff.). In fact, he takes as his basis persons who are more concrete, but still more abstract than people of flesh and blood, and he does so because he wants to arrive at certain results. The circularity of

---

18. At least, one might flatter well-governed people with Fleece's words: "Your woraciousness, fellow-critters, I don't blame ye so much for; dat is natur, and can't be helped; but to gobern dat wicked nature, dat is de pint. You is sharks, sartin; but if you gobern de shark in you, why den you be angel; for all angel is not'ing more dan de shark well goberned" (Melville [1992], 303 f.).

his procedure is evident.[19] This becomes still clearer when Rawls discusses the principles of justice between generations. It remains a great contribution of his to have formulated this central problem as early as 1971 (128 f., 136 ff., 284 ff.), but Fichte is more consistent when this set of problems does not even come into view on the basis of his contract theory approach—for between temporally separated beings there can be no true contract. For that reason, the talk—arising from the wish to subsume this problem as well under modernity's favorite figure of legitimation—about a generational contract is misleading. The question is precisely whether this figure is sufficient to resolve our problem, and one of Hans Jonas's contributions was to have clearly denied that it is.[20] So far as Rawls is concerned, because he rightly maintains that intergenerational justice is part of justice in the full sense, he assumes first, that the parties to the contract in the original position are representatives of descendants who are at least interested in their descendants, and second, that they could wish that the principles decided upon had been followed by the preceding generations as well. But of course these presuppositions are arbitrary, and the first one alone (which transcends the general egoism originally assumed) is also not strong enough, because it does not lead to justice with regard to the generations following the next one, at least so long as one does not assume that feelings of responsibility for the next generation are transitive.

Once again, Rawls's intuitions concerning justice are not false, but it is not clear what legitimation advantage is gained by a procedure that consists in introducing structural conditions on the basis of which one could, even if one assumes that the contracting parties are selfish, justify those intuitions. This procedure could presumably be followed for most justice-intuitions; if one wanted to have state-sanctioned vegetarianism, one would only have to assume that the persons in the original position believe in interspecies metempsychosis or at least do not exclude its possibility. In short, depending on the construction of the persons in the original position, one can ultimately prove anything one wants. On the other hand, on the basis of his premises, Rawls does not even arrive in a compelling way at religious freedom. Suppose a risk-averse individual who had to reckon only with the possibility of becoming a member of a religion whose god punished eternally in Hell the granting of religious freedom even retroactively with respect to the original position: he would—according to the criteria of Pascal's wager

---

19. Against Rawls's hypothetical contract theory approach, Dworkin rightly observes (1978), 151: "A hypothetical contract is not simply a pale form of an actual contract; it is no contract at all. . . . Your main argument is that your solution is fair and sensible, and the fact that I would have chosen it myself adds nothing of substance to that argument." Dworkin is repeatedly important for my subsequent remarks, because he clings to a strong concept of super-positive rights, even if he erroneously believes he can do without the category of natural law, whose caricature he adopts from its opponents. The concept of natural law set forth in the following also presupposes that there is an argumentative procedure for grasping natural law norms, and is therefore not intuitionist.

20. (1984), 38 ff.

(which is so repulsive because, like Hobbes's philosophy of the state, it argues purely in terms of instrumental rationality)—in that case consider wordly persecution by another religion as the lesser evil; and therefore he would have to approve of a state religion, if there were even the slightest possibility that his later religion would be the state religion.[21] Obviously, one can construct the original position in such a way that this case is impossible,[22] but then the circularity, which can be overlooked only by modernity's senseless wish to reduce natural law to rational selfishness, becomes even clearer.

Unfortunately, I have to admit that in the following I have only inadequate considerations to offer concerning the positive solution of the problem of drawing a dividing line between the obligations of individual ethics and those of natural law—no matter how clear the failure of the contract-theory model. This is unsatisfactory, but it seems to me better than the sharp delimitations that cut out too much—beheading is not always the best way to deal with headaches, even if admittedly it does away with them more effectively than any other.

I will first discuss the proposed solutions that are clear and precise, but also too short-winded. Fichte is the classical German representative of this kind of reduction of natural law, and therefore his theory should be briefly presented here. This is not because of its historical interest—Fichte was the first to have made explicit what was ultimately implicit in the liberal legal philosophy of the seventeenth century, and indeed with a radicality and consistency (proverbial German characteristics) compared with which positions such as Joel Feinberg's seem almost innocuous.[23] For Feinberg attributes rights only to beings having interests, but to all of them, whereas Fichte attributes rights only to beings with self-consciousness. Fichte takes the autonomous *I* as the foundation of natural law and thereby radically limits the state's actions, even if the tasks assumed by his state are relatively numerous compared with those assumed by Humboldt's or Nozick's state. However, in his principles, Fichte is clearer and more philosophically reflective than Humboldt, for instance in his clear statement that the principle of natural law is fundamentally different from that of morals. His main argument for the het-

---

21. It is presupposed that there is only one religion that is so illiberal. (Pascal also has to make an analogous presupposition.)

22. Thus one could point out that this kind of religion is not rational and that persons in the original condition would make only rational assumptions. On the other hand, it can be objected that most religions are not rational and that religious freedom is concerned with the protection of religions, including and especially irrational ones. Furthermore, it can certainly be rational for a person to consider that he himself will someday cease to be rational, and to take steps to prepare for this case.

23. Cf. in particular Feinberg's article "The Rights of Animals and Unborn Generations" (1980; 159–184), in which he considers whether individual animals and plants, species and corporate groups, the deceased, the severely handicapped, fetuses, and future generations can have rights. It is unfortunate that Feinberg does not know Fichte and Hegel; analytical philosophy in general is sometimes in danger of reinventing the wheel. Conversely, my own reflections published in 1989 (from which much of the following was drawn, as well as from the sections on the philosophy of law in my 1987 book on Hegel) were unfortunately not yet informed by writings in English on the philosophy of law.

erogeneity of the two principles is, however, not very convincing; he simply refers to the fact that something that is morally forbidden can be permissible under natural law. This is true, of course, but it is just as compatible with the theory that natural law norms are a proper subset of moral norms, and it still does not prove that the two groups of norms have independent origins. According to Fichte, the (natural) law relationship is a relationship between reasonable beings such "that each is to limit his freedom through the concept of the possibility of the other's freedom, under the condition that the latter likewise limit his freedom through the freedom of the former."[24] From this concept Fichte derives a few important consequences.[25] Since legal duties are strictly mutual, first of all for him, as for German idealism in general, legal relationships can exist only between human beings; even an animal protection act (not to mention more comprehensive demands) would therefore be for him contrary to natural law. Second, legal duties with regard to minors are inconceivable. More consistently than present-day supporters of legalized abortion, Fichte seems to extend temporally the right of parents to kill their children; logically, he should say that it continues until the emergence of self-consciousness, but he thinks that parents themselves have the right to decide when maturity has been achieved.[26] On the basis of Fichte's views there can be a fortiori no norms of intergenerational justice (even if Fichte did not explicitly express himself on this point); for on one hand, those not yet born do not yet have any actual self-consciousness, and on the other, what has posterity done for those living today? On Fichte's principles, things do not look good for the mentally handicapped either, though he does not raise the question. Third, neither can there be any duties toward the dead; succession law therefore cannot be based, according to Fichte, on any rights of the deceased, but only on the interest of those presently alive in increasing the likelihood of their own last wills and testaments being respected, when the time comes, by respecting the wills of the now deceased.[27] Fourth, there can be no legal duties to oneself; one can do with oneself what one will, and with others, everything to which they willingly consent. "Volenti non fit iniuria" is one of the principles of Roman law that Fichte (like Mill) accepts. Note, however, that Fichte does not deny that there are corresponding moral duties; his extremely liberal legal philosophy is not, as it is in Hobbes, accompanied by moral cynicism, but rather by a very rigorous ethics. But for him, the recognition of purely moral duties is a wholly private matter, and the cruelest sado-masochistic relationships by mutual consent, as well as the abuse of one's own children and cruelty toward animals, may not be punished by the state.

---

24. ". . . , dass jedes seine Freiheit durch den Begriff der Möglichkeit der Freiheit des anderen beschränke, unter der Bedingung, dass das erstere die seinige gleichfalls durch die des anderen beschränke" (1971; 3:52). Trans. M. Bauer (2000), 48. Cf. also Kant, *Metaphysik der Sitten, Einleitung in die Rechtslehre* § B (1976 f.; 8:337).

25. (1971), 3:53 ff.

26. Cf. §§ 39–61 (3:353 ff.).

27. 3:259, 367.

Fichte's restriction of the scope of natural law differs from another proposal—with which it is nevertheless compatible—which might be called the "libertarian" solution.[28] Fichte rejects the tempting distinction between natural law and morals in the narrower sense, which claims that the former is concerned, so far as possible, with omissions, the latter also with actions. For Fichte teaches that according to natural law there is a duty to provide assistance in an emergency;[29] and in his later *Rechtslehre* (*Doctrine of Right*), he even argues for the construction of a welfare state. But according to extreme libertarianism, as developed by Humboldt, and, in our own age in a particularly radical form by Nozick, the welfare state is contrary to natural law.[30] According to this position, the morally legitimate minimal state may demand from the individual no further restriction of freedom than is necessary to ensure the other's freedom of action; taxation of the rich in order to support the poor already exceeds these limits. The state may use coercion to prevent killing; it cannot compel one in a specific case to save a drowning person, or to support the starving through taxes. The libertarian conception of natural law does not necessarily deny that moral duties of this kind exist—but it sees them precisely as only moral, not as based on natural law. Nonetheless, the real development toward the welfare state, which had not yet begun in Humboldt's time, caused Nozick's position based on Locke to become a brilliant anachronism, even in the United States, whereas some aspects of Fichte's program were first realized (and fortunately, up to now only in part) in the twentieth century. Yet the real imposition of a certain notion of law is still no argument for its validity, so that Nozick's approach (which he later abandoned) can in no way be considered as having been made obsolete by political developments alone.

7.2.2.2. Natural Law as the Nucleus of Morals

The following discussion follows essentially from the reflections developed in chapters 3 and 5. Natural law can be imposed by coercive means; but coercion is a form of interaction that is far more problematic morally than offering positive sanctions or convincing. It may be used only where not using it would result in a greater evil. That is certainly the case if without the threat of legal coercion another use of coercion would result; legal coercion is thus at least permissible, and even a duty, when it is necessary in order to prevent illegitimate coercion. Coercion is illegitimate when it violates subjec-

---

28. Sometimes—and especially in Germany—the concept of "liberalism" is used in such a way that only positions that largely reject a welfare state fall under it. But according to the definition given above, Rawls's and Fichte's approaches are also liberal theories. In the following pages, the conception in legal philosophy that rejects a right to positive benefits will be termed "libertarian," even if in fact there are left-libertarians who defend the welfare state.

29. (1971), 3:252 f.

30. The fact that Nozick is more "liberal" than Fichte on some points does not mean that he would be more "liberal" on all points; thus he considers rights to freedom from interference for animals (1974; 35 ff.).

tive rights guaranteed by the legal order. Subjective rights do not depend on the grace of others, but must be respected. The awareness of having subjective rights (which was denied many people in pre-universalist legal systems) increases one's own self-respect more than almost anything else: consider the average United States citizen. However, one can personally renounce most subjective rights (for instance, property), and there can often be moral grounds for doing so. Someone who is not prepared to do this is not a moral person; and there are grounds for suspecting that it is mainly insecure people who do not want to give up their rights, because they draw their sense of self-respect from them alone. But the purely selfish exercise of one's own rights, which is morally reprehensible, is permissible under natural law, at least insofar as it is not carried out with the sole purpose of harming another person.[31]

The decisive norm of (objective) natural law states that coercion may be used to protect the (subjective natural law) rights of the persons in whom they are vested. However, since on one hand individual protection is less effective than public protection, and on the other hand mutual fear and mistrust only too easily lead to an erasure of the line between defensive and aggressive behavior, the delegation of this protection to a public authority, if it is reliable, is a moral duty. From this it follows that coercive measures taken by the state to ensure the safety of every individual are permissible and even obligatory. Therein lies the state's first, elementary task. The state must not protect only those who could protect themselves and delegate this task to it; if a contract-theory legitimation of natural law is rejected, coercion may and should also be used to protect the helpless—for instance, children or handicapped people—against force. The claim of basic rights to be protected naturally holds not only with regard to private individuals, but also with regard to the state. Nevertheless, the state may be granted, on the basis of its protective function, rights that rank higher than some rights of private persons, even if no other private person is allowed to violate them.

What rights are there, and how are they to be subdivided? Rights can be classified from *formal* and from *substantive* points of view. So far as the formal classification is concerned, "Jellinek's theory of statuses, . . . despite its numerous obscurities and a few lacunae, remains the most splendid example of analytical theory construction in the realm of basic rights,"[32] and should be taken as a starting point. Thus a distinction must first be drawn between pre-political and political rights, the latter meaning the right to help shape positive law. Furthermore, rights to omissions (rights to freedom from interference) should be distinguished from rights to actions; of particular interest in this respect are rights with regard to the state. Within rights to positive actions on the part of the state— rights to positive benefits in the broader sense—the right to the state's protection of one's own right to freedom from interference by other people should be distinguished from

---

31. Thus many legal systems include a prohibition on the abuse of the law (for example, the prohibition of chicanery in the German Civil Code [*Bürgerliches Gesetzbuch*] § 226).

32. R. Alexy (1985), 243. Alexy's book is itself an important further elaboration of the theory of basic rights.

rights to positive benefits in the narrower sense, that is, from basic social rights; moreover, all basic rights can be protected through rights to organization and procedure.[33]

With regard to the substantive classification, the question arises as to what concrete objects of legal protection are, that is, what may under certain circumstances be defended by the use of force. First of all, the central sphere of the person must be protected. As an organism, the person is for others real in a mortal body that should be protected from all attacks directed against his life or health. But a person would not be a person if he were content with merely preserving his own life; he needs a sphere of action in which he can freely carry out his plans and intentions while maintaining his self-respect. The protection of the individual's freedom of religion and conscience, freedom of speech and action, and freedom of association follows directly from the concept of the person. Duress by imprisonment is a serious violation of rights, and compelling someone to perform acts that, in order to be moral, presuppose love, is a particularly humiliating kind of coercion, whose reprehensibility is increased when the person coerced runs the risk of an unwanted pregnancy. The rights associated with personhood also include protection of a private and intimate sphere into which society must not enter. The inviolability of a person's home and of the secrecy of the mail and telecommunications may be limited only when a serious danger is involved. As an organism, the human person is dependent on food intake, that is, on the incorporation of part of the external world; as a self-determining being it needs a sphere in which it can act on its own responsibility. The protection of property is therefore the second basic state task. However, that does not mean that the state must protect the factually existing property order; unlike factual possession, property presupposes legal recognition, and the latter achieves its highest form only through the state. Whereas as a rule a person's life is an undeniable fact that the state can do nothing but acknowledge, positive law first determines what property is as distinguished from the factual power of disposal. No one can steal his own life, and this fact requires the direct recognition of life as such; on the other hand, this does not mean that what one possesses was gained in a just way. For that reason, there is no pre-state property, but only a pre-state possession. Here we must agree with Hobbes against Locke. However, against Hobbes it must be objected that the state's constitution of a property order is bound to moral principles, including among others the natural law obligation to provide certainty of the law. Thus the state need not retain the factual distribution of possessions (through regulatory law concerning the use of property, it can provide, for instance, validity for restrictions on individual property rights for the benefit of society), but it cannot arbitrarily redistribute property.[34] The right to property means, among other things,

---

33. I largely follow R. Alexy (1985), 395 ff., even if I cannot unreservedly agree with the systematic place he gives to organization and procedure; for these rights include rights to freedom from interference and basic social rights.

34. Cf. Kant's well-considered position in *Metaphysik der Sitten* I §§ 9, 15 (1976 f.; 8:366 f. and 374 ff.). I am citing here the first edition, even though the arrangement of its text obviously deviates from that of Kant's lost manuscript, and transpositions have to be made.

a right to the maintenance of positions guaranteed by positive law, which may not be intruded upon without sufficient justification.[35] Finally, as social beings humans are dependent on the minimum of general recognition that is called "honor" and without which the individual cannot act socially. Coercive measures are also permissible in order to defend it. Insofar as a person's name and image make a significant contribution to his identification, they must also be legally protected.

Respect for the *rights* (and not merely the interests) of others can lead to the restriction of the individual's freedom of action and even freedom of speech—the latter to a lesser extent, since speech is able to injure fewer of the other's basic rights than are actions. Thus one has a right to say stupid things, but the importance of protecting others' self-respect and honor does not allow slander and libel. That means that a few prima facie rights may be sacrificed to higher competing rights of third parties.[36] Thus one can forfeit rights through one's own fault; for example, a criminal condemned to a prison term has lost the freedom of movement. But one's rights can be restricted even without previous guilt of one's own. Consider legal expropriation, for example, in which public interests must far outweigh private interests and compensation must be paid; or restrictions on the freedom of movement of people suffering from an infectious disease. Analogously, a serious endangerment of third parties[37] can justify restrictions of basic rights such as the secrecy of the mails. Naturally, the danger involved must be serious and its probability great, and institutional precautions must be taken to prevent abuse of the restriction of rights, so that it never goes further than is necessary; if these conditions are fulfilled, this restriction can even become a duty, because citizens certainly have a right to be protected from epidemics or from murderous criminal organizations. Not all basic rights are of equal value—it is not permissible to weigh the right to life against any right other than that to life. Interventions in religious freedom should not occur too often, given the importance of even the most irrational religions for the shaping of a morally responsible identity; but they are allowed if the *exercise* of the religion violates more basic rights, for instance in the case of a religiously motivated refusal of the medical treatment necessary for a person's own children, which amounts, as it were, to human sacrifice through omission.[38]

---

35. Cf. R. Alexy (1985), 177 ff.

36. The concept of prima facie rights follows from the fact that there are various legal principles that each appear to support specific rights and that must be weighed against each other. In contradistinction to rules, principles are obligations to optimize that can claim only a prima facie validity. Cf. R. Alexy (1985), 71 ff.

37. It goes without saying that these third parties have to be concrete persons or institutions; the majority has no right to impose its will just because it is its will. Cf. Dworkin (1978), 194 f.

38. On the other hand, German law's prohibition on Jewish and Muslim ritual slaughter was hardly convincing, in view of the pain that may otherwise be inflicted on animals, and not only in terms of natural law, but also on the basis of the order of values in the Basic Law (at least until the change in the Basic Law in 2002, which explicitly mentions animals).

Limitations on freedom of action are often viewed as restrictions of freedom as such, since the latter is understood to include the freedom to do what one wants; but Hegel's paradoxical insight is profound: freedom is first realized in this limitation.[39] Two considerations speak for this view. First, humans are social beings, and for such beings sociality means a fulfillment, not a limitation, of their nature. Second, in its highest form, freedom is an orientation toward the sphere of pure validities, and if this sphere prescribes a limitation on an arbitrariness that is probably determined by its whims, then such a limitation is a manifestation of freedom. The modern, nearly obsessive interest in maximizing the sphere of individuals' arbitrary decisions leads only too easily to disrespect for the rights of the weakest (for instance, those of future generations). In contrast, the moral person gratefully exercises his freedom within the limits set by natural law, and is afraid less of failing to exhaust the permissible area of freedom than of exceeding it. Since he also has pre-social virtues, he finds it easier to restrain himself. Extreme liberalism underestimates the costs of the decision-making process and the relief to be had from restricting the possible options—an unlimited abundance of options can be a torment, because it keeps one from something more important (for instance, choosing among the thousands of new books that flood the market every year can prevent one from reading the few really great books), and because at the same time it overburdens people with responsibility and subjects people to a subtle pressure to adapt to the most various expectations of others. Being able to choose is certainly constitutive for human beings, but the apex of this ability is free restraint of one's own arbitrary freedom.[40]

That according to natural law life, property, and honor are objects of legal protection means, first, that attacks on them may be repelled by means of force. But may the state also force people to make a positive contribution to the preservation of these goods, that is, are there on the level of natural law also *rights to positive benefits* in the narrower sense? The question is not easy to answer. On one hand, we have seen in chapter 3.3.3.3 that within morals there is already a certain asymmetry between action and omission. Killing someone is a more serious crime than letting someone starve to death; and since natural law is a proper subset of moral norms, it is tempting to consider only prohibitions as belonging to natural law. Hegel is one of many thinkers who have represented this position: "The result is that there are only prohibitions in the sphere of right, and the positive form of any command in this sphere is based, in the last resort, if we examine its ultimate content, on prohibition."[41] The second clause acknowledges that there are also legal obligations, such as "you shall honor your contracts"; but since there is no duty to enter into contracts, the obligation in fact means only that the duties assumed must not be violated. In addition, the duty to pay taxes in order to maintain the police force, the courts, the military, etc., results only from the wish, presupposed

---

39. *Rechtsphilosophie* § 29 (1969 ff.; 7:80 f.). See also Locke, *Second Treatise* § 57 (1690; 305 f.).

40. Cf. the excellent essay by G. Dworkin (1982).

41. *Rechtsphilosophie* § 38: "Es gibt daher nur Rechtsverbote, und die positive Form von Rechtsgeboten hat ihrem letzten Inhalte nach das Verbot zugrunde liegen." (1969 ff.; 7:97). Trans. T. M. Knox, 38.

in saying "yes" to the state, to guarantee the enforcement of legal prohibitions. On the other hand, in answering the previously mentioned question, we must take into account not only the difference between action and omission but also the value of the object of legal protection at stake. Since human life is an extraordinarily high good, with which property cannot compare, even extensive taxation is justified in order to help those who lack basic goods; from this follows that there must be restrictions on individual property rights for the benefit of society. To speak of the "freedom" of starving people is merely cynical; surmounting hunger and providing educational opportunities first create freedom and guarantee basic rights.[42] Indeed one cannot maintain that a person who has to steal in order to avoid starving to death, or in order to buy a seriously ill relative the drugs that will save his life, is acting immorally, since he is sacrificing a lower good to a higher one; however, because it is the state's task to avoid anarchy, it must be able to prevent the emergence of such situations through legal redistributions. The richer a society is, the less taxes on luxuries impose restrictions and the more contrary to natural law is state indifference to elementary poverty and hardship. Finally, an increase in state power weakens other institutions that earlier performed tasks of social protection, for which the state now has in fairness to step in. An individual's legal duty to provide concrete assistance when it is necessary and reasonable makes sense; however, since the personal intervention required in such situations represents a greater restriction of freedom than taxation distributed over many individuals, not too much can be regarded as reasonable. A person whose taxes support a just social system ought not to be legally obligated in addition, for instance, to provide further concrete aid to a drunken homeless person whose life is not in danger by taking him to a homeless shelter.

Conservative Christians sometimes oppose the welfare state on the ground that it destroys the culture of individual charitable donations and thereby a subjectively moral structure; and unfortunately it cannot be denied that this is often the case. It is just as undeniable that taking care of family members—for example, a handicapped child—generally differs greatly in intensity from that provided in state facilities. But the contingencies connected with charitable donations and familial love can lead to the grossest injustices—a starving person, however, has a right to receive help even if he does not live near generous people, and the handicapped person has a right to receive care even if he does not have any relatives or if his relatives lack charity. Furthermore, a conscious decision to create or to maintain a welfare state on the part of those who do not profit from it is certainly a moral achievement that does not evaporate by becoming habitual—it is, as it were, the virtue of a community. Conservative Christians who oppose this kind of habitualization would also have to be analogously against a one-time formal self-commitment in marriage, which would have to be renewed every day in order to provide more room for the subjectively moral. Finally, people who do not want to

---

42. This argument was used by P. van Parijs (1995) as the basis for a far-reaching conception of the welfare state.

participate in charitable activities also benefit from them, because more generous people protect social peace—but then it must also be possible to tax the former group.

However, it is true that rights to positive benefits are more difficult for the state to sanction (and usually also to put through politically) than are rights to freedom from interference.[43] As we have said, the protection of rights to freedom from interference also requires a special apparatus;[44] but a welfare state not only must pay the officials entrusted with social tasks, but in addition must deliver the social benefits to the needy. One cannot imagine a realistic situation in which it would be in principle impossible that people inflict no violence on each other, but one can easily imagine a situation in which meeting everyone's basic needs would be impossible, simply because not enough supplies were available. Moreover, it has to be acknowledged that the protection of rights to freedom from interference is more urgent than that of rights to positive benefits in the narrower sense—someone who is reduced to begging may survive thanks to the contributions of a few people, despite the indifference of many others; someone who is pursued by a murderous criminal (not to speak of a murderous state) has it considerably harder. Finally, it should be pointed out that at first glance guaranteeing rights to positive benefits seems to violate equality, since only the wealthier are forced to make certain contributions. Nonetheless, this impression involves a sort of optical illusion, for the violation of legal equality in fact serves to produce a greater factual equality.

Since enforceability—sometimes by means of force—is a necessary part of the concept of a right (which is stronger than the concept of the morally due, not to speak of the merely desirable), it is unfortunate that in recent years all kinds of unbinding declarations of a multitude of rights to positive benefits have been approved. For many developing countries much would already be achieved if classical rights to freedom from interference (by the state, but also by third parties) were truly guaranteed, and the mere declaration that everyone has in addition a right to work is not worth the paper it is written on if it is not simultaneously stated how this right can be institutionally secured; indeed it only endangers the sacredness of the concept of a right, which must be distinguished from mere state goals. It is better to guarantee a few rights than to declare many rights without any consequence. It becomes ridiculous when people talk about rights that cannot in principle be enforced by coercive means. It is certainly desirable that children be loved by their parents, and parents who are not capable of loving their children are usually—if one considers emotions, too, as subjects of moral predicates—morally reprehensible. But it is absurd to talk about children's right to parental love, because someone cannot be forced to love. Few things are sadder than litigations regarding inheritance in which behind the squabbling over some object are hidden the unfulfilled, and now of course unfulfillable, longings for a fairer distribution of parental love, or the legal actions over neighborhood quarrels in which the opposing parties seek

---

43. Rights to positive benefits are mentioned for the first time in the framework of a list of basic rights in the French constitution of 26 June 1793.

44. Cf. F. V. Kratochwil (1989), 170 f.

mutual recognition of their peculiarities of character in the only remaining forum for conflict, given the state monopoly on force—a forum before which they certainly do not belong, because their problem is not justiciable. (Cultures that still have extra-legal mechanisms of conflict resolution, for instance of a religious or even magical nature, are certainly enviable.) It is similarly erroneous to postulate a right to happiness, because it is not even imaginable what things other humans might have to be forced to do in order to make the holder of that right happy.

The concept of a right logically entails a corresponding *legal duty* on the part of others. If someone has a right to life, then no one else may kill him, and everyone must be prevented from doing so—by means of force, if necessary. Thus the corresponding omissions are obligatory for everyone. If the right involved is a right to positive benefits, then there must be someone with a corresponding duty to provide these benefits; under some circumstances, many people would have to be taxed for this purpose, and the state must create a corresponding branch of the administration. Whereas rights to freedom from interference imply a universal operator, an existential operator corresponds to rights to positive benefits. Certainly the number of those who have to contribute to the fulfillment of the corresponding duty may be undetermined (taxpayers, for instance); but there must always be concrete individuals to whose action the holder of the right is entitled. We can grant J. Feinberg[45] that in everyday language rights are sometimes understood as "claims to, . . ." but not necessarily as "claims against . . .": A starving child in Rwanda may have a right to food, without that already determining who should satisfy his hunger. But if we are talking about a right in the natural law sense, then this means that there is a moral duty to construct a political order in which concrete persons—they need not be private individuals, of course, but could also be public officials paid by all—have a legal duty to satisfy this right. Rights would not be rights if they did not entail duties. However, one must distinguish between the (so-called "relative") rights that follow from a concrete legal relationship that binds certain persons together—think of claims for damages—and the absolute rights that are valid for everyone. In the case of the right to life and the right to property (understood as rights to freedom from interference), for instance, it is a matter of absolute rights, for they are to be respected by everyone.

From the correlation of the concepts of rights and duties, it does not logically follow that all holders of rights must necessarily also have duties. Small children and persons who are severely handicapped mentally are possible counter-examples. To be sure, force may also be used on them, if they violate others' rights to freedom from interference, but they have at least no concept of their duty. In particular, however, no specific duties to provide positive benefits correspond to their rights to positive benefits. Yet it must be conceded that an extensive correspondence of those with rights and those with duties is desirable, because it is most likely to lead to the rights being realized. In

---

45. (1980), 130–142.

a world with only a few people capable of working and a large number of handicapped people, for instance, the latter could hardly be fed. But some philosophers of law have wrongly made this desirable correspondence into a logical consequence of the previously mentioned correlation between rights and duties, and thereby obstructed the possibility of conceiving the rights, at least the rights to positive benefits, of the helpless. Similarly, it should be emphasized that the fact that I have a right does not necessarily mean that the duty to respect it concerns others exclusively. The child has a right to go to school, and may not be hindered from doing so by anyone, but he also has a corresponding duty to go to school, because only in that way can he become autonomous. Analogously, one can defend the view that in addition to a right to vote there should also be a corresponding duty to vote, so that democracy might be rooted in society. Feinberg calls such rights "mandatory" (as distinguished from "discretionary rights");[46] they guarantee a narrower freedom of action than do rights in the full sense. But even they are rights, whereas the duties of the other not to hinder my school attendance (and indeed, under certain conditions, even to finance it) do not for him represent *eo ipso* a right.

A direct consequence of the concession of rights to positive benefits in the narrower sense is the rejection of the idea—held by Fichte and Mill, for instance—that according to natural law, everyone can do with himself (or, if he is an adult, allow to be done to him) whatever he wants. It is obvious that already on a moral level suicide—which is not permissible without justifying grounds, which may exist, and which under certain circumstances may even provide the foundation for a right to decide when one will die— is considerably less bad than murder; for even if in both cases a human life is destroyed, in the second case this occurs against the will of another person. Thus someone may sacrifice himself in order to save a work of art that is of special importance to him, but he may not sacrifice anyone else; indeed, in the well-known conflict case, he must save from the burning Prado museum not Velázquez's "Las Meninas," but rather a child. Furthermore, it is clear that natural law must assume, even more than morals, a far-reaching asymmetry between harming (or endangering) oneself and harming or endangering others. For only harm that one voluntarily inflicts on oneself can expand one's own personality, and even if experiments with oneself go far beyond what is morally permissible, for the most part only the person involved can decide how far they are necessary for his development. However, it is a minimal condition of natural law that one must be able to acknowledge its violations intersubjectively. But that does not mean that when this acknowledgment is clearly possible, every individual may do anything with himself—and in particular not when the community has to assume responsibility for the consequences of his inflicting harm on himself or endangering himself. The rejection of paternalism[47] is certainly a position worthy of discussion, but only if one also rejects, as does libertarianism, rights to positive benefits in the narrower sense. If a drug addict has a right to state help, then the state must also have a right to prevent the spread of drug addic-

---

46. (1980), 157 f., 232 ff.
47. See Feinberg's discriminating article (1980; 110–129).

tion. It is obviously unjust to reject, in the name of freedom of action, any use of coercion against those who endanger themselves, while at the same time forcing those who have not put themselves in a situation where they need help to aid those who have done so. Conversely, the assumption of a right to prevent others from harming themselves is far more plausible if it is accompanied by the recognition of a duty to practice solidarity and to help them resolve their difficulties. Moreover, the weak form of paternalism that asserts that everyone can do knowingly whatever he wants with himself, but has to at least inform himself regarding the risks of his self-endangerment, is not very satisfying theoretically. For if a driver who does not put on his seatbelt can be *forced* to watch a film about the grave risks he is running, or just to seek written information regarding them, then we are dealing with a second-level paternalism; on consistent anti-paternalistic bases, nothing more than an offer of such information is justifiable.

But even if self-harm can be a burden on society (especially if one avoids by this means concrete duties such as military service), why should suicide be a problem? Does one not have an unconditional right to commit suicide, even without any justifying ground? It is important to carefully consider the consequences of an affirmative answer to this question. Thus the view that one has an unconditional right to commit suicide, but not to aid and abet it, is awkward, for it is not logical that one should not have the right to help someone exercise his rights, insofar as one does not harm third parties in doing so. The "principle of accessoriness" (*Akzessorietätsprinzip*) in German positive criminal law also holds for natural law. But if one assumes a general right to aid someone to commit suicide (as does German law, for instance),[48] then it is not very plausible to consider killing on request to be fundamentally wrong. Insofar as it is more rational (and it probably is) to wish to put an end to one's own life if one is completely paralyzed than if one can still move about freely, it is absurd that, as in German law, a person who puts a cup of poison to the lips of a paralyzed person who insistently asks him to do so should be punished, while one who only procures poison for a healthy person who is— simply temporarily—weary of living is not punished. Indeed, fundamentally it is also not clear why duels that have not been arranged under coercion should be forbidden, if both of the parties have a right to put their lives at risk. Finally, even a person who uses physical force to prevent someone from attempting to commit suicide would have to be punished because of duress; in German law this is prevented by, among other things, the notorious vagueness of the paragraph on duress. It goes without saying that natural law cannot prescribe the punishment (by death, for example?) of a non-fatal attempt at suicide; but this is still far from proving that one has a right to commit suicide.[49] To be sure, there are many good empirical arguments against strong paternalism,

---

48. According to German law, abetting the mentally ill to commit suicide is punishable; in British law even this is not punishable.

49. Hegel is the most important modern philosopher of law who rejects a right to commit suicide (and indeed entirely independently of the violation of any rights of the nearest relatives). See *Rechtsphilosophie* § 70 (1969 ff.; 7:151).

which can easily lead to an abuse of state power and to the withering away of individual responsibility; here I am concerned only with the fact that it is not refuted by any fundamental argument in legal theory, except by the questionable precedence given to the value of arbitrary freedom over that of human life.

7.3. The System of Natural Law

The fundamental rights possessed by every individual have already been mentioned. However, they have not yet been developed into the concrete order of natural law. This can be structured best in the following way. First, we must discuss the *basic rights* that the individual possesses qua individual, as they are the special subject of a few parts of civil law. Second, from the concept of the law as what can, on moral grounds, be imposed by force, follows the right to defend basic rights against attack, if necessary by means of force; this *right to coerce* is the moral basis of criminal law. However, both basic rights and the right to coerce can be completely realized only within an institution that makes and enforces laws. Third, this fact leads to the *state as the power of the law*, as the institution that springs from the laws' need to be protected, positivizes law, and thereby also organizes itself. At the same time, the state is dependent on other institutions, over which it rises. In chapter 6, we already discussed the most important subsystems of the social; whereas the military subsystem is absorbed by the constitutional state, the *family*, the *economy*, and *religion* must remain independent. But even they need legal regulation. Family law and the law of the society must therefore be dealt with before constitutional law. It may seem surprising that I include the subsystems of economics and religion within the concept of society. Despite the great differences between the two, neither is equipped with the power of coercion—unlike the family, with the parents' right to bring up their children, and unlike the state. If one accepts the principle of the freedom of conscience, religions must compete with each other in the framework of society. On one hand, economics and religion constitute the sphere of difference, in comparison to the natural unity of the family and the unity of the state founded on political will, which alone guarantees the unity of the legal order. On the other hand, at the same time they transcend the reality of the state, which is, not according to its conceptual necessity but in reality, not unique. Economic processes and religions transcend the boundaries of states. From the qualitative difference among the most important social institutions, it follows that in them there are different duties. As a spouse, one has a different responsibility from that which one has as a customer or as a citizen. For this reason the reductionism that conceives the state on the model of a large family or a business enterprise is just as false as the one that subjects the family and economy to the normative principles of constitutional law. To that extent, one can, following Hegel's example, speak of different "spheres of justice." But they are all developments of a *single* universalist idea of justice, even if they have their place in different social subsystems.

7.3.1. Principles of Civil Law: Person, Property, Contract

The basic concepts of civil law are the person, property, and the contract. The *person* is, as it were, the substance of the whole legal system—if there were no holders of rights, the idea of a legal order would be meaningless. *Property*, a concept under which a whole bundle of different rights of disposal is concealed,[50] represents a relationship between subject and object; as we have already said, only this relationship guarantees the person objective reality. Already as an organism, and a fortiori as a thinking being, the human being develops a multitude of needs and plans, in order to satisfy and realize which he must call upon the world around him. The dominion of human beings over lifeless things is unproblematic, insofar as it does not violate the rights of other human beings; on the other hand, with regard to dominion over animals restrictions are appropriate. However, animals themselves cannot hold property, but only possess something, for the category of property presupposes, first, the capacity for long-term planning, for will guided by thought, and, second, usually an ability to recognize the property of others as well. A fortiori, plants and inorganic entities cannot have property, anymore than can nature as a whole, for it has no will. If a nature preserve is closed to economic exploitation by humans, for the most part this happens in the name of third parties, such as future generations; and there must be an individual or collective human will that excludes other human beings who want to appropriate this unexploited nature. For only the will can tame wills. The category of property is just as ultimate as that of the will. Just as property by a thing is excluded by natural law, so is owning a person, that is, slavery. The latter contradicts the symmetry of the legal relationship; rights with regard to a person are always rights to a thing or to certain service from that person. Even one's own body is not one's property in the same way that things are, because it is interwoven with one's own person in an entirely different way than an object. The fascinating thing about property is that it broadens the sphere of the person in unforeseeable ways; on the basis of this institution a person can suffer an injury through an object with which he is not in any way connected physically, and from which he may be far removed.[51] Finally, *contracts* constitute an intersubjective relationship that is nonetheless usually concerned with things. However, the thing may be only a pretext; and even where it is not, the contract constitutes a subject-subject relationship with its own dynamics. Where the intersubjective relationship becomes an end in itself, as in *marriage*, for instance, the nature of the usual contract is transcended; finally, the *state* cannot be conceived on the model of the contract.

---

50. Whether one can speak of "property" only with regard to things or also, for instance, with regard to one's own body or claims is a purely terminological question, as long as a distinction between the individual forms is made.

51. The almost spooky element involved here was very well developed by Kant: *Metaphysik der Sitten* I § 7 (1976 f.; 8:362 ff.).

7.3.1.1. Who Has Rights?

The first and most crucial question of every natural law theory is who has rights. First of all, it is clear that on the basis of a universalist ethics all real persons (in the moral sense) belong to this group, since in everyone something absolute is expressed. Neither race nor sex nor religion can legitimate any kind of inequality in determining basic rights. If there were non-human persons, they would obviously also be legal subjects. Concerning the question at what degree of development someone should count as a legal person, I refer the reader to what was said in chapter 4.4.2. If one abandons the idea of a contract-theory foundation of the doctrine of natural law and recognizes potentiality arguments, there can be hardly any doubt that so-called *potential persons*—that is, *children, fetuses, embryos*—are also legal subjects. Their life as well as their freedom from bodily injury are to be protected; it is not clear why birth or any stage in the development of the fertilized egg should mark a significant turning point in this regard, and the supporters of the view that abortion is legally unobjectionable who, like some pre-universalist cultures, consider even infanticide unproblematic, should be praised at least for their consistency. The fact that today the mother and no longer the father can decide regarding the life of the child does not cancel the injustice. Nonetheless, because of the close connection between mother and unborn child, not only are guilt-mitigating grounds to be taken into account in the case of an abortion, but it may even be that in an early phase of the pregnancy the embryo cannot be protected against the mother's will, and that punitive sanctions are not the most effective means of protecting it; this should be analyzed empirically, but it does not alter the state's fundamental duty to protect the unborn child.

One of the implications of this duty is that the execution of a pregnant woman, no matter how criminal (even if capital punishment were not contrary to natural law anyway) must be impermissible (indeed, it represents a state murder), and that even if the strongest anti-paternalistic option is chosen, a pregnant woman can be forbidden to risk her life. Thus in 1966 the New Jersey Supreme Court forced a pregnant Jehovah's Witness to have a blood transfusion, whereas it left open the question of whether she could have been forced to do so had she not been pregnant.[52] If, like Feinberg, someone attributes only *conditional* or *contingent* rights (such as the ability to inherit in the event of birth) to the unborn child, he cannot agree with these two legal decisions. Feinberg even goes so far as to defend, under certain circumstances, a child's right not to be born, which should under certain conditions be actionable (before the birth, of course, by a representative). To that end, he naturally has to *presuppose* that unborn children have no unconditional rights, with which view the extensive conditional rights he postulates—if to be born,

---

52. Feinberg (1980), 179 f., 212 f. In the case of the Erlangen baby, the decision to continue the brain-dead mother's pregnancy was not unreasonable, if one puts the embryo's right to life above the right of a corpse (or of a still living human body?) not to be instrumentalized. Whether a body should be regarded as a corpse immediately after the occurrence of (total) brain-death, which is not easy to determine, remains an open question here; cf. J. Hoff and J. in der Schmitten (1995).

then to be born under good conditions (however one understands this extremely subjective concept)—do not fit well, even if they do not logically contradict it.[53] In particular, it is not clear why killing the child after birth should not be preferred to allowing it to live as a post facto attempt at redress. Feinberg's argument that if one allows someone to get into a situation in which his rights are violated, one becomes guilty of violating these rights, to which one could have done justice only by preventing the situation from occurring,[54] has a remarkable consequence if it is applied to all legal subjects (which Feinberg would refuse to do): a painless murder would be a lesser violation of rights than merely allowing any other violation to occur. If the argument is applied only to potential entities without rights of their own, it has the consequence that one would have a legal duty to sterilize all human beings if the only alternative were to allow future generations to have the justified feeling that the principles of intergenerational justice had been violated (which will probably be the case). Nevertheless, it must be admitted that at least for the law, an actual person must have greater importance than a potential person—the medical grounds for abortion are therefore a valid justification, and in the case of rapes the question in fact arises to what extent the law can expect a woman who bears not the slightest responsibility for her situation to accept a limitation as extensive as that represented by a pregnancy.[55] (She cannot under any circumstances be expected to bring up the child.) An abortion law allowing abortion up to a certain time after conception violates several natural law principles if at the same time it sets different limits for the permissible abortion of healthy and of handicapped fetuses, for this fundamentally asserts that the life of a handicapped person is less valuable than that of a non-handicapped person. Finally, how social grounds for abortion are to be justified in a welfare state with extensive rights to positive benefits is not easy to understand.

The state's duty to protect can follow only from the individual rights of the potential person, never from the state's demographic ambitions. There can be no legal duty obligating the individual to pass on life, not only because sexual intercourse is one of the things that may not be compelled, but also because raising children costs a great effort, which the law cannot impose on someone who has not assumed responsibility for it through his own action. (On the other hand, it is just to tax more heavily childless individuals whose pensions must later be paid for by the children of others.) But the state has to see to it that persons on this planet can lead their lives with human dignity for the foreseeable future. Intergenerational justice is not only a moral duty in the narrower sense, but also a strict (natural law) legal duty. The state must forbid actions that drastically reduce *future generations'* chances of survival, and it may compel actions that will

---

53. If the unborn child is (as in many legal systems) capable of inheriting in the event it is born, there is an additional motive to abort it; it would therefore be better protected if it did not have conditional rights at all.

54. (1980), 216.

55. We must agree with J. J. Thompson (1974; 14 ff.) that in natural law, abortion in the case of rape has a different structure than in the other cases.

make their survival easier. However, a multitude of difficult questions arises here. Unlike embryos, future generations are not yet present at all; in this case one has to operate with a concept of possibility different from that of the organic. Even if it would be profoundly immoral not to continue the human adventure in the cosmos, since the most valuable finite structure we know would thereby be destroyed, a moral duty would be disregarded by those who so acted, but no subjective rights would be violated, for beings that do not yet exist can hardly have rights. The rights of future generations are, unlike those of embryos, really conditional; but the fulfillment of the condition is first, extremely probable, and second, morally obligatory, so that respect for these conditional rights is a natural law obligation. Here we have the interesting case in which a moral norm in the narrower sense (not to allow humanity to die out by "ebbing away" [*verebben*][56] through a general renunciation of procreation, which would not be directly contrary to natural law) is important for natural law, by way of the additional argument that it is not probable that all human beings act immorally. Even a tiny probability of the existence of coming generations is sufficient, however, to take their conditional rights seriously. In addition to their conditional rights they also have conditional duties, among them the duty to respect the conditional rights of the generations to follow them. The beneficiaries of their conditional duties are not those on whom they impose duties; the usual structure of direct mutuality explodes here and is replaced by a cascade-like structure. Each generation takes from the preceding generation and gives to the following generation.

The precise kind of duties we have to future human beings depends on two factors: their *needs* and their *number*. So far as the first is concerned, any conjecture regarding what future generations would like to have is extremely uncertain. Presumably they will want to live, but even that is not sure; and still less sure is it that they will take pleasure in natural beauty and biodiversity. It is certainly not impossible a priori that human beings might wither away spiritually to the point that they will be completely satisfied with a plastic world in a barren natural world—but what can be excluded a priori is that such a structure of needs would be good. The question is not which needs future human beings *will* have, but which needs they *should* have; and we can thank the problem of future generations for showing us that it is not factual needs that must be the standard of the normative, but rather the normative that must be the guiding star in shaping the future.

So far as the second factor is concerned, it is clear that a finite Earth has room only for a limited number of people.[57] The development of technology and administration has significantly increased the number of people who can be nourished and live together in peace with others; but it cannot be increased as much as one wishes, because, among other reasons, of the environmental damage connected with human technologies. However, even with technology and economic capabilities (which are not the same among

---

56. I borrow this term from K. Akerma's monograph (1995).

57. The settlement of other planets will probably be difficult, but on the basis of this principle it certainly seems desirable. No less fascinating would be an encounter with rational beings with another biological form, which would offer an opportunity for the highest form of overcoming cultural alterity.

all peoples) as given parameters, the number of people whom the Earth can support is not a fixed magnitude; it depends on at least two further parameters: on one hand, people's average level of needs, and on the other, the number of non-human species and organisms that can still exist alongside humans. Even if man has a higher value than other life forms, it can be argued, on the basis of the principle outlined at the end of chapter 3.5.1, that because it realizes a plenitude of differences, a world with fewer people and many species is better than one with more people and only the economically useful animals and plants necessary for survival. It is true that it is not permissible to kill any people or even to let them starve in order to save a species whose individuals are not persons, but it is a reasonable moral demand to limit human population growth for the sake of the survival of other species. In relation to the level of needs, we should recall Parfit's famous "repugnant conclusion" on the basis of classical utilitarianism, which aims at maximizing total utility.[58] Since a philosophy that begins from the concept of subjective rights cannot answer the question how many not yet existing holders of rights there would be in the best case, it seems advisable to resort to utilitarianism to answer this question (no matter how little it might otherwise be able to provide the foundation for a philosophy of law). The answers to this question given by classical utilitarianism and average utility utilitarianism (which are in fact quite different theories in their deep structures)[59] are, interestingly enough, diametrically opposed. According to the latter, the average utility is what counts; and therefore without complex additional assumptions,[60] it must opt for a world with the smallest possible number of people since each of them would then have access to the largest possible number of resources, so long as the population did not fall below the level needed for a complex society with division of labor. According to the criteria of average utility utilitarianism, a world with many people, one group of which had an especially high standard of living, would be worse than a world that consisted exclusively of that privileged group.[61] On the other hand, given two worlds, classical utilitarianism must prefer the one with twice as many people and somewhat more than half the quality of life, since for it what matters is the product of the number of human beings and the quality of life—and with the iteration of the argument one gets to a world with minimal positive quality of life. Parfit is dissatisfied with this conclusion, which goes beyond the most radical Catholic moral teachings regarding demography (therefore he calls it "repugnant"), but he considers it unavoidable. In fact, the conception favored by average utility utilitarianism, which underlies Huxley's

---

58. (1987), 381 ff.

59. Cf. Rawls (1971), 161 ff., esp. 165 f.

60. Of course, how the concept of utility is defined is crucial. I reduce it here to its economic dimension, in order to make the problem emerge as vividly as possible, not because I deny that even an average utility utilitarian could assert that from manifold social interactions a happiness might arise that would compensate for the loss in resources.

61. Despite a slight alteration, P. Singer's suggestion (1976) is also a form of average utility utilitarianism.

Brave New World, is not very attractive, for it is based on purely egoistic premises, and it is hard to deny that a world with many people who consume little has a higher intrinsic value than one with few people who consume a great deal (and who would, moreover, not be happier, nor would any one of them realize more values). However, it is clear that a Darwinian struggle for survival, which could, given human nature, begin with restrictions of a standard of living far above the subsistence level, offends human dignity and must categorically be avoided; therefore it is far better to fall below the questionable threshold value than to risk that struggle. Indeed, in a historical situation with means of mass destruction and an exaggerated level of needs that can nonetheless not be changed in the short term, there is a serious danger that humanity might destroy itself in such a battle or after it vegetate for a very long time at an extremely low level of population; therefore it is legitimate to take steps to stabilize population on the basis of classical utilitarianism as well, for it is not a question of maximizing the sum in a brief historical moment, but rather over the course of the whole of history. I will come back to this point. What matters in the current context is only that ideas of intergenerational justice that assume that the population will be very low in the future must be rejected. It may be that this will happen; but there is little empirical evidence for believing that without a terrible catastrophe it will happen any time soon; in any case, in an ideal world there would be a large number of people, of which each one would put few demands on the Earth.

From the obligation of intergenerational justice follow *conditional rights to freedom from interference and rights to positive benefits for future generations.* Since on grounds that will be discussed later on, nature as a whole cannot simply become private property, but is instead the collective property of the whole succession of generations of rational beings, in a just society only the interest on renewable resources, not the principal, may be used up. That is the meaning of the popular saying, "We have only borrowed the world from our children." Property in nature is in reality only a (heritable) usufruct. An analogous regulation is unthinkable in the case of non-renewable resources, and it would be senseless to claim that they might not be touched out of respect for future generations. For there will always be—let us hope—future generations, so that on that view no one would ever get to enjoy those resources. But then the ground for protecting them would fall away. Instead, taking into account the needs of future generations, it is sensible to raise the price of such resources sharply as they become scarcer, and to invest the profits in research on alternative energy sources or materials. This presupposes a state influence on price formation; more about that later on. Neither may particularly valuable landscapes and works of art be regarded as the private property of an individual or an individual generation. They are part of the common heritage of mankind. In protecting the Egyptian pyramids, for example, not only future generations are respected, but also the ancient Egyptians themselves, whose achievements will also be recognized in the future.

Still more important than protecting scarce resources is stopping the pollution of the environment. In the not too distant future, wasting resources that do not belong to a single generation will presumably be considered, from the point of view of natural law, as theft, and because of its probable consequences, the destabilization of the world climate will be seen, from the same point of view, as a contribution to mass murder, because for this kind of judgment it is not very relevant whether the deaths caused by climatic catastrophes occur now or only in the future. The individual may console himself by reflecting that the deluge will take place after his own death; but since the foundation of natural law is not rational selfishness, this plays no role in the realization that moral law must prevent such things. It is impermissible to discount the future in relation to such negative developments because they will not affect oneself or because one may be careless with regard to one's own future—for other people's future, which there is a moral duty to respect, is also and especially involved. However, it must be admitted that the scenarios of the future are no more than probable, that new and unforeseeable developments are conceivable in the future, and so on.[62] A natural criminal law evaluation of the corresponding behavior must take into account how far the consequences in question could be foreseen. It is obvious that there is a violation of the duty to take care when one could inform himself but did not do so out of laziness; if one expressly avoided information that was offered or even slandered those who made the corresponding knowledge available to the public, the guilt is greater; indeed one is approaching the *dolus eventualis,* if the occurrence of the presumed consequences could have been recognized as probable.

Future generations would already be greatly helped today if their rights to freedom from interference were respected; but they also have certain rights to positive benefits. Of that which can be the private property of a generation, some should be invested, if basic needs are covered, in projects that facilitate life on the planet over the long term. It is also fair that a part of public expenditures be used for long-term investments even if those who are taxed can no longer derive any utility from these investments, and indeed this is all the more so the more they themselves have profited from the investments made by preceding generations. It is true that in this case no express contract is involved; for instance, a child who benefits from the advantages of a good public school system cannot make a good and valid contract in which he commits himself to leave behind him a similar or even a better school system for the generations of his children and grandchildren. But natural law is not to be based on contracts; duties also arise out of the good deeds that one has benefited from—fundamentally, gratitude is even an attempt to win back one's own autonomy by transforming oneself from a donee into a donor. One can best show one's gratitude to earlier generations that are no longer present by continuing their charitable work in the future. Here as well it is not as important—if also not as clear as in the case of future generations (since past generations were real and had real wishes)— to ask for what it was that they wished, as for what it was that they should reasonably have wished. One can also act unjustly intergenerationally by completely sacrificing the legitimate needs of the present generation to the interests of future generations, which

---

62. Therefore Nicholson (1990; 38 ff.) defends taking into account a discount parameter in dealing with the future, which he interprets, however, as a general uncertainty factor.

probably could happen only in a non-democratic state form. This becomes particularly unjust when supposed interests are involved; and the height of injustice is reached when this sort of thing is combined, as for example in the construction of a socialist society, with the greatest environmental destruction in history.[63]

People's rights arise from the fact that the human being as a human being has a certain dignity. Attacks on this *dignity of the species* violate natural law even if they are not directed against a person's individual rights. Thus the reduction of human beings to exclusively animal functions that are explicitly or implicitly extolled, as for instance in brutally violent films or hard-core pornography, is certainly an insult to human dignity, even if those involved have agreed to do so, and even if not a single real person has committed a cruel act in producing it. It is to be supposed that with time, this kind of insult increases the tendency to use force on individuals in real life (someone who has become used to merely virtual child pornography will probably eventually get bored and need pornographic films with enslaved children in order to become sexually excited); however, this kind of proof is, although useful, in no way required in order to grasp the wrongful nature of such behavior. Even a corpse, as a likeness of a human being, participates in human dignity, and one cannot do anything one wants to it without justification. Corpses are not things.

The same goes for *animals and plants*. The strict juridical dichotomy—recently abandoned in German law—of persons and things does not do justice to the intermediate position of the organic, and among the moral principles that underlie dealings with animals, the elementary ones are certainly part of natural law, which cannot be grounded in a contract theory. Thus animals capable of feelings have rights to freedom from interference in the form of cruel types of abuse, and the most highly developed animals probably also have a right not to be killed, even though the violation of these rights under certain conditions can be justified—precisely when this is necessary to save a human life.[64] However, economic advantage alone cannot justify current industrial livestock raising or tormenting animal transport. Higher animals will be granted rights to positive benefits only with regard to their owners, who cannot, for example, abandon them at will; the exploitation of animal labor must be accompanied by special care for them. This duty is the flip side of the human property right, which must also exist with respect to animals if conflicts over them are to be avoided. But this right can be forfeited in case of abuse; to that extent one can rank owning higher animals between owning things and the right to custody of one's own children, for example. On the other hand, species in general have a right to the positive benefit of protection. These rights exist for the sake of animals, and not, for instance, because a neighbor disapproves of cruelty to animals (for if disapproval is unjustified, it does not concern natu-

---

63. I am aware that my remarks are vague. But Rawls also claims that the current state of our knowledge does not permit us to determine with precision a just savings rate (1971; 286).

64. The basic problem of the German Animal Protection Act is the vagueness of the "reasonable grounds" considered sufficient to justify killing.

ral law, and if it is justified, one must give a reason for it), and also not because cruelty to animals promotes cruelty toward humans—this is not proven, and indeed cruelty to animals may even provide an outlet for impulses to be cruel to humans, although the former cannot be justified thereby. Species protection is also based less on the fact that future generations will be interested in biodiversity (partly on scientific and aesthetic grounds, and partly on grounds of a long-term guarantee of the food supply and medical care) than on the fact that they should be interested in it because species realize an intrinsic value.

Juristic persons, that is, certain corporate groups, also have legal capacity. The complicated ontological status of the social was already discussed in chapter 3.4.2.1; within the social phenomena, corporate groups that—unlike a raging mob, for instance— have a clear decision-making structure were discussed in chapter 4.3.2. Insofar as corporate groups are capable of action, there is no reason to deny them legal capacity in civil law—this ultimately follows from the individual's freedom of association. However, a form, that is, particular organs that guarantee the corporate group's responsibility, may be prescribed for them. Even making them subject to criminal law is worth consideration, insofar as the punishment of a juristic person does not result in that of the persons composing it; for there is no collective guilt, and individual guilt must always be proven in each case. Furthermore, since a juristic person has no conscience and therefore is not capable of guilt, there is much to be said for using, in a system like the German one, where punishment presupposes *mens rea,* what in German criminal law are called measures for the prevention of crime and for the reformation of offenders, rather than punishments. These measures can take the form of fines, restrictions on freedom of action on the capital market, or payment for negative advertising—but not of corporal punishment or imprisonment, because a juristic person has no body.

If *communitarianism* rightly points to the great importance of associations for the vitality of a social system, it is still not proceeding in a way that contradicts liberalism, for freedom of association is a liberal basic right. However, one moves beyond liberalism when one emphasizes that there is a moral duty to make use of this right. But this assertion of concrete moral duties that are not sanctioned by coercive means only goes beyond liberal legal philosophy; it does not contradict it. The demand that it be made more difficult to get out of commitments one has made goes still further. Certainly it is to be welcomed when the factual mores evaluate negatively an unjustified withdrawal from commitments, and certainly one can imagine legal forms in which the dissolution of the bond is made difficult from the outset. The most important of these institutions is marriage. But the freedom to enter into contracts would be undermined if withdrawing from an association were fundamentally made extremely difficult. Moreover, it would no longer be necessary for a corporate group to be continually concerned about the loyalty of its members, as every group otherwise is—and that would clearly not be in the interest of those who would like to strengthen the mores of corporate groups. In actuality, it should be emphatically pointed out that the rights of individuals have precedence over those of communities, even if the latter cannot be completely reduced to the former. The individual's partial ontological dependency on the social does not in any way alter his axiological primacy; the individual finds his emancipation only in communities that can be experienced as ends in themselves, but he should decide *voluntarily* to join such a community. Not only do the rights of the individual have an intrinsic value, but the community also benefits when the individual is granted, for instance, the right to make a mistake, because behind supposed errors are often enough hidden truths that can ultimately become the source of a new and more moral community.[65]

Since non-human organisms are no more capable of perceiving their own interests than are future generations, the demand that corporate groups working for environmental protection have the right to institute legal action is only right and proper, and a small contribution to giving them comparable weapons. This kind of right—along with further structures such as a special state organ that acts, as it were, as a guardian of the interests of future generations—transforms the constitutional welfare state into an ecological state,[66] and only an ecological state can claim to correspond to the demands of natural law, because the latter does not recognize solely the rights of the present generation of humans.[67]

---

65. To that extent one can attempt to deny that there is a contradiction between Mill's utilitarianism and *On Liberty*, even if utilitarianism cannot grasp the intrinsic value of individual rights.

66. On this topic, see *Vom Grundgesetz zur deutschen Verfassung* (1991), 41 ff.

67. It will occur to the reader that the ecological state developed here is conceived primarily, though not exclusively, on the basis of the rights of future human generations, for on transcendental grounds the precedence of the life of rational beings over other values is incontestable, even if it is not the only value (cf. G. Scherer [1990], 244). To that extent, I differ considerably from the various physio-centric conceptions, for instance, from Arne Næss's Spinozistic "deep ecology" or K. M. Meyer-Abich's idea (1990) of a natural state grounded holistically in respect for the other beings in the world we share (*Mitwelt*), for the following reasons. First, I don't see how the holistic idea is supposed to ground a normative theory—the whole is given to the same extent in all possible developments of the world, and thus its concept cannot suffice to give preference to one state of the world over another. However, an ethics must at least be able to ground a preference relation. The physiocentrists can only say that the series of values to be recognized in an axiology must be larger than the usual one. This is worth considering in itself, but the inorganic, which unlike the organic has no desired states of its own, must in most cases be axiologically subordinated to the organic. In general, we need a hierarchy of values and, if the ideal approach is to be usable for the philosophy of law, reflections on the distinction between norms in the philosophy of law and moral norms; the works of the holists lack both such a hierarchy and such reflections. (Even Jonas, who has something important to say about the first problem, on the basis of his penetrating insight into the mode of being of the organic, which generalizes Heidegger's analysis of *Dasein*, never attempts to draw a borderline between natural law norms and moral norms in the narrower sense.) A further problem in the holists' approach arises from their normative loading of the concept of nature—as a complement to this, they usually ignore the aspects of nature that are not very pleasant, such as the competitive struggle between organisms. However, for intellectual beings the necessity of law arises from the phenomenon of struggles for power, already familiar from pre-human nature. In general, radical ecological approaches run the risk of underestimating what positive things modernity has achieved in the realms of law and economics, however much they deserve credit for having had a relatively early grasp on the philosophical dimension of the environmental problem. Conversely, it may be the case that the approach represented here is too friendly toward the achievements of modernity.

7.3.1.2. Legitimate Sources of Property

The largest part of civil law has to do with the determination of status. Since it is a truism that humans fight over money more bitterly than over anything else, the determination of the limits of property is one of the most important tasks of positive law. But the relevant natural law principles necessarily remain abstract, since property is one of the externals of human beings. It would be absurd to try to determine a priori the details of the laws of contracts and torts (*Obligationenrecht*); therefore it is no accident that in law schools the philosophy of law is taught by specialists in criminal and constitutional law rather than by specialists in civil law. But not every property order is compatible with natural law. Which principles are to be assumed on the basis of natural law?

It is tempting to posit the principle that in an ideal world one would not need any delimitation of property, since every person would work in accord with his abilities and receive in accord with his needs. Marx dreamed of such an order for the final phase of human history,[68] and it should be acknowledged that it might have seemed that the dynamics of the industrial revolution promised to create the conditions for a society in which the situation of scarcity, which constitutes the subsystem of economics and the necessity of a property order, would disappear. Three factors prevented this hoped-for condition from occurring. First, not only production but also the population increased; second, because of the ecological presuppositions of the economy, the limits to economic growth became apparent; third, the number of needs grew even faster than the possibility of satisfying them. And even without these three circumstances, the dream of a society without defined rights of disposal would not be possible to achieve, because most goods are neither free nor public, but private. Unfortunately, given the structure of human self-consciousness, it is very likely that humans would repeatedly fight over *precisely this* piece of land, even if there were still land of equal value available in the immediate neighborhood; for each individual thing has a quality—no matter how inessential—that distinguishes it from all others. In addition, there are truly unique things, such as important works of art, whose reproduction at will is not possible even in an affluent society. In short, it is impossible to satisfy everyone's needs without limitation; one is far more likely to succeed in making humans happy by teaching them to limit their needs to those that can be satisfied. However, it has to be conceded that a property order is unjust if in it humans are not given access to the means of meeting their basic needs—naturally, only insofar as they can be satisfied. Thus there is a basic need for physical and mental health, but even with a highly developed medical science it is not always possible to satisfy this need. The injustice is particularly great if there is no individual guilt for one's own inability to satisfy basic needs—the unsatisfied hunger of a child is a far greater violation of natural law than the hunger of an adult who is unwilling to work. But even the latter must be helped, after more urgent needs have been met,

---

68. See *Kritik der Gothaer Programm* (1961 ff.; 19:21).

although he should still be encouraged to do the work that can be expected of him.[69] What can be expected depends on the usual mores, insofar as they are not contrary to natural law. In defining poverty we must distinguish between *absolute* and *relative poverty.* Absolute poverty exists when food, clothing, housing, or medical care are not guaranteed; fighting it is a natural law duty, out of which limitations on private property arise. However, fighting absolute poverty is particularly hard if, for example, a drug addiction leads a person to no longer seek the appropriate offices and to spend money given him on drugs that threaten his health. Forms of absolute poverty grounded in such situations cannot be overcome by redistributions alone. On the other hand, relative poverty is defined in relation to the average income of a society—anyone who, for example, has less than half of that average counts as poor. I will come back to this point.

No less erroneous is the conception that there is only a *collective ownership* by humanity of anything that can be property at all. Collectives must be capable of action, and this is the case only if they have an organ capable of making decisions. However, the members of this organ or the majority in this organ would become de facto sole owners of the whole, and such an order would be still more unjust than even the most unequal distribution of property. Certainly forms of collective property are conceivable—one such form will be defended later—but the individual would be deprived of the right of decision were there not also *private property* over which he alone had disposal, for he could then make only a very few decisions for which he would bear sole responsibility. The rule of the majority over the minority, which is inevitable in the public sphere, should not be extended to all spheres of life: It is in the interest of all persons to have an area of action all their own. However, not only does each individual have a *right* to private property, but also the *utility* to society and to the weakest persons in the community of an order that counts strongly on private property should not be underestimated. The delimitation of the areas of action is a necessary (certainly not a sufficient) condition for the possibility of developing a feeling of responsibility for the society in general. Demoralization is a direct result of communist experiments. Only a person who is himself called to account for errors and cannot simply put the responsibility on an amorphous community will learn to treat things respectfully; otherwise, given human nature, getting a free ride is all too great a temptation; prisoners' dilemma situations (for instance, in the form of the tragedy of the commons) are almost inevitably formed, at least in larger and anonymous groups. Privatizing profits and socializing losses is a basic tendency of human nature.

---

69. I assume that what is usually called "the right to work" can reasonably be merely a right to a minimal income usually to be earned through work. Full employment may be a state goal, but not at any price. U. Steinvorth's defense of a strong interpretation of the right to work (1996) seeks to reduce the latter to, among other things, a right to make use of one's own productive abilities, but such a right can also be satisfied through private poietic activities. Work in the economic sense is defined by the satisfaction of others' demand, and this kind of demand can hardly be enforced. To be sure, the recognition of one's own activity by others is central for one's own well-being, and the unemployed person who is fed lacks this kind of recognition. But a recognition that is not sincerely meant is worth very little.

If one accepts the indispensable nature of private property, one could defend the thesis that the greatest possible equality in private property is a requirement of natural law. Nonetheless, it must be granted Rawls that this kind of principle has to be immediately complemented by the difference principle, because no reasonable person would want to cling to equality if even those worst off in the system with inequality were better off than everyone in the state of equality. That in fact West German welfare recipients were in a better position than Soviet workers, quite apart from the inequalities within the Soviet Union, undermined the legitimacy of the latter's economic order. Envy can lead to a few people even accepting disadvantages for themselves if only things are just as bad for others, but envy is not a morally relevant motive to be taken into account in outlining a just property order. However, even with regard to the postulate of equality complemented by the difference principle, doubts remain, if the latter is applied to the property order. On one hand, the idea, still to be discussed, that labor is an important source of legitimate property cannot be dismissed out of hand, and if one recognizes this principle, it is not obvious why the idler and the industrious person should have the same property rights. In objection to this, Rawls argues that according to the difference principle, a legitimate end to redistribution in favor of the idler would occur as soon as the fiscal inflow decreased because the too heavily taxed wealthy people, angered, would also begin to work less; but on the other hand, it can be replied that Rawls leaves unanswered the question of *when* the rich have a moral right to initiate their strategy of refusal. According to Rawls's principles, the earlier the people capable of working threaten to employ this strategy, the more they can justly get out of it for themselves. On one hand, it seems considerably more plausible to argue that the justice of the extent of the redistribution can hardly depend on the organizational and tactical abilities of those from whom something is taken away, and that a role must be played by other arguments, such as the urgency of the needs, the extent of one's blamelessness for one's own need, and the magnitude of the probability that with the help of others one will soon be able to help oneself and others who are in still greater need. These tactical maneuvers become legitimate when, and only when, the redistribution is not guided by these criteria. In fact, history shows that there is no maximum tax rate above which taxation always and everywhere becomes counterproductive—during a just defensive war, taxation can be very high without people's willingness to work being decreased; conversely, a quite low rate can be counterproductive if the taxpayers have the impression that the government is using taxes to construct an inefficient bureaucracy and to take care of its own friends and subordinates. In any case, it must be acknowledged that relative poverty is far from representing a moral problem comparable to that represented by absolute poverty; for if the richer people, and only they, produce more and consume more, then by definition relative poverty increases without anyone necessarily being worse off.[70] One can admit that people can be made insecure as social beings if others

---

70. Cf. Rescher (1972), 92 ff.

consume still more than they did earlier; but the state's reasonable contribution must be directed against the feeling of insecurity rather than against relative poverty. In any case, it is morally unacceptable to do everything to overcome the relative poverty in a wealthy part of the world, and at the same time be indifferent to the greatest absolute poverty elsewhere. This would also hold if it could be proven empirically that the relatively poor person is more unhappy under certain conditions than the absolutely poor person, because the former has more opportunity to think about the fact that he is denied so many of the goods enjoyed by the rich; for only the satisfaction of rational needs, not the production of happiness, can be the task of law.

If one recognizes that unequal achievements justify unequal rights of disposal (among other reasons, because the more industrious people presumably exercise their rights of disposal more reasonably), one can still argue that one must work to give people the same capacity for achievement. One has to agree with that—the demand for equality of opportunity, and in particular for equal opportunities for education, is just and indispensable precisely in a democracy. However, it takes no especially intimate familiarity with human nature to see that even a publicly guaranteed education, that is, extensive equality of opportunity, will lead only to less economic inequality, not to the same results; for the natural differences in talent are too great, whether they are determined genetically or conditioned by upbringing in the family. Genetic engineering to make everyone equal and the abolition of the family would be necessary (but probably not sufficient) to actually achieve an equal capacity for achievement. Three things can be said against doing so. First, such an equality would be purchased at the price of the greatest inequality, because many people would have to be deprived of the possibility of handing on their genes and realizing their values in a family. Second, in order not to make the violation of equality too striking, people would in all probability agree on the golden mediocrity and eliminate all unusual talents. Third, according to the principle at the end of chapter 3.5.1, it is undeniable that plurality and differentiation increase the world's plenitude of values, *if* there is equality in basic rights and in the satisfaction of basic needs.

How precisely is the concrete differentiation of private property to be justified? It is naive to think that the original act of *taking possession* as a real manifestation of a corresponding act of will is the ultimate ground for the legitimation of the distribution of property. Hegel even sees in the act of taking possession by merely marking a thing as one's own a higher form than directly grasping it physically; [71] according to this view, a person who happened to be the first to enter a continent would have been able to take full possession of it, to exclude all other persons from it by means of a simple gesture. To be sure, one can grant Hegel that it is a tautology that a second person cannot take possession of something that is already someone else's property, but it is not a tautology that the first act of taking possession founds ownership.[72] On the other hand, Rousseau's famous statement at the beginning of the second part of the *Discours sur l'origine de l'iné-*

---

71. *Rechtsphilosophie* §§ 54 ff. (1969 ff.; 7:119 ff.). However, see § 51 (7:114 f.).
72. § 50 (1969 ff.; 7:114).

galité surely has a certain justification: "The first man who, having fenced off a piece of land, thought of saying, 'This is *mine*,' and found people silly enough to believe him, was the true founder of civil society."[73] To be taken far more seriously is the view that the shaping of a thing, the *labor* done on it, founds a property right; for on one hand, labor means a subjective sacrifice, which it seems right to compensate, and on the other, it first leads to the existence of products of labor, which would not exist without it.[74] This view was developed with special clarity by Locke, whose theory of property corrects earlier ideas of a divinely founded collective human ownership of the earth.[75] For even if Locke still assumes that God granted humans the Earth as their common property, he thinks that private property rights could be based on individual labor. However, Locke limits the right to ownership of nature, at least initially, in that he maintains that one can appropriate no more than what he is himself in a position to use, and that enough must be left over for others.[76] Furthermore, he recognizes that the value of a product is not completely determined by the labor invested in producing it. Characteristically, he initially limits the exceeding value to a tenth, but then reduces it to a hundredth, and finally to only a thousandth of the total value.[77] This reduction is obviously in Locke's interest, for he wants the broadest possible justification of the order of private property, but it still recognizes that the material of the object in which labor has been invested cannot really become private property, since it is not itself a product of human labor. Only that part of an object that is made by humans can be appropriated at all—not the whole object itself. This insight is still found in Fichte,[78] whereas Hegel explicitly rejects it.[79]

---

73. (1975), 66: "Le premier qui, ayant enclos un terrain, s'avisa de dire: Ceci est à *moi*, et trouva des gens assez simples pour le croire, fut le vrai fondateur de la société civile." The passage goes on: "Que de crimes, de guerres, de meurtres, que de misères et d'horreurs n'eût point épargnés au genre humain celui qui, arrachant les pieux ou comblant le fossé, eût crié à ses semblables: Gardez-vous d'écouter cet imposteur; vous êtes perdus, si vous oubliez que les fruits sont à tous, et que la terre n'est à personne." ("How many crimes, wars, murders, miseries, and horrors the human race would have been spared had someone pulled up the stakes or filled in the ditch, and shouted to his fellows: 'Don't listen to this imposter; you're lost if you forget that the fruits belong to everyone, and the land to no one.'")

74. That does not hold for the discovery of a resource, even if it cannot be denied that its discovery is an achievement that deserves to be honored. The overly subtle notion that independently of human beings there are raw materials but not resources does not alter the fact that without raw materials there can also be no resources, and that the "creator" of resources presupposes the pre-existence of raw materials.

75. On the other hand, the idea of collective ownership is still present in Kant. See *Metaphysik der Sitten* I § 16 (1976 f.; 8:378 f.).

76. *Second Treatise* § 31 (1690; 290).

77. Cf. §§ 40, 43 (1690; 296, 298).

78. (1971), 3:127 ff., 10:546 ff.

79. *Rechtsphilosophie* § 44 (1969 ff.; 7:106). Philosophically interesting is the question already discussed in Roman jurisprudence, whether labor invested in a material that does not belong to oneself founds a right to ownership of it. In the different options of the Proculian and Sabian schools, a role may have been played by the fact that the former followed the Stoics in making matter the crucial

However, Hegel's premises are unacceptable; therefore one must begin from Locke's basic idea, but one should not adopt his metrical determinations, which are not consistent with each other. If the human being can appropriate only what he himself makes, rights to intellectual property are the easiest to ground;[80] the law concerning industrial property and copyrighted materials—patent law, for instance—arises from an implicit contract between the intellectual proprietor and the general population, for which participation in the property produced by him is useful.[81] However, the destruction of natural resources is not allowed human beings insofar as they are not the creators of these resources. The farmer is entitled to the grain that he has sown and grown to maturity, but not to the soil or to the share of the grain that is necessary for the next sowing. Not only is it usually in the farmer's own interest not to deprive himself of the opportunity to continue his activity, but even where this is not his interest, he has a duty—in general—not to do so. (Obviously, there can be situations in which less fertile land can be abandoned, or the number of individuals of a species of animal or plant can be limited, if elsewhere new and more fertile land is opened up or another and more useful species is bred; clearing a forest is permissible when in the long term it increases the number of people that can live on the Earth.) Here we encounter the foundation for the thesis put forward earlier, to the effect that there can be only a collective ownership on the part of the whole series of human generations.[82] For while one can agree with Hegel that things fall under the sovereignty of spirit, and indeed that shaping them ennobles them, in the case of resources the spirit to whom they belong is the spirit of humanity as a whole, not that of the person who happens first to have taken possession of them. This kind of natural law principle in no way implies that there can be no limited private

---

factor in the decision, whereas the latter followed the Peripatetics in making form the crucial factor: cf. M. Kaser (1983), 124. The German Civil Code (BGB) follows, as it were, the Proculians, but only "so far as the value of the labor or the transformation is not considerably less than the value of the material" (§ 950), and recognizes claims for compensation (§ 951).

80. This holds especially for artistic products, and to a lesser extent for scientific knowledge and technical inventions that discover or exploit laws independent of human beings—without Cervantes, *Don Quixote* would not exist, but the process for synthesizing ammonia would exist without F. Haber and C. Bosch; it would simply have been discovered somewhat later.

81. That does not mean that all determinations of the relevant law concerning industrial property and copyrighted materials are reasonable; consider, for example, the long-term favoring of heirs. From the social duty connected with property it follows that regulations should be found that allow the poorest people in the world access to important patented medicines—but these regulations should not be exclusively to the disadvantage of the discoverer; that would be both unjust and counterproductive. Furthermore, it must be admitted that we should find new ways of legally protecting the collective knowledge of archaic cultures, which is frequently exploited by modern business enterprises; because of the greater importance of the community in such cultures, the idea of a tribe's collective ownership in such rights is reasonable.

82. Cf. U. Steinvorth (1993; 14 ff.), who would like to ground only on this idea possible rights to positive benefits.

ownership of land. On the contrary, concrete action to improve a piece of land ought to be rewarded with such a right, and it is naive to assume, for example, that a state proprietor could not also rob future generations of the natural resources to which they are entitled. What is crucial is that the ownership of a forest, for instance, whether as private or public property, involves only the right to do certain things, not the right to do anything one wants with it. Hegel's defense of full property may have been significant in the context of the overcoming of feudal special rights; in a time that has experienced the destructive power of modern capitalism, his concept of property is no longer tenable. The ownership rights of an individual person, and also of a corporate group, to something that ultimately belongs to everyone may not imply an unlimited power of disposal. For example, in general it should be permitted to cut down trees in a forest only if care is taken to replant a like number of trees; fishing, but not overfishing, should be allowed in a body of water. The fruits of the natural capital stock or the share of the non-renewable resources that a given generation may appropriate could and should in fact become for the most part private property—but not the capital stock itself, of which each generation is only the *trustee.* "From the standpoint of a higher socio-economic formation, the private property of particular individuals will appear just as absurd as the property of one man in other men. Even an entire society, a nation, or all simultaneously existing societies taken together, are not the owners of the earth. They are simply its possessors, its beneficiaries, and have to bequeath it in an improved state to succeeding generations, as *boni patres familias.*"[83] The concept of the *environmental space*—used by the Wuppertal Institute[84]—makes sense in this context: the number of fish that may be caught without overfishing must be divided by the number of people that currently exist; each person thus has a corresponding environmental space, which on universalist grounds must be the same for all healthy people, larger for disadvantaged ones. (Each person can, of course, exchange his environmental space for other goods.) Analogously, the same goes for the amount of the emission of a certain pollutant that nature can still cope with— the quotient of this amount divided by the number of people in the world represents the corresponding environmental space.

A limitation of the power of disposal through regulatory laws concerning the use of property must also exist where the property in question has a special importance for the whole of humanity because of the impossibility of reproducing it and because of its intrinsic worth. The owner of great works of art may enjoy them, but he may not destroy them or allow them to be damaged, not even if he is their creator, for talents are not private property. After Kafka's death, Max Brod was right not to respect his will, and he would even have had a right to steal Kafka's manuscripts during the latter's lifetime if this had been the only way to save his work—it being assumed, of course, that

---

83. Marx, *Das Kapital* bk. 3, chap. 46 (1961 ff.; 25:784). Trans. D. Fernbach (1981), 3:911.
84. Cf. BUND/MISEREOR (1996), 26 ff.

he would always have acknowledged Kafka's own intellectual property rights. Were it Augustus's only achievement to have saved the *Aeneid*, one would still have reason to remember him with gratitude.[85]

The goal of property is the *use* to which it may be put, and which sometimes implies using up the object. If over a long period of time no concrete use occurs at all (apart from use for speculative reasons, for instance), the property rights become questionable. The destruction of foodstuffs while other people go hungry is therefore not only deeply immoral, but also contrary to natural law. Use can also consist in renting the object concerned, in which, in return for something, the direct use is passed to another person, whose rights are, of course, limited by those of the owner. That factual possession does not yet imply a full right to a thing (that is, ownership in the sense of civil law) presupposes the human mind's high capacity for abstraction; nonetheless, possession is a presumption of property. Acquisitive prescription is therefore a sensible principle, and indeed not only on the ground of the certainty of the law, but also because ownership that does not at least occasionally make a claim to use is an abstraction.[86] But the argument on the grounds of the certainty of the law is not to be underestimated, especially since in a capitalist society the undoubted certainty of property is a necessary condition for long-term investments, which would be endangered by drawn-out legal battles. (One must therefore question whether the decision that "a specific restitution of property ought to be preferred to compensation" after German reunification was really reasonable.) Particularly dangerous is the refusal of property rights on the basis of acquisitive prescription when this results in conflicts not in court, but on the battlefield—that is, between sovereign states—for in the latter case human lives are being risked for the sake of supposed property rights. Even the constant maintenance of a claim can no longer provide the basis for property rights after the passage of a certain period of time, which might most reasonably coincide with the length of a generation. Setting aside the fact that otherwise the boundaries of quite a few states would be up for grabs, it would not be just to force the children of the occupier of a country to leave their homeland because it was illegally occupied, since they are not in any way to blame.[87] If someone thinks that a piece of land belongs to a state because it was *conquered* (and

---

85. "No es justo ni acertado que se cumpla la voluntad de quien lo que ordena va fuera de todo razonable discurso. Y no le tuviera bueno Augusto César si consintiera que se pusiera en ejecución lo que el divino Mantuano dejó en su testamento mandado," Cervantes has Vivaldo say in *Don Quixote* (1994; 1:188). ("It is neither reasonable nor right to obey the wishes of someone who commands you to do that which goes beyond all reason. Who would have thought it right had Augustus Caesar consented to the divine Virgil's dying wish?" Trans. B. Raffel, 66.)

86. Cf. Kant, *Metaphysik der Sitten* I § 33 (1976 f.; 8:406 ff.); Hegel, *Rechtsphilosophie* § 64 (1969 ff.; 7:138).

87. Analogously, justice does not demand that the descendants of former black slaves in the United States be guaranteed claims for compensation for damages, for they themselves were not enslaved. To be sure, they may be entitled to broad rights to positive benefits in the narrower sense, but that also holds for other less-favored social groups.

later illegally taken away by others) *a few thousand years earlier* by a political structure with which a continuity is *constructed,* he is thinking neither logically nor in a way that serves the cause of peace.

From the determination of the end of property it follows further that it must be possible to acquire what is really at stake, that is, pure use, and that the normal purchase must be reducible to the acquisition of pure use if such a legal regulation facilitates the environmentally acceptable disposal of the object used. For just as the first owner of a forest is not allowed by natural law to plunder it at will—precisely because it cannot belong to him as a whole—so he is not allowed to *throw away* the remains of the things he has used if they can no longer be absorbed into the natural cycle, because he does not have the right to pollute nature. Since in modern industrial production the producer is most likely to know how the material basis of the object used is to be re-incorporated into nature, only the use of the car or television set should be for sale, and there should be a duty to take back the discarded product. Few things better symbolize the extreme individualism of our time than the abundance of non-recyclable packaging whose goal is to delimit the product bought as sharply as possible from others, and few things are a clearer expression of a disrespectful attitude toward being than the production of an enormous number of non-repairable throw-away products. The broadest possible recycling economy is demanded by natural law, because it combines the mind's right to shape things with the maintenance of the possibility of nature being shaped.

7.3.1.3. The Importance and Limits of Contracts

Most property rights are not derived directly from one's own labor—we do not usually make the paper on which we write, and even the paper producer did not himself plant and raise the trees used to make the paper. The *contract* is the most important institution for the transfer of property rights and other rights (in addition to succession law, which can be understood only to a limited extent by reference to the figure of the contract). Its affirmative nature arises on one hand from its voluntary nature, which already characterizes the alienation of property, and on the other hand from the agreement with another party's will. As a rule, the contract is mutual, as, for example, in an exchange or purchase, or renting or lending for a fee. In this case Hegel's definition makes sense: "that each in accordance with the common will of both, ceases to be an owner and yet is and remains one."[88] However, one can also conceive of unilateral (*einseitig*) contracts such as donations, in which only one party performs something, or imperfectly bilateral (*unvollkommen zweiseitig*) contracts such as gratuitous loans.[89] In a contract the property rights of the contracting party are acknowledged, and, basically,

---

88. *Rechtsphilosophie* § 74: ". . . , daß jeder mit seinem und des anderen Willen *aufhört*, Eigentümer zu sein, es *bleibt* und es *wird.*" (1969 ff.; 7:157). Trans. T. M. Knox (1942), 58.

89. [I translate the German terms literally here, although their English equivalents mean something different from the terms used in American contract law. Trans.]

also those of his contractual partner, because the former's property rights depend on the latter's; therefore the contract leads to a general recognition of property rights. Nevertheless, from the point of view of the philosophy of law, it is erroneous to assume that it is the contract that first constitutes property rights. On the contrary, the contract already presupposes the institution of property; therefore it is not possible to found property rights on a general contract, for the latter would imply at least that the contracting parties collectively own what they distribute to each other.

Contracts must be fulfilled. Every commitment one makes, even a one-sided promise, must be taken seriously, but a reciprocal contract is one of the strongest commitments one can imagine. However, the goal of the contract is mutual performance; to that extent my duty to perform exists only so long as the other is willing to perform in turn. Within a state, there is a guarantee for the other's performance of the contract, which is actionable. Where this is not guaranteed, as for instance in international law, breaking a contract (that is, a treaty) is under some circumstances easier to justify, namely if one can determine with a high degree of probability that the other side will break it, and if waiting for its concrete violation by the other side would entail an unreasonable disadvantage. That certainly does not mean that contracts acquire their validity only within a state; on the contrary, the wish to provide their merely normative validity with a greater degree of reality is a reason for establishing a state.

Since one's own commitment must be comprehensible to the other in order to elicit his own commitment, the decisive factor is not the subjective intentions of the person making the commitment, but rather—possible exceptions granted—only the objective meaning of his words, that is, the meaning derived from normal linguistic usage. A radical will theory (*Willenstheorie*) would once again destroy the medium of intersubjectivity that the contract is supposed to constitute; however, the *person making the declaration* must expressly seek to exclude the possibility of plausible misinterpretations on the part of the recipient of the declaration if there is to be an agreement of *wills*. A declaration of one's will can also be made in the form of behavior implying a specific intention, even by keeping silent, if a corresponding action or omission can be interpreted as a declaration of one's will in accord with a specific agreement or the relevant common usage; participation in the social world determines what counts as a declaration of one's will. The principle of *good faith* in the interpretation of contracts demands that the legitimate interests of the parties to the contract be respected, and excludes the exploitation of formal possibilities that the letter of most laws allows, even against their own goals, their spirit. In more complex contracts such as the transfer of real estate, keeping to prescribed forms is sensible, in order to avoid later problems of interpretation that burden the courts, and thus the population as a whole; otherwise the principle of the *autonomy of private individuals* should be defended so long as the contracts do not infringe on the rights of third parties or too greatly violate the substantive justice of contracts. There is not much to be said for following French civil law and Hegel in considering property to be already transferred at the moment of the agreement of wills. In the case of contractually agreed-upon services, the Hegelian conception cannot be maintained in any case; the distinction between the act by which one commits oneself and the disposition (*Verpflichtungsgeschäften* and *Verfügungsgeschäften*) cannot be denied. The law regulates the sphere of external things; physical delivery ought thus to be necessary in order to complete the transfer of property. This criticism does not imply that in a normal sale three contracts (one *Verpflichtungs-geschäft* and two *Verfügungsgeschäfte*) should be involved, as in German law; the principle that the transfer of property presupposes its delivery does not exclude the possibility that, as for instance in the General Prussian Code (*Allgemeines Preußisches Landrecht*), a sale represents a single contract.

Since a contract already presupposes property, conversely the object of a contract cannot be something that the individual has no right to alienate. If one assumes that someone has the right to kill himself, then it is hard to see why he should not also have the right to sell himself—for example, for money that his family members could then inherit—to someone who would kill him and use his organs. We have already seen that the assumption that someone has rights does not imply that only others have a duty to respect these rights; it is certainly sensible to assume that this duty also concerns the person himself. Thus it is directly self-contradictory to sell oneself into slavery, because the proceeds could not become one's own property, since slaves have no property rights. But donating oneself into slavery (even if it is spiritual slavery, as by joining certain sects) can also not be the content of a legally valid contract, because one's own legal capacity is not at one's own disposition. One can hardly have a right to give up what provides rights for oneself in the first place.[90] One's own life and one's own freedom are not commodities. Only limitations of one's own freedom, such as through contracts for services or to produce a result, are permissible, not its complete relinquishment—and even services are not commodities to the same extent as things, because their complete objectivization contradicts the person's dignity. The commitment that takes place in a contract may not undermine freedom, which is the foundation of the contract; to that extent even the legal limitation of supply contracts to a certain period of time is reasonable. The destruction of one's own capacity for economic action also cannot be permissible if other people—whether one's family or the state—have to care for one; in the long run, placing compulsive spendthrifts under the control of a guardian protects their right to property even if it limits their concrete power of disposal. Indeed, one cannot dispose of even one's own body in the same way as one can things; a trade involving important organs of one's own requires very different justifying grounds than does the sale of houses. Moreover, it is not contradictory, as is sometimes claimed, when a person is allowed to donate one of his kidneys to a relative (insofar as the donor was well informed regarding the risks), but not to sell it. One can take certain risks out of love, but comparing these risks with finite things is absurd, because the two are incommensurable. To the extent (and only to the extent) that the factual mores recognize

---

90. Cf. Locke, *Second Treatise* § 23 (1690; 284); Kant (1976 f.; 11:147); Hegel, *Rechtsphilosophie* § 66 (1969 ff.; 7:141 ff.).

objective differences between what is external and can be exchanged for other external things, and what may spring only from inner conviction, inclination, and the like, it is right to deny effectiveness to contracts that are against public policy.[91] But whether such actions are punishable by law is another question.

The recognition of basic rights can generally lead to a limitation of the liberty to contract. However, a concrete weighing is always necessary, since the ability to make contracts at will is also a basic right that should not be restricted without a pressing reason. The state is obligated to protect basic rights in an entirely different way than is the private individual, because the state has a monopoly on legislation; from this duty does not follow a *direct effect of all basic rights on third parties,* which are supposed first of all to protect the individual from the state. Nonetheless, the classical rights to freedom from interference must also be valid with respect to third parties; and even the effect on third parties of a basic right like that of equality becomes more worth considering the greater the dependency on the third party in question (for instance, because of a monopoly position). If the state acts as a private entrepreneur, it should not have a status different from that of other private persons, because otherwise this would only disadvantage it.

The state's restriction of child labor, of working in life-threatening situations, and so on did contradict the liberal ideology of the free contract; but it was reasonable not only because the persons concerned were often not adequately informed of the risks, or could not correctly assess them. Even with sufficient information there is, as already pointed out, no right to run risks with regard to life and limb that are irresponsible because they are in no relationship to the good to be attained. In addition, in commutatively just trade contracts of exchange, something *of equal value* should be exchanged, so that, for instance, usorious contracts are rightly not considered valid in German and Austrian law.[92] But on what is the value of a commodity based? The labor theory of value is obviously absurd, on both the descriptive and the normative levels; and it is deplorable that decades that could have been used for an urgently needed intelligent critique of capitalism were wasted because a large share of the critical intelligence professed this untenable theory. First of all, the labor theory of value cannot explain why scarce but unwrought natural resources should have a high price, which is the only way to motivate people to treat them with care. Second, labor may be an end in itself anthropologically, but certainly not economically—I have a moral claim to the satisfaction of my needs above the subsistence level only if I also take the needs of others seriously, which my labor must therefore serve (which I can do, obviously, only if the price of the product covers my costs). The value of a product or a service cannot be determined by the producer's labor, but must rather be determined by the needs of consumers, whom Marx underestimated

---

91. Unlike common usage, *boni mores* are not determined solely by sociological research. However, the judge needs to be familiar with a good moral theory if his decisions are not to become arbitrary.

92. Cf. German Civil Code (BGB) § 138 II. The Austrian Civil Code § 934 (*Allgemeines Bürgerliches Gesetzbuch*) additionally makes indemnification possible if the diminution (of the value) exceeds half the total value.

along with traders. Here, however, a problem arises that was already mentioned in chapter 5.1.2.2.4.2. It is obviously in the interest of a person who wants to make an exchange to conceal his needs; someone who immediately makes it clear that he absolutely wants to have something will have to pay more for it. For if someone is certain that the other person is dependent on him and he himself knows that the other knows this, without there being a corresponding symmetrical situation, he is in a very favorable position, and it seems odd that the contingency of his superiority in knowledge should justify such advantages. However, the situation improves if the person who wants something can go to another seller, that is, when the two-sided situation of exchange is broadened into a *market* with several sellers and buyers. But this does not mean that the price that is established on the market is by definition just—any more than a law can claim to be just simply because it is valid. In any case, the latter position has a trace of plausibility only when the legislative procedure corresponds to certain formal criteria; analogously, one can concede that the market leads to a fair price structure only when certain structural conditions are met.[93] More about that later.

Just contracts may not be made at the expense of third parties, and since exchange in itself does not prevent passing on internal costs and producing negative externalities, that is another justification for limiting contracts of exchange. For it is clear that every passing on of costs is a violation of the property rights of others; therefore it is illegal and provides a basis for a claim to compensation. In actuality, I am responsible for damages I cause to the person or property of the other, and I have a duty to compensate him so far as possible—so far as possible, because the transformation of the most subjective feelings into claims for cold cash not only has problematic economic consequences, but also ultimately does not do justice to the incommensurability of emotions. It is lunacy when the greatest stroke of good fortune one can have consists in having a misfortune, and a small accident brings in more than the labor of a whole life. That there can be a *liability* (of course also of the state) not only for damages that one causes intentionally or negligently, that is, in the case of a provable violation of the duty to take care, but also for risk or strict liability, is a principle grounded in natural law that is becoming increasingly important in an industrialized world.[94] Someone who has things or animals that are dangerous has the advantage, but he is also responsible for the risk: individual freedom of action and liability are two sides of the same coin. He does not have the right to shift the risk to someone else, even if he has committed no concrete offense—at least so long as it is not the case that his possession of these things or animals is in the general interest. The liability of a person who keeps animals may be different in the case of a cow than in

---

93. The well-known argument that all parties always win in exchanges, and therefore the search for a fair price is pointless (see, for example, J. M. Buchanan and G. Tullock [1965], 250), rightly points to certain differences between a market and state domination. But it is still necessary to ask whether what the parties win is also fairly distributed.

94. On the historical development from fault liability to risk or strict liability, cf. H. Barta (1995), 27 ff. The idea of risk liability is implied in Hegel, *Rechtsphilosophie* § 116 (1969 ff.; 7:216).

the case of a snake.[95] It has to be admitted that in many cases, the extraordinary inter-connection of the modern world makes it difficult to determine the concrete causes; how-ever, with good will, they can be partially tracked down, and the refusal to do so can, when individual autonomy is emphasized at the same time, only lead to distortions that can be worse than the injustices of societies that did not know modern individualism at all. The obligations derived from liability are only one example of the risks one runs in life, and since these risks can endanger an existence to a large degree, it is sensible to *insure* oneself against them—that is, to accept in common a certain but small disadvantage in order to be protected against an unexpected big one. In a society in which rights to positive benefits in the narrower sense exist, the individual has a duty to insure himself against risks that would under certain circumstances cause him to make a claim on the services of others, even if there should be room for individual preferences concerning the specific form of the insurance. But what was said earlier in opposition to communist ideas also holds here. Insurance *can* lead to a decline in the individual's feeling of responsibility, to the so-called moral hazard phenomenon; and its very foundations will be shaken espe-cially if the attitude that one must get at least as much out of it as one has paid in be-comes widespread. This attitude is relatively tempting on the basis of rational egoism, if one no longer understands that the elimination of life-threatening risks is a moral achieve-ment, whoever profits from it; however, a necessary consequence of this tempting atti-tude is a prisoners' dilemma situation that has to lead to a constant rise in the price of in-surance and ultimately to the breakdown of the idea of insurance.

7.3.2. Principles of Criminal Law

From the fact that rights may be defended by coercive power, it immediately fol-lows that in addition to the previously mentioned rights, everyone also has a *right to use coercion to defend them.* To be sure, a society in which even the threat of force would be unnecessary is desirable; but that does not change the fact that the threat, indeed, even the use of force, is permissible, insofar as rights (and only insofar as rights) are threat-ened; given human nature, this possibility has constantly to be reckoned with. The pro-tection of every person against violence must therefore be guaranteed by the threat of force—this also holds for any possible pre-state condition. If Robinson Crusoe is at-tacked by a stranger on his island, he is allowed to defend himself and to use force, even if the stranger could not be considered guilty because he is mentally ill. Not only self-defense, but also the defense of others from immiment attack is moral. Whether the person unjustly attacked is myself or another holder of rights is irrelevant. Speaking strictly morally, I may even accept my own abuse rather than allow that of another per-son, so long as the latter does not expressly approve of the attack. However, the right to

---

95. Cf. German Civil Code (BGB) § 833.

use coercion extends only so far as is necessary for the defense of the legal state. The measures taken must be *required* in order to defend the law; whatever goes beyond this, that is, excessive self-defense, is not permissible. An interesting question is whether the measures taken must also *be proportionate to the violation.* It is obvious that anyone whom one wants to kill may defend himself with all necessary means—even the killing of several rogues is permissible when that is the only way to save one's own life. But does this also hold when it is only a matter of defending property? Fichte said it did; in other words, he defended the claim that it was permissible under natural law to shoot a fleeing thief, if that was the only way to get one's own property back.[96] German criminal law, unlike Italian criminal law, follows Fichte; and it is certainly true that violations of the law must be prevented as much as possible. But it is not permissible to pay any price for this. The thief also has rights; and such a fundamental right as that to life cannot be forfeited by violating another person's property rights, but only by endangering his life. Quite apart from the fact that theft might even be justifiable in terms of natural law in certain political systems that do not recognize rights to positive benefits in the narrower sense, Fichte's notion that the recognition of rights is a mutual affair is first of all one-sided, and second, a thief's violation of my property would then mean only that I was not required to respect his property, not that I was no longer required to respect his right to life. The lawbreaker does not get outlawed. However, there may be situations— for example, before the founding of a state—in which it may be permissible to use means that are not commensurate with the object of legal protection violated in the specific case, but rather are commensurate with all those objects of legal protection whose violation would be a highly probable result of accepting that specific violation of the law, which can be prevented only by the use of disproportionate means. For it cannot be denied that under certain conditions successful crimes set precedents.

However, the individual right to use coercion against lawbreakers is accompanied by special difficulties. Thus a specific right may be violated in the sincere belief that one is acting within the law, for however clear it is that murder or rape is unjust, the concrete interpretation of a contract may be difficult. A violation of the contract by the other side may be accompanied by the sincere intention to respect the law in itself; and this possibility must make one skeptical with regard to the supposed infallibility of one's own good will. This kind of wrong—which essentially corresponds to an offense in *civil law*—is of a fundamentally different kind from that which is directed not against a concrete form of the idea of law, which can be debatable, but rather against the idea of law itself—*a wrong in criminal law.*[97] Offenses in civil law usually occur openly, because

---

96. (1971), 3:250 f., 10:595 ff. The early Fichte even teaches that there is a moral duty to act in this way: 4:307 ff.; cf., however, 10:596.

97. Here we are concerned with the delimitation of the basic character of the two forms of offense in the philosophy of law; in the interpretation of positive law, decisions that could also have been made otherwise are often unavoidable. In addition, sometimes civil law sanctions have a sufficient deterrent effect.

they are committed with a certain good conscience. A sign of this good conscience is the fact that one is prepared to turn to a third person to establish the law at issue. Only a third person who is not himself a party to the dispute can claim to judge objectively; mutual submission to the authority of a judge represents an important step toward avoiding an outbreak of violence that is almost inevitable, given human nature, when someone considers his rights threatened. Since diminishing the use of force is for the most part in one's own interest and is always a moral duty, those who agreed, for the first time in history, to accept the judgment of a third person, no matter what it was, did humanity a great service. Insofar as there are such reliable third persons, and insofar also as the opposite side is also prepared to follow this route, there is a legal duty to do so; and a person who refuses to follow it forfeits his right to use coercion. After the judge's determination of the law, it is permissible to use coercive means for the purpose of restoring the legal state, so far as possible, but only for this purpose. Enforcement of the law by means of force is not yet a punishment.

The problem becomes more difficult when the violation of the law is clear and willed as such by the other side. In this case, it is naive to hope that the two sides will agree to submit to the judgment of an arbitrator; for that reason, with regard to this wrong, individual coercive measures are morally less questionable. However, they are also more difficult—on one hand because the other side will defend itself, and on the other because the problem is not over with the restoration of the legal state. Taking his loot away from the thief is not enough, since the thief—unlike a person who has misinterpreted a contract—has shown that he is fundamentally prepared to break the law. Therefore a more obvious solution is to do something to him that will deprive him of the desire to steal, that is, to punish him. But how, precisely? We have already seen that the lawbreaker does not lose all his rights, and therefore it is entirely possible that the punishment inflicted on him might go beyond what may be justly inflicted on him. In that case, the punishment itself is a violation of the law that must also be punished, whether by himself, or, if he has been killed, by his family members—and so on, under some circumstances *ad infinitum,* as in the terrible cycles of blood revenge in archaic times. Orestes avenged the murder of Agamemnon by killing the latter's adulterous wife, Clytemnestra, who had not forgiven Agamemnon his sacrifice of their daughter Iphigenia. But in the eyes of the Furies, Orestes' matricide also represents a stain, and only the judgment of a rational, not directly involved authority, the Areopagus, can lead Aeschylus's trilogy out of murder and revenge—which cannot always be clearly distinguished—toward a positive ending. Violating the law and defending the law against violation are not so easily kept distinct from one another, also because a right to use coercion against presumptive threats cannot simply be denied. Let us suppose that two strangers, who deeply disliked and felt uncomfortable with each other from the moment they met, and also perceived each other's feelings, are shipwrecked on a desert island with very few resources. It seems likely that each would relatively soon form the suspicion that the other was only waiting for the right moment to eliminate him, and that this suspicion would cause the first one to commit an act of aggression to see it as an act of preventive self-defense. Of course, such an act would be immoral, and certainly each of them would have a duty to avoid any provocation and to take confidence-building measures—for example, by telling the other person something about himself that makes certain basic moral values clear or by creating a situation in which mutual cooperation would be in the interest of both parties. In such a case, for example, even an ascetic ought to encourage the emergence of more complex needs that it would be possible to satisfy only by working together. If the mistrust did not subside, one should pretend to be asleep, for instance, in order to see whether the other would exploit this situation, and before doing so arm oneself secretly against a possible attack. And yet, if one or the other finally struck first in an atmosphere poisoned by mutual suspicion, that act would not be equivalent to the usual murder.

However, everything must be done to prevent situations such as these, which are typical of civil wars. This is done by delegating the right to self-defense to a reliable authority with a monopoly on the use of force. This is as a rule both more efficient and more objective than the individual defending himself. Ultimately, only it can claim to transform subjective revenge into just punishment. Its right to punish violations of the law is derived from the individual right to use coercion, which exists in a subsidiary way where the individual is attacked and state power is not available to provide protection. An individual right to use coercion in such cases does not imply that in a constitutional state every person must have the right to carry arms, as the Second Amendment to the United States Constitution provides. If the risks entailed by the freedom to buy weapons are greater than those entailed by limiting them, then respect for the individual's right to life provides the basis for such a prohibition backed by force. However, one may legitimately ignore such a prohibition if the state is too weak to fulfill its task of protecting, so that only criminals would have an illegal, but de facto free access to weapons; for the right to life implies the right to use coercion in its defense—a right that can be delegated, but never surrendered. A fortiori, no one can expect this kind of delegation if there are serious grounds for assuming that the state not only will not fulfill its task of protecting, but will abuse the monopoly on the use of force entrusted to it for all the more uninhibited violations of the rights of individuals. Only a state with broad guarantees against the horrible abuses of power that are possible within it can expect the right to use coercion to be delegated to it.

An important guarantee is the limitation of its coercive power, which may be used exclusively for the creation and protection of the law. The enforcement ordered by a civil court and a police arrest of a robber are two examples of the justified coercive power of the state. Most decisive for the individual are, however, the measures that are called "punishments." Someone who commits a criminal offense has first of all a duty to provide compensation under civil law, and may derive no advantage from his violation of the law (this is the legal idea that forms the basis of the institution of the forfeiture of the pecuniary benefits gained by committing the crime); second, he will also be subject to punishment. Why should punishment take place? Theories of punishment essentially differ according to whether they justify punishment by reference to the act committed or to future acts that must be prevented; the first kind of theory is called "absolute," the second "relative." The most important modern representatives of an *absolute* theory of punishment are Kant[98] and Hegel;[99] *relative* theories of punishment are found in such varied thinkers as Plato, Hobbes,[100] Fichte, and Mill.[101] Within relative theories of punishment, one can differentiate between theories of *individual* and *general deterrence:* According to the former, the legitimate end of punishment is the prevention of further criminal acts only by the offender; according to the latter, it is the prevention of criminal acts in general. What is difficult about deciding between the two kinds of theories of punishment is that the criticisms each of them makes of the other are more plausible than their own positions. Thus the classical arguments against the theory of general deterrence are absolutely convincing. If the punishment is justified by the utility that consists in deterring others, then obviously the punishment of innocent people (for example, the children of an escaped offender) is also justifiable, if only it serves this end. Indeed, the severity of the punishment must be guided by the urgency of the prevention, that is, by the spread of the corresponding offense; shoplifting would probably have to be more strictly punished than murder, which is comparatively rare. The claim that the utility for others justifies punishing a person presupposes a utilitarian model; however, in chapter 3.2.1 and 3.2.3, we saw that the most elementary principles of justice cannot be founded on such a basis. There may be situations in which the limitation of an individual's rights is justified for the sake of a higher good; taking hostages in a just war might be defensible under certain circumstances, if this forces the other side to exercise restraint and if what is done to the hostages remains within bounds. But these are exceptional situations, for the most part lasting only for short periods, and the reputation of the hostages is not damaged. It would obviously be absurd to interpret punishment in accord with the same model.

At the same time, it is not difficult to make fun of absolute theories of punishment that can hardly avoid capital punishment for murder (and even a cruel execution in the case of a cruel murder). The execution of a murderer does not undo his murder, and why the elimination of another life is supposed to represent something intrinsically valuable is not easy to see. Especially if the offender has in the meantime sincerely repented his act, punishing him as an end in itself hardly seems sensible. There is certainly a human drive toward retribution; it can be explained at least in part by the evolutionary stability of "tit for tat" strategies. But precisely for that reason Scheler's view[102] that this drive is more vital than spiritual in nature is not implausible. The idea of a God who punishes without having any improvement in view has something repel-

---

98. *Metaphysik der Sitten* I § 49E (1976 f.; 8:452 ff.).

99. *Rechtsphilosophie* §§ 90 ff., esp. 99 ff. (1969 ff.; 7:178 ff., esp. 187 ff.). In § 218 (7:371 ff.), however, elements of a relative theory are also recognized.

100. *Leviathan* chap. 28 (1651; 353 ff.).

101. (1972), 47 ff.

102. (1980), 359 ff.

lent about it. However, Scheler says that retribution is in fact a legitimate goal of punishment, not because it is just in itself, but rather because it prevents the emergence in the victim of an aggressivity and ressentiment damaging to society. But if these feelings could also be stopped by punishing the offender's children,[103] would the latter be legitimate? The most plausible argument still seems to be Kant's and especially Hegel's: by committing a crime, the offender has, as it were, set the standard to which he will now be himself subjected; in fact, the murderer who is put on the scaffold can hardly complain. But even if *he* cannot complain, that is far from meaning that others cannot complain about it. Precisely if one does not want to interpret crime as an expression of reason, it remains unclear why it should be reasonable to make a criminal act the standard of a just punishment. Since in addition a complete determination of human actions is at least not to be excluded, the noble person will as a rule feel a certain compassion for even the greatest criminal, if the latter can no longer do any harm to other people. The verses at the beginning of Annette von Droste-Hülshoff's *Judenbuche* (*The Jew's Beech*) are the most perfect expression of the appropriate attitude toward criminals.

Therefore the most satisfactory position is the following. First of all it should be acknowledged that the *ground for punishment* can only be the act committed. This is the greatest guarantee against the abuse of the power to punish, which would be at its most terrible where everyone could be instrumentalized in order to deter others. One's own offense is a necessary condition for punishment, and it sets limits to the severity of the punishment. Furthermore, it should be acknowledged that the idea of retribution can become plausible if it is brought closer to that of the duty to provide compensation in civil law. Someone who causes harm must do what he can to undo it. However, a thief has not only harmed a specific piece of property, he has also manifested a cast of mind that disrespects the law as such. Through his offense, he has himself given an infectious example that it is his legal duty to undo. His atonement consists now partly in having to serve as a deterrent example for others, and partly in having to strengthen others' positive feeling of the power of the law. Thus the basic idea of the theory of deterrence is recognized, but on another argumentative basis than the utilitarian one. At the same time, the absolute theory is also corrected: a criminal offense is a necessary but not a sufficient condition for punishment, since the latter is not an end in itself—it is supposed to have an effect on the criminal and on the society, and the possibility of this effect is what first makes punishment a duty. Thus deterrence is certainly *one* of the *goals of punishment*, if not the only one; but the offender can be used to deter others only because the ground for punishment is to be found in his act.

The general deterrence grounded in a duty to provide compensation is not the only goal of punishment. As much as possible, punishment should lead the offender himself to recognize the law. In the case of the theory of individual deterrence, most of the

---

103. Given the pathological nature of the human thirst for revenge, this certainly cannot be excluded—one has only to read the story in Herodotus, VIII 105.

arguments used against theories of general deterrence fall away. Thus according to the theory of individual deterrence, the guilty person is punished for his own sake, not for that of others, and society certainly has a right to protect itself against further acts on the part of an offender (for instance, a habitual offender) by taking steps against him. So far as the determination of the severity of the penalty goes, it is sensible to allow oneself to be guided by points of view based on individual deterrence. Someone who steals for the third time will rightly be punished considerably more severely than for the first time, when a suspension of sentence on probation could make sense, providing the effect of general deterrence did not evaporate. Points of view based on general deterrence also speak for a statute of limitations on criminal prosecution and especially on the execution of the penalty.[104] In particular, punishment should serve to improve the offender, at least to resocialize him—insofar as this can be attained. However, it must be admitted that this goal of punishment is not easy to achieve. But this objection may speak more against the specific form of a penal system that sometimes first makes offenders into real criminals than against the principle, and moreover it is never permissible to make a final judgment that a person cannot be reformed, no matter how great the temptation to do so may be.[105] However, if the ultimate goal of punishment is the *reintegration* of the offender, then he must have a chance to be rehabilitated—and that means that capital punishment, unlike the killing of an aggressor that saves a life in a specific case, cannot be legal. (Further grounds are that this punishment cannot be undone and that judicial errors can never be excluded with absolute certainty, that access to attorneys of differing quality on the basis of differing financial conditions leads to a particularly unacceptable unequal treatment in the case of capital punishment, and that participating in an execution has a brutalizing effect. Moreover, its deterrent effect is very dubious.)[106]

Life sentences, too, are affected by the first argument (as well as by the further argument that they are of differing lengths for every individual); but society's interest in security, which must have priority over the offender's wishes, justifies them in a few cases. If the offender is inwardly reformed (which cannot always be determined with certainty), then release from the rest of the sentence after serving part of it (parole) is reasonable. But it is a lesser evil that a sexual murderer, for instance, who has really reformed, but about whose reform serious doubts remain, must spend his whole life in prison than that another child be killed. An offender who has committed serious crimes will always have to serve part of his sentence, even if he has fully repented; for this kind of repentance must find its expression in the wish to provide compensation for his

---

104. Normative principles of the law of criminal procedure, and especially the difficulty of attaining clarity regarding acts committed in the distant past, also speak for the first kind of limitation.

105. Think of the capital punishment frequently imposed on such grounds in Plato's *Laws* (e.g., 854c).

106. Solely in wartime and emergency situations could arguments for capital punishment be given that are not out of the question from the start; but the state that forgoes it even in this case is morally superior.

crime, and punishment contributes to that compensation through the general deterrent effect. The most plausible kind of punishment is one that has a concrete relationship to the offense committed, and makes the value of the injured object of legal protection as perceptible as possible—making environmental offenders do environmental community service, prohibiting traffic offenders from driving, and prohibiting physicians who have grossly violated their duty from practicing medicine are such sensible punishments. However, it must be conceded that reasons of practicability on one hand, and the structure of modern subjectivity on the other, impose major restrictions on the concrete forms of punishment. Punishments that violate the offender's human dignity are never acceptable. In a highly mobile society, banishment would hardly be felt as punishment any longer; punishments relating to honor, money, and freedom force themselves on us because of their abstract nature and their quantifiability. On grounds of social justice, fines should be calculated as a number of days' earnings; since the condition of isolation in prison (as in the army) facilitates abuses of power, the prisoner must furthermore have certain opportunities for communication with the outside world, which may, however, be restricted if they are used for criminal purposes. The probability that a criminal act will be discovered and punished has a greater deterrent effect than the severity of the punishment.

Finally, so far as the possibility that we live in a deterministic universe is concerned, it in no way follows from this possibility that punishments should be abolished, and, as in the case of persons not criminally responsible for their actions, that they should be replaced by *measures for the prevention of crime and for the reformation of offenders* (*Maßregeln der Besserung und Sicherung*), the German alternative to punishment, when *mens rea* cannot be assumed. For even if every act, and even every idea, is predetermined, then the normal person is also predetermined to raise himself, even if by detours, to an understanding of the sphere of validities, and in this sense to become free. However, humans can become free only if they are treated by others as having this ability, and therefore nothing is more counterproductive than the transformation of criminal law into psychological analyses and operations.[107] Of course, the criminologist will always find social and psychological causes whose elimination is a prominent task of preventive policies. But one of the most important causes of violations of the law is precisely the undermining of the belief in individual responsibility, and if the program of "prevention instead of repression" ultimately leads to this kind of undermining, then it has become pretty counterproductive. A person who feels compassion for the offender is precisely the one who must not show compassion for him. The victim, on the other hand, should be helped as much as possible by the state.

---

107. Cf. the magnificent observations in Fichte (1971; 10:623 f.), whose theory of punishment markedly differs from the Kantian-Hegelian one, and contains the most substantial philosophical criticism of capital punishment of which I am aware—a criticism that is possible on the basis of neither an absolute nor a general deterrence theory of punishment.

Punishment presupposes, first of all, that all the facts constituting an offense are present. Since punishment represents a particularly massive infringement on the individual's sphere of freedom, the threat of punishment should precede the punishment (even if naturally it cannot ground its legitimacy); furthermore, it should be determined as clearly as possible. In the early twentieth century, the Supreme Court of the Reich (*Reichsgericht*) did not subsume electrical energy under the category of things, and thus refused to allow punishment for the unauthorized tapping of electrical power until a corresponding law was passed. In so doing, it acted, in view of the triviality of the offense, reasonably, and it spurred the legislators to close the loopholes in criminal law. The principle *nulla poena sine lege* (no punishment without a law) cannot, however, mean that serious state crimes must remain unpunished if the power-holders have been careful enough (which they often are not) to create a legal basis for their misdeeds. For criminal law is also based on natural law: injuries to the body, health, freedom, sexual self-determination (for instance, by exploiting dependencies), property, or honor of individuals; cruelty to animals; damaging or endangering the environment, the internal or external security of a just state, its constitutional organs, or the public order (including criminal offenses while in office); and finally, promoting a war of aggression—all these offenses require punishment on natural law grounds. The justice of the punishment proceeds from the conscious violation of the law as such; legal wrongdoing is also a violation of the law, only of natural law. To be sure, it would be absurd to punish members of foreign cultures for violating certain norms to the level of which they have not yet raised themselves.[108] But that does not hold for modern anti-universalism, which should be evaluated morally in an entirely different way than pre-universalist ethics. The Nazis were, of course, well aware that one must not kill innocent people and that the Führer's decrees to do so did not change anything in this regard.[109] It is an insult to justice when petty thieves must go to prison but mass murderers who held state power are not bothered. However, there can be situations in which it is not expedient to prosecute wrongdoing by earlier regimes (for instance, because doing so would increase the risk of a civil war); but prosecuting such crimes is not in itself unjust. Nevertheless, one should overlook them if the legal wrongdoing was not too great, since deviating from the principle that the punishment must be legally determined before the act too easily leads to abuse of power and new wrongdoing.

The illegality of an act does not mean that it must be punished in every case—not, for instance, when punishment would be *counterproductive.* Thus according to the principles developed above there is absolutely no right to injure oneself; but that alone does not mean that the consumption of mild drugs should be prohibited. For that kind of prohibition creates a black market in which the drugs are sold at much higher prices than if they were sold legally, and this promotes crimes whose goal is to acquire drugs.

---

108. Cf. Montesquieu, *Esprit des lois* 26.22 (1748; 2:199 f.).

109. This is also recognized in positive law; cf. the provision in the European Convention for the Protection of Human Rights and Fundamental Freedoms, Art. 7 II.

Americans are rightly prouder of few things than the stability of their constitution, which has been amended only a few times in over two hundred years; but it is a point in their favor that they had the courage to repeal an amendment to the constitution (the only time in their history that they have done so) when it turned out that the consequences of Prohibition were disastrous.[110] In such cases, the means provided by civil law are far more efficient than those provided by criminal law. In any case, in making a decision regarding criminal law policy it is an elementary prudential obligation to take into account empirical criminological knowledge, and not only knowledge of dogmatic criminal law and philosophy of law. However, it should not be forgotten that the threat of punishment, which must be rooted in the mores in order to be effective, can itself have a strengthening effect on mores, and that in a time of destructive morality criminal law often maintains the last kernel of mores.

When a criminal law is passed, then it follows from the postulate of universalizability that all acts meeting the statutory definition of the same offense must be punished in the same way. Therefore *pardons* of individuals, unlike general amnesties, are not compatible with this principle. Since a criminal offense represents a violation of the law as such, its prosecution may not be based on the individual: the principle of public prosecution of offenses is entailed by natural law. The public prosecutor must act on the basis of the law alone. Only in exceptional cases can discretion be allowed to deviate from the principle of mandatory prosecution. Something that represents a violation of the law only if it is subjectively perceived as such (libel, for instance), or something that occurs in a private sphere in which an individual pardon would be the best way to eliminate the wrong and bring the offender back to reason, can be regarded as an offense prosecutable only if the victim files a request for it. Someone who steals in a public place endangers public security partly through the example he sets, and partly because his victim could have been anyone; on the other hand, someone who steals from his parents in their house does not fulfill these two conditions, and therefore whether a prosecution is instituted may depend on whether the parents file a request for prosecution. If the person concerned demands a prosecution, the public prosecutor should have to act; the archaic legal form of the private prosecution is unjust, because it favors people who are more versed in the law.

The fact that an act corresponds to the statutory definition of a crime does not yet lead to punishment. For criminal laws correspond (even if they are directed only indirectly to the offender) to prima facie prohibitions, and we have already seen that there can be exceptions to these prohibitions. A killing may be in self-defense, and then it is legal, because it is based on the right to use coercion. Obviously, a penal code should itself mention the valid *grounds of justification;* and it will make use of a general formula according to which, for instance, violation of an inferior object of legal protection is permissible, so far as it is an appropriate means of preserving a significantly higher object

---

110. Cf. the Eighteenth and Twenty-first Amendments.

of legal protection from a direct danger that cannot be otherwise averted. However, the question arises what higher objects of legal protection are. The priority of human life is incontestable. In order to save a human life, violations of property must be allowed; indeed, it is to be demanded that the claims for damages resulting therefrom should be paid by the state, since someone who saves a human life should not even have to pay for his act according to civil law.

But should the killing of a human being also be allowed if it is necessary to save several other people? Most systems of criminal law hold that it is not, but nevertheless find themselves forced to judge against this principle in certain cases—which is, to say the least, not satisfactory from the point of view of the theory of criminal law. Just as in a state there should be no area outside the law, so no case should escape the conceptual scope of the law: exemption theories are a capitulation of reason. The railroad switchman example is well known: A train threatens to run into a station platform with a hundred people on it; the switchman diverts it onto another track where a vagrant is illegally sitting; the train kills him, and the switchman cannot justify his act because human lives cannot be weighed against each other; there are also no grounds for excuse, so long as a close relative is not among those threatened. The case is made up, but theoretically analogous cases are not rare in the history of unjust states. For example, the physicians who during the Third Reich occasionally killed a handicapped child because if they refused they would have been dismissed (not executed), and their position would have been filled by a Nazi who would have murdered virtually all the children in the institution, were not punished after the war, even if this extra-statutory state of emergency (*übergesetzlicher Notstand*) has, as its name suggests, no real basis in the German penal code. If one does not abandon the principle that humans cannot be weighed against each other, there can be no question of a justifying state of emergency (*rechtfertigender Notstand*, which according to German law would entail that the act committed in such a situation is not wrongful), or of an excusing state of emergency (*entschuldigender Notstand*, which according to German law means only that there is no culpability, given extenuating circumstances, even if the act itself is wrongful), since the physicians themselves were not directly threatened (for which reason it is objectively wrong to subsume the extra-statutory state of emergency under the category of mitigating circumstances, as German teachers of criminal law do, in order to preserve the appearance of legality). Fundamentally, I see only two conceivable possibilities: either letting these physicians get off scot-free is contrary to natural law, or the principle that human lives cannot be weighed against each other is not always valid, and we are confronted with a case of a justifying state of emergency. To be sure, there is a duty to do everything one can to prevent the occurrence of such situations, and every decent person will hope to be spared such a test; but that is no solution to the problem that arises if one finds oneself in such a situation through no fault of one's own.

Certainly, there are some cases in which most people are willing to give up that principle: in an assassination attempt on a murderous tyrant, innocent people may also be killed whose death is accepted; bombing a militarily important industrial plant inside a city in a just war will also cause, with a degree of probability approaching certainty, the loss of civilian lives. It is true that the latter case differs from the one described earlier in that as a rule, a just war represents an international situation of self-defense, or one in which other states are defended from attack (and we have already seen that this principle is not valid in cases of self-defense), whereas those poisoned children in Nazi Germany were guilty of no violation of the law. But what offense had been committed by the children killed in the bombing (whose death was not intended, but still voluntarily accepted, so that a *dolus eventualis* is involved), even if their parents might be reproached for not having prevented the rise of this tyrant? It is clear that from the point of view of the theory of criminal law, killings in war are subject to different principles, but from the point of view of natural law, these cases are not so different that doubts concerning this principle might not spread.[111] However, there are enough cases in which one feels an intuitive repugnance at the thought of deviating from that principle—think of killing an innocent person in order to use his organs to save the lives of several seriously ill people. Certainly essential differences between the two cases are obvious, especially because in the latter example there is the possibility that one of the seriously ill people who would otherwise soon have to die might sacrifice himself in order to donate to others his healthy organs, or that they might all voluntarily agree to draw lots; in addition, the two examples mentioned above have in common that the victims associated with the assassination or the bombing are, on the one hand, not expressly warned beforehand, which avoids situations of fear and resistance, and, on the other, have to expect a dangerous exceptional situation in any case, whereas the innocent person to be killed would have to be selected in peacetime, in accord with a certain procedure, his health would have to be checked, and so on. But enough concern remains. A conception that starts out from individual rights will justify killings in self-defense, but not the killing of innocent people, for in killing an aggressor it is, as it were, only his own right, the principle that he has recognized, that strikes back at him—he can, in a certain sense of the word, feel that he is taken seriously. On the other hand, the innocent person killed is not respected as an end in himself, but rather instrumentalized. Even if this occurs, as in the supposed case, for the sake of a higher end, his autonomy will still be sacrificed to the latter. The situation is different if one considers life to be a higher value than autonomy (and in any case, in the framework of a utilitarian approach, whose absurd favoring of factual preferences is, however, not at all necessary in order to have doubts about the principle that human lives cannot be weighed against each other).

---

111. Here I am concerned only with the principle that human lives cannot be weighed against each other with regard to quantity; if quality is taken into account, it is still more difficult to defend the idea that lives may be weighed against each other. All the same, one could understand someone who, having lifted a person into a lifeboat that has room left for only one person, realizes that he has taken a mass murderer on board and that out there is a noble person swimming without any hope of survival, and then throws the murderer back in the water in order to take in the other person. Furthermore, in allocating scarce medical goods (e.g., organs) it is reasonable to consider the life expectancy of the persons waiting for them, which may correlate with age.

An interesting case intermediary between a self-defense situation and the killing of innocent people in order to rescue other innocent people is represented by General W. Jaruzelski's declaration of martial law in Poland in 1981 (which cost a few people their lives), insofar as one assumes that in all probability this was the most effective way of preventing a Soviet invasion, which would have greatly endangered not only Poland but the whole world political situation, and insofar as Jaruzelski's motive was in fact to prevent the invasion. (Whether these two conditions were met cannot be determined by a philosopher, but at best by a historian.) Certainly the declaration of martial law did not have to lead to deaths, and certainly the victims broke positive laws. For that reason their killing is not equivalent to killing innocent children, and to that extent the differences with the case of the physicians mentioned are obvious. But probably it was likely that these deaths would occur, and a deeper right was on the side of the victims, so that, on the basis of both the principle that human lives cannot be weighed against each other and a strict distinction between action and omission, pursuing a policy that would presumably have led to the Soviets marching into the country would have been morally compulsory. But that is counterintuitive, for Jaruzelski's behavior seems morally at least worthy of discussion.

An act can be contrary to the law; on the basis of an intentionalist ethics, in order to be punished, *mens rea,* individual *culpability* (the lack of which also limits the individual right to self-defense) is also required. Thus in a just legal order a debtor may not be put in prison, because his debts as such do not yet constitute culpability. For culpability to be present, the actor must be able to know (not necessarily know in fact) that his action is contrary to the law; an unavoidable error as to the prohibited nature of his act excludes culpability. Even an error regarding the circumstances of the act—for example, in the case of putative self-defense—excludes wrongful intent. The actor must have had alternatives and to that extent have been free. Certain mental illnesses exclude culpability; in a system like the German one, they lead only to measures for the prevention of crime and for the reformation of offenders, but not to punishment. In the case of acts committed in the heat of passion, there is no exclusion from culpability, but a diminution of culpability to differing degrees is plausible. Intoxication also constitutes a factor diminishing culpability; but one is responsible for having intoxicated oneself, and if one has even done so in order to commit a criminal offense, then because of this *actio libera in causa* one can rightly be punished as if one had purposefully and knowingly committed the offense. A threat to one's own life or to that of a family member certainly diminishes culpability: a soldier who shoots innocent people in an unjust war when he is commanded to do so, because he would otherwise be himself shot, is acting in a way that is contrary to law and morally not respectable; but it is clear that he cannot be punished like an ordinary murderer. In German law, pushing someone off Carneades' famous plank, which can carry only one shipwrecked person, in order to save one's own life, would be a case in which the excusing state of emergency excluded any punishment.[112] As a rule, this

---

112. Cf. Kant, *Metaphysik der Sitten,* Appendix to the Introduction to the Doctrine of Right II (1976 f.; 8:343 f.); Fichte (1971), 3:252 ff., 10:598 f.

kind of behavior cannot be *justified* even if one abandons the principle that human lives cannot be weighed against each other; but fear for one's own life often counts as a ground for *excluding culpability.* In actuality, it must be granted Kant that in such a case punishment has no great practical meaning, for no threat of subsequent punishment can compete with a direct threat to one's life. However, if one does not see the purpose of punishment as being primarily deterrence, but rather the strengthening of a positive image of what constitutes moral duty, then punishment, even if only symbolic, is justified, for the feeling of shame could lead a larger number of people to refuse orders in the case of an unjust war, and the greater the number of those who might be prepared to do so, the more difficult the abuse of power becomes. In fact, according to German law not everyone enjoys the privilege of the excusing state of emergency; someone who is committed to a particularly dangerous profession or has himself caused the danger cannot appeal to it, although the Kantian argument would also apply to this case. The use of the threat of punishment to maintain a norm's claim to validity can also be sensible, even if, given human nature, it is not to be assumed that it will lead to many people observing it, if only it leads to more people observing it than would be the case without that threat.

If someone causes a person's death, he can be punished only if he has done so deliberately or has at least accepted it, that is, if it involves a specific or general *intent,* or if he has violated a duty to take care, that is, acted *recklessly* or *negligently.* If a child runs into the car of someone who is driving carefully, the latter can be liable in civil law, but he cannot be punished. However, it is not easy to explain why a person who is driving inattentively, but is lucky enough not to hit a child, can be punished only for endangering traffic, while someone who is just as inattentive, or even less inattentive, and is unfortunate enough to have an accident, is subject to a significantly more severe punishment. (Usually, but not always—as in Germany in the case just mentioned—offenses consisting only in the endangerment of others, or oneself, are considered only infringements of police and administrative regulations, which are threatened by milder sanctions.) "Moral luck" is not an acceptable category in moral philosophy—so why should it be acceptable in criminal law? A possible reason is that a person who causes an accident *proves* that he was not sufficiently attentive, whereas a person who is not guilty of any concrete property damage or bodily injury might perhaps have really avoided an accident had he been in an analogous situation, because he would have recovered his attentiveness much more quickly than the other person. In fact, there is a consciousness of one's capacities concerning which only the individual can decide *ante factum.* However, it is clear that negligent acts must be more leniently punished than intentional acts, even if repeating the same negligent act several times almost amounts to *dolus eventualis,* that is, to acting knowingly. Someone who has caused several automobile accidents should give up driving. Furthermore, it is obvious that in a technological world the number of offenses consisting only in the endangerment of other people (or oneself) and the severity of their punishment must increase.

To some degree, turning this problem around raises the question as to why the *attempt* at a criminal act is not always punished just as severely as the consummated act.

Sometimes it is not punished at all, and even if it is, the punishment is usually milder than for the consummated act. It is evident that a malicious intention as such does not fall within the purview of the law; the act, not the actor, is the subject of criminal law, even if the judge, when the act has been committed, cannot forgo an evaluation of the actor's motives, or even if, particularly according to the conception of punishment as individual deterrence, an outline of the actor's character must be drawn up. But the mere preparation of an act can hardly be punishable, except perhaps in the case of the most serious crimes, if only because the actor could always break it off. But if a criminal act is attempted (which is not easy to distinguish from preparing it), why should it be counted to the offender's credit that he was not successful? Here as well one can only argue that the successful conclusion of the act usually reveals a greater criminal energy, whereas a failure *may* indicate inconclusiveness. The lesser necessity of general deterrent measures in the case of unsuccessful crimes (especially in the case of attempts with completely inadequate means), as well as the wish to relieve the courts of a burden, may justify not punishing a mere attempt at a minor offense; the state's right to punish still exists. Normatively, it is hardly relevant that the need for revenge is usually less in the case of unsuccessful attempts. From the fact that natural law is a proper subset of morals, it follows that only a few true omissions can be punishable. Things are different with respect to so-called specious crimes by omission, which were discussed in chapter 3.3.3.3. It is a point in favor of criminal law that some of the categories it has elaborated prove useful for general ethics.

7.3.3. The Law of the Most Important Social Institutions

In the preceding text the state has already been discussed at length. Guaranteeing rights to positive benefits in the narrower sense asks too much of the individual and is possible only if there is a central redistribution authority; one can count on contracts being adhered to only if breaking a contract is threatened by an almost infallibly imposed sanction; passing costs on to future generations, that is, producing negative externalities for them, is an obvious temptation, if their rights are not publicly protected; the difficulty of an objective interpretation of contracts makes impartial judges necessary; mutual distrust can result, through a preventive use of the right to use coercion, in unpredictable violence. For all these reasons, the establishment of an authority with a wideranging monopoly on legislation and a complete monopoly on the use of force, which alone can lead out of prisoners' dilemma situations, is morally obligatory. But that is easier said than done. For the establishment of such an authority is exceptionally risky, and it is not obvious why one should trade a bird in the hand for two in the bush, especially since the latter could turn out to be predatory. *Quis custodiet custodes*, who guards the guardians? The greatest expense of acumen in designing mechanisms of the separation of powers cannot change the fact that constitutional law cannot be protected in the same way as civil law, because it is a system that must support itself. But why I can trust my fellow man more when he has become a state official and I am defenseless before him than when we encounter each other in an equally weak condition in the state of nature is the insoluble problem for all descriptive and normative contract theories; and it is characteristic that at this stage of his argument, Fichte makes a *salto mortale* from an atomistic to an organicist model (3:202 ff.). Not only must I myself recognize moral principles in order to come to a Pareto-optimal result in a prisoners' dilemma situation, but I must also be able to reasonably believe that the other person also recognizes these principles and himself trusts that I am also moral. The phenomena of decay in late-modern societies have much to do with the fact that this trust is dissolving; and in fact it is one of the greatest problems of modern philosophy of law (with the exception of Hegel), that it does not reflect on how one can institutionally construct or at least maintain this trust. If the importance of *socialist* movements in comparison with *liberalism* lay in the fact that they rightly refused to resign themselves to the factually existing inequalities, then the truth of *conservatism* lay in the acknowledgment that pure liberalism cannot support itself, for the latter lives off institutions that grasp human beings in a deeper way than the mere idea of individual rights can. Certainly conservatism often idealized these institutions, especially marriage, family, and church, in a way that had little to do with reality, and therefore understandably provoked a liberal protest.

A philosophy of law can be complete only if it also discusses the institutions that support trust. However, that does not mean that the basic ideas of modern liberalism should be abandoned; there is no going back on the idea of individual basic rights, which was alien to the ancients. It is also clear that the state's right to use coercion must not extend to the sphere of inwardness; the inward recognition of the principles on which law is based and which are more than prudent selfishness cannot and should not be coerced. But that does not mean that the state, as the power of the law, can be indifferent to the sphere of conviction. Fortunately, we have seen that power is not limited to the system of negative sanctions; political philosophy must also deal with the other forms of power. Behavior that, on moral grounds, is not coercible is, or can be, a political matter of the first importance; the people who live most fully the plenitude of the moral (and not only the limited subset of it known as "law") not only are the salt of the earth, but also maintain the legal system, and they are especially indispensable in times when the factual mores must elevate themselves to meet higher demands of the moral law.

7.3.3.1. Principles of Family Law

No area of the law is more difficult to subject to norms than family law. This is connected with the fact that the most various aspects are bound together in the institution of the family: the sex drive, emotional needs, economic necessities, the procreation of life, the education of future generations. This mixture is already complicated enough in itself (even if it is perhaps also appropriate, precisely because of its complicatedness, to the complex nature of human beings), but the element of the emotions alone poses a sufficient threat to the law, because it completely eludes coercion. At the same time, for sociological observation the family remains one of the most fascinating human in-stitutions, indeed, the ideal framework for the development of various virtues and the nucleus of the social: the feeling of immediate acceptance that the child experiences in a happy family is one of the most important sources of moral behavior, which can hardly be replaced by anything else. The Italian *Codice Civile,* unlike the German *Bürgerliches Gesetzbuch,* rightly begins with family and succession law, which are important for the new citizen of the Earth far earlier than is his ability to make contracts. For the state, the family is interesting for two reasons. On one hand, it is usually the framework for pass-ing on human life, in which the state, as an institution stretching over generations, has a special interest (it is obvious, for instance, that the breakdown of traditional marriage has demographic consequences); on the other hand, within it forms of self-transcendence can develop that make it possible to overcome the symmetry of rational egoism, even if the limited form of altruism peculiar to this institution is often able to obstruct the higher altruism of the state. Responsibility for a common structure leads beyond natural ego-ism, although it can easily remain stuck in an egoism involving two (or three, or four, etc.) people. Altruism restricted to the family has a biological basis that has a stronger effect on human beings than the feeling of pure duty—love for one's own children is, *ceteris paribus,* stronger than that for children of complete strangers. However much this love may also lead to one's giving priority, against all principles of justice, to one's own offspring in distributing offices, it can also be the germ of a responsibility for fu-ture generations that cannot arise from a balance of rational egoism.

To be sure, the natural character of an institution is still no argument in its favor; nature is not a ground of validity, and rising above natural feelings is a necessary con-dition of moral behavior. Modern rationalism is surely right when it emphasizes, against traditionalism, that rational insight is the sole source of legitimate institutions. But here one must understand reason as moral reason, not strategic rationality maximizing self-interest; if the latter is left a free rein, as has happened in modernity, the moral level achieved by naturally developed institutions or even biological evolution may be un-dercut (I remind the reader of my interpretation of sociobiology). With profound in-sight, Aeschylus made the *Oresteia* end not simply with the triumph of the court of reason over the powers of blood, but with the integration of the Furies into Athens's po-litical system—transformed into Eumenides, they remain, in accord with their essence but in a benevolent form, indispensable for the state's well-being. In a similar way, in a reasonable state the family must be "sublated" (*aufgehoben*).

The nucleus of the family is *marriage.* In regulating it legally, two mutually opposed ideal-typical approaches are conceivable. On one hand, marriage can be interpreted *individualistically,* that is, as a contract between two, or if one wishes, several persons, whose more detailed form is completely up to them. Thus Humboldt continued to favor monogamy morally, while at the same time demanding that legally, the state leave it en-tirely to the "free and arbitrary choice of the individuals, and of the manifold contracts that they make, in general and in their modifications" (1903; 122). Soviet marriage law in the initial phase of the Soviet Union (before its reform by Stalin) came closest to

Humboldt's ideas, but they were never realized in a pure form. Thus in most legal systems contracts concerning sexual services are considered void; the obligation to comply with legal formalities is particularly pronounced in family law, and a marriage limited in duration from the outset is hardly accepted by law, which is not compatible with an individualistic, contract-theory interpretation. Temporally limited contracts for services are normal; indeed, in some contracts an unlimited temporal extension is not even permissible. It is clear that a purely individualistically conceived marriage could not claim any special favor on the part of the state, since it is important only for those concerned (as such, it might nonetheless provide the basis for damage claims), and it does not produce the binding forces that every society needs.

On the other hand, there is the *supra-individual* conception of marriage, according to which the partners enter a state of marriage that has its own gravity, not dependent upon the will of the spouses; and the marriage is dissolved only on the death of one of the spouses. Catholic canon law is still based on this conception, and the civil law in many Catholic states was long based on it as well. Since marriage conceived in this way now has hardly any social reality in wealthy industrial states, except perhaps in rural areas, piety obliges us, so to speak, to briefly mention the grounds that can be advanced in favor of this conception of marriage. Its starting point is the idea that morally legitimate sexual relations presuppose love. But love is the feeling of having found a valuable and at the same time complementary person, for whom one would like to take a responsibility similar to that one takes for oneself. Polygyny and polyandry are not compatible with the symmetry that characterizes just institutions. Asymmetry could indeed be overcome in a relationship among four people (and in the case of bisexuality, also in a relationship among three people); but in these cases the element of total dedication to the other person would be lacking. Since one remains responsible for oneself during the whole of one's life, love furthermore implies a life-long bond with the beloved as one's alter ego. To be sure, there may be loveless people, but the sentence, "I love you now, but someday I will no longer love you" is performatively self-contradictory as a declaration of love. A person can be spoken of in this way in the third person; but if the person concerned acknowledges to himself that this is the case, one can be sure that he is also not in love at that moment. People who frequently change partners either know that they are not in love or are extremely forgetful; if each time they hope they have at last found the right partner, they must at least have forgotten that they have already had this hope several times in the past. According to the absolutist conception of love, marriage as a bond of life-long partnership is an extremely affirmative institution, the legal counterpart, as it were, to the phenomenon of mutual love. It leads to a merging of the lovers in a new unity, and is therefore so different from usual contracts that it would be misleading to understand it as a contract, even if it begins with an act of the will. Finally, it is obvious that the relationship between parents and children cannot be conceived as a contract.

Even a society in which extended families reaching over generations have not only largely disappeared, but the nuclear family is also in severe crisis, ought to acknowledge that a happy, monogamous marriage deserves moral admiration—Philemon and Baucis are moving, and even demand respect. Furthermore, it is clear that every marriage goes through crises and that without a certain self-discipline that must be strengthened precisely through respect for the institution of marriage, a life-long partnership cannot be maintained. Nonetheless, at the same time it should be noted that the law can do no more than offer such a form, and that it cannot prescribe that it should be carried on if the foundation on which it was shaped has collapsed. If marriage's economic necessity, its social recognition, and its religious sanction are lost (if today a church clings to the indissoluble nature of marriage, it has to expect an increased number of people to leave the church), the law has to more or less adapt itself, even if it should at least not accelerate this development. Thus every legal system must recognize that marriage as the legal counterpart of love is essentially precarious. For love is one of those things that are not coercible—even for oneself. (Therefore there cannot be a right to sexual services to be provided by the spouses, and for that reason the crime of rape should be extended to marriage.) Even if there are possibilities of preventing or encouraging the development of one's own emotions (possibilities that one has a moral duty to perceive), the extinction of affection cannot be excluded any more than the emergence of a new passion. Certainly it is important that the validity of marriage not be based, in the consciousness of the spouses, exclusively on the continuation of love and even less on the continuation of being in love. A deep friendship as well as a fundamental reflection on the scope of the institution should precede the wedding, no matter how strong the erotic attraction. Certainly infidelity remains problematic, not only morally, but also legally, because the other has relied upon a commitment and made his life plan in accord with it—even if it is an infidelity grounded on a new, and perhaps for the first time, true love (who would want to condemn Jamila?) and may be more excusable than all other cases. For example, the spouse who has been chiefly concerned with raising the children has given up chances for a professional career that can no longer be retrieved. Nonetheless, people cannot be forced to go on living together, and although the law should make difficult the *dissolution* of the old marriage, which can only be declared by a family court, as well as the entry into a new marriage (especially if there are minor children), it cannot fundamentally obstruct it. Precisely in modernity, with its highly complex, often self-absorbed characters who develop in unforeseeable ways, and with the economic independence of each of the spouses, the divorce rate will inevitably rise. To be sure, this devalues also the nature of the normal marriage commitment, which is hardly any longer characterized by the dignity of a life-long self-commitment, which is the greatest expression of freedom one can imagine—an expression of freedom that justifies a religious ceremony. But although this ceremony may be refused, for instance in a remarriage after a divorce, a constitutional state cannot make the institution of marriage dependent on that ceremony. However, it is doubtful that the general abandonment of the principle of divorce on the grounds of fault alone that has spread in most Western legal systems over the past few decades was prudent, even if one concedes that the breakdown of a marriage is almost never the fault of one of the partners alone. The disappearance of the consciousness that a continuation of the marriage is a duty to be taken seriously—a consciousness that can be important precisely in times of crisis—is favored by the shift to the principle that for divorce it is sufficient that the marriage has broken down.

If a society has a high divorce rate and marriage is no longer an almost necessary condition or even only a probable transitional phase for procreation, marriage loses a large part of its meaning for the state. Marriage, like the state, is rightly counted among those institutions that can also be protected by means of criminal law—think of the prohibition on bigamy.[113] But the state's interest in the family, indeed even in groups of persons organized in non-familial ways that are involved in the domestic realm with the raising of children or caring for those who need help (the elderly, for instance), must be greater than its interest in childless marriages. Therefore it is absurd when greater tax advantages are associated with getting married than with the raising of children on whom depend the future of a state and, in old age, even those who are currently child-less. In fact there is something to be said for the view that the conservative critics are right, and that the overall social price to be paid for decoupling reproduction from monogamous marriage will yet turn out to be a high one. But the possibility cannot be excluded that new, small social groups will become the functional equivalent of mar-riage in socializing young people. Even someone who regards recent developments with great skepticism must hope this will happen, for the sake of future generations.

A marriage can be made only voluntarily; conversely, *the impediments to marriage should be as limited as possible.* In view of the importance of this step, majority is gen-erally to be required. Marriage with the very closest relatives is rightly forbidden be-cause it cannot be an expression of freedom—part of becoming an adult is breaking away from one's own family. (A conceivable exception is the encounter of siblings who were separated after birth.) In *Der Erwählte* (*The Holy Sinner*) Thomas Mann aptly showed how the double incest in the story springs from an arrogance that sees everything foreign as of less value; in less exceptional cases the fear of the new will replace this motive. The social utility of exogamy is an argument that is not sufficient for marriage prohibitions,

---

113. It is a difficult question whether immoral sexual behavior between consenting adults can be punishable at all. (For behavior that is wrongly regarded as immoral by the majority of the popu-lation, the answer must be a categorical no.) The question, even in the case of adultery, will probably be answered in the negative (unequal treatment of the two sexes is of course contrary to natural law), but still makes the seduction of minors subject to punishment, because the preservation of sexual self-control is a value that can be given up only after mature reflection. Child prostitution is a serious crime that, in view of its increasing frequency, should certainly be actively prosecuted in accord with the active personality principle, if not indeed in accord with the universality principle. The sexual ex-citement of third parties, for instance through sexual intercourse in public, need not be tolerated, ei-ther, and certainly not the transmission of diseases through sexual intercourse. Someone who has rea-son to suppose, on the basis of his behavior, that he has such a disease, has a duty to be cautious; if he acts contrary to this duty and infects a sex partner, he should be punished on the ground of know-ingly inflicting bodily injury (this being a case of the *dolus eventualis*). Human health and human life are higher objects of legal protection than sexual permissiveness—as the AIDS problem ought to re-mind us once again.

since the philosophy of law should not be based on considerations of utility, but rather on the idea of freedom.[114] Possible genetic damage to the progeny is equally insufficient as an argument, if care is taken not to conceive children, and moreover it is no more probable than under other conditions that commonly do not represent impediments to marriage. In fact, most legal systems have not made the possibility of the birth of children a condition of marriage; one can get married even at an advanced age or when both partners know one of them is sterile, and after the development of means of contraception it is within the discretion of every married couple to determine the number of their children. Therefore every moral argument for limiting marriage to people of different sexes falls away. If morally legitimate sexual intercourse presupposes only love, then there can be morally respectable sexuality between members of the same sex; permitting marriage among people of the same sex is sensible precisely in order to limit promiscuity.

This is even more true since in an industrial society the peculiar *differences between the sexes* are steadily becoming less marked. To be sure, there are deep, biologically based differences between the sexes in social behavior and emotional life, which will always remain; to be sure, the traditional attribution of different tasks to the two sexes made superfluous many tiresome discussions that currently represent a burden for many marriages—asymmetries are often functional. But the integration of women into the economic sphere is an obligation of justice, and it undeniably means the dissolution of many of the differences that used to be presented as timeless essential differences. A man must blush with shame if he considers, for instance, the sufferings to which talented women were subjected for thousands of years because they were largely refused the possibility of an intellectually active life; and it is self-evident that every unequal treatment of man and woman, including, for instance, the husband's having the last word in marital disagreements, is against natural law. But that does not mean that the acquisition by women of male vices would represent progress; there are values and virtues traditionally associated with women that should not be sacrificed to women's liberation, but instead should be adopted by men.

As a community of life, marriage also requires *provision for material existence.* The wish to construct a life-long unity of common action makes community property or at least a sharing of the economic advantages of marriage appear as the most appropriate arrangement; separate property makes sense when one partner's liability for the debts of the other is to be limited. The legal form of a community of property acquired in common acknowledges that both partners, including the one who remains at home, participate in the economic success of a household. Few things in modern industrial societies are more unjust and more counterproductive in the long run than a one-sided recognition of gain-

---

114. Even Montesquieu's reflections in *Esprit des lois* 26.14 (1748; 2:189 ff.) do not grasp the morally relevant point, however much he is right that it depends in part on the cultural framework conditions (for instance, on whether cousins live together), whether or not a certain family relationship is considered as an impediment to marriage.

ful work (for instance, as the only thing entitling an individual to a pension) at the expense of unpaid work. Raising children and caring for elderly relatives are also kinds of work, of course, and where these are not recognized financially and in the system of social prestige, one should not be surprised that they are declining. Taking into account the years spent in raising children when determining old-age pensions is today more important than the benefits paid to widows capable of working. Certainly, the idea of monetarizing every service is not particularly attractive; the disappearance of grace in capitalistic societies has much to do with the fact that in them disinterested goodness is not recognized, and the fear that the economization of non-gainful work will lead to a further decline in the spontaneous willingness to provide aid is only too well founded. However, there is no alternative to taking steps in this direction, if the logic of capitalism is not to lead to a complete drying up of both convictions and actions that are crucial for the survival of a society. For that reason, few state interventions in the structural conditions of the work world are as justified as those that help maintain a family culture worthy of the name.

Of special importance are the relationships between family law and *succession law*. So far as the legal philosophy of inheritance goes, we must clearly distinguish two different strategies of argumentation, between which some legal systems (for instance, the German one) make a compromise that is not always plausible.[115] On one hand, one can defend the position of unrestricted freedom of testation and base it on the idea of an absolute right of disposal over one's own property. Two objections to this may be made. First, the testator is dead, so that the question arises how the will of a dead person can obligate his descendents at all.[116] Fichte emphatically disputes this obligation (1971; 3:257ff., 10:602 ff.); according to his view, it is only the interest of the living in having their own testaments respected that leads them to respect the testaments of the dead. If this interest disappeared, the validity of the testament would no longer be guaranteed. Second, it should be pointed out that acquiring property through inheritance (not through hereditary pacts) is not compatible with the principle that property rights have to be grounded in individual achievements: one has not worked for what one inherits. The latter argument speaks a fortiori against the second strategy, which does not proceed from a right of the testator's, but rather from the legal heirs' right to their share of the estate, entirely independently of the testator's will, which could disinherit them only in exceptional cases.[117] The legal heirs are the members of the family up to a certain degree of relationship, whose right to an

---

115. Radbruch (1973; 253 f.) rightly complains "that contemporary succession law is an unfathomable compromise between opposed systems and principles, that it combines the succession forms of freedom of testation with those of intestate succession, and on the other hand, compulsory division of the inheritance with compulsory maintenance of unpartitioned inheritance, and that in it individualistic, social, and family goals are . . . almost inextricably intertwined."

116. Much the same holds for the denigration of the deceased's memory. Cf. Kant, *Metaphysik der Sitten* I § 35 (1976 f.; 8:410 ff.).

117. Hegel defends this position in an exemplary way. See *Rechtsphilosophie* §§ 178 ff. (1969 ff.; 7:330 ff.).

inheritance is based on such conceptions of law or the idea that ultimately the family is the true property owner. As we have already said, this conception conflicts even more strongly with the principle that property rights have to be grounded in individual achievements, because the heirs by intestate succession have usually contributed nothing to the inheritance, whereas according to the first strategy at least the testator whose will is respected has achieved something himself (unless he inherited his wealth).

The following principles seem to me the most reasonable. First of all, we should note that no way of acquiring property is more problematic than inheriting it. Nothing can be taxed, even heavily, with a clearer conscience, if (and only if) the state needs funds for legitimate tasks. However, two exceptions must be made. Close members of the deceased's family who are no longer or not yet capable of working—spouses and children—should be cared for out of the inheritance, either until their deaths or until they are themselves capable of working, for in the case of spouses and minor children one can in fact agree with the Hegelian notion that they are co-owners of the family resources. Furthermore, the testator should have a chance to decide for himself how his money will be used, if he dedicates it to goals in the common interest: endowments should be favored in estate tax law. Second in importance, there is the principle of freedom of testation, which is more compatible with the principle that property rights have to be grounded in indidivual achievements, and on which it would be counterproductive to impose excessively strict limitations, because it could prevent greater efforts to work. Moreover, care should be taken that gifts are taxed in the same way, since as unilateral contracts, gifts also contradict the principle that property rights have to be grounded in indidivual achievements, and since otherwise inheritance and estate taxes could be evaded. Third, if there is no will, the claims of the next family members should be respected in a subsidiary way; they can be primary only if the family is the main support of a society. In such a case as well, the claims of the family one has oneself established should have priority with respect to those of the family into which one was born, and all children, even illegitimate ones, should be treated equally.[118] If the welfare office, not myself, has a maintenance obligation with regard to my cousins, then it is not clear why I should be able to inherit from them; these days, it is ridiculous to consider valid inheritance regulations that go back to the law of a culture that was based on *gentes* (extended family). Indeed, even inheriting from one's own parents, if it occurs when one is an adult, should at least be subject to heavy taxation. When one has brought up one's children, one's duty to them has been fulfilled, and it is not easy to see why it should not be possible to disinherit children who have hardly cared for their parents. (The main argument against it, on the other hand, remains the danger of weak-willed elderly people being exposed to legacy hunting.) Certainly, there are a few things to be said for the continuation of family traditions, but where they have dissolved by themselves, a succession law whose legitimacy depends on

118. Entailed estate can be legitimate only in a society with an aristocracy of birth; if the latter is not desired, then entailed estate should be abolished.

their existence is meaningless. With the transition from owner to managerial capitalism, a further important argument in favor of intestate succession by family members has collapsed, insofar as the entrepreneurial tradition is hardly confirmed by a family anymore; private bequeathing of publicly subsidized property is even absurd.

Marriage attains its completion in the *family*. In children, the parents' love has become objective, as it were; raising children constitutes a task that gives many marriages a central content. However, only in unfortunate cases does raising children fill the whole duration of the marriage. The new orientation of the marriage after the departure of the last grown child—who has a moral right to leave the family and usually also a moral duty to do so, because this is the only way for him to become independent—proves to be a notoriously difficult task that is made still more difficult when one of the spouses has given up his or her professional life during the period of child raising. With regard to those who are responsible for their existence, children have claims to support (to which correspond, when they have grown up, obligations to maintain and support parents who have claims to maintenance and support—obligations that the children acknowledge by continuing to live, since this action implies that they accept having been born). The immaturity of children justifies their having only later on certain rights that could be used to their own harm, and acquiring a few of them only when they have reached maturity. Despite individuals' very different rates of development, in order to avoid conflicts and major injustices all people should acquire individual rights at the same age. The point at which maturity is reached has repeatedly changed through history, and it is not clear that in late modernity human beings become mature earlier than in preceding epochs, because today one must know more in order to act responsibly in a highly technologized world. The rights to parental custody are not absolute, but rather subordinate to the child's right to an appropriate upbringing, in which limited means of coercion may also be used: Children are not private property, but they may not do anything they want—paradoxically, they have a right to have their arbitrary freedom restricted, in order to be led toward rational autonomy.[119] Compulsory school attendance for children also follows from their right, on one hand, to acquire the abilities that will allow them to survive independently in modern civil society and establish a certain social equality, and on the other hand to become acquainted with the values on which the state is based. This includes a culture's factual mores, which should be respected, so long as it does not conflict with basic moral norms, because it makes everyone's behavior more predictable; the greater the state's homogeneity, the fewer explicit legal regulations it needs. At the same time, the young pupil ought to acquire as much as possible the morality that allows him to distance himself in a critical but not destructive way from the faulty norms of his own culture's mores and also of its legal system, and thus work toward better norms.

---

119. It will hardly be found surprising that in order to provoke their parents, children who have been allowed to do almost everything hit upon the idea of breaking the most extreme taboos that still remain—in Germany, for instance, they may become neo-Nazis.

If a reasonable upbringing is not guaranteed, then the children can be taken away from the parents—even if only in exceptional cases should it be assumed that as a result the children will experience more good than bad. If children lose their parents, the appointment of someone to represent their personal and property interests, that is, of a *guardian*, is indispensable. The guardian has a duty to promote their interests, not his own, and therefore is subject to state supervision. In case of a divorce, both parents should be granted as extensive joint custody for the child as possible, not so much because of the parents' right to their children's affection, but rather because there is much to be said for the view that continued contact with both parents strengthens the child's sense of self-respect. Only if the relationship to one of the parents endangers the child morally may his custody be radically restricted. The precedence given the woman in modern divorce law, sometimes without regard to the wishes of the children, who often enough know with astonishing precision what they need, is merely a reversal of earlier injustices and not therefore itself just. Equally unconvincing is German law's assignment of the custody of illegitimate children exclusively to the mother.

If contraceptive means have separated *sexual intercourse* from *reproduction*, then modern reproduction technologies will increasingly make procreation independent of sexual intercourse and perhaps even of pregnancy. Genetic engineering interventions in somatic (and under some circumstances, even germ) cells are defensible if this is the only way to eliminate terrible diseases (and inherited diseases, of which it cannot be presumed that any descendant has an interest in them), and if it can be guaranteed that the interventions are directed solely against the diseases. On the other hand, the production at will of a person, and even more cloning, would cause the breakdown of the view that recognizes in every person an end in himself, and therefore that of the foundation for the sense for the moral as well. To be sure, there are some things about human nature that arouse anxiety; but precisely for that reason, as well as because of the unpredictability of the effects of such activities, man should not be granted the right to use genetic engineering to change his own nature. It is certainly meritorious to help people who could otherwise have no children to satisfy their desire to have children, if this is not done by violating the rights of others (for instance, those of embryos or of spouses who have not given their consent). In view of the unimaginable misery of already existing children, adoption is doubtless a significantly more moral way of achieving this goal, however, and it would be desirable to change the law to make adoption easier. Making it possible for single people or same-sex couples to adopt is all the more worth considering the more horrible the alternatives are that will otherwise threaten children.

One has a right to bring children into the world only if one is capable of feeding them, either by oneself or with state help.[120] In particular, there is a *duty to practice preventive birth control*, in order to prevent the population from attaining the point at which

---

120. On the following, cf. in greater detail V. Hösle (1994). Also see S. L. Isaacs's convincing article (1995).

a Darwinian battle for survival would necessarily ensue. It goes without saying that infanticide and abortion are not permissible as means of birth control, and drugs and devices that inhibit implantation are probably also subject to potentiality arguments.[121] But all other means are morally permissible, even irreversible ones such as sterilization, in particular after the birth of a second child. As much as possible, the main responsibility for contraception should not be limited to one partner.

Is the duty involved a moral or a legal duty? The question may seem surprising, because the whole tradition of the philosophy of law has naively assumed, as though it were a matter of course, that there is an unlimited right to reproduce; and in fact it will be conceded that at least the child can hardly complain about being brought into the world. Nonetheless, there are two objections to the general validity of this alleged right. First, if couples in a "Malthusian" situation bring into the world on average more than 2.1 children each (or whatever the replacement level may be in the country concerned), they are increasing the likelihood that a battle for survival will break out, and thus they are endangering the lives of others (under certain circumstances, those of their own children). But there cannot be a right to do so. Second, it should be considered that children have rights to positive benefits in the narrower sense, which, if they are not fulfilled by the parents, must be satisfied by the community, since no child can be blamed for having been born. However, since the assumption by others of the parents' responsibility would lead only too easily to a breakdown of individual responsibility, in an extreme case the community must have the right to force parents not to bring further children into the world.

It need hardly be said that coercion must be the *ultima ratio,* and the system of positive sanctions must first be exhausted; equal rights for women, the construction of a system of retirement benefits that does not presuppose a high number of children in order to be cared for when one is old, and, in the medium term, the lowering of infant mortality are known to be the most efficient ways of limiting population growth (which, because of so-called population momentum, can only be influenced relatively slowly). But there can be situations in which there is not enough time and the means are not available to put these strategies into effect. In such cases, very heavy taxation of families with many children, for example, is justified, if only because children make demands on resources. Moreover, compulsory sterilization (which represents a less extensive infringement on the personal rights of adults than does abortion on those of the embryo, even if it is incomparably more difficult to put through politically) could even be supported as a last-ditch means, if, and only if, the following conditions were fulfilled. First, this kind of sterilization must take place after the elementary right to bring children into the world has been satisfied, that is, as far as possible after the birth of the second or third child. Second, this sterilization must take place in accord with the basic principle

---

121. The possibility of the formation of multiple embryos or of chimeras before implantation hardly makes the killing of fertilized egg cells any better.

of equal treatment. Special regulations make sense in the case of representatives of cultural minorities, in order not to make permanent the demographic advantage of individual peoples. On the other hand, one should reject the view that someone could sell on the free market his right to a certain number of children, since such an important element of a fulfilled life is involved that he would probably quickly regret it, and no price can be put on the person as such; this kind of trade is subject to the same objections as trading in human organs. Third, it should be pointed out that a community that sterilizes parents who are not in a position to feed their children must assume part of the responsibility for the children already born; sterilizations without such a benefit in return are absolutely contrary to natural law in non-Malthusian situations.

I am well aware that many of my last remarks may seem outlandish and even repellent. I ask the reader to consider that my remarks follow from the subordination of the right to procreate to the right to life. It is to be hoped that these two rights never contradict each other. But it is irresponsible, after events like those in Rwanda, to try to deny that possibility; and it serves no one to draw up a list of basic rights without ever asking whether they are always compatible with each other and which right has precedence in case of a conflict.

7.3.3.2. Principles of the Law of Society

Even if the state alone makes laws, such as family law or the regulations that allow the construction of private juristic persons, it still has a duty to acknowledge in its legislation the moral principles that precede it, from which follows, among other things, the independent existence of extra-state institutions—a form of the division of power that is at least as important as the separation of powers within the state.[122] Because the state delegates certain tasks to groups that can fulfill them better than it can, it can devote itself to its own tasks all the more unreservedly; the principle of subsidiarity protects not only the other institutions, but also the state itself. Without a culture of free, responsible associations, such as is promoted by communitarianism, a mentality that reduces citizens to clients of the state will necessarily spread, for which the state itself will ultimately have to pay a high price. A state that completely absorbs society into itself not only violates elementary rights to freedom, but also suffocates the sources of energy that alone can grant it the means it needs to pursue its own ends; on the other hand, a state that completely emancipates the sphere of society will soon destroy itself. In society, the natural impulses toward sympathy and the feeling of belonging together that characterizes the family are lacking; on one hand, systematic rational self-interest, which must, however, take into account the self-interest of others, and on the other hand the striving for

---

122. [The German text distinguished here between the *Machtteilung* characteristic of extra-state institutions and the *Gewaltenteilung* characteristic of the state, as the corporate group that holds a monopoly on the use of force. Trans.]

the satisfaction of the needs for transcendence, determine the two most important sub-systems of society. The economy is guided more by instrumental rationality than is the family, and so far as this is in one's own interest, it is more universal; whoever can be useful will be sought out, beyond one's own family and national boundaries. Whoever is not useful will be avoided—despite family or national bonds that do not count in the economy: Its power to cross boundaries can not only broaden horizons but also be destructive. On the other hand, religion has to satisfy the needs for meaning that the economy cannot satisfy. It can motivate sacrifices that go far beyond what is common in a family; at the same time, it can contain a principle of fanaticism that has an effect far more directly and rapidly destructive than does egoism in the economy.

7.3.3.2.1. The State and the Economy

A morally acceptable economic order must be guided by the following principles: It must satisfy everyone's *basic needs,* guarantee the individual extensive freedom of action and choice, and acknowledge the principle that property rights have to be founded on individual achievements. Economic needs are most efficiently satisfied by a system of the division of labor, even if it is accompanied by a loss of the unity of production and consumption characteristic of subsistence economies—a loss that can increase to become a feeling of alienation. A system of the division of labor can be based either on a *central administration* or on the *market.* The advantages of the latter have not only been confirmed by historical development, but can also be grasped theoretically.[123] They consist in the fact that in a market economy producers and consumers have *more* options for action, which lead *more quickly* to the establishment of an equilibrium of supply and demand than in a centrally administered or command economy, in which exchange takes place not directly between two parties, but rather through a bureaucracy. Such a central administration can under certain circumstances have criteria for determining prices reasonably;[124] but it is a mistake to suppose that it has a more detailed acquaintance with the needs of the people concerned than they themselves have, just as it is naive to assume that this kind of bureaucracy will at least be guided by what it believes to be the common good. Only in exceptional situations such as wars may elements of a command economy (such as rationing, for example) make sense. To be sure, demand for a scarce commodity in a market economy will drive up its price until a corresponding increase in supply succeeds in lowering the price again. But that is also sensible, because artificial price controls can only increase the scarcity of the commodity in question (because the commodity will be used up even more quickly), and because they will usually create a black market characterized by even more unpleasant dependencies than those that characterize the public market. The possibility of choosing between a

---

123. Cf. P. Koslowski (1995).
124. Cf. J. A. Schumpeter (1959), 172 ff., in opposition to L. von Mises.

career as a dependent and one as an independent person, a possibility that exists only in a market economy, and the extensive freedom to choose one's own vocation in the modern world, are not only values in themselves but also give the economy greater energy and a stronger innovative potential; the flip side is, however, the periodic unemployment caused by the obsolescence of earlier methods of production. Nonetheless, everyone can benefit from a capitalist economy, *if* the profits are appropriately distributed. More important morally is the argument that points to the greater efficiency of the market than the one that emphasizes the individual's freedom of action. In the event of a conflict, arbitrary freedom would have to be subordinated to justice; arbitrary freedom may also be restricted for the sake of social security.

It is true that the price to be paid for a market economy is greater *competition* among people, but it is also inevitable. In any case, forms of competition that are disrespectful of human beings, such as those based on deception and lies, can be prevented by laws against unfair competition. Moreover, less efficient and more leisurely enterprises can certainly survive in a market economy if there is enough demand for the advantages connected with this kind of entrepreneurial culture; furthermore, competition does not exclude the possibility of forms of cooperation that do not eliminate competition — consider large Japanese firms' practice of holding each other's stock. On the market, products that are relatively little in demand have a chance if production costs are not too high or if consumers are very willing to pay for them, whereas even in a democratic command economy a majority decision would be required in order to put such a commodity into production. Those who were outvoted would have to pay for a commodity in which they had no interest at all. On the other hand, the "dollar vote" offers possibilities of differentiation that are denied the ballot (even if the latter is equally available to all in a democracy). It may well be that the individual would be prepared to accept the loss of individual freedom for the sake of even so slim a chance of exercising collective power (as perhaps the average Frenchman would in contrast to the average Englishman);[125] but the natural law question is not which preferences the individual has, but rather which preferences he ought in justice to have, and it is not clear why the majority should prescribe for the minority when this is not necessary. The individual consumer's power of decision should be maintained as much as possible.

The foregoing is not incompatible with the state itself being active as an entrepreneur, so long as it subjects itself to the competition of the market and does not burden the taxpayers by its inefficiency or even distort competition by subsidizing itself. Still more compatible with this is the state setting developmental trends by means of fiscal policy and the like in a long-term industrial policy, meeting the needs of future generations and fighting unemployment through intelligent investments, and seeking to diminish the negative consequences of fluctuations in the rate of economic activity through a counter-cyclical stabilization policy. Furthermore, it should be acknowledged

---

125. Cf. Mill (1972), 226 f.

that in the case of public goods proper, which are characterized by non-rivalry in consumption and especially by the failure of the exclusionary principle, the market cannot function, because free-riders would be rewarded. For instance, since it is impossible to defend only a few citizens, either everyone must pay for defense or those who did so voluntarily would be fools, because the others who refused to pay would also benefit from it. In the case of such goods, no individual choice can be allowed, but that does not mean that in weapons production, for instance, market mechanisms must be fundamentally abandoned. All other things being equal, the state should spend its tax money on the lowest bid.

The advantages of the market appear only when certain *structural conditions* are present. Just as the voluntary nature of an exchange is a sufficient condition for the latter's justice only if the structural conditions of the society are just, so the logic of the market can lead to good results only if the market is supported by a structure that does not itself function in accord with the principles of the market. All the advantages of the market would disappear if the highest bidders were favored by judgments in the legal system and by decisions in monetary policy, for all property that one has produced by one's labor would be insecure, the transaction costs would increase unpredictably, and every motive for working would disappear. Strict laws against bribing officials and official corruption, as well as scrutiny of party financing, are indispensable—not only on grounds of justice, but also solely for the sake of the maintenance of the market. The market presupposes courts and a central bank that is directed by values external to the market—thus a central bank should prevent inflation even if it is in the interest of wealthy landowners and currency speculators and harms only those with small savings accounts and pensioners. Paradoxically, the complete triumph of the market's value system would mean its destruction. Because of humans' striving for profits, natural markets have a tendency to produce cartels, and even monopolies and monopsonies; it is therefore necessary that a structure external to the market limit the freedom to enter into contracts, in order to maintain the market's advantages for consumers. However, it is more reasonable to use state cartel offices to stop this development than to increase the disadvantages of an economic monopoly by combining the latter with a monopoly on legislation. A state takeover of the branch of the economy concerned (which need not imply that those who work in it have the privileges of public officials), or at least strict controls of the corresponding private enterprises, is indispensable only where there can be no economically efficient alternative to monopolies. Monopolies or oligopolies in the area of the media are dangerous not only economically, but also politically, since in a mass democracy control of the media makes possible the strongest influence on the formation of public opinion and thereby on the political process. Legal regulation of media cartels is particularly urgent in order to maintain the division of power. This holds particularly for television, the medium that has the strongest influence on people, partly because it is not directed primarily at the faculty of reason and affects two senses at the same time. If it is correct that the length of the attention span of schoolchildren in the United States correlates with the length of a film clip between two commercial interruptions, then this medium influences not only content, but also formal structures of elementary importance for all intellectual, and therefore for all political, activities of human beings; and if this kind of influence undermines people's ability to make responsible political decisions, then the corresponding legal restrictions are just as permissible as the privileging of public television, insofar as the latter maintains certain standards of quality.[126] For public culture is no doubt a public good.

Furthermore, it is obvious that neither the negotiating power nor the knowledge of the parties to a contract should be too unequal. If elementary rights to positive benefits are not guaranteed, then in order to feed himself and his children the poor man can be forced to sell all his labor power at a far lower price than it would bring if his need were not clear; if all classes do not have, whether legally or because of different educational opportunities, rights and possibilities of association, one side has extraordinary advantages in setting the exchange value. From this follow various duties *of the state as the guardian of the market.* First of all, it must protect the individual's rights of association and broaden them by creating special legal forms. Forms of social property—cooperatives, for instance—permit the economically weaker, by joining together, to diminish the advantage of the economically stronger; in a labor struggle, employers and employees should have equal weapons; consumers should be helped to form corporate groups. Protection against wrongful dismissal is reasonable with regard to both housing and jobs, for without it the socially weaker have less freedom. Family policy considerations can justify special protection for families. However, the freedom of the weaker is to be weighed not only against the freedom of the owners or employers, but also against that of those who have no housing or jobs, partly because in concrete, individual cases, housing and jobs remain with those who cannot be dismissed, and partly because the owner or employer does not rent the housing or fill the job that has become available because strict laws against wrongful dismissal deter him. In such a case, laws of this kind become counterproductive and socially unjust. (Much the same goes for minimum wages that are set too high.) In general, one cannot exclude the possibility that groups of what were once the weaker might in time become power-clusters that significantly restrict the freedom of individuals (for instance, to engage in part-time or periodic activity in their profession) and do not consider at all the interests of those who do not belong to these groups—for instance, the unemployed; in this case, the state must protect individuals against such groups. Second, the state should supply, for instance, through labor employment agencies, the information that alone can lead to an equilibrium between supply and demand and that many people are always interested in repressing; here it may be not only possible but even desirable that there be private employment agencies operating under state supervision.

Third, in order to produce far-reaching equal opportunities, the training and further training of the individual (and if necessary, his retraining) should be financed in

---

126. Cf. N. Postman (1985).

accord with the needs of the market. Schools attended by all should be free, or the state should distribute school vouchers that make it possible to attend various private schools. Private schools may be in a position to react more quickly to parents' and children's needs than public schools, but they must be supervised by the state, which has a special responsibility for children. It is true that influencing the needs of children is an important task of the state, but there is no reason to suppose that this must necessarily take place with its direct collaboration. Experience shows that an extensive state monopoly on education becomes disastrous if state pedagogy goes off track, a possibility that cannot be excluded a priori. Surely a system with school vouchers would favor the children of parents who make a more intelligent choice; but it is absolutely legitimate to want to promote the interests of one's own children, and in the current situation the children of richer, not more prudent, parents often benefit from good private schools, which is hardly preferable. In the case of higher education, the cost-free principle is scarcely justifiable, since it is not clear why the taxes of those who do not attend such institutions should pay for the study of those who do. It is just and proper that colleges and universities be financed in large part by the later higher income of their students (which currently occurs in Germany only to a limited extent, through progressive taxation), if, and only if, *all* those who want to study *and* are capable of doing so have a claim to the necessary loans, and if the conditions for repaying these loans are not too much of a deterrent. An argument in favor of cost-free higher education could only be that everyone would ultimately be able to benefit from it, because a higher level of education would have beneficial effects on the whole society. Whether this is the case depends on the society's stage of development and on the kind of education offered; and one may have strong doubts that the present-day knowledge industry can claim that it does not primarily serve particular interests.

The fourth legitimate intervention by the state concerns the policy of redistribution to the advantage of the worst-off segment of the population (not to the advantage of the voters of the currently governing party), for trickle-down effects on the poorest people do not automatically ensue; indeed, they are even unlikely if, for instance, the people concerned belong to a despised social group. A right to social aid is indispensable, and follows directly from human dignity; realistically, one should even reckon with the possibility that in a highly complex society part of the population may no longer be capable of establishing itself in the market. But there is much to be said for creating options for individual recipients of benefits—and that presupposes a multiplicity of benefit providers, all of which need not be financed directly by public funds (think of neighborhood aid groups); a plurality of this kind will probably even be cheaper for the state. Furthermore, a democratic state should avoid strong polarizations in society and promote the middle class; in particular, land should not be concentrated in a few hands. It is important that just redistributions not take place through subsidies to business firms, which send misleading signals to the market and make it harder to construct more efficient branches of the economy. To be sure, subsidies that balance out the disadvantages that come about through externalities caused by other people are indispensable. In addition, during a transitional period, the construction of important long-term branches of the economy should be supported, preferably in the framework of laws valid for a limited length of time, so that people do not get used to subsidization. Furthermore, it is certainly just that so far as possible, everyone should participate in the blessings of a brilliant innovation. Should the latter make a professional area superfluous, then those who are at the beginning negatively affected should have a claim to compensation by the general population—for instance, to adjustment assistance in the form of retraining. On the other hand, an unlimited continuation of their profession cannot be reasonably demanded.

From the recognition of the individual's rights to positive benefits follows the state's right to oblige people to *insure themselves against unemployment and old age.* For this purpose individual efforts and differentiations beyond a certain minimum are reasonable, because needs are different and because parasitism necessarily results if people do not make any contribution of their own. Since health is closely related to the basic good of life, healthcare may not be left to the market alone, but it is just as important to prevent the individual from having no options. It is reasonable to leave the provision of every luxury in medical care and perhaps also the prolongation of a vegetative state at an advanced age to the individual choice of a more expensive insurance policy; but it cannot be permissible to forgo insurance against a life-threatening illness that only seldom occurs, but whose treatment is expensive, if one assumes that the individual ought not to put his life at risk. Moreover, culpable damage to health should be taken into account in determining contributions. The idea of justice forbids, for instance, allowing the results of genetic tests to lift the veil of ignorance, thus leading to a major financial burden for people with inherited diseases, but the same idea makes it appear sensible to make alcoholics and others pay more. The idea of a mutually supportive group breaks down as soon as the unfortunate and the guilty are no longer distinguished (which can be difficult to do in individual cases).

The protection of the rights of the owners, the employees, the creditors, and the customers of a business as well as of the society as a whole justifies the multitude of regulations that characterize the private law of all civilized peoples and that necessarily multiply with the increase in human interactions and technological possibilities of having an impact on the world, as well as with the decline of mores. Indeed, all other things being equal, individual possibilities for shaping things must be greater in groups formed by adults than in the family, in which the defenselessness of children makes particularly extensive regulations necessary; but the complexity of the modern world endangers those living in it in such a way that protecting them is indispensable. This protection may be provided only by a power that has no direct interest at stake and that can be trusted. In particular, it must establish *duties to ensure information and to maintain safety.* Not everyone who wants to may open a medical practice or a bank, or even drive a car, if the health and property of innocent people are not to be endangered. Even contracts in which the individual forgoes the protection to which he is entitled— for instance, the leisure time required for revitalization after work—have to be considered null and void. Since because of his superior knowledge the producer is in a better position to discern the deficiencies of a complex object than is the unsuspecting customer, it is reasonable to establish a product liability that cannot be escaped even in the fine print of the sales contract. A fortiori, the state should require producers to inform their customers regarding the data relevant to their own well-being, including their moral well-being in particular, and thus to make them capable of comparing a product to others; a bank customer, for instance, ought to be able to find out in what kind of projects his money is invested, and a consumer ought to be able to find out whether his food has been altered by genetic technology.

The market also needs a state framework, insofar as it tends to *externalize internal costs.* It is particularly tempting to pass on costs when the people affected cannot defend themselves—for instance, future generations. In any case, the market is the most reasonable means of allocation only in satisfying the needs of people with purchasing power; it in no way helps those without purchasing power, of whom there are certainly a great number in many states that are not welfare states. Analogously, the market does not help to respect the needs of coming generations. If the latter's future demand were already equipped with purchasing power, then prices for non-renewable resources that are already becoming scarce would shoot up; and since their needs are legitimate, the state has a duty to intervene on their behalf in the pricing process—for instance, by establishing environmental taxes (this was discussed in chapter 7.3.1.1). Furthermore, the state should set limits to the using up of the capital stock of renewable resources as well as to the pollution of the environment—and do this by taking preventive measures, not by undertaking repairs after the fact. Here there are two possible solutions: either the state determines the acceptable *quotas* that may be extracted from nature or that may be emitted into it; or it determines the *prices* for such extractions or emissions. The other parameter in each case will then be determined by the market.[127] A blend of both systems is probably ideal for environmental protection. Naturally, the limitation of the quantities must be the goal of state policy (even if there are no absolutely correct threshold values). But this is not always best achieved through a quota solution, since only the price solution creates an incentive to undershoot the thresholds prescribed in the quota solution, although overshooting them is also compatible with the price solution. In making a decision for the quota solution, one also should not forgo tools using market forces (for instance, negotiable emissions licenses), because they make possible a more efficient allocation of resources than do detailed regulations. If the current environmental destruction is not stopped, then the universal market that has developed in modernity will become one of the most destructive institutions in world history, because the collapse of all limits to exchange takes the constantly occurring externalities into unforeseeable dimensions. For instance, if the costs of transportation do not correspond to the true costs, that is, those that result if we oblige those who cause environmental damages to

---

127. Cf. H. Bonus (1992) and U. E. Simonis (1996), 184 f.

pay the costs of environmental repair, then the great increase in transportation is a disaster. An environmental policy conceived as a integral part of economic policy must hinge on the polluter-pays principle and the principle of prevention.

Foreign trade must be controlled by specific legal regulations. On one hand, arguments in favor of the market are also valid for the world market. If a product can be produced more cheaply in one place than in another, and the price differential is greater than the (objectively correct) transportation costs, then it makes more sense for consumers that it be produced at the first location; indeed, even if all goods are produced more cheaply domestically, it is economically rational to export the relatively cheapest goods and to import the relatively most expensive. This is not in contradiction to the fact that it may be reasonable, if it is a matter not of natural but of the man-made advantages of a location, to make structural changes in one's own country in order to eliminate the comparative advantage of the foreign country. To be sure, the macroeconomic costs of free trade on the national level (for instance, in the form of temporary unemployment) can be large. But the loss of jobs at home is hardly a morally relevant argument—even if it is cratically a very strong one—so far as cheaper positions are created elsewhere and so far as in this way people poorer than one's own unemployed are helped to raise their standard of living; for the principle that one should first help those most in need is morally compelling. The sensible reaction to this loss would rather be for a country to find new market niches. Furthermore, there is much to be said for the view that the creation of stable and many-sided mutual dependencies decreases the risk of war; world trade can be a way of creating peace, especially if there is an equitable balance of payments.[128] On the other hand, trade with states that represent a danger to one's own security or to that of other states must not strengthen the dangerous state militarily; a just state ought therefore to prevent this, just as it should prevent the export of goods that could be used for criminal ends in the countries concerned. It would also be risky to become completely dependent for basic food supplies and other vital products (these could also be high-technology products) upon a foreign country with which one is not allied through a stable friendship. Furthermore, importing goods from other countries can make it harder to build up one's own industry, because the advantage of a powerful competitor is not easy to overcome given economies of scale and the like; in this case tariffs are legitimate during a transitional period. Finally, the comparative advantages in another country may result from its producing environmental externalities in a more uninhibited way and violating elementary social rights; against this it is permissible to defend oneself by means of (environmental) tariffs.

In order to limit environmental destruction it is indispensable to turn away from the unqualified growth tendencies of the modern economy; at least *economic growth*

---

128. This was rightly emphasized by Kant. On the other hand, in his book *Der geschlossene Handelsstaat* (*The Closed Commercial State*) Fichte pleads for a closed mercantile state. Even if his choice should be rejected, it should still be recognized that a great gap between political and economic power can lead to problems of governance and injustices.

should be disassociated from using up resources and environmental destruction. That the GNP has become the most important economic indicator of the progress of the richer countries is absurd, among other reasons because it does not include damage to and destruction of natural resources and because defensive expenses are included in it; illnesses, accidents, and environmental destruction increase the need for labor and thus increase the GNP. It is urgently necessary to learn to assess the "net economic welfare" of a society; in the current situation, despite, or precisely because of, their quantitative objectivity, assertions about the GNP massively mislead the public. Thus in Germany the net economic welfare, that is, the NNP minus the real economic costs of prosperity, stopped increasing in 1970; in 1990, the costs of prosperity were already 53 percent of the NNP.[129] Even full employment cannot be the primary economic goal, if it results in pressure for growth. A world in which a large part of the work would be performed by machines and most people would enjoy guaranteed rights to positive benefits and a modest life of leisure is a desirable ideal if, and only if, a meaningful leisure can be relearned; otherwise aggressivity arising from the feeling of emptiness is inevitable. Given the current state of the human soul, work is often not so much an economic necessity as a psychological need. Unpaid work in the family and the society should be socially and financially supported; in order to do so, it is indispensable to establish in Europe a greater flexibility in the supply of gainful employment. Growth cannot be an end in itself; instead, it must serve the achievement of the level of prosperity that is necessary for a life with dignity. Thus in order to overcome absolute poverty, economic growth is often indispensable, and for the most part easier to establish politically than are redistributions. Nevertheless, if that level is achieved, an economy of quasi-equilibrium should be given preference, precisely because, quite independently of the ecological consequences, it avoids the inner restlessness that is characteristic of economies in the growth phase and that makes the search for higher, non-material values more difficult. To be sure, again and again new discoveries will be made that result in a restructuring of production; it is certainly desirable, for instance, that there be further progress in medicine. But growth rates can and should decrease if needs and the population stop increasing; if a certain degree of saturation is reached, a society is to be envied, not pitied. The just state should be a *welfare state* in the sense that it should seek to overcome absolute poverty and inequalities that endanger the market and democracy; but it does not need to be a welfare state in the sense that it implies the support for constantly increasing prosperity. Since a person's feeling of happiness is determined essentially by the relationship between fulfillment and expectation, an economy of growth with its constant increase in people's expectations does not necessarily lead to greater happiness.[130] On the contrary, if economic growth suddenly encounters its limits, but the expectation of "always more" remains, the result is likely to be a phase of general unhappiness that

---

129. Cf. G. Scherhorn, H. Haas, F. Hellenthal, and S. Seibold (1996), 23 ff. The reflections in this work deviate from those that led to the Index of Sustainable Economic Welfare.

130. Cf. Rescher (1972), 42 ff.

can perhaps also lead, for the same reason, to greater aggressivity than does the real un-happiness of painful, absolute poverty, since those concerned ultimately know that they have no right to be unhappy.

In an economy of quasi-equilibrium, *interest rates* will fall greatly; people might regain an understanding for those cultures that banned lending at interest. Today, this means of directing the economy cannot yet be forgone, since investments in the future—in the realm of the environment, for instance—are crucial for survival, and without interest there would hardly be a sufficient motive for saving. In fact, *technological progress* should not be generically rejected. It can contribute to the prolongation of human life, to overcoming diseases or at least to diminishing their consequences, to augmenting food production, to the lessening of environmental pollution, to increasing efficiency in the use of resources—all of which is in the interest of fundamental objects of legal protection. Therefore the state has a duty to support the development of such technologies precisely when they are considered not profitable by a market that calculates in the short term (no matter how important the research that is conducted essentially within private corporations). The same goes for the promotion of the sciences based on instrumental rationality, for which the state can set relevant questions, even if they have to be able to work out the answers independently and freely—of course, while respecting other basic rights. But technology and the sciences based on instrumental rationality are value-neutral; they can also attain the exact opposite of the goals just mentioned, directly as well as through their side effects—acceleration in using up resources and environmental poisoning as well as the breakdown of the human intellectual and social abilities without which a society cannot exist. Learning to distinguish between the two is the first task of a reasonable technology policy. The ecological, social, and mentality-related consequences and risks of a new technology should be anticipated as much as possible through testing for environmental compatibility (whose cost should be borne not by the population at large, but by those with an interest in the technology) as well as through technology assessments, within the framework of institutions that themselves have no interests at stake and that need not adhere to the subjective perceptions of risk on the part of the majority of the population, since these are often irrational and have a compensatory function.[131] Important criteria against a technology are, for instance, the lack of reasonable error tolerance (which makes excessive demands on people), the long-term nature of threatening consequences (the half-life of plutonium is and remains a strong argument against nuclear fission), and still more the irreversibility of the changes they cause. The extinction of a species, for instance, cannot be undone, since a species is the product of millions of years of evolution. We will

---

131. In the context of the philosophy of law, it is evident that probability assessments should not be merely subjective; for an authority to coerce can be no more based on mere subjective expectations than on mere subjective preferences. When there are significant differences in the risk assessments of various experts (which are in any case not easy to aggregate), one should assume that a decision has to be taken in uncertainty.

also want to avoid developments at whose end the individual's right to security forces the state to take steps that increasingly limit rights to freedom. Of special interest is the question of which risks arising from certain technologies can be imposed on people who do not benefit from their advantages and who do not expose their fellow humans to risks that differ in kind but are equally great. Contemporary motorized individual transportation, for instance, is not only contrary to natural law because of the effects of its emissions on the climate, but also because of the many traffic fatalities that by no means involve solely those who themselves drive cars and voluntarily subject themselves to this risk. (Traffic accidents on superhighways are for this reason less problematic from a natural law point of view than are those in the city.) It is true that one can without difficulty argue for ambulances, since they save considerably more lives than they destroy in individual cases; but there is no comparably strong ground of justification for normal private vehicle traffic—the increase in individual mobility does not outweigh the death of so many people. The far-reaching consequences for the mores of a society of accepting individual automobile driving should not be underestimated. Ulrich Beck rightly points out that "undistanced internalization of the daily brutality of our traffic system is the best training for accepting the next maximum credible accident. Transport policy is cultural policy."[132]

An interesting example of externalities is *advertising*. The market presupposes a comparison of various offers; this requires a free flow of information, and comparative advertising that limits itself to objective information is relatively unobjectionable. However, information must be distinguished from manipulation, and it is not in any way a requirement of the market that people also be manipulated in it. The main argument for the market, namely that only in it is production guided by needs, begins to totter when so much energy is obviously invested in the *creation* of needs. If freedom consists in having only modest needs, then the incitement of needs is an infringement on freedom; and just as sending unsolicited advertising can be stopped (sending unsolicited pornography is already a criminal offense in some countries), so it would be worth considering whether posting manipulative advertising in public places constitutes an infringement of the observer's rights to freedom, since it has a subliminal effect on him even if he does not recognize it. Since manipulation is obviously addressed to the more primitive instincts whose restraint constitutes the wonder of human culture, it is certainly justifiable to ask whether, for instance, advertising that makes violence appear to be something positive is not partly responsible for the increase in violence in a society— especially since it also makes it appear that the only respectable lifestyle is one that a few people can afford only by engaging in criminal activity (and others by going into debt). This is already true of advertising for harmless things. But when advertising promotes harmful things such as cigarettes, then it is clear that it has at least a partial responsibility for the illnesses that afflict those who began smoking in their youth. Advertising can

---

132. (1991), 25.

hardly be entirely without effects, for then so much would not be spent on it. In this case, a change in liability law could be considerably more fruitful than the use of detailed environmental regulations.

But even if the property rights of future generations are acknowledged and if extensive controls on externalities are imposed, the market can still lead only to a structure in which people who satisfy more needs for goods with higher marginal utility—which must be sharply distinguished from total utility—and who are more talented in bargaining (which is not always an attractive quality) receive greater rewards. On one hand, this is just, for a person's own economic rights of disposal should depend on how far he shows himself to be useful to others. The market rightly does not reward efforts that do nothing for anyone; and compared with rights to disposal that are based on gifts or inheritances, for instance, those that are produced by the market should in general be regarded as the result of *achievement*. Accidents that themselves have nothing to do with achievement in the broadest sense of the term also play a role in profits—think of windfall profits; however, the profits of a dynamic entrepreneur should be regarded as the equivalent of an achievement. On the other hand, in the economy, the achievement concerned is of a special kind. First of all, it is compatible with good luck in the sense of an undeserved accident. A fashion model with a good figure satisfies the needs of millions, although the attractiveness of her body is in large part a gift of nature; but one can say much the same of intellectual gifts and perhaps even of a demonic will to work. Certainly there are certain achievements to which one can rise through hard work, but this is not possible in other cases, and the economic advantages derived from them are therefore easily perceived as unjust. At least, it will be conceded that heavier taxation of such achievements, and especially of windfall profits, would be less counterproductive than increasing taxes on achievements based on hard work, because if the problem of distinguishing between the two could be solved, higher taxes would hardly lead to a decline in an activity not seen as demanding. Furthermore it is obvious that those who are favored by the market in this way have a special moral duty to be generous to the least advantaged and to coming generations. Thus they can transform their good luck into an act of their own, as it were, and thereby prove their gratitude to fate, on one hand, and regain their autonomy, on the other—for the mysterious gift of a talent can, like any ungrounded gift, be felt to be a peculiar form of humiliation.[133] Among the forms of generosity, foundations are particularly noteworthy, because they constitute a fascinating intermediate area between private and public. On one hand, they arise from private successes, and on the other, they serve the common good, in forms that are marked by the concrete experiences of the donor and that can range from quite particular to the most sublime tasks. As the still-existing endowments from the Middle Ages show, they can be a way to achieve perpetuity among human beings that is otherwise granted only to creative individuals.

---

133. This argument pursues further an idea of Schweitzer's (1932; 70).

Second, the needs whose satisfaction the market rewards are the factually existing ones, and can be of the most ordinary kind. A fashion model's appearance will usually please more people than the most important philosophical discovery or the most noble act of individual charity; this can be seen by examining the bank balances of the people concerned, about which those who make these profits possible by buying the corresponding magazines have no right to complain. But the dignity of intellectual or moral activity is shown precisely by the fact that it is not motivated primarily by economic concerns, and it is pure envy that waxes indignant over the success of those who are guided by the more primitive needs of consumers. Moreover, in a market society there is also, for instance, the possibility of making great *works of art* palatable. Very wealthy people often develop peculiar needs in order to distinguish themselves from others, and the art market shows at what exorbitant prices even mediocre products by charlatans are sold. And that is precisely the problem: after the decline of an aristocracy with a certain taste there is no guarantee that really good works of art will succeed in the market; in fact, it is even unlikely, since creative abilities are seldom accompanied by marketing abilities— a divergence that produces the whole tribe of gallery owners, middlemen, and agents. Later generations' legitimate interest in great art—which satisfies higher needs, strengthens moral feelings, and fortifies the collective identity of a community that has developed historically—justifies state support of the arts as well as a state cultural policy (which intersects with policy concerning construction projects, among other things), insofar as the people responsible for it proceed in accord with criteria that can be rationally grounded. What these criteria are cannot be discussed here; for the most part, the conservation of the great art of the past is uncontroversial, since the aesthetic value of a work is easier to recognize later on. Schiller's aesthetics still remains one of the best foundations for a justification of state support for art, because Schiller, recognizing its autonomy, attributes to art a mediating role between moral reason and sensuousness, which is of great importance for motivating people to moral action. It is true that in the meantime, a revolution in art has taken place that has relativized to a large extent Schiller's concept of art; but with regard to modern art one can argue that the capacity for a critical perception of the reality in which man lives is morally and politically relevant.

In addition to the argument that great art contributes to a public good, namely the mores of a community, or is itself such a good (for instance, a beautiful public square), there is the further argument that art is, according to R. A. Musgrave's concept, a meritorious good, that is, one with an intrinsic value that goes beyond what people are usually prepared to pay for it. The assumption of the existence of meritorious goods is plausible, precisely on the basis of a substantive value ethics: not all needs have equal rights. But this assumption is never a sufficient argument for state promotion of the arts, because it must in addition be shown that this kind of promotion discovers meritorious goods, that is, truly great art, sooner than the market does. This can be the case, but it is not necessarily so; if the state cultural bureaucracy is in the hands of people who are selected primarily because of their party membership, it is even very improbable that they will have better taste than the market, which is more pluralistic by nature. If a society

has been convinced that there are not immanent aesthetic criteria and that even indirectly, art has nothing to do with the moral foundations of a community, then a qualified
protection of artistic freedom that goes beyond that of the usual freedom of opinion (as
in the German Basic Law) makes no sense, and taxing those who are not interested in
art for the purpose of promoting the arts is illegitimate and merely a form of social policy
with excessive rates; in such a case, the whole sphere of art should be left to the market,
in whose niches something substantial has at least a chance of surviving. Naturally, more
important works will then be honored more than popular works and mediocre ones
only in exceptional cases; but one must be satisfied with this. The world of economics
is not the most sublime sphere of reality, and insofar as the basic needs of everyone
are met, one has to accept with equanimity the inequalities that result from the market.
However, this equanimity may change into anger if economic success becomes the criterion of nearness to God, for this attitude is nefarious.[134]

Egoism should have its place in the system of the social, for human beings are first
of all *I*'s, and even taking care of others is taking care of *I*'s; and since people know their
own needs best, all other things being equal, people should take care of themselves
rather than others. But if it is to be legitimate, egoism must be limited by the obligations of justice and a sense of responsibility for colleagues, customers, and all those affected by one's activity; and if the cult of the most uninhibited egoism is celebrated as
the condition for the flourishing of the market, then the market will eventually break
down as a result of general corruption. The feeling of the honor of one's profession
(which often accompanies life-long membership in a self-governing professional group
that can sometimes impose painful negative sanctions) long maintained certain limitations on the individual striving for profit that were rooted in traditional mores. The corrosion of this feeling and the rapid transformation of the modern world, which, on one
hand, made many of the old mores seem no longer to be in the interest of the general
good and, on the other, increased social and professional mobility, have led, in addition,
not only to the diverse professional ethics in which the modern need for argumentation
is combined with the concrete practice of a particular economic activity in ways that
vary from profession to profession, but also to the programmatic formulation of "corporate identities" through which worldwide enterprises seek to construct within themselves a collective identity and solidarity that spans the class differences between those
working in it. Forms of co-determination (especially within work units) can contribute
to this identity and solidarity, as can employee participation in the enterprise's assets
(which is to be promoted in the case of privatization). Long-term planning in business
firms will take place only if the amount of the annual dividend payments is not the decisive criterion of success, but instead the board of directors and the employees identify
with goals of the firm that extend over greater periods of time. In any case, it is clear

---

134. Only in economic situations in which hard work is a moral duty, namely in order to
put a society in a position to satisfy basic needs, can legally earned wealth be an index of a higher
moral value.

that although the sphere of the economy as a whole is part of the social type of a society, in individual enterprises experiences of community must be possible if people are to be happy—even if only the economy is supposed to flourish.[135]

7.3.3.2.2. *The State and Religions*

We have now approached ideas about the moral principles that sustain the market. These principles are a very special commodity—because only they allow us to evaluate commodities, and indeed the forms of economic activity and the social world. These principles rise above the world of society but are at the same time part of society. We have already encountered this complementary structure in chapter 2.1.2; it forces us to subsume under society what Hegel called "absolute spirit," a sphere that must conclude a complete system of philosophy, since in the framework of natural law what is outside the state must be considered as preceding the state. Certainly the state can and must seek its ultimate justification in religion (in the broad sense of the word, that is, including philosophy), but at the same time it must reduce all concrete religions to the sphere of society if the idea of an established state church is to be avoided.

However, this idea must be avoided for two reasons. First, *religious freedom* is an absolute basic right. This would still be valid even if a religion could be proven to be the true one. From positive religious freedom follows the right to free exercise of worship, insofar as the latter does not infringe upon the basic rights of others or even on one's own: religions whose members make it a duty to murder others or to commit collective suicide, who sell themselves into intellectual slavery, as it were, or reject the basic principles of natural law liberalism, may however be prohibited; and even contesting general duties of the citizen, such as paying taxes, need not be accepted. (If one uses a broader concept of religion, one can therefore say that religious freedom cannot be absolute, because the civic religion of natural law must remain superior to the other religions.) Even tolerance for religions that would not tolerate other religions if their members were to have state power in their hands is in no way a natural law duty, and in some cases it is even an irresponsible betrayal of those who cling to the idea of tolerance. There can certainly be cases, however, in which generosity toward an innocuous minority is reasonable, because it contributes to this minority's intellectual opening-up and integration into a pluralistic society. Negative religious freedom implies, for instance, that no one be compelled to listen to polemical sermons (or perhaps, to see in public spaces symbols that stand for a specific religion). The right to proselytize also follows from the freedom of religion and can be restricted only where criticism of the dominant religion would necessarily cause the collapse of a culture. It is self-evident that it goes against freedom of religion when officials or the head of state alone must belong to a specific religion or denomination.

---

135. On business ethics, see K. M. Leisinger (1997).

Second, it can hardly be denied that no single religion can claim a monopoly on truth. Christianity may have a special affinity with the idea of basic rights founded in natural law, and therefore be more appropriate as the religion of a state that understands itself as a realization of natural law; but there is a great deal in Christianity that has no necessary connection with that idea, and therefore cannot be interpreted as an ideological presupposition of the natural law state. Someone who denies the Virgin Birth is not necessarily an opponent of natural law; in general, criticism of religion is a presupposition for intellectual progress and often for moral progress as well. The denominational schism at the beginning of the modern age for the first time opened up a larger scope of action for the state. Often enough, Christianity (not to mention other religions) has resisted changes that follow from the idea of natural law as well as from scientific knowledge; and unfortunately even in Europe the era when religious hatred endangers the carrying out of the state's most elementary task, that of ensuring internal peace, is not yet over forever.

In chapter 6.1.2.5, we have also seen that there is much to be said from both sides against a direct identification of the state and religion. In fact, the example of the United States splendidly demonstrates that even a clear *separation of church and state*, if it does not arise from hatred (as it did in France in 1905), can be in the interest of both parties, and does not present an obstacle to a social presence of religion. Religion often does not have a sense for instrumental rationality in politics and the indispensability of power struggles; on the other hand, a state that directly subordinates to itself the creators of legitimation may have an advantage in the short run, but in the long run it undermines its social legitimacy—for an extorted or even a purchased justification is not particularly credible. The same also holds for science and philosophy. The wish to become an official philosophical advisor for politics, or even perhaps the head of a special ministry that produces legitimating expert knowledge, may be understandable, but it is not prudent. For such certificates would be worth nothing if the authority of the philosopher who wrote them was recognized only because he held the office of state philosopher. That authority, which is never a guarantee of truth, can be earned only in society; it cannot be prescribed by the state.

And yet all this does not mean that the state should be indifferent to the sphere of religion. This would be nothing less than suicidal. A state composed of devils cannot function, and therefore institutions that give the state the moral force without which the society would dissolve are indispensable. One of these institutions can be art: Damon even thought that the style of music is never disturbed without the most important political laws being disturbed as well.[136] But the systems that communicate to human beings the conviction that natural law is to be respected not only because of its utility, but because of its sacredness as well, are even necessary for survival, because they alone create the basic trust that overcomes prisoners' dilemma situations—consider

136. Plato, *Republic* 424c.

the meal of brotherhood that is common to so many religions and that confers the feeling of participating in a divine substance transcending the individual and thereby binding to others. Although neither that conviction, nor especially any of the many conceivable concrete forms in which it may be communicated, may be coerced,[137] the state can and should use its other means of power to support these systems. Even if the moral ideas of a given religion contradict the demands of natural law on certain points, one should carefully consider whether the religion's respect for the sacredness of the other elements of natural law does not make up for this lack. A so-called culture struggle (*Kulturkampf*) whose end result is a society of calculating egoists should be avoided even if a religious community shows a lack of understanding regarding a few less essential demands of natural law. A religious community should be largely left to manage its own internal legal organization. Perhaps it is even in the interest of the separation of powers if in a democratic state with a monopoly on the use of force there are extra-state institutions that have certain elements of aristocracy and elected monarchy, so far as these presuppose relevant objective achievements and do not contradict universalist principles, for they make more difficult the triumph of mere majority opinion, which not only has no guarantee of truth, but can also represent a dangerous threat to the rights of minorities. The organizational principles of the Catholic church, for instance, may under no circumstances be transferred to constitutional law, but it takes no special acumen to predict that a thorough democratization of the Catholic church would limit the multitude of ideas in modern societies more than is already the case without it. From the sociology of knowledge's insight that certain social systems favor certain convictions, it follows that a multiplicity of organizational principles promotes intellectual pluralism. However, the framework of the whole social system must correspond to the principles of natural constitutional law; thus membership in a church must obviously be based on the individual's free choice.

The idea of the social role of religions being replaced by *philosophy* is illusory, because the majority of people have neither the gift nor the time indispensable for studying philosophy in a fruitful way, and because there is consequently no reason to assume that philosophy would produce a more comprehensive consensus than religions, even if there were stringent arguments for a *single* philosophy. The idea is also false because what matters for the state is not that there be good talk, but good action, and because the acquisition of virtues has much more to do with early childhood experiences and the reformation of emotions than with the study of ethical arguments, which is not necessarily accompanied by an exemplary way of life. Certainly the extent to which religions are accessible to philosophical comprehension and even encourage it is a crucial criterion in evaluating them; but that is not the same thing as the replaceability thesis. Formulating a

---

137. Even the prohibition of working on Sunday cannot be justified on religious grounds at least in a society that includes many non-Christians and in which most Christians also pursue non-religious leisure activities on Sundays.

prudent policy regarding philosophy is one of the state's most important tasks in a post-Enlightenment period; but it can neither be conceived as an alternative to a policy regarding religions nor consist in the establishment of a state monopoly on philosophy.

Thus it is certainly sensible for schools to provide instruction that communicates the basic values of the constitutional state governed by law and endows them with a religious foundation. To entrust this instruction solely to private provision could be reckless, because the constitutional state needs a kind of civic religion that is more or less closely approximated by the individual religions. Obviously, instruction in a specific religion cannot be prescribed; instead, it is one of the state's tasks to guarantee free state instruction in *all* religions that have communities with a significant number of members. On one hand this follows from the principle of equal treatment for all religions, and on the other, it guarantees the state the possibility of participating with the religious communities in the supervision of instruction. Obviously, this supervision cannot concern the dogmatic differences between individual religions, but rather the moral ideas that influence the attitude toward the constitutional state. In a pluralistic state, it is imperative that worldviews that are non-religious (in the narrower sense) be presented on an equal footing with religions; they are subject to the same supervision with regard to their compatibility with the principles of the state as are the religious communities, and it is not clear that a Nietzschean nihilism would do any better in this respect than Buddhism, for instance. At a higher level of education, the state should certainly provide means of influence for the philosophical orientations that have won respect in the society and in science, and that at the same time have a special affinity with the principles of the constitutional state, even if their influence will be great only if they at the same time retain their independence.

The means that the state should use to promote religions and moral ways of life are of various kinds. Using criminal law to protect symbols of religions and worldviews against attacks is conceivable, unlike the punishment of blasphemy, but it is by far not the most important action to be taken. Other important means are, for instance, creating legal forms such as granting a public corporation, under certain circumstances, even the right to tax its own members (grounds of social justice favor this, while theological grounds speak against it); recognizing, in the public law concerning church-state relations, the special tasks of the churches, for instance in the area of education and the healthcare system; granting tax advantages for support and direct promotion of religious communities' activities that are useful to all, which are often less expensive than the corresponding state activities because of the greater commitment of the religious communities' members; considering and giving more importance to the participation of religious committees in the process of state decision making; limiting social developments that necessarily result in the corrosion of a society's religious and moral feelings; distinguishing and granting prizes to individuals who live in a morally exemplary way—for instance, those who do volunteer work for good causes; and finally, politicians' openly acknowledging their own moral and religious bonds, while at the same time proving their respect for religions to which they do not themselves belong. However, it is clear that the sovereignty of the state with regard to the society also includes the churches. To be sure, a church representative, like any other person, can arrive after conscientious examination at the conclusion that the state's law is unjust and that resistance to it is justified, indeed morally obligatory. But he must be able to pay the price of this resistance just like anyone else.

The recognition that religious communities play a special role for the state does not entail a surrender of the basic liberal principle that convictions may not be subject to any coercion. This principle must not be questioned, even if it implies that "the free, secularized state . . . [lives on] presuppositions that it cannot itself guarantee."[138] This recognition implies only a rejection of the idea that the state's tasks are limited to the use of means of coercion. It is characteristic that Mill, who in *On Liberty* argued for a radical limitation of the state power to punish, recognizes in *Considerations on Representative Government* that "the most important point of excellence which any form of government can possess is to promote the virtue and intelligence of the people themselves."[139] Doesn't this reference to virtue contradict the ideas in the earlier essay? That would be the case only if one conceived punishment solely as a way of promoting virtue.[140] Religions are, if not the sole means of promoting moral behavior, certainly one of the strongest means of doing so, even if Mill would probably not have granted this. They make it possible to feel the absoluteness of the moral law, of which natural law is a subset, even if it remains the task of philosophy and the sciences to give this feeling concrete form in the system of the law of reason and the most expedient norms. It is precisely the social question that shows the enormous importance of religions. One can imagine a world in which everyone's basic physical needs were met on the basis of efficient production and just distribution. But it would be rather naive to think that in such a society people would also be happy. Human beings do not live on bread alone, and therefore in a society in which no one has learned to show other people that he loves them—and the latter is hardly possible without a culture of renunciation—the deepest frustrations inevitably result. However, this result will sooner or later change into an aggressivity compared with which the aggressivity found in archaic cultures will seem innocuous; in the latter, ritualized, bloody sacrifices maintained, in a barbaric way, the idea that the meaning of human life is not exhausted by pleasure.

---

138. E.-W. Böckenförde (1976), 60.

139. (1972), 193.

140. One of the more interesting debates in the German parliament was ignited in 1980–1981 precisely by the question, crucial for all modern democracies, of a "spiritual and moral leadership" role for politics, whose necessity was supported by the then leader of the opposition, Helmut Kohl, and whose possibility was denied by the chancellor, Helmut Schmidt. On this debate, see J. Rüttgers (1993), 116 ff.

7.3.3.3. Principles of Constitutional Law

The state is the institution with the greatest potential for realizing that which is objectively right, and constitutional law is the fulfillment of the idea of law. In the latter natural law catches up with itself, so to speak, because the former establishes the secondary norms in accord with which the positivization of natural law has to take place, and without which it cannot achieve social effectiveness. That natural law become positive law and that in order to identify the latter the sources of law be unambiguously defined is an obligation of natural law itself, for otherwise the unity and sovereignty of the state cannot be maintained. But conversely, this means, on grounds of consistency, that positive law must avoid as far as possible contradicting natural law: it should be just and expedient. One of the criteria for a rational constitutional law is how far it contributes to establishing just and expedient law. In addition, there are immanent criteria for the justice of constitutional norms that differ from those already mentioned. The existence of these two types of criteria, which is rooted in the difference between intrinsic and extrinsic value, is not peculiar to constitutional law; however, it is a specific difference that the *expediency* of constitutional norms is related to, among other things, how far this constitutional law makes the establishment of *just* laws probable. It is true that one can also ask how far a private legal order can provide the foundation for a just (e.g., democratic) constitutional law. But this dependency is social and therefore more or less relative, whereas the inverse interdependency is a legal one that can be evaded only by breaking the law. A person who dominates constitutional law dominates law as a whole; therefore the greatest care is appropriate in regulating it.

The following remarks are thematically close to the theory of the state set forth in chapter 6.1.3, which, however, was purely descriptive or was limited to the proposal of instrumentally rational norms such as those of organizational law. In the following, it will be a question of the normative evaluation of a few of the countless historically realized forms of the elements of the state on the basis of natural constitutional law principles.

7.3.3.3.1. *The Problem of the State Form*

The first decision involved in elaborating constitutional law concerns the question who should have political rights. There is no doubt that on universalist bases the answer must be "everyone." The government of a people in the sense of the *genitivus objectivus* should not be solely a government for the people, but also a government of the people, in the sense of the *genitivus subjectivus*—a government by the people—partly because each individual's feeling that he can participate in decision making can lead to a special commitment to the common good, and partly on grounds of justice. But it is just as certain that natural constitutional law cannot be reduced to this simple answer. First of all, it is not so easy to decide whom the word "everyone" should include. Up to now, children have not enjoyed direct political rights in any state (even in hereditary monarchies, the rights of a head of state who is still a minor are assumed by a regent), not to mention future generations. Is this limitation sensible, and if so, why? Perhaps because children are not yet able to decide what is best for them? If this is a valid argument, why should it not be applied to certain adults? Second, it goes without saying that no political system can count on unanimous decisions made by all those entitled to vote; it would quickly dissolve, and in fact could not even be said to exercise domination, the forms of which include state power. Thus a form of the majority rule principle is inevitable, and that of a simple majority is often the most practical. (A principle of minority rule is obviously absurd; in addition, through strategic voting it would end up being a principle of majority rule.) The principle of majority rule—no matter how qualified—means, however, a partial disempowerment of those who are outvoted. To be sure, they have participated in the voting; but if they have been outvoted on the crucial issues, this is a poor consolation. Third, it has already been pointed out that because of the relevant state organs' power over all law, constitutional law should be subject to restrictions that do not permit the violation of natural law. A reasonable constitutional law should lead to reasonable laws and to a just politics, and there may very well be situations in which the rule of the majority does not guarantee this. In hardly any other area of the law does natural law have to deal with conditional obligations as it does in the area of constitutional law. Whereas the violation of elementary rights to freedom from interference is permissible only for the sake of other rights to freedom from interference, the restriction of democratic rights can be justified if the social conditions that a democracy needs in order to succeed do not obtain—so long as every effort is made to produce those conditions. (I will come back to this in chapter 8.1.4).

However, it is clear that even the greatest intelligence in constitutional law can always think up only institutions that reduce the possibility of an abuse of power (a form of which is the neglect of the duties assumed along with an office); the abuse of power can never be eliminated entirely. Institutions are sustained by human beings, and just as even poor institutions can benefit the community through a good holder of the office, so the best institutions can lead to catastrophe if they fall into the hands of the wrong people. The Weimar Constitution was not a good constitution, but it was not worse than most of the previous constitutions of the German states; nonetheless, only it made possible the legal seizure of power by the greatest criminal in the history of mankind. Through the educational system, the state can have a certain influence on the shaping of people, the spirit of the nation, its ethical life and its mores, but it can always do so only within certain limits. In any case, these possibilities of influence must be taken into account in evaluating a state form. Therefore Mill rightly mentions two criteria that are to be considered in evaluating many political institutions: "A government is to be judged by its action upon men, and by its action upon things; by what it makes of the citizens, and what it does with them; its tendency to improve or deteriorate the people themselves, and the goodness or badness of the work it performs for them, and by means of them. Government is at once a great influence acting on the human mind, and a set of organized arrangements for public business: in the first capacity its beneficial action is chiefly indirect, but not therefore less vital, while its mischievous action may be direct."[141]

From what has been said up to this point, at least three conclusions may be drawn. First, at a certain degree of maturity of the population, the just form of the state should be a *democracy*. This means that as far as possible, the whole citizenry should have political rights; indeed, it should constitute the fundamental organ entitled to constitute other organs: This follows on one hand from the postulate of universalizability, and on the other from the fact that democratic institutions can contribute to a special expansion of the feeling of responsibility for the common good and to the protection of pre-political basic rights. It should also be demanded that extensive opportunities for differentiation be allowed in voting, insofar as they are not too impractical. The exclusion of children from the enfranchised citizenry is understandable but far more problematic than the temporary loss of political rights by prisoners convicted of crimes. It is unacceptable when the duty to perform military service begins before the voting age, because this means that someone can be forced to risk his life in a war that is the result of a policy for which he cannot have the slightest responsibility. It is true that this possibility also arises otherwise, because someone can be outvoted, or because the policy leading to the war can have been introduced, or the declaration of war taken place, before the first time he was able to vote in an election, but in all these cases he has at least the opportunity to oppose as a citizen the measures with which he disagrees. Someone who is mature enough to fight must also be mature enough to vote and to be taken seriously as a citizen. Since for obvious reasons directly guaranteeing children the right to vote is not a possibility, there seem to be two solutions to this problem. A conceivable suggestion is to entrust the child's vote to his parents (and that of adults placed under the control of a guardian to their nearest relatives), since the parents can also assume the child's other rights; parents of minor children would thus be given additional voting rights, which would lead to a plural voting system. It can be argued against this option that the administration of children's money by their parents is subject to state supervision; this kind of supervision is not possible in the case of voting, if the people is to be the primary organ entitled to constitute other organs. Furthermore, it is not clear why only children who have already been born (or conceived) should be represented, and not also future generations, if they also have (conditional) rights. A truly comprehensive representation should also allow them to have their say, though of course this would have to happen through representatives that they could not have elected themselves. Only a constitutional law counterpart of the civil law figure of the guardian can represent their legitimate future interests. The demand for such an institution cannot be seen as an attack on the basic idea of democracy, but rather as an extension of the universalizing tendency that has found expression in modern democracy. Certainly, such an organ must ultimately be grounded in the already existing enfranchised citizenry,

---

141. (1972), 195.

but through several intermediary steps that will prevent its addition from being redundant. (I will come back to this in chapter 7.3.3.3.4.) Not incompatible with the basic idea of a formal universalism is the restriction of voting rights on certain issues to those who are directly affected by the decision to be made. Thus there is an unmistakable spark of justice in the correlation between the right to vote and the duty to perform military service found in some ancient polities, insofar as the decisions to be made had mostly to do with foreign policy. (However, it is no more than a spark, since wars also affect women, for instance.) Analogously, a plural voting system would be worth considering when decisions have very long-term effects—a system favoring young people, who will in all probability be affected by them for a considerably longer time. This would be an interesting turnabout of the historically realized gerontocracies, which were based on the argument that the elderly had greater experience and wisdom.

This last argument is one of many that were adduced until well into the twentieth century to justify restricting the universality and especially the equality of voting rights on paternalistic grounds (by Mill, for instance). According to this conception, unequal abilities justify—and are ultimately even in the interest of those thereby excluded or disadvantaged—unequal political rights, the relevant inequality being discerned in physical characteristics such as age or sex, or in social differences such as education, income, or property. The first group of characteristics, which were interpreted, on the basis of false empirical assumptions, as indices of more intellectual characteristics, is not worth confuting. Even economic abilities, not to speak of inherited wealth, are not criteria for greater responsibility for the common good, and there are grounds for suspecting that in such a system the recognition of universal basic social rights would be prevented by the more wealthy. Only in the case of voluntary organizations that are concerned primarily with the distribution of money may it be just to make voting rights proportional to the amount paid in; but the state is not that kind of organization, because it has coercive power. Only the criterion of education holds water. However, it is first of all difficult to measure; second, it does not exclude malice and sometimes stupidity as well; third, only very great differences in education, such as hardly exist in modern societies, could count. Moreover, there would be no relationship between the offense to people's feelings that is involved in any plural voting system and that makes its abolition irreversible, on one hand, and the quite narrow differences in the outcome of voting, on the other. However, it is correct that eligibility for some positions can be made dependent on qualifications. Certain offices, such as judgeships, even in a "political" court such as the federal constitutional court, presuppose legal studies; much the same goes for the bureaucracy, and it seems in no way absurd to suggest that the head of a department ought to have some of the objective knowledge of his subordinates. Tiered age limits for eligibility for certain offices are found in many constitutions; they can be justified only if one assumes that certain intellectual, moral, and volitive abilities increase with age.

The likelihood that those who are most just and most capable with regard to knowledge and carrying out actions for the common good will attain positions of responsibility is, in addition to the democratic principle, a second important criterion in justifying a political system. It could be called the *"aristocratic-elite"* criterion; it limits the democratic idea, but it is not fundamentally incompatible with it. On the contrary, in a good democracy there is a greater chance that the best people will be dominant than in an oligarchy of birth. In this sense, true democracy should be an aristocracy. In a democracy, few things are more important than the maintenance and promotion of the endeavor and the ability to recognize and acknowledge the most qualified people; no vice poses a greater threat to the success of democracy than envy, just as no vice more greatly undermined the legitimacy of the aristocracies of birth than arrogance.[142] Only if a culture of appropriate self-assessment, acknowledgment of moral and intellectual authorities, and admiration for exemplary persons is cultivated is it possible to diminish the number of power struggles that must otherwise necessarily be greater in a universalist democracy than in an aristocracy of birth, because in the former there are more competitors, and only in this way can the development of a mediocratic politics of the smallest common denominator be avoided. Plato and Al-Farabi never understood the greatness of the democratic state form, but there is much to be learned from their criticism of it that should be taken into account precisely by those who are dedicated to this state form. For like all state forms, it is also threatened by decay, and only conscious moral and intellectual efforts to rationally aristocratize it can protect it against decay. Since moreover, as we will see, there is much to be said for a monocratic executive power, the constitution demanded by natural law can be seen as a mixed constitution.

The third criterion concerns the *prevention of the abuse of power,* which is a terrible danger for an institution with a monopoly on force. This means, for instance, protecting the rights of minorities, which is particularly urgent when the state population is not sufficiently homogeneous, because in this case a situation easily arises in which a certain group is always (and not, as it would be otherwise, only sometimes) outvoted, if it does not have guaranteed rights to have a say or even a veto right in the parliament, the administration, and the bureaucracy. Given man's nature and the nature of his striving for power, this point of view is the most crucial; therefore, in choosing between a democracy without separation of powers and a politically liberal system without full democracy, one should not hesitate for a moment to elect the latter, insofar as the mechanisms of the separation of powers do not cancel the state's ability to act and its sovereignty with respect to society. Fortunately, the democratic and liberal principles are mutually compatible, albeit not without concessions—thus the number of decisions to be made democratically must be limited for the sake of the separation of powers. In no case is it possible to reduce one principle to the other. They are both rooted in natural law liberalism, that is, in the idea that all human beings have certain basic rights. These basic rights include political rights, which must not, however, present a danger to pre-political basic rights: both of them to-

---

142. Cf. Hamilton and Madison, *Federalist* 57 (1787 f.; 289): "The aim of every political Constitution is or ought to be first to obtain for rulers, men who possess most wisdom to discern, and most virtue to pursue the common good of the society; and in the next place, to take the most effectual precautions for keeping them virtuous, whilst they continue to hold their public trust."

gether lead to a democracy with separation of powers. It is one of the most dangerous errors of our time to think that the limitation of absolute democracy by means of the mechanisms of the separation of powers exists by the grace of this absolute democracy; that it is just, for instance, because a constitution was adopted by majority vote that grants a court supervisory control over the legislative branch. For that would mean that a majority vote could repeal the mechanisms of the separation of powers. One can concede that many another institution is legitimated by the majority: the occupation of the office of head of state by a hereditary monarch in fact exists by the grace of democracy and not by the grace of God. Certainly the specific arguments for and against hereditary monarchy are not reasonable because a majority considers them so; but it is in any case rational that the (under certain conditions qualified) majority should make the ultimate decision regarding the validity of those arguments, and thus regarding the possible abolition of the monarchy. However, this in no way holds for the question of the separation of powers.

The thesis that the establishment of liberal democracy leads to a cultural decline because the greatest intellectual achievements are hardly conceivable without an aristocratic consciousness has been defended again and again at least since Tocqueville, and with special emphasis by Nietzsche, who sharpened it into a negation of universalist ethics. This is not the place to examine this thesis more closely, and I will limit myself to two observations. First, even if it were true, it could not be a morally relevant argument against modern democracy, since justice is a far more central task of the state than is the promotion of culture. There is no doubt that slavery would be too high a price to pay for the recovery of Greek tragedy, even if hardly anything can produce such sublime aesthetic experiences as the enjoyment of those works of art. Second, a liberal democracy certainly has room for great achievements. It may be that such achievements have less chance of winning general recognition, but geniuses find niches even in an egalitarian society, at least to the extent that they have the strength to resist the pressure to adapt to the average. If they do not have this strength, then they should complain, not about democracy, but rather about themselves.

7.3.3.3.2. *The Special Status of Constitutional Norms*

It is a direct expression of the limits of the democratic principle that constitutional norms often cannot be changed by a simple majority, and that in some constitutions a few norms are considered absolutely inalterable.[143] Is this sensible? On the basis of the

---

143. For instance, Articles 1 and 20 in the German Basic Law (according to Article 79 III). Cf. also Article 139 of the Italian Constitution, concerning the inalterability of the republican state form. The American Constitution, in which the mechanisms for amending the constitution are more complex than in most other constitutions, declared in Article 5 only two provisions to be inalterable for a limited length of time (until 1808); furthermore, it says that no member state may be deprived, "without its consent," of equal suffrage in the Senate. This is a weaker guarantee than that provided by the corresponding articles in the German and Italian constitutions.

principle of majority rule, the question can be answered only in the negative; it is not without good reason that in Great Britain, a country without a written constitution, constitutional scholars debate whether the parliament may pass a statute that limits the omnipotence of the parliament, and stipulates that from that point on, certain norms may be changed only by a qualified majority.[144] For if such a statute were passed by a simple majority, then a simple majority would subject later majorities to the domination of a minority, which seems to fly in the face of formal principles of justice. The situation would not be fundamentally different if a law requiring a two-thirds majority (of the members) for amending certain norms were itself passed by a two-thirds majority. Indeed, during that same parliamentary term no sufficient number of members of parliament could complain about no longer being able to repeal these norms by a simple majority, for at least a third of them would have themselves agreed to this limitation on their power. But with what right can they limit the power of later parliaments? (Analogous problems would arise if it were not the parliament but the people who were voting.) Particularly after a generational change (and good constitutions are constructed to last several generations) it seems outrageous, on the basis of the principle of majority rule, that the will of the dead should be able to hem in later majorities, or—as in the case of "eternity clauses"—even prevent future *unanimous* decisions from being legally valid. Is it not a self-evident principle that no generation should be able to deprive a future generation of its freedom?[145] However, it is worthwhile to reread this statement, for it may well be performatively self-contradictory. It applies to *all* generations, and that means that it denies other generations certain rights. To be sure, what is involved here is the right to restrict the rights of other generations; but if one had the right to establish this proposition, could one not also say that no individual or group of people, and thus no future generation, has the right to violate any person's basic freedoms? And is a restriction imposed on future generations not permissible if it consists precisely in forbidding the violation of any person's fundamental rights? Of course, an affirmative answer to this question presupposes that we have a suprahistorical claim to truth that allows us to know what fundamental rights are, for otherwise we could not exclude the possibility that in the future it might be rightly acknowledged that simple majorities have a fundamental right to persecute minorities in any way that pleases them.

This defense of requiring a qualified majority to change a constitution agrees only in part with the arguments put forward by J. M. Buchanan and G. Tullock. Both authors transfer economic categories to the state. Thereby they seek to legitimate governmental rule by claiming that unanimity is required at the highest level; at that level, they

---

144. Hart (1961), 144 ff.; Dworkin (1978), 61 ff.

145. Cf. Article 28 of the French "Déclaration des droits de l'homme et du citoyen de l'an I," approved on 26 June 1793: "Un peuple a toujours le droit de revoir, de réformer, et de changer sa Constitution. Une génération ne peut assujétir à ses lois les générations futures" *La conquête des droits de l'homme* (1988), 73. ("A people always has the right to revise, reform, and change its constitution. One generation cannot subject future generations to its laws.")

add, it may nonetheless be decided to adopt the principle of majority rule (possibly in some cases with qualifications).[146] One reason for adopting the principle of majority rule, they argue, would be that the costs of a unanimous decision process could be higher than those of being outvoted.[147] Now, just as it would be absurd to interpret the requirement of unanimity as the rule of one individual over all others, so must we avoid interpreting the requirement of a qualified majority as the *domination* of a minority— in reality, it represents only a form of protection for minorities.[148] We can certainly concede that the conclusion drawn by these authors is correct: the need to protect the individual against the majority is the ground that legitimates requiring qualified majorities; and it would be ridiculous to equate this protection with the direct exercise of power. The individual's right to veto injustices is far from meaning that he can arbitrarily dispose of others in the way a monocrat can. However, the foundations in moral philosophy on which Buchanan and Tullock base their justification are very different from those on which this book is based. Both authors are Hobbesians; for them, the point is to justify, not the legitimate, but the factual preferences of individuals; they assume that each individual could simply break out of the social contract if he were willing to run the corresponding risks. For that reason, however, they cannot explain why, save in exceptional cases, there is a *moral* duty to obey the state; indeed, it even remains hard to understand why the founders of the state would have an interest or even a right to ensure protection for minorities after their own deaths. Ultimately, on their premises each new generation should be able to return to the state of nature and to re-negotiate the constitution, with whatever kind of protection for minorities it saw fit to provide.[149]

From what has been said, it follows that it is certainly just to include in a constitution norms that can be altered only by a qualified majority, as well as some norms that cannot be changed at all. However, these must not concern inessential matters, such as traffic regulations—only the fundamental principles of natural law, which in fact no one has the right to change, are possible candidates. Since the concrete application of these principles nonetheless depends on the situation, and since one cannot exclude the possibility that future generations might interpret them differently, such norms have to be deliberately limited to a few general propositions, such as those concerning the inviolability of human dignity and the right to life; the inviolability of the person and the home; freedom of action, opinion, religion, profession, and association; the rights to

---

146. (1965), 6 f., 249 f.

147. Cf. 62 ff., 97 ff.

148. See 259: "The distinction between the power of taking action and of blocking action proposed by others is an essential one; it represents the difference between the power *to impose external costs on others* and the power *to prevent external costs from being imposed*."

149. One could object that since according to the position being criticized each person in fact has the right to resist at his own risk, his failure to do so amounts to consent. However, in this sense every existing political constitution is based on consensus—a tautology that is not particularly enlightening. Certainly, there is behavior implying a specific intention, such as a silent "consent"; but when the alternative is violent subjection, then it is difficult to speak of "consent."

free choice of residence, to equality before the law, to marry, to own property; and finally, the right to emigrate as the final act through which the outvoted individual can escape the power of the state, provided that he can find another state that will take him
in.[150] On grounds of the systematics and pedagogy of law, it is desirable that alongside
rights the corresponding duties should be listed: property ownership, for example,
should involve social and environmental responsibilities; the duty to attend school, pay
taxes, and provide general aid (under certain conditions, the duty to perform military
or community service) should be expressly cited as the conditions of the functioning of
the state. Since the restriction of individual basic rights for the sake of other basic rights
may prove necessary, it would be desirable, even if it should not be accompanied by an
"eternity clause" declaring it to be inalterable, to draw up a hierarchy or weighting of individual rights, such as is implicitly presupposed by the *Wesengehaltsgarantie* (the guarantee of the essential content of a right) in the German Basic Law[151] (this guarantee receives little support from a philosophy that has abandoned the concept of essence).
Among natural constitutional law provisions, the principles of due process of law and
the welfare state, the separation of powers, and the democratic principle (with an institutional anchoring of the rights of future generations) should be mentioned; the principle of federal government is not on the same level, and should not be guaranteed to be
inalterable. The constitutional government must be prohibited from eliminating itself,
for example by passing an enabling act authorizing exceptional powers, and this corresponds, at the constitutional level, to the prohibition against individuals selling themselves into slavery; this is even easier to justify, since by such an act legislators would
deprive not only themselves but also their voters of their basic rights. In the case of a
plurality of states, elementary natural international law principles such as the prohibition on aggression against other countries should count among the inalterable provisions. Of course, one must be very careful in dealing with "eternity clauses"—but also
in dealing with basic rights. In any case, in weighing matters it is a reasonable rule to assign, when in doubt, a guarantee of inalterability to too few rather than to too many
norms, in order not to tempt future generations to break the law.

The status of specific provisions concerning state organs differs from that of such
general natural law principles, and for that reason they must never be protected by inalterability clauses. In their case, it is also harder to explain why any special protection
should be accorded them at all, since for example there is no a priori reason for choosing a parliamentary democracy over a presidential democracy. The protection of the
individual is not connected with this issue, as it is with basic rights. Which system is the
better will depend on circumstances that can change, and if the legislative majority

---

150. The right to leave a country does not entail a right to be accepted in another country, any
more than the right to get divorced entails a right to marry someone else against his or her will. See
B. Barry's criticism of R. E. Goodin in B. Barry and R. E. Goodin (1992).

151. Article 19 II.

can be prevented from doing the right thing by 35 percent of the legislature, this will understandably be perceived as illegitimate rule by a minority.[152] The constitution of the United States is, as the level of the argumentation in the *Federalist Papers* shows, one of the most important achievements of the political mind, and the obstacles put in the way of changing it have proven to be beneficial. But when a poor constitution can be altered only by a two-thirds vote of both houses of the legislature, this can produce even in persons of integrity a tendency to violate the constitution, if this appears to be the sole way of keeping political forces from paralyzing each other.[153] Nonetheless, even in the case of the most important positive constitutional law provisions there are grounds for making amendment difficult. The strength of the protection of such provisions should, however, be distinguished from the protection of basic rights: an "eternity clause" is out of the question, and even the requirement of a two-thirds majority for changing the provisions may be too restrictive. However, constitutional law is cratically very important, and it therefore makes sense, for example, in a constitution to set on the period of office of a national president precise limits that are difficult to change, even if there are no rational arguments against shortening or lengthening it by a year—so long as one can thus prevent it from being suddenly tripled, by a simple majority vote, which in certain situations can pave the way for tyranny. Just as general laws should not be too frequently changed because this diminishes their authority, the law on which everything else depends should, a fortiori, enjoy special stability. Patriotism with regard to the constitution, or even an understanding of the concrete interplay of state organs, cannot develop if changing majorities can constantly tinker with the constitution.

A defender of the principle of majority rule might reply that this is all very plausible—for the majority of a people or a legislature as well. In fact we cannot exclude the possibility that a legally omnipotent legislature might use its power wisely, as the British parliament, for instance, confirms (even today, however, the House of Lords and the Crown represent certain mechanisms of the separation of powers). But the question remains whether one should rely on this wisdom, or whether instead constitutions that explicitly forestall abuse of power are more reasonable. It is clear that the second alternative is preferable, because blind trust is not appropriate in matters of constitutional law. This also comes close to providing an answer to the question as to what grounds the validity of the constitution. If the latter limits the principle of majority

---

152. See Hamilton, Madison, and Jay, *Federalist* 58 (1787 f.; 298 f.).

153. The Articles of Confederation of the United States of America provided in Article XIII a guarantee of the union's perpetuity, and made agreement by the United States Congress as well as by the legislatures of every state a requirement for any alteration of the articles. Just a few years later, however, the Thirteenth and the Sixth Articles of Confederation were nonetheless violated by the Seventh Article of the proposed Constitution of the United States, according to which ratification by nine states was sufficient to put the constitution into effect.

rule, it would be self-contradictory to try to ground its validity on this same principle;[154] and even approval by a two-thirds vote would lead us back to the question raised at the outset: why should this two-thirds majority be able to impose its will on later generations in such a way that slightly more than a third of those voting can restrict the freedom of action of the rest? Nor are periodic new votes with a return to the state of nature in the event of a refusal particularly attractive. Of course this does not mean that it is not politically prudent to propose a new constitution to the people for a vote. It was a mistake to pass up this opportunity after German reunification, even if it was certainly no violation of the constitution, since the Basic Law foresaw two possibilities for the reunification, one of which was the one that was chosen (via Article 23 or via Article 146).[155] But it is not true that such a vote would have resolved the problem of the validity of the constitution in a way that was not circular or self-contradictory. This problem can be solved only if we transcend the sphere of positive law and the world of the social and rise to the level of the ideal norms of natural law, which is not valid because it is recognized, but rather must be recognized because it is valid. Showing the reasonable character of most of the norms included in a constitution, as well as of their metaphysical and ethical presuppositions, is incomparably more important for their social acceptance than a further vote or historical research into its genesis.[156]

7.3.3.3.3. The Federal Principle

In chapter 6.1.3.5, the respective advantages of centralization and decentralization were mentioned. We opted for decentralization, although with certain qualifications: even if the center should retain the right to supervise, it is important to delegate as much as possible to those immediately affected. (Admittedly, situations may occur in which primarily centralization is required, because a sense of the mechanisms of the separation of powers without detriment to a simultaneous respect for the sovereignty of the state has not yet developed.) The less the equalization of revenue and costs between the central government and the states or local authorities operates in accord with a complete

---

154. This also holds for the mode of voting used by the constituent power, especially (but not solely) when it has to decide about ratifying the constitution. In his pamphlet, Sieyès very wrongly defends the thesis that the principle of the simple majority is self-evident, and basically suggests that the constituent power needs no previous principles in accord with which to proceed, because it would constitute them itself (1970; 185). But a law-free space cannot exist, if matters are to proceed in a way that can be acknowledged—it must at least be clear how a valid agreement is supposed to come into existence. The insolubility of this problem is evident in Sieyès's contribution first to the revolutionary self-constitution of the Third Estate as the National Assembly on 17 June and to the National Constituent Assembly on 6–9 July 1789, and finally to the coup d'état of 18 Brumaire in the revolutionary year VIII (9 November 1799): Napoleon Bonaparte's military dictatorship provided the real answer to the problem related to the constituent power.

155. On this problem, see the excellent discussion by E. G. Mahrenholz (1992).

156. Cf. Hegel, *Rechtsphilosophie* §273, n. (1969 ff.; 7:439).

compound system (*totales Verbundsystem*) in which the central government receives all tax income and then distributes part of it, and the more independent financial sources subordinate bodies have, the more scope for action these bodies have. Cities and municipalities must have the right to govern themselves. Direct election of the mayor is an elementary precept of democracy. Politicians who prove themselves at the municipal level are often also well known as private individuals, and this promotes the development of the confidence that alone can provide a way out of prisoners' dilemma situations and overcome the feeling of the anonymity of politics. Although they extend beyond the family and the neighborhood, municipalities are still relatively manageable wholes— but much less, of course, the modern metropolises, whose advantages in efficiency are often lost as a result of the corrosion of the basic trust and feeling of responsibility that are easier to maintain in small groups. The federal principle represents a form of decentralization that is particularly radical because it shares out the competence of defining competencies. This principle not only suggests itself when several previously independent states unite, but is also generally commendable—at least when the state has a certain size. To encourage relationships among the member states to flourish, a federal state should consist of at least three member states. If there are only two member states, and each has equal weight in the federal organ that represents the member states, the result is likely to be a constant stalemate; and if the two states do not have equal weight in this organ, the larger member state will always be able to outvote the smaller one.

Three arguments can be given in support of the federal principle. First, it represents a form of the separation of powers, namely a *vertical separation of powers* that complements the horizontal one. Madison writes: "Hence a double security arises to the rights of the people. The different governments will controul each other; at the same time that each will be controuled by itself."[157] It is much more difficult for a polarization between the government and the opposition to develop in a federal state, because as a rule the opposition controls at least one of the member states and thus will be obliged to collaborate with the federal government. Responsibility is more equally divided between the two, and in the event of a change of government, an abrupt change of policy is less likely. The Spanish Civil War might have been prevented had the country been transformed into a federal state in the early 1930s.

The second argument concerns *regional, historically developed differences,* whose preservation is a very important task, and whose dimensions partly determine how many competencies should remain with the member states. To be sure, the rights of cultures are not of the same importance as the rights of individuals—the latter must have the right to abandon their own culture, if they discover a superior one; thus there is no doubt that the Christianization of Celtic and Germanic peoples transformed their culture, and (if we define the elusive concept of culture on the basis of religion) destroyed it. But whereas there are moral arguments for historically moving beyond certain religions—

---

157. Hamilton, Madison, and Jay, *Federalist* 51 (1787 f.; 264).

though this does not imply that religious homogeneity is the goal of history—there is no rational ground for eliminating customs that are largely indifferent from a moral point of view, and certainly not for eliminating languages. On the contrary, there are many reasons for preserving them, because all languages and many mores contain insights and values that are not to be found in others. Just as monoculture is economically foolish because, among other things, a single pest suffices to destroy, for example, the food supply, so it is absurd to pin one's hopes on a single world culture (which would most probably represent the lowest common denominator of the world's various mores), because humanity would have no chance of survival should this world culture prove to be struck by a fatal disease. Isolation is a factor that promotes biodiversity, and it also promotes cultural diversity. Thus indigenous peoples should have the right to prevent others from entering their territory. In culturally more homogeneous states, the federal principle is the appropriate constitutional mechanism for maintaining a certain isolation. The fact that over the past two or three decades Bavaria has not participated in all the mistakes in educational policy committed by other German states is not only to its advantage, but it may also show other Germans a way that would otherwise no longer be rooted in living traditions.

The third point presupposes later observations. The problem of ensuring peace cannot be definitively resolved if there is a plurality of sovereign states; therefore there is a categorical duty to work toward a *world state*. However, because of its size and because of the diversity of individual cultures, such a government will necessarily take the form of a multi-leveled federal state, and it would certainly be sensible to become familiar already at the national level with this form of organization required by historical development. This is not meant to suggest, of course, that all actually existing member states in a federal state have an intrinsic value and must be preserved. The abandonment of a federal division for the purpose of producing a more comprehensive federation may be reasonable—in this way the first ground for a federal structure would be equally satisfied, and the concessions on the second point would be more than compensated for by the progress on the third point.

The question as to how far the member states are to be regarded as being on the same footing is a morally important one. Insofar as they are seen as states, they are equal, for they are all equally states; yet since the dignity of states is based not solely, but mainly, on the rights of their individual citizens, the number of people they represent must be taken into account as well. To treat China and Liechtenstein in the same way within a worldwide federal state would be an obvious injustice. Conversely, if two or three member states with very large populations overruled by their majority many smaller member states, this would violate the principle of the preservation of diversity that the federal state is supposed to promote. A compromise between these two extremes is not easy to find, because there are no stringent arguments that allow us to determine precisely where the ideal middle ground lies; but a compromise is nonetheless indispensable.

7.3.3.3.4. *The Legislative*

Legislating is the crucial function of the state from a legal point of view, if not always from the cratic point of view. Requiring the administration and the bureaucracy to abide by the law satisfies a minimum demand of morality, namely a certain form of the postulate of universalizability: similar cases must be treated in a similar way; *ad personam* laws are not permitted; the general has priority over the individual. This achievement is guaranteed, however, only if one rejects an exclusively formal conception of law (of the kind criticized in chapter 6.1.3.7), and even this qualification does not yet exclude laws such as the Nuremberg race laws or provisions regarding slavery—for that, a constitutional *principle of the equality of all human beings* is indispensable. And even such a principle offers no guarantee against massive violations of natural law, because it is compatible with everyone being treated equally unjustly: a principle of equality will still not suffice to prevent the death penalty for theft.

Moreover, in interpreting such a principle the question arises as to what normatively relevant equality is, for unequal treatment of unequal cases would not be precluded by this principle, and rightly so (sometimes it would even be prescribed by the principle). However, since all entities, and a fortiori all persons, are equal in at least one respect (namely, insofar as they are entities or persons), and in at least one respect different (if we assume the *principium identitatis indiscernibilium*), additional arguments are always required in order to recognize in laws that are conceived relatively generally, but nonetheless cover only a specific group of people, a violation of the principle of equality. (In reality there might even be only one individual who falls within the purview of the law, without the latter necessarily being an *ad personam* law.) A law that offers tax breaks to people who build a house before a qualifying date does not violate the principle of equality if the state's interest in promoting the construction of housing continues only up to a certain point, for instance, the point at which the housing market is saturated or other tasks will take priority, and if this interest is the normative ground for the tax breaks involved. On the other hand, a law that offered such tax breaks only to people with blonde hair would violate the principle of equality, since no normative ground is conceivable for giving blondes priority. Of course, the burden of proof has to lie with those who maintain that laws resulting in unequal treatment do not violate the principle of equality.[158] In restricting basic rights and duties one would have to argue that for a given population group, the exercise of a right or the fulfillment of a duty is not possible, is not in its interest, or is not in the interest of those who would otherwise profit from the fulfillment of this duty. The principle of equality is also violated if the execution of the law leads to unequal treatment of normatively like cases, as occurs, for instance, when the wealthy have opportunities to break the law that are de facto protected from criminal prosecution.

---

158. As R. Alexy rightly points out (1985), 370 ff.

The law can be obeyed only if it is made public and thereby known. However, the main problem of modern times differs from that of archaic times. Whereas then the people did not know the law, because those in power kept it secret so that they could change it and execute it arbitrarily, today it is the abundance of legal regulations that produces for the ordinary citizen a similar obscuring effect, and that even legal experts find difficult to categorize. Of course it is naive to wish to check the flood of legislation, for the more manifold the interactions and possibilities for conflict are, the more laws are required. Nonetheless, making the laws clear and simple is a legitimate and realizable goal. Concern with trivial details is a burden on legislatures, which are thereby prevented from dealing with more essential tasks;[159] and against superfluous regulations one may also cite Montesquieu's profound insight that laws that treat as necessary what is in itself a matter of indifference have the disadvantage of soon making what is in reality necessary come to be seen as a matter of indifference.[160] The only thing still more dangerous are laws that are not respected.[161] What is crucial here is that the citizen grasp the principles that underlie the law in its manifold branches. A reading of large parts of the constitution and an explanation of the most important categories of civil and criminal law should therefore be made part of the school curriculum, at least at the higher levels. Respect for the law can result only from the insight that it is more than a means of wielding power, that it serves justice. Plato laid down the requirement that the legislator should first provide a justification of the laws;[162] anyone who deals with a law should at least be capable of deducing this justification if he is to respect it.

In its crucial areas, the legislative function must be exercised either directly by the people or by a state organ that is elected by the people and that is also responsible for the ratification of international treaties and for declarations of war. It is not easy to decide to what extent the people should have direct democratic voting rights. However, the difference between *parliamentary* and *direct* democracy is not so great as it is sometimes supposed to be, for the organ entitled to constitute other organs is the same in both systems. In a direct democracy as well, the people can decide to rely on the expertise of the legislature; and in a parliamentary democracy a party can be elected that promises to introduce the right to direct democratic participation (insofar as this is not precluded by the constitution, which would certainly be contrary to natural law). It goes without saying that in modern states with an extended territory, a parliament is indispensable. A particularly strong reason for having a parliament is that there should be a political center that continually works on certain problems and is characterized by a constant culture of discussion. But that does not by itself imply that the people should not also enjoy direct legislative rights, which, given the greater costs of direct democracy, must remain optional, except perhaps in the case of amendments to the constitu-

---

159. See E. Forsthoff (1971), 102.
160. *Esprit des lois*, 24.14 (1748; 2:149 f.).
161. See Don Quixote's wise remarks in Cervantes' novel (1994; 2:412).
162. *Laws* 719e f.

tion. Arguments for a purely parliamentary democracy usually emphasize the legislators' superior knowledge and experience; in examining the results of referenda in Switzerland, for instance, it often seems that laws proposed by the Federal Council or by the Federal Assembly would have been better than those approved by the people (for instance, the latter's repeated refusals to extend the franchise to women). Moreover, parliamentary systems tend to encourage legislators to base their political decisions not on their own interests, but rather on their own conception of the common good, because their election constituted a delegation that can strengthen the feeling of responsibility.

On the other hand, there are the following arguments in favor of providing an opportunity for referenda. In many situations legislators have also proven unable or unwilling to represent the people's legitimate needs, and in such cases a greater injustice is done an individual than when he has to atone for having done something foolish for which he is himself responsible. Moreover, in a direct democracy it is impossible to whine about "those in power." One has an indisputable co-responsibility for bad decisions, and this makes projecting the blame onto others more difficult; however, when the right decision is made, the majority of the people will support it with conviction. Nonetheless, it is clear that the element of direct democracy must be limited. It can play a role only in a system with a separation of powers that cannot itself be abolished by direct democratic means. Certain delicate questions (in foreign policy, for example) that cannot be competently decided without access to information that must remain confidential should be outside the reach of direct democracy. A constitutional court should also review laws passed in a direct democratic manner (or better yet, it should determine the constitutionality of such proposed laws before they are presented to the voters). Amendments to the constitution should have to be approved by a majority of the people *and* a majority of the legislature (in the latter case, perhaps even by a qualified majority). The number of voters required to petition an initiative to referendum should be quite high. A second, confirming vote after a year has passed might even be required before the law goes into effect—a process analogous to the basic idea of the bicameral legislature. It is important to distinguish the absolutizing of the democratic principle, such as that on which the theory of Swiss constitutional law is based, and which we have already rejected, from the issue of direct democratic rights to participation, which are certainly not a patent remedy, but are a reasonable instrument in the concert of the separation of powers. In any case, it is an unacceptable distortion of history when in the contemporary German debate the experiences of the Weimar Republic are sometimes used as arguments against referenda. They played a minor role in the Weimar constitution, and an evanescent role in its constitutional reality. The Weimar Republic was destroyed by a parliamentary system that was incapable of taking action and by antidemocratic forces.

Even when direct-democratic elements are included in a constitution, the chief legislative power must lie in the parliament, which each individual can *petition*. The principle of the separation of powers favors a bicameral system, possibly with restricted rights for the second chamber, but the two chambers must be constituted in accord with different principles if the second is not to be a superfluous obstacle (as the Italian Senate is). The political focus must be on a chamber that is elected, on the basis of universalist principles, in accord with *general* and *equal* voting rights. The *directness* of the vote is not of the same importance; but on one hand, since direct voting is more democratic, it has greater intrinsic value, and on the other hand, the long-assumed advantages of indirect voting are minimal.[163] The freedom of voting must be taken for granted, because otherwise it could just as well be abolished, and since the *secrecy* of voting contributes to its freedom, that must also be defended, especially after the terrible experiences of the twentieth century. And yet Mill's polemic against secret voting[164] is not so implausible; it is seldom the most courageous and most honorable persons who appeal to the secrecy of voting. But since such people exist, we have to grant that without secrecy the dangers to freedom would be greater. However, within a parliament there are good reasons for opposing secret votes on substantive legislative matters, because this can encourage irresponsibility. Voting by representatives of the people is a public act by which these representatives should stand, because only in this way can the voter know whether he should re-elect them.

Should *majority* or *proportional* voting be given priority? Proportional representation where the voters have no other choice than the choice of a list gives the people who draw up these lists extraordinary power; the individual candidate becomes less important than his party. This does not promote a feeling of self-worth and responsibility on the part of legislators, although it gives the voter an opportunity to vote for a comprehensive program rather than for a person about whom he often knows very little. One advantage of this system is that the seats in the legislature are proportional to the votes cast, whereas in a majority vote, a party that wins 30 percent of the votes in the whole country may not get a single seat; the individual votes as a citizen of his electoral district, not of his country. This can be detrimental to the feeling of responsibility for the whole country, and moreover, this outcome seems unfair since it makes it more difficult for minorities to gain representation and for new political forces to arise.[165] However, we must consider that proportional voting does not necessarily lead to a proportional distribution of power in the parliament. To be sure, a party that has won 6 percent of the votes gets 6 percent of the seats; but its chances of participating in the government may be just as great as those of much stronger parties, and under certain circumstances amount mathematically to a third, and in real terms even more.[166] Why? Imagine a parliament with three parties, one with 48 percent of the seats, a second with 46 percent,

163. Cf. Mill's criticism (1972), 293 ff. We would do well to keep in mind that in the original (1787) American Constitution two of the most important state organs—the Senate (until 1913) and the Presidency—were to be elected by indirect voting.

164. (1972), 298 ff. Cf. Montesquieu, *Esprit des lois* 2.2 (1748; 1:135).

165. See Mill's severe criticism of the majority voting system, which persists in his homeland to the present day: (1972), 256 ff.

166. See M. D. Davis (1983), 213 ff.

and a third with 6 percent. Since legislating and, for the most part, the forming of governments presuppose a majority, two parties are necessary, and in the three possible alliances of two parties each party is represented twice, and thus equally often; yet since a coalition of the two larger parties is inappropriate in democracies based on competition, this means that the smallest party is more likely to participate in the government than are the other two. This hardly seems just, even if the smallest party has fewer portfolios in the government than its larger partner, for its power in the cabinet remains significant, since it can constantly threaten to leave the coalition and thus bring down the government. Since one of the parliament's crucial tasks is to form a government, it must be further emphasized that a majority voting system generally leads to strong governments, because it favors a two-party system. However, if a certain threshold vote is required for representation in the legislature, the number of parties in a proportional voting system can be decreased, thereby making it easier to form governments. These threshold requirements contradict the principle of proportional voting, but can be justified on the ground that without an enduring government, no one's rights, not even those of minorities, can be protected.[167]

The most reasonable solution is probably a *mixed system* like Germany's, which is, however, closer to proportional representation than to the majority vote system. For the purpose of strengthening individual responsibility and diminishing the power of parties, *list systems with the right to cumulative vote and to panachage* (i.e., to vote for candidates from differing lists) or proportional representation with the single transferable vote are advisable. There is no reason to deprive the voter of opportunities for differentiating— he should be able to vote for the candidates in whom he has the most confidence, even against the will of the party leadership (even if this inevitably increases the power of the media favorites and thus of the media themselves), and express his preferences for a coalition by *panachage*. In voting on issues in a direct democracy, it should also be possible to give some weight to one's own acceptance or refusal.

The *quality* of legislators is far more important than their *quantity*. It was a mistake, which fortunately was later corrected, to increase the number of seats in the German parliament in proportion to the increase in population after reunification. Madison rightly points out that qualititative increases may imply qualitative changes: "Nothing can be more fallacious than to found our political calculations on arithmetical principles. Sixty or seventy men, may be more properly trusted with a given degree of power than six or seven. But it does not follow, that six or seven hundred would be proportionally a better depositary. And if we carry on the supposition to six or seven thousand, the whole reasoning ought to be reversed. . . . Had every Athenian citizen been a Socrates, every Athenian assembly would still have been a mob."[168] The number of seats in the

---

167. In addition to threshold requirements, the larger parties can be favored in the proportional voting system through the procedures for calculating seats in the legislature (for instance, d'Hondt's highest average rule, as opposed to Niemeyer's largest remainder rule).

168. *Federalist* 55 (1787 f.; 281).

parliament should not be less than is required to ensure representation of the most important interests of the society and fruitful discussion, but neither should it be so great as to prevent legislators from getting to know each other during their term of office. It would be wrong to see in this kind of limitation a danger to the principle of democracy; on the contrary, an unmanageable number of persons tends precisely to concentrate power in the hands of a small clique.[169]

Even though legislators should be familiar with affairs of state even before they are elected, they nonetheless learn many things only when they begin concrete legislative work. For this reason the legislator's *term of office* must not be too short, but also not so long that he forgets those to whom he is accountable. Even if there is no unambiguously ideal span of time between these two extremes, it is plausible that with the increasing complexity of society the term of legislative office should be lengthened. Today, the greater danger is impotence in the face of the problems to be dealt with rather than abuse of power, since more than before, public opinion controls the legislature, which should in general debate in public, and as a rule electoral campaigns lead to a decrease rather than to an increase in responsibility for the common good. Long-term projects, which always harm someone, cannot be undertaken at the end of a parliamentary term, and since at the beginning of a term expertise is still often lacking, the time in the middle is of special importance; thus it should not be too short. In addition, there should be no limit on re-election, for more complex societies are difficult to govern without professional politicians. The latter have a right to an *appropriate emolument;* denying it only favors the wealthy classes. It is also inevitable that the law providing for legislative salaries will be passed by the legislature itself; almost sovereign organs must be judges in their own cases, if an infinite regress is to be avoided. Delegating in such a law the specific determination of emoluments to an independent committee is, however, a matter of good style.

Parliamentary representation is best interpreted as a *relationship of trust,* which on one hand links the representative to his voters through periodic elections, and on the other opens up a sphere of personal responsibility, which must include the right to change parties—especially on relevant grounds, such as shift in policy on the part of the representative's own party—without this affecting the legitimacy of his claim to his seat in the legislature. (Only in a pure proportional voting system without the right to cumulative vote and to *panachage* might one see this differently.) If legislators are to be autonomous, there can be no mandate, which is compatible only with direct democracy, and of course the latter has more effective means at its disposal. It is not only possible but desirable that legislators learn something new in legislative debates, and that the knowledge acquired might influence their decisions. Furthermore, legislators are not representatives of their electoral districts, but of the whole people; and a legislator who is prepared to sacrifice the interests of his electoral district, not to mention private

---

169. Cf. *Federalist* 58 (1787 f.; 297 f.): "It is, that in all legislative assemblies, the greater the number composing them may be, the fewer will be the men who will in fact direct their proceedings."

interests, to the common good is only doing his duty. To be sure, the common good is not completely separate from particular interests; their articulation is indispensable, and an ideology is totalitarian if it turns against their articulation (in order, of course, to pursue all the more shamelessly the particular interests of the power-holders in the state, under cover of the alleged common good). But it is superstitious to believe that out of the mere collision of particular interests the common good will emerge by itself. The common good has a chance of being recognized only when a sufficient number of persons are ready to forgo their own interests for the sake of a higher interest. Even purely procedural regulations, which are supposed to preclude emotional decision making—for instance, the requirement that proposed bills be read several times—can preclude only certain forms of injustice, but they are absolutely compatible with systematic violations of the rights of minorities or those of future generations.

In what does the *common good* consist? Its basis is the safeguarding of fundamental rights, including and especially those of minorities. If these rights are guaranteed, then all interests have to be considered as having equal weight, including the probable interests of those who cannot themselves vote, such as future generations. The greatest happiness of the greatest number is a legitimate criterion in economic policy if it does not result in the sacrifice of any rights. However, one has to take care that so-called external preferences are not deemed as important as personal preferences—someone can have a certain wish only in order to harm someone else, and not because he himself has an interest in the matter. Dworkin rightly observes that if it respects such external preferences, utilitarianism defeats itself.[170] In any event, in such questions utilitarianism has its role to play, and a vote that articulates one's own interest would be generally justifiable, if all those equally affected by the decision had an equal voice in making it. No decision in social policy can satisfy everyone, but it should satisfy the largest possible number as much as possible. Here we should start out from the assumption of a decreasing marginal utility of money; the same amount will do more to make a poor man happy than a rich one. Obviously, absolute poverty should always be avoided, for there is a fundamental social right to surmount it, and rights cannot be put on an equal footing with the welfare of others. Ultimately, the common good involves respect for certain values, even if they are at the moment rejected by a large majority; the encouragement of meaningful art and science can hardly be seen as a right of the artists and scientists concerned, but it remains a legitimate responsibility of the state even when it is recognized as such by only a minority.

The voting behavior of delegates should also be oriented toward their concept of the common good when they are judging what constitutes the greatest happiness of the

---

170. "Suppose many citizens, who are not themselves sick, are racists in political theory, and therefore prefer that scarce medicine be given to a white man who needs it rather than to a black man who needs it more. If utilitarianism counts these political preferences at face value, then it will be, from the standpoint of personal preferences, self-defeating, because the distribution of medicine will then not be, from that standpoint, utilitarian at all" (1978; 234).

greatest number. As we have said, it is usually just when in pursuing collective goals the majority of votes expressing individuals' particular interests determines the outcome, so long as these goals do not contradict basic rights and so long as the interests of those who cannot vote are respected. But the majority of those entitled to vote in the legislature does not always reflect the majority in the country, and certainly not the interests of future generations. The delegate has to take into account the opinion held by the majority of the population, not only for obvious strategic reasons, but also with the sincere intention of learning from the current debates. But it is very possible that he will arrive at the conclusion that their arguments are not cogent, and in this case he is duty bound first to act in accord with his conscience, and second to persuade as many of his constituents as he can that he has made the right decision.

A person would not be serving the common good by being the only one who renounced the expression of an individual preference; one certainly has the right to demand that others make the same renunciation. This does not mean that when one fails with this demand, politics can be reduced to the negotiation of particular interests; quite the contrary. However, *strategic voting* is permissible and even obligatory, if it is the only way to bring others to act reasonably. We can and should vote against the legitimate interests of others if this is the only way one can teach them to respect others' interests; one may and even should forgo voting for the morally best solution if doing so is very likely to lead to the third-best solution, whereas the second-best has a good chance of being adopted if one votes otherwise.[171] A person who can make no compromises will be able to achieve nothing in a collegial organ or in a system with a separation of powers (although he may be able to make the state incapable of acting). But first of all, compromises that are farther removed from the common good than either of the original proposals are absolutely to be avoided (in such a case it is better to agree on tossing a coin); second, in order to be respectable, a legislator must make it clear that he has worked out his own position, and that on certain basic issues he would rather let himself be outvoted, and even become unpopular, than yield out of opportunism. However, he must take into account the members of the party with which he wants to achieve long-term goals.

Today, the *role of political parties* in democracy is increasingly criticized, and rightly so. Parties are not state organs; the political power of party leaders, who themselves hold no state office, contradicts the constitutions of most modern states,[172] and the use of employees of the state chancelleries for the purposes of political parties is unacceptable. Nonetheless, it would be hard to get along without parties. A legislature that consisted of atomic individuals would be unpredictable, and if individual candidates did not begin to

---

171. On strategic voting, see S. J. Brams (1975), 51 ff.

172. G. Amato reports that in 1992, after finally winning a long battle as Prime Minister to reduce the influence of party secretaries on the composition of the cabinet, he told journalists: "Somehow Paragraph 92 of the constitution has been applied" (1996; 72). Conversely, one must welcome it when a head of government makes his decisions more through discussions with the members of parliament supporting him and with the cabinet than with his own party.

form coalitions until after they were elected to the legislature, it would be even harder for voters to choose among them. Only when the candidate joins a party and in general submits in the legislature to a party's discipline (which need not, however, be as rigid as it is in Germany) does coherent law making become possible; for even if everyone voted rationally and with an eye to the common good, the result might very well be laws that were wanted by different majorities and were incompatible with each other. Nonetheless, parties lose their legitimacy when they leave no room for the rise of strong and uncommon personalities, and end up becoming a pack of opportunistic sinecure hounds. The fact that a person who has done hard cratic work in a party wants to be rewarded for this work is certainly understandable; but it is equally easy to understand that trust in the parliament must decrease if the voter does not have the feeling that more expertise is collected there than in any average group in society. In the latter case, a direct democracy with a part-time and unpaid legislature would be the most reasonable solution. Only a parliament that recruits from the various strata of society representatives who are above average in intelligence, honesty, and eloquence can in the long run claim more legitimacy than direct democracy. Parties that do not understand this or do not behave in accord with it harm parliamentary democracy. In particular it is not hard to see that the tasks of the legislator cannot consist merely in shaping public opinion, legislating, and controlling government; he has somehow to function as a model within the society, because norms that are seen in life are much more effective than norms that are merely prescribed. The constitution must be more than a piece of paper, more even than a legal form; it must be anchored in the people's customs and sense of values.

The inalterability of certain constitutional provisions necessarily entails that *associations and parties may be prohibited* if they do not respect these provisions. However, this kind of prohibition is not always expedient for achieving the goal, since it can lead to an increase in prestige for the prohibited parties; it should be proclaimed only when it is both just and expedient. Thus a country like the United States, in which government by laws is strongly rooted in the mores of the people, can allow itself to be very tolerant with regard to fascist movements. In general, one can say that democracy must not open the way to its own abolition; it must be prepared to defend itself energetically. Of course, it cannot be the legislature that decides whether a party is opposed to the constitution, because there would be too great a temptation to eliminate parties that were legitimate but were felt to be dangerous competitors. The organ that makes such a decision can only be a constitutional court whose task is to protect the constitution against the legislator as well. Laws can be valid only when they do not violate the constitution; the increased difficulty of altering constitutional norms is sensible only if the ordinary legislator cannot get around it. Admittedly, this alone still does not entail that the legislature itself should not be the protector of the constitution; but the additional argument that is required to demonstrate this is extremely simple—namely that no one can serve as judge in his own case.[173]

---

173. Cf. Dworkin (1978), 141 ff.

The most reasonable solution would probably be to entrust *the protection of the rights of future generations* to an analogously constructed state organ. This should consist of proven professionals who try to anticipate the long-term ecological and social effects of certain laws on future generations and see themselves as representatives of the latter's legitimate interests. Certainly it is right for every legislator also to feel himself bound to serve the common good, and to think about coming generations himself; but it is not very likely that this will happen, because the pressure exerted by those who can express their interests directly is significantly greater. The German Federal Republic made a wise decision in sheltering the German Federal Bank from direct legislative pressure, because in monetary policy as well, short-term advantages only too easily divert attention from long-term goals. It is a good idea to prescribe in the constitution the limits of public debt, because there is a temptation to be generous to present-day voters at the expense of those who will have to pay the debt later on. The establishment of independent audit offices is an indispensable protection against the waste of state revenues. Analogously, the protection of the rights of future generations should be entrusted to an organ that enjoys an autonomy comparable to that of a court or at least to that of the German Federal Bank. Whether such an organ should be merely consultative, having a voice in the consideration, not of all laws, but of all those that have a significant influence on future generations (which laws would belong to this category must not, of course, be ultimately decided by the legislature itself), or whether it should even have the right to a veto, is not easy to decide. It would be most effective if the opinion of this organ were forwarded to the constitutional court, which would be bound by the constitution to declare void laws that violated the rights of coming generations. If this solution were adopted, in some cases (as is necessarily the case already in protecting rights to positive benefits) the court would have to be granted positive legislative powers—naturally, so long as we adhere to the ideal of the separation of powers, these powers would be only temporary—until the legislator found solutions that were compatible with these rights. The members of the proposed state organ should be chosen by the legislature, and perhaps also partly by other organs, such as the constitutional court or the head of state, from a list of qualified candidates; so that they are not in any way dependent upon the organs entitled to constitute them, their term of office should not be extendable, and it should not be possible to remove them from office.

Earlier we mentioned a *second chamber.* The principle of the composition of the second chamber is clear in the case of a federal state.[174] If the member states already have extensive rights in decision making, the members of the second chamber should not also be delegated by the state administrations. A corporatist composition of the second chamber guarantees something that is otherwise not ensured, namely that the largest possible number of elements in the society have a voice, whereas in the first

---

174. In a state in which tribal structures play a role, the heads of these tribes will also, or chiefly, belong to the second chamber.

chamber public officials or jurists are likely to be over-represented, and in this way the principle of the separation of powers is strengthened on the substantive level as well. However, such a chamber can exercise only an advisory, or at best a suspensive, function, because the mechanism governing its composition excludes too many citizens from representing or even being represented.[175] Analogous considerations would apply to a second chamber that was composed, at least in part, in accord with the third principle worth considering, namely, one that gathers together people who have achieved special merit.[176] Such a chamber, which would resemble in many ways the Roman Senate or the British House of Lords after the withdrawal of the elements of an oligarchy by birth, would guarantee a certain continuity of policy and the public expression of political opinions by individuals who have proven their worth and who need not be concerned with being re-elected—a concern that does not always promote sincerity. A crucial issue involved in constituting this chamber would be whether formal criteria (such as holding an important office for a certain length of time) would suffice, or whether a separate state organ (the head of state is an obvious possible choice) should choose among formally qualified candidates. The latter is the better alternative, but it presupposes a consensus in the society regarding substantive criteria for determining qualification. Such a chamber would represent an aristocracy compatible with universalism, and it is not hard to see that such an aristocracy would be good for modernity.

7.3.3.3.5. *The Executive*

Carrying out the laws must be entrusted to a state organ other than the one that makes them. However, this does not mean that it should have no influence on the parliament's work nor that it should not be dependent on the parliament. In a democracy, it must be elected either by the parliament or directly by the people; its appointment by a head of state without executive power can be no more than a formality. There is something to be said for both approaches. *Direct election by the people* gives the president a greater ability to act and guarantees the stability of the administration during its term of office. To be sure, it must be determined how the state president can be removed from office under certain circumstances; however, not disapproval of his policies, but only a violation of the law or his inability to discharge the powers and duties of his office can empower the parliament to begin such a procedure if the president has been put in office, not by the parliament, but by the people. Nonetheless, every head of government,

---

175. The fact that the Bavarian Constitution combined in a coherent way direct democratic, parliamentary, and corporate organizational principles made it one of the best in the world.

176. This kind of bicameral system was suggested in particular by Mill: "If one House represents popular feeling, the other should represent personal merit, tested and guaranteed by actual public service, and fortified by practical experience. If one is the People's Chamber, the other should be the Chamber of Statesmen; a council composed of all living public men who have passed through important political offices or employments" (1972; 328).

even one elected directly, is dependent upon the cooperation of the parliament, and the danger of presidential democracy consists precisely in the fact that a harmonious relationship between the parliament and the administration is not guaranteed. In contrast, this harmony is guaranteed *if the parliament elects the head of government,* although the latter must then pay much more attention to the opinions of the parties supporting him, and in many constitutions he can be replaced in the middle of a parliamentary term. This is for the most part possible even if the party (or parties) that cause his removal from office went into the campaign with him as its candidate for the the office of prime minister. In such a case, and only in other, analogous cases such as the inability to work with the parliament, it seems reasonable for the head of government to have the right to dissolve parliament in order to allow the people to decide regarding his removal from office. A mere vote of no confidence without a majority for a new premier should have no consequences so far as the premier's position is concerned—for just as one does not abandon a scientific theory as soon as it is falsified, but only when a better one is available (because one cannot pursue further research without a theory), so a poor administration is better than no government at all.

The arguments for and against the two systems almost balance each other out, and it is essentially the spirit of the people that determines which system is better in a given situation. A presidential democracy is better after a long phase of administration not democratically legitimated, because it can more easily satisfy the need for a leadership figure, at least insofar as such a figure exists. In a country with such an outstanding culture of compromise as the United States, the advantages of presidential democracy have proven themselves without its disadvantages having become discernible. On the other hand, in countries in which no comparable culture exists and, moreover, no natural authority is generally recognized, presidential democracy can easily lead to serious conflicts between parliament and president that may culminate in coups d'etat and putsches. The latter must be distinguished from the legal self-restraint of the parliament's legislative power in *states of emergency,* that is, the grant (in the worst case, after the fact) of exceptional powers to the administration, a grant that should always be permissible only for a limited length of time and for a clear and limited goal. The declaration of a state of emergency need in no way threaten the foundations of the constitutional state, especially if this means is used only infrequently and solely in obvious crisis situations. It is a splendid sign of the discipline and democratic conviction of the British people that it was able to withstand even the battles of the Second World War largely within the framework of the usual parliamentary democracy.

However, the call for a presidential democracy is understandable in parliamentary democracies in which the mode of election and the degree of the population's polarization make it difficult or nearly impossible to form a stable administration. For one thing is clear: No state can get along without a strong executive branch, and a democracy that proves incapable of producing one will in the long run lose its legitimacy. The executive is the central state organ, out of which the others have crystallized, and an important criterion for determining whether a people has the talent for democracy is precisely the presence of this capability.[177] (Another, still more important, criterion is a sense for the mechanisms of the separation of powers that is compatible with the democratic option.) In addition to the mode of electing the administration, little contributes so much to its ability to act as a clear assignment of responsibilities—for there is responsibility only if individuals are responsible.[178] In accord with the cratic maxim that one should reflect at length but act quickly once one has made a decision, the parliament must allow all the important opinions existing in a society to be presented, and therefore it must be large while yet manageable; on the other hand, the administration should either, as in the United States, be a *monocratic* organ, or else grant the head of government clear *authority to determine the general policy guidelines.* Switzerland can permit itself to have a collective organ as an administration because the latter is not dependent on the confidence of parliament and no minister has to fear being dismissed; moreover, the country is not exposed to the kind of foreign policy pressure that often enough makes rapid and secret decisions indispensable. It is misleading to think that an organ with a clear concentration of power in the hands of a single person is more likely to lead to an abuse of power—this is not the case if, as is presupposed here, he is controlled by public opinion, which can make his resignation nearly inevitable, and if another organ has the power to replace him. On the contrary, the diffusion of responsibility makes concrete criticism more difficult, for each person can excuse himself by attributing his own bad decisions to the pressure put on him by others. If one analyzes Italian politics after the Second World War, one cannot conclude that the head of government's weak position kept the administration from abusing its power (which can also consist in leaving criminal organizations alone out of weakness). The obscurity of the context of decision making in collegial organs that are dependent on powerful bureaucracies is one of the chief causes of the current crisis of confidence in politics. There is certainly a danger that this crisis could eventually lead to a powerful explosion that would take the pressure off, since as a means of exercising power, violence is at least apparently connected with clearer imputations.

To be sure, the head of government will be dependent upon the cooperation of the ministers, each of whom should have extensive responsibility for his own portfolio; but the head of government should be able to select them and dismiss them. On the other hand, it is not as sensible that the head of government, or even the parliamentary majority, should be able to determine the number of departments. There is something scandalous about a situation in which new ministries can be created or others abolished, depending on the number of people to be provided with a ministerial office, which

---

177. No one has expressed this more clearly than Hamilton, at the beginning of *Federalist* 70: "There is an idea, which is not without its advocates, that a vigorous executive is inconsistent with the genius of republican government. The enlightened well wishers to this species of government must at least hope that the supposition is destitute of foundation; since they can never admit its truth, without at the same time admitting the condemnation of their own principles. Energy in the executive is a leading character in the definition of good government" (1787 f.; 354 f.).

178. Cf. Mill (1972), 352: "Responsibility is null when nobody knows who is responsible."

leads partly to the establishment of new departments and partly to elevated expenditures for sinecures and pensions. The state's tasks only rarely change radically; therefore an almost complete determination of the number of ministries in the constitution helps increase the dignity of the ministerial office and is cheaper for the taxpayers. A concentration of tasks that by nature belong together makes much more sense than dividing them into independent ministries, which often compete more than they cooperate. The external dimension of politics makes a ministry of foreign affairs and, subordinate to it, a ministry of defense indispensable, and a preventive security policy must also include a development policy. The ministries of justice and the interior correspond, respectively, to the tasks of further developing the law and protecting it against violation. The state can finance its activities only through a system of taxation that must, along with other tasks, be subordinate to the finance ministry. The natural environment, healthcare, the family, the educational system, and the economy, as the framework and presuppositions of the state, should be the responsibility of separate administrative units; much the same holds for the tasks of distributing and organizing collective goods. Whether these units should be independent ministries depends basically on the extent to which there are conflicts of interest between the individual tasks or the extent to which these tasks can be separated from each other at all. It makes sense to grant a veto right to cabinet ministers who have special responsibility for future generations, such as the finance and environmental ministers.

Furthermore, it should be required that a minister be in charge of the same ministry for an extended period of time. Certainly a minister must have competencies that go beyond those of the ministerial bureaucracy. He must coordinate decisions made in his department with the guidelines of the administration's policy as a whole; he must deal respectfully but decisively with the parliament and interest groups, and have a sense for possible alliances; he must be able to select and lead people, and in particular he must be able to run a bureaucracy. But he must also have objective competencies in the area for which he is responsible, as well as the imagination necessary to conceive better alternatives. In view of the rapid changes in the modern world, a minister should regularly take time to get further training and leave, as much as he can, the show-business aspects of the business to under-secretaries[179]—the number of speeches that must be delivered by a minister in a modern democracy is ridiculously high. The appointment of a few ministers who do not come from the party machine is a clear index of the responsibility that the head of government feels for the common good. But it would certainly be naive to deny that for the most part the ministers and always the head of government need cratic abilities. This is not merely a descriptive statement; they *should*

---

179. Offices without their own responsibility, which are basically proxies for another, are not unproblematic, because for the most part they are frustrating—think of the office of vice-president in the United States. If one has already decided for under-secretaries and does not follow Bavaria's sensible example of granting them cabinet rank, then one should at least use them so that they really unburden the minister.

have these abilities. Otherwise, since there is no power vacuum, either a splintering of the decision-making mechanisms will result, or an *éminence grise* not democratically legitimated will draw power to himself; neither of these consequences is desirable. However, these cratic abilities should serve the common good (for that is what "ministry" ought to mean). Understanding government as public service leads to a readiness to forgo positions to which one cannot do justice, to give up one's office when the time for doing so has come, and, under some circumstances, to continue to work for the state in a subordinate position.

No less important than the premier's authority to determine the general policy guidelines is the *length of the administration's term of office.* In order to increase the probability of a better correspondence to the majority relationships in parliament, even in the case of a presidential democracy it should correlate as much as possible with the parliamentary term, and it should be possible to re-elect the head of government. As a rule, it is in a country's interest to have its policy guided by the same individual over a long period of time; therefore there must be good grounds for replacing him. The governing party's loyalty to the premier should be great; criticism of him should initially always be internal and not immediately released to the media; excusable errors should even be concealed if a significantly better alternative to him is not in view—an alternative that was only slightly better would not make up for the loss of stability that would be connected with a change in premiers. Only if it has become clear that the premier is the wrong person for the job, a long time in power has corrupted him, or new political issues have arisen with which he is incapable of dealing, should his own party instigate his dismissal—but obviously only if a better successor can be found. Then, however, swift and decisive action should be taken.[180] It goes without saying that violations of the law, as well as serious political errors for which he is personally (even if indirectly) responsible must result in a premier's or a minister's resignation. So far as offenses against public morals (offenses against private morals, and especially sexual morals, should play no role) are concerned, it is important that a parliamentary committee set general guidelines before the appearance of questionable cases; otherwise there is a very great danger that the population's moods, or antipathies in the media, will determine the outcome of the affair, and that has nothing to do with justice. The quality of public opinion is one of the most important guarantees of public law, and just as it is difficult to imagine a functioning democracy in a state that has an extensive territory but no mass media, it is important to understand that a hectic exchange of information without concern for the essential and without a consensus regarding basic values in no way helps a democracy to succeed.

---

180. Churchill aptly formulated the relevant maxim: "The loyalties which centre upon number one are enormous. If he trips he must be sustained. If he makes mistakes they must be covered. If he sleeps he must not be wantonly disturbed. If he is no good he must be poleaxed. But this last extreme process cannot be carried out every day; and certainly not in the days just after he has been chosen" (1948 ff.; 3:13).

There is debate as to the constitutional permissibility of *re-electing* the head of government. Tocqueville rightly pointed out that before elections a president (or, analogously, the head of government) who is once again a candidate almost inevitably loses his status as a person responsible for the whole country and becomes one party among others.[181] With this is connected a contamination of the idea of the state that is cause for concern and that moved the great Tocqueville to advise that re-election be prohibited. However, most constitutions have not followed his advice; a *one-time* re-election of the head of state is permissible almost everywhere. But since Tocqueville's argument applies to this case as well, another argument must be given against re-electing the head of state *more* than once, and this is naturally the fear of an abuse of power. However, there are several replies to this argument. First, it is anti-democratic, since it deprives the people of the possibility of re-electing the person who has proven most worthy of its trust. Second, it diminishes the head of government's willingness to work, since his hope of being re-elected can stimulate him to exceptional achievements (even if sometimes also to ridiculous concern about public opinion). Third, in dangerous historical situations it excludes the person who may be the only one capable of dealing with them—world history might have gone quite differently, and not better, had the Twenty-Second Amendment to the United States Constitution already been in effect in 1940. Fourth, it is not very convincing in the framework of a system that already has various guarantees against the abuse of power and different mechanisms of the separation of powers (such as regulations regarding the ineligibility of office-holders for other offices, especially when there are conflicts of interest between them); indeed, it can, as Louis Bonaparte's 1851 coup d'état shows, even be counterproductive, because it invites popular personalities to break the law in a way easily justified in terms of the theory of democracy.[182] The prohibition of re-election is more in the interest of second-rate politicians who are thinking of their own chances of being elected than in that of the state. Moreover, the argument against abuse of power relates only to a president with real power or to the premier, not to the state notary. The prohibition or limitation of the latter's re-election—as in Article 54 II of the German basic law—makes no sense. Nonetheless, Germany owes to this the fortunate fact that at the end of his second term, Richard von Weizäcker, the Federal President, dared to tell a few truths that did not please the country's political elites.

Oversight of the administration is the task of public opinion (which should have a right to extensive information, particularly in matters of internal politics), the judiciary (which can do so more easily if the public prosecutors are also part of the third, judiciary power), ombudspersons appointed by the parliament, and the opposition. (The influence of parliamentary investigating committees is rather limited so long as the majority relationships in them mirror those in the parliament, which in parliamentary democracies supports the government.) The integration of opposition forces into the

---

181. (1835 ff.), 1:208 f.
182. Cf. Hamilton's *Federalist* 72, which I follow here to a great extent (1787 f.; 367 ff.).

state is one of the greatest achievements of democracy and gives this system a great stability, because it fills everyone with the hope that he might himself someday be in line
for power. The expression "Her Majesty's Opposition" is a fine manifestation of this
aspect of democracy. Hegel aptly writes that precisely what the opposition is often
charged with, as if it were something bad, "namely, that all it wants is to form a ministry itself," is in fact its greatest justification.[183] However, the dialectic and the intellectual level of the debate is of an entirely different kind if the opposition hopes only to
take over the reins of administration—that is, if it is not brought into the administration from the outset (and thus ceases to be an opposition). Just as competition in the
market stimulates production, so in weighing alternatives a democracy based on competition is more productive than a consociational democracy based on concordance or
a grand coalition (which can, moreover, end up strengthening the fringes of the political spectrum). However, in situations of historical crisis, and especially in wars, the latter can be the only way to get the population as a whole behind a policy that asks individuals to risk even their lives. Loyalty to the common state, the recognition of the
administration's positive achievements (which is not only demanded by decency, but is
also usually more worthwhile cratically than petty grumbling), the elaboration of a
convincing conceptual alternative that makes it clear that more is involved than an exchange of benefice-holders, the preservation of party discipline, and finally the will to
power arising from responsibility (without which a party will long be left in the opposition, because the actual administration has an advantage in the voters' favor as well as
other important means of power)—all these are virtues that the opposition needs and
that it is not always easy to balance. Since in a democracy the administration is not a
benefactor but a trustee, the people always has the right to vote out an administration if
it thinks the opposition would be better able to act in accordance with the people's
wishes in dealing with the tasks that have to be faced in the future, no matter how capable the administration has proven itself in the past; when the historical situation has
changed, past achievements are no guarantee of future results. It is possible to think
that the British people were not prudent when they voted Churchill out of office in 1945,
because the policy he represented would have been better for Great Britain and the
world; but it is a disturbing category mistake when people speak of ingratitude. It is still
more absurd when people retain unquestioning faith in a party whose leadership has
changed or whose program has become obsolete. The morally responsible citizen is a
floating voter, and if he is fortunate enough to live in a federal state, he should certainly
support different parties at the same time if, for instance, he finds one of them more
convincing in internal policy and the other more convincing in foreign policy.

Here, we can only touch on the question of the *head of state*. In a presidential democracy, the office is identical with the chief executive, and represents in concrete form the
unity of real power and state power at its formal apex; in a parliamentary democracy, it is

---

183. (1969 ff.), 4:476. Trans. T. M. Knox (1964), 258.

a separate state organ without real power, which, depending on the case, either is insignificant to the point of being ridiculous, or can assume a position above the parties and mediate in a quite different way from a president, who is (co-)responsible for the government. A purely representative office should not be misused to provide a home for failed politicians, but rather filled by a reflective person who can bring people together, and who needs fewer cratic instincts than any other government official. It is justifiable to have this position filled by a *hereditary monarch* if such a figure is seen by the great majority of the people as a living symbol of the state and instills patriotism in them, along with a feeling for traditions that could otherwise not be achieved.[184] To be sure, this violates the right of others who might otherwise become head of state; but since the real power of the head of state in this system is limited to a minimum, and since the most intensive symbolic functions can be assumed only by a monarchical head of state, a violation of Rawls's principles is justifiable in this one case. After phases of monocratic administration, a monarch can seem to guarantee the continuity of the state form, and thus strengthen the new democracy, as Juan Carlos succeeded in doing in Spain. Had Germany succeeded in making the transition to a parliamentary monarchy, it—and the world—might have been spared Hitler. A further advantage of hereditary monarchy is that it illustrates the importance of the family for the state. However, this advantage is squandered when members of royal families show the whole world that they are no more capable of conducting a dignified marriage than are ordinary citizens, or when, for example, a successor to the throne complains publicly about the strict way his father raised him, even though such an upbringing alone would have been appropriate to his privileged status; thereby they do considerable damage to the legitimacy of an institution that, once abolished, is in recent times for the most part lost forever.

The *bureaucracy* is not the head, but rather the backbone, of a modern state. Together with the judiciary, it guarantees the continuity of the state during the re-election of the parliament and a change of administration. The work of the bureaucracy must be regulated by law, even if general clauses and discretionary powers are unavoidable. The police administration and the administration concerned with ordinances regulating businesses are responsible for the society's security, but the latter must also be protected against the former's intervention, because otherwise the former could be a greater evil than the one they were created to eliminate. It must be possible to bring complaints about violations of the laws or the constitution before an independent court—given the executive's power, it is indispensable that it be subject to control by the courts. The complexity of modern societies makes the idea of changing the bureaucracy every time the administration changes seem absurd; moreover, it is of the utmost importance that positions in the bureaucracy not be used to provide for fellow party-members. The criteria for promotion in the administration must be professional competence, eagerness

---

184. An example of the strength of this need is the integration of hereditary monarchy elements into a formal democracy in the form of the Nehru clan in India.

to serve, and personal integrity, not acquaintance with those holding offices in the administration and loyalty with respect to their whims. In addition to knowledge of a specific area, a member of the upper levels of the bureaucracy should also have a general education, which alone makes it possible to fit his work into the larger context that makes it, depending on the case, beneficial or disastrous; the ideal bureaucrat should thus be not only a specialist, but also a generalist. Responsibility for the common good must become a habit, and insofar as it contributed to the formation of this habit, the German system of public officials (*Berufsbeamtentum*) was the appropriate bearer of this responsibility in the development of modern bureaucracies. But if the privileges connected with such a position are not accompanied by a corresponding sense of the state, then they are not only unjustified, but even harmful, because they represent forms of parasitism in a place where it can least be afforded. It must be a cause for concern that for the most part the efficiency of private administration is today greater than that of state administration, for it is a state's duty, as the entity responsible for the common welfare, not to fail to meet the standards of private administration. It goes without saying that not demanding individual achievement as a condition for promotion makes no sense; in the modern world, the principle of seniority has no moral basis. In a rapidly changing society the continuing education of a dynamic bureaucracy is just as important as the habitualization that stands in a certain contradiction to it, at which it arrives only through long exercise of the same activity, and which sometimes promotes hostility to innovation and obstinacy. No less important, in a society in which communication between the individual subsystems is poor, is the increase of what might be called "inter-systematic competence," that is, the ability to understand from the inside the logic of spheres outside the state—for in a pluralistic democracy, hardly anything can be done without intensive cooperation among the state, the economy, and shapers of opinion. Having members of the public bureaucracy work for a time in private enterprises and having their positions filled by colleagues from private bureaucracies is a very promising way of achieving this competence.

The tendency to grow is marked in all bureaucracies; it is particularly strong in state bureaucracies, because they are not restrained by the market. Exceptional efforts are necessary in order to fight this growth. To be sure, the readiness to make a just contribution to the fulfillment of state tasks is an elementary necessary condition for one's being considered a moral person; cheating on one's taxes is no venial sin, and a finance minister who praises as a gift to voters a tax law that makes tax evasion easier is shameless. But the readiness to serve the state rightly depends on how legitimate the state's tasks are felt to be. In the modern age, an individual's contribution to the fulfillment of the state's tasks is increasingly reduced to the duty to pay taxes, to which is added in some states the duty to serve in the military and sometimes the duty to act as a lay assessor or juror. On one hand, it is right that the abstract means of money allows people to do the concrete work they like best and probably are most competent to perform, and that because of its quantitative nature the tax burden is, relatively speaking, the easiest thing to distribute fairly. On the other hand, it should not be overlooked that the main problem, especially among young people of both sexes, is that they no longer know that rights imply duties without which freedom remains barren; for example, calling upon them to make a concrete contribution in the framework of a year's community service can offer an opportunity for an experience of meaning and community from which the state can benefit to a large degree, even if from a purely economic point of view the allocation is not the most efficient.

So far as the question of *military service* is concerned, the state must have the right to call upon its citizens to defend the community (also within the framework of collective security organizations)—otherwise it is not following an evolutionarily stable strategy. Such a right exists only in the case of a just war. Asking a citizen to put his life at risk for the sake of justice cannot be justified on the grounds of his self-interest. This is a heroic act that demands respect, insofar, and only insofar, as such acts take place for the sake of a just goal. Risking one's own and others' lives, for instance, in order to escape the boredom of a consumerist way of life, is deeply immoral. On the other hand, it is acceptable to arrange military service in such a way that it becomes primarily a means of social bonding within the country, as for instance in the Swiss system of retraining courses. It goes without saying that the military must be subordinate to the civil executive branch; and universal military service helps prevent the army from becoming autonomous and makes it easier to control democratically. Moreover, abolishing the duty to serve in the military definitely involves the danger that the risk of death will fall largely on the poorer classes, who have fewer alternatives to a military career than do the wealthy. However, military reasons and the principles of equity in conscription may suggest limiting oneself to a professional army composed of highly motivated and qualified soldiers who bear the main burden in the event of war; but in addition it must be possible to call upon every citizen capable of performing military duty when necessary. In view of the great importance of moral prima facie norms for a culture's mores and morality and, within such norms, the extreme importance of the prohibition on killing, a refusal to perform military service on grounds of conscience is acceptable if it is not based on the—unjust—refusal to take the same risk of death that others take, but rather on a serious wish, confirmed by other behavior, not to kill another human being under any circumstances. A state's decision to use conscientious objectors as medics in case of war is compatible with respect for this wish. Certainly there can be cases in which the individual recognizes in principle the right to self-defense, but comes to the conclusion that the war currently being waged is not justified; but a state can hardly recognize such an opinion, because it would thereby deprive itself of the right to conduct the war at issue. On one hand, in such a case at least the option of passive resistance remains open to the individual—with all the consequences connected with it, which in a good state should not be too severe, because it can turn out later on that the war waged really was unjust. On the other hand, the state should allow people to leave the state corporate group as a legal way of avoiding military service.

The greatest part of most citizens' contribution to the maintenance of the state consists in conscientiously paying their *taxes;* a refusal to pay taxes on grounds of conscience cannot be recognized by the state under any circumstances. Taxes can be interpreted at most as equivalent to a general service by the state, which varies according to the wealth of the taxpayer, but certainly not as equivalent to a special source in exchange for which the taxes are paid (as in the case of fees and contributions). More plausible than the benefit principle is the idea that taxes represent a sacrifice that is determined by each person's ability to pay,[185] because the duty to pay taxes also concerns the financing of those activities of the state from which the individual does not directly benefit, even if he participates in the collective identity of the citizenry. However, the individual must be able to see that his contributions serve meaningful ends and not the expansion of a superfluous bureaucracy. The principles with which a good system of taxation should be in accord are the following.[186] The taxing entity must have an interest in tax income being sufficient for its ends, and in the possibility of adapting taxation to changing state tasks. At the same time, taxation must be just, that is, general, and it must correspond to the individual's ability to pay; it can also serve the state's legitimate redistribution goals. The structural conditions of a market economy should not be affected by the system of taxation. Using taxes to pursue particular ends must be avoided, interventions in the private sphere must be limited, and the state's economic goals must not be endangered; in order to avoid the flight of capital, international coordination of tax law is urgently needed in the era of globalization. Tax law should be free of contradictions, as continuous as possible, transparent and practicable, and financial offices should work cheaply and without avoidable expense for the taxing entity and the taxpayers. The transparency of tax law is ultimately part of justice, since an excessively complex system with an abundance of unnatural possibilities for deductions favors those who can afford clever tax advisors and for whom more loopholes are open because of their more complex financial affairs. Only expenses that the individual incurs while serving the common good and that, for instance, relieve the state's burden of caring for those in need should be deductible.

In a modern society, the basic forms of taxation are income, property and net worth, corporation, inheritance, and consumption taxes. The most problematic is the wealth tax, because wealth has usually been taxed once already, and this kind of tax can have, under certain circumstances, confiscatory effects; moreover, it can deter the accumulation of wealth that is in the state's interest because it makes recourse to social benefits less likely; in addition there are problems relating to the determination as well

---

185. This theory is already implicit in Rousseau (1966), 347: "On trouvera que pour repartir les taxes d'une maniere équitable & vraiment proportionelle, l'imposition n'en doit pas être faite seulement en raison des biens des contribuables, mais en raison composée de la différence de leurs conditions & du superflu de leurs biens." ("It will be found that in order to impose taxation in an equitable and truly proportional way, assessments should not be made solely in proportion to the goods of taxpayers, but in a proportion composed of the difference between their condition and the superflueity of their goods." Trans. J. R. Masters [1978], 232).

186. Cf. F. Neumark's outstanding book (1970).

as the evaluation of various kinds of wealth. In the case of consumption taxes, it makes sense to have lower taxes on goods indispensable for life, such as basic foodstuffs, rentals, and medical care (and in some cases still higher taxes on luxury goods). Indirect taxes such as the sales tax, which de facto taxes consumption by passing on the tax burden, are frequently preferred to direct taxes, on the argument that on one hand, they can be collected with more certainty and are perceived less as an intervention on the part of the state,[187] and that on the other hand, taxation of consumption that goes beyond what is necessary for survival is less counterproductive economically than taxing labor; moreover, they also tax consumption by foreigners staying in the country. However, an exclusive tax on consumption would be an unjust burden on those who cannot yet or cannot any longer work (and on those who have obligations to maintain and support them), and would at most lead to proportional, but not progressive, taxation. Taxes not only serve to meet the financial needs of the state, but are also a way of steering the economy. This holds in particular for so-called environmental taxes, which in no way impose a special burden on the citizen for debatable goals, but only internalize externalities and protect the rights of future generations. For the purpose of decreasing administrative costs, it makes sense to combine these distribution authorities with the fiscal authorities and to conceive social aid as a negative income tax.

7.3.3.3.6. *The Judiciary*

Few things are more important for a constitutional state than the *independence of the judiciary* from the other branches. Whereas the executive must be controlled by the parliament, an analogous control of the judges is unnecessary because they have less power, and it would moreover mean the end of the separation of powers, which is already imperiled when judges are elected (not to mention re-election). The qualifications required for judgeships must be all the more rigorous. Procedural law is almost as important as substantive law, which without it remains a dead letter, for substantive law achieves the ultimate degree of reality only in concrete legal findings. This does not mean that a large number of trials is a criterion for the quality of a polity; on the contrary, in the wasps in his play of the same name Aristophanes found a superb symbol for people for whom engaging in trials is an end in itself; and there is a well-grounded fear that insurance against legal costs, together with the attitude toward insurance described earlier, will lead to a rapid increase in the number of trials. Trials should not be playgrounds; to this end, high fees for those who lose their cases can make sense. If conflicts can be resolved in a pre-trial procedure—through a settlement in civil law and through the imposition of a fine in cases involving offenses against police and administrative regulations—or through arbitration tribunals, so much the better.

---

187. However, against this "principle of inconspicuousness," see F. Neumark (1970), 37 ff., who argues for the precise opposite, partly on grounds of political pedagogy.

The concept of law necessarily includes that of its *public nature,* and whereas consultations must by their very nature be secret because one can often achieve the right results only if one allows the playing out of intellectual scenarios that afterward prove to be absurd, the court business should (save in exceptional cases) be public. All parties should be heard, the legally appointed judges should not be biased, the witnesses should be examined. So far as possible, everyone should have the services of a lawyer he can trust; in cases where a lawyer is reasonably required, the state should grant a court-assigned defense for the poor. Lawyers should consider themselves not primarily as serving all possible needs, but rather as organs of the administration of justice whose obligation is to serve the common good. Since law is general, everyone has a legal duty to make his contribution to the legal finding: witnesses can rightly be forced to testify. *Omertà* is no trifling offense; it is incompatible with the respect for the law without which no constitutional state can long survive. However, the state has a corresponding duty to protect witnesses.

From the particularly massive character of the interference represented by punishment, it follows that the decision-making procedures that lead to the imposition of punishment, that is, those of *criminal trials,* are subject to restrictions entirely different from those put on *civil trials.* Because of the qualitatively different legal consequences involved, different standards of evidence are indispensable. (Nonetheless, it is not unproblematic for the unity of the legal order if a criminal court acquits someone for lack of proof of an act for which he is held liable in a civil court in the same country.) Indeed, arrest and pre-trial confinement must already be subject to clear restrictions and controls. Before judgment is passed, the innocence of the accused should be presumed; indeed, the confidentiality of the investigation, which is dangerously threatened by the media, should be strongly protected. In the event of an acquittal, appropriate compensation should be paid for the time spent in prison during the pre-trial confinement. Extorting testimony through violence not only constitutes an extreme violation of human dignity, but is also an unreliable means of arriving at the truth. The principle *in dubio pro reo* ("of the benefit of the doubt") follows from the fact that it is a far greater evil that an innocent person should be punished than that several guilty persons remain unpunished; but within the limits of the permissible, every effort should be made to convict the guilty, and as quickly as possible. The violation of the idea of law in itself prevents the use in criminal cases of the adversarial principle of party presentation, which is appropriate in most areas of civil law, where only conflicts of interest between adult private individuals are concerned. It is a matter of great concern when, as in the United States for instance, the public prosecutor and the accused agree on a so-called plea bargain regarding the charges brought against the latter. However, in exceptional situations, when the police and the judicial system are overloaded, and in order to more successfully fight a form of criminality that poses an existential threat to the state, procedures such as offering immunity for turning state's evidence may be justified; for it is better to forgo punishment of only one criminal than to forgo punishment of all.

On one hand, the desire to better protect the accused who is to be judged by people he regards as his peers, and on the other, the democratic idea of a greater participation of the people also in the third, judicial power are strong arguments for *jury trials* where the question to be decided does not presuppose any specific legal expertise, that is, especially in a criminal proceeding concerned with determining the factual issues. This holds, of course, only so long as a people's intellectual and moral level and a culture's structural conditions (for instance, the system of the media) do not make miscarriages of justice more probable than in a judgment made by a professional judge. Choosing lay assessors and jurors by lots is the most reasonable procedure. An election, as in the case of creating the legislature, is not reasonable, since majority feelings must not determine the outcome of the process; aptitude tests, like those administered to candidates for members of the bureaucracy and professional judges, would contradict the presupposition of a greater democratization. Choosing by lots is in this, and almost only in this, public area the procedure most compatible with universalist principles. S. Lumet's *Twelve Angry Men* is perhaps the most accomplished film dealing with the way common responsibility for the law can be achieved by different people from various classes within the framework of the institution of the jury trial.

The jurisdiction of a constitutional court cannot be justified democratically, but only with regard to the separation of powers. Someone who bases the normative principles of constitutional law solely on ideas of democracy cannot accept an institution that can declare void laws that have been approved by the majority of the parliament and that under some circumstances are also desired by the majority of the population (and in the case of "eternity clauses," even constitutional amendments that have been passed by a unanimous vote of the parliament). Nevertheless, it is not hard to see that this is precisely the institution's goal—the protection of the constitution, and that means, among other things, the protection of the individual rights guaranteed by the constitution. One can hold the view that minorities should have no rights with regard to the majority; but one cannot approve of minority rights and at the same time wax indignant when these rights are defended by a state organ that is not bound by the opinions of the majority. However, the court is well advised to use its power sparingly—under no circumstances should personal preferences be confused with the letter and the spirit of the constitution. The court should have a sense of what is necessary for the state's survival; respect for the in part constitutionally recognized will of the majority, as well as a cratic instinct, should keep the court from contradicting the lawmakers in cases that for good reasons should not be seen as unambiguously decidable.[188] Conversely, it is an obligation of elementary political culture that the members of parliament not openly disqualify the court's decisions, even if they find them in specific cases lamentable or even absurd, just as it is a violation of a constitutional judge's moral duty when he gives interviews in which he declares that a possible constitutional amendment (that would

---

188. On the other hand, the constitutional court may very well come the conclusion that a law contradicts constitutional norms, for example basic rights, only under certain empirical conditions, with which it must therefore make itself familiar. Forsthoff's polemic against this case (1971; 142) ignores the essence of conditional obligations.

be compatible with the constitution) considered after an unpopular ruling will not find a majority in parliament, for it is not his business to concern himself with majorities in parliament. The structure of the separation of powers is imperiled when such reactions are thought to be normal.

Because of its special importance in constitutional law, the jurisdiction of the constitutional court raises in the highest degree a problem that also arises for every jurisdiction, and that is of great philosophical interest. The question is how far the decision of the judge is predetermined by the law or the constitution, and how far a *law-making* element is involved or may be involved in it. First, it is clear that in the majority of cases the judge's decision is predetermined by the letter of the law and the characteristics of the case; moreover, it is clear that there are hard cases in which competent judges arrive at different conclusions. Does it follow from this alone that the judges are acting in a law-making way? It is in particular the contribution of Dworkin's work to have shown that this is in no way the case.[189] In actuality, the overwhelming majority of judges are convinced that they are discovering existing rights, not inventing new ones, even if they differ from the opinions of their colleagues. However, this conviction can be interpreted as a useful (self-)deception; additional arguments are required. Dworkin points out that for an ideal judge, whom one has the duty to approximate, the analysis of the logical implications of the law (or the constitutional norms) and, in Anglo-American law, of precedents, as well as taking into account various general legal principles and giving them the correct weight, would for the most part predetermine a single decision. However, Dworkin himself must concede that there can be *a few* difficult cases in which the judge can, after examining all the relevant criteria for decision, come to the conclusion that a decision on the basis of the given materials is not possible; how often such a situation occurs will depend partly on the complexity of the legal system in question.[190] In his theory of interpretation, Dworkin recognizes only the moral principles incorporated into positive law, but he emphasizes that the concepts intended by the framers of the constitution and the legislators must be distinguished from the concrete conceptions that they have connected with them, and that only the former are binding.[191] On the basis of this distinction Dworkin can maintain that it might be possible, for instance, to declare capital punishment incompatible with the Eighth Amendment to the United States Constitution, which prohibits cruel and unusual punishments, even if he has no doubt that in their own time those who approved the amendment did not regard capital punishment as cruel and unusual punishment. However, it is not their conception, but their concept that counts for present-day constitutional lawyers and judges.

---

189. (1978), 81 ff.

190. 279 ff., esp. 287.

191. "When I appeal to the concept of fairness I appeal to what fairness means, and I give my views on that issue no special standing. When I lay down a conception of fairness, I lay down what I mean by fairness, and my view is therefore the heart of the matter. When I appeal to fairness I pose a moral issue; when I lay down my conception of fairness I try to answer it" (1978; 135).

Dworkin's argument is in my opinion convincing, and indeed all the more convincing the more abstract the relevant concepts are (for example, that of human dignity); however, it is clear that it presupposes a platonizing, anti-Wittgensteinian theory of meaning. It is not the factual opinions of those who use a concept that constitute its meaning, but rather its ideal, normative content.

But if one therefore grants that there is a normative element that transcends positive law in the narrower sense, then one can also concede that there are certainly more difficult cases that cannot be decided on the basis of existing law than Dworkin thinks, without being for that reason forced to draw the conclusion that the judge must use his own discretion in an arbitrary way. In cases in which positive law does not predetermine a decision, the judge is required to apply *natural law principles,* and in some cases even those that have not yet been acknowledged by positive law, but that must not contradict it. (However, it is conceivable that the legal system is not consistent with itself; in this case, a positive law principle for the solution to the conflict must first be sought and a natural law solution only if no positive law solution is found.) But there may also be situations in which neither positive nor natural law provides a decision, and in which the judge—but not a judge on the constitutional court—may, indeed must, use his own arbitrary discretion, since one cannot live without a decision and the lawmaker obviously has delegated it to the judge.

From the previously outlined norms of the theory of the interpretation of the law in general and of the constitution in particular follows an important consequence with regard to the *composition of the constitutional court.* Certainly it is an error to demand an "open" constitutional court that mirrors the various elements of the society; that would make it only a miniature parliament, and it is not clear how such an organ homogeneous in its principle of composition should exercise a supervisory function with regard to the parliament, which is its task. The court must consist of people who have devoted many years to interpreting the constitution and its normative implications. But there need not necessarily be jurists who are qualified for a seat on the bench—philosophers of law (who do not adhere to legal positivism) and philosophers of the state could also be among them, and perhaps even should be, in order to make clear the super-positive ground of the constitution's validity, which alone justifies restricting the principle of majority rule and ties the law-making element back to the objective arguments of ethics.

7.3.3.3.7. *A Universal State or a Plurality of States?*

If humans learned to limit their needs and their number, the economic sphere could be reduced to a minimum. But it would still not be possible to do away with the political sphere—a legislating authority with a monopoly on the use of force would remain indispensable. To be sure, one can imagine a world in which people are so good that even the threat of negative sanctions would be unnecessary; but a coordination of some of their activities, binding on everyone, would still be needed. A human society without criminal law (which in any case consists only of implications and therefore would not even have to be abolished formally; instead, it would simply go out of use) is very improbable, but conceivable. But a society without civil law and constitutional law or mores that were the functional equivalent thereof is inconceivable—the total anarchy of the state of nature would be the result. How about international law? Of all spheres of law it is the hardest to norm in accord with natural law—and precisely because the ultimate goal of international law must be its own abolition. This follows from the anomaly noted in chapter 6.1.3.4, which consists in the fact that international law comes into being in a decentralized manner and that there is no legal guarantee that it will be enforced. If constitutional law is, as it were, the resolution of tensions that arise from civil and criminal law, then international law falls back to a level we thought we had long since overcome—autonomous structures facing each other without a common judge and without common decision-making mechanisms. The fact that these structures have internal legal systems can make conflict resolution easier; however, it can also make it harder if the legal systems differ widely from one another, and if they strengthen each side's feeling that it is right. A clash between two states that owe their power to a highly efficient internal organization is far bloodier than one between two individuals, and it is also far more problematic morally, because it not only affects a large number of innocent people, but also induces people to kill who are not always involved directly in the conflict, at least when there is compulsory military service.

Even if there are situations in which wars are justified, there is a moral obligation to create a world in which not even justified wars take place. This obligation is all the more urgent in a world like ours, where weapons of mass destruction mean that a war can be far more destructive than in the past, and could even lead to an annihilation of the human race and many other higher species. Kant thought that eternal peace could be achieved in the framework of a confederation of republics. But confederations are not stable structures—they either fall apart, like the League of Nations, at the first conflict of interests, or they are transformed into federal states. M. W. Doyle (1983) defended the thesis that there would be no war between liberal states; and it must be granted, first, that in general a constitutional homogeneity diminishes the risk of war between states (partly because of the greater community of values, and partly because distrust is less, since one knows from one's own experience how decisions are made on the other side), and second, that democracies are less inclined to wars because in them the people makes the decision about whether to get involved in a war and to that extent is more cautious than a monocrat, who often runs hardly any personal risk, but merely sacrifices his subjects. Nonetheless, Doyle is far too optimistic. There is sufficient empirical evidence against his thesis;[192] and one can argue that democracies will especially be found waging wars with non-democratic states, so long as there are any, but that even in a world that consisted only of liberal democracies, conflicts between them would probably break out before long. A still more insecure guarantee of peace than a confederation is a balance of

---

192. Cf. M. Mann (1986 ff.), 2:766 ff. Cf. *Federalist* 6 (1787 f.; 21 ff., esp. 24).

sovereign powers, as we have seen in chapter 6.1.3.6. The hegemonic position of a single state provides a considerably stronger protection for peace, but it is connected with great inequality between the hegemonic state and other states, an inequality that not only is in itself morally problematic, but will also be felt to be unjust, at least in a world with egalitarian values, and can easily lead to attempts to undermine it.

The only enduring solution is a *universal state with a monopoly on force*.[193] That this must be a federal state follows from what was said earlier, in chapter 7.3.3.3.3: If even considerably smaller states should be federal states, then this holds a fortiori for a state that includes the whole planet, which must, of course, include more than two levels of statehood (there should be a right to emigrate from any member state, possibly after paying a fee for the education received). The chief objection to the idea of a universal state is sometimes the fear that once it exists, there will no longer be any hope of escaping it, as soon as it turns into a totalitarian monocracy. But the objection does not hold water. First, it would be just as possible that given a plurality of states, all of them would become totalitarian; and then the evil of totalitarianism would be combined with that of wars between such structures. Second, totalitarianism is even more likely with a plurality of states than in a universal state. It is true that in connection with the debates on the ratification of the United States Constitution, Montesquieu's opinion that a republic was possible only on a small territory[194] was cited; but Hamilton and Madison refuted this in theory by referring to the principle of the federal state,[195] and the United States has refuted it in practice. Quite to the contrary, it is plausible that only a threat by another state favors and seems to legitimate the establishment of a monocratic executive. It is hardly an accident that the homeland of Western liberalism was an island that could be considerably less concerned about external dangers than could Russia or Germany, for instance. "Thus internal and external injustice mutually affect each other, the external is produced by the internal, the internal by the external."[196]

That it alone can prevent wars is not the sole argument in favor of a universal state. In addition, only a universal state can carry out the positive tasks that produced modernity, with its expansion of the economy and technology over the round and therefore finite Earth. The *ecological problem* concerns the whole globe, and individual state solutions find themselves in prisoners' dilemma situations from which only a common decision-making authority with the right to enforce its decisions can provide an escape. The *divergence of the state's area of influence and economic expansion* deprives the state of control over the economy, which can make it more difficult to carry out a socially just policy. Again and again, this leads to protectionist reactions that arise from the justified desire to make state and economy coincide, but that choose the wrong way of achieving this.

---

193. On the following, see for instance C. Horn (1996).
194. *Esprit des lois*, 8.16 (1748; 1:255 ff.).
195. Cf. *Federalist* 9 and 14 (1787 f.; 37 ff., 62 ff.), and Montesquieu, *Esprit des lois* 9.1 (1748; 1:265 f.).
196. Fichte (1971; 10:646 f.): "So stehet die innere und äussere Unrechtlichkeit in Wechselwirkung, die äussere wird hervorgebracht durch die innere, die innere durch die äussere."

This divergence should usually be temporarily accepted, since it is the sole way of making world society ripe for a universal state.

Furthermore, the multitude of states prevents *the establishment of universal basic social rights.* Are there such rights? First, we must note that for individuals there is certainly a strong moral duty to fight absolute poverty abroad as well as at home if the poorest people in the world are left in the lurch by citizens of their own country, just as there is also a duty to save a drowning child if his father is sitting indifferently on the beach. Limiting basic social rights to a closed group, even if it is one's citizenry, cannot be justified on the basis of universalist principles. P. Singer (1972) made up for some of his errors by emphasizing this important point. On the other hand, it is inappropriate to object that such moral duties would collide with the right of an inhabitant of a wealthy country to pursue his lifestyle; first of all, our lifestyle itself requires justification, and second, universalist ideas are part of precisely our way of life.[197] Someone who has fought for the idea of the welfare state when he himself could benefit from it, but argues for limiting it when extending it is not in his own interest, shows that earlier he was already acting on behalf of this idea, not out of a sense of social justice, but out of pure egoism; and such a person is even less respectable than one who has always for principled reasons rejected basic social rights. Indeed, this duty is even a legal duty insofar as there is a *right* not to have to starve to death. Nonetheless, one can hold the view that this legal duty concerns primarily (even if not exclusively) people who are, along with those they support, subject to the same state power as those they support. (I will come back to this in chapter 8.2.1.3). But this means that these rights to positive benefits could be most fully realized in a universal state.

However, why has there thus far been no universal state, and why is it, despite the moral arguments in its favor, so extraordinarily difficult to establish such a state? A *fusion* of states presupposes either constitutional homogeneity or the willingness of one party to adopt the other's political system, at least for federal organs. (An agreement on a system alien to all parties is, although conceivable, improbable.) Where neither of the presuppositions is met, the offer of a fusion is empty talk; and even the fulfillment of one of the two conditions is still far from sufficient for a successful fusion. Let us assume that a state with tribal structures is willing to unite with a democracy and to adopt its political order, because it expects to gain advantages from it. What would happen? In a very short time the united state would break down, especially if the majority of the population came from the less-developed country, for they would be able, in accord with the common constitutional principle, to overrule the others and force decisions upon them that sprang from a mentality not compatible with a democratic constitutional state. Every state presupposes certain shared basic values, but above all a democracy, which therefore has special difficulties in tolerating cultural differences (cf. chapter 6.1.3.1).

---

197. Cf. A. Belsey (1992), 46: "So far from calling for an abandonment of 'our' way of life, global justice is a demand to take its moral bases seriously, and to rectify its present decrepitude by rebuilding it on its original, genuine foundations."

At the same time, democracy is the state form more in accord with the principles of natural law, and one cannot simply expect people to make concessions concerning democracy for the purpose of coming closer to a universal state; surrendering freedom for the sake of sheer survival is not always reasonable. Therefore we are confronted by the disturbing conclusion that precisely the constitution that is ideal with regard to constitutional law makes the road to the universal state demanded by natural law longer and harder than it would have been, for instance, for pre-modern empires, within which, however, democratic structures could never have developed.

The recognition that democracy presupposes an especially large degree of homogeneity among the population is not an argument for *nationalism*, by which I mean the theory that every people should have its own state. (The theory that only one's own people should have rights is not universalizable and does not deserve to be discussed.) In certain historical situations nationalism has diminished the number of states, and if an approach to a universal state is one of the normative criteria on which the evaluation of events in foreign affairs should be based, then in those situations and times nationalism can be seen as having had a secret rationality that nonetheless deviated considerably from the intentions of the actors involved. Today, however, nationalism is almost everywhere a centrifugal force that leads away from that historical goal. Even if it can be easily *explained* why it has such a great attraction as a compensation mechanism for the least developed countries, that does not *justify* it. Naturally, its rational core, the demand for the preservation of cultural diversity, should be respected, partly through federal mechanisms, partly through the recognition of cultural rights of minorities. Certainly it would be a bad thing if the Catalan and Basque languages were to disappear; but it is to the moral and political credit of the Catalonian people that it has been content with its autonomous status within Spain, whereas Basque terrorists are pushing for secession.

The binding elements that a democratic state needs are neither a single common language (though there should be a *lingua franca*) nor a common religion or common ethnic descent. On the contrary, a state with a great diversity of languages, religions, and ethnic groups can be especially rich culturally, and the home of extraordinary intellectual achievements; it can even be loved very deeply by the whole citizenry; all other things being equal, it is clearly preferable to a monocultural state because of the abundance of cultural values realized in it. Conversely, when there are other differences, commonality in these three parameters may not produce the slightest feeling of belonging together. Many northern Italians would prefer to live in a Swiss canton rather than in a part of Italy.[198] What are the truly indispensable elements on which the great majority of a citizenry must be in agreement? First, there must be a consensus that conflicts are to be resolved without the use of force; few things are more detrimental to living together than differing ideas regarding the legitimacy of the private use of force. An ethnic group

---

198. A fortiori, pan-Slavism failed because the linguistic relationships among the Slavs did not at all make up for the differences in mentality, partly based on religious denomination.

that sees in private revenge a heroic virtue cannot live on an equal basis with another that recognizes the state's monopoly on the use of force. Second, everyone must fundamentally recognize the legal order; an ethnic group without the concept of private property will have difficulties if it enters into a political unit with another in whose value system private property has a central place—at least so long as it does not even recognize the private property of the members of the second ethnic group. Third, so far as basic social rights go, differing work ethics arouse ressentiment if the country has a redistribution system that not only battles absolute poverty, but also sets as a goal the eradication of relative poverty. Inevitably and perhaps also justly, the more productive will have the impression of being exploited by parasitic individuals if through their help the poorer people do not succeed in increasing their productivity within a reasonable length of time. In such a case, a lower level of redistribution should be preferred, because it makes living together considerably easier, at least if the poorer people enjoy the same respect and the wealthier do not excite their desires through advertising and the like. With respect to political rights, agreements, or better yet, regulations in constitutional law should be used to ensure that not all political or military offices fall into the hands of the ethnic group constituting the majority of the population. An active promotion of various minorities and disadvantaged groups by using quotas in allocating university admissions, party and governmental offices, etc., may contradict the principles of equality and the principle according to which property rights have to be founded in indivudal achievements. Such a policy can therefore be accompanied by contempt for the successful members of those minorities as mere "quota students," and for the most part entails the injustice that all of the relevant minorities are seldom taken into account, attention being focused instead on those that are relatively strong, and thus actually are least in need of help. But it can be defensible as an ultimate resort during a transitional period so long as there is strong empirical evidence that equally qualified individuals belonging to a minority have, because they belong to this minority, not been chosen or admitted. However, this way of proceeding becomes counterproductive if it leads to ethnic and other differences compared to the common citizenship, not gradually melting away, but rather becoming stronger and stronger.[199] Fourth, in actuality no state can do without a feeling of belonging together that transcends rational egoism and motivates sacrifices where they are required. Patriotism would be indispensable even in a universal state; it in no way necessarily implies delimitation from other political structures, but only the sublime feeling that one's own value arises from one's action on behalf of something greater than oneself. At its most comprehensive, this something greater would be a universal state; it would be at its most morally valuable if one's own state were structured in accord with the principles of natural law. Certainly it is fine when someone loves the landscapes of his homeland, and the peculiarities of his country's citizenry and his native language; but more valuable yet is love for a just constitution, because only it is the

---

199. On this problem, see B. Gräfrath (1992).

result of a free moral decision. This love must be expressed in the readiness to act on be-half of the state in which one lives—and that includes criticizing one's state, when criti-cism is objectively justified, for example by getting involved in citizens' action groups that reveal the errors of official policy.

From what has been said follow the principles that should govern the granting of *citizenship* to those who are not themselves children of citizens. Neither ethnic kinship nor even the mastery of the country's language or the *lingua franca* to a degree higher than is sufficient for conducting everyday affairs may be the decisive criterion, but only the internalization of the basic values of the constitution, which is to be promoted by a policy of integration. Admittedly, it is more difficult to determine this kind of internali-zation than kinship relations; but something as important as citizenship may not be granted in accord with simple criteria. Neither can it be objected against the proposed criterion that in Germany French nationals find it easier to get citizenship than do Al-gerian nationals, for instance, and that this is unjust; for the premise on which this ob-jection is based is precisely the abstract universalism that was criticized above. In any case, it was a mistake that Germany more easily granted citizenship to the descendants of people who emigrated three hundred years earlier than to others who were born in modern Germany, for participation in a culture is not transmitted genetically, but rather through upbringing and the social environment in which one moves. Even if in a foreign environment the children of those emigrants might have remained true to the German culture of three hundred years ago, that would be far from meaning that they are more likely to have internalized the principles of the modern constitutional state than are the children of Turkish guest-workers who were born in Germany. What mat-ters is not ethnic tradition, but loyalty to the constitution. It must be acknowledged that states may, or even should, make the definitive granting of citizenship conditional on the surrender of previous citizenship, in order to avoid conflicts in loyalty.

Citizenship should be distinguished from *transit* and *residence rights* for foreigners, even if a lengthy, successful residence naturally entails the right to become a citizen. These rights must, especially with modern transportation, be subject to restrictions, pre-cisely because a state would collapse if anyone could immigrate into it at will. The popu-lation density of the country, its wealth, the nearness of its culture to that of the poten-tial immigrants, and finally the extent of their need are the morally relevant parameters to be taken into account in the concrete legal regulations. Expelling or turning away people who are threatened with death is morally unacceptable.[200] This holds in particular for political refugees, but also for people fleeing civil wars. On the other hand, those flee-ing economic conditions cannot be tolerated, not out of hard-heartedness, but rather because with the same money that their residence costs, considerably more people who are suffering from need at least as great could and should be aided in their own country. The foreigner must at least enjoy all the citizen's rights to freedom from interference in the

---

200. As Kant says in *Zum ewigen Frieden* (1976 f.; 11:213).

country in which he is a guest, for they follow from human dignity, not from the rights of the citizen, which do not constitute the other rights but merely complement them. So far as basic social rights are concerned, the question may and should be answered in the affirmative only with limitations, for even if elementary rights to positive benefits must be made available to all those who have a right to reside in the country, making them too generous can be counterproductive, in the sense that only a few people will be allowed to come in because on average they represent a greater burden. (Moreover, asylum seekers are for the most part a special burden for the poorer strata of society.)

Since natural law demands a universal state, the concept of *natural international law* is somewhat misleading. To be sure, there must be normative principles that make it possible to distinguish a just from an unjust foreign policy in a situation with a plurality of states; but such principles essentially belong to the theory of politics under non-ideal conditions, and will concern us in the following chapter. Nonetheless, the following very general principles can be stated as the core of natural international law. Since according to the presupposition made above there should be no central legislative authority, states have to recognize one another as independent; and from this it follows that, in addition to customary international law, *treaties* must be the most important source of law. Customary international law may be objectively absurd and unjust, but one should not deviate from it without very strong justification, since the certainty of the law generally reduces conflicts and since conflicts in international law are often accompanied by bloodshed. So far as treaties are concerned, it goes without saying that they must be adhered to. Nevertheless, in international law there are two justifications for violating a treaty that do not exist in civil law concerning contracts. One was already mentioned in chapter 7.3.1.3: the anticipation, *on good grounds,* of an impending violation of the treaty by the other party that could put oneself at a serious disadvantage. The other justification has to do with the problem (mentioned in chapter 7.3.3.3.2 in connection with constitutional law) of binding future generations. We have seen that this kind of binding is legitimate if it is reasonable. But what if it is not reasonable, or at least can be perceived as unreasonable? Why should nineteenth-century Denmark consider itself *morally* bound to adhere (apart from prudential reasons, which we are not discussing here) to treaties made in 1460? A satisfactory justification for considering it bound by such treaties would depend on the assumption that each generation has tacitly renewed them. But even in the same generation an analogous problem arises if not a change of administration, but a revolution, takes place. For since what is morally crucial for a state is its state form, it is not easy to explain why after a change in its state form, a state should be considered the same, even if the citizenry and the state territory have not changed. For instance, why should a people pay state debts run up by an overthrown autocrat, if only he and not the people benefited from them?[201] The debts of a normal corporate group continue to be valid, because the members confirm the

---

201. Cf. Aristotle, *Politics* 1276a10 ff., though he only asks the question without answering it.

acknowledgment of them through their continued membership in the corporate group; but states are ruling corporate groups from which one cannot simply withdraw, especially if they are monocracies.

The objections become even stronger if the treaty does not proceed from a consensus, but rather had to be accepted after a defeat in war—as, for instance, in the case of the Unequal Treaties between China and the Western powers. Roman private law already recognized the interdict *unde vi* (under duress); and of course still today civil law contracts made under duress are not valid. Whereas Hobbes clings to the idea that subjugation out of fear of death is binding, Locke emphatically defends the right of every people that has been forced to capitulate to throw off its yoke at the first opportunity.[202] Locke's position seems immediately plausible—the concept of a valid treaty implies voluntary agreement on both sides. But his position has a dreadful consequence. If an attitude in accord with it were always to be expected, under certain circumstances a people following its own rational self-interest, instead of seeking a capitulation on which it could not rely, would be forced to annihilate its adversary. Rather, the recognition of a factual legal situation that has come about through treaties promotes peace and maintains trust in the institution of treaties for the future. Therefore it is not so much the supposed intrinsic disvalue of violating a treaty that has been made under duress or by an exploitative tyrant as the negative consequences for humanity of such a violation that provide the decisive moral argument for a prima facie obligation to abide by treaties. In the case of debts, for instance, one can say that it is not so much respect for the rights of creditors (who knew what they were getting into when they offered loans to an illegitimate autocrat) as the hope of getting further loans that is an argument for paying them. If one does not cherish this hope and does not want to support loans to future monocrats, a refusal to pay such debts can certainly be just.

One condition for states' being able to make treaties is reliable communication by their representatives in each others' countries; diplomatic immunity is, as it were, a transcendental condition of the possibility of states' ability to make treaties. If opposed interests cannot be reconciled through treaties, or if conflicts regarding the interpretation of treaties cannot be jointly resolved, going before a common arbitrator is morally obligatory. But that does not mean that one can agree on such an arbitrator; and in any case the arbitrator will not have enforcement power if the parties to the conflict are sovereign states. To be sure, even if a joint solution cannot be found, the use of force is to be avoided; a positive international law prohibiting the use of force, such as is found in the Briand-Kellogg pact or in Article 2, 4 of the United Nations Charter, is a great step forward compared with a legal system that lacks such a prohibition. But this kind of prohibition must be generally valid, and there must be general trust that it will be respected in reality as well. The wholly problematic nature of such a prohibition, given the continu-

---

202. Contrast Hobbes, *Leviathan* chaps. 14 and 20 (1651; 198 and 252) and Locke, *Second Treatise* chap. 16 (1690; 384 ff.).

ing existence of sovereign states, results from the following reflection. No doubt all law and all state policy is bound by basic moral values, especially life, freedom, and property, which are endangered by any war. From this it follows that if it comes to a war, the war should be waged in such a way as to cost as few human lives as possible; and that there is a duty to take confidence-building steps in order to make entry into the war as unlikely as possible; indeed, it follows that there can be *no sovereign right to wage war* at all.

But this also means, conversely, that there is a right to use force to prevent wars waged by others; and that means that there is a right to self-defense and to defend others against aggressors. However, if they proceed from states, self-defense and the defense of others against attack inevitably take the form of warfare. Since most states will easily be perceived as potential aggressors if there is a lack of trust that the prohibition on the use of force will be generally respected, attacks on them can be presented as preventive defensive wars or as punishment for earlier wars of aggression; once one has recognized that war can ultimately be prevented only in a universal state, one might even imagine that for the purpose of establishing such a state, wars (history's last) are justified. Not all, but very many wars would be justifiable in that way. Their number increases further if one acknowledges that the principle that no state should meddle in the internal affairs of another is not very convincing. Of course, most of the justifying grounds just mentioned are, at least without qualification, sophistic; they will be examined more closely in chapter 8.2.2.1. Here I am concerned only to show how natural wars seem precisely when one wants to avoid wars. The moral quality of a positive international legal order is to be gauged in any case by the degree to which it serves peace and other goals necessary for the survival of the human race. It does this best if it is used to abolish in a peaceful way the sovereignty of states. This presupposes political decisions that must be made under very different non-ideal conditions. The moral nature of such decisions is the subject of the next chapter.

8

Just Politics

W hat is a good and just politics? This question certainly cannot be answered without a conception of natural law. But such a conception is only a necessary, not a sufficient condition for a satisfactory answer. For actions that in the context of power struggles are directed toward the determination and implementation of state goals never take place in the framework of an order that already corresponds to all the demands of natural law; the conditions under which politics occurs are always more or less non-ideal, and every politics that does not want to be condemned to fail must take these structural conditions into account and respect them at least partially and in an external way. Classical natural law theory has often enough ignored the moral problems arising from the non-ideality of historical conditions. The following passage from Fichte on the genesis of modern states is symptomatic of this: "1) It is true that the states of modern Europe came into being as a result of *conquest*. . . . 2) It is true that they also cannot reasonably come into being otherwise: For that reason law must first develop in such an *emergency constitution*. 3) But it is also true that this does not concern us."[1] We can grant Fichte that the development of natural law must in fact disregard genetic observations; but the question of whether the conquest of foreign territories at the beginning of the modern age was morally justifiable is legitimate, and a political philosophy that does not consider such questions is incomplete.

The non-ideality of structural conditions is not only a misfortune. It is true that it raises additional moral problems that are often difficult to resolve; that under non-ideal conditions fundamental objects of legal protection such as human life are endangered; and that under such conditions the most terrible vices can find full expression. But only under such conditions can the higher moral virtues develop that in an ideal world would

---

1. (1971), 10:548: "1) Es ist wahr, daß die Staaten des modernen Europa so entstanden sind, durch *Eroberung*. . . . 2) Es ist wahr, daß sie auch nicht füglich anders entstehen können: daß darum in einer solchen *Nothverfassung* sich das Recht erst entwickeln muß. 3) Es ist aber auch wahr, daß uns dies Nichts angeht."

not be needed. Times that need no heroes may be praised as happy times, and there is certainly a duty to work toward such times. But the deepest experiences of happiness are possible only because the misery of the *conditio humana* repeatedly spurs at least a few people to achievements that let us glimpse a reflection of the divine. Someone who has decently lived through a difficult historical period will think back again and again with a certain melancholy to that time, which was hard, but which also made demands on him that allowed him to become better acquainted with himself and with others than would otherwise have been the case, and, if he was lucky, gave him the finest experience a human being can have—the experience of unconditional fidelity and friendship. Finite beings are not granted the possibility of reckoning up the happiness and unhappiness of historical periods; but what I mean will become clear if I mention that the turmoil of the first century BC nonetheless made the *Laudatio Turiae* possible. Probably only during the Roman civil war would Turia (or whoever the matron eulogized was) have had a chance to prove how much she loved her husband and at the same time to have a husband who loved her in a way that can still move the reader of the literarily clumsy epitaph.

Politics is situated in a field of tension between two tasks. First, it must be concerned with moral state goals; second, it must have a chance of attaining the latter, that is, of being carried out with cratic competence, and the means used in doing so must also be evaluated morally. On one hand, good politics should work toward fulfilling natural law obligations—or what can be seen at a certain time as required by natural law; on the other, it may not endanger what has already been achieved. Thus, for instance, violations of existing positive law are morally acceptable only in exceptional cases. For even if no social and political order completely corresponds to the demands of reason, most orders are better than anarchy, and it would be irresponsible to imperil them for the sake of a merely possible improvement. In addition, the room for maneuver granted politics is considerably narrower than it is thought to be, at least by those infantile people who think that all the world's problems would be resolved if *they* held the reins of power; politics depends on factual mores, from which not even the moral power-holder can deviate too much. This is obvious in a democracy, for otherwise he would not be re-elected. But even in a monocracy, the risk connected with this kind of behavior is significant: someone who cannot be voted out of office can still be assassinated, and even if in certain situations the monocrat himself runs little risk, and is himself the only one who can murder someone in the struggle for a higher law, this kind of politics can hardly elicit respect.

In the following pages, I will mention a few of the moral principles that allow us to evaluate a politics under non-ideal conditions. The first distinction to be considered concerns domestic politics and foreign policy. (A triadic classification would result if we took the politics of international institutions into account. But since such politics became an important factor only in the twentieth century, it has no place in the relatively general discussion in this chapter; instead, it will be discussed in the next chapter.) It is immediately clear that because of the lack of a common legal order with coercive power, there are morally relevant distinctions between the two forms of politics; indeed, within foreign policy one must make a further distinction between the normative principles applied to the relations between states in peacetime and those applied when a war between them is being waged. A distinction orthogonal to this one concerns the norms relevant to relationships between states that have similar mores and the norms relevant to relationships between states and political corporate groups with very different systems of norms. So far as internal politics is concerned, we should distinguish between the moral principles to be applied to politics within a given set of mores and those to be applied to a politics in situations of historical crisis. Just as when founding an enterprise one has to act differently than one does after it is established, so both the founding of states and the transformation of their structure that is sometimes required in times of upheaval are subject to different normative principles than the givens of normal politics.

8.1. Moral Principles of Domestic Politics

Domestic politics is in general easier to norm morally than is foreign policy, even if it should be granted that the boundaries between the two basic types of politics are not always easy to draw. Should Prussia's policy with regard to the Holy Roman Empire be regarded as a domestic or a foreign policy? Is the abolition of feudal privileges in the wake of the emergence of modern territorial states an act of domestic politics or foreign policy? Despite all the smooth transitions, the morally relevant difference is that in general the degree of threat is higher in foreign policy than in domestic politics and that the common legal system promotes greater mutual trust. However, only in general: A situation of civil war or a bloodthirsty tyrant can be a significantly greater threat than a peaceful or weak neighboring state; and between citizens of the same—heterogeneous—state there may be greater mistrust than between neighboring peoples that belong to the same cultural area. In any case, common mores and a common legal system are two morally relevant parameters that should be taken into account in norming politics.

8.1.1. The Morals of Mores

A politics whose prospects of success are not to be considered vain from the outset must be aware of the factual mores, and the behavior of competent politicians must be in general determined by these mores, or at least seem to be so, because that is the only way they can win the people's extensive trust. But in addition to this we must note that mores usually have an intrinsic value. For all mores, even the most barbarian, achieve something that is morally relevant: they stabilize mutual expectations, make the individual's behavior predictable, and give him the possibility of adapting himself to the wishes of others; they diminish conflicts and thereby protect human lives. Without them, for most people the moral law would not be perceptible at all; the conviction that something is a moral duty first arises from the customs of one's own group. Just as one can expand a language only if one already speaks it and has mastered its grammar, so one must be familiar with the social grammar of a set of mores in order to lead people beyond it. In addition, mores can motivate people to achieve things, and these achievements demand respect even if they are achieved for the sake of something that is bad in itself: someone who courageously and chivalrously risks his life in a war that is unjust, but which he almost inevitably considers just, deserves the respect even of those who consider his behavior to be objectively wrong. Someone who is rooted in a set of mores generally has feelings of empathy which, even though they are limited to his own group, nonetheless at least transcend himself. He recognizes something higher than himself and tries to be guided by something that does not coincide directly with his self-interest. Furthermore, it is a point in favor of the morals of mores that they avoid the vices that may be connected with morality. At the same time, mores are as such incapable of insight into their own defects. The most terrible customs are considered legitimate, simply because they are and always have been customs; certainly, a standard for evaluating them that transcends customs is recognized in more detailed reflection, but it remains meaningless for concrete dealings at least with the customs that form the center of the factual mores. Someone who is imbued with the mores of his culture is less complicated than someone imbued with morality; and depending on the situation, this can be an advantage or a shortcoming. Nevertheless, most mores permit different modes of behavior depending on the rank to which one belongs; thus moving from one rank to another (for instance, by joining a monastic order) has often provided a way out for people who observe *both* morals and mores.

The ambivalent morals of mores explains why a "progressive" and a "conservative" politics are the two most obvious political alternatives, at least in relatively complex societies, quite independently of the content of the corresponding politics. All mores have lacks that at a certain level of reflection awaken a desire for change; at the same time, also and especially with increased reflectiveness, it becomes plausible to assume that too rapid a change in mores could lead to a disintegration of society. It is completely impossible to begin over from zero. To do that, one would have at least to follow Plato's recommendation[2] that all people above the age of ten be exiled; indeed, one would have to set the age limit even lower. Since a large part of human behavior depends not only on education but also on genes, a demand for a genetic tabula rasa would be the ultimate consequence of this abstract utopian stance that sets natural law norms against factual mores. The decisive argument against a politics that requires us to ignore factual mores cannot be a moral skepticism that denies that there is a recognizable normative criterion above and beyond factual mores; on the contrary, such a conservatism based on moral skepticism is in the long run extremely detrimental to the strength of mores handed down by tradition. The argument can only be that without traditional mores natural law norms could not take root, that a stance that fails to recognize the achievements of factual mores destroys more than it creates—indeed, that distrust of any set of

---

2. *Republic* 540ef.

mores at all is even self-canceling because every reform or even revolution, if it seeks to have an effect on history, must itself strive to found a new set of mores. Aristotle is a classical representative of this sociologically based conservatism, which cannot be too sharply distinguished from anti-Enlightenment, cynical, and all too often even nihilistic conservatism, and he rightly pointed out that a law should not be changed if the new one suggested was only a little better than the law in force up to that point. For, he argued, the legal advantage is more than counterbalanced by the disadvantage that consists in the fact that the citizens lose trust in the stability of the laws and the wisdom of the lawmakers, while the laws lose their anchorage in the power of mores, without which they would have no social validity.[3]

8.1.2. The Morals of Positive Law

If these reflections are valid even for a legal change in the law, they are still more valid for violations of the law. The factual legal system deserves respect to a special extent, at least so long as it is a proper subset of mores, for because of the sanctions connected with it, positive law is a particularly important control system for a society. This does not mean merely that it is prudent to avoid violating the law because one incurs risks by doing so; someone who liked to take risks or was willing to accept negative sanctions would sometimes have, on the basis of the logic of rational self-interest, no ground for respecting the law. My thesis is rather that there is a prima facie moral obligation to respect the legal order of a state and of the community of states. To be sure, only a prima facie obligation is involved, but the violation of such an obligation also requires significant justifying grounds. This moral obligation is valid—unlike one based purely on self-interest—even if hardly any danger is connected with the violation, whether because the social validity of the law is weak or because the lawbreaker is in a privileged position: Coups d'etat or disregard for certain international treaties are also prima facie immoral if the person who commits them does not run any real risk because he holds all the means of power in his own hands. This obligation proceeds from the fact that without law no society can survive; disregard for the law often threatens a society enough, and even if it does not because the population, on the basis of its factual mores, gets along more or less without law, a situation in which explicit legal norms are less respected than factual traditions is a cause for concern.

Even if in the normal case the law is a proper subset of mores, there can still be divergences between the two. Thus someone can put in force, in a manner completely legal, norms that contradict the reigning mores, and someone can violate valid law in the name of traditional mores. If one compares the two violations from a purely formal point of view, without taking the relevant content into account, it is not easy to say which

---

3. *Politics* 1268b26 ff., esp. 1269a17 ff.

is worse. On one hand, all other things being equal, the public nature and the formal rationality of most legal orders seem to be more affirmative than the often muffled power of mores. On the other hand, the law is by definition intended to have social validity—a law that enjoys no social validity is a miserable thing. Respect for legality, that is, the conscious guidance of one's own behavior by the valid law even where it deviates from previous mores, is a typical achievement of modernity; if one wishes, one can say that this is a main element of modern mores. If on the contrary a set of mores does not imply that one formally recognize law legislated as the guideline for one's own behavior, it is a mistake to expect rapid general recognition of a new legal norm. In this case, having such an expectation would be imprudent; but moreover, disrespect for a legal norm that is not socially valid is—once again, all other things being equal—morally less problematic than disrespect for a socially valid law, since most (not all) legal norms derive their legitimacy from the mutual nature of a behavior in conformity with norms; if others do not respect a norm, it may be morally permissible and even obligatory to violate it as well, in accord with a "tit for tat" strategy, because this may be more likely to make the other see reason. Thus in a country where no one correctly pays his taxes, tax evasion is less reprehensible than in a land with a high fiscal morality, not only because unethical behavior is infectious and a certain moral exoneration occurs when a concrete alternative is not experienced, but also because a person who has no illusions about the moral duty to pay his taxes correctly can argue that through his illegal behavior he is more likely to force the state to construct an efficient and just investigation into tax evasions. Thus there are not only certain grounds for a diminution of culpability but also—partial—justifying grounds for behaving contrary to the law in this way. On the same grounds, violations of international law are, *ceteris paribus,* less bad than violations of internal state law, precisely because the social validity of international law is weaker than that of internal state law.

In many moral discussions, the argument that was just given in a partial defense of tax evasion in countries with a low level of fiscal morality—an argument that refers to the behavior of others, whether illegal or legal—plays a role in very different forms that are not subject to the same moral evaluation. For instance, today it is unacceptable when people repeatedly say that in principle they oppose environmentally damaging behavior and support an increase in aid for development but that since this involves state tasks, no one can expect them to be active in this regard as private individuals (or to omit doing certain things). It is true that in these fields the individual cannot achieve any fundamental change, but first, that does not alter his duty to do what he can, and second, it is obvious that in modern democracies such measures as environmental taxes have a significantly greater chance of being introduced if a sufficient number of individuals have shown that they are prepared to accept the limitations connected with them. How such evidence should be collected if individuals do not begin to live in a more moral way is unclear, for it is only too well known that the positive results of mere opinion surveys do not indicate a genuine readiness to change behavior. The situation is entirely different in the case of "grade inflation," which should be rejected on good grounds. Any teacher who laments this inflation may not therefore disadvantage his students by giving them lower grades for certain levels of achievement than they would get from his colleagues for worse performance (at least so long as his different standards are not generally known), because grades are relative. In this case it is certainly morally consistent to oppose a grading practice that at the same time one follows temporarily. The case of tax evasion occupies a middle ground between the two others, for on one hand it sets a bad example, and on the other justice does not oblige individuals to bear burdens that are by their nature general but that most other people evade. In a moral decision, how seriously the state tries to fight tax evasion will play a role—not because on this depends the risk of being discovered oneself, but because a generous toleration of tax evasion by the state suggests that the state is not interested in justice and therefore will not deal justly with tax income either. It goes without saying that the money saved by tax evasion must be devoted to meaningful charities or ecological tasks.

Sometimes the legal order is more distant from moral demands than are factual mores are, and sometimes it is nearer. Evidently, this substantive aspect must also be taken into account if violations of the law and of mores are to be compared with each other. Antigone's refusal to recognize Creon's command with regard to Polyneices' corpse has a different moral status than some Indians' refusal to respect the British prohibition on suttee (the self-immolation of a widow on her husband's funeral pyre), at least if one considers the dimension of the objectively right. However, in such a comparison another dimension has to be taken into account. A norm can be valid law even though the person who set the norm is not socially recognized; in this case the lawbreaker can imagine that he is breaking a law that is not even formally legitimate. Thus, to come back to the example just mentioned, Antigone has no doubt that Creon is the formally legitimate power-holder of Thebes, but some Indians could believe that the occupation of their country by the British was not legitimate and that they therefore did not have a duty to obey them. Whether this specific view on the part of some Indians was right is not the question here; but in any case we must recognize that the violation of a primary norm has more weight morally if the secondary or competence norms are recognized. Where these are rejected, disregard for the primary norms is tempting. However, it is not compelling if the validity of substantive norms is not reduced to that of procedural norms (which will be argued for in chapter 7.2.1). Thus one can reject an absolute hereditary monarchy and still believe that the laws made by the monarch are right, just as conversely one can accept democracy on grounds of natural constitutional law and yet consider unjust a law passed by the parliament and confirmed by the constitutional court. Nonetheless, the difference regarding the dimension of procedural norms is important: in one case only a single norm is rejected, whereas in the other the source of all norms is rejected. In the latter case, resistance is more comprehensive and more dangerous, but *ceteris paribus* less problematic in subjective-moral terms because it does not contradict the recognition of the norm-setter fulfilled in the other case. For if the norm-setter is recognized, then one has in principle a duty to obey the norms set by him even if one considers them substantively wrong; otherwise the concept of the norm-setter would have no meaning. If one had to obey legal norms only if one agreed with them in the specific case, no central legislative authority would be needed; *ad hoc* agreements between all those concerned in an individual case would be the only legitimate procedure for putting legal norms in force. Someone who considers such a conception false on natural law grounds will have to limit resistance in cases in which at least the secondary norms correspond to a large exent to principles of natural constitutional law.

8.1.3. The Subjectively Moral in Immoral Mores

On the basis of an intentionalist ethics one has no choice but to recognize that someone who obeys the immoral norms of his culture bears no guilt, insofar as he has had no opportunity to reflect on a possible alternative. There can certainly be impressive people who take for granted living off the work of their slaves—although one can call them "impressive" only to the extent that they do not have the possibility of conceiving another social order and that they treat their slaves as justly and humanely as is possible within the framework of their mores. The actions of a politician must therefore be measured first of all by the norms of his own mores; this insight of historicism cannot be surrendered. The moralizing judgments of Enlightenment historiography, which waxed indignant over those who did not behave in accord with the humanitarian norms of the Enlightenment, were rightly abandoned—rightly, however, only on the basis of a differentiating intentionalism, not on that of a historical relativism which, if it were consistent, could not criticize at all, thus not even in the style of Enlightenment historiography. Genghis Khan was a great man when judged by the norms of his own culture, and it is these norms, rather than Genghis Khan himself, that should be criticized.

Two things are compatible with the recognition of the subjective guiltlessness of those who act in accord with what is usual in their mores. First, it is obvious that their guiltlessness does not imply that these actions were objectively right. Therefore there can be a right to use coercion to prevent such actions, even if those who commit them cannot be reproached: One can very well maintain that one may and should save a person from a head-hunter without thereby judging that the latter is making himself subjectively guilty by his activity. Second, the recognition of the inner standards of a culture should not lead to an underestimation of the moral level that this culture itself has already attained. Thus it is an unacceptable slander on Islam when a sadistic murderer like Saddam Hussein is excused on the ground that this behavior corresponds to what is usual in his culture (not to mention the fact that under the conditions of modernity he must have heard of other norms). It is true that one cannot expect pre-modern cultures to act against against their opponents in accord with the prinicples of a constitutional state founded on the rule of law, but chivalry is a virtue they were certainly familiar with, and someone who lacks it is worse, according to the axiology immanent in their factual mores, than someone who has it. In legitimist monarchy there may be lickspittles, but also people who out of a deep feeling of loyalty to their king criticize him when they think he is wrong and at the same time would defend him with their lives when he is in danger; a figure such as Malesherbes, who against the advice of his friends returned from exile in Switzerland to defend Louis XVI—whose policies he had more than once opposed—even though he knew full well that doing so could be dangerous to him, commands respect. Whether an aristocrat is worthy of respect depends on whether he combines his special status with an unfounded arrogance or justifies it by a lofty feeling of responsibility for the less fortunate. If one of traditional Christianity's least acceptable ideas was the assumption that all the unbaptized were necessarily damned, few things are less attractive in classical modernity than the refusal to recognize those to whom modernity's moral principles have still remained alien. However, one can certainly understand in retrospect why precisely at the beginning of the establishment of a new set of mores there is a temptation to demonize those who challenge one's own not-yet-secure enterprise,[4] and to someone familiar with late modern relativism it may sometimes seem that this attitude of classical modernity is the lesser evil.

It is consonant with what has been said that brutal despots who are morally repellent, not only when judged by the criteria of a higher set of mores but even when judged by those of their own set of mores, may be able to perform an objectively right function—for instance, that of eliminating other rogues and centralizing state power. For an objectively right behavior can result not only from moral grounds but also from quite different grounds, and this holds for private life as well as for politics. However important the differentiation of motives may be in evaluating the corresponding political personalities (and for an omniscient moral judge it will be the sole criterion that counts), it should not prevent a moral person from supporting the right policy, even if he knows that the person who is fulfilling it with a good chance of success is doing so for questionable motives. Naturally, this holds only so long as there is no reason to fear that these questionable motives will ultimately—for instance, after the elimination of control mechanisms—lead to objectively wrong decisions. It is important to have a sense of how far one can go in supporting a morally questionable person without putting him in a position to give his immoral motives free rein.

Culpability is always diminished, even if not completely excluded, when someone does something objectively wrong out of fear of death. In certain historical situations someone can actually have only the choice between killing or being killed, without being himself responsible for the social structural conditions into which he was born. (Naturally, this excuse is not valid if by committing a crime one has put oneself in the position of having to commit other crimes in order to avoid just punishment.) A clear example is the heir of a family involved in a bloody cycle of revenge with another family. Certainly he should seek to abolish the principle of revenge, but that is often easier said than done, partly because the other side will not necessarily agree to do so, and partly

---

4. In *De l'esprit des lois*, Montesquieu brilliantly seeks to discern as much as possible that is positive in the various state forms and to outline for each a system of conditional obligations.

because behavior interpreted as a sign of weakness can trigger murderous intent on the part of one's own allies. To be sure, it is more noble to sacrifice oneself magnanimously, but someone who fights for his own life in such a situation cannot be considered an ordinary criminal. History creates dependencies from which one cannot simply escape, because along with an office one assumes the responsibilities created by one's predecessors. This also holds for the modern world. A new premier who considers unjust a war being waged by his own state, and who would therefore like to end it, cannot do so on the day he takes office; he must at least try to negotiate favorable withdrawal conditions for his soldiers, and to do that it may be necessary to order military actions that can cost human lives. Of course, the person concerned would have the option of giving up the office of premier or giving up political activity in general, but then the unjust war would continue significantly longer than if he sought to put an end to it in such a way that the continuity of his state's policies was not entirely interrupted.

It is a terrible tragedy when a man of higher morals has to grow up within a set of immoral mores with which he cannot identify to the slightest degree. In such a situation, he would be well advised to emigrate outside the country or within it; if he considers it his duty to do something for his people, he should follow Plato's example[5] by concentrating on pedagogical activity with subliminal and long-term effects. In such a case, direct political activity is usually doomed to fail, and the person involved should be grateful if, like Don Quixote, he is only beaten and scorned[6] and does not suffer the fate of Anacharsis, the Scythian prince who had to accept Greek customs and was killed by his people for doing so. It is dubious that Anacharsis existed historically, but in any case his figure expresses a deep truth about essences: namely, that the *Volksgeist*—and its core, religion—must change before there can be any question of communicating to it a new political order, no matter how superior it may be. For a form of government to last, a majority of a people must be prepared to stop doing certain things, and a minority must be committed to doing certain things; a democracy with an overwhelming majority of politically apathetic citizens cannot endure. Certainly, politics can change a society, but within a given period of time it can never change it beyond a certain limit that is essentially defined by the *Volksgeist,* which is stabilized by educational traditions. This *Volksgeist* is not inalterable—contemporary Germans differ considerably from the ancient Germanic peoples—but it is tenacious. Peter the Great achieved more in the area of foreign affairs than in that of internal affairs, and even political cataclysms such as the establishment of a communist dictatorship produced astonishingly little change in Russia over many decades; today, the Russian national character is not very different

---

5. See *Seventh Letter* 324b ff. Plato's attempts to have a more direct influence were not exactly successful.

6. A good example would be Koshkaryov in Gogol's *Dead Souls* (pt. 2, chap. 3), who makes a ridiculous attempt to force Russian peasants to follow German organizational forms (which Gogol did not, of course, consider superior) that results only in the peasants using these forms to lead him by the nose.

from what it was at the end of the nineteenth century. Changes that are not expressly desired or recognizable as desired, such as those induced by modern industrialization, are often more crucial than the ones striven for politically, which can arouse resistance,[7] but these changes, too, take quite different forms depending on the *Volksgeist.* "Thus such laws fail, even if their content is true, on colliding with the conscience, whose spirit differs from the spirit of the laws, and does not sanction the latter. It is to be considered only a folly of the modern age to change a system of corrupt mores, its constitution, and its legislation without changing its religion, to have made a revolution without a reformation," we read in one of the most profound paragraphs of Hegel's *Enzyklopädie.*[8] Therefore in seeking to change political culture it is important to hook up with the indigenous religion in at least an external way. If monogamy is introduced in an Islamic country such as Turkey or Tunisia, it is sensible to argue that the Prophet allowed as many as four wives, but only if one loved each of them equally, and that since this is hardly compatible with human nature, the abolition of polygyny is clearly in line with the Prophet's intention. The example of Turkey shows how many changes under certain circumstances can be made (even if perhaps not in a lasting way); among the favorable conditions were, paradoxically, the defeat in the First World War, which made the necessity of reforms obvious, and the great figure of Kemal Ataturk, who is certainly one of the most impressive politicians of the twentieth century.

Mere participation in a developed set of mores is not yet a moral achievement of which one should be particularly proud: Many of the great deeds of famous politicians would have been inconceivable without the qualities of bureaucrats who remained unknown but whose contribution was crucial, and even without those of the whole *Volksgeist.* Analogously, it is unjust, for example, if, without a detailed analysis of the case, one reproaches on moral grounds a politician who tolerates corruption (without himself being corruptible) in a country where corruption is endemic; it can very well be the case that with the best will in the world he cannot change anything and that only by accepting this evil central to the mores of his people can he improve at least a few things that without his action would go on being bad. In view of his impotence, it may be that he would have done better to resign—that question has to be examined in each individual case—but it is completely naive to think that a politician can transform the mores of a people in a short time. If he wants to achieve something, he must be able to make compromises that should not come easily to him, so that he does not get too used to making them, but

---

7. Cf. Montesquieu, *Esprit des lois* 5.5 (1748; 2:172): "Il est bon quelquefois que les lois ne paraissent pas aller si directement au but qu'elles se proposent." ("Sometimes it is good that the laws not seem to go so directly toward the goal that they seek.")

8. § 552, n. (1969 ff.; 10:360): "So scheitern solche Gesetze, wenn ihr Inhalt auch der wahrhafte wäre, an dem Gewissen, dessen Geist verschieden von dem Geiste der Gesetze ist und diese nicht sanktioniert. Es ist nur für eine Torheit neuerer Zeit zu achten, ein System verdorbener Sittlichkeit, deren Staatsverfassung und Gesetzgebung ohne Veränderung der Religion umzuändern, eine Revolution ohne eine Reformation gemacht zu haben." Cf. also 12:535.

which he must still ultimately accept. In his story "Das Gesetz," Thomas Mann brilliantly discussed this problem in the framework of a conversation between Moses and his brother-in-law Jethro. Moses feels that he is not up to dealing alone with the quantity of conflicts to be judged, but he does not want to bring in other judges, as his corpulent brother-in-law recommends, because he rightly fears that they will accept bribes. "'I know that,' answered Jethro, 'I know it quite well. But one has to close one's eyes to that, just a little. Wherever order reigns, wherever law is spoken, wherever judgments are made, they become a little involved through gifts. Does that matter so much? Look, those who accept presents, they are ordinary folk. But the people themselves are ordinary folk; therefore they understand the ordinary and the ordinary is comfortable to the community. . . .' Thus did Jethro discourse with even gestures, gestures which made life easier if one but saw them. . . . With a heavy heart did Moses listen and nod. His was the pliable soul of the lonely spiritual man, the man who nods his head thoughtfully at the cleverness of the world, and understands that the world may well be in the right. He followed the counsel of his deft brother in law—it was absolutely necessary."[9]

8.1.4. Fundamental Moral Tasks of Politics within Stable Mores

The most important tasks of a moral politics within stable mores are first, *defending the existing social order* against internal and external threats, and second, doing the moral best that is possible within that social order. The social order itself may be unjust, but the instruction the politician receives from those who support his power never includes the social order's destruction, but only at most its transformation. Therefore the politician must be thoroughly familiar with the order in question and the *Volksgeist* that sustains it, and indeed he must not only have studied them from the outside but have experienced them from the inside, that is, he must identify with them. For he can motivate people to act on behalf of their social order only if he himself, despite his reservations, is devoted to it. He must feel certain values of this order so deeply that he is willing to work, to fight, and even to die for their preservation. The subsystem of the social order with which he must make himself particularly familiar is naturally the political one. He must have a precise understanding of its legal structural conditions—that is,

---

9. (1976), 2:649 f. "'Weiß ich auch', erwiderte Jethro. 'Weiß ich ganz gut. Aber etwas davon muß man in den Kauf nehmen, wenn nur Recht gesprochen wird überhaupt und eine Ordnung ist, werde sie auch etwas verwickelter durch Geschenke, das macht nicht soviel. Siehe, die da Geschenke nehmen, das sind gewöhnlichen Leut', aber das Volk besteht auch aus gewöhnlichen Leuten, darum hat es Sinn fürs Gewöhnliche, und wird ihm das Gewöhnliche gemütlich sein in der Gemeinde. . . .' So äußerte Jethro sich, mit ebenen Gebärden, die einem das Leben erleichtern, wenn man sie nur sah . . . Schwermütig hörte Mose ihm zu und nickte. Er hatte die bestimmbare Seele des einsamen, geistlichen Mannes, der nachdenklich nickt zu der Klugheit der Welt und einsieht, daß sie wohl recht haben mag. Auch befolgte er wirklich den Rat des gewandten Schwähers—es war ganz unumgänglich." Trans. G. R. March (1943), 40 f.

the principles of the constitutional law in force, and especially of the share of power as-signed to him; he must be able to categorize the social forces that support or oppose specific political goals and to assess their power; and finally he must know the individ-uals active in the political arena in order to be able to judge who the most important power-holders are and whether it makes sense to work with them. He must have a sense for public opinion and for the cycles of conservative and innovative phases, and he must be especially able to sense when a people want to move on to new tasks and when they are exhausted and find the consolidation of what they have already achieved a sufficiently absorbing task. He must be aware of the objective constraints that virtually dictate certain political decisions without allowing any alternatives, and he must rec-ognize where there is room for maneuver, where real interests are connected to what is morally obligatory—and for that he must be a realist (*Realpolitiker*). The abstract the-orist of natural law is seldom a great statesman, since his normative knowledge does not correspond to an adequate sense for social reality; and although it is important that there be political philosophers who elaborate their normative theories in a consistent form undisturbed by objective constraints, and who partly exercise an influence on public opinion and partly advise politicians, it remains true that they should usually not be directly active in politics, for in general this would serve neither philosophy nor politics. Ideological or utopian doctrinaires who go into politics with two or three poorly digested abstract philosophical ideas are even dangerous. Only in times of crisis do they have a chance, but then they can wreak considerable damage—like that Rous-seauian provincial lawyer, Robespierre, for whom Mirabeau predicted a great career be-cause he really believed everything he said. In actuality, a certain naiveté in politics can be a great advantage (and a conscious or unconscious will to power may underlie its cultivation) if there is a widespread aversion to people with ulterior motives or at least nothing more is expected from such people because they have succeeded in mutually paralyzing each other.

The good statesman must have perceived which of the *social subsystems outside politics* is the most important in his time. A medieval ruler in the West without a sense of the logic of religion was in serious danger; today, in contrast, economics is the sub-system most important for politics, because in the meantime economic gratifications have acquired greater motivational power than the promise of salvation. The military's direct physical force should never be underestimated; only in historical situations in which a constitution characterized by the priority of civilian power over military power is deeply rooted in the mores of a people can one afford to pay less attention to the mili-tary subsystem. In general, the military is in a privileged position to seize power, and it is certainly advisable to ensure that one can rely on the leaders of the armed forces. That means that these leaders should be dismissed, as inconspicuously as possible, if there is reason to fear that they are disloyal, though this should of course be done on some pretext, since it is cratically imprudent to show fear. The way in which Fritsch and Blomberg were sidelined in 1938 was only further proof of Hitler's diabolical cratic intelligence—as were his decisions in favor of the regular army (*Reichswehr*) and against the storm troopers (SA) in 1934 and, under the Weimar Republic, his wooing of officers who were discharged after the First World War frustrated and impoverished, but with cratic know-how. Furthermore, since not only the army but also the police have access to force as a mode of power, as the new chancellor, Hitler transferred the interior ministries of the Reich and, in an acting capacity, of Prussia, to the other National Socialists in his government (of which there were initially only two). In addition to a sense for the crucial social subsystem of the period, a mastery of the currently dominant media is indispensable, for a politics can be effective only if it is suitably represented. Given modern journalists' search for new information, as well as the disloyalty of many collaborators (even public officials), in modern democracies there is an increasing danger that some partial aspects of great political projects will be talked to death in public before the comprehensive conception can be presented at all, with the result that the latter no longer has any appeal. In particular, someone who has not understood how television functions and does not know how to deal with it has hardly any chance as a politician today—and that is certainly deplorable but in no way alters the duty of someone who wants to exercise political influence to make an effort to master the medium. A significant power advantage is gained by someone who is the first to learn to use a new medium, as Hitler learned, for instance, to use radio. Indeed, the fascinating phenomenon of the political aesthetics of fascism, National Socialism, and communism shows how cleverly the new masters were able to meet the masses' formal needs for meaning, which were no longer satisfied in a secularized world, and thus to use the masses for their own ends.

The external threats to a state order will be discussed later on. The inner threats can be of very different kinds. On one hand, they may be direct violations of the legal order; on the other, they may be insidious changes that gradually corrode the social system and shake its foundations—for instance, legal economic processes that inevitably rob the state of its ability to act, as in the case of environmental damage. A good politician is someone who recognizes both threats and averts them, so far as possible. Recognizing insidious changes represents a greater intellectual achievement, for if one is rooted in one's own set of mores it is often not easy to grasp dangers arising from the fact that the historical surroundings are constantly changing while one's society's mores remain the same. In such a case the only chance for salvation lies in adapting one's own set of mores, in innovation; and that is difficult for the naive representative of a society's mores. Without an eye for the developmental tendencies of one's own society and its environment, one can hardly consciously make history. The fact that in the seventeenth century the Spanish elites did not understand the logic of the process of modernization that the rest of Western Europe was undergoing is the most profound reason why a world power became an underdeveloped state that rejoined the rest of Europe only in the twentieth century.

No set of mores prescribes a single politics; the most admirable politics is one that seeks, while considering the existing ethics and with the most thoroughgoing respect for existing law, to achieve the *moral optimum*. The protection of life and of the basic rights to freedom of those who are recognized as citizens is the moral minimum of every politics, which alone can legitimate something like the obedience of those subject to it. The main tasks of a moral politics consist in increasing the number of those who are at least partially protected by the law and in guaranteeing ever more concrete rights (and the corresponding duties). Thus in Rome of the fifth century BC, putting patricians and plebeians on an equal footing politically was inconceivable because the social order would have collapsed and those who had worked on its behalf would have been eliminated earlier; but the codification of the law, which at least produced the certainty of the law, was then already possible, and those who supported it deserve great respect. The situation can be improved even for slaves: Protecting them from cruel treatment can often be achieved within traditional mores as well.

Naturally, in every period there is a *plurality of moral goals* whose realization is cratically conceivable; hence various moral politics are possible. If all the goals of these various politics are moral, the latter must be in principle compatible; nonetheless, *conflicts in goals* may arise because not all justified goals can be pursued at the same time. Without comparative normative concepts there can be no ethics, and therefore no political philosophy, but there can also be no politics. One of the main problems of contemporary politics consists precisely in the fact that the media daily introduce new political desiderata into the discussion without society or politics being able to hierarchize these desiderata, which sometimes are not even compatible with each other. In order to master such a situation, one must be capable of deciding which goals are objectively more important; in addition, one must have a sense for which goals must be sought first, as necessary means for a higher goal, or which goals develop their own dynamics after being achieved—for instance, because new interests arise from them and lead to the formation of habits whose power to shape human behavior must not be underestimated. However, making a rational choice is difficult in that what is involved is not only the moral urgency of political goals but also their feasibility—and that means, among other things, the possibility of forming a consensus in support of them. It may be better rapidly to achieve an unimportant goal that sends a signal and has directly plausible positive consequences for the majority of citizens than to waste time and energy on vain attempts to achieve a higher goal. Wasting time and energy in this way is not only deplorable in itself but sometimes extremely counterproductive because for the individual it can lead to a loss in prestige, and even to being excluded from active politics, while for the state it can lead to collapse: Brüning's financial policy was correct in itself, but was hardly responsible given the threat posed by the National Socialists, who harvested its fruit. Particularly in election years, democratically legitimated politicians have to have something concrete to show for their labors and cannot afford any conflicts that wear them down. For this reason it is important not to set goals so high that one ends up sacrificing a good that could be produced for the sake of a higher one that cannot. The ideal is to pursue moral goals over the long term, while skillfully staging unimportant but popular achievements that will win votes for continuing one's substantial politics.

The authors of the *Federalist Papers* repeatedly acknowledge that the constitution proposed for ratification is adequate but not perfect, since it resulted from compromises,[10] and at the same time they point out that it would be absurd to postpone ratification because of the lack, for instance, of a bill of rights, which could still be drawn up later on.[11] Hardly any of Gorbachev's mistakes was more serious than postponing the signing of the rewritten union treaty, rather than wrapping it up in the first half of 1991, when the time was most propitious; by doing so, he might have been able to save the Soviet Union. (Of course, we can speak of a "mistake" here only if we assume that it would have been a good thing to preserve the Soviet Union.) After Yitzak Rabin's assassination, Shimon Peres should have immediately called for new elections, which he would surely have won, or at least he should have postponed them to the last possible minute, when the peace process would have made further progress; setting them for May 1996 was extremely imprudent. (In a democratic politician, the sense for the ideal timing of elections corresponds to a general's sense of the right moment [*kairos*] to engage the enemy in battle.) One can deem noble Peres's desire not to exploit the emotions that raged after Rabin's death, but if one considers a political goal to be morally obligatory, then the use of a means such as steering noble emotions in a certain direction is unobjectionable; they may contain more truth than cold calculation, which is not necessarily guided by moral principles. What has been begun should be finished;[12] unfocused activity that starts all sorts of things but completes none of them is unworthy of a good politician. However, it is not always easy to decide when time and energy would have simply been wasted and when they would have been a subliminally effective investment in a politics successful in the future. Superficially, Alexander Dubček might not seem to have been a successful political crat—his reform-communism was crushed by Warsaw Pact tanks, and even his political visions were doomed to fail. But without his experiments and his defeats, the later political successes would not have been possible. Those who benefit from such earlier efforts should remember with gratitude those who are not among the victors of history, but without whom there would be no moral victories in history.

This historical development of the modern state, as interpreted by M. Kriele, for instance, offers a few hints regarding the *moral ranking of political desiderata.* Human life is the fundamental object of legal protection; and insofar as hardly anything threatens human life as seriously as war and civil war, preventing them is one of the primary duties. Civil war produces even greater moral evil than does normal war, because it sows

---

10. Cf. esp. *Federalist* 37 (1787 f.; 175 ff.).

11. "I should esteem it the extreme of imprudence to prolong the precarious state of our national affairs, and to expose the union to the jeopardy of successive experiments, in the chimerical pursuit of a perfect plan. I never expect to see a perfect work from imperfect man," Hamilton aptly writes in *Federalist* 85 (1787 f.; 446).

12. Cf. Einhard, *Vita Karoli Magni* 8 (1971; 22 ff.), and Montesquieu, *Esprit des lois* 31.18 (1748; 2:390 f.), on Charlemagne's staying power.

mistrust, corrodes a people's mores, and invites the closest family members to betray one another—and not only the number of the dead is an evil but also the constant fear of a violent death. The creation and preservation of a stable state that can defend itself against plundering by its neighbors and against muggers and terrorists within is the first task of politics; although it does not obliterate other duties, the latter must be considered subordinate. Within a state with a monopoly on power, the citizens' rights to freedom from interference should be protected, and here too the right to life comes first; it is followed by the right to freedom of conscience and the right to own the products of one's own labor. Since in the long run such rights can be protected only through the mechanisms of the separation of powers, the latter, especially the independence of the judicial branch, are almost as important as the rights themselves. Basic social rights, whose realization is dependent on more presuppositions than the realization of the rights to freedom from interference, are subordinate to the latter. A prolongation of life expectancy, a decline in infant mortality, and the overcoming of absolute poverty in the whole population are possible only with development in the modern sense, that is, with industrialization and the adoption, *within certain limits,* of modern technology and science; to the extent, and only to the extent, that it is a means for realizing basic social rights, support for development is a moral duty of politics. Insofar as there is a conflict between the most elementary rights to positive benefits and the rights to democratic participation in decision making (which is not necessarily the case), the former take precedence over the latter, but this holds only for the most fundamental rights to positive benefits, since a welfare state without political freedoms or even with totalitarian control over convictions, such as is defended by the Grand Inquisitor in Ivan's famous narrative in Dostoevsky's *The Brothers Karamazov,* reminds us more of a zoo than of a human society.

The hierarchy proposed here contradicts the ideas of Habermas, for whom the political rights are fundamental.[13] In reality, the latter are only the culmination of the development of the constitutional state, and introducing them too soon can be extraordinarily counterproductive because under certain circumstances that imperils basic social rights and can even result in states falling apart in a civil war—in 1994 a stable monarchy was urgently desirable in Rwanda. With a very heterogeneous population and serious underdevelopment, a party democracy can be contraindicated, and under certain circumstances its positive intrinsic value has to be weighed against its negative extrinsic value. Before judging as objectively wrong successful and also socially relatively just dictatorships for development (*Entwicklungsdiktaturen*), such as that of General Park Chung Hee in South Korea,[14] one should consider that the overwhelming majority of European

---

13. Cf. the interesting debate between Habermas and Rawls (1995; 127 f.).

14. Here I set aside the fact that it was the result of a putsch; naturally, the violation of the law is an additional moral problem that will be discussed in the next section. The international situation should also be considered as a relevant parameter, and after the traumatic experience of the Japanese occupation and the North Korean invasion, it is entirely understandable that South Korea sought military strength.

states started down the road to democracy after the process of modernization had been mastered. A set of mores cannot cope with too many changes at once, and probably the great majority of people, if they had to choose under the veil of ignorance, would prefer to live in a country like General Park's Korea or even post-Mao China, with its relatively successful, moderate command economy, than in India, the largest democracy in the world (assuming, as I said, that one did not know in advance that one would belong to a privileged caste). Formal rights to participate in decision making are of little help if the most elementary basic social rights are not guaranteed, or important rights to freedom from interference are denied de facto to some people, as is the case with the Indian "untouchables." Naturally, my choice does not imply that, for instance, Park acted in a subjectively moral way; his motives are not my subject here. In general, one must acknowledge that Machiavelli, a committed republican, was right that in situations in which limiting democracy can be objectively justified, people driven by moral motives very seldom have a chance.[15] It is also obvious that the most important function of a dictatorship for development consists in making itself superfluous[16]—and Park's policies did just that with amazing rapidity. Naturally, it does not often happen in history that a monocrat achieves this insight by himself: his penchant for power, his pride in what has been achieved under his rule,[17] and perhaps also fear regarding his ulterior fate generally prevent him from doing so. Pressure to move him to resign is indispensable if the real economic conditions have been created without which a modern democracy can hardly survive, and it goes without saying that the moral right is then on the side of the demonstrators and victims. However, it speaks well for the latter if, once they have won, they

---

15. *Discorsi* I.18.27 (1984; 111): "E perché il riordinare una città al vivere politico presuppone uno uomo buono, e il diventare per violenza principe di una repubblica presuppone uno uomo cattivo, per questo si troverà che radissime volte accaggia che uno buono, per vie cattive, ancora che il fine suo fusse buono, voglia diventare principe; e che uno reo, divenuto principe, voglia operare bene e che gli caggia mai nello animo usare quella autorità bene che gli ha male acquistata." ("And as the reformation of the political condition of a state presupposes a good man, whilst the making of himself prince of a republic by violence naturally presupposes a bad one, it will consequently be exceedingly rare that a good man should be found willing to employ wicked means to become a prince, even though his final object be good; or that a bad man, after having become prince, should be willing to labor for good ends, and that it should enter his mind to use for good purposes that authority which he has acquired by evil means." Trans. C. E. Detmold, 171.)

16. Cf. Hegel (1969 ff.; 12:316 f.), on the reign of Peisistratos and his sons.

17. Think, for instance, of the increase in the population's life expectancy by twenty-three years achieved under Suharto's thirty-one-year rule; during the same period, the rate of illiteracy fell from 61 percent to 17 percent, and per capita income increased nearly twenty-fold. Naturally, these successes do not justify his crimes in East Timor, for instance, or his family's corruption, but if one considers that in Russia male life expectancy fell by seven years between 1989 and 1994, one will not consider these successes routine and underestimate their significance. I take the data from the *DSW Newsletter* no. 16, August 1996, 5, which refers to *Population Today*, July 1996, and *Demographic and Health Surveys Newsletter* 8/1 (1996). (Since we are not concerned here with this specific case, I have not further checked the data, which may be exaggerated.)

are able to recognize that the morally superior system they have now achieved would not be comparably stable without the work of the successful dictator for development. But a further problem of the modern world is that in it several peoples have in large part realized the democratic natural law state and that its central ideas enjoy formal legitimacy almost everywhere, even if they are still far from being anchored in the mores of all peoples. This creates difficulties for the social acceptability of even successful dictatorships for development,[18] difficulties that were still spared the European monarchies of the seventeenth century, which could count on unconditional belief in the divine right of kings—a belief that was at that time socially useful in many cases but cannot be revived today merely because it could still be beneficial in some cases. In any case, it is completely unacceptable to announce democratic elections and then to cancel their result or to refuse a second ballot if they turn out differently than one had hoped they would, for thereby one is acknowledging the principle of democratic legitimacy in general and at the same time violating it in the specific case. Since 1992, the Algerian people has been paying a terrible price for this kind of politics.

So far as the means of power to be used in politics go, what was said in chapter 5.3 is fundamentally valid, even though it was not specifically related to political power. Even if every set of mores is accompanied by social oppositions and tensions, and even if politics is nourished by contradictory ideas and thus by struggles, it is nonetheless based on a fundamental consensus. Activating this consensus is the duty of every politics: as many commonalties as possible must be discovered before dealing with the differences. It is an elementary obligation of cratic prudence to make use of the more risky and expensive forms of power only when doing so is indispensable. But even if one's own power were ensured without a broad consensus, exercising it would as a rule be immoral because it would be demoralizing—no less for the power-holder than for the power subjects.[19] In an objective order of values, not only should consensus have priority over all other forms of power, but most factual mores recognize this fact. The processes of constructing and strengthening a consensus are therefore always to be encouraged. But this does not necessarily mean that comprehensive discourses should be organized. In traditional cultures, the consensus need not be achieved through argument; instead, it can be based on authorities, in which the power-holder must himself believe, however, even if with reservations; in the ideal case he would himself have personal authority. To construct a personal authority, a politician has to connect the attainment of certain goals with his own name. Dominating the discussion on a subject is strongly recommended, since personal authority without an objective basis or at least without the perception of

---

18. Cf. V. Hösle (1995b), 25.

19. Tocqueville rightly remarks that "Ce n'est point l'usage du pouvoir ou l'habitude de l'obéissance qui déprave les hommes, c'est l'usage d'une puissance qu'ils considèrent comme illégitime, et l'obéissance à un pouvoir qu'ils regardent comme usurpé et comme oppresseur" (1835 ff.; 1:63). ("It is not the exercise of power or the habit of obedience that corrupts people, it is the exercise of a power they consider illegitimate, and obedience to a power they regard as usurped and oppressive.")

such a basis will hardly last;[20] conversely, an objective issue acquires a quite different attractiveness when it is represented by people who are convincing as personalities or at least seem to be so in the dominant system of the media. However, since defeats often, but not always, damage the construction of a person's authority, one should, so far as possible, not make it known already in the preliminary phase of working toward a political goal that one has set out to attain it; instead, one should pursue several goals at once. An interesting intermediate form between argument and authority is represented by a fable such as Agrippa Menenius Lanatus is supposed to have told the plebeians after their first secession.[21] He spoke (according to the story, which if not true is in any case at least well-invented) in a language intelligible to the plebeians and at the same time laid out a valid argument in the form of a fable. He did the best that was at that time possible: he avoided any use of force by convincing the people in their own language. In modern societies, formal and substantive rationality is indispensable to a greater extent, and the Delphic method, which consists of several rounds of questioning various experts who remain anonymous but are informed regarding the median and the interquartal range of the responses, is certainly particularly advisable, because it is a means of consensus building that promotes objectivity. But even in modernity not all discourses lead to a broader consensus, and especially not to the discovery of the true or the morally right; that depends on the structure of the discourse and those participating in it, etc., and establishing discourses that do more to undermine consensus than to strengthen it is seldom politically prudent. Symbolic actions that directly convince and elicit emulation can be more effective: consider Brandt's going down on his knees in Warsaw, which meant a great deal more than a series of conferences and declarations on foreign affairs. In general, mobilizing all emotional energies that go beyond rational self-interest and serve the common good is more important than a merely intellectual discussion of political guidelines.

A great statesman certainly has the right to conceal complex political strategies whose revelation would at the moment still be counterproductive and to make them known only bit by bit if this contributes to their being ultimately accepted; he should avoid overt lies, but there is no moral duty to reveal one's own plans from the outset. In 1916 Woodrow Wilson won the presidential election in part by arguing that he had succeeded in keeping the United States out of the war. But this kind of assertion about the past did not logically imply that he would do the same in the future; and even if in 1916 Wilson had already decided that the United States would have to enter the war under certain conditions that he considered quite probable, one can hardly reproach him for

---

20. A cratically interesting form of dominating the discussion on a subject was Mitterand's leaving open for a long time the question as to whether he would be a candidate for re-election in 1988. In that way he managed to concentrate public attention on himself for months and to keep it off his opponents. Of course, this tactic functions only when it is accompanied by great loyalty within one's party.

21. See Livy, 2.32.

referring to his peace policy up to 1916 during the campaign. (This judgment does not imply a position on the question of whether the United States' entry into the war in 1917 should be evaluated positively.) The constitution of a collective identity between con-sensus and negative sanctions mediates by marking a difference from foreigners, and especially by repelling an internal or external threat. However, if the threat has been concocted only in order to produce internal cohesion, this generally violates elementary principles of justice.

Positive sanctions should be used as the second means of power. Naturally, the state should acquire them in a just way, for instance through legal taxation; taking money from some people in order to give it to others (especially if the former belong to a foreign people) was considered morally unproblematic by many mores, but even within those mores it hindered the development of a productive economy. Even if the redistributions in favor of the poorest people take place voluntarily, the humiliation felt by most people on accepting a gift can be counterproductive; therefore such redistribu-tions must take place through general mechanisms of restructuring. The practice of in-curring debts that one has no intention of repaying is situated between robbery and legal taxation. In modernity, economic growth made it possible for a time to give to all without taking anything away from anyone; in such situations, politics is considerably easier than in those in which money must be taken from a few or from all through tax in-creases, or in which certain benefits can no longer be continued. For people think they are entitled to what they have become accustomed to, and even if, from a moral point of view, relative poverty and relative impoverishment do not represent a great problem, people fight a relative worsening of their situation, even if it is completely justified ob-jectively, with a bitterness that is often repellent. At least in times when funds are short, there is a chance to actually do away with certain harmful parts of the state apparatus by halting their financing, thanks to the plausible explanation that there is simply no more money—an explanation that can avoid arousing enmities. For the most part, one has to use foreign financial means that were given voluntarily and under acceptable and legal conditions; a politician can hardly forgo seeking the support of the economically more powerful. The formation of alliances is usually connected with an exchange of mu-tual advantages; the ability to recognize non-Pareto-optimal situations and to lead the way out of them often allows the statesman to avoid the use of force. He must have a sense for who would benefit from morally desirable developments and must seek his al-lies among them, for he cannot presuppose too much idealism, and he has to be capable of making reasonable compromises.

Third, in cases in which it is authorized by law, the statesman has to be prepared to use force to prevent the collapse of society. Not using force where it is necessary to prevent a greater explosion of violence contradicts the specific duties of the politician. However, the use of force to defend the law must be complemented by preventive measures; just as important as the decisive use of negative sanctions is the effort to analyze the causes that lead to the violation of the law and to combat them. Perhaps none of Pompey's measures is more impressive than his handling of the pirates after the vigorous and successful elimination of this plague that radically threatened navigation on the Mediterranean. Some twenty thousand pirates surrendered, whom he could have executed or enslaved. "But he had won his rapid victory not least because they counted on his mercy. For he declared that he did not consider them criminals, but rather unfortunate men who carried on their activity because they were in need. So it was a matter of creating better living conditions for them. . . . We hear that in Rome this generous treatment was criticized; it disturbed people that former pirates should be provided for in this way."[22]

As rule, only the political man (*Machtmensch*) can succeed. His motives may be immoral, but his will to power can also arise from a high sense of responsibility—for instance, from the desire to prevent someone significantly worse from attaining political office, whether because this second person himself seeks power or because he has been promoted by others who want to put a weak, mediocre candidate in office so that they can pursue their machinations all the more undisturbed. A political man can certainly seek power, not as an end in itself, but rather only as a means, and no one can be reproached for seeking an indispensable means to a goal if the latter is moral and the intrinsic disvalue of the means is not greater than the value of the goal. Someone who can be sure that he would be a better power-holder may, indeed should, seek power; he may even try to centralize power if there are objective arguments for believing that such a centralization is in the general interest. The fact that he would himself benefit most from such a centralization is no argument against these objective grounds, even if it is advisable, naturally, to check out with special care grounds that are offered by someone to whose advantage they would work. A fortiori, it should be acknowledged that the power-holder has the right, and even the duty, to defend himself against attacks on his power position, which is, as an office, somewhat more general than his private interest, and, if these attacks are illegal, to repel them by imposing punishments and, under some circumstances, by using military force. The fact that Victor Emmanuel III yielded to the pressure of the rabble and appointed Mussolini prime minister in 1922, instead of ordering the army to shoot, was a betrayal of the Italian people, especially since at that time the risk of civil war was not great (even if this judgment is obviously easier to make ex post facto than it was in the concrete situation).

The struggle for power should be conducted as much as possible in an objective manner, preferably with reference to the fact that one's own political ideas are better and that one is the more capable politician. In democracies, the struggle for power is concentrated on election campaigns for state and party offices. It is certainly moral to point out one's opponent's political weaknesses, within the limits of the truth—because political competition concerns precisely the question of political capabilities and, if one's adversary has himself moved to this level of contest, he is only getting what he deserves and is regarded as an end in himself by being attacked on this same level. However, complaining about one's political opponent by referring to qualities that have

---

22. M. Gelzer (1973), 72.

nothing to do with politics is immoral.[23] This holds for any conflict; pointing out to a person offering defective goods that his wife is unfaithful to him is tasteless, even if his goods contradict all standards, because the behavior of his wife has nothing to do with the performance he owes. One can go to court, but the line that delimits the private sphere should not be crossed. Similarly, rummaging around in the private lives of opposing politicians is only a diversion from the real problems and very quickly leads to a decline in political culture. However, striking back is permissible if the opponent has begun to shift levels and if he continues his attacks after having been explicitly warned: tit-for-tat strategies have well-known advantages.

It goes without saying that moral responsibility for the policies pursued by a state is primarily borne by those who have made the corresponding decisions or should have made them, according to the constitutional law in force. In a monocracy, obedient subordinates who carry out an unjust policy can be reproached only for not having violated the law or emigrated; in a democracy, the additional reproach can in some cases be made that the person involved put the unjust government in power or simply failed to vote against it. As a rule, one should exercise the constitutional power that one has; one may be justified in not voting only if one comes to the conclusion that of two parties between which one has to choose, each has the same number of strengths and weaknesses. But in order to arrive at this conclusion, one must be concerned with politics; at least one must seek out someone on whose competent judgment one believes one can rely. In crisis situations, there is a moral duty not only to vote but to vote strategically; one can afford to give one's vote to a splinter party only if strengthening it in the long run is more important than the short-term avoidance of a somewhat worse government. In the run-off between Hitler and Hindenburg in 1932, one had to vote for Hindenburg, even if there was previously a duty to be politically engaged to avoid its ever coming to such a run-off vote between two unattractive, but not really equally unattractive, candidates.

8.1.5. The Morals of Violations of the Law within Stable Mores

Violations of the law can be of various degrees of generality. The most general are attempts to overthrow the whole social order; these are not possible within stable mores but are conceivable only when an ethic is dissolving and entirely different ideas of order are present in a people. I will examine this point later. More limited are attempts to change the constitution—for instance, to replace a monocracy with a democracy, or to overturn a democracy by replacing it with an autocracy. A still smaller degree of generality characterizes the removal of a monocrat by another monocrat, in a palace

---

23. Cf. Nagel (1979), 65 f., in the important essay "War and Massacre," 53–74.

revolution, for instance. All the violations of law mentioned thus far are directed against the institution setting the norms. From these we must distinguish violations of individual norms. How are such violations of the law to be evaluated?[24]

We have already said that there is a prima facie obligation to obey the law. However, this obligation can be challenged on the basis of justifying grounds. Too many important steps forward in human history have resulted from violations of the law, a few of which—and these are obviously harder to justify—were even accompanied by a great deal of bloodshed. The United States owes its existence, first, to an illegal secession that resulted in a war, and second, to an illegal calling of the Constitutional Convention in Philadelphia to adopt a constitution under conditions that contradicted the Articles of Confederation. Both Jefferson, in the *Declaration of Independence,* and Madison, in the *Federalist Papers,* were honest enough to acknowledge that they were violating valid positive law;[25] but they considered themselves morally justified in doing so, although they simultaneously admitted that such moral rights could be claimed only in exceptional historical situations. Their argumentation presupposes a conception of natural law, namely the idea that positive law is bound by anterior normative principles; in the framework of most forms of legal positivism, there is in fact no question of morally legitimating violations of the law. Hardly anyone has proposed a more comprehensive right to freedom from interference than did Locke, and especially important is his argument that a view like his does not increase the number of violations of the law in history but rather decreases it because his view warns the government not to commit those violations of natural law that almost inevitably lead to resistance.[26] It is true that the creation of a view that initially recognizes a moral duty to obey positive law is a necessary presupposition for the genesis of the modern state, whose foundations were threatened by knights errant like Don Quixote and noble robbers like Robin Hood. But the profound truth of Locke's position is evident if one compares the history of England or the United States with that of Germany: The denial of a moral right to freedom from interference, such as is found in many German political philosophers,[27] did not reduce the amount of bloodshed but on the contrary favored the rise of the bloodiest tyranny. The will to resist state injustice can be strengthened by embodying in the constitution a positive right to resist (as in the German Basic Law, Article 20 IV). On grounds of political pedagogy it makes sense, even if it will very seldom be relevant in practice: if the attempt to abolish the free,

---

24. On the following, see Rawls (1971), 363 ff. (who, however, deals only with the simpler cases), and A. Kaufmann (1994), 186 ff.

25. (1787 f.), 189, 199 ff., 224 f. (38, 40, and 43).

26. See *Second Treatise* § 226 (1690; 415 f.): "*This Doctrine* of a Power in the People of providing for their safety a-new . . . is *the best fence against Rebellion,* and the probablest means to hinder it. . . . [T]he properest way to prevent the evil, is to shew them the danger and injustice of it, who are under the greatest temptation to run into it."

27. One has only to read Kant, *Metaphysik der Sitten* I § 49A (1976 f.; 437 ff.).

democratic order fails, an appeal to this right to resist is normally superfluous, and if the attempt succeeds, an appeal to this right would not help.[28] However, the task of a constitution is not only to judge human behavior legally but also to shape legal consciousness and to motivate people to adopt a certain kind of behavior.

Violating the law is subjectively moral only if it is based on such moral grounds and does not use them as a pretext for dishonest ends. The mere subjective conviction that a state law or a state measure is unjust is not a sufficient moral ground. A conscientious study of the arguments for the law or the measure in question is morally obligatory, and, especially if the norm at issue is the result of a mixed syllogism, the acquisition of empirical knowledge is indispensable. Even if one comes to the conclusion that the empirical assumptions on which the legislator based its decision are false, the resistance must have a quality different from the one it has when the legislator openly contravenes fundamental moral principles. The argument that NATO was preparing a nuclear first strike against the Soviet Union, which served to heat up the atmosphere during discussions on deploying the Pershing II missiles, was not only empirically absurd but dangerous because it transformed the German government's position, which may have been based on criticizable empirical premises, into an a priori reprehensible one. To be sure, when fundamental moral principles are violated, resistance is permissible to a very different degree, but for precisely that reason one must be particularly careful in stating that such is the case, and it is immoral to express such opinions publicly without detailed knowledge. Resistance to norms concerning which it is only important that any decision be taken, not which decision, is always inadmissible; resistance to what is decided is not.

Various parameters should be taken into account in deciding in favor of resistance; a few of these were already mentioned in chapter 8.1.2. These are, first, the (natural) objects of legal protection that are violated through positive law; second, those that are violated by one's own breaking of the law; third, the probable consequences of one's own act and its prospects of succeeding. Violent resistance against a murderous state is easier to legitimate than violent resistance to a state with an unjust property order; sit-ins opposing a military decision considered irresponsible are morally less problematic than the use of violence against things or especially against people; if the establishment of a constitutional state is its most probable outcome, assassinating a tyrant makes more sense than if it can be anticipated that a still more bloodthirsty rogue will succeed him or that a civil war will break out. Maintaining a proportionate relationship between one's own violation of the law and the state organ's violation of natural law is an elementary demand (which Kleist's Michael Kohlhaas, for instance, fails to meet), even if it is not easy to weigh violations of freedom against the loss of human lives; this problem comes up especially in the case of violent defenses of freedom in civil wars (and analogously in wars between states). Furthermore, one should consider what alternatives to

---

28. Cf. F. E. Schnapp in I. von Münch (1985), 1:838.

breaking the law exist. Breaking the law must in general be an *ultima ratio* to which one should resort only after all legal means have been exhausted.

8.1.5.1. Violations of the Law in a Constitutional State Founded on the Rule of Law

Legal remedies against state decisions are far more differentiated in a modern democratic constitutional state than in pre-modern states because, among other reasons, everyone can in principle become part of the government. Therefore it can be said that in this state form, violating the law is morally more problematic than in other state forms; if the competence norms are just, obedience even to unjust primary norms is demanded to a higher degree. However, in a constitutional state, violating the law is often less risky than in traditional states, and therefore if the law is regularly violated in such a state, there are grounds for suspecting that it is violated as a result not so much of moral feeling as of the wish to be above the law, if this is not connected with negative sanctions that are too painful. A lawbreaker in a constitutional state should ask himself, for the purpose of testing his conscience, whether he would have the courage to do something analogous in an unjust state. There is much to be said for the psychological theory that in the Federal Republic of Germany, violations of the law are commonly attempts to compensate for an earlier generation's failure to resist. The lack of broad resistance during the Third Reich is truly not something Germans can be proud of, but violations of the law under very different circumstances, and in cases in which it is surely questionable whether the positive law is really contrary to natural law, unfortunately do not have the moral quality of the resistance that was then required.

All other things being equal, the *omission* of a legally obligatory action—for instance, a soldier's obligation to salute the flag—is easier to justify than the commission of an *act* contrary to the law. Analogously, an illegal action that directly results in something good is less problematic morally than one that does so only indirectly—consider hiding an innocent person pursued by state power in contrast to acts of sabotage against one's own state when it is waging an unjust war, if these acts directly endanger one's comrades. Moreover, in a constitutional state, *public* violations of the law are to be preferred to *secret* ones, for in the former case the motive for the violation is made clear, the violation can trigger an open discussion, and the lawbreaker thereby indicates that he accepts the negative sanctions associated with his act because he considers them a lesser evil than the acceptance of a political injustice. (I assume that his act was really a violation of the law and not, for instance, that the highest courts determine that a right to commit them is guaranteed by the constitution or by regulations regarding the justifying state of emergency.) Such acts of *civil disobedience* should forgo direct violence as far as possible, they should have the strongest possible symbolic quality, and they should be directed primarily against state power or against those who benefit from the legal injustice in question, not against innocent third parties. However, this does not mean that one must break the law considered unjust. Someone who considers punishment for adultery to be contrary to natural law should not himself commit adultery in order to draw public attention to the problem; participating in prohibited demonstrations is quite enough. The violation of the law should be limited to the strict minimum required. Since civil disobedience is not an end in itself but should rather produce an effect, it is morally obligatory to deal with this means (1) prudently—that is, sparingly, since inflation is counterproductive; (2) without slandering the majority on which one is dependent in order to change the law; (3) with efforts to see to it that one's acts are favorably reported in the media; and (4) as much as possible in the pose of the weak David, since this elicits sympathy. Greenpeace has made such skillful use of these strategic principles that it is still seen as a powerless David even though many a Goliath has already suffered at its hands. Since the interests of this organization are among humanity's most important, these successes are to be welcomed, but one has to concede that the heroic age of Greenpeace is past.

Secret violations of the law are acceptable in a constitutional state only if they are the only feasible way of preserving an important, directly threatened object of natural legal protection: think of setting free animals on which cruel experiments are to be performed for the sake of developing cosmetics, or concealing political refugees who are to be deported because of an inadequate right to asylum. However, when contemplating such actions, one must consider the fact that they *set an example*. Since the lawbreaker, unlike someone engaging in civil disobedience, is not acting publicly, he should not be surprised if other individuals whose moral ideas are significantly different from his own also soon break the law; they will be rightly able to appeal formally to his example, even if substantively they seek the opposite. This consequence, whose extent may vary depending on the historical situation, must be taken into account and weighed against the arguments in favor of breaking the law. Obviously, if the lawbreaker makes it clear that he believes in no objective moral order, in no natural law, even the most criminal offenders will begin to present themselves as resistance fighters: for instance, when they beat up, in the name of their entirely subjective conscience, the very asylum seekers that the other lawbreaker sought to protect. At a minimum, argumentative efforts must be made, at least after the fact, to demonstrate the necessity of one's own violation of the law; but in particular a lawbreaker must show that he is not afraid to make major sacrifices himself in order to live in accord with the moral principles he considers binding. Someone who does a great deal for the world's poorest people is more credible when he conceals rejected asylum seekers than someone who gets interested in the poorest only when he has an opportunity to break the law. Furthermore, one must consider the likelihood of one's own action succeeding; if concealment can only postpone deportation briefly, it makes less sense than if it can provide the person concerned with long-term protection against unjust deportation.

Violations of the law by members of the judicial or executive branches require special consideration, since these individuals have accepted a duty to be particularly loyal to the law in force. It goes without saying that judges are bound by the valid laws and that a desirable political commitment to changing a law does not release them from their fidelity to the law currently in force; questions *de lege ferenda* and those *de lege lata* must absolutely be distinguished. But judges may and must make use of all the room for maneuver at their disposal (for instance, via the constitutional court's judicial review); indeed, they deserve respect if they resign their office because they consider current law to be so immoral that its application is not compatible with their conscience. Bending positive law can be morally permissible (and then obligatory as well) only if it is the only promising way of preventing massive injustice on the part of the state—consider the non-imposition of death sentences that are prescribed by the law, toward the end of an authoritarian regime.[29] A hard case to judge is one in which a member of the state bureaucracy commits a violation of the law on grounds of conscience or even just becomes guilty of a disloyalty that strongly conflicts with the interests of his agency. For instance, one should consider "whistle-blowing,"[30] in which a member of a firm or a state department informs, for example, the media regarding irregularities or even illegalities committed by his superiors or colleagues, under some circumstances violating a formal legal duty (such as confidentiality). It is obvious that engaging in this sort of activity is no way to make friends, but here we are concerned with the moral question of whether such behavior is permissible. In this context we must first acknowledge that it is certainly more problematic when an official of the agency concerned, rather than a private individual, reveals something improper, for no enterprise, either private or public, can survive if a minimum of loyalty is not guaranteed. From daily collaboration in a corporate group, which is often continued even in leisure activities with the goal of increasing social cohesion (think of company-sponsored excursions), arise special obligations that must be fulfilled by first speaking with those concerned before the public is informed. Such a duty certainly exists, at least so long as no unreasonable risks are connected with it, and so long as there is some hope of improving the behavior criticized. But if attempts at internal reform fail, then even an official should remember that he has stronger duties to his country than to his colleagues and superiors and that by putting the interests of the office over those of the persons holding it he can show himself to be a faithful civil servant. Thus he should certainly inform the media of corruption, waste of public monies, and so on. This can be an incentive for the agency to construct internal mechanisms that make it possible to articulate moral concerns and to discuss them.

Let there be no mistake: Even if psychopathic malcontents sometimes unjustly bring their own agencies into disrepute in the media, dependency on the institution that employs and feeds one is much more likely to cause one to overlook reprehensible things. Moreover, James Waters (1978) worked out the organizational structures that favor *blindness to injustice within one's own firm* and analogously also in a government agency. A socialization that acquaints a person with certain illegal practices from the outset, the recognition of a duty to the cohesion of the group, the fear of external interventions that might damage the firm's or even one's own state's image, a lack of clarity regarding priorities in

---

29. In this connection, the tradition used to speak of "epiky." Cf. Thomas Aquinas, *Summa theologica* II/II, q.60 a.5 and esp. q.120.

30. Cf., for instance, P. A. French (1983), 134 ff.

the firm's guidelines and a lack of a conceptual apparatus that makes it possible to categorize morally problematic cases, being subject to directions given by superiors, the splitting up of decisions, and finally the division of labor often lead precisely to one's ultimately feeling no concrete responsibility for the overall result of the activities of one's own firm or agency—even and precisely in the most horrifyingly unjust states. The organizer of Nazi transportation of the Jews, Adolph Eichmann, who completely rejected any responsibility for what happened to the people transported, is a particularly repellent example of the structure just analyzed. And yet one must admit that in institutional frameworks like the one just outlined, most people fail morally. There is a duty to educate people to react more sensitively to collective injustice, but one must also change the institutions in such a way that they provide more room for critical questions about the factual mores. For human behavior depends on two factors, a person's character and the social environment, and an approach that judges a person's guilt without taking into account the social structural conditions is just as abstract as one that makes any individual responsibility dissolve into these structural conditions.

8.1.5.2. Violations of the Law and Cooperation in States That Are Not Constitutional States

The moral evaluation of violations of the law changes radically when the lawbreaker lives in a thoroughly unjust system that is not even rooted in the people's mores. Consider a monocracy headed by a *tyrant* who does not hesitate to show contempt for human life. It goes without saying that an innocent person who is about to be killed has a right to defend himself, and it is equally clear that in such a system resistance usually has no chance of succeeding. If the tyrant is prudent enough to exploit his subjects in a limited way, to allow vague hopes, and to not kill people indiscriminately, then his position is very strong, so long as all people pursue rational self-interest;[31] for on this assumption, hardly anyone will risk his life by participating in resistance, especially since as a rule a great number of resisters is required in order to achieve anything, and the individual thus has the impression that it does not depend on him at all. A good political system is a public good proper, and we have already seen that in dealing with such goods prisoners' dilemma situations can be avoided only if coercive force is used; but by definition, the potential revolutionaries do not yet have access to such force. That tyrants are nonetheless overthrown again and again results from the fact that there are always people, sometimes even in the required number, who are prepared to risk their lives in order to do their moral duty, and who moreover have organizational abilities. (In addition, it should be pointed out that a few tyrants kill so indiscriminately that the risk connected with an assassination attempt is not much greater than that run by people not involved in it.) However, it cannot be said that one always has a duty to risk

---

31. Cf. G. S. Kavka (1982).

one's life; there is a prima facie duty to preserve one's own life, which becomes even stronger if one has children. On the other hand, one can expect people with a special moral obligation—for instance, Christian clergymen—to risk even their lives for the sake of justice. But prudence can require that one wait until one's own resistance has a better chance of succeeding, although of course the chance of success could also decrease the longer the tyrant holds power. In a remarkable dialectic, the degree of justification of resistance, indeed, of the obligation to resist, increases in the same measure as the weight of the excusing grounds for those who do not do their duty: violations of the law under National Socialism were morally more urgent than in the German Democratic Republic, but they were also riskier, because the former system was significantly more unjust than the latter and therefore also more brutal in dealing with resistance. Passive resistance is, however, seldom risky, and is therefore always a duty. The more one is subjected to harassment within the country and the less chance there is that one can work to improve the situation, the more attractive becomes the option of emigrating. On the other hand, if, within a state that is not truly murderous, one has more possibilities of working toward a slow but effective subversion of the system than one would have abroad, then it is more moral not to emigrate.

In order to ground the right to freedom from interference, it does not matter whether it is oneself or another that is endangered in life and limb; the rights to self-defense and to defend others from attack go hand in hand, and it is even especially noble when someone helps an innocent person who is being persecuted, although he is not himself subject to any threat. These rights are also valid with regard to a state that is not persecuting one but is not able to provide effective protection against aggressors. Nonetheless, even in a thoroughly unjust state, a weak prima facie duty to observe the law arises from the fact that even such a system guarantees a certain stability. Furthermore, a few of this system's norms will be valid—for instance, the prohibition on killing—and these may be violated only if the overthrow of the unjust order can thereby be achieved or the life of an innocent person saved. In the Third Reich, concealing Jews was obviously morally permissible, and even obligatory, but terroristic acts against passersby were not. (It goes without saying that terrorism can under no circumstances be justified in a constitutional state.) On the other hand, the attempt to kill Hitler was morally admirable, and in view of the crimes committed by his regime, if one does not recognize the principle that human lives cannot be weighed against each other, one will have to concede that even accepting the death of innocent people was morally permissible if it was the only way of eliminating Hitler. Georg Elser (a carpenter who, acting on his own, attempted to assassinate Hitler on 9 November 1939) deserves posterity's admiration more than Hindenburg (and, if they are just, even the admiration of the members of the families of the people he killed), and all the more so as there was surely some chance that the assassination of Hitler would cause the system to collapse or at least be crucially modified, since it was very dependent on the person of the *Führer*. On the other hand, assassinating an unjust despot or autocrat is not reasonable if it cannot positively change the system. In such a case the overthrow of a system can for the most part proceed only from several people within the power apparatus, and especially in the military, which bears a special responsibility in this respect because it is often the only institution that can change the system; however, *ought* presupposes *can*. Let there be no illusions: Given the modern state's means of power, only in exceptional cases can the overthrow of an unjust government be achieved by an individual or even by a group of people outside the power apparatus, especially without external help; at least part of the armed forces must go over to the side of the resisters for the latter to succeed. Of course, as a rule the resisters must convince or persuade a majority of the citizens, or at least of the elites, in order to gain an enduring hold on state power, and under the conditions of modernity, that means that they must control the mass media; but access to the latter usually has to be won with tanks. Obviously, this does not mean that the rest of the population does not have some possibilities for resistance and therefore a corresponding duty: Consider only the diverse forms of protest and counter-propaganda. A. T. Wegener's open letter to Hitler and the "White Rose Letters" show what courageous people can do even in an unjust state—even if they directly affect little, they maintain the claim of humanity.

However, it can also be morally permissible to make one's career within the power apparatus of a state that is recognized to be unjust if, and only if, one's motive is to improve or even to reform the system, and if there is a realistic chance of doing so. Guicciardini famously defended the thesis that a good citizen should serve a tyrant, not only on selfish grounds, but because of his responsibility to the state; for he could keep his fellow citizens from suffering worse, and it would not be better for the state if the tyrant had only evil collaborators.[32] There are, of course, enough situations in which *collaborating with an unjust state* does more evil than good; indeed, precisely a person who enjoys special moral prestige should always take care to keep his moral authority from contributing to the legitimation of an unjust system. But Guicciardini is right: in certain situations it is important that in an unjust political system rogues not be the only ones in the government. It is absurd when people fail to make distinctions when morally assessing Ribbentrop and Ernst von Weizsäcker, or Ceaușescu and Jaruzelski. The peaceful victory over Soviet totalitarianism would not have been possible had not a few of the *Sest'desjatniki*, the members of the generation that was educated and came to political consciousness in the 1960s, decided to go into politics. At the same time, the pressure for radical changes would not have been great enough if there had not been uncompromising dissidents who denounced, at great personal sacrifice, the injustice of the system. The paths taken by Sakharov and Gorbachev were very different, but one can surely say that the wonder

---

32. See *Ricordi* B 108 (1977; 220): "[P]erché governandosi così gli viene occasione co' consigli e con le opere di favorire molti beni e disfavorire molti mali. E questi che gli biasimano sono pazzi: perché starebbe fresca la città e loro, se el tiranno non avessi intorno altro che tristi!" ("For if he does, he will be able, through word and deed, to help many good causes and to hinder many evil ones. Those who censure him are mad; they and their city would be in a fine situation if the tyrant had no one but wicked men around him." Trans. M. Dornandi, 122.) See also C 220 (1997; 183).

of *perestroika* would not have occurred had there not been people of both types in the country. That does not mean that Gorbachev went into politics with the express goal of reforming the system. On the contrary: he liked power and he was a convinced communist, but he accepted that worldview because he considered it compatible with a few of the basic moral values of pre-revolutionary Russia that he had internalized as a child. Indeed, one can even say that Gorbachev would not have achieved the successes that were granted him in foreign policy had he been an opponent of the system from the outset. For someone who has spent his whole life simulating does not arouse trust; only the naive combination of integrity and a will to power schooled in Leninism that Gorbachev emanated could convince and even bewitch the West. A figure such as János Kádár, to whom Hungary owes a great deal, despite his infamous role in the Soviet invasion of 1956 (which was preceded by his imprisonment by the Stalinists in 1951), was more opportunistic, more reflective, and probably subtler; but greater complexity is not always a plus in politics. In chapter 3.5.1, we discussed the encounter between Napoleon and Myriel in Hugo's *Les Misérables;* it would have been marvelous had Gorbachev and Sakharov been able to respect each other in a similar way.

More unproblematic than *making a career* in the offices of an unjust state is limited *cooperation* with such a state from a position within a relatively independent institution. For instance, the only too justified disgust felt in communist states for informers who tried to create a significance for themselves (to which they were not entitled by despicably betraying acquaintances, friends, relatives, and even spouses, thereby imagining that they were collaborating, like a little *deus absconditus,* in the shaping of world history) should not be extended to those who saw themselves, for instance, as servants of their church and were at the same time prepared to overcome prisoners' dilemma situations of both adversaries—that is, to accept compromises that were more or less in the interests of both.[33] Not all interactions in unjust states are zero-sum games (not even all encounters with the State Security [*Staatssicherheitsdienst*] of the former German Democratic Republic); and it is not clear why one should refuse an exchange that is useful to both sides. Even the secret services of states that are hostile to each other repeatedly exchange information, and someone can be suspected of being a double agent only if he receives much worse information than he hands on. Even if he does so, the intention to commit treason is not yet proven; the person concerned can also be irresponsibly stupid. Since the intention is what counts most morally, one should not consider abhorrent those who were outmaneuvered against their will, for instance, by the GDR's State Security; however, such people are of no use as politicians because someone representing others' interests must not allow himself to be outmaneuvered. To make a concrete judgment as to whether someone who had contacts in East Germany should be prime minister of a new, unified state of Germany, nothing less is necessary than a precise assessment of the advantages and disadvantages of these contacts for the various sides.

---

33. Cf. the important essay by J. C. Joerden (1993).

After the downfall of an unjust state, only a differentiated observation of the behavior of each individual can claim to be just. The usual grounds for justification and excuse (for example, remorse and an effort to avert the effects of one's wrongful acts in the final days of a regime) are to be taken into account; at the same time, however, as we saw in chapter 7.3.2, the punishment of the true political criminals must not be omitted. Political grounds, such as the achievement of internal peace when confronted by an external threat, can justify amnesties, but the way Germany handled, under Adenauer, the crimes of the National Socialists remains a moral disgrace, especially since there was no compelling political reason for this kind of policy with regard to the past; on the contrary, in the medium term it inevitably aroused sympathy for communism.[34] It goes without saying that punishment of political criminals may take place only on the basis of just procedures; revenge-justice (as for instance in the "trials" of Elena and Nicolae Ceaușescu) is fundamentally even worse than immediate execution because judicial form is misused for purposes that are incompatible with the idea of justice. (In the case mentioned it also distracted attention from the share of the guilt borne by the Ceaușescu' political heirs.) Someone who has become morally guilty should, if he sincerely repents, be able to receive moral forgiveness. However, the principle of self-respect usually precludes recognizing one's guilt before a broad public, or even on live television. Such a procedure, which is in tune with modern media democracy, would only favor those who do not take themselves seriously, and such persons cannot be depended upon in the future.

Hardly any reasonable person will deny that the vague intentions of Generals Halder, Beck, et al. to arrest Hitler and his accomplices on 4 September 1938, and also the assassination attempt of 20 July 1944, were moral performances without which German history would look even more dismal. The fall of the Portuguese prime minister Caetano, brought about by the "Armed Forces Movement" in April 1974, was objectively right, whatever the motives of the officers involved in the putsch may have been; morally, this putsch was justified not only because it took place for a good goal but also because it was largely bloodless. Can there also be *legitimate putsches or coups d'état* against a democratically elected government? Surely only in rare, exceptional cases, since democracy is legitimate according to natural constitutional law; but on the basis of what was said earlier, the question cannot be fundamentally answered in the negative. For in addition to the procedural aspect, substantive objects of legal protection have to be taken into account; and if a democratically elected government proves incapable of maintaining order, protecting human lives, and defending the country against foreign threats, the illegal introduction of a non-democratic state form can be legitimate insofar as it takes place only for a transitional period intended to prepare the country for a more efficient democracy. The violations of human rights by the Turkish military are not to be justified morally under any circumstances, but the question of whether General Evren's

---

34. Nonetheless, Germany later compensated for its mistakes, which one cannot say about Japan or many another state.

military putsch in 1980 was morally reprehensible, in view of the chaotic situation in the country, which had cost thousands of lives, the hopeless deadlock of the democratic politicians, and the repeated warnings made by the military, cannot be answered a priori in the positive; it can be answered only after careful examination of the alternatives that then existed. It is obvious that not every illegal overthrow of an incapable democratic government is legitimate: the new government may be just as incapable of resolving the problems, the situation may get even worse and thus add to the substantive injustices a formal injustice as well, or the putsch itself may be connected with a great deal of bloodshed or may even trigger a civil war.

Avoiding *civil wars* is clearly an elementary obligation for every politics and can be contravened only when it is a matter of preventing a terrible evil, such as the establishment of a totalitarian state. One may forgive Marcus Junius Brutus for murdering in Caesar the benefactor who pardoned him after the battle of Pharsalus and even made him praetor: it can be permissible to betray criminals, and Brutus did not make his decision lightly. The moral assessment of Brutus made by Dante, who puts him, along with Cassius and Judas, in the final circle of Hell, where he is chewed up by Lucifer himself,[35] and thus counts him among the three worst figures of history, is certainly unjust. But what one cannot excuse is that through his behavior, Brutus threw his country into a new civil war; it is harder to forgive him the death of soldiers and civilians than that of Caesar. In particular, his inability to foresee the probable consequences of his act reveals an unacceptable lack of responsibility; his opposition to the elimination of Antony was not a moral achievement but rather a criminal weakness. Machiavelli is right on one point: if one decides to use force (though when one may decide to use it, Machiavelli cannot say), then one should be consistent.[36] *Si peccas, pecca fortiter* (if one sins, one should really sin); or, since here we are concerned with morally justifiable violations of the law, if one commits one such violation, then one must have the strength of will to carry out those that necessarily follow from it. Someone who does not have the personality to do so should avoid committing the first violation. Brutus must also be reproached for not sufficiently understanding that Caesar was a man of an entirely different stature than he was and that after the great internal and external political changes to which Rome was exposed, his own ideas of political order were inadequate. After Caesar's murder, the Senate proved to be incapable of taking power into its own hands, and its panic once again confirmed that the replacement of the senatorial oligarchy by Caesar was not rooted solely in his will to power but also had objective grounds. The condemnation of Brutus's act does not imply that he was a rogue; that Caesar thought highly of him suggests otherwise. It does not follow from all this that I condemn Caesar's violations of the law any less than Brutus's behavior; Caesar bears an even greater co-responsibility for the civil war of 49 BC than Brutus bears for the one that broke out

---

35. *Inferno* 34.55 ff.
36. *Discorsi* I.26.4 f. (1984; 121).

in 44 BC.[37] Even if by his intellect and personality Caesar towered above his opponents, most of whom were mediocre and driven by petty personal interests as well as by envy of him, he had no right to put thousands of human lives at risk for the sake of his *dignitas*.[38] But to provoke a second civil war out of revenge is morally impermissible. Only a relationship to the future, not that to the past, can justify such an act, and Brutus had not in the least understood the developmental tendencies of the future.

Finally, with respect to *palace revolutions* or the overthrow of a legal monocrat by an autocrat or an oligarchic clique, it should be said that they are permissible if the legal ruler is a tyrant—that is, if he tramples on basic principles of his own people's mores and if the new rulers truly possess different moral and political qualities. (If there is no clear order of succession, then it is no violation of the law in the narrower sense when one of the possible heirs seizes power; rather, it is usually an act of self-defense.) Nonetheless, the new autocrats should be careful; by acting as they did, they have set an example that can boomerang on them. If the legal ruler is merely less capable than his competitor, his overthrow is considerably more problematic; if in addition he enjoys great support or is considered to hold a right to rule by the grace of God, one is running the risk of igniting a civil war, which is much too high a price to pay even for a better ruler. Richard II was not a great king, but the Wars of the Roses were far more terrible than his reign, and Henry VI, the usurper's grandson, was even more incapable than Richard and could therefore be deposed with the same and even greater justification. Charlemagne ignored his nephews' succession rights and thereby preserved the unity of the Frankish empire; in addition, there are good reasons for believing that his nephews were not men of the same stature, for in all of history there have been few who were his equal. But Charlemagne was unable to alter the inheritance right of the Frankish royal house, and soon after his death the unity of the Frankish empire was lost again, so that it certainly makes sense to ask whether his violation of the law, which only postponed the problem for two generations, can really be justified, although it at least provided his subjects with relatively good administration for several decades. The fact that in early modern Europe the succession rights of kings, even incapable ones, were taken more seriously than they were in earlier periods did much to promote the stability of European politics and the genesis of the modern state.

It is hardly surprising[39] that in legitimist systems the *elimination of the legal ruler and his progeny* is usual after a revolution,[40] and no matter how immoral it is, it cannot

---

37. See the devastating judgment of Caesar made by Machiavelli (who is the author of the *Il Principe!*). *Discorsi* I.10.12 ff. (1984; 89).

38. Nonetheless, it is a point in Caesar's favor that regarding the men killed at Pharsalus he felt the need to justify himself—even if he did so with the rather simple claim that the opposite side wanted this war (Plutarch, *Caesar*, 46).

39. Great Britain's refusal to take in the Romanovs after they were deposed therefore made it virtually an accessory to their murder, since the latter was only to be expected given the rules of politics.

40. Cf. for instance, Guicciardini, *Ricordi* B 149 (1977; 234), who urgently recommends the assassination of at least all male progeny of an overthrown tyrant and makes differentiations only among the female progeny.

be equated with the usual sort of murder, because through this act a later risk of civil war is supposed to be forestalled (this holds even for fratricide among the Ottomans); at the end of the twentieth century, more than fifty years after the monarchy had been abolished, Italy still refused to allow male descendants of its last king to enter the country. To be sure, this is a violation of less essential basic rights than killing them would be; but it clearly shows how deep the fear of a ruler considered by some as legitimate still is. However, in earlier times it was also possible to avoid murdering the deposed monarch and to be content with putting him in confinement or in a monastery; thus murdering him cannot be justified even if one abandons the principle that human lives cannot be weighed against each other. Killing, in the name of reasons of state, princes' wives who lack the required social rank also belongs to this context, and while it cannot be justified, a character like Ernst in Hebbel's *Agnes Bernauer* cannot be considered a common criminal—though the drama is not very convincing because it presents the problem of the reason of state too simplistically. At least Agnes knows what she's getting involved in, whereas the children of a legitimate ruler cannot be reproached for anything; hence murdering the latter is a still greater crime.

The judgment of history concerning a coup d'état or a putsch will depend on the success granted the (potential) new ruler. This cannot hold for the judgment of morals. Respect for Goerdeler is not diminished by the fact that the attempt on Hitler's life failed; the fact that the Bolshevists' coup d'état succeeded and that they long helped shape world history would not make them great men even if they had succeeded in subjugating the whole world. All that is morally relevant is the prospect of success with which a violation of the law is committed; if it can be assumed on the basis of cratic know-how that a coup d'état or revolution against an unjust regime can succeed without bloodshed, one has a strong moral justification for one's own undertaking. The Glorious Revolution deserves its name, whereas blind and counterproductive heroism is irresponsible.

8.1.5.3. Secession

A coup d'état or a putsch usually seeks only to change the *government* or the *constitution;* it does not put in question the *unity of the state.* What about political efforts to dissolve state unity? Hardly any state recognizes a right to secession; if it does so expressly, it is a confederation and not a federal state. But even if almost every secession contravenes positive law, is it therefore to be condemned from a natural law point of view? Is there a morally relevant difference between the secession of the United States from Great Britain and the secession of the southern states from the United States? Sympathies for a right to secede are implicit in the doctrine of the self-determination of peoples. According to the latter, an ideal world would be one in which each people has its own state. But this doctrine is untenable, as was demonstrated in the discussion of nationalism in chapter 7.3.3.3.7. It contradicts in the crudest way the goal of working toward a universal constitutional state. If the seceding part of the state were to seek annexation to another state, at least the number of states would remain unchanged, but against such secessions we must weigh foreign policy considerations and even the original state's right to self-defense: Czechoslovakia's loss of the Sudetenland was followed in less than six months by its subjugation under the Third Reich. The doctrine of a people's right to self-determination (which, unfortunately, can be asserted by particularly deplorable forms of catch-up nationalism that compensate in a primitive way for the humiliations connected with a people's underdevelopment) would justify dividing up most currently existing states, because there are many peoples without a state and in most states there are ethnic minorities; and it would thus also justify countless wars that would be all the more bitter because it is not easy, indeed, almost impossible, to define what counts as a people. If, on the basis of the existence of a Georgian people, Georgia had a right to state independence and secession from the former Soviet Union, then according to the same principle the Abkhasians have a similar right to secede from Georgia. A person who did not consider Yugoslavia a viable state and granted the member states a right to secede should not have been surprised that Bosnia-Herzegovina would also have problems existing as a state, for in this member state there was the same ethnic mixture as in the nation as a whole. Conversely, there can be a moral right to dissolve a state bond, even if the seceding group belongs to the same people as the rest of the state: in only a few regions did the North American settlers of the 1770s differ ethnically from Britons, and in those regions their readiness to secede was no greater than it was in New England.

The only valid moral argument for secession is that the legal government violates natural law principles and that only the seceding areas, whether on the basis of more highly developed mores or geographical peculiarities, have a real chance of constructing a state that will realize those principles. If there is a genuine possibility of achieving the changes sought in the framework of the nation as a whole, one must seek to make such changes rather than to divide up the state. Only if it turns out that this possibility does not exist in the long term may one think about secession. The object of natural legal protection threatened by the state must be very great to justify secession, for secession injures an important good, namely, the unity of the state. Whereas emigration deprives a state only of part of its citizens, secession always involves a part of the state territory as well, and therefore it raises moral problems quite different from those raised by emigration. Even if objections are often made to both on the basis of principles of distributive justice, one case still involves only human resources, while the other involves natural resources as well and in some instances also strategically important areas that the state loses.[41] If asking emigrants to repay the costs of their own education is an idea worth discussing, then this holds a fortiori for the payment of a secession tax by an area seceding from the rest of the state with the latter's agreement.

The unity of the state is naturally not the highest good of just politics, since the state receives its legitimation from the fact that it protects individual rights. The fundamental right is the *right to life,* and if this right can be protected only through secession,

---

41. Cf. A. Buchanan (1991), 10 f. Buchanan's is the most fundamental study of current political philosophy regarding succession.

there is no doubt a derived right to secession. It is relatively unimportant whether the life of the population of part of one's state is threatened directly by the latter or by another state against which one's own state is not able or willing to provide protection; in these cases one will not be able to deny the affected population the right to establish its own state. Second comes the *right to just political institutions:* if one cannot transform an unjust state as a whole, then one may at least try to construct a free political order in a part of it. Third is the *right to preserve one's own culture:* a people that is, for example, not allowed to use its own language is done a great injustice (even if it is ludicrous to suggest, by using a term such as "cultural genocide," that this kind of injustice is even approximately comparable to physical genocide);[42] and it is *this kind* of injustice, not the violation of an alleged right to *political* self-determination, that can justify resistance. However, if cultural minorities are protected, have their own member state within a federal state, or have veto rights, then there can be no right to secede. Last come *property rights,* which are violated by unjust redistributions, though not every redistribution in favor of the poorer parts of the country is unjust, and at most manifestly unfair redistributions (such as those that do not help the poorest people but rather support local criminal organizations) can provide the basis for a right to secede. Conceptually, a secession need not proceed from the most disadvantaged but can also proceed from the more prosperous groups that want to free themselves from burdensome care for the poor—a wish that is acceptable morally only if the former are unscrupulously overruled by majority vote of the latter. In this context, the argument previously discussed in connection with the principle of acquisitive prescription (chapter 7.3.1.2), according to which past injustice is supposed to be undone by secession, is weak. Most states came into being through violence; according to the principles of natural constitutional law recognized today, even princes' marriages could not provide the basis for any kind of fusion; indeed, even a fusion approved democratically a generation ago cannot be unquestionably binding on the present-day inhabitants—in short, according to that argument, almost every political organizational unit right down to the municipality would have a presumptive right to secede.

For example, the Baltic states had a moral right to secede[43] from the Soviet Union, so long as the latter was a totalitarian state; however, under these circumstances they were unable to exercise it. On the other hand, they would no longer have had such a right had the transformation of the Soviet Union into a constitutional federal state succeeded. Only at the time of the gravest crisis of the *perestroika* policy did they have both a certain right and the real possibility of exercising it. I have deliberately referred to the Baltic rather than to the Caucasian or Central Asian republics of the former Soviet Union because it has to be admitted that a right to secede is easier to assume in the case

---

42. Cf. A. Buchanan (1991), 64.

43. Speaking of "secession" in no way implies that the annexation of the Baltic states by the Soviet Union during the Second World War was lawful. Here the term is used in the sense it has in political science, not the one it has in international law.

of peoples who are more highly developed than the people that determines the policy of a state; Czar Alexander II himself is supposed to have explained to Bismarck that Russia could not dominate Poland because "the Russian does not feel the necessary superiority."[44] However, even the recovery of independence after a long period of occupation does not give a state the right to limit the political rights of the population living within it that is ethnically connected with the former occupying power if the latter bears no guilt for the subjection of this state and if, for instance, their ancestors, partly against their will, were transferred there. In actuality, a concrete evaluation of a secession must always consider the moral principles that guide the state that is seceding and those that guide the state from which it is seceding. In 1776, the American colonies subscribed to the principles of democracy and the separation of powers, which had never before determined a community in this form and with a like degree of clarity; in 1860, the chief motive for the southern states' secession was fear that Lincoln would adopt an abolitionist policy: It is not hard to discern the difference in moral levels. It is true that Lincoln's primary goal was actually to preserve the Union, but the Civil War ultimately gave him the opportunity to abolish one of the most disgraceful institutions in history, which crassly contradicted the principles of 1776.

Of course, in deciding to secede, one must also take into account the *prospect of success* and *the price to be paid*—not only by oneself but also by all those concerned. Slovenia and Croatia bear a certain co-responsibility for the sufferings is Bosnia-Herzegovina. Correspondingly, in another situation, the Baltic states could have been expected to forgo secession if it would have resulted, through secession by other Soviet republics, in a bloody civil war in the whole territory of the Soviet Union;[45] and in particular, other countries would have been well advised not to recognize too quickly the sovereignty of the seceding areas. However, when Yeltsin openly worked to dissolve the Soviet Union and thereby rose to the highest power, there was no longer any moral ground for maintaining the unity of that state. To be sure, it is difficult to predict the consequences of a secession; at the beginning of the American Civil War, both sides thought it would be short and bloodless, and they were terribly mistaken. But there is certainly a duty to carefully assess all possible risks, and anyone who fails to do so is acting immorally and irresponsibly. All other things being equal, secession is easier in the case of a federal state than in that of a unitary state because organizational units already exist; and it is well known that organizing resistance within an already existing state is the chief technical problem that often causes attempts to overthrow a criminal regime to fail. In addition, spatial separation, such as that between East and West Pakistan or between a mother country and its colonies, makes secession significantly easier.

----

44. Bismarck (1898 ff.), 1:308: "der Russe [fühlt] nicht die nöthige Ueberlegenheit."

45. Even if in the case of the Baltic states there were special conditions that justified secession more than in the other republics of the Soviet Union, one would have had to ask whether these special conditions were recognized by the others; in assessing the consequences, one should consider not so much what others should do as what they will in all likelihood actually do.

Even if a secession is not justified, this does not mean that force should be used to prevent it; a civil war is a very great evil, and it may well be more just to accept the division of a state than to expose oneself to a civil war. One may consider the divorce of Czechs and Slovaks lamentable and foolish, but the civilized way in which they handled it deserves admiration. Both states remained constitutional states, and they hope to be included in the supra-national institutions of the European Union and NATO. Conversely, reservations regarding a secession may exist, but the countermeasures taken by the state being seceded from may be of such a kind that one can no longer defend the view that it is conducting a just war. This holds all the more if this state, like the rump of Yugoslavia from 1991 on, makes it clear that it is concerned, not with preserving the nation as a whole, but with incorporating those parts of the seceding member state that have an ethnically welcome population—thereby itself acknowledging the collapse of the original federal state, and thus the independence of the former member states, which now have the right to defend their borders. Certainly, democratic elections are a reasonable means of settling conflicts regarding secession. But the philosophical question that arises in connection with such elections is *who* should be allowed to vote: the whole enfranchised citizenry, the population of the area that wants to secede, or those in the immediate vicinity? Basically, any answer to this preliminary question already anticipates a large part of the ultimate answer, for if one leaves the decision to the area that wants to secede, one has already acknowledged that it is an independent unit. If the area that wants to secede votes against secession, the vote is all the more convincing, and if such a result is foreseeable, it can be prudent for opponents of the secession in the central government to allow such a vote.

8.1.6. The Morals of Morality

Not only violations of the law need to be justified, but also *violations of mores*. The latter are often committed lightly because, at least since the development of the modern state, they are not threatened with sanctions as severe as those imposed on violations of the law; being shunned may be unpleasant, but imprisonment is generally worse. The individual risk run by someone who undermines a set of mores in an intelligent way is usually slight; it is not easy even for a totalitarian system, not to mention traditional mores, to defend itself against an insidious withdrawal of recognition, for instance through political jokes. If it employs brutal repressive measures, it is often doing precisely what morality wants to achieve—it lets its mask fall to allow a hideous face to be seen that it would do better to conceal. Therefore external defeats suffered by morality often turn out in the long run to be victories because thereby it appears as a victim, even if it has provoked its own repression. By the late eighteenth century, the *ancien régime* in France had lost its legitimacy for a great part of the population, including the socially and politically powerful, because, among other reasons, a group of persistent intellectuals deliberately made feudalism and Catholicism seem ridiculous—always an effective way of delegitimizing a social system, that is, of depriving it of social recognition—and because the elites even publicly applauded people like Beaumarchais. On one hand, deliberately delegitimizing a set of mores is morally permissible and even obligatory because otherwise higher moral ideas cannot find a way into the hearts of men and ultimately into social institutions. On the other hand, as we have seen, mores are no less important for a society than is law, and therefore attacks on mores can lead to the collapse of a society; conservatives' reservations regarding a figure like Voltaire are not completely without foundation. But at least one thing should be clear: In certain historical situations, writing pamphlets like Tom Paine's *Common Sense* or Emmanuel Joseph Sieyès's *Qu'est-ce que le Tiers état?* can have a *direct* political effect. One may reject or welcome the American War of Independence or the French Revolution, but the co-responsibility of these pamphleteers should not be denied, however it is assessed.

It is obvious that among *young people* a critical attitude toward their own mores is natural after the onset of puberty; the function of this attitude is to sharpen their eye for injustices, irrationalities, and contradictions in the factual mores, as well as for possible ways of progressing beyond them. Even—and especially—the most venerable traditions become sclerotic, and the desire for a more "authentic" expression of one's own feelings outside the forms laid down by the traditional mores is not only understandable but can also lead to a true revival of tradition. Indeed, it is important that young people be given room to distinguish themselves, for example, from the culture of their family; ultra-critical people who are always outdoing their children in progressive ideas not seldom drive them into despair (or into the arms of right-wing radicals). It is not a point in favor of a young person going through puberty if everything about traditional usages pleases him; a certain distrust of mores is healthy, especially if it is combined with an idealism that is prepared generously to sacrifice one's own interests to those one considers just. As Aristotle already recognized, idealism is a mark of youth because the latter has not yet had much experience with evil and because it is primarily oriented toward the future—the dominant focus is on hopes and not memories.[46]

However, the young people of a period also show whether *the positive or the negative aspects of morality* are predominant: that is, whether criticism of the usually accepted is nourished by a more elevated moral insight into new values or by hatred for one's own origins. Without morality, there would be no progress in world history; cultures that hinder its development are condemned to immobility. Without Socrates and Jesus, the dynamics of Western culture could not be explained. Improvements presuppose critical distance, and this holds for the development of science as well as for that of mores. Indeed, some forms of human greatness are not conceivable at all within the framework of a functioning set of mores. Anyone who is thoroughly imbued by the values of his culture and does his best to protect these values deserves the highest respect; but the battles of innovators in morals—in which these innovators acquire for the first time, and in

---

46. *Rhetoric* 1389a3 ff.

complete isolation, the certainty that despite their rejection by the majority of their contemporaries, they are right—approach the divine. It was already said that Islamic monotheism seems to be more attractive for theoretical reasons than the more complex Christian conception; but no religion has granted morality a greater dignity than the one whose God became a man who was crucified, at the behest of his own people, like a criminal, and was denied by his closest disciples. A culture for which Gethsemane is the paradigmatic event will produce people of an entirely different kind from those produced by a culture whose gods are always on the side of the stronger, and especially from those produced by one that has inherited the achievements of the first-mentioned culture without having acquired them, that is, without having appropriated them internally.

Moral innovators almost inevitably become the objects of *hatred*. First of all, criticizing factual mores almost always disturbs massive interests, at least in the long run, since the recognition of certain institutions is derived from socially recognized values, and these institutions will no longer be socially acceptable if the values on which they are based are felt to be questionable. Second, seen from the old point of view, the new values appear negative, as an unheard-of innovation or an unacceptable relapse (the latter especially from modernity, which gives the category of progress a positive value and therefore has to denigrate as "reactionary" truly substantial changes that affect its interests). Third, an offense, or at least a failure of recognition, is implicit in the rejection of one's own values in the name of higher ones, and therefore morality's battle with mores is always simultaneously a battle for interests, recognition, and values. Even figures as capable of love as Jesus and Gandhi could not help eliciting the most dreadful hatred as well as enthusiasm. "The story of Barabbas and Jesus is also informative here: Jesus' charismatic personality as a leader was enthusiastically applauded, but when the chips were down, meanness showed its solidarity: Society would rather forgive the criminal than respect nonconformists whose standards frighten it. The cacophonous cry of the people for the liberation of the criminal Barabbas sealed Jesus' fate."[47]

However, the fate of Christianity shows that the condition of morality is necessarily transitory. Morality must *transform itself into mores* if it is to be successful; paradoxically, it must give up its form if its contents are to endure, if its ideas are to be made flesh. However, because of the inevitable mutual interaction of form and content, the contents also necessarily change at the same time. The radical pacifism of early Christianity had to be abandoned when Christianity assumed the form of a church that had to be concerned with its own preservation and to try to exercise influence on the state, for corporate groups that want to have an impact on history must be evolutionarily stable. The institutionalization of every morality involves the danger of inverting and perverting its original ideas; in this change Eduard Meyer saw the essence of the *tragic element in history*. "The loftiest thing individuality can create is an idea. It is the creation of an individual person; but it acquires its historical form through the collaboration of several persons who modify it

---

47. K.-M. Kodalle (1994), 48 f.

and fully develop it. . . . [I]t has moved from the world of ideas into the real world of appearances, and is therefore subject to the conditions that rule that world. That is why every idea, as soon as is realized, turns into its contrary: for no idea can comprehend within itself the whole of reality. This change of ideas appears in all historical life: on it is based the tragic element in history, which has often become, namely among the creators of the highest ideas, a tragic element in individual life as well."[48] Certainly it must be granted Meyer that in the course of history the ideas of morality have again and again changed into their opposites: It is obvious that Jesus would have been shocked by the persecution of heretics carried out in his name. And yet Meyer's tragic conception is one-sided. Not all central ideas of the Gospel were betrayed by the triumph of Christianity; for instance, the Christian doctrine of the just war, which represented a significant advance even with regard to the Roman theory, is a splendid compromise between institutional necessities and the key ideas of Jesus' teaching.[49]

In fact, we must also disagree with the alternative conception that fundamentally rejects an institutionalization of morality because it thereby loses its purity and that therefore denies any concrete responsibility. Hegel, who understood better than any other thinker the dangers of morality, which had in the eighteenth century acquired entirely new possibilities of development (even if he did not always do justice to its achievements), aptly grasped this mentality in the figure of the *beautiful soul* ("schöne Seele") that protects at any price its interiority from the encounter with external reality, cannot endure Being, and therefore dissolves in self-pity.[50] Instead of exposing himself to reality through concrete actions and maturing through it, many a representative of morality revolves exclusively around himself; empty reasoning and utopian dreams replace the encounter with reality. There are in fact situations in which inner emigration is prescribed by prudence, but there are almost always ways of having a long-term effect. In contrast, the "beautiful soul" does not want to have an impact on history—but it is a moral duty to communicate new moral insights. Fichte writes: "The blind go on in their blindness, and no injustice happens to them, since they do not see injustice. The wise and virtuous man . . . is thereby obligated to do everything he can to make everyone else worthy and susceptible of this better order, in which he could live with them

---

48. (1981) 1:182 f.: "Das höchste, was die Individualität zu schaffen vermag, ist die Idee. Sie ist die Schöpfung eines Einzelnen; aber sie gewinnt ihre geschichtliche Gestalt durch das Zusammenwirken Mehrerer, die sie modifizieren und voll ausbilden. . . . sie ist aus der Welt der Gedanken in die reale Welt der Erscheinungen eingetreten und untersteht damit den Bedingungen, welche diese beherrschen. Darauf beruht es, daß jede Idee, sobald sie sich verwircklicht, in ihr Gegenteil umschlägt: denn kein Gedanke vermag die Wirklichkeit in ihrer Totalität zu umfassen. Dieser Umschlag der Ideen tritt in allem geschichtlichen Leben hervor: auf ihm beruht die Tragik der Geschichte, die oft genug, eben bei den Schöpfern der höchsten Ideen, auch zu einer Tragik des Einzellebens geworden ist."

49. I thank Jennifer Herdt for a stimulating conversation and many suggestions regarding this subject.

50. (1969 ff.), 3:483 f.

only together."[51] But however right Fichte's demand for action on behalf of new moral convictions may be, the language of this statement, and even more, the rest of Fichte's work, shows the complementary danger of morality. The refusal to recognize already realized reason in factual mores, which appear to be only the work of blind men, can increase to become a rage to destroy that certainly has an impact on history, even if it leaves little but ruins in its wake. In another famous chapter of the *Phänomenologie des Geistes*,[52] Hegel analyzes the transformation of the *law of the heart* ("Gesetz des Herzens") into the *frenzy of self-conceit* ("Wahnsinn des Eigendünkels") with a penetration that is all the more astonishing if we reflect that the new experience of Jacobinism then lay only a few years in the past and that an abundance of illustrative material was first produced only by the nineteenth and especially the twentieth centuries.

Thus it cannot be denied that many forms of criticism of one's own mores do not arise primarily from a new experience of values; instead, the pretension to new moral insights is only the effort to produce a *secondary rationalization* of a mentality that wants to appear, at any price, superior to others or that wants to destroy its own mores simply because they are its own mores. This attitude is repellent and, as a form of self-hatred, pitiable. For only higher moral insights can legitimate a battle against traditional mores; one should not throw oneself into new ethical theories out of hatred of one's own heritage or of human beings in general. It is not always easy to recognize at first glance which motive lies behind a person's deviation from his own customs, but usually it is helpful to observe whether he lives in accord with the newly professed norms even when they contradict his own interests. Many, but far from all, of those who professed socialistic values did so as long as the demand for redistributions was favorable to them or at least did not burden them—that is, so long as they could be generous at other people's expense; but once they became prosperous, they forgot those values and thus showed only too clearly that they did not really believe in them but only appealed to them to gain advantages or to appear better than the rest of society. (It may well have been a matter of self-deception.) Not everyone who demonstrates for broadening the right to asylum would be prepared to take an asylum seeker into his house for a time. It is immoral when someone who benefits from an unjust social system tearfully complains that his own privileges cannot be justified but that because of the immorality of the system he lacks the strength to give them up; in this nineteenth century, the greater part of the Russian intelligentsia found itself in the situation, aptly caricatured in Maxim Gorky's *The Summer People*. Such complaints are cratically imprudent if they are made in the presence of those who are exploited; in fact, if self-accusation is mixed with contempt for the poor because the latter are thought to be unable to help themselves,

---

51. (1971), 10:636: "Die Blinden gehen hin in ihrer Blindheit, und es geschieht ihnen kein Unrecht, da sie das Unrecht nicht einsehen. Dem Weisen und Tugendhaften . . . wird dadurch die Pflicht aufgelegt, aus allen Kräften zu arbeiten, um auch alle Andren dieser bessern Ordnung, in der er nur mit ihnen zugleich leben könnte, würdig und empfänglich zu machen."

52. (1969 ff.), 3:275–283.

morality can easily produce a bloody revolution.[53] It is true that in many historical situations the progress of morality toward more universalistic mores can proceed only from the more privileged; among the exploited the general human aversion to change is particularly strong because they know no situation other than their own, have no opportunity to reflect, and are crippled by fear.[54] But even effective help given by representatives of the wealthier classes is often felt by the poor to be condescending, and even the former's ability to be generous is seen as a proof of their adherence to the unjust system; if the system has finally broken down, wealthy benefactors can be met with the most terrible hatred rather than with gratitude. Of course, even fanatical self-sacrifice is no proof that one is devoted to the new values for their own sake; martyrdom can be based on self-hatred. A sure sign of the presence of the negative motives of morality is the Thersites-like hatefulness that rejoices in the moral weaknesses of other people and ignores positive values in contemporary reality—a spitefulness on which whole newspapers and radio programs currently thrive. This is no way to become happy, and since malice is essential to this kind of carping criticism, the *Schadenfreude* felt at the unhappiness connected with it, which Hegel once confessed feeling,[55] though it may not be noble, is still only a venial sin.

A further moral problem of morality consists in its relationship to *intersubjectivity.* The point of morality is to establish a reference to one's own conscience, but changing an order perceived as unjust can be achieved only if a majority of the people commit themselves to the new values. It is therefore indispensable to seek a consensus with regard to the new moral demands. In times of historical crisis, peculiar ways of being convinced that are not argumentative, but rather transmitted by emotional infection, crystallize with amazing swiftness; in this case, one can speak of a "collective morality." But precisely the stress on individual subjectivity makes it exceptionally difficult to arrive at a stable consensus, for each person guided by the principle of morality will emphasize his entirely special peculiarity. In a period in which mores are dissolving, there is never only *one* competing alternative but rather a great abundance of them, which may feud with each other even more passionately than with the traditional mores. The plurality of diverse moralities in contrast to a relatively compact set of mores lies in the nature of the thing—it is far more difficult to work out a new conception that has not yet been tested in reality than to defend the traditional one; reality is less ambivalent than possibility. Indeed, it would be almost ridiculous to adopt a new position without testing it; young people who rebel against their parents but blindly accept the authority of a group of other young people seldom thereby promote intellectual and moral progress (not to speak of those who, after revolting against their parents, papered their walls with pictures of Stalin and other communist leaders whose crimes they simply refused to acknowledge because they had to idealize mores opposite to their own, even if these states-

53. Cf. Tocqueville (1856), 270 ff.
54. Cf. T. Veblen (1899), 203 ff., and Sieyès (1970), 156 ff.
55. (1969 ff.), 12:48.

men's victory over their own country would have meant that their culture of morality would have been eliminated). That inevitable, peculiar trait of morality has an important negative consequence. In general, a long time passes before a fermenting morality finds a convincing expression capable of competing with the mores that have been dominant, and during this time the conservative defenders of the old mores have a significant strategic advantage: they have only to seek to deepen the divisions of the morality opposing them and to strengthen its self-destructive tendencies. Deepen and strengthen— for these tendencies are not first created by the adversaries, as morality likes to think, but are already present in morality itself.

Although an immoral morality, because of the pretensions necessarily connected with it, is ultimately more irritating than immoral mores, and anti-Enlightenment reactions against it are sometimes absolutely understandable, and although the destructive rage of a bad morality is often greater than that of bad mores that have at least proven themselves in the past, in the case of the maddest superstitious morality one has to acknowledge as well as in the case of mores that the *subjective guilt* of someone who is caught by the wave of a morality that has become socially powerful is not always as great as it seems in hindsight. It is only just to expect from a representative of morality a higher degree of critical capacities than from a representative of mores; indeed, he is responsible for underestimating what has already been achieved morally by his own mores, in an entirely different way, obviously, from that in which the representative of mores is responsible for his inability to anticipate later moral developments. Nonetheless, one should always acknowledge as a ground diminishing his culpability the attractive force exercised by morality in certain periods. Someone who has lived through revolutionary times knows that a general mood that expects great things can work even the soberest minds into a state of excitement that makes them partly ignore the most obvious facts and partly demonize as enemies of the human race those who think differently. The feeling of subjective specialness and indignation against the existing order mix in a horrible dialectic with dissipation into the mass, in which there is no longer any individual responsibility. This kind of psycho-social structure was probably able to establish itself in the evolution of human social behavior because by awakening enthusiasm (although the latter is sometimes blind), it generally has more good than bad effects: the elimination of reason in collective morality can go hand in hand with a readiness for sacrifice that transcends rational egoism and thus surmounts the prisoners' dilemma situations that make revolutions so difficult in unjust states. But the depression that overwhelms a misguided morality after the recognition of its failure is terrible. Happy is he who participates in a collective morality that truly contributes to the progress of morals in reality! Otherwise cynicism is the normal reaction—as many a veteran of 1968 vividly demonstrates today.

One of the most remarkable forms of morality is *modern immoralism:* The thesis that the moral does not exist at all is presented as a new moral discovery that finally overcomes all previous mores. The contradiction immanent in this idea is combined with the usual ills attendant on morality in a mixture that is certainly interesting but still distressing. The criticism of a set of mores can claim to be taken seriously only if it appeals to objective morals; otherwise, it is, according to its own principles, only an arbitrary protest, which usually refers with great volubility and vanity to its own irreducible peculiarity. At the same time, the need to hold onto something is so innate to the human soul that modern morality, which no longer believes in anything, clings to external things that serve as a shibboleth for distinguishing between good and evil persons. Individuals firmly convinced that slavery in other cultures can no more be considered objectively wrong than the environmental damage done by modern societies also think that the salvation of the world depends on doing away with an allegedly sexist language and that reformulating the constitution to read "Der Bundespräsident oder die Bundespräsidentin" (or, analogously, to amend the United States Constitution to read "he or she" in referring to the president) is the most urgent task of politics. Those who have something better to do than thinking and speaking in a "politically correct" manner, because they believe that the question about the morals of politics requires a more complex answer than the demand for capitulation to those who dominate public opinion, will encounter undying hatred that can go hand in hand with the profession of an unconditional pacifism—except, of course, with regard to those who represent a somewhat more differentiated doctrine concerning the conditions under which defense by military means might be permissible.

8.1.7. Fundamental Moral Tasks of Politics in Times of Radical Change

So long as only a small, uninfluential minority finds itself no longer at home in the mores of its own culture, there are hardly any threatening consequences. However, this changes when the social delegitimation of the factual mores expands to a broader circle and the citizens of a state no longer have common ideas of justice. If all or the great majority of the people change their views in the same way at the same time, then the replacement of the old system, which at the slightest shock will collapse as quickly as a building internally gutted by termites, is relatively unproblematic; on the other hand, the situation will become dangerous if, for example, the majority of the bourgeois in Paris have republican ideas while the peasants in the Vendée have royalist ideas. In such situations the outbreak of a historical crisis is inevitable, and since the production of a comprehensive consensus has become more difficult, explosions of violence are probable. "When a new belief does sprout, / Often love and loyalty are / like a noxious weed torn out."[56] A Hobbesian attitude toward the state is no longer sufficient if a great commitment must be expected from the citizens; but if the risk of a civil war is great, it can be considered a stroke of luck if the citizens draw back before chaos for whatever reason, even selfish fear.

---

56. Goethe, "Die Braut von Korinth" vv. 12 ff.: "Keimt ein Glaube neu, / Wird oft Lieb' und Treu' / Wie ein böses Unkraut ausgerauft."

Exercising political responsibility during a great *historical crisis* is one of the most difficult tasks that can confront a person, and only a few politicians have been truly capable of handling it. Even considerably greater monarchs than Louis XVI would hardly have been able to control the French Revolution "because the educated classes were inspired by a Utopia and the masses by an accumulated store of hatred and revenge."[57] Naturally, the success of a policy does not depend on the persons that conceive it and the collaborators whom they choose (in no period is personnel policy more important than in one in which character structures are particularly unpredictable); a people's mores, the international climate, recent historical experiences, the legal structural conditions, and finally, trivial accidents decide whether a historical crisis results in bloodshed or is peacefully resolved. It is clear that there is a moral duty to do everything possible to bring the crisis to a good end without bloodshed. One must concede that in wars and civil wars, bloodshed often enough has an important social function: in view of the general catastrophe, particular interests that would otherwise be tenaciously defended for decades are rapidly abandoned. But even if this argument may play a role in a theodicy, it goes without saying that every politician has a duty to avoid bloodshed as much as possible, even in times of historical crisis. But what means are to be used to achieve this end? The question can be answered only by empirical means, and so far as I know, Burckhardt's famous chapter is the only investigation comparing various epochs that is conducted by a historian with an eye for structural commonalties. Therefore the following considerations are even more abstract and tentative than the rest of this chapter; and I am even more painfully aware than usual that I can mention only a few of the relevant parameters. But the attempt must nonetheless be made, in the hope that it will be pursued further by a more competent person, for it is only too clear that the consensus that has supported the politics of recent decades is in the process of dissolving, in a way that recalls the collapse of the *ancien régime* (which, like every great crisis, did not allow only honorable figures to emerge).

Simplifying, one can say that success in mastering a historical crisis depends on at least the following factors. First, those who are politically responsible must be capable of *understanding each side's value attitudes in accord with their internal logic.* This does not mean that they must approve of these attitudes—opposing moral positions cannot be considered morally right at the same time. It means only that they must think themselves into the mentality of the respective other and especially recognize what is and what is not negotiable for the other side. A person with a rigidly dogmatic attitude is generally not capable of this; to demand, like Cato in 156–55 BC, the expulsion of the Greek philosophers is seldom an adequate response to the challenge of morality, which must be understood before it is fought. Second, it is desirable that the position of the other side be *not only analyzed hermeneutically but also,* so far as possible, *respected.* Much of the bitterness of such a conflict will be removed if it is made clear that while one does

---

57. Burckhardt (1905), 169: "Weil in den Gebildeten eine Utopie und in den Massen ein aufgespeicherter Schatz von Haß und Rache lebendig war." Trans. Nichols, 268.

not share the other side's views, there is nonetheless a common normative basis that makes mutual respect possible. For example, Lincoln repeatedly emphasized, most notably after the Battle of Gettysburg, the consensus regarding values shared by the opposing sides in the Civil War, without which reconstruction after the victory of the Union forces and the restoration of *one* nation would have been impossible. Someone who refuses the other side a basis for self-respect makes a later reconciliation almost impossible. Third, understanding the other side can lead to the development in oneself of a *sense for unconventional alliances.* For the most part, in the chaos of times of radical change the old friend-foe polarizations rapidly become obsolete, and given the tendency of morality to fall apart into trends fighting with each other, it is often not at all difficult for groups that support the old mores, and are prepared to compromise, to find new allies, though these can become lasting friends only if not only common interests but also common values underlie the alliance. Fourth, this intellectual openness must be accompanied by the legal power-holder's *energetic defense of the legal order in force,* for in a historical crisis in which morality has not yet achieved a clear opposing conception, a surrender out of weakness can only lead to further demands that lack any inner restraint and can ultimately lead to the collapse of the state. Louis XVI neither understood the justice of the demands raised against him nor had the strength to oppose those that were unreasonable; the opposite would have been required in both respects to deal with the crisis without bloodshed.

If the representatives of morality gain power, the disputes among them frequently cause enough difficulties; the fanatical hatred for the traditional mores often leads to positions being attacked whose elimination is neither morally or cratically necessary but arouses resistance among the representatives of the old mores. In his masterly analysis of the short-lived Parthenopean Republic, in which he himself had taken part, Vincenzo Cuoco rightly noted the foolishness of the measures taken by the revolutionaries that squandered the trust of the people, who clung to their mores.[58] Cuoco, who was thrown in prison for nine months after the collapse of the republic and then exiled, returned to Naples in 1806 with Joseph Bonaparte and saw in Napoleon the historical figure who had achieved what the French Revolution had sought in vain to achieve: the casting of the new ideas and principles in a firm and enduring form.[59] In fact, Beethoven's disappointment at Napoleon's coronation as emperor was naive, insofar as the adoption of the

---

58. "Non vi curate degli accessori quando avete ottenuto il principale. Io . . . ho visto che il più delle volte il malcontento nasceva dal volersi fare talune operazione senza talune apparenze e senza talune solennità che il popolo credeva necessarie. . . . I riformatori chiamano forza di spirito l'audacia colla quale attaccano le solennità antiche; io la chiamo imbellicità di uno spirito che non sa conciliarle colle cose nuove" (1975; 182). ("You have no concern about the accessory when you have obtained the principal. I . . . saw that most of the time discontent arose from wanting to do certain things without certain appearances and without a certain solemnity that the people believed necessary. . . . The reformers call the audacity with which they attacked the ancient solemnity strength of mind; I call it the foolishness of a spirit that does not know how to reconcile it with the new things.")

59. (1975), 53 (in the foreword to the second edition of 1806).

external forms of the *ancien régime* made a decisive contribution to the stability of the new rule and to the acceptance of revolutionary ideas inside and outside France; unlike the Parthenopean revolutionaries, Napoleon did not hesitate to reconcile the old and the new.[60] Just as the transformation of the Consulate into a hereditary empire was objectively a concession to the forms of the old order, whatever Napoleon's subjective motives may have been, so the formal restitution of the old Roman republic was the way in which Augustus set his seal on the political changes that had occurred in the first century. "On one hand, Augustus avoided producing an alternative, since he claimed that he had restituted the *res publica*. On the other hand, he was able to transform the society and the state in such a way that people were ultimately prepared to respect his principate as an alternative."[61]

It is a sign of pettiness when a morality insisting on its own originality rejects a *synthesis of the old and the new*. In reality only such a synthesis can make history. On one hand, the inertia of traditions is so great that it is unwise to wear oneself out fighting against them; one can at best only steer traditions in a more favorable direction. On the other hand, the new also needs social legitimation, and it is extremely risky to give up the legitimating potential of the old order. It is obvious that Stalin was one of the greatest criminals of history and that he significantly weakened the effectiveness of the Red Army through the so-called purges, as 1941 showed. But his decision to return to tradition during the Great Patriotic War, to revive traditional Russian nationalism, and to seek reconciliation with the Orthodox church,[62] was correct and showed a sense for the connections in question here; Bolshevists with more moral integrity probably would not have been in a position to make such a decision.

The synthesis of old and new need not proceed from those who are to be counted among the innovators. *Persons who stand for the old order* can also adopt principles of morality—partly consciously and partly through cultural osmosis, as it were—and work for them all the more convincingly in that they can count on the loyalty of the representatives of the old mores and often have superior organizational capabilities. Bismarck realized a few ideas that belonged to the program of the progressive parties, and probably in the situation at that time he was the only one who had a chance to realize them. Only de Gaulle was able to let Algeria become independent because only he could do so without its being interpreted (except by the fanatics in the French "Secret Army Organization") as high treason. It probably would have been harder for a Democratic president of the United States or a Mapai prime minister in Israel than for Reagan or Begin to put

---

60. In his ode "Il cinque maggio" ("The Fifth of May"), Alessandro Manzoni aptly emphasized this synthetic aspect in Napoleon's work and personality: "Ei si nomò: due secoli, / l'un contro l'altro armato, / sommessi a lui si volsero, / come aspettando il fato; / ei fé silenzio, ed arbitro / s'assise in mezzo a lor" (vv. 49 ff.). "And he said his name: two centuries, / one armed against the other, / turned submissive to him, / as if awaiting fate; / he commanded silence, and as an arbiter he / sat down between them.")

61. C. Meier (1980b), 274.

62. Cf. G. von Rauch (1977), 379 ff.

an end to the Cold War or to make peace with Egypt, respectively. Whether the change in attitude is due to later insight, the altered historical situation, or mere opportunism, or whether there was a brilliant pretense right from the outset, is often hard to judge, even for the person involved, in whom motives are strangely mixed. For no one is a great statesman who is not prepared to learn new things, to apply the old principles to new situations in such a way as to produce new normative results, to acknowledge the pressure of the conditions, and to play-act, if need be.

The happiest way of bringing a conflict between mores and morality to a peaceful and lasting conclusion is for a government perceived as conservative to carry out a "progressive" reform demanded for decades by a more developed morality, or for a champion of the more developed morality to restore the old forms. To be sure, a solution to a historical crisis that comes "from above" lacks the enthusiasm of a great revolution, which is able to mobilize the masses in a quite different way and usually occurs at the beginning of the crisis, but instead it has a significant advantage: It is usually less bloody, and that is a point whose importance should not be underestimated. However, peace between mores and morality is always only temporary; after a certain time, during which people can recover from this conflict, the transformation of morality into mores necessarily calls forth a new morality (and thus a new conflict). One might wish that it could also be united with the old morality that has become mores in a morally higher form, but this kind of progress is never guaranteed; the conflict between morality and mores can also end in pure destruction.

8.1.8. The Morals of Violations of the Law in Times of Radical Change

Violations of the law in times of radical change have a quality entirely different from the one they have in periods of stable mores. Since law is in general a subset of mores and therefore by definition a conservative power, the rejection of a set of mores usually implies that one also rejects the positive law justified by its principles. Just as it would have been naive to remind the revolutionary representatives of the Third Estate in June 1789 of the constitutional rights of the king and the three estates, it is of little help to point out that a valid law has been passed by a foreign ruler if it is felt to be illegitimate: in both cases there is no recognition of the valid order, and only fear of negative sanctions can motivate people to obey. Nonetheless, there is an important moral motive to respect a legal system that one considers substantively immoral, namely, the fear of a civil war. Insofar as this motive is moral, it cannot involve primarily fear regarding one's own death; concern about the survival of the state and the lives of many innocent people must also be at stake. Conversely, one can feel little respect for those who tumble into a civil war out of fanaticism; the fact that at the end of the eighteenth century the most important British intellectuals took a path different from the one taken by their French counterparts is admirable, even if it should not be forgotten that Great Britain also owed its superior political order to an earlier civil war and that the admonitory example of France had a stabilizing influence. The more hope there is of attaining the political changes regarded as morally obligatory by legal means, at least in the medium term, the more irresponsible it is to accept the risk of civil war.

The prevention of a civil war is such an important goal that it can justify *violations of the law by the government* if these can truly avoid the outbreak of a civil war—though it can be determined only empirically under which conditions this is the case, for in certain situations violations of the law by the government could also unleash a civil war. If, for example, a constitution does not allow the resolution of a historical crisis because it condemns the government to passivity, a coup d'état is a lesser evil than allowing a civil war to occur. The Russian parliament's dismissal of Yeltsin in the fall of 1993 was constitutional, and his attack on the parliament was not; but even someone who did not consider him a great politician and thought that he himself owed his power to a coup d'état (namely, the illegal dissolution of the Soviet Union) could hardly conclude otherwise than that his act was justified, for the Russian Constitution in force at that time was muddled and not adequate to deal with the historical situation of the country, and the alternative power-holders were significantly less capable of solving the country's problems or even merely preventing the collapse of state power. After ten years that saw numerous violations of the constitution and repeatedly revised constitutions, Bonaparte's coup d'état of 18 Brumaire 1799 involved, not the abolition of a stable order, but on the contrary a decisive step toward the construction of such an order; its moral assessment must therefore turn out entirely differently from that of coups d'etat that overthrow a proven constitution or throw a country into chaos.

If overcoming chaos and creating order are the greatest acts of which the human mind is capable and which in the myths of many peoples were attributed to beneficent gods, then the *establishment of states,* within which a lasting legal order can first develop, also has a positive moral value. That does not mean that all means to this end are allowed; however, the transition from the sphere of political corporate groups to that of the states of advanced cultures or from pre-modern to modern states was an important achievement that should not be judged by criteria that become meaningful only after the establishment of a common legal condition. In this connection, Hegel speaks of a "*right of heroes*" ("Heroenrecht") with regard to the state of nature;[63] and even if we have seen that the pre-state condition cannot be interpreted as a war of each against all, the arguments introduced in chapter 7.1 justify the establishment of states, and it is obvious, on the basis of the aporias described in chapter 6.1.1.3, that they cannot have been established by peaceful means alone. The morally ideal form of the founding of a state will, however, limit violence: The plausible necessity of protection against attack by another state and the charismatic authority of the founder of the state, based on the communication of new religious ideas, will in the ideal case reduce the use of internal force.

---

63. *Rechtsphilosophie* § 93, n. (1969 ff.), 7:180. In the first edition, the word is given as *Herrenrecht* (the right of lords), but the correction is more than plausible.

The foundation of a political organization in early history can hardly have been much less violent than it is described as being in Exodus or in Thomas Mann's story *Das Gesetz* (*The Ten Commandments*); it is not without a deeper meaning that today a religion still views this foundation as the starting point for its moral ideas. Thomas Mann aptly compares his Moses to a sculptor who inscribes the ABCs of human behavior in the flesh and blood of his people; in a very realistic way, his hero is characterized by a sensibility for art, for new moral demands, and for violence.

Much the same holds for *the construction of modern states.* The violation of principles—as when modern monarchs violated feudal rights, for instance—was often formally a violation of the law, but Machiavelli is absolutely right that only such violations of the law could have saved Italy from subjugation by foreign states. The more acute the external threat, the more legitimate the goal of constructing a modern state, which is the only one that can be evolutionarily stable. But even this does not mean, of course, that all means to this end are permissible; the emerging modern state must also be a constitutional state. At the beginning of the modern age, prudent marriage politics and compliant courts could achieve many of the partial goals of the modern state. And in certain situations one can conclude that given a people's existing ethic, founding or modernizing a state would involve so many sacrifices that it would be more reasonable to emigrate or to accept the imminent subjugation of one's own people by another capable of constructing a modern state.

8.2. Moral Principles of Foreign Policy

In a rational state there would be no foreign policy, only a global domestic policy (*Weltinnenpolitik*).[64] But until we get that far—if we ever do—the regulation of foreign policy is one of the most important and most difficult tasks of any moral politics. This results on one hand from the fact that the existence of a state depends on external structural conditions that can change more rapidly and unpredictably than internal ones—what Belgium encountered in 1914 and in 1940 could hardly have happened so quickly as a result of internal processes. Therefore much energy must be devoted to observing and influencing external changes. On the other hand, the moral principles that determine foreign policy are far more complex than those that determine domestic policy, precisely because the outbreak of violence, when there is no common judge with coercive power, is more likely than in the internal context, and the moral situation becomes still more difficult if the opposing political corporate groups do not have common mores. One should not underestimate the number of civil wars, but several of them are also intertwined with international conflicts—just think of the Spanish or the Greek civil wars. The differing nature of domestic and foreign policies has induced a few theoreticians of international relations to interpret foreign policy as an area outside morals, whereas in

---

64. I take this expression from C. F. von Weizsäcker (1964), 8.

reality a universalist ethics can only maintain that because of different structural conditions, the same general moral principles have to lead to diverse concrete norms.[65] Still more erroneous is the view that moralizing foreign policy is almost dangerous because it can lead to wars. In chapter 2.3, what is to be said about this was already said on a more fundamental level. Certainly during the Cold War there was a form of foreign policy that complained too shrilly about respect for human rights, for instance, and thereby lost a chance to make substantial progress through discreet backstage diplomatic efforts, and even endangered world peace. Carter was not particularly successful in foreign policy; his activity after he was no longer involved directly in politics deserves only gratitude and admiration, but as president of a world power one has duties that differ from those of a morally committed private individual. This type of foreign policy, however, can be criticized only either for not having correctly weighed the moral goods that are involved in foreign affairs or for being more interested in enjoying its own excellence than in effecting real changes. We owe to the realist school of foreign policy important insights into the mechanisms of the political world, and the normative recommendations that it makes are also often more worth consideration than those of the abstract moralists, since one cannot arrive at the right concrete norms without correct descriptive premises. "In such dangerous things as war, the errors which proceed from a spirit of benevolence are the worst."[66] But clear insights into the nature of moral duties will be sought in vain among the realists. Hans Morgenthau and Kenneth Thompson's *Politics among Nations* is one of the great books of the twentieth century, but too many of its normative and especially its meta-ethical statements are so manifestly false, and even self-contradictory, that it becomes clear that even major social scientists cannot rely on their moral instinct but must explicitly study ethics.[67]

Precisely in the modern world, with its far-reaching globalization of the economic and ecological problem, a certain *primacy of foreign policy* must be assumed as the starting point—at least for states that have a wide range of foreign policy options, that is, the great powers and superpowers. For the latter, an isolationist policy—that is, one that forgoes an active foreign policy—is not morally acceptable because justice and order in international politics are still less likely to result by themselves than in a market embedded in a legal order protected by coercive force. The catastrophic consequences of the United States' isolationist policy after the First World War speak for themselves. Someone who has power must use it for the general good, at least insofar as his renunciation of power is not a feasible alternative because it would increase chaos. However, power in foreign policy needs a foundation in domestic policy, and one must reproach Reagan, who was certainly successful in foreign policy, for having endangered the domestic foundation through his dismantling of the welfare state.

---

65. Cf. M. Maxwell (1990), who enumerates the most important arguments for and against a moralization of foreign policy.

66. C. von Clausewitz (1832 ff.), 192. Trans. J. J. Graham (London, 1949), 1:2.

67. I mention only the delimitation of morals and politics (1985), 6.

At the same time, foreign policy is particularly difficult from a cratic point of view. First of all, a policy must be based on internal agreement, especially in a powerful state; the inhabitants of other states are not a direct factor in the power of the power-holder of a politically sovereign state. In a democracy, for instance, the votes of enfranchised citizens count—but foreigners are not citizens of the state, and a policy that represents even elementary principles of justice with regard to them at the expense of the interests of the voters will not always be appreciated. In any case, for this a high sense of justice is required, not merely the often unclear mixture of the feeling for justice and rational egoism to which a successful domestic policy can and must appeal. Second, since collective identities can be strengthened by distinguishing oneself from other people and nations, there is a great temptation to overcome an internal crisis by creating or exacerbating external tensions. Bismarck was one of the greatest masters of this tactic, and although it must be recognized that he always resorted to limited war only as an ultimate means and for clearly defined political goals, he cannot be spared the reproach that he regarded this means as appropriate even for goals that could hardly justify it. At least Bismarck considered his foreign policy goals to be correct, and while he gladly accepted their tendency to produce internal solidarity, he did not unleash war for the sake of this side effect; this would have been far worse. One can hardly reproach Margaret Thatcher for having used the British prime minister's privilege to dissolve parliament in 1983 after the Falklands War, but it would have been unacceptable had she decided to go to war solely in order to win the election.

8.2.1. Moral Foreign Policy in Times of Peace

The *avoidance of war* is the first task of foreign policy, though not the only one. Someone who limited foreign policy to that task would be asking both *too much* and *too little* of it. Too little, because an active peace policy involves more than avoiding war, since a good politician concerned with foreign affairs should discover and make use of opportunities for positive cooperation between states, and even work in the long term toward a fusion of states and the construction of supranational organizations. Too much, because there are certainly situations in which avoiding war means losing what peace is supposed to preserve—human lives. This is true, in any case, when a war is only delayed until a time in which it must be conducted under considerably less favorable conditions. But even if one later surrenders to the enemy without a battle, that does not mean that more human lives are thereby saved. The blood toll of totalitarian systems is terribly high, and in order to save Jews in one's own country a bloody war against Hitler was not too high a price to pay, but rather an elementary duty of decency; a non-violent defense against Hitler would have achieved nothing. Even if one is threatened not with death but only with enslavement, a war may make sense. In chapter 5.3.4.4 we have already seen that human life is not the sole value but rises above animal life only because human life is the basis for freedom—that is, for behavior guided by moral principles. If fundamental moral principles are violated, it can be a very rational decision not to choose to live at any price, especially if this gives other people an opportunity to live once again in a civilized world that respects the idea of law. Hardly any question is more important in a moral theory of foreign policy than this one: When is a war just, or, since war is always an evil, even if sometimes a lesser one than not going to war, when is it at least justified?[68]

Just as a good domestic politician must not only know the factual power relationships within his country but also have a moral vision, so a capable politician concerned with foreign affairs must have an adequate assessment of the distribution of power in the international force field as well as a perspective regarding the ways in which the international status quo could be further developed in accord with moral demands. His moral duties in no way concern solely the citizens of his own country: This idea is to be firmly rejected on universalist grounds, even if humanity only recently rose to the level of recognizing universal human rights. The exploitation of another people is always unjust, and the fact that it is approved by one's own people does not make it just. Only subjective culpability is diminished if one lives within mores that do not recognize any principles of international justice; the objective injustice of such a policy does not disappear. However, it can be said that an aggressive policy within the framework of international mores that approve of such acts and even consider them unproblematic acquires a certain justification insofar as in the context of such mores an attack can very easily be interpreted as anticipating an attack by the opponent; and in fact it must be granted that in case of conflict a statesman has a greater duty to his own people than to a foreign nation. This follows from the special relationship of trust that binds him to his people. In a democracy, his office is expressly a charge given him by the people, and even in a monocratic state form the ruler draws his legitimacy from the fact that he cares in a special way for his subjects (at least according to the ideology), whom he would be betraying if he sacrificed, without external pressure or moral necessity, their legitimate interests to those of others. A good politician concerned with foreign affairs must be able to negotiate aggressively—but only within the framework of what can be justly demanded. In any case, politicians to whom we owe a humanization of the law of war, from which all peoples benefit, deserve far more respect than those who have enlarged their state territory through bloody wars of aggression. In doing so they can violate not only the rights of their neighbors but also those of their own subjects—for some of the latter also lose their lives in acts of war, and moreover the financial burden on the state treasury is by no means always counterbalanced by the conquests. Louis XIV's foreign policy may be leniently judged because of the value conceptions in his time, but it was not objectively right, and it did not pay off even for his own dynasty.

---

68. The grounds that led to the term "justified war" are certainly plausible. Nonetheless, the connection with tradition is such an important matter for me that I continue to cling to the old term. Words are not concepts, and one should not waste much time on decisions regarding the politics of words but should instead follow common usage.

8.2.1.1. Cultural Relations Policy

Since, precisely on the basis of a universalist ethics, the preservation of a multiplicity of cultures is morally obligatory, as was shown in chapter 3.5.1, two of the most important tasks of foreign policy are the *representation of one's own culture* and the *effort to understand the cultures of foreign countries.* It cannot be a moral goal to give up one's own cultural identity, insofar as it does not contradict elementary moral principles, just as conversely it cannot be a rational goal of foreign policy to seal itself off from foreign cultures, for that would mean making oneself incapable of learning as much as possible from the latter's achievements. Even in the case of contacts between individuals, the correct determination of the relationship between nearness to the other and distance from him is crucial for the construction of a stable identity; this holds still more for intercultural relationships. However, there can be conflicts between the two goals of self-preservation and openness. Many a pre-modern culture could maintain its own mores only by withdrawing from engagement with others. In such situations the obligation of self-preservation can justify a limitation of cultural contacts with other countries. In a few chapters of *De l'esprit des lois*[69] that annoyed some of his contemporaries, the Catholic Montesquieu showed understanding for states that refused to admit missionaries from foreign—that is, also Christian—states because this would necessarily lead to a destabilization of their own society. But there are two things to say about that. First, it is a sign of successful development when a culture can allow itself to engage another culture and can do so at a high level. Japan owes its special status among the modern non-European states to a deliberate analysis and imitation of achievements of Western cultures in the fields of instrumental rationality, which it had the strength to undertake after its violent opening up by the West. Foreigners were invited to come in, and Japan urged its own specialists to visit foreign countries. Second, a certain rapprochement of cultures is a presupposition for a real recognition of international legal norms, and however much Europe may have sinned in this respect in the course of its history by grafting its own culture onto that of others, often through the use of force, it would be naive to deny that one of the reasons for Europe's success was its common religion, which reduced the number of conflicts on the Continent and moderated them; to that extent, the missionary work of the Middle Ages, which was often promoted by the state, was also, and especially when viewed politically, an investment in the future, at least from the standpoint of the more successful culture.

An ideal cultural relations policy should surely be based on *mutuality.* But only an ideologue could deny that not all cultures have equal achievements, from point of view of either instrumental or value rationality. But every culture has a terrain on which it has produced something significant, and the sincere will to become acquainted with these works and to learn from the values of the culture concerned creates trust and allows

---

69. 25.10 and 15 (1748; 2:170 and 175 f.).

the communication of one's own culture without this being perceived as imperialistic. In view of the importance of the intercultural dimension of foreign policy, one has to consider it a wise decision when states choose to make use of leading intellectuals as ambassadors, at least to states with which there is no reason to fear military entanglements; the professionalization of the diplomatic corps is indispensable, but it is better to have an ambassador with personal and intellectual charisma supported by competent professionals than to appoint a solid but colorless bureaucrat to the office—at least so long as the communication of one's own culture is felt to be a goal. That should be the case, however, for two reasons. On one hand, productive intercultural encounters have an intellectual value; often enough, they have promoted cultural development, since the true secret of creativity consists in the synthesis of different things. On the other hand, the political utility of mutual cultural understanding is obvious. Even mere objectivizing understanding makes it possible to anticipate the other side's behavior and can therefore reduce friction, although it can also be a means of domination; true communication regarding the fundamental values that bind parties together, despite all the differences between them, creates trust more than almost anything else. Fear of the other is not the sole cause of war, but it is one of the causes. Overcoming prejudices and stereotypes, explaining the logic of the other, and still more, recognizing in the other a form of the human striving for truth, justice, and beauty are important contributions to ensuring peace. A foreign guest of the state who shows that he has read with profit a few of the books written in the country he is visiting earns a significant bonus in good will; the contrary is the case, however, if it becomes clear that his cultural assistant has looked up a few names just for the purposes of the trip. It goes without saying that cultural relations policy is all the more difficult, but also more important, the more alien the other culture is; when the parties involved belong to the same cultural area, the points of friction may be more numerous because of greater spatial proximity, but the existential distrust that sometimes characterizes relationships with wholly foreign cultures is absent.

To be sure, the weaknesses of human nature lead to there being something strange and even repellent, in every culture, even and especially in its center, that is, in every religion. Not the repellent but the strange should be *tolerated,* and not condescendingly, but with the consciousness that quite a few things about one's own culture must appear just as ridiculous when viewed from the other side and that even ridiculous symbols can point to sublime truths. When a state calls in peacetime for the murder of citizens of another state who are on their own territory, it is a violation of the most elementary principles of natural international law that must be met with the toughest response, especially if the threat is carried out; but that a scholar like Annemarie Schimmel, who, without in the least justifying the *fatwa,* urged people to consider the violation of religious feelings represented for faithful Muslims by Salman Rushdie's *Satanic Verses,* should be the object of the most hateful attacks by a certain portion of the German intelligentsia, is all the more shameful to the extent that part of this same intelligentsia's morality is usually the claim that it is committed to multicultural interests. Verbal multiculturalism is something different from an important person's life-long work on understanding a foreign culture. It is certainly to be feared that after the end of the Cold War human aggressivity might be fixed on cultural differences, so that the latter, and no longer differences in economic systems, become a cause of conflicts and wars.[70]

Openness with regard to other cultures cannot mean that the violation of absolute moral principles is accepted. Human rights are universally valid, and their disrespect by other states should be criticized and not tolerated in the name of an ethical relativism. Naturally, this is especially true if a foreign government fails to meet the standard of its own people's mores or does not respect its duties under international law. But even if it continues traditional barbarities, criticism is reasonable, especially under the conditions of modern globalization. Criticism is particularly effective when it can be communicated directly to the people by means of radio and television. Even the limitation of cultural exchange and economic relationships is a legitimate means of pressure in order to emphasize the importance of human rights, but only insofar as the state concerned consistently pursues clear goals. An administration's oscillation between kowtowing to powerful economic partners and in parliament condemning the same states lacks credibility and cannot be taken seriously. In general, a foreign policy guided by concern for human rights has to respect the following principles. First, basic goods are sacrificed in war as well, and *military steps* taken to impose human rights are therefore rarely appropriate and should never cost too many lives. It would be not only extremely imprudent but also deeply immoral to risk a third and last world war for human rights, because the tortured and unjustly imprisoned cannot be helped by a worldwide nuclear firestorm.[71] Moreover, in deciding to impose economic sanctions one must make sure that it is not precisely the victims of the system that suffer most from them—at least so long as their representatives do not expressly declare that they accept this worsening of their situation because in the long run external pressure will improve their lot. Second, what must always be taken into account is the *real interests* of those whom one wants to support through a policy guided by concern for human rights, and not one's own electorate's needs for moral indignation. Sometimes—but not always—more can be achieved by quiet diplomacy than by noisy protests that may lead to the complete isolation of the country being denounced from the moral culture of the world; in this case, and only in this case, quiet diplomacy is to be preferred. Which strategy will be more effective can be determined only empirically; relevant parameters are national traditions and the individual character traits of those bearing political responsibility. A compromise worth considering is often to limit relationships with governments and at the

---

70. This is S. Huntington's famous thesis (1993).

71. Thus Las Casas objected, against the argument (still accepted by Vitoria) that saving innocent people from being sacrificed by the Aztecs was a justifying ground for the Spanish conquest of the Americas, that the conquest had resulted in incomparably more victims than the natives had been responsible for—"así como si por ella podrían padescer más innocentes, en cuerpos y en ánimas, que librarse pretendían" (1965; 1:509). (" . . . as if it could cause more innocent people to suffer, in body and soul, than they claimed to liberate.")

same time to seek to establish contacts with municipal organs or private organizations, contacts that could promote an integration of the population into one's own value system. Much the same holds for the question of whether to recognize a government that has come to power in an illegal and illegitimate way, or even a new state that has emerged, for instance, as a result of illegitimate secession. If there is no longer any realistic hope that the new government will fall, prudence as well as morals require that it be recognized, because that usually means that one can have more influence on it. However, it can be difficult to arrive at an adequate assessment of the future prospects of such a government, as German history after the Second World War indicates. It remains remarkable that without recognizing East Germany as a foreign country, the German Federal Republic succeeded in constructing forms of cooperation that helped people of the German Democratic Republic and at the same time subtly made its political system dependent on the West and thereby weakened it.

Third, a sense for the *hierarchy of human rights* is essential, especially for the conditional character of many a norm characterized as a "human right" by positive law. A better knowledge of one's own history would often suffice to see that democratic rights to participate in decisions do not make sense at every level of development, whereas on the other hand torture practiced on a daily basis cannot be legitimate on any level, even if in a country that has a serious problem with terrorism it may not be as repellent as it is in a country at peace. Fourth, a plea for human rights must not contradict the fundamental *norms of the ethics of ethics.* Thus it should be accompanied, for one thing, by a readiness to help institutionalize the rights called for, since only this can prove that one's goal is not to humiliate the foreign government but to alleviate suffering. For another thing, the criticizing state should concede its own weaknesses and make clear that it is open to justified criticism. Finally, in criticizing foreign mores, one should always seek to connect one's comments with the values already recognized in it. Human rights' genesis was in the West, to be sure, but anyone who believes that they can be transcendentally grounded must try to discover traces of them in other cultures as well.[72] Above all it must be made clear that one is insisting on the principles of universalist ethics not because they happen to be one's own interest but rather because they are universal, because respect for them is in the interest of all, and because they represent the best possible foundation for respecting members of foreign cultures. Merely imposing even the highest moral norms from outside has no prospect of success; indeed, it will encounter fierce resistance. One should have no illusions about this. A large part of the relations between states, just like those between individuals, consists in battles for recognition; but unlike those between individuals, battles for recognition between states can escalate into bloody wars. As one does not point at the ailments of one's fellow humans in order to avoid deepening their feelings of inferiority, so diplomacy must have a sense for the psychology of foreign collective identities.

---

72. L. Kühnhardt's (1987) remarkable book is unfortunately inadequate in this respect.

If finances permit, cultural encounters should not be limited to contacts between the elites of the countries concerned. International athletic competitions can serve to promote mutual good will and channel human aggressivity into orderly paths, but they can also excite the most primitive national instincts and even lead to wars (consider the Soccer War between Honduras and El Salvador in 1969–70). Youth exchange programs can be an important way of awakening understanding of foreign cultures at an early age. The ability to live in another culture, that is, *real cosmopolitanism,* which a few elites of traditional cultures possessed to an admirable degree, cannot be acquired merely by reading books proceeding from the other culture because it presupposes not only a knowledge of the language but also a sensitiveness to the values of the other way of life and their inner connection; it is one of the abilities that is most needed in a world that is rapidly becoming more and more interconnected. However, an encounter with foreign wealth that will probably be denied oneself for one's whole lifetime is depressing, and under the conditions of modernity, which on one hand presents economic values as the most important and on the other claims to believe that everyone is equal, it is even demoralizing and corrupting; it is well known that after studying in a foreign land, returning to one's own country, in which the same standard of living cannot be continued in a legal way, invites corruption.

8.2.1.2. Policy regarding Transnational Economic and Environmental Issues

Since at least Montesquieu's *De l'esprit des lois,* one of the basic ideas of liberalism has been the conviction that economic interactions between different states—in the ideal case, *free trade*—have a positive value. In chapters 7.3.3.2.1 and 7.3.3.3.7, we briefly discussed the problems connected with this, so this section can be particularly short. In principle, this evaluation is correct: in addition to the economic grounds for having stable trade relationships, the latter also have a pacifying effect because they show that peaceful contacts are in the interest of both parties. To be sure, wars are sometimes waged on economic grounds, for instance, over the control of resources (classic examples are the War of the Pacific between Chile on one side and Peru and Bolivia on the other, as well as the Chaco War between Bolivia and Paraguay), but in general most businessmen have an interest in continued peace because it facilitates trade. The mutual economic interconnection can even become so great that a war between the two countries is no longer possible at all, and that was also one of the reasons that the European Community got underway after the Second World War. No doubt it was a step forward when trade began replace the plundering raids of which economic relationships between states had earlier consisted. It can fairly be said that initially world trade did not differ too much from plundering raids (think only of the slave trade), and even today, they still do not differ too much in some parts of the world; but in time world trade is overcoming at least the domination of sheer force and transforming negative sanctions into positive sanctions, even if it often shamelessly exploits economic inequalities. Montesquieu rightly pointed out that with the arrival of the spirit of trade, virtues of the traditional world such as hospitality to strangers disappeared;[73] but if the flipside of this generosity was the view that one was allowed to steal what one needed, then we should accept its disappearance.

Certainly, being at the mercy of the world market means a certain limitation of a state's sovereignty, but so long as it is controlled and mutual, this limitation is an important goal of moral foreign policy. The globalization of the economy cannot be undone; the observation of the host country's economic development by foreign missions, as well as the handing on of the corresponding information to the political centers making decisions regarding the economy at home, is a much better presupposition for intelligent and long-term economic improvement than protectionist reactions. It is clear that given the inappropriate structural conditions of the global economics, world trade is resulting in terrible damage to the environment, but this is a reason only for making a change in the structural conditions of the world economy, not for a fundamental elimination of world trade (even if it is also a reason for limiting it in cases where the damage done has no relationship to the utility derived from it). An *environmental foreign policy*[74] must accompany economic foreign policy. The limitation of environmental pollution and of the exhaustion of resources must be negotiated in international treaties—for instance, among the states bordering on a sea; indeed, the construction of a special international institution that determines ecological threshold values is indispensable. I will come back to this point.

The promotion of trade happens on one hand through *tariff reductions* and on the other through the *battle against nontariff barriers to trade;* the latter include, for instance, quantitative restrictions or measures setting prices, or state favoring of domestic producers. A *system of fixed exchange rates* is, *ceteris paribus,* to be preferred to one with floating exchange rates because major oscillations in exchange rates can endanger long-term trade; however, such a system presupposes agreement between the states concerned regarding financial policy, which can even extend to a currency union. A special tax on the—very high—profits from currency speculation, such as has been proposed by J. Tobin, is just and reasonable not only as a source of income but also because of its steering effect.[75] We should also mention the further development of international private law, which makes it possible to resolve conflicts between trading partners in different countries. The fundamental principles of the General Agreement on Tariffs and Trade (GATT), and now of the World Trade Organization (WTO), are most-favored-nation status, which allows bilateral steps taken toward liberalization to become effective multilaterally, and nondiscrimination, according to which permissible exceptions to the prohibition on quotas must hold for all partners. This is intended to ensure that facilitations of trade have equal effects and do not lead to the construction of new trade blocs. In

---

73. *Esprit des lois* 20.2 (1748; 2:10).

74. On this concept, see E. U. von Weizsäcker (1994), 164 ff. This book can already be considered a classic.

75. Cf. D. Felix (1995).

actuality, the splendid thing about the idea of the WTO is its universalist character: In principle, all states can join in the agreement, which long ago established itself, if not de jure, at least de facto, as an international organization. Of the exceptions recognized by WTO regarding the most-favored-nation clause, which concern, among other things, trade within customs unions and free-trade zones, the most interesting are industrial countries' general preferential tariffs in favor of developing countries, in which the principle of reciprocity is also relinquished; they are based on the correct insight that the insistence on formal equality in a situation characterized by a massive initial inequality is an injustice. Let there be no illusion—the apparently generous preferential treatment of developing countries occurs only in areas in which they cannot really compete—but nonetheless this principle expresses the recognition of a more complex concept of justice.

8.2.1.3. Aid for Development

A classical view of the morals of foreign policy assumes that moral duties in relations with other countries are based exclusively on a nation's self-interests and, in the ideal case, on the concord of the interests of several states. According to this position, not only is there no moral duty to perform a one-sided act in favor of another nation, but doing so ultimately amounts to betraying the interests of one's own people. Thus a *duty to even out material inequalities between states* was rejected in the past and continues to be rejected today by international law. The agreement concluded within the framework of UNCTAD (United Nations Conference on Trade and Development) stipulating that industrial countries should invest 0.7 percent of their GNP in aid to development was never considered binding under international law and thus was hardly observed. However, this position is not compatible with a universalist ethics, and especially not with the recognition of basic social rights. In view of the factual inequality between states the idea that no state has a duty to help other states, unless in its own interest, corresponds to the fundamental error of extreme libertarianism, namely, its reduction of the idea of law to the protection of equal rights to freedom from interference in the framework of the status quo. On the other hand, it is clear, according to morals and to natural law, that all people have a right not to starve to death, and after the recognition and implementation of basic social rights within wealthy states, it makes no sense to refuse aid for the battle against absolute poverty abroad. Resigning oneself to the current inequality of states is even less possible because equality is one of the basic values of modernity and because the extent of international economic cooperation makes exceptionally urgent, from a moral point of view, the development of mechanisms for reducing inequality between states.

Nonetheless, there is an important, morally relevant argument for treating citizens of one's own state differently from members of another state, namely, the fact, which we have already mentioned on several occasions, that a multiplicity of states itself represents a threat; and it can hardly be a duty to help potential enemies. For instance, before peace is made with Syria, one cannot expect Israel to aid a country that it is at the same time threatening.[76] But where there is no external threat and none is anticipated, there is a duty to help other states, and all the more if one bears a concrete responsibility for the current situation (for example, as a former colonial power). Moreover, under the conditions of modernity, with the increasing interlinking of states, aid of this kind could contribute to the maintenance of a lasting peace, and even to the formation of the structures of a universal state, because it strengthens the idea of a general human solidarity; thus it is in the aiding state's rational self-interest. Therefore it should certainly be promoted by means of general taxes—for *peace is a collective good*. And the more aggressively advertising praises the Western way of life on satellite television beamed all over the planet, the more likely it is that in the long run the wretched of the earth will not be satisfied with the present distribution of goods. The burden of absolute poverty is increased if one is fully aware of how the rich people of the world live. It is true that the military power of the poor is small so long as a proliferation of weapons of mass destruction can be prevented; but the fact that the poorest people have nothing to lose is a factor that increases the threat they pose. Furthermore, the moral power of the weak should not be underestimated. Who would consider himself morally authorized to give the order to fire on the hundreds of thousands of environmental refugees who are ready to cross the straits of Gibraltar? In antiquity, "aid for development" was already an attempt to avert movements of peoples; but *migrations* are increasingly part of the reality of the late modern period, and they will shake the state structure of modernity that is determined by territoriality just as the great migrations in late antiquity did if they cannot be prevented by prudent developmental policies.

However, for various reasons this kind of help is considerably more difficult than it at first seems, and not only because it is not so easy to sell domestically as are redistributions to the advantage of voters. First of all, as we have just said, aid for development is often also, or even primarily, in one's own self-interest. This makes it more possible to justify it in one's own country, but at the same time it entangles it in a web of dependencies that do not exactly make it credible that aid for development is something other than a form of disguised trade. Thus, for instance, clear selfish interests stand behind a third of Western aid for development since the Second World War.[77] These interests can be directly economic but also military or ideological. Already in antiquity, an important role was played by payments and ideological services given by more developed countries—for instance, the Roman Empire—to less developed countries in order to work toward certain foreign policy goals.[78] Now, the pursuit of goals is not bad in itself; it always depends on what the concrete goals are. But the suspicion easily arises that

---

76. See M. W. Doyle (1986), 338 ff., esp. 342.
77. Cf. D. H. Lumsdaine (1993), 4.
78. Cf. F. Altheim (1962).

they are exclusively in the interest of the donor country, and this suspicion often poisons the relationship; it is well known that in German, *Gabe* (gift) and *Gift* (poison) are closely related etymologically. Second, every kind of aid is problematic insofar as it represents an infringement on the autonomy of the other, and therefore it often can (but need not) increase the dependencies it was intended to overcome and cripple the donee country's ability to help itself. But since the modern concept of development is based on the idea of autonomy, T. Kesselring's pointed remark that the concept of development aid is almost self-contradictory is apt.[79]

Third, a more developed society's influence on the one to be helped, no matter how well meant, can profoundly shake up the factual mores of the latter—and the greater the distance between the two societies, the more profound this destabilization can be. On one hand, such destabilization is inevitable, because the traditional mores are usually the deepest reason for underdevelopment; on the other hand, not every sort of destabilization is salutary, because it can destroy self-respect, without which a productive change is not possible. An exogenously induced morality sometimes has even greater difficulties than the one of endogenous origin in being accepted by representatives of the old mores, especially when they encounter the foreign country with distrust; on the other hand, if it is part of traditional mores that one looks up to the foreign country, then it is easier for the morality promoted from outside because it can point to the success of the new recommendations there. Destabilization of the factual mores is, as we said, inevitable because there can be hardly any doubt that the chief impediments to development are not so much a lack of resources and the colonial past as certain mentalities, bad constitutions, and incapable and corrupt governments. But how one can criticize them while at the same time recognizing the international law principle of sovereign equality is the fourth problem. Basically, this principle is violated by any asymmetrical relationship, and every kind of aid constitutes such a relationship. Aid is welcomed, but its flipside, the prescribing of conditions, is considered unjustified. Nonetheless, it is not hard to see that conditions can be legitimate—it depends on their content. Even in private relationships, giving aid without conditions makes sense only if there is reason to believe that the person aided will use the help provided to make an objective improvement in his situation: giving a drunkard money is not a good idea if one cannot be sure that he will use it for a detoxification treatment. In the case of aid between states, however, there is the further argument that aid should go to the most needy, and the latter are seldom identical with those to whom the aid is initially paid out. In short, conditions that are in the long-term interest of the receiving country or the poorest people are legitimate, while those that seek only to promote the economy of the wealthier country are not.

The possibility cannot be excluded that a few countries may not in a position to administer themselves under the conditions of modernity. Just as there is a prima facie

---

79. (1995), 229.

prohibition on intervention against the will of a state, so there is a duty for wealthier and better-organized states to assume a kind of *political guardianship* for underdeveloped states if the latter ask for it, even if such a guardianship results in redistributions from the wealthier state to the advantage of the poorer people of the other country. (However, the situation becomes more difficult if there is reason to expect partial resistance against the new administration, resulting in loss of life.) The sole argument against such redistributions, the possible threat by a foreign state, does not hold here; and although such an asymmetry is intended to last for the shortest possible time, it is still morally acceptable if it is the only way of achieving a greater symmetry, or if it is intended ultimately to lead to a union of member states with equal rights. Vertical responsibility is better than horizontal indifference toward the most massive material inequality, which is entirely compatible with formal equality. If such mandate or trust territories are established conjointly by the international community, there is not much to object to morally in it; but the refusal of wealthier states to assume their administration is morally highly objectionable. Such a refusal corresponds, though at the level of omission, to the desire of the wealthier areas of a state to secede.

8.2.2. Just Wars

No decision is more difficult for a statesman to make than one regarding a war (or civil war). Anyone who is not capable, after the end of hostilities, of going to disabled soldiers and to the families of the fallen, looking them in the eye, and saying, "Your sacrifice was terrible, but it was necessary in order to avoid a greater evil" has no moral right to vote for a war. Nothing is more repellent in Napoleon than his cynical statements about his soldiers, whom he ultimately regarded as cannon fodder; and one of the strongest passages in Tolstoy's *War and Peace* occurs at the beginning of the third volume, where war is explicitly described as an event in which countless evil deeds such as deception, betrayal, theft, forgeries, robberies, arson, and murder are committed, and all with a good conscience. What is particularly eerie about war is the alteration of the relationships between individuals. Persons who previously got along well together can suddenly come into situations in which they have to shoot at each other, and the power of the machinery destroys every direct human warmth toward other people.[80] Nevertheless, the good conscience with which war is usually waged is not always unfounded, since there are just wars, and one can also become guilty by not taking up arms. Hitler's expansion could have been halted, perhaps even without bloodshed, by a vigorous reaction to his occupation of the Rhineland in 1936, and had the Allies declared

---

80. Cf. the description of executions by firing squad in *War and Peace* 4:1 11 (1971; 434 ff.), in which it is particularly remarkable that Tolstoy feels no less sympathy for the executioners than for the victims because even the executioners are only cogs in the mechanism of the situation.

war in 1938 they would probably have been in a more advantageous military situation; finally, no reasonable person can deny that the attack on Poland could no longer be accepted by the civilized world. There is no doubt something useful in the figure of Hitler, and that is that it makes it difficult for even a relativistic *Zeitgeist* to put everything and everybody on the same level: unlike the First World War, the Second World War is the paradigm of a just war.

When is a war *just,* that is, when is it morally permissible (or even obligatory) to wage it? Scarcely any other question in political philosophy is so hard to answer, and in scarcely any other do intellectuals who are satisfied with an easy answer bear greater personal guilt. The answer cannot be guided simply by the regulations of current international law, though of course they are to be respected, and one must be grateful that one lives in a time in which international law prohibits the use of force. But positive international law is not, any more than other positive law, the ultimate standard of morals. On one hand, most wars of aggression were immoral even in a time in which international law did not prohibit them; on the other hand, measures to defend one's own existence are usually justified, even if they contradict positive international law. So long as the international community, for example, is not in a position to guarantee the existence of a state, it cannot deny the latter the right to self-defense and to the measures that self-defense requires. Far from all that the state of Israel has done since it was founded is morally justifiable, but it does not suffice to base criticism of its foreign and defense policies solely on the argument that it has repeatedly violated valid international law. Fortunately, some important thinkers have concerned themselves with the theory of a just war.[81] In particular, it is one of Christianity's immortal achievements to have developed, in the Middle Ages and especially in the early modern period, an impressive doctrine of just war. Thus in Francisco de Vitoria[82] we already find the criteria for a just war categorized into *grounds for war, the conduct of war,* and *post-war policies;* and since these correspond to the three temporal modes, the categorization is so plausible that I will use it as the basis for the following discussions. The first two points of view, which concern the *ius ad bellum* and the *ius in bello,* are only apparently more important than the third, which is often neglected in modern works: for instance, in Michael Walzer's *Just and Unjust Wars,* the most important recent study on the subject, which is impressive by its clear categorial grasp and also by the abundance of historical examples it offers. The following reflections owe a great deal to this book.

It follows directly from the concept of just war that both sides cannot have a just ground for going to war for the one against which there is a just ground for war has a moral duty to yield to the demand made on it, which can, if it does not yield, be imposed by coercive means. Wars can occur only if at least one side has acted unjustly;

---

81. Many peoples have felt that war requires a special justification; the Romans did so to a particularly marked extent.

82. (1952), 170.

otherwise one would have to defend the thesis that even in a world that consisted solely of just persons, the latter could get into a situation in which they had to kill each other.[83] The doctrine of just war does not endanger the chivalrousness of war; on the contrary, it provides a guarantee that a war will not be started solely because it is in the interest of one's own state and that it will be conducted decently—for the justice of a war depends, among other things, on the justice of the way it is waged, and the victim of an aggression that itself systematically kills civilians cannot lay the blame for their death on the aggressor. It is true that the conviction that one is on the right side can give one special strength. But if this conviction is justified, then it is first of all only to be welcomed (should one wish the opposing side more strength?). Also, the doctrine of just war can be used to critique all purely ideological justifications that are introduced in support of wars and that cannot withstand rational examination. Moreover, three things are compatible with the doctrine that only one side can wage a just war. First, there can be, of course, wars *that are unjust on both sides.* Two despots battling for world domination would be an excellent example; presumably quite a few past wars belonged to this category. Russian soldiers' fraternization with the enemy and the mass desertions of the Czechs toward the end of the First World War implied, not that the respective opposing sides were conducting a just war, but rather that it appeared—correctly—that there was no point in continuing the slaughter.

Second, the objective injustice of a war *does not already entail a subjective guilt* on the part of those fighting for the wrong side, or even necessarily of the politicians who made the decision to go to war, because the latter could have been trapped partly in immoral mores and partly in erroneous assumptions regarding the other side's aggressive intentions: there is putative self-defense between individuals as well as between states. A fortiori, those obeying commands are even less often morally guilty. Officers cannot be held responsible for a declaration of war, but they can be held responsible for the violations of the *ius in bello* they have ordered. Soldiers who follow such orders can, *if* they are threatened by the most severe punishment for refusal to perform military service or to obey orders, also appeal to a large extent to grounds that diminish culpability. Furthermore, it will be granted that personal danger and becoming mutually accustomed to killing in war lower the threshold for war crimes as well. This surely does not provide an excuse, because soldiers have a special duty to put their own lives at risk, but it does provide a certain diminution of culpability. Someone who, in the heat of the moment, shoots a prisoner of war who has surrendered

---

83. A conceivable exception (which would have similarities to an excusing state of emergency) would be a strategically crucial neutral country's battle against a state that must itself mount a defense against an aggressor and seeks to occupy the neutral country for this purpose. But it can be replied that there is merely a prima facie right to neutrality and that the neutral country has a duty to defend the state from attack if only its help can save the state under attack. Finland's behavior in 1941 is excusable but not justifiable.

should be severely punished, but, at least if the punishment is not immediately carried out for the purpose of setting a deterrent example, he should not be punished like a common murderer. In any case, the ordinary soldier cannot be held responsible for the violation of the *ius ad bellum:* soldiers do not always have an opportunity to clearly understand the injustice of the war being waged by their country, especially since it is natural to have a basic trust in one's own state and since the feeling of solidarity with one's own comrades can cloud one's perception. However, if after conscientious examination a person arrives at the conviction that his state is waging an unjust war, he has a duty to refuse military service, so far as possible; indeed, he has the moral right (but not necessarily the duty, because not all risks are reasonable) to go over to the other side, even if this means breaking the law (insofar as the war is not unjust on both sides). The fact that in 1933 Hans Jonas left Germany, declaring that he would return only as a soldier in an opposing army, shows that his greatness as a man was no less than his greatness as a philosopher. The desertion of German soldiers or officers during the Second World War was of course also justified (and this ought to have been legally recognized much earlier by the German Federal Republic); until a favorable opportunity to surrender to the British or the Americans was found, it was a moral duty to shoot into the air. Indeed, it seems to me that even the following action, which was reported to me by an eyewitness, can be justified as self-defense. In 1943, a company of German soldiers fighting the Allies in Sicily was ordered by the officer in charge, a fanatical Nazi, to hold a position to the last man. Shortly thereafter, he was shot, and the company could surrender. He had not been hit by enemy fire. A fortiori, an ally is morally allowed and even obliged to change sides if he has seen that he is fighting on the wrong—that is, the unjust—side.

Third, judgment concerning the justice of a war is difficult in that a role is played by *several factors* that are not necessarily connected with each other. The victim of an aggression may systematically violate the *ius in bello;* the aggressor may fight chivalrously; after winning a victory, a victim that has fought chivalrously can pursue an irresponsible post-war policy. Thus it is certainly conceivable that the justice of a defensive war might be lost as a result of the way it is waged, and one could not wish the victim to win, because the peace conditions it would dictate would be unjust; in such a case, one would be dealing with a mutually unjust war. However, it is always a matter of weighing the injustices committed by each side. For example, there was no plausible justifying ground for the bombing of Dresden on 13–14 February 1945, and yet this did not change the duty of all moral persons to fight for an Allied victory. All the greater, therefore, is the admiration deserved by those members of a people fighting a defensive war who, like Lev Kopelev, point out, at great personal risk, violations of the *ius in bello.* It is far more difficult to evaluate morally those who have fought chivalrously in a leading military position, but without political decision-making power, in an unjust war. Erwin Rommel cannot be denied respect because, among other things, he burned Hitler's command, issued on 28 October 1942, to shoot enemy prisoners of war, and in 1944 he joined the resistance; but he might have earned still more respect had he deserted to the Allies early on[84]—no matter how difficult it was, unfortunately, to make such a decision in the time of nationalism. One of the most tragic figures in history is Nicias, who as a politician warned against Alcibiades' Sicilian adventure and then had to be responsible as a strategus for the latter and to pay for it with his own life, whereas Alcibiades defected to Sparta, Athens's enemy in the war.

8.2.2.1. Just Grounds for War

By far the most important moral grounds for war are *self-defense* and *defense of other states under attack.* From these follows immediately the legitimacy of a defense policy that pursues the goal of warding off attacks or preventing them as much as possible through clear deterrence and express warnings; for the concrete use of force should always be only an *ultima ratio.* It is very implausible to assign a right to self-defense only to private individuals but not to states, for states represent the interests of private individuals. At most, one can object that the morally problematic aspect of a state's self-defense is compulsory military service, since even persons who are not themselves immediately threatened are forced to put their lives at risk. The objection cannot be dismissed out of hand, but one can meet it either by abolishing compulsory military service or by guaranteeing a right to emigrate. The latter suffices, especially since there are good arguments for universal military service (cf. chapter 7.3.3.3.5). A right to self-defense generally already exists when the borders of one's own state are crossed by force, for the modern state is essentially defined by territoriality, without which individuals could not be effectively protected. To be sure, borders are often unreasonable and themselves the product of past uses of force; but they are nonetheless the only clear criterion for demarcating states, and if one is not content with the factual borderlines because one does not recognize an acquisitive prescription or even because one is dreaming about natural boundaries,[85] a series of wars is inevitable. To that extent it should be acknowledged that a violent transgression of a state's borders generally grounds a right

---

84. The limiting "might have" is related to the fact that the probability of the resistance's success has to be taken into account; moreover, one has to consider that the subjective risks involved in an attempt at desertion might have been less.

85. It is worth noting that in his sermons and speeches against the First Gulf War, E. Drewermann emphasizes the point that the borders in the region are not natural (1991; 13). This argument, which is not very strong, is moreover superfluous on the basis of his premises because he apparently considers every war unjust, even a British-French defense of Poland from German attack (52 f.). His book, like F. Alt's book against deploying the Pershing II missiles, is a cautionary example of a certain well-intentioned but ethically dilettantish moralism. However, it should be granted that the existence of even an irrational peace movement can have a positive role to play, so long as it does not have to make political decisions, because it can represent a counterweight to the far greater evil of warmongering.

of self-defense for the state that is under attack.[86] Attacks against one's own citizens in another country are not a comparable violation of state sovereignty, since residence abroad involves a risk that the citizens concerned have voluntarily run; one can oppose such attacks with fitting retorsions. Insults are never a ground for war, and someone whom they lead to declare war, as did Napoleon III after the Ems telegram, is waging an unjust war, even if the opposing side cannot on that basis alone make the claim to a just war.

The *right* to self-defense in no way implies that every state has a *duty* to defend itself to the last man against aggressions. On the contrary, there must be a *realistic hope* of achieving the political goal that one has set—for example, of repelling the attack or weakening the aggressor; using force must be *necessary* to achieve the goal; and as much as possible the degree of force used should be proportionate to the threatened evil.[87] In order to decide whether these conditions are fulfilled, the military, which often assesses risks more soberly than do civilian politicians, must be consulted, even if weighing political goals is not its task. So far as the necessity of using force is concerned, there can be cases in which the aggressor can be moved to withdraw only by economic sanctions imposed by third parties; but it is obvious that the country directly under attack cannot use them as a threat, and even third parties should prevent the aggressor from using the interim to gain strategic advantages that make his position incontestable. With regard to being proportionate, I say "as much as possible" because this requirement makes defense of small states from attack by large ones more difficult, although aggressions against them should certainly not always be accepted. What seems crucial is that in even in the context of international law, the good in relation to which self-defense or the defense of another state from attack should be proportionate is not only the concrete, individual case directly concerned; the probable consequences of accepting the aggression must also be taken into account (as in the so-called "domino theory," for instance). Nonetheless, this requirement is important. A state that could defend itself against an aggressor that did not seek to destroy its substance as a constitutional state only by launching a nuclear first strike that would kill countless civilians would have no fundamental right to defend itself; at least it would have to have explicitly threatened its opponent beforehand, so that the latter might give up its plan to attack; and even then the moral question would remain difficult to answer: Would responsibility for the deaths of civilians in the aggressor country—civilians that would be used as hostages, as it were—fall exclusively on the blackmailing aggressor country?[88] However, in normal cases one can say that even if it is clear from the outset that one will ultimately have to

---

86. This also holds for colonial territories. Thatcher's decision to go to war in the Falklands was morally obligatory, given the human rights policy of the Argentinean military junta and Great Britain's responsibility for the population of the Falkland Islands—quite apart from the fact that without the resulting military defeat, Argentina and other Latin American countries would not have been freed from their criminal military dictators.

87. Cf. chapter 7.3.2 on the subject of self-defense. See also J. E. Hare and C. B. Joynt (1982), 57 ff.

88. Cf. chap. 3.3.2.

capitulate, it makes sense to mount a resistance that makes it clear to the aggressor that he will have to pay a certain price—not only to be able to negotiate better conditions of surrender for oneself, because those who simply give in to force are seldom respected, but also in order to move other states to resist injustice. The fact that Finland did not yield to the Soviet ultimatum in 1939 deserves respect; on the other hand, Emil Hácha's behavior in 1939 was not heroic, no matter how little right Great Britain, not to mention France, had to condemn him morally. There can certainly be cases in which one can wear down the aggressor by non-violent resistance after he has occupied one's own country and thereby can achieve as much as with a defensive war; but to be honest one has to admit that this is seldom the case and that a brutal aggressor can easily break non-violent resistance on the part of the majority of the population.

Easier to support than a *renunciation of a meaningful possible self-defense* is the *refusal to defend another country from attack,* for putting one's own citizens' lives at risk is such a difficult decision that one cannot simply condemn those statesmen who avert their eyes from the injustice that occurs elsewhere in the world. This kind of reaction is especially understandable if the country under attack is partly responsible for its situation (for instance, because it has not taken sufficient care to prepare its defense) or if there is no reason to suppose that in a corresponding situation it would itself defend another country. Such a reserved policy is almost morally obligatory if intervention would be suicidal—in 1956 and 1968 the Western powers had no reasonable military options, especially since being guided by the status quo, even if the latter is unjust, is a plausible principle for avoiding conflicts. Since one cannot help everyone, on the basis of human nature it is likely that the cases in which one decides to help will be those in which one's own interests are also involved. If Kuwait had not had oil reserves, the United States would probably have accepted its occupation by Iraq. But that does not mean that the defense of another country becomes illegitimate if there are selfish as well as humanitarian grounds for providing it. Though a world in which every aggression could be resisted would be most desirable, that would be possible only if a large enough number of sufficiently powerful states that were also united on fundamental moral principles committed themselves to such a policy. But even if not defending another country from attack is under certain circumstances morally defensible or at least excusable, moral decency demands that one at least tell the truth—that is, openly admit in the majority of such cases that one is acting out of national egoism; its concealment under pseudo-moral pacifistic ideologemes significantly increases the guilt, first because this is hypocritical and second because it can cripple those who have a more elevated conception of their duties to the international community. In general, it is disagreeable when someone who does not act generously defames those who are better than he because he cannot bear being surpassed morally; but when it is a matter of life or death, this attitude reaches the apex of irresponsibility. (The "parasitical pacifism" that forgoes efforts to defend itself only because it can rely on others for protection is not very attractive either.) If one decides against defending another country against attack, then clearly laying out one's own policy is generally better than making vague promises that one does not intend to fulfill or engaging in saber rattling that is not meant seriously. British behavior after the Italian attack on Ethiopia was extremely inept because it did not help Ethiopia, annoyed Italy (which might have been won as an ally against Hitler), and further weakened Great Britain's credibility.

However, there are two situations in which the refusal to defend another country from attack can hardly be justified morally. First, it goes without saying that *obligations based on treaties* must be met (naturally, only so long as one's own allies are not waging an unjust war). One can see in the defeat of France in 1940 just retribution for its betrayal of Czechoslovakia, which had been its ally since 1924, even though it was to the honor of the French nation that it had a man like General Faucher, the leader of the French military mission in Prague, who, after the Munich accord, became a Czechoslovakian citizen and made himself available to the Czechoslovakian army.[89] There is no positive law duty, but rather a moral one, to join institutions of collective self-defense such as the League of Nations or the United Nations and then also to participate in their peace-keeping and peace-enforcing measures. Second, assistance in an emergency is in general demanded by prudence and duties to one's own people if it represents a *preventive self-defense;* for thus the case is reducible to the one already discussed. The conditions under which a policy of neutrality is cratically imprudent were already enumerated in chapter 5.2.3.2; if imprudence is accompanied by indifference to the fate of others, this is certainly bad politics, as when, like the Benelux countries in 1939–40, one risks occupation by a state that is waging an unjust war rather than join the opposing side. In a few cases such as when another state waging a defensive war can win only by occupying the neutral country, one has to say that there cannot be even a right to armed defense of one's own neutrality. In any case, a crucial task of foreign policy is that of recognizing when yielding will necessarily strengthen the other side's aggressive intentions.[90] Hitler's strategy of territorial expansion was disguised in a minimal way because after two steps forward he took one step backward and shamelessly oscillated between using force and lying; but it did not demand a superior intelligence to see through his game, had one only *wanted* to see through it. Munich was therefore a betrayal not only of Czechoslovakia but also of the French and the British people.

A classic question, admittedly not easy to answer, for the proponent of the theory of just war concerns *preventive war.* If one means by this the anticipation of an immediately imminent attack (which is currently being prepared and has been announced, for instance, through an ultimatum) for the purpose of gaining strategic advantages, there is

---

89. Faucher's decision recalls Clausewitz's entry into Russian service after Prussia's alliance with Napoleon in 1812. At the end of that year, Clausewitz played a role in the conclusion of the Tauroggen Convention, a great example of a correct decision by the military without authorization by the responsible state organs.

90. See R. Gilpin (1981), 207: "Perhaps the greatest task of the prudent and responsible statesman is to be able to judge when appeasement will and will not lead to peaceful resolution of disputes."

hardly any doubt about its justice, even if under certain circumstances it could be prudent to wait for the attack in order to show the whole world that one is oneself the victim;
the mobilization of sympathies can sometimes certainly outweigh the military losses.
Whatever Roosevelt might have known, in the medium term the Japanese attack on
Pearl Harbor helped the United States more than harmed it. But even if the United States
had struck first, while the Japanese air force was on the way to Hawaii, that could not
have altered the fact that Japan would have been the aggressor; the external event of beginning the war is only prima facie evidence for aggression, not the ultimate criterion.[91]
It is worth considering L. Strisower's terminological suggestion that in such a case we
speak of "preventive defense" and call "preventive war" the anticipation of possible later
attacks that are expected on the basis of a negative attitude on the part of the other side.
According to this definition, however, depending on one's concept of possibility, almost
every war could be presented as a preventive war.[92] For instance, even Hitler's attack on
Poland could be called preventative, because he could fear an attack, not by Poland itself,
but by other states that could have allied themselves with Poland; for the assumption
that his domination would not be unconditionally accepted so long as there were decent people anywhere was not ungrounded. A power-obsessed person can easily be persuaded that all wars that precede his achievement of world domination are preventive
wars. Thus it is all the more urgent to distinguish between "preventive defensive wars"
and "preventive offensive wars" if one wants to have an ethically useful language; for
hardly any term has been more grossly abused, and is still abused, than "preventive war."
Against merely possible threats only one response is permissible: preparation for war
through alliances and armament. This threat serves the goal of preventing war and is
therefore justified, so long as it is accompanied by readiness for mutual disarmament, limitation to purely defensive weapons (insofar as this is feasible in terms of military technology), confidence-building mechanisms, and the construction of collective security organizations. In peacetime, confidence-building mechanisms in the broader sense include
secret service activities as well, since these bring into international relationships a kind of
publicity, as it were, and can significantly reduce fear of the opponent.[93] Indignation at
the discovery of individual spies should be accompanied by gratitude for the existence
of the institution of spying and the generous treatment of agents by both sides.

However, with regard to the theory of preventive war it should be admitted that
there are difficult limit cases, of which the *endangering of the balance of power* is probably

---

91. This is also recognized in positive international law; cf. A. Verdross and B. Simma (1984),
288 f.

92. Hegel's explanations in the *Rechtsphilosophie* §§ 335 f. (1969; 7:500 f.), lead in the same
direction.

93. Sometimes it can also increase it and thereby be helpful in that it deters attempts to change
the status quo. Xerxes not only pardoned three Greek spies who had been caught but showed them
his whole army (Herodotus VII, 147 f.).

the most important.[94] The modern state system was almost dominated by concern about the maintenance of the balance of power, as we have seen in chapter 6.2.3.3.3, and several wars were waged in its defense. The War of the Spanish Succession is an excellent example, which is in fact not easy to evaluate morally.[95] If the effort to acquire hegemonic status begins with attacks on smaller states, then the latter have a right to self-defense and other states have a right to defend them from attack, which they have a self-interest in exercising, as we have said; for the incorporation of smaller states strengthens the aggressor for the conflict with its larger neighbors. But what should be done if there is a voluntary fusion of two states? Naturally, Charles II's testamentary nomination of the Duke of Anjou as his successor in Spain did not correspond to the principles of natural constitutional law, but the opposing powers could hardly complain about it because they were not republics either. Charles II acted in accord with the principles of the *ancien régime,* and Louis XIV's refusal to exclude the Duke of Anjou from the succession to the French throne was not contrary to the law. To be sure, a French-Spanish monarchy could have become dangerous to the other European great powers, although the danger was overestimated at the time, but one would have had to wait until a superpower of that kind had actually made preparations for war; up to that point, the other powers would only have been allowed to strengthen their cooperation.

In fact, it is not hard to see that the *voluntary fusion* of two states (for instance, through skilful marriage policy in the age of dynasties), and even more of two democratic states through a treaty, can offer *no ground for war.* If a universal state is the goal of history, and if at the same time, at least under the conditions of modernity, it is not permissible to use violence to construct such a state, then there can be no alternative to the voluntary fusion of individual states—at least if one does not indulge in the illusion that all states would unite simultaneously into a universal state. It is politically prudent to give guarantees to those who are not part of a fusion, and especially to offer them at least in the medium term an opportunity to join in the union; but the other European countries could no more have a veto right with regard to German reunification than Russia can have one with regard to NATO's expansion toward the east.[96] However, it was extremely prudent to strengthen, simultaneously with German reunification, the supranational European and Atlantic institutions, and it remains a central task to invite Russia to join collective security systems. But even if this demand of prudence is not met, the opposite side still has no *ius ad bellum,* however understandable it would be if the citizens of the state attacked, were there a military strike on it because of its exces-

---

94. Another one concerns armament with weapons of mass destruction. Consider the Israeli bombardment of the Iraqi nuclear reactor Osiraq in June 1981, which was an isolated act that did not even lead to a war and would therefore be easier to justify—especially if Israel itself had no nuclear weapons.

95. Cf. M. Walzer (1977), 78 ff.

96. Even an explicit violation of a treaty, such as was committed by the Convention in Philadelphia in 1787, is defensible for this purpose.

sive power, felt almost as much aversion for the wrong politics of its own government as for the aggressors. There is no *ius ad bellum* even when the achievement of hegemonic status by the new state resulting from fusion is inevitable, at least so long as the latter does not directly attack other states. For the existence of a hegemonic power (or even of an extensive empire) is a possible guarantor of freedom, just as is a balance of powers,[97] and even if the peace owed to a hegemonic power is accompanied by significant restrictions on other states, it can be far better than a phase of bloody wars. It is not always cowardice, but often wisdom, when one resigns oneself to a hegemonic power, especially if the latter has the morally more elevated mores for the time in question. In his short essay "Of the Balance of Power,"[98] David Hume painted, like a good Briton, a picture of the bogey of universal monarchy and praised the foreign policy of his country, which aimed at a balance of power, even though he recognized that Great Britain often should have been content with more modest political goals and had waged too many wars (from which, moreover, its own imperial status finally resulted). But one need not agree with Hume's options. The pacifying achievement of the Roman Empire was considerable, and even if one were to admit that a more vigorous policy against its rise at the time when such a policy was still possible would have made sense (an admission that is in no way compulsory, since Roman domination was not without its positive aspects for the Hellenistic kingdoms), that is far from meaning that after the achievement of hegemony one should not have resigned oneself to the status quo or made protectorate treaties with the Roman Empire.

Indeed, *for past times* one can even defend the view that an aggressive foreign policy directed toward achieving hegemony could have represented a contribution to a long-term peace and could understand itself as such.[99] At least this held true so long as the *rise to a hegemonic role* could be relatively quick and bloodless because of the inattention of other powers and because of various vicissitudes. The fact that Philip II exploited the opportunity that was offered to Macedonia in the fourth century bc should not be praised, but it can hardly be held against him. In fact, a fair judgment of expansionist foreign policies must take into account the historical and domestic structural conditions within which they took place. Thus a war against a people with a government it has chosen by itself is a far greater injustice than one against a monocracy that is not beloved by its people. In the age of dynastic limited warfare the people often cared relatively little about who ruled them; the injustice of aggression wronged the opposing monarch and the victims of the war, who were often mercenaries, not so much the civilian subjects. The injustice was diminished still further if the area conquered became a part of the conquering state with equal rights. The injustice disappeared almost completely if a large part of

97. See the well-known distinction of three types of peace—balance, hegemony, and empire— in R. Aron (1962), 157 ff.

98. (1987), 332–341.

99. In the twentieth century, Mao Tse-Tung defended the thesis that the imminent, most ruthless of all wars would serve to put an end to war (1966; 80 f).

the population desired annexation but was not able to express its own will. Prussia's annexation of Hanover and Hessel-Kassel and Italy's annexation of the Kingdom of the Two Sicilies—the latter sanctioned by popular vote—are good examples that received a further legitimation through the main ideology of the time, nationalism. For the annexation of Alsace-Lorraine, which occurred against the will of the majority of the population and paved the way for the next war, there was no justification at all.

But even if a few aggressions of the past can perhaps be excused, the age of legitimate expansion is definitely over since humanity has risen to the idea of collective security systems. It is profoundly unjust when one mentions in the same breath, for instance, Hitler's imperialism and that of Napoleon. The latter was unjustifiable as well, but Napoleon represented a superior legal order, whereas Hitler was the exponent of one of the most barbarous legal systems in the history of humanity. Napoleon could think the monocracies in Spain and Russia he was battling were less just than his own, whereas in 1938 Czechoslovakia, for example, had a highly developed democratic and constitutional culture. Finally, after the catastrophe of the First World War, humanity had created in the League of Nations an organ that there was a duty to further develop; in Napoleon's time, on the other hand, international law recognized a sovereign right to wage war, and almost all his contemporaries found (though today one can hardly consider them right in doing so) the execution of the Duke of Enghien more outrageous morally than the Russian campaign. Similarly repellent is a comparison of Saddam Hussein with Bismarck. It is not just success, which does not count morally, that distinguishes the two foreign policies: Saddam Hussein's Iraq was not a constitutional state founded on the rule of law; none of the neighboring states wanted Saddam to play a leading role in the Arab world, since a federal state solution did not lie within the scope of his imagination; the international law and foreign policy structural conditions are today completely different from what they were in the nineteenth century; and, finally, during its brief occupation of Kuwait, Iraq behaved in a way entirely different from the way Prussia behaved after the annexation of Hanover.

We have mentioned several times the internal political structure of states that are waging wars—can it also be a ground for war? Positive international law still in force rejects *interventions* that cannot be interpreted either as self-defense or as defense of another state from attack, on the basis of the principle of noninterference in internal affairs.[100] Among the reasons for supporting this principle are that it can reduce the number of conflicts, that outside interventions are often counterproductive, and that such interventions can almost always take place solely in weak states, not in the ones that are the most brutal because they are the most powerful oppressive states. But the idea that this principle has an intrinsic value, or is even absolutely valid, is absurd.[101] Most of the principles of modern international law proceed from the transfer of civil law principles

---

100. This principle is recognized in Art. 2 (7) of the United Nations Charter, but humanitarian intervention was justified by Resolution 688 of the Security Council (April 1991).

101. See M. Walzer (1977), 86 ff., which I follow extensively.

to states, which assume, as it were, the place of persons; the principle of noninterference corresponds to respect for the autonomy of the individual. But it is not hard to see that the parallel leads us away from the truth. For harming oneself, even if on principle it is not permissible, is considerably less problematic in natural law than harming someone else; but the latter is concerned when the executive branch of a state abuses its own population. To be sure, in this case one's own citizens are concerned, but they are still other people, and there is no natural law right to abuse them; however, there is a right to defend them from attack, in view of the violation of their human rights.[102] Voluntary associations must in general be respected because they spring from the individual's freedom of association, but states are in general not voluntary associations.[103] In Kant's work *Zum ewigen Frieden* (*Perpetual Peace*), there is a characteristic tension between the fifth preliminary article, that no state ought to interfere by force in the constitution and government of another state, and the first definitive article, according to which the civil constitution of every state ought to be republican; for if the "ought" in the latter invites efforts on the part of all people of good will, then the violent transformation of an autocratic state into a republic is obviously tempting as an *ultima ratio*.

Only states that recognize elementary principles of natural constitutional law have a claim to have their decisions respected and to expect other countries to forgo any intervention, whereas a foreign power's overthrow of a bloodthirsty tyrant who murders his own people or even a minority of them can hardly be considered unjust. It is true that prudence often, and perhaps even usually, requires the avoidance of such actions (especially if the other state is very strong) and that there is certainly a danger that this principle might be terribly abused by states that are more powerful but not necessarily more lawful. Moreover, there is much to be said for the argument that a people must first have shown by its rebellion that it is itself prepared to fight for its own freedom, before others should hasten to help it, since the political virtues required by a free constitution cannot be imposed from without.[104] But all this does not alter the fact that neither those concerned nor anyone within the country or abroad has a natural law duty to look idly on while a population group is annihilated by its legal government; and one cannot fail to give legitimate help where it is possible to do so only because there are cases in which it is impossible to give it, and because even where it would be possible in the individual case, one cannot help all those who are being oppressed. What was said

---

102. From this follow also the morals of the principle of universality in criminal law.

103. See C. R. Beitz (1979), 77: "the objection [to this parallel] is simply that there are few, if any, governments to which all (or even some) of the governed have actually consented, and therefore that there are few, if any, governments that are in fact free associations." Beitz is cited with approval by no less a figure than Rawls (1993; 221 f.), who even explains that "We must reformulate the powers of sovereignty in light of a reasonable law of peoples and get rid of the right to war and the right to internal autonomy" (49).

104. On this subject, see Mill (1867), 173: "The only test possessing any real value, of a people's having become fit for popular institutions, is that they, or a sufficient portion of them to prevail in the contest, are willing to brave labour and danger for their liberation."

earlier about the defense of other states from attack truly holds even more for humanitarian intervention: Russia would not have been so passionate about protecting Christians in the Ottoman Empire had it not been so interested in the Dardanelles; Spain's exploitation of the Cuban population would not have so enraged the United States had Cuba not had such great strategic importance because of its location. But whereas the Russian demand had no objective foundation, because the protection of Christians could also have been undertaken by the other European powers that were defending the Ottoman Empire against Russia in the Crimean War, the Cubans' situation could hardly have been improved without intervention by the United States—even if after its victory the United States did not make any special attempt to satisfy the rebels' wishes.

In dealing with interventions, attempts are repeatedly made to argue that the domestic policy of the country concerned also endangers its neighbors in the middle term, and it is certainly right that internal and external aggressivity often go hand in hand: military dictatorships are more inclined to go to war than are democracies. Nonetheless, this argument is misleading, even though it must obviously be introduced if one seeks to justify an intervention under current international law and therefore plays an important strategic role. First of all, there are enough countries in which the power-holders would be satisfied with butchering their own populations if only they were allowed to do so and that are small enough so that one need not fear that they might attack other countries; but even with respect to them there is a natural law right to intervene, which should be exercised all the more since, given their smallness, it is possible to do so without running any great risk. And second, even in the case of large states, the danger to neighbors is always only a *possibility*—but preventive offensive wars are, as we have seen, immoral. A state's self-imposed duty under international law to protect human rights is not a necessary condition for the legitimacy of an intervention against it, even if it increases that legitimacy.

Naturally, interventions can be justified only if the most fundamental human rights are being violated by the legal government—that is, if a great number of people are being murdered or enslaved; furthermore, military intervention must be *necessary* in order to save people, it must have *prospects of success,* and its moral costs must be *proportionate* to the desired result. The moral justification of an intervention is, *ceteris paribus,* even easier if a civil war is raging or anarchy prevails; in the latter case, there is no longer any state whose rights would be violated. An additional argument for intervention is a successful and morally legitimate secession of a part of the state territory. As was shown in chapter 8.1.5.3, not all secessions are justifiable, only secessions from an unjust state; however, if it is on principle permissible to intervene against such a state, then a fortiori it is permissible to intervene against an unjust state from which a part of the population has already begun to separate itself. In such a case, it is best to recognize the new state, to whose aid one can then come in the framework of defending it from attack. Furthermore, an intervention is easier to justify if it represents a reply to the unjust intervention of another state; it was understandable that the Western European democracies remained neutral in the Spanish Civil War, in view of their weakness and their other concerns, but one cannot seriously maintain that in view of Italian and German support for the rebels, help for the republicans would have been immoral. Naturally, in order to support one side in a civil war it is not sufficient that it is battling an unjust opponent; it must itself maintain certain minimum moral standards. This is not self-evident, since there can be several forms of injustice, and a battle for power between two equally repellent ideologies is not unusual—consider contemporary Algeria. In such a case, intervention cannot be justified. In the Vietnam War the enemy was dangerous, but the side supported by the United States was far too unattractive and far too little rooted in its own people to make it possible to justify supporting it, especially considering the sacrifices it cost. It is obvious that it is immoral to use promises that will not be kept, in an effort to get a group to attack its opponent and thereby to draw an advantage out of the damage done to both; consider the encouragement of the Kurds and the Shiites in their revolt against Baghdad in 1991, without any intention of actually helping them.

It is possible that in the future *interventions on ecological grounds* will also be discussed. They occupy a strange intermediate position between humanitarian interventions and self-defense, for the effects of certain forms of environmental destruction are not limited to the country in which they occur but extend to the whole world—consider the far-reaching climatic changes resulting from CO_2 emissions. A country that has to fear that it will be swamped by a rise in the sea level seems to have at least as great a right to defend itself against this threat as one that is under attack and "only" risks losing its political independence. However, there is no doubt about two things. First, the threatened state has the right to be indignant about another state's environmental destruction only if it does not use more than its own environmental space and is willing to help pay excessive costs involved in maintaining the environment in the other country; however, it is only too likely that the states capable of such interventions will be precisely those that do the greatest environmental damage. Second, so far as the environmental destruction in question involves all or most states, such measures must be sanctioned by the world community; no state may in such a matter, which does not concern it alone, take the law into its own hands. It need not be emphasized that even more than in other cases, the use of force can here be only the last resort, which must be preceded by long negotiations.

If one reviews the criteria just mentioned, one will see that there are not many legitimate interventions; still fewer will be the cases in which an intervention that is justified in itself can be expected of one's own people.[105] Military intervention by a "more advanced" culture in a less developed one cannot be justified merely on the basis of the

---

105. The situation changes if a defensive war against a state that is massacring parts of one's own population is being waged anyway. Bombardment of the roads leading to the gas chambers and of the gas chambers themselves in Auschwitz was certainly to be expected of Allied flyers, and the fact that the Allies failed to do this and many other things that might have saved the lives of Jews and Romany is still in dire need of justification.

difference in development. Even with regard to peoples living as hunters and gatherers there is no generic right to appropriate their land, no matter how true it is that the more advanced culture could feed significantly more people. (Whether the land is appropriated by conquest or through deceitful treaties does not make much difference morally.) Only if the new settlers guarantee the natives the maintenance of the status quo in terms of food supplies and the survival of the central components of their culture can such a right to appropriate land be discussed, especially if the emigrants are themselves in an emergency and cannot be fed at home. An invasion in order to survive can be excused—and even justified *if* at the same time the physical and cultural survival of the people invaded is guaranteed. The culture's survival must, however, be desired by its members; individuals should not be prevented against their will from abandoning an archaic culture. In the abstract, Europeans had no right to be in North America; but one can hardly blame the Irish who fled the famine in their own country, insofar as they believed that North America could feed them as well as the indigenous population (and in fact, could do so only if political power was in the hands of the whites). However, many of the wars waged in modern *colonial history* lacked even the appearance of being motally justifiable (think only of the Opium Wars), and the crimes that were committed by Europeans during these wars and after their victories are patently obvious. But the following qualifications are in order. First, defense of another state against attack remains a justifying ground for war; and if an imperialist power responds to a plea for help issued by a state under attack, it is less a matter of the former acting unjustly than of the latter acting foolishly. Cortés would never have conquered the Aztec empire without the help of native peoples who initially hated the Aztecs far more than they did the Spaniards. However, incorporating the country one allegedly wanted to help after a victory has been won remains unjust. Second, sometimes—not always—colonial domination has protected and promoted objects of legal protection such as human life more extensively than did the preceding political corporate group; once colonial domination was established, its continuation was not necessarily immoral. The crucial thing was what was done with the natives; the Jesuit state in Paraguay may have represented an advance over the indigenous political corporate groups. Third, from the injustice of colonization it does not follow that after the injustice was perceived, the quickest possible decolonization was morally obligatory; in the meantime things had been done and responsibilities assumed. The view of some Britons that their withdrawal from India would result in a bloodbath between Moslems and Hindus was unfortunately not a mere attempt to justify staying there, as the events of 1946–47 showed. In political decisions, it should be the future that counts, not the past. But even if a rapid decolonization of the British Empire could not have been reasonably demanded in the 1930s, that did not mean in the least that other countries had a right to pursue a policy of conquest in order to catch up. Italy's attack on Ethiopia was an unacceptable injustice, even if Mussolini sought to justify it by referring to the earlier colonial policies of other European powers.

It may be asked what meaning moral judgment on world-historical *res actae* such as the extensive destruction of hunter and gatherer cultures and many pre-modern advanced cultures might have. Isn't *world history* the *world court?* It is trivially true that history is mainly written by the victors and that the normative discourse accepted in a society depends on the factual power relationships in that society—in Turkey, one still cannot report on the Armenian genocide. But however appropriate these sociological statements may be, their moral-metaphysical legitimation is unacceptable; this legitimation is already implicit in Hegel and finds its clearest expression in Marx.[106] To be sure, the injustice that the Spaniards, for example, committed against Native American peoples cannot be undone—at least not in this world, which is perhaps not the only one. But it will remain an injustice until the end of history, and even if it would be naive to ignore the fact that this injustice was often vigorously pointed out by Spain's enemies, who thereby sought to promote, not the Native Americans' interests, but their own, there nonetheless remains an indispensable duty to remember the victims in history, even, indeed especially, if one is oneself a descendant of the victors. One thereby gives them the respect they deserve, and perhaps in this way one can help prevent such things from happening again, no matter how great human nature's inclination to evil may be. The Assyrians did not lament their victims; more than two thousand years later, Spain produced at least a Las Casas and can be infinitely more proud of him than of all its conquerors.

8.2.2.2. Just Conduct of War

The decision to go to war ought to be so difficult because one cannot indulge in any illusions regarding its nature: Wars are for the most part horrible, and one can only be deeply grateful if one is spared concrete experience of them. The most fundamental moral principles, which law protects, are trampled upon in wars; and in particular the destruction of human lives is almost inevitable. In the first half of the nineteenth century, Clausewitz already correctly pointed out that it was vain to hope that modern civilization would lead to a humanization of war. The goal of every war, he wrote, is to force the opposing state to do what one wants it to do; and although for that purpose hostile feelings are not necessary, as they were among barbaric peoples, hostile intentions remain indispensable, and these would increase each other until the extreme exertion of all forces was achieved. "Therefore, if we find civilized nations do not put their prisoners to death, do not devastate towns and countries, this is because their intelligence exercises a greater influence on their mode of carrying on War, and has taught

---

106. One has only to read the article "The British Rule in India" in the *New York Daily Tribune*, 25 June 1853, which, despite all its criticism of British policy, ends with a quotation from Goethe's "An Suleika" in the "Timur Nameh" of the *Westöstlicher Divan:* "Sollte diese Qual uns quälen, / Da sie unsre Lust vermehrt? / Hat nicht Myriaden Seelen / Timurs Herrschaft aufgezehrt?" ("Should this torment torment us, / Since it adds to our pleasure? / Has not Timur's rule / myriad souls consumed?")

them more effectual means of applying force than these rude acts of mere instinct. The invention of gunpowder and the constant progress of improvements in the construction of firearms are sufficient proofs that the tendency to destroy the adversary which lies at the bottom of the conception of war is in no way changed or modified through the process of civilization."[107] Certainly there have been a few wars that have cost hardly any human lives, but these battles were fought between mercenary armies that felt no hatred for each other and that were led by officers who had no interest in killing enemy soldiers, since the latter could instead be immediately recruited for one's own army.[108]

The democratization of politics has almost inevitably made wars bloodier, and since the early nineteenth century, national hatred has produced partisan and guerrilla wars that undermine the *clear distinction between combatants and non-combatants*—the fulcrum on which the theory of just war pivots. Let there be no mistake: If hatred for the enemy becomes overpowering, then the capitulation of one's own government, and especially a government with which one has never identified, is not a sufficient ground for putting an end to hostilities; and so long as there is any hope of forcing the enemy to his knees by means of a guerrilla war, it requires especially high moral standards to decide against it, particularly if one is convinced that a victory is absolutely indispensable in order to make progress toward the just goal. All attempts to limit war are open to this objection: If we can agree, for instance, to renounce certain weapons, why shouldn't we agree to reject any use of force to resolve our conflicts, or at least to limit ourselves to a duel between two chosen champions? And since the latter is clearly not the case, why should we accept a certain limitation if it puts us at a unilateral disadvantage? In fact, a people that is hopelessly inferior in terms of weapons technology in an open war against a great power must inevitably ask why it should renounce the use of partisans, even if using them contradicts the valid law of war. Only in a case in which both parties can count on benefiting equally from a limitation on the use of force, or in which they have common values, can one assume that they will adhere to agreements. Wars between culturally heterogeneous peoples and wars for recognition are frequently particularly cruel; on the other hand, if we are dealing with limited conflicts of interest within a common value system, force can often be limited.

This skeptical prognosis concerning human behavior does not affect the moral duty to allow as little bloodshed as possible in the conduct of a war—for which, by the way, an iron discipline in the army is indispensable. Any use of force that goes beyond what is *absolutely necessary* for victory is unacceptable; and the concept of the absolutely necessary should be defined narrowly. For instance, committing rapes might give a few soldiers vital energies, but they are never absolutely necessary; allowing soldiers to rape women is therefore always a crime. Indeed, if one comes to the conclusion that the necessary force is *disproportionate* to the good threatened by the opponent, one must in general, as we have already said, decide against war. The goal of war is to force the enemy to surrender

---

107. 1832 ff.; 193 f. Trans. Graham, 1949, 1:4.
108. See H. J. Morgenthau and K. W. Thompson (1985), 392 f.

his will; since this will is manifested in the *armed forces* and its body consists, as it were, in the *territorial basis* of the state, the goal is victory over the armed forces and, if one wants to be thorough, the occupation of the enemy's territory. However, the latter is morally permissible only if it is necessary in order really to break what is unlawful in the alien will. I say *unlawful* because the whole will may not be coerced by force, but only those elements within it that represented a legitimate reason for using counterforce. However, there can be cases in which unlawfulness is, so to speak, the essence of the alien will, and if there are good reasons for thinking that only an unconditional surrender would provide security against renewed attacks, this is a reasonable war goal—thus the Allies could hardly pursue any other goal in their struggle against Nazi Germany. Otherwise, more modest goals are morally obligatory if they are more in accord with the requirement of *proportionality* than are more ambitious ones. Thus it is worth discussing the thesis—even if I lack the empirical knowledge necessary to judge it concretely—that in the case of Japan the Allies did not need to insist on an unconditional surrender; and in any case to justify dropping the atom bomb on Hiroshima and especially on Nagasaki it is not sufficient to say that a landing on the Japanese main islands would have cost more human lives, because this was not the only alternative; more generous surrender conditions might have been offered, for instance, or one could have merely threatened to use the bombs. However, it is correct that had there been only the first two alternatives mentioned, it probably would have been permissible to choose to drop the atom bomb, as the lesser evil; the spectacular element in the new weapon should not lead us to ignore the fact that the conventional bombs dropped on Tokyo killed even more people than were killed in Hiroshima. (Nonetheless, there is something especially insidious about the long-term effects of nuclear weapons, which affect—for instance, through radiation damage to the genetic makeup—even the next generation, whose victims must be taken into account in making a decision. Something analagous is true for land mines, which cause casualties among civilians, especially among children, long after hostilities have ended.) Naturally, in making such a cost-benefit analysis, deaths in the civilian population and deaths among soldiers must be considered separately; soldiers have to risk their lives in order to save civilians. But one can hardly expect people to accept much greater sacrifices among their own soldiers solely in order to save a few civilians on the enemy side; in the situation of the struggle at that time, the distinction between soldiers and civilians was in any case blurred, since there were good grounds for assuming that a gradual landing on the islands would have led most civilians, including women, to engage in military resistance. The internal victims of a criminal system, whom it might under some circumstances be possible to save by forcing the opponent to capitulate quickly, should also be taken into account in making such decisions.

Clausewitz's famous thesis that war is "a mere continuation of policy by other means"[109] is a great realization insofar as it rejects the disgraceful notion that war is an

---

109. (1832 ff.), 210. Trans. J. Graham (1949), 1:23.

end in itself; his formulation that war has "a grammar of its own, but its logic is not peculiar to itself"[110] hits the essential point on the head. War must serve *political goals*, and these co-determine the *basic strategic decisions*, namely, those regarding the conduct of the war, which in turn determine the *framework for tactics*, namely, the use of the armed forces in individual engagements. But what Clausewitz overlooks is that not only the logic of politics but also the grammar of war is subject to moral judgment; war is not a neutral means of doing politics but rather one that has a negative intrinsic value, and therefore the goals must be changed if the price to be paid in the form of means is too high. The moral price should be calculated on the basis of the presumed number of dead and wounded—and not only one's own but also those of the opposing side. It is true that after the decision to go to war, during the hostilities themselves, there is a duty to minimize the risk to one's own side, at least so long as one's one success is at stake; one's own defeat cannot be casually risked if one believes one is waging a just war. But that does not mean that all means are permissible in order to win; in particular, limits set by the law of war are in general to be respected, in fact on the basis of the conviction that even one's own defeat would represent a lesser evil than the consequences of a breakdown of limitations on war in future conflicts. Exceptions are conceivable, however, if they are the only way of winning a war against a state that has espoused systematic violations of the most elementary human rights—and indeed all the more if this state is on the point of gaining world domination. Walzer has suggested four possible determinations of the relationship of morally justifiable acts of war to positive law of war, which stand in tension between a more Kantian and a more utilitarian framework.[111] Between the extreme standpoint that accepts defeat solely in order not to violate the chivalrous aspects of the law of war[112] and the other extreme, which always disrespects positive law of war when doing so serves its own interest (which is considered good, of course), one can imagine, with Walzer, two intermediary positions: on one hand, a gradual abandonment of all the standards of the law of war in the course of conducting the war, and on the other a fundamental decision in favor of a limited violation of the conventions in order to avert an impending catastrophe. As we have said, there is much to be said for the latter position: to avoid being subjected by a totalitarian state, one can also deviate from positive law if it is necessary to do so and if the evil inflicted stands in a relationship of proportionality to the good achieved. These moral principles are not negotiable, and insofar as the valid law of war usually serves to concretize them, it should be respected. But it has only a prima facie validity because the historical structural conditions can change in such a way that observing it unconditionally favors the aggressor (especially, but not solely, if the latter does not observe it).

---

110. (1832 ff.), 991. Trans. J. Graham (1949), 3:122.

111. (1977), 231 f.

112. A representative of this position is Duke Hsiang of Sung, whom Mao merely laughed at: "We are not like Duke Hsiang of Sung and have no use for his asinine ethics" (1966; 240).

The law of war regulates *who may kill whom when and how*. A *formal symmetry* between the two sides in the war is fundamental: Even though in a just war both states cannot be morally equally justified, this principle of formal symmetry certainly holds for the soldiers fighting; even if its own cause is manifestly justified, no state can expect its own soldiers to be spared by the opposing side if it itself takes no prisoners. In addition to this formal equality, there is also a substantive principle. Only a certain group of people, the combatants, may kill and be killed; they are not necessarily members of state armed forces, but they must at least carry their arms openly or an insigne must make them recognizable at a distance as combatants. The right to kill proceeds from the opposing combatants' presumed intention to kill, not from their personal guilt. During the Second World War, a German soldier may have constantly thought about how he could have himself captured, but the other side could not tell that; a German civilian might have welcomed the Nazis' most terrible crimes, but that did not yet make him a legitimate target of the intent to kill. Soldiers who surrender—and the side waging a just war should encourage soldiers on the other side both to surrender and to desert—have, like the wounded, the ill, and the shipwrecked, a right to the protection of their lives, even if a restriction of their freedom until the end of the war is inevitable.[113] However, as much as possible, such regulations must be mutually accepted and thus represent the result of explicit treaties or behavior implying a specific intention. The moral question, what should be done in waging a war with states that do not adhere to such a principle, is difficult to answer. Thus in 1944 the Germans shot partisans of the "French Forces of the Interior" despite the protests of the Provisional Government, which they did not recognize, until the partisans, after giving a warning, killed eighty German soldiers who had fallen into their hands. After that, no other French partisan was shot. Could this killing, which contravened the Geneva Convention Regarding the Treatment of Prisoners of War (27 July 1929), although the Convention had been recognized by the French Forces of the Interior, be justified? It goes without saying that revenge, which springs from a mere reference to the past, is under no circumstances legitimate. But how are we to judge if, first of all, a reference to the future is the motive, and second, the retribution is proportional to the injustice that has already occurred? Unfortunately, one cannot deny that "tit-for-tat" strategies can be successful, in general and also in this specific case; the French Forces ultimately had a greater responsibility to their own partisans than to the Germans. Nonetheless, the killing of innocent people is so grave an evil that at least alternatives should have been sought, such as falsely reporting that all the prisoners had been shot[114] or limiting the shooting to a considerably smaller number of people or to those who had committed provable crimes. Killing eighty soldiers at once was not a military necessity and was therefore not defensible.

---

113. This right to life is also violated by handing them over to their state, if the latter is a totalitarian power which is very likely to execute them. One need feel no sympathy for Vlasov in order to disapprove of the handing over of his troops to the Soviet Union.

114. This is M. Walzer's suggestion (1977; 208).

As for the *protection of the lives and health of civilians* (who also cannot be used for forced labor and whose property may not be plundered), modern weapons technology (whose precision in hitting the target has to be increased) and modern conduct of war unfortunately make it considerably more difficult to achieve this protection than one would wish. The production of weapons for the armed forces can decide the outcome of a war, and bombing the factories where they are made is justified, even if doing so endangers civilians, as long as this action on the whole saves human lives. On the other hand, attacking factories that produce things for the armed forces that are also essential for the whole population in peacetime cannot be morally justified—not to mention bombing city centers (which is also for the most part counterproductive). Sieges and blockades in particular directly affect the civilian population. Civilians are usually not allowed to leave a city under siege because the result would be that food supplies would last longer for the soldiers that remained; but an extension of the law of war in this direction would be a reasonable demand.[115] It is difficult to say how one should deal with innocent hostages used as shields; even if the guilt for their death is borne far more by those who use them in this way—for example, by building military installations next to hospitals— there remains a duty to seek alternatives (and it does not speak well for humanity's moral level if the death of hospital patients is more easily accepted than the destruction of works of art, which are now also used as hostages, so to speak). However, in general it is a reasonable maxim, which pays off in the long run, not to yield to blackmailers. Blackmailing by threatening to do significant environmental damage is now also one of the options in waging a war—environmental damage that on one hand affects the civilian population and on the other has a high intrinsic disvalue. For it is certain that the destruction in war of animal and plant life is also an evil, no matter how embarrassing it was that during the First Gulf War a picture of a bird dying in a pool of oil upset considerably more people than reports of the death of civilians—reports that were not accompanied by pictures because in 1991 the United States deliberately prevented the social delegitimation of its policy at home by ensuring that pictures of cruelties like those that played a great role in delegitimating policy during the Vietnam War would not be seen. War in the narrower sense is accompanied by a battle for public opinion, which must be convinced that its own side is waging a just war that deserves every kind of support.

Protecting civilians corresponds, on the inter-state level, to *respect for the rights of neutral countries.* As has already been said, there is in general no duty to defend another country waging a just war against an aggressor, and since it is fundamentally desirable that there remain observers who are not affected and are therefore as impartial as possible, it is even good if there are neutral parties during a war, although it is not always in the direct interest of the state defending itself when third countries decide to remain neutral. An attack on a neutral state is prima facie unjust, even if it is made by a state that is itself under attack or defending another state from attack; yet one can imagine extreme

---

115. Cf. M. Walzer (1977), 169 f.

situations in which it can be justified. Churchill's intention to mine Norwegian waters was apparently convincingly grounded in his memorandum of 16 December 1939[116] (even if the final sentence, the appeal to history as the final judge, is unacceptable for reasons that have already been mentioned several times). In particular, Churchill can be granted that Great Britain, which was fighting for the rights of smaller states, had moral rights that differed from Hitler's. Nonetheless, the objection is certainly plausible that precisely someone who is fighting for the rights of smaller states should not violate those rights; that moreover, these measures were not absolutely necessary (before the fall of France, Great Britain was not in a state of supreme emergency); and finally that the mining, which was carried out in April, provoked the German attack on Norway, which could hardly be seen as a *new* German guilt—after the decision to attack Poland, it was only a strategically consistent reaction. Easier to justify is the attack on the war materiel of former allies that is likely to fall into the hands of the enemy. The British sinking of the French fleet off Oran on 3 July 1940 was morally defensible, since the French were unwilling to keep it from falling into the hands of the Germans or Italians. Firing on former allies was certainly not easy; however, Admiral Somerville, who carried out the sinking, cannot be condemned but only pitied and at the same time respected for his action. Still more admirable, however, are the two French farm families who each lost a son during the British attack and insisted that on their coffins the Union Jack should lie alongside the Tricolor. "In this we may see how the comprehending spirit of simple folk touches the sublime," Churchill wrote,[117] and in fact this insight into necessity, this subordination of private grief to a common good that transcends one's own people, deserves to be called sublime.

In my opinion, deliberately assassinating civilian members of the enemy's government who are responsible for an unjust war is morally unproblematic if in that way the war can be quickly brought to an end; it is not clear why soldiers, who must in part serve against their will, should be endangered more than those who bear the responsibility for an unjust war. Such actions can be called "terroristic" in the wider sense, but they are to be sharply distinguished from those that are directed against the civilian population at large, which can under no circumstances be justified—as we already saw in chapter 8.1.5.2. What one's moral response to *terrorism* in the narrower sense should be is one of the most difficult questions to answer. Naturally, punishing the direct offenders is legitimate, on the basis of constitutional procedures, in some cases after they have been abducted from a foreign country; and killing them is to be considered only *if* there is no possibility of bringing them to justice and *if* they would otherwise commit further terroristic acts. But are military sanctions against states that support or at least tolerate terrorists (perhaps not out of ill will but out of weakness) permissible? In terms of positive international law such sanctions are for the most part unacceptable, but positive international law is not the final criterion of morals. Nonetheless, it goes without

---

116. (1948 ff.), 2:129 ff.
117. (1948 ff.), 3:215.

saying that military measures must be the *ultima ratio*. First of all, economic sanctions should be imposed, and states that do not join in the sanctions are making themselves co-responsible for terrorism (and also bear a co-responsibility for any finally resulting countermeasures). Weak states should be offered aid in fighting terrorism. Furthermore, one must distinguish among violence against things, against regular soldiers, and against uninvolved civilians. The first two can be appropriate, but the latter can never be legitimate: Killing innocent civilians of a foreign country that hides terrorists is a kind of reprisal that cannot even be discussed. If a country *systematically* trains terrorists, however, this has to be regarded as an attack against which there is a right to defend oneself by war.

The curious gray area between war and peace is inhabited not only by terrorism but also by *guerrilla warfare*. When individuals continue fighting after their legal government has capitulated, this is not always reprehensible, and neither does it contravene positive international law; however, it should be insisted upon that such individuals be recognizable as combatants. What is morally unacceptable in the phenomenon of guerrilla warfare, because it is directly self-contradictory, is that on one hand, the distinction between combatants and non-combatants is erased, since the guerrilla is indistinguishable from a civilian (in Mao Tse-Tung's well-known phrase, he swims in the mass of the people like a fish in water), and that on the other hand, this distinction is exploited, since it is presupposed that civilians are treated differently than combatants. The guerrilla is, as it were, a free-loader on this essential distinction, and therefore the phenomenon of guerrilla warfare raises serious moral objections. In the case of individual efforts to save third parties, one may conceal one's aggressive intentions; but elevating ruse to a crucial principle of the conduct of war is morally questionable and can be allowed only in defending oneself against the most extreme injustice. However, it should be recognized that guerrillas can usually succeed only in their own country; they are therefore fighting a mainly defensive war and thus usually have a just ground for war. Their indifference to death also usually presupposes that they have nothing to lose; guerrilla warfare is, as it were, the revenge taken by the poor on economically stronger states that are superior in weapons technology. However, guerrilla fighters bear a moral co-responsibility for the suffering caused the civilian population by their activity; for in order to strike the guerrillas, the opposing side will also accept the repression of the civilian population, among which the guerrillas hide and that has to conceal them, if they are to be successful, and it will even use completely uninvolved persons as hostages (think only of the Nazis; however, the example of Carlo Schmid shows that even there the individual German could save innocent people if he was courageous enough). Therefore, far from all the partisans' actions are justifiable, even if their ground for war is just, especially if there are alternatives that do not harm innocent people. The civilian population will not always whole-heartedly support guerrilla warfare; in this case, it will suffer reprisals by both sides until a decision is made. Insofar as the guerrillas have sufficient support among the people this decision will be in their favor, and that is why it is politically imprudent to get into a war with guerrillas (who are almost impossible to strike if they can hide not only among the people but also in a mountainous and forested natural environment). However, there are also serious moral objections to a war against guerrillas, even if one has a just ground for war, because the moral price is too high. The Vietnam War was unjust, not only on the North Vietnamese side, but also on the U.S. side, and all the more unjust since there was hardly any strategic necessity to defend South Vietnam, and since the South Vietnamese government did not deserve support. The decision to go to war was not only objectively wrong but also subjectively immoral because the people responsible for it had made a completely insufficient effort to acquire familiarity with the local situation.[118] Nonetheless, the injustice of this war, putatively conducted to defend another country under attack, cannot in any way be compared with that of Hitler's wars of aggression.

Victory over a guerrilla force could be achieved by *using weapons of mass destruction* to produce, not a willingness to cooperate, but rather a thorough extinction of the population. But it is obvious that modern weapons of mass destruction, which like guerrilla warfare erase the distinction between combatants and civilians, must not be used: In most conceivable cases, their use is profoundly immoral. Is it also immoral to threaten the use of such weapons? Or even to possess them? The question is one of the most difficult moral problems the human mind has ever faced, and it would be naive to assume that with the end of the Cold War it has lost its relevance. On one hand, the breakdown of the Soviet Union has favored nuclear proliferation, and on the other, even the most extensive disarmament measures—which are certainly sensible—do not alter the fact that technological knowledge cannot be disarmed and that if one has the necessary raw materials, atom bombs, for instance, can be produced again relatively quickly. Is it morally permissible to threaten to strike back with nuclear weapons if one is attacked with them, or even attacked by superior conventional armed forces? This question is so difficult to answer because a threat is credible only if one is prepared to carry it out in the event that the opposing side acts accordingly; at the same time, however, killing civilians in such great numbers as are connected with the use of nuclear weapons can hardly be justified. The problem grows larger if one imagines a situation in which a state threatens to unleash a nuclear holocaust (that is, to destroy all higher life) if others do not accept its domination: Must one give in to such a blackmailer, or should one die—without, as in all other wars, leaving to one's descendants a world that may have more freedom and fewer blackmailers, because there will no longer be any descendants? The claim has repeatedly been made that in the face of such a dilemma, the only moral decision would be to yield; and in fact it is hard to see how one could decide otherwise if one could be sure that rejecting the other's demands would lead to the destruction of the world. For even the most terrible dictatorship contains within itself the hope of

---

118. Cf. R. McNamara's list of the mistakes made by American policy (1995), 321 ff., esp. 322: "Our misjudgments of friend and foe alike reflected our profound ignorance of the history, culture, and politics of the people in the area." Thus it is all the more impressive that McNamara recognized and was able to admit the erroneous decisions made at that time.

improvement; on the other hand, a planet after a nuclear holocaust would be barren and void. But can one be sure that a nuclear war would lead to a holocaust (in the literal sense)? R. Aron points out that someone who, like Bertrand Russell, upholds the greater rationality of capitulation when confronted by such a threat, is overlooking the fact that not every threat that one firmly resists will be carried out, and that in addition, even the outbreak of a nuclear war would not necessarily lead to the destruction of humanity.[119] Indeed, one can add that such a terrible threat would probably not be made at all if it were made clear from the outset that such reflections would not be entertained; a mad dictator who endangered the entire world would be, for instance, removed from power by his own people if they had reason to fear that his threat would not be acceded to. (The psychological aspect of threatening, which should be distinguished from the military effect of its being carried out, was moreover the only one relevant in the debate about deploying the Pershing II missiles, for in fact over-kill abilities are militarily meaningful only to a very limited degree (for striking back after a first strike by the enemy). But showing the Soviet Union a clear will to defend oneself and *at the same time a readiness to cooperate* was important and right, as later history has shown, just as one must recognize in general that without the existence of nuclear weapons the Cold War would probably not have remained cold.

Nonetheless, the philosopher cannot subject himself to any prohibition on thought; and against Aron he can, in a kind of secularization of Pascal's wager, object that even if a nuclear holocaust were only a weak possibility, its disvalue must be assessed as being so high that the moral expected value of the alternative "resistance" is under all circumstances much less than that of the alternative "capitulation." Against this, one can object only that capitulation is also accompanied by risks. If this kind of behavior is adopted by others, the next blackmailer will soon appear, indeed perhaps even several of them, so that the expected value of the second alternative falls considerably because it is also infected by the possibility of a holocaust. This possibility is associated with the *conditio humana* in the late modern period; and far more important than reflecting on the question of which of the two alternatives should be preferred—which responsible politicians cannot in any case discuss in public—is the search for a solution that offers a way out of the dilemma. Thus one should seek by all means to prevent an unjust state from acquiring a first-strike capacity that deprives the opponent of the possibility of striking back, because then the situation of stable mutual threat breaks down; the proliferation of nuclear weapons should be slowed as much as possible, because an n-person game develops in a less predictable way than a two-person game; one should work on overcoming the hatred that alone can drive people to threaten each other with a nuclear holocaust; and finally, in the medium term, a just institution with a monopoly on weapons of mass destruction should be established. For one thing is clear: Threatening with weapons of mass destruction can be acceptable only in a transitional period of human history, and no period must

---

119. (1962), 603 f.

seek more urgently to establish structures of a universal state than one that trembles on the edge of the nuclear abyss.

8.2.2.3. Just Post-War Policy

The goal of war must be to defeat the injustice that constituted the ground for war. In extreme cases of aggressivity, the just victor can demand a *guarantee* that he will not be attacked again. Whereas ceding territories is problematic under the conditions of modern nationalism, because for the most part it takes place against the will of the local population, and the latter is often even driven out, a transformation of the constitutional law of the subjugated state is legitimate if the new state form corresponds to principles of natural constitutional law and for that reason is more likely to predispose people to peace. It can be a far greater blessing for the civilian population than oppressive conditions like those under which the Iraqi population has had to suffer since 1991. The victorious powers' policy after the First World War was also cratically absurd (not to mention its morals) because it humiliated Germany and would have tormented it for several generations without being able to significantly weaken it; it produced a hatred that was capable of quickly becoming dangerous. The reparations demanded of Germany were damaging not only to the German economy but also to that of the whole world; and the one-sided attribution of blame to a country whose guilt was great, but not so clear that the opponents could claim to be waging an obviously just war, made it difficult to achieve rapprochement with neighboring countries whose sense of moral superiority could not be taken seriously without qualification. A sharp distinction was not made between the enemy government and the defeated people. The Versailles Treaty could hardly be considered just, and the seriousness of the defeat was not made experienceable in everyday life through an occupation that could in addition have led to familiarity with the achievements of modern liberal bureaucracies. Finally, the bad conscience produced by this peace treaty led to the erstwhile enemies being indulgent at the wrong point—namely, with regard to Hitler.

On the other hand, the Western powers' post-war policy after 1945, especially that of the United States, with regard to Germany and Japan was exemplary, no matter how much it did not result exclusively from moral motives and no matter how much fear of the Soviet Union played a central role in it. The occupation of both countries proved to be a blessing for the population because it made possible the construction of democratic and constitutional institutions; in Japan, in addition, distribution of large estates to small farmers and breaking up of holding companies provided the bases for greater social justice. Reparations were not demanded, and economic reconstruction was generously supported; within a short time, the losers in the war managed to get on their feet again, whereas the succeeding states of the victorious Soviet Union today appear as latter-day losers. A clear distinction was drawn between the people and its criminal government, and the former enemies in war were actively brought into common supranational institutions. In the United Nations, an organ was created that was supposed to serve the purpose of preventing war more effectively than had the League of Nations. Through symbolic gestures, youth exchange programs, and economic cooperation, the Western European peoples laid the foundations of a lasting reconciliation that today makes a war between Germany and France as unlikely as a war between Bavaria and Prussia would have been eighty years ago.

Of special interest is the question of whether *war crimes trials* are morally justified. The answer should be a decisive "yes". It is true that such trials can smack of victor's justice and that, for instance, after the Second World War Allied violations of the *ius in bello* went unpunished. Kant, who truly pleaded for a moralization of politics, even defended the notion that an amnesty was connected with a peace treaty and that the victor might make many demands, but not present the opponent's war as unjust, because this constitutes an insult.[120] But Kant was writing at a time when a generic sovereign right to wage war was still recognized; this idea was partly already abandoned in 1945, and partly overcoming it was the goal of the new development of international law, so that planning a war of aggression, which in any case contradicts natural international law, could be rightly punished—not to mention violations of the *ius in bello,* which one cannot allow to go unpunished if at the same time one wants to punish with a good conscience for lesser crimes such as theft. The deterrent effect of such trials should not be underestimated either, for although it is correct that among those participating in war the fear of death, and a fortiori lesser punishments, is seldom a strong motive, a peculiar conception of honor plays an important role, and no would-be hero likes to live with the risk of being considered a criminal later on, even if he might have been militarily successful. Law is only what can be coerced; without the development of an international criminal law, international law cannot be called "law" in the full sense of the term. However, a formally convincing international criminal law must avoid the defects of the Nuremberg and Tokyo war crimes trials. In particular, the judges must come from states that have not themselves been involved in the war.

---

120. *Metaphysik der Sitten* I § 58 (1976 f.; 8:472).

9

Outline of a Political Ethic
for the Twenty-First Century

T he main difficulty for a political ethic for the twenty-first century[1] is the thorny question: From what vantage point should the conse-quences of our action be evaluated? What is central—the interests of the current generation of one's own people, those of one's own people in general, or those of humanity over time? On the basis of a universalist ethic it is obvious that a morally relevant answer must affirm the last alternative. However, from the point of view of *Realpolitik*, it is clear that a politician who, although acting within an individual state, bets exclusively on the universalist dimension is doomed to fail. The admirable and unfortunate Erhard Eppler is a good German example of this, and Gorbachev's fall also had much to do with the fact that his successes in foreign policy had no comparable equivalents in domestic policy. Indeed, not only in a *Realpolitik* perspective, but also morally, there can be a certain tension between the different standpoints from which the situation is evaluated—consider population growth, which has to be slowed on the global level and encouraged in most wealthy industrial countries. At least, there is an increasing, worldwide awareness that the extensive networking of the world demands a new definition of political goals, and no intelligent person with responsibility can any longer avoid anxiously wondering "to what extent the western concept of order could unintentionally and surreptitiously be transformed into a trigger for disorder if the realization of its premises, that is, the surmounting of the scarcity of goods and a humane (i.e., democratic) redistribution of sufficient goods on the planetary level is not achieved."[2] In view of the dangers that threaten humanity, maintaining a course that

---

1. Even if the perspective of the future is dominant, this chapter will repeatedly introduce ex-amples taken from the late twentieth century, for it goes without saying that the turn of a century is not a natural turning point and that during the final decades of the twentieth century, the fate of the twenty-first century was already being shaped in a general way.

2. P. Kondylis (1992), 49 f.

has been proven to contribute to these dangers (for example, economic growth at any price in the rich countries) should be rejected, along with the pursuit of ludicrous goals (for example, trivialities such as the elimination of the dominance of the masculine in our language, which distract attention from the real problems we face). There is no greater lack in our currently highly reactive political subsystem than a reasonable and moral list of priorities. The following pages will be concerned with such a list, though not with its details, a full discussion of which cannot be provided by a philosopher.

Even if there is great uneasiness about contemporary politics, one does not yet sense much of a readiness not merely to rethink matters (which is unfortunately insufficient) but to change behavior as well. The current world-historical situation can be pointedly conceptualized as follows: Because of the manifold economic and ecological interconnections, in the late twentieth century the realization of universalistic ideals, which began with the universal religions and were rationally articulated in the Enlightenment, became a question of pure survival; but human nature, the result of a natural evolution over millions of years, is still far from meeting demands that are abstractly recognized as right. Despite the creative potential of hypocrisy (repeatedly acknowledged in the part of this book on the philosophy of history), there is certainly a danger that late modern morality can no longer stand the extent of its own hypocrisy and that the latter is either collapsing in cynicism or degenerating into a fanatical search for scapegoats in order to project this self-hatred onto them. Consider Schiller's warning "that the moral motives, which are taken from *an ideal of excellence to be achieved*, do not lie naturally within the human heart, and, precisely because they were first brought there through art, do not always have beneficial effects, but are even often exposed, in a very human transition, to damaging misuse."[3] The truly fateful question today is how modernity's mores can be transformed without depriving them of self-respect, the loss of which no culture can survive.

9.1. THE POLITICS OF INTERNATIONAL ORGANIZATIONS

In view of the global nature of the problems threatening humanity's survival, it is clear that it would be one-sided to assume that states are the sole actors of a sensible politics. To be sure, a large part of the power available on this planet remains in their hands (or rather, in the hands of a few of the almost two hundred members of the United Nations); but since the state lags behind social development, certain changes in

---

3. "... [,] daß die moralischen Motive, welche von *einem zu erreichenden Ideale von Vortrefflichkeit* hergenommen sind, nicht natürlich im Menschenherzen liegen und eben darum, weil sie erst durch Kunst in dasselbe hineingebracht worden, nicht immer wohltätig wirken, gar oft aber, durch einen sehr menschlichen Übergang, einem schädlichen Mißbrauch ausgesetzt sind" (1959), 2:260 (from the Eleventh Letter on *Don Carlos*).

the society can be far more productive politically than power struggles within state organs, even when the latter are successful. Because economics and religion are more international, these two subsystems are destined to play a leading role in resolving a few—though certainly not all—world problems; the Marxist-Leninist view that power must be first won in the state before dealing with social wounds has been shown, through the catastrophe of the Soviet experiment, to be such an enormous error that it is no longer necessary to refute it. Nonetheless, the state's monopoly on the use of force is such an important power factor that one cannot do without it for long; and even if the global nature of the problems requires crossing national boundaries, the simultaneous inevitability of institutions with a monopoly on the use of force means only that supra-national institutions (ideally, of course, just one such institution) must be established, which might one day possess the decisive characteristic of statehood. The following analysis will concentrate on the most comprehensive, even if not the most powerful, of these supra-national organizations.

9.1.1. The United Nations

It is clear that the United Nations is not a world government—it cannot directly impose duties on any citizen of its member states; indeed, it has only as much power as its members are willing to delegate to it in each situation. During the Cold War, its range of action was extremely limited, because every permanent member of the Security Council had the right to veto any resolution, and only in the short time between the end of the Cold War and the breakdown of the Soviet Union was there a realistic hope that the United Nations might be able to make a decisive contribution to the construction of a new world order and do away with aggressive wars throughout the world. After the Gulf War, the UN's first peace-enforcement action since the Korean War, the United Nations' weakness has become increasingly clear—just think of Somalia. However, this weakness can only be a reason to strengthen the United Nations; for if there is a moral obligation to avoid wars, and if the avoidance of war can be ensured only through a world government or, lacking the latter, through collective security organizations, then there is no alternative to a further development of the United Nations. If this development fails, one should certainly not be surprised if individual states take the law (or what they consider their right) into their own hands; the renunciation of violence according to Article 2 (4) of the United Nations Charter is reasonable only in view of the right, ascribed in Articles 42 and 43 of the Charter, to use force against those who break the peace. If this right is not exercised, a right of individual or collective self-defense naturally takes its place (Article 51). In short, only so long as Article 42 is actually put into action in case of need is there a chance to achieve a real monopoly on the use of force for the United Nations on the international level; for a real monopoly on the use of force by the superior authority, and a renunciation of the use of force by the subordinate authority, are two sides of the same coin.

To that extent, it is obvious that the United Nations should be allowed to *use force against aggressors*—because of its deterrent effect, among other things; anyone who rejects this possibility is promoting a relapse into international anarchy. What could be criticized in the First Gulf War was not Security Council Resolution 678, which authorized the states cooperating with the government of Kuwait to use all means necessary to carry out Resolution 660, but rather that the war was not waged under the strategic command or at least the political command of the Security Council.[4] (Furthermore, the morally problematic aspects of the First Gulf War also included the fact that Iraq had long been provided with weapons by the Soviets and the Western powers and had not been warned clearly enough by the United States. But however great a mistake the latter was—or if it was intentional, however immoral an omission—it did not give Iraq the right to attack Kuwait. Moreover, Iraq was given enough time to make an orderly withdrawal. It is obvious that such a withdrawal would not have been achieved by economic sanctions alone—one has only to consider how Saddam Hussein was able to cope with the consequences of the blockade after the war. Embargoes are hard to impose, except in the case of islands, and they affect the weakest people in the population most.) But even if it were desirable that the United Nations have its own armed forces, in accord with Article 43, it would still be wrong to give up the establishment of the program of collective security, so long as the United Nations did not have such forces—one must do what good one can, while continuing to work for the ideal solution. Since in the short and medium term, a United Nations military command over the armed forces involved in such actions cannot be attained, much would already be gained if at least a political command determining the precise goals of the war—the operational control—were established in the United Nations Security Council.[5] An opportunity was missed when, after the defeat of the Iraqi aggression, the victory was celebrated, not as a victory of the United Nations, but only as a victory of the individual states that took part in the coalition against Iraq; a victory celebration by the United Nations could have promoted the construction of a collective identity, without which the United Nations will not be capable of acting in the long run. It must not be made easy for aggressors to present themselves as suffering at the hands of imperialistic powers rather than of a world community defending itself. The First Gulf War is also open to the criticism that military action obviously took place only because major Western interests were at stake—but from this it does not follow that the Iraqi aggression should have been accepted, rather that in the future, analogous measures should perhaps be taken against all aggressors. This is possible, of course, only if there is agreement between the members of the Security Council.

Certainly it should be admitted that *prevention of wars* is still more important than militarily repelling aggression (even if it would be false to conclude that errors made in

---

4. On this subject, see E.-O. Czempiel (1994), 96 ff. This book has provided me with much information and stimulation, even if I cannot always endorse its value judgments.

5. Cf. B. Russett and J. S. Sutterlin (1991), 81.

pre-war politics result in a weakening of the right to self-defense and to defend other states from attack). Recognizing growing conflicts early on, using the local presence of powers that have the ability to limit conflicts, disarmament negotiations, limiting the arms trade, preventing the proliferation of weapons of mass destruction through treaties such as the Nuclear Non-Proliferation Treaty, mediation and good offices in the sense of the sixth chapter of the Charter, and finally, economic and social cooperation that creates mutual dependencies are all to be promoted. As much as possible, this should take place within the framework of the United Nations and its various organs and agencies, whose administrative efficiency must be increased because only in this way can one seriously expect member states to pay their dues and bear part of a necessary increase in the budget. *Subjection to an international jurisdiction* is certainly also desirable. But it is not clear how this is supposed to happen without limiting state sovereignty, to which most states jealously cling and will continue to cling, at least so long as that limitation does not take place on all sides. In order to become active, an international court presupposes individual states' agreement to subject themselves to its jurisdiction— always a general agreement, and often a special agreement in regard to the individual case at issue. Article 36 of the Statute of the International Court of Justice created the possibility of fundamentally acknowledging the jurisdiction of the court and the binding character of its decisions even without an agreement in the individual case, but most states accepted this clause only with reservations that make it possible for them to withdraw from it at any time.[6] Nonetheless, the International Court of Justice is a permanent court with full-time judges (who ought reasonably to represent the most important legal system in the world); as such, it has, more than the Permanent Court of Arbitration, for instance, a chance to develop a continuous jurisprudence, even if it is not bound by its own decisions and if the latter have no legal force for other international courts. Fundamentally, it should be remarked that courts are only rarely in a position to resolve the conflicts that usually lead to wars—for a party that acknowledges them has accepted the valid legal order, but one that does not accept it will not be particularly impressed by the decision of such a court.[7]

Between peaceful conflict resolution and peace enforcement, an intermediate position is occupied by the United Nations' *peacekeeping missions,* which are desired by the parties to the conflict and in which UN forces supervise a cease-fire, for instance. One of Dag Hammarskjöld's enduring achievements was to have conceived in 1956, beyond the peace enforcement discussed in the seventh chapter of the UN Charter, the idea of peacekeeping. Hammarskjöld was one of the most moral and at the same time most tactically gifted politicians of the twentieth century, and his greatness is shown even, or rather especially, by the fact that he occasionally exceeded his mandate in the direction

---

6. Concerning the United States' declaration on this matter, H. J. Morgenthau and K. W. Thompson (1985; 305) aptly remark: "It is hard to visualize an international dispute that might not be interpreted so as to be covered by either reservation b. or c."

7. Cf. H. J. Morgenthau and K. W. Thompson (1985), 463 ff.

of a higher responsibility. However, peacekeeping is much easier in wars between states than civil wars, not to mention the situation after a collapse of statehood, because especially in the latter case, the parties to the conflict, whose agreement is by definition a presupposition of peacekeeping, can be determined only with difficulty. It is obvious that a complete consensus of all parties to the conflict is not given even in the case of peacekeeping after conflicts between states; if all those concerned were really for peace, the provocations that alone make the presence of UN troops necessary could not occur. Thus what is meant here is only that there must be a *basic* consensus between *governments*, whereas by the very nature of the thing, deviations from it by individual persons or in questions of detail will certainly occur. If this is acknowledged, one sees that between peacekeeping in inter-state conflicts and in civil wars, there is no fundamental, but only a quantitative, difference in the degree of deviation from the absolute consensus that would make peacekeeping missions superfluous. Finally, in practice the transition between peacekeeping and peace-enforcing actions is also fluid, as the concept of "robust peacekeeping" suggests; where else but in the middle of the spectrum should we situate enforcing the continued maintenance of a cease-fire or the securing of aid measures? This does not mean that those quantitative differences could not also legitimate different decisions; the prospect of success and the proportionality of the measures must be taken into account not only in the United Nations' peace-enforcing actions but also in its peacekeeping actions, and in these respects things are generally worse in civil wars than in conflicts between states. However, the prospect of success also depends upon the political will with which such actions are undertaken; if it is lacking, as in the case of UNOSOM II (the United Nations Operation in Somalia), it is better to forgo it altogether, not only because through its failure the expenditure made in the particular case loses its legitimacy, but also because such operations undermine the authority of the United Nations. Above all, half-hearted operations such as those long pursued during the Yugoslavian crisis should be avoided, since they increase the international prestige of the aggressors and serve to confirm them.

The involvement of the world's most powerful states in peacekeeping and a fortiori in peace enforcing can easily arouse resentment; therefore in such actions it is desirable to use soldiers from neighboring regions, whose intervention will in many cases be more likely to be considered helpful. *Regional suborganizations of the UN* (such as, since 1992, the Conference on Security and Cooperation in Europe) are expressly authorized in the eighth chapter of the Charter, even if they may not resort to peace-enforcing actions without the authorization of the Security Council (Article 53 [1])—a limitation that is certainly indispensable if the United Nations does not want to give up a legal monopoly on the use of force in conflicts between states. Nonetheless, it should be soberly noted that not all regions of the world have the political and organizational know-how to collaborate competently in peacekeeping and peace-enforcing operations; in such cases, the choice is between intervention by the most powerful states and leaving alone countries that already owe their misery in part to wars and will deepen it through further wars. Rejecting earlier Western colonialism should not become a cheap way of protecting oneself against sanctions on one's own crimes. The truth may and must be told. In many of Africa's problems, for instance, local potentates and mentalities hostile to development are more to blame than the colonial past. The denial of this truth, like any false diagnosis, makes an effective therapy more difficult and takes the indigenous population less seriously than a sober analysis of the causes of conflicts—anyone who puts the whole blame for African poverty on the West is thinking in an extremely Eurocentric way because instead of internal causes he assumes that there are only external, that is, Eurogenic, causes.

Of course, the United Nations' greatest moral problem consists in the *special role of the five permanent members of the Security Council that have veto rights.* Is this special role compatible with a universalist ethics? At first, it seems that the answer must be "no." However, it is not hard to see that without a consensus on the part of the most important states, peace-enforcing actions could not take place or might even lead inevitably to a world war. The Security Council's ability to work and its stability also depend on the number of its members remaining manageable and some of its members being permanent. But even if a veto right for the most powerful states is unavoidable, doesn't the postulate of universalizability require that decisions be unanimous? It is equally obvious that such a requirement would make the Security Council incapable of acting—for not only the aggressor but also his allies would be able to block peace-enforcing operations legally. If the concept of domination involves more than complete consensus, then the Security Council can claim to exercise domination (no matter in how limited a form) only if it does not presuppose unanimity. A three-fifths majority including all the permanent members is amply sufficient as a presupposition. To be sure, this rule privileges the permanent members. But it would be completely illusory to think that the problem of peace could be solved in any way that did not involve the cooperation of the world's most powerful states—the League of Nations failed because it fell victim to this illusion. It is certainly possible that these states might cooperate in exploiting the others, but there is no conceivable means of power for preventing this except international public opinion and protests within the powerful states. Nonetheless, there is hope that the legal self-obligation in the Charter will pave the way for a gradual overcoming of war. It is no more than a hope, but there is no better alternative means of achieving the goal of peace, unless it is the construction of a universal state, for which the time is not yet ripe. Non-ideal peacekeeping is still better than none at all; the sole chance for further developing the United Nations in the direction of an elementary world government lies in long-term, institutionalized cooperation on the part of the great powers.

Nonetheless, this does not mean that the current rules—which may very well soon be changed in accord with Article 108—are optimal. In a greatly changed world, it is hard to justify giving in perpetuity a special role to the victorious powers of the Second World War. A general rule that prescribed giving states a permanent seat on the Security Council when they met certain conditions would be crucial. (More difficult is the question of whether these new permanent members should also have a veto right. On one hand, the veto right makes it more difficult to construct a global political unit; on the other, having permanent members without a veto right alongside members with a veto right creates a further inequality, and such a status would not be particularly attractive.)

Which conditions could justify unequal treatment of the different states, whether in the Security Council or in other international organizations?[8] We have already discussed *unequal power;* and even if it is not in itself a normatively relevant criterion, in a non-ideal world we must resign ourselves to it, while not failing to recognize that states' differing levels of power are partially based on superior organizational achievements that could benefit not only their own populations but also the rest of the world. Thus we arrive at a second criterion, a state's *political and technological know-how,* which corresponds to the educational criterion that was used in the nineteenth century by the opponents of universal and equal voting rights. Even if this criterion is better than that of sheer power, it can be misused to make differences in education permanent and therefore can be employed for a transitional period at most. Still more important is the criterion of *the proximity of a state's politics to natural-law norms.* What corresponds to natural law in detail is debatable; but there is not the slightest reason for giving a permanent seat on the Security Council to a state that commits such basic violations of human rights as does Nigeria, especially since it can make no claim to such a seat either cratically or *de lege lata.* Furthermore, we should not underestimate the criterion of the *service provided* in international organizations that assume primarily economic tasks; *so long as* poorer states' rights to positive benefits are not recognized under international law, things cannot go on very differently in such organizations than in joint-stock companies. The annoyance in the United States at having to finance a fourth of United Nations' operations, which the United States considers unreasonable on grounds that are sometimes objective, is thoroughly understandable, even if it does not sufficiently justify the United States' behavior in regard to paying its share of the costs. In military actions as well, it is not unjust for those who bear the main military burdens to want a larger voice than others. In addition to competence and performance, the *extent to which a state is affected* is a further criterion that may go hand in hand with the others but need not do so—the marginal utility of redistribution measures is greatest in the poorest states, but their positive contribution to them is the smallest, and they do not always have the competence necessary to deal efficiently and justly with the funds received. Finally, the criterion of *population size,* already discussed in chapter 7.3.3.3, is very important. In accord with what has just been said, only heavily populated states with economic capability and constitutional structures could be considered for additional permanent seats on the Security Council, and a seat should be connected with a duty to participate especially extensively in military and economic commitments. An equitable geographical distribution of the permanent members would be desirable (Article 23 [1] in fact requires it for the non-permanent members), but this cannot be a decisive criterion, only one among others. If one had to choose between Germany and Japan, Japan should cer-

---

8. On this subject, see M. Hartwig (1995), 205 ff.

tainly be given precedence—among other reasons because through its history Japan has shown the non-European world that it is also possible, on the basis of another tradition, to adopt the main ideas of modernity.

In electing the *Secretary-General* of the United Nations, there is much to be said for concentrating the search on honest and capable people from the so-called developing countries. The office is enhanced when a former prime minister or president makes himself available to serve in it, instead of former Secretaries-General conversely returning to politics in their homelands. It is obvious that the Secretariat must remain a monocratic organ; the troika recommended by the Soviet Union, which France also supported in 1958, would have deprived the secretariat of the ability to act. It is certainly cratically plausible that states that want to hang on to their sovereignty under any circumstances want a weak, and perhaps even blackmailable, Secretary-General; but that only means that responsible statesmen, who have understood the necessity of the United Nations, must oppose such efforts. It is certainly sensible also to give a voice in the General Assembly to peoples without a state and to powerful organizations in world society; that could be a first step toward constructing a chamber whose members are not delegates from individual states but rather elected directly by the world population; such a chamber could constitute a forum for world public opinion. In the current situation, the fact that San Marino and India have equal votes in the General Assembly does not seem just and is acceptable only because the General Assembly has less power than, for example, the Security Council.

In chapter 8.2.1.2, we have already mentioned an institution that would determine the ecological limits to the extension of human power over the planet. In fact, an *environmental council* similar to the Security Council is urgently needed, no matter how difficult it will be to arrive at an agreement regarding the power relationships within such a council. Ecological know-how as well as an exemplary environmental policy should be the crucial criteria to be taken into account in selecting the permanent members of such an organ; but a strong interconnection between the Environmental Council and the Security Council will realistically have to be sought if the recommendations of the former are to be more than well-intentioned but not binding—in other words, if in the medium term an *international environmental police* is envisaged. It goes without saying that the limitations on environmental pollution and using up resources cannot take the status quo as their starting point, for the status quo is clearly unjust, and there is not the slightest reason why the states that have already committed the worst exploitation of nature should be favored. At first glance, only guaranteeing the same environmental space for every person seems compatible with the principles of justice; however, in order to create incentives to limit population growth, it would be conceivable to presuppose, for the future as well, the current population numbers. A mixed system would probably be the most just, and more precisely one that presupposed every individual's right to a certain environmental space, but on the basis of a new population census carried out every ten years (for instance); it would grant individual *states* (*not individuals* directly) the right to certain resources and environmental damage during the corresponding period of time, so that population growth during that period would burden, not the whole world population, but only the individual state concerned. Realistically, however, it would already be satisfactory to see the first steps in the direction of the solution just sketched out, for the renunciation of long-standing privileges is significantly more difficult to impose than a confirmation of the status quo.[9]

It is implicit in my argument that natural resources in principle belong to all of humanity, not to individual persons, and also not to individual states; we have already discussed this point in chapter 7.3.1.2. In fact, this conception is presupposed by the notion of a *common heritage of mankind*, which has recently become part of positive international law; however, it has been used only in the 1982 United Nations Law of the Sea Convention's regime for deep-sea mining and was one of the most important reasons for the heavy opposition to putting this convention into effect.[10] Moreover, against the logic of that principle, through the establishment of the exclusive economic zone and the regime for the continental shelf, the same convention "carried out the greatest nationalization of parts of the earth's surface since colonialization"[11]—a nationalization that protects a few developing countries from being plundered of offshore resources by technologically more advanced countries but at the same time increases the inequalities between states by reinforcing geographical accidents since it privileges countries with long coastlines and in any case leans far away from the idea of a common heritage with regard to natural goods. If this idea were truly recognized, it would have two important consequences. On one hand, the list of grounds for intervention by the United Nations would be extended. On the other hand, it is obvious that to a common right would have to correspond a common duty for all countries—for instance, a duty to assume the costs of species protection. For of course the countries that have the remainder of rain forests, which are especially rich in species, cannot be expected to pay all the costs of maintaining them if the species that ought to be protected "belong" to the whole of mankind.

In view of the connection between ecological and demographic development, it is good that the United Nations has organized conferences devoted specifically to *population growth*. In the current situation, supplying families that are interested in morally acceptable forms of family planning but have no direct access to them with information and actual contraceptive devices is extremely sensible, for it helps decrease the potential for conflict on Earth. Particularly important would be a contribution to the construction of a system of retirement benefits that did not depend on a high number of

---

9. T. Pogge (1995), to whom we owe important contributions to the theory of international justice, developed the idea of a global raw materials dividend but wants to use it to battle absolute poverty. However, it should be noted that ecological taxation and social redistribution are subject to separate moral principles, and only reasons of practicability speak in favor of connecting the two questions. (I thank T. Kesselring for stimulating comments on this subject.)

10. Cf. A. Verdross and B. Simma (1984), 737 ff.

11. M. Hartwig (1995), 203.

children, and to which people would have a right if they limited the number of their children to two or three. So far as the conflict between the various ideological camps is concerned, a great deal would be gained if it were possible to agree on a rejection of abortion and a responsible use of contraceptives. The recommendation that population growth be limited is all the more justified the more the wealthy nations are willing to limit the environmentally damaging aspects of their way of life, and the more substantial the contribution they make to fighting absolute poverty. It has already been conceded that good aid for development is not easy; but the guarantee of the minimum necessary for subsistence for all people on the planet in the sense of worldwide social aid is a task that the world community will not be able to avoid in the medium term and that would best be handled by the United Nations if only it could function more efficiently. However, to this end, independent financial sources will have to be provided for it, such as a share of the proposed Tobin tax on currency trading.

Just as it is naive to think that peace can be maintained without the threat of force and the use of force, it is one-sided to try to make peace solely by the use of negative sanctions. We have already discussed the importance of policy concerning transnational economic issues and cultural relations policy, and it is clear that the United Nations should promote *economic and cultural exchange*. The Economic and Social Council (ECOSOC) is an independent organ, indeed, an integral component of the conception of the United Nations, and UNESCO is one of its important specialized agencies (whose rapid increase at the same time as the United Nations' central organ remains weak is not necessarily a blessing). The responsibility of such institutions concerns—at least in theory—not the interests of an individual state but rather the preservation and promotion of the economic welfare and the cultural heritage of mankind as a whole. Since the development of a feeling of responsibility for the whole of humanity is an important step on the way to the creation of the structures of a universal state, the existence of these organizations is certainly to be approved. The concrete value of their work depends, however, on two presuppositions. First, concentration on the essential, and especially on what cannot be done by individual states and individual persons alone, is crucial—the inflation of some of these UN organizations into bureaucracies that serve primarily to provide the elites of many countries with absurdly high incomes is a well-known problem, and the battle against it is by no means a Eurocentric demand but rather a presupposition for these organizations' realization of the goals that are actually their purpose. Second, in allocating their means, fundamental principles of social justice must be respected—UNICEF's promotion of education for poor children in developing countries is far more important than organizing colloquia for the international smart set. Thus one must realistically acknowledge that in many cases economic and cultural aid must ignore the governments of the respective countries and go directly to the poor people concerned or to capable local non-governmental organizations. Robber states are not to be supported; fundamentally, one can even maintain that the modern state is often too small to deal with global problems and at the same time too large to deal with local demands.

9.1.2.　Religions

In addition to supra-national organizations that have limited political and military functions, two social subsystems play a major role in the international domain: economics and religion. To begin with the latter, we must not fail to recognize that it can significantly increase the potential for conflict—think only of the manifold forms of fundamentalism. Nonetheless, it is clear that without the help of the traditional religions, it will not be possible to alter human behavior, for the individual's motivational system is highly correlated with the value systems transmitted by religions, and it is also clear that the secular late-modern religion of rational egoism will not be capable of solving the urgent problems. The necessary coordination between individual cultures can only be achieved if the majority of people, or at least of the elites that lead them, agree on a certain normative course of action. Taking a cue from Hans Küng,[12] one can speak of the necessity of shaping a *world ethos,* and it is obvious that the world religions can and must contribute a great deal to that enterprise. However, we must forestall a few tempting misunderstandings that might be connected with the program of constructing a world ethos. Unlike an unbinding declaration of good will, an ethos cannot be produced out of thin air, and conferences on the world ethos can under no circumstances replace the difficult task of integrating into one's own life the new norms in the ecological, demographic, or international social domains. One has to start doing this early on, and it takes moral will power—but intellectuals' weakness of moral will is a subject that has often been discussed.[13] There is certainly a danger that under the rubric "world ethos" only encounters between the already largely interconnected international elites will take place, without these having the slightest effect on the masses fascinated, for instance, by fundamentalist ideologies.

No less to be feared is that only the smallest common denominator of all cultures will be presented as a world ethos—it is well known that everyone is for the good, the true, and the beautiful, without such vague notions being able to create commonalties. On the other hand, part of a world ethos that is really intended to help the world progress must be a consensus regarding very controversial questions: Think only of population growth. Here, achieving a consensus is possible only if the representatives of the various mores and religions are prepared to separate themselves from a few of the central components of their ways of life and their faiths; and we all know that this is not easy to do. However, it is equally evident for every religion that the other religions will be willing to make concessions only if it is itself able to move; this insight can result in openness. In order for such a dialogue between differing religions and mores to be fruitful, two presuppositions (not mutually incompatible but only seldom present at the same time) must be fulfilled. First, *reason* must be involved in distinguishing between what

---

12.　(1990, 1995).

13.　On the sociology of intellectuals, chap. 13, pt. 2 of J. A. Schumpeter's book (1959: 145 ff.) remains impressive.

can be given up and what cannot; for the *logos* represents something common that is more than the smallest common denominator. Second, a good rationalistic philosophy can be helpful in conducting an intercultural dialogue, but only if it has a *sense* for the *sensitivities of historically developed cultures.* Sometimes progress on the issues is possible only if one makes far-reaching concessions regarding the form, and this can be difficult precisely for an abstract rationalism.

To be sure, the result of a comprehensive dialogue between religions cannot be anticipated; a great deal would already be achieved if the present regained the culture of inter-religious discussion that existed in the Middle Ages and in the early modern period. On the basis of what was said above, it is not hard to suppose that religions that have been influenced by the Greek philosophy of the *logos* could deal with each other without great difficulty, were family resemblances not sometimes a ground for special aversions: Think only of the relationship between Islam and Judaism. However, a special opportunity in the current historical situation consists precisely in the fact that the disastrous aspects of Western rationalism are becoming ever clearer, and the entirely different determination of the relationship between nature and man in Indian and East Asian religions is also increasingly attractive for persons from the West. Speculations in the philosophy of history are not prognoses, but one could offer the following suggestion: Just as the Word, which gave late antiquity a unifying ethos, was a synthesis of Greek and Jewish thought formulated in such a way that it also spoke to barbarian peoples, so a *unification of Western rationalism with the tradition of Eastern holism* could be the germ of a world ethos for the twenty-first century. What would be good about such a world ethos would be not only that it would provide a common basis for action but also that through it the humiliation that the triumph of Western culture means for the rest of the world could be overcome. A culture that achieved a standard of living that was really universalizable without implying the destruction of the planet would have every reason to be proud, and it should even be hoped that this is not first achieved by Western culture, at least if one considers desirable a more uniform distribution of great cultural achievements over the whole earth.

So far as Christian denominations are concerned, it is plausible to suggest that they will survive only if, instead of fleeing into ritualism, they work out a rational ethic suited to the time and do not simultaneously completely abandon authority as a means of power—for the time being, there is no alternative to the latter. Religious needs for meaning (which are still very strong even in the late modern period) must be connected with the demands of a rational ethics if the former are to withstand rational examination and the latter is to have an effective motivational basis. For imposing moral norms is still more important than giving them a theoretical foundation; for this, the model provided by the leadership of the churches is essential. Thanks to its presence in very different cultures, its connection of a very subtle culture of the emotions with a rationalism shaped in the pre-modern age, its ambivalent attitude toward modernity, and finally its strict hierarchy, which does not necessarily stand in contradiction to universalist ideals, *Catholicism* has possibilities of having an effect of which it is desirable that

it should make use. Because of its hierarchical structure, this depends in part on the occupant of the papal office, who should have both the ability to take a critical distance on
the merely relative norms of his own faith and an instinctive certainty and imperturba-
bility in positions that can claim more wisdom than can all the possible fashions of the
late modern period.

9.1.3. Economics

If religions are the protectors of *value rationality,* then today economics can most
plausibly claim to have access to the heart of modern *instrumental rationality.* On one
hand, it has made the planet into a single unit far faster than would have been possible
for the political subsystem; on the other hand, it bears the chief responsibility for the
ecological disaster toward which we are moving. For both good and evil it is a power of
the first order, and it is no exaggeration to see in the leading managers, who are transferred from one place to another in the world, a functional equivalent of the old aristocracies, which were comparably international.[14] Their economic and technological
expertise is just as impressive as their intercultural competence often is. Their influence
on politics is all the greater the more the latter bases its power on positive sanctions;
and that is to a large extent the case, at least in the most powerful countries in the
world. If economics refuses it, ecological reform cannot be achieved; conversely, the
discovery of economic opportunities in the ecological domain will make it significantly
easier to realize a reasonable environmental policy. Analogously, a sensible development
in the poorest countries of the world is unlikely without the use of international capital;
however, the intervention of multinational firms, which want to skim off profits as
quickly as possible, can under certain circumstances contribute to the destruction of indigenous cultures and to the spread of corruption. How great is the probability that at
least a few business enterprises will become allies of a better politics?

First of all, it is obvious that no businessman can risk insolvency; if that is the
probable consequence of environment-friendly production, the latter cannot be expected.
But business can work to see to it that the *structural conditions of the market* are framed in
such a way that environment-friendly behavior is not disadvantaged, or it can at least
stop torpedoing efforts in this direction. Moreover, within the given system one can expect a renunciation of certain legally possible profits, and since the law of decreasing
marginal utility applies to money as well, one can certainly expect decision makers in
business, especially those who have very high incomes, to forgo further profits for the
sake of the environment—partly out of moral motives and partly because, for an entrepreneurial personality, solving particularly difficult problems can be an attractive chal-

---

14. P. Anderson notes (1974; 31 f.) that while feudal rulers were mobile and their land immobile,
in modernity capital is mobile, and capitalists are nationally fixed—but that holds only for the nineteenth century, no longer for the late twentieth century.

lenge. Let there be no illusion: without the organizational know-how and the institution-alized capacity for innovation that are far easier to find in private business than in a state bureaucracy, a change in the social structures that are causing rapid environmental de-struction is inconceivable. Some measures for environmental protection are neutral in their effect on a business firm (and in that case it unquestionably has a moral obligation to undertake them); indeed, some can even be economically profitable—for instance, through savings made by increasing efficiency, through greater motivation of employees, and finally, if consumers prefer products compatible with preserving the environment and if savers invest their money in accord with moral criteria.

In fact, a transformation of economics can take place essentially on two levels (set-ting aside for a moment the level of state economic policy, which is not the subject of this section)—on the *supply* side and on the *demand* side. To begin with the first, the tasks of the business firm are the following.[15] First of all, the leadership team must be prepared to count among the firm's goals an orientation toward a sustainable develop-ment of the planet. In order to realize this goal, establishing institutions of aid for de-velopment and environmental protection within the firm and staffing them with the right people is indispensable; in general, environmental training for workers (even and especially in subsidiary firms in developing countries, which should not fall beneath the environmental standards in the firm's home country) is desirable. In addition, alterna-tives must be comparable with regard to their ecological costs; for this purpose, ecologi-cal balance-sheets are indispensable. The latter are admittedly not easy to produce be-cause there is no easy means of weighing, for instance, air pollution, and the using up of a rare raw material, the extinction of a species, or an increase in noise pollution;[16] but with good will, usable guidelines can be found that would already be a blessing, even if they were only approximate. Environmental costs are incurred in procuring the components of the product, in producing it, and usually also during its lifetime and in disposing of it; moreover, the environmental costs of office and factory buildings and transporting the product have to be considered. Relatively speaking, it is easiest to increase efficiency in the area of energy and water consumption, as well as in the use of resources that go into the final product; through recycling, both materials costs and en-vironmental pollution can be diminished. If a retrenchment is not possible, environment-protecting materials should be used as much as possible; environmentally polluting materials should be either reused or transformed into a condition in which they can be overseen with the smallest possible risks; for this purpose it is best to capture them at the moment that they emerge from the plant or the product.

However, no matter how important it is,[17] *increasing efficiency* is not a panacea. Given the infinitist structure of the needs of modern people, the ecological advantages

---

15. Cf. G. Winter (1989), 64 ff.

16. Thus F. Schmidt-Bleek (1994) emphasizes the material-input per service unit (MIPS), a pa-rameter that must be distinguished from the consumption of energy.

17. Cf. E. U. von Weizsäcker, A. B. Lovins, and L. Hunter Lovins (1995).

gained in this way would quickly be nullified by a corresponding increase in the level of needs: if people had cars that used half the amount of gasoline to cover the same distance, they might drive twice as much. Only if an increase in efficiency is accompanied by a *revolution in sufficiency* will it be possible to undo the violation of elementary principles of intergenerational justice. Politics and economics can certainly promote such a change in direction: through limiting advertising, through public relations work that informs people of the negative consequences of certain products, or through honoring a environmentally conscious way of life. But in a market economy the consumers, and in a democracy the enfranchised citizenry, which consists of all adults, has the final word; and if the citizenry resists a reasonable environmental policy and any change in the structural conditions of the economy, and if consumers cling to the most senseless and environmentally damaging products and services, there will be no change. The success of a revolution in sufficiency depends crucially on the readiness not to define one's own success by the level of one's needs but, on the contrary, to draw from the limitation of one's needs the feeling of one's own dignity. If according to the model of the neoclassical theory of equilibrium the order of preference is a given that economics has to take as its starting point (which is only partly correct, as the phenomenon of advertising shows), then it must be the task of the opinion makers, particularly of the religions, to communicate universalizable preferences to people.

Much would already be gained if people limited their consumption out of a simple feeling of decency and justice, in a way that did not violate duties to coming generations and to the weakest people in the developing countries; but on the basis of an ethics that also positively evaluates the emotions, one would certainly have to prefer a world in which people strictly limit their use of cars, for instance, not only because using cars is connected with negative consequences for others, but also because they see in riding a bicycle or taking public transportation direct opportunities to experience intrinsic values—whether in a deeper contact with nature or in the encounter with other people, or at least to concentrate on activities other than steering a car. It is crucial that an *imitable way of life* be represented, one that will be accepted by the factual mores and become habitual among many people; the bizarre peculiarities of an ecologically excited morality are natural in a time of transition, but they do not solve the problem that faces us. Because of the example-setting character of elites in politics, economics, and culture, they should lead the way with ecologically defensible behavior, and indeed, only people who are able and ready to internalize the new norms should be considered members of a true elite. Obviously, the remarks just made complement those on the construction of a world ethos. Whereas in the latter case we were primarily concerned with the formal aspect of the production of an interculturally recognized basis for action and with its abstract foundations in value rationality, here we are concerned with the concrete content. This content cannot leave uninfluenced the daily conduct of life—even if it would be an atrocity to prescribe a single form of eating, clothing, dwelling, traveling, working, and reproducing, an ethos that had nothing to say about these spheres would not be worth much. We would be fortunate to have the functional equivalent of the stoic philosophy of late antiquity, whose greatness consisted in the fact that it was not only a theoretical system but also a movement that provided the elites of the whole empire with a moral foundation that enabled them to endure the historical turmoil of their time with admirable dignity.

9.2. FOREIGN POLICY IN THE BROADER SENSE

Despite the reactivity of present-day politics, states still have a monopoly on the use of force; the decision between war and peace continues to depend on them. Therefore, a political ethics must next deal with states. However, the following pages will deal first with the international dimension of state politics, that is, with foreign policy, and only then with domestic policy. In view of a major war's consequences for humanity in the current situation, the doctrine of the primacy of foreign policy has seldom been in any period more convincing than in our own, in which, however, the great simplification that a bipolar world represented for foreign policy has recently dissolved. This primacy is also and especially valid on the basis of a universalist ethics, for a Third World War would have catastrophic consequences for everyone. Nonetheless, it is not easy, on such a basis, to determine the principles of foreign policy. For the concept of foreign policy presupposes a multitude of sovereign systems of self-assertion, so that even more directly than in the case of the other forms of politics we must ask, "Foreign policy for whom?" No doubt domestic policy in Germany must be different from domestic policy in Indonesia, for instance; but in this area there are general criteria that determine a system of conditional obligations for every state at a certain level of development. In contrast, foreign policy seems to be a zero-sum game, so that recommendations on one side necessarily collide with those on the other side. This objection can be answered only by saying that a universalist theory of foreign policy cannot regard this field as a pure zero-sum game but must instead assume that a just foreign policy has to be capable in principle of a consensus, among other reasons because some of its important components are in the long-term interests of all parties. A situation of competition in economic life in no way excludes a common recognition of the market as the most efficient mechanism of allocation; analogously, the avoidance of violent conflicts can be considered to be in the fundamental interest of the whole international community. At the present time, war must be avoided even more than in the past, and under no circumstances can it be used as a means of resolving internal political crises; however, the painful truth still holds that sometimes major wars can be avoided only through an intelligent and limited use of force.

9.2.1. Foreign Policy in the Narrower Sense

In view of the inordinate production of negative externalities connected with transporting commodities, it is easy to see why an increasing number of environmental protectionists are demanding a re-regionalization of world politics (which sometimes goes so far as a rejection of European integration). There is no reason for Europeans to eat fruits from overseas or for masses of German tourists to go to Norway; indeed an ecologically justified protectionism is legitimate. However, this kind of protectionism can have only one goal, namely the elevation of environmental standards in other countries by offering to open oneself to free trade as soon as the passing on of environmental costs in general is halted. In fact, we should beware of the illusion that the global problems could be solved if the European Union, not to mention just Norway, merely went its own way and sealed itself off from the rest of the world. Environmental problems can be dealt with only on the international level; even if the United States and all of Western Europe adopted an ecologically more rational ecological line of conduct, this would not help much if at the same time the newly industrializing countries sought to continue along the current path without restraint. Naturally, the industrialized countries have a moral right to demand that other states take more rigorous measures to protect the environment only if they themselves first set a good example; indeed, even if one came to the conclusion that a great catastrophe would probably be necessary in order to teach the surviving people a better way of proceeding, the individual person and the individual state would certainly still have a duty to limit their consumption to the environmental space allocated to them. (They could have no duty to accelerate that catastrophe, even if it was supposed to be salutary, so long as they did not *know* that it would be salutary, and so long as they could not conclude with *certainty* that the path of exemplary reason no longer had any chance of succeeding.) But morals do not demand merely that humanity die out with decency; a reasonable environmental policy in domestic affairs must be interconnected with a corresponding environmental foreign policy. To be sure, many international conferences produce little more than another burden on the environment; however, that is not an argument against environmental conferences but only an argument for better organizing them. From what has been said it follows that the environmental and foreign ministries need to work together institutionally more intensively and that the environmental minister must have, in addition to his other manifold competencies, international experience as well.

Today, every country's foreign policy has to take as its starting point the recognition of an elementary fact: *the hegemonic status of the United States.* This recognition does not mean that the United States will keep this hegemony in the future—the international distribution of power is notoriously unstable—and certainly not that it *ought* to retain this hegemony. What should be said about these two questions? To begin with the first, the duration of the United States' hegemony will obviously depend also on developments in the rest of the world (which we will discuss later), for power is a relative concept. So far as the contribution of the United States itself is concerned, the following factors seem to me particularly relevant. Since stable power cannot be based on negative sanctions alone but instead requires consensus, the decisive factor will be whether the United States succeeds in calming the aversion that any hegemonic status arouses. In order to do so, two steps are indispensable, and because of its history and traditions, they will be difficult for the United States to take. First, the United States must develop a *universalizable way of dealing with nature*—but the environmental space that the average United States citizen currently claims is several times greater than is permissible. Given the American tradition of the most pronounced possessive individualism, it is not easy to see how a limitation on using up natural resources, which would not be possible without increasing the power of the federal government and that of various international organizations, could be imposed. Nonetheless, ever since its foundation, the United States has had a strong sense of justice; and unlike Western Europe, it is not yet entirely eaten up by historical relativism. If it proves possible to broaden the concept of justice by including elements of intergenerational and international justice within it, the American people might go about establishing, with the same enthusiastic energy and the same moral self-confidence with which it has borne the banner of modernity, a more just way of dealing with nature. However, the recognition of a more comprehensive concept of justice will have to be won through a long and wearing two-front war—on one hand, against fundamentalist individualism, and on the other, against the immoral forces that are spreading in the society of the United States, as they do in all periods of decline.

The second problem with which the United States must deal is its *relationship to other cultures.* The way the United States takes it for granted that the norms of modernity are the only right ones is a source of strength for its politics that should not be underestimated; and it is obvious that a world power cannot afford the kind of tormenting feeling of insecurity still dominant in Germany fifty years after the end of the Second World War (which is on one hand a good thing, and on the other leads to a peculiar intellectual climate in which it is possible, for example, to give as an argument against vegetarianism the fact that leading Nazis were also vegetarians). Lines of thought based on cultural relativism cannot convince the average American that genocide is acceptable anywhere on Earth; and in this power of resistance of common sense, as opposed to pseudo-intellectual bluffs, lies one aspect of the greatness of the character of the American people. Nevertheless, the price paid for this immunity is high—a thorough lack of sensitivity to the logic of foreign cultures and to the values that exist in them as well. (Consider the refusal of average Americans abroad to learn even a basic vocabulary in the language of the country they are visiting.) The Vietnam debacle, for instance, can be explained only by a deep-seated inability to understand the conflict there primarily in terms of its own cultural roots, rather than immediately transposing it into the system of Cold War categories. When they had a hegemonic status, the British were far more capable of entering into the sensibilities of other cultures, partly because they made intelligent use of their great anthropologists in the framework of their imperialism— something that is harder to do for a country that is in some ways very proud of its anti-intellectualism—and partly because they had preserved pre-modern traditions in their own social system and in their government (a conservatism that was compatible with carrying out the first industrial revolution and parliamentary government in the world). The achievements of America's art, music, and literature are considerably less impressive than those of its politics, and the displacement of old and venerable cultures by the onslaught of American popular culture is certainly not a blessing for the world (even if it contributes to the construction of a universal culture and forcefully transmits a few values of abstract universalism). It is bad enough that not much can be done to resist this process; aggressively promoting it is immoral, indeed, extremely imprudent, since it arouses ressentiment to an extent that will unpleasantly surprise the United States; against suicide squads consisting of fanaticized terrorists, even hegemonic powers are relatively defenseless. (The last sentence, written in 1996, proves that the events of 11 September 2001 should not have come as a surprise.)

The hope that the United States will succeed in resolving these two questions is all the more sincere in that the second question can be answered only by saying that American hegemony is absolutely good for the world. The existence of a hegemony is a far better guarantee of world peace than an always unstable balance of power; and one will long for the bipolar structure of the post-war order if having overcome it leads not to the emergence of a hegemonic power but to a multipolar world in which every one of the various great powers has nuclear weapons and alliances change as quickly as they did in the classic era of the European system of states, but this time without the shared basic values that from 1648 to 1914 saved Europe from destroying itself. To be sure, one should not be willing to pay any price for any peace; but among the conceivable candidates for hegemonic status, there is none better than the United States. No other state has a constitution that comes comparably close to the principles of natural law and at the same time has the will and the ability to act worldwide on behalf of these principles, by military means if necessary. The world would pay a high price for a new isolationism in the United States (an isolationism that is entirely possible because the exercise of power is demanding and expensive), a price that might this time even have to be paid in a currency whose units are weapons of mass destruction. However, it is clear that a hegemonic status can endure over time only if the hegemonic power provides for the participation of the rest of the world's states in decision-making processes, as well as in the burden of carrying them out; unilateralism cannot work. This holds also and especially for today, not only because otherwise resistance by others has to be expected, but also because it would be too much to expect the United States to act as the world's only policeman. *Cooperation between the United States and the United Nations is the fulcrum on which the future of the world turns.* On it will depend whether the United States will become more than one of the numerous, always transitory hegemonic powers in world history or whether it will succeed in making its hegemonic role the springboard for a responsible world government that might be able to moderate the battles for environmental resources that the twenty-first century must expect.

As a step toward constructing an efficient world government, the creation and strengthening of just regional *systems of alliances, economic unions,* or even *federal states,* such as the Commonwealth of Independent States, the Association of South East Asian Nations, or the European Union, are desirable. However, these will lead to a new emergence of a multipolar system of states unless they accept the basic idea of the United Nations and see themselves as building stones for a multi-layered universal federal state. If they do so, they should be encouraged by the United Nations and the United States, because it is completely impossible for the United Nations, in its current form, to ensure peace all over the world; to do that, it must depend on regional organizations. The autonomization of such regional organizations is, however, a real danger; therefore as their power grows they must be integrated into the work of the United Nations. Thus it would be good if the world community could agree to grant such supranational organizations a permanent seat on the Security Council if they met the conditions mentioned in chapter 9.1.1. The presence of two members of the European Union as permanent members with veto rights on the Security Council contradicts a development that could culminate in a thoroughgoing European integration.

Despite the possible loss of a seat on the Security Council, true political union—or even a unified foreign policy, the lack of which made Europe co-responsible for the Yugoslavian crisis—would be a great advantage for the whole of *Europe*. It was certainly a mistake for Germany alone to recognize Slovenia and Croatia. It remains one of the construction errors of the process of European unification that the emphasis was put one-sidedly on the economic sector, while the foreign policy (and cultural) sector was neglected. On the other hand, traditional confederations and federal states have rightly sought, on the basis of a deep insight into a certain primacy of foreign policy, to integrate the latter, whereas economic policy has often remained a matter for the member states. It is true that under the conditions of the modern global economy, economic (and social) unification has an entirely different status than it had in earlier periods and that NATO has provided for a common defense policy; but it is a naive error to believe, on the basis of a long period of peace, that foreign policy is of comparatively secondary importance. Germany and France are the most powerful of the states willing to advance the process of European unification, and they can and must do so. Everything suggests that the weakest and most rebellious members of the system should not be allowed to determine the speed of the process of unification; instead, a series of concentric circles of supra-national European institutions should be constructed, so that broadening and deepening can be pursued simultaneously on various levels. In its draft constitution of 1787, the Convention in Philadelphia departed from the principle of unanimity of the currently still valid constitution, which was consciously violated in order create the new federal state; and in fact, it is clear that no state can have a moral right to prevent the further integration of other states that are willing to do so. Great Britain should be in a position to recognize that after the collapse of the Empire, it can help shape world politics only within the European Union; if it continues to reject this recognition because it cannot assume its new role, it should at least not be able to limit the deepening of the Union, which should not have to pay for Great Britain's identity crises.

Crucial for such a deepening is the introduction of the principle of majority rule in the central organs of the European Union. The Council of Ministers will have to be transformed into a second chamber rather like the German *Bundesrat,* and the Commission will have to be elected by the European Parliament. The fact that most of the decisions made by the European bureaucracy lack democratic legitimation is a problem on whose resolution the future of Europe crucially depends. Since democracy presupposes a public sphere, the construction of a public opinion involving all countries of the European Union is a central task—the most important contributions of the European media should be made accessible to a broader public in every country, in its own language.[18] The establishment of a *lingua franca* that should, so far as possible, be spoken by all citizens of the Union is indispensable; it would not prevent the cultivation of the national languages, especially if it was accompanied by a realistic assessment of their consequences (Sardinian is certainly less important than Italian). It is not the mere power of the factual that designates English as a European *lingua franca*, and indeed even as a world language. Hardly any other language in the world combines in the same way easiness at an elementary level with a wonderful complexity of syntax and vocabulary for those who know how to make use of it. In addition, it has two linguistic roots—one more than many other languages, even if less than most international artificial languages, whose deserved fate shows that so fundamental an institution as language cannot be planned out at a desk.[19] Youth exchange programs in Europe should be further intensified; they can promote intercultural marriages whose children are most likely to have a European consciousness. The construction of a collective European identity will not be possible, however, without an explicit reference to common values and a common task. In a post-Christian society, Christianity can no longer represent this common basis, and for that reason the inclusion of an Islamic country, so long as it has become a more or less constitutional state—for instance, Turkey or Tunisia—is possible and even desirable, because it would be an important sign of the openness of Western culture. A rejection of Turkey, for example, because of a parameter it certainly cannot change would only increase the fundamentalist forces there. It is now evident that economic growth cannot be the kind of goal that creates a collective identity. Only the vision of an ecological transformation of the society that does not surrender the great achievements of European political history, but rather continues and completes them, will have the intellectual attractiveness without which the process of European unification will necessarily come to a halt. A trend toward political union will emerge from the common currency, whose rapid introduction was prudent on political grounds, even if all the criteria for stability were not fulfilled. Political unity is a higher value than limiting inflation. It was right that the institutions for which the latter is a primary goal issued warnings, but it was also right that these institutions did not have to make the final decision.

In every foreign policy calculus, the most important successor state to the Soviet Union, namely *Russia*, must play a crucial role—its temporary weaknesses should not

---

18. I am adopting here a suggestion made by E. G. Mahrenholz.

19. Almost as unwise as drafting an artificial language is the attempt made by the Indian federal government to establish Hindi as the official language at the expense of English. On one hand, Hindi has not developed a comparable richness, and on the other, the South Indian population in particular cannot help feeling that they are overruled by majority vote and forced to learn a language that they cannot use in as many countries as they can English.

prevent us from seeing that by its size, population, scientific level, and military power, it remains a great power, and that disregarding it on the international scene might trigger internal political developments that could, given the terrible humiliation that the collapse of the communist experiment has meant for Russia, endanger world peace. Naturally, there is an understandable fear of the wounded colossus among its western neighbors, but it would be terrible if fear of Russia became a self-fulfilling expectation by unleashing chain reactions that would make the country far more frightening than it already is. The eastward extension of NATO, which is reasonable and just in view of the past sufferings of Eastern Europe, must be calibrated with an integration of Russia into European organizations and eventually into NATO. There must be a certain understanding of Russia's need to take its own way internally; establishing the rule of law is there still an elementary task that is indispensable for the development of a just form of capitalism, a task that cannot be fulfilled without democratic and constitutional structures but does not require all the guarantees of the separation of powers that a more developed society can afford. Hardly anything is more important for stabilizing Russian democracy than the construction of an efficient civil society with a large middle class that renounces the use of force (such as was achieved in Spain while it was still under Franco), and for that purpose the spread of denominations other than the Orthodox would be helpful. Only religions that recognize capitalism and at the same time set moral limits on it have a chance of contributing to a stable modernization. It is true that Russia will have to come to terms with the fact that its mentality is less compatible with modernity than the Western European or East Asian mentalities, for example, but giving Russia a political and economic culture at the level of that of Greece is certainly a feasible goal. It could help stabilize the Russian sense of self-respect to realize that a lower level of "development" comes closer to the one that is to be preferred on normative grounds because it is universalizable. The strengthening of the relationships within the Commonwealth of Independent States and the transformation of the latter into a genuine economic community would be absolutely sensible, and there is no fundamental objection even to a reunification of individual states, such as especially Russia and Belarus. Preventing the threatened breakup of the Russian Federation is also a legitimate goal, but one that should not be pursued at any price. Continuing to ignore Chechnya's declaration of independence would have been far more rational, even cratically speaking, than military intervention. Such interventions can distract attention from internal problems only if they are successful; otherwise, they intensify the legitimacy crisis. Even without the bloody use of force, it would have been possible to avoid the danger that Chechnya's factual independence might send a signal to the other autonomous republics within the Russian Federation. However, it is correct that no one should have had any illusions regarding the nature of the Chechen power-holders. Nevertheless, so long as the population favorable to the Russians had been allowed to immigrate into Russian territory, the toll in human life would still have been incomparably lower than it was in the war, which in addition resulted in a significant decrease in Russian political and military prestige.

A country with a great desire to be a world power is *China*. If it succeeds in making a peaceful transition from a party dictatorship to a democratic system—which is not guaranteed but because of the size of the country is one of the most important tasks of a moral politics in the twenty-first century—East Asia will probably become, at least until the breakdown of late modernity, the economic center of the world. Its population and especially its mentality, which is manifested, for example, in the economic success of Chinese outside the country, predispose it to this development. Japan once seemed on its way to becoming the first economic and technological power in the world (it was already the first financial power and is still the country that provides the most aid for development);[20] but the Japanese population is small in comparison with the Chinese, who have similar economic abilities and will hardly accept the same military abstinence as Japan. Conflicts among the three East Asian states—China, Japan, and Korea—cannot be excluded any more than economic wars between the East Asian economic sphere and that of the United States or the European Union; tensions between Japan and the United States are an omen of far more violent conflicts. However, a shift in the United States' primary concern from the Atlantic to the Pacific realm is also a possibility, and it is certainly in Europe's interest to protect itself against such a shift, for example by proposing a North Atlantic Free Trade Zone. Of course, what would make the most sense would be for the trilateral group of the United States, the European Union, and Japan to assume long-term responsibility for the solution of global problems.

The fundamental change of direction that the economic growth of East and Southeast Asia implies for world politics has not yet been adequately grasped. While twenty years ago, the Green movement could still hope to set a standard for the rest of the world by achieving an ecological change of course in the rich industrial countries, in the meantime Europe and the United States have long since lost the initiative. The *globalization of the economy* now forces them to practice a reactive policy with regard to the lower social and ecological standards of the newly industrialized countries. The central task of foreign policy toward the latter countries can only consist in developing an environmental foreign policy whose goal is to promote a globally acceptable and sustainable form of development. One thing is clear: there is not the slightest reason why the average Chinese should give up cars if Europeans and North Americans are not willing to do so; and it is no less incontestable that the Earth will react quite strongly to the spread of the Western lifestyle to over a billion additional consumers.

While East and Southeast Asia upset Westerners through their astonishing success in realizing the ideas of modernity, most countries in sub-Saharan *Africa* depress them because of the misery in which the majority of these countries' population lives and because of the periodic, extremely bloody wars—wars that are all the more detestable when they are not fought for the sake of just goals, as would be, for instance, a possible future uprising on the part of the dalits in India, but rather primarily for the supremacy

---

20. Cf. P. Glotz, R. Süssmuth, and K. Seitz (1992), 59 ff.

of one or another tribe or of one or another religious group. (Moreover, the criteria in accord with which wars are perceived by the media are arbitrary. Hardly any reporting was done on one of the bloodiest wars of recent years, that in Sudan.) The most important hope that the southern part of the continent can offer is the development in South Africa. If it succeeds, even after Mandela's departure, in creating a stable and just state, it could provide an important model for the rest of the continent's states and make South Africa the center of a regional organization that could deal successfully with some of the continent's problems and thereby avoid the odium that outside interventions arouse. Support for the continuing peaceful development of South Africa remains a central task of every moral African policy. If the South African experiment fails, in a few decades many a country in Africa might ask for forms of trusteeship by more developed countries (always only for a transitional period, of course, which might turn out to be rather long); one should then have enough respect for the expression of the will of foreign peoples to take such wishes seriously and at least not silence them. R. Neudeck reports that in 1983, during a civil war that was estimated to have cost a million human lives, he heard Ugandans say, "We were better off under the English." "At the time," Neudeck says, "this seemed to me obscene. The uneducated Ugandans, Baganda, and Kakwa couldn't know any better. But Heaven forbid that it be reported in Europe."[21] Neudeck, who devoted his life to humanitarian aid, now considers his reaction in 1983 to be a mistake. One might say that he has understood that his antipaternalistic reaction was based on a subtler and, in terms of its consequences, perhaps even more terrible form of paternalism—a typical intellectual meta-paternalism, which one can and must criticize, even if this criticism is currently not viewed as politically correct. At least, one should consider that in traditional societies the transfer of political domination, for instance after civil wars, to neutral foreigners was a recognized means of pacification. It is true that it has been discredited by modern nationalism, but that says more about nationalism than about the rationality of this means.

There are grounds for hope, even if they are weak, that the intellectual traditions of East and Southeast Asia could make their cultural area able to develop a *form of modernity* that is *less destructive than that of Western Europe;* strengthening and reviving such traditions should be a goal of Western foreign policy at least as important as promoting exports. Once again, as was already indicated in chapter 8.2.1.1, since a significant portion of relationships between states consists in battles for recognition, much would be gained if it proved possible to give direction to attempts to overcome the humiliation that the unprecedented extension of the European cultural area's power over the whole planet means for other cultures—a direction that did not consist in imitating the Western life style but outlined instead a universalizable alternative. The reason that Gandhi must be seen not only as one of the greatest persons of the twentieth century but also as one of its greatest politicians, even if one does not approve of all his political goals, is

---

21. (1993), 115.

that with a naturalness that was as naive as it was reflective, he succeeded in continuing to live according to many of the traditional norms of his own culture while at the same time incorporating the central universalistic ideas of British culture. On the other hand, the corruption of most of the elites in current developing countries is directly attributable to the fact that they imitate not the virtues but the vices of modernity. The composure with which Gandhi wore simple Indian clothing he had woven himself when meeting with the highest British officials, and refused, in a way that was simultaneously friendly and provocative, to adopt their not exactly morally grounded clothing norms, deserves the greatest respect, and all the more so in that Gandhi used highly expressive symbolic gestures to criticize his own culture as well—just consider his cleaning latrines. Furthermore, Gandhi was able to interpret into the fundamental texts of his own culture the central ideas of modern universalism, and even if there are historical and philological objections to his way of doing so, the latter are fully compensated for by the political gain, namely the strengthening of his own people's self-respect through the simultaneous further development of the traditional mores.

Only an analogous combination of both elements will protect Islamic and other cultural areas against the rise of fundamentalist forces. The causes of *fundamentalism* are, as was already noted in chapter 6.3.1, a decrease in social status and the striving for justice for the economically weaker, the feeling that one's own culture is being taken by surprise by Western hegemony and is being betrayed by one's own elites, and finally, the often accurate perception of phenomena of decline in the Western world. Fundamentalist ideologies have great attraction for the losers in the world-historical process of modernization, even if their teachers certainly recommend the use of modern technology's tools of power because they have understood that otherwise the West's power advantage cannot be overcome: The fundamentalist terrorist combines an apparently old-fashioned piety with significant know-how in ultra-modern explosive technologies. The following methods for combating fundamentalism suggest themselves. It is clear that terrorists must be met with countervailing force; it is a dangerous mistake to think that fanatics are impressed by generosity. They feel that they are recognized only if they are met on the battlefield that they have themselves chosen. Cooperation between states, and perhaps even an international organization that is expressly devoted to fighting terrorism, are absolutely necessary; states that support terrorism must be isolated and suffer economic disadvantages; even merely tolerating terrorist organizations within a constitutional state is unacceptable; their finances have to be drained. It is depressing that the energetic actions of the United States against international terrorism have not been sufficiently supported by the other OECD states, even if the United States can be reproached for not always giving adequate consideration to the interests of its allies in making its decisions, or even consulting them. At the same time, all other means of power should be used to weaken the terrorist milieu—partly on moral grounds (for the use of force must be limited to what is necessary) and partly on cratic grounds: A war against a population, half of which consists of fundamentalists, cannot be won with morally justifiable means. One of the morally more questionable means of power consists in turning the aggressiveness of the various fundamentalisms against each other—in analogy to Tacitus's famous plea that in view of the threat to the Empire, the discord among the Germanic tribes might be maintained.[22]

But the real task involved in dealing with fundamentalism consists in fighting its causes. Decreasing the luxury enjoyed by the local elites, which is often felt to be a provocation, is an important factor; the extravagant Achaemenid jubilee celebrations in Iran in 1971, through which the Pahlavi dynasty sought to appropriate the immemorial dignity of the ancient Persian rulers, in fact marked the beginning of the end of its rule. An income distribution policy that is more socially just is crucial, and wealthier countries should contribute to it in the framework of aid for development. However, the latter can be counterproductive if it passes through a local government that is both corrupt and hated by its own people. In the framework of such aid for development, there is much to be said for supporting steps to stabilize population growth; for inevitably, in a country like Egypt, the positive results of economic growth and foreign aid are quickly wiped out by population growth. Of course, this kind of policy can be carried out only with the agreement of the local religious authorities; foreigners' desires to limit the population seldom meet with approval, and even less, the more relationships between the countries involved are poisoned by the feeling that the wealthier side seeks world domination.

In addition to *economic* measures, cultural measures are indispensable. The return to indigenous culture in a conscious rejection of the West is often a result of the feeling that in the framework of the Western system, the indigenous culture has no chance of expressing itself, that it is not recognized and taken seriously—a feeling that is certainly intensified by the dominant mode of Western tourism. An institutionalization of religious dialogue might promote the construction of a world ethos, and even if it did not produce that result, it could be helpful as a sign of sincere interest in non-Western cultures. For on one point, the fundamentalists are absolutely right: the question of God cannot be bracketed out of human thought and life, and a culture that tries to do so can hardly claim to be a model. Moreover, the opponents of Westernization must always be granted that modernization undermines virtues such as chastity and hospitality, of which they have every reason to be proud. However, this must be combined with the observation that this has been the price to be paid by the West for the realization of modern virtues and values such as justice and equality. At the same time, both sides should acknowledge that everyone would owe a great debt of gratitude to a culture that managed to find a better balance between pre-modern and modern virtues than the West has so far achieved. Thus in cultural dialogue, it must be conceded, for instance, that cultures that do not allow pornography have a better claim to safeguard *one* aspect

---

22. "Maneat, quaeso, duretque gentibus, si non amor nostri, at certe odium sui, quando urgentibus imperii fatis nihil iam praestare fortuna maius potest quam hostium discordiam" (*Germania* 33). ("Long, I pray, may foreign nations persist, if not in loving us, at least in hating one another; for destiny is driving our empire upon its appointed path, and fortune can bestow on us no better gift than discord among our foes." Trans. H. Mattingly, 129.)

of women's human dignity. So far as Islam is concerned, an opportunity for reconciliation with it consists precisely in its relatively close proximity to the Western cultural area—a proximity that is presumably the reason why Islamic fundamentalism is stronger than any other (cf. chapter 4.3.3). The rational theology of medieval Islam is one of the greatest creations of the human spirit; it should be taken as a starting point if one seeks real dialogue with Islamic culture.

9.2.2. Defense Policy

The crucial task of defense policy in the twenty-first century must be to integrate it into a global domestic policy. The goal of a global defense policy must be less to defend one's own country (not to speak of waging aggressive wars) than to increase the United Nations Security Council's monopoly on the use of force. The limitation of arms and armies on all sides (for instance, by means of an extensive ban on arms exports) is no doubt a better way of responding to the desire for security than engaging in an arms race—not only because the funds are urgently needed for ecological and social ends but also because increasing armaments is no way to build confidence. Nonetheless, it would be an error to adopt the standpoint of formal symmetry and claim that the *nuclear powers* would have a right to try to prevent the proliferation of nuclear weapons only if they completely scrapped their own nuclear arsenals. It is unrealistic to expect them to do so, and in view of the enormity of the dangers threatening humanity the principle of equality must be secondary to the goal of preventing a nuclear war. Unfortunately, this cannot be achieved by having all states give up nuclear weapons—since know-how cannot be "disarmed," there would still always be concern that one's neighbor was secretly preparing to construct nuclear weapons. In this situation, the lesser evil is for a few states, whose governments can be somehow relied upon to act justly, to have a monopoly on nuclear weapons. There is hardly a situation in which Hobbes's argument for subjection to Leviathan is more convincing than it is in the current stage of world history, in which there is a real possibility not merely of a normal war but rather of the annihilation of a large part of humanity. In view of the threatening battles over the allotment of the last resources, even the hegemonic position of a country that is certainly not an ecological model is the lesser evil. It is true that a just institution with a monopoly on weapons of mass destruction is not yet possible; but the fewer states have such weapons, the closer we come to it. The thesis has been proposed that a quite large number of nuclear powers would make the outbreak of a war less likely than a limited number of nuclear powers because then the number of the possible alliances would be so huge that fear of a war would be yet greater; but the probability of a misuse of nuclear weapons by dictators not acting in even a rationally egoistic manner is directly proportional to the number of states that possess them. Therefore one can say with a clear conscience that limiting the number of nuclear powers is in the general interest of the world—that is, in the interest even of those states that do not belong to the nuclear club. However, it is of great importance psychologically that the nuclear powers decrease the size of their arsenals, and renounce nuclear testing, for example; this kind of policy significantly increases the acceptability of the status quo.

It is certainly understandable that people want to find a technological means of protecting themselves from modern weapons of mass destruction, but such means will never do away with the feeling of being threatened, since by its very nature, the escalation of technology and countertechnology leads to an infinite regress. Thus the development of a nuclear defense shield would be desirable if it were possible—but its feasibility is extremely questionable. Naturally, such a shield would have to be made available to all states in order to eliminate generally the fear of a nuclear war; but it would be naive to assume that it would put an end to all wars—on the contrary, more conventional wars would probably break out again because there would be less fear that they might escalate into nuclear wars. To be sure, weapons that quickly put out of commission the enemy's decision-making centers are to be welcomed; intrusions into the enemy's information systems can make it possible to forgo more lethal weapons. But it will not be possible to fight future wars by computers alone. If the will to kill is given, the elimination of computer-supported weapons systems means only that the battle will be continued with knives. Nonetheless, since such "meta-weapons" would decrease the number of people killed, because it would be more difficult to kill, their development can be approved morally.

Military alliances are among the supra-national institutions that produce a subtle limitation of the sovereignty of the states involved in them and make international politics more manageable by limiting the number of possible alliances. They are to be welcomed if they have purely defensive goals. It can hardly be denied that the foundation of NATO after the Second World War was a blessing not only for Europe but also for the whole world. The Atlantic alliance is one of the most important factors for stability in the world today, and there can be no question of doing away with it but only of broadening it, possibly to include Russia. The reintegration of France into NATO was long overdue; dreams of going it alone as a national state should now be abandoned by all former European great powers. For the latter, it makes sense only to concentrate on cooperating with the developing countries with which they have a special relationship on the basis of earlier colonial history, a common language, and common values—France can achieve more in francophone Africa, or Great Britain in the Commonwealth states, than can other countries.

Since state expansion, if it is supposed ever to have been a legitimate goal of politics, is in any case no longer one today, the chief task of a possibly globally approved defense policy is *early recognition of hot spots* and *controlling them internationally*, naturally under the aegis of the current hegemonic power. The conflict in the Middle East and that between India and Pakistan remain threatening, and mediation efforts on the part of states that have the means of power consisting in authority and positive sanctions, and can make express threats that they can carry out if necessary, are more important. A concentration of power in the United States is, as we have already said, not too high a price to pay for establishing a world order in which wars become increasingly rare. In particular, public opinion in Germany and Japan must understand that the history of these countries does not release them from the duty to cooperate in such a world order—quite the contrary. If this history teaches anything, it is that an international system that consists of sovereign powers that close their eyes to aggression is dangerous. Drawing lessons from the period between the World Wars means recognizing that one can also become guilty by omission. The German Greens, for instance, became capable of governing at the federal level only after grasping this elementary ethical truth. Neither a generic pacifism nor specific aversions to United States hegemony are a moral basis for a politics that claims to be responsible. To be sure, one cannot deal with all the world's hot spots (thus it is thoroughly understandable that on 7 October 1993 President Clinton declared that it was not the United States' task to rebuild Somalia's society), but it is crucial to recognize that the legitimate interests of the United States, not the fundamental injustice of intervening in a country ravaged by civil war, morally justify this decision. Acknowledgment of a moderate egoism is more moral than an inconsistent and dishonest moralism that uses noble words to deceive itself and others regarding its own motives.

In chapter 7.3.3.3.5, we gave the arguments in favor of establishing a general duty to perform military service. It is reasonable, for instance in order to avoid military dictatorships; and in a war between a democratic constitutional state and an unjust state, such as the Second World War, it is the only right thing to do. In the present situation, in many states there is much to be said for concentrating on the construction of an efficient professional army. The primary task today is not defending Western democracies against threats on the part of totalitarian states but rather competent and moderate cooperation in United Nations peace-enforcing and peacekeeping operations. Just as fighting terrorism should be entrusted to groups specially trained for this purpose, so should cooperation in UN military operations be based on smaller but highly professional, intrinsically motivated, and technologically well-equipped armies. One should not for that reason forgo asking young people to do a year of service, which can play an important role in socializing them; but it should take the form of a year of social service within the country, or, better yet, abroad, in the context of aid for development. Intelligent aid for development is a crucial contribution to a preventive defense policy. Today, the greatest threat to world peace does not come from other economically successful states; prosperity decreases the readiness to put one's life at risk. Neither does it come from communist ideology, which has irretrievably failed. Nor from the poorest of the poor, because wars are expensive. The threat comes from poor states that can afford weapons of mass destruction, even if only chemical and biological weapons, and in which a large portion of the people are consumed by a hatred such that they would not hesitate to sacrifice their own lives or those of others.

9.2.3. Development Policy

Development and environmental policy are the two central tasks of a moral politics in the twenty-first century. What is disturbing about this fact is that they seem, at least at first glance, to be in tension with each other—for the universalization of our level of "development" is ecologically impossible. Hence there can be a great potential for conflict between these two tasks, so that ecologists who want to establish intergenerational justice at the expense of international justice and are indifferent to the poverty of the Third World are not a rarity. In reality, this conflict entails something that is theoretically very easy but practically very difficult to deal with: the fact that development policy must begin in the wealthy countries. If "development" is to be more than a descriptive concept referring to the factual process of modernization in industrialized countries, if it is to be understood as a normative concept that refers to an ideal condition, then only a country that does not, for example, claim more than the environmental space it is entitled to can be called "developed." It may be that in this sense, Costa Rica is more developed than Germany, although or precisely because the per capita GNP corresponds to about one-thirteenth of Germany's (whereas life expectancy, although only for men, is higher).[23] What was most deeply unsatisfactory in German unification was that it expanded a non-universalizable standard of living when it had the opportunity to reduce it. In contrast, development policy must become a cross-sectional task.

Fundamentally, there are three objections to the *usual understanding of "development"* underlying development policy since the Second World War. First, it has often been assumed that the goal of world history is an extensive homogenization of the world. On the other hand, there is the view that a plurality of cultures makes the world richer and more beautiful than does the universal monoculture that is threatening to establish itself everywhere. Monocultures, in agriculture for instance, not only lead to the disappearance of species, which is intrinsically a disvalue, but also have a negative extrinsic value in that when they decline, possibilities for doing things otherwise no longer exist. The same holds for human cultures (cf. chapter 7.3.3.3.7); therefore it is important to preserve a multitude of languages, religions, ways of life, and modes of dwelling and dressing, to the extent that they do not contradict elementary principles of natural law. It is depressing when development policy leads, for instance, to the same food being consumed everywhere; indeed, this tendency becomes a crime if the advertising produced by Western companies for white bread in Africa, for example, drives out local species of grain that are the only ones that can be produced with economic success and at prices affordable for everyone in the countries in question. However, this argument presupposes that all people should be fed, and if there are cultures that

---

23. I take these data for the year 1991 from *Webster's New Encyclopedic Dictionary* (1993 ed.). I am also indebted for some of the following information to I. Hauchler (1993).

accept with indifference the fact that part of their population is going hungry, then this is an element of those cultures that must be overcome. If the discussion on development long remained under the spell of an abstract, Eurocentric monism, today there is the inverse threat: the demand, in the wake of the later Wittgenstein, for instance, for an unlimited cultural diversity. However, this would necessarily involve throwing out the idea of an development policy based on an international consensus, along with the idea that the Earth's poorest people have fundamental rights to positive benefits. But not only is cultural plurality to be preferred—with the just mentioned qualification—to a global monoculture; the second problem area in the earlier concept of development has to do with the fact mentioned at the beginning of this section, namely that the Western level of development is not universalizable. However, if Western culture has been so obviously moving in the wrong direction for several decades, its right to set the standards for reasonable development is questionable. Nonetheless, it must be recognized that some of the central ideas of the Western world remain correct; but a cultural area that succeeds in realizing a universalizable level of development, whatever that cultural area might be, will probably attain cultural hegemony if it is able to pursue an appropriate cultural relations policy. Third, the descriptive thesis of many traditional theories of development, according to which all cultures move toward a "modern" level of development, at least when they are supported, is false. The transition to the sphere of statehood is already not "natural," as we saw in chapter 6.2.2.1, and this means a fortiori that some cultures are not compatible with the principles of modernity at all. But then one must ask what development policy can mean for them concretely.

The first task of a theory of reasonable development policy consists in discerning the elements in the modernization project that are justified by practical reason and in distinguishing them from those that are morally indifferent or even to be evaluated negatively from a moral point of view. Among the latter are certainly the expansion of the individual's consumption beyond the environmental space to which he is entitled, the corrosion of the traditional virtues that lead beyond rational egoism and make experiences of community possible, and the loss of cultural diversity compatible with natural law. Even if it were possible to decouple economic growth from the exhaustion of resources and environmental pollution, it would still be absurd to consider the per capita and annual GNP (even if related, with the help of the PPP, or purchasing power parity, to purchasing power in the country concerned) as the crucial index of development; this point was already discussed in chapter 7.3.3.2.1. Not only is absolute poverty among a large part of the population compatible with a high per capita GNP, but even if the constant increase in consumption were general and compatible with the environment, it would necessarily lead to a breakdown in temperance and therefore to the destruction of one of the most important sources of legitimate self-respect. On the other hand, *fighting absolute poverty* is a reasonable task—but therefore so is a *qualified* growth. Since human life is the most fundamental object of legal protection, an *increase in life expectancy* is the most important index of the kind of development to be promoted—or rather an *increase in health expectancy,* since overcoming physical pain makes life considerably more pleas-

ant and a long final phase of life with a great deal of pain or even without full consciousness is not really desirable.[24] *Decreasing infant mortality* is to be promoted on the same
ground; objecting to such efforts by saying that they promote a population explosion is
immoral in itself and also because in the medium term these efforts certainly promote a
limitation of population growth. However, the mere physical life of an intellectual being
is not an end in itself; it is valuable as the basis of free and intellectual activities. In order
to pursue such activities, education is indispensable; the *literacy rate* must therefore also
be recognized as a morally important index, even if literacy is always only a means (and
only a useful means, not an indispensable one) to achieve the kind of education that has
an intrinsic value. Part of "development" in the normative sense must also involve moving closer to elementary principles of natural law. Equal treatment for all citizens, guaranteeing crucial rights to freedom from interference, rights to positive benefits, political
rights, and, finally, a stable condition of peace, are far more important normative parameters of development than is the GNP.[25]

How can a prudent development policy help move us closer to these goals? Unfortunately, it cannot be denied that aid for development has often had exactly the opposite effect, and it is obvious that halting such failed development aid (including private
aid) is an urgent moral obligation. Aid for development should serve not the donor
countries' good conscience but rather the morally acceptable and universalizable needs
of the donee countries, and sometimes considerably more can be achieved by not doing
anything than by a bunch of inconsistent actions. A Marshall Plan can yield positive effects only if there is a mentality that can deal productively with aid. Thus the list of the
mistakes made by a good part of aid for development to date is a long one. The aid has
often gone for the most part into the pockets of the local elites, who bear the chief
blame for the misery of their countries, and it has even allowed them to continue their
injustices and to extend them further; by promoting senseless projects, it has contributed
to enormous environmental destruction and to the displacement of traditional virtues;
it has destroyed local markets, weakened the donees' will to help themselves and their
trust in their own culture, and led the local elites to adopt the way of life of the wealthy
countries. Even if corruption is endemic in many developing countries and often goes
back to old traditions, contact with Western business firms and governments has given
it wholly unimagined opportunities for expansion. It was a formal error to assume
naively that all cultures naturally develop in a linear path toward modernity, for it is

---

24. Not all causes of death can be attributed in the same degree to politics—the destruction of
one's own health, by taking drugs, for instance, represents less of a reproach to state health policy
than death as a result of an infectious disease that could be eliminated by immunization, because the
latter is easier to prevent than the former.

25. In this connection, the Human Development Index (HDI) used since 1990 is important; it
involves a complex calculation including life expectancy, educational attainment, and standard of living (in some cases taking into account inequalities in income distribution). Cf. Human Development
Report (1994), 90 ff. However, a calculation of a society's net economic welfare is still lacking.

obvious that Africa will take a different path from that taken by East Asia and that aid for development must be adapted to the cultural as well as to the geographic and economic possibilities of the country receiving it.

Since prosperity is more dependent on organizational abilities than on resources, one must assume that different cultures will achieve different levels of prosperity, even and especially in the long run, even if every individual is allotted the same environmental space. This may be lamentable, but it contradicts the principles of justice only if part of humanity is living in absolute poverty or another part claims more than the environmental space it is entitled to. Differences that remain within these extremes should be accepted: The decision to work less and thus to earn less deserves every respect, whether it is made by an individual or a culture, and it is far better to recommend as a model for a poor African country a relatively successful neighbor such as Botswana than a European country because too great a cultural and economic difference tends to be discouraging and makes it difficult to build the healthy self-respect that people certainly can and should have, especially at a lower level of prosperity. There is much to be said for multilateral development projects in which the absolute wealthiest and the relatively "most developed" states in a region work together in order to fight absolute poverty in donee countries.

Obviously, there are three ways of fighting absolute poverty. The first is *direct support for the poorest people;* it has already been shown that a broadening of the principles of the welfare state to the global level is morally obligatory on universalist bases.[26] Laziness should not be encouraged, but a contribution, for instance, to the education of children who have lost their parents or who are forced, because of their families' poverty, to do labor damaging to their health or to prostitute themselves can hardly be seen as supporting laziness, especially if education makes these children capable of taking care of themselves and earning their livings in a moral way. On the contrary, the inability of the world community to ensure every child a basic education (to do which only a relatively small sum would be required) is a moral scandal. It is crucial to strengthen poor people's sense of self-respect, their consciousness that they have *rights* and that their poverty is not a matter of fate but rather the result of specific social structures. Aid to stabilize population growth can and should accompany such measures in countries in which population growth is outstripping economic growth and in which the limits of what is ecologically sustainable have already been reached.

The second way of fighting absolute poverty consists in *improving a country's infrastructure* in order to enable it as soon as possible to care for its own poor; this includes loans on favorable terms. Such projects have long been the core of aid for development, and they remain indispensable; but they were often counterproductive insofar as a technology imported from outside is only rarely congenial to the mentality of those who are

---

26. Cf. U. Menzel's chapter, "Globale Sozialpolitik statt Entwicklungshilfe" (1992, 202 ff.). I have learned a great deal from Menzel's book.

supposed to make use of it. Even if "big technology" is partly desired by the donee countries as a mark of prestige, and is partly connected with great economic advantages for the donor countries, exporting it should be refrained from, and there should be a concentration on training people in the intellectual capacities required for effective economic activity. A machine that is unlikely to be maintained by the indigenous population either is a wasted investment or produces a humiliating dependency. This holds a fortiori for major loans to a nation that cannot deal with them productively. On the other hand, there should be support for the construction of the most efficient possible healthcare system, in which efficiency is measured by the relation between the costs and the years of healthy life saved by medical intervention. Moreover, there should be support for the development of an economy oriented toward meeting basic needs, and especially for the development of agriculture, whose poor condition is often attributable to an unjust policy on the part of the local elites, who have their power base in the urban population, for which they want to retain supplies at prices below what the market would justify. Furthermore, it is crucial that the technologies and procedures offered damage the environment as little as possible. Environmental technologies should be made available at highly subsidized prices; indeed, given the current conception of property rights to nature, the purchase of large parts of the rainforest by governmental and private environmental protection organizations is certainly to be welcomed, partly in order to preserve biodiversity; with the funds thus acquired, the developing countries involved could pay off their debts.

The third way of fighting absolute poverty is to *facilitate free trade*, which is in the interests of both sides in the medium term, even if during a transitional period it can cause problems that will have to be absorbed by welfare measures. But these problems are no justification for protectionist barriers raised by the rich with regard to the poorer countries—barriers that are all the more unjust in that the poorer countries' natural resources and capital are flowing into the wealthier countries. There is no objection in principle to capital being allocated where it can produce the most; this can spur the developing country concerned to create more rational structural conditions. But the moral problem of a large part of this flight of capital is that it involves illegally acquired or at least illegally transferred funds; a state has the right to make it more difficult for its citizens, who claim its protection, to invest money abroad. Furthermore, there is much to be said both economically and morally for orienting one's own economy primarily toward domestic demand before opening it to the world market on a wide scale; but this means only that the poorer countries, not the richer ones, have a right to take protectionist measures for a transitional period.

Exporting weapons to potential aggressors is a crime; and it is absolutely legitimate to cease cooperating with the government (but not with the non-governmental organizations) of a country if an indefensibly large share of its budget is devoted to military expenditures. It is true that the present power advantage of the militarily better-equipped states will thereby be maintained; but if the production of a United Nations monopoly on the use of force is a goal of world politics, then this must be accepted, especially since today wars affect mainly the poorest people. In general, a failed policy in a developing country should be denounced in public forums such as the United Nations General Assembly as well. For poor governance in many developing countries must be considered one of the main causes of their poverty,[27] and since it violates human rights, it is not a situation that concerns governments alone. It is obvious, for instance, that Brazil needs land reform and broad redistribution to the poorest people; pointing out to the local elites the inevitability of such steps is a greater service to the country, and in the medium term to the elites themselves, than continued support for the status quo. In any case, many governments of developing countries are legitimated neither democratically nor by objective success, and it is not at all clear that the interests of the Burmese people, for instance, are better represented by their government, which has masked its traditional Oriental despotism with a socialist ideology, than by the world public. However, in criticizing bad governments, the principles mentioned in chapter 8.2.1.1 must be observed. Thus it is possible that the shortcomings are due more to a lack of knowledge and organizational abilities than to ill will; in this case, help in improving governance should be offered. Nonetheless, it would be naive to think that the problems are never caused by an irresponsible egoism, which one certainly has a right, and indeed a duty, to combat. For that reason, despite the creditors' moral co-responsibility for the current situation, the demand for a generic debt cancellation for developing countries is unreasonable—unlike the demand for an international law regarding insolvency and the supervision of bank operations—if there is no guarantee that the financial room for maneuver thus gained will really benefit the poorest people. Otherwise, debt cancellation often enough means only that the creditor countries have lost the opportunity to prescribe reasonable conditions, and it is not clear why the middle class in the wealthy countries should protect the foreign bank accounts of corrupt kleptocrats. The business firms and governmental departments of the wealthier countries should instead see to it, through strictly supervised agreements, that they do not promote corruption in developing countries (and doing so would be not only morally but also financially advantageous for them). If a country is being ruined by a criminal despot, then it makes sense to support the opposition—insofar as there is one, as it really represents a better alternative, and as it is more or less united, or at least a large part of the population supports a part of the opposition. There is also much to be said for providing logistical help for indigenous forces seeking to overthrow criminal governments. As a last resort, a humanitarian intervention legitimated by the United Nations should be considered. We have already discussed such interventions, as well as the establishment of trust territories.

The main problem of aid for development is that not everyone can be helped at the same time. Drawing up lists of priorities is here even more indispensable than in other

---

27. On the problem of governance in developing countries, see K. M. Leisinger's fundamental essay (1995).

areas of politics. What are the morally relevant criteria? Four should be noted. The first has already been mentioned several times: One must *start with the poorest.* However, the number of the latter is unmanageable, and it is often not possible to compare the needs of those who live in absolute poverty. Since moreover on the foregoing assumption not all can be helped, one has to concentrate on those who will as soon as possible no longer need help, partly because it can then be given to others and partly because the people who have become independent can themselves help others. Thus we have given the second criterion, which can be in a certain tension with the first: Aid should pursue the goal of making itself unnecessary. Among the points in favor of making aid as much as possible *help for self-help,* there is not only the possible expansion of aid that it makes possible, but also the fact that autonomy has an intrinsic value. From this criterion follows the right to give more support, in the event of conflict, to families that do not perpetuate the need for aid through their demographic behavior, even if in an ideal world the rights of children of large families to positive benefits should remain uninfringed. But we do not live in an ideal world, and however defensible one might find a major increase in governmental and private aid for development and environmental protection on the part of wealthy countries in order to finance a global Marshall Plan if conditions were such that the aid would be used sensibly by the donee countries, this is very unlikely to take place in the foreseeable future; therefore selections may and should be made on the basis of the second criterion. Even if the two criteria do not always single out the same groups, there is a group whose promotion can be supported on the basis of both: women. For on one hand, they are among the most disadvantaged, and on the other, the economic and moral strengthening of women—for instance, through minor loans—is an important factor in limiting population growth.[28] The third criterion concerns the *guilt* of those who are living in poverty. This cannot be applied to children, for instance, but it can be applied to those who have thrown themselves into poverty and are not willing to let themselves be helped in a rational way. Not only does this criterion have an intrinsic value, but it would be counterproductive not to take it into account because that would quickly further increase the number of those who would have to be helped, even if in a given case aid led to self-help. (To that extent, this criterion is not identical with the second one.) Instrumentalizing a person in order to deter others is, as we saw in chapter 7.3.2, permissible if he is personally guilty; if this holds even for punishments, then it holds a fortiori for the omission or restriction of aid. The fourth criterion has to do with the concrete position of a donee country in the *general international political situation.* Enemies will not be supported; however, failing to offer comprehensive aid to a country can also first encourage a development that makes it dangerous. Thus at present, support for Russia is more important than support for Ukraine because Russia is bigger and the fate of the whole world, including Ukraine, depends on the road it takes. At the same time, one should avoid making aid for development

28. Cf. K. M. Leisinger (1993), 269 ff.

appear to be given out of fear in order not to be subjected to blackmail. But in a world that still has no central authority with a monopoly on the use of force, concern for the preservation of peace cannot be disregarded, no matter how little a just development policy can be reduced to this point.

9.3. Domestic Policy in the Broader Sense

The domestic tasks that states such as Burundi and the United States must undertake today are extremely different (and the following pages will be concerned primarily with the tasks of Western industrial countries). But they agree in one respect: Both countries must put environmental policy at the center of the political efforts. In fact, it would be a mistake to see environmental policy as just one sector among other areas of politics. In the present situation, just as peace is the first task of foreign policy, the preservation of the environment must become the generating principle of domestic policy because no other area of politics is currently farther removed from what is demanded by natural law than is environmental policy and because violations of these demands put in question the physical possibilities of life for future generations. In Western countries, for instance, further reforms of criminal law are incomparably less important than a new conception of environmental policy; indeed, it is this new conception from which reasonable innovations in criminal law must emerge. It has been rightly pointed out "that the best environmental protection is one that never becomes necessary. . . . To put it technically, we want to transform environmental policy from a subordinated concept into an integrated one, from a longitudinal task to a cross-sectional task."[29]

This is not intended to mean that what is affirmative in the achievement of real historical development up to this point should be thrown overboard; on the contrary, the only environmental policy that has a chance is one that tries to integrate the environmental problem into the existing legal system and has a sense for the inner logic of the particular political domains, especially foreign policy. It is not impossible that in a crisis situation an ecological policy might prevail that put the achievements of the liberal, democratic state at risk; but one should not imagine that the way of life in such a political system would be exactly attractive, even if it were really to solve the environment problems. Far more probable would be a takeover by hate-filled, power-obsessed individuals who misused the ecological issue as a pretext for satisfying their own thirst for power. However, the triumph of an eco-dictatorship is all the more likely the less successful efforts to change course are in coming years; and those who resist these efforts—mainly in the name of basic liberal values—will be morally co-responsible if

---

29. M. Hustedt, R. Loske, G. Nacken, T. Stein, and B. Ulrich (1990), 45. This text, which appeared remarkably early, is one of those that has the most to say about the opportunities and dilemmas for ecological politics.

that dictatorship should ever come to pass. Conversely, a reasonable ecological policy must have a sense of consistency and cut its ties with some beloved traditions that are part of the identity of those from whom the ecological movement has long been recruiting its members. The result is that the social and political alliances necessary to impose a more comprehensive ecological policy must include all possible groups; only if environmental groups, business firms, churches, opinion shapers, parliamentarians from various parties, the judicial system, and the bureaucracy provide a common impetus for an ecological *perestroika* will it be possible to put the required pressure on a generally immobile politics. In hardly any other historical period has "interstitial emergence" been both as possible and as necessary as it is today. This contributes to the chaos in current politics clearly discernible behind its façade of orderly respectability, but it is also what makes the current era stimulating. Two things are conceivable in the coming decades: Either modern welfare democracy will not survive a period in which there is less to distribute, because it has founded its legitimacy exclusively on economic benefits, or humanity will find a way out of the prisoners' dilemma situation in which it finds itself with regard to natural resources. The second outcome is possible, however, only if a sufficiently large number of people are guided not solely by rational egoism and are convinced that this is also true of others—in short, only if a new, value-centered collective identity develops.

9.3.1. Environmental Policy

Because of the dominance of the subsystem of economics in modernity, economic policy is today the central task of domestic policy in wealthy countries. This may change again in the future; given the analysis of the ways of using the forms of power in the modern state offered in chapter 6.3.2, we must currently assume that the ministry of economics is far more important cratically than is, for instance, the interior ministry. Therefore it would be much more important that an ecologically committed politician be appointed as minister for economics than that he or she be appointed as minister for the environment; for only if economic activity becomes compatible with preserving the environment will environmental policy become more than a mechanism devoted to repairing damage already done, and yet helpless and reactive in view of the enormity of the destruction. Environmental damage can be prevented only if there is a change in the way business is done; a unification of the economics and environmental ministries would therefore make sense if this did not mean, in the present phase, that environmental concerns would be completely sacrificed to those of the national economy, or— to be more exact and to tell the truth—to short-term particular economic interests. In actuality, an ecological turnaround is not conceivable without a great alliance of economic and environmental groups; and in terms of election strategy, it is of the utmost importance that parties that have set ecological goals both have an objective knowledge of economics and also be perceived by the public as having that knowledge.

Not only must economic activity become *compatible with preserving the environment,* but environmental policy must be *compatible with economic activity.* This means, for instance, the following: The environmental policy conception may only determine a framework within which every individual firm may and should freely make its own decisions; the long-term and stable nature of environmental policy must provide the certainty of the law without which economic activity cannot develop; international harmonization (or as a second option, eco-tariffs) should not be forgone if a country is not to suffer disadvantages in international competition; the governmental organs determining the framework must come to an agreement with business and cooperate with it; finally, the criteria of economic rationality must be applied to all dealings with scarce resources,[30] that is, also to a responsible environmental policy, which must not expect too much readiness to sacrifice from those who are supposed to support it. "One measure is twice as 'efficient' as another if twice as much environmental protection can be purchased' for the same money. . . . As long as environmental policy was a relatively small-scale activity it could afford a low level of efficiency, but as the goals become more ambitious . . . this will have to change." [31] Concretely, this means that a list of priorities is indispensable in environmental policy, and there is little doubt which measure should come first on this list—the introduction of environmental taxes or emissions licenses (and not much time should be wasted debating the relative advantages of the two solutions). In addition, prohibitions on poisonous chemicals are indispensable; but they cannot have such far-reaching consequences as generic taxes on the consumption of resources. Given the importance of egoism for organic nature in general, human nature in particular, and especially that of late modern human beings, the only system that has a chance is one that does not leave the person who acts morally in the position of the "dummy" (with regard to rational self-interest). In a society in which money has become the central medium of communication, environmental resources will be handled with care only if their use is correspondingly expensive. It remains true that the decision to introduce environmental taxes or licenses requires a moral impetus that transcends rational egoism, especially among older people who do not feel directly threatened by subsequent historical developments. But in times of crisis a not inconsiderable number of people are absolutely capable of such achievements, even if a daily appeal for sacrifice is obviously too much for the majority. The importance of stable mores lies in the fact that they create a framework within which selfish and moral actions are in a certain balance; and a society compatible with preserving the environment could make a far greater claim to the predicate of moral mores than present-day industrial societies. It is demanding to live in a time that sees through the deficient morals of its mores, but periods in which morality becomes especially necessary are also unusually exciting, and on the whole one should be grateful to live in an era that is one of the most interesting in human history.

---

30. See above, chap. 2, n. 47.

31. E. U. von Weizsäcker (1994), 144, and especially 143 ff., which I have largely followed. In the following pages I return again and again to this book.

What should be considered in introducing *environmental taxes* or *licenses?* The resources for which price solutions are to be given precedence over quota solutions can be determined only empirically; in chapter 7.3.3.2.1 we already saw that a mixture of the two approaches is desirable. Thus it is not impossible that even with high environmental taxes too much may still be demanded of the environment; in this case, they can be raised until the desired effect takes place, but that may be politically more difficult to achieve than a clear quota solution (particularly in the United States, where taxes are feared). But in favor of a price solution—that is, of environmental taxes—there is the existing incentive to remain below the acceptable threshold values; moreover, raising taxes is cheaper than determining whether threshold values have been maintained. In many cultures the state can still reliably raise only taxes on consumption; and environmental taxes are one—objectively especially legitimate—form of taxes on consumption. Taxes should be imposed on the use of energy and of the basic elements water, air, and land, as well as on the production of waste. In such a system there may well be overlaps, for instance, in the case of energy-related air pollution, but someone who uses two resources should pay for both of them. The advantage of environmental taxes over duties (which should not be abandoned, because of their greater precision in steering economic behavior, but which do not suffice to limit the destruction of the environment) consists in the fact that the latter, because they have to be used for specific purposes, turn out to be much lower than is necessary; for it is a question not of bringing in money in order to repair the environment but rather of anticipating and preventing environmental destruction. Ideally, environmental taxes should not raise the state's tax revenues at all—they have instead the task of steering economic behavior, and they will be most successful in attaining their goal if they bring in scarcely any additional revenue because the economy has shifted over to a more environment-friendly mode of production.

For the time being, however, one thing is necessary. The introduction of environmental taxes must result in the state having the same level of revenue, that is, it must be accompanied by a reduction in other kinds of taxes. This is all the more clear in that in Germany, for instance, the taxation of labor (especially in the form of non-wage labor costs such as pensions and healthcare) is counterproductively high; people should be deterred not from working but from destroying the environment. In order to give the economy time to adjust, the introduction of these taxes cannot be too sudden but must instead take place gradually. However, it does not take much acumen to see that the main problem of current politics in many countries consists in the fact that environmental taxes cannot even get off the ground, although they have been recognized for at least a decade as the most effective means of preventing destruction of the environment and although in the meantime all German political parties have endorsed them at least in theory. The failure to introduce such taxes should be assessed in the framework of a political ethic as a spurious omission on the part of the politicians responsible; the extent of the guilt involved in this omission corresponds to the enormity of its consequences. Resistance to environmental taxes does not stem solely from the captains of industry; the latter are not a homogeneous bloc in any case, and it is clear that under changed conditions many a branch of the economy that was less resource-intensive or was even able to offer a thriftier way dealing with resources would reap significant profits, while other branches would suffer great losses and might even disappear from the market. The resistance also proceeds from the labor unions representing employees in these branches of the economy, and from their political arm. In fact, in relation to environmental policy, the opposition between capital and labor, or, more precisely, between employers and employees, is relatively unimportant, since they can easily—especially in a time of rising unemployment—come to an agreement at the expense of the environment; the distribution of interests cuts straight across both camps. (The distribution of interests should be distinguished from moral insight, since of course a loser can also acknowledge that the new development is morally obligatory and work on its behalf. Such just persons are rare, but they exist.) On the whole, the more "intelligent" branches of the economy are likely to profit more from a system of environmental taxes; the tertiary sector will expand further at the expense of the secondary sector.

But is that not in conflict with social justice? Here we touch upon a fundamental objection that refers less to interest groups than to moral value convictions. There are two replies to this objection. One result of environmental taxes will certainly be—so long as it is not possible to reduce the environmental damage that is connected with use of cars—that people will drive less; and in a society with an unequal distribution of income, that means that only the rich will be able to afford a level of consumption of natural resources equivalent to that of present-day average citizens in industrial countries. This does not contradict the idea of an equal environmental space for everyone, since the corresponding certificates must be negotiable in order to achieve an optimal allocation; and it corresponds precisely to the current situation, in which wealthy people can also afford relatively more flights than poor people can. However, in the future both the poor and the rich will be able to afford fewer flights in absolute numbers—that is the goal of environmental taxes. Calling this "unjust" is a strange categorical mistake, since justice never determines the absolute level of consumption but has rather to do with determining relationships; and if one is looking for injustice in the current situation, one ought to focus on the intergenerational and international injustice that accompanies that level of consumption. To be sure, one must act on behalf of the weaker, but the weakest are currently the future generations and those living in absolute poverty in developing countries. Making all citizens in industrial countries, including the relatively poor, pay more for the waste they produce would surely be more just than exporting it to developing countries, where it damages the health of innocent people, and would be an incentive to avoid producing waste; analogously, making water more expensive—which would necessarily lead to distinguishing between drinking water and industrial water—would be more just than endangering ground water for coming generations. In addition, demands for justice between classes in one's own country remain; they should be dealt with in the framework of social policy, and there is no reason, after introducing environmental taxes, not to increase social and unemployment aid, pensions, and so forth, even if the increase may not go so far that the desired effects do not occur. However, one thing is clear: just as pursuing a social policy by means of certain tools of economic policy—such as subsidizing businesses that are justifiably not competitive—is a mistake, so it is absurd to pursue social policy by not developing a reasonable environmental policy. It is true that this is the easiest way to proceed because one need not make changes either in environmental policy or in social policy and thereby avoids tiring battles over distribution; but one should be ashamed to try to legitimate such procedures by references to justice— "justice" is far too noble a concept for such an abuse to be permissible.

However much changing the price structure is the crucial task facing an integrated economic, financial, and environmental policy, there remain plenty of individual problems that a concrete environmental policy must attack. They are all well known: the *stabilization of the world climate* and the *prevention of the depletion of the ozone layer,* which protects life from most ultraviolet radiation, are two of the main challenges that must be tackled by a responsible Earth politics, and they are interconnected, insofar as the destruction of stratospheric ozone could also have consequences for the climate, and as both threats have, in addition to differing causes, one common one, namely greenhouse gases.[32] It is of little help to point out that in the course of its history, and even of modern history, the Earth has already undergone several radical changes in its climate; if these changes are inevitable, we must accept them, but insofar as they are caused by humans, the human behavior that is responsible for them can also for the most part be changed, and if that can be done, we have a strong moral duty to do so (and this duty is absolutely a natural-law duty). Even if all predictions regarding the development of the world climate do not get beyond probabilities, and we are perhaps dealing with a decision under uncertainty, one thing is clear: the extent of the damage that threatens to result from the greenhouse effect is so great that even a far smaller probability or the maximin rule suffice to found a duty to act.[33] The moral weight of this duty is all the greater because the consequences of a further heating up of the atmosphere imperil especially the innocent—not only future generations but also, for instance, people living in island countries, whose contribution to carbon dioxide and methane emissions is negligible but who would be directly affected by a rise in sea level caused by the melting of ice at the poles, or the populations of countries closer to the equator, in which deserts would grow larger and fertile land would be destroyed. It can already be said that we should not forgo adaptive strategies such as thinking about protecting coastal areas and an orderly resettlement of millions of environmental refugees; for even if emissions could be reduced radically right away, the long-term consequences of emissions up to this point could not be prevented, and it is in addition not particularly likely that the required limits will go into effect any time soon. But it goes without saying that in addition to strategies of adaptation there must also be strategies of limitation, and indeed that the latter

---

32. On the following, see the contributions in P. J. Crutzen and M. Müller (1989), from which I have taken the crucial data.

33. Cf. R. Loske (1996), esp. 67 ff.

are more urgent morally; for even if a resettlement of environmental refugees succeeded (although given the nature of the human race, one should not be too surprised if
those responsible for the climatic catastrophe refused to receive their victims in a hos-
pitable manner), the latter would be deprived of their homelands, and that is certainly a
crime, especially if it occurs as a result of continuing a superfluous consumption. Without a very significant *reduction* in emissions the climatic *status quo* cannot be maintained,
and this is an interesting example of the peculiar interconnection of preserving and
changing: It is *conservative* goals that result in a radical *change;* the change in question is
partially a *return* to earlier conditions. The reduction of carbon dioxide emissions can
be attained only by consuming far less fossil fuels and by limiting clear-cutting, especially in the rainforests, which are in addition the sole habitat in which many species
can survive; to some extent, these emissions could be compensated for by massive re-
forestation programs. The production of CFCs must be prohibited, and the output of
methane strictly limited—for instance, by reducing the number of cattle around the
world and developing new methods of growing rice.

From what has been said it follows that *energy policy* is a crucial component of environmental policy.[34] Whereas for a long time the level of energy consumption was considered a parameter of progress, and economic growth depended on growth in the energy supply, today there is a consensus that the consumption of energy must be reduced.
Not only does the use of non-renewable resources at the current rate violate the rights
of future generations, but this is just as true of the environmental damage that goes
hand in hand, for example, with the consumption of fossil fuels (partly also because
drilling for oil and natural gas results in methane being emitted into the atmosphere).
What can be done about this? By far the most important way out of this dilemma is to
save energy. Only through increasing efficiency—for instance, by co-generation, higher
standards in housing construction more in accord with Swedish standards, or recycling
of materials produced by energy-intensive processes—can energy needs be significantly
reduced, even if, as was explained in chapter 9.1.3, only a combination of a sufficiency
revolution and an efficiency revolution can achieve the desired effect over the long term.
An increase in efficiency is encouraged by raising the price of energy, just as, conversely,
there can be no doubt that the electrical rates in force until recently in Germany—
which decreased with elevated consumption—encouraged wasting energy. In addition,
the economic structure of energy companies does not promote energy saving because
it is in the interest of every company to sell as much of the commodity produced as
possible (apart from the question of who is to pay for the costs of dismantling excess
capacity). It makes sense to separate energy producers from energy distributors, and
care should be taken that energy companies can make profits by providing services
in the area of energy saving; a decentralization and recommunalization of the energy
supply is desirable. In addition to savings, alternative energy sources must be sought—

---

34. In the following, I owe several insights to conversations with my friend Dr. Thomas Unnerstall.

sources that in recent decades have been indefensibly neglected to the advantage of nuclear energy. One should have no illusions: solar, wind, water, and geothermal energies are also connected with certain kinds of environmental damage, or at least would be if used to the extent that would be necessary in order to satisfy humanity's current thirst for energy; nevertheless, they do not raise the moral problems that are raised by using up non-renewable energy sources. So far as nuclear fission is concerned, its dangers have rightly been stressed again and again;[35] from the standpoint of responsibility for the future, the half-life of plutonium is already reason enough for concern, especially since a satisfactory solution to the problem of disposing of nuclear waste has still not been found, and the number of terrorists who would like to use radioactive waste for criminal ends is growing. Nuclear fusion avoids some of the problems of nuclear fission, but because they involve fewer risks, alternative energy sources and especially energy saving should be given priority over it. However, it is not easy to say whether in the current situation fossil fuel or nuclear energy is the greater evil. The threatening greenhouse effect makes some people regard nuclear energy as a comparatively minor evil because it is less likely to result in a global catastrophe than is the use of fossil fuels; and it is certainly correct that it is irresponsible to refuse to accept a lesser evil if the morally best alternative (energy saving) simply cannot be carried out. But in this case the factual situation is more complicated because the further development of nuclear energy (or, in Europe, the maintenance of the status quo) would lead to the best alternative being neglected; the pressure to save energy would disappear if people pinned their hopes on greater (or continued) reliance on nuclear energy. However, it would be a great misfortune if the ongoing conflict between supporters and opponents of nuclear energy resulted in carbon dioxide emissions continuing unabated; tactical concessions regarding nuclear energy, if they can be used to achieve major energy savings and funds for alternative energies, are more moral than the anti-nuclear fundamentalism that caused the collapse of discussions seeking to reach a consensus concerning energy policy in Germany.[36] Such discussions can succeed only if each side is able to think itself into the premises of the other—that is, if a discursively rather than a positionally oriented politics is practiced.[37] *Transportation* is one of the main sources of environmental destruction: "In Germany transport accounts for almost a quarter of total energy consumption, 60 per cent of nitric oxides pollution and 70 per cent of carbon monoxide pollution. . . . Road and other transport construction may be responsible for half the area covered by concrete, bitumen etc. and for some 80 per cent of the cutting through of natural habitats causing biotope shrinking and isolation dangerous to the survival of

---

35. Cf. K. M. Meyer-Abich and B. Schefold (1986).

36. Much the same holds for genetic engineering, which can be desirable even and especially on ecological grounds, if care is taken that it does not lead to a reduction of biodiversity and if at the same time public funds are made available to achieve targeted goals such as resistance to pests in ways that do not involve genetic engineering.

37. Cf. R. Ueberhorst (1986), esp. 219 ff.

many species."[38] Therefore in general restriction of the transportation of people and goods is necessary, especially since a not inconsiderable part of modern mobility has more to do with running away from oneself than with the pursuit of reasonable goals.[39] In terms of *Realpolitik*, however, much would already be gained if the forms of transportation changed. In particular, reducing motorized individual transportation, strictly limiting airplane flights, and shifting much of the transportation of people and goods from roads to rails are important short-term goals—a shift that becomes all the more urgent the more transportation of goods is liberalized. The central means of achieving this goal are, of course, making energy more expensive and taxing pollution of the environment (including noise pollution). Moving from taxes on vehicles to taxes on fuels (which must also include airplane fuel); using a leasing system, as was suggested in chapter 7.3.1.2, to include the fixed costs of a vehicle in the miles driven; imposing tolls, high parking fees, and limited prohibitions on driving private vehicles and trucks; making train travel and public transportation cheaper; and finally orientating road construction toward public transportation such as streetcars are further measures, some of which could be implemented on the communal level. It is a slap in the face to elementary principles of justice when tax breaks are given for mileage driven back and forth to work, which is a typical example of socializing costs at the same time that profits are privatized: someone who prefers a bigger and relatively less expensive home outside the city should not be able to escape the resulting transportation costs at public expense. Through a different kind of urban planning that did not so sharply distinguish the places where people live from those where they work, and through use of modern means of communication to increase the amount of work done at home, transportation related to work could be reduced. In the same way, a more settled leisure and vacation culture must be found; however, it presupposes a recovery of autonomy that cannot be achieved without basic changes in the educational system. Long-distance travel is obviously enjoyed by many people as a subtle form of experiencing power, to which people become more addicted in proportion as they cease to be well-balanced individuals.

So that taking vacations closer to home becomes more attractive, agriculture must change. It can only be considered extremely unfortunate that an economic sector that traditionally had a special closeness to nature has become one of the greatest sources of environmental destruction. The decline in biodiversity (the primary cause of which is modern agriculture and forestry), erosion, overgrazing, poisoning the water with fertilizers, liquid manures, and pesticides are the consequences of modern industrial agri-

---

38. E. U. von Weizsäcker (1994), 144.

39. Cf. Lucretius, *De rerum natura*, III 1057 ff.: "ut nunc plerumque videmus / quid sibi quisque velit nescire et quaerere semper / commutare locum, quasi onus deponere possit." ("as we see them now for the most part do, not knowing any one of them what he means and wanting ever change of place as though he might lay his burden down." Trans. H. A. J. Munro, 135.) See also Seneca's 28th letter to Lucilius.

culture, which is increasingly driving out small farms and the values connected with their way of life—consequences that in view of overproduction lack even the appearance of a justification. In fact, the theory that a consistent ecological agriculture could not feed everyone in Germany is false.[40] It is true that the consumption of meat would have to be reduced, but in view of the moral arguments in favor of vegetarianism (cf. chapter 4.4.1) and its advantages for individual health, this would hardly be a misfortune. Ecological agriculture would profit from the negative externalities of agricultural chemistry being internalized; in addition, express governmental supports for efforts to protect nature (for instance, cultivating rare varieties) and providing payment for good water, good air, and so forth are desiderata. To make small farms economically viable, a combined income policy is crucial: there should be an additional profit-making activity (such as housing vacationers). In fact, it is undeniable that in the current situation cities, which were once the centers of higher cultural development, particularly metropolises, have become almost parasitical on the countryside. "Water, air, food, space for dumping rubbish and for recreation, raw materials and biological diversity are all products of the land from which the city benefits, and for which it pays practically nothing."[41] It is true that the introduction of environmental taxes would change this situation a great deal, but Weizsäcker rightly wonders whether far-reaching compensation mechanisms would not be necessary in addition to environmental taxes. In any case, in the current situation, and especially in developing countries, promoting rural areas is a crucial task of environmental policy. The smaller number of stimuli to which people are exposed in the countryside as compared with the city also indicates its importance—for the health of a society is endangered by excessive consumption not only of material goods and social relationships but also of intellectual goods, as the bucolic poetry of the ancients already rightly perceived.

9.3.2. Economic Policy and Social Policy

It does not fall within the competence of a philosopher to make concrete recommendations regarding economic policy. But common sense can recognize which leading ideas must underlie a moral economic policy at the present time. We have already noted that making the economy compatible with the preservation of the environment constitutes the central task of the twenty-first century; in this context what is crucial is to distance ourselves from the idea that the GNP is the ultimate justifying ground of economic policy and to base our calculations on net economic welfare. It is no less important to accept the *challenge of globalization*. It would be unjust (and economically counterproductive) if industrial states in the West, which owe much of their prosperity

---

40. Cf. A. Bechmann (1993).
41. E. U. von Weizsäcker (1994), 154.

to the export of their commodities throughout the world, were to take refuge in protectionist reactions because they are no longer the economic center of the world. Such reactions can be justified by foreign environmental standards that deviate still further from what is morally obligatory than do those at home; but this holds for lower standards of social welfare only if they contradict fundamental principles of justice, as in the case of the exploitation of child labor—otherwise, both egoism and justice favor employing the poorer people. To be sure, a worldwide unification of social policy is desirable; flanking the common market with a common social policy was an important step in the history of the European Union. But so long as there is no will to establish worldwide social aid, it is false to believe that the particularly high standards of social welfare in Germany, for instance, are inalienable human rights. It may very well be the case that these standards could be funded only during a time in which Germans had it unusually good because of singular structural conditions in the world economy and in domestic politics—conditions that are not likely to recur, at least so long as a relationship between performance and rights to positive benefits different from the current one has not been constructed. It is clear that some social privileges must be given up on purely domestic policy grounds. With the increase in life expectancy, the working life must also be proportionally extended if people want their pensions to remain as high; in absolute numbers, a gain in years of work-free life would remain, but even this cannot be considered guaranteed with sharply decreasing birth rates, for it is obvious that justice to the younger generation will not be done if the solution is always to raise pension contributions rather than to reduce pensions. It would be desirable to establish legally such conditional norms from the outset in order to avoid painful conflicts in individual cases. Unless non-wage labor costs such as payments for pensions and healthcare are limited, German business cannot remain competitive, and there are not sufficient incentives to hire new employees; however, without a functioning economy and a certain number of people working, a long-term social policy is inconceivable, for it is obvious that one can distribute only what exists to be distributed.

It is obvious that Western European welfare states are living beyond their means—consider only the extent of their *public debt,* which violates the rights of future generations to the same extent as environmental destruction, and the share of welfare expenditures in the state budget. Public debt cannot be reduced by further raising taxes but only by reducing state expenditures—in all sectors, including the most expensive one, that is, in the area of social welfare. Furthermore, the state, like a business, must reduce the size of its bureaucracy and make it cheaper and more efficient; there should be government officials only in the core area of the state performing sovereign functions, and even they should make their own contributions to their old age care. The state will have to cease its involvement in many public enterprises; after the postal service and the railroads, universities should also be largely privatized. As was mentioned in chapter 7.3.1.2, there is no "absolute" maximum tax rate; should great, directly experienceable environmental catastrophes occur, raising taxes would be unavoidable and would meet with acceptance. But anyone who wants to introduce environmental taxes today must decrease other taxes; raising existing taxes at the same time is unthinkable. However, everything possible should be done to prevent tax evasion, which in Germany amounts to (at least) tens of billions of euros a year (not to mention a country like Italy). Since experts agree that hiring additional tax auditors would be economically advantageous, it is remarkable that this has not yet been done; a role may be played in this not only by the—sometimes counterproductive—equalization of revenue and costs among the German federal states that does not always make it desirable for a state to have a higher tax income at its disposal but also by a certain accommodation of tax evaders for which one can have only a little understanding, and not only in times of tight budgets.

A *welfare state that has gotten out of hand,* and which seeks to satisfy the desires of the most diverse clienteles—which, unlike rights to freedom from interference, have no immanent limits—has no future; indeed, insofar as its expenditures are guided, not by recognizable principles of justice, but instead by the power of the corresponding clienteles in the market of votes, it actually undermines the substance of the constitutional state, which depends upon the *generality* of the laws. In a work that can claim to be one of the first to remind us of the state's fundamental ecological tasks, Forsthoff (1971), who very clearly perceived the relationship of tension between the constitutional state and the welfare state, even if he sometimes exaggerated, raised the question of the extent to which the state was still capable of limiting industrial society at all after it had contracted such manifold dependencies on the latter. In fact, the state can recover its scope of action and concentrate on major problems only if it shakes off responsibilities that are not really its own. If the United States had a social welfare policy at the level of Germany's, it would immediately cease to be able to play a central role in world politics because such a policy is associated with an extreme political immobility. In addition, to the extent that they are triggered by identity crises, for instance, some social problems cannot be dealt with by legal means, especially by transferring monies, at least not directly; indifference to social problems ("soziale Kälte") can be fought only through institutions with an emotional background, such as the family and the church, and those who have weakened these institutions should complain about the new climate only if they at the same time recognize their own mistakes.

This does not mean that according to natural law there are no rights to positive benefits in the narrower sense. On the contrary, precisely because they exist for every person, the welfare state must concentrate on people who are truly in need, and even in its own country (not to mention internationally) it can do so only if it does not undertake too many tasks at once. The first task of a welfare state must be *the battle against absolute poverty in its own country,* and it is depressing when a rich country like the United States is not willing or able to do so—even if it is admittedly not easy to deal with people who have gotten into trouble, for instance by abusing drugs (including alcohol). But there must continue to be an incentive to return to the working world (for instance, by cutting off aid or negative income tax credits if suitable work is refused), and it would certainly be worth considering a symbolic "taxation" of even the poorest people in rich countries in order to promote development projects in poor countries, so as to increase the awareness that in rich countries like Germany even the unemployed are better off economically than many hard-working people in developing countries. However, one should start limiting the income of the socially weakest only when the special privileges granted the economically stronger—for instance, in the form of subsidies, arbitrary tax deductions, and bureaucratic prerogatives—have been eliminated. In particular, it is self-evident that in times in which saving is a moral duty, representatives of the people must set a good example: Raising legislative salaries in such times is not a good idea (just as abolishing property and net worth taxes, for which there are certainly good arguments, should not be done at a time when social benefits are being cut). The counter-argument that legislative salaries account for only a tiny percentage of the state budget and that they have not been raised for a long time is misleading because it ignores the example-setting function of the state elites; even if an increase were objectively justified, in certain situations it should be forgone in order to achieve political credibility for the reduction in expenditures (which has been begun).

In Western European countries, *unemployment* is increasingly becoming a problem that cannot be solved even through economic growth, and these countries will have to resign themselves to being unable to do anything about a certain part of this problem. Nonetheless, because of its inflationary effect, full employment is not always only a blessing; but even if it is a higher good than monetary stability, one should not accept a higher rate of inflation if in the long run it cannot change the rate of unemployment because over time, the responsible economic actors lose the money illusion—the elements of Keynesianism that rely on belief in the money illusion are dead. (The deepest reason for this is to be found in the ambivalence of cratology discussed in chapter 5.2.2) Technological developments decrease the quantity of work (at least if one is thinking of many traditional kinds of work), and producing short-lived and even unneeded commodities solely in order to create work is not an acceptable counter-measure within the framework of an ecological market economy. In addition, giving up technically possible labor savings is seldom a satisfactory solution and may even be economically damaging if competitors do not do the same thing. People should work in order to satisfy reasonable needs, not maintain a given standard of consumption or technology in order to justify work. No matter how important it may be, even a general limitation of the number of hours worked—naturally, with a corresponding reduction in salary and non-wage labor costs—is not a solution to all problems, since certain jobs cannot be shared, and increasing the number of its employees can considerably alter the specific quality of a firm. Hence the expansion of the service sector should be promoted all the more; for example, it is absolutely reasonable to make the cost of domestic help tax-deductible, for jobs are thereby created. Moreover, it is crucial to offer more flexible jobs, for many people who have jobs would like to work less if only they could. A world in which many people work part-time not only is not necessarily a worse one but can be even better than a world with full employment, insofar as basic needs are met and being temporarily out of work is not felt to be a stigma. Today, unemployment is a problem of prestige at least as much as an economic problem, and much would be gained if there were more respect for unpaid work or for contemplative activities again. The high esteem for work as an end in itself is not an anthropological constant; it emerged at a certain point in history, in which it was indispensable for getting industrialization underway, and will presumably become less important in a later phase of history. If in certain situations it is the state's task to encourage its citizens to do productive work, in another it can become its duty to encourage them do other things; but it will be crucial to develop leisure activities that are both meaningful and cheap. Phases of gainful work should alternate with phases of unpaid work—although that will mean lowering the level of consumption as well. One may mock those who derive their identity from what they have only if one has already made the necessary change in one's own behavior. It would be good if there were today a type of politician who already represented the kind of consumer behavior that will be generally established in an ecologically adapted society—one who rode a bicycle to parliament, for instance.

However, two things are clear. First of all, even in an ecological state, and especially in the transitional phase, there is *a huge amount of meaningful work* to do. Second, in times of radical economic changes—as at the beginning of industrial capitalism and probably also now, since the introduction of an ecological market economy is on the agenda—a *major difference in the distribution of income* is probably inevitable because only a few people have the ability to adapt to the rapidly changing structural conditions. This adaptation is difficult enough, and it is counterproductive if it is made more difficult from the outset by the pressure of extensive redistributions. After the new economic structure has been stabilized, one can and indeed should make even stronger efforts to overcome the newly emerged differences. At the beginning, however, the state must encourage those who, as dynamic entrepreneurs (in Schumpeter's sense), discover market niches and run personal risks, whether it does so through incentive programs (for instance, by offering venture capital) or by passing an insolvency law that makes it easier to get a new footing after a failure. Without a good educational and further training policy, especially for young people, adaptation to the world market and the creation of new jobs cannot be attained. In view of East Asian progress in computer technology, telecommunications, industrial robotics, and semiconductors, states that want to keep up with East Asia or simply avoid too great a dependency on it must pursue a more resolute technology policy. If this involves environmental technologies, that will be expressly welcomed; if it involves environmentally neutral technologies, the higher tax revenues they produce can at least be incorporated into environmental policy. For environmental policy is expensive. If industrial societies are successfully transformed, in an ecological state there will still be differences in income, and even a kind of luxury that is compatible with preserving the environment. But to the extent that it is expressed in the form of the possession of art works or in using especially exquisite intellectual services, for example, there is nothing to object to in it from an ecological point of view, and from a socio-political point of view (but not from the point of view of individual ethics), it should be accepted if it is the flipside of special achievements for the common good, as for instance in the case of the discovery of environmental technologies.

9.3.3. Domestic Policy in the Narrower Sense

An intelligent ecological policy in economic policy can learn much from the libertarian critique of an attitude, based on a crude understanding of social justice, that the state should provide everything one needs. Likewise, it must internalize in domestic policy in the narrower sense the conservative conviction that the state cannot give up the means of negative sanctions and that it must defend its monopoly on the use of force. Thus in a world in which international crime organizations control a significant part of economic life and an increasing part of state bureaucracy, *fighting crime* is one of the state's most important duties. In view of German history, it is understandable that there is a deep mistrust with regard to state force; but it remains odd for someone in the current historical situation to be more afraid of a democratic constitutional state than of gangs who care nothing about human life and a fortiori the interests of future generations. Much the same goes for terrorism; it is curious when the public is more upset about a terrorist killed in a shootout with police than about the police officers he has murdered (however unrelentingly one must investigate the terrible suspicion the terrorist was killed after he had been disarmed). In states like Russia, Colombia, and Italy, in which the fight against crime must have first priority, it can already be waged only with difficulty because of the close-knit penetration of the state apparatus by Mafia-like structures on whose financial support almost everyone somehow relies (which makes it possible to blackmail even relatively decent politicians); therefore it is all the more urgent to fight them at the outset and to use all necessary means to prevent the spread of such criminal groups. The police must not be more poorly equipped in terms of technology and personnel than these groups are; and the extent of the threat absolutely permits the limitation, under judicial supervision, of basic rights such as the secrecy of telephone conversations, not to mention the secrecy of bank accounts.

It is obvious that the emergence of an area outside the law represents a particularly great burden on the economically weaker classes; someone who lives in a suburban house and drives a car can afford to be less concerned about the condition of many subway stations in modern metropolises than are those who live in the cities and are dependent on regular use of subways. A *vigorous domestic policy* is therefore also a matter of *social justice*, and since it puts a lighter load on the state treasury than a welfare policy that has gone out of control, there is no reason to forgo it. In most societies, and especially in those with economic problems, referring to criminals who get off scot-free is an effective way of winning the votes of persons who normally draw their self-respect from the legality of their behavior, since they are denied subtler intellectual or pseudo-intellectual pleasures; it can be abused by political parties that care little about the constitutional state. Thus it is all the more important to remove this theme from public debate by seriously addressing it. It is alarming, for example, when criminal prosecution of foreigners must be abandoned because the fear of being murdered leads interpreters to refuse to serve in court. In addition, early release of prisoners should under no circumstances be at the expense of the citizens. The expulsion of asylum seekers who have committed a crime is just if they are not threatened by death or torture in their homelands; one forfeits one's right to hospitality in a country whose legal system one is not willing to respect.

However, it is obvious that the problem of criminality cannot be resolved by repression alone. It is crucial to prevent the recruitment of young people who maintain the traditions of criminal organizations. Since one of the most important causes of criminal behavior is the idea that acquiring certain material goods is more important than abiding by the law, one must wonder whether a world in which enormous sums are spent on getting people to buy all sorts of silly things at the same time that there is no advertising for the intrinsic worth of moral principles, and in which sex and violence receive ample opportunities for development in the media, is not co-responsible for the rise of criminality—in a highly sexualized society the number of sex crimes will presumably increase. If a society establishes a consensus that the sole ground for obeying the law is the fear of negative sanctions, then this means that the weaknesses of the state can be unscrupulously exploited; indeed, even if there is a relatively great probability that one will be caught, in the framework of such a value order committing a crime can be a way of proving to oneself and to one's friends that one has courage or at least a willingness to take risks. Without a broad consensus that crimes are also violations of the moral law, the growth of criminality is inevitable, and today one must ask oneself with concern what social forces could rebuild such a consensus after the crisis in the family and religions. According to Montesquieu, if virtue and the sense of honor are lacking, the alternative to anarchy is the state form whose *principle* is fear—that is, despotism.[42]

The *drug problem* cannot be solved without what might be called a policy that tries to communicate meaning (*Sinnpolitik*).[43] Someone who finds nothing in reality that is worth loving, and does not even recognize a logic that reflects a higher reason, will want to escape this reality, and drugs are an effective means of doing so. To be sure, one can and should also try to deal with the supply side of the drug problem, but given the existence of individual sovereign states, it is not clear how the United States, for instance, is supposed to prevent coca from being grown in Peru and processed in Colombia. The construction of other branches of the national economy should be supported, even if the profits can hardly compete with those to be made from drugs (and even if these profits go far more to processors and middlemen than to the producers); and the extradition of drug dealers from countries that are not in a position to prosecute them to efficient constitutional states like the United States is a useful means of pressure. But so long as the United Nations has no international drug police force that can intervene in individual countries, efforts will have to focus primarily on the demand side and will probably have to be content with modest successes. Whether a legalization of drugs (which would have to be, of course, distributed in a controlled manner) would be a lesser evil than a higher level of criminality and an additional danger to the health of drug addicts (for example,

---

42. *Esprit des lois* 3.9 (1748; 1:150 f.).
43. On the following, cf. M. Wöhlcke (1996), 102 ff.

using dirty needles), which seem to be the consequences of the current situation, is not easy to decide, and no general answer can be given to this question. In chapter 7.2.2.2 it was shown that there is no right to harm oneself or to encourage others to harm themselves, and it goes without saying that it makes sense to use vigorous punitive measures to prevent the consumption of drugs from getting started—Singapore's drug policy is correct, apart from the imposition of capital punishment. But once drug consumption has reached the extent it has in many Western industrial countries, legalization may prevent a greater evil, and the political forces that have to enforce the prohibition of drugs could be devoted to more urgent tasks; state taxes on drug consumption could prevent the profits of the drug trade from going exclusively to criminal organizations. To be sure, at least in the short run more people would become addicted to drugs, but that does not necessarily mean that more would die. In addition, the hunger of an African child and the misery of environmental refugees deserve more compassion than a person who is responsible for destroying himself by using drugs.

Even if referring to the afflictions of late modern societies provides no moral excuse for criminals, one should certainly acknowledge that the *moral credibility of a legal order* is significantly damaged if it violates fundamental natural-law principles. For example, the fact that a large part of the profits from the trade in drugs and weapons ends up in rich industrial states, and that respectable financial centers such as Hong Kong and Switzerland help launder the money involved,[44] considerably reduces the morals of these states' indignation about drug imports; fences should not complain about thieves. Similarly, the fecklessness of current politics with regard to massive environmental damage necessarily diminishes respect for positive law. It is naive to expect young people, who regularly hear on television that in the course of their lives terrible environmental catastrophes will probably still occur, to show great respect for objects of legal protection that their state shows itself incapable of protecting in the future. That does not mean that television ought not to communicate such information, for the latter is not unfounded, and without such reports a change will certainly not take place. But the spread of an apocalyptic mood cannot promote obedience to the law because the latter depends on belief in the long-term social effectiveness of law. Indeed, it cannot be denied that many actions of civil disobedience, such as are committed by environmental protection movements, for instance, are absolutely justified morally—they remain within the bounds of proportionality and sometimes have a far quicker effect than tedious negotiations between politicians and interest groups, which are obviously more afraid of arousing negative echoes in the media than of that toothless old lion, the state. But the anxious question remains, when such morally defensible violations of the law will be replaced by actions that are no longer morally defensible—indeed, when a resolute minority will finally arrive at the view that a violent overthrow of the government is morally justified. That time may be nearer than we think.

---

44. Cf. R. T. Naylor (1987).

In order to prevent this kind of development, constitutional policy is one of the most important requirements. The construction of an organ that articulates the interests of the coming generations is the most urgent of these constitutional changes that could lead to an ecological state, even more urgent than giving (in a country like Germany) corporate groups working for environmental protection the right to institute legal action. If staffed with people who have great professional and personal authority, it could play a significant integrative role, for the disrespect that a large part of the population feels for politicians has reached a dangerous degree. People talk of "confidence-building measures" mainly in relation to foreign policy, but in most Western countries, *confidence-building measures* are urgently needed domestically as well, despite or precisely because of the democratic structure, which is a form of political self-rule: The distrust of politicians is a form of disguised distrust of oneself. It is not going too far to suggest that in the not too distant future, the politicians who will be trusted by the people (if not by their contemporary colleagues) will be those who speak very directly about the people's co-responsibility for environmental problems, instead of currying their favor and adapting to their views, and who openly talk about the limits of their power. Honesty, which can certainly be accompanied by rudeness; an eye for the essential; didactic abilities; a certain personal charisma; and an uninhibited recognition of the fact that every society, even and especially a complex one, needs elites will probably soon once again be prized as qualities, even if they were long neglected.

Integration is all the more important for Western industrial countries to the degree that they will inevitably become multicultural structures. It is depressing that Germany still has not reached consensus about an adequate immigration law; but a country that has de facto become an immigrants' country needs an explicit integration policy, which has obviously not been formulated because the facts are not acknowledged. In chapter 7.3.3.3.7, the criteria to be considered in granting citizenship were discussed; an uncontrolled acceptance of immigrants would make as little sense as rejecting the immigration on which the member states of the European Union are all the more dependent in that without it, their social security systems cannot be saved because of the decline in the population.[45] It is true that the state must contribute far more extensively to the high costs of raising children (which consist partly in a lack of income for a parent busy raising the child), and childless individuals must be much more heavily taxed, since in the future support payments for people no longer able to work will have to be provided by these children;[46] but since in an extremely individualistic society even the non-economic costs of lost life opportunities caused by children are considered high, to be realistic one has to assume that even with greater state support for families, the decline in population can only be moderated. This only makes the promotion of immigration more indispensable, no matter how little it may by itself suffice, even if immigrants are

---

45. On the following, see H. Birg's outstanding essay (1995).

46. Such a policy promoting domestic population growth should be combined with support for population control measures in over-populated developing countries.

mainly of the right age, to finance the social security systems at the current level. That the trust in life shown by giving birth to children is less common in rich peoples than in poorer ones provides food for thought; however, in view of the fact that the growth of the world population is the greater problem, from a global standpoint the European development is not a catastrophe. In any case, if globalization already means that the competition among states has increased, the immigration issue means that now states are competing for the most gratified residents and future citizens.

Nonetheless, as was already said, this only makes a resolute integration policy all the more important. Integration into a multicultural society is thus a *two-sided* affair. Naturally, the immigrant must first assimilate the culture of the country that has taken him in, its language and especially the spirit of its laws. (For this purpose, giving immigrants a right to vote in local elections even before they have been granted citizenship may be useful.) But the host country must also learn something about the culture of the immigrants in order not to be alienated by their difference and in order to distinguish more easily between what is in fact not compatible with the substance of a constitutional state and what is worthy of respect. A certain elasticity in one's own mores—as in the United States—makes the integration of others considerably easier. One should expect that in the foreseeable future, some metropolises in the European Union will have more practicing Muslim inhabitants than practicing Christians; and that is not a bad thing. It would be irresponsible to assume, without any concrete debate, that a religion such as Islam, with its tradition of religious tolerance (in comparison to which the Christian Middle Ages do not cut a very good figure), is fundamentally incompatible with the principles of the constitutional state, tolerance, and respect for human life. In any case it is shameful how little information German schools offer regarding Turks, the largest group of foreigners living in the country. Z. Şenocak rightly remarks that a multicultural society cannot emerge without promoting bilingualism and interest in the cultures of other peoples, or without granting Islamic religion the same legal status as Christianity, and he puts forward the plausible thesis that the deepest cause of German difficulties in perceiving Turkish culture is—German self-hatred.[47] For one thing is surely true: a culture that does not love itself cannot love another, any more than an individual can.

As we saw in chapter 3.1.1, given human nature, fundamental political changes in direction can be achieved only if in addition to idealists, who are indispensable, there is a large group of people whose egoistic interests would be promoted by the change sought. What is this latter group in the case of the transition to an ecological state? It was already noted that wholly new alliances no longer based on class membership are possible and necessary in order to achieve an ecological turnaround. A relatively homogenous group offers itself as a driving force for such a change: *youth.* The future of every society depends upon this most innovative group; it is of special importance for a society that has to come to terms with its ability to deal with the future in a historically unprecedented

---

47. (1993), 74, 86.

way. For ecologically committed politicians, the ministry of youth is almost as important as the economics ministry. But dealing with contemporary youth is not an easy task. Ortega y Gasset already discerned in the twentieth century's cult of youth a symbolic expression of its basic problem—the infantile demand for more and more rights without recognizing the corresponding duties.[48] Torn between the temptations of a lifestyle that is unique in world history, so far as opportunities for consumption, freedom of movement, economic independence, and opportunities for self-realization, as well as existential loneliness, are concerned, on one hand, and on the other, the oppressive burden of anxiety about a future for whose gloomier aspects it can hardly escape a co-responsibility because of its own way of life, modern youth is an explosive mixture of overestimation of itself and despondency, of cynicism and a need for warmth, a mixture that does not always arouse respect but always arouses pity. Even if it is more natural to respect the older generation than coming ones because people are well aware that they will themselves someday be part of the older generation, it can very well be that the feeling of having been ignored, as well as the extensive isolation of generations from one another, will end up producing a terrible violation of the rights of the older generation. Giving young people an inner compass to guide them through the turmoil of our time is not the only task of educational policy, but it is certainly the central one.

9.3.4. Educational and Research Policy

Even if in coming decades questions of sheer survival will repeatedly arise, and in both domestic and foreign policy the system of negative sanctions will acquire an importance that we would have preferred to limit to past history, and even if without a sober understanding of economic policy successful politics will become impossible, the

---

48. "Esta esquividad para toda obligación explica, en parte, el fenómeno, entre ridiculo y escanadaloso, de que se haya hecho en nuestros dias une plataforma de la 'juventud' como tal. Quizá no ofrezca nuestro tiempo rasgo mas grotesco. La gentes, cómicamente, se declaran 'jovenes' porque han oído que el joven tiene más derechos que obligaciones, ya que puede demorar el cumplimiento de esta hasta la calendas griegas de la madurez. Siempre el joven, como tal, se ha considerado eximido de *hacer o haber hecho* ya hazañas. Siempre ha vivido de credito. . . . Pero es estupefaciente que ahora lo tomen estos como un derecho efectivo, precisamente para atribuirse todos los demás que pertenecen sólo a quien haya hecho ya algo" (1930; 199 f.). ("This evasion of all obligation explains in part the phenomenon, half ridiculous and half disgraceful, of the promulgation of the platform of 'Youth,' of youth per se. Perhaps our times offer no spectacle more grotesque. Almost comically, people call themselves 'young,' because they have been told that youth has more rights than obligations, since the fulfillment of obligations can be postponed until the Greek calends of maturity. Youth has always considered itself exempt from *doing* or *having done* great deeds or feats. It has always lived on credit. . . . It is astounding to behold that nowadays these juniors take it as a definitive right precisely in order to lay claim to all the other rights which belong only to those who have already accomplished something." Trans. A. Kerrigan, 173–174.)

real problem of modern society is intellectual, indeed, ultimately religious. The failed model of development whose imitation throughout the world would bring catastrophe on the Earth is based on false normative and false descriptive assumptions, and without changing these assumptions a fundamental transformation in policy is inconceivable. Changing these assumptions is only a necessary, not a sufficient, condition for that transformation because human behavior is not determined solely by theoretical assumptions. But without a change in the goals of research and education in modern societies, a political change of direction is impossible. Only children who have been educated differently from the majority today will support a policy that promises them something other than a further increase in the GNP. Only people who care more about saving, if not their souls, at least about a hard-to-define functional equivalent thereof, than about conspicuous consumption will voluntarily refrain from environmental destruction before nature's revenge forces them to do so. If one considers how long it took for the ecological dangers of modern industrialization to be recognized by official science, and how hesitantly society has reacted to this recognition, then one cannot avoid having the impression that the scientific system of knowledge in modern societies is not appropriate to their needs. What are the main flaws in the current educational and scientific systems, and what can be done about them?

Schools transmit an abundance of knowledge that has little to do with the central problems that young people have to solve in their lives; as a result, they neglect theoretical and practical abilities that will be urgently needed in order to prevent late modernity from destroying itself. Formally, *educational policy* must first of all acknowledge that individual students have very different talents and that an educational system that pursues a policy based on the smallest common denominator of intelligence does justice neither to the individual nor to the population as a whole. The strategy of making it harder for gifted children to develop their talents not only deprives them of some of the deepest experiences of happiness that are granted human beings but also deprives society of intellectual achievements that would be in the interest of all. Instead of concentrating, out of envy, on the question of how to prevent the development of particularly evident gifts, one should think about what each individual's potential consists in, for the number of different talents is large. Certainly it serves the common good when the state fosters especially gifted children, and to that extent the use of public funds for this purpose is justified. But it would already help if the state at least did not keep them from being fostered through an excessively homogeneous educational policy. Alongside public schools, private schools must be maintained and even further developed; and in particular, schools whose teachers set a moral example, which is ultimately in the interest of all, should at least have a claim to extensive state support, if one does not go even further to institute a system of school vouchers that offers parents broad opportunities for choice without putting children of poorer families at a disadvantage. In any case, it makes no sense to claim that social justice can be promoted by decreasing scholastic and academic standards every year and practicing "grade inflation"—that is as inappropriate an educational policy tool as minting money in order to resolve social problems.

So far as the content of school education goes, the following emphases may be mentioned. All pupils should become proficient in speaking and writing their own language; learn English as the global *lingua franca* (starting, as much as possible, in elementary school); train their formal intelligence through mathematics; discover the special position of the modern within the historically realized periods; gain a certain familiarity with the fundamental principles of their own legal and economic order, without which a constructive critical attitude is impossible; learn about nature, of which human beings are a part (with biology and ecology as the foci), and about the human body; and, finally, acquire an elementary understanding of the global problems that the twenty-first century has to solve. On the basis of this knowledge of *instrumental rationality,* the knowledge specific to various professions should later be developed. At the same time, the schools must also communicate *value judgments;* they should, in the naive and apt words of the Bavarian Constitution, "not only communicate knowledge and skills, but also shape hearts and characters."[49] The shaping of character, which cannot be achieved without discipline, can take place only partly in a theoretical way; respect for personally exemplary teachers, who should be given priority in hiring, and gratifying socialization experiences with schoolmates—experiences that can be facilitated by the class group—are more important than subtleties of argumentation in producing the balance of autonomy and readiness to help others that characterizes a morally valuable person. Physical education and cultivating a sense for the beautiful in classes on art and music are also helpful. Artists who make the problems of a time experienceable in a particularly vivid way and demonstrate moral alternative actions should be given priority; thus Dickens deserves credit for making a significant contribution to the solution of the social problem by opening people's eyes and hearts to it, and a Dickens who could do the same for the environmental problem would certainly be a blessing for humanity.

Given the importance of *religions* emphasized in chapter 7.3.3.2.2, there is much to be said for incorporating religious instruction into the public schools, where this is constitutionally possible; in view of equal legal rights for all religions, this means that in many European schools instruction in Islamic religion should also be offered—this could cut the ground from under fundamentalist Koranic schools, and it would make an important contribution to an integration policy in the sense defined above. For students who belong to no religion, there can of course be no requirement to study any religion at all, but that does not mean that substitute instruction in a philosophical discipline such as ethics should be limited to them, since acquiring argumentative competence in moral questions is so important that it would be a great shame if students were given an opportunity to acquire it only if they forwent religious instruction. In fact, instruction in philosophy should be offered to a greater degree, at least in secondary schools. However, this cannot involve merely the communication of formal skills; young people whose concept of God acquired in their childhoods (if they have one at all) is

---

49. Art. 131 I. Cf. also the list of educational goals in Art. 131 II.

deeply shaken by the encounter with modern natural and historical sciences (and also with historical theology, for instance), which is not without the most serious consequences for their spiritual stability and for the morals of the mores of human cultures, should learn that there is also a philosophical concept of God that can "sublate" the earlier one. In an age when traditional value systems are obviously in difficulty, much would be gained if children and young people were given an orientation that did not depend on recognizing a revealed scripture. The movement of so-called "children's philosophy" has strikingly shown that children ask philosophical questions early on and that they are prevented from pursuing these questions more by social structures than by the nature of the child's mind.[50]

Certainly, in a society whose knowledge is constantly growing, the ability to acquire knowledge should be fostered as much as learning concrete educational contents. But the formalistic pedagogy that maintains that formal skills can be learned without applying them to concrete subjects is wrong. On graduating from high school, a student should have a content-related knowledge that will probably survive further developments and allow him to distinguish the essential from the inessential. This latter ability is what matters in a society whose main problem is an *overproduction of information* — this is the real problem of the so-called "information society," whose technological possibilities should absolutely be utilized but can be utilized fruitfully only if people are trained to have a sense for the rank order of information. Thus, to give one example, something has gone wrong if a high school graduate can remember all sorts of data about elephants and algae but has not understood that plants are autotrophic and animals are heterotrophic and that this has important consequences for their structure. In the higher grades, learning additional foreign languages must play an important part. Europe will not grow together if its elites cannot converse with each other in several languages, and since languages, after their basic grammatical structures have been mastered, are best learned in a country where they are spoken, educational exchange programs should be intensified, so long as the students involved already have the personal maturity required to get along in a foreign culture. So far as *ancient languages* are concerned, not everyone should be expected to learn them; but is important for the identity of Western culture that a sufficiently large number of people still know them. One can hardly imagine what a turning point in the European educational tradition is represented by the fact that today fewer and fewer people can read Thucydides, Plato, Euclid, Cicero, Vergil, and Livy in the original; from the fifteenth to the twentieth centuries, familiarity with these authors was part of the central core of Western education. It is in itself already disturbing when traditions that have endured for hundreds of years are dismantled in two decades, but there are also content-related grounds for clinging to that tradition. Antiquity, often in an idealized form, has always been a counter-image to modernity, and an inner distance with regard to modernity can hardly be constructed

---

50. Cf. Nora's letters in N. K. and V. Hösle (1996).

without such a counter-image (which is infinitely more concrete than the utopian fantasies of an excited morality). Fostering such a distance should be the concern of movements that are critical of modernity. However, it must be admitted that modern classical philology is chiefly to blame for the fact that a classical education has largely disappeared from school curricula; its special status can be maintained only if it tries to communicate normative knowledge, and if representatives of modern classical philology no longer feel capable of doing so, or if they do it at a very low level, they should not be surprised if ancient authors are no longer read. It is not what Plato and Thucydides meant that deserves our interest, but rather their contribution to our understanding of the world in which we live. This contribution is still important, and for that reason it is better to study the classics than to busy oneself with all the changing fashions in the culture industry. Integrating their contribution into one's own worldview, and personally appropriating, for instance, the basic principles of Platonic ethics and even giving it concrete form in an ecological way of life suitable to one's time, deserves to be called education (*Bildung*) in the emphatic sense of the word.

But doesn't this conception of education stand in contradiction to a strong trend in contemporary science's self-concept? The answer is "yes," but this is more an objection to contemporary science than to this concept of education. In fact, every intelligent *policy regarding research* must recognize that in our century a revolution in the concept of scientific knowledge has taken place, which has not left scientific institutions unimpaired. The institutions in which the system of scientific knowledge manifests itself differ considerably in the various countries of the world; universities in the United States are obviously superior to those in Germany, and they will further extend their advantage if German universities are not reformed on the American model (also because good German scientists will not reject interesting offers from the United States). Nonetheless, university reformers who think they identify the key problem of the German scientific system in failed institutional structural conditions are short-sighted. The problem lies deeper; the institutional defects only increase the difficulties that arise from changes in the concept of scientific knowledge—changes that in 1936 already moved Husserl to speak of a "crisis of European sciences." This crisis now rages everywhere, even in countries where the institutions are significantly better than they are in Germany. The problem of the modern system of knowledge is essentially that it is doomed to an ever-increasing *specialization* that on one hand is a condition for acquiring new knowledge but on the other hand only too easily leads to a loss of orientation with regard to the place of the specific problem with which one is concerned in knowledge as a whole. From a certain point on, specialization can be counterproductive, for only the determination of this place can lead to a correct assessment of the scope of a research project and an understanding of its meaning. A major researcher must combine breadth of interests and precision in his own work; both requirements can be adequately met only if one has an eye for what is essential, and one can have this only by sovereignly ignoring everything that is inessential. However, the large number of people who earn their livelihoods in the system of knowledge significantly increases the difficulty of this attitude, for these people, who are actual or potential colleagues, want to be noticed, and a career in the system of knowledge increasingly depends on reading—or at least citing—works that do not always provide new knowledge.[51] In addition, there is the growth of bureaucratic work, which is the fate of all quantitatively inflated institutions, and from which earlier scholars were protected.

Specialization in the broader sense also includes a special peculiarity of modern science, namely its *disconnection from knowledge about values*. The scientists of antiquity were deeply convinced that knowledge of the cosmos concerned an ordered and valuable whole and that this knowledge itself had intrinsic worth; both assumptions were given up in the course of the twentieth century, and with them the most important intrinsic motive for committed research, which cannot be replaced by financial bonuses. Indeed, in the meta-theory of the sciences—and especially the human sciences, which cannot show the same practical success as the natural sciences—a skepticism is spreading that ultimately abandons the idea of truth. In his last book Husserl writes: "A definite ideal of a universal philosophy and its method forms the beginning; this is, so to speak, the primal establishment of the philosophical modern age and all its lines of development. But instead of being able to work itself out in this fact, this ideal suffers an inner disso-lution. . . . But this is to say that, ultimately, all modern sciences drifted into a peculiar, increasingly puzzling crisis with regard to the meaning of their original founding as branches of philosophy . . . This is a crisis which does not encroach upon the theoreti-cal and practical successes of the special sciences; yet it shakes to the foundations the whole meaning of their truth."[52] However, if science is not a privileged place for know-ing the truth, in all honesty one will have to draw the conclusion that its special status with respect to other systems of opinion is unfounded. In particular, the privileging of science by the state is then no longer justified, and Paul Feyerabend's demand for a sepa-ration of state and science is only logical.[53]

Even if one rejects Feyerabend's theory of science, one should allow oneself to be stimulated by his ideas about the politics of science. The contemporary European state is much too closely interwoven with the social subsystem that calls itself "science."

---

51. On the contradiction between the idea of philosophy and the current social subsystem, cf. V. Hösle (1996b).

52. *Die Krisis der europäischen Wissenschaften und die transzendentale Phänomenologie* § 5 (1992), 8:10: "Ein *bestimmtes Ideal einer universalen Philosophie* und einer dazugehörigen Methode macht den Anfang, sozusagen als *Urstiftung der philosophischen Neuzeit* und aller ihrer Entwicklungsreihen. Aber anstatt daß sich dieses Ideal in der Tat auswirken konnte, erfährt es eine innere Auflösung. . . . Das sagt aber, daß schließlich alle neuzeitlichen Wissenschaften nach dem Sinn, in dem sie als Zweige der Philosophie begründet wurden . . . , in eine eigenartige, immer mehr als rätselhaft empfundene Krisis hineingerieten. Es ist eine Krisis, welche das Fachwissenschaftliche in seinen theoretischen und prak-tischen Erfolgen nicht angreift und doch ihren ganzen Wahrheitssinn durch und durch erschüttert." Trans. D. Curr (1970), 12.

53. P. Feyerabend (1975), 295 ff. Even if Feyerabend exaggerates and provokes, he has something important to say; unfortunately, I myself was slow to recognize the relative justice of his demands.

Since art has come to understand itself differently than it did in earlier times—that is, since the crisis of classical modernity—the state must reflect on its policy with regard to art because the classical arguments in favor of state sponsorship of the arts are related to the earlier concept of art. Analogously, we must ask in a very fundamental way which goals are still pursued today through state sponsorship of science. The freedom of science in the sense of a right to freedom from interference is largely unproblematic; but science can make a claim to positive state support only if it gives something back to humankind as a whole. In an era increasingly tormented by the suspicion that science may not only not solve but even increase the problems of modernity, a *new reflection on the utility of science* is indispensable. So far as the sciences of instrumental rationality are concerned, the answer is relatively easy. Someone who wants an end must want the means necessary to achieve it. A state that wants to remain competitive in its economy and to defend itself must, for instance, be interested in developing complex technologies that will be in demand only in later generations, and especially military technologies. But since such technologies depend on basic research in the natural sciences (think of nuclear physics), support for the latter is indispensable. To be sure, this research also has an intrinsic value, but it is not very logical to support basic research in the name of this intrinsic value while at the same time financing—probably also under the rubric of "basic research"—a philosophy that maintains that pure knowledge has no intrinsic value. Much the same goes for the good of health, which scientific medicine no doubt serves. However, scientific medicine is not the sole way of increasing public health; alternative medical traditions that have proven themselves can do the same (and often more cheaply), even if the mechanisms by which they do so remain mysterious—and healthcare policy is concerned only with healing. Analogously, alternative forms of ecological agriculture should also be supported, even if the grant applications do not use the technical terminology of agricultural science, which obviously has not prevented the modern agro-chemical industry from damaging the environment. The flipside of state financing for science must be its contribution to resolving political problems such as those connected with development and the environment; the knowledge sought must be relevant to such problems, it must be communicated in a language comprehensible to the intelligent layperson, and it must be in proportion to what it costs. The autonomy of science cannot mean that taxpayers must pay for insights that even in the future will interest only a few people other than those who produce them. The questions asked by science must in be large measure determined in advance by those who finance it; the answers have to be found by science itself, but it may very well turn out that its answers show that the branch of science concerned is no longer interesting for the state. In this case, restricting or even halting state support is only natural, especially if trust in scientific research's ability to regulate itself on the basis of the use of criteria based on the common good has faded. However, it is not always easy to distinguish between basic research oriented toward the future, which the market will not demand soon enough, and which must therefore be supported by the state, on one hand, and academic self-gratification on the other; and the more mediocrities sit on the evaluation committees, the more difficult this task becomes: An expert in the sociological sense of academic power is not necessarily an expert in the sense of knowledge of the truth, and the less negative sanctions threaten him if he is wrong, the less an expert in the first sense will care about knowing the truth.

But if the natural sciences cannot by themselves ground the legitimacy of their inquiries, should one then not lend especially extensive support to the *human sciences* (*Geisteswissenschaften*)? Unfortunately, the modern human sciences are still less capable of a normative discourse than are the natural sciences. One might be willing to overlook the fact that a large part of what goes on today in the academic culture industry neither produces important knowledge nor even meets elementary demands for consistency (without which one cannot speak of rationality); but the fact that it also dissolves the basic moral convictions that have governed ethical life up to this time without proposing a substitute is far more cause for concern and makes limits on state support seem well worth considering. *Nota bene:* the state cannot prescribe the answers to be given by any science, even and especially the human sciences, but it is only fair to inform the schools of thought that teach that it is impossible to have rational knowledge of values that the implicit purpose of the cooperation that alone justified state support for them has disappeared; at least such scholars can hardly protest against this decision. There is much to be said for the thesis that important achievements in the human sciences and the arts are awarded, in times that need innovation, by the market rather than by state institutions, whose members tend to be rigid and given to class conceit, as well as to co-opting mediocre people like themselves; the idea of modern science emerged in the seventeenth century outside public universities, and in the twenty-first century original ideas will probably also proceed from institutions outside the universities. The state should, if not support these extra-university institutions, at least not handicap them through the distortion of competition that is represented by the existence of a university system as inefficient as the German one is.

In fact, the following point provides food for thought: It is hardly surprising that in Germany the relative number of important scientists and scholars is now far smaller in relation to the number of professors than it was under the Weimar Republic; but the fact that this also holds in absolute numbers must be taken as a sign that something is wrong. (Naturally, the expulsion and murder of Jewish and critical intelligence under National Socialism, which set Germany back intellectually by at least a century, continues to have effects, but that is not the only cause.) What has led to the *decline of the German university,* that once so famous institution, which was supposed to combine research and teaching and was therefore a crucial interface between educational policy and research policy? First of all, the lack of competition between the various universities should be emphasized. Not all universities are equally good, and of course neither are all departments in a given university (for instance, there are significant differences in the intellectual and moral levels of the—too numerous—professors holding chairs), and supporting universities in accord with the principle of "equal shares for all" cannot favor exceptional achievements. A society cannot be proud of having overcome socialism and at the same time adopt a planned-economy university policy. The latter will sooner or later inevitably transform the universities into self-service stores for a cratically talented mediocracy that is not afraid of anything except superior achievement and that behaves with all the greater, sometimes almost hierocratic arrogance, the more it is tormented by the suspicion that it constitutes a parasitical and scheming class. Most universities must therefore be private; state universities, whose teachers' performance should be regularly evaluated, should have autonomy in matters of personnel and financing; in particular they should be allowed to choose their students themselves—for the idea of a general readiness for university, thanks to the Abitur (the final examination in German secondary schools), is a fiction. If the only way to improve one's own position is to negotiate a new position elsewhere, one should not be surprised that professors are more concerned about other universities than about their own institutions.

So far as the *evaluation of research* goes, there is no alternative to peer review, but this criterion does not tell us very much if, as in the German system of letters of recommendation, the dependencies are mutual or a decline in quality has begun among most of the recommmenders. It makes sense to complement peer review with international and interdisciplinary reviews. Regarding the *evaluation of teaching,* it goes without saying that it must proceed from the students, who should have far more influence in determining their teachers than they currently do in Germany; for in the present system bad teachers fear a successful teacher as a competitor. The flipside of this influence must be that the students have to pay for their studies (and not only for room and board during their study). Cost-free higher education has nothing to do with social justice, especially since kindergartens and adult evening classes also cost the user something; on the contrary, in German society cost-free education is one of the most obvious forms of redistributing wealth from the poor to the rich. To be sure, a generous system of scholarships and loans must be provided so that capable students from socially disadvantaged groups can also study at universities; but using the taxes paid by a baker who cannot himself study at a university without a high school degree in order to finance a higher education for the head physician hardly seems right or fair. For university students who come from wealthy families and are studying because they hope thereby to gain a higher income, a university education must not be a gift. This is all the more true since in a society in which money is the ultimate criterion for making differentiations, something that doesn't cost anything is worth nothing. In view of the favorable social conditions connected with going to a university in Germany, one should not be surprised that many students spend a great many years there that serve neither to train them for a practical occupation nor to develop their personalities, which are seldom developed by forms of parasitism and irresponsibility. In Germany, educational policy is in the process of degenerating into part of welfare policy.

The differentiating tendency of modernity suggests that the state should support institutions that pursue separately the various tasks that present-day universities fulfill together, or rather claim to fulfill—*research, teaching, training in accord with the needs of industrial society,* and *general education;* and a fortiori, the demand that every institution of higher education should teach every discipline should also be resisted, because many disciplines ignore each other. Research is not easy in a mass university, and the claim to achievements in research that are not always produced often damages teaching. The achievements of specialized colleges (*Fachhochschule*) are, in relation to their claims, generally more impressive than those of universities. Everyone knows that the grade a student gets on his master's exam counts for considerably less when he enters the job market than does the number of practicums he has done in the course of his study; but only a few human sciences departments arrange practicums for their students because German universities do not see themselves as providing services (just as Germans generally provide poor service). The over-emphasis on research in training for practical occupations such as being a physician or a lawyer is inappropriate; if the courses taught by private tutors preparing students for law examinations are fuller than those taught by law professors (not to mention courses on the philosophy of law), then the system of training in universities is clearly not functional. In addition to institutions for professional training, there should be others where general educational needs are met and which must, of course, be open to working people and retirees as well. Furthermore, first-rate research institutes such as the Max Planck and Fraunhofer Institutes should be more strongly supported. Naturally, there should also be institutions in which research and teaching are combined with each other; but to be realistic, one must admit that there are not many persons who are equally good as researchers and as teachers, and not many students who can fruitfully participate in research tasks from the beginning of their course of study. Since it is always easier to introduce new ranks than to do away with old ones, in Germany a few elite universities should be founded in which the Humboldtian ideal of a unity of research and teaching can still be truly realized, instead of giving further means to the present-day mass universities, since giving them these means will not make them into Humboldtian institutions. P. Glotz, R. Süssmuth, and K. Seitz have recently recommended that institutions be created to train European elites, for instance, a European school of government;[54] and in fact it is obvious that the development of a European political class that is bound together by common values and acquaintances would significantly promote European unity: the Oxbridge system was long a pillar of the British Empire. However, since the political problems of the twenty-first century are global in nature, a *World College* that really includes all the nations in the world and practices a new form of elite-building should be contemplated. For even and especially democracy cannot do without effective elites, insofar as these elites do not claim economic privileges but rather only make available their greater insight for a more competent solution to political problems. For this purpose, however, elites must have more moral integrity; the shaping of their character, indeed, their acquisition of a truly universalizable way of life and their education for a real cosmopolitanism, should go hand in hand with teaching and an appropriation through research of the knowledge indispensable for the survival of a humane culture.

---

54. (1992), 238 ff.

The tasks that the twenty-first century must fulfill are enormous, and it is not at all clear that humanity is up to meeting them. This orients philosophical thought toward a principle that is higher than humans, and without which any humanism becomes a vain overestimate of humans and a childish denial of their fallibility and guilt. It is the knowledge of this principle that saves humans from an existential vulnerability to natural forces and to other humans—the latter can only kill, nothing more; they cannot reach the higher sphere in which humans participate. However, humans can hope that this principle, which in humans brought forth a creature that can know it, will not let its voice be drowned out by all the turmoil of the twenty-first century—and thus will not allow human beings, as the only entity known to us that can perceive this voice, to become extinct. Whether this hope will be fulfilled, however, is known only to God.

Bibliography

For primary texts, I have not always cited complete editions or critical editions, that is, I have not hesitated to quote Hobbes's *Leviathan,* for instance, in the Penguin edition. I have done so partly because it was more convenient, but with a good conscience since this book is not primarily a work of history; and I have done so partly in order to make it easier for the general reader, who probably does not have those expensive editions around the house any more than I do, to look up the passages quoted. For this reason I have, wherever possible, also given the corresponding chapter or section number, or even the pagination of canonical editions such as those by Stephanus or Bekker. In order to forestall any impression that I know more than I do, I want to emphasize that I have read in full many but not all of the works cited. But even when I owe my knowledge of, say, decision theory or game theory to more simple introductory expositions, it seemed to me right to refer to the works that have developed the corresponding theories in a more fundamental way. So as to give some order to the bibliography, I have divided the works listed into five categories, although it was not always easy to decide to which group a given work should be assigned. Thus Schmitt and Weber are classics of philosophy as well as of the social sciences, and in the case of influential philosophers who are still living, it is debatable whether they should be put in category I or category II. In order to contain the length of the bibliography, I have preferred to assign such works arbitrarily rather than to list them twice. Works to which reference is made only in general, but which are not cited explicitly, do not appear in this bibliography.

The majority of translated quotations that appear in the text are the translator's own. I include the original text in the case of classic works of philosophy, history, and world literature and of passages in which the original wording is particularly important. The citation that follows a quotation in the footnotes will, therefore, generally refer the reader to a given text in its original language. Where a standard English translation has been used in place of my own, a reference appears in the footnote and a full citation in the bibliography. When a passage quoted is paraphrased in the body of the text, I have not always given a translation in the footnote. Trans.]

I. Classics in Philosophy and Political Theory

Al-Farabi on the Perfect State. A revised text with introduction, translation, and commentary by R. Walzer. Oxford, 1985.

Apel, K.-O. 1973. *Transformation der Philosophie.* 2 vols. Frankfurt am Main.

———. 1988. *Diskurs und Verantwortung.* Frankfurt am Main.

Arendt, H. 1963. *On Revolution.* New York.

———. 1970. *On Violence.* New York.

Aristotelis Ars rhetorica. Recognovit W. D. Ross. Oxford, 1959.

Aristotelis De anima. Recognovit W. D. Ross. Oxford, 1956.

Aristotelis De animalium motione. De animalium incessu. De spiritu. Recognovit W. Jaeger. Leipzig, 1913.

Aristotelis Ethica Nicomachea. Recognovit I. Bywater. Oxford, 1894.

Aristotelis qui ferebantur librorum fragmenta. Collated by V. Rose. Leipzig, ^{3}1886.

Aristotelis fragmenta selecta. Recognovit W. D. Ross. Oxford, 1955.

Aristotelis Metaphysica. Recognovit W. Jaeger. Oxford, 1957.

Aristotelis Politica. Recognovit W. D. Ross. Oxford, 1957.

Aristotelis Topica et Sophistici Elenchi. Recognovit W. D. Ross. Oxford, 1958.

Arnim, J. von. 1954. *Stoicorum veterum fragmenta.* 4 vols. Stuttgart, ^{2}1954.

Sancti Aurelii Augustini episcopi de civitate Dei libri XXII. Recognovit B. Dombart and A. Kalb. 2 vols. Darmstadt, 1981. English translation, *The City of God.* Translated by M. Dodds. New York, 1950.

Ayer, A. J. 1936. *Language, Truth, and Logic.* London.

Bacon, F. 1857 ff. *The Works.* Edited by J. Spedding, R. L. Ellis, and D. D. Heath. London, 1857–1874.

Bodin, J. 1576. *Les Six Livres de la République.* Paris, 1583. Reprint, Aalen, 1977.

Burckhardt, J. 1905. *Weltgeschichtliche Betrachtungen.* Stuttgart, 1978. English translation, *Force and Freedom.* Translated by J. H. Nichols. New York, 1955.

———. 1949 ff. *Briefe.* 10 vols. Basel and Stuttgart, 1949–1986.

Burke, E. 1790. *Reflections on the Revolution in France.* In E. Burke and T. Paine, *Reflections on the Revolution in France* and *The Rights of Man,* 11–266. Garden City, N.Y., 1973.

Canetti, E. 1960. *Masse und Macht.* 2 vols. N.p.

Cassirer, E. 1960. *Was ist der Mensch? Versuch einer Philosophie der menschlichen Kultur.* Stuttgart.

M. Tullius Ciceronis De legibus libri tres. Recognovit C. Büchner. Milan, 1973.

M. Tullius Ciceronis De officiis. Recognovit K. Atzert. Leipzig, ^{5}1971.

M. Tullius Ciceronis De re publica. Recognovit K. Ziegler. Leipzig, 1969.

Constant, B. 1872. *Cours de politique constitutionelle.* 2 vols. Paris. Reprint, Geneva and Paris, 1982.

Dante Alighieri. 1950. *Monarchia.* Edited by G. Vinay. Florence.

Descartes. 1964 ff. *Œuvres.* Edited by C. Adam and P. Tannery. 11 vols. Paris, 1964–1967.

Diels, H., and W. Kranz. 1954. *Die Fragmente der Vorsokratiker, griechisch und deutsch.* Edited by W. Kranz. 3 vols. Berlin, ^{7}1954.

Diogenes of Oinoanda. *The Epicurean Inscription.* Edited by M. F. Smith. Naples, 1992.

Dworkin, R. 1978. *Taking Rights Seriously.* Cambridge, Mass.

Epicteti Dissertationes ab Arriano digestae. Recognovit H. Schenkl. Leipzig, ^{2}1916.

Feinberg, J. 1980. *Rights, Justice, and the Bounds of Liberty.* Princeton.

Feyerabend, P. 1975. *Against Method.* London.

Fichte, J. G. 1971. *Werke.* Edited by I. H. Fichte. 11 vols. Berlin, 1834–1846. Reprint, Berlin, 1971.

———. 2000. *Foundations of Natural Right.* Translated by M. Bauer. Cambridge.

Filmer, R. 1991. *Patriarcha and Other Writings.* Edited by J. P. Sommerville. Cambridge.

Freund, J. 1965. *L'essence du politique.* Paris.

Fukuyama, F. 1989. The End of History? *The National Interest* (Summer 1989): 3–18.

———. 1992. *The End of History and the Last Man.* New York.

Gadamer, H.-G. 1975. *Wahrheit und Methode.* Tübingen, ⁴1975. English translation, *Truth and Method.* Translated by J. Weinsheimer and D. G. Marshall. New York, 1997.

Gehlen, A. 1957. *Die Seele im technischen Zeitalter.* Hamburg.

————. 1966. *Der Mensch.* Frankfurt am Main and Bonn (⁸1966). English translation, *Man.* Translated by C. McMillan and K. Pillemer. New York, 1988.

————. 1975. *Urmensch und Spätkultur.* Frankfurt am Main.

Gewirth, A. 1978. *Reason and Morality.* Chicago and London.

Gracián, B. 1655. *Oráculo manual.* Heidelberg, 1946.

Guicciardini, F. 1977. *Ricordi.* Milan. English translation, *Maxims and Reflections of a Renaissance Statesman.* Translated by M. Domandi. New York, 1965.

Habermas, J. 1983. *Moralbewußtsein und kommunikatives Handeln.* Frankfurt am Main.

————. 1992. *Faktizität und Geltung.* Frankfurt am Main. English translation, *Between Facts and Norms.* Translated by W. Rehg. Cambridge, 1996.

————. 1995. Reconciliation through the Public Use of Reason: Remarks on John Rawls's Political Liberalism. *Journal of Philosophy* 92 (1995): 109–131.

Hamilton, A., J. Madison, and J. Jay. 1787 f. *The Federalist Papers.* Toronto, 1982 (¹1787 f.).

Hare, R. M. 1952. *The Language of Morals.* Oxford, 1972.

————. 1963. *Freedom and Reason.* Oxford.

Hart, H. L. A. 1961. *The Concept of Law.* Oxford, 1972.

Hartmann, N. 1935. *Ethik.* Berlin and Leipzig, ²1935.

Hegel, G. W. F. 1942. *The Philosophy of Right.* Translated by T. M. Knox. Oxford.

————. 1964. *Hegel's Political Writings.* Translated by T. M. Knox. Oxford.

————. 1969 ff. *Werke in zwanzig Bänden.* Frankfurt am Main, 1969–1971.

————. 1975. *Natural Law: The Scientific Ways of Treating Natural Law.* Translated by T. M. Knox. Oxford.

Heidegger, M. 1979. *Sein und Zeit.* Tübingen, ¹⁵1979.

Heine, H. 1835. *Zur Geschichte der Religion und Philosophie in Deutschland.* In *Heines Werke in fünfzehn Teilen,* pt. 9, 159–278. Berlin, n.d.

Hempel, C. G. 1965. *Aspects of Scientific Explanations and Other Essays in Philosophy of Science.* New York and London.

Hobbes, T. 1651. *Leviathan.* London and Harmondsworth, 1987.

————. 1682. *Behemoth or the Long Parliament.* Edited by F. Tönnies. Chicago and London, 1990.

————. 1839 ff. a. *The English Works.* Edited by W. Molesworth. 11 vols. London, 1839–1845.

————. 1839 ff. b. *Opera philosophica quae latine scripsit omnia. . . .* Collated by W. Molesworth. London, 1839–1845.

Humboldt, W. von. 1903. *Ideen zu einem Versuch die Grenzen der Wirksamkeit des Staats zu bestimmen.* In *Gesammelte Schriften,* pt. 1: *Werke,* edited by A. Leitzmann, vol. 1, 97–254. Berlin.

Hume, D. 1977. *A Treatise of Human Nature.* London.

————. 1987. *Essays Moral, Political, and Literary.* Indianapolis.

Husserl, E. 1970. *The Crisis of European Sciences and Transcendental Phenomenology.* Translated by D. Carr. Evanston, Ill.

————. 1992. *Gesammelte Schriften.* 9 vols. Hamburg.

Joly, M. 1864. *Dialogue aux enfers entre Machiavel et Montesquieu.* Paris, 1968.

Jonas, H. 1966. *The Phenomenon of Life.* New York. German edition, *Organismus und Freiheit.* Göttingen, 1973.

————. 1979. *Das Prinzip Verantwortung.* Frankfurt am Main. English translation, *The Imperative of Responsibility.* Translated by H. Jonas and D. Herr. New York and London, 1984.

————. 1988. *Materie, Geist und Schöpfung.* Frankfurt am Main.

Kant, I. 1927. *Kant's gesammelte Schriften.* Vol. 15, pt. 2. Berlin and Leipzig.

————. 1956. *Critique of Practical Reason.* Translated by L. W. Beck. New York

———. 1976 f. *Werkausgabe.* Edited by W. Weischedel. 12 vols. Frankfurt am Main.

———. 1996. *The Metaphysics of Morals.* Translated by M. Gregor. Cambridge.

———. 1998. *Groundwork of the Metaphysics of Morals.* Translated by M. Gregor. Cambridge.

The Kauṭilīya-Arthaśāstra. 1988. 3 vols. Edited and translated by R. P. Kangle. Delhi.

Kierkegaard, S. 1963. *Samlede Værker.* 20 vols. Copenhagen.

La Rochefoucauld. 1967. *Maximes.* Paris.

Las Casas, B. de. 1965. *Tratados.* 2 vols. Mexico.

Leibniz, G. W. 1965. *Kleine Schriften zur Metaphysik.* Darmstadt.

———. 1978. *Die philosophischen Schriften.* Edited by C. J. Gerhardt. 7 vols. Hildesheim and New York (^{1}1875–1890).

Locke, J. 1690. *Two Treatises of Government.* Edited with an introduction and notes by P. Laslett. Cambridge, 1990.

———. ^{5}1706. *An Essay Concerning Human Understanding.* Edited with an introduction by J. W. Yolton. London, 1961.

Löwith, K. 1949. *Meaning in History: The Theological Implications of the Philosophy of History.* Chicago.

Lucreti De rerum natura libri sex. Recognovit C. Bailey. Oxford, ^{2}1922. English translation in W. J. Oates, ed., *The Stoic and Epicurean Philosophers.* Translated by H. A. J. Munro. New York, 1957.

Machiavelli, N. 1984. *Discorsi sopra la prima deca di Tito Livio.* Milan. English translation in *The Prince and the Discourses.* Translated by L. Ricci, E. R. P. Vincent, and C. E. Detmold. New York, 1950.

———. 1986. *Il Principe.* Milan. English translation in *The Prince and the Discourses.* Translated by L. Ricci, E. R. P. Vincent, and C. E. Detmold. New York, 1950.

MacIntyre, A. 1981. *After Virtue.* London.

Malthus, T. R. 1798. *An Essay on the Principle of Population.* London.

Mandeville, B. de. 1714. *The Fable of the Bees: or, Private Vices, Publick Benefits.* London.

Mao Tse-Tung. 1968. *Selected Military Writings.* Peking.

———. 1974. *Five Essays on Philosophy.* Peking.

Marci Antonini Imperatoris In semet ipsum libri XII. Edited by H. Schenkl. Leipzig, 1913.

Marsilius of Padua. 1932 f. *Defensor pacis.* Edited by R. Scholz. 2 vols. Hannover, 1932–1933.

Marx, K., and F. Engels. 1961 ff. *Werke.* 27 vols. Berlin, 1961–1965.

———. 1981. *Capital.* Translated by D. Fernbach. New York.

Mead, G. H. 1967. *Mind, Self, and Society: From the Standpoint of a Social Behaviorist.* Chicago and London, ^{14}1967.

Mill, J. S. 1867. A Few Words on Non-Intervention. In *Dissertations and Discussions,* vol. 3, 157–178. London.

———. 1972. *Utilitarianism. Liberty. Representative Government.* London.

M. Minucius Felix. *Octavius, lateinisch-deutsch.* Edited by B. Kytzler. Munich, 1965.

Montesquieu. 1734. *Considérations sur les causes de la grandeur des Romains et de leur décadence.* Paris, 1968.

———. 1748. *De l'esprit des lois.* 2 vols. Paris, 1979.

———. 1949. *Œuvres complètes.* Vol. 1. Paris.

Moore, G. E. 1903. *Principia Ethica.* Cambridge, 1976 (^{1}1903).

Musashi, M. 2000. *The Book of Five Rings.* In *Classics of Strategy and Counsel,* 263–379. Boston and London.

Nagel, T. 1979. *Mortal Questions.* Cambridge.

Nicholas of Cusa. 1964 ff. *Philosophisch-theologische Schriften.* Edited by L. Gabriel. 3 vols. Vienna, 1964–1967.

Nietzsche, F. 1980. *Sämtliche Werke. Kritische Studienausgabe.* 15 vols. Edited by G. Colli and M. Montinari. Munich.

———. 1990. *Twilight of the Idols and the Anti-Christ.* Translated by R. J. Hollingdale. London.

————. 1998. *Twilight of the Idols.* Translated by D. Large. Oxford.

Nizam al-Mulk. 1960. *The Book of Government; or Rules for Kings.* New Haven.

Nozick, R. 1974. *Anarchy, State, and Utopia.* New York.

Ortega y Gasset, J. 1930. *La rebelión de las masas.* Madrid, 1986. English translation, *The Revolt of the Masses.* Translated by A. Kerrigan. Notre Dame, Ind., 1985.

Otto, R. 1971. *Das Heilige.* Munich (¹1917).

Paine, T. 1776. *Common Sense.* Harmondsworth, 1980.

————. 1791. *The Rights of Man.* In E. Burke and T. Paine, *Reflections on the Revolution in France* and *The Rights of Man,* 267–515. Garden City, N.Y., 1973.

Parfit, D. 1987. *Reasons and Persons.* Oxford.

Pascal, B. 1966. *Les Provinciales.* Paris.

————. 1982. *Les Pensées.* Edited by F. Kaplan. Paris.

Platonis Opera. 5 vols. Recognovit I. Burnet. Oxford, 1900–1907.

Plessner, H. 1961. *Lachen und Weinen.* Bern and Munich, ³1961.

Poincaré, H. 1912. *Science et Méthode.* Paris.

Popper, K. 1945. *The Open Society and Its Enemies.* 2 vols. London.

————. 1960. *The Poverty of Historicism.* New York.

Popper, K. R., and J. C. Eccles. 1977. *The Self and Its Brain.* Berlin, New York, and London.

Pufendorf, S. von. 1667. S. de Monzambano (S. von Pufendorf), *De Statu Imperi Germanici.* Edited by F. Salomon. Weimar, 1910.

Radbruch, G. 1973. *Rechtsphilosophie.* Edited by E. Wolf and H.-P. Schneider. Stuttgart, ⁸1973.

Rawls, J. 1971. *A Theory of Justice.* New Haven, Conn.

————. 1993. The Law of Peoples. In *On Human Rights,* edited by S. Shute and S. Hurley, 41–82 and 220–230. New York.

Rescher, N. 1972. *Welfare.* Pittsburgh.

Rousseau, J.-J. 1966. ECONOMIE ou ŒCONOMIE. In *Encyclopédie ou dictionnaire raisonné des sciences des arts et des métiers,* vol. 5, 337–349. Facsimile. Stuttgart and Bad Cannstatt. English translation, *On the Social Contract, with the Geneva Manuscript and Political Economy.* Translated by J. R. Masters. Boston and New York, 1978.

————. 1975. *Du contrat social et autres œuvres politiques.* Paris. English translation, *On the Social Contract, with the Geneva Manuscript and Political Economy.* Translated by J. R. Masters. Boston and New York, 1978.

Sartre, J.-P. 1943. *L'être et le néant.* Paris.

————. 1966. *L'existentialisme est un humanisme.* Paris (¹1946).

Scheler, M. 1974. *Wesen und Formen der Sympathie.* Bern and Munich, 1974 (¹1913). English translation, *The Nature of Sympathy.* Translated by T. Heath. New Haven, 1954.

————. 1978. *Das Ressentiment im Aufbau der Moralen.* Frankfurt am Main, 1978 (¹1912).

————. 1980. *Der Formalismus in der Ethik und die materiale Wertethik.* Bern and Munich, ⁶1980 (¹1913/16).

————. 1988. *Die Stellung des Menschen im Kosmos.* Bonn, ¹¹1988 (¹1928). English translation, *Man's Place in Nature.* Translated by H. Meyerhoff. New York, 1961.

Schmitt, C. 1922. *Politische Theologie.* Berlin, ⁶1993.

————. 1927. *Der Begriff des Politischen.* Berlin, 1979.

————. 1928. *Verfassungslehre.* Berlin, 1970.

————. 1934. *Über die drei Arten des rechtswissenschaftlichen Denkens.* Hamburg.

————. 1938. *Der Leviathan in der Staatslehre des Thomas Hobbes.* Cologne-Lövenich, 1982.

————. 1958. *Verfassungsrechtliche Aufsätze aus den Jahren 1924–1954.* Berlin.

————. 1963. *Theorie des Partisanen.* Berlin.

————. 1970. *Politische Theologie II.* Berlin.

Schweitzer, A. 1932. *Aus meinem Leben und Denken.* Leipzig.

L. Annaei Senecae epistulae morales. Recognovit L. D. Reynolds. 2 vols. Oxford, 1965.

Sepúlveda, J. Ginés de, and B. de Las Casas. 1975. *Apologia.* Edited by A. Losada. Madrid.

Sieyès, E. 1970. *Qu'est-ce que le Tiers état?* Geneva.

Sorel, G. 1908. *Réflexions sur la violence.* Paris.

Spinoza. N.d. *Opera.* Edited by C. Gebhardt. 4 vols. Heidelberg.

Sun-tzu. 1988. *The Art of War.* Edited by J. Clavell. New York. German edition, *Über die Kriegs-Kunst.* Translated by K. Leibnitz. Karlsruhe, 1989.

Q. Septimii Florentis Tertulliani Apologeticum. Recognovit J. Martin. Bonn, 1933.

Divi Thomae Aquinatis De regimine principum. Turin and Rome, 1948.

Sancti Thomae Aquinatis, Summa theologiae. 5 vols. Madrid, 1961–1965.

Tocqueville, A. de. 1835 ff. *De la démocratie en Amérique.* 2 vols. Paris, 1981 (^{1}1835–1840).

———. 1856. *L'ancien régime et la révolution.* Paris, 1988.

———. 1953. *Œuvres complètes.* Vol. 2, pt. 2, *L'ancien régime et la révolution; Fragments et notes inédites sur la révolution.* Paris.

Tönnies, F. 1887. *Gemeinschaft und Gesellschaft.* Darmstadt, 1979.

Toynbee, A. J. 1965. *A Study of History.* 2 vols. New York.

Vico, G. B. 1953. *La scienza nuova seconda giusta l'edizione del 1744.* Edited by F. Nicolini. 2 vols. Bari, ^{4}1953. English translation, *The New Science of Giambattista Vico.* Translated by T. G. Bergin and M. H. Fisch. New York, 1961.

Vitoria, F. de. 1952. *De Indis recenter inventis et de jure belli Hispanorum in barbaros relectiones.* Edited by W. Schätzel. Tübingen, 1952.

Voegelin, E. 1952. *Die Neue Wissenschaft der Politik.* Munich, 1959. English translation, *The New Science of Politics.* Chicago, 1952.

Weber, M. 1917. Der Sinn der "Wertfreiheit" der soziologischen und ökonomischen Wissenschaften. In *Gesammelte Aufsätze zur Wissenschaftslehre,* 489–540. 1973.

———. 1919a. Wissenschaft als Beruf. In *Gesammelte Aufsätze zur Wissenschaftslehre,* 582–613. 1973.

———. 1919b. Politik als Beruf. In *Gesammelte Politische Schriften,* edited by J. Winckelmann, 505–560. Tübingen, ^{5}1988.

———. 1965. *Die protestantische Ethik.* Munich and Hamburg, 1965 (^{1}1905). English translation, *The Protestant Ethic and the Spirit of Capitalism.* Translated by T. Parsons. Los Angeles, 1996.

———. 1973. *Gesammelte Aufsätze zur Wissenschaftslehre.* Tübingen, ^{4}1973 (^{1}1922).

———. 1980. *Wirtschaft und Gesellschaft.* Tübingen, ^{5}1980 (^{1}1922). English translation, *Economy and Society.* Translated by A. R. Henderson and T. Parsons. London, 1947.

Williams, B. 1981. *Moral Luck.* Cambridge.

Windelband, W. 1894. *Geschichte und Naturwissenschaft.* In *Präludien,* vol. 1, 136–160. Tübingen, ^{4}1911.

Wright, G. H. von. 1977. *Handlung, Norm und Intention.* Edited by H. Poser. Berlin and New York.

Xenophontis Opera omnia. Recognovit E. C. Marchant. 5 vols. Oxford, 1900–1920.

II. Recent Philosophical and Secondary Studies

Akerma, K. 1995. *Soll eine Menschheit sein?* Cuxhaven and Dartford.

Barry, B. 1970. *Political Argument.* London and New York, ^{4}1970.

Barry, B., and R. E. Goodin. 1992. *Free Movement.* University Park, Pa.

Bayertz, K. 1993. *Evolution und Ethik.* Stuttgart.

Belsey, A. 1992. World Poverty, Justice and Equality. In *International Justice and the Third World,* edited by R. Attfield and B. Wilkins, 35–49. London and New York.

Berlin, I. 1980. The Originality of Machiavelli. In *Against the Current,* 25–79. London.

Bernstein, R. J. 1976. *The Restructuring of Social and Political Theory.* Oxford.

Binswanger, H. C. 1990. Abschied von der "Restriskio-Philosophie": Herausforderung der neuen Gefahrendimension. In *Risiko und Wagnis: Die Herausforderung der industriellen Welt,* edited by M. Schütz, 257–275. Pfullingen.

Birnbacher, D. 1988. *Verantwortung für zukünftige Generationen.* Stuttgart.

———. 1995. *Tun und Unterlassen.* Stuttgart.

Braithwaite, R. B. 1969. *Theory of Games as a Tool for the Moral Philosopher.* Cambridge.

Braungart, W. 1989. *Die Kunst der Utopie.* Stuttgart.

Buchanan, A. 1991. *Secession.* Boulder, Colo., San Francisco, and Oxford.

Buchanan, J. M., and G. Tullock. 1965. *The Calculus of Consent.* Ann Arbor, Mich.

Coady, C. A. J. 1993. Dirty Hands. In *A Companion to Contemporary Political Philosophy,* edited by R. Goodin and P. Pettit, 422–430. Oxford and Cambridge, Mass.

Doyle, M. W. 1983. Kant, Liberal Legacies, and Foreign Affairs. In *Philosophy and Public Affairs* 12: 205–235, 323–353.

Dworkin, G. 1982. Is More Choice Better than Less? In *Social and Political Philosophy,* edited by P. A. French, T. E. Uehling, Jr., and H. K. Wettstein, 47–61. Midwest Studies in Philosophy, vol. 7. Minneapolis.

Elster, J. 1983. *Sour Grapes.* Cambridge.

Finnis, J. 1980. *Natural Law and Natural Rights.* Oxford.

Forke, A. 1964. *Geschichte der alten chinesischen Philosophie.* Hamburg, ²1964.

French, P. A. 1983. *Ethics in Government.* Englewood Cliffs, N.J.

Fritz, K. von. 1954. *The Theory of the Mixed Constitution in Antiquity.* New York.

Gaiser, K. 1968. *Platons ungeschriebene Lehre.* Stuttgart, ²1968.

Gethmann, C. F., and M. Kloepfer. 1993. *Handeln unter Risiko im Umweltstaat.* Berlin.

Goebel, B., and M. Wetzel. 2001. *Eine moralische Politik? Vittorio Hösles Politische Ethik in der Diskussion.* Würzburg.

Goodin, R., and P. Pettit. 1993. *A Companion to Contemporary Political Philosophy.* Oxford and Cambridge, Mass.

Gräfrath, B. 1992. *Wie gerecht ist die Frauenquote?* Würzburg.

L. Hanke. 1974. *All Mankind Is One: A Study of the Disputation between Bartolomé de Las Casa and Juan Ginés de Sepúlveda in 1550 on the Intellectual and Religious Capacity of the American Indians.* De Kalb, Ill.

Hare, J. E., and C. B. Joynt. 1982. *Ethics and International Affairs.* London and Basingstoke.

Hoff, J., and J. in der Schmitten, eds. 1995. *Wann ist der Mensch tot?* Reinbek.

Honneth, A. 1992. *Kampf um Anerkennung.* Frankfurt am Main.

Horn, C. 1996. Philosophische Argumente für einen Weltstaat. *Allgemeine Zeitschrift für Philosophie* 21: 229–251.

Hösle, V. 1984a. *Wahrheit und Geschichte. Studien zur Struktur der Philosophiegeschichte unter paradigmatischer Analyse der Entwicklung von Parmenides bis Platon.* Stuttgart and Bad Cannstatt.

———. 1984b. *Die Vollendung der Tragödie im Spätwerk des Sophokles.* Stuttgart and Bad Cannstatt.

———. 1986. Eine unsittliche Sittlichkeit. In *Moralität und Sittlichkeit,* edited by W. Kuhlmann, 136–182. Frankfurt am Main.

———. 1987a. *Hegels System.* 2 vols. Hamburg.

———. 1987b. Carl Schmitts Kritik an der Selbstaufhebung einer wertneutralen Verfassung in "Legalität und Legitimät." *Deutsche Vierteljahrsschrift* 61: 3–36.

———. 1988. Tragweite und Grenzen der evolutionären Erkenntnistheorie. *Zeitschrift für allgemeine Wissenschaftstheorie* 19: 348–377.

———. 1989. Was darf und was soll der Staat bestrafen? Überlegungen im Anschluß an Fichtes und Hegels Straftheorien. In *Die Rechtsphilosophie des deutschen Idealismus,* edited by V. Hösle, 1–55. Hamburg.

———. 1990a. Etica e politica: Riflessioni sul *Principe* di Machiavelli. In *La legittimità del politico*, 11–39. Milan. German in Hösle (1996a), 129–152.

———. 1990b. Vico und die Idee der Kulturwissenschaft. In G. Vico, *Prinzipien einer neuen Wissenschaft über die gemeinsame Natur der Völker*, translated by V. Hösle and C. Jermann, xxxi–ccxciii. 2 vols. Hamburg.

———. 1990c. *Die Krise der Gegenwart und die Verantwortung der Philosophie*. Munich.

———. 1991. *Philosophie der ökologischen Krise*. Munich.

———. 1992a. *Praktische Philosophie in der modernen Welt*. Munich.

———. 1992b. Kan Abraham reddes? Og: Kan Søren Kierkegaard reddes? Et hegelsk oppgjør med "Frgyt og Bæven." *Norsk Filosofisk Tidsskrift* 27: 1–26. German in Hösle (1996a), 206–239.

———. 1993. Hva er de viktigste forskjellene mellom den antikke og den moderne filosofien? *Norsk Filosofisk Tidsskrift* 28: 1–20. German in Hösle (1996a), 13–36.

———. 1994. Moralische Ziele und Mittel der Weltbevölkerungspolitik. In *Dokumente. Tagungsberichte der Deutschen Welthungerhilfe e.V.*, vol. 4, *Weltbevölkerung und Welternährung*, 127–136. Bonn.

———. 1995a. Macht und Moral/Replik. *Ethik und Socialwissenschaften* 6: 379–387, 427–432.

———. 1995b. Soll Entwicklung sein? Und wenn ja, welche Entwicklung? In *Entwicklung mit menschlichem Antlitz*, edited by K. M. Leisinger and V. Hösle, 9–38. Munich.

———. 1996a. *Philosophiegeschichte und objektiver Idealismus*. Munich.

———. 1996b. Philosophy in an Age of Overinformation, or: What We Ought to Ignore in Order to Know What Really Matters. *Aquinas* 39: 307–320.

———. 2003. *Philosophie und Öffentlichkeit*. Würzburg.

Huber, G. 1995. *Eidos und Existenz*. Basel.

Jermann, C. 1986. *Philosophie und Politik. Untersuchungen zur Struktur und Problematik des platonischen Idealismus*. Stuttgart and Bad Cannstatt.

Jermann, C., ed. 1987. *Anspruch und Leistung von Hegels Rechtsphilosophie*. Stuttgart and Bad Cannstatt.

Joerden, J. C. 1993. Gerechtigkeit im "Fall Stolpe"? In *Rechtsphilosophische Hefte* 2: 87–94.

K., N., and V. Hösle. 1996. *Das Café der toten Philosophen*. Munich. English translation, *The Dead Philosophers' Café: An Exchange of Letters for Children and Adults*. Translated by S. Rendall. Notre Dame, Ind., 2000.

Kaufmann, A. 1994. *Grundprobleme der Rechtsphilosophie*. Munich.

Kesselring, T. 1995. Entwicklungshilfe—ethische Aspekte. In *Entwicklung mit menschlichem Antlitz*, edited by K. M. Leisinger and V. Hösle, 226–262. Munich.

Klein, H.-D. 1989. Philosophie der Gegenwart—Versuch einer Begriffsbestimmung (200 Jahre nach 1789). *Wiener Jahrbuch für Philosophie* 21: 47–63.

Kodalle, K.-M. 1994. *Verzeihung nach Wendezeiten?* Erlangen and Jena.

Kondylis, P. 1992. *Planetarische Politik nach dem Kalten Krieg*. Berlin.

Koslowski, P. 1995. *Ethik des Kapitalismus*. Tübingen, ⁵1995.

Krämer, H. 1992. *Integrative Ethik*. Frankfurt am Main.

Kratochwil, F. V. 1989. *Rules, Norms, and Decisions*. Cambridge.

Kullmann, W. 1980. Der Mensch als politisches Wesen bei Aristoteles. *Hermes* 108: 419–433.

Kutschera, F. von. 1973. *Einführung in die Logik der Normen, Werte und Entscheidungen*. Freiburg and Munich.

———. 1982. *Grundlagen der Ethik*. Berlin and New York.

Leist, A. 1990. *Eine Frage des Lebens*. Frankfurt am Main and New York.

Losurdo, D. 1997. *Hegel e la Germania*. Milan.

Lübbe, H. 1986. *Religion nach der Aufklärung*. Graz, Vienna, and Cologne.

———. 1987. *Politischer Moralismus*. Berlin.

Lumsdaine, D. H. 1993. *Moral Vision in International Politics*. Princeton.

Lyons, D. 1965. *Forms and Limits of Utilitarianism*. Oxford.

Macpherson, C. B. 1962. *The Political Theory of Possessive Individualism: Hobbes to Locke*. Oxford.

Maxwell, M. 1990. *Morality among Nations.* Albany, N.Y.

Meinecke, F. 1924. *Die Idee der Staatsräson in der neueren Geschichte.* Munich and Berlin.

Meyer-Abich, K. M. 1990. *Aufstand für die Natur.* Munich and Vienna.

Meyer-Abich, K. M., and B. Schefold. 1986. *Die Grenzen der Atomwirtschaft.* Munich.

Nida-Rümelin, J. 1987. *Entscheidungstheorie und Ethik.* Munich.

Oesterreich, P. L. 1994. *Philosophen als politische Lehrer.* Darmstadt.

Øfsti, A. 1988. *Das "Ich denke" und Kants transzendentale Deduktion im Lichte der sprachphilosophichen (pragmatischen)Wende.* Trondheim. (=Det Kongelike Norske Videnskabers Selskab, Skrifter 3/1988).

Parijs, P. van. 1995. *Real Freedom for All.* Oxford.

Pogge, T. 1995. Eine globale Rohstoffdividende. *Analyse und Kritik* 17: 183–208.

Primas, H. 1992. Umdenken in der Naturwissenschaft. *Gaia* 1: 5–15.

Qviller, B., and B. Thommessen. 1991/2. The Political Realism of Machiavelli. *Collegium Medievale* 4: 129–175.

Roetz, H. 1992. *Die chinesische Ethik der Achsenzeit.* Frankfurt am Main.

Sasso, G. 1980. Niccolò Machiavelli—Storia del suo pensiero politico. Bologna, [2]1980.

Scherer, G. 1990. *Welt—Natur oder Schöpfung?* Darmstadt.

Schramm, M. 1991. Symmetrie—zur Geschichte von Wort und Sache. In *Bozner Treffen 1990: Symmetrien-Dynamik-Strukturen,* 17–38. Bolzano.

Schütrumpf, E. 1980. *Die Analyse der Polis durch Aristoteles.* Amsterdam.

Singer, P. 1972. Famine, Affluence, and Morality. *Philosophy & Public Affairs* 1: 229–243.

———. 1976. A Utilitarian Population Principle. In *Ethics and Population.* Edited by M. D. Bayles, 81–99. Cambridge, Mass.

Spaemann, R. 1982. *Moralische Grundbegriffe.* Munich.

Steinvorth, U. 1993. Menschenrechte und Sozialstaat. *Rechtsphilosophische Hefte* 1: 9–21.

———. 1996. Das Recht auf Arbeit. *Rechtsphilosophische Hefte* 5: 77–95.

Stern, S. M. 1968. *Aristotle on the World State.* Oxford and Columbia, S. C.

Sternberger, D. 1978. *Drei Wurzeln der Politik.* 2 vols. Frankfurt am Main.

Stolleis, M. 1990. *Staat und Staatsräson in der frühen Neuzeit.* Frankfurt am Main.

Strauss, L. 1952. *Persecution and the Art of Writing.* Chicago and London, 1998 ([1]1952).

———. 1953. *Natural Right and History.* Chicago.

———. 1958. *Thoughts on Machiavelli.* Washington.

Taylor, C. 1989. *Sources of the Self.* Cambridge.

Thompson, J. J. 1974. A Defense of Abortion. In J. Finnis et al., *The Rights and Wrongs of Abortion,* 3–22. Princeton.

Todorov, T. 1991. *Face à l'extrême.* Paris.

Walzer, M. 1977. *Just and Unjust Wars.* New York.

Wandschneider, D. 1995. *Grundzüge einer Theorie der Dialektik.* Stuttgart.

Warrender, H. 1957. *The Political Philosophy of Hobbes: His Theory of Obligation.* Oxford.

Wilhelm, F. 1960. *Politische Polemiken im Staatslehrbuch des Kautalya.* Wiesbaden.

Willer, D. E. 1967. Max Weber's Missing Authority Type. *Sociological Inquiry* 37: 231–239.

Wolf, U. 1990. *Das Tier in der Moral.* Frankfurt am Main.

Wyller, E. A. 1970. *Der späte Platon.* Hamburg.

III. Other Studies

Adler, A. 1947. *Menschenkenntnis.* Zurich, [5]1947.

Alexy, R. 1985. *Theorie der Grundrechte.* Baden-Baden.

Altheim, F. 1962. *Entwicklungshilfe im Altertum.* Reinbek.

Amato, G. 1996. Ein Übergangskabinett. Meine zehn Monate als Ministerpräsident von Italien. In *Politikversagen? Parteienverschleiß? Bürgerverdruß?*, edited by M. Schmitz with A. Trägler. Regensburg, 67–79.

Anderson, P. 1974. *Lineages of the Absolutist State.* London.

———. 1978. Passages frm Antiquity to Feudalism. London (¹1974).

Arnason, J. P. 1993. Comparing Japan and the West-Prolegomena to a Research Programme. *Development and Modernity*, edited by L. Gule and O. Storebø, 167–195. Bergen.

Aron, R. 1962. *Paix et guerre entre les nations.* Paris.

———. 1972. Macht, Power, Puissance: Prose démocratique ou poésie démoniaque? (1964). In *Études politiques*, 171–194. Paris.

Arrow, K. J. 1951. *Social Choice and Individual Values.* New York.

Asch, S. E. 1951. Effects of Group Pressure upon the Modification and Distortion of Judgments. In *Groups, Leadership, and Men*, edited by H. Guetzkow, 177–190. New York.

Assmann, J. 1992. *Das kulturelle Gedächtnis.* Munich.

Axelrod, R. 1984. *The Evolution of Cooperation.* New York.

Bachrach, P., and M. S. Baratz. 1970. *Power and Poverty.* New York.

Balandier, G. 1967. *Anthropologie politique.* Paris.

Baldwin, D. A. 1971/72. The Power of Positive Sanctions. *World Politics* 24: 19–38.

Bandura, A. 1986. *Social Foundations of Thought and Action.* Englewood Cliffs, N.J.

Barta, H. 1995. *Medizinhaftung.* Innsbruck.

Bechmann, A. 1993. *Landwirtschaft 2000 — Die Zukunft gehört dem ökologischen Landbau.* Edited by the Zukunfts-Institut, Projektleitung A. Bechmann. Barsinghausen.

Beck, U. 1991. *Politik in der Risikogesellschaft.* Frankfurt am Main.

Beitz, C. R. 1979. *Political Theory and International Relations.* Princeton.

Berman, H. J. 1983. *Law and Revolution.* Cambridge, Mass.

Binswanger, H. C. 1991. *Geld und Natur.* Stuttgart.

Birg, H. 1995. Globale und nationale demographische Entwicklung und Wanderungen als Rahmenbedingungen für die sozialen Sicherungssysteme in Deutschland. *Zeitschrift für die gesamte Versicherungswissenschaft* 4: 593–616.

Bloom, A. 1987. *The Closing of the American Mind.* New York.

Böckenförde, E.-W. 1976. *Staat, Gesellschaft, Freiheit.* Frankfurt am Main.

Bonus, H. 1992. Marktwirtschaftliche Lösungsansätze: Ein neuer Interventionismus ante portas? In Bonus et al., *Umweltzerstörung und Ressourcenverschwendung*, 11–32. Chur and Zurich.

Boulding, K. E. 1973. *The Economy of Love and Fear.* Belmont, Calif.

Brams, S. J. 1975. *Game Theory and Politics.* New York and London.

Brinton, C. 1965. *The Anatomy of Revolution.* New York , ¹1938.

BUND/MISEREOR. 1996. *Zukunftsfähiges Deutschland.* Basel, Boston, and Berlin.

Calhoun, C., ed. 1994. *Social Theory and the Politics of Identity.* Cambridge, Mass.

Claessens, D. 1974. *Rolle und Macht.* Munich, ³1974.

Clausewitz, C. von. 1832 ff. *Vom Kriege.* Bonn, ¹⁸1973 (¹1832 ff). English translation, *On War.* Translated by J. J. Graham. 3 vols. London, 1949.

La conquête des droits de l'homme. 1988. Textes fondamentaux. Paris.

Crutzen, P. J. and M. Müller, eds. 1989. *Das Ende des blauen Planeten?* Munich.

Czempiel, E.-O. 1994. *Die Reform der UNO.* Munich.

Davis, M. D. 1983. *Game Theory.* New York.

Dawkins, R. 1976. *The Selfish Gene.* Oxford and New York.

Dehio, L. 1948. *Gleichgewicht oder Hegemonie.* Krefeld.

Doyle, M. W. 1986. *Empires.* Ithaca and London.

Drewermann, E. 1991. *Reden gegen den Krieg.* Düsseldorf.

Edelman, G. M. 1989. *The Remembered Present: A Biological Theory of Consciousness.* New York.

Eibl-Eibesfeldt, I. 1975. *Krieg und Frieden aus der Sicht der Verhaltensforschung.* Munich and Zurich.

———. 1980. *Grundriß der vergleichenden Verhaltensforschung.* Munich, ⁶1980.

Eliade, M. 1966. *Kosmos und Geschichte.* Reinbek. French edition, 1949.

Emmett, D. 1972. *Function, Purpose and Powers.* London and Basingstoke, ²1972.

Engisch, K. 1935. *Die Einheit der Rechtsordnung.* Heidelberg.

Erikson, E. H. 1959. *Identity and the Life Cycle.* New York.

Felix, D. 1995. The Tobin Tax Proposal: Background, Issues and Prospects. *The United Nations: Policy and Financing Alternatives.* Edited by H. Cleveland, H. Henderson, and I. Kaul, 195–208. Washington, D.C.

Forsthoff, E. 1959. *Rechtsfragen der leistenden Verwaltung,* Stuttgart.

———. 1971. *Der Staat der Industriegesellschaft.* Munich, ²1971.

Freud, S. 1913. *Totem and Tabu.* Frankfurt am Main and Hamburg, 1971. English translation. *Totem und Taboo.* Translated by J. Strachey. New York, 1950.

Frey, B. S. 1978. *Modern Political Economy.* New York, 1978.

Furet, F. 1995. *Le passé d'une illusion.* Paris.

Fustel de Coulanges, N. D. 1864. *The Ancient City.* Boston, 1873. French edition, 1864.

Galbraith, J. K. 1984. *The Anatomy of Power.* London.

Ganshof, F. L. 1964. *Feudalism.* New York.

Gellner, E. 1981. *Muslim Society.* Cambridge.

———. 1983. *Nations and Nationalisms.* Oxford.

———. 1988. *Plough, Sword and Book.* London.

Gelzer, M. 1973. Pompeius. Munich (¹1949).

Giddens, A. 1990. *The Consequences of Modernity.* Stanford.

Gilpin, R. 1981. *War and Change in World Politics.* Cambridge.

Glotz, P., R. Süssmuth, and K. Seitz. 1992. *Die planlosen Eliten.* Munich.

Grewe, W. G. 1988. *Epochen der Völkerrechtsgeschichte.* Baden-Baden, ²1988.

Hall, J. A., and G. J. Ikenberry. 1989. *The State.* Minneapolis.

Hall, J. A., ed. 1994. *The State: Critical Concepts.* 3 vols. London and New York.

Hartwig, M. 1995. Die Gleichheit und Ungleichheit von Staaten. Das völkerrechtliche Verhältnis zwischen den industrialisierten und den Entwicklungsländern. In *Entwicklung mit menschlichem Antlitz,* edited by K. M. Leising and V. Hösle, 187–217. Munich.

Hauchler, I., ed. 1993. *Globale Trends 93/94.* Frankfurt am Main.

Heller, H. 1934. *Staatslehre* (¹1934). In *Gesammelte Schriften,* 3 vols., 3: 79–406. Leiden, 1971.

Hennen, M. 1995. Versuch sozialwissenschaftlicher Begriffsarbeit für Macht und Moral—kritisches Koreferat. *Ethik und Sozialwissenschaften* 6: 401–403.

Herzog, R. 1971. *Allgemeine Staatslehre.* Frankfurt am Main.

Hess, R. D., and J. V. Torney. 1968. *The Development of Political Attitudes in Children.* Garden City, N.Y.

Hintze, O. 1929. Wesen und Verbreitung des Feudalismus. In *Feudalismus-Kapitalismus,* edited and introduced by G. Oestreich, 12–47. Göttingen.

Hockett, C. 1973. The Origin of Speech. *Scientific American* 203/3: 88–96.

Human Development Report. 1994. *Human Development Report 1994.* New York and Oxford.

Huntington, S. P. 1993. The Clash of Civilizations? *Foreign Affairs* 72/3: 22–49.

Hustedt, M., R. Loske, G. Nacken, T. Stein, and B. Ulrich. 1990. Ökologisches Manifest für eine grüne Zukunft. *Kommune* 6: 39–46.

Isaacs, S. L. 1995. Incentives, Population Policy, and Reproductive Rights: Ethical Issues. *Studies in Family Planning* 26: 363–367.

Jackson, R. H., and C. G. Rosenberg. 1994. Why Africa's Weak States Persist: The Empirical and the Juridical in Statehood. In *The State: Critical Concepts,* edited by J. A. Hall, 2: 267–286. London and New York.

Jeffrey, R. C. 1965. *The Logic of Decision.* New York.

Jellinek, G. 1922. *Allgemeine Staatslehre*. Berlin, ³1922.

Jones, E. L. 1987. *The European Miracle*. Cambridge, ²1987.

Jouvenel, B. de. 1945. *Du pouvoir*. Geneva.

Kavka, G. S. 1982. Two Solutions to the Paradox of Revolution. In *Social and Political Philosophy*, edited by P. A. French, T. E. Uehling, Jr., and H. K. Wettstein, 455–472. Midwest Studies in Philosophy, vol. 7. Minneapolis.

Kaser, M. 1983. *Römisches Privatrecht*. Munich, ¹³1983.

Kelsen, H. 1928. *Der soziologische und der juristische Staatsbegriff*. Tübingen, ²1928.

Kennedy, P. 1993. *Preparing for the Twenty-First Century*. New York.

Klemperer, V. 1969. *"LTI." Die unbewältigte Sprache*. Munich.

Kluckhohn, C., and W. H. Kelly. 1945. The Concept of Culture. In *The Science of Man in the World Crisis*, edited by R. Linton, 78–105. New York and London.

Knights, D., and J. Roberts. 1994. The Power of Organization or the Organization of Power? In *Power: Critical Concepts*, edited by J. Scott, 2: 168–184. London and New York.

Kohlberg, L. 1983. *Moral Stages: A Current Formulation and a Response to Critics*. Basel.

Köhler, M. 1982. *Die bewußte Fahrlässigkeit*. Heidelberg.

Krickeberg, W. 1961. Die Religionen der Kulturvölker Mesoamerikas. In *Die Religionen des alten Amerika*, edited by W. Krickeberg, A. Trimborn, W. Müller, and O. Zerries, 1–89. Stuttgart.

Kriele, M. 1975. *Einführung in die Staatslehre*. Reinbek.

Kühnhardt, L. 1987. *Die Universalität der Menschenrechte*. Munich.

Küng, H. 1990. *Projekt Weltethos*. Munich and Zurich.

Küng, H., ed. 1995. *Ja zum Weltethos*. Munich and Zurich.

Lapierre, J.-W. 1968. *Essai sur la fondement du pouvoir politique*. Aix-en-Provence.

Lasswell, H. D., and A. Kaplan. 1969. *Power and Society*. New Haven and London, ⁸1969 (¹1950).

Le Bon, G. 1934. *Psychologie des foules*. Paris, ³⁸1934 (¹1895).

Leisinger, K. M. 1993. *Hoffnung als Prinzip*. Basel.

———. 1995. Gouvernanz oder: "Zu Hause muß beginnen, was leuchten soll im Vaterland." In K. M. Leisinger and V. Hösle (1995), 114–172.

———. 1997. *Unternehmensethik*. Munich.

Leisinger, K. M., and V. Hösle, eds. 1995. *Entwicklung mit menschlichem Antlitz*. Munich.

Lévi-Strass, C. 1961. *Race et histoire*. Paris.

Liddell, H. G., and R. Scott. 1961. *A Greek-English Lexicon*. Oxford.

Lorenz, K. 1977. *Die Rückseite des Spiegels*. Munich.

Loske, R. 1996. *Klimapolitik*. Marburg.

Luce, R. D., and H. Raiffa. 1957. *Games and Decisions*. New York.

Luhmann, N. 1975. *Macht*. Stuttgart.

———. 1986. *Ökologische Kommunikation*. Opladen.

Lukács, G. 1920. *Die Theorie des Romans*. Berlin.

Lukes, S. 1974. *Power: A Radical View*. London and Basingstoke.

Luttwak, E. N. 1976. *The Grand Strategy of the Roman Empire*. Baltimore.

Mahrenholz, E. G. 1992. *Die Verfassung und das Volk*. Munich.

Maine, H. S. 1861. *Ancient Law*. London, 1918.

Malinowski, B. 1926. *Crime and Custom in Savage Society*. London and Henley, 1978.

Mann, M. 1986 ff. *The Sources of Social Power*. 2 vols. Cambridge.

———. 1994. The Autonomous Power of the State: Its Origins, Mechanisms and Results. In *The State: Critical Concepts*, edited by J. A. Hall, 1: 331–353. London and New York.

Marty, M. E., and R. S. Appleby, eds. 1991. *Fundamentalisms Observed*. Chicago and London.

Marx, S. 1994. *Beispiele des Beispiellosen*. Würzburg.

Mauss, M. 1973. *Sociologie et Anthropologie*. Paris.

Maynard Smith, J. 1982. *Evolution and the Theory of Games*. Cambridge.

McNamara, R. 1995. *In Retrospect: The Tragedy and Lessons of Vietnam.* New York.

McNeill, W. H. 1963. *The Rise of the West.* Chicago and London.

Meier, C. 1980a. *Die Entstehung des Politischen bei den Griechen.* Frankfurt am Main.

———. 1980b. *Die Ohnmacht des allmächtigen Dictators Caesar.* Frankfurt am Main.

Menzel, U. 1992. *Das Ende der Dritten Welt und das Scheitern der großen Theorie.* Frankfurt am Main.

Meyer, E. 1981. *Geschichte des Altertums,* 5, in 8 vols. Darmstadt (^{3}1910 ff.)

Meyer, T. 1992. *Die Inszenierung des Scheins.* Frankfurt am Main.

Mommsen, T. 1974. *Abriß des römischen Staatsrechts.* Darmstadt (^{1}1893).

———. 1976. *Römische Geschichte.* 8 vols. Munich (^{1}1854–1885).

Morgenstern, O. 1935. Vollkommene Voraussicht und wirtschaftliches Gleichgewicht. *Zeitschrift für Nationalökonomie* 6 (1935): 337–357.

Morgenthau, H. J., and K. W. Thompson. 1985. *Politics among Nations.* New York, ^{6}1985.

Münch, I. von. 1985. *Grundgesetz-Kommentar.* 3 vols. Munich.

Münch, P. 1992. *Lebensformen in der frühen Neuzeit.* Frankfurt am Main and Berlin.

———. 1996. The Growth of the Modern State. In *Germany: A New Social and Economic History,* vol. 2, *1530–1800,* edited by S. Ogilvie, 196–232. London.

Naraghi, E. 1991. *Des palais du Chah aux prisons de la révolution.* Paris.

Naylor, R. T. 1987. *Hot Money.* New York.

Neudeck, R. 1993. Nachwort. In S. Kohlhammer, *Auf Kosten der Dritten Welt?,* 115–121. Göttingen.

Neumann, J. von, and O. Morgenstern. 1944. *Theory of Games and Economic Behavior.* Princeton.

Neumark, F. 1970. *Grundsätze gerechter und ökonomisch rationaler Steuerpolitik.* Tübingen.

Nicholson, M. 1990. *Formal Theories in International Relations.* Cambridge.

Paris, R. 1995. Die Politik des Lobs. In *Politische Institutionen im Wandel,* edited by B. Nedelmann, 83–107. Opladen.

Parker, G. 1988. *The Military Revolution.* Cambridge.

Parsons, T. 1969. *Politics and Social Structure.* New York and London.

Piaget, J. 1932. *Le jugement moral chez l'enfant.* Paris.

Portinaro, P. P. 1986. *Il terzo.* Milan.

Portmann, A. 1956. *Zoologie und das neue Bild vom Menschen.* Hamburg.

Postman, N. 1985. *Amusing Ourselves to Death: Public Discourse in the Age of Show Business.* New York.

Rauch, G. von. 1977. *Geschichte der Sowjetunion.* Stuttgart, ^{6}1977.

Riesman, D. 1950. *The Lonely Crowd.* New Haven.

Rigotti, F. 1992. *Il potere e le sue metafore.* Milan.

Riker, W. H. 1962. *The Theory of Political Coalitions.* New Haven and London.

Russett, B., and J. S. Sutterlin. 1991. The U. N. in a New World Order. *Foreign Affairs* 70/2 (1991): 69–83.

Rüttgers, J. 1993. *Dinosaurier der Demokratie.* Hamburg.

Sahlins, M. 1972. *Stone Age Economics.* London.

Sartori, G. 1987. *The Theory of Democracy Revisited.* Chatham, N.J.

Schapera, I. 1967. *Government and Politics in Tribal Societies.* New York.

Scherhorn, G., H. Haas, F. Hellenthal, and S. Seibold. 1996. *Informationen über Wohlstandskosten.* Stuttgart, ^{2}1996.

Schmidt-Bleek, F. 1994. *Wieviel Umwelt braucht der Mensch?* Basel.

Schnur, R., ed. 1975. *Staatsräson.* Berlin.

Schönke, A., and H. Schröder. 1982. *Strafgesetzbuch Kommentar.* Munich, ^{21}1982.

Schumpeter, J. A. 1959. *Capitalism, Socialism, and Democracy.* London. ^{8}1959.

Schwartz, M. J., V. W. Turner, and A. Tuden, eds. 1976. *Political Anthropology.* Chicago, ^{3}1976.

Scott, J., ed. 1994. *Power: Critical Concepts.* 3 vols. London and New York.

Şenocak, Z. 1993. *Atlas des tropischen Deutschland.* Berlin, ^{2}1993.

Service, E. 1975. *Origins of the State and Civilization.* New York.

Sigrist, C. 1979. *Regulierte Anarchie*. Frankfurt am Main.

Simon, H. A. 1955. A Behavioral Model of Rational Choice. *Quarterly Journal of Economics* 69: 99–118.

Simonis, U. E. 1996. Elemente einer globalen Umweltpolitik—Eine institutionell-ökonomische Perspective. In *Nachhaltige Entwicklung*, edited by H. B. Kastenholz, K. H. Erdmann, and M. Wolff, 173–186. Berlin.

Smend, R. 1928. *Verfassung und Verfassungsrecht*. Munich.

Sombart, W. 1987. *Der moderne Kapitalismus*. 3 in 6 vols. Munich, 1987 ([2]1916).

Stein, L. 1850. *Geschichte der socialen Bewegung in Frankreich von 1789 bis auf unsere Tage*. 3 vols. Leipzig.

Stern, D. 1977. *The First Relationship*. Cambridge, Mass.

Sternberger, D., G. Storz, and W. E. Süskind. 1968. *Aus dem Wörterbuch des Unmenschen*. Hamburg and Düsseldorf, [3]1968.

Strayer, J. 1970. *On the Medieval Origins of the Modern State*. Princeton.

Tilly, C. 1993. *European Revolutions, 1492–1992*. Oxford.

Tönnies, F. 1922. *Kritik der öffentlichen Meinung*. Berlin.

Touraine, A. 1994. *Qu'est-ce que la démocratie?* Paris.

Uberoi, J. P. S. 1978. *Science and Culture*. Delhi.

Ueberhorst, R. 1986. Technologiepolitik—was wäre das? In *Die ungeklärten Gefahrenpotentiale der Gentechnologie*, edited by R. Kollek, B. Tappeser, and G. Altner, 202–227. Munich.

Veblen, T. 1899. *The Theory of the Leisure Class*. New York, 1934.

Verdross, A., and B. Simma. 1984. *Universelles Völkerrecht*. Berlin, [3]1984.

Vogel, C. 1989. *Vom Töten zum Mord*. Munich and Vienna.

Vom Grundgesetz zur deutschen Verfassung. 1991. Berlin.

Waltz, K. N. 1979. *Theory of International Politics*. Reading, Mass.

Wasser, H. 1984. *Die Vereinigten Staaten von Amerika*. Frankfurt am Main, Berlin, and Vienna.

Waters, J. A. 1978. Catch 20.5: Corporate Morality as an Organizational Phenomenon. *Organizational Dynamics* (1978): 3–19.

Weizsäcker, C. F. von. 1964. *Bedingungen des Friedens*. Göttingen.

Weizsäcker, E. U. von. 1994. *Earth Politics*. London. German edition, *Erdpolitik*. Darmstadt, 1989.

Weizsäcker, E. U. von, A. B. Lovins, and L. Hunter Lovins. 1995. *Faktor Vier*. Munich.

White, L. A. 1959. *The Evolution of Culture*. New York.

Winter, G. 1989. *Das umweltbewußte Unternehmen*. Munich, [3]1989.

Wöhlcke, M. 1996. *Sociale Entropie*. Munich.

Wrong, D. H. 1979. *Power*. Oxford.

———. 1994. Some Problems in Defining Social Power. In *Power: Critical Concepts*, edited by J. Scott, 1: 62–71. London and New York, 1994.

Zimbardo, P. G. 1988. *Psychology and Life*. Glenview, Ill., [12]1988.

Zippelius, R. 1991. *Allgemeine Staatslehre*. Munich.

IV. Classics in Historiography

Bismarck, O. von. 1899 ff. *Gedanken und Erinnerungen*. 3 vols. Stuttgart, 1898–1921.

C. Iuli Caesaris Commentarii. Edited by A. Klotz. 2 vols. Leipzig, 1950–1957.

Churchill, W. S. 1948 ff. *The Second World War*. 12 vols. London, 1964 ([1]1948 ff.).

———. 1974. *His Complete Speeches 1897–1963*. Edited by R. Rhodes James. Vol. 5, *1928–1935*. New York and London.

Cortés, H. 1985. *Cartas de relación*. Madrid.

Cuoco, V. 1975. *Saggio storico sulla rivoluzione napoletana*. Turin.

Díaz del Castillo, B. 1986. *Historia Verdadera de la Conquista de la Nueve España*. Mexico.

Einhard. 1971. *Vita Karoli Magni. Das Leben Karls des Großen, lateinisch und deutsch.* Translated by E. S. Coleman. Stuttgart.

Frederick the Great. 1920. *Die politischen Testamente Friedrich's des Grossen.* Edited by G. B. Volz. Berlin.

Havel, V. 1997. *The Art of the Impossible.* Translated by P. Wilson et al. New York and Toronto.

Herodoti Historiae. Recognovit C. Hude. 2 vols. Oxford, 1927. English translation, *The Histories.* Translated by A. de Sélincourt. London, 1996.

Lincoln, A. 1969. *His Speeches and Writings.* Edited by R. P. Basler. Cleveland and New York.

Titi Livi ab urbe condita. Edited by G. Weissenborn and M. Museller. 4 vols. Leipzig, 1926.

Plutarchi Vitae Parallelae. Recognovit C. Sintenis. 5 vols. Leipzig, 1860–1873.

Polybii Historiae. Edited by T. Büttner-Wobst. 5 vols. Leipzig, 1882–1904.

C. Sallusti Crispi Catilina. Iugurtha. Historiarum fragmenta selecta. Appendix Sallustiana. Recognovit L. D. Reynolds. Oxford, 1991.

Suetonius. *Kaiserbiographien, lateinisch/deutsch.* Translated by O. Wittstock. Berlin, 1993.

Cornelii Taciti libri qui supersunt, . . . Edited by E. Koestermann. 3 in 2 vols. Leipzig, 1965–1970.

———. *The Complete Works of Tacitus: The Annals.* Translated by A. J. Church and W. J. Brodribb. New York, 1942.

———. *The Agricola and the Germania.* Translated by H. Mattingly and revised by S. A. Handford. Harmondsworth, 1970.

Thucydidis Historiae. Recognovit H. S. Jones and J. E. Powell. 2 vols. Oxford, 1942.

V. World Literature

Bolt, R. 1970. *A Man for All Seasons.* London.

Camões, L. de. n.d. *Os Lusíadas.* Rio de Janeiro.

Cervantes, M. de. 1994. *El Ingenioso Hidalgo Don Quixote de la Mancha.* 2 vols. Madrid. English translation, *Don Quixote.* Translated by B. Raffel. New York, 1995.

Chesterfield. 1963. *Lord Chesterfield's Letters to His Son.* London.

Conrad, J. 1988. *Lord Jim.* New York.

Dante Alighieri. 1910. *La Divina Commedia.* Edited by T. Casini. Florence, ⁵1910.

Fontane, T. 1974. *Werke, Schriften und Briefe.* Pt. 1., vol. 4. Munich.

Frisch, M. 1975. *Andorra.* Frankfurt am Main.

Goethe, J. W. 1991. *Sämtliche Werke nach Epochen seines Schaffens.* München edition. Vol. 17. Munich.

———. 1998. *Maxims and Reflections.* Translated by E. Stopp. London and New York.

Havel, V. 1991. *Angst vor der Freiheit.* Reinbek.

Q. Horatii Flacci Opera. Recognovit E. Curotto. Turin, 1957.

Hugo, V. 1963. *Les Misérables.* Paris.

Huxley, A. 1977. *Brave New World.* London.

Ibsen, H. 1978. *Samlede Verker.* 3 vols. Oslo, ³1978.

Kolitz, Z. 1995. *Yossel Rakover Speaks to God.* Hoboken, N.J.

Maass, J. 1965. *Die Stunde der Entscheidung. Drei Dramen.* Basel.

Mann, T. 1943. *The Ten Commandments.* Translated by G. R. March. New York.

———. 1975. *Joseph und seine Brüder.* 3 vols. Frankfurt am Main. English translation, *Joseph and His Brothers.* Translated by H. T. Lowe-Porter. London, 1959.

———. 1976. *Die Erzählungen.* 2 vols. Frankfurt am Main.

———. 1982. *Königliche Hoheit.* Frankfurt am Main. English translation, *Royal Highness.* Translated by C. Curtis. Berkeley and Los Angeles, 1992.

Manzoni, A. 1973. *Tutte le opera.* Edited by M. Martelli. Vol. 1. Florence.

Melville, H. 1986. *Billy Budd, Sailor and Other Stories.* New York.

———. 1992. *Moby Dick.* Ware.

Musil, R. 1989. *Nachlaß zu Leibzeiten.* Reinbek.

Orwell, G. 1984. *Nineteen Eighty-Four.* Oxford.

Schiller, F. 1959. *Sämtliche Werke.* 5 vols. Munich.

The Complete Works of William Shakespeare. 6 vols. Toronto, 1988.

Tolstoy, L. N. 1971. *War and Peace.* Translated by R. Edmonds. 2 vols. London.

Verdi, G. 1986. *Falstaff.* Reinbek.

P. Vergili Maronis Opera. Recognovit M. Geymonat. Turin, 1973.

———. 1981. *The Aeneid of Virgil: A Verse Translation.* Translated by A. Mandelbaum. New York.

Wagner, R. 1978. *Die Musikdramen.* Munich.

Yourcenar, M. 1974. *Mémoires d'Hadrien.* Paris.

Zamyatin, Y. *We.* Translated by B. G. Guerney. London, 1976.

Index of Names

Abelard, P.: *Ethica*, 93
Adams, J., 523
Adenauer, K., 533, 804
Adler, A., 217, 253n.117
Aeschylus, xviii, 9; *Oresteia*, 424, 680, 694; *Prometheus Bound*, 424, 470
Aesop, 192
Akerma, K., 658n.56
Akhenaton, 513n.
Alcibiades, 360–61, 841
Alexander I, 146n.136, 392
Alexander II, 601, 810
Alexander the Great, 16n.49, 19n.66, 22, 22n.82, 547, 554, 563–64, 567
Alexy, R., 645n.32, 646n.33, 647nn.35, 36, 737n.
Alt, F., 841n.85
Altheim, F., 835n.78
Amato, G., 744n.172
Ambrose, St., 24, 24n.91
Amphitryon, 253n.116
Anacharsis, 781
Anderson, P., 479n.69, 554n.204, 564n.220, 566n.223, 567n., 573n.232, 576, 577n.241, 578n.243, 587, 595n.282, 878n.
Andreae, J. V., 29
Anouilh, J.: *Antigone*, 94–95
Anschütz, G., 491
Antonius, M., 378n.147, 805
Apel, K.-O., xx, 108, 114n.63, 128n.97, 129, 175
Appleby, R. S., 606n.
Aquinas, St. Thomas, 16n.50, 125n.93, 399n.261, 421n.332, 639, 799n.29; on ambition, 289n.180; on means and ends, 131n.101; on natural law, 26; on vices, 299
Archimedes, 565

Arendt, H., 45n., 54, 67n.14; on American vs. French Revolution, 590; on natality, 235; on power and force, 339n.63
Aristophanes: "Clouds," 9; "Wasps," 758; "Women at the Ecclesia," 9
Aristotle: "Constitution of Athens," 15n.41; on corporate groups, 457n.33; on democracy, 15, 17, 17n.57; on education, 17; on ethics, 91n.9, 106; on the family, 15–16, 475; on friendship, 17–18, 292; on happiness, 16–17, 43; vs. Hegel, 51; on human beings as political animals, 189, 189n.1; on law, 518, 518n.143, 776; vs. Machiavelli, 13; *Metaphysics*, 25n.93, 125n.93; on military and political functions, 462, 462n.; *Nicomachean Ethics*, 5n.4, 81n.40, 125n.93, 289nn.179, 181, 459n.34; vs. Plato, 14–15, 16, 17, 18; and political handbooks, 149; *Politics*, 4n.3, 15n.41, 17, 17n.57, 18nn.62, 64, 43n.160, 106n.43, 189, 189n.1, 387n.193, 455n.29, 457nn.32, 33, 462n., 472n.53, 474n.59, 483n.77, 518n.143, 588, 639n.16, 769n., 776n.; on popular decisions vs. laws, 518, 518n.143; on potentiality, 279n.163; on practical syllogisms, 125n.93; on praxis, 219n.53; on revolution, 588; *Rhetoric*, 75, 356, 356n.93, 812n.; on size of state population, 474; on slavery, 4, 27, 336, 444; on the state, 15–18, 17n.57, 18nn.62–64, 19n.66, 455n.29, 462, 462n., 474, 475, 588, 639n.16; on suicide, 639n.16; on theology, 25n.93; *Topics*, 295n.; on vices, 295, 299; on virtues, 289n.181, 295, 295n.; on youth, 812
Arnason, J. P., 577n.240
Aron, R., 309n.9, 847n.97, 862
Arrow, K. J., 120n.83
Asch, S., 252n.115
Aśoka, 398, 513, 513n.

Assmann, J., 273n.156
Atatürk, K., 782
Augustine, St.: on Alexander the Great, 22; on ambition, 289n.180; on child development, 452n.; *De civitate Dei*, 21, 21n.77, 22, 24n.91, 25n.93, 31n., 119n.80, 193n.12, 301n.201, 367n.117, 368n.119, 412n.315, 422n.335, 452n., 455n.28, 507n.; on envy, 301n.200; on history, 24n.89; on human beings, 28, 193n.12, 221n.58, 454–55, 455n.28; on incest taboo, 454–55; on original sin, 22; on peace, 506–7, 507n.; on pride, 367n.117; on Roman Empire, 22; on Sermon on the Mount, 422n.335; on the state, 22, 22n.86; on virtues of Christian princes, 321n.
Augustus, 331, 363, 364, 364n.109, 378n.147, 398, 513, 514, 569, 589, 672, 672n.85, 821
Aurelius, M., 381n.160, 413, 422
Axelrod, R., 138n.114, 269n., 335n.58
Ayer, A. J., 89n.3

Bach, J. S.: *St. John Passion*, 153
Bachrach, P., 309n.8, 350n.86
Bacon, F.: *New Atlantis*, 42, 42n.155
Balandier, G., 268n.146
Baldwin, D. A., 342n.71
Bandura, A., 235n.83, 248n.104
Baratz, M. S., 309n.8, 350n.86
Barry, B., 111n., 732n.150
Barta, H., 677n.94
Bayertz, K., 203n.25
Beaumarchais, C. de, 812
Bechmann, A., 911n.40
Beck, L., 804
Beck, U., 715
Becket, T., 377, 377n.143
Beethoven, L. van, 820–21
Begin, M., 821–22
Beitz, C. R., 849n.103
Belsey, A., 765n.
Benjamin, W., 546n.
Bergengruen, W., 367; *Der Großtyrann und das Gericht*, 186
Bergman, I., 326n.41
Berlin, I., 181
Berman, H. J., 574n.234
Bernstein, R. J., 155n.
Binswanger, H. C., 140n.121, 583n.257
Birg, H., 919n.45
Birnbacher, D., 137n.112, 144n.131
Bismarck, O. von, 133, 392, 392n.226, 491, 533, 587, 600–601, 810, 821, 826, 848

Blomberg, W. von, 784
Bloom, A., 610
Böchenförde, E.-W., 723n.138
Bodin, J., 15, 15n.43, 33, 586n.
Boethius, 417
Boito, A.: *Falstaff*, 353
Bolt, R.: *A Man For All Seasons*, 330n.46, 361n.102
Boniface VIII, 407–8
Bonus, H., 711n.
Borgia, Cesare, 31, 31n.114, 401
Boris I, 414
Bosch, C., 670n.80
Botero, G., 29n.109
Boulding, K. E., 340n.66
Braithwaite, R. B., 136n.110
Brams, S. J., 744n.171
Brandt, W., 386n.191, 791
Brinton, C., 588n.265
Brod, M., 671–72
Brüning, H., 786
Brutus, L. J., 381
Brutus, M. J., 805–6
Buchanan, A., 808n., 809n.42
Buchanan, J. M., 677n.93, 730–31
Burckhardt, J., 46n.167, 178, 405, 546n., 549n.194, 553, 819, 819n.
Burke, E.: *Reflections on the Revolution in France*, 47–48, 48n.171, 57, 589, 589n.271
Busch, W., *Die fromme Helene*, 144n.132
Butler, J., 231n.74
Bynkershoek, C. von, 483n.79

Caesar, Julius, 20n.75, 161n., 171, 331, 359, 362–63, 364, 372n.129, 378n.147, 392, 421, 547, 569, 806nn.37, 38; assassination of, 805–6; *De bello civili*, 156–57, 156n.153
Caetano, M., 804
Calhoun, C., 591n.276
Calhoun, J. C., 487n.89
Caligula, 146n.136, 366, 366n.112, 399, 404
Callippus, 385
Camões, L. de, 400n.262
Campanella, T., 29
Canetti, E., 339n.63, 361n.103, 594
Caracalla, 18, 370, 370n.123, 569
Caravaggio, 359
Carlos, J., 754
Carter, J., 825
Cassirer, E., 256
Cassius, C., 805
Castro, I. de, 327

Cato the Elder, 570, 819
Cato the Younger, 421
Catullus, 19
Ceauçescu, N., 393n.231, 802, 804
Celestine V, 407–8
Cervantes, M. de: *Don Quixote*, 301n.204, 378–79, 402–3, 586, 670n.80, 672n.85, 738n.161, 781, 795
Chamberlain, N., 139, 152n.150, 412
Charlemagne, 401n.273, 513, 787n.12, 806
Charles II, 846
Charles the Bold, 461, 575
Charles V, 107, 107n.47, 313, 414
Chautemps, C., 392
Cheng Ho, 555n.205
Chesterfield, P. D. S., Earl of, 379n.152
Churchill, W., 139, 142n.125, 152n.150, 192n.7, 353n., 382, 388, 390, 392, 412, 414, 420, 533, 533n.173, 751n., 753, 859
Cicero, 20n.73, 32, 118n.75, 290n.183, 346n.76, 363, 363n.108, 430n., 924; on law, 20n.74, 632n.9; on rhetoric, 75; on the state, 13n.34, 19–20, 473
Cincinnatus, 526
Claessens, D., 445
Clausewitz, C. von, 64, 825n.66, 844n.89, 853–54, 855–56
Clinton, B., 148, 894
Coady, C. A. J., 88n.
Coelho, P., 327
Coke, E., 523n.
Commodus, 422
Comte, A., 45, 306, 620
Conan Doyle, A., 374n.132
Conrad, J.: *Lord Jim*, 95n.22, 191, 303n.208, 407
Constant, B., 566
Constantine, 513, 571
Cortés, H., 107n.47, 128n.97, 328, 392n.222, 599, 852
Cossiga, F., 525
Crassus, M. L., 346, 420n.329
Cromwell, O., 590, 628
Crutzen, P. J., 907n.32
Cuoco, V., 428, 428n., 820–21, 820n.58
Cyrus, 563
Czempiel, E.-O., 868n.4

Dante Alighieri: *De Monarchia*, 13n.34, 27; *Inferno*, 299, 407–8, 805; *Purgatorio*, 296n.189, 299n.193
Darwin, C., 162, 191, 197, 201–2, 202n., 203, 209, 227n.67, 270–71, 619, 660
David, King of Israel, 359, 402, 447, 563n.219
Davis, M. D., 136n.109, 740n.166

Dawkins, R., 197, 199n., 208, 214n.43, 456n.
Dehio, L., 599n.289
Descartes, R., 30n.112, 42, 150; *Discours de la méthode*, 83n.41; on foundation for ethics, 82; mind-body dualism of, 4, 30, 76n.28, 202, 621; on provisional ethics, 83, 83nn.41, 42
Destutt de Tracy, A. L. C., 305–6
Díaz del Castillo, B., 107n.47
Dickens, C., 923
Diebschlag, E., 218
Diocletian, 414, 565n.220, 570–71
Diogenes Laertius, 19n.69
Diogenes of Oenoanda, 19n.66
Dion, 385
Dollfuss, E., 528n.162
Dostoyevsky, F., 304, 361, 595n.283; *Crime and Punishment*, 369n.121; *Demons*, 326; *The Idiot*, 408; *The Brothers Karamazov*, 104n.38, 428, 788
Doyle, M. W., 506nn.127, 129, 763, 835n.76
Drewermann, E., 841n.85
Droste-Hülshoff, A. von: *Judenbuche*, 683
Dubček, A., 787
Durkheim, E., 469, 556, 590, 619
Dürrenmatt, F.: *Der Besuch der alten Dame*, 109; *Die Physiker*, 141n.123
Dworkin, G., 648n.40
Dworkin, R., 641n.19, 647n.37, 730n.144, 743, 743n., 745n., 761–62, 761n.191

Eccles, J., 202n., 231n.73
Edelman, G., 227n.67
Eibl-Eibesfeldt, I., 197, 212n.39, 214nn.45, 46, 215n., 217n.50, 218, 242n.94
Eichmann, A., 800
Einhard, 401n.273, 787n.12
Einstein, A., 142–43
Eisenstein, S.: *The Battleship Potemkin*, 339n.
Eliade, M., 24n.89
Eliot, T. S.: *Murder in the Cathedral*, 95
Elser, Georg, 801
Elster, J., 307n.4
Emmet, D., 229n.72
Engels, F., 56n.196
Enghien, Duke L. of, 848
Engisch, K., 464n.42
Epictetus, 106n.42, 328n.
Epicurus, 19n.69
Eppler, E., 865
Erikson, E. H., 224n.
Euclid, 20, 34n.126, 106n.44, 118n.75, 924
Eugene of Savoy, 600

Eulenspiegel, T., 331
Euripides, xviii, 9; *Iphigenia in Aulis*, 368n.118
Eusebius, 22n.86
Evren, K., 804–5

Fabius Maximus Verrucosus, Q., 323
Fahd, King, 606
Farabi, Al-, 13n.34, 25, 25n.96, 728
Faucher, L. E., 844, 844n.89
Feinberg, J., 642, 642n.23, 651, 652, 656–57, 656n.
Felix, D., 833n.75
Festinger, L., 245n.100
Feyerabend, P., 926, 926n.53
Fichte, J. G., 77n.30, 282, 631n.6, 642n.23, 644n.30,
    690n.112, 693; on the closed commercial state
    (*Der geschlossene Handelsstaat*), 130n., 712n.; on
    contracts, 641; on foreign trade, 712n.; on gene-
    sis of modern states, 772; vs. Hegel, 50, 52, 669;
    on history, 544, 549; on internal and external
    justice, 764n.196; vs. Kant, 48, 50, 52; on moral
    insights, 814–15; on moral responsibility, 407;
    on natural law, 632, 640, 642–44; on normative
    vs. descriptive statements, 48; on property, 669,
    679, 679n.96; on punishment, 682, 685n.; vs.
    Rawls, 641, 644n.28; *Rechtslehre*, 644; *Reden an
    die deutsche Nation*, 54; on selfishness, 640; on
    suicide, 652; *System der Sittenlehre*, 106n.42, 114;
    on testation, 699; on the welfare state, 644
Filmer, R., 35, 43, 442
Finnis, J., 632n.7
Flaubert, G.: *Madame Bovary*, 584
Fontane, T.: *Effi Briest*, 324n., 416n.326
Ford, John: *Young Mr. Lincoln*, 361–62
Forke, A., 6n.5
Forsthoff, E., 511n., 512, 610n.305, 738n.159, 760n., 913
Francis I, 313
Francis of Assisi, St., 24n.88, 83
Franco, F., 371, 389, 887
Frederick II: *Antimachiavel*, 372, 373n.128
Frederick the Great, 111, 365n., 373n.130, 374n.133,
    380n.158, 384n.178, 388n.199, 390n.210,
    394n.233, 395nn.240, 241, 397n.249; on
    alliances, 387nn.194, 196; on moral respon-
    sibility, 407
Frege, G., 158n.156
French, P. A., 799n.30
Freud, S., 97, 100, 216, 217, 217n.48, 229–30, 243, 402
Freund, J., 325n.39, 359n.99, 383n.172
Frey, B. S., 611n.
Frisch, Max: *Andorra*, 249n.107
Fritsch, W., Baron von, 784

Fritz, K. von, 19n.71
Fukuyama, F., 59, 594
Furet, F., 596n.284
Fustel de Coulanges, N. D., 21n.76

Gadamer, H.-G., 86n.50, 101n.35, 558
Gaiser, K., 12n.30
Galba, 346–47, 347n.77
Galbraith, J. K., 340, 340n.66
Galileo Galilei, 171
Gandhi, M., 432–33, 813, 889–90
Ganshof, F. L., 575n.235
Gaulle, C. de, 396–97, 821
Gehlen, A., 41–42, 220n.54, 222n.59, 233, 236, 241,
    248n.106, 255n.120, 256n.121, 261, 464n.41, 557;
    on agriculture, 584n.258; on archaic social
    structures, 270n.148; on institutions, 267,
    267n.141; on monuments, 272n.; on non-
    binding authority, 262; on reciprocal relation-
    ships, 270n.148; on representative rites, 257;
    on stabilized tension, 242
Gellner, E., 340n.66, 535n.178, 545, 555, 560n.213, 574,
    590n.273, 591, 591n.277
Gelzer, M., 793n.
Genghis Khan, 779
Genscher, H.-D., 414n.321
George I, 544, 545
George III, 544
Geronimo, 556, 630
Gethmann, C. F., 626n.
Gewirth, A., 114, 114nn.62, 63
Giddens, A., 582n.254
Gide, A., 383n.172
Gilpin, R., 505n.124, 603n., 844n.90
Ginés de Sepúlveda, J., 26–27, 122n.87
Glotz, P., 888n., 930
Goerdeler, C. F., 807
Goethe, J. W., 83n.43, 299n.195, 301n.203; "An
    Suleika," 853n.; *Die Braut von Korinth*, 818n.;
    Egmont, 31, 383; *Faust*, 401n.271; on love, 294n.
Gogol, N.: *Dead Souls*, 781n.6
Gonçalves, A., 327
Goodin, R. E., 732n.150
Gorbachev, M., xxi, 68, 133, 394, 417, 503, 596, 605,
    608, 787, 802–3, 865
Göring, H., 139
Gorky, M.: *The Summer People*, 815
Gracchi, the, 569
Gracián, B., 372n.129, 374, 374n.133, 379n.154,
    381nn.161, 165, 384n.177, 388n.198, 389n.207,
    392n.221, 393nn.228, 230, 400n.264, 403n.284

Gräfrath, B., 767n.

Grewe, W. G., 96n.27

Griepentrog, H., 305n.1

Grillparzer, F.: *Weh dem, der lügt*, 373

Grotius, H., 480–81

Guicciardini, F., 29n.109, 141n.122, 379nn.150, 154, 156, 383n.175, 388n.202, 389n.205, 391n.217, 396, 802, 802n., 806n.40

Guillaume, G., 386n.191

Haas, H., 713n.129

Haber, F., 670n.80

Habermas, J., 54n., 108, 175, 177n.182, 282n.169, 306, 464, 788, 788n.13

Hácha, E., 843

Hadrian, 527

Hadrian VI, 354n.89

Halbwachs, M., 273n.156

Halder, F., 804

Hall, J. A., 552, 562n.216, 582n.253, 593n.280

Hamilton, A., 41, 342n.70, 497n.111, 522n., 523n., 728n., 733, 749, 752n.182, 764, 787, 787n.11

Hamilton, W. D., 198

Hammarskjöld, D., 869–70

Han-fei-tzu, 6n.5

Hannibal, 323, 323n.34, 545

Hare, J. E., 842n.87

Hare, R. M., 72n., 91n.11, 116n.67, 117n.71, 125n.93, 139n.116

Hart, H. L. A., 436n., 465n.43, 632, 633, 730n.144

Hartmann, E. von, 100

Hartmann, N., 91

Hartwig, M., 604n., 872n., 874n.11

Harun ar-Rashid, 394

Hašek, J., 431

Hauchler, I., 895n.

Havel, V., xxi, 410n.

Haydn, J., 412

Hebbel, F.: *Agnes Bernauer*, 807

Hebel, J. P., 418

Hegel, G. W. F., 45, 84, 87n.51, 116, 153, 208n., 322n., 325, 642n.23, 816; on the absolute, 51, 719; vs. Aristotle, 51; on Christianity, 21n.78, 59, 545; on civil society, 50–51; on constitutions, 474n.59; on contracts, 673, 674–75; on corporate groups, 379n.155; *Encyclopedia of the Philosophical Sciences*, 98n., 305, 631n.5, 782; vs. Fichte, 50, 52, 669; on freedom, 648; on Greece, 566n.223; on history, 51–52, 183, 470, 544, 545, 546n., 554, 554n.204, 593, 621, 853; vs. Hobbes, 51; on India, 572n.; on inheritance, 699n.117, 700; vs. Kant,

50, 52, 117n.69, 119n.77; on law, 474n.59, 636, 639, 693; vs. Locke, 51, 639n.15; on morality (*Moralität*), 73, 88, 814, 815; on mores (*Sittlichkeit*), 50–51, 73, 88, 580n.247; on natural law, 486n., 632, 648; on opposition forces in the state, 753; on Peisistratos, 789n.16; *Phänomenologie des Geistes*, 815; on philosophy of law, 50–51, 50n.179; on power-holders, 393n.229; on property, 668–71, 672n.86, 674–75, 675n., 699n.117, 700; on punishment, 682, 682n.99, 683, 685n.; on reason, 52, 58–59; *Rechtsphilosophie*, 12n.29, 50–52, 119n.77, 167, 526n.158, 541n.183, 626–27, 636n.13, 648n.39, 653n.49, 668nn.71, 72, 669n.79, 672n.86, 673n.88, 677n.94, 682n.99, 699n.117, 734n.156, 823n., 845n.92; on religion, 470, 782; vs. Rousseau, 51; on spheres of justice, 654; on the state, 29n.108, 50–52, 58–59, 442, 473n.58, 526n.158, 545, 823; on state of nature, 823; on suicide, 653n.49; on technology, 578n.242

Heidegger, M., 167, 180, 232n.76, 235, 282, 298n.192, 305, 306, 621n., 664n.67

Heine, H., 50, 96

Hellenthal, F., 713n.129

Heller, H., 437, 461n.36, 477n.67, 481n.74, 482n.76, 488n., 540n.181, 542n.184

Hempel, C. G., 170

Hennen, M., 404n.285

Henry I, 575

Henry II, 376–77

Henry VI, 806

Henry VIII, 330, 330n.46, 361, 369, 369n.122

Herder, J. G.: *Ideen zur Philosophie der Geschichte der Menschheit*, 194

Herdt, J., 814n.49

Herodotus, 9, 9n.17, 64, 93, 142n.127, 390n.213, 683n., 845n.93

Herzog, R., 464n.41, 477n.65, 487n.87, 494n.103, 500n.117, 503n.123, 520n.146

Hesiod: *Theogony*, 443

Hess, R. D., 479n.70

Hieron I, 403

Hindenburg, P. von, 794, 801

Hintze, O., 576

Hitchcock, A., 312

Hitler, A., 143, 329, 434–35, 547, 826, 837–38, 845, 861, 863; assassination attempts on, 388–89, 598n., 801, 804, 807; cruelty of, 58, 78, 398, 398n.252, 597, 686, 725, 840; and Enabling Act of 1933, 516, 527, 528n.162; *Mein Kampf*, 141–42, 141n.124; vs. Napoleon I, 848; as politician, 70,

230, 343, 351, 353, 371, 384, 396, 420, 527, 594, 598, 725, 784–85, 794, 844; relations with the military, 784–85

Hobbes, T., 8, 9n.17, 11n.26, 15n.43, 32–44, 46, 53, 271, 488, 642, 770, 818, 892; axiomatic method of, 34, 34n.126; on Christianity, 36, 37–38, 39–40, 39n.145; and civil war, xix, 34, 37, 38, 88, 628, 629; on commands, 325; on contracts, 35–36, 38–39, 630, 638–39, 731; on death, 39–40, 770; *De Cive*, xix, 156; on distinction between private and public, 35; on domination, 441n.11; on equality, 36, 36n.137; vs. Fichte, 643; vs. Hegel, 51; on human beings, 42–43, 193, 233; on justice, 13, 37, 37n.139; vs. Kant, 43–44, 48–49, 48n.172; vs. Locke, 32–33, 34, 34n.128, 40–41, 42–44, 43n.160, 639n.15, 646, 770; vs. Machiavelli, 28, 33–34, 37; on morals and politics, xv, 13, 28, 37, 88; on natural law, 37–39, 37n.139, 38n.143, 39n.145, 40n.150, 636, 639, 640; on peace, 34–35, 36; vs. Plato, 13, 32, 36, 42, 43; on positive law, 13, 35, 37, 37n.139, 626, 627; on power, 310, 310n.11, 313n.18, 375n.135; on property, 646; on punishment, 682; vs. Rousseau, 44; on self-interest, 28, 36, 37–39, 38n.143, 40n.151, 42–44, 48–49, 51, 58, 105–6, 106n.42, 268, 449, 619, 628, 639, 640; on the social contract, 35–36, 630, 638–39, 731; as social scientist, 156, 225, 268; on sovereignty, 24n.91, 33–35, 34n.129, 40–41; on state of nature, 38, 40, 40n.151, 316, 448–49, 628–29, 638–40; on Thucydides, 81n.38; on truth, 33; and universalism, 105–6, 106n.42; on universal state, 40n.151; on value of human beings, 42–43

Hockett, C., 257n.125

Hoff, J., 656n.

Hofmannsthal, H. von: *Elektra*, 332n.53

Holbein, H., 330

Honecker, E., 393n.231

Honneth, A., 317n.25

Horace, 570n.228

Horn, C., 764n.193

Hsiang of Sung, Duke, 856n.112

Huber, G., 288n.174, 546n.

Hugo, V.: *Les Misérables*, 181–82, 433, 803

Humboldt, W. von, 55, 55n.194, 56, 642, 644, 694–95, 930

Hume, D., 48; on causality, 170; on *Is* and *Ought* (Hume's Law), 89n.4, 90, 90n.6, 276; "Of the Balance of Power," 847; on social contract theory, 447n.21

Huntington, S., 830n.70

Hussein, S., 399, 779, 848, 868

Husserl, E., 74, 925, 926

Hustedt, M., 902n.

Huxley, A., 59, 179n.186, 621n.; *Brave New World*, 165n.164, 280, 351, 370, 620, 659–60

Iambulus, 29n.110

Ibsen, H.: *Peer Gynt*, 282; *Rosmersholm*, 326

Ikenberry, G. J., 552, 562n.216, 582n.253, 593n.280

Isaacs, S. L., 702n.

Ivan the Terrible, 534

Jackson, A., 521

Jackson, R. H., 438n.4

Jaruzelski, W., 690, 802

Jay, J., 41, 787

Jefferson, T., 523, 795

Jeffrey, R. C., 135n.108

Jellinek, G., 437, 437n.3, 438, 473, 484, 487, 489n.91, 494nn.103, 105, 500n.118, 519n., 520n.147, 645

Jenner, Edward, 68–69

Jeremiah, 427

Jermann, C., 10n.21, 50n.178

Jesus of Nazareth, 23n., 24n.89, 85, 94n.19, 153, 288, 359, 422n.335, 571, 812, 814, 833; as Incarnation, 24, 39, 545, 572, 574, 579, 813; Sermon on the Mount, 422n.335, 432–33

Joerden, J. C., 803n.

John of Salisbury: *Policraticus*, 27

Johnson, A., 532n.170

John XXIII, 395

Joly, M.: *Dialogue aux enfers entre Machiavel et Montesquieu*, 372, 375n.135, 381n.166, 382n.171, 394n.238, 399n.259, 400n.265

Jonas, H., xx, 114n.63, 115, 131n.103, 153, 195n.16, 226n., 247n.103, 292n., 425, 546n., 620n., 641, 664n.67, 840; on *Ought* (*Sollen*) and volitive act (*Wollen*), 280n.165; on plants vs. animals, 211, 226

Jones, E. L., 555

Jouvenel, B. de, 192n.9, 529n., 552

Joynt, C. B., 842n.87

Judas Iscariot, 805

Justinian, 514

Kádár, J., 803

Kafka, F., 671–72; *Metamorphosis*, 229; *The Trial*, 331, 444

Kahr, G., 398n.252

Kāmandaka: *Nītisāra*, 6n.6

Kangle, R. P., 6n.6, 7n.9

Kant, I., 30, 116, 144, 417, 675n., 856; on a posteriori judgments, 121; on a priori synthetic judgments, 121; on autonomy, 100; on the categorical imperative, 48, 49–50, 93, 113–14; *Critique of Judgment*, 153, 209n.35; on cruelty to animals, 115, 115n.64; vs. Fichte, 48, 50, 52; on foreign policy, 849; on foreign trade, 712n.; on God, 48; on the good will, 96; on head of household, 444n.14; vs. Hegel, 50, 52, 117n.69, 119n.77; on helping others, 108; on history, 52, 544; vs. Hobbes, 43–44, 48–49, 48n.172; intentionalism of, 48, 92, 93–94, 108, 124, 174–75; on intrinsic value, 96; on lies, 94, 108, 108n.49, 109, 112, 117, 117n.69; vs. Locke, 43–44; on mathematics, 118n.76; on maxims, 93, 106; *Metaphysics of Morals*, 49–50, 483n.79, 643n.24, 646n.34, 655n.51, 669n.75, 672n.86, 682n.98, 690n., 699n.116, 795n.27, 864n.; on moral feelings, 101–2; on moral obligations, 44, 101–2, 102n., 105–6, 108, 112, 117, 117n.69, 153, 209, 282n.169; on morals and politics, 48–50, 49n.176; on normative vs. descriptive statements, 48, 50, 57, 121, 125, 129, 153, 209; on noumenal vs. phenomenal *I*, 290; on peace, 49, 763, 864; on perfect vs. imperfect duties, 108, 112; vs. Plato, 11; on practical reason, 48, 50, 134; on property, 646n.34, 655n.51, 669n.75, 672n.86; on punishment, 682, 683, 685n., 690n., 691; on rationalization, 370; on realm of ends, 114, 129; vs. Robespierre, 50; on the state, 48–49, 52, 473n.58; on unity of apperception, 224; universalism of, 92, 105–6, 106n.42, 108–9, 112, 113–14, 118–19, 174–75; on wanting the same thing, 313n.19; *Zum ewigen Frieden*, 49, 49n.176, 763, 768n., 849
Kaplan, A., 62n.3, 85n.47, 156n.152, 168–69, 247n.102, 260n.129, 271n.150, 342, 355n.91, 362n.105, 449n., 491–92, 528n.163
Kapp, W., 528
Kaser, M., 669n.79
Kaufmann, A., 795n.24
Kauṭilīya, 6–8, 6n.6, 7n.9, 19n.67, 64, 323n.33, 340, 348, 348n.81, 371n.125, 374n.133, 375n.134, 381n.159, 383n.174, 385n.181, 386n.190, 388n.200, 391n.215, 392n.225, 397n.248, 399n.256, 502n., 508
Kavka, G. S., 800n.
Kelly, W. H., 255n.118
Kelsen, H., 37, 437, 491n.97
Kennedy, P., 609n.303
Kepler, J., 194n.15
Kesselring, T., 836, 874n.9

Kettner, M., 404n.290
Keynes, J. M., 914
Kierkegaard, S., 177n.183, 282, 621; *Either/Or*, 326n.41; *Fear and Trembling*, 79n., 142n.126
Klein, H.-D., 597n.287
Kleist, H. von, 247n.101; *Michael Kohlhaas*, 796; *Penthesilea*, 332
Klemperer, V., 256n.123
Kloepfer, M., 626n.
Kluckhohn, C., 255n.118
Knights, D., 552n.198
Kodalle, K.-M., 813n.
Kohl, H., 391, 394, 723n.140
Kohlberg, L., 175, 573
Köhler, M., 99n.30
Kojève, A., 59
Kolitz, Z., 598n.
Kondylis, P., 865n.2
Kopelev, L., 840
Koslowski, P., 705n.123
Krämer, H., 282n.169
Kratochwil, F. V., 386n.188, 496n., 650n.44
Kreft, B., 514n.138
Kreft, W., 514n.138
Krickeberg, W., 175n.181
Kriele, M., 473n.56, 484, 487n.88, 489n.92, 626, 787
Kubrick, S.: *Dr. Strangelove*, 116–17; *2001: A Space Odyssey*, 234n.81
Kuhn, T., 237, 549
Kühnhardt, L., 831n.
Küng, H., 876
Kutschera, F. von, 89n.1, 98n., 108n.49, 135n.108

La Fontaine, J. de, 192
Lao-tzu, 563
Lapierre, J.-W., 189n.2, 472n.52
La Rochefoucauld, F. de, 96n.26, 290n.184, 301n.200, 373n.131, 382nn.167, 169, 580n.246
Las Casas, B. de, 26–27, 122n.87, 830n.71, 853
Laslett, P., 33n.123, 43n.161
Lasswell, H. D., 62n.3, 85n.47, 156n.152, 168–69, 247n.102, 260n.129, 271n.150, 342, 355n.91, 362n.105, 449n., 491–92, 528n.163
Le Bon, G., 594, 609n.304
Le Carré, J., 369; *Smiley's People*, 434n.347; *The Spy Who Came in from the Cold*, 7, 373–74
Leibniz, G., 80n.36, 168n.168, 179, 179n.187, 202n., 227, 231n.74, 288n.178, 544, 551n.196, 588, 632
Leisinger, K. M., 719n., 900n., 901n.
Leist, A., 279n.162
Lenin, V. I., 22n.82, 70, 139, 320, 601, 620

Lenz-Medoc, P., 395n.239

Lessing, G. E.: *Minna von Barnhelm,* 288n.175

Levinas, E., 288

Lévi-Strauss, C., 270, 454, 548, 548n.191, 607n.

Lincoln, A., 120, 810; Gettysburg Address, 820; second inaugural address, 185

Livy, 20n.75, 161n., 382n.171, 392n.224, 393n.227, 402n.276, 404n.289, 535, 791n.21, 924; on Herennius Pontius in Second Samnite War, 150–51, 150n.142, 151nn.144–46, 173; on Lucius Valerius Flaccus, 173; and Machiavelli, 553; on Maharbal and Hannibal in Second Punic War, 323n.34; on meeting between Marcius and Perseus, 336; on Philip V, 348n.82, 385n.183; on Romulus and Remus, 463n.38; on Tullus Hostilius's punishment of Metius Fufetius, 270n.149

Locke, J., 53, 231n.74, 271, 644; on concepts, 168n.168; *Essay Concerning Human Understanding,* 43, 229n.71; on family and state, 442; on freedom from interference, 795, 795n.26; vs. Hegel, 51, 639n.15; vs. Hobbes, 32–33, 34, 34n.128, 40–41, 42–44, 43n.160, 639n.15, 646, 770; vs. Kant, 43–44; on money, 459n.35; on natural law, 43, 43n.161, 44, 632; on property, 43, 646, 669; vs. Rousseau, 44; on self-interest, 42–44, 51, 512; on speciesism, 278n.161; on the state, 55, 517; on state of nature, 40; *Two Treatises of Government,* 33, 34n.128, 40, 43, 43n.161, 306, 517n.142, 648n.39, 669n.76, 675n., 770, 795n.26

Lorentz, K., 171, 197, 220n.55, 273n.155

Loske, R., 902n., 907n.33

Losurdo, D., 52n.187

Louis XIII, 587

Louis XIV, 598, 827, 846

Louis XVI, 780, 819, 820

Lovins, A. B., 879n.17

Lovins, L. H., 879n.17

Löwith, K., 25n.92

Lübbe, H., 152n.149, 184n.191

Luce, R. D., 134n.

Lucretius, 19, 910n.39

Luhmann, N., 47n.168, 141n.123, 164, 306, 311n.16

Lukács, G., 561n.215

Lukes, S., 350n.85

Lumet, S.: *Twelve Angry Men,* 760

Lumsdaine, D. H., 835n.77

Luther, M., 581, 581n.250; two realms theory, 28, 28n.107

Luttwak, E. N., 570

Lvov, G. Y., 408

Lynch, D.: *The Elephant Man,* 123n.

Machiavelli, N., 46, 57, 181, 323, 333, 374n.133; on alliances, 388n.197; vs. Aristotle, 13; on aspirants to power, 378n.148, 379n.151; attitudes toward, 6–7, 8, 31, 31n.117; on Borgia and Ramiro de Lorqua, 401; on Caesar, 806n.37; on Christianity, 21; on combination of fear and love, 394, 394n.235; on compromises, 150, 150n.143; on concealment of talent, 381; on conspiracies, 371–72; on contracts, 421; on democracy, 789; on dictatorship, 526n.159; *Discorsi,* 21n.76, 32, 64, 346n.75, 347n.78, 364n.110, 371n.125, 372n.129, 377n.146, 387n.196, 390nn.208, 212, 391n.214, 392n.222, 396n.243, 397n.248, 398n.255, 429n., 526n.159, 789n.15, 805n.36, 806n.37; on envy, 382n.168; on ethics, 87; on flattery, 380n.157; on force, 30, 31, 192n.10, 390, 398, 401, 805; vs. Guicciardini, 141n.122; on happiness, 31; on hereditary monarchies, 377n.145; vs. Hobbes, 28, 33–34, 37; on law, 824; and Livy, 553; on money, 348; on morals and politics, xv, 6–7, 13, 21, 28, 29–32, 37, 42; on patricians and plebeians, 568; vs. Plato, 13; on power, 29–32, 31n.118, 33, 64, 87, 171n.176, 348, 349n.84, 376, 376n.141, 396, 397nn.247, 248, 399n.257, 400n.263, 401, 405, 410; *Il Principe,* 29–32, 29n.109, 42, 65n.12, 71, 192n.9, 203, 323n.36, 347n.80, 349n.84, 372, 377n.144, 378n.148, 386n.187, 388n.201, 389, 392n.225, 394n.235, 397nn.247, 248, 398nn.250, 254, 255, 399n.257, 401, 421n.333, 478n., 806n.37; on revenge, 398, 398n.255; on ruses, 372n.129; on ruthlessness, 398, 398n.255; on strategic rationality, 30–31

MacIntyre, A., 68n.18

Macpherson, C. B., 42n.157

Madison, J., 41, 497n.111, 639–40, 728n., 733, 735, 741, 764, 787, 795

Mahavira, 563

Mahrenholz, E. G., 514n.137, 734n.155, 886n.18

Maimonides, M., 25n.95

Maine, H. S., 467n.45

Malesherbes, C. G. de, 780

Malinowski, B., 270, 270n.148

Malthus, T., 456

Mandela, N., 421

Mandeville, B. de: *Fable of the Bees,* 42

Mann, H.: *Der Untertan,* 419n.

Mann, M., 165, 255n.119, 338n., 340, 539n., 552, 560n.214, 570n.227, 575n.237, 584n.260,

588n.266, 590, 590n., 592n., 763n.; on cultural
    evolution, 556; on history, 554, 554n.204; on
    interstitial emergence, 263, 547, 547n.188;
    on irrigation, 559n.212; on power, 263n.138;
    on rights, 593; on sources of social power,
    264; on the state during Middle Ages,
    573n.231
Mann, T., 80n.34, 525n.156, 550; *Die Bekenntnisse des
    Hochstaplers Felix Krull*, 284n.172; *Der Erwählte*,
    415n.325, 697; "Das Gesetz," 783, 824; *Joseph and
    His Brothers*, 185n.193, 186, 217n.49; "Royal
    Highness," 525–26
Mannheim, K., 306
Manzoni, A., 821n.60; *I promessi sposi*, 330–31, 333,
    335–36, 337, 354, 358, 361n.103
Mao Tse-Tung, 387n.192, 580, 847n.99, 856n.112,
    860
Marcius Philippus, Quintus, 336
Marius, 569
Marlborough, John Churchill, Duke of, 379n.152
Marlowe, C.: *The Jew of Malta*, 31n.117
Marshall, J., 523
Marsilius of Padua: *Defensor pacis*, 27, 27n.105
Marty, M. E., 606n.
Marx, K., 56–57, 97, 306, 347n.78, 593, 609, 609n.304;
    on classes, 459, 538–39; on commodities,
    676–77; *Communist Manifesto*, 56n.196; on his-
    tory, 547, 554n.204, 595–96, 853; on labor, 236,
    676–77; on private property, 665, 671n.83; on
    the state, 22n.82, 56, 538
Marx, S., 247n.101
Maslow, A., 241n.92
Mass, J.: *Das Eis von Cape Sabine*, 143n.129
Mauss, M., 236n.87, 270n.148
Maxwell, M., 825n.65
Maynard Smith, J., 199, 214n.43
McNamara, R., 861n.
McNeill, W. H., 596n.285
Mead, G., 249, 250
Meier, C., 9n.14, 821n.61
Meinecke, F., 29n.109
Melville, H.: "Benito Cereno," 393n.231, 492; *Billy
    Budd*, 300n.199, 339n.62; *Moby Dick*, 315n., 413,
    434, 640n.
Menenius Lanatus, Agrippa, 791
Menzel, U., 605n., 898
Meyer, C. F.: *Der Heilige*, 377n.143
Meyer, E., 255, 455n.29, 813–14
Meyer, J. J., 7n.9
Meyer, T., 396n.245
Meyer-Abich, K. M., 626n., 664n.67, 909n.35
Michels, R., 528

Mill, J. S., 349n.83, 495n.108, 520n.149, 530, 563n.219,
    586n., 706n., 849n.104; on bicameral systems,
    747n.176; *Considerations on Representative
    Government*, 723; on evaluating political insti-
    tutions, 725–26; *On Liberty*, 55, 56, 664n.65,
    723; on pleasure, 113; on punishment, 682;
    on responsibility, 749n.178; on the state, 55;
    on suicide, 652; on voting, 740, 740n.165
Minucius Felix, 22n.83
Mirabeau, H. de, 784
Mises, L. von, 705n.124
Mitterand, F., 791n.20
Mobuto Sese Seko, 606
Mohammed, the prophet, 177, 450n., 572, 782
Mommsen, T., 20n.73, 156n.153, 392n.218, 499n.115,
    501n.119, 527n.160; *History of Rome*, 156–57
Montesquieu, 46n.165, 309n.6, 335n.57, 366n.113,
    381n.162, 382n.170, 388n.201, 394, 397n.247,
    403n.281, 419n., 474n.59, 495n.106, 505n.124,
    534n.176, 553, 559n.211, 686n.108, 740n.164,
    780n., 787n.12, 828; on Ambrose, 24n.91; on
    despotism, 917; on European power, 552n.199;
    on feudalism, 576; on foreign trade, 832–33; on
    institutions, 540; on the judiciary, 521, 522; on
    law, 438, 465, 633n., 634, 636n.12, 738, 782n.7;
    on marriage, 698n.; on mores, 485n.85,
    534n.175; on patricians and plebeians, 568; on
    power vs. freedom of the people, 531n.168; on
    punishment, 485n.84; on separation of powers,
    41, 517; on territoriality of the state, 764; vs.
    Tocqueville, 54
Montezuma II, 107, 328
Moore, G. E.: on human life, 112n.; on naturalistic
    fallacy, 90, 90n.6; on organic wholes, 119n.78,
    182; *Principia Ethica*, 90n.6, 106n.42, 112n.,
    119n.78, 131n.102
More, T., 330n.46, 361, 361n.102, 369; *Utopia*, 29–30,
    57
Morgenstern, O., 136n.109, 157n.154, 374n.132
Morgenthau, H. J., 66n., 309n.7, 335n.56, 389n.204,
    497n.111, 505n.125, 506, 508nn.131, 132, 524n.,
    601n.295, 825, 854n.108, 869nn.6, 7
Mosca, G., 528
Moses, 450
Mozart, W. A., 302, 412
Müller, M., 907n.32
Münch, I. von, 796n.28
Münch, P.:, 554n.200, 578n.244, 582n.255
Musashi, M., 64
Musgrave, R. A., 717
Musil, R.: *Geschichten, die keine sind*, 302n.206
Mussolini, B., 329, 343, 371, 397, 534, 793, 852

Nacken, G., 902n.

Nagel, T., 86n.49, 794n.

Napoleon I, 181–82, 380, 392, 527, 547, 589, 598, 600, 803, 820–21, 821n.60, 823, 844n.89, 848

Napoleon III, 372, 530, 752, 842

Næss, A., 664n.67

Naylor, R. T., 918n.

Necho II, 555n.205

Nerva, 422

Neudeck, R., 889

Neumann, J. von, 136n.109

Neumark, F., 757n.186, 758n.

Nicholas of Cusa, 25n.96

Nicholson, M., 150n.140, 169n., 505n.126, 661n.

Nicias, 841

Nida-Rümelin, J., 121n.85

Nietzsche, F., 22, 72, 84, 97, 178, 282, 288n.176, 301n.200, 307, 354n.88, 722, 729; on architecture, 514; on Christianity, 299n.196, 619n.; on the Dionysian and Apollonian, 314n.21; *Geburt der Tragödie*, 314n.21; *Genealogy of Morals*, 73, 297; on human beings, 298n.191; on life and spirit, 223n.62; on power, 58, 305, 405, 429; on ressentiment, 297; on vices, 290n.184

Nossack, H. E.: *Das Testament des Lucius Eurinus*, 549n.192

Nozick, R., 642, 644, 644n.30

Octavian. *See* Augustus

Odysseus, 324

Oesterreich, P. L., 356n.94

Øfsti, A., 250n.110

Oppenheim, P., 170

Ortega y Gasset, J., 477n.66, 525n.155, 594, 617n., 921, 921n.

Orwell, G.: 1984, 59, 78n.31, 260, 260n.130, 275n., 326, 326n.40, 331, 370; *Animal Farm*, 192

Otto, R.: *Das Heilige*, 468–69

Pahlen, P. von, 146n.136

Paine, T., 47n.169, 48, 48n.171; *Common Sense*, 812

Pāṇini, *Aṣṭadhayāyī*, 20

Papinian, 369–70, 370n.123

Pareto, V., 306, 307, 528, 619; Pareto-inclusiveness, 120, 120n.82; Pareto-optimality, 111, 111n., 137, 161, 448, 630, 693, 792

Parfit, D., 659

Parijs, P. van, 649n.

Paris, R., 342

Park Chung Hee, 606, 788–89, 788n.14

Parker, G., 599n.290

Parsons, T., 334, 340, 342, 342n.69

Pascal, B., 77n.30, 133n.105, 191n.4, 225n.65, 250n.109, 320, 347n.79, 416n.327, 580n.248, 641–42, 642n.21, 862

Paul, St., 22

Paul I (Czar), 146n.136, 527

Peisistratus, 390n.213

Peres, S., 787

Pericles, 566

Perperna, 412n.313

Perseus of Macedonia, 336

Peterson, E., 22n.86

Peter the Great, 527, 781

Philip II (Macedonia), 847

Philip II (Spain), 598

Philip V (Macedonia), 348n.82, 385n.183

Piaget, J., 175

Pico della Mirandola, G., 191n.4

Pilsudski, J., 528nn.162, 163

Pirandello, L., 251n.112

Plato, 9n.18, 11n.24, 25, 26, 29n.110, 82, 424, 762, 924, 925; allegory of the cave, 11, 12n.28; *Apology*, 10nn.21, 22; vs. Aristotle, 14–15, 16, 17, 18; on art, 148; communism of, 12, 15; on democracy, 566, 728; doctrine of Ideas, 10–11, 12, 12n.28, 18, 143, 158n.156, 163; on education, 14, 18; *Gorgias*, 36, 68; on happiness, 43; *Hippias Minor*, 99n.31; vs. Hobbes, 13, 32, 36, 42, 43; on intergenerational conflict, 548; on judges, 510n.; on justice, 13–14; vs. Kant, 11; on law, 514, 738; *Laws*, 12n.29, 15, 612n.308, 684n.105, 738; vs. Machiavelli, 13; on mathematics, 11, 11n.25, 42, 74, 118n.76, 158; on morality, 565; on music, 720; on power, 14, 15, 67, 321, 412, 419n.; on punishment, 682, 684n.105; on reason, 14; *Republic*, 5n.4, 7n.10, 10–16, 12n.28, 17, 18n.65, 20, 29, 36, 42, 131n.102, 163, 367n.116, 399n.257, 412, 419n.328, 457n.32, 462n., 510n., 548, 720n., 775; on rhetoric, 75; *Seventh Letter*, 14n.38, 781n.5; on slavery, 4; *Statesman*, 15, 514n.138; *Symposium*, 361; and totalitarianism, 15, 15n.50; on truth, 14; on virtues and vices, 295; on women, 4, 12

Plessner, H., 223, 223n.61

Plutarch, 327n., 412n.313, 421n.331

Poe, E. A.: *The Purloined Letter*, 373, 384n.176

Pogge, T., 874n.9

Poincaré, H., 148n.139

Polo, M., 577

Polybius, 19n.71, 404n.289, 548n.189

Pompeius, 327n., 792–93

Pontius Pilate, 153

Popper, K. R., 15n.40, 127n.96, 171n.174; falsification-
    ism of, 140n.118; on memory, 231n.73; on mind
    and body, 202n.; theory of the three worlds, 158
Portinaro, P. P., 332n.50
Portmann, A., 219n.52
Postman, N., 708n.
Primas, H., 201n.22
Procopius, 514
Prusias, 404n.289
Pufendorf, S. von, 29n.108
Pulcher, P. Clodius, 24
Pushkin, A.: *Mozart and Salieri*, 302, 302n.205

Quinctius Flaminius, 259
Qviller, B., 28n.106

Rabin, Y., 787
Racine, J., 402n.275
Radbruch, G., 635n., 699
Raiffa, H., 134n.
Ramiro de Lorqua, 401
Rapoport, A., 138n.114
Rauch, G. von, 821n.62
Rawls, J., 115n.66, 118, 129, 133n.104, 290n.182,
    644n.28, 659n.59, 754, 788n.13; on the difference
    principle, 667; on equality, 110–11, 110n., 667;
    on the good and the right, 90n.9; on justice,
    107n.46, 110–11, 110n., 115n.65, 129, 301,
    640–41, 662n.63; on maximin principle, 110–11,
    110n.; on the original position, 92n.14, 290,
    640–41; on reflective equilibrium, 91; on sav-
    ings rate, 662n.63; on sovereignty, 849n.103; on
    teleological theories, 90n.9; on universalism,
    106n.41; on utilitarianism, 110–11, 115n.66; on
    violations of law, 795n.24; on the welfare state,
    xix, 54n.
Reagan, R., 821–22, 825
Rescher, N., 667n., 713n.130
Ribbentrop, J. von, 802
Richard II, 806
Richardson, L. F., 169
Richelieu, Cardinal, 32n.122, 587
Riesman, D., 560, 585n., 594, 614, 615
Rigotti, F., 192n.7
Riker, W. H., 387n.194
Roberts, J., 552n.198
Robespierre, M., 45, 45n., 50, 620, 784
Roetz, H., 7n.10
Röhm, E., 398n.252
Rommel, E., 840–41
Roosevelt, F., 143, 146n.135, 845

Rosenberg, C. G., 438n.4
Rosenkranz, K., 305–6
Ross, W. D., 16n.49
Rousseau, J.-J., 56, 371n.126, 372, 480n.72, 534, 598,
    784; on Christianity, 21, 44–45; on democracy,
    44, 44n.162, 488, 531; and French Revolution,
    46, 46n.165; on the general will, 44, 44n.162;
    on goodness of human beings, 46, 46n.167, 136;
    vs. Hegel, 51; vs. Hobbes, 44; vs. Locke, 44; on
    morals and politics, 21; on the noble savage, 179;
    on property, 668–69, 669n.73; on taxation,
    757n.185
Rushdie, S.: *Satanic Verses*, 829
Russell, B., 862
Russett, B., 868n.5
Rüttgers, J., 723n.140

Sahlins, M., 557
Saint-Exupéry, A. de: *Le petit prince*, 474
Sakharov, A., 802–3
Salieri, A., 302
Sallust, 20n.75, 156n.153, 161n., 275n., 372n.129,
    420n.329
Sargon of Akkad, 562
Sartori, G., 531n.169
Sartre, J.-P., 119, 167, 316n.24, 332n.50
Sasso, G., 32n.120
Scelzo, D., 63n.5
Schapera, I., 472n.51
Schefold, B., 909n.35
Scheler, M., 81n.38, 84n.45, 93n.18, 101, 113n.61, 121,
    179n.185, 241n.91, 258, 282n.168, 284n.171, 300;
    on asceticism, 223; on feelings, 239–40; on
    pleasure, 281; on principle of solidarity,
    104n.38; on ressentiment, 297, 297n.; on retri-
    bution, 682–83; *Die Stellung des Menschen im
    Kosmos*, 223; on value ethics, 72; *Wesen und
    Formen der Sympathie*, 239
Scherer, G., 91n.10, 571n., 664n.67
Scherhorn, G., 713n.129
Schiller, F., 268n.145; on aesthetics, 717; *Die Braut
    von Messina*, 368n.118, 400n.267; *Don Carlos*,
    174, 404; on grace (*Ammut*), 296n.188; on
    Hadrian VI, 354n.89; *Maria Stuart*, 402; on
    moral motives, 866; *Wallensteins Tod*, 139n.117,
    323, 345, 378, 387n.195, 393, 393n.229
Schimmel, A., 829
Schlosser, F. C., 405
Schmid, C., 860
Schmidt, H., 723n.140
Schmidt-Bleek, F., 879n.16

Schmitt, C., 22n.86, 43, 192n.6, 389n.206, 439n.7,
    494n.103, 602n.296; on constitutions, 489nn.91,
    93, 490n.96, 516–17, 516n., 517n.140, 518–19;
    Der Begriff des Politischen, 58, 67, 383; on
    dictatorship, 526–27, 526n.159; on friend-foe
    distinction, 307, 383, 383n.172, 406n.; on law,
    465n.44, 473n.54, 518, 518n.144; on Machiavelli,
    372; on modernity, 601; on religion and public
    law, 467n.46; on states of emergency, 490, 603;
    Verfassungslehre, 437
Schmitten, J. in der, 656n.
Schnapp, F. E., 796n.
Schneider, R.: *Schlafes Bruder*, 547
Schnur, R., 29n.109
Schönke, A., 118n.74, 145n.133, 484n.80
Schopenhauer, A., 100
Schramm, M., 106n.44
Schröder, H., 118n.75, 145n.133, 484n.80
Schüle, W., 219n.52
Schumpeter, J. A., 705n.124, 876n.13, 915
Schürmann, R., 81n.37
Schütrumpf, E., 15n.41
Schwartz, M. J., 68n.16
Schweitzer, A., 716n.
Scipio Africanus maior, P. Cornelius, 385n.183
Seibold, S., 713n.129
Seitz, K., 888n., 930
Sejanus, L. A., 403, 403n.283
Sen, A.: on Pareto-inclusiveness, 120, 120n.82
Seneca, 19n.68, 21, 910n.39
Şenocak, Z., 920
Service, E., 556n.207
Severus Antoninus, 20n.73
Seyss-Inquart, A., 528n.162
Shah, G., 177n.182
Shakespeare, W., xviii, 174, 374n.133; *Antony and
    Cleopatra*, 378n.149, 381n.161; *Coriolanus*,
    391n.216; *Hamlet*, 378, 385n.180, 410; *Henry IV,
    Part 2*, 368n.118, 376n.138, 399, 399n.258;
    Henry V, 376, 376n.139, 394, 400, 410; *Henry VI,
    Part 1*, 397n.248, 408–9; *Henry VI, Part 2*, 409;
    Henry VI, Part 3, 366, 368n.118, 408; *Henry VIII*,
    369n.122, 414–15; *Julius Caesar*, 378n.149,
    385n.182, 407n.293, 427; *King John*, 400–401;
    King Lear, 359n.97, 410, 422n.334; *Macbeth*,
    127n., 413n.318; *Measure for Measure*, 367;
    Othello, 351; *Pericles*, 403n.284; *The Rape of
    Lucrece*, 396n.244; *Richard II*, 376, 376n.141,
    401n.269, 408; *Richard III*, 394n.237, 396;
    Romeo and Juliet, 410; *The Tempest*, 367,
    415, 416

Shang Yang, 6n.5
Sieyès, E. J., 734n.154, 816n.54; *Qu'est-ce que le Tiers
    état?*, 812
Sigrist, C., 445n.17, 556n.208
Simma, B., 475n.60, 476n.63, 483n.78, 845n.91,
    874n.10
Simmel, G., 332n.50
Simon, H. A., 147
Simonis, U. E., 711n.
Singer, P., 659n.61, 765
Smend, R., 540
Socrates, 10, 10n.20, 14, 68, 81n.38, 82, 245, 286, 296,
    360, 427, 812
Sombart, W., 583
Somerville, J., 859
Sophocles, xviii, 9; *Antigone*, 94–95, 315, 778; *Oedipus
    at Colonus*, 93, 413; *Philoctetes*, 413
Sorel, G., 58n.200, 306
Spaemann, R., 434n.436
Spinoza, B. de, 26n.97, 201n.20, 240, 282n.168,
    371n.126, 637n.; on mind-body parallelism,
    74–75; on natural law, 631n.5; on sovereignty,
    24n.91
Spranger, A., 362n.105
Stalin, J., 339, 367, 388–89, 392, 424, 634, 694, 816; as
    politician, 70, 139, 396, 398, 420, 547, 597;
    purges of, 580, 821
Stein, K., Baron of, 600
Stein, L. von, 55
Stein, T., 902n.
Steinvorth, U., 158n.155, 666n., 670n.82
Stern, D., 236n.85
Stern, S. M., 18n.63
Sternberger, D., 22n.82, 256n.123
Stolleis, M., 29n.109
Storz, G., 256n.123
Strauss, L., 25n.95, 31n.119, 36n.135, 60n.
Strayer, J., 575n.236
Strindberg, A.: *Miss Julie*, 326n.41
Strisower, L., 845
Sudoplatov, P., 388–89
Suetonius, 331n.47, 363n.107, 364n.109, 366n.112,
    399n.260, 404n.286
Suharto, 789n.17
Sulla, 327n., 414
Sun-tzu, 64–65, 192n.8, 381n.163, 392n.222, 507–8
Süskind, W. E., 256n.123
Süssmuth, R., 888n., 930
Sutterlin, J. S., 868n.5
Swift, J.: *Gulliver's Travels*, 298n.191
Szilard, L., 142–43

Tacitus, 161n., 179, 403, 403n.283, 550, 891, 891n.;
   Agricola, 20n.75, 303n.208; *Annals*, 146n.136;
   Historiae, 347
Taft, W. H., 522
Tarquinius, L., 420n.329
Taylor, C., 582n.252
Teresa, Mother, 206n.
Thatcher, M., 826, 842n.86
Themistocles, 566
Theodoric, 479
Theodosius I, 24, 24n.91
Thommessen, B., 28n.106
Thompson, J. J., 657n.55
Thompson, K. W., 309n.7, 335n.56, 389n.204,
   497n.111, 505n.125, 508nn.131, 132, 524n.,
   601n.295, 825, 854n.108, 869nn.6, 7
Thucydides, 9, 161n., 172n.177, 173, 344n., 374n.133,
   382n.171, 387n.196, 388n.201, 392n.221,
   393n.227, 567, 924, 925; on alliances, 386n.189;
   on Athens, 9n.18, 160–61, 517n.141; on civil war
   in Corcyra, 260; Hobbes on, 81n.38; on insults,
   556; on Megara, 387n.193; on Pericles, 364n.109;
   vs. Tocqueville, 9n.18
Tiberius, 403
Tilly, C., 588n.265
Tinbergen, N., 242
Titus and Berenice, 402
Tobin, J., 833, 875
Tocqueville, A. de, xxi, 502–3, 553, 589n.270,
   594n., 615n.310, 816n.53; on democracy,
   53–54, 53n.189, 590n.272, 729; on federalism,
   497n.113; on French Revolution, 46n.165,
   588, 588n.268, 591n.275; on Native
   Americans, 590n.272; on power, 790n.19; on
   re-electing head of government, 752; on satis-
   faction of needs, 613n.; vs. Thucydides,
   9n.18
Todorov, T., 433n.345
Tolstoy, L., 299n.196, 408; *Anna Karenina*, 615n.311;
   War and Peace, 171–72, 267n.143, 339n.62,
   413n.318, 445n.16, 543, 837n.
Tönnies, F., 267n.142, 541; *Gemeinschaft und
   Gesellschaft*, 167, 168
Torney, J. V., 479n.70
Touraine, A., 535n.177
Toynbee, A., 555n.206, 579n.
Trajan, 422
Tuden, A., 68n.16
Tullock, G., 677n.93, 730–31
Turgeniev, I., 378–79
Turner V. W., 68n.16

Uberoi, J. P. S., 581n.251
Ueberhorst, R., 67n.14, 909n.37
Uexküll, J. von, 211
Ulrich, B., 902n.
Unnerstall, T., 908n.
Usener, H., 469

Varro, C. Terentius, 391–92
Veblen, T., 316n.23, 816n.54
Verdross, A., 475n.60, 476n.63, 483n.78, 845n.91,
   874n.10
Vico, G., 54, 179, 444n.15, 553, 634; on customs,
   262–63; on historical development, 51, 557; on
   language, 257; on law, 438; on marriage, 453;
   on patricians and plebeians, 568, 568n.226;
   on Roman jurists, 568; on sexuality, 283; on
   theology, 25n.93
Victor Emmanuel III, 793
Virgil, 19n.70, 270n.149, 390, 390n.211, 398n.250,
   402n.276, 420n.330, 514, 672, 672n.83, 924
Viśākhadatta, 8; "Mudrārākṣasa," 421
Vitoria, F. de, 26, 838
Viviani, F., 329n.
Vlasov, A., 857n.113
Voegelin, E., 13n.32, 60n., 162n.162, 170n.170
Vogel, C., 204n.27, 220, 228n.
Voltaire, 812

Wagner, R.: *Der Ring des Nibelungen*, 312, 366–67
Waltz, K. N., 533n.172
Walzer, M., 838, 846n.95, 848n.101, 856, 857n.114, 858n.
Wandschneider, D., 167n.166, 195n.16
Warren, E., 522
Warrender, H., 39n.145
Wasser, H., 523n.
Waters, J., 799–800
Weber, M., 72, 262n.134, 451n., 468n., 470n.,
   501n.120, 520n.150, 619; on Arthaśāstra litera-
   ture, 6; on corporate groups, 264, 264n.139,
   484–85; on domination, 440, 445, 449–50,
   562n.217; on ideal types, 168; on patrimonial
   domination, 562n.217; *Politik als Beruf*, 62n.3; on
   power, 310–12, 311n.15, 313; on rationalization,
   179; on the social, 160n.159; on the state, 62n.3,
   69n.20, 437n.2, 484–85, 485n.82; on values,
   57–58
Wegener, A. T., 802
Weizächer, E.-U. von, 210n., 833n.74, 879n.17, 904n.31,
   910n.38, 911
Weizäcker, C. F. von, 824n.
Weizäcker, E., 802

Weizäcker, R. von, 752
Welles, O.: *The Lady from Shanghai*, 374
White, L. A., 194n.13, 270n.148, 551n.197
Wilhelm, F., 6n.6
Willer, D. E., 450n.
William I, 587
Williams, B., 86n.49, 143n.128; "Politics and Moral
    Character," 120n.81
William the Conqueror, 388, 575
Wilson, E. O., 197
Wilson, W., 791–92
Windelband, W., 170n.171
Winter, G., 879n.15
Wittgenstein, L., 177n.182, 228, 762, 896; *On
    Certainty*, 81n.39; on private language,
    250n.111
Wöhlcke, M., 551n.195, 917n.43

Wolf, U., 115n.65
Wright, G. H. von, 125n.93
Wrong, D. H., 309n.10, 310n.12, 312n.
Wyller, E., 11n.24

Xenophon, 10, 403; *The Education of Cyrus*, 18n.64
Xerxes, 845n.93

Yeltsin, B., 354, 516, 810, 823
Yourcenar, M., 398

Zamyatin, J., 59, 118n.76, 179n.186, 370
Zarathustra, 177, 563
Zeno of Elea, 10n.20
Zimbardo, P. G., 100n.32, 235n.84, 243n.96
Zippelius, R., 441n.10, 480n.71
Zwingli, U., 581, 581n.251

Index of Subjects

abortion, 122, 260, 279, 279n.162, 617, 643, 656, 657, 657nn.53, 55, 703, 875

absolute, the, 51, 234, 424, 470, 489n.93, 621, 719

abstraction, 240, 256, 289–90

acedia, 298–99

actions, 240–47; and collective attention frames, 247; and compartmentalization, 243; and displacement activities, 242–43, 243n.97, 618; and emotional isolation, 243; flexibility in, 245; goal-directed vs. non-goal-directed actions, 244–45; as habitual, 244, 246, 286, 294; impulse actions, 244; and omissions, 144–46, 145n.134, 166, 644, 648, 649, 690, 797; redirected behavior, 242, 243; relationship to knowledge, xix; relationship to power, 309; and repression of drives, 243; substitute actions, 243–44, 243n.97; and willpower, 245, 246

addictions, 297, 913, 917–18

adolescent crisis, 274, 304, 317

advertising, 351, 355, 429, 430, 585, 715–16, 767, 835, 880, 895, 917

aesthetic values, 79–80, 80n.34, 117n.72, 154, 276, 285, 717–18

aesthetic virtue, 285, 286–87

Africa, 180, 438n.4, 543, 555n.205, 606, 871, 888–89

agents provocateurs, 390–91

agriculture, 551, 574, 582, 583, 895, 899, 910–11, 927; agrarian societies, 555, 558–64; irrigation, 559, 628

AIDS, 697n.

Alamo, the, 432

Algeria, 790, 821, 851

alienation, 56, 705

alliances, 505–6, 537, 564n.221, 569, 792, 820, 845; based on friendship, 385–86, 387, 392–93, 420; based on interests, 344, 385, 386, 387–89, 393, 420, 611; during power struggles, 337–38, 343, 344–45, 346, 382–83, 385–89, 387nn.194, 195, 419, 432

Alsace-Lorraine, 848

altruism, 235n.84, 242, 288, 619; in the family, 694; and sociobiology, 197–200, 203–4, 206–10, 206n., 213

ambition, 289, 397

American Civil War, 185, 460, 488n., 497, 535n.177, 552, 599, 601, 807, 810, 820, 869n.6, 882

American Revolution, 33n.124, 47, 47n.169, 96, 590, 599, 795, 807, 810, 812

anarchism, 59, 69n.19, 73, 628–29

anarchy, 348, 548

Andean culture, 556

anger, 302–3

animals, 210–22; and liability, 677–78; locomotion in, 211, 216, 268; rights of, 277–78, 277n., 278n.161, 643, 644n.30, 662, 798; treatment of, 647n.38, 655, 662–63, 662n.64, 686, 798

Appenzell, 530n.166

Archimedean axiom, 118, 118n.75

architecture, 514, 558, 629

Argentina, 432, 606, 842n.86

Arianism, 479n.69

Armenians, 591, 853

arrogance, 302, 303, 395, 395n.240

Arrow's paradox, 120n.84

art, 219, 239, 241, 256, 266, 558, 585, 619, 629, 858, 915; aesthetic values, 79–80, 80n.34, 117n.72, 154, 276, 285, 717–18; and education, 923; as intellectual property, 670, 670n.80, 671–72; Plato on, 148; relationship to death, 234; relationship to truth, 173–74; in Renaissance, 578; state support

of, 513–14, 717–18, 743, 927; in United States,
883–84

Arthaśāstra literature, 29, 156; *Kauṭilīya-Arthaśāstra*,
6–8, 6n.6, 7n.9, 10, 19n.67, 64, 323n.33, 340,
348, 348n.81, 371n.125, 374n.133, 375n.134,
381n.159, 383n.174, 385n.181, 386n.190,
388n.200, 391n.215, 392n.225, 397n.248,
399n.256, 502n., 508

artificial intelligence, 228

asceticism, 223, 245, 262, 281, 284, 285, 286, 368, 614

Asia, East, 543, 597n.286, 605, 606, 877, 884, 888,
889–90, 915

Asia, Southeast, 597n.286, 605, 888, 889–90

assassination, 388–89, 598n., 688, 773, 796, 800,
801–2, 804, 805–7, 806nn.39, 40, 807, 859

Association of South East Asian Nations, 884

Assyrian empire, 562, 563, 853

asymmetry, 204, 214, 214n.44, 232, 266, 288, 293, 360,
401n.273, 425, 427, 454, 538, 652, 698, 836, 837;
of action and omission, 144–46, 648; of power
relationships, 310, 310n.12, 311, 342, 343,
359n.98, 367, 371, 395, 404, 573, 577

atheism, 589, 619n., 621

atonement, 249, 302–3

attention frames, 247, 260, 351

Australia, 552

Austria, 477–78, 528n.162, 597, 676, 676n.92; Austro-
Hungarian Empire, 480, 598, 839

authority, 357–61; of age, 614–15; of a leader, 441,
449–51, 790–91, 823; delegation of, 338–39,
380, 400–401, 681; as moral authority, 100–101,
101n.34, 426–27

automobiles, 715, 880, 888, 906, 910

Baltic states, 809–10, 809n.43, 810, 810n.45

The Battleship Potemkin, 339n.

Bavaria, 531, 736, 747n.175, 750, 864, 923

Belarus, 887

Belgium, 824

Bernoulli's principle, 135

biodiversity, 210, 277, 899, 909n.36, 910

biologism, 191

birth control, 585, 702–4, 874–75

Black Death, 576

blackmail, 398n.251

blandishments, 341

bluffs, 328–29, 382, 432

Bolivia, 832

"Bonham's Case," 523n.

Bosnia-Herzegovina, 808, 810

Botswana, 898

Brazil, 900

Briand-Kellogg pact, 770

Bruce-effect, 456n.

Buddhism, 23, 470, 513n., 563, 722

Burma, 900

Byzantine empire, 571

Calvinism, 579–80

Canada, 552

Cannae, battle of, 391–92, 545

cannibalism, 213

capitalism, 98, 104n.39, 113, 294, 334, 512, 552, 572,
582–84, 587, 601, 605, 613, 635, 671, 672, 699,
701, 878n., 887; automization in, 585; class
structure of, 591–92; and economic growth, xiv,
60; entrepreneurs, 583, 915; vs. feudalism, 574,
577; and Hobbes, 42–43; and law, 587; and
Locke, 42–43; unemployment in, 613, 706,
708, 710, 712, 713, 914–15. *See also* economic
activity

capital punishment, 636, 656, 684nn.105, 106, 685n.,
761, 799, 918

Carneades' plank, 690

Carolingian empire, 577

Carthage, 480, 569; Hannibal, 323, 323n.34, 545

Casablanca, 318n.

castes, 458, 559, 560

Cataline conspiracy, 420n.329

catastrophe theory, 169–70

categorical imperative, 39, 48, 49–50, 78, 91–92, 93,
94, 113–14, 437n.3

Catholicism, 144, 297n., 371, 543, 572, 580, 587, 592,
609, 631, 659, 721, 811–12, 877–78; canon law,
574, 695; Jesuits, 117n.70, 133n.105, 416n.327,
852; and marriage, 695; natural law in, 26, 632,
632n.8

causality, 153, 170–72, 197, 230, 237, 238, 581, 678

censorship, 351–52

Central America, 556

Chaco War, 832

chaos theory, 170

charisma, 359–61, 359n.99, 449–51, 450n., 463, 547,
813, 823, 829, 919

charity, 582, 596, 661; in Christianity, 289n.181,
293–94, 572, 619, 649–50

chastity, 891

Chechnya, 887

chemistry, 158

children, 214, 216–17, 221, 362n.106, 643, 662, 898,
919; adolescent crisis, 274, 304, 317; adoption of,
702; child prostitution, 697n.; and the family,

children (*cont.*)
258, 268, 425, 443, 452, 650–51, 654, 693, 694, 695, 697, 699, 700–702, 701n., 703, 710, 801, 816; infant mortality, 788, 897; labor of, 676, 912; rights of, 279, 645, 647, 650, 651–52, 656–57, 703, 724–75, 726, 901

Chile, 832

China, 556, 559, 562, 563, 577, 580, 605, 608, 613, 736, 789, 888; Opium Wars/Unequal Treaties, 770, 852; political thought in, 6, 6n.5, 7n.10, 8; technology in, 565, 578, 581

Christianity, 14, 42, 100, 189n.1, 212, 349, 549, 550, 600, 813–14, 828, 886; *acedia* in, 298–99; baptism in, 780; Catholicism, 117n.70, 133n.105, 144, 297n., 371, 416n.327, 543, 572, 574, 580, 587, 592, 609, 631, 632, 632n.8, 659, 695, 721, 811–12, 852, 877–78; charity in, 289n.181, 293–94, 572, 619, 649–50; forgiveness in, 36; fundamentalism in, 606; God in, 23, 24, 26, 28, 37, 39, 43, 44, 367, 415n.325, 545, 563, 572, 574, 578, 579, 580–81, 619n., 813; Hegel on, 21n.78, 59, 545; and history, 24–25, 24n.89, 25n.92; Hobbes on, 36, 37–38, 39–40, 39n.145; and hypocrisy, 180, 580, 589; Incarnation of God, 24, 39, 545, 572, 574, 579, 813; and individual rights, 22, 23; and intentionalism, 93; vs. Islam, 23, 25, 563, 572, 920; Jesus, 23n., 24, 24n.89, 39, 85, 94n.19, 153, 288, 349, 422n.335, 432–33, 545, 571, 572, 574, 579, 812, 813, 814, 833; vs. Judaism, 23, 25; just war doctrine in, 26, 814, 838; love as a virtue in, 181, 289n.181, 293–94; and modernity, 23–25, 578–81, 585; and natural law, 720; and nature, 24, 24n.88, 37; Nietzsche on, 299n.196, 619n.; original sin, 22, 23, 46–47, 47n.168; Orthodox church, 24n.88, 574, 821, 887; and pacifism, 813; and political philosophy, 21–27, 37; predestination in, 579–80; Protestantism, 28, 58n.199, 555, 577, 579–80, 580n.248, 585, 589, 594, 614; and Roman Empire, 570, 571; Rousseau on, 21, 44–45; and salvation, 23, 571, 579; and science, 572, 577, 581; Scripture in, 581; sin in, 296n.189, 298–99; and the state, 30, 51, 575; and subjectivity, 23, 30; and universalism, 22, 23, 27, 105, 293, 493, 578, 582

citizenry, 473–80, 475n.62, 482, 834–35; citizenship requirements, 768; enfranchised citizenry, 476, 476n.64, 479, 480, 528–29, 530, 566, 573, 573n.232, 723–24, 726–27, 739, 811, 826, 880

civil disobedience, 797–98, 918

civil law, 482, 487, 626, 654, 710–11, 738; compensation in, 677, 683; vs. constitutional law, 692;

contracts in, 448, 655, 673–78, 673n.89, 679, 769; vs. criminal law, 93n.16, 679–80, 679n.97, 687, 759, 762–63; in Germany, 510, 645n.31, 669n.79, 675, 676, 678n., 694; in Italy, 694; juristic persons in, 498, 501, 511, 663, 704; liability in, 93n.16, 610, 677, 677n.94; marriage in, 695; persons in, 655, 656–64; property in, 655, 665–73; vs. public law, 464; relationship to international law, 848–49; in Roman Empire, 20–21, 20nn.73, 75, 38n.144, 498, 568–69, 572–73, 579, 593–94, 770, 773; trials under, 759

civil society, 485; relationship to the state, 50–51, 442, 513, 533–34, 533n.174, 536–42, 593, 704, 704n., 887

civil war: American Civil War, 185, 460, 488n., 497, 535n.177, 552, 599, 601, 807, 810, 820, 869n.6, 882; disvalue of, xix, 34, 38, 88, 399, 540, 548, 627–28, 628, 629, 681, 686, 787–88, 796, 805, 807, 810, 811, 818, 822–23, 837, 850, 889; English Civil War, xix, 34, 628, 822–23; and Hobbes, xix, 34, 37, 38, 88, 628, 629; vs. normal war, 787–88, 870; Roman Civil War, 773; Spanish Civil War, 735, 824, 850–51

classes, socioeconomic, 457–58, 459, 537, 538–39, 560, 591–93, 597; bourgeoisie, 583, 585–86, 587–88, 587n.264, 592; class struggle, 568; middle class, 887; working class, 592–93

classificatory vs. comparative concepts, 117, 117n.71, 167–68

coercion. *See* negative sanctions

cognitive dissonances, 245, 245n.100

Cold War, 57, 466, 602, 796, 825, 843, 862, 863, 883; end of, xiv, 508, 603, 608, 821–22, 830, 861, 867

collaboration with unjust state, 802–3

collegiality, 501–2, 526, 533, 535, 744, 749

Colombia, 916, 917

colonialism, 599–600, 600nn.292, 293, 601, 602n.297, 613, 835, 842n.86, 870–71; and moral evolutionism, 176, 180; of Spain, 26–27, 122, 122n.87, 128n.97, 175, 599, 830n.71, 850, 852, 853

comic drama, 9, 353

Commodus, 422, 527

common good, 31, 411, 417, 430, 705, 716, 724, 859, 915, 922; defined, 743; in the just state, 726, 727–28, 728n., 739, 742–44, 746, 750–51, 755, 759; and politicians, 17, 611–12, 791, 825; relationship to competition, 406; relationship to individual preferences, 121; relationship to positive law, 26

Commonwealth of Independent States, 884, 887

communism, 165n.164, 354, 527, 530, 594, 595–96, 666, 678, 894; Bolshevism, 68, 151, 471, 595–96,

595n.283, 806n.39, 807, 821; collapse of, xiv, xxi,
57, 58–59, 68, 78, 133, 349, 466, 483, 592, 596,
596n.285, 602, 604–5, 613, 619, 802–3, 804; vs.
National Socialism, 57, 139, 345, 389, 396, 597; of
Plato, 12, 15
communitarianism, 663, 704
community, 104, 104n.38, 162, 269, 559, 590, 594, 649,
896; duty to perform community service, 756;
relationship to individualism, 12, 112, 191, 259,
267–68, 314; rights of communities, 663–64; vs.
society, 267–68; and values, 164, 320–21
compensation (defense mechanism), 253, 541, 594,
597, 604–5, 618, 766, 808
compensation (economic), 672n.87, 677, 683, 710, 911
competition, 136, 274, 386–87, 928; in economic
activity, 459, 706, 881; in politics, 753, 793–94;
relationship to common good, 406; role in
organic evolution, 197, 205–6, 209, 213, 217,
664n.67. *See also* capitalism; power struggles
compromises, 33, 149–51, 316, 389–90, 389n.206, 535,
539, 744, 748, 782–83, 787, 792, 803, 830–31;
Machiavelli on, 150, 150n.143
concepts, 166, 168n.168, 237–38; classificatory
concepts, 117, 117n.71, 167–68; comparative
concepts, 117, 117n.71, 167–68, 786; Locke on,
168n.168; metrical concepts, 118, 118nn.75, 76,
134; normative vs. descriptive, 259–60
Condorcet's paradox, 120n.84
confederations, 487–98
Conference on Security and Cooperation in Europe,
870
conflict avoidance and resolution, 214, 268, 291, 405,
406, 466, 582, 680, 766–67; avoidance of war,
504, 557–58, 712, 763–64, 770–71, 826, 829, 844,
844n.90, 867, 868–69, 881, 892–94, 899–900;
moral obligations related to, 763, 884; role of
the state in, xiv, 34–35, 36, 472, 473, 503–4, 627,
720, 902
Confucianism, 471, 563
Congress of Vienna: *Déclaration contre la traite des
nègres,* 96
conscience, 128n.98, 654, 788
consciousness, 194, 227–29, 230–40, 231n.73, 250,
272. *See also* self-consciousness
consensus, 128, 298, 357, 406, 423–26, 427, 502,
731n.149, 751, 766–67, 786, 816, 908, 917; as
international, 870, 871, 876, 881, 896; vs.
positive sanctions, 430; public opinion as,
541–42; and social orders, 424–25; as source
of power, 331, 485, 790–91, 882
consent, mutual, 643

consistency, 238, 418, 426, 464, 635–36, 928
constitutional courts, 523–24, 739, 745, 746, 760–62,
760n., 778, 799; German Supreme Court, 686;
United States Supreme Court, 497n.113, 522,
523, 524
constitutional law, 437–38, 439, 439n.7, 463, 494n.105,
578n.244, 618, 639, 654, 665, 784, 824; amendment of constitution in, 465–66, 516–17,
527–28, 528, 687, 729–31, 729n., 730n.145, 733,
738, 739, 760–61; vs. civil law, 692; concept of
sovereignty in, 487–93, 495; constituent power,
515–17, 734n.154; constitutional courts,
497n.113, 522, 523, 524, 686, 739, 745, 746,
760–62, 760n., 778, 799; and equality, 737, 767;
federation principle, 734–36; and future generations, 725, 726–27, 730, 730n.145, 732, 734, 769;
in Great Britain, 463n.39, 510, 730; *Marbury vs.
Madison,* 523; principle of democracy in, 725,
726–27, 728, 730–31, 733–34, 734n.154, 739,
739–41, 742, 760, 762, 766; as public law,
510–11; relationship to international law, 732,
763; relationship to natural law, 625, 626, 627,
632–33, 721, 724, 725, 731–32, 767–68, 779–80,
804, 846, 863, 884; role of common good in,
727–28; in Rome, 499. *See also* constitutions
Constitution of Athens, 10
constitutions, 474n.59, 500, 535, 544, 545, 807, 913;
Basic Law of German Federal Republic, 489,
497, 515–16, 517, 647n.38, 718, 729n., 732, 734,
752, 795–96, 818; Bavarian constitution,
747n.175, 750n., 923; French constitution of
1793, 650n.43; general norms in, 514–17; Italian
constitution, 729n.; Mexican Constitution of
1824, 515; Prussian constitution, 491, 533;
Russian constitution, 516, 823; Schmitt on,
489nn.91, 93, 490n.96, 516–17, 516n., 517n.140,
518–19; Soviet constitution, 497n.110; United
States constitution, 41, 53, 487n.89, 515, 681,
687, 729n., 733, 740n.163, 750n., 752, 761, 764,
787, 795, 818, 846n.96, 884, 885; Weimar constitution, 490n.96, 516–17, 517n.140, 725, 739.
See also constitutional law; *Federalist Papers*
contemplative values, 79, 284–85, 414n.322, 417
continuity, 263, 273
contraception, 585, 702–4, 874–75
contracts, 112, 116, 441, 458, 462, 559, 568–69, 648,
679–80, 692, 708, 710–11; contract theory of
the state, 35–36, 447–48, 630, 638, 639–41,
641n.19, 655, 693, 731, 731n.149, 769; defined,
673; and domination, 441, 446–50, 451; and
duress, 770; Hobbes on, 35–36, 38–39, 630, 638,

contracts (*cont.*)
731; Machiavelli on, 421; and marriage, 694–95; relationship to labor, 673; relationship to natural law, 655, 661, 662, 673–78; relationship to property, 569, 673–74, 675; regarding sexual services, 695

convincing, 450, 485, 537, 644; vs. persuading, 340n.64, 352–57

cooperation, 137–38, 215–16, 266–67, 269–71, 269n., 291–92, 316, 344, 446, 451, 535, 559, 629, 706. *See also* alliances

corporate groups, 263–64, 379n.155, 457–58, 574, 708, 799, 919; as juristic persons, 498, 501, 511, 663; ownership of property by, 666, 669, 670, 670n.81, 671; as political, xvii, 265, 436, 437, 438, 444, 446–48, 451, 464, 481, 484–85, 485nn.82, 83, 486–87, 498–99, 498n., 628, 704n., 769–70, 823, 852

corruption, 423, 430, 782, 799, 832, 878, 890, 897, 900
Costa Rica, 895
coups d'état, 776, 788n.14, 804–7, 823
courage, 285–87, 290, 295–96, 295n., 321, 325, 461, 775; of one's convictions, 286, 291, 294, 295, 298, 406
cowardice, 298, 299
cratic, the: defined, 63; relationship to politics, xv, 62–68, 62n.3, 66n., 439–40, 750–51, 773, 790–94

cratology, xvii, 126; ambivalence of, 370–74, 914; as amoral, 65; defined, 63; maxims for fighting enemies, 382–93, 419–22; maxims of aspirants to power, 375–76, 377–81, 417–19; maxims of power-holders, 375–77, 393–401, 422–23; relationship to morals, 65; rules of power, 371, 374–401. *See also* power; power-holders; power struggles

creation (theology), 153
Crimean War, 850
criminal law, 510, 610, 626, 633, 654, 663, 697, 697n., 722, 738, 902; vs. civil law, 93n.16, 679–80, 679n.97, 687, 759, 762–63; and pardons, 687; principles of, 678–92, 684n.104, 849n.102; proportionality in, 679, 684–85; punishment under, 681–87; relationship to natural law, 686, 687, 688–89; trials under, 759–60

criminal law, German, 116, 636, 653n.48; actions vs. omissions in, 144–45; active personality principle in, 484, 697n.; conscious negligence vs. unconscious negligence in, 99; defense of property in, 679; *dolus directus* vs. *dolus eventualis* in, 99; measures for the prevention of crime and the reformation of offenders in, 663, 685, 690;

principle of accessoriness in, 653; protection principle in, 484; spurious crimes of omission in, 144–45, 692; and states of emergency, 688, 691; universality principle in, 484, 697n.

critical theory, 306
Critolaus, scale of, 118n.75
Croatia, 810, 885
cruelty, 115, 115n.64, 191, 193, 217, 222, 246, 303, 303nn.207, 208, 304, 368, 398, 398n.252
Cuba, 850
culture, 5–8, 254–55, 442, 542–43, 550–51, 883–84; archaic cultures, 5–6, 171n.175, 172, 175–76, 178, 180, 263, 268, 269–70, 270n.148, 274, 279, 288n.177, 452, 454, 458, 465–66, 467, 555–58, 670n.81, 723, 852, 853; cold vs. hot, 548; cultural evolution, 162, 174–82, 202, 204, 205, 205nn.29, 30, 207, 212, 219, 221, 262–63, 270–71, 555–56; cultural norms, 10–11, 12, 12n.29, 18, 21–22, 50, 129, 164, 174–82, 202, 204, 267, 449, 465, 466, 477; cultural relations policy, 828–32, 891–92, 896; defined, 255, 255n.119; multiculturalism, 562, 591, 610–11, 828–30, 895, 896, 919–20; preservation of, 182, 735–36, 809, 828, 851–52, 895; subcultures, 255. *See also* language; mores

customs, 260–63, 261, 270–71, 294–95; customary law, 463, 463n. *See also* mores (*Sittlichkeit*)
cybernetics, 169, 202
cynicism, 615–16, 817, 866
Czechoslovakia, 598, 787, 808, 811, 843, 844, 848

deception, 216, 228–29, 252, 259, 299, 373n.131, 421n.332, 432; ruses, 323–24, 345, 361, 372–73, 372n.129, 373, 860. *See also* lies
decision theory, 92, 133–53, 135nn.107, 108, 417
defense mechanisms, 243, 246, 249, 249n.107, 251, 253
democracy, 34–35, 46, 60, 259–60, 378, 398n.251, 416, 432n., 460–61, 495, 591, 591n.276, 626, 629, 723n.140, 773, 781, 787, 827, 880; Aristotle on, 15, 17, 17n.57; compromises in, 150; demagogues in, 355, 355n.92, 424, 428, 518, 536, 567, 616; vs. dictatorship, 374, 788–90; direct democracy, 528–29, 530, 530n.166, 532n.171, 565–66, 738–39, 741, 742, 745, 747–48, 747n.175; election laws/voting rights in, 515, 530, 531, 592–93, 726, 727, 730–31, 732–34, 739–40, 826; floating voters in, 753; in Greece, 9–10, 15, 17, 397, 528, 565–67, 569, 573, 573n.232, 593; Habermas on, 54n.; indirect vs. direct voting, 740, 740n.163; the just state as, 726–29, 730–31, 732, 765–66, 766–67; and law, 465, 778; Machiavelli on, 789; majority voting, 85, 120n.84, 480, 529, 538, 539,

611–12, 616, 706, 725, 729, 730–31, 733–34, 734n.154, 739–41, 760, 762, 809; as mediocratic, 536; vs. oligarchy, 528–30; opposition forces in, 752–53; parliamentary democracy, 525, 526, 532–33, 732–33, 738–39, 747–48, 753–54; Plato on, 566, 728; political parties in, 62, 63, 85–86, 492, 525, 533, 533n.172, 534, 537–38, 612, 616, 740–41, 741n.167, 744–45, 744n.172, 748, 750, 751, 751n., 754; power struggles in, 307, 793–94; presidential democracy, 525, 532, 532n.170, 606, 732–33, 747–48, 749, 750, 751, 753–54; proportional representation, 530, 740–41, 741n.167, 742; public opinion in, 541–42; relationship to economic equality, 54–55; relationship to natural law, 632–33, 766, 790; restrictions on, 666, 725, 745, 831; rights to cumulative vote and *panachage*, 741, 742; role of elites in, 528–29, 536, 728, 930; Rousseau on, 44, 44n.162, 488, 531; and separation of powers, 531–32, 531n.167, 535n.177m, 535, 638, 721, 728–29, 810; strategic voting, 744, 794; Tocqueville on, 53–54, 53n.189, 590n.272, 729; and universalism, 726–27, 729; violations of law in, 797–800, 804–5, 823; and war, 763–64, 850, 854

denial of reality, 246, 249

descriptive statements vs. normative statements, 7–8, 16, 48, 57, 70–79, 89–90, 92, 121, 125, 129, 153, 154–55, 156, 167, 202, 209, 219, 246, 261, 276, 438–39

despotism, 534, 552, 573, 917

determinism, 103, 141, 685

dictatorship, 374–75, 490, 501, 526–27, 530, 788–90, 788n.14, 789n.17, 800–807, 842n.86, 850, 861–62, 902–3. *See also* monocracy

diplomacy, 508–9, 559, 829, 830–31; language of, 329, 432, 432n.; and power struggles, 343–45. *See also* foreign policy

discourse ethics, 106n.45, 128, 152n.147, 357, 424, 632

discretion, 383

divide and rule principle, 388, 397, 397n.248

divorce, 696–97, 702

doctrinaires, 355–56

domination, 335, 357, 361–62, 370–71, 425, 439–51, 441n.12, 506, 871; from charisma of strong leader, 441, 449–51, 450n.; and collective identity, 441; by contract, 441, 446–50, 451; defined, 440, 445; in the family, 441, 442–44, 447, 449–50, 450, 628; of masters over slaves, 441, 444–46, 447, 475, 634; as political, 439–41, 442, 451, 464, 472–73, 476, 483–93, 498, 517, 526, 530, 559, 575, 629; as pre-political, 442–51; role of communication in, 478; traditional

domination, 449–50, 450n.; Weber on, 440, 445, 449–50, 562n.217. *See also* power; state, the

double effect, doctrine of, 124n.90

Dr. Strangelove, 116–17

drug abuse, 913, 917–18

dualisms, 238; form and matter, 195, 196; general and particular, 514–15; individual and community, 191; *Is* and *Ought*, 4, 5, 11–12, 16, 27–28, 50, 52, 89–90, 89n.4, 90n.6, 92, 125, 153, 183, 184, 544; life and spirit, 191; male and female, 204–5, 284; mind and body, 23, 30, 74–75, 202, 202n., 240, 240n., 257, 547n.187; monism and dualism, 563; nature and consciousness, 4; nature and freedom, 209n.35

ecological issues: ecological crisis, 4, 45, 60, 82, 104, 115, 193–94, 481, 482, 548, 602–3, 607, 608–9, 612, 616–18, 711–12, 764, 878–81; the ecological state, 626, 626n., 664, 664n.67, 915, 919, 920–21; environmental damage, 818, 851, 858, 905, 906, 908–11, 912, 918, 922; environmental protection, 660–61, 664, 671, 673, 685, 686, 711, 712–13, 714–15, 750, 758, 785, 873–74, 878–79, 881–82, 902–11; environmental taxes, 758, 777, 874, 904–7, 911, 912–13. *See also* environmental policy

economic activity, 79, 85n.47, 190, 270, 282, 346–47, 375, 430, 436, 446–47, 453, 456–59, 507, 588, 762; advertising, 351, 355, 429, 430, 585, 715–16, 767, 835, 880, 895, 917; central administration of, 459, 705, 789; competition in, 459, 706, 881; division of labor in, 457, 705; economic equality/inequality, 54–56, 59–60, 110n., 556, 650, 834, 837; economic growth, 60, 66, 512–13, 583, 583n.257, 592, 605, 609, 612, 613, 619, 665, 712–14, 792, 866, 886, 896, 908, 914; economic virtues, 285, 294, 298, 482; foreign trade, 555, 558, 564, 565, 587, 712, 832–34, 882, 888, 899, 911–12; globalization/world economy, 582–83, 607, 612, 613, 654, 712, 757, 764, 825, 830, 833–34, 865, 878, 885, 888, 899, 911–12, 920; and GNP, 713, 895, 896, 897, 911, 922; good luck in, 716; and interest rates, 714; markets, 458–59, 542n.185, 558, 613, 676–77, 677n.93, 705–8, 715–18, 753, 878, 880, 881, 899, 928; in Middle Ages, 573–74; monopolization, 352, 707–8; relationship to the environment, 878–81, 903–4; as social subsystem, 79, 264, 265, 266, 268, 340, 341n., 456, 513, 547, 784, 867, 876, 903; and unemployment, 613, 706, 708, 710, 712, 713, 914–15. *See also* capitalism; state, the, economic policy

Economic and Social Council (ECOSOC), 875

education, 265, 346, 535, 561, 668, 727, 732, 738, 872, 897n.25; Aristotle on, 17; in Germany, 709, 925, 928–30; grade inflation, 777–78, 922; in languages, 924–25; literacy rate, 897; Plato on, 14, 18; public vs. private, 709, 922, 929; and religion, 923–24; and the state, 14, 17, 35, 55n.194, 290, 513–14, 590, 610, 693, 701, 708–9, 722, 725, 750, 808, 898, 910, 921–25; in United States, 610, 925

egoism. *See* self-interest

Egypt, ancient, 479, 513n., 555n.205, 556, 558, 562, 563, 660

Egypt, modern, 822, 891

Einstein-Podolsky-Rosen correlations, 201n.22

elderly, the, 234, 453, 699, 700, 703, 710, 921

The Elephant Man, 123n.

El Salvador, 832

embryos, 656–57, 656n., 658, 703n.

England, 587, 795; Charles II, 846; Civil War, xix, 34, 628, 822–23; War of the Roses, 806; William the Conqueror, 388, 575

English language, 886, 886n.19, 923

Enlightenment, the, xiv, xv, 80–81, 176, 180, 468, 544, 565, 581–82, 619, 779; and moral authority, 101, 101n.34; vs. Sophists, 10; universalism of, 96–97, 866

entailed estate, 700n.

environmental policy, 608–9, 616–17, 711–12, 902–11, 902n., 914, 915, 916; emissions licenses, 904–7; energy policy, 907–10; environmental taxes, 661, 711, 758, 777, 874, 904–7, 911, 912–13; and foreign policy, 833, 881–82, 895, 904; price solutions vs. quota solutions in, 711, 905; relationship to economic activity, 903–4, 911. *See also* ecological issues

environmental space, 671, 873–74, 882, 895, 898, 906

envy, 101, 102, 300–302, 300nn.199, 204, 303, 382n.168, 389, 615, 667, 728, 816, 922

Epic of Gilgamesh, 233n.79, 332n.51

equality, xiv–xv, 17n.57, 23, 53, 287, 447, 573, 700, 892; and constitutional law, 737, 767; economic equality, 54–56, 556, 650; economic inequality, 59–60, 110n., 834, 837; gender equality, 572, 585, 697n., 698, 702, 703, 704, 818, 901; Hobbes on, 36, 36n.137; before the law, 35, 48, 519, 638–39, 732, 737; in modernity, 581, 587–88, 591, 593, 596, 616, 764, 832, 834, 891; of opportunity, 668, 708–9; in private property, 667–68; relationship to justice, 106–7, 107n.46, 289, 290; societies based on, 556

erotic, the, 332n.52, 453, 461, 462, 584–85, 590; essence of, 332; as form of power, 359, 359n.98; vs. politics, 190; vs. sexuality, 332, 332n.51, 584–85

Eskimos, 558

essences, 166, 167, 173, 174, 193, 231, 732, 781–82, 924, 925–26; essence of action, 244; essence of justice, 289–91, 303; essence of law, 437, 466; essence of man, xvii, 222–25, 262, 280; essence of power, 308–13, 312n., 342–43; essence of the erotic, 332, 359; essence of the state, xvii, 439, 485–86

ethical principles, xvi–xvii, 424; categorical imperative, 39, 48, 49–50, 78, 91–92, 93, 94, 113–14, 437n.3; consensus regarding, 424; hierarchy of goods and values, 117–21; in practical syllogisms, 125–26; relationship to moral feelings, 75, 101–3; universalizability, 39, 48, 49–50, 78, 91–92, 93, 94, 106, 107–12, 113–14, 139, 205–6, 271, 437n.3, 602, 607, 616, 687, 726–27, 737, 871, 877, 880, 883, 887, 895, 896

ethics, 413, 582; as deontological, 90–91, 90nn.8, 9, 116–17; grounding of, 89, 89n.1, 90n.6, 94, 153–54; individual vs. political, 5, 13–15, 16, 16n.50, 23, 30–31, 50–51, 52, 71–72; objectivity of, 174–82; relationship to descriptive sciences, 92, 149; relationship to historical situations, 32; relationship to natural events, 144, 144n.130, 153–54, 183; relationship to natural law, 144–46, 632, 637–38, 642–54, 657, 658, 664n.67, 692; relationship to public framework, 32; relationship to sociobiology, 197, 202–10, 214–15; relationship to state power, 87, 491; relationship to truth, 77, 125; role of empirical knowledge in, 92, 101n.34, 121, 122–55, 796, 819; role of intellectual and practical abilities in, 99, 100–101; as science, 91; as teleological, 90–91, 90n.9, 115–16, 115n.66, 180–82. *See also* decision theory; ethical principles; ethics of ethics; game theory; universalism; utilitarianism

ethics of ethics, 80–87, 307; ethical virtue vs. moral virtue, 82–83; ethicist's own actions, 81–83, 425; ethicist's reflection, 82–84, 147–48; ethicist's relationship to audience, 81–82, 81n.38, 85–87, 85n.48, 87nn.51, 52, 180; and human rights, 831; principle of autonomy, 86–87, 180, 288, 290; spontaneity, 84–85; tact, 86–87, 86n.50

Ethiopia, 390, 599n.291, 844, 852

ethnology, 162, 162n.163, 477

ethology, 190, 192–93, 197–98, 198n., 201, 203, 206, 242

Europe, Eastern, 575, 603

Europe, Western, 176, 554–55, 575, 598–99, 604, 828, 912–13; vs. United States, 603, 609, 610

European Community, 494–95, 832

European Convention for the Protection of Human Rights and Fundamental Freedoms, 686n.109

European Union, 495, 604, 811, 882, 884, 885–86, 888, 912, 919, 920

euthanasia, 145, 145n.134, 279

evil, 130, 179, 184, 186, 319

evolution, cultural, 162, 174–82, 202, 204, 205, 205nn.29, 30, 207, 212, 219, 221, 262–63, 270–71, 555–56

evolution, organic/biological, xvii, 100n.32, 154, 197–222, 205nn.29, 30, 218n., 227, 227n.67, 262, 263, 264, 620–21, 866

evolutionary stability, 459, 544, 607; relationship to morals, 199–201, 205–7, 205n.29, 209, 214–15, 214n.44, 270, 296, 406, 431, 682, 813; of the state, 460, 543, 575, 589, 630–31, 756, 824

exchange, 270, 341–42, 430, 446–47, 458–59, 673, 677, 677n.93

executive, the, 488, 500, 515, 519–21, 524–26, 737, 747–58, 849; demagogues, 355, 355n.92, 424, 428, 536, 567, 616; in direct democracy, 530–31, 530n.166, 532n.171, 565–66, 747–48, 747n.175; head of state, 443, 525, 530–31, 729, 747, 752, 753–54; vs. judiciary, 515, 521–23, 522n., 534; in parliamentary democracy, 525, 526, 532–33, 732–33, 747–48, 753–54; in presidential democracy, 525, 532, 532n.170, 606, 732–33, 747–48, 749, 750, 751, 753–54; relations with ministers, 749–51; violations of law by, 518, 798–99. *See also* monarchy; monocracy

extravagance, 298

fame, 289

family, the, 459, 913, 917; altruism in, 694; Aristotle on, 15–16, 475; and children, 258, 268, 425, 443, 452, 650–51, 654, 693, 694, 695, 697, 699, 700, 701–2, 701n., 703, 710, 801, 816; collective identity in, 441, 444; domination in, 441, 442–44, 447, 449–50, 450, 628; and education, 693; law related to, 458, 627, 638, 693–704, 698n., 710; as patrilineal vs. matrilineal, 454; relationship to morals, 694; relationship to the state, 15–16, 35, 50–51, 71–72, 441–42, 443, 455, 472, 475, 513, 536, 694, 708, 750, 754, 919; and reproduction, 221, 264–65, 451–55, 452–53, 693, 697; as social

subsystem, 266, 268, 451–55, 513, 654, 705; vs. the tribe, 443, 453–55; unity of, 654. *See also* marriage

fanaticism, 320, 589, 590

fascism: in Austria, 597; in Italy, 286–87, 302, 329, 390, 397, 534, 599, 793, 844, 851, 852; in Spain, 371, 389, 597, 887. *See also* National Socialism

fashions, 261n.133

fear, 394–95, 394n.237

Federalist Papers, 742n.169, 763n.192, 842n.; Hamilton in, 41, 342n.70, 497n.111, 522n., 523n., 728n., 733, 749, 752n.182, 764, 787, 787n.11; Madison in, 41, 497n.111, 639–40, 728n., 733, 735, 741, 764, 787, 795

feudalism, 27, 500, 562, 572–74, 573n.232, 576–77, 579, 587, 594, 606, 618, 811–12, 824, 878n.; vs. capitalism, 574, 577; defined, 576; Montesquieu on, 576

Finland, 388, 839n., 843

First World vs. Third World, xiv–xv, xvii, 59–60, 605–7, 834–37, 865, 888–90, 895, 897–99, 911–12, 914, 919n.46, 920

flattery, 378, 380

force, 58, 165, 192, 200–201, 213–14, 218, 262, 265, 357, 431, 449, 792–93, 823–24, 875; degree of, 434, 842, 854–55; Machiavelli on, 30, 31, 192n.10, 390, 398, 401, 805; vs. persuasion, 405; relationship to power, 309, 321–22, 338–39, 339n.63, 347, 347n.79, 361, 362, 374, 432, 485; as *ultima ratio*, 321–22, 339n.63, 347, 432, 485, 703, 841, 849, 851, 860. *See also* military, the; state, the, monopoly on force; war

foreign policy, 66, 66n., 329, 385–86, 475, 495, 503, 508, 509, 512, 539, 566, 567, 739, 749, 881–92; aid for development, 834–37, 888, 891, 894, 895–902; cultural relations policy, 828–32, 896; vs. domestic policy, 773–74, 824–26, 827, 881; economic sanctions, 348, 405, 830, 860, 868, 890; and environmental issues, 833, 881–82, 895, 904; Hobbes on, 40n.151; and human rights, 830–31; intervention in other countries, 837, 848–53, 894, 900; and justice, 826, 883, 895, 906, 912; in modernity, 598–602, 603–9; and natural law, 773–74, 849, 850; relationship to morals, xvii, 769, 773–74, 824–64, 883, 906, 912; of Rome, 569; and secession, 808; security policies, 504–9; unilateralism in, 884; and universalism, 825, 827, 828, 830, 831, 834, 881. *See also* international relations

foreign trade, 555, 558, 564, 565, 587, 712, 832–34, 882, 888, 899, 911–12 forgiveness, 87, 184, 193, 291, 420–21, 428

France, 309, 392, 600n.293, 604, 720, 791n.20, 873, 885, 893; Charles the Bold, 461, 575; De Gaulle, 396–97, 821; Louis XIII, 587; Louis XIV, 598, 827, 846; Louis XVI, 780, 819, 820; the modern state in, 397, 478, 531, 532, 535n.177, 540, 552, 575; Napoleon I, 181–82, 380, 392, 527, 547, 589, 598, 600, 803, 820–21, 821n.60, 823, 844n.89, 848; Napoleon III, 372, 530, 752, 842; relations with Germany, 426, 546, 841n.85, 844, 857, 864; relations with Great Britain, 859. *See also* French Revolution

Fraunhofer Institute, 930

freedom, xv, 259, 315, 444, 633, 685; of action, 368, 371, 644, 646, 647–48, 653, 677, 705–6, 731; of association, 646, 663, 708, 731, 849; of conscience, 654, 788; and human life, 431–32, 826–27; from interference, 644n.30, 645–48, 646n.33, 650, 651, 660, 661, 662, 676, 725, 768–69, 788, 789, 795, 795n.26, 801, 834, 897, 913, 927; of opinion, 731, 788; relationship to institutions, 267; relationship to morals, 304, 318, 826–27; relationship to reason, 238–39, 357; relationship to the state, 17n.57, 48–49, 566, 627, 629, 637, 644, 704, 715, 788; of religion, 641–42, 642n.22, 646, 647, 654, 719, 731; of speech, 646, 647; of testation, 699, 700; of the will, 102, 205n.28, 221, 232–33, 235, 544. *See also* human beings, autonomy of

French Revolution, 550, 588–91, 600, 811–12, 818, 819, 822–23; Burke on, 47–48, 48n.171, 57, 589, 589n.271; Jacobins, 46, 534, 589, 590, 815; and the modern state, 52, 586, 594; and Napoleon I, 47, 380, 589; and nationalism, 590–91; Paine on, 47n.169; Reign of Terror, 46, 47, 580; and Robespierre, 45, 45n., 50, 620, 784; and Rousseau, 46, 46n.165, 534; Tocqueville on, 46n.165, 588, 588n.268, 591n.275

friendship, 112, 254, 291–94, 300, 332n.51, 385n.185, 401n.273, 403–4, 773; alliances based on, 385–86, 387, 392–93, 420; Aristotle on, 17–18, 292; friend-foe distinction, 307, 337, 382–83, 385–86, 387, 406n., 820; and marriage, 453, 461, 696; as social virtue, 289; and symmetry, 293, 538

frustration, 243

functionalism, 161–62

fundamentalism, 478, 579, 595n.283, 606–7, 876, 890–91, 892, 923

future generations: and constitutional law, 725, 726–27, 730, 730n.145, 732, 734, 769; rights of, 137, 648, 657–58, 660, 661–62, 664, 664n.67, 670–71, 692, 711, 716, 725, 726–27, 730, 730n.145, 731, 732, 734, 743, 746, 750, 758, 769, 880, 902, 906, 908, 912, 919

game theory, 136–38, 169, 199, 206, 337, 862; chicken situations, 138, 317n.26; equilibrium points in, 380; mixed strategy in, 373; prisoner's dilemma situations, 137–38, 161, 269n., 448, 448n., 449, 666, 678, 692, 693, 720–21, 735, 764, 800, 803, 817, 903

gender equality, 572, 585, 697n., 698, 702, 703, 704, 818, 901

gender roles, 205–6, 251, 452, 453, 557, 560, 585, 698, 702

General Agreement on Tariffs and Trade (GATT), 833

generosity, 288, 392, 716

genes, 197–201, 203n.25, 204n.26, 205, 218n.; genetic engineering, 612, 620, 668, 702, 711, 909n.36; genetic testing, 710; and human behavior, 197, 203, 207, 212–13, 221–22, 235, 235n.84

Geneva Convention Regarding the Treatment of Prisoners of War, 857

genocide, 306–7, 307n.3, 363, 389, 433, 433n.345, 590, 591, 597–98, 598n., 800, 801, 809, 826, 851n., 853, 883

Georgia (former Soviet republic), 808

Germany, 499n.116, 545–46, 723n.140, 764, 872–73, 916; Animal Protection Act, 662n.64; Basic Law of Federal Republic, 489, 497, 515–16, 517, 647n.38, 718, 729n., 732, 734, 752, 795–96, 818; Bavaria, 531, 736, 747n.175, 750, 864, 923; bureaucracy in, 521, 539, 755; citizenship in, 768; civil law in, 510, 645n.31, 669n.79, 675, 676, 678n., 694; concept of liberalism in, 644n.28; economic conditions in, 604, 895; education in, 709, 925, 928–30; Enabling Act of 1933, 516, 527, 528n.162; environmental issues in, 617, 905–6, 908, 909–10, 911, 919; executive in, 443, 533; expressionist films in, 351; family law in, 702; Federal Bank, 746; Federal Constitutional Court, 517, 524; Federal Republic, 466, 488–89, 497, 517, 533, 667, 746, 797, 804, 804n., 831, 840; German Democratic Republic, 466, 801, 803, 831; Greens in, 894; head of state in, 443; immigrants in, 919, 920; intellectuals in, 253, 591n.275, 609, 829; judiciary in, 517, 523, 524, 686; labor law in, 509; legislature in, 741; NNP in, 713; party discipline in, 745; the political official (*politischer Beamter*) in, 421; Reich of 1871, 495, 495n.107, 501; relations with Austria, 477–78, 528n.162; relations with France, 426, 546, 841n.85, 844, 857, 864; relations with Great

Britain, 426, 432, 841n.85, 844, 859; relations with Slovenia and Croatia, 885; relations with Soviet Union, 344, 345, 388, 420, 601, 821; relations with United States, 344, 345, 863; reunification of, 394, 604, 672, 734, 803, 846, 895; Supreme Court of, 686; taxation in, 709, 905–6, 913; unification of, 133, 497, 575; vs. United States, 3–4, 54n., 353, 883, 913, 925; universities in, 925, 928–29, 930; Weimar Republic, 490n.96, 516–17, 517n.140, 528, 725, 739, 785, 786, 928; welfare state in, 54n., 593, 611, 912–13, 914, 929. *See also* criminal law, German; National Socialism

globalization. *See* economic activity, globalization/world economy

Glorious Revolution, 33, 590, 807

gluttony, 297, 299

Gnosticism, 209

God, 48, 283, 305, 305n.2, 309, 368, 368n.120, 489n.93, 618, 621, 669, 682–83, 891, 923–24, 931; in Christianity, 23, 24, 26, 28, 37, 39, 43, 44, 367, 415n.325, 545, 563, 572, 574, 578, 579, 580–81, 619n., 813; love of, 304

goods, 90n.5, 153, 175, 176; basic goods, 278–81, 290; economic, 118, 911; happiness, 16–17, 31, 43, 102, 245, 284, 285, 424, 586, 609n.309, 629–30, 651, 659n.60, 660, 665, 713–14, 719, 723, 743–44, 773; health and healthcare, 131, 131n.101, 584, 665, 710, 713, 714, 750, 896–97, 897n.24, 899, 927; hierarchy of, 115n.66, 117–21, 132, 148, 697n., 787–88; human dignity, 276n., 278–80, 280n.164, 283, 293, 294, 302, 303, 315, 316–17, 318, 322, 324, 418, 430, 507, 515, 541, 657, 660, 675, 685, 709, 713, 731, 759, 762, 769, 892; human life, 112–13, 112n., 113n.60, 114–15, 118, 121, 137, 278, 280–81, 286, 291, 324, 405, 429, 431, 434, 633, 645, 646, 647, 648, 649, 652, 653–54, 656–57, 662, 679, 688–90, 689n., 697, 772, 785–86, 787, 801, 804–5, 807, 819, 826–27, 850, 852, 858, 896–97, 920; intellectual goods, 911; personal honor, 281, 647, 648, 685, 686, 864, 917; public goods, 707, 708, 717–18, 800, 835; Rawls on the good, 90n.9; relationship to ethics, 113–15, 116; relationship to evil, 184, 186; relationship to values, 113; *summum bonum*, 39. *See also* common good; property, private; values

grace (*Anmut*), 296, 296n.188

gratitude, 288, 301, 422, 469, 638, 661

Great Britain, 535n.177, 604, 653n.48, 748, 764, 806n.39, 843, 893; British Empire, 20, 598, 600n.293, 602n.297, 778, 847, 852, 883, 890, 930; bureaucracy in, 521; Churchill, 139,

142n.125, 152n.150, 192n.7, 353n., 382, 388, 390, 392, 412, 414, 420, 533, 533n.173, 751n., 753, 859; Civil War, xix, 38, 628, 822–23; constitutional law in, 463n.39, 510, 730; executive in, 532, 533; and Gandhi, 433; George I, 544, 545; George III, 544; Glorious Revolution, 33, 590, 807; House of Lords, 531, 733, 747; Industrial Revolution in, 584; intellectuals in, 591n.275; Labour Party, 593; monarchy in, 526, 528, 552, 733; relations with Argentina, 432, 826, 842n.86; relations with China, 852; relations with European Union, 885; relations with Finland, 388; relations with France, 859; relations with Germany, 426, 432, 841n.85, 844, 859; relations with Ireland, 592; relations with Japan, 353n.; separation of powers in, 590; and slave trade, 96

Greece, 7, 554, 845n.93; art in, 578; Athens, 9n.18, 160–61, 517, 517n.141, 528, 565–67, 568, 841; Civil War, 824; comic drama in, 9; democracy in, 9–10, 15, 17, 397, 528, 565–67, 569, 573, 573n.232, 593; influence on Roman Empire, 570; the polis in, 4–5, 10, 11, 18, 19, 29, 43, 45, 51, 62, 63, 455n.29, 564, 565–67; religion in, 513; science in, 564, 565; slavery in, 566, 566n.223, 729; Sophists in, 8–9, 36, 75, 565, 567; Sparta, 461, 567; as stage in history, 564–67, 593; tragic drama in, xviii, 9, 163, 729

greed, 298, 299

greenhouse gases, 907–8, 909

Greenpeace, 798

guilt, 100, 103–5, 186, 205n.28, 223, 249, 251, 251n.113, 288–89, 410n., 663, 779–84, 800, 817, 839–40, 843, 901. *See also* intentionalism; responsibility, individual

gypsies, 306–7, 389

habit, 246; relationship to virtue, 244, 286, 294

handicapped, the, 645, 649, 651–52, 657, 688

haplodiploidy, 198, 201

happiness, 102, 245, 284, 285, 424, 586, 609n.309, 651, 659n.60, 660, 665, 713–14, 719, 723, 743–44, 773; Aristotle on, 16–17, 43; vs. justice, 629–30; Machiavelli on, 31

hatred, 224, 239, 303–4, 317, 332, 332n.53, 389, 394, 398, 419, 434, 616, 813, 818

Hawaii, 600n.292

head of state, 443, 525, 530–31, 729, 747, 752, 753–54

health and healthcare, 131, 131n.101, 584, 665, 710, 713, 714, 750, 896–97, 897n.24, 899, 927

hermeneutic abilities, 128n.97, 288, 328, 385, 579, 599

Hinduism, 470, 478, 550, 606

Hiroshima, 142–43, 855

historicism, 3, 24–25, 175, 258–59, 553, 581, 619, 634–35, 779

historiography, xviii, 9, 9nn.17, 18, 156–57, 160–61, 161n., 165–66, 167, 170–72, 173, 174, 436, 439, 514, 545–46, 779

history, 3–4, 96; accident and necessity in, 543–45; battles in, 545; and Christianity, 24–25, 24n.89, 25n.92; crises in, 547–50, 548n.189, 774, 794, 818–24; and Europe, 554–55; Hegel on, 51–52, 470, 544, 546n., 554, 554n.204, 593, 621, 853; Kant on, 52, 544; laws of development in, 172; Marx on, 547, 554n.104, 595–96, 853; philosophy of, xvi, 3, 12–13, 25n.92, 51–52, 57, 179, 183, 194n.13, 543–53, 593–94, 595–96, 609, 621, 853, 866, 877; progress in, 551–53, 551n.196, 593–94; relationship to values, 12–13; the tragic in, 813–14

history, stages in, 554–602; agrarian societies, 555, 558–64, 589, 592, 620; Greece, 564–67, 593; hunters and gatherers, 555–58; Middle Ages, 562, 571–77, 594; Phoenicia, 564; Roman Empire, 568–71, 572–73, 593–94. *See also* modernity

Holocaust, 306–7, 307n.3, 389, 433, 433n.345, 591, 597, 598n., 800, 801, 826, 851n.

Holy Roman Empire, 27, 28–29, 29n.108, 573, 578n.244, 598, 774

Homer, 163, 252n.114, 324, 462, 551

Honduras, 832

honesty, 378, 418, 919

Hong Kong, 918

honor, personal, 281, 486, 614, 647, 648, 685, 686, 864, 917

hospitalism, 314n.20

hospitality, 461–62, 833, 891

hostages, 327, 328, 561, 860

human beings: aggressivity in, 213–15, 235n.84, 243, 247, 268; aging of, 234, 699, 700, 703, 910, 921; Aristotle on, 189, 189n.1; Augustine on, 28, 193n.12, 221n.58, 454–55, 455n.28; autonomy of, 86–87, 100–101, 180, 191, 288, 290, 314, 338–39, 357, 360, 413, 414, 423–24, 423n.337, 425, 431, 441–42, 443, 459, 462, 544, 621, 642, 652, 661, 674, 689, 701, 849, 901, 910; cruelty in, 191, 193, 217, 222, 303, 303nn.207, 208, 304, 368, 398; curiosity in, 219; dignity of, 276n., 278–80, 280n.164, 283, 293, 294, 296, 296n.188, 302, 303, 315, 316–17, 318, 322, 324, 418, 430, 507, 515, 541, 657, 660, 662, 675, 685, 709, 713, 731, 759, 762, 769, 892; as ends in themselves, 114, 127–28, 702; feelings/emotions of, 75, 84, 87, 128, 128n.98, 179, 239–40, 255–56, 270–71, 548,

550, 717; genetically determined behavior in, 197, 203, 207, 212–13, 221–22, 235, 235n.84; Hobbes on, 42–43, 193, 233; human nature, xvii, 46, 46n.167, 191, 191n.4, 210, 222–26, 262, 264–65, 280, 281, 321, 439–40, 544–45, 549–50, 553, 556, 627, 631, 660, 666, 668, 678, 680, 691, 702, 728, 782, 829, 843, 866, 904, 908, 920; imagination of, 219, 238; instrumentalization of, 114, 220, 283–84, 297, 303, 316, 345, 396, 413, 585, 683, 689, 901; intentions/meaning of, 160, 160n.160, 161, 169, 184, 240, 244; interior dimension (*Innenseite*) of, 76, 76n.28, 122–23, 158–60, 161, 169, 194, 217, 227–29, 230–40, 255–56, 314, 693; *I*-self structure in, 223–40, 232n.75, 235n.82, 249–50, 251, 252, 254–55, 256, 263, 271, 282–83, 282n.169, 289–90, 299, 614, 621, 642, 718; killing of other human beings by, 190, 193, 222, 234; mortality of, 190, 193, 222, 233–34, 234, 252, 269, 283, 285–86, 285n., 288, 296, 298, 321–22, 375, 472, 561, 611; natality of, 235, 269, 288; Nietzsche on, 298n.191; and organic evolution, xvii, 3; personal honor in, 281, 647, 648, 685, 686, 864, 917; as political animals, 189–90, 189nn.1, 3, 192; Rousseau on, 46, 46n.167; use of tools by, 220, 222–23, 236; will of, 309, 312, 313–15, 322, 411. *See also* children; human life; identity, individual; reason; recognition; self-consciousness; sexuality

Human Development Index (HDI), 897n.25

human life: and freedom, 431–32, 826–27; principle that human lives cannot be weighed against each other, 688–90, 689n., 801, 807; value of, 42–43, 112–13, 112n., 113n.60, 114–15, 118, 121, 137, 154, 278, 280–81, 286, 291, 293, 324, 405, 429, 431, 434, 633, 645, 646, 647, 648, 649, 652, 653–54, 656–57, 662, 679, 688–90, 689n., 697, 772, 785–86, 787, 801, 804–5, 807, 819, 826–27, 850, 852, 858, 896–97, 920

human rights. *See* rights, human/basic rights

human sacrifice, 175–76, 175n.181

humiliation, 360, 361

humility, 302

Hungary, 803

hunting, 220–21, 257, 315, 315n., 555–58, 852, 853

hymenoptera, 198, 201

hypocrisy, 180, 580, 589, 596, 843, 866

hypothetical imperatives, 7–8, 39, 78, 91–92, 109, 156, 437n.3

ideal being, 158, 193, 194, 195, 196, 237, 238–39, 260, 276, 290, 306–7, 424 idealism, German, 616, 643; and freedom, 315; and human identity, 191; the state in, xviii

identity, collective, 286, 303, 340, 361, 418, 451, 454, 459, 461, 538, 543, 563, 595–96, 604, 718–19, 757, 792, 799–800, 868, 903; crisis of, 274–75, 387, 594; and domination, 441; in Europe, 886; in the family, 441, 444; vs. individual identity, 271–75; and institutions, 272, 274; relationship to education, 513; relationship to enemies, 275, 275n.; relationship to mores, 73; relationship to power, 275; relationship to the state, 44, 271, 449, 475, 495, 717, 826, 831; role of common future in, 477, 477n.66; role of common interests in, 273–74; role of common values in, 273–74; role of descriptive self-images in, 274, 275; role of historiography in, 545; role of language in, 272–73; role of normative self-images in, 274, 275, 282n.169; *We-They* structure in, 271, 302, 335, 348, 356–57, 386, 462, 477. *See also* community

identity, individual, 222–54, 314, 316, 546, 548, 647, 903; vs. collective identity, 271–75; crisis of, xvii, 195, 224–26, 228, 252, 254, 274–75, 303–4, 350, 913; and doubles, 253; *I*-self structure in, 190, 223–40, 232n.75, 235n.82, 249, 249–50, 251, 252, 254–55, 256, 263, 271, 278, 282–83, 282n.169, 289–90, 299, 614, 621, 642, 718; *Me* structure in, 249–54, 262, 274, 300, 316, 365, 456; *principium individuationis*, 235; relationship to power, 275; relationship to recognition, 242, 317–18; relationship to values, 319, 350; relationship to work, 915; role of the body in, 228–29, 272; role of descriptive self-image in, 247–49, 274, 275; role of hatred in, 332, 332n.53; role of historiography in, 545; role of normative self-image in, 247–49, 254, 261, 274, 275, 438

ideology, 305–6, 369, 370–71, 375, 471, 562, 580, 588–89

immigration, 606, 808, 919–20

immoralism, 817–18

imperialism, 506, 506n.129, 509

Incas, 459

incest taboo, 454–55, 631

income: distribution of, 897n.25, 906, 915. *See also* wealth

Index of Sustainable Economic Welfare, 713n.129

India, 177–78, 177n.182, 180, 478, 479, 550, 556, 559, 565, 572n., 576, 581, 605, 754n., 778, 789, 852, 877, 886n.19, 888, 889–90, 893. *See also* Arthaśāstra literature

indirect communication, 329–30

individualism, 482, 498; historical development of, 5, 19, 22, 23, 51; methodological individualism, 164, 448–49, 449n.; in modernity, 369, 441–42, 574, 582, 606, 614, 615, 648, 673, 678, 696; possessive individualism, 42–45, 55, 56, 883; and Protestantism, 579–80; relationship to community, 12, 112, 191, 259, 267–68, 314; and universalism, 112. *See also* self-interest

Indonesia, 789n.17

induction, 140, 140n.118, 166

Industrial Revolution, 512, 534, 548, 555, 583–84, 585, 589, 590, 592, 593, 594, 599, 601–2, 629, 635, 665, 883

infinite, the, 238

inflation, 583n.257, 707, 914

influence: defined, 311n.14; power as, 311, 312, 313, 342, 350–51, 357–58, 441; vs. social effect, 311, 312

information glut, 352, 426, 924

inorganic being, 193, 196, 210–11, 655; value of, 276–77, 278

institutions, 406, 415–16, 544, 547–48, 704; vs. biological systems, 159, 221; and collective identity, 272, 274; function of, 161–62; and interstitial emergence, 263, 547, 547n.188, 903; relationship to freedom, 267; relationship to mores, 813; relationship to political ethics, 95, 98–99, 149; relationship to security, 241; relationship to trust, 692–93; representatives of, 252; symmetry in, 695

insults, 390

insurance, 678, 710, 758

intellectuals, xv, 507, 591, 596, 607, 615, 815, 838, 876, 876n.13; in Germany, 253, 591n.275, 609, 829

intellectual values, 79, 114–15, 281, 282, 284–85

intentionalism, 93–105, 93nn.16, 18, 95n.23, 178, 240, 637–38, 803; and collective responsibility, 103–5; and individual responsibility, 690–91; of Kant, 48, 92, 93–94, 108, 124, 174–75; and self-righteousness, 97–98; the subjectively moral vs. the objectively right, 95–97, 97n., 101–3, 129, 131–32, 432, 779, 780; the subjectively moral vs. the objectively wrong, 143, 143n.129, 184, 789

intercultural relations, 295, 442

interests, 241–42, 246–47, 458, 537–39, 632, 743, 744, 746, 830, 834, 865; alliances based on, 344, 385, 386, 387–89, 393, 420, 611; immediate vs. long-term, 245; power struggles over, 225, 315–17, 319–20, 324, 334, 365, 390, 465; relationship to truth, 33, 157. *See also* needs interior dimension (*Innenseite*), 195, 241; evolution of, 202, 203, 209, 210, 211, 213, 216, 277; of human beings, 76, 76n.28, 122–23, 158–60, 161, 169, 217, 227–28, 255–56, 314, 693; and language, 255–56, 257. *See also* self-consciousness

International Court of Justice, 869, 869n.6

international law, 463, 475n.60, 476, 494n.105, 496n., 504, 607, 828, 838, 845n.91, 856, 869, 900; and inequalities between states, 834, 872; vs. internal state law, 777; international private law, 833; Law of the Sea Convention, 874; and political science, 438, 439; principle of noninterference in, 848–49, 850, 859; prohibition on aggression, 732, 771; relationship to civil law, 848–49; relationship to constitutional law, 732, 763; relationship to natural law, 732, 763, 769–70, 864; and sovereignty, 483, 493–96, 498, 836, 848; and state territory, 481–82, 483; and terrorism, 859–60; relating to war, 848–49, 850, 856–57. *See also* international relations

International Monetary Fund, 607

international organizations, 494–95, 496, 607, 608, 773, 826, 833–34, 846. *See also* NATO; United Nations; World Trade Organization

international relations, 18, 20, 26, 64, 169, 335n.56, 577; balance of power in, 505–6, 599, 763–64, 845–46, 847, 847n.97, 884; in bipolar systems, 505–6, 602, 881; diplomacy, 329, 432, 432n., 508–9, 559, 829, 830–31; hegemonic powers in, 506, 598–99, 764, 846, 847, 847n.99, 882–84, 892, 894; intervention in other countries, 837, 848–53, 900; and mores, 774, 827; in multipolar systems, 505–6; and religion, 876–78; and sovereignty, 493–96, 494nn.103, 105; and treaties, 494, 607, 674, 738, 769–70, 776, 833, 844, 846n.96. *See also* foreign policy; international law; international organizations

interstitial emergence, 263, 547, 547n.188, 903

intersubjectivity, 7, 135–36, 191, 216, 228, 229, 250, 250n.111, 321, 324, 332n.50, 367, 369, 589, 655; and language, 256, 257–58, 260, 314–15, 326, 674; relationship to morality, 816–17; vs. subjectivity, 55. *See also* friendship; identity, collective; love

intolerance, space-related, 214–15, 631

introjection, 251

Iran, 399, 536, 829, 891

Iraq, 399, 608, 843, 846n.94, 848, 851, 863, 868. *See also* war, Gulf War, First

Ireland, 531, 592, 852

Islam, 177, 470, 536, 576, 647n.38, 779, 829, 877, 886; vs. Christianity, 23, 25, 563, 572, 920; funda-

mentalism in, 274, 606, 890, 892, 923; as monotheistic, 572, 813; and war, 582n.253

Israel, state of, 306–7, 787, 835, 838, 846n.94

Italy, 346, 502, 522, 531, 542n.185, 599n.291, 601, 679, 740, 744n.172, 749, 766, 807, 824, 844, 848, 913, 916; civil law in, 694; Constitution of, 729n.; economic conditions in, 604; under fascism, 286–87, 302, 329, 390, 397, 534, 599, 793, 844, 851, 852; political parties in, 525, 604, 608; relations with Ethiopia, 390, 599n.291, 844, 852

Jainism, 470

Japan, 353n., 493, 576–77, 599–600, 604, 788n.14, 804n., 828, 845, 855, 864, 872–73, 888, 894

jealousy, 300, 300n.198

Jehovah's Witnesses, 656

Jericho, 558

Jesuits, 117n.70, 133n.105, 416n.327, 852

Jews, 275, 480; Holocaust, 306–7, 307n.3, 389, 433, 433n.345, 591, 597, 598n., 800, 801, 826, 851n.; state of Israel, 306–7, 787, 835, 846n.94. *See also* Judaism

John, Gospel of: Pontius Pilate in, 153

Judaism, 14, 21, 23, 24, 25, 563, 585, 606, 647n.38, 877

judiciary, 465–66, 488, 503–4, 509, 510, 511, 512, 523n., 566, 680, 727, 758–62; constitutional courts, 497n.113, 522, 523, 524, 686, 739, 745, 746, 760–62, 760n., 778, 799; vs. executive and legislature, 515, 521–23, 522n., 534; in Germany, 517, 523, 524, 686; independence of, 521–22, 754, 758, 788; judicial review of laws, 523–24, 523n., 534, 729, 739, 745, 760–62, 760n., 799; and public prosecutors, 752, 759; in United States, 497n.113, 522, 523–24, 523n.; violations of law by, 798–99

jurisprudence, 438–39, 439n.8, 465, 467, 468, 491, 510–11, 515, 516, 574, 669

juristic persons, 498, 501, 511, 663, 704

justice, 116, 205, 222, 287, 293, 294, 295n., 316, 320, 321, 411, 419, 449, 537, 560, 619, 630, 682, 718, 729, 730, 778, 792, 891, 916; in distribution of wealth, 512–13, 592, 607, 611, 667–68, 906; essence of, 289–91, 303; in foreign policy, 826; vs. happiness, 629–30; Hobbes on, 13, 37, 37n.139; as intergenerational, 618–19, 626n., 641, 643, 648, 653–62, 657, 880, 883, 895, 906; as international, 826, 883, 895, 906, 912; just wars, 20, 26, 119–20, 136–37, 137n.111, 353, 416, 426, 569, 588–89, 667, 682, 688–89, 756, 763, 771, 814, 826–27, 827n., 837–64, 838n.81; maximin principle, 110–11, 110n., 134–35, 140, 143, 907; in modernity, 295; Plato on, 13–14;

Rawls on, 107n.46, 110–11, 110n., 115n.65, 129, 301, 640–41, 662n.63; relationship to equality, 106–7, 107n.46, 289, 290; relationship to law, 37, 290, 303, 466, 473, 631n.6, 724; relationship to self-interest, 291, 300; relationship to social subsystems, 654; and symmetry, 290–91, 293, 695; and universalism, 39, 106–7, 284, 290, 560, 629–30, 654. *See also* virtues

kinship systems, 269, 335, 443, 449, 450, 453–55, 472
Kolmogorov axioms, 138
Kuwait, 843, 848, 868. *See also* war, Gulf War, First

The Lady from Shanghai, 374
language, 222–23, 255–60, 256n.123, 263, 267, 442, 458–59, 542–43, 547n.187; ancient languages, 924–25; of diplomacy, 329, 432, 432n.; English language, 886, 886n.19, 923; indexicals, 106n.45, 278; as instrument of power, 260, 427–28; and interior dimension, 255–56, 257; and intersubjectivity, 256, 257–58, 260, 314–15, 326, 674; learning of, 257–58; and nationalism, 478; nominal definitions, 166; oral vs. written, 257; origin of, 227, 257; preservation of languages, 736, 766, 809, 895; printing, 577–78, 589, 591, 594; relationship to politics, 256n.123; relationship to universalism, 106, 106n.45; role in collective identity, 272–73; sexism in, 818, 866; speech acts, 224, 306–7; and traditions, 221, 258; writing, 257, 558–59, 564, 577, 590
Latin America, 477n.66, 605, 842n.86
Laudatio Turiae, 773
laughter, 223
law, 193, 462–67, 575; administrative law, 510, 626; in archaic cultures, 465–66, 467; Aristotle on, 518, 518n.143, 776; business law, 465; and capitalism, 587; certainty of, 464, 633, 646, 672, 769, 904; Cicero on, 632n.9; codification of, 509–10, 510n., 786; and coercion, 68–69, 71, 262, 290, 437, 462, 463–64, 465, 466, 625–26, 631n.6, 637–68, 644–45, 648, 650, 654, 693, 776; commercial law, 510; and concept of equity, 467; copyright law, 510; due process of, 732; equality before the, 35, 48, 519, 638–39, 732, 737; essence of, 437, 466; family law, 458, 627, 638, 693–704, 698n., 710; in formal sense, 517–19, 737; generality of, 514–15; Hegel on, 474n.59, 636, 639, 693; history of, 438, 634; inheritance law, 458, 479, 643, 657n.53, 673, 694, 699–701, 699n.115; juristic concepts, 72; labor law, 708; legal

positivism, 35, 37, 637, 795; Montesquieu on, 438, 465, 633n., 634, 636n.12, 738, 782n.7; vs. morals, 280–81; norms of competence related to, 465–66, 465n.44; origin of, 462–63, 551, 559, 562; patent law, 670, 670n.81; philosophy of, 37, 50–51, 50n.179, 71, 72, 122, 438, 439, 625–26, 637, 638–39, 642, 642n.23, 663, 664n.67, 665, 674, 679n.97, 687, 693, 698, 703, 714n., 762, 795, 930; presumption of innocence, 759; proceduralist conception of, 518, 632–33; procedural law, 626, 758–60; relationship to economic activity, 451, 462; relationship to justice, 37, 290, 303, 466, 473, 631n.6, 724; relationship to mores, 462, 463–64, 465, 466–67, 478–79, 491, 496, 510, 515, 629, 634, 638, 663, 675–76, 687, 776–79, 822; relationship to power struggles, 664n.67; relationship to religion, 467–68; relationship to reproduction, 451, 462; relationship to the state, 35, 41, 48, 51, 52, 58–59, 180, 378, 405, 416, 437–38, 446, 448, 464, 472–73, 476, 485, 487, 488–90, 498, 502, 509–10, 512, 516, 517–18, 521–24, 536, 540, 544, 625–27, 629, 631, 632–33, 642–44, 645, 646, 648–49, 654, 674, 679, 681, 692, 693, 774, 798–99, 820, 823–24, 887; respect for, 738, 759, 776–77, 795, 801, 822; rule of, 41, 48, 51, 52, 58–59, 180, 378, 405, 416, 446, 472–73, 512, 544, 887; sociology of, 438, 634; state law vs. international law, 496–97; trials, 758–60. *See also* civil law; constitutional law; criminal law; international law; jurisprudence; natural law; positive law
leadership, xvii, 60, 66–67, 67n.15, 70, 218, 264, 289, 334–35, 447, 449, 460, 556, 790–94
League of Nations, 601, 763, 844, 848, 864, 871
legal positivism, 35, 37, 637, 795
legislature, the, 500, 517–19, 587, 737–48, 746n.174, 747n.176, 749; vs. judiciary, 515, 521–23, 522n., 534. *See also* democracy
leisure, 615, 910, 915
lending at interest, 583, 583n.257
leniency, 392
liability, 93n.16, 610, 677–78, 677n.94, 711, 716
libel, 647
liberalism, 55–56, 512, 513, 533, 596, 597, 626, 638–44, 644n.28, 648, 663, 676, 693, 723, 728–29, 763, 764, 832, 902–3; and separation of powers, 534, 593, 638
libertarianism, 644, 644n.28, 652, 834, 916
lies, 30, 77, 291, 299, 299n.196, 324, 383–84, 421n.332, 432; Kant on, 94, 108, 108n.49, 109, 112, 117, 117n.69. *See also* deception

life: life expectancy, 584, 788, 789n.17, 895, 896, 897n.25, 912; negation of, 112, 145, 145n.134, 222, 223, 225–26, 262, 269, 278, 279–80, 372–73, 639n.16, 652, 653, 653nn.48, 49, 675; right to, 647, 656, 679, 681, 704, 731, 788, 800–801, 808–9, 850, 857, 857n.113; and spirit, 191, 222–26, 281; value of, 209–10, 277. *See also* human life

logic, 77

love, 248, 254, 287, 295, 303, 326, 341n., 359n.98, 360, 584–85, 590, 723; in Christianity, 181, 289n.181, 293–94, 572, 619, 649–50; of God, 304; in marriage, 695–96, 698; parental love, 650–51; vs. power, 366–67; relationship to sex drive, 247, 284, 340n.64; relationship to tyrannical behavior, 366–67; relationship to values, 240; Scheler on, 239, 240; self-love, 240; as social virtue, 289; as symmetrical relationship, 367, 394n.235

Macedonia, 348n.82, 567, 847

macroeconomics, 263

Magdalenian culture, 558

magic, 237, 261, 469, 651

malice, 204, 204n.26, 300

Manchus, 563

Manicheanism, 571–72

manipulation, 350–52, 353–54, 357, 358, 361–62, 429, 450, 485, 537, 542, 715

marriage, 385–86, 452–53, 649, 663, 693, 694–99, 701–2, 782, 824, 846; community property, 698–99; vs. contracts, 655, 694–95; and friendship, 453, 461, 696; and procreation, 452–53, 697; role of love in, 695–96, 698; same-sex marriage, 698. *See also* family, the

Marshall Plan, 897

Marxism-Leninism, 45, 56–57, 183, 265, 471, 552, 591, 595–96, 596n.285, 597, 601, 606, 619, 620, 867

mathematics, 140, 148n.139, 581, 620, 923; ability to count, 238, 238n.88; Plato on, 11, 11n.25, 42, 74, 118n.76, 158; vs. practical philosophy, 73, 74, 83n.42, 106, 106n.44, 118n.76, 125; in social sciences, 169–70

Mauss, M., 236n.87

Max Planck Institute, 930

means-end relationship, 58, 94, 94n.21, 123–33, 125n.93, 133n.105, 149–51, 169, 184, 219, 221n.57, 241, 244–45, 244n., 247, 268, 286–87, 298, 364–65, 426, 434, 793, 819; communicative rationality, 128, 149; regarding morals and

power, 405, 410–17; strategic rationality, 30–31, 126–28, 136, 149, 155, 694; technical rationality, 126–27, 136

media, the, 483, 509, 542, 591, 612, 614, 615, 741, 751, 759, 760, 786, 791, 798, 799, 802, 886, 889, 917; monopolization in, 352, 707–8; newspapers, 594; radio, 594, 785, 830; television, 132, 594, 707–8, 785, 804, 830, 835, 918

memory, 231–32, 231n.73, 250, 252; collective memory, 273, 273n.156, 275

mercantilism, 587

Merovingian kings, 492, 571

Mesopotamia, 554, 556, 559, 562

metrical concepts, 118, 118nn.75, 76, 134

Mexico: Constitution of 1824, 515

microeconomics, 263

Middle Ages, 559, 562, 571–77, 578, 586, 587, 594, 621, 716, 828, 838, 877, 920; political philosophy during, 23, 25–27, 28–29, 44, 51

Middle East, 893

middle way, the, 149–50, 150nn.142, 143

migrations, 835

military, the, 270, 340, 341n., 346–47, 453, 512, 538, 599, 607, 830, 842, 851–52; duty to perform military service, 110, 726, 727, 732, 755, 756, 763, 841, 894; military occupation, 483; relationship to politics, 264, 451, 464, 503–4, 508, 559, 562, 575, 654, 784–85, 793, 802; as social subsystem, 79, 264, 265, 266, 451, 459–63, 503–4, 654, 784–85. *See also* war; weapons

mind and body, 23, 30, 257; epiphenomenalism, 202n.; interaction between, 74–75, 202, 202n., 240, 240n., 547n.187

mixed syllogisms. *See* practical syllogisms

moderation, 283–84

modernity, 27n.105, 179, 179n.186, 243, 287, 334, 577–602, 664n.67, 780, 813, 866; vs. agrarian societies, 559–60; and Christianity, 23–25, 578–81, 585; crisis of, xiv, 58–61, 602; equality in, 581, 587–88, 591, 593, 596, 616, 764, 832, 834, 891; foreign policy in, 598–602, 603–9; immorality in, 817–18; individualism in, 369, 441–42, 574, 582, 606, 614, 615, 648, 673, 678, 696; justice in, 295; mobility in, 909–10, 910n.39; and projection, 249; religion in, 468, 577, 589, 609, 618–21, 619n.; and the Renaissance, 578–79; respect for law in, 777; selfishness in, 618–19, 642; social orders in, 263; social subsystems in, 78–79, 266, 468; the state in, xv, 27, 52, 58–61, 439, 468, 484–85, 485n.83, 486–88, 491, 493, 500, 512, 516, 519, 521, 535,

537, 543, 544, 545, 552, 553, 555, 556, 574, 575, 586–608, 610–14, 629–31, 723n.140, 772, 795, 824, 835, 875, 903; subjectivity in, 3, 12, 28, 45–46, 51, 57, 101, 102, 290, 589, 614, 620–21, 685; superstructure of, 41–42; and technology, 41–42, 59, 577–78, 581, 585, 764; trust in, 693; war in, 600–602; Western standard of living, 346, 602–3, 607, 616, 765, 865–66, 879–80, 888, 889–90, 895, 896

modesty, 283, 883

Moldova, 478

monarchy, 15, 17, 35–36, 394, 400n.262, 402, 402n.275, 449, 480, 480n.72, 494n.103, 586–87, 595, 790–91; as absolute, 106–7, 397, 499, 526–28, 778, 779–80; as constitutional/ parliamentary, 495n.107, 526, 528, 532, 754, 754n.; as elective, 526; as hereditary, 111, 146n.136, 377, 377n.145, 410, 412, 500, 521, 525, 526, 527, 534, 724–25, 729, 754, 754n., 778, 779–80, 806–7; as legitimist, 410, 412, 527, 779–80, 806–7

money, xiv, 334, 346–47, 348, 364, 459, 564, 614, 685, 878, 929; fixed vs. floating exchange rates, 833; inflation, 583n.257, 707, 914; marginal utility of, 743; monetary policy, 511, 538, 707, 746; taxes on currency speculation, 833, 875

Mongols, 349, 545

monocracy, 460–61, 495, 501–2, 526–28, 527n.160, 529, 533, 536, 539, 540, 562, 567, 578, 579, 586, 606, 749, 764, 773, 794, 827, 847, 873; as autocracy, 527, 527n.161; dictatorship, 374–75, 490, 501, 526–27, 530, 788–90, 788n.14, 789n.17, 800–807, 842n.86, 850, 861–62, 902–3. *See also* monarchy

monotheism, 563, 571–72, 572, 813

moral authority, 100–101, 101n.34, 426–27

moral evolutionism, 174–82, 209–10, 218–22, 563, 573, 593–94, 634–35; and hypocrisy, 180, 580

moral feelings, 75, 84, 87, 128, 128n.98, 179, 270–71, 717

moralism, 85–86, 85n.48, 152–53, 152n.149, 617–18

morality (*Moralität*): Hegel on, 73, 88, 814, 815; vs. mores (*Sittlichkeit*), 73, 88, 266, 549–50, 565, 617, 811–22, 904; relationship to intersubjectivity, 816–17

moral luck, 86, 87n.52, 103, 104, 691

morally indifferent, the, 85, 85n.46

moral obligations, 549, 663, 691; and communities, 112; conditional obligations, 109–10, 109n.54, 134, 176, 280n.165, 635, 725, 760n., 780n., 881; to the environment, 907; exceptions to, 108–12,

116–17, 116n.67; to future generations, 731; Kant on, 101–2, 102n., 105–6, 108, 112, 117, 117n.69, 153, 282n.169; to obey the law, 634, 731, 776, 795, 797–98; to oneself, 282–83, 282n.169, 407, 424, 643, 686; "ought" implies "can," 90, 675, 802; related to establishing a state, 692; related to poverty, 667–68, 713, 743, 765, 788, 834, 895–902, 898, 913–14; relationship between *Is* and *Ought*, 4, 5, 11–12, 16, 27–28, 50, 52, 89–90, 89n.4, 90n.6, 92, 125, 153, 183, 184, 544; relationship to happiness, 284; relationship to prohibitions/permissions, 90n.8; relationship to rights, 466, 651–52, 675, 732, 756, 765, 874, 921, 921n.; to the state, 634, 726, 727, 731, 732, 755, 756, 763, 841, 894; and universalism, 105–12. *See also* justice

moral relativism, 117n.70, 126, 133n.105, 177, 177n.182, 620, 883

morals, 276–304; defined, 70–71; vs. law, 280–81; metaphysics of, 76–77; moral feelings, 75, 84, 87, 101–3, 128, 128n.98, 179, 270–71, 717; moral intuitions, 17, 72, 84, 91, 120; moral judgment, 245, 246–47; the moral optimum vs. moral minimum, 147, 785–86; vs. mores, 72–73, 78, 82, 84, 84n.44, 88, 106, 176–77, 179, 204, 237, 320, 417–18, 451, 549–50, 693, 701, 756, 774–824, 827, 890, 904, 924; relationship to cratology, 65; relationship to evolutionary stability, 199–201, 205–7, 205n.29, 209, 214–15, 214n.44, 270, 296, 406, 431, 682, 813; relationship to foreign policy, xvii, 769, 773–74, 824–64, 883, 906, 912; relationship to freedom, 304, 318, 826–27; relationship to natural law, 144–46, 637–38, 642–54, 648, 657, 658, 664n.67, 692; relationship to organic evolution, 218–22; relationship to personality, 103; relationship to politics, xv–xvi, xix, xxi, 4–5, 7, 10, 13–14, 15, 16–17, 21–22, 23–24, 29–31, 32, 43, 48–51, 52, 57–58, 60, 61, 62n.1, 63, 70–71, 75, 76–80, 87–88, 504–5, 772–76, 872; relationship to religion, 92, 183–86, 183n., 468–70, 610, 619, 620, 719–21, 723, 781–82; relationship to rhetoric, 75; relationship to self-interest, 91–92, 96–97, 287–88, 291, 300, 645, 661; relationship to symmetry, 108, 137, 138, 270, 290–91, 432, 462, 466, 640, 857; relationship to the family, 694; role of argumentation in, 75, 75n., 114–15, 641n.19; skepticism regarding, 775, 817–18; and volitions, 101–3, 102n.37. *See also* goods; moral evolutionism; moral obligations; power and morals; values mores (*Sittlichkeit*), 267, 323, 456–57, 620, 628, 710, 718, 736, 880, 920; and aid for development, 836; Hegel on, 50–51, 73, 88, 580n.247; and international relations, 774, 827; vs. morality (*Moralität*), 73, 88, 266, 549–50, 565, 617, 811–22, 904; vs. morals, 72–73, 78, 82, 84, 84n.44, 88, 106, 176–77, 179, 204, 237, 320, 417–18, 451, 549–50, 693, 701, 756, 774–824, 827, 890, 904, 924; and politicians, 773, 774–76, 779, 782–83; relationship to collective identity, 73; relationship to customs, 260–62; relationship to law, 462, 463–64, 465, 466–67, 478–79, 491, 496, 510, 515, 629, 634, 638, 663, 675–76, 687, 776–79, 822; relationship to natural law, 773, 774–824, 808; relationship to religion, 469–70, 563; relationship to the state, 449, 471, 472, 485, 485n.84, 491, 534, 534n.175, 536, 547, 586, 625, 629, 631, 725, 745, 751, 765, 773, 774–76, 800; revolutions in, 549; as stable, 774, 783–818, 822; as unstable, 774, 794, 818–22; vs. usual manners of conduct (*Üblichkeiten*), 261; and *Volksgeist*, 781–82

mortality, 196, 212; of human beings, 190, 193, 222, 233–34, 234, 252, 269, 283, 285–86, 285n., 288, 296, 298, 321–22, 375, 472, 561, 611

motion pictures, 351, 594, 662

Mudrārākṣasa, 8

multiculturalism, 562, 591, 610–11, 828–30, 895, 896, 919–20

Munich accord, 808, 844, 848

municipalities, 487, 735, 809

Myanmar, 900

myths, 6, 246, 256, 265, 268, 557

Nagasaki, 142–43, 855

Naples, 820–21

narcissism, 614

Nāstikas, 8n.13

nationalism, 44, 52, 477–78, 591n.277, 597, 601, 766, 807, 808, 821, 841, 848, 854, 863, 889; definition of nation, 477, 477nn.66, 67; and French Revolution, 590–91; and language, 478; vs. universalism, 54, 591

National Socialism, 104, 246, 256n.123, 286–87, 302, 306, 309, 331n.49, 353, 397, 478, 479–80, 528, 580n.249, 591, 596–98, 634, 688–89, 701n., 737, 786, 795, 797, 804n., 851, 855, 860, 883, 928; as anti-universalist, 57, 139, 178, 180, 597, 686; vs. communism, 57, 139, 345, 389, 396, 597; Hitler, 58, 70, 78, 141–42, 141n.124, 143, 230, 329, 343, 344, 351, 353, 371, 384, 388–89, 396, 398,

398n.252, 420, 432, 434–35, 516, 527, 528n.162, 547, 594, 597, 598, 598n., 686, 725, 754, 784–85, 794, 801, 802, 804, 807, 826, 837–38, 840–41, 844, 845, 848, 861, 863; mores of, 73, 78

Native Americans, 556, 590, 590n.272, 599, 630, 852, 853

NATO, 885; deployment of Pershing II missiles by, 151–52, 152n.148, 796, 841, 862; expansion of, 811, 846, 887, 893

naturalistic fallacy, 90, 90n.6, 205

natural law, 32, 473n.54, 631–92, 631nn.4–6, 641n.19, 647n.38, 706, 719, 784, 896, 897; Aquinas on, 26; in Catholicism, 26, 632, 632n.8; defined, 632; and environmental protection, 660–61, 664, 671, 673, 715, 902, 907; and foreign policy, 773–74, 849, 850; and gender equality, 698; Hegel on, 486n., 632, 648; Hobbes on, 37–39, 37n.139, 38n.143, 39n.145, 40n.150, 626, 639, 640; and homosexuality, 148; vs. justice, 631n.6; Locke on, 43, 43n.161, 44, 632; in non-ideal conditions, 772–74; and personhood, 655, 656–64; and property, 655, 665–73; and punishment, 686; relationship to constitutional law, 625, 626, 627, 632–33, 721, 724, 725, 731–32, 767–68, 779–80, 804, 846, 863, 884; relationship to contracts, 655, 661, 662, 673–78; relationship to criminal law, 686, 687, 688–89; relationship to democracy, 632–33, 766, 790; relationship to ethics, 144–46, 632, 637–38, 642–54, 657, 658, 664n.67, 692; relationship to human dignity, 662; relationship to human nature, 631; relationship to international law, 732, 763, 769–70, 864; relationship to legislature, 737–47; relationship to morals, 144–46, 637–38, 642–54, 648, 657, 658, 664n.67, 692; relationship to mores, 773, 774–824, 808; relationship to politics, 772, 872; relationship to positive law, 17, 20, 26, 37, 518, 625–27, 632–38, 686, 687, 688–89, 724, 734, 761–62, 776–79, 795, 796, 797, 799, 807–11, 859–60, 917, 918; relationship to reason, 631–32; relationship to religion, 719–21, 723; relationship to the state, 625–27, 631, 642–44, 769; and rights, 633, 645–48, 650n.43, 655–78, 728–29, 731–32; and secession, 808–10; and the welfare state, 644, 913–14

natural selection, 197–210, 216, 543; evolutionary stable strategies, 199–201, 205–7, 205n.29, 209, 214–15, 214n.44

nature, 209, 923; biodiversity in, 210, 277, 899, 909n.36, 910; and Christianity, 24, 24n.88, 37; climate, 482, 608, 661, 907–8; vs. consciousness, 4; fossil fuels, 584, 908; laws of, 153, 170–72, 194, 194n.15, 543, 544; natural resources, 608–9, 660, 669–71, 669n.74, 673, 676, 711, 712–13, 714, 873–74, 884, 899, 903, 904, 908–9; ownership of natural resources, 669–71, 673, 873–74; ozone layer, 907–8; as profane, 24; rainforests, 899, 908; renewable vs. nonrenewable resources, 660, 711, 908–9; value of, 115, 115n.65, 176–77, 285. *See also* ecological issues; environmental policy

Near East, 493

needs, 241–44, 241n.92, 245, 246–47, 261, 261n.132, 265, 315, 368, 458, 459, 594, 613, 613n., 658, 659, 660, 715–17, 762, 913, 916; basic needs, 665–66, 667, 668, 676, 705, 718, 718n., 723, 899, 914–15; of consumers, 676–77, 715, 767, 879–80; creation of, 430, 456, 583, 715, 767; need for food, 196, 211, 213, 216, 233, 241, 242, 283, 297, 343, 453, 456, 457, 557, 584, 646, 649, 672, 711, 714, 852, 895–96; need for recognition, 191, 193, 217, 242, 289, 361, 361n.102, 365, 404, 419, 442, 647, 648, 666n., 831, 854, 889. *See also* interests; sexuality

negative sanctions, 166, 339, 407, 445, 447, 463, 485–86, 489–90, 492, 503, 522, 534, 547, 629, 718, 792–93, 832, 875, 916, 917, 921, 928; economic sanctions, 830, 860, 868, 890; legal coercion, 68–69, 71, 262, 462, 463–64, 466, 486, 625–26, 631n.6, 637–38, 644–45, 648, 650, 654, 693, 776; in power struggles, 325–26, 326nn.40, 41, 327, 328, 340n.64, 341–43, 344, 346, 347–49, 352, 394, 398, 398n.251, 423, 431–35, 587; in religion, 354, 470; in slavery, 441, 446. *See also* punishment

negligence, 93, 124, 677, 691; conscious vs. unconscious, 99, 99n.30; vs. *dolus eventualis*, 99, 105, 661, 697n.

Neolithic Revolution, 548, 548n.190, 551, 555

Nigeria, 872

nihilism, moral, 57–58, 59, 60, 87, 124, 179, 406n., 580n.249, 597, 598, 610, 722

normative statements: vs. descriptive statements, 7–8, 16, 48, 57, 70–79, 89–90, 92, 121, 125, 129, 153, 154–55, 156, 167, 202, 209, 219, 246, 261, 276, 438–39; as true or false, 89; vs. value judgments, 90–91, 121

North Atlantic Free Trade Zone, 888

North Korea, 788n.14

Norway, 859

nuclear energy, 140, 140n.121, 714, 909

Nuclear Non-Proliferation Treaty, 604, 869

nuclear weapons, 603–4, 842, 855, 861–63, 892–93

objective idealism, 183, 208, 209–10

Old Testament: Book of Genesis, 288n.177; prophets in, 253, 563, 563n.219; story of Joseph, 185

oligarchy, 15, 17, 460–61, 526, 528–30, 534n.176, 537, 538, 562, 568

omissions, 144–46, 145n.134, 166, 644, 648, 649, 690, 692, 797

opinion, 441, 537; freedom of, 731, 788; public opinion, 541–42, 612, 742, 751, 752, 858, 873, 886; role in power struggles, 340, 342n.71, 348–62, 425, 426–29

opportunism, 129

organic being, 193–97, 210–22, 229; value of, 176–77, 276–77, 278, 278nn.160, 161

organization, 338–39, 341, 348

Orthodox church, 24n.88, 574, 821, 887

Ostrogoths, 479, 479n.69

Ottoman Empire, 409n.311, 480, 494n.105, 506, 578, 591, 598, 807, 850

pacifism, 152, 152n.147, 406, 408, 432–33, 813, 818, 826, 843, 889–90, 894

pain, 229, 241, 257, 280

Pakistan, 810, 893

Pan-American Treaty, 475n.60

Pañcatantra, 192

Pan-Slavism, 595n.283, 766n.

Paraguay, 832, 852

Pareto-inclusiveness, 120, 120n.82

Pareto-optimality, 111, 111n., 137, 161, 448, 630, 693, 792

Parthenopean Republic, 820–21

paternalism, 534, 538, 652–54, 656, 889

patricians and plebeians, 568, 568n.226, 786, 791

patriotism, 102, 479–80, 513, 733, 767–68

peace, 129–30, 506–7, 770, 829, 835, 847–48, 847n.97, 871, 875, 884, 897; Augustine on, 507n.; Hobbes on, 34–35, 36; Kant on, 49, 763, 864; and the state, xiv, 34–35, 36, 66, 503–4, 509, 627, 720, 826, 902

Peace of Westphalia, 602

Peripatetics, 95n.25

Permanent Court of Arbitration, 869

Pershing II missiles, 151–52, 152n.148, 796, 841n.85, 862

Persian Empire, 563–64, 566

personhood, 278, 280, 283; juristic persons, 498, 501, 511, 663; and natural law, 655, 656–64; potential persons, 656–57, 656n., 703, 703n.; and rights, 646, 654, 655, 656–64; subsumption problem, 122–23, 122nn.87, 88, 175 persuading, 450, 537; vs. convincing, 340n.64, 352–57; vs. force, 405, 423

Peru, 832, 917

Pharsalus, battle of, 805, 806n.38

philosophy, 239, 256, 259, 266, 305, 565, 581–82, 619, 620, 629, 719, 877, 923–24, 931; analytical philosophy, xviii, 3; empiricism, 166; epistemology, 154, 237; German idealism, xviii, 191, 315, 616, 643; phenomenology, 167; philosophical anthropology, 155; philosophy of culture, 191; philosophy of religion, 468, 470, 782; philosophy of science, 154; positivism, 37, 437n.3, 637, 795; pragmatism, 237; social philosophy, 155, 158, 162–64, 165, 167, 174; social role of, 720, 721–22, 762, 784. *See also* law, philosophy of; philosophy of history; political philosophy

philosophy of history, xvi, 3, 12–13, 25n.92, 57, 179, 194n.13, 543–53, 593–94, 609, 866, 877; of Fichte, 544, 549; of Hegel, 51–52, 183, 470, 544, 545, 546n., 554, 554n.204, 593, 621, 853; of Kant, 52, 544; in Marxism, 183, 547, 552, 594, 595–96, 853. *See also* historicism

philosophy of law. *See* law, philosophy of

Phoenicians, 554, 555n.205, 564

physiocentrists, 664n.67

Pietism, 581n.250

piety, 298

plants, 655; vs. animals, 210–11, 226, 277, 278n.160, 620–21, 924

pleasure, 84, 241, 241n.91, 276, 280, 281, 286, 297, 723

plebeians, 568, 568n.226, 786, 791

poetry, xviii, 19

poietic values, 285, 298

Poland, 488, 506, 528nn.162, 163, 592, 595, 690, 802, 810, 838, 841n.85, 845

politeness, 289, 385, 418

political anthropology, 436

political asylum, 768–69, 798, 815, 916–17

political awareness, 479–80

political correctness, 818

political criminals, 804

political ethics, xvi–xvii, 4–5, 71–72, 87–88, 130–31; and collective responsibility, 103–5; and establishment of ideal state, 625; and exceptional situations, 626, 682; and omissions, 144–46; political strategies, 132–33; relationship to citizens' preferences, 120–21, 120n.84, 129; relationship to individual ethics, 5, 13–15, 16, 16n.50, 23, 30–31, 50–51, 52, 71–72; and resistance to positive law, 634, 731n.149, 756, 795, 797–98, 918

political genius, 149

political magazines, 615

political man (*Machtmensch*), the, 120, 308, 330n.46, 334, 449; advisors of, 380; choice of collaborators by, 380–81; defined, 362, 362nn.104, 105; and the executive, 520; ideals of, 380, 380n.158; maxims of aspirants to power, 375–76, 377–81, 417–19; maxims for fighting enemies, 382–93, 419–22; maxims of power-holders, 375–77, 393–401, 422–23; personality and character of, 230, 358–62, 363–70, 365n., 380, 389–90, 398n.251, 411–12, 413–14, 418–19, 420–21, 422–23, 423n.336, 427, 533, 790–91, 793; as power-obsessed, 362, 365, 366, 367–70, 371, 374, 412, 414n.322, 419, 419n.328, 534, 594, 845, 902. *See also* cratic, the; cratology; politicians

political parties, 62, 63, 85–86, 492, 525, 533, 533n.172, 534, 537–38, 612, 616, 740–41, 741n.167, 744–45, 744n.172, 748, 750, 751, 751n., 754

political philosophy, xv–xvi, xvii–xviii, 5, 68, 154, 515, 547, 786; and capitalism, 42–43; and Christianity, 21–27, 37; in Greece, 4–5, 7, 7n.10, 8–18, 32, 36, 45, 51, 60, 60n., 63, 75; in Hellenistic period, 18–19, 19n.66, 22, 29n.110; vs. jurisprudence, 439; during Middle Ages, 23, 25–27, 28–29, 44, 51; during modern period, 27–61, 58n.199; vs. philosophy of law, 625–26; vs. political science, 7, 155; and power, 305, 693; relationship to philosophy of history, 51–52; relationship to political institutions, 95, 98–99, 149, 784; relationship to science, 32, 34, 57–58, 76; in Roman Empire, 18–21, 32, 75; utopias in, 12–13, 14–15, 29–30, 29nn.110, 111, 57, 59, 129, 418, 471, 609, 775–76, 925

political psychology, 436

political scandals, 307, 541, 615–16, 751, 762

political science, 7, 115, 155, 160, 260, 436, 437, 438, 439, 439n.7, 492, 494

political symbols, 192, 193, 355, 355n.91

political theology, 25–26, 25n.93

politicians: and the common good, 17, 611–12, 791, 825; as demagogues, 355, 355n.92, 424, 428, 536, 567, 616; during historical crises, 818–22, 820n.58; leadership/cratic abilities of, 66–67, 67n.15, 70, 790–94; and mores, 773, 774–76, 779, 782–83; personality and character of, 32n.122, 33, 66–67, 67n.15, 70, 100n.33, 101n.34, 120, 120n.81, 130–31, 144, 145–46, 146nn.135, 136, 148, 148n.138, 152n.150, 192, 218, 230, 358–62, 365, 380, 398n.251, 411–12, 418–19, 420–21, 422–23, 423n.336, 427, 540, 615, 787, 790–94, 823, 919; political moralism among,

152–53, 152n.149; political strategies of, 132–33;
public distrust of, 919; relations with political
opponents, 152–53, 152n.150, 793–94, 819–20;
religious convictions of, 722–23; and social
subsystems, 783–85; as statesmen, 66, 67n.15,
356n.95, 358, 410, 486, 504, 791–93, 821–22; and
universalism, 865. *See also* executive, the; legislature, the; political man (*Machtmensch*), the

politics: and collective attention frames, 247; conservative vs. progressive, 70, 775, 822; definitions of,
62–63, 62n.3, 68, 69n.20, 189, 189n.3; the enemy
in, 190; vs. the erotic, 190; idealism in, 130–31;
and patriotic feelings, 102, 479–80, 513, 733,
767–68; *Politikpolitik*, 67, 67n.14; pragmatism
in, 130–31; and projection, 249; relationship
to common good, 17, 121, 611–12, 791, 825;
relationship to the cratic, xv, 62–68, 62n.3,
66n., 439–40, 750–51, 773, 790–94; relationship
to empirical sciences, 101n.34; relationship to
language, 256n.123; relationship to the military,
264, 451, 464, 503–4, 508, 559, 562, 575, 593,
654, 784–85, 793, 802; relationship to morals,
xv–xvi, xix, xxi, 4–5, 7, 10, 13–14, 15, 16–17,
21–22, 23–24, 29–31, 32, 43, 48–51, 52, 57–58,
60, 61, 62n.1, 63, 70–71, 75, 76–80, 87–88, 504–5,
772–76, 872; relationship to representation, 252;
relationship to rhetoric, 75; relationship to
social sciences, xv–xvi, xviii, 50, 57–58, 76;
relationship to the state, 62–68, 62n.3, 189,
436, 785, 787–88; relationship to violence,
190, 192; substitute actions in, 243–44;
symbols in, 192, 193, 355, 355n.91. *See also*
political philosophy; politicians; state, the

population, 628, 629, 658–60, 670, 736, 762, 872;
growth in, 456, 560, 585, 659, 665, 702–4, 865,
874–75, 876, 891, 898, 901, 912, 919–20, 919n.46

pornography, 662, 715, 891–92

Portugal, 532, 599, 804

positive law, 438, 473, 686n.109, 838; vs. consensus,
430; consistency of, 464, 635–36; Hobbes on, 13,
35, 37, 37n.139, 626, 627; and human rights,
831; Marsilius on, 27, 27n.105; procedural vs.
substantive norms, 778–79, 804; and property,
646–47, 665; relationship to common good, 26;
relationship to natural law, 17, 20, 26, 37, 518,
625–27, 632–38, 686, 687, 688–89, 724, 734,
761–62, 776–79, 795, 796, 797, 799, 807–11,
859–60, 917, 918; right of resistance to, 37, 634,
723, 773, 778–79, 795–807, 918; violations of,
26, 37, 634, 773, 776, 778–79, 788n.14, 794–811,
822–24, 916–18; relating to war, 856–57. *See also*
punishment

positive sanctions, 166, 441, 446, 467, 471, 485–86,
503, 512–13, 522, 537, 547, 610, 611, 644, 703,
792, 832; in power struggles, 307, 340–43,
340n.65, 344, 345–49, 352, 395, 423, 430,
587

poverty, xiv, 56, 56n.196, 537, 538, 592, 605–6, 809;
absolute, 666, 667–68, 713, 743, 765, 767, 788,
834, 835, 871, 874n.9, 875, 896, 898–99, 901,
906, 913–14; moral obligations related to,
667–68, 713, 743, 765, 788, 834, 895–902, 898,
913–14; relative, 666, 667–68, 767, 792, 906;
rights of the poor, 765, 834, 898, 906. *See also*
wealth

power: abuse of, 40, 41, 304, 531, 629, 654, 681, 683,
685, 686, 691, 725, 728–29, 733, 742, 749, 752,
848–51; amorality of, 310; as asymmetrical
relationship, 310, 310n.12, 311, 342, 343, 359n.98,
367, 371, 395, 404; attaining vs. retaining,
375–76, 377; balance of, 505–6, 599, 763–64,
845–46, 847, 847n.97, 884; bases of, 309,
309n.8, 312, 323, 328, 329, 335n.56, 338, 343, 377,
414n.321; collective vs. distributive, 503, 552; as
comprehensive, 338, 338n., 472; delegation of,
338–39, 380, 400–401, 407, 487, 734; essence
and definition of, 308–13, 312n., 342–43; as
extensive, 338, 338n., 472; formal vs. factual,
491–93, 493n.101, 536; and friend-foe distinction, 307, 382–83, 385–86, 387, 406n., 820; as
influence, 311, 312, 313, 342, 350–51, 357–58, 441;
as intensive, 338, 338n., 472; intrinsic vs. extrinsic value of, 405; language as instrument of,
260, 427–28; legitimacy of, 423–24, 423n.337,
425–26; Machiavelli on, 29–32, 31n.118, 33, 64,
87, 171n.176, 348, 349n.84, 376, 376n.141, 396,
397nn.247, 248, 399n.257, 400n.263, 401, 405,
410; necessity of, 405, 406–10, 416; Nietzsche
on, 58, 305, 405, 429; obsession with, 230, 362,
365, 366, 367–70, 371, 374, 412, 414n.322, 419,
419n.328, 534, 594, 845, 902; Plato on, 14, 15, 67,
321, 412, 419n.; relationship to action, 166, 309;
relationship to authority, 357–62; relationship
to collective identity, 275; relationship to expectations, 309; relationship to individual identity,
275; relationship to physical force, 309, 321–22,
338–39, 339n.63, 347, 347n.79, 361, 362, 374,
432, 485; relationship to technology, 310, 322,
338, 341, 351, 534, 598, 599, 601–2, 603–4, 607;
self-representation of, 514, 559; and social sciences, 305, 306–8, 351, 405; weakness as factor
in, 353–54, 354n.89, 522; will to, 217, 217n.49.
See also cratic, the; cratology; domination;
negative sanctions; opinion; political man

power (*cont.*)

(*Machtmensch*), the; positive sanctions; power and morals; power-holders; power struggles

power and morals, 166, 308, 320–21, 324; evaluation of maxims, 417–23; goals of power, 405, 410, 411, 412–13, 434; morals of negative sanctions, 431–35; morals of positive sanctions, 430; morals of power based on opinion, 426–29; moral striving for power, 374, 410–19; necessity of power, 405, 406–10, 416; relevance of common good, 406, 411, 417, 419, 422; relevance of consensus, 423–26, 423n.337

power-holders, 309n.8, 382n.169, 384–85, 393n.229, 492–93, 536; and consensus, 790–94; as feared, 394–95, 394n.237; formal vs. factual, 491–93, 493n.101, 536; loneliness of, 401–4; Machiavelli on, 376, 376n.141, 396, 397nn.247, 248, 399n.257, 400n.263, 401, 405, 410; maxims of, 375–77, 393–401, 422–23; as models, 396; vs. offices held, 498–501; psychology of, 263–70; relations with king-makers, 376–77, 376nn.142, 143, 409, 422, 422n.334; relations with power-subjects, 310, 311, 312–13, 338–39, 342, 349, 386, 393–96, 394n.238, 395nn.239–41, 397–404, 397nn.248, 249, 399nn.256, 258–60, 400nn.262, 263, 401n.273, 413, 417–22, 423–26, 440, 444–46, 445n.16, 475, 541–42, 559, 790–94; self-assessment by, 396–97; self-presentation of, 393–94, 422–23; will of, 309, 312, 351

power struggles, 8, 29–32, 58, 62–68, 70, 301, 313–62, 453, 560, 616, 728, 772; alliances during, 337–38, 343, 344–45, 346, 382–83, 385–89, 387nn.194, 195, 419, 432; between classes, 568; convincing during, 340, 352–57, 358, 361–62; defined, 334, 441; in democracy, 307, 793–94; and diplomatic abilities, 343–45; distinguishing friend from foe in, 307, 382–83, 385–86, 387, 406n., 820; insults used in, 390; over interests, 225, 315–17, 319–20, 324, 334, 365, 390, 465; legal conflicts as, 465, 472; maxims in, 371, 374–401; necessity of, 405, 406; negative sanctions in, 325–26, 326nn.40, 41, 327, 328, 340n.64, 341–43, 344, 346, 347–49, 352, 394, 398, 398n.251, 423, 431–35, 587; persuasion in, 340, 352–58, 361–62, 423; positive sanctions in, 307, 340–43, 340n.65, 344, 345–49, 352, 395, 423, 430, 587; psychology of, 363–70; over recognition, 225, 226, 317–18, 317n.26, 319–20, 320n.29, 321–22, 324, 334–35; relationship to law, 664n.67; role of information in, 322–23, 323–24, 346; role of opinion/belief in, 340, 342n.71, 348–62, 425, 426–29, 465; role of theories in, 307–8; rumors

used in, 390; ruses used in, 272–73, 323–24, 353, 361, 362, 372n.129; between states, 505n.125, 625, 867; third parties in, 331–39, 332n.50, 347–48, 386; threats used in, 327–31, 338, 340, 341, 361, 362, 432, 435, 861; traitors during, 345, 393, 432; over values, 318–21, 322, 334, 337, 353–54, 365, 390, 406, 465; victory vs. defeat in, 391–92

practical philosophy, 71–72; vs. mathematics, 73, 74, 83n.42, 106, 118n.76, 125; vs. sociology, 73–75. *See also* ethics; political philosophy

practical syllogisms, 125–26, 125nn.93, 94, 151–52, 157, 202–3, 246, 248, 635, 796

preferences, 92, 112, 689, 706, 731, 743, 743n.; hierarchy of, 241; individual vs. collective, 120–21, 120n.84; relationship to common good, 121; relationship to political ethics, 120–21, 120n.84, 129; of voters, 611–12

prestige, 335–36, 335n.58, 365, 386, 457, 560, 586, 614, 914–15

pretending, 228, 259

pride, 283, 367n.117

prisoner's dilemma situations, 137–38, 161, 269n., 448, 448n., 449, 666, 678, 692, 693, 720–21, 735, 764, 800, 803, 817, 903

privati, 242, 250, 250n.111, 275, 287

probability, 133–36, 138–44, 140n.120, 142, 149, 150, 323, 380, 417, 661, 714n., 907

progress, 12–13, 46n.167, 563, 593–94, 813

progressive politics vs. conservative politics, 70, 822

projection, mechanisms of, 249, 249n.107, 251, 372, 580, 589

promises, 291

propaganda, 351, 355, 514, 602

property, private, 458–59, 579, 655n.50, 661, 665–73; animals as, 662; in civil law, 655, 665–73; vs. collective ownership, 660, 666, 669, 670, 670n.81, 671; equality in, 667–68; Fichte on, 669, 679, 679n.96; Hegel on, 668–71, 672n.86, 674–75, 675n., 699n.117, 700; intellectual property, 670, 670n.80, 671–72; Kant on, 646n.34, 655n.51, 669n.75, 672n.86; in land, 481, 671, 709; and law, 646, 648, 669, 669n.73, 670–71; Locke on, 43, 646, 669; principle of acquisitive prescription, 672–73, 809; relationship to contracts, 569, 673–74, 675; relationship to individual achievement, 667, 668, 669–70, 699–700, 705, 716–17, 767; relationship to labor, 582, 667, 669–70, 669n.79; rights to, 466, 486, 574, 582, 585, 646–47, 648, 649, 655, 662, 666, 669n.79, 677, 699–74, 705, 716, 732, 767, 788, 809, 899; state protection of, 43, 486, 646, 648, 686 protectorates, 494, 494n.104

Protestantism, 28, 58n.199, 555, 577, 579–80, 580n.248, 585, 589, 594, 614

Protocols of the Learned Elders of Zion, 372

prudence, 286–87, 295

Prussia, 491, 495, 501, 533, 587, 589, 595, 774, 844n.89, 848, 864

psychology, 72, 91, 147, 158; behaviorism, 75–76; moral psychology, 146; motivational psychology, 126; psychoanalysis, 97, 100, 216, 217, 217n.48, 229–30, 243, 246, 402, 585

public goals vs. state goals, 68–69

public law, 464, 467, 487, 498, 515; vs. private law, 510–11. *See also* constitutional law; criminal law

public opinion, 382n.171, 541–42, 612, 742, 751, 752, 858, 873, 886

public relations, 514, 880

punishment, 35, 425–26, 471, 485, 485n.84, 486, 510, 610, 653n.48, 663, 681–92, 697n., 759, 901; absolute vs. relative theories of, 682–84, 685n.; of attempted vs. consummated criminal acts, 691–92; capital punishment, 636, 656, 684nn.105, 106, 685n., 761, 799, 918; and determinism, 685; as deterrence, 176, 635, 679n.97, 680, 682–85, 685n., 691, 692, 840; as individual vs. general deterrence, 682–84, 692; Kant on, 682, 683, 685n., 690n., 691; life sentences, 684–85; and natural law, 686; as retribution, 682–83, 692. *See also* negative sanctions

Puritans, 448

Pyrrhic victories, 335n.56, 388

rape, 634, 657, 657n.55, 696

reason, xv, 164, 222–23, 225, 227–28, 229n.72, 237–39, 281, 298, 321, 383, 411, 544, 549, 550, 565, 566, 581, 619, 621, 701, 876–77; argumentation, 75, 75n., 114–15, 641n.19; communicative rationality, 128, 149; Hegel on, 52; instrumental rationality, 642, 705, 714, 720, 724, 828, 878, 923, 927; Kant on, 48, 50, 134; Plato on, 14; rationalization, 246, 299, 815; relationship to freedom, 238–39, 357; relationship to mores, 815; relationship to natural law, 631–32; and religion, 25–26; strategic rationality, 30–31, 126–28, 136, 149, 155, 694; technical rationality, 126–27, 136. *See also* Enlightenment, the

recognition, 122–23, 123n., 226; desire for, 191, 193, 217, 242, 289, 361, 361n.102, 365, 404, 419, 442, 647, 648, 666n., 831, 854, 889; power struggles over, 225, 226, 317–18, 317n.26, 319–20, 320n.29, 321–22, 324, 334; relationship to

individual identity, 242, 317–18; withdrawal of, 340, 360, 361n.102

recycling, 673, 879, 908

religion, 143, 256, 283, 467–71, 513, 543, 546, 547, 549, 557, 609n.304, 651, 693, 705, 880, 913, 917, 922; in agrarian societies, 561–62; defined, 265–66, 471; and education, 923–24; freedom of, 641–42, 642n.22, 646, 647, 654, 719, 731; fundamentalism in, 478, 579, 595n.283, 606–7, 876, 890–91, 892, 923; Hegel on, 470, 782; and international relations, 876–78; in modernity, 468, 577, 589, 609, 618–21, 619n.; monotheism in, 563, 571–72, 572, 813; national religions, 274, 470, 563; negative sanctions in, 354, 470; priests, 272, 470; prophets, 470; and reason, 25–26; relationship to art, 239; relationship to capitalism, 585; relationship to morals, 92, 183–86, 183n., 468–70, 610, 619, 620, 719–21, 723, 781–82; relationship to natural law, 719–21, 723; relationship to philosophy, 239; relationship to the state, 8, 8n.12, 23–24, 27, 28, 29, 34, 34n.129, 38, 44–45, 45n., 172, 185, 255, 265, 536, 538, 555, 559, 563n.219, 575, 586, 587, 590–91, 600, 629, 654, 719–23, 721n., 784, 813, 823; relationship to truth, 25–26; as social subsystem, 164, 265, 266, 285, 341n., 468, 654, 784, 867; sociology of, 469; universal religions, 274, 470, 555, 570, 571–72, 573, 589, 609, 620, 866. *See also* Buddhism; Christianity; Hinduism; Islam; Judaism

remorse, 87, 143, 143nn.128, 129, 184

Renaissance humanism, 578–79

repression of drives, 243, 272

reproduction, biological, 196–97, 213, 213n.41, 218, 266, 341, 442, 456–57, 457n.33, 658; contraception, 585, 702–4, 874–75; and the family, 221, 264–65, 451–55, 452–53, 693, 697; male/female reproductive strategies, 204–5, 874–75; and marriage, 452–53, 697. *See also* sexuality

reproduction, cultural, 207, 265

reputation. *See* prestige

research policy, 41–42, 714, 720, 743, 788, 915, 925–30

responsibility, collective, 103–5, 246

responsibility, individual, 103–5, 164, 240, 407–8, 561, 614, 615, 647, 654, 678, 685, 690–92, 703, 742, 749, 749n.178, 779–84, 794, 800, 817, 827, 839–40, 901. *See also* guilt; intentionalism

ressentiment, 297, 297n., 366, 541, 683, 767, 884

revenge, 291, 303, 398, 398n.255, 434, 507, 510, 618, 631, 680, 682–83, 683n., 692, 767, 780–81, 804, 857 revolutions, 491, 527–28, 546, 548–49, 588n.269, 769, 794–95, 816; American Revolution, 33n.124, 47, 47n.169, 96, 590, 599, 795, 807, 810, 812; Bolshevist revolution, 151, 471, 595–96, 595n.283, 806n.39, 807; bourgeois revolutions, 587–88, 587n.264, 595; coups d'état, 776, 788n.14, 804–7, 823; Glorious Revolution, 33, 590, 807; Industrial Revolution, 512, 534, 548, 555, 583–84, 585, 589, 590, 592, 593, 594, 599, 601–2, 629, 665, 883; Neolithic Revolution, 548, 548n.190, 551, 555; palace revolutions, 806–7. *See also* French Revolution

rhetoric, 75

rights, 48–49, 280n.164, 290, 613, 675, 701, 736; of animals, 277–78, 277n., 278n.161, 643, 644n.30, 662, 798; of children, 279, 645, 647, 650, 651–52, 656–57, 703, 725, 726, 901; of communities, 663–64; conditional rights, 656–57, 657n.53, 658, 660, 726; Dworkin on, 641n.19; of the elderly, 921; formal vs. substantive, 645–46; to freedom from interference, 592, 644n.30, 645–48, 646n.33, 650, 651, 660, 661, 662, 676, 725, 768–69, 788, 789, 795, 795n.26, 801, 834, 897, 913, 927; of future generations, 137, 648, 657–58, 660, 661–62, 664, 664n.67, 670–71, 692, 711, 716, 725, 726–27, 730, 730n.145, 731, 732, 734, 743, 746, 750, 758, 769, 880, 902, 906, 908, 912, 919; of the handicapped, 645, 649, 651–52; hierarchy of, 831; human/basic rights, 17, 19, 23, 23n., 44, 108, 180, 476, 488, 516, 534–35, 553, 581, 597, 629, 633, 635, 644–54, 650n.43, 655–78, 668, 676, 686n.109, 693, 704, 714, 719, 720, 726, 727, 728–29, 730, 731–32, 733, 743, 760, 765, 767, 769, 785–86, 788–89, 804–5, 807, 808–9, 827, 830–31, 834, 849, 850, 856, 872, 897, 900, 912, 916; of indigenous peoples, 736, 878; of minorities, 721, 743, 760, 767; and natural law, 633, 644–54, 650n.43, 655–78, 728–29, 731–32; to organization, 646; and personhood, 646, 654, 655, 656–64; political vs. pre-political, 645; of the poor, 765, 834, 898, 906; to positive benefits (social rights), 535, 592, 644n.28, 645–46, 646n.33, 648–53, 650n.43, 652–53, 660, 661–62, 670n.82, 672n.87, 678, 692, 703, 708, 709–10, 713, 743, 746, 765, 767, 769, 788, 834, 872, 896, 897, 901, 912, 913–14; prima facie rights, 647, 647n.36, 839n.; to privacy, 646; to property, 466, 486, 574, 582, 585, 646–47, 648, 649, 655, 662, 666, 669n.79, 677, 699–74, 705, 716, 732, 767, 788, 809, 899; protected by the state, 629, 645–51, 656, 692, 726, 785–86, 788; with regard to the state, 516, 645, 676; relationship to legal duties, 651–52; relationship to moral obligations, 466, 651–52, 675, 732, 756, 765, 874, 921, 921n.; restrictions on, 647–48, 649, 725; right not to starve, 765, 834; right of association, 592, 646, 663, 708; right to asylum, 768–69, 798, 815, 916–17; right to coerce, 644–45, 648, 650, 654, 678–81, 687, 689–90, 692, 731n.149; right to defend others, 426, 486, 771, 801, 841, 842, 843–44, 846, 848, 849–50, 852, 869; right to emigrate, 732, 732n.150, 764, 801, 824, 841; right to employment, 650, 666n.; right to just political institutions, 809; right to life, 647, 656, 679, 681, 704, 731, 788, 800–801, 808–9, 850, 857, 857n.113; right to make contracts, 676, 692; right to natural resources, 873–74; right to preserve one's culture, 809; right to reproduce, 703–4; right to resist positive law, 37, 634, 723, 773, 778–79, 795–807, 918; right to self-defense, 426, 486, 678–81, 687, 689–90, 771, 800, 801, 839, 841–43, 844–46, 848, 856, 860, 867, 869; right to self-determination, 807, 808; right to vote, 515, 530, 531, 592–93, 726, 727, 730–31, 732–34, 739–40, 826; to secret mail, 647; and separation of powers, 488; of the state, 487, 498, 645–46, 652–53, 756

risk, 133–36, 135n.107, 138–44, 140n.120, 422, 678–79, 710, 714–15, 714n.

rites, 246, 257, 265, 268, 274, 557

role-playing, 251–52, 299

Roman army, 461, 569, 570

Roman civil law, 20–21, 20nn.73, 75, 38n.144, 498, 568–69, 572–73, 579, 593–94, 770, 773

Roman constitutional law, 490, 493n.101, 499, 501, 527n.160

Roman dictators, 490, 501, 526

Roman Empire, 27, 68, 179, 339, 527, 549, 573n.232, 603, 636, 847; Augustine on, 22; Augustus, 331, 364, 364n.109, 378n.147, 398, 506–7, 513, 514, 569, 589, 672–73, 672n.85, 821; Aurelius, 381n.160, 413, 422; vs. British Empire, 598; Caesar, 20n.75, 156–57, 156n.153, 161n., 171, 331, 359, 362–63, 364, 372n.129, 378n.147, 392, 421, 547, 569, 805–6, 806nn.37, 38; Caligula, 146n.136, 366, 366n.112, 399, 404; Caracalla, 18, 370, 370n.123, 569; and Christianity, 570, 571; Civil War, 773; Commodus, 422; Diocletian, 414, 570–71; fall of, 570; Greek culture in, 570; Hadrian, 527; Justinian, 514; political philosophy in, 18–21, 32, 75; relations with barbarians, 569–70, 571, 835, 891; separation of powers in, 564; Trajan, 422

Romania, 393n.231, 606, 802, 804

Roman jurisprudence, 669

Roman Republic, 344, 480, 535, 567, 568, 786, 821

Romans, xviii, 554; justification for war among,
506–7, 569, 838n.81; patricians and plebeians,
568, 568n.226, 786, 791; patrons and clients, 568,
573

Roman Senate, 527n.160, 747, 805

Romany, 306–7, 389, 851n.

rumors, 390

ruses, 323–24, 345, 372–73, 372n.129, 860

Russia, 495, 575, 576, 587, 593, 595, 595n.283, 598,
602n.297, 764, 781–82, 806n.39, 815, 821,
839, 848, 850; Alexander I, 146n.136, 392;
Alexander II, 601, 810; after Cold War, 604–5,
606, 608, 789n.17, 846, 886–87, 893, 901, 916;
Ivan the Terrible, 534; Paul I, 146n.136, 527;
Peter the Great, 527, 781; Yeltsin, 354, 516, 810,
823. *See also* Soviet Union

Rwanda, 704, 788

Saudi Arabia, 605, 606

Schadenfreude, 300, 816

Schröder, H., 118n.74

science, xiv, xv, 106, 113, 256, 259, 266, 558, 561, 564,
565, 572, 670n.80; Bacon on, 42, 42n.155;
and causality, 170–72, 197, 230, 237, 581; and
Hobbes, 34, 34n.126; and modernity, 41–42, 59;
relationship to ethics, 92, 149; relationship to
philosophy, 154–55; relationship to political philosophy, 32, 34, 57–58, 76; relationship to truth,
74, 163–64, 926, 928; scientific values, 79; specialization in, 925–26; state policies relating to,
41–42, 67n.14, 714, 743, 788, 925–30; technical
vs. strategic rationality in, 126–27; as value-
neutral, 714, 926; and *verum-factum* principle,
34, 581, 582. *See also* mathematics; psychology;
sciences, natural; sciences, social

sciences, natural, 149, 153, 158, 175, 285, 368, 558, 579,
927–28; biology, 158, 619; and Christianity,
572, 577, 581; vs. philosophy of nature, 154–55;
physics, 158, 201n.22, 619; relationship to
engineering sciences, 156; vs. social sciences,
126–28, 157, 165, 170–71, 172, 172n.178, 926,
928; technical rationality in, 126

sciences, social, 149, 158n.157, 436, 438, 546; and
causality, 170–72; as empirical, 140, 165–67;
mathematics in, 169–70; methodology of,
155–72; vs. natural sciences, 126–28, 157, 165,
170–71, 172, 172n.178, 926, 928; and power,
305, 306–8, 351, 405; and problems of identity,
225; relationship to the historical sciences, 165,

165n.165, 167, 170–72, 173; relationship to politics, xv–xvi, xviii, 50, 57–58, 76; relationship to
social technology, 156; and social engagement of
social scientists, 160–61; vs. social philosophy,
155, 158, 162–64, 165, 167; strategic rationality
in, 126–27, 149; theories in, 126–28, 156–57,
172, 307–8, 567; as value-free, 30, 54, 57–58,
167, 619, 926. *See also* social, the

secession, 497, 807–11, 809n.43, 810n.45, 837, 850

secretiveness, 421, 421n.332

secret police, 339, 803

secret services, 7, 117, 145, 369, 432, 507–8, 803, 845

self-actualization, 248

self-consciousness, 191, 281, 314, 315, 324, 665; *I*-self
structure, 190, 223–40, 232n.75, 235n.82,
249–50, 251, 252, 254–55, 256, 263, 271, 278,
282–83, 282n.169, 289–90, 299, 614, 621,
642, 718; of *privati*, 242, 250, 250n.111, 275;
relationship to the absolute, 234; relationship
to socialization, 227, 236, 254–55, 316; role of
the future in, 232–33; role of labor in, 236;
role of memory in, 231–32, 231n.73; role of
mortality in, 233–34, 322, 344n.79; role of
the world in, 235–36; value of, 278–80. *See
also* interior dimension (*Innenseite*)

self-deception, 98, 259

self-defense, 431, 486–87, 678–81, 687, 689, 771, 800,
838, 839, 840, 841–43, 867

self-determination of peoples, 807, 808

self-esteem/self-respect/self-worth, 315, 316, 319, 326,
341, 352, 369, 502, 503, 586, 614, 615, 645, 646,
647, 702, 804, 820, 836, 866, 890, 896, 898,
914–15

self-fulfilling assumptions, 135–36, 157

self-handicapping, 248n.105

self-hatred, 224, 303–4, 403n.281, 616, 816, 866, 920

self-interest, 51, 201, 267, 282, 282n.170, 310, 353, 361,
425, 441, 442, 448–49, 448n., 506, 550, 583, 585,
596, 618–19, 620, 639–41, 660, 678, 693, 694,
704–5, 718, 721, 765, 770, 775, 776, 791, 800,
817, 876, 894, 896, 903, 904, 920; and aid for development, 835–36; Hobbes on, 28, 36, 37–39,
38n.143, 40n.151, 42–44, 48–49, 51, 58, 105–6,
106n.42, 268, 449, 619, 628, 639, 640; vs. interest, 39–40; La Rochefoucauld on, 96n.26; Locke
on, 42–44, 51, 512; vs. moral obligations, 91–92,
96–97; psychological egoism, 98, 98n.; relationship to justice, 291, 300; relationship to morals,
91–92, 96–97, 287–88, 291, 300, 645, 661; and
sociobiology, 197–200, 203–4, 206–10, 213,
269. *See also* individualism

self-presentation, 393–94

self-righteousness, 97–98

self-sacrifice, 6, 40, 51, 94, 207, 268–69, 281, 288, 322

sense experience, 211, 237, 238, 250, 259

separation of powers. *See* state, the, separation of powers in

September 11th attacks, 884

servility, 419, 419n.

sexuality, 79–80, 193, 216–17, 217n.49, 221, 229, 239, 243, 292, 297n., 307, 561, 638, 693; abortion, 122, 260, 279n.162, 617, 643, 656, 657, 657nn.53, 55, 703, 875; bisexuality, 695; contraception, 585, 702–4; vs. the erotic, 332, 332n.51, 584–85; homosexuality, 241, 461; lust, 297, 299; in males vs. females, 204–5, 284, 874–75; promiscuity, 283–84, 584–85; prostitution, 430, 697n.; relationship to love, 247, 284, 340n.64; sex crimes, 917; sexual favors, 378. *See also* reproduction, biological

shame, 225, 251, 251n.113, 278, 288–89, 288n.178, 360

ship travel, 554–55, 564, 564n.220, 577, 578

signs, 256, 256n.122, 259, 260n.131

Sikh fundamentalism, 606

sincerity, 77, 116, 291, 614

Singapore, 918

slander, 647

slavery, 4, 19, 27, 96–97, 122n.86, 325, 336, 338, 364, 424, 431, 507, 560, 569, 574, 655, 675, 737, 779, 786, 810, 818, 832, 850; compensation for, 672n.87; domination in, 441, 444–46, 447, 475, 634; in Greece, 566, 566n.223, 729; negative sanctions in, 441, 446; in United States, 590, 672n.87

Slovakia, 811

Slovenia, 810, 885

social, the: ontology of, 156, 158–62, 158nn.157, 158; organicist models of, 159; pre-scientific knowledge of, 173; relationship to values, 8; self-interpretation of social structures, 162–64; social hierarchy, 217–18, 457–58, 472, 556, 558, 559, 560, 592; social skills, 289; society vs. community, 267–68. *See also* classes, socioeconomic; corporate groups; culture; sciences, social; social orders

social Darwinism, 202, 208

socialism, 45, 58–59, 609, 609n.304, 662, 665, 693, 815, 928–29. *See also* communism

socialization, 229, 261, 319; relationship to self-consciousness, 227, 236, 254–55, 316

social mobility, 458, 560, 568, 582, 587, 590, 718

social orders, 262–67, 575; and consensus, 424–25; and corporate groups, 263–64; evolution of, 262–63, 264, 266, 270; inequalities in, 59–60,

110n., 266; legitimation of, 6, 265–66, 268–69, 436, 467, 468, 470, 471, 561; vs. natural order, 268; state defense of, 265, 436, 783–86, 792–93; subsystems in, xv, 78–79, 264–66, 341, 341n., 451, 468, 513, 536, 539, 546, 547, 550, 654, 704–5, 783–85, 867. *See also* economic activity; family, the; military, the; religion

sociobiology, 190, 192, 197–210, 213, 214, 218n., 269, 288, 694

sociologism, 258–59

sociology, 54, 72, 73–75, 305–6, 307–8

Somalia, 867, 870, 894

Sophists, 8–9, 36, 75, 565, 567

sorcery, 469

South Africa, 421, 599, 889

South Korea, 606, 788–89, 788n.14, 888

sovereignty, 473, 475, 490n.94, 494n.102, 626, 724, 734, 736, 849n.103, 869; in constitutional law, 487–93, 495; external sovereignty, 493–98; vs. factual power, 491–93; Hobbes on, 24n.91, 33–35, 34n.129, 40–41; internal sovereignty, 484–93; and international law, 483, 493–96, 498, 836, 848; and international relations, 493–96, 494nn.103, 105; and legal omnipotence, 489, 495; Marsilius of Padua on, 27, 27n.105; and nuclear weapons, 604; popular sovereignty, 44, 44n.162, 53; Rawls on, 849n.103; and right to wage war, 771, 864; Rousseau on, 44, 44n.162; and separation of powers, 40–41, 53, 55, 587; Spinoza on, 24n.91

Soviet Union, 152, 354, 386, 408, 468, 478, 495, 552, 594, 602n.297, 667, 796, 873; and Baltic states, 809–10, 809n.43, 810, 810n.45; Bolshevist revolution, 151, 471, 595–96, 595n.283, 806n.39, 807; Constitution of 1977, 497n.110; dissolution of, 133, 349, 480, 497n.110, 588, 598, 602, 603, 604–5, 618, 787, 802–3, 808, 809–10, 809n.43, 823, 861, 867, 886–87; Gorbachev, xxi, 68, 133, 394, 417, 503, 596, 605, 608, 787, 802–3, 865; Lenin, 22n.82, 70, 139, 601, 620; marriage in, 694–95; *perestroika* in, 68; relations with Finland, 843; relations with Germany, 344, 345, 388, 420, 601, 821; relations with Great Britain, 388; relations with United States, 344; Stalin, 70, 139, 339, 367, 388–89, 392, 396, 398, 420, 424, 547, 580, 597, 634, 694, 816, 821. *See also* Cold War; Russia

Spain, 477n.66, 543, 590n.272, 598, 754, 766, 785, 846, 848; Civil War, 735, 824, 850–51; colonialism of, 26–27, 122, 122n.87, 128n.97, 175, 599, 830n.71, 850, 852, 853; fascism in, 371, 389, 597, 887; relations with United States, 850 speciesism, 222n.60, 278, 278n.161

speech acts, 224, 306–7

spirit, 285, 621; defined, 238–39; vs. intelligence, 225; and life, 191, 222–26, 281

spiritualism, 191

state, the, xvi, 154, 159, 189n.3, 273, 326n.40; administration of community services by, 511–14; as administrative/regulative group, 437; apparatus and organs of, 498–503, 516, 517, 519, 526; Aristotle on, 15–18, 17n.57, 18nn.62–64, 19n.66, 455n.29, 462, 462n., 474, 475, 588, 639n.16; art supported by, 513–14, 717–18, 743, 927; basic rights protected by, 629, 645–51, 656, 692, 726, 785–86, 788; bureaucracy, 69–70, 519–21, 528, 539, 540, 567, 570–71, 586, 611, 612–13, 702, 727, 737, 750, 754–56, 757, 799–800, 912; centralization vs. concentration in, 502–3; and Christianity, 30, 51, 575; Cicero on, 13n.34, 19–20, 473; citizenry/population, 473–80, 475n.62, 482, 494n.104, 507, 508, 566, 736, 768, 769, 834–35, 880, 919–20; collegiality in, 501–2; and conquest, 672–73, 772; contract theory of, 447–48, 630, 639–41, 641n.19, 655, 693, 731, 731n.149, 769; drug abuse policies, 632–33, 917–18; economic policy, 55–56, 66, 67n.14, 263, 306, 459, 472, 485–86, 512–13, 536, 587, 593, 612, 613, 660, 666n., 705–19, 743, 750, 758, 764–65, 784, 788–89, 792, 903, 907, 911–15, 921–22; and education, 14, 17, 35, 55n.194, 290, 513–14, 590, 610, 693, 701, 708–9, 722, 725, 750, 808, 898, 910, 921–25; environmental policy, 608–9, 616–17, 661, 711–12, 758, 777, 833, 874, 881–82, 895, 902–11, 902n., 912–13, 914, 915, 916; essence of, xvii, 439, 485–86; establishment of a state, 87, 771, 774, 788, 823–24, 885, 896; as evolutionarily stable, 460, 543, 575, 589, 630–31, 756, 824; as federal, 488, 494–95, 497–98, 497n.112, 531, 534, 732, 734–36, 746–47, 753, 764, 810; fiscal policy, 486, 511, 522, 522n., 532, 537, 538, 552, 571, 575, 587, 613, 634, 636, 644, 648–49, 661, 667, 697, 700, 703, 706, 707, 709, 716, 718, 722, 735, 737, 746, 750, 755, 756–58, 767, 777–78, 792, 833, 874, 904–7, 910, 911, 912–13, 914, 918, 919, 929; forms of, 439, 526–36, 724–29, 769; goals of, 66–70, 189, 437n.3, 503, 514, 650, 666n., 713, 772, 773, 856; Hegel on, 29n.108, 50–52, 58–59, 442, 473n.58, 526n.158, 545, 823; Hobbes on, 24n.91, 32–41, 34n.129; honor of individuals protected by, 486, 647, 648, 685, 686; Kant on, 48–49, 52, 473n.58; legitimation of, 7, 8, 15, 24–25, 28–29, 35–36, 37–38, 39–40, 42, 44, 54n., 60, 265, 442, 475,

484–88, 491, 491n.97, 513–14, 589, 590–91, 610, 618, 625, 627–32, 639–40, 692–93, 748, 804, 808–9; Marx on, 22n.82, 56, 538; in modernity, xv, 27, 52, 58–61, 439, 468, 484–85, 485n.83, 486–88, 491, 493, 500, 512, 516, 519, 521, 535, 537, 543, 544, 545, 552, 553, 555, 556, 574, 575, 586–608, 610–14, 629–31, 723n.140, 772, 795, 824, 835, 875, 903; monopoly on force, xiv, 29, 32, 34–35, 37–38, 40, 63–64, 87, 259, 294, 375, 377, 405, 411, 433, 436, 448, 455, 484–88, 493, 510, 537, 552, 586, 611, 627, 651, 681, 692, 693, 721, 762, 764, 767, 780, 788, 862–63, 867, 881, 916; monopoly on legislation, 486, 587, 627, 676, 692; moral obligations to, 634, 726, 727, 731, 732, 755, 756, 763, 841, 894; as multi-ethnic, 476, 480; as nomadic, 481, 481n.74; origin of, xvii, 5, 435, 441–42, 441n.10, 447–49, 451, 455, 471–73, 481, 498–99, 555, 556–57, 559, 626, 629, 630, 674, 692–93, 772, 795, 823–24; and peace, xiv, 34–35, 36, 66, 503–4, 509, 627, 720, 826, 902; Plato on, 7n.10, 10–16, 12n.28, 17, 18, 20; police system, 511, 754, 916–18; as polity, 492n., 515; population policies, 513; private property protected by, 43, 486, 646, 648, 686; redistribution of wealth by, 512–13, 593, 644, 646, 649–50, 666, 667, 692, 709–10, 757–58, 767, 792, 809, 837, 874n.9, 915, 929; relationship to civil society, 50–51, 442, 513, 533–34, 533n.174, 536–42, 593, 704, 704n., 887; relationship to collective identity, 44, 271, 449, 475, 495, 717, 826, 831; relationship to the cosmos, 13, 13nn.32, 33, 34, 44; relationship to the family, 15–16, 35, 50–51, 71–72, 441–42, 443, 455, 472, 475, 513, 536, 694, 708, 750, 754, 919; relationship to freedom, 17n.57, 48–49, 566, 627, 629, 637, 644, 704, 715, 788; relationship to law, 35, 41, 48, 51, 52, 58–59, 180, 378, 405, 416, 437–38, 446, 448, 464, 472–73, 476, 485, 487, 488–90, 498, 502, 509–10, 512, 516, 517–18, 521–24, 536, 540, 544, 625–27, 629, 631, 632–33, 642–44, 645, 646, 648–49, 654, 674, 679, 681, 692, 693, 774, 798–99, 820, 823–24, 887; relationship to mores, 449, 471, 472, 485, 485n.84, 491, 534, 534n.175, 536, 547, 586, 625, 629, 631, 725, 745, 751, 765, 773, 774–76, 800; relationship to philosophy, 720, 721–22; relationship to politics, 62–68, 62n.3, 189, 436, 785, 787–88; relationship to Protestantism, 58n.199, 555; relationship to religion, 8, 8n.12, 23–24, 27, 28, 29, 34, 34n.129, 38, 44–45, 45n., 172, 185, 255, 265, 536, 538, 555, 559, 563n.219, 575, 586, 587, 590–91, 600, 629, 654, 719–23, 721n., 784, 813, 823; right

state (*cont.*)
of veto in, 500, 750; rule of law in, 41, 48, 51, 52, 58–59, 180, 378, 405, 416, 446, 472–73, 512, 544, 887; science and technology policies, 41–42, 67n.14, 482, 714, 720, 743, 788, 915, 925–30; secession from, 497, 807–11, 809n.43, 810n.45, 837, 850; separation of powers in, 40–41, 53, 55, 411, 488, 490, 491, 500, 509, 515, 518, 522n., 529, 531, 531n.167, 534, 535, 535n.177, 539, 552, 564, 587, 590, 626, 638, 692, 704, 728–29, 732, 733, 734, 735, 739–40, 744, 746–47, 749, 752, 758, 788, 810, 887; social order defended by, 265, 436, 783–86, 792–93; vs. the soul, 13–14, 13n.32; territoriality of, 29, 436, 473, 480–84, 480n.72, 482n.75, 483n.79, 507, 526, 562, 575, 654, 672–73, 764, 769, 835, 841, 855, 863; unity of, 486–88, 497–98, 497n.111, 524–26, 539, 568, 654, 724, 807–11; as universal state, xvii, 19, 40n.151, 52, 59, 64, 112, 275, 294, 475, 498, 506, 736, 762–71, 764, 835, 846, 862–63, 867, 871, 875, 884–85, 899–900; Weber on, 62n.3, 69n.20, 437n.2, 484–85, 485n.82. *See also* constitutional law; constitutions; democracy; domination, as political; ecological issues, the ecological state; executive, the; foreign policy; judiciary; legislature, the; military, the; sovereignty; totalitarianism; welfare state
state of emergency, 489, 490, 603, 688, 690, 691, 748, 797, 839n., 859
state of nature, 87, 357, 433, 446, 504, 693, 731, 734, 763; vs. civil war, 627–29; Hegel on, 823; Hobbes on, 38, 40, 40n.151, 316, 448–49, 628–29, 638–40; Locke on, 40
sterilization, compulsory, 703–4
Stern, D., 236n.85
Stoicism, 19, 19n.68, 95n.25, 328n., 473n.53, 570, 669n.79, 880–81
subjectivity, 76n.28, 191, 226; in antiquity, 19; and Christianity, 23, 30; vs. intersubjectivity, 55; in modernity, 3, 12, 28, 45–46, 51, 57, 101, 102, 290, 589, 614, 620–21, 685
subsumption problem, 122–23, 122nn.87, 88, 175
succession law, 458, 479, 643, 657n.53, 673, 694, 699–701, 699n.115
Sudan, 889
suicide, 112, 222, 223, 225–26, 262, 269, 278, 279–80, 372–73, 639n.16, 652, 653, 653nn.48, 49, 675
Sumeria, 562
Sweden, 388, 587, 595, 600, 908
Switzerland, 461, 497, 519, 530, 531, 532n.171, 533, 739, 749, 756, 766, 918

symbols, 256, 256n.122, 259, 272–73, 272n., 275, 513; political symbols, 192, 193, 355, 355n.91
symmetry, 106n.44, 114, 214, 270n.148, 276, 301, 317, 317n.26, 324, 336, 372, 429, 447, 557, 585, 617, 655, 694, 892; of alliances, 344; of consensus, 357; of exchange, 341–42, 430; and friendship, 293, 538; and justice, 290–91, 293, 695; of love, 367, 394n.235; relationship to morals, 108, 137, 138, 270, 290–91, 432, 462, 466, 640, 857; and universalism, 108, 466
sympathy, 179, 239–40, 288, 288n.178, 292–93, 294, 382n.171, 385–86, 418, 428–29, 462
synthetic a priori judgments, 121, 140n.118
Syria, 835

tact, 86, 86n., 289, 291
Tauroggen Convention, 844n.89
taxation, 35, 472, 486, 512, 552, 562, 566, 571, 574, 575, 587, 626, 634, 636, 644, 648–49, 650, 657, 667, 697, 700, 703, 707, 709, 716, 718, 719, 722, 732, 737, 750, 755, 756–58, 792, 835, 910, 914, 918, 919, 929; on currency speculation, 833, 875; environmental taxes, 661, 711, 758, 777, 874, 904–7, 911, 912–13
Taylorism, 585
technology, xiv, xv, 82, 124, 140, 178, 193, 236, 241, 266, 285, 315, 368, 457, 460–61, 469, 483, 508, 546, 551, 555–56, 565, 574, 618, 670n.80, 854, 898–99, 927; Bacon on, 42, 42n.155; genetic engineering, 612, 620, 668, 702, 711, 909n.36; and modernity, 41–42, 59, 577–78, 581, 585, 764; and population, 658–59; relationship to power, 310, 322, 338, 341, 351, 534, 598, 599, 601–2, 603–4, 607; state policies relating to, 41–42, 482, 714, 788, 915; technological virtue, 285, 294; television, 132, 707–8, 785; and unemployment, 914; as value-neutral, 714
teleological explanations, 153
teleonomic behavior, 229, 229n.72, 244
television, 132, 594, 707–8, 785, 804, 830, 835, 918
temperance, 283–84, 285–86, 287, 290, 294, 295, 295n., 321, 325
terrorism, 132, 801, 859–60, 884, 890, 894, 909, 916
theodicy, 184, 184n., 186
theology, 25–26, 25n.93, 467–68
Third World, 428; debt cancellation for, 900; development policies toward, 834–37, 888, 891, 894, 895–902; vs. First World, xiv–xv, xvii, 59–60, 605–7, 834–37, 865, 888–90, 895, 897–99, 911–12, 914, 919n.46, 920
threats, 327–31, 338, 340, 341, 361, 362, 432, 435, 680–81, 861

time, 165, 165n., 172, 172n.178, 194–95, 230–33, 261, 273, 582

"tit for tat" strategies, 138, 269n., 449, 682, 777, 794, 857

tolerance, 215, 562, 563–64, 566, 569, 719, 765, 829, 920

torture, 42n.155, 326, 434, 759, 831

totalitarianism, 86, 168, 193, 275, 331, 464, 473, 586, 593, 594–98, 597n.286, 601, 637, 764, 811, 856, 857n.113; defined, 533–34; immorality of, 95, 132, 805; and Orwell's *1984*, 78n.31, 260, 275n.; and Plato, 15, 15n.50; vs. pre-state condition, 629; and Rousseau, 44. *See also* communism; National Socialism

totemism, 557

tourism, 512, 615, 615n.311, 891

Tours, battle of, 545

traditions, 273, 275, 351, 561, 758–59. *See also* culture; customs

tragedy of the commons, 666

tragic, the, 119, 253, 813–14; tragic drama, xviii, 9, 21, 31, 163, 174

transcendental pragmatics, 224, 250, 424

transitivity, 114

trust, 97, 135–36, 137, 254, 293, 389, 394, 448–49, 451, 461, 495, 582–83, 692–93, 720–71, 735, 742–43, 745, 774, 827, 829, 919

truth, 238, 258–59, 355, 370–71, 427, 610, 614; vs. correctness, 174; Hobbes on, 33; as normative category, 77, 355n.92; Plato on, 14; relationship to art, 173–74; relationship to ethics, 77, 125; relationship to interests, 33, 157; relationship to religion, 25–26; relationship to science, 74, 163–64, 926, 928; relationship to the whole, 193; truthfulness, 291; *verum-factum* principle, 34, 47, 212, 581, 582

Tunisia, 782, 886

Turkey, 782, 804–5, 853, 875, 886, 920

Twelve Angry Men, 760

tyranny, 774, 780, 796, 800–807, 849–50. *See also* dictatorship

Uganda, 889

Ukraine, 901

unconscious, the, 99–100, 158n.158, 228, 229–30, 272

unemployment, 613, 706, 708, 710, 712, 713, 914–15

United Nations, 602, 617, 863–64, 866–75, 899–900, 917; Charter, 770, 848n.100, 867, 868, 869, 870; and First Gulf War, 867, 868; General Assembly, 873, 900; inequality in, 871–72; Law of the Sea Convention, 874; peace-keeping/peace-enforcement by, 844, 867–71, 894; relations with United States, 872, 884, 885; Secretary-General, 872; Security Council, 604, 605, 608, 848n.100, 867, 868, 870, 871–73, 885, 892; in Somalia, 867, 870; UNESCO, 608, 875

United Nations Conference on Trade and Development (UNCTAD), 834

United States: Articles of Confederation, 733n.153, 795, 846n.96, 885; Constitution, 41, 53, 487n.89, 515, 681, 687, 729n., 733, 740n.163, 750n., 752, 761, 764, 787, 795, 818, 846n.96, 884, 885; Declaration of Independence, 795; drug policies in, 917; education in, 610, 925; electoral college, 532; vs. Europe, 603, 609, 610; the executive in, 532, 532n.170, 748, 749, 750; vs. Germany, 3–4, 54n., 353, 883, 913, 925; as hegemonic power, 506, 603, 882–84, 892, 894; isolationism in, 603, 825, 884; judiciary in, 497n.113, 522, 523–24, 523n.; mores in, 920; New Deal in, 593; plea bargains in, 759; political parties in, 538, 745; popular culture in, 883–84; prohibition in, 631, 687; relations with Germany, 344, 345, 863; relations with Japan, 146n.135, 845, 863, 888; relations with Kuwait, 843; relations with Soviet Union, 344, 602, 863; relations with Spain, 850; relations with United Nations, 872, 884, 885; separation of church and state in, 720; separation of state powers in, 590; slavery in, 590, 672n.87; spoils system in, 521; Supreme Court, 497n.113, 522, 523, 524; taxation in, 905; television in, 707–8; and terrorism, 890; welfare state in, 54n., 524, 825, 913. *See also* American Civil War; American Revolution; Cold War

universalism, 4, 77, 105–17, 137, 149, 175, 176, 178–80, 204, 215, 222, 254, 318–19, 377, 406, 544, 551–52, 566, 589, 593–94, 617, 620, 638, 656, 724, 765, 765n., 768, 816, 849n.102, 884, 890, 898; and Christianity, 22, 23, 27, 105, 293, 493, 578, 582; and democracy, 726–27, 729; and distribution of prosperity, 592, 602, 607, 616; of the Enlightenment, 96–97, 866; and exceptions, 108–12, 116–17, 116n.67; and foreign policy, 825, 827, 828, 830, 831, 834, 881; and individualism, 112; and justice, 39, 106–7, 284, 290, 560, 629–30, 654; of Kant, 92, 105–6, 106n.42, 108–9, 112, 113–14, 118–19, 174–75; and moral obligations, 105–12; vs. nationalism, 54, 591; vs. National Socialism, 57, 139, 178, 180, 597, 686; and politicians, 865; postulate of universalizability, 39, 48, 49–50, 78, 91–92, 93, 94, 107–12, 113–14, 139, 205–6, 271, 437n.3, 602, 607, 616, 687, 726–27, 737, 871, 877, 880, 883, 887, 895, 896; relationship to language, 106, 106n.45; and

universalism (*cont.*)
symmetry, 108, 466; of utilitarianism, 105–6, 106n.42, 108–9, 108n.51
Upper Paleolithic culture, 558
utilitarianism, 93, 102, 112–13, 114n.63, 115, 118–19, 119n.77, 144, 287, 619, 664n.65, 856; act utilitarianism, 108–9; classical vs. average utility, 659–60, 659nn.60, 61; Dworkin on, 743, 743n.; as hedonistic, 84, 112, 113; principle of average utility, 640; and punishment, 682–83; Rawls on, 110–11, 115n.66; rule utilitarianism, 108, 109; and the treatment of innocents, 109, 109n.53, 113, 113n.59, 279, 682, 688–89; universalism of, 105–6, 106n.42, 108–9, 108n.51
utopianism, 12–13, 14–15, 29–30, 29nn.110, 111, 57, 59, 129, 418, 471, 609, 775–76, 925

values, xiv, xvii, 49–50, 153, 245, 246, 300, 344, 514–15, 771, 828–29; aesthetic values, 79–80, 80n.34, 117n.72, 154, 276, 285, 717–18; bourgeois values, 583, 585–86, 588; conflict between, 119, 149, 181–82; contemplative values, 79, 284–85, 414n.322, 417; cultural norms, 10–11, 12, 12n.29, 18, 21–22, 50, 129, 164, 174–82, 202, 204, 267, 449, 465, 466, 477; ecological threshold values, 833; and education, 923; hierarchy of, 79–80, 115, 117–21, 132, 148, 277–78, 281, 282, 285, 286, 294, 297, 562, 654, 657, 659, 662, 664n.67, 687–88, 689, 732, 785–90, 831–32, 866; ideal norms, 10–11, 12, 18, 21–22, 90, 129–31, 158, 164, 175, 180–81, 202, 204, 271, 424, 466, 546; intellectual values, 79, 114–15, 281, 282, 284–85; intrinsic vs. extrinsic, 131–33, 149, 276, 281, 284, 286, 287, 289, 291–92, 405, 410, 662–63, 664, 676–77, 717–18, 724, 788, 793, 895, 927; labor theory of value, 43; maximin principle, 110–11, 110n., 134–35, 140, 143, 907; moral values vs. aesthetic values, 79–80, 80n.34, 117n.72; objectivity of, 89, 304; power struggles over, 318–21, 322, 334, 337, 353–54, 365, 390, 406, 465; relationship to charisma, 360; relationship to difficulty of acquisition, 316, 316n.23; relationship to ethics, 113–15, 116; relationship to goods, 113; relationship to history, 12–13; relationship to individual identity, 350; relationship to love, 240, 319; relationship to the social, 8; role in collective identity, 273–74; role in friendship, 292–93; scientific values, 79; value judgments, vs. normative statements, 90–91, 121; value of inorganic being, 276–77, 278; value of organic being, 276–77, 278, 278nn.160, 161; value of self-consciousness, 278–80; vital values, 281,

282, 284, 285, 286, 297; Weber on, 57–58. *See also* goods; human life, value of; justice; virtues
vanity, 288, 365, 423
Vatican City, 526
vegetarianism, 277, 883, 911
venality, 430
Venice, Republic of, 529
verum-factum principle, 34, 47, 212, 581, 582
vices, 281, 289, 290n.184, 295–304; pre-social vices, 296–99; social vices, 299–304; vs. virtues, 13, 295–96, 296n.189
violence. *See* force; war
virtues, 36, 102, 181–82, 207, 281–95, 469, 721, 723, 772–73, 891, 896, 917; bourgeois virtues, 583, 585–86, 588; pre-social virtues, 281–82, 283–87, 289, 290, 291; relationship to habit, 244, 286, 294; secondary virtues, 286–87; social virtues, 282, 287–95; vs. vices, 13, 295–96, 296n.189. *See also* justice; values
volition. *See* will
voluntary servitude, 312

war, 6, 214, 399n.256, 459–62, 493, 504–7, 630, 672, 727, 753, 774, 781, 824; in archaic societies, 557–58; Austro-Prussian War, 392, 392n.226; avoidance of, 504, 557–58, 712, 763–64, 770–71, 826, 829, 844, 844n.90, 867, 868–69, 881, 892–94, 899–900; civilians in, 842, 855, 857–58, 859–60, 860, 861; compulsory military service in, 726, 727, 732, 755, 756, 763, 841, 894; conduct of, 825, 838–40, 853–63, 864; conscientious objectors during, 756; declarations of, 738; and democracy, 763–64, 850, 854; Falklands War, 432, 826, 842n.86; Franco-Prussian War, 842; grounds for, 434–35, 586, 831, 832, 838–39, 840, 841–53, 854, 864, 888–89; guerilla warfare, 601–2, 630n., 854, 860–61; Gulf War, First, 399, 608, 841n.85, 843, 848, 850, 858, 863, 867, 868; Hundred Years' War, 575; and ideology, 588–89; international law relating to, 848–49, 850, 856–57; and Islam, 582n.253; just wars, 20, 26, 119–20, 136–37, 137n.111, 353, 416, 426, 569, 588–89, 667, 682, 688–89, 756, 763, 771, 814, 826–27, 827n., 837–64, 838, 838n.81; in modernity, 600–602; neutrality in, 839n., 850–51, 858–59; occupation after, 426, 855; Opium Wars, 770, 852; Peloponnesian War, 160–61, 173, 260, 364n.109, 386n.189, 387n.193, 517n.141, 841; post-war policies, 838, 840, 863–64; as preventive, 504, 844–46, 850; Second Punic War, 323, 323n.34; Soccer War,

832; Social War, 18; and sovereignty, 771, 864; Spanish-American War, 850; Thirty Years' War, 600; Vietnam War, 842, 851, 858, 861, 861n., 883; war crimes, 839–40, 857, 864; War of the Pacific, 832; War of the Roses, 806; War of the Spanish Succession, 846; wars of aggression, 130, 434–35, 686, 771, 841–48; and world state, 763–64, 770–71; World War I, 57, 133, 172, 346, 353, 432, 435, 567, 586, 597, 598, 601, 604, 782, 791–92, 824, 838, 839, 848, 863; World War II, 57, 139, 142n.125, 146n.135, 246, 344–45, 383, 388–89, 392, 416, 420, 426, 432, 433, 433n.345, 434–35, 600, 601–2, 608, 748, 809n.43, 821, 824, 837–38, 839n., 840–41, 841n.85, 843, 844, 845–46, 851n., 855, 857, 857n.113, 859, 863–64, 871, 894. *See also* civil war; Cold War; weapons

wealth: distribution of, 430, 512–13, 592, 605–6, 607, 611, 644, 646, 649–50, 666, 667–68, 709–10, 757–58, 767, 792, 809, 837, 874n.9, 897n.25, 906, 915, 929; redistribution by the state, 512–13, 593, 644, 646, 649–50, 666, 667, 709–10, 757–58, 767, 792, 809, 837, 874n.9, 915, 929. *See also* poverty

weapons, 42n.155, 322, 323, 341, 460–61, 508, 551, 599, 707, 854, 858, 860; cannons, 577, 578; export of, 899–900; land mines, 855; of mass destruction, 142–43, 504, 601–2, 603–4, 660, 763, 835, 842, 846n.94, 855, 861–63, 869, 884, 892–93, 894; nuclear weapons, 142–43, 603–4, 842, 855, 861–63, 892–93; and United States constitution, 681

Weimar Republic, 528, 785, 786, 928; constitution of, 490n.96, 516–17, 517n.140, 725, 739

welfare state, 54–56, 55n.194, 59, 60, 144, 290, 511–14, 520, 528, 534–35, 537, 593, 597, 603, 607, 611, 626, 644n.28, 649n., 657, 788, 898, 903, 912–14, 916; and charity, 649–50; Fichte on, 644; in Germany, 54n., 912–13, 914, 929; just state as, 713–14, 732, 765; Rawls on, xix, 54n.; reduction of, 613–14, 617; in United mStates, 54n., 524, 825, 913

whistle-blowers, 799–800

"White Rose Letters," 802

will, 93–94, 195, 313–15, 322, 411, 655; and contracts, 674–75; freedom of the, 102, 205n.28, 221, 232–33, 235, 544; of power-holders, 309, 312, 351; weakness of, 125n.93, 245, 408; willpower, 245, 246. *See also* intentionalism

wisdom, 284–85, 286–87, 291, 298

women, 177, 180, 353–54; equality for, 572, 585, 697n., 698, 702, 703, 704, 901; voting rights for, 531, 593. *See also* gender roles

World Bank, 607

world ethos, 876, 880–81, 891

World Trade Organization (WTO), 607, 833–34

Wuppertal Institute, 671

Young Mr. Lincoln, 361–62

young people, 812–13, 920–21

Yugoslavia, former, 478, 598, 603, 604, 808, 810, 811, 870, 885

Zaire, 606